OXFORD ENGLISH DICTIONARY
ADDITIONS SERIES

VOLUME 3

OXFORD ENGLISH DICTIONARY ADDITIONS SERIES

GENERAL EDITOR

JOHN SIMPSON

———

VOLUME 3

———

EDITED BY

MICHAEL PROFFITT

CLARENDON PRESS · OXFORD

1997

Oxford University Press, Great Clarendon Street, Oxford OX2 6DP

Oxford New York
Athens Auckland Bangkok Bogota Bombay
Buenos Aires Calcutta Cape Town Dar es Salaam
Delhi Florence Hong Kong Istanbul Karachi
Kuala Lumpur Madras Madrid Melbourne
Mexico City Nairobi Paris Singapore
Taipei Tokyo Toronto Warsaw
and associated companies in
Berlin Ibadan

Oxford is a trade mark of Oxford University Press

Published in the United States
by Oxford University Press Inc., New York

British Library Cataloguing in Publication Data
Data available

Library of Congress Cataloging in Publication Data
Data available

ISBN 0-19-860027-5 (v.3)

1 3 5 7 9 10 8 6 4 2

Typeset in Monotype Imprint by
Latimer Trend Ltd, Plymouth
Printed in Great Britain
on acid-free paper by
Biddles Ltd., Guildford

OXFORD ENGLISH DICTIONARY

CHIEF EDITOR   John Simpson

DEPUTY CHIEF EDITOR   Edmund Weiner

EDITORIAL STAFF–VOLUME 3

EDITOR   Michael Proffitt

CHIEF SCIENCE EDITOR   Alan Hughes

CHIEF RESEARCH EDITOR   Yvonne Warburton

SENIOR EDITORS (NEW WORDS)   Peter Gilliver (–1994),
John Paterson (Bibliographical Collation), Sara Tulloch (–1991)

DIRECTOR, NORTH AMERICAN READING PROGRAMME
Jeffery Triggs

SENIOR ASSISTANT EDITORS (NEW WORDS)   Melinda J. Babcock
(Library Research), George Chowdharay-Best (Library Research),
Lynne Doy (Bibliographical Collation), Rosamund Ions, Danuta
Padley, Richard Palmer (–1994), Bernadette Paton (–1994),
Angus Stevenson (–1993)

ASSISTANT EDITORS (NEW WORDS)   Edith Bonner (–1991),
Eric Dann (–1987), Mathew Fletcher (–1996), Neil Fulton, Sarah
Hutchinson (–1994), Emma Lenz, Jennifer Miell,
Gerard O'Reilly (–1994), Judith Pearsall (–1991), Eleanor
Rands, Judith Selfe, Anthony Waddell (–1991)

PROJECT COORDINATOR   Carolyn Garwes

DEPARTMENTAL SECRETARY   Margot Charlton

Working alongside the editorial staff of the Dictionary have been numerous freelance library researchers, concerned principally with tracing the
earliest uses of terms and with the verification of quotations cited in the
volume:

Oxford: David Banks, Julie Bowdler (–1991), Jane Brownlow, Margaret
Davies (–1993), Julia Esplen, Gigi Horsfield.

London: Catherine Malone, Patrick Vasey (–1994).

Washington: Nancy Balz, Melissa Conway (–1991), Daphne Gilbert-Carter (–1991), Dorothy Hanks, Shari Jacobson, Adriana Orr (–1991), Jon Ross Simon.

New York: Rita Keckeissen.

Boston: Sally Hinkle.

New Haven: Lori Bronars (–1993).

Kingston, Ontario: Margery Fee (–1994).

San Francisco: Ken Feinstein (–1993).

Valuable additional assistance has been given by several others not on the permanent staff of the Dictionary:

Compilation of Index: Veronica Hurst.

Proof-reading: Edith Bonner, Hazel Clark, Juliet Field, Hania Porucznik.

Keyboarding: Judi Lancashire, Jennifer Linton, Graham Oliver, Susan Wilkin.

Quotation-file sorting: (*designates a former research assistant): Evadne Adrian-Vallance, Lucy Atkins*, Emma Back, Sue Baines, Alexandra Barratt*, Juliet Field*, Mathew Fletcher*, Giles Goodland, Patricia Greene*, Kirsten Hayman, Rachel Hiley*, David James, Keith Jebb, Peter Jenkins*, Lisa Johnston, Jonathan Jones*, Barbara Levick*, Brian McKenna*, Paul Messerschmidt*, Eric Peyton*, Hania Porucznik, Murray Pratt*, Rob Pursey*, Alastair Ricketts*, Clare Senior, Ian Shiels*, Nicola Smyth*, Catherine Soanes*, Andrew Strachan*, Peter Sweasey, Susan Vickers*.

The following have each contributed over 5,000 quotations to the reading programme since the publication of *OED2*:

Pat Back, Katherine Barber, Janet Begnoche, Alex Bisset, Chris Collier, Sue Cowen, Emma Fontanella, Noel Marie Gaeta, Marybeth Geanious, Alesia Goginsky, Daria Goginsky, Tony Gordon, Charlotte Graves Taylor, Susan A. Hill, Joanne Hindman, Victoria Jansen, Daria Kelly-Uhlig, Anna Kirby, Andrew Lintern-Ball, Ruth Mateer, Andrea Nagy, Jennie Neary, Vivienne Painting, Sir Edward Playfair, Rebecca Pressman, Michael Quinion, Gillian Rathbone, Stephen Redenbaugh, Vivien Redman, Susan Rennie, David Rode, Allan Rostron, Kathy Shock, Trish Stableford, Marcy Stamper, Sara G. Triggs, Peter Wexler, Mary White, Jelly Williams, Wayne Wunderlich.

The following have been responsible for keying material collected by the reading programme:

Charles Blackmore, Diane Diffley, Sally Francisco, Noel Marie Gaeta, Marybeth Geanious, Philip Gerrish, Martin Green, Susan A. Hill,

Joanne Hindman, Daria Kelly-Uhlig, Judi Lancashire, Jennifer Linton, Jessica Maybar, Andrea Nagy, Graham Oliver, David Rode, Marcia Slater, Marcy Stamper, Helen Triggs, Sara G. Triggs, Wayne Wunderlich, Alexandria Zander.

Lauren Busciglio and Sue Cowen have been responsible for the processing of over 100,000 quotations taken from the North American Reading Programme for the reading programme database in Oxford.

The Editors are also indebted to the many others who have contributed information on particular entries in the Dictionary; also to the staff of the libraries, especially the Bodleian Library, the British Library, the Library of Congress, and the New York Public Library, who have unfailingly treated the Dictionary's requests for information and assistance with courtesy and dispatch; and to Bellcore at Morristown, NJ (particularly Dr Michael Lesk and Dr Donald Walker), which generously provided resources throughout the development of the *OED*'s North American Reading Programme.

A number of people have been involved in other aspects of the preparation of this volume. The Editors are particularly indebted to the following, who between them shared the task of reading and commenting on ranges of proofs:

Robert Barnhart, Michael Grose, Dr Philip Hardie, Terry Hoad, Deborah Honoré, Hazel Wright.

Thanks are also due to Katherine Barber and her team of lexicographers working on the *Canadian Oxford Dictionary* for their assistance with entries relating to Canadian English, and also for their important contribution to our reading programmes.

In addition to those listed on p. x of the first volume of the *Oxford English Dictionary* (second edition) and in the first volume of the *OED Additions Series*, valuable specialist comment on individual entries has been provided by the following:

Dr P. Baker, Ms K. Barber, Dr D. Barrett, Mr P. Beale, Mr I. M. Beestin, Dr H. C. Bennet-Clark, Mr A. Bissett, Professor J. Black, Mr R. J. Bowater, Mr A. Carr, Dr L. D. Carrington, Professor V. Castellani, Dr M. Clark, Dr S. V. Clube, Sir Howard Colvin, Ms M.-H. Corréard, Mr A. Credland, Dr Q. C. B. Cronk, Mr A. Davidson, Dr J. H. C. S. Davidson, Dr C. Davies, Dr T. Dean, Professor P. G. Drazin, Dr M. Fee, Mr W. K. V. Gale, Dr W. J. Gould, Mrs J. Harrison, Dr P. G. Hoare, Dr T. S. Kemp, Dr P. Klenerman, Dr A. M. Lackie, Dr R. Lambourne, Mr R. P. W. Lewis, Dr T. W. A. Little, Dr A. M. MacLean, Dr T. Mahoney, Mr J. McAleer, Dr D. W. Minter, Mr C. Mitchell,

Mr B. Moore, Dr D. D. Murison, Dr H. Orsman, Mr R. C. Palmer, Mr D. Parkinson, Professor A. Pawley, Mr G. Pointon, Ms J. Poke, Dr F. N. H. Robinson, Captain A. B. Sainsbury, Mr D. Shulman, Mrs P. Silva, Ms S. Slaney, Professor E. G. Stanley, Professor N. S. Sutherland, Dr S. S. Strickland, Dr G. P. Thomas, Mrs S. K. Tulloch, Dr C. Upton, Lord Walton of Detchant, Mr K. Whyld, Professor J. D. A. Widdowson, Professor M. V. Wilkes, Mr T. Wilson, Professor J. C. Wright, Dr R. Wynne-Davies.

The Editors are sad to record the deaths during the preparation of the volume of Dr H. M. Rosenberg and Mr W. K. V. Gale, long-standing consultants to the Dictionary, and of Dr Donald Walker, formerly of Bellcore at Morristown, NJ, who assisted greatly in the development of the North American Reading Programme.

It is with great sadness that we record the death in June 1996 of Mathew Fletcher of our editorial staff. Much of his work for the Dictionary has still to appear in print, but his contribution to this and future *OED* publications will stand as an enduring testament to his outstanding talents and as a reminder to those fortunate enough to have known him.

PREFACE

THIS third volume in the *Oxford English Dictionary: Additions Series* presents a selection of approximately 3,000 entries and subsenses not previously included in the *OED*.

The principles followed in the preparation of this volume are identical to those used in preparing Volumes 1 and 2. Again, the material is not confined to a particular alphabetical range, permitting a new entry to be included in any volume rather than having to wait for its turn in a publication cycle, and allowing related entries which are alphabetically distant to be included in a single volume. In each volume, however, there are concentrations of entries, reflecting the recent work of the project. In Volume 3, the bulk of the entries lies in the ranges *A-C* and *K-O*, and derives from the systematic analysis of the *OED*'s quotation files (paper and electronic). Other entries reflect the *OED*'s role in providing fully researched new entries for the range of dictionaries produced by the Oxford University Press, notably in this volume the *Oxford English Reference Dictionary* and the *Concise Oxford Dictionary* (ninth edition).

A cumulative index of volumes 1, 2, and 3 is included at the end of this volume.

The Editors would as ever be delighted to hear of suggestions for words or senses which might be treated later in the series.

Oxford, May 1996

Michael Proffitt

KEY TO THE PRONUNCIATION

THE pronunciations given are those in use in the educated speech of southern England (the so-called 'Received Standard'), and the keywords given are to be understood as pronounced in such speech.

I. *Consonants*

b, d, f, k, l, m, n, p, t, v, z *have their usual English values*

g as in *g*o (gəʊ)
h . . . *h*o! (həʊ)
r . . . *r*un (rʌn), te*rr*ier ('tɛrɪə(r))
(r) . . . he*r* (hɜː(r))
s . . . *s*ee (siː), su*cc*e*ss* (sək'sɛs)
w . . . *w*ear (wɛə(r))
hw . . . *wh*en (hwɛn)
j . . . *y*es (jɛs)
θ . . . *th*in (θɪn), ba*th* (baːθ)
ð . . . *th*en (ðɛn), ba*th*e (beɪð)
ʃ . . . *sh*op (ʃɒp), di*sh* (dɪʃ)
tʃ . . . *ch*op (tʃɒp), di*tch* (dɪtʃ)
ʒ . . . vi*s*ion ('vɪʒən), dé*j*euner (deʒøne)
dʒ . . . *j*u*dg*e (dʒʌdʒ)

ŋ as in si*ng*ing ('sɪŋɪŋ), thi*n*k (θɪŋk)
ŋg . . . fi*ng*er ('fɪŋgə(r))

(FOREIGN AND NON-SOUTHERN)

ʎ as in It. serra*gli*o (ser'raʎo)
ɲ . . . Fr. co*gn*ac (kɔɲak)
x . . . Ger. a*ch* (ax), Sc. lo*ch* (lɒx),
          Sp. fri*j*oles (fri'xoles)
ç . . . Ger. i*ch* (ɪç). Sc. ni*ch*t (nɪçt)
ɣ . . . North Ger. sa*g*en ('zaːɣən)
c . . . Afrikaans baardmanne*tj*ie
          ('baːrtmanəci)
ɥ . . . Fr. c*u*isine (kɥizin)

Symbols in parentheses are used to denote elements that may be omitted either by individual speakers or in particular phonetic contexts: e.g. *bottle* ('bɒt(ə)l), *Mercian* ('mɜːʃ(ɪ)ən), *suit* (s(j)uːt), *impromptu* (ɪm'prɒm(p)tjuː), *father* ('faːðə(r)).

II. *Vowels and Diphthongs*

SHORT

ɪ as in p*i*t (pɪt), -*ne*ss (-nɪs)
ɛ . . . p*e*t (pɛt), Fr. s*e*pt (sɛt)
æ . . . p*a*t (pæt)
ʌ . . . p*u*tt (pʌt)
ɒ . . . p*o*t (pɒt)
ʊ . . . p*u*t (pʊt)
ə . . . an*o*ther (ə'nʌðə(r))
(ə) . . . beat*e*n ('biːt(ə)n)
i . . . Fr. s*i* (si)
e . . . Fr. b*é*b*é* (bebe)
a . . . Fr. m*a*ri (mari)
ɑ . . . Fr. b*â*timent (bɑtimɑ̃)
ɔ . . . Fr. h*o*mme (ɔm)
o . . . Fr. *eau* (o)
ø . . . Fr. p*eu* (pø)
œ . . . Fr. b*oeu*f (bœf) c*oeu*r (kœr)
u . . . Fr. d*ou*ce (dus)
ʏ . . . Ger. M*ü*ller ('mʏlər)
y . . . Fr. d*u* (dy)

LONG

iː as in b*ea*n (biːn)
ɑː . . . b*a*rn (bɑːn)
ɔː . . . b*o*rn (bɔːn)
uː . . . b*oo*n (buːn)
ɜː . . . b*u*rn (bɜːn)
eː . . . Ger. Schn*ee* (ʃneː)
ɛː . . . Ger. F*ä*hre ('fɛːrə)
aː . . . Ger. T*a*g (taːk)
oː . . . Ger. S*oh*n (zoːn)
øː . . . Ger. G*oe*the ('gøːtə)
yː . . . Ger. gr*ü*n (gryːn)

NASAL

ɛ̃, æ̃ as in Fr. f*in* (fɛ̃, fæ̃)
ɑ̃ . . . Fr. fra*nc* (frɑ̃)
ɔ̃ . . . Fr. b*on* (bɔ̃)
œ̃ . . . Fr. *un* (œ̃)

DIPHTHONGS, etc.

eɪ as in b*ay* (beɪ)
aɪ ... b*uy* (baɪ)
ɔɪ ... b*oy* (bɔɪ)
əʊ ... n*o* (nəʊ)
aʊ ... n*ow* (naʊ)

ɪə as in p*eer* (pɪə(r))
ɛə ... p*air* (pɛə(r))
ʊə ... t*our* (tʊə(r))

aɪə ... f*iery* ('faɪərɪ)
aʊə... s*our* (saʊə(r))

The incidence of main stress is shown by a superior stress mark (ˈ) preceding the stressed syllable, and a secondary stress by an inferior stress mark (ˌ), e.g. *pronunciation* (prəˌnʌnsɪˈeɪʃən).

For further explanation of the transcription used, see the 'General Explanations' in Volume I of the *Oxford English Dictionary*.

NOTE ON PROPRIETARY STATUS

THIS Dictionary includes some words which have or are asserted to have proprietary status as trade marks or otherwise. Their inclusion does not imply that they have acquired for legal purposes a non-proprietary or general significance nor any other judgement concerning their legal status. In cases where the editorial staff have some evidence that a word has proprietary status this is indicated in the entry for that word but no judgement concerning the legal status of such words is made or implied thereby.

A

A. Add: [III.] **ABH** *Brit. Law*, actual bodily harm (see *ACTUAL *a.* 7).

1980 S. McConville in Michaels & Ricks *State of Lang.* 529 Convenience in the processing of large numbers of prisoners and the frequent repetition of certain operations led to a superabundance of initials. These range from designations of the crimes and characteristics of the prisoners to the routines of institutional life. *ABH stands for actual bodily harm, which is to be distinguished from GBH—grievous bodily harm. **1988** K. Amis *Difficulties with Girls* xviii. 253, I'll be up before him again in a couple of weeks, charged with assault occasioning, as it's familiarly known, meaning occasioning ABH, that's actual bodily harm. **1992** *Independent* 6 Jan. 14/7 If it's going to make anyone feel happy so you can nick me for ABH . ., or whatever you're going to get me nicked for, I'll admit it.

ADA *Biochem.* and *Med.* = *adenosine deaminase* s.v. *ADENOSINE *n.*; esp. in *ADA deficiency*, an inherited deficiency of the enzyme ADA, which can cause severe immune deficiency and other immunological disorders.

1972 *Lancet* 18 Nov. 1069/1 If the *A.D.A. deficiency is causally related to the immunological impairment, then [etc.]. **1980** *Clin. Genetics* XVII. 293 (*title*) Prenatal detection of a probable heterozygote for ADA deficiency and severe combined immunodeficiency disease using a microradioassay. **1988** *Mouse News Let.* Nov. 84 We have developed a highly sensitive biochemical microassay for ADA which is capable of detecting femtomolar amounts of reaction product in a single blastomere. **1992** *Analog Sci. Fiction & Fact* Feb. 78/1 An example of such an enzyme selected for gene therapy is ADA (adenosine deaminase).

ab- (æb), *prefix*². *Electr. rare.* [Shortened form of AB(SOLUTE *a.*] Prefixed to the names of practical units (predecessors of SI units) of electrical and magnetic quantities to form the names of corresponding units in the CGS electromagnetic system, as **abampere, abcoulomb, abfarad, abhenry, abohm, abvolt**.

1905 W. Duddell in *Jrnl. Inst. Electr. Engin.* XXXIV. 172 The second proposition of Dr. Kennelly was that names should be given to each of the C.G.S. units in both the magnetic and the static systems, and he suggested that the prefix *ab* or *abs* should be used with the names of the practical units (Volt, Ampere, Ohm, etc.), to form names for the corresponding C.G.S. electro*magnetic* units, and the prefix *abstat* to form the names for the C.G.S. electro*static* units. **1909** *Cent. Dict.* Suppl., Abcoulomb. *Ibid.*, Abfarad. *Ibid.*, Abhenry. **1930** A. Zeleny *Elem. Electr.* 402 The abcoulomb is the quantity of electricity that passes any plane in a circuit in 1 second when the current is 1 abampere. **1940** F. A. Fish *Fund. Princ. Electr. & Magn. Circuits* (ed. 3) iii. 28 The absolute unit, or abvolt, is that e.m.f. which will cause 1 abampere of current to flow in 1 abohm of resistance. *Ibid.* iv. 90 If e_s is expressed in abvolts, and i is in abamperes, L is given in abhenries; the abhenry is, therefore, equal to 1 henry divided by 10^9. **1963** Jerrard & McNeill *Dict. Sci. Units* 13 The inconvenience of having three systems of electrical units, ab units, stat units and practical units has been overcome by the introduction of the metre, kilogramme, second, ampere units. **1966** *McGraw-Hill Encycl. Sci. & Technol.* I. 332/1 The abampere (10 amperes) is seldom used. **1970** *Amer. Jrnl. Physics* XXXVIII. 421 The relationships among corresponding symbols are given and applied to precise statements about the relation between the oersted and the ampere per meter, the abampere and the ampere, etc.

abapical (æb'eɪpɪkəl, æb'æpɪkəl), *a. Biol.* [f. AB-¹ + APICAL *a.*] Pertaining to or designating the side or part that is remote from or opposite to the apex.

1940 *Chambers's Techn. Dict.* 1/2 *Abapical*, pertaining to, or situated at, the lower pole: remote from the apex. **1967** *Oceanogr. & Marine Biol.* V. 364 Dividing cells in the frontal epithelium were concentrated in the central and abapical regions of the bud.

Abbe ('æbə), *n.*² *Optics.* Also *misspelt* Abbé. [The name of Ernst *Abbe* (1840-1905), German physicist, introducer or popularizer of the instruments and concepts.

The form *Abbé* (with pronunc. ('æbeɪ)) prob. arises from a misconception that the name is French.]

Used *attrib.* and in the possessive to designate optical instruments and concepts relating to optical theory, as **Abbe condenser**, a condenser for compound microscopes in the form of a wide-aperture compound lens; **Abbe number**, the reciprocal of the dispersive power of a substance; **Abbe refractometer**, an instrument for directly determining the refractive index of a small sample of liquid.

1882 *Jrnl. R. Microsc. Soc.* II. 411 Abbe's Condenser.—This apparatus as originally devised was not easily applicable to any stand but that of Zeiss for which it was specially made. **1883** *Ibid.* III. 581 Abbe's Refractometer. **1924** R. A. Houston *Treat. Light* (rev. ed.) vii. 109 The Abbe refractometer is an instrument of this type. Such instruments are usually calibrated with liquids of known refractive index. **1937** G. S. Monk *Light* vi. 65 It is customary for glass makers to give the value of $1/\omega$, sometimes called the Abbe number *v.* **1937** *Discovery* Jan. p. vii/1 Polariscopes, Abbe Condensers, etc. **1964** N. G. Clark *Mod. Org. Chem.* iv. 49 This can be accomplished with the Abbé refractometer, an instrument designed to give a direct reading of the refractive index to four decimal places with speedy manipulation. **1973** B. J. Ford *Optical Microscope Man.* iii. 53 We now call this form, as a rule, an Abbé condenser. **1988** M. Pluta *Adv. Light Microscopy* I. i. 60 For many practical purposes some standard dispersion quantities are in use. Among them the most important are the mean dispersion . . and the Abbe number.

abducens (æb'djuːsɛnz), *n. Anat.* [ad. L. *abdūcens*: see ABDUCENT *a.*] Either of the sixth pair of cranial nerves. Also *abducens nerve*.

1822 J. Shaw *Man. Anat.* (ed. 3) I. 212 Sixth, or Abducens. **1920** S. W. Ranson *Anat. Nervous Syst.* viii. 123 The abducens emerges between the pons and the pyramid. **1967** *Arch. Neurol.* XVII. 81/1 Paralysis of the abducens nerve may be a consequence of intracranial hypertension of whatever cause. **1980** *Gray's Anat.* (ed. 36) VII. 1068/2 The abducens nucleus consists of large and small multipolar neurons.

Abell ('eɪbəl), *n. Astron.* [The name of George O. Abell (b. 1927), U.S. astronomer.] Used (*a*) *attrib.* and in the possessive (esp. in *Abell*('s) *catalogue, cluster*) with reference to Abell's catalogue of clusters of galaxies which satisfy certain criteria of richness (the number of galaxies in the central region of a cluster); (*b*)

with a following numeral to denote a particular cluster in this catalogue.
1959 *Astrophysical Jrnl.* CXXIX. 269 Separating it into an 'early' and a 'late' one.., we take from Abell's catalogue the empirical frequencies of our Table 1. *Ibid.* CXXX. 629 It has been listed by Abell (1958) (No. 2151 in his catalogue), and there is another irregular cluster, Abell No. 2152, 1°.3 south of it. **1962** *Ibid.* CXXXV. 8 A very poor clustering surrounding NGC 3158—so poor that it is not eligible for inclusion in the Abell catalogue. **1964** *Monthly Notices R. Astron. Soc.* CXXVIII. 106 In neither analysis was any allowance made for the variation of the apparent size of Abell's clusters with distance. **1977** *Astrophysical Jrnl.* CCXV. 714 According to Abell's richness criteria, R=2 clusters should have 1.6 times as many galaxies as R=1 clusters.., at least at r ≤ 1.5h⁻¹Mpc, the Abell radius. **1989** J. SILK *Big Bang* (rev. ed.) xii. 266 (*caption*) The cluster is Abell 370 at a redshift of 0.17.

abient ('æbɪənt), *a. Psychol.* [ad. L. *abiens*, *abient*- pres. pple. of *abīre* to depart: see -ENT.] Exhibiting, involving, or pertaining to a tendency to avoid or withdraw from a stimulus.
1931 E. B. HOLT *Animal Drive & Learning Process* I. vii. 41 Since there is no satisfactory adjective already in use to characterize these responses which give the organism *more* of the stimulus, I shall adopt the very apt term *adient*, which has been kindly suggested by Prof. H. C. Warren. The immediate effect of an adient response..is to give the organism *more* of the stimulus that elicits the response; and of its opposite, the avoidance or *abient* response, the immediate effect is to give the organism *less* of the exciting stimulus. **1946** P. M. SYMONDS *Dynamics Human Adjustment* ii. 32 Abient..drives are those which secure riddance of the stimulus by avoiding [it]. **1951** *Brit. Jrnl. Psychol.* XLII. 114 [Social] attitudes, in this context, are defined as verbal responses to statements implying adient or abient reactive patterns towards the issues.. defined. **1977** M. L. HUTT *Hutt Adaptation of Bender-Gestalt Test* (ed. 3) vi. 158 Abient individuals tend to block out new experiences and profit less from such exposures. **1977** *Jrnl. Personality Assessment* XLI. 492 The delinquent group was more abient than normal children.

So **'abience** *n.*
1931 E. B. HOLT *Animal Drive & Learning Process* xv. 137 If..an object for which it has a pronounced adience happens to stimulate the senses of a restless animal, this adience will be re-enforced by the (random) annoyer:..thus abience from the mild annoyer and adience to some other stimulus will become one act. **1977** M. L. HUTT *Hutt Adaptation of Bender-Gestalt Test* (ed. 3) vi. 158 Field dependence..may also be related to perceptual abience.

abiological, *a.* Add: Hence **abio'logically** *adv.*
1893 in *Funk's Stand. Dict.* **1979** *Proc. Grassland Soc. Southern Afr.* XIV. 15 On a global basis it has been estimated that annually 200 million tons of N are fixed abiologically (e.g. by lightning). **1986** *Sci. Total Environment* LIII. 133 Methylation occurs abiologically in the dark and is influenced by reaction temperature, inorganic mercury concentration and solution pH.

abiotrophy (eɪbaɪ'ɒtrəfɪ), *n. Path.* [f. A- + Gr. βιοτρόφος life-sustaining, f. βίος (see BIO-) + τροφή nourishment: see -Y³.] Degeneration or progressive loss of function in a tissue or organ; a condition characterized by this.
1902 W. R. GOWERS in *Lancet* 12 Apr. 1003/1 Here the simplest mode of obtaining what we need is to insert the root of βίος after the negative particle in 'atrophy' which gives us 'abiotrophy'. But it is generally better, if you can, to appropriate what you need than to make it afresh, and we find the word βιοτρόφος used in the sense of 'vital nutrition'. If we prefix the negative particle we have the same word, 'abiotrophy'. **1938** J. H. PARSONS *Dis. Eye* (ed. 9) xvii. 343 Treacher

Collins, however, has advanced the theory that the disease is due to abiotrophy of the neuro-epithelium. **1976** *Brain* XCIX. 459 (*title*) Neurotransmitter-related enzymes and indices of hypoxia in senile dementia and other abiotrophies. **1979** *Adv. Human Genetics* IX. ii. 93 The term abiotrophy is usually reserved for an apparently nonmetabolic disturbance of function in an organ previously apparently normally developed and functioning.

So **abiotrophic** (-'trɒfɪk, -'trəʊfɪk) *a.*
1902 W. R. GOWERS in *Lancet* 12 Apr. 1007/2, I would especially impress upon you the fact which is illustrated by the lad whom I have shown you—the sporadic occurrence of these abiotrophic diseases. **1962** A. SORSBY in A. Pirie *Lens Metabolism Rel. Cataract* 297 The distinction between congenital and abiotrophic defect is not readily applied to cataract. **1991** *Cosmetics & Toiletries* Mar. 74/1 Microcirculatory activation is indicated..for the management of the aging skin..and of the regressive abiotrophic pannicular disease of the lower limbs and the female breast secondary to venous stasis and/or chronic venous insufficiency.

Abipon ('æbɪpɒn), *n.* and *a.* Also **Abipón**, **Abipone**. Pl. unchanged or with -s. [ad. *Abipón*, self-designation.] **a.** A member of an extinct native S. American people formerly inhabiting the Gran Chaco area of Paraguay. **b.** The extinct Guaycuruan language of this people. Also *attrib.* or as *adj.*
1822 S. COLERIDGE tr. *Dobrizhoffer's Acct. Abipones* I. 125 The equestrian nations remaining in Chaco, and still formidable to the Spaniards, are the Abipones, ..and Oekakalots, Guaycurus, or Leguas. **1898** D. G. BRINTON in *Proc. Amer. Philos. Soc.* XXXVII. 184 (table) *Guaycuru Dialects* Mocovi,..Toba,..Mbaya, ..Abipon,..Caduveo,..Quiniquinas,..Upper Tobas. **1912** S. A. LAFONE QUEVEDO *Great Chanca Confederacy* i. 6 Table II..serves to shew how intimately the *Toba*, *Mocoví*, *Mbayá* and *Abipón* tongues are related to each other. *Ibid.* iii. 9 The *Abipón* nation..claimed nobility for their head men. **1950** J. H. STEWARD *Handbk. S. Amer. Indians* VI. III. 280 D'Orbigny (1839) insisted that the *Mascoi* were *Guaicurú*, like the *Toba*, but Lafone-Quevedo (1896-97) compared the vocabulary with *Abipon* with a negative conclusion. Brinton (1898a) found a few similarities with *Chon*. **1961** W. BRANDON *Indians* 56/1 Eastern neighbors of the Diaguita were the Guaicuruan hunters of the Chaco region, some of whom, notably the Abipon, developed striking parallels to the hunting tribes of the North American plains. **1995** E. S. MILLER *Nurturing Doubt* 105 Furlong knew..little about the Toba except that they had killed the Jesuits who sought to 'pacify' them. Thus, he loved the Abipon, long deceased, but considered the Toba a belligerent and treacherous people.

So **Abiponian** (æbɪ'pəʊnɪən) *n.* and *a.*
1788 *Encycl. Brit.* I. 19/2 They are a strong and hardy race of people; which our author [*sc.* Dobrizhoffer] attributes to their marrying so late, an Abiponian seldom or never thinking of marriage till 30 years of age. **1822** S. COLERIDGE tr. *Dobrizhoffer's Acct. Abipones* II. xvi. 160, I am going to treat compendiously of the Abiponian language. *Ibid.* 171 This is the extent of the Abiponian arithmetic.

abled ('eɪb(ə)ld), *ppl. a.* [f. ABLE *v.* + -ED¹.]
†**1.** Capable; vigorous, thriving. *Obs.*
1576 F. CLEMENT *Petie Schole* (1587) 4 How fewe be there under the age of seauen or eight yeares, that are towardly abled, and praysablie furnished for reading? **1597** T. MIDDLETON *Wisdome of Solomon* ii. 11 Wee are the cedars, they the mushromes bee, Vnabled shrubs, vnto an abled tree. **1605** B. JONSON *Sejanus* II. i. sig. D, For this potion, we intend to Drusus, ..whom shall we choose As the most apt, and abled Instrument, To minister it to him?

2. [formed in contradistinction to DISABLED *ppl. a.*] Able-bodied; not disabled. Freq. used *euphem.* as the second element in Combs. to avoid perceived negative connotations of the prefix *dis-*, as in *differently abled*, disabled. Also *absol.* orig. and chiefly *U.S.*

1981 *Washington Post* 30 Oct. III. 8/4 The disabled vary like the abled. Some are terminally ill, some are teen-agers paralyzed by car accidents. **1985** *Los Angeles Times* 9 Apr. V. 1/4 In a valiant effort to find a kinder term than handicapped, the Democratic National Committee has coined differently abled. The committee itself shows signs of being differently abled in the use of English. **1987** V. MOLLENKOTT *Godding* iii. 39 Predominantly middle-aged, fully abled, self-consciously heterosexual married membership. **1990** *San Francisco Chron.* 4 July (Briefing section) 7/1, I was aware of how truly frustrating it must be to be disabled, having to deal not only with your disability, but with abled people's utter disregard for your needs. **1990** *Amateur Stage* Sept. 5/2 All the young members of this group suffer from cerebral palsy but insisted 'We are not disabled, we are differently abled.' **1992** A. MAUPIN *Maybe the Moon* i. 16 They were gentle, surprisingly naive kids, who took endless pains to guard against what they referred to as 'the exploitation of the differently abled'.

ableism ('eɪb(ə)lɪz(ə)m), *n.* orig. *U.S.* Also able-ism. [f. ABLE *a.* + -ISM, after RACISM *n.*, SEXISM *n.*², etc.] Discrimination in favour of able-bodied persons; prejudice against or disregard of the needs of the disabled.

1981 *Off our Backs* May 39/1 'Ableism'—that is, the systemic oppression of a group of people because of what they can or can not do with their bodies or minds—is the result of . . ignorance. **1985** S. E. BROWNE et al. *With Power of each Breath* 92 Sexism and able-ism work in concert to disqualify us from vast areas of social life. **1986** *Daily Tel.* 8 Nov. 15/2 The Labour party in Haringey has come up with the 'ism' to cap the lot . . . 'Ableism', presumably coined to describe those sinners who discriminate in favour of able-bodied persons for jobs on building sites. **1993** R. HUGHES *Culture of Complaint* iii. 162 But certainly clause (3) made it clear that he was against racism, sexism, ableism, lookism and any of the other offences against social etiquette whose proscription by PC was already causing such mirth and laughter among the neo-conservatives.

So **'ableist** *a.*

1981 *Off Our Backs* May 35/1 One must imagine trying to show a woman with lower body paralysis that she is 'accepted' by saying, 'We're all less strong than we'd like to be,' to realize how *ableist* it is to say 'We're all crazy'. **1990** *Rouge* Winter 27/1 The cover design appears to be rather male-dominated, white, ableist and playing right into the homo-sexuality - only - leads - to - isolation - and - unhappiness brigade.

abnormal, *a.* Add: **2.** Special collocation. **abnormal psychology**, the branch of psychology that deals with unusual behaviour, mental processes, and personality, esp. mental pathology and maladaptive behaviour.

1906 J. JASTROW *Subconscious* II. i. 174 May we follow the trail of the subconscious in its meanderings through the realms of *abnormal psychology. **1911** I. H. CORIAT *Abnormal Psychol.* p. vii, Abnormal psychology, or the study of abnormal mental phenomena, is one of the late developments of scientific medicine. **1926** W. McDOUGALL *Outl. Abnormal Psychol.* i. 1, I ask the reader to pardon my use of the expression 'abnormal psychology' in the restricted sense of psychology of functional disorders. **1972** I. G. SARASON *Abnormal Psychol.* i. 3 The term 'abnormal psychology' has traditionally referred to the types of human failures and inadequacies that we shall call the 'personal maladaptations'. **1987** A. M. COLMAN *Facts, Fallacies & Frauds in Psychol.* i. 13 Case studies are especially useful in the field of abnormal psychology, where detailed descriptions of the background, symptoms, and responses to treatment of individuals with unusual mental disorders can be illuminating.

aboral, *a.* Add: Hence **a'borally** *adv.*, in an aboral position or direction.

1883 *Jrnl. Linn. Soc.* XVI. 228 Mouth-plates rather broad, prominent aborally, having 5 or 6 short mouth-spines attached to the lateral aliform extensions, and directed horizontally. **1903** *Proc. R. Soc.* LXXI. 117 Sources of aborally-running fibre-systems. **1910** *Encycl. Brit.* VII. 675/1 The shell is similar to that of *Loligo*, but ends aborally in a little hollow cone. **1974** *Nature* 8 Feb. 395/2 The arms were always seen to recurve aborally through almost 270°. **1992** *Age & Ageing* XXI. 1/1 Under normal conditions, the major factor that limits the concentration of bacteria in the upper small intestine is intestinal motility, sweeping gut contents aborally.

aborted, *ppl. a.* Add: **3.** *fig.* Brought to a premature or fruitless termination; frustrated, thwarted, abandoned. Cf. ABORTIVE *a.* 2.

1907 *N.E.D.* s.v. *Monster sb.* and *a.*, *Monster-love*, a deformed or aborted love. **1924** *Glasgow Herald* 9 Apr. 10/3 Mr Wheatley having apparently availed himself of Mr Simon's bill to construct the second clause of his aborted measure. **1951** W. FAULKNER *Requiem for Nun* I. 17 Nor did it take the settlement long to realise that it was not the escaped bandits and the aborted reward, but the lock, and not a simple situation which faced them. **1958** A. SILLITOE *Sat. Night* xv. 200 It was hardly a stream, but an aborted branch-line of the nearby canal. **1976** *Billings* (Montana) *Gaz.* 7 July 3-A/2 Sudanese President Jaafar Numeiry broke off diplomatic relations with Libya Tuesday in reprisal for what he said was its role in last week's aborted coup against his regime. **1985** W. SHEED *Frank & Maisie* vi.131 The kid did look funny, and all it took was one repressed giggle or aborted twitch to have everyone shaking.

abortee (əbɔː'tiː), *n.* [f. ABORT *v.* + -EE¹.] A woman who undergoes an abortion.

1942 *N.Y. Suppl.* 2nd Ser. XXX. 732 There is a striking analogy between the female contemplated within the provisions of Section 2460, Penal Law, under consideration and the abortee mentioned in Section 80, Penal Law. **1963** *Amer. Jrnl. Psychiatry* CXIX. 982/1 Abortion represents psychological traumata to the abortee on many levels. **1976** in *1st Rep. Sel. Comm. Abortion* II. 51/1 in *Parl. Papers 1975–6* XV. 51 If somebody proved to me that all abortees were happy. **1979** T. KENEALLY *Passenger* xiii. 128 The partisan women on the islands of Dalmatia who were . . his last abortees.

above, *adv.* and *prep.* Add: [A.] **9.** *spec.* Above zero (on a temperature scale), *esp.* above freezing point. Cf. BELOW *adv.* 5.

[c**1840** D. THOMPSON *Narr. Explorations W. Amer. 1784–1812* (1916) vi. 120 The first and most changeable mirage is seen in the latter part of February and the month of March, the weather clear, the wind calm, or light; the Thermometer from ten above to twelve degrees below zero.] **1944** E. B. WHITE *Let.* Mar. (1976) 251 There was a snow squall the first night, and next morning it came off cold—one above. **1974** *National Skat & Sheepshead Q.* Mar. 11 Our winter so far has been mild with about one week of a cold snap. It was around 20 degrees above.

abrasion, *n.* Add: Hence **a'brasional** *a.*, pertaining to or formed by abrasion.

1932 *Bull. Nat. Res. Council* (U.S.) No. 89. 100 (*heading*) A study of the abrasional work of river ice and of glaciers. **1942** *Jrnl. Geol.* L. 731 Flutes are believed by the writer to be solutional rather than abrasional forms. **1986** D. J. DREWRY *Glacial Geologic Processes* iv. 61/1 Does this indicate that ice, frozen to bedrock under cold conditions, will have absolutely no abrasional potential?

abrogate, v. Add: **3.** *Immunol.* To suppress or prevent (a physiological process).

1959 [implied in *ABROGATION *n.* below]. **1965** *Science* 2 July 82/2 The inhibition of cell growth in the hybrids.., which is detected by tumor transplantation into mice, could be abrogated by treatment of the recipient mice with cortisone acetate. **1974** *Nature* 10 May 161/1 (*heading*) Lymphocytes from human newborns abrogate mitosis of their mother's lymphocytes. **1990** *EMBO Jrnl.* IX. 3821/2 PT application abrogates interleukin-2 (IL-2) secretion from a murine hybridoma.

abrogation, n. Add: (Example in sense 3 of *ABROGATE *v.*)

1959 *Nature* 5 Dec. 1815/1 (*heading*) Abrogation by injected mouse blood of protective effect of foreign bone marrow in lethally X-irradiated mice.

‖**abruptio placentae** (æˈbrʌptɪəu pləˈsɛntiː, æˈbrʌpʃɪəu pləˈsɛntiː), *n. Gynaecol.* [mod.L.: see ABRUPTION *n.*, PLACENTA *n.*] The premature separation of the placenta from the uterine wall during pregnancy, which can cause a haemorrhage.

1913 J. B. DE LEE *Princ. & Pract. Obstetr.* xxxiv. 445 Rigby, in 1775,.. most clearly distinguished between placenta prævia and abruptio placentæ... Rigby gave the name unavoidable hemorrhage to the former, and that of accidental hemorrhage to the latter, condition. **1977** *Lancet* 19 Nov. 1088/1 The second patient, aged 18, was admitted unbooked at 30 weeks of 'pregnancy' with a suspected abruptio placentæ. **1987** *Brit. Med. Jrnl.* 10 Oct. 896/2 The incidence of deaths from antepartum haemorrhage (all due to abruptio placentae) was 2.9/1000 births.

absence, n. Add: **[3.] b.** *Med.* Sudden, temporary, and unexpected loss of consciousness of which the subject is subsequently unaware, esp. in *petit mal*; an occurrence of this. Freq. in *absence seizure*.

1753 RICHARDSON *Grandison* V. iii. 21 In that space, Lady Clementina's absences were stronger, but less frequent than before. **1928** W. S. DUNN tr. *L. Muskens's Epilepsy* xi. 296 In many of these 'absences' automatic movements such as chewing.. may be continued. **1930** F. B. TALBOT *Treatm. Epilepsy* vi. 68 Minor attacks of epilepsy... In some patients they consist merely of momentary loss of consciousness, so-called 'absence', while in others they appear as fainting spells or periods of dizziness. **1957** *Encycl. Brit.* VIII. 654/2 Such episodes are frequently referred to by parents, teachers or classmates of the afflicted child as 'staring attacks', 'little absences', 'fainting turns', 'dizzy spells', or 'little blackouts'. **1966** *Epilepsia.* VII. 147 The most frequent combination is that of tonic seizures with variant of petit mal absences. **1968** *Brain Res.* IX. 372 Behavioural components of the absence seizure. **1987** M. J. NEAL *Med. Pharmacol.* xxiii. 52/2 Absence seizures are usually treated with ethosuximide.

absorptance (əbˈzɔːptəns), *n. Physics.* [f. L. *absorpt-* (see ABSORPT *ppl. a.*) + -ANCE, after REFLECTANCE *n.*, etc.] The proportion of incident radiation absorbed by a surface or object.

1934 in WEBSTER. **1937** W. E. FORSYTHE *Measurem. Radiant Energy* i. 23 If.. none of the radiation is transmitted, the incident radiation.. is equal to the sum of the part absorbed and the part reflected... If φ is the incident radiant flux, $\phi = \rho\phi + \alpha\phi$ or $1 = \rho + \alpha$ where ρ is the reflectivity and α the absorptance of the material. **1978** *Nature* 14 Sept. 95/2 Proprietary coatings include various Ni/Cr oxides/sulphides, which can have solar absorptances of up to 0.98 and infrared

emittances of less than 0.2. **1986** C. P. LO *Appl. Remote Sensing* v. 199 The behaviour of infrared reflectance or absorptance is largely dependent on the optical characteristics of the air-water interface within the cells.

absorptiometer, n. Add: **absorpti'ometry** (also †absorp'timetry) *n.*, the measurement of absorption of radiation.

1950 M. G. MELLON (*title*) Analytical absorption spectroscopy. Absorptimetry and colorimetry. **1955** C. R. N. STROUTS et al. *Analytical Chem.* II. xxi. 648 Absorptiometry may be defined as the measurement of optical density or of percentage transmission of light. **1973** *Nature* 20 July 186/1 Emission applications are far more important and consequently reduced the discussion on absorptiometry—a technique with important but limited applications. **1989** *Brit. Med. Jrnl.* 19 Aug. 478/1 The trabecular bone contents of the lumbar spine and the total skeleton, measured by dual photon absorptiometry, are roughly 60% and 20%, respectively.

absorption, n. Add: **[III.] [6.]** **absorption costing** *Comm.*, a method of calculating the cost of a product or enterprise by taking into account all production expenses, including overheads.

1953 *Nat. Assoc. Cost Accountants Bull.* XXXIV. 1081 This company has continued to use *absorption costing in arriving at inventory costs. **1969** D. C. HAGUE *Managerial Econ.* xiii. 290 There is nothing absorption costing can do that marginal costing, properly handled, cannot. **1990** R. IZHAR *Accounting, Costing, & Managem.* II. xix. 294 In the UK the official recommendation is to use absorption costing... It would be fair to say that financial accountants are more concerned with absorption costing, management accountants with marginal costing.

abutment, n. Add: **[4.] b.** *Dentistry.* A tooth that anchors or supports a prosthesis. Also *abutment tooth*.

1895 *Brit. Jrnl. Dental Sci.* XXXVIII. 550 Bridgework in dentistry is the building of an artificial denture.. depending upon the abutments for its stability and position. **1930** G. M. HOLLENBACK in I. G. Nicholls *Prosthetic Dentistry* xlii. 653 It.. does not provide as good retention, nor as good support for the abutment tooth as a partial veneer. **1963** C. R. COWELL et al. *Inlays, Crowns, & Bridges* xi. 129 The inclination of the abutments will determine the path of insertion of the bridge. **1975** H. THOMSON *Occlusion* xi. 215 With the exception of the canine an abutment tooth for a partial denture should have two roots.

Abwehr (ˈæbvɛə(r), ‖ˈapveːr), *n.* (and *a.*) *Ger. Hist.* [a. G. *Abwehr*, lit. 'defence, resistance'.] An intelligence agency founded in 1921 as a division of the German Ministry of Defence and expanded in 1934 by the ruling Nazi party. Also *attrib.* as *adj.*

1946 *Amer. Hist. Rev.* LI. 623 The activities of Oster, Hansen, Josef Mueller, and other *Abwehr* officials were never altogether unknown to Himmler. **1957** *Times Lit. Suppl.* 20 Dec. 771/1 The *Abwehr's* so-called Brandenburg Division was cannibalized, and five further Commando Battalions were formed. **1964** L. DEIGHTON *Funeral in Berlin* (1966) App. 2 Gehlen went to the Abwehr Archives at Zossen and burned every document there. **1979** *Summary World Broadcasts: USSR* (B.B.C.) 4 Apr. C2 During the Third Reich, the OUN bandits served as agents of the Gestapo and Abwehr. **1990** *Daily Tel.* 23 May 18 His task was to check that another Abwehr agent, codenamed Tate by MI5, was still at liberty operating independently.

Abyssinian, a. and n. Add: **[A.] [b.] Abyssinian banana** = ENSETE *n.*

1881 *Gardeners' Chron.* 2 Apr. 434/3 (*heading*) The *Abyssinian Banana in Jamaica. **1989** *Atlantic* Sept.

28/1 Seven to eight million Ethiopians eat the starchy center of the stem of the ensete, or Abyssinian banana.

abzyme ('æbzaɪm), *n. Biol.* [f. A(NTI)B(ODY) *n.* + EN)ZYME *n.*] An antibody that has been altered to give it some of the catalytic properties of an enzyme.

1986 A. TRAMONTANO et al. in *Science* 19 Dec. 1566/3 We now describe how these antibodies are capable of true enzyme catalysis when their proper substrates are identified. These findings portend the emergence of a class of proteins, having the antibody-enzyme dichotomy, for which the term 'abzyme' is suggested. **1989** *Economist* 18 Nov. 109/3 These catalytic antibodies—or 'abzymes'—look promising to doctors for such tasks as gobbling up blood clots or scar tissue, and to industry for producing certain sorts of bulk chemicals. **1990** *New Scientist* 24 Mar. 38/1 The new 'artificial enzymes'—catalytic antibodies which some researchers nicknamed abzymes.

acallosal (eɪkə'ləʊsəl), *a.* (and *n.*) *Anat.* [f. A-14 + CALLOSAL *a.*] Having no corpus callosum. Also as *n.*, (a person with) a brain lacking a corpus callosum.

1925 *Jrnl. Nerv. & Mental Dis.* LXII. 469 (*caption*) Partial acallosal brain. **1965** *Electroencephalogr. & Clin. Neurophysiol.* XVIII. 524/2 (*heading*) Visual and tactile responses in acallosal patients. **1965** M. A. JEEVES in E. G. Ettlinger *Functions of the Corpus Callosum* (Ciba Foundation) 92 Unlike most other studies of acallosals or sectioned callosals the studies have concentrated on the .. performance of acallosals. **1990** *Brit. Jrnl. Developmental Psychol.* VIII. 7 Children with callosal agenesis *are* able to develop perceptual and cognitive perspective taking. Thus, acallosal children do not perform in a comparable way to children with autism.

acanthocephalan (ə,kænθəʊ'sɛfələn), *a.* and *n. Zool.* [f. mod.L. *Acanthocephala* (C. A. Rudolphi 1809, in *Entozoorum sive Vermium Intestinalium Hist. Nat.* II. I. 5): see ACANTHOCEPHALOUS *a.*, -AN.] **A.** *n.* A member of the phylum Acanthocephala, comprising parasitic worms which have recurved hooks on their proboscis for attachment to the gut of vertebrates but have no gut themselves. **B.** *adj.* Belonging to or characteristic of this phylum.

1889 *Cent. Dict.*, Acanthocephalan, *n.* **1909** WEBSTER, Acanthocephalan, *a. & n.* **1916** *Trans. Amer. Microsc. Soc.* XXXV. 228 A long list of Acanthocephalan genera. **1917** *Jrnl. R. Microsc. Soc.* 126 New acanthocephalan... H. J. van Cleave gives a careful description of *Filicollis botulus* sp. n. from the intestine of an eider-duck. **1951** L. H. HYMAN *Invertebrates* III. xii. 1 The acanthocephalan worms were noticed about the beginning of the eighteenth century but were not clearly distinguished from other intestinal worms until 1771 when Koelreuther proposed the name *Acanthocephalus* for one from a fish. **1980** *Parasitology* LXXX. 407 The acanthocephalan *Moniliformis dubius*. **1987** R. D. BARNES *Invertebr. Zool.* (ed. 5) ix. 250/1 The acanthocephalan proboscis and neck can be retracted into a muscular proboscis sac in the anterior of the trunk.

acanthocyte (ə'kænθəʊsaɪt), *n. Path.* Orig. †acanthrocyte. [f. ACANTHO- + -CYTE. The earlier form represents a blend with ERYTHROCYTE *n.*] An abnormal erythrocyte having irregularly spaced, spine-like protoplasmic projections.

1952 K. SINGER et al. in *Blood* VII. 577 Since the most conspicuous feature of these abnormal erythrocytes is their distorted 'thorny' appearance in wet preparations and in the film, we have called them acanthrocytes. **1960** *Lancet* 13 Aug. 329/1 To recognise the acanthocytes it is essential to examine

fresh undiluted blood. **1967** *Arch. Neurol.* (Chicago) XVII. 8/1 Retinitis pigmentosa, night blindness, and acanthocytes (thorny erythrocytes) are present. **1987** *Oxf. Textbk. Med.* (ed. 2) II. xix. 139/2 Several variants of this condition have been reported; notably, the association of the acanthocytes and mental retardation with normal β lipoprotein levels.

acanthosis (ækæn'θəʊsɪs), *n. Path.* [f. ACANTH(O- + -OSIS.] Abnormal thickening of the prickle-cell layer of the epidermis. **acanthosis nigricans**, a form of this which is associated with darkening of the skin and hyperkeratosis in the affected areas (often a sign of an underlying carcinoma).

1889 in *Cent. Dict.* **1890** S. POLLITZER in P. G. Unna et al. *Internat. Atlas Rare Skin Dis.* IV. x. 1 (*heading*) Acanthosis nigricans. **1929** *Brit. Jrnl. Dermatol. & Syphilis* XLI. 122 The skin shows some acanthosis and parakeratosis, with a very dense round-celled infiltration of the superficial half of the corium, with a slight excess of deposit of pigment. **1966** WRIGHT & SYMMERS *Systemic Path.* II. xxxix. 1500/2 The clinical picture of acanthosis nigricans is characterized by thickening and deep pigmentation of the skin of the flexures, with hyperkeratosis of the palms and soles, and areas of depigmentation and warty tumours elsewhere. **1988** *Brit. Med. Jrnl.* 20 Feb. 547/1 In psoriatic skin mitosis is reduced and acanthosis diminished.

acanthrocyte *n.*, obs. var. *ACANTHOCYTE *n.*

accelerant (æk'sɛlərənt), *n.* and *a.* Chiefly *Sci.* [f. L. *accelerant-*, pr. pple. stem of *accelerāre* to accelerate.] **A.** *n.* A thing that causes a process, etc., to go faster; an accelerator. **B.** *adj.* Having an accelerating effect; accelerating.

1909 *Cent. Dict. Suppl.*, Accelerant, *a.* and *n.* **1933** *Federal Reporter* (U.S.) 2nd Ser. LXIII. 365/1 The doctor testified that appellant was then suffering from tuberculosis; that a bad cold would break down the system and act as an accelerant; that there are many other predisposing factors. **1951** *Proc. Soc. Exper. Biol. & Med.* LXXVIII. 281 Accelerant factors for a transplantable mouse mammary carcinoma of inbred .. mice are equally effective whether derived from fresh (unfrozen) or frozen homologous cancerous tissues. **1970** A. TOFFLER *Future Shock* xx. 406 In a world of accelerant change, next year is nearer to us than next month was in a more leisurely era. **1979** *Forbes* (N.Y.) 3 Sept. 94 The fact is, arson is not that tough to spot—by trained eyes. Such factors as point of origin and the type of accelerant used can tell much about a fire. **1990** *Cosmetics & Toiletries* Dec. 101/1 A general theory is presented for accelerant activity based on the possible alterations, at the molecular level, of the components of the horny layer.

accept, *v.* Add: [1.] **c.** Of an inanimate thing: to take into itself, to receive and hold fast; (of a substance, etc.) to admit, to absorb; (of an electronic device) to receive and respond to (data, etc.); (of an electrical or mechanical device) to allow to be inserted, connected, or attached.

1925 [implied in *proton-accepting* s.v. PROTON *n.* 3]. **1950** W. W. STIFLER *High-Speed Computing* xv. 386 An analog-to-digital converter is a device which accepts instantaneous values of continuously variable quantities. **1950** W. SHOCKLEY *Electrons & Holes in Semiconductors* 14 Impurities with a valence of five are called 'donor impurities' because they donate an excess electron to the crystal; those with a valence of three are called 'acceptor impurities', since they accept an electron from somewhere else in the crystal .., thus leaving a hole to conduct. **1962** *B.S.I. News* Mar. 24/2 Socket-outlets requiring fused plugs must not accept unfused plugs. **1967** KARCH & BUBER *Offset Processes* ii. 40 The RCA-301 computer accepts punched paper tape and produces a new tape, adding justification (otherwise keyboarded by the Teletypesetter operator). **1976** *Railway Mag.* Aug. 391/2 The ceiling of pre-formed Melamine-surfaced panels is designed to accept the fluorescent lighting tubes. **1982** *Brit. Telecommunications Engin.* Apr. 9/1, 200 payphones which accept..a phone card. **1989** *Q* Dec. 96/2 (Advt.), The distinctive loading facility accepts 3-inch CD singles without calling for an adaptor. **1991** *Photo Answers* Apr. 36/2 Matt or semi-matt papers accept dyes the best.

accessory, *a.* and *n.* Add: **A.** [1.] **d. accessory mineral** *Petrogr.*, a mineral whose presence or absence in a particular rock is disregarded for purposes of identification.
1882 A. GEIKIE *Text-bk. Geol.* 61 Minerals may either be essential or accessory, original or secondary constituents of rocks. **1931** A. JOHANNSEN *Descr. Petrogr.* I. ii. 28 In some cases the accessory minerals are of unusual interest or they have become so prominent that they are conspicuous. **1971** *Sci. Amer.* Oct. 50/3 A number of other minerals, including metallic iron, are found in concentrations below 1 percent. Eight of these 'accessory' minerals are the most important. **1990** C. PELLANT *Rocks, Minerals & Fossils* 11/2 Accessory minerals found in granite include sphere, magnetite and apatite.
e. accessory cell, (*a*) *Bot.* = *subsidiary cell* s.v. SUBSIDIARY *a.* and *n.* A. 1 c; (*b*) *Immunol.*, any of various cells of the immune system that interact with T lymphocytes in the initiation of the immune response.
1892 A. A. CROZIER *Dict. Bot. Terms* 2/2 *Accessory cell*, the sister-cell of a guard-cell; subsidiary cell. **1965** K. ESAU *Plant Anat.* (ed. 2) vii. 158 In many plants two or more of the cells adjacent to the guard cells appear to be associated functionally with them... Such cells are called subsidiary, or accessory, cells. **1974** *Jrnl. Immunol. Methods* V. 239 Passage of mouse spleen cells through a column of Sephadex G-10 beads results in the selective retention of antibody-forming cells and of accessory cells required for in vitro induction of primary and secondary humoral immune responses. **1981** *Jrnl. Exper. Med.* CLIV. 1005 Our interest centers on defining the immunogenic unit recognized by primed T cells, as distinct from any accessory cell requirements for stimulation by these two forms of antigen.

accidental, *a.* and *n.* Add: [B.] **e.** *Ornith.* = *VAGRANT *n.* 4.
1952 J. FISHER *Fulmar* xiii. 303 There is a March fulmar record from the coast of Maine, clearly an 'accidental'. **1954** R. T. PETERSON et al. *Field Guide Birds Brit.* p. xix, An additional 100 species have occurred in Europe fewer than twenty times: these are described briefly in the appendix as 'Accidentals'. **1973** *Biol. Abstr.* LVI. 693/2 The significance of records of accidentals and the possibility of indications of shifting range of the species is discussed.

accretion, *n.* Add: **9.** Special Comb. **accretion disc** *Astron.*, a rotating disc of matter which forms around a massive body such as a black hole or neutron star owing to the gravitational attraction of the latter.
1972 *Astron. & Astrophysics* XXI. 1 It is emphasized that *accretion discs can display a wide range of properties (depending on the accretion rate, viscosity, etc.). **1988** *Sci. Amer.* Apr. 15/3 The models suggest that some accretion disks could be sufficiently dense and hot for thermonuclear fusion to occur. **1990** W. R. PELTIER in Mungall & McLaren *Planet under Stress* (1991) 80 The 'accretion disc' of gas and dust that was probably created from this explosion was later the context for the Earth-formative events that began over 4.5 billion years later.

acerebral (eɪˈsɛrɪbrəl, eɪsəˈriːbrəl), *a.* [f. A- 14 + CEREBRAL *a.*] Lacking a brain; unintelligent, unthinking.
1968 *Punch* 31 July 157/2 Some urge in accordance with the principles of Darwinism has merged it [*sc.* the public] into one worldwide, multicelled, acerebral organism. **1990** *Chicago Tribune* 27 May XIV. 6/4 Should he corner you later, you can explain that your remark was merely an example of acerebral abecedarianism—brainless alphabetization.

acetal, *n.* Add: **3.** = *polyoxymethylene* s.v. POLY- 2 c.
1957 *Materials & Methods* XLV. 153 Called Delrin acetal resin, the polymer is still in an early stage of development. **1986** *Early Music* Aug. 419/3 (Advt.), A harpsichord jack...Made in low friction acetal (similar to Delrin). **1990** *New Cyclist* Summer 47/1, 90% of the freewheel is plastic, a very durable, rigid polymer known as Acetal.

acetate, *n.* Add: [2.] **b.** Cellulose acetate in the form of a clear plastic film, used in photography, in graphic design, as a display medium, etc.; also, a sheet of such film.
1934 *Plastic Products* Feb. 58 (*heading*) Applications of 'Acetate'. A review of typical uses of this molding material. **1940** *Chambers's Techn. Dict.* 6/2 *Acetate film*. Positive or negative film consisting of emulsion carried on a base of cellulose acetate. **1973** E. WILSON *Embroidery Bk.* ii. 136 Trace round its outlines with a black permanent marker on tracing paper or acetate (that marvelous plastic material which is as clear as glass, enabling you to trace your design perfectly). **1975** *Language for Life* (Dept. Educ. & Sci.) xxii. 319 Letters and words can be written on transparent acetates and then cut out. **1978** *Sci. Amer.* Dec. 138/3 The transparent screen is acetate ruled with closely spaced lines. **1989** *Brit. Jrnl. Orthodontics* XVI. 281/2 The lateral skull radiographs taken at the different magnifications are traced as usual on acetate sheets.

acetoacetate (ˌæsɪtəʊˈæsɪteɪt), *n.* [f. ACETO- + ACETATE *n.*] The anion, or an ester or salt, of acetoacetic acid.
1881 *Jrnl. Chem. Soc.* XL. 409 (*title*) Decomposition of polybasic aceto-acetates by alkalis. **1902** *Ibid.* LXXXI. 1527 On subsequent treatment with acetic acid, an oil was obtained from the benzene extract which..was identical in every respect with ethyl acetoacetate. **1970** *Nature* 25 July 384/1 We have..studied the effect in man of raising the blood ketone body levels by ingestion of sodium acetoacetate (NaAcAc). **1988** L. STRYER *Biochem.* (ed. 3) xx. 479 The odor of acetone may be detected in the breath of a person who has a high level of acetoacetate in the blood.

acetobacter (əˈsiːtəʊˌbæktə(r), ˌæsɪtəʊˌbæktə(r)), *n.* [mod.L. genus name *Acetobacter* (coined by M. W. Beijerinck 1898, in *Zentralblatt f. Bakteriol., Parasitenkunde, Infektionskr. und Hygiene* II Abt. 211): see ACETO-, BACTERIUM *n.*] A bacterium that oxidizes organic compounds to acetic acid, *esp.* one belonging to the genus *Acetobacter*.
1959 L. E. & A. M. REEVE *Gift of Grape* 105 But acetobacter is just one of the raiders. Putrefactive vandals of all sorts now join in the looting. **1975** P. V. PRICE *Taste of Wine* x. 181/1 The worst type is *acetobacter*, the bacteria which turns wine into vinegar. **1990** *Food Engin.* Apr. 32/1 The production of vitamin C starts with fermentation of D-sorbitol by an acetobacter organism to L-sorbose. **1991** *San Francisco Chron.* 10 Apr. (Food section) 2/2 Add 1 to 2 cups of unpasteurized vinegar that contains a live vinegar 'mother', or acetobacter.

acetogenic (ə,siːtəʊ'dʒɛnɪk, ,æsɪtəʊ'dʒɛnɪk), *a.*
Microbiol. [f. ACETO- + -GENIC.] Causing the
formation of acetic acid; producing acetic acid
as a metabolic by-product.
1981 *Arch. Microbiol.* CXXIX. 275/1 Hydrogen-
oxidizing acetogenic bacteria in pure culture are
presently represented by the two mesophilic species,
Acetobacterium woodii and *Clostridium aceticum.* **1984**
Science 9 Mar. 1022/2 A second group of acetogenic
bacteria converts hydrogen and carbon dioxide to
acetate and sometimes other acids. **1988** *BioFactors* I.
147/1 Acetate synthesis by the acetogenic bacterium,
Clostridium thermoaceticum.

acetoin (ə'siːtəʊɪn, 'æsɪtəʊɪn), *n. Chem.* [f. ACETO-
+ -IN[1], after BENZOIN *n.*] A hydroxyketone,
$C_4H_8O_2$, which gives butter and cream their
characteristic aroma; 2-hydroxybutan-3-one.
*c*1919 *Decennial Index Chem. Abstr. I-X,* 2015
Acetoin, see 2-Butanone, 3-hydroxy-. **1935** *Jrnl.*
Chem. Soc. 704 Acetylmethylcarbinol, or acetoin..the
aliphatic analogue of benzoin, is one of the simplest
unsaturated optically active compounds. **1976** *Ann.*
Rev. Microbiol. XXX. 561 If..fumarate is provided as
a hydrogen acceptor, acetoin (acetylmethylcarbinol) is
excreted, attended by a corresponding reduction in
formate and ethanol production.

acetolysis (æsɪ'tɒlɪsɪs), *n. Chem.* [f. ACETO- +
-LYSIS *n.*] The decomposition of a molecule
under the action of acetic acid; simultaneous
acetylation and hydrolysis.
1911 *Jrnl. Chem. Soc.* C. 1. 179 Acetolysis..is less
quickened by the sulphoacetic acid produced in the
acetylating mixture at high temperatures. **1923** *Chem.*
Abstr. XVII. 3098 Acetolysis of α-celluloses isolated
from 10..woods under carefully controlled conditions
yielded appreciable amts. of cellobiose octaacetate from
all. **1955** *Jrnl. Amer. Chem. Soc.* LXXVII. 3747
Acetolysis stops cleanly with cleavage of the first alkyl
group, cleavage of the second group being extremely
slow. **1973** *Microscopy* XXXII. 322 The technique of
acetolysis, which enables pollen to be concentrated
from deposits rich in cellulosic plant debris, was
outlined. **1990** *Glycobiology* I. 88/2 Deuterated
derivatives are conveniently prepared by using
deuterated reagents during the acetolysis.

acetoxy- (æsɪ'tɒksɪ), *comb. form* (and *n. attrib.*).
Chem. [f. ACET- + OXY-.] **a.** As an inseparable
formative element in chemical names: =
*ETHOXY- *a.*
1861 *Q. Jrnl. Chem. Soc.* XIII. 237, I have named
the new substance acetoxybenzamic acid. **1901** *Jrnl.*
Chem. Soc. LXXX. ii. 408 Aspirin (*o*-acetoxybenzoic
acid) does not increase the flow of urine, but somewhat
raises the total output of solids. **1990** *EMBO Jrnl.* IX.
3828/1 Thermocyte suspensions..were loaded with
acetoxy-methyl ester of indo-1.
b. Without hyphen, in *attrib.* use: = *ETHOXY-
b.
1945 *Jrnl. Amer. Chem. Soc.* LII. 1191 In acetic acid
solution the epoxy ring [of peracetic acid] is opened
and mixtures of hydroxy-acetoxy compounds are
obtained. **1981** *Sci. Amer.* June 72/1 The
cephalosporin molecule could be further modified
without altering its essential ring system by means of
chemical procedures that exchange the acetoxy group
(-OCOCH₃) attached to the carbon atom designated 3′
projecting for the six-membered ring for other groups
or for a hydrogen atom.

acetyl, *n.* Add: [b.] **acetyl CoA** [abbrev.] =
acetyl coenzyme A below.
1951 *Biol. Rev.* XXVI. 438 Adenosinediphosphate
+ *acetyl CoA + orthophosphate. **1974** *Jrnl. Amer.*
Chem. Soc. LXXIV. 3205 It would be of considerable
advantage if acetyl CoA were readily available for study
in itself and as a substrate. **1990** *EMBO Jrnl.* IX.
2444/1 The inactivation of HMG-CoA reductase and
acetyl-CoA carboxylase, and the activation of the AMP-
activated protein kinase.
acetyl coenzyme A, the acetyl ester of
coenzyme A, involved as an acetylating agent in
various biochemical processes.
1952 *Jrnl. Amer. Chem. Soc.* LXXIV. 3205 The
separation of *acetyl coenzyme A (CoA) from respiring
yeast. **1974** M. C. GERALD *Pharmacol.* vii. 127 Choline
acetyltransferase..mediates the transfer of an acetyl
group from acetyl coenzyme A to choline. **1988**
BioFactors I. iv. 267/1 Ten years ago Stewart and
Wieland (1978) synthesized acetonyldethia-coenzyme
A (acetyl-CH₂CoA), i.e. an analogue of acetyl-
coenzyme A in which the sulphur has been replaced
by methylene.

acetylation, *n.* Add: **a'cetylator** *n.*, a person
or animal capable of acetylation at a specified
characteristic rate.
1965 *Clin. Pharmacol. & Therapeutics* VI. 430 There
is a clear polymorphism for the acetylation of isoniazid,
sulfamethazine, and hydralazine, so that human beings
are clearly divisible into either slow or rapid
acetylators. **1973** *Gut* XII. 631 The metabolism of
salicylazosulphapyridine was studied in 16 patients with
ulcerative colitis admitted to hospital. The acetylator
phenotype was determined on admission. **1990**
Mutagenesis V. 553/1 C57BL/6J mice..are rapid
acetylators relative to the A/J mice. **1992** *Independent*
27 Oct. 13/5 To their relief, while the controls fell
equally into slow and fast acetylators, an amazing 10
out of 11 cancer patients fell into the slow category.

acetylcholinesterase (ə'siːtaɪlkəʊlɪ'nɛstəreɪz,
,æsɪtaɪlkəʊlɪ'nɛstəreɪz), *n. Biochem.* Formerly
acetylcholine esterase. [f. ACETYLCHOLIN(E *n.* +
ESTERASE *n.*] A cholinesterase that causes rapid
hydrolysis of acetylcholine after the
transmission of a nerve impulse.
1938 *Acta Ophthalm.* XVI. 157 This inactivation
consists in a hydrolytic splitting of acetyl-choline into
choline and acetic acid by the action of an enzyme,
acetyl-choline esterase. **1943** *Chem. Abstr.* XXXVII.
7354 (Index), Acetylcholinesterase. **1977** *Sci. Amer.*
Feb. 115/1 Carbachol (an agonist that experimenters
often use because it is not broken down by
acetylcholinesterase). **1987** *Oxf. Textbk. Med.* (ed. 2)
I. VI. 62/2 The nerve agents, a group of the most toxic
chemicals currently recognized as chemical warfare
agents, are irreversible inhibitors of acetylcholinesterase.

achiasmate (eɪkaɪ'æzmeɪt), *a. Cytol.* [f. A- 14
+ *CHIASMATE *a.*] = *ACHIASMATIC *a.*
1965 *Chromosoma* XVI. 542 A possible additional
genus with achiasmate bivalents is *Mantoida.* **1977** J.
COHEN *Reproduction* v. 108 Some mites have haploid
or achiasmate males. **1991** *Jrnl. Evol. Biol.* IV. 259
The strong trends for achiasmate meiosis do not apply
to quantitative sex differences in recombination.

achiasmatic (eɪkaɪəz'mætɪk), *a. Cytol.* [f. A-
14 + *CHIASMATIC *a.*] Occurring without the
formation of a chiasma (CHIASMA *n.* 2); having
no chiasma.
1962 *Chromosoma* XIII. 526 The occurrence of
achiasmatic meiosis..in the female prompted detailed
study of the behaviour of their meiotic
chromosomes. **1984** *Human Genetics* LXVII. 372 In
mouse and man..normal disjunction of the X and Y
is assured by an achiasmatic end association. **1989**
Jrnl. Heredity LXXX. 10/1 Most species show sex
differences in autosomal recombination, including
many examples of achiasmatic males as well as
achiasmatic females.

achievable, *a.* Add: Hence a,chieva'bility *n.*
1926 A. N. WHITEHEAD *Sci. & Mod. World* x. 226
Possibility is that in which there stands achievability,
abstracted from achievement. **1988** *Tennis* June 12/2

The problem is that the achievability of the requisite level of success almost never bears any relation to the realistic prospects of attainment.

achievement, *n*. Add: [4.] **b.** Special Comb. **achievement motivation**, motivation to attain a desired end or level of performance, esp. where a degree of competitiveness is involved; the drive to excel through addressing and succeeding at difficult tasks.

1949 McCLELLAND & LIBERMAN in *Jrnl. Personality* XVIII. 247 Our measures of n Achievement are not reflecting simply a temporary motivational state but do in fact represent . . the level of *achievement motivation a subject maintains over a period of months. **1953** D. C. McCLELLAND et al. *Achievement Motive* v. 145 As achievement motivation is increased, the imaginative stories that subjects write become increasingly more concerned with achievement. **1962** *Listener* 11 Jan. 61/1 Tests of what is known as 'achievement motivation' do discriminate between over- and under-achievers. **1982** *Psychol. Rep.* L. 51 One aspect of training children that seems instrumental in the development of achievement motivation is maternal expectancies for achievement.

achieving (ə'tʃiːvɪŋ), *ppl. a.* [f. ACHIEVE *v.* + -ING².] **1.** As the second element in Combs., either objective (e.g. *fame-achieving, deed-achieving*; now *rare*) or (esp. in *Educ.*) with adjs. or advbs. denoting a level of achievement (e.g. *over-achieving*): see the first element.
2. That achieves, in various senses of the verb; applied esp. to people who (work to) attain their goals (cf. ACHIEVER *n.* b).

1905 J. C. HEDLEY *Wisdom from Above* (1934) xiv. 174 The world — the great universe of intelligent man — the kingdoms, the races, the generations, of thinking, seeking, aspiring, and achieving humanity. **1952** H. H. MORGAN in *Jrnl. Consulting Psychol.* XVI. 291/1 This paper considers . . personality traits . . and motives of achieving and nonachieving college students of high ability. **1958** F. L. STRODTBECK in D. C. McClelland et al. *Talent & Society* iv. 142 In the nineteenth century there was a slightly different image of the achieving man. **1961** D. C. McCLELLAND (*title*) The achieving society. **1977** *N.Y. Rev. Bks.* 14 July 3/1 The achieving female of a hundred years ago has presented problems as a model for her achieving feminist successors of our times. **1993** *Times Educ. Suppl.* 5 Mar. 49/4 (Advt.), We are a happy achieving School where children and adults are valued and their personal growth celebrated.

Achimenes (ə'kɪməniːz), *n*. [mod.L. (P. Browne: see below), f. Gr. ἀχαιμενίς, the name of some plant.] A genus of herbaceous perennials of the family Gesneriaceae, native to Central America but cultivated elsewhere (freq. as hybrids) for their tubular or trumpet-shaped flowers; (also **achimenes**) a plant of this genus.

1756 P. BROWNE *Civil & Nat. Hist. Jamaica* II. ii. 270 *Achimenes.* i. Major, herbacea, subhirsuta . . . The larger hairy *Achimenes.* **1860** *Proc. R. Hort. Soc.* I. 163 The following kinds of flowers: — Verbenas . . Fuchsias, Tydæas and Achimenes, Bouvardias and Variegated Begonias. **1931** 'L. KENT' *Hills of St. Andrew* 2 A bank beside the Coratoe I see at my desire, Where scarlet achemenes [*sic*] grow. **1939** L. H. BAILEY *Stand. Cycl. Hort.* I. 206/2 The garden achimenes are much confused by hybridization, and it is doubtful whether any of the pure species are in general cultivation in this country. **1990** *Amat. Gardening* 3 Nov. 12/4 Dry off achimenes, cannas, tuberous-rooted begonias.

achlorhydria, *n*. Add: Hence **achlor'hydric** *a.*, exhibiting or characterized by achlorhydria.
1930 *Guy's Hosp. Rep.* LXXX. 253 Simple achlorhydric anæmia is a form of anæmia which is

not uncommon in women and occasionally occurs in men. **1943** H. L. BOCKUS *Gastro-Enterol.* I. xx. 247 Knud Faber . . claims to have found microscopic evidence of gastritis in all achlorhydric stomachs which were properly fixed at death. **1976** *Lancet* 25 Dec. 1369/1 Recurrent ulcers in an achlorhydric patient are very rare.

achlorophyllous (eɪklɔ'rɒfɪləs), *a. Bot.* [A- 14 + *chlorophyllous* s.v. CHLOROPHYLL *n.*] Lacking chlorophyll.
1889 in *Cent. Dict.* **1952** C. J. ALEXOPOULOS *Introd. Mycol.* i. 1 We restrict . . the term fungus to the nucleated, achlorophyllous organisms which typically reproduce sexually and asexually. **1991** *Nature* 10 Jan. 109/3 *Astasia longa* (a morphologically similar achlorophyllous alga that . . retains a plastid genome depleted of genes for photosynthetic proteins).

achondrite, *n*. Add: Hence **achon'dritic** *a.*
1920 A. HOLMES *Nomencl. Petrol.* 119 *Howardite*, an achondritic meteorite. **1965** *Science* 19 Feb. 858 The K/Rb ratios for both chondritic and achondritic meteorites . . are also shown in Fig. 2. **1989** *Nature* 11 May 127/1 IDP pyroxene data differ greatly from achondritic pyroxenes because major and minor elements do not display correlations like those seen in, for example, Pasamonte or Shergotty pyroxenes.

achromatopsia, *n*. Add: Hence **achroma'topsic** *a.*, pertaining to or characterized by achromatopsia; also as *n.*, a person with achromatopsia.
1980 *Neurology* XXX. 1064 Cerebral evoked responses produced by pattern shift stimulation were normal for black and white but abnormal for red and green, when stimulation was given in the achromatopsic field. **1986** *Times* 12 May 12/2 Claustrophobics, hysterics and achromatopsics. **1990** *Brain* CXIII. 1727 One is the central nature of the achromatopsic defect in every case, regardless of the extent of the scotoma, a fact rarely commented upon.

achromatous (eɪ'krəumətəs), *a. rare.* [f. Gr. ἀχρώματος (see ACHROMATIC *a.*) + -OUS.] Colourless; lacking in colour.
1882 R. QUAIN *Dict. Med.* I. 9/2 An achromatous or colourless state of an usually coloured tissue. **1889** in *Cent. Dict.*

achronological (ˌeɪkrɒnə'lɒdʒɪkəl), *a.* Chiefly *Lit. Theory.* [ad. F. *a-chronologique* (C. Metz *Essais sur la signification au Cinéma* (1968) v. 127): see A- 14, CHRONOLOGICAL *a.*] = UNCHRONOLOGICAL *a.* 1.
1973 C. METZ in *Screen* Spring/Summer 62 The filmic discourse, with its particular forms of montage (flash-back, a-chronological montage, etc). **1983** *Times Lit. Suppl.* 9 Dec. 1383/1 He admits to being achronological, but . . he claims that his book is not ahistorical. **1985** *N. & Q.* June 258/2 The achronological approach fails to make the distinction between the early *Roland* and late contamination of epic by romance.

achy, *a.* Add: Hence **'achiness** *n.*
1973 in *Webster's New Collegiate Dict.* **1988** G. NAYLOR *Mama Day* 259 At first it felt as if I had a virus: the achiness in my head, the fever.

acicular, *a.* Add: Hence **acicu'larity** *n.*
1956 *Nature* 17 Mar. 518/2 A further series of electron micrographs showed that during the reduction much of the acicularity of the particles was lost. **1982** in D. Francois *Adv. Fracture Res.* III. 1209 The degree of acicularity was estimated by measuring the grain size and also by comparison of dislocation densities.

acid, *a.* and *n*. Add: [A.] [3.] [f.] Similarly *acid air, precipitation.*

1955 *Tellus* VII. 253/2 The principal features of the chart of Fig. I are: (a) the region of acid precipitation along the west coast. **1974** *Water Resources Res.* X. 1134/2 Evidently, acid precipitation was occurring in the Northeast as early as 1952. **1982** *Washington Post* 3 Aug. A10/2 The suspected culprit is 'acid air', made up of sulfuric acid and related pollutants. **1991** *N.Y. Times* 18 Feb. 4/3 The striking figure of St. Mark..its marble nose has been stunted by acid air and water potent enough to destroy parts of the figure's fingers and of the Bible in its hand.

[**B.**] [**1.**] [**b.**] *spec.* in *Comm.* (further example); hence **acid test ratio**, a liquidity ratio used esp. in estimating the ability of an enterprise to meet its current obligations, usu. calculated as the ratio of liquid assets to current liabilities. **1928** WALL & DONING *Ratio Anal. Financial Statements* v. 90 A great many analysts have supplemented their measure of the total current assets against the total current liabilities by a comparison in which the inventory does not play a part. This has been called the 'acid test'. **1936** MACFARLAND & AYARS *Accounting Fundamentals* xxx. 477 The acid test ratio is the expression of the relationship of cash, receivables, and marketable securities.., to the current liabilities. **1978** *Business Week* 11 Dec. 112 The acid-test ratio — cash, cash equivalents, and receivables divided by current liabilities — declined to .94 from 1.3 the year before.

[**4.**] **acid-loving** *Biol.*, thriving in acid conditions. **1910** *Jrnl. Med. Res.* XXII. 155 Moro believed that it was in reality an '*acid-loving' organism. **1985** A. TYLER *Accidental Tourist* xix. 307 For azaleas and what else do you have, andromeda, acid-loving plants. **1994** *Daily Tel.* 11 Oct. 4/6 The bog..is home to the sundew, a rare acid-loving carnivorous plant, cotton grass, bog rosemary and rare mosses.

acidimetric (əˌsɪdɪ'mɛtrɪk, ˌæsɪdɪ'mɛtrɪk), *a.* [f. ACIDIMETR(Y + -IC.] Of or pertaining to acidimetry.
1844 *Mech. Mag.* XL. 335/2 Instead of using beads for preparing the alkalimetric and acidimetric test liquors..hydrometers may..be employed. **1938** *Thorpe's Dict. Appl. Chem.* (ed. 4) II. 644/1 (*heading*) Typical acidimetric and alkalimetric estimations. **1977** *Lancet* 29 Oct. 906/1 A new rapid acidimetric test for the detection of β-lactamase production by *H. influenzæ.*
Hence **acidi'metrically** *adv.*
1937 *Ann. Rev. Biochem.* VI. 38 The determination of ammonia in an absorption liquid may be made acidimetrically.

acidize, *v.* Add: Hence **acidi'zation** *n.*
1959 *Petroleum Handbk.* (Shell Internat. Petroleum Co.) (ed. 4) 136 The process of acidization has long been established and is used chiefly for limestone reservoirs. **1973** J. W. JENNER in Hobson & Pohl *Mod. Petroleum Technol.* (ed. 4) iv. 142 There are many ways of cleaning up and stimulating a well, the main ones being acidization and hydraulic fracturing. **1977** *Chem. Engin. Sci.* XXXII. 339/2 A model has been developed..which predicts the movement of the acid and permeability fronts..during matrix acidization.

acidosis, *n.* Add: Hence **aci'dotic** *a.*, of, exhibiting, or characteristic of acidosis.
1925 *Jrnl. Biol. Chem.* LXIV. 320 We believe that in anoxemia the true acidotic nature of diminished oxidation is merely masked at the beginning by the initial alkalosis. **1941** *Physiol. Rev.* XXI. 424 In acidotic conditions such as those just named, at least three closely related factors can be cited. **1961** *Lancet* 16 Sept. 664/1 He was drowsy, severely dehydrated, and wasted; his breathing was acidotic. **1985** M. F. MYLES *Textbk. Midwives* (ed. 10) xxxii. 554 The infant becomes acidotic.

acidulous, *a.* Add: Hence (in *fig.* sense) **a'cidulously** *adv.*

1889 B. WHITBY *Awakening M. Fenwick* I. xi. 283 Then she acidulously added, as the carriage drove off, 'You never remember what an old man you are.' **1986** A. POWELL *Fisher King* v. 29 He described himself rather acidulously as..the sort of child whose nose was always buried in a book.

aciduric (æsɪ'djʊərɪk), *a.* [f. ACID *a.* and *n.* + EN)DUR(E *v.* (or L. *dūr-āre* to hold out, last) + -IC.] Acidophilic; tolerant of acid conditions.
1910 A. I. KENDALL in *Jrnl. Med. Res.* XXII. 155 The writer proposes the name 'aciduric' in place of 'acidophilic' as the type name for these bacteria..keeping in mind..their ability to 'endure' acid. [*Ibid.* 166 The writer is indebted to Miss Anne Marjory Day for the coining of this word.] **1935** *Times Lit. Suppl.* 19 Sept. 583/2 Stabilizing of a predominantly aciduric flora by the oral administration of cultures of *Lactobacillus acidophilus.* **1964** M. HYNES *Med. Bacteriol.* (ed. 8) xii. 176 The members of this group are often..termed aciduric from their ability to survive in concentrations of acid that kill other non-sporing bacteria. **1989** *Oral Microbiol. & Immunol.* IV. 57 The possibility that S[treptococcus] mutans was capable of aciduric adaptation during a biologically-generated pH reduction was examined.

acidy ('æsɪdɪ), *a.* [f. ACID *a.* and *n.* + -Y¹.] Resembling or reminiscent of acid; sharp, vinegary.
1961 in WEBSTER. **1970** G. F. NEWMAN *Sir, You Bastard* 261 James had been too desperate to appreciate the acidy taste of revenge. **1972** D. KENNEDY *Cuisines of Mexico* i. 36 A Mexican brand of canned *chiles poblanos*..were..too acidy to be of real use. **1981** WILCOX & RANTZEN *Kill Chocolate Biscuit* vi. 113 A great many rather sad-looking vol-au-vents and sandwiches with curling edges accompanied by acidy white plonk. **1987** D. HALL *Seasons at Eagle Pond* iv. 81 A ripe McIntosh that detonates with the sweet-sweet yet acidy harsh texture of the accurate apple, Autumn's bounty.

acinus, *n.* Add: Hence **a'cinic** *a.*, of an acinus (ACINUS *n.* 4).
1953 *Cancer* VI. 1119/2 Franssen derived his tumor from acinic cells of the parotid. **1975** *Year Bk. Ear, Nose & Throat* 227 The mucoepidermoid and acinic cell tumors. **1992** *ENT News* May-June 22/2 Acinic cell carcinoma is an unusual form of salivary gland malignancy.

Ackermann ('ækəmæn), *n.* Also *misspelt* Ackerman. [The name of Rudolph *Ackermann* (1764-1834), German-born coach-builder and publisher.] Used *attrib.* with reference to steering systems designed in accordance with the principle (the *Ackermann principle*) that in order to minimize lateral skid while turning, the extensions of the centre lines of the wheel axles must intersect at the centre of the arc on which the vehicle turns.
1898 *Judges' Rep. Liverpool Trials Motor Vehicles* (Liverpool Self-Propelled Traffic Assoc.) 45 The steering is accomplished by means of a steering handle connected to the pivoted axles..on the well-known Ackermann system. **1902** W. W. BEAUMONT in A. C. Harmsworth et al. *Motors* x. 211 (*caption*) Typical Ackerman steering axle. **1906** —— *Motor Vehicles & Motors* II. xxxiv. 567 The front wheels run on pivoted axles, the steering being on the Ackermann principle. **1959** *Motor Manual* (ed. 36) v. 100 Translating this requirement into a mechanical linkage between the two wheels might appear to involve considerable complication. Fortunately, there is a simple method (generally known as the Ackerman principle) of achieving it. **1975** J. DAY *Bosch Bk. Motor Car* 170 The system is known as Ackermann steering, because Lenkensperger arranged for Rudolph Ackermann, a London bookseller and publisher, to

have sole rights to benefit from the invention in England and Wales. **1989** *Classic & Sportscar* Feb. 55/3 The 19th century carriage trade was fairly quick to take up Ackermann steering.

acme, *n.* Add: **3.** Used *attrib.* to designate (a screw having) a type of modified square thread whose grooves have sides inclined at an angle of 29°.

1895 *Amer. Machinist* XVIII. 2 Mr. Handy has named the new thread the 'Acme Standard'. **1920** *Ibid.* LIII. 105 The Acme thread was not designed for any particular ratio of pitch for a given diameter although W. S. Dix..recommended that the ratios of pitch to diameter be in the proportion of one half the number of threads or twice the pitch of the U.S. standard screw. **1930** *Engineering* 6 June 721/1 A narrow thread must throw up less metal in its thread than a Vee-thread, or an acme thread. **1964** S. CRAWFORD *Basic Engin. Processes* (1969) v. 116 Travel of the cross-slide is controlled by a screw, usually of square or acme thread form.

a contrario *adv. phr.*, var. ***E CONTRARIO** *adv. phr.*

acorn, *n.* Add: **[2.] c.** In the proverb *great* (or *tall*) *oaks from little acorns grow* and varr.; hence used allusively to suggest the significant (and often unforeseen) consequences arising from small beginnings.

1584 A. FLEMING *Withals's Dict. Lat. & Eng.* (rev. ed.) sig. D4, Of a nut springes an hasill, and of an Akorn an hie or tall oke. **1732** T. FULLER *Gnomologia* 197 The greatest Oaks have been little Acorns. *a***1795** D. EVERETT in C. Bingham *Columbian Orator* (1797) 58 Large streams from little fountains flow, Tall oaks from little acorns grow. **1923** *Times* 13 Oct. 7/2 Here in England, as nowhere else in the world, 'great oaks from little acorns grow'. **1976** *New Yorker* 1 Mar. 81/2 It is from such embarrassing acorns that Parkers grow. **1995** *Wire* Jan. 20/1 Great oaks from tiny acorns: in 1994 alone, Guy's output has been overwhelming, with the albums *After The Rain, Portraits* [etc.]..containing some of the most compulsive music to be heard all year.

acorn ('eɪkɔːn), *v.* Now *dial.* or *rare.* [f. ACORN *n.*] *intr.* To hunt for or gather acorns. Only as *vbl. n.* and *pres. pple.*, esp. in phr. *to go acorning*.

1821 R. WILBRAHAM *Cheshire Gloss.* in *Archaeologia* XIX. 18 To go aitchorning is to go gathering Acorns. The pigs are gone o' aitchorning. **1842** W. P. HAWES *Sporting Scenes* I. 152 It might be an unmanageable colt,..or a stray porker acorn-ing. **1932** *Times Educ. Suppl.* 29 Oct. (Home & Classroom section) p. iv/1 At this time of the year many children have a half-day off from school..to 'go acorning', and sell what they collect to pig keepers.

acourse (ə'kɔːs), *adv. colloq.* Also **a course, a-course.** [Repr. colloq. pronunc. of *of course* s.v. COURSE *n.* 37 c: see A *prep.*² 1.] Of course, naturally.

1895 S. CRANE *Red Badge of Courage* xiv 147, I thought a course they was all dead. **1906** E. DYSON *Fact'ry 'Ands* xvi. 214 Acourse, I parted me arf jim — couldn't have ther brick face t' do less under the circs. **1962** N. MARSH *Hand in Glove* iv. 103 'Lamps? ...Was there one here?' 'A-course there was.' **1983** W. KENNEDY *Ironweed* vi. 159 He give me a hefty wad of cash and acourse I blew it all.

acoustic, *a.* and *n.* Add: **[A.] [1.] [a.] acoustic hood,** a sound-absorbent cover, usu. used to reduce the noise from a machine or appliance; **acoustic microscope,** a microscope that relies on the reflection of sound waves to produce an image of the magnified object.

1962 *Acustica* XII. 139/2 Enclosures of this kind, known as *acoustic hoods.., do nevertheless involve problems of their own. **1985** *Practical Computing* Aug. 92/2 You do not need to buy an acoustic hood as the laser printer is inherently quieter. [**1970** METHERELL & LARMORE *Acoustical Hologr.* II. x. 117 Other topics explored include (1) theoretical performance characteristics of a 1-GHz scanning acoustical microscope.] **1971** *Nature* 9 July 110/2 We report on initial experiments with an *acoustic microscope operating at 100 MHz with a resolution of the order of 25μm. **1984** HOLTZMAN & NOVIKOFF *Cells & Organelles* (ed. 3) I. ii. 25 Acoustic microscopes detect differences in 'elasticity'— various materials reflect sound waves to varying degrees and show changes in such reflections under different conditions. **1992** S. S. HALL *Mapping Next Millennium* (1993) xii. 245 Calvin Quate at Stanford, as venerable a figure in the field as Binnig and Rohrer, has developed the scanning acoustic microscope, which applies something like sonar on a nanometer scale to map surfaces.

acquaintance, *n.* Add: **4.** Special Comb. **acquaintance rape,** rape of a woman by a man who is known to her.

1980 S. TROTT *When your Lover Leaves* (1981) 212, I'd fallen into the trap of so many women..who..could not bring themselves to report *acquaintance rape. **1984** *Gainesville* (Florida) *Sun* 28 Mar. 1C/1 Bright street lights won't prevent acquaintance rape. **1991** *N.Y. Times* 2 Jan. A1/5 The growing prominence of the phenomenon, acquaintance rape or date rape, raises as many questions about subtleties in male–female relationships as it does about criminality on campus. **1992** *Premiere* Feb. 94/2 After a charged battle of wits, Dino..initiates an acquaintance rape of the misguided missy (yeah, sure—she's crazy about him).

acquiree (ə,kwaɪə'riː), *n.* Chiefly *Comm.* [f. ACQUIRE *v.* + -EE¹.] A person or thing that has been acquired; the subject of an acquisition.

1969 *Financial Executive* May 36/2 Harassment of the acquiree's personnel by the investigator is minimized. *Ibid.* 36/3 Attention should be given to the competence..of the acquiree's auditors. **1976** *Harvard Business Rev.* July 80/1 The prospective acquiree's management may transmit the offer on the buyer's behalf. **1981** *Forbes* (N.Y.) 22 June 141/1 Pretty soon every bank will have to decide whether to be an acquirer or an acquiree. **1989** *Times* 22 Sept. 13/4, I have been involved in a number of corporate acquisitions (both as acquirer and acquiree).

acral ('ækrəl), *a. Med.* [f. ACR(O- + -AL¹.] Of, pertaining to, or affecting the extremities of the body.

1929 in DORLAND & MILLER *Med. Dict.* (ed. 15) 40/1. **1974** *Helvetica Paediatrica Acta* XXIX. 59 The case differs from most of the previously reported cases by the presence of acral dysostosis. **1988** *Brit. Med. Jrnl.* 5 Mar. 705 Acral melanoma occurs on the soles and palms. **1992** *Independent* 3 Mar. 17/1 Doctors..compare his disorder to 'canine acral lick', a compulsive disorder in which dogs obsessively lick their forepaws to the point of ulceration.

acraniate (eɪ'kreɪnɪət), *a.* and *n. Zool.* [f. A- 14 + CRANIATE *a.* and *n.*] **A.** *adj.* Lacking a skull or cranium; acranial; *spec.* belonging to the subphylum Cephalochordata (formerly Acrania), of the phylum Chordata, which contains the lancelets. **B.** *n.* An acraniate organism.

1879 A. S. PACKARD *Zool.* viii. 401 The Vertebrates are divided into the skulless or *acraniate..and the skulled or *craniate* (*Craniata*). **1893** *Stud. Biol. Lab. Johns Hopkins Univ.* V. 213 (*title*) An undescribed acraniate: asymmetron lucayanum. **1894** A. WILLEY *Amphioxus & Ancestry of Vertebrates* II. 46 Amphioxus, while possessing the general facies of a fish..has no skull, or, in other words..is Acraniate. **1977** *Compar. Biochem. & Physiol.* B. LVII. 167/1 The phylogenetic interrelationships between the three chordate subphyla, namely the tunicates, the acraniates, and the vertebrates, are still quite obscure. **1987** *Gen. & Compar. Endocrinol.* LXVI. 40 Of the four groups of chordates, tunicates,..appendicularians, acraniates, and craniates, the first three groups are suspension feeders.

acrasia (ə'kreɪzɪə, ə'kræsɪə), *n.*[1] *Obs.* exc. in *Med.* dicts. Also 7-8 **acrasie**, 6-9 **acrasy**. [f. Gr. ἀκρᾱσία bad mixture, f. ἄκρᾱτος unmixed, untempered, intemperate, applied by Hippocr. to meats.
   In certain (esp. med.) sources there is app. some confusion (both etymological and semantic) with *ACRASIA *n.*[2]]
   Irregularity, disorder; morbid intemperance, excess. In Spenser's *Faerie Queene*, intemperance or excess personified as an enchantress.
   1590 SPENSER *Faerie Queene* II. xii. 362 (motto), Guyon..Doth ouerthrow the Bowre of blisse, And Acrasy defeat. *Ibid.* II. xii. 381 Here wonnes *Acrasia*, whom we must surprise, Els she will slip away, and all our drift despise. S. DANIEL *Coll. Hist. Eng.* (1617) 156 A time [reign of Henry III] that hath yeelded notes of great varietie with many examples of acrasie, and diseased State, bred both by the inequality, of this Princes manners, and the impatience of a stubborne Nobility. **1707** PHILLIPS, *Acrasia*, Indisposition, Disorder. [Also as in BAILEY.] **1731** BAILEY, II. *Acrasy* (with Physicians) the Excess or Predominancy of one Quality above another in Mixture, or in the Constitution of a Human Body. **1743** R. JAMES *Med. Dict.* I. 2/2 *Acrasia*,..intemperance. **1780** CORNISH *Life of Firmin* 84 (T.) A little prone to anger, but never excessive in it, either as to measure or time; which acrasies..occasion great uneasiness. **1818** TODD, *Acrasy*, Excess, irregularity. **1826** J. S. FORSYTH *New London Med. & Surg. Dict.* 10/1 *Acrasia*, (From α, and κεραω, to mix) unhealthiness. The same with *Acratia*. **1853** R. G. MAYNE *Expos. Lex.* 14/2 *Acrāsia*, incontinence, or intemperance in food, drink, or any other thing; excess; also applied to weakness, or inability to move; or to want of tone, and so like *Acrateia*. **1953** HINSIE & SHATZKY *Psychiatric Dict.* (ed. 2) *Acrasia, acrasy*, morbid intemperance in anything; at one time it was synonymous with *acratia*, debility, impotence, inefficieny. **1981** *Dorland's Illustr. Med. Dict.* (ed. 26) 24/2 *Acrasia*, lack of self-control; intemperance.

acrasia (ə'kreɪzɪə, ə'kræsɪə), *n.*[2] *Philos.* Also 20 **akrasia**. [a. Gr. ἀκρᾱσία f. ἀ- privative prefix + κρᾱτός power, strength.
   In certain (esp. med.) sources there is app. some confusion (both etymological and semantic) with *ACRASIA *n.*[1]: see quot. 1853.]
   The state of mind in which one acts against one's better judgement; weakness of will, 'incontinence'. (Used esp. with reference to Aristotle's *Nichomachean Ethics* VII.)
   [**1836** J. S. BREWER tr. Aristotle *Nicomachean Ethics* 259 ἀκρασία and ἐγκράτεια are not perfect Habits, and consequently the former cannot be properly considered in the light of perfect Vice, nor the latter in that of perfect Virtue.] **1853** R. G. MAYNE *Expos. Lex.* 14/2 *Acrāsia*, incontinence, or intemperance in food, drink, or any other thing; excess; also applied to weakness, or inability to move; or to want of tone, and so like *Acrateia*. **1889** in *Cent. Dict.* **1952** R. M. HARE *Lang. Morals* 169, I shall not here inquire farther into the fascinating problem which has been called, ever since Aristotle's masterly exploration of it, the problem of *Akrasia* or 'weakness of will'. **1969** G. VLASTOS in *Phoenix* XXIII. 75 Most cases of acrasia occur when the agent is only half convinced of the goodness of an action. **1978** J. McDOWELL in Hookway & Pettit *Action & Interpretation* 149 There is a full cognitive equivalent to akrasia and it is at the heart of the

experience of thinking. **1980** *Pacific Philos. Q.* LXI. 245 Since the time of Plato, philosophic theories of practical reasoning have been such as to render the phenomenon of acrasia, or weakness of will, problematic, if not impossible. **1983** *Proc. Amer. Cath. Philos. Assoc.* LVII. 50 Aristotle's analysis of acrasia also points to the manner in which a state could become continent. **1984** *Times Lit. Suppl.* 21 Sept. 1056/2 It fails to convey the ghastliness of his continual backsliding, the miserable drama of his perpetual akrasia. **1986** A. E. MELE in *Philos. & Phenomenol. Res.* XLVI. 673 In eating the pie, Fred seems to exhibit weakness of will or what Plato and Aristotle called *akrasia*.

acrasie *n.*, var. *ACRASIA *n.*[1]

acrasy *n.*, var. *ACRASIA *n.*[1]

acratic (ə'krætɪk), *a.* and *n. Philos.* Also **akratic**. [As if formed on Gr. *ἀκρᾱτικ(ός, f. ἀκρᾱτ(ής powerless + -IC: see *ACRASIA *n.*[2]] **A.** *adj.* Exhibiting weakness of will or 'incontinence'. **B.** *n.* An acratic person.
   1969 G. VLASTOS in *Phoenix* XXIII. 75 Gallop.. clings to the notion that the people to whom the question is being put are somehow merged with the acratic man whose soul is 'the seat of conflict' between good and evil. **1969** R. ROBINSON *Ess. in Greek Philos.* vii. 142 The second solution as well as the first consists in showing that the acratic both knows and does not know that his act is wrong. **1975** *Canad. Philos. Jrnl.* Oct. V. 232 Though acratic action may be involuntary and indeed may entail the loss of one's normal self, it does not entail the loss of moral or legal liability to penalty. **1980** A. O. RORTY in *Social Sci. Information* XIX. 908 If philosophers who deny acrasia are self-deceptive and akratic, so are those who deny the integrative functions of the varieties of rational strategies. **1985** *Times Lit. Suppl.* 27 Dec. 1485/2 The akratic's failure consists in forming such an all-out evaluative thought despite his considering that, relative to all his evidence, something else is best. **1993** *Jrnl. Med. Ethics* XIX. 206/2 Declaring an akratic agent autonomous classifies him together with an ordinary non-akratic agent; declaring him non-autonomous involves putting him in with non-rational beings such as animals, comatose patients and those in advanced stages of Alzheimer's Disease. Neither classification is comfortable.
   Hence a'**cratically** *adv.*
   1975 *Canad. Philos. Jrnl.* Oct. V. 224 When you act acratically, it is not your normal self that acts. **1986** A. E. MELE in *Philos. & Phenomenol. Res.* XLVI. 678 If John had correctly gauged 'the amount of effort required,' he would not have acted akratically.

acro-, *comb. form.* Add: **acrocya'nosis** *Path.* [ad. F. *acrocyanose* (coined by J.B. Crocq 1896, in *Arch. de Neurologie* II. 218)], cyanosis of the extremities.
   1897 *Index Medicus* XIX. 864/1 (Index), *Acrocyanosis.* **1907** *Jrnl. Nerv. & Mental Dis.* XXXIV. 746 Perhaps the simplest form of vasomotor neurosis is simple acrocyanosis. **1930** *Heart* XV. 240 Acrocyanosis presents distinct contrasts with the variety of Raynaud's malady previously investigated. **1982** D. E. BAYLY *Reflexol. Today* (rev. ed.) ix. 32, I have seen many old people suffering from acrocyanosis (blueness of the extremities).
   acrodynia (-'daɪnɪə) *Path.* [ad. F. *acrodynie* (coined by M. Chardon 1830, in *Rev. Med. Française et Étrangère* III. 51), f. Gr. ὀδύνη pain], (*a*) (now *rare*) a painful erythematous disease, chiefly affecting the hands and feet of children; (*b*) = *pink disease* s.v. PINK *n.*[4] and *a.*[1] C. c.
   1839 DUNGLISON *Dict. Med. Sci.* (ed. 2) 12/1 *Acrodynia*, a painful affection of the wrists and ancles especially. **1920** *Arch. Pediatrics* XXXVII. 518 What knowledge we possess of acrodynia is derived chiefly

from the..Paris epidemic..first observed in June, 1828. **1922** *Brit. Jrnl. Children's Dis.* XIX. 23 The cases in young children in America, described during 1920 and 1921 as acrodynia.., are of the same nature as the Australian 'erythrœdema' [*sc.* pink disease] cases. **1987** *Oxf. Textbk. Med.* (ed. 2) I. VI. 14/2 Acrodynia in infancy, or 'pink disease', has been associated with the use of mercury-containing teething powders.

acroclinium (ækrəʊ'klɪnɪəm), *n.* [a. mod.L. genus name *Acroclinium* (coined by A. Gray 1852, in *Hooker's Jrnl. Bot.* IV. 270), f. ACRO- + Gr. κλίνη couch, with reference to the acutely conical receptacle.] A herbaceous plant, *Rhodanthe* (formerly *Acroclinium*) *roseum*, of the family Compositae, native to Australia but cultivated elsewhere for its pink, everlasting flowers.

1854 *Curtis's Bot. Mag.* LXXX. 4801 (*heading*) *Acroclinium Roseum.* The rose-coloured acroclinium. **1873** *Young Englishwoman* Nov. 547/1 The everlasting flowers—Acroclinium, Xeranthemum, and..Helichrysums. **1962** *Amat. Gardening* 24 Mar. 9/2 My own favourite hardy annuals are..phacelia, acroclinia [*sic*]..eschscholtzia [*sic*]. **1991** *Shepherd's* (Felton, Calif.) *Garden Seeds Catal.* 78/2 Also called Acroclinium, these classic crafters' flowers have strong stems and large semi-double daisy-like blooms.

acron ('ækrɒn), *n. Zool.* [a. F. *acron* (coined by C. Janet 1899, in *Mém. de la Soc. Zool. de France* XII. 295), f. Gr. ἄκρον extremity.] The unsegmented region at the anterior end of the body of an arthropod; *spec.* the prostomial region of an arthropod embryo.

1901 *Jrnl. R. Microsc. Soc.* Apr. 147 It is not difficult to distinguish six divisions..; but Janet raises the total to nine by analysing the acron into four somites. **1934** A. D. IMMS *Gen. Textbk. Entomol.* (ed. 3) II. 177 It is not regarded as a true segment but rather as a pre-oral outgrowth—the acron of Heymons. **1964** R. M. & J.W. Fox *Introd. Compar. Entomol.* ii. 43 The antennae are thought to belong to the acron and thus not to be true segmental appendages. **1992** *Development* CXV. 239/1 The anterior system controls the gnathal and thoracic regions..i.e., the acron (defined here as the brain and parts of the head skeleton).

Hence a'**cronic** *a.*

1964 R. M. & J. W. Fox *Introd. Compar. Entomol.* vi. 184 Holmgren, Hanström and others..erred in concluding..that the entire protocerebrum is acronic.

acrosin ('ækrəʊsɪn), *n. Biochem.* [f. ACROS(OME *n.* + -IN[1].] A proteolytic enzyme found in the acrosome of mammalian spermatozoa, which is thought to facilitate penetration of the ovum at fertilization by digesting the outer protein coat of the ovum.

1970 L. J. D. ZANEVELD et al. in *FEBS Lett.* XI. 345 The acrosome of the mammalian spermatozoon is a cap over the anterior end of the sperm head containing digestive enzymes...One of these enzymes..has been assigned the name acrosin. **1984** L. W. BROWDER *Developmental Biol.* (ed. 2) ix. 385 Penetration of the zona..has been ascribed to the action of an acrosomal proteolytic enzyme, acrosin, which has been proposed to digest a path through the zona in advance of the sperm. **1988** *Nature* 6 Oct. 546/1 Proteins previously tested as contraceptive immunogens include the sperm enzymes hyaluronidase, acrosin and lactate dehydrogenase C-4. **1992** *Jrnl. Assisted Reproduction & Genetics* IX. 34/2 The significant differences detected between filtrates in terms of spermatozoan motility and acrosin content cannot be accounted for by changes in the membrane integrity.

acrylamide (ə'krɪləmaɪd), *n. Org. Chem.* [a. F. *acrylamide* (coined by M. Moureu 1893, in *Bull.*

Soc. Chimique (Paris) IX. 417): see ACRYL *n.*, AMIDE *n.*] The amide of acrylic acid, a toxic, colourless, crystalline solid, $CH_2=CHCONH_2$, which readily yields water-soluble polymers.

1893 *Jrnl. Chem. Soc.* LXIV. I. 695 Acrylamide is prepared by saturating a cooled benzene solution of acrylic chloride with dry ammonia. **1945** *Jrnl. Soc. Chem. Industry: Trans.* LXIV. 233/2 When the hydrogen sulphate was heated to $130°-140°$, no significant conversion into acrylamide was observed. **1988** L. STRYER *Biochem.* (ed. 3) iii. 44 Their [*sc.* polyacrylamide gels'] pore sizes can be controlled by choosing various concentrations of acrylamide and methylenebisacrylamide (a cross-linking reagent) at the time of polymerization.

actinian, *n.* Substitute for entry: **actinian** (æk'tɪnɪən), *a.* and *n. Zool.* [f. ACTINI(A *n.* + -AN.] **A.** *adj.* Belonging to or characteristic of the order Actiniaria (the sea anemones) or the genus *Actinia.* **B.** *n.* A member of the order Actiniaria or the genus *Actinia*; a sea anemone.

1888 ROLLESTON & JACKSON *Forms Animal Life* (ed. 2) 742 It [*sc.* the ciliated larva] usually assumes the Actinian condition while in the free-swimming stage. **1888** *Athenæum* 30 June 830 A tube-forming actinian (*Cerianthus membranaceus*). **1889** *Proc. R. Soc. Victoria* I. 112 The discovery of three parasitic Actinian larvae on a Scyphomedusa. **1928** T. A. STEPHENSON *Brit. Sea Anemones* I. p. viii, I acknowledge the debt which I owe..for invaluable assistance during the early part of my study of Actinians. *Ibid.*, The present monograph deals primarily with Actinian morphology. **1992** *Copeia* III. 902/2 The host actinian represents the territorial center and primary source of defense for anemonefish.

actinin ('æktɪnɪn), *n. Biochem.* [f. ACTIN *n.* + -IN[1].] Either of two proteins found associated with actin microfilaments in striated muscle fibres and certain other cells.

1965 S. & F. EBASHI in *Jrnl. Biochem.* (Tokyo) LVIII. 7 (*title*) α-Actinin, a new structural protein from striated muscle. **1969** *Biophysical Jrnl.* IX. A12 We have prepared α-actinin by extraction directly from myofibrils at 2°. **1982** T. M. DEVLIN *Textbk. Biochem.* xxi. 1007 β-Actinin is found associated with the F-actin molecules and is a length-determining factor for the assembly of the thin filaments. **1992** *Proc. Nat. Acad. Sci.* LXXXIX. 9282/1 α-Actinin appears to occupy a strategic role in the assembly and maintenance of stress fibres of nonmuscle cells.

actinon ('æktɪnɒn), *n. Chem.* [f. ACTIN(IUM *n.* + -ON[2].] **1.** An isotope of the radioactive gas radon, of mass number 219, occurring in the actinium decay series. Now *Hist.*

1920 E. Q. ADAMS in *Jrnl. Amer. Chem. Soc.* XLII. 2206 The names 'radium emanation', 'actinium emanation' and 'thorium emanation' have been shortened, respectively, to 'radon', 'actinon' and 'thoron', names which suggest that the element in question is an inert gas. **1932** *Proc. R. Soc.* A. CXXXVI. 412 The transformation actinon-actinium A is accompanied by weak β-rays and strong γ-rays. **1938** R. W. LAWSON tr. *Hevesy & Paneth's Man. Radioactivity* (ed. 2) xvii. 165 The molecular weight of the emanations (radon, thoron, actinon) can be approximately determined by observation of the velocity with which they flow through small orifices. **1959** *Chambers's Encycl.* XI. 484/2 Its [*sc.* radon's] isotopes thoron and actinon are also radioactive emanations.

2. = ACTINIDE *n.*

1947 *Q. Rev. Chem. Soc.* I. 126 The term 'lanthanon' (Ln) is proposed to denote any element of the group from lanthanum to lutecium inclusive.., and to bring them into conformity with their new analogues the 'actinons'. **1962** P. J. & B. DURRANT *Introd. Adv. Inorg. Chem.* xxvi. 1130 The actinons are the elements following actinium in the seventh Period of the periodic table. **1984** GREENWOOD & EARNSHAW *Chem. of Elements* (1986) xxxi. 1450 The 'actinides' ('actinons' or 'actinoids') are the fourteen elements from thorium to lawrencium inclusive.

active, *a.* and *n.* Add: [A.] [8.] **active immunity** *Immunol.*, acquired immunity which is induced in an individual by exposure to an antigenic stimulus.
1897 MUIR & RITCHIE *Man. Bacteriol.* xix. 426 *Active immunity is obtained by (*a*) injections of the organisms either in an attenuated condition or in sub-lethal doses, or (*b*) by sub-lethal doses of their products. **1928** L. E. H. WHITBY *Med. Bacteriol.* ii. 16 In active immunity the defensive mechanisms of the body have been created either by a response to a previous infection or artificially by inoculation with vaccines. **1985** M. F. MYLES *Textbk. Midwives* (ed. 10) xxviii. 485 Some weeks elapse before the baby produces an active immunity to various organisms.

active matrix *Electronics*, pertaining to or designating a form of liquid crystal display in which each pixel is controlled by its own transistor, thus improving contrast.
1980 *Information Display* Nov. 9/2 To overcome addressing problems, an *active matrix silicon MOS wafer was used to address the display (one transistor and one capacitor per element). **1984** *Fortune* 28 May 76/3 While laboratory samples of active-matrix screens exist..the production process is still a question mark. **1992** *IEEE Spectrum* Mar. 3/1 Experts said the technology..could produce displays that are lighter..and more energy-efficient than the active-matrix liquid-crystal displays.

active site, (*a*) *Biochem.*, the region of an enzyme which binds specifically to the substrate and participates directly in catalysis; (*b*) *Chem.*, a region of a solid surface possessing catalytic activity.
1957 *Jrnl. Amer. Chem. Soc.* LXXIX. 2657/1 The substrate is assumed to be absorbed with a precise fit into an area called the '*active site*' of the protein. **1984** J. PENNINGTON in C. A. Heaton *Introd. Industr. Chem.* viii. 294 The term *active sites* was coined to describe those localities on the surface which would induce the desired chemical reaction. **1990** *Protein Engin.* IV. 117/1 The glutamine and tyrosine are the only polar, non-liganding residues present in the active site of the enzyme at close enough proximity to the iron atom to play a direct role in catalysis.

active transport *Biochem.*, the transport of molecules or ions across a cellular membrane against an electrochemical gradient.
1937 *Trans. Faraday Soc.* XXXIII. 912 *Active transport of a substance is brought about by some kind of *dynamic machinery* working within living cells. **1964** G. H. HAGGIS et al. *Introd. Molecular Biol.* vi. 155 Movement against the concentration gradient or, more generally, movement of the transported molecule or ion to a state of higher thermodynamic potential energy, is termed active transport. **1989** *Sci. Amer.* Nov. 51/3 Concentrations of micronutrients in blood plasma are usually low; to scavenge them from the blood, the choroid plexus relies on active-transport mechanisms.

actual, *a.* Add: **5.** As an intensifier. **a.** Placed before a noun to emphasize its exact or particular identity; (the thing) itself. In weakened use: precise, exact. Cf. VERY *a.* 10 b.
1869 'M. TWAIN' *Innoc. Abr.* lv. 601, I touch, with reverent finger, the actual spot where the infant Jesus lay, but I think—nothing. **1892** *Pall Mall Gaz.* 18 Aug. 1/3 The actual form on which the message was written is put into a little cloth box, called a carrier, and blown through a tube to the central telegraph office. **1914** S. LEWIS *Our Mr. Wrenn* xvi. 211 He was already 'getting right down to brass tacks on it',..he had already investigated four more plays and begun the actual writing. **1934** J. B. PRIESTLEY *Eng. Journey*

vii. 213 For most of the people engaged in it, excluding the technical men in charge, the actual work here is not so interesting as that in the factories I explored later, where the domestic and more decorative earthenware and porcelain are manufactured. **1976** G. GORDON *100 Scenes from Married Life* 37 Look, I'm sorry, friend of Ferdy Linden, at this actual moment I think you look idiotic and I find you boring. **1991** *N.Y. Times Mag.* 13 Oct. 51/1 They are some of Paris's most formidable fashion weapons—the embroiderers, button makers, jewelry and handbag craftsmen and the all-important *les mains*, 'the hands' that make the actual garments.

b. *your actual* (..): placed before a noun to emphasize its authentic or archetypal status; genuine, real, typical. *colloq.* (sometimes *iron.*).
1966 TOOK & FELDMAN in *Round the Horne* (1974) 97 Well chacun à son goût—that's your actual French you know. *Ibid.*, Well there's not really enough to build a career on in that. What you want to be is your actual TV personality. **1973** *Time Out* 2 Mar. 14/1 My impression is that when the surge of violence was on..quite a few teachers got messed about. It was somewhere beyond extreme rudeness, but short of your actual NAS physical assault. **1976** *Times* 23 Mar. 19/4 There won't be any room for your actual horny-handed sons of toil in the TUC; there'll be too many sharp-suited managers. **1986** R. SPROAT *Stunning the Punters* 103 One, since you ask, is too many Waverley novels. Whereas your actual Wild Romantic Gael was lying out on the hill after Culloden getting his Wild Romantic Arse frozen off. **1994** *Observer* 16 Oct. (Life Suppl.) 93/2 Several newspaper columnists..were let loose on the Net and decided it was full of silly little people and that 'yer actual human contact' was much better than online communication.

6. Phr. *in actual fact*: in reality, contrary to expectation or appearance; *gen.*, really, actually, as a matter of fact. Cf. FACT *n.* 6 b.
1900 in *N.E.D.* s.v. *Indeed advb. phr.* 1, In actual fact, in reality, in truth. **1947** *Sporting Mirror* 7 Nov. 8/1, I must add that in actual fact there was not much scientific football. But the dizzy paced thrills made up for that. **1959** P. BULL *I know Face* iii. 54 In actual fact we should have been sitting pretty, as the get-out was only £663 a week. **1980** R. QUIRK in Michaels & Ricks *State of Lang.* 9 We have come to insist that the different styles of language (or dress) required for different occasions and purposes are neither immutable nor even absolutely obligatory. Not that we have in actual fact levelled out to a 'unistyle', of course, any more than to a unisex. **1991** A. A. AIDOO *Changes* ix. 73 He would sit behind his desk at Linga Hide Aways after office hours, pretending he was working. In actual fact he was thinking about Esi.

7. *actual bodily harm* (*Brit. Law*), physical injury, such as bruising, broken bones, etc., inflicted intentionally on a person, but less serious than grievous bodily harm (cf. GRIEVOUS *a.* 3 b) under the terms of the Offences Against the Person Act 1861; also, in some instances, emotional trauma so inflicted. Abbrev. *ABH*.
1851 *Act 14 & 15 Vict.* c. 100 §29 Any indecent Assault, or any Assault occasioning actual bodily Harm. **1945** *Weekly Notes* 24 Mar. 71/1 Humphrey J. said that persons who were not acquainted with the jumble into which sentences in this country had got might be surprised to learn that an assault with intent to commit rape was not punishable by nearly as heavy a sentence as an assault occasioning actual bodily harm. **1977** *Abingdon Herald* 17 Mar. 17/2 At Didcot on Friday, McDermott,..admitted assaulting Mr William Collins and causing him actual bodily harm. **1991** A. ASHWORTH *Princ. Crim. Law* viii. §5 301 If the man uses force or inflicts emotional shock on his wife in order to obtain sex, he is liable to conviction for assault occasioning actual bodily harm or some other offence against the person.

8. *actual size* phr. used *attrib.* and *absol.* to denote plans, drawings, models, etc., which represent objects at full scale, or which are reproduced without reduction or enlargement. Also occas. as *advb. phr.*

1893 S. H. WELLS *Engineering Drawing & Design* II. xiii. 156 Dimensioning a Drawing.—All the parts of working drawings should be fully dimensioned the actual size of the part, blue ink being used for the dimension lines. **1901** T. WALTON *Steel Ships* vii. 180 His domain is the mould loft, where..he proceeds to reproduce the 'lines' plan upon the loft floor to actual size. **1953** *Radiology* LXI. 88/1 The point-by-point technique of plotting the frontal area occupied by the thyroid gland..has been simplified by the introduction of the 'scintiscanner' for obtaining an actual size scintigram of the gland. **1987** *Graphics World* Nov./Dec. 31/2 When drawing up the artwork it should be done at actual size (or reduced to actual size) to ensure that the image will work on such a small scale. **1990** *Artist's & Illustrator's Mag.* May 23 (*caption*) Because of the simple nature of these illustrations I worked actual size throughout the book for the first time.

actualité (ˌæktʃuːælɪˈteɪ, ‖aktyalite), *n.* [a. F. *actualité* topicality, news.] **a.** *sing.* Topical interest, relevance, immediacy; also, truth (this sense not found in French). Also *attrib.* **b.** *pl.* News, current affairs, events from real life.

1839 THACKERAY in *Fraser's Mag.* June XIX. 747/1 We are not going to praise it: it wants vigour, to our taste, and what you call *actualité*. **1884** *Athenaeum* 5 Jan. 30/1 French dramatists lose little time in the production of *actualités*. **1952** *Scrutiny* XVIII. 191 The *actualité* of those issues is apparent in the essay by him to be found in the present number. **1989** *Independent* 5 Dec. 19/6 Then—*actualité* radio at its finest—Goodey got arrested. **1992** *Independent* 10 Nov. 1/4 When asked why the company had not been advised to include the potential military use, he [*sc.* Alan Clark] said it was 'our old friend economical..with the *actualité*.'

actuarily (ˈæktʃuːˈɛərɪlɪ), *adv.* [f. ACTUARY *n.* + -LY².] = ACTUARIALLY *adv.*

1936 *N.Y. Suppl.* CCLXXXVI. 145 The actual contract is..for the payment to the beneficiaries of installments readjusted actuarily so as to impose upon the insurance company no greater burden. **1968** *Punch* 21 Aug. 261/2 Forty years ago a professional friend of mine, a Liberal and anti-Socialist, had it calculated actuarily that, for 1*d.* on the current income tax, everyone could have free travel all over the country. **1989** *Guardian* 26 July 23/6 The Heir Apparency is now Mr Major's to cherish or, like Jellicoe at Jutland, to lose in an afternoon. Actuarily speaking his chances must be fragile: he is her heir apparent, not theirs.

actus reus (ˈæktəs ˈreɪəs), *n. Law.* [L., = guilty act.] The action or conduct which constitutes a crime, as opposed to the mental state of the accused (see MENS REA *n.*).

1902 C. S. KENNY *Outlines Crim. Law* iii. 44 In these cases, from the difficulty of obtaining legal evidence of the offender's knowledge of one portion of his *actus reus* (*e.g.*, the adulteration, or the drunkenness), something much less than actual knowledge is allowed to suffice in respect of that portion. **1953** G. L. WILLIAMS *Crim. Law* i. 16 If I carry off my own umbrella thinking that I am stealing somebody else's, there are the *mens rea* of larceny and an act, but not the *actus reus* of larceny. **1992** *All England Law Rep.* III. 674 Lord Diplock described the actus reus of the offence as driving a vehicle in such a manner as to create an obvious and serious risk of causing physical injury.

acumentin (ækjuˈmɛntɪn), *n. Biochem.* [f. L. *acūmen* point + -*tin* (prob. after *VIMENTIN *n.*)] A protein which binds selectively to the pointed end of actin filaments.

1982 SOUTHWICK & HARTWIG in *Nature* 27 May 304/2 We propose to name this protein acumentin, from the

Latin *acumen* meaning the point. **1985** *Jrnl. Biol. Chem.* CCLX. 7404/2 Acumentin reversed profilin's effects on actin in both ionic conditions. **1988** P. W. KUCHEL et al. *Schaum's Outl. Theory & Probl. Biochem.* v. 125 Only one such protein has been described so far, namely, acumentin from macrophages.

acute, *a.* Add: [**2.**] [**b.**] Also *acute-care*.

1971 *N.Y. Times* 17 Feb. (Late City ed.) 32/3 The Department of Health, Education and Welfare..would provide $16.4 million this year for construction of new acute-care hospital facilities. **1985** *Times* 21 Mar. 37/4 (Advt.), Greenslopes is an acute-care teaching hospital of 417 beds.

ad (æd), *n.*³ *Tennis colloq.* [Abbrev.] = ADVANTAGE *n.* 2. Freq. *attrib.*, in *ad court, point.*

1928 in *Funk's Stand. Dict.* **1979** J. KRAMER *Game* (1981) viii. 134 In the final set, when I was ahead only 4-3, I hit the chalk with a backhand volley to save an ad Frankie held against my serve. **1986** *New Yorker* 13 Oct. 137/3 Mecir, with Becker serving, fought off three ad points that Becker held. He then went to ad himself with a tremendous backhand return. **1990** *Tennis* July 80/2 His serve spins away in the ad court, forcing you to change the direction of the ball.

ad (æd), *n.*⁴ *slang. rare.* Also **add**. [Abbrev. of ADDICT *n.*] A drug addict.

1938 *Amer. Speech* XIII. 180/1 *Ad.* or *add.*, a narcotic addict, especially a needle-addict. **1951** *Evening Sun* (Baltimore) 27 Mar. 4/1 Depending on the type of 'junk' he was using and the place and method of administration, he was an 'ad'. **1976** *Amer. Speech* 1973 XLVIII. 208 With the drug explosion, large hospitals have increasingly admitted more *ads* 'addicts' who have taken an *OD* 'overdose'.

adamancy (ˈædəmənsɪ), *n. U.S.* [f. ADAMANT *a.*: see -ANCY.] = ADAMANCE *n.*

1952 *New Jersey Superior Court Rep.* XIX. 145 The additional indubitable circumstance of plaintiff's election to disaffirm shows credible corroboration of her adamancy. **1963** H. BRODKEY in *New Yorker* 23 Nov. 122/2 The concern he pretends has a vast adamancy, a coldness of spirit, and the grace Oskar cannot help but display in his attempt to appear a gentleman. **1980** *Fortune* 17 Nov. 108/3 His adamancy dismayed Rosen, but Schwartz firmly supported it, even though in the short run it may have cost the company several million dollars. **1993** G. DONALDSON *Ville* 231 Maybe Jesse was about to come up with his own jammy, his own piece of adamancy.

Adamless (ˈædəmlɪs), *a.* [f. ADAM *n.*¹ + -LESS.] In phr. *Adamless Eden*: designating a situation or way of life from which men are absent or excluded and which is regarded, often *iron.*, as a variety of paradise.

See also the earlier *Adamic Eden* in quot. 1839 s.v. ADAMIC *a.*

1883 *Sat. Rev.* 23 June 795/2 It is not every young lady even in China, who desires to live in an Adamless Eden. **1895** *Daily News* 18 May 7/2 Only two males—a couple of professional players to strengthen the double basses—invaded this otherwise Adamless Eden; but an excellent performance testified to the fact that the ladies had spared no pains at preliminary rehearsals. **1936** O. NASH *Primrose Path* 218 Lonely Eve in an Adamless Eden. **1995** P. A. PALMIERI (*title*) In Adamless Eden: the community of women faculty at Wellesley.

Adams–Stokes (ˌædəmzˈstəʊks), *n. Path.* [The names of Robert *Adams* and William *Stokes*: see STOKES-ADAMS *n.*] *attrib.* = STOKES-ADAMS *n.*

1906 *Jrnl. Amer. Med. Assoc.* 3 Feb. 361/2 A case of Adams-Stokes' disease which I had the opportunity to observe presented symptoms of heart block. **1940** S. A. LEVINE *Clin. Heart Dis.* (ed. 2) i. 7 A patient may have a history of serious syncopal attacks with complete heart block (Adams-Stokes disease) and yet..will show..no..pain whatever. **1988** *European Heart Jrnl.* IX. 1008 An important finding..is the high percentage of sudden death in patients paced for Adams-Stokes attacks (12%) and Adams-Stokes equivalents (13%).

adaptationalism (ædæp'teɪʃənəlɪz(ə)m), *n. Biol. rare.* [f. ADAPTATIONAL *a.* + -ISM.] = *ADAPTATIONISM n.

1985 A. ROSENBERG *Struct. Biol. Sci.* viii. 243 Adaptationalism must be compatible with the possibility, indeed the actuality, that many evolved structures have a present function, but were 'not built by natural selection for their current roles'. **1988** *Amer. Zoologist* XXVIII. 200/2 They go on to allege that all sorts of problems with evolutionary theory, including a blind adherence to adaptationalism..can be laid at the door of reductionism.

adaptationism (ædæp'teɪʃənɪz(ə)m), *n. Biol.* [f. ADAPTATION *n.* + -ISM.] A reductionist approach to the study of biological adaptations which considers each character or feature of an organism as having evolved in isolation to fulfil a specific function.

1983 *Acta Biotheoretica* XXXII. 217 The conceptual analysis in the present paper has a preliminary character. It is meant primarily as a basis for criticizing various arguments against 'adaptationism'. **1988** *Times Lit. Suppl.* 19 Aug. 911/4 He enlists the somewhat dubious help of biological 'adaptationism' to make the point that assigning a purpose to a biological trait doesn't require knowledge of how the trait fulfils that purpose. **1991** *Nature* 11 July 117/3 In the English scientific context,..the complexities of conventional adaptationism may be underestimated by Gould.

adaptationist (ædæp'teɪʃənɪst), *a.* and *n.* [f. ADAPTATION *n.* + -IST.] **A.** *adj. Biol.* Of, pertaining to, or holding a view of the evolution of morphological features which stresses adaptation by natural selection.

1978 *Sci. Amer.* Sept. 161/1 Their work is informed by the adaptationist program, and their aim is to explain particular anatomical features by showing that they are well suited to the function they perform. **1983** *Man* XVIII. 786/2 La Fontaine may well choose not to identify with the adaptationist paradigm..but this should not lead her to characterise the biological approach as in any sense pitted against cultural explanations. **1987** *Nature* 9 July 121/2 Foley's approach to evolution is strictly neo-darwinian and (despite his protestations) equally strictly adaptationist. **1988** J. GLEICK *Chaos* 201 So an adaptationist explanation for the shape of an organism or the function of an organ always looks to its *cause*, not its physical cause but its final cause.

B. *n.* **1.** *Biol.* One who stresses the role of adaptation in evolution, *esp.* one who holds that every morphological feature of an organism is the result of adaptation for a specific purpose.

1982 R. DAWKINS *Extended Phenotype* iii. 31 History seems to be on the side of the adaptationists, in the sense that in particular instances they have confounded the scoffers again and again. **1982** *New Scientist* 6 May 360/2 The cladist uses his method to construct a taxonomy; the comparative adaptationist inverts the technique. **1983** THORNHILL & ALCOCK *Evolution Insect Mating Syst.* i. 11 An extreme adaptationist would interpret this behavior in the following way.

2. *Ecol.* One who believes that human beings will adapt their behaviour to accommodate changing climatic conditions. Chiefly *N. Amer.*

1991 *Washington Post* 22 Sept. C1/2 A temperature rise of two or three or four degrees spread out over 50 or 60 years? No big deal, say these adaptationists. **1991** *Gazette* (Montreal) 16 Oct. B2/5 The point of view of the so-called 'adaptationist' is not only shortsighted but also stupid. **1992** *Washington Times* 19 June F2/5

Stephen Schneider was one of the first 'adaptationists' (i.e., moderates) in the global warming debate.

adapter, *n.* Sense 3 in Dict. becomes 4. Add: **3. a.** Used *attrib.* to designate components and fittings intended to adapt one fixture, device, etc., to another, as *adapter board* (*BOARD *n.* 2 h), *card* (*CARD *n.*² 12), *ring*, etc.

1860 *Ure's Dict. Arts* (ed. 5) I. 8 An adapter tube is then fitted to the lateral cylinder. **1963** M. CAIDIN *Man-in-Space Dict.* 11/1 *Adapter skirt*, a flange or extension of a booster rocket stage or section that provides a ready means of fitting another stage or section to it. **1978** *Washington Post* 11 June F14/4 Accessory elements used in photography—specifically an antique lens, color filters, an adapter ring for the lens, a 5,000 watt studio light bulb, and a photo album. **1981** *Electronics* 20 Oct. 270/3 A universal adapter card that translates the 9516 bus structure into the bus structure of Millennium's 9508 microsystem emulator. **1986** *Byte* May 273/2 The plus sign cannot be displayed in graphics mode or by some display-adapter boards. **1991** *Airforces Monthly* Oct. 7 (Advt.), Features include a helical (rubber duck) antenna with an aircraft type BNC connector, a variable squelch control, earphone adaptor jack and crystal clear high fidelity speaker.

b. Special Comb. **adapter molecule** *Molecular Biol.*, a molecule of transfer RNA.

[**1957** F. H. C. CRICK in *Struct. Nucleic Acids* (Biochem. Soc.) 25 The combination between each amino acid and its own specific adaptor could be made by a special enzyme, or enzymes.] **1958** — in *Symp. Soc. Exper. Biol.* XII. 155 It is therefore a natural hypothesis that the amino acid is carried to the template by an '*adaptor*' molecule. **1983** B. LEWIN *Genes* vii. 103/1 Transfer RNA occupies a pivotal position in protein synthesis, providing the adaptor molecule that accomplishes the translation of each nucleotide triplet into an amino acid.

adaptive, *a.* Add: **2.** Special collocations: **adaptive control**, a form of control in which the control parameters are automatically adjusted as conditions change so as to optimize performance.

1958 *IRE Trans. Automatic Control* Dec. 102 (*title*) A survey of *adaptive control systems. *Ibid.* 108/1 In answers to these questions may lie the fundamental principles of adaptive control. **1968** *Brit. Med. Bull.* XXIV. 251/1 A self-optimizing (also called 'adaptive control') system is one that operates by continuously maximizing an overall performance index by adjusting the characteristics of the system. **1984** J. F. LAMB et al. *Essent. Physiol.* (ed. 2) i. 13 Adaptive control systems are those which change to meet changing needs.

adaptive optics, a system for the automatic adjustment of reflecting surfaces in some astronomical telescopes so as to compensate for varying distortion caused by atmospheric turbulence.

1976 *Jrnl. Optical Soc. Amer.* LXVI. 193/1 A considerable degree of interest has developed in the area of *adaptive optics to be used for correction of wave-front distortion induced by atmospheric turbulence. **1987** *New Scientist* 17 Dec. 16/3 A new system called 'adaptive optics' will take care of atmospheric effects. It has to adjust the shape of the mirror 20 to 100 times per second.

adaptogen (æ'dæptədʒən), *n. Alternative Med.* [ad. Russ. *adaptogen* (used by N. V. Lazarev): see ADAPT *v.*, -OGEN.] Any of a class of natural substances, of which ginseng is the best known, which in herbal medicine are considered to help the body adapt to stress and to exert a normalizing effect upon bodily processes.

1969 *Ann. Rev. Pharmacol.* IX. 419 The theoretical basis for separation of a new group of medicinal substances was laid down by Lazarev... The medicinal substances causing SNIR [*sc.* state of nonspecifically increased resistance] were named 'adaptogens'. **1980** J. H. APPLEBY tr. *Brekhman's Man & Biol. Active Substances* iii. 59 Eleutherococcus root extract, the most studied and widely used of the adaptogens. **1991** *Musclemag* Mar. 102/1 Russian athletes..have relied for years on adaptogens—biologically active substances, derived from natural plant and animal sources, which reduce training stress and speed recovery.

So **adapto'genic** *a.*
1969 *Ann. Rev. Pharmacol.* IX. 419 This comparatively recent history of the discovery of adaptogenic action of dibazol and its analogues had been preceded by attainments of folk medicine of long standing. **1988** R. MABEY et al. *Compl. New Herbal* v. 189 Ginseng has an overall adaptogenic effect.

add *n.*, var. of *AD *n.*[4]

add back ('ædbæk), *n. phr. Accounting.* Also **addback, add-back.** [f. ADD *v.*, BACK *adv.*] A method of accounting in which items not affecting working capital are added to or deducted from net income; an item thus added or deducted.
1972 *N.Y. Times* 4 June v. 9/6 Part of the regular entry fees in all shows go for administrative expenses, so the exhibitor rarely has a chance to break even. With the add back system, he can come out ahead. **1989** *Times* 17 Apr. 28/7 After discounting for drought 'add-backs,' the real gross national product of the US may have shown negligible growth in the first quarter.

adder, *n.*[2] Add: [5.] **adder-tongue** *N. Amer.* = ADDER'S-TONGUE *n.* 1, *3.
1817 A. EATON *Man. Bot.* 124 *Ophioglossum.* Capsules round, 1-celled, opening transversely; they are placed on a somewhat jointed spike in two close rows..(*adder-tongue fern). **1898** D. C. SCOTT *Labor & Angel* 52 The adder-tongue swinging its golden bells As the light wind swoops. **1927** A. C. PARKER *Indian How Bk.* (1931) xli. 187 Leaves like those of the adder tongue, wild mustard, [etc.]..are all good as greens or pot herbs. **1967** B. J. BANFILL *Pioneer Nurse* x. 122 The earthy carpet, cushioned with pink and white flowers and yellow adder tongues.

adder's-tongue, *n.* Add: **3.** Any of various dog's-tooth violets (genus *Erythronium*) native to N. America, *esp.* (more fully *yellow adder's-tongue*) *E. americanum. N. Amer.*
1818 A. EATON *Man. Bot.* (ed. 2) 242 *Erythronium...dens-canis* (dog tooth violet, adder's tongue..) leaves oblong-ovate, glabrous, spotted. **1820** in *Mass. Hist. Soc. Coll.* (1832) 2nd Ser. IX. 150 Plants, which are indigenous in the township of Middlebury, [Vermont, include].. *Erythronium lanceolatum,* (*Pursh.*) Adder's tongue. **1894** J. BURROUGHS *Riverby* 25 *Erythronium*... How it came to be called adder's-tongue I do not know; probably from the spotted character of the leaf, which might suggest a snake. **1947** *Amer. Midland Naturalist* July 37 Yellow Adders-tongue [is] abundant in bottomland forest. **1962** A. LURIE *Love & Friendship* xiii. 249 Thin green grass grew in the clearings, and adder's-tongues with their leopard-spotted leaves. **1968** PETERSON & MCKENNY *Field Guide Wildflowers Northeastern & North-Central N. Amer.* 102 Trout-lily, adder's-tongue *Erythronium americanum*... March–May.

add-in ('ædɪn), *a.* and *n.* Chiefly *Computing.* [f. ADD *v.* + IN *adv.* Cf. ADD-ON *n.* (and *a.*)] **A.** *adj.* Designating something added to a system internally to improve its capabilities or performance.
1984 *InfoWorld* 8 Oct. 61/2 If you have a substantial investment in add-in hardware and software for the IBM PC that will not work (or work well) on the IBM PC AT, then the Deskpro is a good bet for you. **1985** *Practical Computing* May 31/3 We have an add-in drive for the IBM PC which allows a low-cost upgrade to the XT level. **1988** *Washington Post* 29 Feb. F47/3 It [*sc.* Quattro] produces beautiful charts in a variety of styles that 1-2-3 can't duplicate, even with graphics add-in programs. **1991** *Personal Computer World* Feb. 128/3 Choosing a Micronics 80486 motherboard with nothing but computer and RAM and adding the interfaces and peripherals it wants using add-in boards.

B. *n.* An add-in device.
1988 *Computer Weekly* 14 Apr. 6 Turning PCs into workstations for Cad or engineering applications means expensive add-ins. **1988** *PC Mag.* Oct. 99/1 A special menu option whereby users can install all the add-ins that Computer Associates hope will be produced. **1989** *PC World* Oct. 62/3 Hundreds of software houses have written add-ons and add-ins for the spreadsheet. **1991** *Choice* Mar. 75/2 There are less costly ways to provide revitalising water therapy, from simple bathtub air-mat add-ins to double-sized, air-jetted baths.

Addisonian (ædɪ'səʊnɪən), *a. Path.* [f. ADDISON *n.* + -IAN.] **1.** **Addisonian (pernicious) anaemia** = *pernicious anaemia* s.v. PERNICIOUS *a.*[1] a.
1910 *Practitioner* Jan. 126 The appearance presented by the tongue described by Dr. W. Hunter as specific for Addisonian anæmia. **1933** *Discovery* Mar. 83/1 Pernicious anaemia, or as it is more generally known, Addisonian anaemia, was first described by Addison, a physician at Guy's, in 1856. **1960** *Lancet* 27 Aug. 458/2 (*title*) Cerebral manifestations of Addisonian pernicious anæmia. **1984** M. J. TAUSSIG *Processes in Path. & Microbiol.* (ed. 2) ii. 200 Antibodies which inhibit a biologically active secreted molecule are found in pernicious (Addisonian) anaemia, an anaemia which results from insufficient uptake of vitamin B_{12} by the stomach.

2. Also **addisonian.** Characteristic of or affected with Addison's disease. **Addisonian crisis,** a state of shock in a person with Addison's disease.
1929 M. A. GOLDZIEHER *Adrenals* v. 272 The hypoglycemia and increased glucose tolerance of the Addisonian patients. **1946** L. J. SOFER *Dis. Adrenals* v. 98 An increase in cyanosis associated with Addisonian crisis and vascular collapse. **1977** *Lancet* 5 Nov. 955/2 Mean A.C.T.H. levels were raised $(107 \pm 12 \text{ pmol/l})$ in addisonian outpatients on cortisone acetate. **1983** *Oxf. Textbk. Med.* II. xxi. 125/2 Addisonian crisis may be accompanied by generalized convulsions, which are attributed to hyponatraemia and water intoxication.

addition, *n.* Add: [3.] †**b.** *U.S.* An adjacent piece of land added to an existing holding. *Obs.*
1636 *Official Rec. Springfield, Mass.* (1898) I. 159 [A lot with] an adition..of as much marish as makes the wholel twenty fouer acres. **1721** *Mass. House of Representatives Jrnl.* (1922) III. 12 A Petition..Praying for an Addition of 3700 Acres of Land, to be added to their former Grant.

c. *U.S.* An area laid out as an extension of a town.
1786 *Maryland Jrnl.* 6 Jan. (Advt.) (Th.), Found, in Howard's new Addition to Baltimore-Town, 127 panes of glass. **1885** *Harper's Mag.* Apr. 694/2 The centre of an important new quarter of the town, or 'addition', as the trans-Mississippi word is. **1941** *Morgantown* (W. Va.) *Post* 18 Mar. 10/3 The Guardian Investment Company deeded a lot in Norwood Addition, Town of Sabraton, to Vinnie Sanders.

d. A wing, room, etc., added as an extension of an existing building. orig. *U.S.*
*c*1638 *Harvard College Rec.* (1925) I. 172 Ffor unloading the Timber prepard for y[e] Addition: [£]3. 10[s.]. **1679** MOXON *Mech. Exercises* I. 130 If either a Quirk or any Addition be added to the building..you must describe it also proportionably. **1887** M. E. WILKINS *Humble Romance* 120 Hiram Arms never

ought to have put on them additions. **1978** *Lancashire Life* July 37/3 Instead of being tied-in to the building next-door this 19th century addition was simply slapped-up alongside it. **1991** *Atlantic* Oct. 121/2 An ill-conceived and weirdly imitative addition to the Kimbell Art Museum was about to be built. **1992** *Down East* Feb. 80/3 (Advt.), Comfortable, well-kept original home, well-built mother-in-law addition, spacious decks overlooking back yard, mountain views.

additive, *a.* and *n.* Add: [**B.**] **2.** *Comb.* **additive-free**.

1975 *Business Week* 17 Mar. 82/2 But these additive-free materials are difficult for converters to handle. **1982** D. CANTER et al. *Cranks Recipe Book* (1985) 12 James More-Molyneux, whose ready response resulted in Loseley becoming one of the largest suppliers of additive-free yoghourt and ice-cream for the whole of the south of England. **1990** D. MABEY et al. *Thorsons Organic Consumer Guide* I. i. 27 Organic food should be additive-free, but not all additive-free produce is organic.

address, *v.* Senses 8 e, f, g in Dict. become 8 f, g, h. Add: [**II.**] [**8.**] **e.** *trans.* To pay one's addresses to (a woman); to woo, court. Cf. ADDRESS *v.* 8 c. *arch.*

1775 SHERIDAN *Rivals* III. v. 57 To prevent the confusion that might arise . . from our both addressing the same lady . . I shall expect the honour of your company . . to settle our pretensions . . in King's Mead Fields. **1814** JANE AUSTEN *Mansfield Park* III. i. 19 You may live eighteen years longer . . without being addressed by a man of half Mr. Crawford's estate. **1835** *Fraser's Mag.* XII. 68/1 It appears that when little more than a girl, she had been addressed by a young gentleman abroad. *a* **1927** *Star of Logy Bay* in G. S. Doyle *Old Time Songs & Poetry of Newfoundland* 68 If you address my daughter, I'll send her far away, And she never will return again, While you're in Logy Bay.

addressin (ə'drɛsɪn), *n. Biochem.* [f. ADDRESS *n.* + -IN¹.] Any of a group of substances which appear to act as position markers and to mediate cellular interactions; *spec.* in **vascular addressin**, such a substance occurring in specialized blood vessels.

1988 P. R. STREETER et al. in *Nature* 7 Jan. 43/1 Because its apparent role is to convey position (tissue address) information to circulating lymphocytes, we propose to call this mucosa-specific antigen and related tissue-specific determinants in other sites 'vascular addressins'. **1990** *Glycobiol.* I. 33/2 ELAM-1 . . , a vascular addressin that acts from the endothelial cell surface and increases the adherence properties of neutrophils. **1990** *Laboratory Investigation* LXIII. 476 The addressin MECA-325, a marker of mouse lymph node high endothelial venules.

adelphophagy (ˌædɛl'fɒfədʒɪ), *n.* Also **adelphophagia** (æˌdɛlfəʊ'feɪdʒɪə) [ad. F. *adelphophagie* (coined in sense 1 by A. Giard 1899, in *Cinquantenaire de la Soc. de Biol.* (Paris) *Volume Jubilaire* 656), f. Gr. ἀδελφός brother: see -PHAGY.]

1. *Genetics.* The fusion of gametes of the same sex. *rare.*

1901 *Jrnl. R. Microsc. Soc.* 56 The author adopts Giard's term *adelphophagy* for a union of gametes of the same sex. **1982** R. J. LINCOLN et al. *Dict. Ecol., Evol. & Systematics* (1983) 4/2 *Adelphophagy*, the fusion of two gametes of the same sex.

2. *Zool.* The ingestion by a developing larva of other eggs or larvae from the same brood.

1965 B. E. FREEMAN tr. *Vandel's Biospeleol.* xxii. 354 The ovum . . grows at the expense of the other cells of the 'nest' which nourish it. This is an example of the phenomenon of adelphophagia. **1979** *Jrnl. Exper.*

Marine Biol. & Ecol. XXXVI. 41 Nutrient transfer probably involves nurse eggs and parental body fluids and does not occur by placentation or adelphophagia. **1981** *Amer. Zool.* 1019/1 (*title*) Embryonic oophagy and adelphophagy in sharks. **1989** *Jrnl. Molluscan Stud.* LV. 67/2 Adelphophagy is ingestion by a developing larva of nurse eggs or sibling embryo(s)/larva(e) in the same egg capsule.

adendritic (eɪdɛn'drɪtɪk), *a. Anat.* [f. A- 14 + DENDRITIC *a.*] Of a nerve cell: lacking dendrites. Of any other cell: lacking cytoplasmic processes.

1898 E. A. SCHÄFER *Essent. Histol.* (ed. 5) xviii. 107 Dendrons may be absent; the cell is then said to be adendritic. **1972** *Jrnl. Heredity* LXIII. 19 (*title*) Adendritic melanocytes: a mutation in linkage group II of the fowl. **1990** *Jrnl. Compar. Neurol.* CCXCVIII. 237 In contrast to the adendritic spherical cell of other species, the spherical neuron in *Sternopygus* exhibits an extensive basilar dendrite.

adeno- ('ædɪnəʊ), *comb. form.* [Gr. ἀδήν gland + -o¹.] Used in *Biol.* and *Med.* in terms relating to glands, *spec.* the adenoids, as **adenolym'phoma** *n.* (pl. -omas, -omata), †(*a*) a tumour-like enlargement of a lymph node (*obs.*); (*b*) a benign encapsulated tumour composed chiefly of lymphoid tissue and usually occurring in the salivary glands of men.

1881 *Syd. Soc. Lex.*, *Adenolymphoma, a synonym of *Lymphadenoma*. **1900** DORLAND *Med. Dict.* 24/1 Adenolymphoma, adenoma of a lymph-organ. **1966** WRIGHT & SYMMERS *Systemic Path.* I. xi. 449/1 The adenolymphoma is very slowly growing, and presents as a soft, lobulated mass. **1974** PASSMORE & ROBSON *Compan. Med. Stud.* III. i. xix. 14/1 Adenolymphomata arise from heterotopic salivary gland tissue within lymph nodes in or around the parotid gland, and are rarely malignant. **1989** *Clin. Otolaryngol.* XIV. 205/1 Adenolymphoma is the second most common tumour of the major salivary glands and arises almost exclusively in the parotid gland.

ˌ**adenomy'oma** *n.* (pl. -omas, -omata), a non-malignant myoma containing glandular elements, usually occurring in the uterus.

1889 *Cent. Dict.*, *Adenomyoma. **1904** *Jrnl. Obstetr. & Gynæcol.* V. 251 We conclude that we have to deal with an adenomyoma of the uterus, the name adenomyoma denoting a new formation composed of glandular and muscular elements. **1978** *Dis. Colon & Rectum* XXI. 259/1 Adenomyoma of the stomach is an uncommon lesion.

ˌ**adenosar'coma** *n.* (pl. -omas, -omata), a complex sarcoma containing glandular elements.

1881 *Syd. Soc. Lex.*, *Adenosarcoma. **1895** *Brooklyn Med. Jrnl.* IX. 33 Dr. Wilson . . reported it to be 'Adeno Sarcoma of rapid growth'. **1989** *Obstetr. & Gynecol.* LXXIII. 510/1 Müllerian adenosarcoma is a distinctive type of müllerian mixed tumor, consisting of benign-appearing neoplastic glands and a sarcomatous stroma.

ˌ**adenotonsi'llectomy** *n.*, surgical removal of the adenoids and tonsils.

1941 DORLAND & MILLER *Med. Dict.* (ed. 19) 52/1 *Adenotonsillectomy. **1967** *Jrnl. Laryngol. & Otol.* LXXXI. 777 Surgeons specializing in E.N.T. since World War II have found themselves the innocent inheritors of an extremely controversial operation, adenotonsillectomy. **1987** *Brit. Med. Jrnl.* 29 Aug. 541/2 (*caption*) Early adenotonsillectomy in children with failure to thrive, enlarged tonsils, and associated obstructive apnoea will lead to dramatic improvement in weight gain and general wellbeing.

adenosine, *n.* Add: [**b.**] **adenosine deaminase**, an enzyme which catalyses the deamination of adenosine to inosine; abbrev. *ADA* s.v. *A III.

1937 *Nature* 10 Apr. 627/1 All the *adenosine deaminase previously found in muscle and liver may have been really contained in the residual blood in these tissues. **1991** *U.S. News & World Rep.* 4 Nov. 69/1 The disease Anderson and his colleagues..chose to investigate was adenosine deaminase (ADA) deficiency, an inherited disorder that destroys the body's immune cells.

adenovirus, *n.* Add: Hence **adeno'viral** *a.*
   1966 in WEBSTER Add. **1968** *Folia Microbiologica* XIII. 573/2 (*title*) Study of adenoviral infection of pig foetus. **1982** *Jrnl. Virol.* XLII. 488 Early RNA..selected by hybridization to adenoviral DNA fragments spanning the region from 14.7 to 31.5 map units.

adenyl, *n.* Add: **2.** Special Comb. **adenyl cyclase** = *adenylate cyclase* s.v. *ADENYLATE *n.* 2.
   1962 E. W. SUTHERLAND et al. in *Jrnl. Biol. Chem.* CCXXXVII. 1220/1 For simplicity, the term *adenyl cyclase or cyclase will be used to describe the enzyme system until other evidence..is available. **1968** *Science* 2 Feb. 545/1 The purpose of this report is..to show that the renal adenyl cyclase sensitive to parathyroid hormone is anatomically distinct from that sensitive to vasopressin. **1988** *Nature* 3 Nov. 17/2 These results suggest slow steps in the coupling of hormone receptors to the enzymes responsible for generation of the second messenger, phospholipase C or adenylcyclase.

adenylate (ə'dɛnɪleɪt), *n. Biochem.* [f. ADENYL *n.* + -ATE[1].] **1.** A salt of adenylic acid.
   1937 *Jrnl. Biol. Chem.* CXXI. 153 The white, powdery material..had the following composition, agreeing fairly well with that for barium adenylate. **1976** *Ann. Rev. Microbiol.* XXX. 8 The five- and three-prime adenylate was readily deaminated by the enzyme. **1984** J. F. LAMB et al. *Essent. Physiol.* (ed. 2) iii. 56 (*caption*) A practically irreversible reaction catalysed by adenylate deaminase.
   2. Special Comb. **adenylate cyclase**, an enzyme that catalyses the formation of cyclic AMP from ATP.
   1969 *Proc. Nat. Acad. Sci.* LXIV. 113 The depolarizing effect of norepinephrine is interpreted as being at least partially associated with biochemical events terminating in the activation of *adenylate cyclase. **1989** B. ALBERTS et al. *Molecular Biol. Cell* (ed. 2) xii. 696 At least four hormones activate adenylate cyclase in fat cells, and all of them stimulate the breakdown of triglyceride (the storage form of fat) to fatty acids.

adenylating (ə'dɛnɪleɪtɪŋ), *vbl. n.* and *ppl. a. Biochem.* [Back-formation from *ADENYLATION *n.*: see -ING[2], -ING[1].] **A.** *ppl. a.* That causes the introduction of an adenyl moiety into a molecule.
   1969 *FEBS Lett.* III. 263 (*heading*) Independent genetic regulation of glutamine synthetase and its inactivating (adenylating) enzyme in *E. coli.* **1988** MYRVIK & WEISER *Fund. Med. Bacteriol. & Mycol.* (ed. 2) vi. 87 A variety of enzymes which inactivate aminoglycosides have been identified. These include acetylating, phosphorylating and adenylating enzymes.
   B. *vbl. n.* The action of adenylating something; adenylation.
   1977 *Biochem.* XVI. 2570/2 Coupling between ligands..has been observed within the adenylating site of several aminoacyl-t RNA synthetases.
   Hence (as back-formations) **a'denylate** *v. trans.*, to introduce an adenyl moiety into; **a'denylated** *ppl. a.*
   1972 *New Scientist* 14 Dec. 623/3 The maternal mRNA in the unfertilised egg is unadenylated or partially adenylated. **1976** *Arch. Biochem. & Biophysics* CLXXIII. 204/2 Some of the mRNA

present in the zoospore was adenylated subsequent to germination.

adenylation (ə͵dɛnɪ'leɪʃən), *n. Biochem.* [f. ADENYL *n.* + -ATION.] The covalent attachment of an adenylate moiety to a molecule.
   1967 *Biochem. & Biophysical Res. Communications* XXVIII. 740 The interconversion of the two forms of glutamine synthetase is an 'adenylation' of glutamine synthetase by ATP. **1968** A. WHITE et al. *Princ. Biochem.* (ed. 4) xxiii. 537 Adenylation provides a mechanism of regulation of glutamine synthetase. **1975** *Bio Systems* VII. 179/2 Adenylation, as a step of activation of pABA. **1989** *Nature* 13 Apr. 599/1 The mechanism of this reaction involves the adenylation of firefly luciferin.

adenylic (ædɪ'nɪlɪk), *a.* (Formerly at ADENYL *n.*) *Biochem.* [f. ADENYL *n.* + -IC.] **adenylic acid**, a nucleotide composed of a phosphoric acid ester of adenosine, present in most DNA and RNA; = *adenosine monophosphate* s.v. ADENOSINE *n.* b.
   1894 *Jrnl. Chem. Soc.* LXVI. i. 156 The nuclëic acid prepared from the thyroid gland of calves yields adenine on boiling with water, and is therefore termed adenylic acid. **1936** *Ann. Reg. 1935* 54 Muscle study showed that the chemical changes accompanying contraction are a complicated chain of linked reactions involving creatine, adenylic and phosphoric acid, and carbohydrates and the complexity grows. **1946** *Nature* 23 Nov. 746/2 Here also the hydrogenation would be accompanied by a hydrolysis of the coenzyme molecule followed by a transfer of the phosphate of adenylic acid to other phosphate acceptors. **1975** *Sci. Amer.* May 25/2 There are four kinds of nucleotide, named for their bases: adenylic acid, uridylic acid, guanylic acid and cytidylic acid, better known as *A, U, G* and *C.* **1989** B. ALBERTS et al. *Molecular Biol. Cell* (ed. 2) ix. 528 A poly.A polymerase enzyme adds 100 to 200 residues of adenylic acid (as poly A) to the 3′ end of the RNA chain to complete the primary transcript.

adenylyl ('ædənɪlɪl, -laɪl), *n. Biochem.* [f. ADENYL(IC *a.* + -YL.] = ADENYL *n.* Chiefly in **adenylyl cyclase** = *adenylate cyclase* s.v. *ADENYLATE *n.* 2.
   1976 *Britannica Bk. Yr.* 471 Many tissues contain membrane-bound adenylyl cyclases, which are activated only by specific hormones. **1984** T. E. CREIGHTON *Proteins* ii. 84 A modification related to phosphorylation is one in which the adenylyl moiety of ATP is transferred to..a tyrosine residue in a phosphodiester linkage. **1988** L. STRYER *Biochem.* (ed. 3) xxiv. 590 An interesting feature of these reactions is that they are catalyzed by the same enzyme, adenylyl transferase. **1992** *Sci. Amer.* Sept. 81/2 Serotonin released from the modulatory neuron..activates adenylyl cyclase in the sensory neuron.

adenylylation (ə͵dɛnɪlaɪ'leɪʃən), *n. Biochem.* [f. ADENYL(IC *a.* + -YL + -ATION.] = *ADENYLATION *n.*
   1967 *Proc. Nat. Acad. Sci.* LVIII. 648 The physiological significance of the adenylylation mechanism. **1969** *Federation Proc.* XXVIII. 467/2 (*title*) Enzymatic adenylylation of pyrophosphate by 3′, 5′ cyclic AMP; reversal of the adenyl cyclase reaction. **1986** M. KOGUT tr. *Schlegel's Gen. Microbiol.* xvi. 498 The modifications (so far discovered) can be adenylylation, phosphorylation, and acetylation of the enzyme protein.
   Hence (as back-formations) **ade'nylylated**, **ade'nylylating** *ppl. adjs.*
   1967 *Proc. Nat. Acad. Sci.* LVIII. 648 Intracellular concentrations of the adenylylated and unadenylylated forms of glutamine synthetase vary widely. **1988** L. STRYER *Biochem.* (ed. 3) xxiv. 590 The covalently attached AMP unit is removed from the adenylylated enzyme by phosphorolysis.

adherend (æd'hɪərənd), n. [f. ADHER(E v. + -END.] An object or surface bonded to another by an adhesive, or to which an adhesive adheres.

1955 Rubber World Aug. 626/2 The conservative assumption of linearity does not invalidate the value of the work with its indications of the nature and distribution of stresses in adhesive joints as functions of the geometry of the joint and the mechanical constants of adhesive and adherend. **1972** Materials & Technol. V. iv. 65 In most cases there is little difference between the adhesive/adherend forces involved whether the adhesive substance is a conventional adhesive or a lacquer or paint. **1990** Jrnl. Adhesion XXXI. 177 Gent and Lewandowski presented an approximate solution for the case of a very thin blister adherend in which membrane stiffness is significantly larger than the bending stiffness.

adhesin (æd'hi:sɪn), n. Microbiol. [f. ADHES(ION n. + -IN[1].] A molecular structure on the surface of a bacterium which mediates attachment to other cells or surfaces.

1959 J. P. DUGUID in Jrnl. Gen. Microbiol. XXI. 272 The responsible agent is therefore termed the mannose-sensitive (MS) fimbrial haemagglutinin or adhesin. The alternative name 'adhesin' is introduced because the fimbriae adhere to many substrates other than red cells. **1989** Microbial Pathogenesis VII. 373 Adhesins such as the filamentous hemagglutinin . . and the pertussis toxin . . are considered as major determinants of pathogenesis and efficient immunogens.

adiabatic, a. and n. Add: Hence **adiaba'ticity** n., the condition of being adiabatic; the degree to which something is adiabatic.

1965 Jrnl. Chem. Physics XLIII. 1605/2 In the activated-complex expression . . vibrational adiabaticity was assumed only in the immediate vicinity of the activated complex. **1983** M. S. RABINOVICH in Galeev & Sudan Basic Plasma Physics I. i. 7 The adiabaticity parameter. **1989** Nature 29 June 691/1 Giving a correction to adiabaticity of the order of $(k/\mu)/(1/r) \cong (r/\mu)^{1/2} \ll 1$.

adiathermanous (ædɪə'θɜːmənəs, ˌeɪdaɪə'θɜːmənəs), a. Physics. rare. [f. A- 14 + DIATHERMANOUS a.] = ADIATHERMIC a.

1855 J. SCOFFERN in Orr's Circ. Sci.: Pract. Chem. 103 Hence, we have transcalent and non-transcalent substances, — otherwise called diathermanous and a-diathermanous. **1884** A. DANIELL Princ. Physics xv. 448 A body impervious to light is opaque, impervious to dark heat it is adiathermanous. **1925** J. JOLY Surface-Hist. Earth 179 The continents offer a nearly adiatherminous [sic] covering to the magma. **1958** H. J. GRAY Dict. Physics 15/1 Adiathermanous, not transparent to [sic].

-adic ('ædɪk), suffix. [f. -AD[1] 1 a + -IC. In sense 1 after G. -adisch (K. Hensel Zahlentheorie (1913) iii. 51); in sense 2 f. POLY)ADIC a. Cf. also MONADIC a., DYADIC a. (n.), etc.] **1.** Math. Used with a preceding symbol or numeral, esp. the generalized symbol p (denoting a prime number), to designate numbers expressible as a sequence of digits in the base represented by the symbol (or more generally as a power series in this quantity). Cf. -ARY[1].

1939 Amer. Jrnl. Math. LXI. 894 In our case the ring of all p-adic integers o takes the place of the field of all real numbers. **1974** Encycl. Brit. Macropædia XIII. 362/2 A simple illustration of the efficiency of using p-adic numbers is the statement that − 1 has a square root in the 5-adic numbers. **1990** Proc. London Math. Soc. LX. 37 (heading) Cell decomposition and local zeta functions in a tower of unramified extensions of a p-adic field.

2. Logic. Used with a preceding symbol to designate a relation having the number of arguments represented by the given symbol. Cf. *-ARY[1] 2.

1940 W. V. QUINE Math. Logic 225 A range of n-argument functionality . . is itself an n-adic relation. **1975** Notre Dame Jrnl. Formal Logic XVI. 87 An arbitrary k-adic operator over $X(n)$ defined by an expression with S as the sole operator. **1990** Mind Cl. 137 Fusion of n singletons to form a plural class is a complex type of conjunction which conjoins n monadic universals to form an n-adic relation.

adient ('ædɪənt), a. Psychol. [ad. L. adiens, adient- pres. pple. of adīre to approach: see -ENT.] Exhibiting, involving, or pertaining to a tendency to seek out or maximize the impact of a stimulus.

1931 E. B. HOLT Animal Drive & Learning Process I. vii. 41 Since there is no satisfactory adjective already in use to characterize these responses which give the organism more of the stimulus, I shall adopt the very apt term adient, which has been kindly suggested by Prof. H. C. Warren. The immediate effect of an adient response . . is to give the organism more of the stimulus that elicits the response; and of its opposite, the avoidance or abient response, the immediate effect is to give the organism less of the exciting stimulus. **1938** KATZ & SCHANCK Social Psychol. II. viii. 227 Although adient responses are the normal reactions which children acquire to most objects in their environment, children also learn to avoid or withdraw from certain harmful stimuli. **1946** P. M. SYMONDS Dynamics Human Adjustment ii. 32 Adient . . drives are those which are reduced by going toward the stimulus or bringing the stimulus toward oneself. **1969** M. L. HUTT Hutt Adaptation of Bender-Gestalt Test (ed. 2) vii. 130 Individuals differ in the degree to which they are . . receptive to perceptual stimulation (adient). **1973** Jrnl. Personality Assessment XXXVII. 78 Alcoholics tend to be more adient and environmentally focused than the other groups.

So **'adience** n.

1931 E. B. HOLT Animal Drive & Learning Process xv. 137 If . . an object for which it has a pronounced adience happens to stimulate the senses of a restless animal, this adience will be re-enforced by the (random) annoyer: . . thus abience from the mild annoyer and adience to some other stimulus will become one act. **1985** Jrnl. Clin. Psychol. XLI. 506 The two psychologists who scored the BGT protocols did so by applying the Hutt Psychopathology Scale and the complete Hutt Adience-Abience Scale.

adipate ('ædɪpeɪt), n. Chem. [f. ADIP(IC a. + -ATE[1].] A salt or ester of adipic acid.

1857 H. WATTS tr. Gmelin's Hand-bk. Chem. XI. p. xx, Adipates, $C_{12}H_8M_2O_8$. **1863** — Dict. Chem. I. 58 The adipates, $C_6H_8M_2O_4$, are for the most part soluble in water and crystallisable; insoluble in alcohol. **1957** L. KELLEY Org. Chem. (ed. 2) xxi. 367 The same ketone [sc. cyclopentanone] is obtained when calcium adipate is heated alone. **1973** Materials & Technol. VI. viii. 606 The most important plasticizers of this group are the adipates, sebacates, and azelates. **1990** New Age Jrnl. June 34/2 A British government study showed that the plasticizer di-(2-ethylhexyl) adipate . . migrates into fatty food.

adipo- ('ædɪpəʊ), comb. form. [a. L. adeps, adip-fat + -O[1].] Used in Biol., Chem., and Med. to form terms relating to fat or fatty tissue, as *ADIPOCYTE n, *ADIPOKINETIC a.

adipocyte ('ædɪpəʊsaɪt), n. Histol. [f. *ADIPO- + -CYTE.] A type of cell found in connective tissue which is specialized for the synthesis and storage of fat.

1934 in WEBSTER. **1967** Amer. Jrnl. Physiol. CCXII. 777/2 Possible changes in the cytoplasmic mass of the adipocyte during fat deposition. **1982** T. M. DEVLIN Textbk. Biochem. xxi. 1019 The rate of entry of glucose into the adipocyte is a rate-determining step in glucose metabolism. **1988** *New Scientist* 22 Sept. 40/1 Another fuel, triglyceride, is stored in fat cells, or adipocytes, each of which contains a droplet of triglyceride that occupies almost the whole cell.

adipokinetic (ˌædɪpəʊkɪ'nɛtɪk), *a. Biol.* [f. *ADIPO- + KINETIC *a.*] Esp. of a hormone: producing or causing the mobilization of stored lipid.
1954 A. WHITE et al. *Princ. Biochem.* xviii. 477 Efforts have been made to identify the hypophyseal fraction responsible for this depot lipid mobilizing, or adipokinetic, action. **1969** MAYER & CANDY in *Jrnl. Insect Physiol.* XV. 611 This hormone ('adipokinetic hormone') is assumed to act by stimulating the release of diglyceride from the fat body. **1979** *Nature* 22 Nov. 420/2 The adipokinetic hormone (AKH) of the locust has been isolated, characterised and synthesised. **1987** LAVERACK & DANDO *Lect. Notes Invertebr. Zool.* (ed. 3) xxiii. 127/2 The red pigment-concentrating hormone (RPCH) of crustaceans is structurally very similar to locust adipokinetic hormone.

adiponitrile (ˌædɪpəʊ'naɪtrɪl), *n. Org. Chem.* [f. *ADIPO- + NITRILE *n.*] A liquid dinitrile derived from adipic acid, used primarily in the manufacture of nylon; 1,4-dicyanobutane, $C_6H_8N_2$.
1950 L. F. & M. FIESER *Org. Chem.* (ed. 2) xxxvii. 950 Adiponitrile. **1953** ASTLE & SHELTON *Org. Chem.* xxxiv. 710 In this case both adipic acid and hexamethylenediamine are obtained from adiponitrile as a common intermediate. **1965** *New Scientist* 21 Oct. 188/1 The new Monsanto electrochemical process for converting acrylonitrile to adiponitrile for the manufacture of nylon-66. **1988** COTTON & WILKINSON *Adv. Inorg. Chem.* (ed. 5) viii. 249 Industrial uses of HCN are for synthesis of methyl methacrylate and to form adiponitrile.

aditus, *n.* Sense in Dict. becomes 2. Restrict *Zool.* to sense in Dict. and add: 1. *Anat.* An entrance to a duct or cavity; *esp.* the irregular aperture which connects the tympanic cavity of the ear to the air spaces of the mastoid process (more fully *aditus ad antrum*: cf. ANTRUM *n.*).
1839 DUNGLISON *Dict. Med. Sci.* (ed. 2) 15/1 *Aditus*, the entrance to a canal or duct. **1890** BILLINGS *Med. Dict.* I. 24/2 Aditus ad antrum. **1902** A. THOMSON in D. J. Cunningham *Text-bk. Anat.* 116 The middle ear or tympanum..opens into the mastoid antrum and mastoid air-cells by the aditus ad antrum. **1962** *Gray's Anat.* (ed. 33) 1295 On the upper part of its anterior wall is an opening, the aditus to the mastoid antrum. **1970** D. WOLFF et al. *Surg. & Microsc. Anat. Temporal Bone* (1971) vii. 386 The medial wall..of the aditus ad antrum is formed by the eminentia canalis semi. lateralis. **1989** COLLIER & LONGMORE *Oxf. Handbk. Clin. Specialties* (ed. 2) vii. 530 Posteriorly, there is communication via the aditus and tympanic antrum to the mastoid air cells.

adjustment, *n.* Add: 6. Special Comb. **adjustment centre** *U.S.*, part of a prison reserved for the solitary confinement of refractory or unstable prisoners.
1955 *Proc. Congr. Amer. Correctional Assoc.* LXXXV. 147 The term *Adjustment Center has been introduced in the nomenclature of the prison system..to describe a facility with positive and constructive treatment objectives..quite the opposite of what..is designated..'The Hole', 'The Shelf', 'Siberia'. **1974** *Black Panther* 9 Feb. 3/2 Prison officials claimed George Jackson and the six brothers killed two White guards and three White inmate-trustees while trying to escape from the prison's Adjustment Center. **1987** A. H. VACHSS *Strega* xlviii. 145 They put me in the hole... Guys spend fucking *years* in the hole. Only they call it the 'Adjustment Center'.

adless ('ædlɪs), *a. U.S. colloq.* Also **ad-less**. [f. AD *n.*² + -LESS.] Of a newspaper, radio station, etc.: carrying no advertisements.
1929 *Chicagoan* 17 Aug. 22/2 When *The Day Book*, an adless newspaper for the masses, was started in Chicago, Sandburg was a staff writer. **1984** *Listener* 15 Mar. 7/1 WDST sounded like subscription-supported ad-less public radio.

administration, *n.* Add: [6.] **b.** *Law.* The control and direction of the property of an insolvent company, bankrupt individual, etc., by an administrator, esp. under the terms of an administration order.
1870 *Felony Act 33 & 34 Vict.* c.23 §18 All such property shall be preserved and held in trust by the said administrator..for the use and benefit of the said convict.., and the possession, administration and management thereof, shall re-vest in and be restored to such convict upon his ceasing to be subject to the operation of this Act. **1883** *Bankruptcy Act 46 & 47 Vict.* c.52 §122 When a judgement has been obtained in a county court and the debtor is unable to pay the amount forthwith..the county court may make an order providing for the administration of his estate. **1927** A. ROPER & G. L. HAGGEN *Ringwood's Princ. Bankruptcy* (ed. 15) xii. 204 All payments in the course of the administration must be made into or out of the Bank of England. **1959** *Dict. Eng. Law* I. 59/1 Administration also means..dealing according to law with the property of bankrupts and persons of unsound mind. **1982** *Insolvency Law & Practice* (Rep. Rev. Committee) (Cmnd. 8558) ix. 122 An Administration, once confirmed, should continue until either: (a) a resolution has been passed for a Liquidation of Assets; or (b) the Court has made an order discharging the Administration Order or making a Protection Order. **1992** *Economist* 30 May 112/2 Companies can emerge from administration as going concerns. Randsworth Trust, which owns £350m of British property, went into administration in March... But survival depends on finding new investors willing to stump up fresh money.

8. Special Comb. **administration order** *Law*, a court order requiring the proper administration of the property of a deceased or bankrupt individual, insolvent company, etc.
[**1854** F. S. WILLIAMS *New Pract. Court of Chancery* (Appendix of Forms) 184 (*heading*) Special form of order for administering the estate of a married woman.] **1883** in R. Ringwood *Princ. Bankruptcy* (1884) (ed. 3) xii. 136 Power for county court to make 'administration order instead of order for payment by instalments. **1908** A. R. INGPEN *Conc. Treat. Law Executors & Administrators* xxviii. 355 A decree for administration of assets is in the nature of a judgment for all creditors..and stops all proceedings...A creditor, however, who has obtained judgment against the executor before the administration order, will not be restrained from pursuing his remedy against the executor personally. **1935** *N. Y. Suppl.* CCLXXVII. 253 It may..be said that the complaint is defective for failure to allege a compliance by the plaintiff with Administration Order No. X-36, of May 26, 1934. **1989** *Guardian* 27 July 11/6 Kentish announced that it had applied for an administration order which, if successful, will give the troubled firm a breathing space.

administrator, *n.* Add: 6. *Law.* An agent appointed by the courts to administer the affairs of a company under the terms of an administration order.
1982 *Rep. Rev. Comm. Insolvency Law & Pract.* (Cmnd. 8558) ix. 117 We propose that in all cases..provision should be made to enable a person (whom we shall call an Administrator) to be appointed..with all the powers normally conferred upon a receiver and manager appointed under a floating charge, including power to carry on the business of the company and to borrow for that purpose. **1987**

Financial Times 19 May 9/5 Administrators are 'an entirely new concept within the framework of the insolvency legislation in Great Britain,' say PW. **1989** *Guardian* 1 Aug. 11/8 An attempt by the company to have its own administrator appointed to try to save the business. **1992** *Independent* 9 July 7/2 The Commons Social Security Committee is to call administrators of the Maxwell companies to give evidence.

admirant (æd'maɪərənt), *a. rare.* [f. ADMIR(E *v.* + -ANT[1], or ad. L. *admīrans, admīrant-* pres. pple. of *admirari.*] = ADMIRING *ppl. a.*

1866 J. B. ROSE tr. *Ovid's Metamorphoses* VI. 159 The envy then Of crowds admirant—now of pity's gaze: Amidst the corpses of her sons she strays. **1893** F. ADAMS *New Egypt* iv. 166 No Anglo-Egyptian seemed to believe that the composer of so ingenuously an admirant illustration of their idol could have the faintest taint of 'disloyalty' about him.

admission, *n.* Add: [1.] **d.** An instance of being admitted, esp. to an educational or medical institution. Now freq. *attrib.* (usu. in *pl.*), esp. in *admissions tutor.*

*a***1635** R. NAUNTON *Fragmenta Regalia* (1641) 5 Charged by her expresse command, to look precisely to all admissions into the Privy-Chamber. **1882** *Admissions Coll. St. John, Cambr.* I. p. iii, For earlier admissions recourse must be had to university matriculations..and..to some scattered admissions belonging to the reign of Elizabeth. *Ibid.* p. ix, The facts recorded in the admissions seem to rest on oral testimony, rather than on written documents. **1891** *Cambr. Univ. Cal.* 22 A fee of £2 2s. is paid to the Common Chest by every student on each admission to a Special Examination. **1942** *Ann. Internal Med.* XVI. 655 Many cases have repeated hospital admissions and form a long line of 'follow-ups' in the out-patient department. **1965** *Listener* 18 Feb. 278/1 Nowadays colleges in the United States send out their admissions counsellors to the high schools and private secondary schools. **1966** *Ibid.* 24 Nov. 767/2 That 'spark of originality' for which the university admissions tutor is looking. **1976** *National Observer* (U.S.) 30 Oct. 1/1 Such administrators as Richard W. Haines, director of admissions at Lafayette College in Easton, Pa. **1988** *Oxford Today* Michaelmas 46/3 There seemed no clear call for a further review of our admissions policies at this stage.

e. A person admitted to a medical or educational institution.

1961 *Lancet* 29 July 238/2 This would explain why our present admissions are more severely ill than the earlier group. **1982** *Financial Times* 12 Oct. 23/4 We are making every effort to encourage patients to share at reduced rates. Approximately 90 per cent of our admissions refuse point blank. **1989** *Guardian* 25 July 30/1 Figures are hard to come by. UCCA provides some clues, analysing candidates and admissions by social class.

admitting (æd'mɪtɪŋ), *ppl. a.* Chiefly *Med.* [f. ADMIT *v.* + -ING.] That admits; *spec.* designating a person responsible for admitting people to a hospital, police station, etc., and that part of a hospital reserved for the accommodation of recently admitted patients.

1913 HORNSBY & SCHMIDT *Mod. Hospital* 340 It shall be the duty of the admitting physician to take cultures from throat and vagina, and send them to the..laboratory..for final treatment and report. **1949** *Hospitals* Aug. 54/2 As soon as the patient has been examined by the admitting physician, he is sent with an attendant to take a shower and change into hospital clothing. **1978** *N.Y. Times* 29 Mar. A12/5 They then took him to the police station, but the admitting sergeant refused to book him because of his battered condition. **1989** *Nursing* 26 Oct. 17/3 In a busy admitting ward the constraints of time must also be considered, less time being required when only the staff plan the care.

adrenergic, *a.* Add: Hence **adre'nergically** *adv.*, by means of adrenergic nerves.

1968 *Jrnl. Pharmacol. & Exper. Therap.* CLXIV. 322/1 Adrenergically induced arrhythmias. **1976** *Nature* 18 Mar. 210/3 The responses of the various adrenergically innervated tissues to drugs.

adreno-, *comb. form.* Add: **a'drenoceptor** *n. Physiol.,* an adrenergic receptor.

1970 *Brit. Jrnl. Pharmacol.* XXXVIII. 13 The effects of the beta *adrenoceptor blocking agents on the spontaneous spike potentials..were studied. **1989** *Adverse Drug Reactions & Acute Poisoning Rev.* VIII. 92 Serious effects on the respiratory, cardiovascular, and central nervous systems have been attributed to the wide use of timolol maleate, a non-selective β-adrenoceptor blocking agent, in eye drops for glaucoma.

adreno'doxin *n. Biochem.,* a ferredoxin found in mitochondria of the adrenal cortex.

1965 KIMURA & SUZUKI in *Biochem. & Biophysical Res. Communications* XX. 373 We would propose to give the trivial name '*adrenodoxin', for the non-heme iron protein isolated from adrenal mitochondria. **1988** *Arch. Biochem. & Biophysics* CCLXIV. 376 Adrenodoxin..participates in cholesterol side chain cleavage and in steroid 11β- and 18-hydroxylation.

adsorptive, *a.* Add: **ad'sorptively** *adv.*

1932 FULLER & CONARD tr. *Braun-Blanquet's Plant Sociol.* vi. 187 The resultant soil scarcely differs from the adsorptively saturated, mild humus of lime soils. **1989** *Soap, Cosmetics, Chem. Specialties* May 96/2 What is the chemical structure of certain polar LAS degradation products that become affixed adsorptively to components of the topsoil?

advance, *n.* Sense V. 12 in Dict. becomes VI. 13. Add: **V. 12.** Chiefly *Photogr.* The mechanism which moves the film forward in a camera; esp. in *film advance* [orig. the infin. of ADVANCE *v.* in *attrib.* use. Also *transf.*]

[**1957** J. DESCHIN *Exakta Photogr.* 20/2 The simultaneous film-advance and shutter-wind knob.] **1978** EMANUEL & MANNHEIM *All-in-One Camera Bk.* 106 The film advance..winds the exposed piece of film out of the camera's film window to bring a fresh section into position. **1984** J. PARTRIDGE *One Touch Photogr.* 46 It is easy, with the automatic advance, to take extra pictures which will be considerably cheaper than reprints. **1986** *Camera Weekly* 15 Nov. 33 (Advt.), A quality slide projector—includes auto slide advance. **1992** *Buying Cameras* July 81/3 Classy model with razor sharp lens, but it's rather large and has an unusual film advance.

adventitial, *a.* Add: **2.** *Anat.* Of or pertaining to the tunica adventitia of a blood vessel or lymphatic.

1890 A. HILL tr. *Obersteiner's Anat. Cent. Nerv. Organs* III. 137 Between the adventitia and the muscularis a considerable space is seen in all isolated arteries, the adventitial lymph-space. **1901** *Jrnl. Exper. Med.* VI. 69 The adventitial lymphatic sheath is in most cases distended. **1928** *Anatomical Rec.* XXXIX. 45 The designations Rouget cells, adventitial cells, and pericytes are used indiscriminately on the assumption that they connote the same structures. **1967** *Jrnl. Pediatrics* LXX. 253/2 Vascular changes consisting of thickening and collagenization of the vessel wall with adventitial proliferation.

aero ('ɛərəʊ), *a.* [Abbrev.] **a.** *colloq.* Aerodynamic, streamlined: used chiefly with reference to motor vehicles.

1988 *Bicycle Guide* Mar. 70/2 He wears an aero helmet and uses a streamlined wheel. *Ibid.* 70/3 His new aero bike makes an additional half-minute improvement. **1989** *Sunday Express Mag.* 17 Sept. 21/2 Five years earlier, Heffernan had gone to Audi in Germany, where he contributed to the current Audi

100, a benchmark in the 80s 'aero' style. **1991** *Harper's Mag.* May 22/2 For 1991 Dodge Caravan and Plymouth Voyager have a lower, more aero front end. **1992** *New Republic* 18 May 12/1 (Advt.), We lowered the front end for more visibility, and softened the lines for a more aero look.

b. *Comb.* **aero bar** *Cycling*, an attachment to or replacement for the handlebars of a racing bicycle, allowing the cyclist to adopt a more aerodynamic, forward-sitting posture.

1988 *Bicycling* May 202/3 (*caption*) *Aero bars can cut more than a minute from a 25-mile time trial. **1992** *Bicycle* Feb. 59/2, I wanted to make a bike that is really comfy in the drops (handlebars) and also when the rider is stretched out on the aero bars.

Aerobie (ɛəˈrəʊbɪ), *n.* [f. AERO- after FRISBEE *n.*] A proprietary name for a thin plastic ring which is spun through the air in a catching game. orig. *U.S.*

1985 *Official Gaz.* (U.S. Patent Office) 7 May TM139/1 *Aerobie*...For aerial toy...First use 8-3-1984. **1986** *Trade Marks Jrnl.* 26 Mar. 752/2 *Aerobie*...Toys... — 11 March 1985. **1988** *Kitchener-Waterloo* (Ontario) *Rec.* 8 June E6/1 World Frisbee champion eight of the last nine years, Zimmerman also holds the record for an Aerobie throw of 377 metres. **1990** *New Scientist* 28 July 40/2 In the late 1970s, Alan Alder..began to investigate the possibilities. Nearly a decade later, he had abandoned the disc for a ring, which he calls the Aerobie ring.

aerospace, *n.* Add: **c.** Special Comb. **aerospace plane**, a space vehicle able to take off and land like an aeroplane.

[**1960** *Aviation Week* 31 Oct. 26/1 Air Force is requesting $20 million..for research and development on Space Plane, a radically different manned, winged vehicle that would fly both in the atmosphere..and into space as far as the moon.] **1962** *Ibid.* 1 Oct. 17/2 Another judgment that could simplify the technical task of designing and building *Aerospace Plane. **1965** E. SÄNGER *Space Flight* 103 The common goal of this project is to create aerospace planes. **1987** *Spaceflight* Oct. 51/1 Development of an air-breathing Aerospaceplane is planned for the 1990's but operation of such an advanced runway-launched craft is not expected until well after 2001.

aetosaur (ˈiːtəʊsɔː(r)), *n.* Palaeont. Also **aëto-** (eɪˈiːtəʊ-). [f. mod.L. genus name *Aëtosaurus* (coined by O. Fraas 1877, in *Jahreshefte des Vereins f. Vaterl. Naturkunde Württemb.* XXXIII. III. 12), f. Gr. ἀετός eagle: see *-SAUR.] Any member of the extinct suborder Aetosauria or family Aetosauridae, comprising predominantly herbivorous thecodont reptiles which resembled heavily armoured crocodiles.

1893 in *Funk's Stand. Dict.* **1904** *Amer. Jrnl. Sci.* CLXVII. 382 In the Aëtiosaur [*sic*] (*Stegomus longipes*)..we find a form whose stilted limbs and comparatively narrow body give it just the proportions one would suppose Batrachopus to have. **1974** *Nature* 8 Mar. 168/2 The thecodontian hand, known in phytosaurs, aetosaurs, [etc.]..was crocodile-like with five long digits. **1979** A. CHARIG *New Look at Dinosaurs* xi. 101 Four other new groups of archosaurs had become firmly established by Late Triassic times. Two of these, the phytosaurs and the aetosaurs, are considered to be specialised suborders of the order Thecodontia, dying out at the end of the Triassic. **1985** D. NORMAN *Illustr. Encycl. Dinosaurs* 186/2 In the early part of the late Triassic the first dinosaurs had caused the extinction of all the herbivorous mammal-like reptiles and a few other aberrant groups of herbivorous reptiles (e.g. rhynchosaurs and aëtosaurs).

affective, *a.* Add: [**7.**] [**b.**] *spec.* (of a disorder) having an abnormally depressed or elevated mood as the main symptom. (Further examples.)

1937 E. MAPOTHER & A. LEWIS in F. W. Price *Textbk. Practice of Med.* (ed. 5) xxi. 1844 The predisposition to an affective disorder may be latent in persons who have not been subjected to the stresses that would make it manifest. **1941** *Brit. Med. Jrnl.* 1 Mar. 308/2 A distinction..can..be made between 'affective disorders', comprising cases in which either the mental and physical symptoms of anxiety or depression is the main feature, and hysterical reactions. **1965** *Brit. Jrnl. Psychol.* CXI. 1141/2 This simple salt..also has a therapeutic action on affective disorders. **1988** A. STORR *Solitude* (1989) ix. 142 The writers interviewed had a much greater prevalence of affective illness (i.e. of severe recurrent depression or of manic-depressive illness) than did a marked control group.

afferent, *a.* and *n.* Add: **B.** *absol.* as *n.* Anat. and *Physiol.* An afferent structure, such as a nerve or vessel.

1927 W. KEILLER *Nerve Tracts Brain & Cord* III. 315 Afferents to the vermis also come from the optic and auditory nerves. **1951** *Jrnl. Physiol.* CXIII. 450 The carotid sinus nerve is a mixed afferent nerve containing afferents from the baroreceptors of the carotid sinus. **1990** *Brain* CXIII. 531 The capacity of peripheral somatosensory afferents to modulate or even to generate burst discharges of striatal neurons seemed to be negligibly small.

Hence **ˈafferently** *adv.*, in an afferent direction; involving afferent structures.

1961 in WEBSTER. **1969** J. S. BRUNER in *Beyond Information Given* (1974) xv. 271 The play of attention alters in time from being afferently dominated to being efferently relevant. **1991** *Clin. & Exper. Immunol.* LXXXIV. 383 In transfer experiments, the function of afferently acting suppressor cells was blocked by local treatment with Z7557 or systemic CY.

affinity, *n.* Add: [III.] **affinity (credit) card** (orig. *U.S.*), (*a*) a credit card available to members of a particular affinity group and entitling them to a range of discounts and other benefits; (*b*) a credit card whose issuer donates a proportion of the money spent through use of the card to a particular charity or other organization.

1979 *Amer. Banker* 13 June 7/4 Mr. Shelton argues, on the other hand, that the *affinity card concept is being made available to hundreds of public organizations. **1986** *N.Y. Times* 9 Aug. 31/1 [He] said that added pressures on the big banks were coming from new affinity cards — those issued by banks through voluntary associations. **1988** *Which?* Dec. 560/2 While these 'affinity' credit cards may be a good way of giving to charity, there are cheaper credit cards around. **1991** *National Trust Mag.* Spring 9/1 Only six months after the launch of the affinity card in April last year, the Trust and Midland Bank announced that over 36,000 National Trust Visa cards were in circulation. **1993** *Canad. Living* (Toronto) Sept. 23/2 In Ontario, ..Dominion, Ultra Mart and Miracle Mart..are providing shoppers with 'affinity' or 'loyalty' cards, which, when scanned through computerized checkouts deduct savings on advertised specials.

affinity chromatography *Biochem.*, a form of chromatography which utilizes the tendency of some molecules in solution to bind specifically to immobilized ligands.

1968 P. CUATRECASAS et al. in *Proc. Nat. Acad. Sci.* LXI. 636 In *affinity chromatography, the enzyme to be purified is passed through a column containing a cross-linked polymer or gel to which a specific competitive inhibitor of the enzyme has been covalently attached. **1975** *Nature* 3 Apr. 441/2 Affinity chromatography..has been used extensively in the purification of soluble proteins. **1990** *EMBO Jrnl.* IX. 3938/1 We were unable to separate individual BPc species further by heating, non-denaturing gel filtration, ion exchange chromatography or lectin affinity chromatography.

affinity labelling *Biochem.*, a technique for labelling molecules, esp. enzymes or antibodies, at their active site; cf. *photoaffinity* s.v. PHOTO-1.

1962 L. WOFSY et al. in *Biochemistry* I. 1031 A general method, termed *affinity labeling, is proposed to achieve the labeling of the active sites of antibody and enzyme molecules. **1981** L. STRYER *Biochem.* (ed. 2) viii. 162 The importance of a second residue in catalysis was shown by affinity-labeling studies. **1988** P. W. KUCHEL et al. *Schaum's Outl. Theory + Probl. Biochem.* ix. 281 The technique of affinity labeling is widely used to establish the nature of the amino acid residues in the active site of an enzyme.

affluential (æfluːˈɛnʃəl), *a.* and *n.* orig. and chiefly *U. S.* [Blend of AFFLUENT *a.* and INFLUENTIAL *a.*] **A.** *adj.* Prominent or socially influential on account of wealth; rich and powerful. **B.** *n.* An affluential person.

1975 *Forbes* (N.Y.) 15 Mar. 13/1 New York City's influential, affluential, liberated *Village Voice* reports. **1983** *N.Y. Times* 18 Dec. VI. 13/1 *Spa*..has become a word for 'watering place' associated with the weight-conscious affluentials around the world. **1985** *Houston Business Jrnl.* 8 Apr. 1A In the past two months two new banks have opened in the most affluential part of Houston. **1987** *Arizona Republic* (Phoenix) 6 Sept. (Final ed.) F6 Unlike 'yuppies', who have become so ubiquitous that they no longer merit study, affluentials have not received very much attention in Phoenix. **1994** *Evening Standard* 22 June 13/1 The clientele will be very much as it is in America. That is, the corporate male, very successful in his business, affluential. Not the sort of people who can handle rejection.

affluenza (æfluːˈɛnzə), *n.* [Blend of AFFLUEN(CE *n.* or AFFLUEN(T *a.* + IN)FLUENZA *n.*] A psychological malaise supposedly affecting (esp. young) wealthy people, symptoms of which include a lack of motivation, feelings of guilt, and a sense of isolation.

1979 *Washington Post* 25 Oct. D1/6 A Boston paper even referred to the people she [*sc.* Ann Beattie] writes about, usually disenchanted orphans of Affluenza, as the Beattie Generation. **1984** *N.Y. Times* 15 May C4/6 'Affluenza' is the name coined by one researcher for the maladies wealth can bring. **1986** *Omni* Jan. 28/2 Levy believes that affluenza is a peculiarly American affliction. **1990** *Times* 12 June 3/3 'Affluenza' is defined as 'that nauseous guilty feeling that creeps over people who make more money than they think they are worth'. **1991** *Mother Jones* Sept.-Oct. 4/1 Stand up for children..living in poverty and too many others the victims of 'affluenza', neglect, and alienation.

aflagellar (ˌeɪfləˈdʒɛlə(r)), *a. Microbiol.* [f. A- 14 + FLAGELLAR *a.*] = *AFLAGELLATE *a.*

1913 *Ann. Trop. Med. & Parasitol.* VII. 187 The macronucleus may actually be situated behind the micronucleus at the aflagellar end of the trypanosome. **1970** *Nature* 18 Apr. 268/1 After 3 or 4 days of cultivation, the formation of large irregular, aflagellar cell masses..can be observed. **1989** *Hybridoma* VIII. 355 Sonicates..from flagellar and aflagellar strains of *S. typhi.*

aflagellate (ˌeɪˈflædʒəleɪt, ˌeɪˈflædʒələt), *a. Microbiol.* [f. A- 14 + FLAGELLATE *a.*] Lacking flagella.

1924 *Bull. Entomol. Res.* XIV. 273 The shorter forms are aflagellate, or almost so, and feebly undulant. **1968** *Jrnl. Cell Biol.* XXXIX. 96a/2 The aflagellate but motile spermatozoon of *Steatococcus tuberculatus* is a long, pencil-like structure. **1991** *Infection & Immunity* LIX.

2733/2 Paralyzed mutants with the flagellar structure were no more virulent than the aflagellan mutants.

African, *n.* and *a.* For 'Special collocation' read 'Special collocations' and add: [**B.**] [**2.**] **African horse disease** = **African horse-sickness* below.

1912 LADY A. BLUNT *Jrnl. 1878-1917* 20 Feb. (1986) 353, I got one interesting piece of information from the Duke of Westminster about that swelled head disease of which we have lost two or three foals. It *is* the *African horse disease. **1961** *Spectator* 3 Feb. 135 The Ministry of Agriculture..advised on the matter of African horse disease..was able to tell Moscow that the Russian horses will be allowed to compete in the Grand National.

African horse sickness = *horse-sickness* s.v. HORSE *n.* 28 a.

1899 D. HUTCHEON *Dis. Horse* (Index), *African (South) horse sickness. **1974** *Stand Encycl. S. Africa* X. 301/1 Horse-sickness, better called African horse-sickness, is an acute infectious disease of horses, mules and sometimes donkeys. **1991** *Sci. News* 5 Jan. 4/3 Other reoviruses, called orbiviruses, pose a significant veterinary threat, causing an equine disease called African horse sickness.

African swine fever, a usu. fatal viral disease of pigs, originating from sub-Saharan Africa and characterized by high fever, haemorrhages in the skin, and partial paralysis.

[**1921** R. E. MONTGOMERY in *Jrnl. Compar. Path. & Therapeutics* XXXIV. 159 The diagnosis of what is herein termed East *African swine fever dates from June 1910.] **1957** SMITH & JONES *Vet. Path.* ix. 297 Changes grossly evident in African swine fever are similar in many respects to those of hog cholera, but are generally more severe. **1993** *New Scientist* 17 July 35/2 Some say that the threat of African swine fever was nothing more than a rumour generated by Duvalier to justify killing the pigs.

African violet = SAINTPAULIA *n.*

1902 L. H. BAILEY *Cycl. Amer. Hort.* IV. 1598/1 *Saintpaulia...ionantha...*African Violet. Usambara violet. **1941** F. L. MULFORD *House Plants* 25 The so-called African-violet (*Saintpaulia ionantha*) is a blue-flowered, constant-blooming plant under house culture. **1990** *Garden News* 21 Nov. 5/4 A new but yet unnamed African violet raised by Tony Clements caught the attention of the enthusiasts.

Africanized (ˈæfrɪkənaɪzd), *ppl. a.* Sense 1 formerly at AFRICANIZE *v.* in Dict. **1.** Made African in character or form.

1865 *Cincinnati Commercial* 4 July 1/2 A Yankee voice with Africanized accent. **1905** *Tablet* 21 Oct. 649/2 They have become thoroughly Africanised, speak only the Ethiopian language. **1958** *Economist* 13 Dec. (African Suppl.) 7/2 The fate of Africa in the next decade, therefore, depends upon economic advance catching up with political advance in the 'Africanised' north and west. **1991** P. SWEENEY *Virgin Directory World Music* 238 In 1975, a new Africanised variant on the Rio-style samba school was born in the form of the big percussion marching bands known as 'Afro-blocos'.

2. Designating an unusually aggressive type of honeybee originally produced by crossing an African subspecies with a European one. Of a colony, population, etc.: containing such bees.

[**1964** *Bee World* XLV. 119 The 'Africanization' of our European strains of *A. mellifera* was astonishingly rapid.] **1970** *Amer. Bee Jrnl.* CX. 460 'Selected' Africanized bees produce large amounts of brood, resulting in rapid colony building. **1976** *Sci. Amer.* Jan. 63/1 The African bees are unable to survive the cold season in temperate climates as other honeybees do by forming winter clusters, and the Africanized hybrids share this behavioral handicap. **1989** *Nature* 18 May 182/1 These authors maintain that European bees have not contributed significantly to the feral, Africanized gene pool. **1992** *New Scientist* 4 July 45/1

Once this breeding stock is tainted with even a few aggressive, unmanageable Africanised colonies, orders will dry up overnight.

Afrocentric (ˌæfrəʊˈsɛntrɪk), *a.* orig. and chiefly *U. S.* Also **Afro-centric.** [f. AFRO- + -CENTRIC.] Centring on African or Afro-American culture; regarding Africa as the source of black or Afro-American culture.

1967 *Freedomways* VII. II. 170/2 In the end our Eurocentric, rather than Afrocentric, conclusions merely confirm our pathological communion with the well-known .. 'fallacy of misplaced concreteness'. **1973** *Black World* June 49 The Atlanta University Summer School .. will offer 'a group of advanced Afrocentric courses'. **1976** *Economist* 28 Feb. 108/3 Good examples of demolition are Mr Martin's critique of Mr Bodelsen's anti-imperialism thesis and Mr Hyam's critique of the 'afrocentric' thesis of late-Victorian empire. **1984** *Washington Post* 26 Aug. B3/2 (*caption*) Howard University students organized and sponsored an 'Afro-Centric Unity' event yesterday at Meridian Hill Park in Washington. **1992** *Ebony* Mar. 120/2 I've always thought of myself as an enlightened, Afrocentric person who considered *all* Black people beautiful.

Hence **Afrocen'tricity** *n.*, **Afro'centrism** *n.*, **Afro'centrist** *n.* and *a.*

1977 N. GORDIMER in *S. Afr. Outlook* CVII. 181 (*heading*) From Apartheid to Afrocentrism. **1980** M. K. ASANTE (*title*) Afrocentricity: the theory of social change. **1988** *Times Lit. Suppl.* 3 June 616/4 Eurocentrics attempted to curb the tide of Afrocentrism with vague pleas for cultural 'universalism'. **1989** *Washington Post* 7 Feb. B3/4 The importance of Afrocentricity is that it begins to let us know that we, as black Americans, are normal in the context of African people. **1989** *New Republic* 11 Dec. 40/1 'Afrocentrists,' thundered the Nigerian critic Chinweizu at a recent literary gathering 'see the Nobel Prize as [etc.]'. **1990** *Washington Post* 29 Sept. A21/2 Most parents .. believe that an Afrocentrist view in urban American education is a necessary, though not sufficient, precondition for addressing those dire ailments. **1991** *Utne Reader* July-Aug. 55/1 Black conservative Shelby Steele worries .. that Afrocentrism legitimizes a sense of difference and victimization among blacks. **1993** *Playboy* Feb. 17/1 Even before Afrocentricity became a catchphrase in the Nineties, the band invoked Egyptian and African cultures in its music.

after-care, *n.* Add: [**2.**] **b.** Support facilities, such as free servicing and advice, available to a customer following the purchase of a product.

1976 *Economist* 15 May 101/2 The fund launched on Thursday .. originally .. was to have had four roles: providing equity finance; giving after-care until the company aided had reached a sounder position .. and assisting the institutional shareholders' committee. **1983** *Which?* Sept. 392/3 One firm recommendation from users is to make sure that the company you buy from can offer a comprehensive and convenient after-care service. **1989** *Franchise Mag.* Summer 35/3 In these days of careless drivers and hazardous urban driving where the odd chip and scrape is not easy to avoid, he has found a niche in the car after-care market.

afterglow, *n.* Senses a, b in Dict. become 1 a, 2. Add: [**1.**] **b.** *spec.* A warm or pleasant feeling following sexual intercourse.

1928 S. BROWNE tr. T. H. Van de Velde *Ideal Marriage* viii. 146 At the conclusion of sexual union or communion, begins the *after-glow*, the epilogue. **1973** E. JONG *Fear of Flying* ix. 168 'How to Manage the Sex Act', penetration, foreplay, afterglow. **1977** E. J. TRIMMER et al. *Visual Dict. Sex* (1978) x. 107/2 They may often experience what is sometimes called the *after glow*. This is a stage of physical and emotional warmth and love. **1979** R. JAFFE *Class Reunion* (1980) I. vii. 96

Annabel had her first orgasm ... 'How's your afterglow?' he asked. **1991** S. FRY *Liar* ix. 270 Adrian had never been able to luxuriate in the afterglow ... 'Why do you always want to have a bath the moment after you've made love to me?'

afterload ('ɑːftələʊd), *n. Physiol.* [f. AFTER- 6 + LOAD *n.*] The load which must be overcome by the cardiac muscles at the beginning of systole. Cf. PRE-LOAD *n.*

1941 *Amer. Jrnl. Physiol.* CXXXIV. 643 To define work, oxygen consumption and efficiency, it is necessary to consider the nature of the load as regards initial load (venous return), and after load (resistance to emptying), as well as in regard to heart size. **1961** *Circulation Res.* IX. 1152/2 The only variable was the increase in the afterload, which was instituted at a time during which the aortic valves were closed. **1989** *Brit. Med. Jrnl.* 27 May 1431/2 Reduction in afterload enhances performance of the failing ventricle by decreasing myocardial wall tension and oxygen requirements.

So **'afterloaded** *ppl. a.*, subjected to an afterload.

1966 *Circulation Res.* XVIII. 742/1 These workers utilized lightly afterloaded control beats. **1970** *Ibid.* XXVI. 279 Isometric, afterloaded and isotonic contractions of cat right ventricular papillary muscle were studied in vitro at 30°C or 37°C. **1987** *Oxf. Textbk. Med.* (ed. 2) II. XIII. 10/2 The contraction of the intact heart can be visualized as being similar mechanically to the afterloaded contraction of an isolated muscle strip.

afterpotential ('ɑːftəpəʊˌtɛnʃəl), *n. Physiol.* [f. AFTER- 6 + POTENTIAL *a.* and *n.* B.] A (usu. slow) fluctuation in the electrical potential of a nerve cell or heart muscle cell, which sometimes follows an action potential.

1930 GASSER & ERLANGER in *Amer. Jrnl. Physiol.* XCIV. 248 After considering various possibilities we have decided upon 'spike' and 'after-potential' ... The latter term has the double advantage that it refers only to a potential and that, while it is entirely non-committal as to whether or not this potential is continuous with the spike, it covers the situation satisfactorily if, as is probably the case, the after-potential is separate. **1935** *Jrnl. Physiol.* LXXXV. 464 In the non-medullated vagal fibres the spike is followed by a short positive after-potential. **1968** *Ibid.* CXCVII. 86P The amplitude and duration of the after-potential is dependent on the duration of the preceding stimulus. **1987** M. J. NEAL *Med. Pharmacol.* xvii. 41/1 If the afterpotential reaches threshold, an action potential is generated causing an 'ectopic beat'.

aftosa (æfˈtəʊzə), *n. Vet. Sci.* [ad. Sp. (*fiebre*) *aftosa* aphthous fever.] = *foot-and-mouth disease* s.v. FOOT *n.* 35 a.

1947 *Amer. Milk Rev.* Sept. 4 (headline) Aftosa — Mexican tragedy; a story of the foot and mouth disease. **1950** *Sci. News Let.* 15 Apr. 227/1 If it hit American herds, 'aftosa' as the Mexicans call it .. would almost certainly disrupt the nation's entire livestock industry. **1972** *Buenos Aires Herald* 1 Feb. 9/1 The census is linked to the campaign against foot-and-mouth disease as vaccination against 'aftosa' also starts today. **1989** HECHT & COCKBURN *Fate of Forest* vi. 98 With aftosa .. endemic and rife among its herds, Amazonian beef is prohibited from sale on international markets.

agamospecies (əˈgæməˌspiːʃiːz, eɪˈgæməˌspiːʃiːz, əˈgæməˌspiːsiːz, eɪˈgæməˌspiːsiːz), *n. Bot.* [f. Gr. ἄγαμος unmarried + SPECIES *n.*] A species that reproduces only asexually.

1929 G. TURESSON in *Hereditas* XII. 332 The species in the Linnéan and in the ordinary sense of the word represents units of very different nature, including the ecospecies, the coenospecies .. and the agamospecies, defined below. **1947** *Acta Univ. Lundensis* XLIII. 226 The Scandinavian population should, from Turesson's point of view, be said to form an agamospecies, rather than a forma apomicta. **1971** *Nature* 1 Oct. 309/1 The special case of the almost totally apomictic *Alchemilla*, many of whose agamospecies are narrow endemics yet show some ecotypic differentiation. **1988** *Evolution* XLII. 289/2 Because the natural clones behave largely as independent genetic entities ('agamospecies'), it is reasonable to expect the biochemical variability of the parasite to be statistically correlated with other features.

agarose ('ægərəuz), *n. Biochem.* [f. AGAR *n.* + -OSE².] **1.** A polysaccharide which consists of alternating residues of D-galactose and 3,6-anhydro-L-galactose and is the main constituent of agar.

1953 C. ARAKI in *Mem. Faculty Industr. Arts Kyoto Techn. Univ.* II. B. 22 From these analytical data, the experimental formula of $C_{18}H_{26}O_{14}$ or $C_{19}H_{30}O_{14}$ seems to be suitable for the part 'agarose', which occupies about 70% portions in whole agar. **1956** *Bull. Chem. Soc. Japan* XXIX. 543/2 Agar is composed of two polysaccharides, agarose and agaropectin. **1971** *New Scientist* 30 Sept. 739/1 Hormone effects are produced by insulin attached to beads of agarose, which certainly cannot penetrate the cell membrane. **1990** *EMBO Jrnl.* IX. 3846/1 DNA was then isolated by melting the agarose . . and extracting it twice with phenol.
2. Special Comb. **agarose gel**, a gel composed chiefly of agarose for use in gel electrophoresis or other experimental procedures.

1965 *Jrnl. Chromatogr.* XX. 157 Separations were made in agarose gel over-laying a tissue slide cover-glass held flat on a glass lantern slide. **1984** *Science* 22 June 1287/1 (Advt.), The resulting fluorograms are fully comparable to those obtained using other fluorographic techniques, with either polyacrylamide or 2% agarose gels.

agboin ('ægbəʊɪn), *n. Bot.* [Yoruba.] = *DAHOMA *n.*

1920 *Nature* 29 July 692/1 Other heavy constructional woods which resist the white and and show good promise for the future are . . Agboin (*Piptadenia africana*), and Apa (*Afzelia africana*). **1951** W. J. EGGELING *Indigenous Trees Uganda Protectorate* 228 *Piptadenia africana* . . . Dahoma, Agboin (Trade names). **1974** *Nomencl. Commerc. Timbers* (*B.S.I.*) 41 *Piptadeniastrum africanum* . ., agboin (Nigeria) . . dahoma (Ghana).

age, *n.* Add: [III.] **age-dating** *n.*, a process of establishing the age of geological deposits, archaeological remains, etc., by means of scientific examination of samples of them; also, a date ascertained by such a process.

1959 *Bull. Geol. Soc. Amer.* LXIX. 1574 (*title*) Radioactive *age dating and its petrologic implications for some Georgia granites. **1963** *Special Paper Geol. Soc. Amer.* No. 73 95 More than 1000 age datings on precambrian rocks of North America have been compiled. **1974** F. J. SAWKINS et al. *Evolving Earth* iii. 65 The ⁴⁰K–⁴⁰Ar method has been a favorite for age dating.
    hence (as a back-formation) **age-date** *v. trans.*
1984 *Oil & Gas Jrnl.* 15 Oct. 154/1 The Nonesuch formation, whole rock Rb-Sr *age dated by Chaudhuri and Faure (1967) as 1075 ±50 million years. **1988** T. FERRIS *Coming of Age in Milky Way* (1989) I. xiii. 251 The scientist who comes along years later to age-date their remains is . . reading a clock that started when the host died.

age-dated *ppl. a.*, (*a*) classified or classifiable by age; *spec.* marked with a date that enables a person to know the age of a product; (*b*) dated by means of age-dating.

1983 *N. Y. Times* 26 Dec. A18/1 Americans' speech is *age-dated. **1984** A. C. & A. DUXBURY *Introd. World's*

Oceans iii. 84 Research done on age-dated layers of volcanic rock shows that the polarity . . reverses. **1991** *Los Angeles Times* 28 Nov. (San Diego County ed.) (N. County Focus section) 3 Items are shipped within days of manufacture to ensure freshness. In fact each item is age-dated and the spa will replace any unused product after one year.

age spot = *liver spot* s.v. LIVER *n.* 7; also *fig.* and *transf.*, a sign of age.

1955 *Mademoiselle* Jan. 44/3 (Advt.), These horrid *age spots . . . Weathered brown spots on the surface of your hands and face . . . Fade them away with new Esoterica. **1989** B. MUKHERJEE *Jasmine* (1990) ii. 12 Then I took his big pink hand, speckled with golden age spots. **1990** *San Francisco Chron.* 16 Feb. E20/5 Nelder says that it's a 'seriously flawed' bit of legislation, although if it's that flawed it's hard to understand why she wanted to delay its consideration back in September. Did it develop age spots? **1992** *Atlanta Jrnl.* 11 Sept. 3/1 For age spots on antique mirrors, rub with a wad of paper moistened with denatured alcohol.

agglomerator (ə'glɒməreɪtə(r)), *n.* [f. AGGLOMERATE *v.* + -OR.] An apparatus or device that causes agglomeration. Also, a binding agent.

1962 *Engineering* 12 Jan. 43/1 The desired properties of agglomerator and filter elements are similar. **1975** *Chem. Week.* 3 Sept. 31/2 The mixture also contains an agglomerator, which binds ash particles together, and a catalyst. **1992** *Oil & Gas Jrnl.* 6 July 77/3 If an agglomerator vane or fibrous filter is used, then a viscosity term must be added to the above equation.

aggregate, *ppl. a.* and *n.* Senses B. 5, 6 in Dict. become B. 6, 7. Add: [A.] **10.** *Bot.* Designating, constituting, or considered as an aggregate (sense *B. 5 below).

1870 H. C. WATSON *Compendium Cybele Brit.* III. 427 When aggregate species AB comes to be made into two by the severance of B from it, leaving A equally alone, what are we to do with all its old recorded localities? **1937** A. H. WOLLEY-DOD *Flora Sussex* 58 Arnold says that aggregate [*Viola*] *tricolor* is rare in West Sussex, and all segregates of *arvensis* are rare in Div. VI.

[B.] **5.** *Bot.* A group of several closely related species formerly (and still occasionally for convenience) not distinguished from each other. Opp. SEGREGATE *n.* 2.

1859 H. C. WATSON *Cybele Britannica* IV. 52 He must consult records in which the segregate species of the present day are treated as unit-species under names which are now the names of aggregates. **1870** —— *Compendium Cybele Brit.* III. 427 Some pages will be devoted to expositions of the manner in which the aggregates (the recognized species of the older botanists, and still accepted in the same character by influential botanists of the present time) have passed into the modern segregates. **1912** J. W. WHITE *Flora of Bristol* 405 The old [*Hieracium*] *murorum* aggregate has long been split into many 'species'. **1957** *Proc. Bot. Soc. Brit. Isles* II. 220 When the + sign is placed in parentheses, this indicates that Trail recorded an aggregate which now includes the species, e.g. he recorded *Caux flava* but not *C. demissa*. **1978** *Watsonia* XII. 113 The history of the taxonomic treatment of the *Juncus bufonius* L. aggregate is surveyed. Five species within it are recognized in Europe.

aggressive, *a.* Sense 3 in Dict. becomes 4. Add: **3.** *Agric.* and *Med.* Designating or pertaining to diseases and pathogens which spread vigorously within an organism.

1937 A. R. WILSON in *Ann. Appl. Biol.* XXIV. 269 It became increasingly evident that infection [*B. cinerea*] was of two types, 'aggressive' and 'non-aggressive'. The former causes blackening and death of part or the whole of the shoot system . . . The latter merely causes the death of localized areas of tissue. **1953** F. T. Brooks *Plant Dis.* (ed. 2) x. 150 From January to April..the fungus may resume activity in suitable weather and again become aggressive. **1961** R. D. Baker *Essent. Path.* xiii. 304 Gliomas may be exemplified by glioblastoma multiforme, the most aggressive variety. **1977** *Ann. Internal Med.* LXXXVI. 33/1 None of the subjects in the current investigation had evidence of distant metastases or aggressive invasion in the neck. **1991** *Garden* Mar. p. xx (Advt.), These trees..have proved resistant to both aggressive and non-aggressive strains of the disease.

agmatine ('ægmətiːn), *n.* Biochem. [ad. Ger. *Agmatin* (coined by A. Kosselin 1910, in *Zeitschr. für Physiol. Chem.* LXVI. 257), prob. f. *A(mino-* AMINO- + *G(uanidin* GUANIDINE *n.* + *Ptomain* PTOMAINE *n.*] An amine produced by the decarboxylation of arginine during the degradation of proteins; aminobutylguanidine, $H_2N \cdot (CH_2)_4 \cdot NH \cdot C(NH) \cdot NH_2$.

1919 *Jrnl. Amer. Chem. Soc.* XLI. 681 Agmantine [*sic*] picrate crystallized out first upon fractionally crystallizing the lysine picrate fraction. **1972** *Jrnl. Bacteriol.* CIX. 44/1 In recent years evidence has accumulated that agmatine can replace arginine as an energy source for the growth of certain strains of *S. faecalis.* **1986** M. Kogut tr. *Schlegel's Gen. Microbiol.* xiv. 434 The best known of these bases (formerly called ptomaines) are cadaverine, putrescine, and agmatine.

agnogenic (ægnəʊ'dʒɛnɪk), *a.* Path. [f. Gr. ἄγνω-στος or ἀγν-ώς unknown, f. ἀγνοῦν be ignorant + -GENIC.] Not attributable to a specific cause; of unknown aetiology; = CRYPTOGENETIC *a.*

1941 Dorland & Miller *Med. Dict.* (ed. 19) 62/2 *Agnogenic,* of unknown origin or etiology. **1971** *Lancet* 9 Oct. 811/2 The most serious exceptions I can think of are three words for disease causation—iatrogenic, cryptogenic, agnogenic. They should according to the rule proposed be -genous, or drop the -gen- suffix altogether. **1987** *Oxf. Textbk. Med.* (ed. 2) II. xix. 40/1 Primary myelosclerosis is a myeloproliferative disorder... The condition has many alternative names, including..agnogenic myeloid metaplasia, and megakaryocytic splenomegaly.

agnolotti (ˌænə'lɒtɪ), *n. pl.* [a. It., pl. of *agnolotto,* prob. related to *agnellotto* stuffed meat dumpling, f. *agnello* lamb.

An alternative etymology, from *anello* 'ring', has been suggested by some commentators (see S. Battaglia *Grande Dizionario della Lingua Italiana* I. (1961)).]

A variety of pasta in the shape of small half-moons or squares, filled with minced meat, and served either in broth or with a sauce. Cf. RAVIOLI *n. pl.*, TORTELLINI *n. pl.*

1953 M. La Rosa tr. *A. Boni's Talisman Italian Cook Bk.* ix. 145 (*heading*) Agnolotti or ravioli. **1954** E. David *Italian Food* 96 There is great rivalry between the different provinces of central and northern Italy as to the merits of their respective traditional stuffings for *tortellini, agnolotti, anolini, ravioli* and the rest. **1970** Simon & Howe *Dict. Gastron.* 14/1 Stuffed pasta should only be called ravioli when it is stuffed with eggs, ricotta and other cheeses. When the small squares of pasta are stuffed with any of the meat fillings,..they should be called agnolotti. **1992** *Gourmet* Feb. 156/2 Not only can the restaurant turn out..*fettuccine,* broad *pappardelle,* ravioli and *agnolotti*—but it can also produce round pasta.

agonistic, *a.* Add: **4.** Physiol. Designating a muscle that is an agonist, and its mode of action.

1932 *Jrnl. Bone & Joint Surg.* XIV. 7 In these cases the balance between agonistic and antagonistic muscle groups is extremely labile. **1971** H. O. Kendall et al. *Muscles* (ed. 2) i. 3/1 A comprehensive..knowledge of muscle function..must include a knowledge of joint motion, the origin and insertion of muscles, their

agonistic and antagonistic action, as well as their role in fixation and substitution. **1989** *European Jrnl. Appl. Physiol.* LVIII. 426/1 The reinforcement of dynamic force may be produced by the pre-stretch of agonistic muscles.

5. Pharm. Of or pertaining to an agonist (AGONIST *n.* 5); having the effect of an agonist.

1955 *Arch. Internat. de Pharmacodynamie et de Thérapie* C. 308 The substance...has an affinity as well to the receptors on which the agonistic as to those on which the antagonistic effect is initiated. **1967** *Pharmacol. Rev.* XIX. 464 Analgesics whose pattern of pharmacological and agonistic effects is similar to that of morphine. **1991** *Jrnl. Pharmacy & Pharmacol.* XLIII. 857/2 Agonistic activity on the presynaptic dopamine receptors in the central nervous system in-vivo has been reported.

agribiz ('ægrɪbɪz), *n.* colloq. (orig. *U.S.*). [Abbrev.: cf. BIZ *n.*] = AGRIBUSINESS *n.*

1977 *Time* 28 Nov. 111/3 Pretty soon Leroy finds himself in Los Angeles..working as a painter for an arm of the same agribiz octopus that chased him away from home. **1985** *New Yorker* 29 Apr. 62/3 Captains of agribiz and manufacturing. **1992** *Daily Tel.* 13 May 18/6 Consider for a moment what sort of countryside we have made in the last 40 years—one ravaged by agribiz, sterilised and poisoned by chemical bombardment, marshes and woodlands destroyed.

agrimi (əg'riːmɪ), *n.* Zool. Pl. agrimia, agrimi, agrimis. [mod.Gr. ἀγρίμι.] The wild goat, *Capra aegagrus,* as found in Crete and depicted in Minoan art.

1865 T. A. B. Spratt *Travels & Researches in Crete* I. i. 13 When we first sighted it [*sc.* Mount Ida], a group of Agrimia, a species of Ibex.., were standing motionless upon its pinnacle. **1924** H. R. Hall in J. A. Hammerton *Countries of World* III. 1507/2 For the sportsman [Crete]..is perhaps losing its charm, as the ibex (or 'agrimi') is rarer than it was. **1977** R. F. Willetts *Civilization Anc. Crete* v. 87 Over the doorway sit four heraldically placed agrimi. **1984** *Canad. Jrnl. Zool.* LXII. 419/1 The total population of 89 agrimi was captured. **1986** *Jrnl. Mammal.* LXVII. 757 The agrimi (*Capra aegagrus cretensis* Lydekker) is an endangered subspecies of wild goat that lives in reduced numbers in the White Mountains of Crete and two other small Greek islands.

agro-, comb. form. Add: [b.] **agroe'cology**, ecology as applied to agriculture.

1930 *Internat. Rev. Agric.* Aug. 280 In *agroecology there will be taken into consideration all the factors which have an influence on the development and success of the crop. **1987** S. B. Hecht in M. A. Altieri *Agroecology* i. 5 At the heart of agroecology is the idea that a crop field is an ecosystem in which ecological processes found in other formations..also occur. **1991** *New Age Jrnl.* Apr. 12/2 She has gone to England to learn biodynamic gardening, apprenticed at local organic farms, and studied at the agro-ecology program at the University of California at Santa Cruz.

agroe'cologist, an expert in or student of agroecology.

1930 *Internat. Rev. Agric.* Aug. 279 All the kinds of plant adaptations occurring should be most carefully studied by the *agroecologist. **1987** R. B. Norgaard in M. A. Altieri *Agroecology* ii. 21 Agroecologists are fascinated by agricultural systems that have evolved over centuries. **1991** *Discover* Dec. 47/3 Agro-ecologists look for solutions to farmers' problems that are less ecologically and socially disruptive.

agromyzid (ægrəʊ'maɪzɪd), *a.* and *n.* Ent. [f. mod.L. family name *Agromyzidae,* f. genus name *Agromyza* (coined in C. F. Fallén *Specim. Entomol. Novam Diptera Disponendi Methodum* (1810) 21), f. Gr. ἀγρός field + μύζειν to suck: see -ID[3].] **A.** adj. Of or belonging to the family

Agromyzidae of dipteran flies, whose larvae are characterized by their habit of tunnelling within the leaves of plants. **B.** *n.* An insect of this family.
1928 *Funk's Stand. Dict.*, Agromyzid, *a.* & *n.* **1933** *Ann. Appl. Biol.* XX. 498 The following paper deals with the morphology and bionomics of an interesting Agromyzid fly which mines or tunnels in the cambium of basket willows. **1951** COLYER & HAMMOND *Flies Brit. Isles* 235 Apart from various *Phytomyza* species which turn up quite frequently when sweeping grasses and low herbage..adult Agromyzids are not met with very commonly. **1972** SWAN & PAPP *Common Insects N. Amer.* 631 Most agromyzids are leaf miners, and a species usually feeds on only one genus of plant. **1979** *Nature* 11 Oct. 425/2 Lawton and Price were unable to determine any significant difference in the number of agromyzid species associated with annual, biennial or perennial umbellifers.

Agulhas (ə'gʌləs), *n. Oceanogr.* [The name of Cape *Agulhas*, the southernmost point of Africa.] **Agulhas Current**, a fast, warm ocean current that flows down the eastern coast of southern Africa.
[*a* **1830** J. RENNELL *Currents Atlantic Ocean* (1832) i. 20 There is a real Stream off the Cape of Good-Hope, which is a portion of the well known *Lagullas Current*.] **1881** *Encycl. Brit.* XII. 822/1 When the Agulhas Current is at its strongest, it carries a temperature of 79° as far west as the meridian of 15°E. **1973** *Stand. Encycl. S. Afr.* VIII. 283/1 One may assume that the continuations of these two elements..meet somewhere north of Durban to form the Agulhas Current. **1984** A. C. & A. DUXBURY *Introd. World's Oceans* viii. 255 One region that is noted for such [episodic] waves is the area where the Agulhas Current, sweeping down the east coast of South Africa, meets the storm waves arising in the southern ocean.

Aharonov–Bohm (ə'hærənɒv bəʊm), *n. Physics.* [The names of Yakir *Aharonov*, 20th-cent. Israeli physicist, and David *Bohm* (1917–92), U.S.-born physicist.] Used *attrib.* (esp. in *Aharonov–Bohm effect*) with reference to a phenomenon predicted by Aharonov and Bohm in 1959 (*Physical Rev.* CXV. 485), whereby electrons propagating around a region containing magnetic flux acquire a phase-shift of their wave function proportioned to the linked flux.
1961 *Ann. Physics* XVI. 177 The conventional Schrödinger treatment of the Aharonov-Bohm effect of inaccessible magnetic fields postulates the use of single-valued wave functions, even in a multiply connected region. **1987** *Nature* 22 Oct. 676/1 Even more surprising..is the appearance of Aharonov-Bohm oscillations in some non-superconducting solid-state devices. **1989** A. LEGGETT in P. Davies *New Physics* ix. 283/2 A macroscopic version of a quantum-mechanical effect, known as the Aharonov–Bohm effect.

ahermatypic (ˌeɪhɜːmə'tɪpɪk), *a. Zool.* [f. A- 14 + *HERMATYPIC *a.*] Designating corals that lack symbiotic zooxanthellae and are not reef-forming.
1943 VAUGHAN & WELLS *Special Papers Geol. Soc. Amer.* No. 44. 1 Certain aspects of the ecology of the ahermatypic or non-reef-builders are here extensively considered for the first time. **1967** *Oceanogr. & Marine Biol.* V. 455 One may point to the flourishing Quaternary population of deep-water ahermatypic corals. **1984** *Pacific Sci.* XXXVIII. 205/1 The ahermatypic coral fauna of 16 genera and 19 species is one typical of sandy or silty bottoms in moderately deep water (220m) and consists mainly of small free-living caryophyllids and flabellids.

ahuehuete (ˌæhweɪ'hweɪteɪ), *n.* [Mex. Sp., ad. Nahuatl *ahuehuetl*, f. *huehue* old + *atl* water.] A Mexican swamp cypress, *Taxodium mucronatum* (family Taxodiaceae), which can attain great girth and is important for the production of medicinal resins and timber.
1828 G. F. LYON *Jrnl. Residence Mexico* II. ix. 113 A white hoary lichen..hangs like long waving locks from all the gigantic branches, and gives to these trees a most indescribably majestic appearance. The Baron de Humboldt considers these 'Ahūahüetes' [*sic*] as the *Cupressus disticha* Linn. **1893** W. THOMPSON tr. *A. Garciay Cubas's Mexico* 143 The ahuehuetes (*Taxodium distichum* [*sic*]). **1965** J. DIDION in *Sat. Even. Post* 14 Aug. 78 There had been *ahuehuete* trees in Durango; a waterfall, rattlesnakes. **1990** T. CHRISTENSEN tr. *La Desdichada* in *Fuentes's Constancia & Other Stories* 105 The *pirul* and the ahuehuete trees, calla lilies.

aileron, *n.* Add: **2.** *attrib.* and *Comb.* **aileron roll**, a roll (ROLL *n.*² 1 d) executed by means of ailerons.
1930 R. DUNCAN *Stunt Flying* ix. 88 An *aileron roll is easy of accomplishment for the pursuit type of airplanes, no rudder being necessary. **1987** *Kentucky Poetry Rev.* Fall 54, I remember things done wrong: an aileron roll too close to the ground..a thunderstorm full of hail.
aileron turn = *aileron roll above.
1942 *Tee Emm* (Air Ministry) II. 65/2 Do a quick barrel half roll with plenty of skid,..and then rudder into a steep dive with *aileron turns. **1986** *Pilot* Aug. 54/3 Others believe they saw the Pitts fly several downward 'spirals', which might be interpreted to mean aileron turns.

ainhum ('eɪnhəm), *n. Path.* [a. Pg. *ainhum*, perh. ult. f. Yoruba *eyun* saw.] A condition in which progressive fibrous constriction about the base of a toe or finger results in its loss, most commonly affecting Negroid males in the tropics and associated with going barefoot.
1872 FOX & FARQUHAR *Scheme Better Knowl. Endemic Skin Dis. India* 20 The name 'Ainhum' signifies 'to saw', and is the term applied to a disease which is said to exist amongst the Africans...The disease consists of spontaneous amputation of the little toes, with hypertrophy of the amputated part. **1898** P. MANSON *Trop. Dis.* vii. 599 Ainhum is very rare in women or children, being most common in adult males. **1981** *Arch. Dermatol.* CXVII. 228/2 Cole believes that the primary factor underlying ainhum is an abnormal and excessive keratinization.

air, *n.*¹ Add: [**B.**] [**II.**] **air battery**, a dry cell or battery in which current is generated by the oxidization in air of an electrode (usually one of zinc).
1943 *Chem. Abstr.* XXXVII. 3354 In practical performance such '*air batteries' have excelled the best pyrolusite (Leclanché) batteries. **1975** D. G. FINK *Electronics Engineers' Handbk.* vii. 51 Air batteries...This system, using bulky zinc anodes, a carbon-air electrode, and a potassium hydroxide electrolyte in a glass jar, has been used successfully for railway signals and similar applications.
air bearing, a bearing that consists of a jet of air.
1949 SHAW & MACKS *Analysis & Lubrication of Bearings* viii. 330 Although Hirn first mentioned the possibility of using air as a lubricant in 1855, Kingsbury was the first to carry out an actual experimental investigation of the hydrodynamic lubrication of an *air bearing. **1991** *Professional Engin.* July-Aug. 57/1 The new high accuracy 750 series has a ceramic spindle, 'A' frame design, low friction air bearings and Kemco's *PC3D* software package.
air-brake: hence **air-braked** *a.*

1952 *Jrnl. Inst. Locomotive Engineers* XLII. ii. 151 The corresponding figure for air loss for *air braked trains was 50 cubic feet of free air per hour. **1984** 'TIRESIAS' *Notes from Overground* 10 For Use On Merry-Go-Round Air-Braked Trains Only.

Airey ('εərɪ), *n.* [The name of Sir Edwin *Airey* (1878-1955), of William Airey & Son Ltd., a Leeds engineering company.] Used *attrib.* (esp. in *Airey house*) with reference to a system of constructing houses from precast concrete sections, which was devised by Airey in the 1920s.

1945 *Builder* 14 Dec. 478/3 The 'Airey' system of house construction comprises essentially precast concrete external wall-posts clad with precast vibrated concrete slabs tied back to the posts and lined with plasterboard or similar wallboard. **1947** *Times* 18 Aug. 2/5 By the end of June only 3,600 of the 20,000 Airey houses were in approved contracts. **1973** M. FOOT *Aneurin Bevan* II. ii. 81 Bevan..in the Spring of 1946 settled on two types—the British Steel House and the Airey House, a construction of precast concrete. **1982** *Daily Tel.* 8 Sept. 2/6 Council tenants who have bought their 'Airey' homes, which have been found to contain structural defects, will be compensated by the Government.

Airy ('εərɪ), *n.* *Math.* and *Physics.* [The name of Sir George Biddell *Airy* (1801-92), English astronomer and physicist.] Used *attrib.* and in the possessive to designate concepts introduced by Airy or arising out of his work, as **Airy('s) disc** [described by Airy in *Trans. Cambr. Philos. Soc.* (1835) V. 285], the circular diffraction pattern formed when plane light waves pass through a point aperture; the bright central region of this. **Airy('s) function**, each of the functions satisfying the differential equation $d^2y/dx^2 - xy = 0$, which are usually expressed in the form of an indefinite integral. **Airy('s) integral** = *Airy('s) function* above. **Airy points**, the points along the length of a bar at which it must be supported for the amount of bending (for a given number of points) to be minimized. **Airy('s) spiral**, each of the spirals of light visible when polarized light which has been passed through two plates of left-handed and right-handed quartz is viewed through crossed Nicol prisms; also, these spirals collectively.

[**1889** G. M. HOPKINS *Exper. Sci.* xii. 258 By superposing a right hand quartz on a left hand quartz, the beautiful spirals discovered by Airy, and named after their discoverer, may be exhibited.] **1895** T. PRESTON *Theory of Light* xvii. 447 (*heading*), 272 Isochromatic lines—Airy's spirals. **1911** *Proc. R. Soc.* A. LXXXV. 441 Now the Airy points of support are so arranged that the ends of the bar are horizontal. **1922** G. N. WATSON *Treat. Theory Bessel Functions* vi. 189 The reader will observe that Stokes' differential equation for Airy's integral is identical with one of the transformed forms of Bessel's equation. **1929** A. E. CONRADY *Appl. Optics & Optical Design* I. iii. 131 (*heading*) The Airy spurious disk. **1936** H. H. EMSLEY *Visual Optics* ii. 42 The sizes of the central Airy disc and surrounding rings can be calculated. **1968** *IEEE Trans. Antennas & Propagation* XVI. 691/1 A more accurate approximation is obtained by replacing spherical Bessel functions..by Hankel functions..or by Airy functions. **1968** *Jrnl. Photogr. Sci.* XVI. 250 The relation of various image properties to the line width and to the aperture of a diffraction-limited lens can be computed from the light distribution in the Airy disk. **1975** BRAM & DOWNS *Manuf. Technol.* i. 24 Supporting at the Airy points will reduce the deflection and out of plane of bar ends. **1983** *Sci. Amer.* Feb. 66/1 The function that describes the relation between the optical length and the transmission of the interferometer (defined as the ratio of the strength of the transmitted beam to that of the incident beam) is called an Airy function and is quite important in the construction of an optical transistor. **1990** *Jrnl. de Physique* LI. 2095 For a quartz plate observed in transmission with a circular analyzer, an Airy spiral with two branches can be observed, whereas Airy spirals with four branches occur if two quartz plates with the same thickness and opposite handedness are observed between crossed linear polarizers.

Ajuga (ə'dʒuːgə), *n.* *Bot.* [mod.L., a. med.L. *ajuga* (Diefenbach), adopted by Linnaeus in his *Species Plantarum* (1753) II. 561 as the name of a genus.
App. a var. of L. *abiga* a plant having the power to induce abortion (f. *abigere* drive away: see ABIGATE *v.*).]
A genus of plants of the mint family which lack the floral upper lip characteristic of other labiates and include several species (esp. bugle, *A. reptans*) cultivated as ornamental ground cover; (also *ajuga*) a plant of this genus.

[**1597** GERARD *Herball* 422 Ground pine is called in Greek χαμαιπίτυς: in Latine *Ibiga, Aiuga & Abiga.*] **1793** SOWERBY & SMITH *Eng. Bot.* II. Plate 77 The true Ajugas are distinguished from the Teucriums by not having the calyx swelled on one side as the fruit ripens. **1864** L. H. GRINDON *Brit. & Garden Bot.* 392 The blue pagodas of the Ajuga rank with the prettiest ornaments of the springing hay-field. **1903** *Garden* 11 Apr. 243/3 Several of the Ajugas are rather aggressive in their ways. **1961** *Amat. Gardening* 18 Nov. 1/1 The ajuga keeps quite flat on the soil and even the attractive little blue flower spikes only grow a few inches tall. **1992** *Century Home* (Canada) May 66/3 Invasive plants like ajuga are almost impossible to eradicate.

Akebia (ə'kiːbɪə), *n.* [mod.L. (coined in Fr. by J. Decaisne 1837, in *Compt. Rend.* V. 394), ad. Jap. *akebi.*] An East Asian genus of twining shrubs of the family Lardizabalaceae, which have purplish flowers and palmately divided leaves and are cultivated esp. as wall cover; (also *akebia*) a plant of this genus.

1855 *Curtis's Bot. Mag.* LXXXI. 4864 (*heading*) Five-leaved Akebia. **1868** S. HEREMAN *Paxton's Bot. Dict.* 20/1 *Akèbia*..From a name one of the species bears in the gardens of Japan. **1924** *Jrnl. R. Hort. Soc.* XLIX. 150 The shrubs of the middle forest include, besides the rhododendrons..akebia, smilax, and lonicera. **1966** M. FISH *Carefree Gardening* (1972) 85 The flowers of the akebia never show up very well, being dark chocoate-red. **1985** *Homes & Gardens* Dec. 98 The façade was further softened by planting espaliered pear trees, the five-leaved akebia (*Akebia quinata*) and English boxwood.

akermanite ('ækəmənaɪt), *n.* *Min.* [ad. G. *Åkermanit* (coined by I. H. L. Vogt 1890, in *Arch. for Math. og Naturvidenskab* XIII. 323), f. the name of Richard *Åkerman*, 19th-cent. Swedish metallurgist: see -ITE[1].] A silicate of calcium and magnesium, $Ca_2MgSi_2O_7$, belonging to the melilite series of minerals and occurring as transparent or translucent crystals of the tetragonal system.

1890 *Amer. Jrnl. Sci.* CXL. 336 Åkermanite.—A lime-magnesia silicate, containing no alumina, and belonging to the tetragonal system like melilite... It is not known in nature but has been obtained by Vogt. **1920** *Ibid.* CC. 131 The compound $2CaO.MgO.2SiO_2$ was discovered by Ferguson and Merwin... The mineral åkermanite was thought by them to consist essentially of this compound. **1975** *Sci. Amer.* Feb. 33/1 Melilite is a mineral whose composition can vary continuously between $Ca_2Al_2SiO_7$, known as gehlenite, and $Ca_2MgSi_2O_7$, known as akermanite. **1990** *Jrnl. Petrol.* XXXI. 557 Many of these minerals, including wollastonite, monticellite, and akermanite, are characteristic of low pressure.

akinete (eɪ'kaɪniːt), *n. Biol.* [ad. G. *Akinet* (coined by N. Wille 1883, in *Bot. Centralblatt* XVI. 217), f. A- 14 + Gr. κινητ-ός movable.] In certain algae, a thick-walled non-motile resting cell or spore, formed asexually by the differentiation, without division, of a vegetative cell.

1902 *Encycl. Brit.* XXV. 267/1 Akinetes are ordinary thallus cells, which on account of their acquisition of a thick wall are capable of surviving unfavourable conditions. 1945 F. E. FRITSCH *Struct. & Reprod. Algae* II. 808 In many instances akinete-formation depends on the realisation of certain external conditions. 1955 G. M. SMITH *Cryptogamic Bot.* I. ii. 22 An akinete is not a zoospore or a stage in formation of zoospores. 1986 M. KOGUT tr. *Schlegel's Gen. Microbiol.* iii. 128 Akinetes are 'survival' forms. They are recognised by their size, intense pigmentation, and thick cell walls.

akrasia *n.*, var. of *ACRASIA *n.*[2]

akratic (ə'krætɪk), *a.*[1] *rare*−1. [f. as if on Gr. *ἀκρᾱτικ(ός, f. ἀκρᾱτ(ος unmixed + -IC: see *ACRASIA *n.*[1]] ? Failing to mix, irregular.

1851 *Fraser's Mag.* XLIV. 154/2 Among the akratic, or 'chemically indifferent', spas, Teplitz, in Bohemia, is that which combines the largest quantity of solid ingredients with the highest temperature.

akratic *a.*[2] and *n.*, var. *ACRATIC *a.* and *n.*

aktashite ('æktəʃaɪt), *n. Min.* [ad. Russ. *aktash* (V. I. Vasil'ev 1968, in *Voprosy Metallogenii Rtuti* 125), f. *Aktash*, name of a town in the Altai Mountains in southern Russia where the mineral was discovered: see -ITE[1].] A rhombohedral sulpharsenite of mercury and copper occurring as xenomorphic grains and isotypic with nowackiite.

1970 *Mineral. Mag.* XXXVII. 954 *Aktashite*... Sulpharsenite of Cu and Hg, with Cu around 24%, Hg 33%, As (+ Sb) 20%, and S 23%, occurring at Aktash in the high Altai. 1982 *Soviet Physics: Crystallogr.* XXVII. 26/2 Aktashite was discovered in 1968...Chemical analysis led to the formula $Cu_6Hg_3As_5S_{12}$, which as a result of structural determination was changed to $Cu_6Hg_3As_4S_{12}$.

alamethicin (ælə'mɛθɪsɪn), *n. Biochem.* [f. *alamethic-*, of unknown origin, (perh. a reference to the predominance of methyl alanine residues in the peptide) + -IN[1].] A macrocyclic peptide which is produced by strains of the fungus *Trichoderma viride* and acts as an ionophore and antibiotic.

1968 *Nature* 24 Feb. 713/1 The electrokinetic and chemical data suggest that six or more alamethicin molecules form either carriers or tubular channels through which ions flow across the membrane. 1969 *New Scientist* 17 Apr. 127/2 The macrocyclic peptide alamethicin had a similar effect upon the BLM [*sc.* bimolecular lipid membrane]. 1979 *Nature* 15 Nov. 336/2 Alamethicin, a polypeptide of molecular weight ~2,000, induces voltage-dependent conductance phenomena in artificial lipid bilayer membranes.

Alaska, *n.* Add: [a.] **Alaska Current**, a surface ocean current that flows anticlockwise in the Gulf of Alaska.

1880 S. JACKSON *Alaska & Missions N. Pacific Coast* i. 54 The former stream flowing northward has been named 'the 'Alaska Current', and gives the great southern coast of Alaska a winter climate as mild as that of one third of the United States. 1984 A. C. &

A. DUXBURY *Introd. World's Oceans* vii. 226 The Alaska Current, fed by water from the North Pacific Current and moving in a counterclockwise gyre in the Gulf of Alaska.

alaskaite (æ'læskəaɪt), *n. Min.* [f. the name of the *Alaska* mine in Colorado where the mineral was discovered + -ITE[1].] A substance originally identified as a mineral but now recognized as a mixture of sulphosalts of lead, silver, copper, and bismuth.

1881 G. A. KÖNIG in *Proc. Amer. Philos. Soc.* XIX. 473 Very prominent among its neighbors is the *Alaska* vein...The breast of the lower adit showed beautiful ore. Nests of gray copper and Alaskaite in a gangue of quartz and barite. 1927 *Amer. Mineralogist* XII. 21 The alaskaite, which is an argentiferous variety of galeno-bismuthinite, was found in the Saxon mine. 1944 C. PALACHE et al. *Dana's Syst. Min.* (ed. 7) I. 476 Alaskaite has been variously classed as an argentian galenobismutite..but the mineral is not sufficiently characterized to permit a definite opinion. 1980 G. C. AMSTUTZ et al. tr. *Ramdohr's Ore Minerals & Intergrowths* (ed. 2) II. 716 Over the mineral 'alaskaite' hovers an unlucky star.

alata (ə'lɑːtə), *n. Ent.* Pl. **alatae**. [f. mod.L. *migrans ālāta* winged migrating (generation) (adopted by O. Nüsslin 1903, in *Naturwiss. Zeitschr. für Land- und Forstwirtschaft* I. 27), f. L. *ālāta*, fem. of *ālātus* winged: see ALATE *a.*] A winged female aphid.

1922 *Proc. Acadian Entomol. Soc. 1921* VII. 10 In the case of..monophagous species.., the control of the production of alatae was even more perfect. 1938 *Trans. R. Entomol. Soc.* LXXXVII. 166 During July the alatae become increasingly scarce and finally disappear. 1992 FINCH & THOMPSON in R. G. McKinlay *Vegetable Crop Pests* iv. 88 In mid-May alatae disperse to colonise new host plants on which further batches of apterae and, later, alatae are produced parthenogenetically.

alba ('ælbə), *n.*[2] [a. L. *alba*, fem. of *albus* white, in *Rosa alba* (adopted by C. Linnaeus in his *Species Plantarum* (1753) I. 492), now called *Rosa × alba*.] A shrub rose derived from *Rosa × alba* (an old white garden rose now thought to be a hybrid), distinguished by grey-green leaves and pinkish-white, sweet-scented flowers; also, a flower of such a plant.

1848 W. PAUL *Rose Garden* I. iv. 51 Summer Roses: Provence, 8. Moss, 10. Damask, 6. Alba, 6. Gallica, 75. 1869 S. R. HOLE *Bk. about Roses* xi. 161 It was patent to their shrewder sense why pink Roses were called Albas. 1962 I. MURDOCH *Unofficial Rose* xxii. 219 Snipping off here a faintly blushing alba and here a golden-stamened wine-dark rose of Provence. 1962 *Amat. Gardening* 24 Mar. 4/3 The species and older shrub roses such as the albas. 1990 *Pract. Gardening* Nov. 69/1 (Advt.), Their form of flower, delicacy of colouring and particularly their rich fragrance, can be compared with the Damask, Gallica and Alba roses of years gone by.

albariza (ælbə'raɪzə, -'riːzə), *n.* [a. Sp. *albariza* whitish (usu. of the ground or soil), f. L. *albus* white.] A whitish loam of the Oligocene epoch, characteristic of the sherry-producing region around the town of Jerez de la Frontera in southern Spain.

1824 A. HENDERSON *Hist. Anc. & Mod. Wines* II. iii. 190 The soils of the district have been divided..into four orders: viz 1st, *Albariza*, which consists chiefly of carbonate of lime. 1833 C. REDDING *Hist. Mod. Wines* vi. 189 The soil of the Xeres vineyards..consists of what is called 'albariza' and 'barros'. 1959 W. JAMES *Word-bk. Wine* 4 The best vineyards in the Spanish sherry country lie in extremely chalky soil called albariza. **1991** *Wine & Spirits* Apr. 40/2 The best vineyards are comprised of albariza soil, a chalky, powdery soil type.

albendazole (æl'bɛndəzəʊl), *n. Pharm.* [f. *al-* of unknown origin + THIA)BENDAZOLE *n.*] An anthelminthic drug, $C_{12}H_{15}N_3O_2S$, effective against most nematode and some cestode worms, used in veterinary and human medicine.
1976 *Experientia* XXXII. 702 Albendazole is methyl [5-(propylthio)-1H-benzimidazol-2yl] carbamate and has the chemical formula $C_{12}H_{15}N_3O_2S$. **1984** *Jrnl. Pharm. & Biomed. Anal.* II. 73 Albendazole is a potent member of the benzimidazole group of anthelmintics. **1991** *Lancet* 14 Sept. 686/2 Helminth infections no longer needed to be dealt with one by one, since albendazole, a single-dose oral medication, would simultaneously treat all geohelminth infections—hookworm, ascariasis, trichuriasis, and enterobiasis.

albino, *n.* Add: Hence **al'binic** *a.* = ALBINISTIC *a.*
1903 *Science* 9 Jan. 75/2 Two of the sons, apparently, married wives who were 'pure dominants', *i.e.*, who were entirely free from the recessive (*albinic*) character. **1910** *Amer. Naturalist* XLIV. 727 Two albinic parents have only albinic offspring. **1984** *Zool. Sci.* I. 309/2 Three produced albinic tadpoles together with nearly the same number of wild-type tadpoles.

albite, *n.* Add: '**albitize** *v. trans.*, to convert into a form containing albite, by the alteration of alkali feldspar or plagioclase feldspar to the albite end-member; '**albitized** *ppl. a.*
1909 *Geol. Mag.* Decade V. VI. 253 In the lavas which have been most completely albitized, there was still a surplus left. **1946** *Bull. Geol. Surv. Nigeria* No. 17. 11 A new tin-zinc mineral..occurs.. associated with the albitized pegmatites. **1965** G. J. WILLIAMS *Econ. Geol. N.Z.* viii. 87/2 Thin marginal dykes of albitized, carbonated and epidotised porphyry. **1988** *Geol. Mag.* CXXV. 229/1 The original feldspars were antiperthites in which the K-feldspar lamellae were albitized.

albomycin (ælbəʊ'maɪsɪn), *n. Pharm.* [ad. Russ. *al'bomitsin* (coined by Gause & Brezhnikova 1951, in *Novosti Med.* XXIII. 3), f. L. *albus* white: see -o[1], -MYCIN.] A siderochrome antibiotic produced by the bacterium *Actinomyces subtropicus*, which has been used against bacteria resistant to penicillin.
1955 *Brit. Med. Jrnl.* 12 Nov. 1177/1 Albomycin, a new antibiotic, has been manufactured during recent years by the pharmaceutical industry of the Soviet Union. **1960** M. E. FLOREY *Clin. Applic. Antibiotics* IV. iv. 88 Albomycin was brought to the notice of the medical world in 1951... It was found to inhibit Gram-positive cocci readily, particularly the pneumococcus and the staphylococcus. **1972** *Materials & Technol.* V. xviii. 633 Albomycin is an antimicrobial agent with a similar spectrum to penicillin.

Albright ('ɔːlbraɪt), *n. Path.* [The name of Fuller *Albright* (1900-69), U.S. endocrinologist.] **a. Albright('s) syndrome, Albright's fibrous dysplasia** [described by Albright et al. in *New England Jrnl. Med.* (1937) 29 Apr. 727], a rare disease characterized by fibrous dysplasia of bone tissue, brownish patchy pigmentation of the skin, and endocrine disturbances, including precocious puberty in females.
1940 *Q. Cumulative Index Medicus* XXVI. 974/2 *Osteitis..fibrosa*, case with precocious puberty and cutaneous pigmentation (Albright syndrome). **1965** R. H. DURHAM *Encycl. Med. Syndromes* 19 Differential diagnosis should exclude hyperparathyroidism.., for

in Albright's syndrome considerable portions of the skeleton are unaffected. **1987** R. WYNNE-DAVIES in S. P. F. Hughes et al. *Orthopaedics* xix. 420/1 Polyostotic fibrous dysplasia.. is characterized by the development of fibrous tissue within bone at multiple sites. In Albright's fibrous dysplasia this feature is associated also with patches of brown skin pigmentation and, in girls, with gonadal dysfunction and precocious puberty.
b. Albright('s) (hereditary) dystrophy [tr. F. *dystrophie d'Albright* (coined by P. Seringe & S. Tomkiewicz 1957, in *Ann. de Pédiatrie* XXXIII. 1099/1); described by Albright et al. in *Endocrinology* (1942) XXX. 922 and *Trans. Assoc. Amer. Physicians* (1952) LXV. 337], **Albright('s) (hereditary) osteodystrophy**, the conditions pseudohypoparathyroidism and pseudopseudohypoparathyroidism.
1957 *Current List Med. Lit.* XXXII. 313/2 Albright's dystrophy: pseudo-pseudo-hypoparathyroidism of other authors. **1962** *Ann. Internal Med.* LVI. 335/1 The ossification or calcification of Albright's hereditary osteodystrophy is subcutaneous. **1993** *Jrnl. Clin. Endocrinol. & Metabolism* LXXVI. 1560/2 Activity of $G_s\alpha$ protein is reduced in most subjects with Albright hereditary osteodystrophy (AHO), an inherited disorder characterized by a constellation of somatic and developmental defects.

Albucid (æl'bjuːsɪd), *n. Pharm.* [Invented name.] A proprietary name for the sodium salt of sulphacetamide.
1938 *Trade Marks Jrnl.* 23 Nov. 1428/2 *Albucid*...Pharmaceutical preparations. **1941** *Pharm. Jrnl.* 29 Nov. 188/3 Sulphacetamide is a name which it has been proposed should be adopted for the preparation now known under the trademark 'Albucid'. **1964** S. DUKE-ELDER *Parsons' Dis. Eye* (ed. 14) xiv. 143 The most effective for general application because of its complete lack of irritability is sodium sulphacetamide (albucid). **1971** *Deutsche Gesundheitswesen* XXVI. 76/1 The treatment was carried through by applying Albucid eye ointment.

album, *n.*[2] Add: **3. album graecum** ('graɪkəm, 'griː-) [L. *graecum*, neut. sing. of *graecus* Greek], the excrement of dogs, hyenas, etc., after it has dried and whitened, formerly used medicinally.
1607 TOPSELL *Foure-f. Beastes* 189 The dung of dogges (called by the Apothecaryes *Album Græcum*) because the white is best,.. is verye profitable.. against inflammations in the brests of Women. **1804** SOUTHEY *Let.* 5 Mar. (1965) I. 355, I have called him [*sc.* Malthus] a dog by implication—having mentioned his *album græcum*. **1877** *Encycl. Brit.* VI. 353/1 Buckland's conjecture that they were of fæcal origin, and similar to the *album græcum* or excrement of hyænas, was confirmed by Dr Prout.

alchemilla (ælkə'mɪlə), *n. Bot.* Also †alchimilla. [ad. med.L. *alchimilla* lady's mantle, poss. ad. Arab. *iklīl al-malik*, lit. 'the crown of the king', infl. by med.L. *alchim-ia* alchemy + dim. suffix *-illa*, from the belief of the alchemists that dew from the leaves of this plant could turn base metals to gold. Adopted as a genus name by Linnaeus in his *Species Plantarum* (1753) I. 123.] Any of numerous herbaceous perennials of the genus *Alchemilla* of the rose family, whose members are widely distributed in the north temperate zone and mountainous regions of tropical Africa and are distinguished by palmately lobed leaves and cymes of tiny green or yellowish flowers; also **Alchemilla**, the genus itself. Cf. LADY'S MANTLE *n.*
1548 W. TURNER *Names of Herbes* (E.D.S.) 82 Alchimilla, other wyse called Pes leonis, is called in

english our Ladies Mantel or syndow. **1754** *New &*
Compl. Dict. Arts & Sci. I. 87/2 *Alchemilla*, in botany,
the same with *alchimilla. Ibid.* 88/1 The *alchimillas*
belong to the *tetrandria monogynia* class of Linnæus,
and are esteemed powerful vulneraries and
incrassants. **1885** *Encycl. Brit.* XIX. 46/1 Drops are
frequently to be found on the margins and at the apices
of the leaves.., of many plants, such as Grasses, Aroids,
Alchemillas, Saxifrages, &c. **1915** H. H. THOMAS *Bk.*
Hardy Flowers 19 The Alchemillas are valued as much
for their foliage..as for the flowers. **1985** *Gardening*
from 'Which?' Nov. 374/3 The yellow-flowered
alchemilla also goes well with *Sedum maximum*
'Atropurpureum'.

Alcian ('ælsɪən), *n.* Also **alcian.** [Perh. f.
PHTH)AL(O)CYAN(INE *n.*, with phonetic
respelling.] A proprietary name used with
following colour name to designate various
pigments derived from copper phthalocyanine,
esp. in **Alcian Blue**, a water-soluble blue dye
originally used in textile printing and later as a
histological stain for glycosaminoglycans.

1947 *Jrnl. Soc. Dyers & Colourists* LXIII. xvi.
(Advt.), Announcing Alcian Blue 8G. A new, fast,
water-soluble, blue printing dyestuff. **1959**
Chambers's Encycl. IV. 694/1 These beautiful colours
include the novel calico-printing Alcian blue 8G. **1961**
Lancet 30 Sept. 734/2 It..was weakly positive with
alcian blue. **1970** *Acta Histochem.* XXXV. 411 The
latter group comprises the copper phtalocyanines [*sic*],
i.e. Alcian Blue, Alcian Yellow, Alcian Green and Astra
Blue. **1989** *Jrnl. Zool.* CCXIX. 23 Toluidine blue and
alcian blue..at different pH values..for differentiating
acid from neutral mucopolysaccharides.

alcid ('ælsɪd), *n. Ornith.* [f. mod.L. family name
Alcidae, f. mod.L. genus name *Alca* (adopted
by C. Linnaeus in his *Systema Naturæ* (ed. 4,
1743) 74), f. as AUK *n.*: see -ID.] A bird of the
auk family, Alcidae.

1893 *Funk's Stand. Dict.* s.v. *Alcidæ*, Alcid, *n.* **1934**
R. T. PETERSON *Field Guide Birds Eastern N. Amer.* 82
Brünnich's Murre... This is the only Alcid one is likely
to encounter in the interior. **1958** E. T. GILLIARD
Living Birds of World 193/2 There are 22 species of
alcids, most of them inhabitants of the colder regions
of the Northern Hemisphere. **1972** L. HANCOCK
There's a Seal in my Sleeping Bag v. 76 Little is known
about puffins, or indeed about any of the alcids in
British Columbia.

Alclad ('ælklæd), *n. Metallurgy.* Also **alclad.** [f.
AL(UMINIUM *n.* + CLAD *ppl. a.*] A proprietary
name for a composite material consisting of
sheets of aluminium alloy coated with pure
aluminium (or an aluminium alloy different
from that of the core) to increase corrosion
resistance.

1927 *Official Gaz.* (U.S. Patent Office) 19 July 550/2
Alclad...Duplex aluminum and aluminum-base
alloys. **1933** *Jrnl. R. Aeronaut. Soc.* XXXVII. 698
Essentially, alclad is duralumin sheet sandwiched
between aluminium. **1984** E. P. DEGARMO et al.
Materials & Processes in Manuf. (ed. 6) viii. 185 Where
both high strength and superior corrosion resistance
are needed, the wrought aluminum is often produced
as Alclad.

alcohol, *n.* Add: **6.** *Comb.* **alcohol-free** *a.*, (*a*)
prohibiting, restricting, or avoiding the sale or
consumption of alcoholic drinks; 'dry' (DRY *a.*
11 a); (*b*) (esp. of a beer, wine, etc.) containing
little or no alcohol.

1913 E. GORDON *Anti-Alcohol Movement in Europe*
iv. 134 The fencing associations also exhibited, in
recognition of the alliance between athletics and the
alcohol-free life... Indirect methods of fighting drink
were represented by..an exhibition by thirty firms of

alcohol-free wines. **1978** *Washington Post* 2 Nov. 11/5
Maintain, develop proven programs for 'average',
handicapped, gifted/talented students. Require
disciplined, drug/alcohol free, learning
environment. **1979** *Ibid.* 23 June D9/6 The Saudis
have oil, which the world wants. Now C. Schmidt &
Sons, a Philadelphia brewery, has something the Saudis
want — alcohol-free beer. **1986** *Summary of World*
Broadcasts: Soviet Union (B.B.C.) 17 May C2/2 Already
in the first quarter of this year we have a growth rate
of 37% over last year for alcohol-free drinks. **1990** W.
BOYD *Brazzaville Beach* 47 Apart from his new alcohol-
free life, there were no other significant changes in
John's life that Hope could easily discern. **1991** B. E.
ELLIS *Amer. Psycho* ii. 27 One should use an alcohol-
free antibacterial toner with a water-moistened cotton
ball to normalize the skin.

alcoholic, *a.* and *n.* Add: [**A.**] **2.** Chiefly *Path.*
Produced or caused by the consumption of
alcohol, or by alcoholism.

1850 W. B. CARPENTER *Use & Abuse Alcoholic Liquors*
i. 9 The term Intoxication..is commonly applied to
alcoholic intoxication alone. **1882** *Med. Temp. Jrnl.*
No. 50. 77 Symptoms of chronic alcoholic
poisoning. **1916** E. V. LUCAS *Vermilion Box* 141 He
was, as the slang phrase has it, 'oiled'; which is a
condition of alcoholic comfort well on this side of
inebriety. **1968** *Brit. Jrnl. Psychiatry* CXIV. 1549/1 A
short list would include..depression in sexual
perversion, alcoholic depression, and depressive
symptoms resulting from organic disorder. **1991** J.
DISKI *Happily ever After* i. 4 He listened, in an alcoholic
torpor, from the depths of his armchair, to the sounds
of the house.

3. alcoholic fermentation, the type of
fermentation occurring in yeast, in which
glucose is broken down to produce ethanol and
carbon dioxide (earlier called *vinous*
fermentation); contrasted with *lactic*
fermentation.

1852 T. R. BETTON tr. *Regnault's Elem. Chem.* II. IV.
511 We shall be satisfied with stating what is known
concerning alcoholic fermentation. **1879** J. TYNDALL
Fragments Sci. (ed. 6) VI. xii. 260 The true alcoholic
fermentation. **1947** C. E. SKINNER et al. *Henrici's*
Molds, Yeasts & Actinomycetes (ed. 2) xi. 323 This
investigator concluded that the production of alcoholic
fermentation does not require as complicated an
apparatus as the living yeast cell. **1988** K. LYNCH
Adventures on Wine Route (1990) v. 152 The alcoholic
fermentation occurs within the skin of each uncrushed
grape.

alcoholysis (ælkə'hɒlɪsɪs), *n. Chem.* [ad. F.
alcoolyse (coined by A. Haller 1906, in *Compt.*
Rend. CXLIII. 657): see ALCOHOL *n.*, -LYSIS.]
Decomposition of a compound by reaction with
an alcohol.

1907 *Jrnl. Chem. Soc.* XCII. 1. 9 The author applies
the term 'alcoholysis' to the breaking down of a fat into
glycerol and an alkyl ester..by heating it with the
corresponding absolute alcohol. **1910** *Chem. Abstr.* IV.
597 Addition of Zn or Sn to the HCl mixture during
alcoholysis of oils..will serve to prevent
oxidation. **1967** I. L. FINAR *Org. Chem.* (ed. 5) I. ix.
219 Alcoholysis is carried out by refluxing the ester
with a large excess of alcohol. **1992** *Tetrahedron Lett.*
XXXIII. 3232 We studied the enzymatic alcoholysis
of the diester in organic solvent.

alcometer (æl'kɒmɪtə(r)), *n.* Also **Alcometer.** [f.
ALCO(HOL *n.* + -METER.] An instrument for
determining the level of alcohol in the breath.

[**1941** *Q. Jrnl. Stud. Alcohol* II. 58 The purpose of
the Alcoholometer..is to fulfill all these conditions
through a portable robot which collects a sample of
expired air..and registers the results in terms of alcohol
concentration of the blood.] **1950** *Jrnl. Amer. Med.*
Assoc. 18 Feb. 523/1 The Alcometer, a breath-testing

apparatus recently developed by the Department of Applied Physiology of Yale University. **1974** *Telegraph* (Brisbane) 6 Feb. 37/1 Dr. Piga claimed that the balloon-type alcometer issued to Spanish police.. was inaccurate and unreliable. **1991** *Lancet* 7 Sept. 607/1 In the early studies patients were awake and breathed spontaneously into the alcometer; now the method has been applied to unconscious patients.

aldicarb ('ældɪkɑːb), *n.* [f. ALDE(HYDE *n.*, with phonetic respelling, + CARB(AMIDE *n.*] A carbamate derivative used as a systemic agricultural pesticide against some mites, insects and nematodes; 2-methyl-2-(methylthio)-propionaldehyde *O*-methylcarbamoyloxime, $C_7H_{14}N_2O_2S$.

1970 *Jrnl. Econ. Entomol.* LXIII. 651/1 Aldicarb (formerly Temik®) has been reported to be effective against.. the two-spotted spider mite. **1977** *Jrnl. R. Soc. Arts* CXXV. 567/1 Two very toxic substances, aldicarb and oxamyl, with a strong systemic action, have been of considerable benefit as soil applications. **1990** *N.Y. Times* 7 May D11/5 Most people are far more frightened of the threat of cancer than of the flulike symptoms that they associate with food poisoning. Fanning their anxieties are frequent alerts: about dioxin in milk, aldicarb in potatoes, Alar in apples.

aldol, *n.* Add: **2.** Special Comb. **aldol condensation, reaction**, a condensation reaction between two carbonyl molecules to yield a single molecule with one hydroxyl and one carbonyl group (exemplified by the conversion of acetaldehyde to aldol).

1901 *Jrnl. Chem. Soc.* LXXX. 450 This reaction takes place so much more slowly than the ˙aldol condensation that the former is practically entirely concealed. **1936** W. J. HICKINBOTTOM *Reactions Org. Compounds* iv. 139 The simplest type of reaction is that exemplified by the ˙aldol reaction. **1968** A. WHITE et al. *Princ. Biochem.* (ed. 4) xviii. 397 This enzyme can catalyze an aldol condensation between dihydroxyacetone phosphate and a wide variety of aldehydes. **1988** L. STRYER *Biochem.* (ed. 3) xi. 271 The aldehyde derivatives of two lysine residues undergo an aldol condensation. **1992** *Organometallics* XI. 350 Cerium enolates.. undergo aldol reactions with ketones or sterically hindered aldehydes.

aldolization (ˌældɒlaɪˈzeɪʃən), *n.* *Org. Chem.* [f. ALDOL *n.* + -IZATION.] Conversion of an aldehyde or ketone to aldol or a structurally related molecule.

1934 in WEBSTER. **1938** ALLEN & BLATT in H. Gilman *Org. Chem.* I. vi. 569 Schiff's bases add organic compounds containing an active α-hydrogen atom by a process which is analogous to aldolization. **1975** *Nature* 25 Sept. 303/2 Although the kinetics of aldolisation reactions have been studied, no observations have been reported concerning the effect of oxygen on their rates and kinetics. **1987** *Chem. Engin. Jrnl.* XXXV. 25/2 Gerritsen et al. performed some orienting aldolization experiments and found that the aldolization activities of RhHCO(PPh₃)₃ and PPh₃ are negligible.

aldonic (ælˈdɒnɪk), *a.* *Chem.* [f. ALD(OSE *n.* + -ONIC.] **aldonic acid**, any of a class of carboxylic acids obtained from aldose sugars by oxidation of the aldehyde group.

1929 *Jrnl. Amer. Chem. Soc.* LI. 2225 (*title*) Improvements in the preparation of aldonic acids. **1938** M. L. WOLFROM in H. Gilman *Org. Chem.* II. xvi. 1404 On hypobromite oxidation, the aldoses produce the corresponding aldonic acids. **1967** I. L. FINAR *Org. Chem.* (ed. 5) I. xviii. 473 Aldonic acids, in aqueous solution, are largely in the form of the γ-lactone. **1988** P. W. KUCHEL et al. *Schaum's Outl. Theory & Probl. Biochem.* ii. 40 Oxidation of the

aldehyde group of an aldose to a carboxylic acid group gives a derivative known as an aldonic acid.

alethic (əˈliːθɪk), *a.* *Logic.* [f. Gr. ἀλήθ-εια truth + -IC.] Designating modalities of truth, e.g. the possibility or impossibility of something being true.

1951 G. H. VON WRIGHT *Essay in Modal Logic* i. 1 Alethic modes or modes of truth... can conveniently be divided into two sub-kinds. Sometimes we consider the modes in which a proposition is (or is not) true... Sometimes we consider the modes in which a property is present (or absent) in a thing. **1982** R. QUIRK *Style & Communication in Eng. Lang.* iii. 50 A fourth modality, alethic.., can be disregarded in ordinary linguistic communication, concerned as it is with purely logical necessity ('Since he is unmarried, he must be a bachelor'). **1987** L. W. SUMNER *Moral Found. Rights* ii. 22 The analogy between the two kinds of constraints serves to remind us that deontic categories (required/forbidden) are counterparts, or perhaps special cases, of alethic modal categories (necessary/impossible).

Aleutian, *a.* and *n.* Add: [A.] **2.** Special collocation: **Aleutian disease** *Vet. Sci.* [see quot. 1977], a frequently chronic, systemic viral disease of mink and ferrets.

1956 *National Fur News* XXVIII. 10/2 The possibility of two or more unrelated conditions occuring as 'Aleutian disease' must be given consideration. **1977** *Sci. Amer.* May 140/2 It is the Aleutian disease of mink, so named because it is in time invariably fatal to a mutant strain of mink with a fashionable light-hued fur resembling the pelage of the Aleutian blue fox. **1989** *Microbial Pathogenesis* VII. 319 Parvoviruses cause well defined, sometimes life threatening diseases such as myocarditis and enteritis (canine parvovirus), leukopenia (feline parvovirus), and immune complex disease (Aleutian disease virus).

Alexandra, *n.* Add: [**2.**] Special Comb. **Alexandra palm** (also **Alexander palm**), a tall ornamental palm, *Archontophoenix alexandrae*, native to Queensland, Australia, which has a bulbous trunk and large feathered leaves.

1880 F. VON MUELLER *Sel. Extra-Tropical Plants* 264 *Ptychosperma Alexandræ*, f. v. Mueller. The Alexandra Palm. Queensland... The tallest of Australian Palms, and one of the noblest forms in the whole empire of vegetation. **1908** E. J. BANFIELD *Confessions of Beachcomber* II. i. 252 The heart of the Alexandra palm.., the long root-stock of *Curculigo ensifolia*.. would stand as vegetables. **1967** A. M. BLOMBERY *Guide Native Austral. Plants* ii. 208 Alexandra Palm. A tall palm, similar to *A. cunninghamiana*, but with a trunk showing distinct ringed ridges. **1988** *Courier-Mail* (Brisbane) 3 Mar. 18/5 Toowong fruiterer Mr Tom Paridissas.. has given four 6.7m Alexander palms to help beautify Expo's amusement park.

alfacalcidol (ælfəˈkælsɪdɒl), *n.* *Pharm.* [f. *alfa*, phonetic respelling of ALPHA *n.* + CALCI(FEROL *n.* and -*idol*, perh. alteration of *DIOL *n.*] An analogue of vitamin D_3 used in the treatment of vitamin D deficiency; 1α-hydroxychole-calciferol.

1978 *Approved Names 1977* (Brit. Pharmacopoeia Comm.) Suppl. III, Alfacalcidol. **1985** *Brit. Med. Jrnl.* 26 Oct. 1153/2 The lack of toxicity of alfacalcidol makes a clinical study feasible. **1989** COLLIER & LONGMORE *Oxf. Handbk. Clin. Specialties* (ed. 2) iii. 280 Vitamin D (50 nanograms/kg of alfacalcidol/day PO) is helpful in reducing phosphate excretion.

alfalfa, *n.* Add: **2.** Special Comb. **alfalfa sprouts** *n. pl.* (also *attrib.* in *sing.*), the edible sprouting seeds of alfalfa.

1972 *Sunset* May 230 *Alfalfa sprouts are good raw or may be butter-sautéed to emphasize flavor. **1979** *Tucson Mag.* Apr. 78/1 Try one of their special alfalfa sprout, avocado and jack cheese open face sandwiches. **1989** W. BELASCO *Appetite for Change* Epilogue 245 In 1970 who would have thought that yogurt, tofu, 2-percent milk, herbal tea..would now be supermarket norms, or that salad bars would offer alfalfa sprouts?

Al Fatah *n.*: see *FATAH *n.*

aliteracy (eɪ'lɪtərəsɪ), *n.* [f. A- 14 + LITERACY *n.*] Disinclination to read, despite having the ability to do so. Cf. ILLITERACY *n.*

1981 *Presstime* Sept. 5/1 'Aliteracy' might be our largest literacy problem. **1982** *Publishers Weekly* 1 Oct. 34/1 The nation's decision-making process..is threatened by those who can read but won't, Townsend Hooper, president of the Association of American Publishers, told some 50 persons attending an 'a-literacy' conference. **1984** *Washington Post* 8 Dec. A. 12/2 Illiteracy and aliteracy, described as the unwillingness to read, are the major threat to the culture of the book. **1990** *Times* 18 Apr. 13/5 The process is due, of course, to the triumph of television, and the vast aliteracy of our time—people can read but don't.

aliterate (eɪ'lɪtərət), *a.* (and *n.*) [f. A- 14 + LITERATE *a.* and *n.*] Of a person: unwilling to make use of any reading ability he or she may possess; disinclined to read. Hence, of a society: characterized by aliteracy. Also as *n.*, an aliterate person.

1966 *Sat. Rev.* (U.S.) 25 June 10/1 The student body there consisted of boys who hated books, boys who had gotten into trouble. 'They were not only illiterate,' Fader says, 'they were a-literate.' **1981** *Presstime* Sept. 4/1 'Aliterates'—those people who can read but who, for whatever reasons, choose not to. ('Aliterate' is a term ignored by Webster's but used here, and in the jargon of most reading specialists, to mean one who can but won't read.). **1985** *N.Y. Times* 12 June 26/4 We live in an *aliterate* society. **1991** *Wilson Q.* Summer 81/1 As an English teacher it is particularly disturbing to see fewer and fewer of even the brightest students reading, except when a grade is involved. The new term for these nonreaders is 'aliterate'.

all, *a., n.*, and *adv.* Add: [E.] [III.] [13.] **all-sky** *a.*, covering the entire sky (either both hemispheres or just the visible hemisphere); **all-sky camera**, a camera, now usu. one with a wide-angle lens, capable of photographing all or most of the visible hemisphere of the sky in one exposure.

1955 *Tellus* VII. 510/2 An *all-sky camera is doubtless an ideal tool for the study of auroral forms and their changes. **1973** C. SAGAN *Cosmic Connection* (1975) vii. 50 (*caption*) Composite photograph by all-sky cameras of our Milky Way Galaxy. **1989** *Nature* 13 July 111/2 The lack of all-sky visibility. **1992** *Financial Times* 11–12 Apr. II. 1/6 The Set: plan involves two complementary modes. First, there will be an all-sky search covering nearly 500m channels in the 1,000–10,000 MHz range. **1992** S. P. MARAN *Astron. & Astrophysics Encycl.* 314/1 A highly successful series of flights, called *Hi Star*,.. provided the first all-sky map of the sky at thermal infrared wavelengths.

Allen ('ælən), *n.*[2] [The name of Joel A. *Allen* (1838–1921), U.S. zoologist.] **Allen's rule**, an ecogeographical rule first formulated by Allen in 1877 (*Ann. Rep. Smithsonian Inst. 1905* (1906)), according to which the protruding body parts of a warm-blooded animal are smaller in populations occupying the cooler parts of its geographical range. Cf. *BERGMANN *n.*

1937 ALLEE & SCHMIDT *Hesse's Ecol. Animal Geogr.* xx. 389 We find that mammals of cold climates have

their heat-radiating surfaces decreased by a reduction in size of the ear and tail, by a shortening of the neck and in general by a more compact form. This has been referred to as Allen's Rule. **1954** G. L. CLARKE *Elem. Ecol.* 158 These simple ecological relationships, in addition to underlying Bergmann's principle and Allen's rule, undoubtedly account in part at least for the fact that no extremely small mammals or birds exist, that is, as small as the majority of insects. **1973** B. J. WILLIAMS *Evolution & Human Origins* xiii. 221 Allen's rule is concerned with changes in shape to achieve the optimal volume-to-surface area ratio. **1992** *Cambr. Encycl. Human Evolution* (1994) x. i. 389/1 Body form also obeys certain rules, like Allen's rule..: Inuit (Eskimos) are short-limbed, and Africans of the sunny tropics are the opposite.

allene, *n.* Substitute for entry: **allene** ('æliːn), *n. Chem.* [ad. Fr. *allène* (coined by L. Henry 1875, in *Bull. Soc. Chim. Paris* XXIII. 350): see ALLYL *n.*, -ENE.] **1.** = *PROPADIENE *n.*

1877 H. WATTS *Fownes' Man. Elem. Chem.* (ed. 12) II. 63, β Allylene, or allene, $CH_2=CH=CH_2$ [*sic*], is formed..by the electrolysis of itaconic acid. **1930** *Jrnl. Amer. Chem. Soc.* LII. 4540 No record exists concerning the behavior of methylacetylene, $CH_3-C\equiv CH$, at high temperatures. Except for Lebedev's work, the same may be said for allene, $CH_2=C=CH_2$. **1968** A. A. BAKER *Unsaturation in Org. Chem.* vii. 89 In 1891 Vaubel prepared allene..and he found that it readily isomerized on heating to propyne. **1979** *Nomencl. Org. Chem.: A–F, H* (I.U.P.A.C.) 11 The following non-systematic names are retained: Ethylene $CH_2=CH_2$. Allene $CH_2=C=CH_2$. **1988** *New Scientist* 22 Oct. 57/2, I can think of allene in the traditional way as a molecule of formula $CH_2=C=CH_2$ with double bonds between its three carbon atoms.

2. A substituted derivative of allene; a hydrocarbon having two double bonds in adjacent positions.

1899 *Jrnl. Chem. Soc.* LXXVI. 1. 658 The various allene hydrocarbons can be distinguished..(i) Mono-substituted allenes give dibromotrimethylenes. **1937** *Thorpe's Dict. Appl. Chem.* (ed. 4) I. 79/2 The allenes are non-conjugated diolefinic hydrocarbons..which are obtained by..isomerization of certain alkylacetylenes on heating. **1972** A. DEMPSTER tr. *Natta & Farina's Stereochem.* iv. 113 A class very similar to the allenes consists of the spirans—bicyclic compounds whose rings are attached to only one atom.

allergic, *a.* Add: **2.** Special collocation. **allergic rhinitis**, rhinitis caused by allergy, e.g. to pollen or the house dust mite, and typically accompanied by sneezing and running of the nose.

1924 *Amer. Rev. Tuberculosis* IX. 79 The sneezing and nose symptoms had never existed to the degree to arouse even a suspicion of *allergic rhinitis. **1966** *Ann. Allergy* XXIV. 150/1 One of the most difficult of the allergic diseases to control adequately is perennial allergic rhinitis. **1976** R. MACKARNESS *Not all in Mind* (1980) iv. 80 Most doctors now call hay fever 'allergic rhinitis'.

allergy, *n.* Add: **aller'genically** *adv.*; **allergenicity** (ˌælədʒə'nɪsɪtɪ) *n.*, the capacity to elicit an allergic response.

1943 *Jrnl. Immunol.* XLVII. 443 The proteic component segregated in the allergenically active polysaccharidic-protein fraction..passed readily through a collodion membrane. **1965** *Ann. Allergy* XXIII. 47/1 Recently we reported initial observations concerning the possible allergenicity of airborne algae. **1978** *Clin. Allergy* VIII. 135 An allergenically important mite. **1980** *Chem. in Brit.* Nov. 605/1 Sulphoxide, epoxide and quinone formation from aromatic compounds is a recognised pathway of drug metabolism and the products would react with proteins, but allergenicity has not been firmly linked with them. **1988** *Fitness* May 30/1 Some people are allergic to specific foods and for this reason Quorn was tested for allergenicity and intolerance in human volunteers.

allethrin (ə'li:θrɪn), *n.* [f. ALL(YL + PYRE)THRIN *n.*] A pyrethroid compound, $C_{19}H_{26}O_3$, used as a contact insecticide against household pests.
1950 J. B. MOORE in *Jrnl. Econ. Entomol.* XLIII. 207 Seven samples of the allyl analog of cinerin I (hereafter referred to as allethrin) were received from five different sources and were assayed. **1962** *New Scientist* 6 Dec. 577 A somewhat similar synthetic compound, allethrin, ..has partially replaced natural pyrethrum. **1991** WORTHING & HANCE *Pesticide Man.* (ed. 9) 19 Formulations show higher efficacy than those of natural pyrethrins. In the case of liquid formulations, insecticidal activities of allethrin are enhanced by pyrethrin synergists.

alliance, *n.* Sense 2 b in Dict. becomes 2 d. Add: [2.] **b.** Used collectively of the parties to an alliance. Occas. const. as *pl.*
1708 J. ADDISON *Present State War* 20 The Grand Alliance have innumerable Sources of Recruits..in *Britain* and *Ireland*. **1849** MACAULAY *Hist. Eng.* I. ii. 207 Apprehensions..which, in our age, induced the Holy Alliance to interfere in the internal government of Naples. **1883** *Manchester Guardian* 17 Oct. 5/2 The step which the United Kingdom Alliance wants Parliament to take is on their own showing a momentous one. **1965** A. J. P. TAYLOR *Eng. Hist. 1914–45* xi. 382 The Labour party remained what it had been before—an alliance of men with widely differing views, not a disciplined army. **1987** *Methodist Recorder* 29 Oct. 1/3 Horoscopes, Hallowe'en celebrations and ouija boards are doorways to evil and destruction, says a report just published by the Evangelical Alliance.
c. *Ecol.* [First used in this sense in Fr. by Braun-Blanquet & Pavillard in *Vocabulaire de Sociol. Végétale* (ed. 2, 1925) 20, app. tr. Ger. *Verband.*] In phytosociology, a grouping of closely related associations.
1930 F. R. BHARUCHA tr. *Braun-Blanquet & Pavillard's Vocab. Plant Sociol.* 21 The associations (and fragments of associations) which show floristic and sociological affinities between themselves, form an 'Alliance' or a group of associations. **1961** HANSON & CHURCHILL *Plant Community* vi. 179 These attributes—kinds of species, abundance, frequency, dominance, and fidelity—have been used to make a hierarchical system of classification, including the association with its subdivisions and variants to alliance, order, and class. **1974** MUELLER-DOMBOIS & ELLENBERG *Aims & Methods Vegetation Ecol.* ix. 210 As examples of alliances may be named, among others, the *Arrhenatherum* meadows (*Arrhenatherion*), the *Phragmites* water grass communities (*Phragmition*) and the moist alder forest communities (*Alnion glutinosae*) and the therophytic *Salicornia* marshland communities (*Salicornion europaeae*).

allicin ('ælɪsɪn), *n. Biochem.* [f. L. *allium* garlic (mod.L. *Allium*, genus name) + -c- + -IN[1].] An antibacterial substance in garlic which is an oily yellow liquid with the characteristic odour of garlic; S-2-propenyl-2-propene-1-sulphinothioate, $(C_3H_5S)_2O$.
1944 CAVALLITO & BAILEY in *Jrnl. Amer. Chem. Soc.* LXVI. 1950/1 The garlic antibacterial, hereinafter called allicin, showed a sharp zone of inhibition with the periphery accentuated by a line of heavy growth. **1964** W. G. SMITH *Allergy & Tissue Metabolism* v. 66 Enzyme inhibitors which react with sulphydryl or amino groups—iodoacetate, allicin,..and acetic anhydride blocked the release of both histamine and SRS-A. **1990** *Here's Health* Dec. 30/2 (Advt.), The best garlic for you (but not for your breath) is raw garlic. It provides a substance called allicin which has important benefits but is also very smelly.

alligator, *n.* Add: [4.] [a.] **alligator snapping turtle**, the larger of two species of snapping turtle, *Macroclemys temminckii*, having crests on its tail which resemble those of an alligator.
1882 H. C. YARROW in *Bull. U.S. Nat. Mus.* No. 24. 5 Macrochelys Lacertina (Schweigger) Cope. *Alligator Snapping Turtle; 'Caoune'. **1989** WILSON & FERRIS *Encycl. Southern Culture* 325/2 The alligator snapping turtle is the largest freshwater turtle in the world.

allochronic (æləʊ'krɒnɪk), *a. Biol.* [f. ALLO- + SYN)CHRONIC *a.*] Of species, populations, etc.: existing at different points in (geological) time; breeding or flourishing at different seasons. Of speciation: occurring through the development of different breeding seasons in populations which are not geographically separated.
1953 E. MAYR et al. *Methods & Princ. Systematic Zool.* i. 37 It has therefore been proposed to use two sets of terminology, one for the synchronous allopatric subspecies of the neontologist and one for allochronic subspecies. **1966** *McGraw-Hill Encycl. Sci. & Technol.* XII. 572/2 Species which occur together in time, more particularly at the same geological level, are designated as synchronic; those which are separated in time are allochronic. **1977** *Science* 5 Aug. 592/3 Proposed cases of sympatric speciation through seasonal isolation (that is, allochronic speciation) are not as well supported. **1983** THORNHILL & ALCOCK *Evolution Insect Mating Syst.* xiii. 409 There are few well-documented cases of nearly identical songs..among allopatric or allochronic (seasonally segregated) species of acoustical insects.
Hence **a'llochrony** *n.*, seasonal segregation.
1978 *Environmental Entomol.* VII. 708 *Podosesia syringae* (Harris) and *P. aureocincta* Purrington and Nielsen are sympatric sibling clearwing moths reproductively isolated by adult allochrony. **1988** *Nature* 3 Nov. 66/1 This allochrony is potentially important in serving to isolate sympatric populations on the two host plants. **1992** *Environmental Biol. Fishes* XXXIII. 173/1 *V. vimba* also spawns somewhat earlier in the season than *B. bjoerkna* and so spawning allochrony further safeguards their reproductive isolation.

allodapine (æləʊ'deɪpaɪn), *a.* and *n. Ent.* [f. mod.L. genus name *Allodape* (coined in P. A. Latreille et al. *Encycl. Méthodique* (Histoire Naturelle) (1825) x. 19/1), f. Gr. ἀλλοδαπός foreign: see -INE[1].] **A.** *adj.* Of or belonging to the genus *Allodape* or the subfamily Allodapinae of primitively social bees, which rear the broods of several females communally in unsealed burrows and some of which are parasitic in other bee colonies. **B.** *n.* An allodapine bee.
1969 *Jrnl. Kansas Entomol. Soc.* XLII. 248 Eversible ventrolateral projections or pseudopods occur and serve to hold and manipulate food in some species of *Braunsapis* and other allodapines. *Ibid.* 289 To permit publication of materials on the ecology, behavior, and systematics of allodapine bees.., certain new genera are described. **1975** D. V. ALFORD *Bumble Bees* iv. 57 Larvae of allodapine bees, which are primitively social, ..continue to receive food after they have hatched.

allometry, *n.* Add: **allo'metrically** *adv.*
1966 DAVIS & ZANGERL tr. *Hennig's Phylogenetic Systematics* ii. 100 In positive allometry, 'the larger the body becomes, the larger does the allometrically growing organ become'. **1978** *Nature* 10 Aug. 583/1 Differences between males are exaggerated by the horns, the length of which increases disproportionately (allometrically) with body length. **1992** *Amer. Jrnl. Physical Anthropol.* LXXXVII. 206/2 In a sample of cercopithecids..the lengths of the major segments of the hindlimb and foot scale allometrically with body mass.

allomone ('æləʊməʊn), *n. Biol.* [f. ALLO- + -*mone* after PHEROMONE *n.*] A chemical secreted and released by an organism which, when detected by an organism of another species, evokes a specific response, *esp.* one that adaptively favours the releasing organism (cf. *KAIROMONE *n.*).

1968 W. L. BROWN in *Amer. Naturalist* CII. 190 *Allomone*: a chemical substance produced or acquired by an organism which, when it contacts an individual of *another species* in the natural context, evokes in the receiver a behavioral or developmental reaction adaptively favorable to the transmitter. *Ibid.* 191 Allomone has been used in informal discussions in the United States for two or three years. **1971** *Nature* 2 Apr. 315/2 The importance and potential economic application of naturally occurring chemicals, including pheromones and allomones, for controlling the spatial and temporal structure of [insect] populations have long been realized by some ecologists. **1982** J. B. HARBORNE *Introd. Ecol. Biochem.* (ed. 2) vii. 179 Volatile chemicals used for communication *within* species are termed 'pheromones', while chemicals used *between* different species are called 'allomones'. **1987** *Times* 1 Oct. 16/6 The waterpepper plants produce an allomone which prevents insect pests from eating them.

allonal ('ælənəl), *n. Pharm.* Also **Allonal.** [f. ALL(YL *n.* + -O[1] + -AL[2], with inserted *n.*] A derivative of barbituric acid which has been used as a sedative and hypnotic; 5-allyl-5-isopropylbarbituric acid, $C_{10}H_{14}N_2O_3$.

1922 *Trade Marks Jrnl.* 11 Oct. 1830 A pharmaceutical product. Allonal. **1927** *Glasgow Herald* 24 Dec. 10/5 The death of a nurse as a result of taking a new German drug known as 'Allonal'..has resulted in the revelation that there is in this country 'a very considerable demand' for dangerous German drugs. **1938** 'N. SHUTE' *Ruined City* (1951) 14 He must sleep...He..shook out three tablets of allonal, and swallowed them. **1949** M. LOWRY *Let.* 16 Feb. (1967) 168 By this time I had run out of sonoryl and switched to allonal, a sleeping medicine prescribed for Margerie.

allopatric, *a.* Add: **allo'patrically** *adv.*

1961 WEBSTER, Allopatrically. **1968** *Science* 8 Mar. 1069/1 In the case of a chromosomal rearrangement which first establishes itself near the edge of a species distribution, one can imagine it spreading both inwards through the range of the species (stasipatrically) and outwards into previously unoccupied territory (allopatrically). **1987** *Bull. Brit. Ornith. Club* CVII. 150 The presumption is that the 2 forms speciated allopatrically by the subdivision of a single parental form. **1992** *Jrnl. Plankton Res.* XIV. 555 It appears to have evolved allopatrically during the Cretaceous as a result of continental drift.

allophenic (ælə'fiːnɪk), *a. Biol.* [f. ALLO- + *phen(otyp)ic* s.v. PHENOTYPE *n.*] = *tetraparental* adj. s.v. TETRA- 1.

1967 B. MINTZ in *Proc. Nat. Acad. Sci.* LVIII. 349 The mice produced by aggregating eggs will henceforth be called *allophenic* mice. **1979** *Nature* 25 Jan. 300/1 It may be predicted that the agar embedding method will prove useful, not only for culture *in vivo* of micromanipulated sheep eggs whether they be of the 'single blastomere' or the 'allophenic' variety, but also in opening the way for similar experiments in other species. **1992** *Exper. Hematol.* XX. 470/1 Day-2 embryos from C57BL/6 and DBA/2 strains were fused to produce allophenic chimeric mice.

alloplastic (ælə'plæstɪk), *a.* [f. ALLO- + PLASTIC *a.* and *n.*[3]] **1.** Orig. *Psychoanal.* (Concerned with) altering or manipulating the external world, as opposed to altering the person, e.g. through psychological or evolutionary adaptation.

1924 J. RIVIERE tr. *Freud's Coll. Papers* II. xxiv. 280 This expedient normal attitude leads naturally to some active achievement in the outer world and is not content..with establishing the alteration within itself; it is no longer auto-plastic but allo-plastic. **1927** S. FERENCZI *Further Contrib. Theory & Technique Psycho-Anal.* xii. 164 Catalepsy and mimicry..would be regressions to a much earlier primitive method of adaptation of the organism..while flight and defence aim at an alteration in the environment (allo-plastic adaptation). **1954** W. LA BARRE *Human Animal* v. 90 Man's evolution..is through alloplastic experiments with objects outside his own body and is concerned only with the products of his hands, brains, and eyes—and not with his body itself. **1986** G. K. WOLFE *Crit. Terms for Science Fiction & Fantasy* 5 Technological societies use 'alloplastic' means, manipulating the environment to make it more hospitable.
2. *Surg.* Pertaining to or of the nature of alloplasty.

1965 *Bull. Acad. Polonaise des Sci.* (Biol.) XIII. 611 (*heading*) Ascites formation from abdominal organs placed in alloplastic bags. **1976** *Jrnl. Laryngol. & Otol.* XC. 699 A variety of alloplastic and natural substances have been utilized for support of the orbital floor following a blowout fracture. **1976** *Lancet* 30 Oct. 968/2 Alloplastic repairs, in common with other forms of cranioplasty, involve the introduction of foreign material.

alloplasty ('æləʊplæstɪ), *n. Surg.* [ad. G. *Alloplastik* (coined in F. Marchand *Der Process der Wundheilung* (1901) xxvii. 373): see ALLO-, -PLASTY.] Surgical repair or replacement of natural tissues and organs with synthetic materials.

1929 *Ann. Surg.* XC. 926 With respect to the grafting of inorganic and foreign materials, the procedure has had the term alloplasty applied to it by Marchand. **1966** *New Scientist* 12 May 342/3 Though internal, plastic hearts make headlines for alloplasty—the surgical technique of replacing natural organs by man-made substitutes—unsung progress is also being made externally. **1966** *Jrnl. Dental Res.* XLV. 1221/1 (*heading*) Titanium metal in alloplasty.

allosaur ('æləʊsɔː(r)), *n. Palaeont.* [Anglicization of *ALLOSAURUS *n.*] A dinosaur of the genus *Allosaurus*.

1934 WEBSTER, Allosaur. **1949** R. C. MOORE *Introd. Hist. Geol.* xvi. 383 The tyrannosaur is not merely a larger, more ferocious edition of the allosaur. **1989** *Guinness Bk. Records 1988* 43/1 Some of the allosaurs..of North America, Africa, Australia and China also reached exceptional sizes.

Allosaurus (æləʊ'sɔːrəs), *n. Palaeont.* Pl. **Allosauri.** [mod.L. (coined by O. C. Marsh 1877, in *Amer. Jrnl. Sci. & Arts* CXIV. 515): see ALLO-, *-SAUR.] A genus of large bipedal carnivorous theropod dinosaurs known from remains discovered in rocks of the Late Jurassic in North America; (also **allosaurus**) a dinosaur of this genus.

1886 *Encycl. Brit.* XX. 443/2 Order 4. Theropoda...Fam. *a*...Genera: *Megalosaurus* (European): *Allosaurus, Cælosaurus,* [etc.]. **1911** *Ibid.* XX Plate facing p. 581 (*caption*) Skeleton of *Allosaurus.* **1955** *Sci. News Let.* 5 Feb. 94/2 Cavemen had enough to face, what with mastodons, cave bears and woolly rhinoceroses; it is just as well that they were spared casual allosauri and diplodocuses. **1966** A. S. ROMER *Vertebr. Paleont.* (ed. 3) xii. 153/1 *Allosaurus* was an animal with a total length of about 34 feet. **1975** *N.Y. Times* 3 Oct. 16/1 Anyone who can shell out $29,995 for the store's 'Saurian Safari' is guaranteed a skeleton of an allosaurus. **1986** G. CULVERWELL tr. *Arduini & Teruzzi's Macdonald Encycl. Fossils* No. 218, The genus *Allosaurus* has been discovered in Upper

Jurassic sediments (160 million years ago) in the U.S. **1991** *Sydney Morning Herald* 28 Sept. 21/1 Palaeontologists believe a 150-million-year-old allosaurus skeleton..could lead them to a vast dinosaur graveyard.

allylene, *n.* Substitute for etymology and def: [ad. Fr. *allylène* (coined by M. Berthelot in *Chimie Organique* (1860) II. iii. i. 160): see ALLYL *n.*, -ENE.] **1.** = PROPYNE *n.*

1862 MILLER *Elem. Chem.* III. (ed. 2) iii. § vi. 243 The representative of this class of hydrocarbons is acetylene, but a second (C_6H_4), allylene, has lately been announced. **1921** *Jrnl. Amer. Chem. Soc.* XLIII. 1227 The disappearance of the blue color shows the formation of sodium acetylide; subsequent addition of methyl iodide brings about the formation of allylene. **1965** PHILLIPS & WILLIAMS *Inorg. Chem.* I. xvii. 612 A magnesium carbide Mg_2C_3 is said to give largely allylene..on hydrolysis, suggesting that its lattice contains C_3^{4-} units.

†**2.** = *PROPADIENE *n.* Cf. *ALLENE *n.* 1. *Obs. exc. Hist.*

[**1872** *Jrnl. Chem. Soc.* XXV. 144 The authors hope to obtain different allylenes, whereof theoretically at least, three isomeric forms are possible.] **1889** *Jrnl. Chem. Soc.* LVI. Abstracts 840 The author's attempts to prepare allylene, $CH_2:C:CH_2$..were unsuccessful. **1968** A. A. BAKER *Unsaturation in Org. Chem.* vii. 88 For a number of years there was a great deal of confusion surrounding the name allylene. Some chemists used it..in describing propadiene, but others used it synonymously with propyne and were convinced that propadiene, which they called allene, did not exist.

allylestrenol, *n.*, var. *ALLYLOESTRENOL *n.*

allyloestrenol (ælaɪl'i:strənɒl, -'estrənɒl), *n. Pharm.* Also **allylestrenol.** [f. ALLYL *n.* + OESTR(OG)EN *n.* + -OL.] A synthetic progesterone analogue, $C_{21}H_{32}O$, given orally in cases of threatened or habitual abortion.

1961 *Lancet* 21 Jan. 135/1 Allylestrenol ('Gestanin', Organon)..seems to be completely free from androgenic activity. **1962** *Med. Jrnl. Austral.* 8 Sept. 375/2 Each tablet of the combined hormone preparation, 'Premenquil', contains 5 mg. of allyloestrenol. **1976** *Acta Paediatr. Acad. Sci. Hung.* XVII. 263/2 Allyloestrenol has no hypophysis inhibiting effect and does not depress the action of the ovary. **1992** *Life Sci.* LI. 309 Steroid hormones (diethylstilbestrol, allylestrenol) have been commonly used to preserve pregnancy, and contraceptives to prevent it.

alnico ('ælnɪkəʊ), *n.* [f. AL(UMINIUM *n.* + NI(CKEL *n.* + CO(BALT *n.*] Any of several steel alloys which typically contain nickel and aluminium, with smaller amounts of cobalt and copper, and are used for permanent magnets.

U.S. usage can be especially variable: see quot. 1969. **1935** *N.Y. Times* 22 Oct. 6/2 The alloy is called 'alnico' because it is a combination of aluminium, nickel and cobalt, which three metals are added to iron. **1948** R. S. YOUNG *Cobalt* viii. 112 Production of small Alnico magnets by casting. **1969** E. N. SIMONS *Dict. Alloys* 9 The Americans include Alnic, Alnico, 20 nickel, 5 cobalt, 12 aluminium, 63 iron, and Alcomax Alloys under the general name of Alnico. **1974** *Sci. Amer.* Dec. 92/3 Columnar structures have other uses. One of them is to attain improved magnetic properties…Many alnico magnets are therefore made with at least a partly columnar structure. **1994** *RIP* June 77/2 The Power Blade and Dual Blade pickups..retain the clarity and (dare we say it?) romance usually attributed to the elderly alnico-magnet-wearing Fender single coils.

aloe vera, (ə‚ləʊɪ 'vɪərə), *n. phr.* [f. the mod.L. taxonomic name *Aloe vera* (Linnaeus *Species*

Plantarum (1753) I. 320), lit. 'true aloe'.] An aloe, *Aloe vera*, native to the Mediterranean and cultivated in the Caribbean, which is a major source of the drug aloes and also yields a gelatinous substance used (esp. in cosmetics) for its emollient and skin-repairing properties; also, the extracted gel itself.

1980 *Jrnl. Amer. Animal Hosp. Assoc.* XVI. 768 (*title*) The therapeutic efficacy of *aloe vera* cream..in thermal injuries. **1985** *Woman's Own* 22 June 18/3 Revlon's new Dry Skin Relief with aloe vera, £2.69, is quickly absorbed. **1989** A. TAN *Joy Luck Club* 192 A cutting of aloe vera that Lena gave me did not belong anywhere because we had no other succulents. **1992** *Gourmet* Feb. 49/3 And Sol y Luna is the place to drink a Pisco sour, a Machu Picchu (Tequila with cranberry and aloe vera juices).

alprazolam (æl'preɪzəʊlæm), *n. Pharm.* [f. al- of unknown origin + P(HENYL *n.* + T)R(I)AZOL(E *n.* (elements of the systematic name) + *-AZEP)AM.] A long-acting benzodiazepine, $C_{17}H_{13}ClN_4$, with properties similar to those of diazepam, given orally in tablet form in the treatment of anxiety.

1973 *Jrnl. Amer. Med. Assoc.* 26 Nov. 1116/1 The following nonproprietary names for the drugs described have been adopted by the United States Adopted Names (USAN) Council…Alprazolam. **1974** *Current Therapeutic Res.* XVI. 1010 Alprazolam..is a new benzodiazepine compound. **1987** M. J. NEAL *Med. Pharmacol.* xxii. 51/2 Intravenous benzodiazepines..are used in status epilepticus..and in panic attacks (however, oral alprazolam is most effective for this latter purpose).

alprenolol (æl'prɛnəlɒl), *n. Pharm.* [f. AL(LYL + ISO)PREN(ALINE *n.* + *-OLOL.] A beta blocker given orally as the hydrochloride in the treatment of hypertension, angina, and cardiac arrhythmias; 1-(2-allylphenoxy)-3-isopropyl-aminopropan-2-ol, $C_{15}H_{23}NO_2$.

1968 *WHO Chron.* XXII. 112 Alprenolol. **1969** *Amer. Heart Jrnl.* LXXVII. 598/1 Alprenolol was introduced in 1966 by A. B. Hassle Laboratory of Sweden and has had limited clinical trial. **1970** *Brit. Jrnl. Pharmacol.* XL. 380 The stimulant effects of alprenolol were also blocked by propranolol. **1977** *Lancet* 22 Oct. 850/1 Propranolol, alprenolol, and oxprenolol block the peripheral β-receptors mediating vasodilatation at lower concentrations than are required to block cardiac β-receptors. **1980** *Brit. Med. Jrnl.* 29 Mar. 888/2 Beta-blockade may have harmed some patients and helped others: the recent alprenolol study has shown a differential effect in patients aged under and over 65.

altered, *ppl. a.* Add: [**3.**] Special Collocation. **altered state** (in full *altered state of consciousness*) [tr. G. *veränderte Bewusstsein* (Breuer & Freud 1893, in *Neurol. Centralbl.* XII. 10)], any state of mind that differs from the normal state of consciousness or awareness of a person, *esp.* one induced by drugs, hypnosis, or mental disorder; also *attrib.* or as *adj.*

[**1924** J. RICKMAN tr. Breuer & Freud in *Freud's Coll. Papers* I. ii. 33 When a trauma effective enough in itself occurs during a state of seriously disabling affect or of altered consciousness.] **1941** *Jrnl. Abnormal & Social Psychol.* XXXVI. 489 Hypnotic behavior, the striving to behave as if hypnotized, takes place in an *altered state of the person. **1965** *Jrnl. Amer. Med. Assoc.* 11 Jan. 104/1 The use of hallucinogenic..substances to produce altered states of consciousness is not new. **1968** *Brit. Jrnl. Psychiatry* CXIV. 1209/2 Altered-state subjects who appear to minimally attend to their surroundings. **1989** D. KOONTZ *Midnight* I. lvi. 230 They seek an altered state in which complex emotions and pleasure aren't linked — the life of an unthinking beast.

alternant, *ppl. a.* and *n.* Add: [A.] **3.** *Chem.* Designating or pertaining to a conjugated hydrocarbon whose rings each contain an even number of carbon atoms.
1947 COULSON & LONGUET-HIGGINS in *Proc. R. Soc.* CXCII. 19 As we move along any chain of unsaturated bonds the atoms will belong alternately to one set and to the other. For this reason we shall refer to such a hydrocarbon as an alternant hydrocarbon. **1952** *Jrnl. Amer. Chem. Soc.* LXXIV. 3345/1 Most of the present discussion will be confined to alternant mesomeric systems. **1967** I. L. FINAR *Org. Chem.* (ed. 5) I. xxx. 808 Pyridine is an even-membered ring, and so is an alternant compound. **1980** M. ORCHIN et al. *Vocab. Org. Chem.* iii. 64 This classification of hydrocarbons is significant in molecular orbital theory because alternant hydrocarbons possess complementary bonding and antibonding orbitals.

Alternaria (ælta'nɛərɪə), *n.* [mod.L. (coined in Ger. in C. G. Nees von Esenbeck *Das System der Pilze u. Schwämme* (1816) 72), f. L. *altern-us*: see ALTERN *a.*, -ARY.] A genus of hyphomycetous fungi which cause various plant diseases; (also **alternaria**) a fungus of this genus. Freq. used *attrib.* to designate a disease caused by such a fungus.
1899 G. MASSEE *Text-bk. Plant Dis.* 110 The dead heart-leaves are often more or less covered with greenish-brown velvety patches consisting of *Alternaria*..spores. **1914** *Jrnl. Agric. Res.* I. 475 Helminthosporiums, Alternarias, Cladosporiums, and Fusariums were obtained. **1924** *Ibid.* XXIX. 421 Alternaria leafspot has a very wide distribution, both here and abroad. **1953** F. T. BROOKS *Plant Dis.* (ed. 2) xx. 389 *Alternaria citri*..Alternaria rot of citrus. **1986** *Power Farming* Oct. 22/3 An early dose of fungicide is applied to the rape if alternaria is considered a threat. **1988** *Farmer's Weekly* (S. Afr.) 24 June 43/1 Purple or Alternaria blotch is well known in South Africa.

alternative, *a.* and *n.* Add: [A.] **[7.]** *alternative therapy.*
1978 *Washington Post* 6 May A3/4 When specialists ordered radiation treatments, the Greens decided to seek alternative therapy. **1989** R. COWARD *Whole Truth* (1990) i. 15 This sense of the virtue of being natural is by no means confined to alternative therapies. It is a widespread and prevalent feeling: if it's natural, then it must be good for us. **1992** *N.Y. Times Mag.* 17 May 46/1, I don't rule out alternative therapy: if you want to try other things like acupuncture or diet, feel free to explore them.

8. Special Collocations. **alternative birth** (or **birthing**) orig. *U.S.*, any method of childbirth in which the delivery occurs at home or in a similar environment, often without the use of painkilling drugs or obstetric instruments.
1978 *Time* 24 Apr. 60/3 Illinois Masonic's *alternative birthing center is a small, completely independent unit with two bedrooms, a nurses' station with rolltop desk, and a small lounge where family and friends can wait. **1981** *N.Y. Times* 21 Sept. B14/1 Sibling preparation classes, pioneered in 1976 at the Alternative Birth Center in San Francisco's Mount Zion Hospital and Medical Center. **1987** *Los Angeles Times* 14 Sept. v. 2/1 The alternative birth movement of a decade ago forced hospitals to expand delivery departments to include birthing centers. **1992** J. MITFORD *Amer. Way of Birth* IV. xiii. 209 Dotted around the country are scores of 'freestanding' or 'alternative' birth centers, organized to provide maternity care for low-risk women who want to avoid the impersonal, sterile atmosphere of a hospital.

alternative comedy, a style of comedy first popular in the 1980s which seeks to reject certain established (esp. racist or sexist) comic stereotypes, and is typically characterized by aggressively physical performance, and a leftist political stance; so **alternative comedian**, **comedienne**.
1980 *Time Out* 17 Oct. 30/5 *Alternative comedy has come of age and you have nothing to use but your chains. **1981** *Sunday Times* 13 Sept. 32/5 The final run-through was completed... Throughout, Alexei Sayle, the alternative comedian, had sat in the aisle spurning the bourgeois comfort of a seat. **1986** *Melody Maker* 19 Apr. 9/2 Alternative comedian Ade Edmondson and alternative comedienne Jennifer Saunders introduce their alternative sprog. **1989** WILMUT & ROSENGARD *Didn't you kill my Mother-in-Law* p. xiii, In another way, 'alternative' comedy is simply a rejection of the preceding fashions in comedy — just as each new generation of comics has sought to build their own style rather than stay in the well-established mould. **1993** *Guardian* 10 Dec. II. 3/4 Pre-alternative comedians cracked mother-in-law jokes. Alternative comedians cracked Margaret Thatcher jokes. Post-alternative comedians don't crack jokes about either.

alternative fuel, a fuel for motor vehicles other than the usual ones of petrol and diesel oil.
1924 *Nature* 14 June 866/2 Excluding benzol.. *alternative fuels of greatest promise include 'tetralin' (tetrahydronaphthalene), which, mixed with benzol and alcohol, was used considerably by the Germans during the war. **1990** *Sci. Amer.* May 60/3 In many ways, being the first on the scene with an alternative-fuel vehicle might not be an enviable position. **1991** *Impact* (*UNESCO*) XLI. 98 Alternative fuels such as ethanol and methanol have gained ground in California as part of a strategy to achieve air quality standards.

alternative technology, technology designed to conserve natural resources and avoid harm to the environment, esp. by harnessing renewable energy sources such as wind- or solar power. Cf. SOFT *a.* IV. 28 d.
1972 E. GOLDSMITH et al. in *Ecologist* Jan. 8/2 The invention, promotion and application of *alternative technologies which are energy and materials conservative. **1984** *Forbes* (N.Y.) 12 Mar. 174/2 What about alternative technologies such as magnetic levitation ('maglev'), where the train floats friction-free above the rails? **1991** *Whole Earth Rev.* Summer 133/3 Computers are not alternative technologies. They are energy consumptive and lock a person into the system of Earth destruction.

[B.] 6. One who or that which represents an unorthodox style or approach (see sense 7 of the adj.).
1984 *Times* 31 July 10/3 The soft punks and the new romantics and the alternatives and the posers.. are massaged by music which depends for its impact as much upon producer as upon the artist. **1988** *Courier-Mail* (Brisbane) 27 Sept. 17/2 Jennifer is a 20-year-old Alternative, with short platinum hair jelled and sprayed into a cone, bright face, smart casual clothes and heavy worker's boots. **1990** *Catholic Herald* 30 Nov. 7/1 Clare was not a down-and-out. She was an alternative, whatever that was supposed to mean. **1990** *Health Guardian* Nov.-Dec. 1/1 This was not an alternatives versus the medics debate. **1992** *Buffalo News* 23 Aug. G5/1 This is music that is out of the commercial mainstream. Alternative includes the gothic sound of Peter Murphy, the humour of the Barenaked Ladies and everything in between.

alternobaric (ɔːlˌtɜːnəʊˈbærɪk), *a. Med.* [f. ALTERN(ATE *a.* and *n.* + -o + BARIC *a.*[2]) Of vertigo: caused by an imbalance of pressure between the right and left middle ears.
1965 C. E. G. LUNDGREN in *Brit. Med. Jrnl.* 28 Aug. 512/2 Vertigo is sufficiently common among divers.. to deserve a wider recognition... I would suggest that it should be known as 'alternobaric vertigo (vertigo

alternobarica)'. **1966** *Aerospace Med.* XXXVII. 180/2 Alternobaric vertigo occurred almost exclusively in the fast jet planes. **1976** *Undersea Biomed. Res.* III. 403 Pressure vertigo..or alternobaric vertigo..is a type of transient vertigo normally accompanied by a feeling of bodily rotation,..apparent movement of the visual scene, and..nystagmus.

altigraph (' æltɪgrɑ:f, -græf), *n. rare.* [f. ALTI- + -GRAPH.] An altimeter which produces a graphical record of its measurements.

1927 *Daily Express* 20 May 1/3 A sealed altograph [*sic*]..recorded a height of sixteen thousand feet when they returned. **1937** C. G. PHILP *Conquest of Stratosphere* x. 83 The equipment consisted of special ventilators, altigraphs, thermographs, photographic cameras and other apparatus.

altimetric, *a.* Add: Hence **alti'metrically** *adv.*

1893 in *Funk's Stand. Dict.* **1958** F. E. ZEUNER *Dating Past* (ed. 4) 167 Altimetrically, the surface of this fluviatile aggradation runs into the Tyrrhenian (32 metres) sea-level of the Penultimate Interglacial. **1990** *Earth, Moon & Planets* L/LI. 343 The equatorial latitudes of Venus are characterized by several altimetrically high-standing regions.

aluminian (ælju:'mɪnɪən), *a. Min.* [f. ALUMINIUM *n.* + -IAN.] Of a mineral: having a small proportion of a typical constituent element replaced by aluminium.

1930 W. T. SCHALLER in *Amer. Mineralogist* XV. 572 Aluminian chromite for a chromite with a minor quantity of aluminium replacing part of the chromium. **1964** *Mineral. Abstr.* XVI. 549/2 This newly characterized mixed-layer mineral consisting of unusual aluminian chlorite and montmorillonite is named tosudite. **1990** *Jrnl. Petrol.* XXXI. 1203 Large..megacrysts of aluminian augite ($Wo_{49}Fs_9En_{42}$), olivine (Fo_{82}) and pleonaste spinel..occur.

ambience, *n.* Add: **2.** *Audio.* The acoustic quality of a particular environment, as reproduced in a recording; *spec.* a sense of some specific or individual atmosphere, esp. an impression of live performance, created or enhanced by recording techniques (such as added reverberation), or by the presence of background noise.

1961 G. A. BRIGGS *A to Z in Audio* 15 For domestic use a reasonable amount of ambience in most records is desirable to give the listener a sensation of being in the concert hall, but too much blurs the fine detail. **1971** *Hi-Fi Sound* Feb. 71/3 The shape and the furnishing of the listening room, modifying the ambience that is built-in by the recording engineer, can broaden and smudge the stereo image. **1977** *Gramophone* Sept. 512/2 In quadraphony the back speakers make the contribution..of added ambience, to add a subtle extra dimension to the realism of the orchestral image at the front. **1986** *Electronic Musician* Aug. 29/1 How would you like to beef up the sounds you already have by adding a software-controllable dose of ambience or punch? **1993** *Rolling Stone* 14 Oct. 54/2 We were starting to lose trust in the conventional sound of rock and roll.., those big beautiful pristine vocal sounds with all this lush ambience and reverb.

3. = *ambient music* s.v. *AMBIENT *a.* 3 c.

1991 *Vox* Sept. 66/3 If we were to talk Brian Eno, The Blue Nile and ambience, the picture would be clearer...This is dance music without the wild agitation. **1995** *Face* Jan. 47/1 Ambience doesn't have its immediate roots in the chill-out rooms of danceterias: its connection to the original vision of Cage and Eno is far more explicit.

ambient, *a.* and *n.* Add: [A.] [3.] **b.** *Audio.* Designating atmospheric sound occurring naturally or at random in a particular environment at a particular time, esp. (unwanted) background noise picked up by a microphone. Usu. in *ambient noise* or *sound*. Also (of recorded sound), engineered in such a way as to create or reproduce a specific acoustic quality: cf. *AMBIENCE *n.* 2.

1959 *Proc. Inst. Electr. Engin.* CVI. B. Suppl. No. 14. 257/1 When operating in a stereophonic manner, the ambient studio sound appears to fill the whole space between the loudspeakers with positional accent on the individual sound sources. **1961** G. A. BRIGGS *A to Z in Audio* 16 Deaf people are often worried by ambient noise which covers a wide frequency range, as it probably includes the register in which they hear best. **1964** *Oceanogr. & Marine Biol.* II. 431 The clicking of snapping shrimp..is a form of ambient sound when one is concentrating on the sounds of fish. **1975** D. G. FINK *Electronics Engineers' Handbk.* xxv. 125 Self-noise has many directional characteristics..; ambient noise generally has an omni-directional distribution. **1990** *Gramophone* May 2086/3 The remastering is effective overall: the Concerto has lost only a little of its original ambient bloom and certainly sounds vivid. **1992** *Videomaker* Feb. 65/2 (Advt.), By putting the microphone 'where the action is', the Nady 151 VR Wireless System delivers crisp, clear, precise professional quality audio. No more ambient noise problems.

c. (Orig. in *ambient music*.). Designating or relating to a style of largely instrumental music, characterized by its predominantly electronic textures and the absence of a (persistent) beat, which is designed to create or enhance a particular atmosphere or mood, esp. of relaxation or contemplation. Also used in *comb.* with the names of other types of popular music (as *ambient house*, *ambient techno*, etc.) to denote various hybrid styles, mostly associated with the dance-music and rave culture of the late 1980s and 1990s.

1978 B. ENO *Music for Airports* (record sleeve note), Over the past three years I have become interested in music as ambience...To create a distinction between my own experiments in this area and the products of various purveyors of canned music, I have begun using the term Ambient Music. *Ibid.* Whereas the extant canned music companies proceed from the basis of regularizing environments by blanketing their acoustic and atmospheric idiosyncrasies, Ambient Music is intended to enhance these. **1980** *Melody Maker* 5 Jul. 18/1 'The Plateau of Mirror' continues the development of ambient music — background music for a supermarket society. **1989** *Blitz* Dec. 126/2 What's overwhelming is the soft-throb chorus of sandbanked synths, matched only by the sound of waves breaking against the shore...What we're talking about here is 'ambient house' — a new phenomenon that appears to be a natural development. **1991** *Vox* Apr. 77/1 Fans of the Ambient Rap sound that 808 represent won't be disappointed with these semi-instrumentals. **1992** *DJ* 26 Nov. 24/2 The DJ Sven was playing heavy techno just two months ago, but now we hear..more ambient sounds. **1994** *Rolling Stone* 30 June 72/3 *Selected Ambient Works 85-92*..established the Cornwall ..native as the pioneer of ambient techno, a musical style that converts the energized electrobeats and keyboard surges of dancefloor techno into slower, more tranquil washes of sound. **1995** *GQ* Jan. 27/2 'In Dub', the six-track bonus CD that accompanies it, is better still: fresh slices of ambient dub, spiralling improvisation and space-trippy lyrics.

[B.] **4.** *ellipt.* for *ambient music* above.

1993 *Wire* Feb. 64/1 Electroacoustic, tape collage, post-industrial, ambient and various polystylistic unclassifiables are weird and sometimes wonderful bedfellows for nearly 75 minutes. **1994** *N.Y. Times* 13 Mar. II. 32/4 Initially popular as music for ravers coming down after a night's mayhem, ambient has become a booming album-based genre.

ambilateral (æmbɪˈlætərəl), *a.* [f. AMBI- + LATERAL *a.*] **1.** Two-sided, bilateral; *spec.* in *Med.*, affecting equally both sides of the body or a part; also, ambidextrous.

*a*1832 J. BENTHAM *Deontol.* (1834) I. i. xvi. 233 Resentment may be used in an ambi-lateral sense; a man may resent a kindness as well as an unkindness. **1960** H. T. LAMBRICK *John Jacob of Jacobabad* App. B. 408 So far from 'not allowing' such ambilateral occupation, Jacob permitted part of the formerly predatory section of the Dombkis..to return as they wished to their former homes. **1975** *Cor et Vasa* XVII. 183 In renovascular hypertension caused by panarteritis of the aorta, very often..an ambilateral affection of the main renal arteries occurs. **1979** *Ann. Internal Med.* XC. 709/2 Ambilateral harmfulness, the term I have coined for the capacity of certain microorganisms to associate antagonistically with both plants and animals. **1990** *Internat. Jrnl. Neurosci.* L. 196 According to the level of significance..of the difference between the frequencies of the right- and left-paw use, the animals were designated as right-preferent, left-preferent, and ambilateral.

2. *Anthropol.* Pertaining to or designating a kinship system in which an individual may claim membership of either the father's or the mother's lineage group, or both.

1929 R. FIRTH *Primitive Econ. N.Z. Maori* iii. 98 The admission to membership through descent from either males or females — or both conjoined — shows that the *hapu* is not a unilateral group of the strict type. It may be called, in fact, an *ambilateral* group, since both parents are eligible for the purposes of kinship affiliation. **1956** *Man* CLXX. 148/1 The formal definition of 'ambilateral'..admits the possibility of rights in both parental groups, while 'utrolateral' explicitly excludes the possibility. **1968** M. HARRIS *Rise Anthropol. Theory* (1969) xi. 301 The concept of ambilateral descent, which has subsequently turned out to be the key to the understanding of Kwakiutl social organization. **1989** *Encycl. Brit.* IV. 30/1 Ambilateral (or ambilineal) descent systems are those in which membership in a kinship group may be claimed through either parent.

Hence **ambilate′rality** *n.*; **ambi′laterally** *adv.*

1934 WEBSTER s.v. *Ambilateral*, Ambilaterality. *Ibid.*, Ambilaterally. **1936** R. FIRTH *We, the Tikopia* xvi. 596 The ambilaterality of the Maori. **1950** E. R. LEACH *Social Sci. Res. Sarawek* App. B. 68 A non-exogamous unilaterally or ambilaterally descended clan. **1957** *Man* LVII. 6/2 A corporate descent group of a non-unilinear (ambilineal) character, membership being obtained ambilaterally..according to circumstances. **1964** M. CRITCHLEY *Developmental Dyslexia* viii. 53 Both cerebral ambilaterality and dyslexia are to be equated with immaturity of cerebral development. **1991** *Internat. Jrnl. Neurosci.* LVI. 187 Testosterone administered intramuscularly may..induce ambilaterality in right-preferent female cats.

ambilineal (ˌæmbɪˈlɪnɪəl), *a. Anthropol.* [f. AMBI- + LINEAL *a.*: cf. MATRILINEAL *a.*, PATRILINEAL *a.*] Designating or pertaining to a kinship system in which an individual may choose to claim membership of either the father's or the mother's lineage group, but not both.

1950 E. R. LEACH *Social Sci. Res. Sarawak* App. B. 62 In the 'ambilineal' systems of Borneo and Polynesia, descent through the father still usually counts for more than descent through the mother. **1957** R. FIRTH in *Man* Jan. ii. 6/1 It would seem useful to include among such terms the following:..*Ambilineal* for the maintenance of group continuity through the generations by using male or female links without set order. **1968** BUCHLER & SELBY *Kinship & Social Organization* iv. 90 In cases where ancestor-based groups are formed out of people who are related through *either* male or female ascendants *concurrently*, we refer to them as ambilineal. **1989** *Encycl. Brit.* XIX. 72/2 There are some societies that recognise an ideal of patrilineal descent but in which persons may opt for tracing descent through a female link. This arrangement, known as ambilineal descent..bears some relation to the cognatic descent system of egalitarian hunter-gatherers.

Hence **ambiline′ality** *n.*

1984 BARNARD & GOOD *Res. Practices in Study Kinship* vii. 148 Both hierarchy and ambilineality are characteristic of Polynesian descent groups.

ambilocal (æmbɪˈləʊkəl), *a. Anthropol.* [f. AMBI- + LOCAL *a.*: cf. MATRILOCAL *a.*, PATRILOCAL *a.*] Designating or pertaining to a system of residence after marriage in which a couple may choose to live in either the husband's or the wife's home or community.

1956 R. NEEDHAM in *Man* Feb. xxx. 31/1 'Ambilocal' refers to marital residence in either the husband's or the wife's group. **1960** G. P. MURDOCK *Social Struct. Southeast Asia* i. 2 Residence is ambilocal — more often patrilocal than matrilocal among the Yami. *Ibid.* 157 'Ambilocal' is..preferable for a rule of residence which permits a choice between two unilocal alternatives, the one uxorilocal..and the other virilocal. **1985** *Bull. Inst. Ethnol. Acad. Sinica* LIX. 167 The kinship system of ancient society as represented by the Shilla dynasty was characterized by cognatic descent, including ambilocal residence. **1988** *Ethnology* XXVII. iii. 260 Although both factions of Cheyannes..had preferred unilocal residence, the Dawes Act forced them to become bilateral and ambilocal. **1992** SILVERBERG & GRAY *Aggression & Peacefulness in Humans & Other Animals* 193 Residence is ambilocal, and residence units vary from single households scattered over a band's territory to hamlets where the entire band resides.

Hence **ambilo′cality** *n.*

1973 *Ethos* Spring 41 The patterns considered most likely to expose a significant proportion of young males to conditions of low adult male salience were matrilocality.., uxorilocality.., and ambilocality. **1984** BARNARD & GOOD *Res. Pract. in Study Kinship* v. 81 Ambilocality permits a couple to reside either uxorilocally or virilocally.

ambiophony (æmbɪˈɒfənɪ), *n.* [f. AMBI(ENT *a.* + -o¹ + -*phony*, after STEREOPHONY *n.*] Sound reproduction in which a three-dimensional effect is produced by feeding signals from two sources to four or more speakers with slight time differences.

1959 *Philips Techn. Rev.* XX. 322/2 The solution to this problem by means of ambiophony has already been described. **1963** *Radio Times* 10 Jan. 32/1 Studio 4 uses a new device called 'ambiophony'...The 'dead' orchestral sound is..played back to the studio through..sixty-two loud-speakers at several different very small time-delays, calculated in thousandths of a second. **1975** *Which?* Sept. 274/2 This can create a four-channel effect from stereo records, tape or radio; how pleasing you find this effect (called ambiophony) will depend on you.

So **ambio′phonic** *a.*, of the nature of or pertaining to ambiophony.

1959 *Philips Techn. Rev.* XX. 323/2 An ambiophonic installation can also be used to suggest to listeners that they are seated in a hall of greater size. **1975** G. J. KING *Audio Handbk.* xii. 260 Terms often used for the 2-2-4 arrangement are 'ambiophony' and 'ambiophonic'. **1975** *Gramophone* Jan. 1416/3 There may be a facility for giving a quasi-quadraphonic or 'ambiophonic' effect. **1978** *Ibid.* Apr. 1796/3 There is a switch which introduces a Hafler-type circuit, using the second pair of loudspeakers as an ambiophonic rear channel.

amblypod (ˈæmblɪpɒd), *n. Palaeont.* [f. mod.L. *Amblypoda* (coined in E. D. Cope *Syst. Catal. Vertebrata Eocene New Mexico* (U.S. Army Engin. Dept.: Geogr. Explorations & Surveys) (1875) 28), f. Gr. ἀμβλύ-ς blunt + πούς, ποδ- foot.]

A mammal of the former order Amblypoda (now separated into the orders Pantodonta and Dinocerata), comprising large, mainly hoofed ungulates which were widely distributed in North America, Europe, and East Asia in the Early Tertiary.

[**1887** E. D. COPE in *Amer. Naturalist* XXI. 987 All ungulates, in passing from the taxeopodous to the diplarthrous stages, traversed the amblypodous.] **1893** *Funk's Stand. Dict.* s.v. *Ambly-*, Amblypod. **1927** HALDANE & HUXLEY *Animal Biol.* xi. 243 (*caption*) Herbivorous forms with defensive horns or other weapons...Amblypod. **1933** *Amer. Jrnl. Sci.* CCXXV. 423 Gidley's conception of a titanothere relationship has not been sustained, in fact, he later abandoned the idea in favor of amblypod affinities. **1985** D. LAMBERT *Cambr. Field Guide Prehist. Life* viii. 170 Amblypods ('slow footed') were early, ponderous hoofed herbivores with broad, low, ridged cheek teeth.

Ambu ('æmbuː, 'æmbjuː), *n. Med.* Also **ambu**. [Sortened form of AMBULANCE *n.* or Da. *ambulance.*] A proprietary name for a type of resuscitator consisting of a face mask connected by a valve to a self-inflating bag, which, when squeezed, inflates the patient's lungs with air or oxygen. Usu. *attrib.* in *Ambu bag.*

1959 *Trade Marks Jrnl.* 22 Apr. 426/2 *Ambu*...Medical apparatus and instruments; airpumps for use in the resuscitation of persons suffering from asphyxiation. **1960** *Official Gaz.* (U.S. Patent Office) 12 July TM71/1 *Ambu*...For lifesaving apparatus and instruments—namely, respirators for artificial breathing, pressure or suction pumps especially for medical purposes. **1968** *New England Jrnl. Med.* 22 Feb. 456/1 Surely, the physician to whom the book is directed would do better in most circumstances with instruction in closed-chest massage and in positive-pressure respiration either mouth-to-mouth or with an Ambu bag. **1980** *Brit. Med. Jrnl.* 29 Mar. 934/2 An ambulanceman appears. He has an airway, an Ambubag, and a two-man lifting chair. **1991** *Paris Rev.* Fall 39 The ambulance crew waits, their equipment useless, their ambubags and cardiopulmonary cases still scattered over the gravelly grass.

ambulatorium (ˌæmbjʊləˈtɔːrɪəm), *n. Med.* Pl. **-ia**. [Prob. f. AMBULAT(ORY *a.* 5 + -ORIUM, usu. after Russ. *ambulatóriya.* Cf. med.L. *ambulatorium* (see AMBULATORY *n.*).] A place for the treatment of ambulant patients; an out-patients' department; a dispensary. Used chiefly in relation to Russia or the former Soviet Union.

1904 *Appleton's Med. Dict.* 101 *Ambulatorium*, a dispensary. **1937** H. E. SIGERIST *Socialised Med. in Soviet Union* v. 289 In the Soviet Union medical service is given to the working population through health centres. These centres have various names. They are called dispensaries, polyclinics, ambulatoria, preventoria or prophylactoria. **1984** *Brit. Med. Jrnl.* 28 Apr. 1289/1 If the situation is unsatisfactory at the 'ambulatoria' of area doctors there are also many defects in the polyclinics.

ambulatory, *a.* Add: [5.] **b.** Of places or apparatus: intended or suitable for ambulant patients.

1890 BILLINGS *Med. Dict.* I. 47/1 *Ambulatory clinic*, clinic for persons able to walk about; a dispensary. **1973** *Sci. Amer.* Sept. 29/3 The vast bulk of care is provided by physicians in ambulatory settings. **1978** B. PYM *Very Private Eye* (1984) 317 Had an ambulatory electro-cardiogram attached to me for 24 hours. **1981** *Times* 1 Dec. 15/7 The Tracker ambulatory recorder uses a standard C-90 tape cassette running at slow speeds to record a continuous electrocardiograph. **1990** *Brain* CXIII. 1584

Subcutaneous administration of apomorphine by ambulatory minipump.

amethocaine (æ'mɛθəʊkeɪn), *n. Pharm.* [f. *ametho-* (perh. f. Gr. ἀμέθ-υστος not drunken (see AMETHYST *n.*) + -o[1], or a blend of METHYL *n.* and AMINO-, elements of the systematic name) + *-CAINE.*] The hydrochloride salt of a diamino-ester which is used as a local anaesthetic for topical application, esp. in ophthalmology.

1943 *Martindale's Extra Pharmacopœia* (ed. 22) II. 528 *Amethocaine hydrochloride*, (Butethanol),..surface anæsthetic, formerly known as Decicain. **1962** *Lancet* 29 Dec. 1361/2 The method described..seems to permit..the use of 10 ml. of 4% lignocaine in a patient who had previously sucked a lozenge containing an unspecified amount of amethocaine. **1971** D. LAMBERT in C. Bonington *Annapurna South Face* App. G. 299 Amethocaine is an anaesthetic, and our climbers carried it to enable them to open their eyes if they became snow-blind. **1987** M. J. NEAL *Med. Pharmacol.* v. 16/2 Because of their toxicity, amethocaine and cocaine are now only used for bronchoscopy and ENT surgery respectively.

amnio ('æmnɪəʊ), *n. colloq.* [Abbrev.] = AMNIOCENTESIS *n.*

1984 *Sci.* 84 July/Aug. 92/2 (*heading*) Amnio alternative. **1986** *Crain's Chicago Business* 15 Sept. 51 We were apprehensive about the risks,..but there are risks with amnio, too. **1991** *Chicago Tribune* 3 Mar. 1. 5/2 We can now reassure an older woman that if the amnio is OK, she should feel just as optimistic about the outcome of her pregnancy as a younger woman. **1992** *Independent* 11 Feb. 13/2, I agonised for days about whether to have an 'amnio'.

amniote ('æmnɪəʊt), *n. and a. Zool.* [f. mod.L. *Amniota* (coined in Ger. by E. Haeckel in *Gen. Morphol. Der Organismen* (1866) I. p. cxxxii): see AMNIOTA *n. pl.*] **A.** *n.* Any vertebrate whose embryo develops within an amnion and chorion and possesses an allantois, i.e. a reptile, bird, or mammal; cf. AMNIOTA *n. pl.* **B.** *adj.* Designating or pertaining to an amniote.

1887 A. C. HADDON *Introd. Study Embryol.* iv. 95 The epiblastic epithelium lining it is the exact equivalent of the false amnion or serous membrane of other amniotes. **1893** *Funk's Stand. Dict.* s.v. *Amniota*, Amniote. *a.* & *n.* **1926** J. S. KINGSLEY *Outl. Compar. Anat. Vertebr.* (ed. 3) 397 In the amniotes the yolk sac reappears. **1949** A. S. ROMER *Vertebr. Body* xiii. 474 In the amniote heart the left atrium has no proper blood supply in the embryo. **1992** *Atlantic* May 10/1 The explosive evolution of the reptiles was a direct result of the development of the amniote egg.

amobarbital (æməʊ'bɑːbɪtəl), *n. Pharm.* [f. AM(YL)O- + BARBITAL *n.*] The equivalent in the U.S. Pharmacopeia of *AMYLOBARBITONE n.*

1950 *Jrnl. Amer. Med. Assoc.* 2 Dec. 1209/2 (*heading*) Amobarbital sodium and prolonged insulin coma. **1973** T. PYNCHON *Gravity's Rainbow* (1975) 1. 168 Try to remember,..last night amobarbital sodium 0.2 Gm. at bedtime. **1974** M. C. GERALD *Pharmacol.* xi. 204 Deep sedation is induced by the intravenous injection of amobarbital. **1980** *Washington Post* 27 Nov. B1/1 The tests showed two barbiturates in the child's blood—amobarbital and secobarbital.

amorph ('eɪmɔːf), *n. Genetics.* [f. A- 10 + -MORPH.] A mutant allele which has no activity compared with the wild-type allele.

1932 H. J. MULLER in *Proc. 6th Internat. Congr. Genetics* I. 236 The hypomorphs and amorphs are just the kind of mutants which the few remaining advocates of the presence-and-absence hypothesis..require as evidence. **1949** DARLINGTON & MATHER *Elem. Genetics* vii. 152 Far from removing bristles, scute-I helps to produce them. It does the same job as the wild type, but less than half as effectively. Such a gene Muller calls a hypomorph or, in the extreme case, when it does nothing, an amorph. **1993** *Blood* LXXXII. 656/1 The second type of Rh$_{null}$, which was first noted in a Japanese family, is called 'amorph' or 'silent type'.

amorphic (eɪˈmɔːfɪk), *a.* [f. A- 10 + -*morphic*, after POLYMORPHIC *a.*, etc.] **1.** = AMORPHOUS *a.*
1885 A. B. HERVEY tr. *J. W. Behrens' Microsc. in Bot.* v. 429 More seldom they appear as crystals or crystalline forms, or also as amorphic masses in the cell membrane or cell contents. **1987** *Nature* 19 Nov. 253/1 The amorphic ferric oxide is synthesized by neutralizing a ferric chloride solution. **1993** *European Surg. Res.* XXV. 184 No correlation was found between the amount or size of amorphic granules using UW.
2. *Genetics.* Designating, pertaining to, or characteristic of an amorph; (of a mutant or mutation) inactive.
1932 H. J. MULLER in *Proc. 6th Internat. Congr. Genetics* I. 236 This latter type of mutant may..be called 'amorphic'. **1949** DARLINGTON & MATHER *Elem. Genetics* vii. 152 The hypermorph is more efficient than the wild-type gene...The wild-type gene is hypomorphic to its hypermorphic mutant and amorphic to its neomorphic mutant. **1966** E. A. CARLSON *Gene* xiii. 112 Not all mutations could be interpreted by hypomorphic and amorphic activity of genes. **1989** *Nature* 13 July 153/1 We do not know why *Elp* mutations predominantly affect the eye when amorphic mutations are lethal to the embryo.

amoxapine (əˈmɒksəpiːn), *n. Pharm.* [f. AMINO- + OX- + -*apine*, respelling of -*epine*: see BENZODIAZEPINE *n.*] A tricyclic antidepressant drug, $C_{17}H_{16}ClN_3O$, given orally.
1971 *Jrnl. Amer. Med. Assoc.* 25 Jan. 621/1 Amoxapine. **1972** *Current Therapeutic Res.* XIV. 381 Amoxapine seems to possess antidepressant properties, with only a mild degree of adverse reactions. **1976** *Nature* 12 Aug. 597/2 After 4 weeks' treatment with antidepressants (either imipramine or amoxepine [*sic*]) a change in uptake characteristics was observed. **1989** *Pharmaceutical Jrnl.* 16 Sept. 316/1 In comparison with other tricyclic antidepressants, amoxapine is more likely to induce seizures and renal failure.

ampangabeite (ˌæmpænˈɡeɪbɪaɪt, ˌæmˌpæŋɡəˈbeɪaɪt), *n. Min.* [a. F. *ampangabéite* (A. Lacroix 1912, in *Compt. Rend.* CLIV. 1044), f. the name of *Ampangabe* in Madagascar where the mineral was discovered: see -ITE[1].] = SAMARSKITE *n.*
1913 *Mineral. Mag.* XVI. 353 Ampangabeite...A tantalo-niobate (containing but little titanium) of uranium, iron, yttrium, &c., occurring..in pegmatite at Ampangabe, Madagascar. **1920** *Brit. Mus. Return* 145 in *Parl. Papers* XXXVI. 673 A series of specimens from Madagascar including good crystals of columbite, monazite, ampangabeite, and citrine. **1961** *Amer. Mineralogist* XLVI. 770 Ampangabeite is identical with samarskite. **1977** *Canad. Mineralogist* XV. 94/1 The Nb_2O_5 content of the 'ampangabéite' is lower than one would expect of typical samarskites.

Ampère, *n.* Sense in Dict. becomes 2. Add: **1.** Used in the possessive to designate various laws of electromagnetism deduced or derived by Ampère, esp. (*a*) the law relating the current in a conductor to the magnetic flux density it produces; also, the theorem derived from this, which states that the line integral of magnetic flux density around any closed path is proportional to the net current passing through the enclosed area; (*b*) the mnemonic rule that the lines of magnetic force generated by a current in a conductor would appear to run clockwise to an observer looking in the direction of the current.

1861 *Phil. Mag.* XXI. 248 Now, according to Ampère's well-known law of angular currents, the two currents will repel each other. **1862** *Ibid.* XXIII. 142 When the battery was not too strongly charged..the bullets..were seen to approach each other..and gave a confirmation of Ampère's law at once simple and direct. **1884** S. P. THOMPSON *Dynamo-Electr. Machinery* ii. 7 A more usual rule for remembering the direction of the induced currents is the following adaptation from Ampère's well-known rule. **1903** GEE & KINZBRUNNER tr. *Rosenberg's Electr. Engin.* ii. 44 'If we imagine a man swimming in the wire with the electric current and so as always to face the needle, then the north pole will be deflected to the left hand of the swimmer.' This rule is called Ampère's Rule. **1953** E. R. PECK *Electr. & Magn.* vii. 215 Equation (7.67) is a statement of Ampère's circuital law. We may write it more briefly...$\mathbf{B}\cdot\mathbf{dl} = \mu_0\,I_c$. **1966** *McGraw-Hill Encycl. Sci. & Technol.* II. 246/2 The field near a straight conductor can be found by application of Ampere's law. **1984** D. C. GIANCOLI *Gen. Physics* xxix. 564 We now use Ampère's law to determine the magnetic field inside a very long..closely packed solenoid.

amphetamine, *n.* Add: **2.** A tablet containing amphetamine.
1955 *N.Y. Times* 28 Sept. 25/6 A report on a drive against illegal traffic in amphetamines, called 'thrill pills' by teenage users, was made today. **1975** C. JAMES *Fate F. Fark* IV. 37 The parties Where people ate Amphetamines like Smarties. **1990** *Pract. Health* Spring 13/3, I took amphetamines to suppress my appetite.

amphi-, *comb. form.* Add: **amphiʹblastula** *n. Zool.*, a blastula composed predominantly of two different cell types, which constitutes a free-swimming larval form in certain sponges.
1888 *Proc. Boston Soc. Nat. Hist.* XXIII. 76 The walls were either double or single on different sides of the same *amphiblastula in Halichondria. **1940** PARKER & HASWELL *Text-bk. Zool.* (ed. 6) I. iii. 120 The embryo leaves the parent sponge in the peculiar stage to which the name of amphiblastula is applied. **1987** LAVERACK & DANDO *Lect. Notes Invertebr. Zool.* (ed. 3) iii. 25/1 The flagellated embryo is liberated from the parent as an amphiblastula.., and generally swims for a time.
amphiʹcarpic *a. Bot.* = AMPHICARPOUS *a.*
1846 *Florist's Jrnl.* VI. 152 *Amphicarpic, bearing fruit of different forms, or which ripens at various seasons. **1964** *Amer. Jrnl. Bot.* LI. 26 A more detailed investigation of the physiology of the seeds and seedlings of a typical amphicarpic plant.
ʹamphicyte *n. Anat.* = *satellite cell* s.v. SATELLITE *n.* 8.
1925 STRONG & ELWYN *Bailey's Text-bk. Histol.* (ed. 7) ix. 170 The capsule cells (*amphicytes) enveloping the cerebrospinal and sympathetic ganglion cells. **1978** *Acta Anatomica* CII. 238/2 Surrounding individual ganglionic neurons were well-defined satellite cells (amphicytes) to form the 'capsule'. **1985** C. R. LEESON et al. *Textbk. Histol.* (ed. 5) vii. 219/2 Each perikaryon has a 'capsule' formed by a single layer of small, flattened, low cuboidal cells, the satellite cells or amphicytes.
amphiprotic (-ˈprəʊ-) *a. Chem.* [ad. G. *amphiprotisch* (coined by J. N. Brönsted 1930, in *Zeitschr. f. angew. Chem.* XLIII. 231/1)], designating a solvent (or solute) which can act as either a donor or an acceptor of protons; amphoteric.
1931 *Chem. Rev.* VIII. 193 Thus we recognise water as *amphiprotic since it is capable of the acid reaction $H_2O \rightleftharpoons H^+ + OH^-$ and the basic reaction $H_2O + H^+ \rightleftharpoons H_3O^+$. **1966** J. A. TIMM *Gen. Chem.* (ed. 4) xxvii. 369 A solution of sodium hydrogen carbonate contains the amphiprotic hydrogen carbonate ion. **1991** *Chem. & Pharm. Bull.* XXXIX. 2929/1 The solutes having

amphiprotic substituents usually exhibited the acceleration effect.

amphitrichate (-'trɪk-) *a. Microbiol.* = *amphitrichous* adj. below.

1929 TOPLEY & WILSON *Princ. Bacteriol. & Immunity* I. ii. 25 There may be a single flagellum at each pole, the *amphitrichate condition. **1983** *Current Microbiol.* VIII. 234 The genus *Campylobacter*. . contains bacteria that are Gram-negative, motile, amphitrichate.

amphi'trichous (-'trɪk-) *a. Microbiol.*, designating or pertaining to bacteria having one or more flagella at each pole.

1900 DORLAND *Med. Dict.* 38/1 *Amphitrichous. **1928** F. W. TANNER *Bacteriol.* iv. 63 The adjectives used to denote the presence or absence of flagella, and their location when present, are . . amphitrichous-tufts of flagella on both ends. **1986** M. KOGUT tr. *Schlegel's Gen. Microbiol.* ii. 59 Bipolar polytrichous flagellation is called amphitrichous.

amphiarthrosis, *n.* Add: Hence **amphiar'throtic** *a.*

1956 *New Gould Med. Dict.* (ed. 2) 61/2 Amphiarthrotic. **1960** *McGraw-Hill Encycl. Sci. & Technol.* VII. 314/2 In the slightly movable, or amphiarthrotic, joints the opposing bony surfaces are separated by a flattened cartilaginous disk. **1992** *Ann. Zool. Fennici* XXVIII. 396/2 The fossae nudatae are interpreted as grooves or channels through which the liquid synovia [*sic*] is introduced between the amphiarthrotic joints.

amphibolite, *n.* Add: Hence **amphibo'litic** *a.*, of the nature of amphibolite; resembling amphibolite in composition.

1903 A. GEIKIE *Text-bk. Geol.* (ed. 4) II. 804 A conformable series of sericitic, amphibolitic, chloritic, and other schists. **1952** *Norsk Geol. Tidsskr.* XXX. 128 The final product of metamorphism is a crystalloblastic, amphibolitic rock, including biotite, garnet and diopside. **1989** *Nature* 20 July 223/1 A foliated orthogneiss consisting of tonalitic and amphibolitic layers alternating on a centimetre scale.

amphibolitization (æmˌfɪbəlɪtaɪ'zeɪʃən), *n. Petrogr.* [f. AMPHIBOLIT(E *n.* + -IZATION.] The alteration of a rock to form amphibolite, or one more nearly resembling amphibolite in composition.

1918 *Q. Jrnl. Geol. Soc.* LXXIV. 61 W. G. Foye correlates the liberation of alkaline solutions by amphibolitization with the production of nepheline-syenites. **1932** A. HARKER *Metamorphism* xviii. 308 True eclogites . . may be seen in all stages of amphibolization. Amphibolitization is perhaps a more appropriate description; for it is often not a mere replacement of pyroxene by amphibole but a reaction between garnet and pyroxene, yielding an aggregate of hornblende and plagioclase. **1974** *Scottish Jrnl. Geol.* X. 42 Amphibolitization of a granulite-facies terrain involves hydration of essentially anhydrous mineral assemblages.

Hence (as back-formations) **am'phibolitize** *v. trans.*, to increase the amphibolic content of (a rock); **am'phibolitized** *ppl. a.*

1961 WEBSTER, Amphibolitize, *v.t.* **1963** *Jrnl. Petrol.* IV. 356 Sr and An values in plagioclases present in rocks of all stages from fresh to amphibolitized gabbros . . are similar. **1974** *Nature* 4 Oct. 382/1 Paucity of fluids may also explain why large areas of Archaean granulites were not amphibolitized in later times. **1985** *Chem. Geol.* L. 65/2 These rocks have been referred to as 'symplectitic eclogites', 'amphibolitized eclogites', 'retrograded eclogites', 'eclogitic amphibolites' or even 'clinopyroxene–garnet rocks' by previous investigators. **1993** *Jrnl. Geol.* Cl. 358 A . . low-K, calcic amphibolite, collected from an amphibolitized mafic dike.

amphibolization (æmˌfɪbəlaɪ'zeɪʃən), *n. Petrogr.* [f. AMPHIBOL(E *n.* + -IZATION, or by simplification of *AMPHIBOLITIZATION *n.*] = *AMPHIBOLITIZATION *n.*

1932 A. HARKER *Metamorphism* viii. 109 A case of special interest is that of eclogite enveloped in a granite intrusion . . . Amphibolization in this case is to be regarded as a reaction between the two minerals. **1936** *Q. Jrnl. Geol. Soc.* XCII. 530 Much of the amphibolite development belonged to the injection period, but it seemed clear . . that further amphibolization took place at a subsequent stage. **1984** *Indian Jrnl. Earth Sci.* XI. 187 The availability of water has been the main cause for selective amphibolization of the gabbros leading to the formation of amphibolites.

Hence **am'phibolized** *ppl. a.*

1936 *Q. Jrnl. Geol. Soc.* XCII. 507 The structure remains that of an eclogite, so that the rock is best described as an amphibolized eclogite. **1977** *Mineral. Mag.* XLI. 124 (*title*) Tourmaline from amphibolized gabbro at Hanter Hill, Radnorshire.

amphiphilic (æmfɪ'fɪlɪk), *a. Chem.* [f. AMPHI- + -PHILIC.] = *amphipathic* adj. s.v. *AMPHI-.

1948 P. A. WINSOR in *Trans. Faraday Soc.* XLIV. 377 Such species have previously been termed 'amphipathic' by Hartley but . . will here be termed 'amphiphilic'. **1966** *Molecular Crystals* II. 59 The appropriate degree of lipophilic-hydrophilic balance may be obtained by mixing different amphiphilic substances. **1973** *Nature* 26 Oct. 465/2 Amphiphilic gels are produced by introducing a limited number of hydrophobic groups into hydrophilic gel-forming substances. **1991** *New Scientist* 18 May 46/1 The more complex structure of amphiphilic molecules means that they possess an even richer diversity of liquid crystalline structures.

So **'amphiphile** *n.* = *amphipath* s.v. *AMPHI-; **amphiphi'licity** *n.*, the condition of being amphiphilic; the degree to which something is amphiphilic.

1948 P. A. WINSOR in *Trans. Faraday Soc.* XLIV. 377 It is such species, which may conveniently be termed amphiphiles, which typically give rise to such phenomena as hydrotropy, solubilisation and emulsification. **1982** *Nature* 23 Sept. 371/2 (*title*) The helical hydrophobic moment: a measure of the amphiphilicity of a helix. **1989** *Adverse Drug Reactions & Acute Poisoning Rev.* VIII. 75 Numerous other cationic amphiphiles accumulate in lysosomes and induce the development of lysosomal abnormalities similar to those produced by aminoglycoside administration without inducing similar nephrotoxicity.

amphiploid ('æmfɪplɔɪd), *n.* and *a. Biol.* [f. AMPHI- + -PLOID.] = *allopolyploid* s.v. ALLOPOLYPLOIDY *n.*

1945 *Publ. Carnegie Inst. Washington* No. 564. v. 68 The first condition for a successful amphiploid is that the genomes of its parents fit together properly to insure a harmonious development of the F_1. *Ibid.* vii. 120 Not many natural amphiploid species have been artificially synthesized. **1968** *Amer. Jrnl. Bot.* LV. 473 (*heading*) Endogenous beta irradiation and tumor production in an amphiploid nicotiana hybrid. **1983** E. C. MINKOFF *Evolutionary Biol.* xv. 261/1 Grant (1971) reports that 'the vast majority' of well-analyzed polyploid plant species are amphiploids.

amphisbaenian, *a.* and *n.* Add: **B.** *n.* A burrowing, usu. limbless lizard of the family Amphisbaenidae (suborder Sauria or Lacertilia), found in Africa, the Mediterranean region, and North and South America; a worm-lizard.

1865 *Proc. Zool. Soc.* 23 May 442 (*heading*) A revision of the genera and species of Amphisbænians. **1886** *Encycl. Brit.* XX. 461/1 In the *Ophidia* and Amphisbænians and some other Snake-like Lacertilians there is no tympanic cavity. **1968** *Amer. Naturalist* CII. 345 Amphisbaenians are a group of slender, elongate, generally limbless squamates, sometimes classified with the lizards. **1986** ROMER & PARSONS *Vertebr. Body* (ed. 6) vii. 218 Snakes, amphisbaenians, and certain lizards have abandoned limbs and reverted to..locomotion based on body undulation.

amphisbaenid (ˌæmfɪsˈbiːnɪd), *n. Zool.* [f. mod.L. family name *Amphisbaenidae*, f. AMPHISBAENA *n.*: see -ID³.] = *AMPHISBAENIAN n.*

1889 in *Cent. Dict.* **1957** SCHMIDT & INGER *Living Reptiles of World* 161/2 Worm lizards or amphisbaenids. **1965** R. & D. MORRIS *Men & Snakes* iv. 83 The Amphisbaenids, or 'worm-lizards', have blunt tails resembling their heads. **1979** *Acta Anatomica* CIV. 208/2 The amphisbaenids are reptiles very adapted to a burrowing and underground life.

Ampholine (ˈæmfəliːn), *n. Biochem.* Also **ampholine**. [a. Sw. *ampholine*, f. *AMPHOL(YTE n.* + -INE⁵.] A proprietary name for ampholytes used to establish stable pH gradients in isoelectric focusing.

1968 *Trade Marks Jrnl.* 3 July 1077/1 *Ampholine*...Chemical products for industrial and scientific use in the separation, purification and characterization of proteins and like substances. **1968** *Lancet* 20 Apr. 847/2 Mixtures covering the whole pH range of 3-10 or narrower ranges within these limits are commercially available as 'Ampholine' carrier electrolytes. **1976** *Physics Bull.* Aug. 359/3 The separation takes place in a pH gradient of ampholine in a direction parallel with the long edge of the tray. **1989** *BioFactors* II. 107/2 Precast Ampholine PAG Plates, ..pH 3.5-9.5, were used for determination of isoelectric points.

ampholyte (ˈæmfəlaɪt), *n. Chem.* [f. AMPHO(TERIC *a.* + ELECTRO)LYTE *n.*] An electrolyte possessing both acidic and basic groups.

1921 D. BURNS *Introd. Biophysics* vii. 59 Substances which produce both H and OH' ions on dissociation are called amphoteric electrolytes or ampholytes. **1940** GLASSTONE *Text-bk. Physical Chem.* xii. 976 An ampholyte is at its iso-electric point when the extent of ionization as an acid is equal to that as a base. **1982** T. M. DEVLIN *Textbk. Biochem.* ii. 43 In electrophoresis, an ampholyte (protein, peptide, or amino acid) in a solution buffered at a particular pH is placed in an electric field. **1989** *Jrnl. Exper. Bot.* LX. 1017/2 The prolonged, multiple exposures to acid, ampholytes, salts, and other chemicals during sample preparation are a possible cause of this blockage.

amphometer (æmˈfɒmɪtə(r)), *n. Austral.* [f. *amph-* (prob. f. *m.p.h.* s.v. M 6, with arbitrary *a-* prefixed) + -OMETER.] A device for measuring the speed of vehicles passing over the stretch of road on which it is installed.

1964 *Telegraph* (Brisbane) 9 Dec. 39/1 In each case, the amphometer and the police car speedometer had shown the same reading. The amphometer consists of a meter and two tubes which are placed across the road 88ft. apart. **1966** *Courier-Mail* (Brisbane) 26 Oct. 7/5 Queensland should follow Victoria's lead and introduce 'the little black boxes' (amphometers) to cut down the State's tragic road toll. **1980** *Kyabram* (Victoria) *Free Press* 26 Feb. 1/7 An amphometer set up on the Midland Highway at Stanhope also intercepted five speeding motorists.

amphoteric, *a.* Delete *rare-⁰* and for 'neutral, neither acid nor alkaline' read: Chiefly *Chem.*, having or exhibiting both acidic and basic properties.

1906 G. MANN *Chem. Proteids* vi. 216 These compounds are therefore formed by the amphoteric amino-acids. **1984** GREENWOOD & EARNSHAW *Chem. of Elements* (1986) vii. 253 Al(OH)₃ is amphoteric, forming both salts and aluminates. **1988** *Prima* Aug. 36/2 L'Oreal's latest hair care range contains..amphoteric polymers which maintain the spring of the perm.

Hence **ampho'terism** *n.*, the capacity to act as an acid or as a base.

1937 J. H. YOE *Chem. Princ.* xvi. 164 Amphoterism and also the degree of acidic and basic ionization of amphoteric hydroxides are related to the position of their metallic elements in the periodic table. **1957** SIENKO & PLANE *Chem.* xvii. 363 Some elements, such as chromium, show amphoterism in one oxidation state but not in another. **1990** D. F. SHRIVER et al. *Inorg. Chem.* v. 161 An important issue in the *d* block is the oxidation number necessary for amphoterism.

amphotericin (æmfəˈtɛrɪsɪn), *n. Pharm.* [f. AMPHOTERIC *a.* + -IN¹.] Either of two amphoteric polyenes with antifungal properties obtained from the soil bacterium *Streptomyces nodosus*; *esp.* the antibiotic C₄₇H₇₃NO₁₇ (more fully *amphotericin B*), used to treat some serious fungal infections.

1956 J. VANDEPUTTE et al. in *Antibiotics Ann. 1955-6* 587 A *Streptomyces* species (M4575) has been found to produce two antifungal agents that we have named amphotericins A and B. **1964** S. DUKE-ELDER *Parsons' Dis. Eye* (ed. 14) xiv. 144 Many fungi are sensitive to nystatin, amphotericin or trichomycin. **1977** *Ann. Internal Med.* LXXXVI. 47/1 Amphotericin B is a polyene antifungal antibiotic that binds to cholesterol in the plasma membrane of eukaryotic cells. **1989** *Lancet* 3 June 1262/1 Because of the deleterious effects of amphotericin B on renal transplants, he was started on fluconazole 200 mg orally every second day.

amplectant (æmˈplɛktənt), *a.* [ad. mod.L. *amplectans, amplectant-*, alteration of or a mistake for cl. L. *amplectens* pr. pple. of *amplectī*: see AMPLECT *v.*, -ANT¹.] 1. Embracing, clasping; *spec.* in *Bot.*, twining tightly about some support. *rare-⁰*.

[**1826** KIRBY & SPENCE *Introd. Entomol.* IV. xlvi. 331 *Amplectent* (*Amplecteus*), when posteriorly it is so curved as to form a large sinus which embraces the Dorsolum. **1832** J. LINDLEY *Introd. Bot.* iv. 415 *Embracing* (*amplectans*), clasping with the base.] **1857** A. GRAY *First Lessons Bot.* 204 *Amplectant*, embracing. **1954** H. I. FEATHERLY *Taxon. Terminol. Higher Plants* 4/1 *Amplectant*, embracing, clasping by the base.

2. *Zool.* Of a frog or toad: engaged in amplexus.

[**1951** R. RUGH *Frog* iv. 73 As the frog's egg is shed into the water, the male (in amplectic embrace)..sheds clouds of spermatozoa over the eggs.] **1954** *Texas Jrnl. Sci.* VI. 73 Many amplecant [*sic*] pairs of *B. punctatis* were presently found in the water or on the banks. **1979** *Nature* 6 Dec. 611/1 We collected amplectant pairs of toads from several breeding congregations. **1983** A. ARAK in P. Bateson *Mate Choice* viii. 182 (*caption*) Like many other explosive breeders, males 'scramble' for females and attempt to dislodge amplectant males. **1991** *Jrnl. Herpetol.* XXV. 324 Nor was there a correlation between the body size of the amplectant males and their female partners.

amplexus (æmˈplɛksəs), *n. Zool.* [a. L. *amplexus* an embrace, f. *amplex-* pa. ppl. stem of *amplectī*: see AMPLECT *v.*] The mating embrace of frogs and toads, in which the male clasps the female's body tightly from behind.

1932 *Proc. Zool. Soc.* 890 The release appears to occur through the grip of the male relaxing on account of the absence of the necessary stimulus to amplexus. **1951** M. SMITH *Brit. Amphibians & Reptiles* iv. 128 Under normal breeding conditions not more than 24 hours are spent in amplexus. **1972** *Oxf. Bk. Vertebr.* 116/2 He places himself on the female's back and wraps his forelimbs around her body just below the armpits; this position is called amplexus. **1988** *New Scientist* 7 Apr. 41/1 The male does several things during amplexus, one of which is to rub glands on his cheeks against the female's nostrils.

amplitude, *n.* Add: [**6.**] [**d.**] Hence (as back-formations) **amplitude-modulate** *v.* *trans.*; **amplitude-modulated** *ppl. a.*
   1938 G. E. STERLING *Radio Manual* (ed. 3) vi. 353 An analysis of a frequency modulated wave shows that it contains the same side bands that are present in an amplitude modulated wave. **1970** J. EARL *Tuners & Amplifiers* v. 104 The clicks, pops and whistles we commonly have to tolerate on a.m. stations are caused by the received signal being effectively amplitude-modulated by interference. **1982** *Giant Bk. Electronics Projects* x. 463 This video output may in turn be used to amplitude modulate an rf carrier. **1990** *Physiotherapy* LXXVI. 745/2 Both the medium frequency currents themselves, and the amplitude modulated beat frequency, are portrayed as sinusoidal.

ampoule, *n.* Add: Hence 'ampoule *v.* *trans.*, to put into or store in an ampoule; 'ampouled *ppl. a.*
   1946 *Nature* 5 Oct. 487/1 The rabbit anti-sera..had been Seitz-filtered through E.K. pads, ampouled and stored at 5°C. **1969** *Indian Vet. Jrnl.* XLVI. 877 Dehydrated semen extenders..and liquid but ampouled extender..were recommended on the basis of their preservability of bovine spermatozoa. **1977** *Lancet* 17 Dec. 1281/1 The two reference thromboplastins 67/40 and 68/434 were freeze dried and ampouled. **1992** *Thrombosis & Haemostasis* LXVII. 424 An international collaborative study was undertaken to establish the potency and stability of an ampouled pure α-thrombin preparation.

Ampthill ('æmθɪl), *n. Geol.* [The name of a town in Bedfordshire, England.] **Ampthill Clay**, (a bed of) clay, similar to Oxford clay, deposited during the Oxfordian stage of the late Jurassic and cropping out south of the River Humber.
   1877 *Q. Jrnl. Geol. Soc.* XXXIII. 260/1 (*heading*) Ampthill Clay and Elsworth Rock. [*Ibid.* 313 At Ampthill, the place after which Mr Seeley has called the middle division of the clay, we have found in the débris of the railway-cutting a well marked spine of that most characteristic fossil *Cidaris florigemma.*] **1946** L. D. STAMP *Britain's Struct.* xii. 133 North of Oxford the Oxford Clay is succeeded by the similar Ampthill Clay. **1989** *Proc. Geol. Assoc.* C. 353/1 Although it is generally agreed that the section exposed both Ampthill Clay and Kimmeridge Clay, the precise stratigraphy has remained obscure.

amrinone ('æmrɪnəʊn), *n. Pharm.* [f. AM(INO- + PY)RI(DI)N(E *n.* + -ONE.] A drug, $C_{10}H_9N_3O$, with positive inotropic action on the heart muscles, which has been used to treat congestive heart failure.
   1977 *Jrnl. Amer. Med. Assoc.* 25 July 344/1 Amrinone. **1978** *Federation Proc.* XXXVII. 914/2 The positive inotropic activity of amrinone..was tested in the isolated cat atria and papillary muscle. **1987** M. J. NEAL *Med. Pharmacol.* xvii. 41/2 Amrinone directly increases myocardial contraction and is a vasodilator. **1989** *Martindale's Extra Pharmacopoeia* (ed. 29) 822/3 Amrinone produces gastro-intestinal disturbances that may necessitate withdrawal of treatment.

Amur ('æmʊə(r)), *n.* [The name of the *Amur* region in south-east Russia, bordering the river of the same name.] Used *attrib.* to designate plants and animals native to or originating from the Amur region, as **Amur maple**, a small maple, *Acer ginnala*, with creamy-white flowers

and scarlet autumnal foliage, much cultivated as an ornamental shrub; **Amur pike**, a pike, *Esox reicherti*, which has a silvery body with numerous black spots and is a food fish in the Amur basin; **Amur tiger**, the Siberian tiger.
   1934 WEBSTER, Amur maple. **1962** O. RONEN tr. *Berg's Freshwater Fishes U.S.S.R. & Adjacent Countries* I. 492 (*heading*) *Esox reicherti* Dybowski.—Amur pike. **1964** *Biol. Abstr.* XLV. 8085/2 The Amur tiger inhabits Manchurian type forests. **1981** *Northeast Woods & Waters* Jan. 6/2 This is the only lake in the country where an angler can take the Amur Pike, a transplant from Russia and a river of the same name. **1988** *New Scientist* 1 Sept. 69/1 These 68 zoos had 207 Amur tigers between them, including 94 males and 113 females. **1988** *Guinness Bk. Records 1989* 24/3 The largest member of the cat family (Felidae) is the protected long-furred Siberian tiger (*Panthera tigris altaica*), also called the Amur or Manchurian tiger. **1992** *Harrowsmith* Aug. 70/3 Not all maples are huge, and for compact gardens, the Amur maple (*Acer ginnala*) is a rewarding choice.

amusia (ə'mjuːzɪə, eɪ'mjuːzɪə), *n. Path.* [ad. Ger. *Amusie* (coined by A. Knoblauch 1888, in *Deutsch. Arch. f. Klin. Med.* XLIII. 343), f. Gr. ἀμουσία want of harmony: see -IA¹. Cf. APHASIA *n.*] A condition in which there is the loss of a musical ability, such as the comprehension of music, the production of music, or the ability to read or write musical notation.
   1890 A. KNOBLAUCH in *Brain* XIII. 330 To name the motor disorders which correspond to aphasia we would propose the term '*amusia*'. **1912** *Med. Rec.* (N.Y.) 13 Jan. 59/2 Amusia, according to Brazier, may be simple or total or at any rate complex. **1961** R. BRAIN *Speech Disorders* vii. 105 Failure to recognize familiar music is known as sensory amusia; and inability to sing, whistle or hum a tune is motor amusia. **1977** *Times Lit. Suppl.* 10 June 709/3 Arthur Benson then gives a refreshingly systematic account of the multifarious disorders—the 'amusias'—to which musical ability is prone. **1990** *Cortex* XXVI. 470 Loss of the ability to analyze complex tones for pitch extraction may produce some degree of receptive amusia.

amyelia (ˌeɪmaɪ'iːlɪə), *n. Path.* [f. Gr. ἀμύελος without marrow: + -IA¹; cf. A- 14, MYELIN *n.*¹] Congenital absence of the spinal cord.
   1865 *Med. Press* (Dublin) XI. 435/2 The appearance of the spinal nerves at the neural foramina in the absence of the spinal cord (amyelia) has been remarked. **1897** GOULD & PYLE *Anomalies & Curiosities Med.* vi. 281 Foot records a case of amyelia, or absence of the spinal cord, in a fetus with hernia cerebri and complete fissure of the spinal column. **1927** *Anatomical Rec.* XXXVI. 310 The literature does not supply many cases of anencephaly or amyelia in very young embryos. **1979** *Virchows Archiv* A. CCCLXXXIV. 292 In this case of amyelia and anencephaly there were apparently normal neural crest derivatives and vertebral column.

amygdala (ə'mɪgdələ), *n. Anat.* Pl. amygdalae. [a. L. *amygdala*, ad. Gr. ἀμυγδάλη almond: see AMYGDAL *n.*] **1.** A tonsil (TONSIL *n.* 1). Usu. in *pl.* Cf. AMYGDAL *n.* 2 a. Now *rare* or *Obs.*
   1749 J. BARROW *Dict. Medicum Universale*, *Amygdalæ*, almonds. It also sometimes signifies the *Tonsillæ*. **1816** C. BELL in J. Bell *Anat. & Physiol. Human Body* (ed. 4) III. iv. iii. 201 These are the tonsils or amygdalæ The amygdala is a mucous gland. **1843** J. G. WILKINSON tr. *Swedenborg's Animal Kingdom* I. ii. 67 The *amygdalæ* are 2 glandular bodies of a reddish color. **1905** H. GRAY *Anat.* (ed. 16) 1050 The tonsils (*amygdalæ*) are two prominent bodies situated one on each side of the fauces.

2. A lobe on the underside of each hemisphere of the cerebellum; = TONSIL *n.* 2. Now *rare* or *Obs.*

1845 R. B. Todd *Anat. Brain* vii. 195 The cerebellum...On the inferior surface of each hemisphere the following lobes are readily distinguishable...1. The amygdala. **1909** H. Gray *Anat.* (ed. 17) 829 The cerebellum...The amygdalæ, or tonsils are rounded masses, situated in the lateral hemispheres. **1946** W. E. Le Gros Clark *Pract. Anat.* 278 Close to the side of the medulla is a well-defined oval lobule of the cerebellar hemisphere called the amygdala or tonsil.
3. One of the basal ganglia in each cerebral hemisphere, situated towards the front of the temporal lobe and concerned with the control of motivation and aggression.
1889 *Cent. Dict.*, *Amygdala*..a small mass of gray matter in front of the end of the descending cornu of the lateral ventricle of the brain. **1899** F. H. Gerrish *Text-bk. Anat.* 526 The *Amygdaloid nucleus*, this ganglion, otherwise called *amygdala*, is a mass at the tip of the temporal lobe. **1947** H. C. Elliot *Textbk. Nervous Syst.* xviii. 225/1 The formation of the temporal lobe has..been explained...The amygdala and hippocampal formation lie in this region. **1976** Smythies & Corbett *Psychiatry* iv. 40 Small tumors or other irritative lesions of the amygdala can cause violent and aggressive disorders of behavior. **1991** *Lancet* 2 Mar. 559/1 Pathological changes in AD [*sc.* Alzheimer's disease] and ageing are mainly in structures related anatomically to the olfactory system, such as the amygdala and entorhinal cortex.

amygdalar (ə'mɪgdələ(r)), *a.* *Anat.* [f. *AMYGDAL(A n.* + -AR¹.] Of or pertaining to the amygdala of the brain; caused by lesions in the amygdala.
1959 *Amer. Jrnl. Physiol.* CXCVII. 158 Animals of group 3 were bilaterally amygdalectomized..during the dynamic phase of amygdalar obesity. **1960** *Ibid.* CXCVIII. 1315 (*title*) Relationship of the middle hypothalamus to amygdalar hyperphagia. **1979** *Nature* 5 Apr. 562/2 The lesser decreases in amygdalar concentrations might indicate that at least some of the immunoreactive material present in this area could arise locally. **1991** *Jrnl. Clin. & Exper. Neuropsychol.* XIII. 21/1 (*title*) Mnemonic effects of bilateral amygdalar lesions in man.

amygdale (ə'mɪgdeɪl, 'æmɪgdeɪl), *n.* *Geol.* [ad. L. *amygdala*: see AMYGDAL *n.*] A vesicle in a lava filled with secondary minerals.
1897 A. Geikie *Anc. Volcanoes Gt. Brit.* I. iii. 15 As the kernels thus produced are frequently flattened or almond-shaped (amygdales).., the rocks containing them are said to be amygdaloidal. **1916** *Q. Jrnl. Geol. Soc.* LXXII. 232 The amygdales are occupied by agate, jasper, and quartz, and by a variety of zeolites. **1944** A. Holmes *Princ. Physical Geol.* v. 49 The filled 'bubbles' sometimes look like almonds, and so the name amygdale is given to them. **1990** C. Pellant *Rocks, Minerals & Fossils* 23/1 The amygdales are both round and elongated and contain calcite, the rhombic cleavage of which is visible.

amygdalite (ə'mɪgdəlaɪt), *n.* *Petrogr. rare* [f. L. *amygdal-a* (see AMYGDAL *n.*) + -ITE¹.] = AMYGDALOID *n.*
1811 J. Pinkerton *Petralogy* I. 89 *Amygdalite*,..this substance, the *mandelstein*, or almond-stone of the Germans, has a base of coarse trap or basalton. **1983** S. I. Tomkeieff *Dict. Petrol.* 24/1 *Amygdalite*, see *amygdaloid*.

amygdaloid, *a.* and *n.* Add: [A.] **2.** *Anat.* Of or pertaining to an amygdala (see *AMYGDALA n.*).
1836 Todd *Cycl. Anat. & Phys.* I. 583/1 The amygdaloid lobe [in the cerebellum.] **1877** C. Heath *Pract. Anat.* (ed. 4) 511 (Index), Amygdaloid lobe of cerebellum. **1959** *Jrnl. Compar. Neurol.* CXIII. 245 We have called the rostral portion of the amygdaloid complex the anterior amygdaloid area. **1967** *Bull. Acad. Polonaise de Sci.* XV. 304 Fibres of this tract terminate also in the anterior amygdaloid area. **1993** *Pharmacol., Biochem. & Behavior* XLV. 445 Indeloxazine..dose-dependently..shortened the evoked amygdaloid afterdischarge *Ibid.* 449/1 Indeloxazine showed a biphasic action on amygdaloid kindling in rats..
3. Special collocations: **amygdaloid complex** *Anat.*, the amygdaloid nuclei and associated transitional areas of the cerebrum.
1915 *Jrnl. Compar. Neurol.* XXV. 416 It is evident..that what is here described as the medial large-celled nucleus belongs to the *amygdaloid complex. **1980** *Gray's Anat.* (ed. 36) 996/1 The corticomedial amygdaloid complex consists of the central, medial, and cortical amygdaloid nuclei, the nucleus of the lateral olfactory stria, and a transitional poorly differentiated amygdaloid area. **1992** D. G. Amaral et al. in J. P. Aggleton *Amygdala* i. 1 The amygdaloid complex..is a prominent component of the medial temporal lobe in primates, including man.
amygdaloid nucleus *Anat.*, the amygdala (*AMYGDALA n.* 3); any of the nuclei that together make up the amygdala.
1889 *Cent. Dict.* s.v. *Amygdaloid*, Amygdaloid nucleus. **1893** H. Morris *Treat. Human Anat.* V. 740 The *amygdaloid nucleus is a thickening of the grey cortex of the apex of the temporal lobe. **1964** J. Z. Young *Model of Brain* ii. 15 The amygdaloid (nutlike) nucleus among the basal ganglia of the forebrain is concerned with smell. **1990** *Brain* CXIII. 11 (*caption*) Nissl-stained transverse section..showing the location of tritiated amino acids injected into the medial parts of the basolateral amygdaloid nuclei and the deep layers of the entorhinal cortex.

amyl, *n.*² Add: [**2.**] **amyl nitrate**, (*a*) a colourless liquid, $C_5H_{11}NO_3$, added to diesel fuel to increase the cetane number; (*b*) = *amyl nitrite* below.
[**1857** H. Watts tr. *Gmelin's Hand-Bk. Chem.* XI. 65 Nitrate of amyl burns with a faint green-edged flame.] **1911** Webster, *Amyl nitrate. **1927** *Jrnl. Inst. Petroleum Technologists* XIII. Amyl nitrate and nitrite..according to Midgley are pro-knock. **1968** 'A. Diment' *Bang Bang Birds* viii. 142 That Amyl Nitrate, that's dynamite, man. **1979** S. Wilson *Glad Hand* I. i. 10 Oh, Christ! Who's on amyl nitrate? Or have you all just forgotten to change your socks? **1982** *Oil & Gas Jrnl.* 31 May 93/3 A number of diesel-ignition improvers..have been commercially available..and include the following compounds: isopropyl nitrate..amyl nitrate. **1989** *Brit. Med. Jrnl.* 10 June 1566/2 Amyl nitrate is no longer used as a coronary vasodilator but is often abused for 'recreational' purposes by sniffing.
amyl nitrite, a yellowish, volatile liquid, $C_5H_{11}NO_2$, rapidly absorbed by the body on inhalation, which acts as a vasodilator and is sometimes used for its stimulatory effects.
[**1857** H. Watts tr. *Gmelin's Hand-Bk. Chem.* XI. 64 Nitrite of amyl is decomposed by peroxide of lead with the aid of heat.] **1881** *Med. Temp. Jrnl.* 72, I have given up the employment of alcohol as a menstruum for *amyl nitrite in angina. **1938** R. H. A. Plimmer *Organic & Bio-Chem.* (ed. 6) vi. 68 Amyl nitrite is a pale yellow oil boiling at 96°. **1978** *Amer. Jrnl. Psychiatry* CXXXV. 1216/2 Sales of amyl nitrite rose sharply due to its nonmedical use as an agent for getting high and as an aphrodisiac. **1990** *Amer. Jrnl. Epidemiol.* CXXXII. 393/2 Neither the number of sexual partners nor the amyl nitrite usage was significant.

amylin ('æmɪlɪn), *n.* [f. AMYL(O- + -IN¹.] **1.** *Chem.* The water-insoluble fraction of starch, which forms the outer layer of starch granules (cf. AMIDIN *n.* 1); amylopectin. Now *rare.*
1838 T. Thomson *Chem. Org. Bodies* v. 652 The vesicular portion of the grain, which is insoluble in

water, may be distinguished by the name of *amylin*. [*Note*] I have . . been obliged to employ a new term and I have adopted *amylin*, from the Greek word αμυλον starch, as sufficiently appropriate. **1887** *Encycl. Brit.* XXII. 420/2 Reserve cells or thesocytes have been described in several sponges as well as amylin and oil-bearing cells. **1924** T. B. ROBERTSON *Princ. Biochem.* (ed. 2) iv. 94 Thus we have *Amylin, Lavosin, Cerosin* and *Secalin*, etc., found in grain-seeds, some of which yield glucose on hydrolysis, others fructose.

2. *Physiol.* A peptide hormone, found as amyloid deposits in the pancreas in certain types of diabetes, which is thought to decrease the rate of glycogen synthesis in mammalian skeletal muscles.

1988 LEIGHTON & COOPER in *Nature* 13 Oct. 632/2 Amylin is a 37-amino-acid peptide which is a major component of islet amyloid and has structural similarity to human calcitonin gene-related peptide-2. **1989** *Ibid.* 16 Mar. 211/1 Leighton and Cooper recently reported a potential physiological function of a newly discovered pancreatic β-cell hormone which they refer to as 'amylin'. **1990** *Sci. News* 20 Oct. 251/2 To elicit the insulin-blocking effect, . . investigators have had to use 'industrial' concentrations of amylin—about 1,000 times higher than the tiny amounts . . normally circulating in rat or human blood.

amylobarbitone (ˌæmɪləʊˈbɑːbɪtəʊn), *n. Pharm.* [f. AMYLO- + BARBITONE *n.*] A barbiturate drug, $C_{11}H_{18}N_2O_3$, with hypnotic and sedative properties, usu. given in tablet form (freq. as the faster-acting sodium salt); 5-ethyl-5-isopentylbarbituric acid. So *amylobarbitone sodium.* Cf. *AMOBARBITAL *n.*

1945 *Brit. Pharmaceutical Codex 1934* Suppl. 6 Amylobarbitone is 5-*iso*amyl-5-ethylbarbituric acid. **1949** *Brit. Pharmaceutical Codex* 92 Amylobarbitone sodium is the sodium derivative of amylobarbitone, and may be prepared by the action of sodium ethoxide on amylobarbitone. **1965** J. POLLITT *Depression & its Treatment* iv. 57 A barbiturate (such as amylobarbitone sodium) is effective as premedication. **1989** COLLIER & LONGMORE *Oxf. Handbk. Clin. Specialties* (ed. 2) iv. 334 Hypnosis (or IV amylobarbitone) may be used to enable the patient to relive the stressful events.

amyloglucosidase (ˌæmɪləʊgluːˈkɒsɪdeɪz, ˌæmɪləʊgluːkəʊˈsaɪdeɪz), *n. Biochem.* [f. AMYLO- + *GLUCOSIDASE *n.*] An enzyme which catalyses the hydrolytic cleavage of successive glucose residues from the non-reducing end of a glucan molecule; *spec.* one which hydrolyses α-1,6 glycosidic bonds in glycogen, effecting debranching of the molecule.

1950 CORI & LARNER in *Federation Proc.* IX. 163/1 When a protein fraction, obtained from muscle, is added to phosphorylase, the entire glycogen molecule is digested. This fraction contains an enzyme for which the name amylo-1,6-glucosidase is proposed. **1976** *Jrnl. Ultrastruct. Res.* LIV. 115 Treatment of thin sections with the enzyme, amyloglucosidase, led to the disappearance of glycogen particles. **1986** M. K. TURNER in C. A. Heaton *Chem. Industry* vi. 333 One is amyloglucosidase which is isolated from various strains of *Aspergillus spp.* **1994** *Daily Tel.* 9 Feb. 6 In conventional brewing processes used to make diet beer an enzyme called amyloglucosidase AMG is added to the fermentation broth to break down some of the complex sugars.

amyloidogenic (ˌæmɪlɔɪdəʊˈdʒɛnɪk), *a. Path.* [f. AMYLOID *a.* and *n.* + -o¹ + -GENIC.] Giving rise to, or promoting the formation of, amyloid deposits.

1969 *Proc. Soc. Exper. Biol. & Med.* CXXXI. 460 Our studies show that two compounds that are amyloidogenic can diminish the PHA response of

mouse spleen cells *in vitro.* **1985** *Brit. Jrnl. Exper. Path.* LXVI. 140 Upon termination of the amyloidogenic stimulus, some degree of spontaneous regression of amyloidosis does occur. **1992** *Biochem. Jrnl.* CCLXXXV. 151 Several structural features of the amyloidogenic light chains here are worth noting.

amyotonia (ˌeɪmaɪəˈtəʊnɪə), *n. Path.* [f. A- 14 + MYOTONIA *n.*] Lack of muscle tone; *spec.* (in full *amyotonia congenita*), any of several rare congenital diseases characterized by general hypotonia of the skeletal muscles.

1907 *Brain* XXX. 146 (*heading*) Dr. James S. Collier.—A case of amyotonia congenita. **1946** M. R. EVERETT *Med. Biochem.* (ed. 2) vi. 462 Pathological creatinuria occurs during the course of such muscle diseases as amyotonia congenita. **1969** *Developmental Med. Child Neurol.* XI. 381 The features . . used to define the syndrome are: 1 . . emaciation . . followed . . by voracious appetite and gross obesity. 2. Amyotonia and weakness dating from birth. **1987** *Jrnl. Med.* XVIII. 94 These congenital myopathies have been taken from the ill-defined heterogeneous conglomeration known as amyotonia congenita or floppy infant syndrome.

Hence **amyo'tonic** *a.*

1961 *Epilepsia* II. 298 Epileptic seizures . . variously called apoplectic, . . amyotonic, paralytic, etc., have been subdivided into a great number of varieties. **1969** *Developmental Med. Child Neurol.* XI. 381 A syndrome of adiposity, slight growth, cryptorchidism and oligophrenia following an amyotonic onset in the newborn period.

amyotrophic, *a.* Add: **2.** Special collocation: **amyotrophic lateral sclerosis** [tr. F. *sclerose latérale amyotrophique* (coined by J. M. Charcot 1874, in *Progrès Med.* II. 325/1)], a rare degenerative motor neurone disease which results in progressive muscular atrophy, usu. beginning in the hands, and spasticity in the limbs.

1886 *Brain* VIII. 165 Two cases showing during life the typical symptoms of *amyotrophic lateral sclerosis have occurred in the practice of my colleague Dr. Leech. **1946** M. R. EVERETT *Med. Biochem.* (ed. 2) vi. 462 Pathological creatinuria occurs during the course of such muscle diseases as . . amyotrophic lateral sclerosis. **1965** *Jrnl. Indiana State Med. Assoc.* LVIII. 1136/1 A patient with amyotrophic lateral sclerosis is commonly middle-aged or older. **1990** DiMAGGIO & GILBERT *Real Grass, Real Heroes* ii. 24 It took a terminal disease to stop Gehrig—amyotrophic lateral sclerosis—ALS, known ever since as 'Lou Gehrig's disease'.

ancestrula (ænˈsɛstrʊlə), *n. Zool.* [mod.L. (coined in Fr. by J. Jullien in *Mission Scientifique du Cap Horn 1882-83* (1891) VI. III. 27): see ANCESTOR *n.*, -ULE.] The first or founder zooid of a bryozoan colony, formed by the metamorphosis of a sexually produced larva.

1902 *Q. Jrnl. Microsc. Sci.* XLVI. 321 The primary zoœcium, has been termed the 'ancestrula' by Jullien . . , a name which he appears to have used merely to convey the idea that it was the actual ancestor . . of the other individuals of the colony. **1911** *Encycl. Brit.* XXII. 43/1 The ancestrula inaugurates a process of budding, continued by its progeny, and thus gives rise to the mature colony. **1967** *Oceanogr. & Marine Biol.* V. 352 Subsequent growth of the colony . . occurs in a regular manner around the ancestrula. **1987** LAVERACK & DANDO *Lect. Notes Invertebr. Zool.* (ed. 3) xxviii. 161/1 The metamorphosis is complete with the formation of the first zooid or ancestrula.

anchimeric (ˌæŋkɪˈmɛrɪk, ˌæŋkaɪ-), *a. Chem.* [f. Gr. ἄγχι near + μέρος part + -IC.] **anchimeric assistance**, the participation of a functional group of a molecule in a reaction at an adjacent site within the same molecule, producing an increase in the reaction rate; also, the kinetic acceleration that results from such an interaction.

1953 S. WINSTEIN et al. in *Jrnl. Amer. Chem. Soc.* LXXV. 148/1 k_c is the estimated rate constant of ionization with neither anchimeric assistance nor nucleophilic assistance from solvent. [*Note*] This adjective (from the Greek 'anchi' and 'meros'), meaning pertaining to the neighboring or adjacent part..has been suggested to us by Dr. A. P. McKinlay..for use in connection with neighboring group participation. **1964** *Q. Rev. Chem. Soc.* XVIII. 45 If the transition state of a rate-determining step is stabilised in this way, an increased reaction rate results and the neighbouring group is then said to provide anchimeric assistance. **1983** MCQUILLIN & BAIRD *Alicyclic Chem.* (ed. 2) viii. 183 Anchimeric assistance of this kind is clearly geometrically possible for displacement of an *exo-* but not an *endo-* group.

So **anchi'merically** *adv.*, by the participation of a neighbouring functional group in the same molecule.

1953 *Jrnl. Amer. Chem. Soc.* LXXV. 148/1 The rate constant of solvolysis with nucleophilic solvent participation exceeds k_c more than does the anchimerically assisted ionization rate. **1992** *Organometallics* XI. 292/1 It is uncertain..whether the ψ^5-Cr(CO)$_3$ loss is anchimerically assisted by the migrating species.

ancrod ('æŋkrɒd), *n. Pharm.* [Prob. f. mod.L. *Agk(ist)rod(on* (coined by A. M. F. J. Palisot de Beauvois 1799, in *Trans. Amer. Philos. Soc.* IV. 381), lit. 'barb-tooth', f. Gr. ἄγκιστρον fish-hook + ὀδούς, ὀδοντ- tooth, former genus name of the snake from which the enzyme is obtained, with alteration of *-gk-* to *-nc-* following the usual model for Gr. transliteration.] An anticoagulant protease that lowers the concentration of fibrinogen by cleaving fibrin in the blood, and is given intravenously in the treatment and prevention of some kinds of thrombosis.

1970 *Brit. Med. Jrnl.* 5 Dec. 591/1 The defibrinating agent ancrod (Arvin) was used instead of Leparin for intermediate haemodialysis. **1977** *Lancet* 19 Mar. 625/1 Fifteen patients with severe intermittent claudication were treated by therapeutic defibrination with subcutaneous injections of ancrod for 5 weeks. **1984** *New Scientist* 25 Oct. 43/1 Ancrod, an anticoagulant derived from the Malayan pit viper.

AND (ænd), *v.* Chiefly *Computing.* Also **and**. [f. AND *conj.*[1] D.] *trans.* To combine (sets, binary signals, etc.) using a Boolean AND operator.

1969 D. E. KNUTH *Art of Computer Programming* II. 536 If we AND the result with the constant (10.01)$_2$, the desired answer is obtained. **1984** *Personal Software* Winter 12/1 The program for plot ANDs X with 7. **1986** S. P. HARTER *Online Information Retrieval* vii. 179 All three strategies..proceed to reduce the size of this set by ANDing additional concepts or by otherwise limiting it. **1989** *Nature* 9 Feb. 549/2 Consider a set of layers of processors holding the results of multiplying or logical 'anding' image 'features'.

and, *conj.*[1], *prep.*, *n.*, and *a.* Add: [D.] **b.** Special Comb. **AND gate**, a circuit which produces an output only when signals are received simultaneously through all input connections.

1959 *Bell Syst. Techn. Jrnl.* XXXVIII. 50 The operation of the Laddic as an *AND gate. **1984** J. HILTON *Choosing & using your Home Computer* III. 52/2 If the two AND gates have their outputs connected to an OR gate, the output of the OR gate will be true only if one, and one only, of the inputs is true.

androecium, *n.* Add: Hence **an'droecial** *a.*

1909 in WEBSTER. **1951** G. H. M. LAWRENCE *Taxon. Vascular Plants* iv. 68 More recent views..differ in some respects from the..better-known classical theories of androecial origins. **1992** *Canad. Jrnl. Bot.* LXX. 1775/2 The androecial arrangement with four diagonal (here alternipetalous) stamens is a characteristic with a great predictive value.

androgen, *n.* Add: Hence ˌandroge'nicity *n.*, the property of producing a masculinizing effect resembling that of an androgen; the degree to which something produces a masculinizing effect; ˌandrogeni'zation *n.*, treatment with androgens; also, the development of male sexual characteristics, esp. after treatment with androgens; **'androgenized** *ppl. a.*, treated with androgens; also, possessing or having developed male sexual characteristics.

1957 *Cancer* X. 809/2 We have assigned a 2-plus androgenicity to testosterone. **1959** *Proc. Staff Meetings Mayo Clinic* XXIV. 124 Chemical alterations..which decrease androgenicity. **1963** D. C. JOHNSON in *Endocrinology* LXXII. 832/1 We propose to use the term 'androgenized' for those animals which have been subjected to increased amounts of androgen prior to final differentiation of the hypothalamic-hypophysial axis. **1963** *Ibid.* LXXIII. 467/2 Androgenization of females was accomplished by injecting 5-day-old animals with 2.5 mg of testosterone propionate. **1968** *New England Jrnl. Med.* 8 Feb. (Advt. facing p. 344), Mild androgenicity (hirsutism, deepened voice and menstrual irregularity) has been reported rarely. **1977** *Lancet* 24/31 Dec. 1361/2 The use of gonadotrophins after correction of cryptorchidism should not be contemplated until puberty because of the danger of premature androgenisation. **1990** H. J. EYSENCK *Rebel with Cause* vi. 225 Many of the androgenized girls stated they would rather not have children.

android, *n.* and *a.* Add: **B.** *adj.* **a.** Resembling a human being, esp. a man. *rare.* **b.** *Anat.* Esp. of a pelvis: resembling that of a man.

1886 WEBSTER Suppl. 1541/3 *Android, a.*, resembling a man. **1933** CALDWELL & MOLOY in *Amer. Jrnl. Obstet. & Gynecol.* XXVI. 490 The Android Type... These female pelves bear a resemblance to the male sex of man. **1936** H. J. STANDER *J. W. Williams's Obstetrics.* (ed. 7) i. 18 Caldwell and Moloy..divided the female pelvis into four large groups on the basis of morphology. The first group is the normal female or 'gynecoid' pelvis, the second the male or 'android', the third the 'anthropoid', resembling the pelvic form of the great apes, and the fourth group the simple flat or 'platypelloid' pelvis. **1982** E. L. SAFFORD *Handbk. Adv. Robots* i. 28 Android types are hobbyists' toys right now. **1989** *Times* 12 Oct. 18/3 The incidence of android pelvises—a triangular, smaller pelvis—is higher for some reason among tall women than short. **1989** *Internat. Jrnl. Epidemiol.* XVIII. 368/1 In diabetics a male type of subcutaneous fat pattern, called android or upper body obesity, was found more often than a female type.

androstenedione (ˌændrɒstiːn'daɪəʊn), *n. Physiol.* [ad. G. *Androstendion* (coined by Ruzicka & Wettstein 1935, in *Helv. Chim. Acta* XVIII. 988): see ANDROSTERONE *n.*, -ENE, -DIONE.] An androgenic steroid, $C_{19}H_{26}O_2$, from which testosterone and certain oestrogens are derived in humans.

1935 *Nature* 17 Aug. 259/1 The table clearly shows the high activity of androstedione [*sic*] on the seminal vesicles and the penis. **1959** S. L. SIMPSON *Major Endocrine Disorders* (ed. 3) ii. 80 The two important adrenal androgens in man are 11β-hydroxy Δ4-androstene-3-17-dione and Δ4-androstenedione. **1964** L. MARTIN *Clin. Endocrinol.* (ed. 4) viii. 263 The normal ovarian theca-cell contains all the enzymes needed for the conversion of progesterone to oestradiol, an intermediate stage being the substance androstenedione. **1988** L. STRYER *Biochem.* (ed. 3)

xxiii. 568 The side chain consisting of C-20 and C-21 is then cleaved to yield androstenedione, an androgen.

anechoic, *a.* Add: Also, of a coating, building material, etc.: tending to deaden sound.
1960 F. M. WIENER in L. L. Beranek *Noise Reduction* viii. 170 The source may be placed on the hard floor of a room whose five other boundaries are anechoic. **1983** *Listener* 12 May 6/1 The Russians already treat most of their submarines with anechoic coatings to reduce sonar returns. **1986** T. CLANCY *Red Storm Rising* (1988) iii. 47 'What's with the tile on your deck? I never heard of rubber decks on a ship.' 'It's called anechoic tile, sir. The rubber absorbs sound waves.'

Anectine ('ænɛktiːn), *n. Pharm.* [Invented name.] A proprietary name for the drug suxamethonium chloride.
1950 *Trade Marks Jrnl.* 30 Aug. 799/1 Anectine. **1955** *Sci. News Let.* 29 Jan. 73/1 Electroshock treatment of the mentally ill can be 'softened'..by a new drug, succinyl-choline chloride...The drug is trade-named Anectine® by its manufacturers. **1990** *Anesthesiol.* LXXIII. 1253/2 A clinically used brand of Anectine from single-dose vials.

anemone, *n.* Add: **3.** Special Comb. **anemone-fish**, any of various damselfishes that live in a commensal relationship with sea anemones; *esp.* one of the genus *Amphiprion.*
1936 T. C. ROUGHLEY *Wonders Great Barrier Reef* vi. 51 *Anemone fish are always brightly coloured and conspicuously marked. **1955** A. Ross *Australia* 55 xi. 117 These tiny anemone-fish..work in conjunction with the anemone. **1990** *Sea Frontiers* Feb. 47 (*caption*) The twobar anemonefish (*Amphiprion bicinctus*) gains protection from the Stoichactidae anemone.

anephric (eɪ'nɛfrɪk), *a. Med.* [f. A- 14 + NEPHRIC *a.*] Lacking kidneys, or lacking functional kidneys.
1968 *Jrnl. Pediatrics* LXXIII. 708/1 The patient was anephric at the time and clotting was probably secondary to hypovolemia from excessive ultrafiltration. **1977** *Lancet* 15 Oct. 785/2 Circumstantial evidence suggests that inactive renin in plasma is in part derived from the kidney, although..renins have also been found in anephric subjects. **1987** *Oxf. Textbk Med.* (ed. 2) II. XIII. 102/1 The half-life of digoxin..is prolonged in renal failure, being about 96 hours in functionally anephric patients.

anergia (æ'nɜːdʒɪə), *n. Psychiatry.* [a. Gr. ἀνεργία idleness, f. ἄνεργος inactive (f. ἀ(ν)- privative prefix (see AN- 10) + Gr. ἔργον work).] Lack of mental energy, debility; passivity.
1881 *Syd. Soc. Lex.*, Anergia. **1974** J. K. WING et al. *Measurement & Classification Psychiatric Symptoms* 155 Subjective anergia and retardation. **1975** *Acta Psychiatrica Scand.* LI. 93 Flupenthixol decanoate..is claimed to be of special value in schizophrenic patients showing features of apathy, anergia,..and paranoid delusions. **1985** *Psychiatry Res.* XVI. 212 Of the psychopathological changes associated with neuroleptic withdrawal, β-endorphin correlated only with anergia. **1987** *Oxf. Textbk. Med.* (ed. 2) II. xxv. 35/2 A general air of indifference is accompanied by withdrawal, anergia, and defective memory and concentration.

aneurysmectomy (ˌænjʊərɪz'mɛktəmɪ), *n. Surg.* [f. ANEURYSM *n.* + -ECTOMY.] Surgical removal of an aneurysm.
1911 STEDMAN *Med. Dict.* 43/2 Aneurysmectomy, excision of the sac of an aneurysm. **1968** *New England Jrnl. Med.* 25 Jan. 218/2 A 42-year-old woman was initially admitted to the hospital for abdominal aneurysmectomy. **1984** *Brit. Med. Jrnl.* 25 Aug. 451/1 In patients who are not in failure aneurysmectomy with coronary artery bypass for refractory angina carries a low operative mortality.

angel, *n.* Add: [B.] [2.] **angel's trumpet(s)** (also **angels' trumpet(s)**), any of various plants of either the South American genus *Brugmansia* of tree-like shrubs or the genus *Datura* of herbaceous perennials, both of the family Solanaceae and characterized by large trumpet-shaped flowers; also, the flower(s) of any of these plants.
1884 W. MILLER *Dict. Eng. Names Plants* 3/2 *Angel's Trumpets*, the flowers of *Brugmansia suaveolens.* **1915** A. W. LUSHINGTON *Vernacular List Trees, Shrubs & Woody Climbers Madras Presidency* I. 323/1 (Index), Angel's Trumpet..Datura suaveolens. **1955** G. GRIGSON *Englishman's Flora* 294 In Somerset it [*sc. Datura stramonium*] has been called Angel's Trumpets, the name usually given now to the tall, shrubby Thorn-apples from Brazil.., which are hung about with trumpet blossoms. **1961** *Amat. Gardening* 14 Oct. Suppl. 17/1 *Datura*..half-hardy plants..(also known as Brugmansias and Angels' Trumpets)..striking evergreen subjects for the cool greenhouse. **1987** *Courier-Mail* (Brisbane) 12 June 3/7 Police may seek to have the plant datura, or angel's trumpet, prohibited after the drugging of six young people on the Sunshine Coast.

angelin, *n.* Add: **b.** The wood of the angelin tree.
1878 *Anal. Returns Queries Colonial Timber* 41 in *Parl. Papers 1878–79* (C. 2197) L. 557 There are large quantities of valuable timber, such as..angelin, which are inaccessible from want of roads. **1889** G. S. BOULGER *Uses of Plants* VII. 183 The Colonial and Indian Exhibition has called attention to various useful woods of this class, such as..Angelin. **1971** F. H. TITMUSS *Commerc. Timbers of World* (ed. 4) 49 Angelin is rather hard to work but can be brought to a good surface.

angelique, *n.* Restrict *Obs. rare* to sense in Dict. and add: **2.** A leguminous tree, *Dicorynia paraensis*, native to South America; also, the hard, reddish wood of this tree, used esp. in marine construction work.
1875 T. LASLETT *Timber & Timber Trees* xxiv. 159 Angélique...This tree is of straight growth, and yields timber 12 to 22 inches square. **1879** *Encycl. Brit.* IX. 406/1 French Guiana contains valuable forests, and produces 'angelique' (*Dicorynia paraensis*), a timber much employed in naval dockyards. **1937** *Archit. Rev.* LXXXII. 198/1 (*caption*) Main wall panelling is of peroba with base of angelique and prima vera. **1979** *Forest Products Jrnl.* June 34/2 Angelique heartwood can be distinguished..by its rose or russet to dark-gray or purplish-brown color.

Angelman ('eɪndʒəlmən), *n. Path.* [The name of Harold *Angelman*, British doctor who described the condition, in *Developmental Med. & Child Neurol.* (1965) VII. 681.] **Angelman('s) syndrome**, a rare hereditary disorder characterized by mental retardation and hyperactivity.
1972 *Amer. Jrnl. Dis. Children* CXXIII. 72 (*heading*) Angelman's ('Happy puppet') syndrome. **1990** *Sci. Amer.* Oct. 29/1 Nicholls..made a..discovery about patients with Angelman syndrome. (In the past, such persons were often described as 'happy puppets' who exhibited excessive laughter, jerky movements and other symptoms of motor and intellectual retardation.) **1991** *Daily Tel.* 20 June 20/7 Patients with Angelman syndrome are hyperactive, while those with Prader-Willi syndrome are slow moving.

angiitis (ændʒɪ'aɪtɪs), *n. Path.* Also 9 **angeitis**. [f. ANGI(O- + -ITIS. Cf. F. *angiite*, which appears to predate the Eng. form *angiitis*.] Inflammation of blood vessels or lymphatic vessels; vasculitis. **1846** DUNGLISON *Dict. Med. Sci.* (ed. 6) 47/1 Angeitis. *Ibid.* 47/2 *Angiitis*, angeitis. **1951** *Amer. Jrnl. Path.* XXVII. 291 There are valid reasons.. for defining the group here presented under the name of allergic angiitis and allergic granulomatosis. **1966** WRIGHT & SYMMERS *Systemic Path.* II. xxxix. 1557/2 The histological changes are similar to those seen experimentally in the Arthus phenomenon, and this strengthens the belief that this form of cutaneous angiitis is a manifestation of allergy. **1989** *Q. Jrnl. Med.* LXXII. 689 A 53-year-old female was receiving immunosuppressive treatment.. because of necrotizing angiitis.

angiocardiography, *n.* Add: ,angiocardio-'graphic *a.*, of, pertaining to, or involving angiocardiography.
1943 *Amer. Jrnl. Roentgenol.* L. 309/1 (*heading*) Angiocardiographic findings. **1965** *Acta Cardiologica* XX. 350 Two angiocardiographic examinations were performed. **1992** *Singapore Med. Jrnl.* XXXIII. 455 We studied these patients to determine their.. angiocardiographic characteristics.

angiography, *n.* Add: **angio'graphically** *adv.*, by means of angiography.
1965 *Jrnl. Canad. Assoc. Radiologists* XVI. 190/1 Two cases [of arterial occlusion] diagnosed angiographically. **1977** *Lancet* 23 Apr. 901/2 Four patients in whom spontaneous attacks of angina were compared angiographically with ergonovine-induced attacks. **1987** *Brit. Med. Jrnl.* 20 June 1577/1 Other studies of normolipaemic patients with angiographically defined obstructive coronary artery disease.

angioplasty ('ændʒɪəʊplɑːstɪ, -plæstɪ), *n.* (In *OED Additions, vol. 2*). Add: Hence **angio'plastic** *a.*
1960 *Ann. Surg.* CLII. 663/1 In analyzing patency rates, the permanence of patency is a consideration that has a unique importance in angioplastic operations. **1974** *Jrnl. Surg. Res.* XVII. 213/2 We believe regional infusion [*printed* infustion] of heparin is essential for patency in vein angioplastic reconstruction of the coronary artery. **1987** *Oxf. Textbk. Med.* (ed. 2) II. xviii. 154/2 The stenosis is demonstrated by angiography, which also indicates whether the lesion is amenable to surgical or transluminal angioplastic repair.

angiotensin (,ændʒɪəʊ'tɛnsɪn), *n.* Biochem. [f. ANGIO- + HYPER)TENSIN *n.*] **1.** A powerful vasoconstricting polypeptide which stimulates the production of aldosterone and vasopressin and results in an increase in blood pressure (more fully *angiotensin II*); *angiotensin I*, the inactive precursor of this, which is formed in the liver by the action of renin on a plasma protein (angiotensinogen), and is converted in the lungs to angiotensin II by a second enzyme. Orig. called HYPERTENSIN *n.*
1958 BRAUN-MENENDEZ & PAGE in *Science* 31 Jan. 242/3 The peptide received two trivial names, angiotonin and hypertensin...We propose the simplified name, *angiotensin*. **1961** *Lancet* 2 Sept. 510/2 It was found that hypertensive patients had a heightened vascular response to angiotensin and 5-hydroxy-tryptamine. **1968** PASSMORE & ROBSON *Compan. Med. Stud.* I. xxiii. 20/2 Another enzyme converts angiotensin I to angiotensin II by removing two amino acids. **1974** D. & M. WEBSTER *Compar. Vertebr. Morphol.* xvii. 436 It is also thought that these myoepithelial cells secrete the enzyme renin which.. can transform the angiotensin I in the blood to angiotensin II. **1984** TIGHE & DAVIES *Pathology* (ed. 4) xxii. 211 The zona glomerula is stimulated to produce aldosterone by angiotensin. **1992** *Science*

News 1 Feb. 71/1 The fat cells in different parts of the body bind to different amounts of angiotensin II.
2. Special Comb. **angiotensin converting enzyme**, a hydrolytic enzyme which catalyses the conversion of angiotensin I to angiotensin II.
[**1956** *Jrnl. Exper. Med.* CIII. 295 (*title*) The preparation and function of the hypertensin-converting enzyme.] **1960** L. T. SKEGGS in M. Schachter *Polypeptides* 111 Helmer.. had found a factor in plasma which enhanced the activity of angiotensin, and suggested to us that this factor might be *angiotensin converting enzyme. **1988** *BioFactors* I. 177/1 Angiotensin-converting enzyme.. acts on angiotensin I, a decapeptide, yielding angiotensin II, a potent vasopressor agent. **1991** *Sun* (Baltimore) 13 Aug. c5/6 Many experts believe medicines called angiotensin-converting enzyme (ACE) inhibitors are the best choice to treat hypertension in diabetics.

So **angio'tensinase** *n.* [-ASE] = sense *2 above; **angioten'sinogen** *n.* [-OGEN] = *hypertensinogen* n. s.v. HYPERTENSIN *n.*; (now the usual name).
1958 BRAUN-MENENDEZ & PAGE in *Science* 31 Jan. 242/3 We propose the simplified name, *angiotensin*, and its derivatives *angiotensinase* and *angiotensinogen*. **1967** *Jap. Jrnl. Med.* VI. 18 Studies on angiotensinase activity in plasma from normal subjects and from patients with hypertension and liver disease were made. **1978** *Federation Proc.* XXXVII. 602/1 Angiotensinase-A activity was determined with the 2-naphthyl-amides of L-aspartate and L-glutamate. **1985** *Sci. Amer.* Oct. 82/1 In 1983 a Japanese group published the sequence of angiotensinogen, the precursor of a small peptide hormone that regulates blood pressure. **1990** *New Scientist* 9 June 63/2 An example of receptor-based drug design is the inhibition of the angiotensinogen cascade. **1990** *Jrnl. Devel. Physiol.* XIV. 90/1 Complete inhibition of 'angiotensinase' activity was accomplished by the addition of protease inhibitors.

angiotonin (ændʒɪəʊ'təʊnɪn), *n.* Biochem. and Med. Now *rare.* [f. ANGIO- + TON(IC *a.* and *n.* + -IN[1].] = ANGIOTENSIN *n.*
1940 PAGE & HELMER in *Jrnl. Exper. Med.* LXXI. 29 A pressor substance was produced which was heat-stable and which yielded crystalline derivatives. For this substance we suggest the name 'angiotonin'. **1942** *Jrnl. Physiol.* CI. 288 The active substance, hypertensin or angiotonin, is precipitated with ammonium sulphate. **1961** *Lancet* 9 Sept. 602/2 We recently noted that angiotonin (angiotensin) caused a marked diminution of the kidney pulse.

angle, *n.*[2] Sense 8 in Dict. becomes 9. Add: **8.** *ellipt.* for *angle-iron*, sense 9 below; iron or other metal in the form of bars having this shape.
1906 H. ADAMS *Cassell's Engineers' Handbk.* v. 114 (*table*) Angle, tee, channel, and flats of 12in. width and under. **1980** *Amat. Gardening* 4 Oct. 31/2 The supporting frame is usually of aluminium angle bolted together and suitably braced. **1983** J. S. FOSTER *Structure & Fabric* (rev. ed.) I. vi. 143/2 Connections.. are made by means of steel bolts and rivets with angles as cleats. **1990** *Traditional Homes* Aug. 10/3 To cut slates to size or shape.. obtain a length of iron angle and cramp it to the edge of a stout board.

Anglian, *a.* and *n.* Add: **2.** *Geol.* Of, pertaining to, or designating a Pleistocene glaciation in Britain, identified with the Elsterian of northern Europe (and perhaps the Mindel of the Alps). Also *absol.*
1968 *Recomm. Stratigr. Classif.* (Geol. Soc.) 20 It is recommended that for the Pleistocene and Holocene of the British Isles the following ages/stages be adopted as a regional scale...Pleistocene:...Anglian. **1973** *Nature* 25 May 214/2 The 'Anglian' and the Wolstonian glaciations. **1977** F. W. SHOTTON *Brit. Quaternary Stud.* xix. 271 Fossil-bearing lake and estuary muds

and marine sands overlie Anglian rocks and underlie Devensian rocks at many sites in East Anglia and provide ample evidence for interglacial climatic conditions. **1983** T. NILSSON *Pleistocene* ix. 114 According to this system, the oldest and most extensive glaciation is the Anglian.

Angophora (æŋ'gɒfərə), *n.* [mod.L. (coined in A. J. Cavanilles *Icones et Descriptiones Plantarum* (1797) IV. 21), f. Gr. ἄγγος jar + -φόρος bearing, referring to the vase-like fruits of some species.] A genus of evergreen trees and shrubs of the myrtle family, native to eastern Australia; (also **angophora, angophera**) a tree or shrub of this genus.

1827 C. FRASER in *Hist. Rec. Austral.* (1923) 3rd Ser. VI. 580 The Hills are exceedingly barren, but producing an immense variety of Plants; here is seen a magnificent species of Angophora. **1830** —— in *Bot. Misc.* I. 227 Producing a magnificent species of *Angophora*. **1892** 'R. BOLDREWOOD' *Nevermore* III. 14 Beneath a wide-spreading angophora Estelle Challoner seated herself. **1933** H. J. CARTER *Gulliver in Bush* 20 The southern shores of the Harbour were good collecting grounds..with considerable areas of angophora and leptospermum of three kinds. **1959** 'M. NEVILLE' *Sweet Night for Murder* vi. 63 There—did they see? Down there just to the right of that big angophera. **1974** D. IRELAND *Burn* 1 The tall rugged eucalypts and angophora cast little shade.

angular, *a.* Add: **7.** Special collocations: **angular crab**, a crab, *Goneplax rhomboides*, of the sublittoral zone with sharply angled chelae and a reddish-brown rectangular shell.

1844 T. BELL *Hist. Brit. Stalk-Eyed Crustacea* 130 *Angular Crab. *Gonoplax angulata*. **1928** RUSSELL & YONGE *Seas* iii. 67 The angular crab (*Gonoplax*), which has a reddish-brown rectangular shell and eyes on the end of movable stalks. **1988** E. WOOD et al. *Sea Life Brit. & Ireland* 147 (*caption*) The angular crab *Goneplax rhomboides* uses its chelae to pick up and move the mud as it excavates its burrow.

angular leaf spot, (*a*) = *black arm* s.v. BLACK *a.* 19; (*b*) an infectious disease of cucumber caused by the bacterium *Pseudomonas lachrymans*, characterized by translucent, angular spots on the leaves.

1907 W. A. ORTON in *U.S. Dept. Agric. Farmers' Bull.* No. 302. 41 There is a bacterial disease of cotton (*Bacterium malvacearum*)..producing various symptoms and receiving various names, such as *angular leaf-spot, black-arm, boll-spot, etc. **1915** *Jrnl. Agric. Res.* V. 465 The angular leaf-spot of cucumbers (*Cucumis sativus*) has been known in the field for many years. **1933** *Ann. Appl. Biol.* XX. 404 The experiment..was designed to test the possibility of investigating the incidence and spread of the angular leaf-spot disease of cotton. **1953** F. T. BROOKS *Plant Dis.* (ed. 2) iv. 60 Angular Leaf Spot is sometimes a serious disease of outdoor and indoor cucumbers in the United States. **1984** ROBERTS & BOOTHROYD *Fund. Plant Path.* (ed. 2) xxiv. 295 Angular leafspot..occurs in cotton throughout the world.

angulate, *v.* Add: **2.** *trans. Skiing*. To bend (the body or parts of the body) so as to assume an angulated position. Also *absol.*

1970 D. PFEIFFER *Skiing Simplified* v. 86/2 If the slope is steep enough..and you want to keep the legs together, then you must angulate. **1973** C. FOWLER *Skiing Techniques* 20/1 If you come forward and angulate slightly with the knees, the skis will start to turn gradually out of the fall line. **1986** *Skiing Today* Winter 6/2 One of the hardest principles for a beginning skier to grasp is the necessity to..'angulate' the upper half of the body outward, towards the outside of each turn. **1988** *Chicago Tribune* 8 Feb. III. 14/1 As speed increases, body must be angulated to keep outside knee flexed and weight against outside ski. **1991** *Skiing*

Mar. 94/2 No need to press your knees toward the hill, or away; no need to angulate and deangulate.

angulation, *n.* Add: **[1.] b.** *Med.* Angular distortion of a bone, joint, or organ; abnormal curvature.

1900 DORLAND *Med. Dict.* 48/1 *Angulation*, the formation of a sharp obstructive angle in the intestine. **1923** E. W. H. GROVES in C. C. Choyce *Syst. Surg.* (ed. 2) III. 804 Angulation..is by far the most important type of deformity in malunion...It actually shortens the bone. **1976** *European Jrnl. Pediatrics* CXXIII. 184 Fetogram..revealed..twisting of the torso, abnormal shortening of the extremities..severe angulation deformities. **1981** *Times* 12 June 14/2 He has severe angulation of the spine, giving him a pronounced stoop. **1987** *Brit. Med. Jrnl.* 1 Aug. 319/2 The penile curvature on erection may be dealt with surgically, but this must not be undertaken until the degree of angulation has stabilised.

2. *Skiing*. The action of bending sideways at the waist, performed by a skier during a turn, so that the legs lean towards the centre of the turn and the upper body leans outwards, to increase stability; also, the angulated position itself.

1965 SHAMBROOM & SLATER *Skiing with Control* 143/1 *Angulation*, bending of the upper body away from the hill, which counter-balances pressing the knees and hips into the hill. **1970** D. PFEIFFER *Skiing Simplified* v. 87/1 You must remain flexible, always changing the amount of angulation to conform to the demands of the terrain. **1991** F. FOXON *Skiing* iii. 89 In tight turns you may..need angulation right from the start, for effective grip and control. **1991** *Skiing* Mar. 94/1 At normal recreational speeds, angulation—tilting your legs, knees, or hips into the slope..—is not..the main factor controlling edging.

3. *Vet. Sci.* The angle formed at a joint by two bones, esp. two long bones; also, the disposition of the bones of an animal's skeleton (with respect to the normal conformation, or to that considered ideal, esp. in pets).

1968 H. HARMAR *Chihuahua Guide* 231 *Angulations*, angles formed where the bones meet: shoulder, upper arm, hock, stifle. **1985** E. H. HART *German Shepherd Dog* iv. 59 Quanto was a powerful black and red-tan dog with a tremendous gait, iron back and excellent angulation fore and aft. **1986** V. HEARNE *Adam's Task* (1987) viii. 185 Weak shoulders, poor angulation and so on would have meant pain and inflammation stopping him on the trail. **1991** *Avian Dis.* XXXV. 710/1 Table 1 shows the relative distribution of angulation scores of each intertarsal joint and also indicates whether the deviation was valgus or varus.

angwantibo (æŋ'gwɒntɪbəʊ, æŋgwæn'tiːbəʊ), *n.* [Efik, perh. f. *angwá* cat.] A small rare primate, *Arctocebus calabarensis*, related to the potto and loris, and native to western Africa.

[**1860** *Proc. R. Physical Soc. Edinb.* 1859–1862 II. 172 The Calabar people call it *Angwántibo*.] **1864** *Proc. Zool. Soc.* 314 (*heading*) On the Angwántibo (*Arctocebus calabarensis*, Gray) of Old Calabar. **1894** H. O. FORBES *Hand-bk. Primates* I. 28 The 'Angwantibo', as this species is called, is known only from Old Calabar, on the west coast of Africa. **1953** G. M. DURRELL *Overloaded Ark* ix. 163, I carefully tipped the Angwantibo out of the basket...He looked not unlike a teddy-bear. **1978** *Sci. Amer.* Feb. 42/2 The stout potto and the slenderer angwantibo never leap but climb with a silent, deliberate motion.

anharmonic, *a.* Add: Hence **anharmoˈnicity** *n. Physics*, the state or quality of being anharmonic; the extent to which an oscillating physical system deviates from simple harmonic motion.

1936 *Ann. Rep. Progress Chem.* XXXIII. 53 The values of the fundamental frequencies of the molecules have only been given to within 1ocm.⁻¹, since corrections have not been made for anharmonicity. **1940** S. GLASSTONE *Text-bk. Physical Chem.* viii. 558 For most purposes the anharmonicity of the oscillations may be neglected. **1974** GILL & WILLIS *Pericyclic Reactions* vi. 208 Substituents which introduce low-lying excited singlet states can dramatically enhance the rates of such reactions by increasing the anharmonicities of the potential energy curves. **1988** *Nature* 29 Sept. 397/1 The peculiar value of a_H has been ascribed to other causes—anharmonicity and 'zero-point' shifts of energy bands.

anhedonia, *n.* Add: Hence **anhe'donic** *a.*, having little or no capacity to feel pleasure.
1961 in WEBSTER. **1972** *Jrnl. Abnormal Psychol.* LXXX. 44/1 By comparison to their less anhedonic counterparts, highly anhedonic *S*s should be less responsive to rewards than to punishments. **1981** *N.Y. Times* 12 Sept. 1. 13/5 The playwright transforms his despair into whimsical..comedy. His anhedonic characters are always coming up with new ways to express their misery.

anhidrosis (ænhɪ'drəʊsɪs), *n. Path.* Also (now *rare*) **anidrosis** (æni-). [a. Gr. ἀνίδρωσις lack of sweating, f. ἀ(ν)- privative prefix (see AN- 10) + ἰδρών to sweat. Cf. HIDROTIC *a.*] Inability (or reduced ability) to sweat.
1743 R. JAMES *Medicinal Dict.* I. sig. 6.O.2/1 *Anidrosis*, a nullity or privation of sweat. **1842** DUNGLISON *Dict. Med. Sci.* (ed. 3) 47/1 Anidrosis. **1900** *Med. Rec.* (N.Y.) 4 Aug. 197/2 (*heading*) Dermographia and anidrosis. **1948** A. BRODAL *Neurol. Anat.* xi. 402 Immediately after an acute interruption of the pathways the autonomic reflexes will be abolished.., and there will therefore be anhidrosis. **1968** *Jrnl. Pediatrics* LXXIII. 857/2 Lesions of the brain and spinal cord may result in anhidrosis. **1993** *Baillière's Clin. Endocrinol. & Metabolism* VII. II. 479 Impairment of sudomotor function results in hypohidrosis or anhidrosis.

anhistorical (ˌænhɪ'stɒrɪkəl), *a.* [f. AN- 10 + HISTORICAL *a.*] = A-HISTORICAL *a.*
1979 N. LASH *Theol. on Dover Beach* ii. 43 Poetry..is also.., as the immediate articulation of present experience, anhistorical. **1984** *Times Lit. Suppl.* 13 Jan. 31/3 The attraction of the non-archaeological, anhistorical approach to the past is its appeal to faith and belief. **1991** *Guardian* 23 Jan. 20/5 One certain truth about Britain and the US is that we have, lodged in our otherwise anhistorical minds, a great legend of second world war heroics.

anhyd. ('ænhaɪd), *a. Chem.* Also **anhyd** (without point). [Abbrev. of ANHYDROUS *a.*] = ANHYDROUS *a.* 1. Usu. as a written abbrev.
1921 *Chem. Abstr.* XV. 4950/1 (*table*) Abbreviations used in Chemical Abstracts...anhyd. anhydrous. **1940** *Ibid.* XXXIV. 1268 Treatment of the hexahydrates of Ni and Co..with anhyd. liquid NH₃ indicates that 1 mol. of H₂O is bound in a manner different from the others. **1992** *Jrnl. Org. Chem.* LVII. 53/1 To a solution of acetylenic ketone..in anhyd THF..was added a solution of MeLi.

anhydraemia (ænhaɪ'driːmɪə), *n. Path.* Now *rare.* Also (chiefly *U.S.*) **anhydremia**. [f. AN- 10 + HYDRAEMIA *n.*] = haemoconcentration n. s.v. HAEMO-.
1851 DUNGLISON *Dict. Med. Sci.* (ed. 8) 77/1 *Anhydræmia*, a condition of the blood in which there is a diminution in the quantity of the serum. **1920** *Amer. Jrnl. Dis. Children* XX. 473 We were able to demonstrate a state of anhydremia in a number of conditions quite unrelated to diarrhea. **1969** *Minnesota Med.* LII. 655 Clausen..discussed the

acidosis of anhydremia: a clinical syndrome then characterized by the 'acute loss of fluid by diarrhea and vomiting in a previously well nourished person'.
Hence **anhy'draemic** *a.*
1920 *Amer. Jrnl. Dis. Children* XX. 467 Dogs rendered anhydremic by a diminished intake of water are very prone to..diarrhea and vomiting when fed. **1925** *Ibid.* XXIX. 763 Anhydremic acidosis is, under certain conditions, associated with a considerable elevation of lactic acid.

anicteric (ænɪk'tɛrɪk), *a. Path.* [f. AN- 10 + ICTERIC *a.* and *n.*] Not icteric; (of a disease, etc.) not accompanied by jaundice as a symptom.
1935 DORLAND & MILLER *Med. Dict.* (ed. 17) 101/2 *Anicteric*, without icterus. **1965** *Jrnl.-Lancet* (U.S.) LXXXV. 494/1 To these congenital anemias which are not usually accompanied by jaundice may be added anicteric erythroblastosis. **1977** *Lancet* 8 Jan. 82/2 A further 6% had an anicteric hepatitis with hepatosplenomegaly. **1987** SMITH & STANITSKI *Sports Med.* xxi. 157 With such prophylaxis, those that develop hepatitis will have an anicteric, asymptomatic infection.

anidrosis *n.*, var. *ANHIDROSIS *n.*

animatic (æni'mætɪk), *n.* [f. ANIMAT(ED *ppl. a.* + -IC (or possibly a blend with SCHEMATIC *n.*).] A preliminary or test version of a film, esp. of an advertising commercial, produced by shooting successive sections of a storyboard and adding a soundtrack.
1977 *N.Y. Times* 24 June IV. 9/3 He had high praise for animatics, which are rough commercials. **1985** T. DOUGLAS *Compl. Guide Advertising* vi. 144 A TV commercial can use..an 'animatic', which is a video made from the drawings or photographs. **1989** *Commercials* Apr. 25/2 Other competing agencies had produced animatics but it was the whole feel of the idea which impressed Condron—not the presentation techniques. **1990** *Times* 28 Dec. 3/5 A riveting, moody 60-second 'animatic' of the opening witches scene of Macbeth.

animatronics (ænɪmə'trɒnɪks), *n. pl.* orig. *U. S.* [Shortened form of *Audio-Animatronics* n. pl. s.v. *AUDIO-ANIMATRONIC *a.*] A technique of constructing robot models in accurate likenesses of humans, animals, etc., which are programmed to perform intricate, lifelike bodily movements in synchronization with a pre-recorded soundtrack. Cf. *Audio-Animatronics* n. pl. s.v. *AUDIO-ANIMATRONIC *a.*
1971 *Rolling Stone* 24 June 35/1 Animatronics is like television with the screen removed. The event can evoke response, but the response cannot affect the 'performer', for he (or she or it) is pre-recorded. **1983** *Financial Times* 16 Apr. 11/4 A Disney engineer on secondment from California..waxed eloquently on the sophistication of 'animatronics'...Singing bears, drunken pirates and gambolling elephants do not merely look 'realistic'; their programmed movements are uncannily natural. **1989** *Movie* No. 33. 26/2 It's a mixture of actors and animatronics. **1992** A. MAUPIN *Maybe the Moon* v. 70 To me, the kids looked like animatronics figures, robots from a ride at Disneyland.
So **'animatron** *n.*; **anima'tronic** *n.* and *a.*
1971 *Rolling Stone* 24 June 35/1 Animatrons were one of Uncle Walt's last technological enthusiasms. **1979** *Forbes* (N.Y.) 12 Nov. 177/1 'How-about-some-shoes-you'd-pay-twice-as-much-for-anywhere-else,' yells Stein, his mouth seeming to move independently of the words, like one of those eerie Animatronic Disney robots. **1987** *Australian* 24 Nov. 58/1 The robots, known as animatronics, were made famous by Disneyland with such displays as its Pirates in the Caribbean, Abraham Lincoln and Bear Canyon

attractions. **1989** *Creative Rev.* June 54/3 Sitting in their office in a Winston Churchill-style suit is a life-size animatronic of the Prime Minister, which moves and talks according to the taped programme. **1993** *Daily Tel.* 27 Mar. (Weekend Suppl.) p.xxxiii/8 An automatic piano plays, complete with large-as-life animatronic pianist.

Animikie (æ'nɪmɪkiː), *n. Geol.* Also **Animike**. [A North American Indian name (Ojibwa *animikii*, lit. 'thunderer') for Thunder Bay, on Lake Superior, Ontario, Canada, where the rocks are exposed and were first investigated.] Used *attrib.* (esp. in *Animikie Group*) and occas. *absol.* to designate a series of Proterozoic rocks of the Canadian Shield that are rich in iron ore.
  1873 T. S. HUNT in *Trans. Amer. Inst. Mining Engineers* I. 339 This older series of Thunder Bay and its vicinity, which may be named the Animikie group, from the Indian name of the bay, is the lower division of the upper copper-bearing series of Logan. **1888** *Amer. Geologist* I. 14 'Animike' is a term employed to designate an assemblage of strata occupying a position between the Copper-bearing, Nipigon, or Kewenian series of lake Superior and the great gneissic and granitic base commonly designated Laurentian. **1903** A. GEIKIE *Text-bk. Geol.* (ed. 4) II. 904 Animikie.., mainly a sedimentary series, consisting of a lower quartzite and an upper slate formation. **1963** D. W. & E. E. HUMPHRIES tr. *Termier's Erosion & Sedimentation* viii. 176 Concordant with the Gunflint Formation..the Rove (Animikie age, c.1,000 million years B.P.) consists of greywackes..passing into argillites. **1972** SIMS & MOREY *Geol. Minnesota* 5 The Middle Precambrian consists dominantly of clastic rocks and intercalated iron-formations that are assigned to the Animikie Group.

anion, *n.* Add: **2.** Special Comb. **anion gap** *Physiol.*, the difference between the total concentration of (positive) sodium and potassium ions and the total concentration of (negative) chloride and bicarbonate ions in blood plasma.
  1969 *Minnesota Med.* LII. 659 A large increase in the concentration of unmeasured anions, i.e., the '*anion gap'. **1973** *Lancet* 13 Oct. 848/2 It is not necessary to use the anion gap as a routine quality-control device. **1982** T. M. DEVLIN *Textbk. Biochem.* xxiii. 1126 In the plasma of a normal individual the sum of Na+ and K+ is greater than the sum of Cl- and HCO₃-. This difference is called..the anion gap.

  anionic *a.(c)* (as *n.*), an anionic surfactant.
  1952 McCUTCHEON & SPEEL in H. C. Speel *Textile Chem. & Auxiliaries* xv. 299 Certain non-ionics can be sulfonated to anionics. **1970** *New Scientist* 15 Oct. 132/2 Difficulty with perborate and anionics could be foreseen, but the effect of phosphate was unexpected. **1989** *Pharmaceutical Jrnl.* 16 Sept. 341/2 Transitions due to lipid melting that were removed by the anionics alone were protected by the added non-ionics.

anisakiasis (æ,naɪsə'kaɪəsɪs), *n. Path.* [f. mod.L. genus name *Anisakis* (coined in F. Dujardin *Hist. Nat. des Helminthes* (1845) 220), f. Gr. ἀνισάκις an unequal number of times, f. ἀ(ν)-privative prefix (see AN- 10) + ἴσος ISO-: see -IASIS.] Infection of the gut with parasitic nematode larvae of the family Anisakidae, which results from eating raw or undercooked infected fish or squid and is marked by epigastric pain, nausea, and vomiting.
  1962 P. H. VAN THIEL in *Parasitology* LII. (Proc. section) 16P As the excretory tube ends near the ventral larval tooth at the head of the larva and rectal glands are present, the larva is a species of Anisakis. Herring worm disease should therefore be called anisakiasis. **1967** *Amer. Jrnl. Trop. Med. & Hygiene*

XVI. 728/1 Ninety-two cases of larval anisakiasis in the gastrointestinal tract of Japanese people..were studied clinicopathologically. **1988** *New Scientist* 12 Nov. 21/1 A disease called anisakiasis that is caused by a parasitic worm found in raw or undercooked fish.

ankaramite, *n.* Add: Hence **ankara'mitic** *a.*, of the nature of or containing ankaramite.
  1971 *Nature* 23 Apr. 510/2 The lavas comprise a succession of alkali-olivine basalts, basanites, and mugearites; ankaramitic varieties are common. **1975** *Ibid.* 9 Oct. 469/2 All of those rocks are traversed by a swarm of dominantly basaltic and ankaramitic dykes. **1990** *Jrnl. Petrol.* XXXI. 747 The ankaramitic parent magma composition is calculated from the most primitive olivine phenocryst composition.

ankle, *n.* Add: **[3.]** *ankle oedema.*
  1959 W. RAAB in A. A. Luisada *Cardiology* IV. xvi. 114/2 Moderate *ankle edema, exertional dyspnea and sighing respiration must not be mistaken as evidence of congestive failure. **1984** *Jrnl. Cardiovascular Pharmacol.* VI. (Suppl.) s1060/2 Dizziness and ankle oedema each occurred once.

ankyloglossia (,æŋkɪləʊ'glɒsɪə), *n. Path.* [f. Gr. ἀγκυλόγλωσσον contraction of the tongue (f. ἀγκύλος crooked + γλῶσσα tongue): see *-GLOSSIA.] A condition in which the frenum of the tongue is abnormally short, restricting its range of movement; tongue-tie.
  [**1743** R. JAMES *Med. Dict.* I. sig. 6 C 1ᵛ/1, *Ancyloglossum*, a Contraction of the Ligaments of the Tongue, hindering Speech.] **1848** DUNGLISON *Dict. Med. Sci.* (ed. 7) 56/1 *Ankyloglossia*, impeded motion of the tongue in consequence of adhesion between its margins and the gums. **1957** H. H. BLOOMER in L. E. Travis *Handbk. Speech Path.* xxi. 643 Lingual deformities of various sorts include tongue-tie (ankyloglossia). **1987** *Nature* 5 Mar. 91/1 The sub-chromosomal localization of a single gene defect causing cleft palate and ankyloglossia (tongue-tied) in a large Icelandic family.

ankylosaurid (,æŋkɪləʊ'sɔːrɪd), *a.* and *n. Palaeont.* [f. ANKYLOSAUR(US *n.* + -ID³.] **A.** *adj.* Of, pertaining to, or designating the family Ankylosauridae, which as now defined comprises ornithischian dinosaurs of Cretaceous times with body armour, four heavy limbs, a broad head, and a club at the end of the tail.
  The family was formerly defined as including the present family Nodosauridae, whose members had narrow heads and no tail clubs.
  1965 *Fieldiana: Geol.* XV. 1. 72 The osteologic affinities of *Tatisaurus* are to these primitive hypsilophodonts, although the dentition is particularized as ankylosaurid. **1969** *Sci. Jrnl.* July 37/3 The Ornithischia were strongly diversified, represented by a numerous group of two-footed ornithopods and two four-footed groups; the horned dinosaurs and the ankylosaurid dinosaurs. **1985** D. NORMAN *Illustr. Encycl. Dinosaurs* 167/1 Ankylosaurid nasal tubes follow an S-shaped course through the head.
  B. *n.* An ankylosaurid dinosaur.
  1978 *Nature* 17 Aug. 663/1 During the Mid-Cretaceous and Late Cretaceous more groups of big ornithischians were added to the fauna..: parrot-beaked psittacosaurs, protoceratopsids, ceratopsids, ankylosaurids and the duck-bills (hadrosaurs). **1988** M. BENTON *Dinosaurs* 27/1 The tail club was an added protection against meat-eaters for the advanced ankylosaurids.

ankylosing ('æŋkɪləʊzɪŋ), *ppl. a.* [f. ANKYLOSE *v.* + -ING².] *ankylosing spondylitis* [tr. F. *spondylite ankylosante* (Auerbach 1900, in *Gaz.*

hebd. de Méd. et de Chir. 7 June 538/1)], an inflammatory arthritis of the spine, chiefly affecting young males, characterized by inflammation and ossification of the intervertebral discs and ligaments, leading to ankylosis of the vertebral and sacro-iliac joints. **1935** *Rep. Chronic Rheumatic Dis.* (Brit. Comm. Chronic Rheumatic Dis.) I. 77 (*heading*) Ankylosing spondylitis. **1942** S. G. SCOTT *Adolescent Spondylitis or Ankylosing Spondylitis* 2 The term 'spondylitis' will be used .. to denote that particular spinal arthritis which attacks the young adult, usually known as ankylosing spondylitis. **1979** M. J. TAUSSIG *Processes in Path. & Microbiol.* vii. 879 One of the most striking associations discovered to date is that between the HLA antigen B27 and ankylosing spondylitis. **1989** C. CAUFIELD *Multiple Exposures* (1990) xiv. 141 A British survey of more than 14,000 people who were subjected to X-rays .. for a painful, but not fatal, back condition known as ankylosing spondylitis.

ankyrin ('æŋkırın), *n. Biochem.* [f. Gr. ἄγκυρα (see ANCHOR *n.*[1]) + -IN[1].] A globular protein found on the inside of the plasma membrane in certain cells, which mediates the attachment of other proteins, esp. that of spectrin in mammalian red blood cells.
1975 R. E. STEPHENS in *Jrnl. Cell Biol.* LXIV. 419/2 Because of the bifurcating nature and anchor-like function of ciliary rootlets, the generic name *ankyrin*, from the Greek *ankyra* (anchor) is proposed for these characteristic high molecular weight structural proteins of rootlets and rootlet-related organelles. **1984** HOLTZMAN & NOVIKOFF *Cells & Organelles* (ed. 3) II. xi. 287 Via ankyrin and other proteins, the actin-spectrin network is bound to some of the integral proteins of the plasma membrane. **1987** *Nature* 6 Aug. 533/1 In several nonerythroid cell types .. homologues of ankyrin and spectrin (fodrin) are localized in specific membrane domains. **1989** B. ALBERTS et al. *Molecular Biol. of Cell* (ed. 2) vi. 289 By connecting band 3 protein to spectrin, ankyrin links the spectrin network to the membrane.

Anna ('ænə), *n.*[2] *Ornith.* [The forename of the wife of Prince François Massena (*c* 1795-1863), Duc de Rivoli, who procured the original specimen.] **Anna('s) hummingbird** [tr. F. *oiseau-mouche Anna* (named in R. P. Lesson *Hist. Naturelle des Oiseaux-Mouches* (1829) 205)], a North American hummingbird, *Calypte anna*, found chiefly in California, the male of which has a deep rose-red head and throat.
1839 J. J. AUDUBON *Ornith. Biogr.* V. 238 Anna Humming Bird. *Trochilus Anna.* **1895** C. BENDIRE *Life Hist. N. Amer. Birds* II. 206 The breeding range of Anna's Hummingbird .. appears to be a rather restricted one. **1953** E. R. BLAKE *Birds Mexico* 265 Anna Hummingbirds have a similar pattern [to Costa Hummingbirds], but their heads and gorgets appear bright rose-red in suitable light. **1988** *Birder's World* July/Aug. 12/2 Anna's Hummingbird .. is the only hummingbird species that winters extensively in North America, largely in the western coastal states.

annulospiral (,ænju:ləu'spaırəl), *a. Zool.* [ad. It. *anulo-spirale* (coined by A. Ruffini 1896, in *Monitore Zool. Ital.* VII. 50): see ANNULAR *a.*, SPIRAL *a.* (and *adv.*).] Designating a type of sensory nerve ending that winds spirally around muscle fibres in a muscle spindle.
1898 *Jrnl. Physiol.* XXIII. 199 The difference between these two modes of ending .. consists in the former presenting a perfect spiral ... In the latter mode of ending there are a succession of rings ... But there exist forms intermediate between these two endings ... I judged it well therefore to speak of the two together under the single term—annulo-spiral ending. **1948** *Q. Jrnl. Microsc. Sci.* LXXXIX. 172 To distinguish between the two types of sensory ending present in muscle-spindles the terms 'annulo-spiral' and 'flower-spray' are commonly used. **1961** *Lancet* 9 Sept. 583/2 The sudan technique .. clearly shows the annulospiral sensory endings of normal muscle spindles. **1974** D. & M. WEBSTER *Compar. Vertebr. Morphol.* x. 201 The annulospiral endings have a larger diameter and transmit impulses more rapidly.

annus horribilis ('ænəs hɒ'rıbılıs), *n.* [mod.L., lit. 'dreadful year', modelled on ANNUS MIRABILIS *n.*] A disastrous or particularly unpleasant year.
1985 *Guardian* 7 Mar. 10/2 Unlike the earlier Kostelec stories, however, The Engineer of Human Souls is written in exile in Toronto, where he was driven by the annus mirabilis, annus horribilis of 1968, and that projected wartime story has expanded into something far more ambitious and problematic. **1988** *Sunday Times* 7 Aug. B1/1 In the past *annus horribilis*, BT's black and yellow cubicles have sprouted in every town and village in the land. **1990** *Financial Times* 23 June II. 2/7 If last year was the *annus mirabilis* of the oil sector of the unlisted securities market, this year is looking more like the *annus horribilis*. **1992** QUEEN ELIZABETH II in *Times* 25 Nov. 3/2, 1992 is not a year I shall look back on with undiluted pleasure. In the words of one of my more sympathetic correspondents, it has turned out to be an 'annus horribilis'.

ano-, *comb. form.* Add: **anococ'cygeal** *a.*, pertaining to or connecting the anus and the coccyx.
1881 *Syd. Soc. Lex.*, *Anococcygeal. **1910** *Practitioner* Apr. 521 A deeper infection above the anococcygeal ligament may lead to an ischio-rectal abscess on one side. **1962** *Gray's Anat.* (ed. 33) 1212 The anococcygeal nerves arise from this plexus. **1992** *Pflügers Arch.* CDXXI. 43 (*heading*) Relationship between force and Ca²+ in anococcygeal and vas deferens smooth muscle cells.

ano'genital *a.*, pertaining to or involving the anus and the genitals.
1909 *Cent. Dict. Suppl.*, *Anogenital. **1932** S. ZUCKERMAN *Social Life Monkeys* ix. 143 The females repeatedly present and continuously examine their anogenital regions. **1966** DUNLOP & ALSTEAD *Textbk. Med. Treatm.* (ed. 10) 145 If .. the yeast infection persists and causes ano-genital dermatitis, nystatin should be given. **1988** *Amer. Jrnl. Publ. Health* LXXVIII. 1533/2 Knowledge of HIV status had no apparent impact on anogenital intercourse.

ano'rectal *a.* [a. F. *ano-rectal* (coined in A. Fournier *Lésions tertiaires de l'anus et du rectum: syphilome ano-rectal* (1875))], pertaining to or involving the anus and the rectum.
1884 C. B. KELSEY *Dis. Rectum & Anus* ix. 229 *Ano-rectal Syphiloma .. is defined by Fournier as 'an infiltration of the rectal walls by neoplasm'. **1903** *Therapeutic Gaz.* 15 May 344/1 Leeching may be employed as a partial substitute for venesection. This in the anorectal region is .. valuable in the successful treatment of those two organs. **1968** *Jrnl. Pediatrics* LXXIII. 603/2 Anorectal bleeding occurred which was associated with hypoprothrombinemia. **1993** *Brit. Jrnl. Surg.* LXXX. 117/1 There were no significant differences in anorectal pressure between patients with constipation and those with faecal incontinence.

similarly **ano'rectum** *n.*, the anus and the rectum considered as a single structure.
1946 M. G. SPIESMAN *Essent. Clin. Proctology* i. 1 (*heading*) Embryology and applied anatomy of the *anorectum. **1983** *Sci. Amer.* Mar. 110/2 All the organs, beginning with the trachea and extending to the anorectum, the urethra and (in females) the vagina are removed en bloc.

anodal, *a.* Add: Hence **a'nodally** *adv.*, towards the anode; by the anode.

1926 *Amer. Jrnl. Physiol.* LXXVIII. 637 The cathode is not totally blocking the anodally decremented wave. **1942** *Jrnl. Neurophysiol.* V. 149 Unintentional recording of anodally increased negative after-potential..resulted in the misinterpretations of experimental observations. **1990** *Jrnl. Molluscan Stud.* LVI. 317/2 We based loci differentiation on clear differential migration distances. All loci, except *Got-1* and *Mdh* migrated anodally.

anodontia (ænəʊ'dɒntɪə), *n. Med.* [f. AN- 10 + ODONT(O- + -IA¹.] Congenital absence of some teeth.
　1881 *Syd. Soc. Lex., Anodontia..*, an anomaly occasionally observed in man, in which no teeth are developed. **1939** *Amer. Jrnl. Orthodontics* XXV. 69 Partial anodontia..means lack of one or more teeth. **1957** H. H. BLOOMER in L. E. Travis *Handbk. Speech Path.* xxi. 640 Other useful terms.. include..anodontia (congenital absence of teeth). **1965** L. B. AREY *Developmental Anat.* (ed. 7) xiii. 225 Anodontia designates a congenital absence of teeth; its mildest expression is the agenesis of a single tooth like the third molar.

anomia (ə'nəʊmɪə), *n. Path.* [f. A- 14 + L. *nōm-en* name + -IA¹, after APHASIA *n.*, etc.] A form of aphasia characterized by inability to recall the names of objects.
　1900 DORLAND *Med. Dict.* 50/1 *Anomia*, loss of the power of naming objects or of recognizing names. **1949** *Jrnl. Speech & Hearing Disorders* XIV. 9/2 The present authors regard anomia..as a symptom which is commonly associated with either expressive or receptive aphasia. **1974** L. F. SIES *Aphasia Theory & Therapy* i. 46 The failure to find the names desired for expression has sometimes been designated as anomia. **1990** *Brain* CXIII. 398 These authors.. measured the anomia of the patients on a battery of test pictures.
　Hence **a'nomic** *a.*²
　1957 J. EISENSON in L. E. Travis *Handbk. Speech Pathol.* xii. 440 A patient with anomic difficulty..may learn to substitute a synonym or a phrase with approximate meaning for the elusive word. **1975** *Cortex* XI. 353 Two patients with an exceedingly poor verbal memory span were observed, one suffering from anomic aphasia and the other from conduction aphasia. **1990** *Brain* CXIII. 398 Severely demented patients may be anomic due to impaired visual perception.

anonymized (æ'nɒnɪmaɪzd), *ppl. a.* Chiefly *Med.* [f. ANONYM(OUS *a.* + -IZE + -ED¹.] Made anonymous, esp. by the removal of names or identifying particulars; *spec.* designating a form of medical screening, performed chiefly for statistical purposes, in which the identities of the subjects are unknown to the investigators.
　1972 A. MARRE *First Rep. Parl. Commissioner for Admin.* 3 in *Parl. Papers 1972–73* XXVII. 1079, I now lay before Parliament..the full but anonymised texts of..reports on individual cases. **1977** *Sunday Times* 23 Jan. 13/8 What is the point of an outpouring of anonymised findings by these expensive commissioners..when no parties—guilty or innocent—can ever be named? **1987** *Daily Tel.* 5 Feb. 1/1 The possibility of 'anonymised testing' of routine blood samples, was disclosed last night by Sir Donald Acheson. **1991** *Brit. Med. Jrnl.* 9 Mar. 596/2, I would personally advocate anonymised applications for training posts. **1992** *Independent* 3 Dec. 1/8 Thousands of results of anonymised screening for HIV in ante-natal and sexual disease clinics.
　Hence (as a back-formation) **a'nonymize** *v. trans.* (usu. in *pass.*).
　1975 *Sunday Express* 8 June 6/4, I did not reveal who was responsible for the 'horrible' word. I anonymised him, as you (or rather Sir Alan [Marre]) might say. **1991** *Brit. Med. Jrnl.* 1 June 1299/2 Before

samples were anonymised, characteristics as recorded routinely in patients' notes were extracted.

anorak, *n.* Add: **2.** *slang* (*derog.*). A boring, studious, or socially inept young person (caricatured as typically wearing an anorak), *esp.* one who pursues an unfashionable and solitary interest with obsessive dedication. Also *attrib.*
　1984 *Observer* 5 Aug. 5/3 At weekends boatloads of Dutch 'anoraks'—pirate radio fans—come out to cheer on their latest hero. **1988** in T. THORNE *Dict. Contemp. Slang* (1991) 10 An anorak is one of those boring gits who sit at the front of every lecture with their Pringle jumpers asking the lecturer their clever questions. **1991** *Independent* 14 Nov. 26/3 Enthusiasts who hang around the radio station, anxious to fetch and carry, answer phones, and do any amount of unpaid work simply to be involved..[are] sometimes disparagingly referred to as 'anoraks'. **1991** *Straight no Chaser* Winter 11/3 A guide to over three thousand blues records. Essential for scribblers and anoraks. **1993** *Personal Computer World* Apr. 390/2 The one difficult part of Demon's system is the software, which, while inexpensive and reliable once you've got it going, is archetypal anorak software. **1995** J. MILLER *voXpop* xii. 170 The Beatles have almost become an obsession. I try to get studio out-takes and rare records, I'm almost anorak level about it—getting really excited if I can hear John Lennon cough.
　Hence **'anoraked** *a.*
　1965 *Guardian* 13 Aug. 8/3 Anoraked and uniformed men are crowded into a tiny saloon of a fell-side inn. **1990** *Observer* 30 Dec. 15/2 It is as if God had an extra jar of comic talent and for a joke gave it to a nerdy, anoraked, northern chemist.

anorchia (æ'nɔːkɪə), *n. Path.* [f. Gr. ἄνορχος without testicles, f. ἀ(ν)- privative prefix (see AN- 10) + ὄρχις testicle: see -IA¹. Cf. earlier G. *Anorchie, Anorchia.*] = *ANORCHISM *n.*
　1890 BILLINGS *Med. Dict.* I. 73/2 *Anorchia*, congenital absence of testicles. **1933** *Ann. Surg.* XCVIII. 107 Perhaps the cases of anorchia represent a..final degree of separation, with resulting atrophy and disappearance of the testis. **1938** *Surgery* IV. 376 The medical records of the War Department..report only 52 cases of anorchia in the first two million men examined. **1980** *Recent Adv. Surg.* X. 349 Where unilateral, anorchia requires confirmation by operation.

anorchidism (æ'nɔːkɪdɪz(ə)m), *n. Path.* [f. AN- 10 + ORCHID(O- + -ISM, after *cryptorchidism* s.v. CRYPTO-, etc.] = *ANORCHISM *n.*
　1918 STEDMAN *Med. Dict.* (ed. 5) 56/2 *Anorchidism*, absence or failure of descent of testicles. **1966** WRIGHT & SYMMERS *Systemic Path.* I. xxvi. 811/1 Absence of both testes (anorchidism), the presence of one testis only (monorchidism), and the presence of more than two testes (polyorchidism) have been observed occasionally. **1990** *Jrnl. Med. Genetics* XXVII. 200/1 We present a male infant with..severely hypoplastic external genitalia with anorchidism.

anorchism (æ'nɔːkɪz(ə)m), *n. Path.* [f. Gr. ἄνορχος: see *ANORCHIA *n.*, -ISM.] The absence of one or both testicles, usu. as a congenital condition. Also, cryptorchidism.
　1883 HOLMES & HULKE *Syst. Surg.* (ed. 3) III. 462 Dr. Gruber..concludes that unilateral anorchism occurs in subjects otherwise well formed. **1962** *Gray's Anat.* (ed. 33) 1523 A man in whom both testes are retained (anorchism) is sterile, though he may not be impotent. **1989** *Encycl. Brit.* XXVI. 705/1 Anorchism (absence of one or both testes) is rare; it may be associated with the absence of various other structures of the spermatic tract.

anorgasmia (ænɔː'gæzmɪə), *n. Med.* [f. AN- 10 + ORGASM *n.* + -IA¹.] Persistent inability to achieve orgasm despite responding to sexual stimulation.

1975 *Postgrad. Med.* July 95/1 *Anorgasmia.* This term describes the condition of the woman who enjoys foreplay, becomes aroused by it, desires coitus when she is aroused, usually enjoys coitus, but rarely or never reaches a climax. **1977** *Arch. Sexual Behavior* VI. 438 The association of Gelineau's syndrome and anorgasmia has not been previously reported. **1981** *Brit. Med. Jrnl.* 10 Oct. 954/2 Gynaecological surgery may be followed by..anorgasmia and lack of libido. **1991** *Details* Dec. 14/2 Candida Royalle..manages to ridicule a Frenchman about premature ejaculation after years of anorgasmia.

Hence **anor'gasmic** *a.*

1975 *Postgraduate Med.* July 95/1 The woman..is currently anorgasmic. **1977** *Arch. Sexual Behavior* VI. 438 The fourth [woman] was always anorgasmic during intercourse. **1989** *Psychosomatics* XXX. 171/2 The present study involved a relatively large sample of anorgasmic women.

anorogenic (æˌnɒrəˈdʒɛnɪk), *a. Geol.* [f. AN- 10 + OROGENIC *a.*] Not orogenic; (of rock) not formed during a period of orogenesis.

1924 *Geol. Mag.* LXI. 155 In the systems from the end of the anorogenic phases, again, muddy deposits and limestones are predominant. **1974** *Nature* 5 Apr. 497/2 All of these deposits are associated with small alkaline and peralkaline granite plutons of anorogenic character. **1990** *Jrnl. Petrol.* XXXI. 558 These events are suggestive of Wilson-cycle tectonics where anorogenic anorthosite intrusion corresponds to continental rifting.

anorthoclase (ænˈɔːθəkleɪz), *n. Min.* [ad. G. *Anorthoklas* (coined in H. Rosenbusch *Mikroskopische Physiographie der Mineralien u. Gesteine* (1885) I. 550): see AN- 10, ORTHOCLASE *n.*] A triclinic sodium-rich alkali feldspar, (Na, K)AlSi₃O₈, similar to microcline, occurring in many slightly alkalic lavas.

1888 J. P. IDDINGS tr. *Rosenbusch's Microsc. Physiogr. Rock-Making Minerals* 311 The series of triclinic potash-soda feldspars..is to be designated as the series of anorthoclases in distinction to the plagioclases which plainly cleave obliquely. **1903** A. GEIKIE *Text-bk. Geol.* (ed. 4) I. II. 221 From a half to two-thirds of the rock consists of cryptoperthite (soda-orthoclase) and soda-microcline (anorthoclase of Rosenbusch). **1965** G. J. WILLIAMS *Econ. Geol.* N.Z. xi. 167/2 Among these rocks is a tinguaite consisting of a network of aegirine crystals with phenocrysts of anorthoclase. **1993** *Jrnl. Geol. Soc.* CL. 892 The phonolites contain <5% of anorthoclase phenocrysts.

anorthoscope, *n.* Add: Hence **anortho'scopic** *a.*, pertaining to or characteristic of the optical illusion produced by an anorthoscope, or the way in which this illusion is perceived; **anortho'scopically** *adv.*

1900 *Amer. Jrnl. Pscychol.* XI. 240 A movement of the eyes in the same direction as the figure, which would bring the experiment under practically the same principle as the ordinary anorthoscopic illusion. **1925** J. P. C. SOUTHALL tr. J. von Kries in *H. von Helmholtz's Treat. Physiol. Optics* III. 276 Here..should be included also the so-called anorthoscopic phenomena as being characteristic illusions connected with ocular judgement of motions. **1981** *Sci. Amer.* Mar. 106/3 To perceive a figure anorthoscopically it is not enough to know one is looking through a slit; the slit must be seen. **1987** *Jrnl. Exper. Psychol.: Human Perception & Performance* XIII. 344/1 Just such distorted shape is often perceived in anorthoscopic perception.

anosmatic (ˌænɒzˈmætɪk), *a. Zool.* [ad. F. *anosmatique* (coined by P. Broca 1878, in *Revue d'Anthropologie* 2nd Ser. II. 398): see AN- 10,

OSMATIC *a.*] Lacking olfactory organs and, consequently, a sense of smell. Also, = *ANOSMIC *a.*

1890 *Jrnl. Anat. & Physiol.* XXV. 106 He [*sc.* Broca] has classified the Mammalia, in relation to the magnitude of their olfactory apparatus, into two groups: osmatic mammals..and anosmatic mammals. **1970** W. B. YAPP *Introd. Animal Physiol.* (ed. 3) vi. 206 A few [mammals], such as the toothed whales, have no olfactory organ and are termed anosmatic. **1978** *Jrnl. Compar. Physiol.* A. CXXVIII. 303/1 Pigeons made anosmatic by inserting plastic tubes in their nostrils were tested from familiar and unfamiliar release sites. **1986** *Anat. & Embryol.* CLXXIII. 291/2 In toothed whales and dolphins, which are anosmatic animals, the vomeronasal organ does not occur at all.

anosmic (æˈnɒzmɪk), *a.* and *n.* Chiefly *Path.* [f. ANOSM(IA *n.* + -IC.] **A.** *adj.* Affected with anosmia; having no sense of smell. Also (*Zool.*), lacking olfactory organs, anosmatic.

1875 T. S. WATSON *Dis. Nose* xiv. 359 Anosmic individuals should be aware that they run great risks in regard to sewer emanations and other poisonous effluvia. **1926** *Jrnl. Exper. Psychol.* IX. 407 Subject Y is anosmic; and his anosmia is probably complete. **1955** *Jrnl. Amer. Med. Assoc.* 31 Dec. 1722/2 We assembled the normal controls and the anosmic patients in three separate groups. **1973** *Sci. Amer.* Apr. 97/2 Both the blind fish and the anosmic ones exhibited a reduced ability to find the river.

B. *n.* An anosmic person.

1929 *Amer. Jrnl. Physiol.* LXXXVIII. 620 The subjects of these experiments were normal individuals, an anosmic and selected hospital patients under light ether anesthesia. **1938** *N. & Q.* 22 Jan. 68/1 Wordsworth was not an anosmic. **1955** *Jrnl. Amer. Med. Assoc.* 31 Dec. 1722/2 On most occasions, when the test food was correctly identified either by an anosmic or by a normal control, the subject declared that he could perceive the flavor. **1973** *Nature* 23 Mar. 271/2 This complex fruity odour screened out any general anosmics having little or no sense of smell.

anosognosia (æˌnɒsɒgˈnəʊsɪə), *n. Path.* Also **anosagnosia** (æˌnɒsægˈnəʊsɪə). [ad. F. *anosognosie* (coined by M. J. Babinski 1914, in *Rev. Neurologique* XXVII. 846): see A- 14, NOSO-, GNOSIS *n.*, -IA¹. *Anogasnosia* after *agnosia*, *prosopagnosia*, *simult(an)agnosia.*] Unawareness of or failure to acknowledge one's hemiplegia or other disability.

1915 *Med. Rec.* (N.Y.) 27 Mar. 521/2 Recently Babinski observed in two cases of organic cerebral hemiplegia that the patients ignored or appeared to ignore the existence of the paralysis with which they were affected. To this condition he gave the name anosognosia. **1937** *Bull. Los Angeles Neurol. Soc.* II. 103 We have reported six cases in which anosognosia was an important element in the clinical picture. **1961** R. BRAIN *Speech Disorders* xiv. 168 Babinski (1914) first used the term anosognosia to describe unawareness of hemiplegia. Since it means imperception of disease, however, it is now more generally applied to cover unawareness of hemiplegia, blindness, deafness and aphasia. **1985** O. SACKS *Man who mistook Wife* 3 It is impossible, for patients with certain right-hemisphere syndromes to know their own problems—a peculiar and specific 'anosognosia', as Babinski called it. **1991** *New Scientist* 9 Feb. 52/1 Another aspect of awareness is revealed in neurological patients who are unaware of their impairments (anosognosia) and fail to comprehend their problems, or even deny them.

anovulation (æˌnɒvjʊˈleɪʃən), *n. Physiol.* [f. AN- 10 + OVULATION *n.*] Absence of ovulation; failure to ovulate.

1930 *Jrnl. Amer. Med. Assoc.* 22 Mar. 834/1 The changes in the genital canal in the anovulation type of cycle..are not quite similar to those seen when ovulation has occurred. **1963** FORD & KELLY *Contemp. Moral Theol.* (1964) II. xvi. 346 The use of the drugs . . usually involves anovulation with consequent temporary sterilization. **1987** *Oxf. Textbk. Med.* (ed. 2) I. x. 89/1 The clinical problems of the polycystic ovary syndrome are anovulation and hirsutism.

anoxygenic (æˌnɒksɪ'dʒɛnɪk), *a. Biol.* [AN- 10 + OXYGENIC *a.*] That lacks or does not produce oxygen; *spec.* designating or pertaining to a type of photosynthesis, occurring in certain bacteria, which does not generate oxygen.

1975 *Jrnl. Bacteriol.* CXXIII. 860/2 In addition to the anoxygenic photosynthesis, *O. limnetica* is capable of oxygenic photosynthesis and can readily shift from one to the other. **1976** *Nature* 22 Jan. 176/2 Everyone seemed to agree with Siever that the earliest Archaean atmosphere was anoxygenic. **1986** M. KOGUT tr. *Schlegel's Gen. Microbiol.* ii. 70 Anoxygenic phototrophs . . grow in the anaerobic zone. *Ibid.* xii. 369 The photosynthetic bacteria that carry out anoxygenic photosynthesis have been divided into two large groups: the purple bacteria . . and the green bacteria.

ansatz ('ænsæts), *n. Math.* [a. G. *Ansatz* attempt, approach.] A mathematical assumption, esp. about the form of an unknown function, which is made in order to facilitate solution of an equation or other problem.

1942 *Jrnl. Indian Math. Soc.* VI. 41 (*title*) Studies in Fourier ansatz and parabolic equations. **1964** E. A. POWER *Introd. Quantum Electrodynamics* viii. 114 The excited state is assumed to decay exponentially so that its amplitude $a(t) = Ae^{-t_{1/2}}$. This ansatz is assumed, together with the small value of $e^2/\hbar c$. **1968** C. G. KUPER *Introd. Theory Superconductivity* xi. 184 The microscopic theory . . makes a variational *Ansatz*, designed to take maximum advantage of the Cooper condensation. **1979** *Nature* 22 Nov. 369/1 It is possible to predict an exponent of the magnitude by combining the rules of reptation . . with a scaling argument. **1990** *IMA Jrnl. Appl. Math.* XLIV. 102 We eliminate $\psi(x)$ between equations (3) and (4) and substitute the ansatz (6) into the resulting equation.

antagonize, *v.* Add: [4.] **b.** *Physiol.* To inhibit or interfere with the action or effect of (a biologically active substance).

1875 A. S. TAYLOR *Poisons* (ed. 3) viii. 52 Attempts have been made . . to antagonize animal poisons, such as that of rabies. **1906** W. E. DIXON *Man. Pharmacol.* xxxii. 438 Physostigmine . . is . . antagonised by the atropine group of drugs. **1949** H. W. FLOREY et al. *Antibiotics* II. xxi. 812 Glutathione and thiothreonine antagonized the anti-bacterial action of penicillin. **1969** *Times* 7 July 5/7 Drugs known to have an effect in reducing inflammation, presumably because they antagonize various of the substances released in the lungs. **1990** *Jrnl. Developmental Physiol.* XIV. 29/2 Treatment . . with indomethacin has been shown to antagonize the ethanol-induced suppression of fetal breathing movements.

antecedence, *n.* Add: 4. *Physical Geogr.* and *Geol.* The formation of an antecedent drainage system; the persistence of a pre-existing drainage pattern despite later deformation of the land surface.

1942 O. D. VON ENGELN *Geomorphol.* xii. 227 Antecedence is independent of the topographic or structural guidance of a covering mass. **1959** G. H. DURY *Face of Earth* iii. 24 Antecedence is to be expected in regions where the crust is unstable. **1970** R. J. SMALL *Study of Landforms* vii. 251 In some instances the impossibility of antecedence, as a mechanism to account for a discordant river pattern, *can* be easily shown. **1977** A. HALLAM *Planet Earth* 76/1 Antecedence, whereby a rapidly eroding stream

manages to keep on cutting down through a fold rising only slowly across its path.

antecedent, *a.* Add: **3.** *Physical Geogr.* and *Geol.* Designating a river or a drainage pattern which has persisted despite deformation or uplift of the land surface; also, designating valleys formed by such rivers.

1875 J. W. POWELL *Explor. Colorado River* xi. 163, I have endeavoured . . to explain the relation of the valleys of the Uinta Mountains to the stratigraphy . . of the region, and, further, to state the conclusion reached, that the drainage was established antecedent to the corrugation or displacement of the beds by faulting and folding. I propose to call such valleys . . *antecedent valleys*. **1927** *Bull. Geol. Soc. Amer.* XXXVIII. 207 Antecedent streams traverse this uplift through watergaps. **1970** R. J. SMALL *Study of Landforms* vii. 251 Theoretically . ., examples of antecedent drainage should occur frequently, for earth-movements affecting land-areas do not always operate with great rapidity.

antenatal, *a.* Add: Hence ante'natally *adv.*, before birth; before giving birth.

1883 E. L. LINTON *Ione* II. xxiv. 288 One of those miserable beings who are antenatally tainted by their parents' dishonour. **1902** J. W. BALLANTYNE *Man. Antenatal Path. & Hygiene: Foetus* xviii. 319 In foetal ichthyosis the thickening of the epidermis has occurred to its fullest extent antenatally. **1976** *Lancet* 9 Oct. 775/2 Most mothers are seen by doctors antenatally.

anteriormost (æn'tɪərɪəmɔʊst), *a. Biol.* [f. ANTERIOR *a.* + -MOST.] In the furthest forward position; nearest to the anterior.

1965 B. KÄLLÉN in DeHaan & Ursprung *Organogenesis* iv. 107/1 As the neural plate and early tube form, the anteriormost part is wider than that which is posterior, and forms the rudiment of the brain. **1988** *Nature* 11 Feb. 524/1 The crowns of eight postcanine teeth are preserved, the anteriormost of which is badly damaged.

antero-, *comb. form.* Add: **anterodorsally.**

1961 J. E. COLLIN *Empididae* I. viii. 185 Care must be taken to note the presence of small but distinct bristles above front, and *anterodorsally on hind, tibiae.* **1989** *Jrnl. Zool.* CCXIX. 169 The tongue is moved anterodorsally and slipped beneath the food item.

antero-inferiorly.

1907 A. M. BUCHANAN *Man. of Anat.* II. 1025 The digastric or submaxillary triangle is bounded . . *antero-inferiorly by the anterior belly of the digastric.* **1992** *Anat. Rec.* CCXXXIII. 322/2 The lateral posterior ciliary artery . . runs antero-inferiorly along the upper edge of the inferior rectus muscle.

anterolaterally.

1909 *Cent. Dict.* Suppl., *Anterolaterally.* **1967** G. M. WYBURN et al. *Conc. Anat.* iv. 125/2 It [*sc.* the posterior cranial fossa] is formed mainly by the parts of the occipital bone enclosing the foramen magnum with anterolaterally the petromastoid part of the temporal bone. **1992** *Brain Res.* DLXXXVI. 39/2 The axons of the two tap neurons were seen to run anterolaterally.

antheridiol (ænθə'rɪdɪɒl), *n. Biol.* [f. ANTHERIDI(UM *n.* + -OL.] A steroid hormone produced by female hyphae of the filamentous fungus *Achyla bisexualis* which stimulates the male hyphae to produce antheridia.

1967 McMORRIS & BARKSDALE in *Nature* 15 July 320/2 An account of the isolation of this hormone, which we wish to designate 'antheridiol', is given here. **1976** *Ann. Rev. Microbiol.* XXX. 231 The water mold *Achyla bisexualis* forms a sex hormone that was characterized and named antheridiol. **1984** J. W. DEACON *Introd. Mod. Mycol.* (ed. 2) iv. 64 Antheridiol is produced by 'female' branches of *Achyla* . . and it initiates the development of antheridia on 'male' or 'neuter' hyphal branches.

anthozoan (ænθəʊ'zəʊən), *n.* and *a. Zool.* [f. ANTHOZO(A *n.* + -AN.] **A.** *n.* An animal of the class Anthozoa of marine cnidarians, which includes sea anemones, corals, and sea-pens. **B.** *adj.* Of or pertaining to this class.

1877 *Proc. R. Soc.* XXV. 93 (*title*) Preliminary note on the structure of the Stylasteridæ, a group of stony corals which..are Hydroids, and not Anthozoans. **1879** H. N. MOSELEY *Notes by Naturalist on 'Challenger'* xx. 532 In the Anthozoan coral, each radiate system is the skeleton on one polyp animal. **1940** L. H. HYMAN *Invertebr.* I. vii. 538 As stomodaeum is an embryological term, this structure in adult anthozoans is best termed pharynx. *Ibid.*, The anthozoan polyp is thus seen to differ from the hydrozoan polyp. **1979** J. D. & J. J. GEORGE *Marine Life* 27/1 Anthozoans, although very common in tropical waters, occur in all seas of the world. **1987** R. D. BARNES *Invertebr. Zool.* (ed. 5) v. 122/2 Some anthozoan nematocysts have a three-part tip that folds back on expulsion.

anthra-, *comb. form.* Add: **anthra'nilate,** a salt or ester of anthranilic acid.

1845 W. GREGORY *Outl. Chem.: Org. Chem.* 474 The latter [*sc.* anthranilic acid] is purified in the form of *anthranilate of potash. **1924** *Times Trade & Engin. Suppl.* 29 Nov. 243/2 Quite a number of changes have taken place among perfumery chemicals, and eugenol.., methyl anthranilate.., musk xylol.., and phenyl ethyl acetate..have all advanced. **1988** *BioFactors* I. 297/1 A number of mutants were unable to grow on anthranilate.

anthranilate synthetase *Biochem.,* an enzyme that catalyses the conversion of charismic acid to anthranilic acid, which is a precursor of tryptophan.

1965 J. A. DeMOSS in *Jrnl. Biol. Chem.* CCXL. 1235/2 It is proposed that a single enzyme, *anthranilate synthetase, catalyses the conversion of chorismic acid to anthranilic acid in *N. crassa.* **1968** A. WHITE et al. *Princ. Biochem* (ed. 4) xxiv. The activity of anthranilate synthetase from *E. coli*..is inhibited by tryptophan; in yeast, the amino acid both inhibits and represses the enzyme. **1990** *Embo Jrnl.* IX. 2762/1 An antibody was obtained against a hybrid protein consisting of residues 117 to 277..of the *COX11* product fused to the amino terminal 323 residues of *Escherichia coli* component 1 of anthranilate synthetase.

anthropic, *a.* Add: Hence **an'thropically** *adv.,* from an anthropic point of view, for anthropic reasons.

1932 *Times Lit. Suppl.* 8 Sept. 627/2 Dualism, while 'anthropically' necessary so far as the problem of 'the One and the Many' is concerned, is necessary in that field alone. **1933** *Jrnl. Theol. Stud.* XXXIV. 94 We are reading into a deliverance of sense an anthropically derived and interpretative over-belief. **1979** *Nature* 12 Apr. 612/1 It is unclear to what extent these coincidences can be interpreted anthropically.

anthropocentric, *a.* Add: Hence **anthropocen'tricity** *n.,* the quality or state of being anthropocentric.

1958 'E. CRISPIN' *Best SF 3* 13 To say that A is sated with anthropocentricity in fiction, and B not, is only the beginning of an answer. **1960** *Times Lit. Suppl.* 3 June 356/1 Mr. Ordish, with his steady biologist's eye, will have none of this anthropocentricity. **1991** *Times* 14 Sept. (Weekend Times) 5/3 Mr Levin prides himself on anthropocentricity. Why would it matter if there were no bitterns? Because it would matter to people.

anthropogenic, *a.* Add: Hence **anthropo 'genically** *adv.*

1982 *Environmental Sci.* XVI. 23 (*title*) Anthropogenically derived changes in the sedimentary flux of Mg, Cr, Ni, Cu, Zn, Hg, Pb, and P in Lough Neagh, Northern Ireland. **1991** *Forestry* LXIV. 417 The thesis of the American Marshall Institute that a reduction of solar radiation over the coming centuries will effectively offset the effects of anthropogenically induced warming.

anthroponomy (ænθrə'ppnəmɪ), *n. rare.* [f. ANTHROPO- + -NOMY. Cf. F. *anthroponomie* (A. Brillat-Savarin *Physiol. du Goût* (1826) II. 31), which, however, seems to be unconnected with the earliest recorded Eng. use.] A name proposed by several writers for the study of human function or behaviour, in various *spec.* senses.

1857 DUNGLISON *Dict. Med. Sci.* (rev. ed.) 71/1 *Anthroponomy*.., a knowledge of the special laws which preside over the functions of the human body in action. **1884** A. LALAUZE tr. *Brillat-Savarin's Physiologie du Goût* xix. 283 Certain uncommon phenomena accompany sometimes sleep and dreams; their examination may serve to advance the progress of anthroponomy. [*Note*] One of the words coined by our author, meaning 'the knowledge of man'. **1925** W. S. HUNTER in *Amer. Jrnl. Psychol.* XXXVI. 286 In the present paper we shall seek to justify the use of a new name for the scientific study of human nature…Anthroponomy is the science of the laws which govern human action—the science of human nature. **1966** in *Random House Dict.*

anti-abortion (æntɪə'bɔːʃən), *a.* Also **antiabortion.** [f. ANTI-¹ 4 + ABORTION *n.*] Opposed to, or legislating against, induced abortion.

1936 *Discovery* Sept. 300/1 Antagonistic phenomena to population growth are said to be birth control and abortion; remedial measures are anti-contraception and anti-abortion laws and family allowances. **1966** *Time* 28 Oct. (Atlantic ed.) 38/1 It called for the relaxing of anti-abortion laws. **1984** B. FRISHMAN *Amer. Families* i. 15 Some 'pro-family' activists . .noisily pressed their antiabortion and 'morality' platform. **1992** *Economist* 29 Feb. 55/3 In effect, the Irish government persuaded the EC to copper-fasten its anti-abortion law, so as to ensure that EC law could not be invoked at some point in the future to allow abortion in Ireland.

Hence **anti-a'bortionism** *n.,* **anti-a'bortionist** *n.*

1973 *Wall St. Jrnl.* 2 Aug. 1/1 Mr. Mooney is also a militant antiabortionist. **1976** *National Rev.* (U.S.) 6 Feb. 64/2, I think it is a mistake to tie anti-abortionism too closely to sex-is-for-procreation. **1989** *Washington Post* 8 Dec. A19/5 Take away anticommunism and anti-abortionism and you have carved out the heart of Republicanism. **1989** D. LEAVITT *Equal Affections* 92 She hated the antiabortionists, but she was also cowed by the power of their belief.

antibody, *n.* Add: **2.** Special Combs. **antibody-negative** *a.,* lacking the antibodies associated with a particular antigen or disease.

1975 *Laboratory Animal Sci.* XXV. 307/1 The purpose of inoculating the 4 *H simiae* *antibody-negative rhesus monkeys was to determine the *in vivo* behavior of the isolated *H simiae.* **1985** *New Statesman* 27 Sept. 14/3 Without testing facilities.., 'high-risk' donors might give blood simply to find out their antibody-status (and possibly transmit the virus while being antibody-negative). **1989** S. SONTAG *Aids & Metaphors* iii. 31 Concentration on the clinical manifestations of AIDS rather than all stages of HIV infection (i.e., from initial infection to seroconversion, to an antibody-positive asymptomatic stage, to full-blown AIDS) has had..the effect of misleading the public.

antibody-positive *a.*, having, or characterized by the presence of, the antibodies associated with a particular antigen or disease.

1969 *Cumulated Index Medicus: Subject Index* (1970) X. 6804/3 (*title*) Characteristics of *antibody-positive hyperthyroidism. **1974** *Amer. Jrnl. Digestive Dis.* XIX. 113 Thirty-nine blood donors, found on routine testing to be Australia antigen (HB Ag) or antibody (HB Ab) positive, were studied for evidence of hepatic disease. **1986** *Nursing Times* 3 Dec. 6/4 Health care providers who are HIV antibody positive should not be barred from working in the NHS.

anticolour ('æntɪkʌlə(r)), *n.* [f. ANTI-[1] 2 d + COLOUR *n.*[1]] The counterpart to a particular colour; *spec.* in *Particle Physics*, a quantized property of antiquarks analogous to the colour of quarks.

1977 *Biofizika 1976* XXI. 758 A colour complementary in all characteristics to the given colour will be nominally called anti-colour. For example, we shall consider as the anti-colour of black the colour white; the anti-colour of a bright red colour being a black-blue-green colour. **1979** *Physical Rev. Lett.* XLIII. 602/2 The question..is whether we expect different characteristics for quark and/or gluon jets if they fragment with limited momentum transverse to the color-anticolor axis rather than to the jet axis as is usually assumed. **1989** H. M. GEORGI in P. Davies *New Physics* xv. 430/2 The antiquark representation can be built out of pairs of states from the quark triplet in a very simple way, by identifying anticolour states with pairs of distinct colour states.

anti-racist (æntɪ'reɪsɪst), *n.* and *a.* Also **antiracist**. [f. ANTI-[1] 7 + RACIST *n.* and *a.*] **A.** *n.* An opponent of racism. **B.** *adj.* Opposing or inhibiting racism.

1938 *New Statesman* 19 Feb. 302/2 On the other hand, he recognises the importance, as anti-racists, of H. J. Muller, Humboldt, [etc.]. **1971** *N.Y. Times* 12 Jan. 6/6 The recent awarding of $200,000..to 19 anti-racist organizations..had some 'negative results'. **1989** *Social Work Today* 23 Nov. 22/3 The above strategy can be utilised for the development of anti-oppressive practice teaching, that is anti-sexist, anti-classist and anti-racist because it addresses *all* power imbalances.

So **anti-'racism** *n.*

1971 *Black Scholar* Jan. 52/1 Blackness, the black author says, despite his antiracism and despite his belief in the potentialities of man, blackness must not disappear. **1993** *Eagle* (Madison, New Jersey) 29 Apr. 4/1 Hentoff argues why should one victim be more precious than the next under the law? 'It's McCarthyism under the benign umbrella of anti-racism,' he argues.

antisense ('æntɪsɛns), *a. Biochem.* and *Genetics.* [f. ANTI-[1] + *SENSE *n.* 29 c.] Designating or pertaining to the strand of duplex DNA that acts as a template for the synthesis of mRNA in a cell; also, designating or pertaining to RNA produced by the transcription of sense DNA, having a complementary base sequence to mRNA and able to bind with it, thereby preventing translation of the latter into protein. Also *absol.* as *n.*

For an antithetical use see note s.v. *SENSE *n.* 29 c.

1977 *Biochem. & Biophys. Res. Communications* LXXV. 602 The synthesis of the 'anti-sense' strand, and its pairing with globin RNA sequences, are processes that will presumably occur in the absence of Hg-substituted precursors. **1979** *Jrnl. Molecular Biol.* CXXXV. 729 A fraction of h22 transcripts from the oocyte must be considered as erroneous since they are derived from the antisense strand of histone DNA whereas in the sea urchin only the sense strand is transcribed. **1988** *Nature* 30 June 801/1 Anti-sense RNA..is complementary to a given messenger RNA

species, with which it pairs, forming double-stranded RNA. **1990** *Food FIPP* Apr. 2/2 Antisense tomatoes are engineered with a gene that significantly reduces the naturally occurring enzyme polygalacturonase. **1991** *Daily Tel.* 27 May 18/5 The scientists inserted an antisense genetic sequence into the chromosomes of fertilised mouse eggs. **1993** W. BAINS *Biotechnol.* 19 Antisense was discovered as the way that some bacteria naturally regulate the activity of some of their genes.

Anton Piller ('æntɒn 'pɪlə(r)), *n. Brit. Law.* [The name of *Anton Piller* K.G., German manufacturers of electric motors.] Used *attrib.* (usu. as *Anton Piller order*) to designate a court order which requires the defendant in proceedings to permit the plaintiff or his legal representatives to enter the defendant's premises in order to obtain evidence essential to the plaintiff's case. Also *absol.*

Named after the case of Anton Piller K.G. v. Manufacturing Processes Ltd., in which such an order was granted in 1975.

1978 *Solicitors' Jrnl.* 5 May 299/1 His lordship [*sc.* Lord Denning] would say that an *Anton Piller* order might be granted against bootleggers as it had against pirates. **1982** *Observer* 17 Oct. 19/1, I was made subject to an Anton Pillar [*sic*] and a Moravia [*sc.* Mareva] **1983** *European Intellect. Property Rev.* Jan. 11/1 It is clear law that a defendant may elect to appeal an *Anton Piller* order rather than apply to the judge who made it for the discharge of the order. **1986** *Observer* 23 Nov. 13/4 An Anton Piller order that would impound every copy of the book and manuscript. **1988** *Computer Weekly* 29 Sept. 40/1 The Anton Piller order has been described as the nuclear weapon in the lawyer's arsenal.

antrectomy (æn'trɛktəmɪ), *n. Surg.* [f. ANTR(UM *n.* + -ECTOMY.] Surgical removal of the walls of an antrum, esp. of the mastoid or pyloric antrum.

1900 DORLAND *Med. Dict.* 56/1 *Antrectomy*, surgical removal of the walls of the mastoid antrum. **1952** N. C. TANNER in F. A. Jones *Mod. Trends Gastro-Enterol.* xvi. 410 It has been recommended..that only a low gastrectomy, a pyloric antrectomy, should be carried out. **1976** *Lancet* 11 Dec. 1303/1 Jordan compared parietal-cell vagotomy with selective vagotomy and antrectomy. **1987** *Oxf. Textbk. Med.* (ed. 2) I. XII. 62/1 Antrectomy in duodenal ulcer patients reduces the acid secretory response to sham feeding.

Antron ('æntrɒn), *n.* [Invented name: cf. NYLON *n.*, etc.] A proprietary name for a type of strong, light nylon fibre used in the manufacture of carpets, upholstery fabrics, etc.; also used of fabrics made from this fibre.

1960 *Trade Marks Jrnl.* 29 June 786/2 *Antron*... Threads and yarns, all of textile material. **1963** *N.Y. Times Mag.* 17 Nov. 12 (Advt.), 'Antron' makes jersey livelier, lovelier—more radiant than ever! **1965** *Guardian* 31 Mar. 9/3 (Advt.), Lingerie and dresses in Antron will be available. **1976** *Northumberland Gaz.* 26 Nov. 2/4 (Advt.), Recoveries...All types of material. Draylons, Meraklons, Antrons, Vinyls. **1990** J. UPDIKE *Rabbit at Rest* ii. 244 Their bedroom in the limestone house has pale-beige Antron broadloom.

antrostomy (æn'trɒstəmɪ), *n. Surg.* [f. ANTR(UM *n.* + -O[1] + -STOMY.] The operation of making an opening into an antrum, esp. an opening from the nose into the maxillary antrum, usu. for the purpose of drainage; also, the opening so made.

1937 THOMSON & NEGUS *Dis. Nose & Throat* (ed. 4) xiv. 234 Intranasal antrostomy...Originally suggested by John Hunter. **1967** R. S. LEWIS et al. *Essent. Otolaryngol.* xx. 210 Caldwell-Luc operation..to make an antrostomy. **1975** *Year Bk. Ear, Nose & Throat*

173 When there is x-ray evidence of maxillary sinusitis, a middle meatal antrostomy is done. **1989** COLLIER & LONGMORE *Oxf. Handbk. Clin. Specialties* (ed. 2) vii. 554 If this fails, perform antrostomy (a drainage hole from antrum to nose).

ANTU ('æntu:), *n. Pharm.* Also **Antu, antu.** [f. initial and other letters of *alpha-naphthylthiourea*, one form of the systematic name.] An anthracene derivative used in powder form as a rodenticide, esp. against the brown rat; 1-(1-naphthyl)-2-thiourea, $C_{11}H_{10}N_2S$.
1945 McCLOSKY & SMITH in *Public Health Rep.* (U.S.) 21 Sept. 1101 Further unpublished investigations..led him to suggest that alphanaphthylthiourea, which for brevity will be referred to as ANTU, might be used advantageously as a rodenticide. **1946** *Infestation Control: Rats & Mice* (Min. of Food) v. 12 Treatments with antu should be done only in consultation with the Ministry. **1966** *McGraw-Hill Encycl. Sci. & Technol.* XI. 615/2 Rodenticides used as contact poisons in the form of dusts include Antu for Norway rats. **1989** *Encycl. Brit.* X. 129/2 Warfarin, 1080.., ANTU.., and red squill are commonly used rodenticides.

anucleate (eɪˈnjuːklɪeɪt), *a. Biol.* [f. A- 14 + NUCLEATE *a.*] Of a cell or cell fragment: having no nucleus.
1909 in WEBSTER. **1953** *Internat. Rev. Cytol.* II. 477 The nucleus lies within the rhizoid. Thus, cutting off the rhizoid produces anucleate parts. **1963** *Exper. Cell Res.* XXXII. 168 The most interesting..result is the fact that anucleate halves respond to parthenogenetic activation in essentially the same way as whole eggs or nucleate halves. **1977** *Jrnl. Protozool.* XXIV. 24/2 In this section we will review some data, unfortunately scarce, concerning the regulatory possibilities of anucleate fragments. **1979** *Sci. Amer.* June 29/2 The anucleate mammalian red blood cell is the only well-known exception.

anucleated (eɪˈnjuːklɪeɪtɪd), *a. Biol.* [f. A- 14 + NUCLEATE *a.* + -ED¹, after ENUCLEATED *ppl.a.*] = *ANUCLEATE a.
1961 in WEBSTER. **1962** D. G. COGAN in A. Pirie *Lens Metabolism Rel. Cataract* 292 The process of lens fibre formation is analogous to keratinization in the skin where the superficial epithelial cells transmute into anucleated, acidophilic, laminated fibres. **1990** *EMBO Jrnl.* IX. 4029/1 A small fraction of the cell population might be anucleated.

anuria, *n.* Add: Hence a'**nuric** *a.*, affected with or accompanied by anuria.
1881 *Syd. Soc. Lex., Anuric,* suffering from deficiency of urine. **1961** *Lancet* 16 Sept. 631/1 Within forty-eight hours he was anuric, and..was therefore transferred to the artificial-kidney unit. **1987** *Nature* 17 Dec. 663/2 With the development of sepsis in controls there was..anuric renal failure.

anxiogenic (æŋksɪəˈdʒɛnɪk), *a. Pharm.* [ad. F. *anxiogène* (M. Martinez-Almoyna 1971, in *Agressologie* XII. 369): see ANXIETY *n.*, -o¹, -GENIC.] Producing a state of anxiety or the physiological effects characteristic of anxiety.
1972 *Biol. Abstr.* LIV. 6588/1 Anxiogenic reflexes of the upper respiratory tract and anesthesiological training. **1978** *Jrnl. Pharmacy & Pharmacol.* XXX. 109/2 The results would be consistent with the interpretation that ACTH has an anxiogenic action. **1983** *Pharmacol., Biochem. & Behavior* XIX. 412/2 We cannot exclude a selective involvement of each bundle in novel situations which are more or less 'anxiogenic'. **1987** S. M. STAHL et al. *Cognitive Neurochem.* x. 183 Anxiogenic stimuli increase noradrenergic activity.., an effect that is blocked by administration of anti-anxiety drugs.

anyon ('ɛnɪɒn), *n. Particle Physics.* [f. ANY *a.* and *pron.* + -ON¹.] A particle having characteristics intermediate between those of fermions and bosons in two-dimensional space.
1982 F. WILCZEK in *Physical Rev. Lett.* XLIX. 957/1 Since interchange of two of these particles can give *any* phase, I will call them generically anyons. **1986** *Physics Lett. B* CLXXX. 384 Thus Boltzmann statistics does not lie on the anyon interpolation between Fermi and Bose statistics. **1989** *Sci. Amer.* May 18/1 Because anyons exist on two-dimensional surfaces, they are believed to be important in such widely studied phenomena as the quantum Hall effect and high-temperature superconductivity.

Apgar ('æpgə), *n. Med.* [The name of Virginia *Apgar* (1909-74), U.S. anaesthesiologist, who proposed this method of assessment in 1953 (*Current Res. Anesthesia & Analgesia* XXXII. 267).] **Apgar score**, a measure of the physical condition of a newborn infant, obtained by adding points (2, 1, or 0) given for heart rate, respiratory effort, muscle tone, response to stimulation, and skin coloration, a score of ten representing the best possible condition.
[**1959** *Ann. Paediatriae Fenniae* V. 32 Apgar's method of evaluation of the newborn infant was tested when the assessment was made by various persons.] **1964** *Obstetr. & Gynecol.* XXIV. 222 The Apgar score observations are made by trained personnel. **1968** *Jrnl. Pediatrics* LXXIII. 607/1 At birth, the infant was in distress, with an Apgar score of 6. **1988** R. O. PLATT *Letting Blood* ii. 14 She cried when Baby Boy's Apgar score was only 9 instead of the perfect 10 she'd hoped for.

apicectomy (eɪpɪˈsɛktəmɪ), *n. Dentistry.* Also †**apicoectomy** (eɪpɪkəʊˈɛktəmɪ). [f. L. *apic-* (see APEX *n.*¹) or APICO- + -ECTOMY.] Excision of the apical portion of the root of a tooth.
1914 *Items of Interest* XXXVI. 652 *(heading)* Apiocoectomy [*sic*]. **1915** *Dental Cosmos* LVII. 473/1 Apicoectomy.—Root amputation, in the treatment of dento-alveolar abscesses, is an operation of necessity and not of choice. **1931** COLYER & SPRAWSON *Dental Surg. & Pathol.* (ed. 6) xiv. 397 The operation of apicectomy has been devised for the sterilisation of the apical area. **1963** C. R. COWELL et al. *Inlays, Crowns & Bridges* viii. 85 A radiograph may reveal evidence of a periapical condition which necessitates an apicectomy. **1982** *Macmillan Guide Family Health* iii. 439 *(caption)* Occasionally a dentist will perform an apicectomy. This is a small operation by which the infected tissue at the base of the tooth is removed.

appraisee (əpreɪˈziː, əˈpreɪziː), *n.* orig. *U.S.* [f. APPRAISE *v.* + -EE¹.] An employee who receives a formal appraisal or assessment of performance, progress, etc. Cf. *APPRAISAL n.* 2.
1963 *Performance Appraisals* (Found. for Res. on Human Behavior) ii. 5 The subsequent discussion concerns ways to improve the appraisee's performance in his organizational role. **1980** *Washington Post* 7 May c3/1 Guests included congressmen and chemical industry people, as well as the appraiser, namely Barbara Muller... The appraisee, meanwhile, just kept signing pictures of himself. **1984** A. LEIGH *20 Ways to manage Better* 31 Use open ended questions to get the appraisee talking and where appropriate use silence to prompt more response. **1987** *Fortune* 12 Oct. 239/1 If compelled to go through the exercise, they tend to do so with bad grace, confusing the poor appraisee. **1991** in *Times Educ. Suppl.* 11 Jan. 30/4 Interviews appeared to be facilitated when both appraisers and appraisees had had training relating to the interview.

Aqua Libra (ˌækwə ˈliːbrə), *n.* [f. L. *aqua* water + *libra* scales, balance.

So named because the drink is promoted as an aid to good digestion and alkaline balance.]

A proprietary name for a soft drink based on a mixture of mineral water and fruit juices with various herbal and other natural flavourings.

1987 *Trade Marks Jrnl.* 18 Feb. 351/1 Aqua Libra...Non-alcoholic drinks...26 July 1986. **1988** *Financial Times* 31 Dec. (Weekend Suppl.) p. ix/2 Aqua Libra which is completely free of alcohol and I like because it is not as sweet as, say Perrier and orange-juice. **1989** *Forbes* (N.Y.) 25 Dec. 48/1 The smart set in England this season is drinking Aqua Libra. The pale-gold beverage is a blend of sparkling water, passion fruit juice and apple juice, seasoned with sesame, sunflower, melon, tarragon and Siberian ginseng. **1990** *Washington Post* 18 July E3/2 Aqua Libra, described by its makers as the 'champagne for the healthy'.

arachniphobia (ə,ræknɪˈfəʊbɪə), *n. rare.* [f. Gr. ἀράχνη spider + -ɪ- + -PHOBIA.] = *ARACHNOPHOBIA n.

1966 *New Statesman* 30 Sept. 471/1 What ails me..is acute arachniphobia.

Hence a'**rachniphobe** *a.*, afraid of spiders.

1984 *Nature* 5 Jan. 8/3 Last Christmas I bought my arachniphobe family a simple device called a 'Spider Scoop'.

arachnophobia (ə,ræknəʊˈfəʊbɪə), *n.* [f. Gr. ἀράχνη spider + -o[1] + -PHOBIA.] Irrational fear of spiders.

1925 *Blackw. Mag.* Aug. 198/1 The gift was hardly in the category of apes, ivory, and peacocks. Still, as an antidote to nightmare, especially in the form of arachnophobia, I have no doubt it proved 'a sovran remedie'. **1983** *Listener* 11 Aug. 33/2 Luis even made strenuous efforts to overcome his arachnophobia, since it unbalanced his otherwise even-handed view of creation. **1990** *Independent* 16 Jan. 15/6 Mrs Guy lived with arachnophobia from childhood, but it grew worse when her last daughter married and left home.

So a'**rachnophobe** *n.*, a person who is frightened of spiders.

1925 *Blackw. Mag.* Aug. 197/2 Solomon presented the bottle to the Queen of Sheba, or his little Arachnophobe, as he called her. 'Take it home with you,' he said; 'then you won't dream about spiders any more.' **1989** *Daily Tel.* 30 Mar. 19/3 Spiders in the bath need no longer terrify arachnophobes, thanks to a newly invented miniature ladder which allows the insects to clamber to safety over the slippery enamel.

arcology (ɑːˈkɒlədʒɪ), *n.* [Blend of ARCHITECTURE *n.* + ECOLOGY *n.*] **a.** A style of urban planning, orig. proposed by the Italian-born U.S. architect Paolo Soleri (b. 1919), which envisages fully integrated cities, each contained within a massive vertical structure, thereby allowing maximum conservation of the surrounding environment. **b.** A city built on these principles.

1969 P. SOLERI (*title*) Arcology: the city in the image of man. *Ibid.* 31/1 Architecture is in the process of becoming the physical definition of a multilevel, human ecology. It will be arc-ology. Arcology..will be an aesthetocompassionate phenomenon. **1971** *UNESCO Courier* Apr. 7 Soleri calls his style 'arcology', a word coined from the marriage of 'architecture' and 'ecology'. **1985** G. KENDALL *White Wing* (1986) x. 130 He remembered their street in the arcology on Nahi II, the hard-packed dirt just outside the complex where nothing ever grew. **1988** B. STERLING *Islands in Net* v. 178 They're making massive arcologies out of nothing!

Arctic, *a.* and *n.* Add: [A.] [1.] [c.] **Arctic char** [CHAR *n.*[3]], a small trout, *Salvelinus alpinus*, of Arctic waters and northern lakes, much prized as a food fish.

1928 *Funk's Stand. Dict.* s.v. *Char,* The *Arctic char (*S. arcturus*). **1937** E. SHACKLETON *Arctic Journeys* 289, I went to look at a little stream and saw many Arctic charr cruising about at the mouth. **1969** H. HORWOOD *Newfoundland* vii. 47 There are lake trout, pike and arctic char, all plentiful and all in trophy sizes. **1986** B. LOPEZ *Arctic Dreams* ii. 45 The lower jaw of an arctic char, eaten a hundred years ago, still glistens with fish oil.

argument, *n.* Add: [2.] **b.** *Math.* and *Computing.* An independent variable of a function (e.g. x and y in $z = f(x, y)$).

1865 BRANDE & COX *Dict. Sci., Lit., & Art* I. 768 Any trigonometrical function of ϕ is termed an *elliptic function*, having the *argument u* and *modulus k.* **1879** *Encycl. Brit.* IX. 818/1 In each case *u* is the independent variable or argument of the function. **1946** *Nature* 12 Oct. 503/2 The ENIAC has three function tables.., each of which comprises an array of switches on which 6-figure values of two functions, with signs, or a 12-figure value of one function, can be set up for each of 104 values of an argument. **1974** A. V. AHO et al. *Design & Anal. Computer Algorithms* i. 37 After a function procedure has been defined, it can be invoked in an expression by using its name with the desired arguments. **1984** *Computerworld* 5 Mar. 54 Use of Boolean commands to connect a segment search argument with the next argument list in the..search field list.

Arjan *n.*, var. *ARJUN *n.*

arjoon *n.*, obs. var. *ARJUN *n.*

arjun ('ɑːdʒʌn, -dʒuːn), *n. Bot.* Also **arjan,** †**arjoon.** [Hindi *arjun,* f. Skr. *arjuna.*] An evergreen tree of southern India and Sri Lanka, *Terminalia arjuna* (family Combretaceae); = KUMBUK *n.*

1862 E. BALFOUR *Timber Trees India* (ed. 2) 249/1 In Nagpore, the timber of Arjoon is of a deeper red than Bejasar. **1880** V. BALL *Jungle Life in India* viii. 312 Another insect..forms..a white wax, which is found in small masses on the twigs and branches of several trees, more particularly on the arjun. **1955** *Nomencl. Commercial Timbers* (*B.S.I.*) 84 *Terminalia arjuna* Bedd...arjun (India). **1992** N. BHATTACHARYA *Hem & Football* i. 3 Shibu, the smart, trousers-and-T-shirt-clad young barber..had recently set up his shop under an arjun tree in the bazaar outside the colony.

artillery, *n.* Add: [8.] **artillery plant,** a tropical American plant, *Pilea microphylla*, of the nettle family, whose mature anthers throw out clouds of pollen and which is a popular house plant.

1878 E. A. JOHNSON *Winter Greeneries at Home* iii. 41 Pilea (*Artillery-plant). **1941** F. BALTHIS *Plants in Home* xviii. 134/1 Artillery plant (Pilea microphylla)...Grown for the fernlike foliage as pot plants. **1956** X. FIELD *Housewife Bk. House Plants* III. 81 *P. microphylla*, or *muscosa*, is the dwarf of the family. The pilea is known as the artillery plant because the pollen from the flowers appears to explode as it is discharged.

-ary, *suffix*[1]. Add: [A.] **2.** Chiefly *Math.* and *Logic.* [f. *-ary* in *unary, binary, ternary,* etc.] Used with a preceding symbol (usu. *n*) to designate a function, operator, etc., having the number of arguments represented by the symbol. Cf. ARITY *n.*, *-ADIC 2.

1940 E. T. BELL *Devel. Math.* xx. 401 An *m*-ary *n*-ic..is a homogeneous polynomial, with arbitrary constant coefficients, of degree *n* in *m* independent variables. **1964** J. J. KATZ in Fodor & Katz *Struct. of Lang.* 526 The amalgam is assigned to the set of paths associated with the node (i.e., the point at which an *n*-ary branching occurs). **1968** P. M. POSTAL *Aspects Phonol. Theory* iv. 65 A priori, there are two fundamentally different types of relation which could obtain for a particular binary phonological feature F_i and its n-ary (N>2) phonetic correspondent... Suppose that the phonetic feature is 3-ary. **1985** *Computer Jrnl.* XXVIII. 105/1 The present paper also generalises the formulation of the consistent labelling problem as an N-ary constraint satisfaction problem.

assisted, *ppl. a.* Add: **2.** Special collocation: **assisted suicide**, suicide effected with the assistance of another person; *esp.* the taking of lethal drugs, provided by a doctor for the purpose, by a patient considered to be incurable.
1976 *Internat. Jrnl. Health Services* VI. 329 If the Swiss can trust themselves with a law to permit *assisted suicide, it should not be beyond our civic courage to follow their lead. **1981** WALLACE & ESER *Suicide & Euthanasia* 87 The relationship between suicide and euthanasia becomes clear: euthanasia is assisted suicide. **1992** *Via Media/Episcopal Life* Jan. 28/2 Suicide and assisted suicide are two of those exits that ultimately must be viewed with mercy by God.

astro-, *comb. form.* Add: ˌastro-archae'ologist *n.*, an expert in or student of astro-archaeology.
1981 *Sci. Amer.* Oct. 38/1 An Amherst physicist turned *astroarchaeologist.
ˌastro-archae'ology *n.* = ARCHAEOASTRONOMY *n.*
1965 G. S. HAWKINS *Stonehenge Decoded* viii. 121 If any university or foundation is casting about for promising fields of exploration and research, let it consider *astro-archaeology! **1976** *Publishers Weekly* 30 Aug. 330/2 The burgeoning study of astro-archaeology. **1981** G. DANIEL *Short Hist. Archaeol.* v. 196 Von Däniken.. has added astronaut archaeology to the already dubious semi-scholarship of astro-archaeology.

atenolol (əˈtɛnəlɒl), *n. Pharm.* [f. *aten-* (perh. f. A(NGINA *n.* + TEN(SION *n.*) + *-OLOL.] A beta-blocker which is selective for cardiac receptors, and is given orally in the treatment of angina and hypertension; 4-(2-hydroxy-3-isopropyl-aminopropoxy)phenylacetamide, $C_{14}H_{22}N_2O_3$.
1974 *Approved Names 1973* (Brit. Pharmacopœia Comm.) Suppl. III, Atenolol. **1977** *Lancet* 16 Apr. 843/1 Propranolol, which is non-selective, delays the rise in blood-glucose after insulin-induced hypoglycæmia, unlike atenolol which has no such effect. **1986** C. W. THORNBER in C. A. Heaton *Chem. Industry* iv. 183 A second generation of β-adrenergic antagonists characterized by atenolol..and metoprolol..have preferential affinity for the heart receptors. **1991** *Which?* Nov. 647 (*caption*) Tenormin, and its generic equivalent atenolol, is often prescribed to lower blood pressure.

Attila (əˈtɪlə, ˈætɪlə), *n.* [mod.L. (adopted as a genus name in Fr. in R. P. Lesson *Traité d'Ornithol.* (1831) I. 360), a. the name of *Attila* (*c* 406–53), king of the Huns.] A genus of tropical American flycatchers (family Tyrannidae) characterized by a large hooked bill; (also **attila**) a bird of this genus.
1907 R. RIDGWAY *Birds N. & Middle Amer.* IV. 804 (*heading*) Gray-headed attila. **1951** G. M. SUTTON *Mexican Birds* 227/2 The last, sometimes called the Polymorphic Attila (8 inches), varies from olive to rufous above and from white to yellow below, but always has a yellow rump and gray streaking on the chest. **1970** R. MEYER DE SCHAUENSEE *Guide Birds S. Amer.* 296/1 Bright-rumped attila... Differs from other attilas.. by contrasting bright yellow to tawny buff rump and upper tail coverts.

attitude, *n.* Sense 6 in Dict. becomes sense 7. Add: **6. a.** Aggressive or uncooperative behaviour; a resentful or antagonistic manner. In phrs. *to cop an attitude, to give attitude*, etc., to assume such a manner. *slang* (orig. *U.S.*).
[**1962** MAURER & VOGEL *Narcotics & Narcotic Addiction* (ed. 2) 289/2 (Gloss.) *Attitude*, hostile or aloof and uncooperative. **1974** H. L. FOSTER *Ribbin'* iv. 169 *Attitude*, to get mad without a good reason.] **1975** WENTWORTH & FLEXNER *Dict. Amer. Slang* Suppl. 673/2 *Attitude*,..a resentful, hostile manner, either toward people in general or toward a specific group. A person who 'catches a quick attitude' is one who is easily angered and ready to fight. Mostly black and prison use. **1980** *Washington Post* 20 July H3/3 If they wanted to give me 'attitude' about being white, they really could–I'm the token minority in this cast. But the whole company has been really nice. **1982** A. MAUPIN *Further Tales of City* 131 No one could resist the urge to clap along...'I like this,' Michael told Bill. 'Everybody's off guard. It's harder to give attitude.' **1985** *Sunday Times* (Colour Suppl.) 23 June 13/1, I can't believe this restaurant. I ask the waiter for a clean fork and all I get is attitude. **1985** *N.Y. Times* 26 Oct. 31/1 If I'm out there for months with everybody yelling at me, I'm going to cop an attitude. **1990** LANE & ANDREWS *Malibu 90265* ii. 18 No wonder the saleswoman had an attitude...A zero had just dropped off the end of her commission. **1991** *Athlon's Baseball '91* IV. 25/1 Bonds developed what is called an attitude. Underneath it all he is a nice kid.
b. Hence, any highly independent or individual outlook, approach, appearance, etc.; self-possession; style, swagger, front; esp. in *with (an) attitude. slang* (orig. *U.S.*).
1975 *Rolling Stone* 24 Apr. 52/1 Natty dreadlocks means hair with an attitude: kinky, jungle thick and matted into tortuous antibraids. **1986** 'PRINCE' *Kiss* (song) 6 You don't have 2 watch Dy-nas-ty 2 have an attitude. **1988** *Tower Records' Top* Feb. 20/4 You got to go at the business with an attitude or you get nowhere. **1990** *Police Rev.* 28 Sept. 1916/1 In this job, you gotta have attitude, hang loose, ready for anything. **1992** *Face* Feb. 44/1 The not-entirely-unattractive cast – spearheaded by Jason Priestley and Luke Perry as hunks with not much attitude Brandon and Dylan – set a good few pulses racing and hogged the covers of the nation's teen press.
[7.] *attitude problem.*
1977 *Washington Post* 3 Aug. D3/2 No one will argue with Anderson about early *attitude problems. But Rawly Eastwick.. says there's more to it than that. **1992** *Spy* Mar. 55 The more cozily bourgeois a culture becomes, the more its citizenry admires the wary iconoclast, the individual with an 'attitude problem', the bad boy.

attractor, *n.* Add: **3.** *Math.* A point or set of points in phase space which represents the state or states towards which a dynamic system evolves with time.
1960 P. MENDELSON in *Boletin de la Sociedad Matematica Mexicana* V. 274 We have shown thus far that an unstable attractor (and by that is meant a critical point having properties (3.1)) must satisfy the following necessary conditions. **1969** R. THOMIN *Topology* VIII. 316 If this point q is such that the trajectory of any point near q goes to q, and no trajectory leaves q, we shall say that q is an attractor of the system. **1976** *Sci. Amer.* Apr. 75/1 An energy minimum in a physical system..is a special instance of a concept called an attractor. In this case it is the simplest kind of attractor, a single stable state. **1987** *Internat. Jrnl. Non-Linear Mech.* XXII. 351 If the attractor is composed of a closed, invariant set of $fλ$, containing infinitely many unstable periodic groups, then chaotic motion occurs. **1989** G. NICOLIS in P. Davies *New Physics* xi. 331/1 The state of equilibrium is a universal point attractor.

audio-animatronic (ˌɔːdɪəʊænɪməˈtrɒnɪk), *a.* and *n.* orig. *U.S.* Also as one word, and with upper-case initial(s). [f. AUDIO- + ANIMA(TED *ppl. a.* + ELEC)TRONIC *a.*] **A.** *adj.* Of, pertaining to, or designating a technique of constructing robot models in accurate likenesses of humans, animals, etc., which are programmed to perform intricate, lifelike bodily movements in synchronization with a pre-recorded soundtrack.

A proprietary name in the U.K.

1963 *New Yorker* 7 Sept. 108/2 Pretty soon, Walt's going to add onto the Tahitian thing a place called the 'Enchanted Tiki Room'.. which will be full of tikis and of what he calls 'audioanimatronic' talking birds and flowers. **1978** *Trade Marks Jrnl.* 8 Feb. 244/1 *Audio-Animatronic*, .. Electronic apparatus for animating model figures and for use in synchronisation with soundtracks. **1978** *Washington Post* 10 Feb. F1/2 The.. story of the American people.. will be 'brought to life' by audio-animatronic versions of Ben Franklin, Mark Twain and Will Rogers who also will present a message of 'optimism for the future'. **1986** W. WEAVER tr. *Eco's Trav. in Hyperreality* i. 45 The 'Audio-Animatronic' technique represented a great source of pride for Walt Disney, who had finally managed to achieve his own dream and reconstruct a fantasy world more real than reality.

B. *n. pl.* (const. as *sing.*). Usu. as **Audio-Animatronics**. The technique of constructing animatronic models. Cf. *ANIMATRONICS *n. pl.*

A proprietary name in the U.S.

1965 *Pop. Electronics* July 81/1 'Audioanimatronics'. This is the jaw-breaking name given to Walt Disney's fantastic creatures that perform.. at the fair. **1967** *Official Gaz.* (U.S. Patent Office) 14 Feb. TM78 Wed Enterprises, Inc., Glendale, Calif... Filed Apr. 23, 1964. *Audio-Animatronics*... First use on about July 1, 1961. **1972** *Times* 14 Oct. 16/6 Realistic sound and motion is provided by a system known as 'audio-animatronics', a.. mixture of electronics, hydraulics and pneumatics. **1979** *Business Week* (Industr. ed.) 26 Mar. 114/3 A presentation on nutrition delivered by jumbo-size vegetables that move and talk via Disney's Audio-Animatronics technology. **1986** *Financial Times* 12 Apr. (Weekend Suppl.) p. xvii/1 Life-size humanoid puppets who — thanks to 'Audio-Animatronics' — talk, walk, gesture, and grimace indistinguishably from the real thing. **1992** *Time* 20 Apr. 83/3 In the dungeon of Sleeping Beauty's Castle.. reposes a fabulous Audio-Animatronics dragon that snorts steam, flashes its stoplight eyes and bares claws.

So **audio-'animatron** *n.*, a robot of this kind; also **audio-anima'tronically** *adv.*

1967 *National Observer* (U.S.) 3 July 1 Unyielding critics say that Bill Roberts and Stu Spencer 'made' Ronald Reagan and that he is hardly more than an audio-animatron like Abe Lincoln at Disneyland. **1973** *Time* 16 Apr. 75/2 Young Hermie — played audioanimatronically by Gargy Grimes. **1982** *Christian Science Monitor* 21 July 3/2 Disney artists.. demonstrate their latest in 'audio-animatrons', life-size human figures that talk and move.

auto-, *comb. form*[1]. Add: [b.] 'auto-fade, a facility on some video cameras for fading sequences in or out automatically during filming.

[**1983** L. LANGMAN *Video Encycl.* 10 *Automatic Fade Control*, a video camera feature designed to provide fade-outs at the end of scenes and fade-ins at the openings.] **1986** *What Video?* Dec. 47/1 Your machine [*sc.* a camcorder] may have a fade facility as standard. *Auto-fades usually come in fade-to-white and fade-to-black guises. **1990** *PIC* July 60/2 When I am out behind one of my trusty Canons peering through the small rectangular window, nothing else matters save the image in my viewfinder, and then the most monumental problem will disappear as if on autofade.

autogenic, *a.* Add: **2.** *autogenic training* [tr. G. *autogene* (coined in J. H. Schultz *Das autogene*

Training (1932))], a method of learning to induce physiological changes in the body by exercises aimed at inducing a hypnotic state in oneself, esp. as a way of reducing stress or achieving relaxation; any similar technique involving biofeedback.

1954 J. H. SCHULTZ in *Brit. Jrnl. Med. Hypnotism* V. III. 23/1 The fundamental discoveries of Freud and his followers changed the whole field of our working and thinking. Therefore other methods, for instance, hypnosis, or autogenic training, its legitimate offspring, were not given a fair hearing. **1973** *Psychosomatic Med.* XXXV. 130/1 Autogenic training.. involves the simultaneous regulation of mental and somatic functions. **1979** *Sunday Mail* (Brisbane) 29 Apr. 30/4 The Westernised form of yoga known as autogenic training. **1990** *Observer* 6 May 21/2 Liz Ferris uses autogenic training with athletes.

Hence **auto'genics** *n. pl.* (const. as *sing.*), (the study or use of) the system of techniques acquired through autogenic training.

1981 *New Scientist* 5 Nov. 369/1 Adherents of biofeedback, meditation, autogenics and other programmes of behavioural change. **1983** INGLIS & WEST *Alternative Health Guide* 178 Dr. Malcolm Carruthers.. brought autogenics to Britain from Canada in the 1970s. **1985** *She* July 115/1 A new study indicates that autogenics — a form of mental press-ups — are as good for reducing stress.. as physical exertions.

automaton, *n.* Sense 6 in Dict. becomes 7. Add: **6.** *Computing.* A (real or imaginary) machine whose responses to all permissible inputs are specified by a set of states and a set of rules for passing from one state to another.

1951 J. VON NEUMANN in L. A. Jeffress *Cerebral Mechanisms in Behavior* 15 We are very far from possessing a theory of automata which deserves that name, that is, a properly mathematical-logical theory. **1953** *Proc. IRE* XLI. 1234/1 This paper reviews briefly some of the recent developments in the field of automata and nonnumerical computation. **1961** *Adv. Computers* II. 380 It is necessary to begin with some sort of definition of 'automaton'... An automaton is a device of finite size at any time with certain parts specified as inputs and outputs, such that what happens at the outputs at any time is determined, or at least its probability distribution function is determined, by what has happened at the inputs. **1966** M. GROSS in *Automatic Transl. of Lang.* (NATO Summer School, Venice, 1962) 130 This non-deterministic automaton is equivalent to a recognition routine that would look for one 'most probable' solution. **1974** *Encycl. Brit. Macropædia* II. 498/2 The class of general automata includes all-purpose, electronic digital computers the memory-storage units of which are of fixed.. size.

[**7.**] **automata theory** *Computing*, the study of formalized automata (in sense *6 above).

1964 *Information & Control* VII. 485 (*title*) Pair algebra and its application to *automata theory. **1974** *Encycl. Brit. Macropædia* II. 497/2 Original work on the neurophysiological aspect of automata theory was done by Warren S. McCulloch and Walter Pitts at the Research Laboratory of Electronics at the Massachusetts Institute of Technology starting in the 1940s.

autumn, *n.* Add: [**3.**] [c.] **autumn crocus**, (*a*) *Bot.* an autumn-flowering crocus of south-west Europe, *Crocus nudiflorus*, with flowers appearing before the leaves, which is naturalized locally in England; (*b*) any of various crocus-like autumn-flowering plants of the genus *Colchicum*, of the lily family; *esp.* meadow saffron, *C. autumnale*.

1822 J. C. LOUDON *Encycl. Gardening* III. 954 Many botanists.. consider that there is only two species, the

C. vernus, or spring-blowing crocus; and the *C. sativus*, the saffron, or *autumn crocus. **1854** S. THOMSON *Wanderings among Wild Flowers* III. 261 We..turn to..the pretty autumn crocus, or meadow saffron (*Colchicum autumnale*). **1899** *Halifax Naturalist* IV. 21 The Autumn Crocus..ought to be of exceptional interest to anyone studying our local flora...It has been..confused with..the meadow saffron, *Colchicum autumnale*, and the saffron crocus, *C. sativus*. **1956** *Dict. Gardening* (R. Hort. Soc.) (ed. 2) II. 522/2 The similarity of the flowers and the habit of several species of producing them in autumn has gained the name of Autumn Crocuses for several [colchicums], and our own native *C. autumnale* has..been called Meadow Saffron. **1960** *Oxf. Bk. Wild Flowers* 162/1 Autumn Crocus (*Crocus nudiflorus*, family *Iridaceae*). Like Meadow Saffron, this species also flowers in the autumn after the leaves have died down. **1963** R. C. L. & B. M. HOWITT *Flora Notts.* 11 The Spring and Autumn Crocuses..are now nearly extinct. **1985** *Gardening from 'Which?'* Aug. 270/2 Colchicums (often wrongly called autumn crocus) produce large crocus-like blooms between September and November.

B

B. Add: [III.] [1.] **BCD**, binary coded decimal.
1959 E. M. McCormick *Digital Computer Primer* iv. 49 An important characteristic of any *bcd system is the ability to form the nines complement of the digit. **1963** B. W. Arden *Introd. Digital Computing* xviii. 341 Six BCD characters can be stored in an IBM 7090 computer word. **1980** C. S. French *Computer Sci.* xix. 103 BCD addition is longer than Pure Binary addition.

BLT *colloq.* (orig. *U. S.*), bacon, lettuce, and tomato (sandwich).
[**1941** J. Smiley *Hash House Lingo* 13 *B.M.T.* [*sic*], bacon, lettuce and tomato sandwich.] **1952** *Amer. Speech* XXVII. 231 The following items were collected..during the summer of 1949...*B.L.T. Bacon, lettuce, and tomato. **1989** *US Air* Sept. 75/2 He eats at his desk every day, sometimes dining on such delicacies as a hot dog or a BLT.

BNF *Computing*, Backus-Naur (formerly Backus normal) form.
1964 *Proc. AFIPS Conf.* XXV. 61/2 The syntax of the source language is described in a language called *BNF (to suggest 'Backus normal form', denoted B.n.f.). BNF looks much like B.n.f. **1966** *Nordisk Tidskr. Informations-Behandling* VI. 302 The language is a finite ordered set of production-rules, written in Backus Normal Form (BNF). **1987** B. J. MacLennan *Princ. Programming Languages* (ed. 2) iv. 159 The decision to use the BNF notation in the Algol-60 Report resulted from Peter Naur's realization that his understanding of the Algol-58 description did not agree with that of John Backus.

BSE, bovine spongiform encephalopathy.
1987 *Economist* 14 Nov. 92/3 Bovine spongiform encephalopathy (*BSE) twists the tongues of vets and wrecks the brains of cows. **1988** *Vet. Rec.* 6 Feb. 142/1 It is unlikely that bovine spongiform encephalopathy (BSE) is caused by hexachlorophene poisoning. **1993** *Guardian* 30 Oct. 8/8 If man is susceptible to BSE, then at least 8 million adults are likely to have eaten enough to get Creutzfeld-Jakob disease. **1996** *Daily Tel.* 25 Mar. 1 The farming and meat processing industries [are] facing a financial disaster of unprecedented proportions following the warning of a possible link with a human strain of BSE.

-babble ('bæb(ə)l), *comb. form. colloq.* (orig. *U. S.*). [f. BABBLE *n.* after *psychobabble* n. s.v. PSYCHO-, etc.] Used as the second element in combinations denoting various types of confusing or pretentious jargon, esp. that characteristic of a specified field or group. See also *Eurobabble* s.v. *EURO- 2 a; *technobabble* s.v. *TECHNO-.
1988 *Jrnl. Design Hist.* I. 137/1 Pure reversal emerges in design terms as the pseudo-babble of the cult of kitsch, the pursuit of the quaint. **1989** *Los Angeles Times* 2 Apr. 106/5 There is marvelous chutzpah in this essentially conservative art... It reads as an icon of the American West, an impersonal symbol of sterility and renewal... What kind of art-babble is that? **1990** *Ibid.* 1 Feb. E. 1/5 Is the environmental hoopla resonating through the halls of American business 'mere corporate ecobabble intended to placate the latest group of special-interest loonies?' **1990** *Artnews* Apr. 62/2 Their facades..is a remarkable condensation of psycho-babble and docent-babble. They simply psychologize their way through his life. **1991** C. Paglia in *Arion* Spring 150 Sometimes a penis is not a penis. A phallus, in Francobabble, is just a power tool. **1992** Dominguez & Robin *Your Money or your Life* ix. 293 If.. [they] can't agree among themselves, why should

you confuse yourself with trying to understand their econobabble?

backplane ('bækpleɪn), *n. Electronics.* [f. BACK *n.*[1] + PLANE *n.*[3]] A board to which the main circuit boards of a device may be connected and which provides interconnections between them; a motherboard. Freq. *attrib.*
1972 D. Lewin *Theory & Design Digital Computers* viii. 278 The same routing techniques may also be used to produce the card layout and wiring pattern for the panels in the main frame cabinets (called the backplane wiring). **1979** *Personal Computer World* 3 Nov. 48/3 Inspection showed that not all of the PC boards are attached to the backplane of the computer. **1990** *Industry Week* 7 May 46/3 Optical interconnects reduced the backplane wiring in its 16,000-processor Connection Machine from more than 1,000 wires to just two fiber cables. **1992** *Byte* Sept. 171/2 Other researchers are investigating the practicality of different kinds of board configurations that would replace the traditional backplane.

Backus–Naur ('bækəs‚naʊə(r)), *n. Computing.* [The names of John W. *Backus* (b. 1924), U.S. computer scientist, who first proposed the notation (*Information Processing* (Proc. Internat. Conf. Information Processing, UNESCO, 1959) ii.125), and Peter *Naur*, 20th-cent. computer scientist, who revised it (*Communications Assoc. Computing Machinery* (1960) III. 299).] **Backus–Naur form** (formerly *Backus normal form*), a mode of formally describing the syntax of programming languages using a special notation; abbrev. *BNF* s.v. B III. 1.
[**1961** *Communications Assoc. Computing Machinery* IV. 534/2 We now present a mechanical language designed for generative syntactic specification of digital linear sequential mechanical languages. Its use is called 'specification by Backus normal form', because John Backus of IBM introduced it.] **1964** D. E. Knuth in *Ibid.* VII. 736/1 Actually, however, only (i) and (ii) were really used by John Backus when he proposed his notation; (iii), (iv), (v) are due to Peter Naur who incorporated these changes when drafting the ALGOL 60 report...Therefore I propose that henceforth we always say *Backus Naur form* instead of Backus Normal Form, when referring to such a syntax. **1967** *Computer Group News* Jan. 6/2 Programming syntax is commonly described in a notation called Backus-Naur Form (or BNF for short). **1989** *Encycl. Brit.* XVI. 634/1 The most widely used language for syntax description is the Backus-Naur form.

bacterio- (bæk'tɪərɪəʊ-), *comb. form.* [f. BACTERI(UM *n.* + -O[1].] Forming terms (chiefly ns. and adjs.) to do with bacteria, as BACTERIOCIDAL *a.*, BACTERIOPHAGE *n.*, *BACTERIORHODOPSIN *n.*
Where the second element begins with a vowel (as in BACTERAEMIA *n.*, BACTERIURIA *n.*), the word can be regarded as directly f. BACTERIUM *n.*

bacteriophobia (bæk‚tɪərɪəʊ'fəʊbɪə), *n.* [f. *BACTERIO- + -PHOBIA.] Irrational fear or dislike of bacteria.
1894 *Lancet* 3 Nov. 1072/2 Some of your readers will accuse me of bacteriophobia. **1976** *Times* 7 Apr. 16/5

Some said his bacteriophobia allowed him no contact with the 'diseased' outside world.

bacteriorhodopsin (bækˌtɪərɪəʊrəʊˈdɒpsɪn), *n. Biochem.* [f. *BACTERIO-* + RHODOPSIN *n.*] A protein present in the purple membrane of some strains of the bacterium *Halobacterium halobium*, which when illuminated mediates the transport of protons across the membrane in large numbers.

1971 OESTERHELT & STOECKENIUS in *Nature New Biol.* 29 Sept. 152/1 We suggest that the purple membrane may function as a photoreceptor and propose the name bacteriorhodopsin for the purple membrane protein. **1975** *Nature* 20 Mar. 178/2 The three proteins retinochrome, bacteriorhodopsin, and rhodopsin provide an opportunity for comparative studies of the part played by a protein in directing the course of a photochemical reaction. **1984** HOLTZMAN & NOVIKOFF *Cells & Organelles* (ed. 3) III. ii. 329 Each bacteriorhodopsin molecule can pump several hundred protons per second. **1992** *New Scientist* 25 Jan. 30/1 The protein, called bacteriorhodopsin, is similar to the protein rhodopsin, which detects light in a real retina.

badass ('bædæs), *n.* and *a. slang.* (orig. and chiefly *U.S.*). Also **bad-ass**. [f. BAD *a.* + ASS *n.*²] A. *n.* A tough, aggressive, or uncooperative person; a trouble-maker.

1956 *Amer. Speech* XXXI. 191 A marine who postures toughness is sarcastically labeled a *badass*. **1969** D. WIEBE *Skyblue the Badass* vi. 105 By the way, Mr. Badass, it's great of you to come out to our party. Faculty members usually don't come over here to talk to us. **1985** *Chicago Tribune* 11 Nov. v. 3/1, I've been impressed with him since the first time I saw him fight. He's a real badass. **1992** J. & M. STERN *Encycl. Pop Culture* 209/2 The Hell's Angels have become the definitive badasses of the road.

B. *attrib.* or as *adj.* Belligerent or intimidating; tough; bad, nasty. Also used approvingly: formidable, terrific, superlative (cf. BAD *a.* I. 4 b.).

Sometimes acting merely as an intensifier.

1955 J. BLAKE *Let.* 28 Dec. in *Joint* (1971) 110 Wanted to be a hard-nose badass type. **1964** R. D. ABRAHAMS *Deep Down* iii. 79 I'm that bad-ass so-and-so they call 'Stackolee'... I'ma give you a chance to run, 'Fore I reach in my cashmere and pull out my bad-ass gun. **1969** *N.Y. Times* 26 Jan. VII. 38/1 He suffers from the 'badass' syndrome, which is an inability to conform to the lunacy about him. **1972** C. BUCHANAN *Maiden* xxii. 198 An older boy in a thistly beard and a bad-ass jacket followed them. **1974** H. L. FOSTER *Ribbin'* v. 208, I set it up and you fell into my trap And I copped your dumb butt with my bad-ass rap. **1981** *Washington Post* 16 July (District Weekly section) 8/1 We were known as bad-ass hard asses who could fight. **1993** *Guardian* 6 May II. 10/3 And just as you feel that Morrison's tilt at jazz is at the expense of some badass blues he dutifully.. belts out a storming finale.

Hence 'bad-assed *a.*

1971 *Playboy* Aug. 32/3 Bo Diddley has been typed and hyped as.. 'the most outrageous, bad-assed guitar man alive', as the liner notes to his most recent disc have it. **1980** E. A. FOLB *Runnin' down some Lines* iii. 119 Like the pimp and his various alter egos, the *hardhead* or the *bad-assed nigger* or the *badman* has also been a folk hero both in the oral literature and daily lives of blacks. **1989** L. CAMPBELL & '2-LIVE CREW' *Dirty Nursery Rhymes* (song) in L. A. Stanley *Rap: the Lyrics* (1992) 365 Papa Bear said, 'Shit, bitch, you must think I'm sick Just get down here on your knees and suck this bad-assed dick.' **1993** *Face* Sept. 149/3 Geeky middle-class black boys fake up a lucrative career as bad-assed rappers.

bail, *n.*¹ Add: [7.] **bail bandit** *colloq.*, one who commits a crime while on bail awaiting trial.

1991 *Times* 20 July 6/1 The study suggests that 'bail bandits' are responsible for between 24 and 39 per cent of recorded crime. **1993** *Independent on Sunday* 3 Oct. 5/7 After a police campaign against 'bail bandits'.. ministers are considering forcing a suspect to prove he would not be dangerous if allowed to wait at home instead of in jail.

Bajocian (bəˈdʒəʊʃən), *a. Geol.* [ad. F. *Bajocien* (coined in A. d'Orbigny *Cours Élémentaire de Paléontol. et de Géol. Stratigraphiques* (1852) II. II. iv. 477), f. L. *Bajocium* Bayeux: see -IAN.] Of, pertaining to, or designating a stage of the Middle Jurassic in Europe, above the Aalenian and below the Bathonian. Also *absol.*

[**1882** A. GEIKIE *Text-bk. Geol.* 798 Bajocien, or Oolithe Inférieure, well developed in the Department of Calvados.] **1909** in *Cent. Dict.* Suppl. **1910** *Encycl. Brit.* IV. 225/2 The Bajocian stage is practically equivalent to the Inferior Oolite of British geologists. **1947** W. J. ARKELL *Geol. Oxf.* 23 (*table*) Bajocian. **1960** L. D. STAMP *Britain's Struct.* (ed. 5) xii. 133 The Inferior Oolite or Bajocian beds are represented on the west coast of Scotland by limestones. **1969** BENNISON & WRIGHT *Geol. Hist. Brit. Isles* xiii. 305 The Grey Limestone or Scarborough Limestone has an abundant marine fauna which proves that it also belongs to the Bajocian (Inferior Oolite). **1986** G. CULVERWELL tr. *Arduini & Teruzzi's Macdonald Encycl. Fossils* No. 110, It is found in Europe, where it is typical of the English Bajocian.

balafon ('bæləfɒn), *n.* Also **balafo**, **balaphon**, and varr. [a. F. *balafon* (1688 in *Trésor*), f. Manding *bala* xylophone + *fo* to play.] A large xylophone with hollow gourds used as resonators, used in various parts of W. Africa and elsewhere in the performance of W. African music. Cf. *BALLARD n.*²

1797 *Encycl. Brit.* III. 767/2 *Bufalo* [sic], a musical instrument, consisting of several pipes of wood tied together with thongs of leather, so as to form a small interstice between each pipe. It is used by the negroes of Guinea. **1833** F. SHOBERL tr. *Hugo's Hunchb.* iii. 60 The Egyptians played upon their African balafoes and tambourines. **1935** G. GORER *Africa Dances* I. iv. 55 No one who was not a griot would.. play the tomtom, the balafron (a kind of xylophone). **1965** *Economist* 16 Jan. 229/3 The Senegal national anthem.. begins.. 'Strum your koras, strike the balafons'. **1988** *Q* Nov. 123/5 Today Jali plays with a new line-up (though the same format of kora, guitars, balaphon and vocals both lead and chorus). **1991** P. SWEENEY *Virgin Directory World Mus.* 21 A spare, heavy bass guitar and minimal touches of synthesizer added a contemporary feel to the raw simple melodies and traditional ngoni and balafon accompaniment.

balance, *n.* Add: [IV.] [14.] c. Esp. in complementary medicine, a state of healthy equilibrium resulting from a harmonious relationship between various aspects of the person, as body and mind, 'yin' and 'yang', etc.

1964 L. Moss *Acupuncture & You* ii. 21 The distribution and balance are never constant in the human body...An inner rhythm is being stimulated by the Yang. **1978** B. SULTANOFF in M. Blate *Natural Healer's Acupressure Handbk.* p. viii, This 'holistic' perspective on the essence of healing presents us with a practical challenge: How can we best utilize the knowledge and services encompassed by Western medicine while maintaining a 'healthstyle' attuned to principles of order, balance, and self-reliance? **1981** V. KULVINSKAS et al. *Life in 21st Cent.* IV. iii. 187 Are you a 'head' person or a 'body' person or perhaps 'centered' in perfect balance and harmony? **1983** HILLIER & JEWELL *Health Care & Trad. Med. in China* vi. 150 The 'Huangdi Neijing' pays great attention to the achievement of good balance both in one's mental and physical states. **1989** R. COWARD *Whole Truth*

(1990) i. 32 The body is used as a source of ideas about 'wholeness', 'balance' and 'harmony', involving both the body and the mind. **1990** A. STEVENS *On Jung* iii. 49 The psyche, like the body, was a self-regulating system. It strives perpetually to maintain a balance.

†**ballard**, *n.*[2] *Obs.* Substitute for entry:
†**ballard** ('bælɑːd), *n.*[2] *Obs.* [Origin obscure; perh. f. Manding *bala* xylophone (see *BALAFON *n.*) + -ARD.] A xylophone of W. Africa, similar to the balafon.
1623 R. JOBSON *Golden Trade* 106, I would acquaint you of their most principall instrument, which is called Ballards made to stand a foot above the ground. **1625** PURCHAS *Pilgrimes* II. IX. xiii. 1573 Their Ballards are a foot aboue ground, hollow vnder, with some seuenteene Keyes on the top, on which the Player strikes .. with two stickes a foot long, with Balls fastened on the end.

balloon, *n.*[1] Add: [10.] **balloon angioplasty** *Surg.*, the widening of a blocked or narrowed blood vessel, esp. an artery, by means of a small balloon that is inserted into it and then inflated; an operation to perform this.
1980 *Radiology* CXXXV. 571/1 Significant compression or redistribution of atherosclerotic plaques could not be demonstrated histologically following *balloon angioplasty. **1988** *Daily Tel.* 22 Nov. 6/5 [She] needed pioneering heart surgery called balloon angioplasty when she had a heart attack while five months pregnant. **1992** *Wall St. Jrnl.* 25 Nov. B1/2 Balloon angioplasties .. don't require the open-heart surgery of a coronary bypass.
    balloon catheter *Surg.* [tr. G. *Ballonkatheter* (coined by C. Müller 1949, in *Zeitschr. für Urologie* XLII. 4)], a type of catheter incorporating a small balloon which may be introduced into a canal, duct, or blood vessel and then inflated in order to clear an obstruction or dilate a narrowed region.
[**1951** *Jrnl. Thoracic Surg.* XXII. 536 The pulmonary artery was occluded on one side by means of a cardiac catheter provided with an inflatable balloon.] **1952** *Q. Cumulative Index Medicus* LII. 397 (*title*) Problems in wet colostomy management following radical pelvic surgery; use of new giant *balloon catheter. **1963** *Amer. Jrnl. Roentgenol.* XC. 650/2 Tourniquets, balloon catheters and gravity have been employed to achieve the desired distribution of injected contrast agents. **1989** *Jrnl. R. Soc. Med.* Sept. 542/2 A Fogarty biliary balloon catheter was introduced proximally to remove residual stones.

Balonda *n.* and *a.*: var. of *LUNDA *n.* and *a.*

Baluba *n.*, var. of *LUBA *n.* and *a.*

Balunda *n.* and *a.*: var. of *LUNDA *n.* and *a.*

band, *v.*[1] Add: **5.** To subject to banding (*BANDING *vbl. n.*[1] 4, 5); to allocate to a band according to ability, income, etc.
1976 *Times* 31 Jan. 1/3 The Inner London Education Authority's system of 'banding' children from primary to secondary school may be made illegal under the Education Bill. Children are 'banded' as above average, average and below average. **1987** *Financial Times* 2 Nov. 34/5 Interest rates were banded last October in an effort to produce greater inter-bank competitiveness. *Ibid.* 10 Dec. 13/3 The desirability of making the community charge more fair by banding the rate of charge in proportion to ability to pay. **1990** *Daily Tel.* 3 May 18 Even if the Government does decide to 'band' the tax .. the damage will have been done. **1990** *Times Educ. Suppl.* 19 Oct. 15/4 The head .. does not know that the infants are banded in terms of their ability.

banded, *ppl. a.* Add: **5.** *Finance*. Divided into bands (see *BAND *v.*[1] 5); *spec.* with reference to

the accumulation of interest at different rates on different parts of the invested capital.
1987 *Times* 7 Dec. 24/7 Proposals for a banded charge rather than a flat rate. **1989** *Financial Times* 28 Jan. (Weekend Suppl.) p. iii/3 You should ask whether your bank is offering you 'tiered rates' — those paying the top rate of interest applicable on all your funds — or 'banded rates' — those paying .. the higher rates only on funds above a certain level. **1990** *Economist* 31 Mar. 27/2 Other wheezes, like a more elaborately banded community charge, would be unthinkable under Mrs. Thatcher.

banding, *vbl. n.*[1] Add: **4.** The practice of dividing school pupils into broad categories according to ability, for teaching purposes.
1969 *Times* 10 Dec. 2/4 The council's controversial plan .. to start a system of 'banding' by academic ability to ensure that pupils from immigrant backgrounds are evenly distributed throughout the twelve schools. **1970** BENN & SIMON *Half Way There* ix. 148 'Banding' .. can be regarded as a coarse, or modified form of streaming . . . Instead of dividing, let us say, a 12-form entry intake .. into 12 streamed classes .. the intake is divided into 2, or .. 3 .. broad bands of pupils .. based on 'ability'. **1974** *Times Educ. Suppl.* 5 Apr. 4/5 Suggested options include retaining the present system of testing the children and placing them in three ability bands .., removing the testing and banding but leaving the rest of the system alone, or drawing a catchment area round each secondary school. **1976** *Economist* 7 Feb. 14/1 The bill would .. outlaw banding — the device used by some local education authorities .. to try to provide schools with a fair share of bright children. **1991** *Guardian* 26 Feb. (EG Suppl.) 22/4 Throughout its development, advocates of the new curriculum had argued that it would do away with the divisive banding which took place at the end of Year 9 .. as 14-year-olds were assigned to academic or vocational tracks.
    5. *Finance*. The division of a continuous scale of earnings, assets, etc., into bands each of which correspond to particular financial conditions, esp. rates of interest or taxation.
1982 *Financial Times* 30 Jan. 4/8 Its service charge is a straight 6 per cent with no banding, giving a true interest rate of 13.7 per cent. **1985** *Ibid.* 15 Apr. 15/1 With the forthcoming earnings related 'banding' of contributions we appear to have invented an anomaly. **1990** *Economist* 31 Mar. 27/2 This limited banding, which would need legislation, would be intended to respond to complaints about the unfairness of the lump-sum tax. **1991** RIDGE & SMITH *Local Taxation* 42 The perennial problem with any system of banding is that if there are only a few bands then the payment will vary substantially between bands.

bandog, *n.* Senses a, b, c in Dict. become 1 a, 2, 3. Add: [1.] **b.** A cross-breed of large, ferocious dog, produced by crossing American pit bull terriers with (usu.) Neapolitan mastiffs; a dog of this cross-breed.
1984 C. SEMENCIC *World of Fighting Dogs* 209 About 15 years ago a veterinarian by the name of Swinford began a breeding program which was ultimately to produce the greatest of all protection dogs . . . Unfortunately Swinford died at an early age, and his Bandog was never perfected as purebred. *Ibid.*, The Bandog, also sometimes known as the Swinford Bandog, or the American Mastiff, is currently produced in different ways. **1990** *Evening Standard* 6 Mar. 15/1 Dog breeders are mating what the RSPCA describe as the world's most savage dog, the American pit bull terrier with Rottweilers, mastiffs and Rhodesian Ridgebacks to produce terrifying beasts called Bandogs. **1991** *Independent* 22 May 3/1 A ban was imposed at midnight last night on the import of American pit bull terriers, Japanese tosas and ban dogs.

barkevikite ('bɑːkəvɪkaɪt), *n. Min.* Also
†**barkevicite.** [ad. Sw. *barkevikit* (coined by W.
C. Brögger 1887, in *Geol. Fören. Förhandl.*
(Stockholm) IX. 269), f. the name of *Barkevik*
in Norway, where typical specimens were found:
see -ITE¹.] An iron-rich sodium and potassium
amphibole occurring as dark brown or black
monoclinic crystals.

   1892 E. S. DANA *Dana's Syst. Min.* (ed. 6) vi. 403
Other amphiboles from Fredriksvärn..are shown to be
intermediate between barkevikite and ordinary
hornblende. **1895** A. HARKER *Petrol.* iii. 41 Some
augite-syenites contain the soda-amphibole barkevicite
with intense brown absorption and pleochroism. **1962**
W. T. HUANG *Petrol.* iv. 129 Other colored minerals
found in pulaskite include aegirite-augite, barkevikite,
or arfvedsonite. **1993** P. KEAREY *Encycl. Solid Earth
Sci.* 86/2 Phenocrysts of amphibole (barkevikite and/or
kaersutite.

barnacle, *n.*² Add: [**1.**] [**b.**] Now *barnacle
goose.*

   1840 *Cuvier's Animal Kingdom* 263 The Barnacle
Goose..with a grey mantle. **1910** *Brit. Birds* IV. 344
The author discovered a number of Barnacle-Geese
in a marsh some ten or fifteen kilometres from the
sea. **1959** F. BODSWORTH *Strange One* (1960) I. i. 3
The barnacle goose..had been restless and more than
normally alert since the last of the flock moved out
the day before on the flight to the Greenland nesting
fiords. **1983** *Birds* Spring 5/1 The barnacle goose was
given full protection throughout the whole of Britain.

bartonellosis (bɑːtənɛ'ləʊsɪs), *n. Path.* [f.
mod.L. *Bartonell-a*, genus name of the causative
organism, f. the name of A. L. *Barton* (1871-50),
Peruvian physician: see -OSIS.] = *CARRION'S
DISEASE *n.*

   1928 *Jrnl. Trop. Med. & Hygiene* XXXI. 30/1 He
[*sc.* Noguchi] considered..that the name 'Carrion's
disease' could be used to designate both varieties of
'Bartonellosis'. **1940** *Trop. Dis. Bull.* XXXVII. 270
Patiño Camargo..describes the clinical features of an
outbreak of bartonellosis in Colombia, hitherto
unaffected by this disease. **1942** *Jrnl. Exper. Med.*
LXXV. 65 Bartonellosis is endemic in certain regions
of Peru, and has more recently been found to be so in
Colombia and Ecuador. **1978** *Nature* 22 June 599/2
Intensive DDT spraying campaigns against
Lu [*tzomyia*] *verrucarum*, which had been indicated as
the vector of human bartonellosis (Carrion's disease)
in the Peruvian Andes.

BASE (beɪs), *n.*⁷ orig. *U. S.* Also **base.** [Acronym
f. the initial letters of *B*uilding, *A*ntenna-tower,
*S*pan, *E*arth (see quot. 1983).
   The strong formative and semantic influence of BASE
*n.*¹ is reflected in increasing occurrence of the acronym
in lower case.]

   In *Comb.* as **BASE jump**, a parachute jump
from a fixed point, esp. a high building or
promontory, rather than from an aircraft; also
as *v. intr.* So '**BASE jumper** *n.*', '**BASE jumping**
vbl. n.

   1983 *Atlantic* May 22/3 He came up with the acronym
BASE — for Building, Antenna Tower, Span (meaning
bridges), and Earth (meaning cliffs). *Ibid.*, To date,
the lowest BASE jump probably belongs to Phil
Smith — a 190-foot drop from the ceiling of Houston's
Astrodome (a publicity stunt). 'That's about as low as
possible,' says Phil Mayfield, another BASE
jumper. **1989** *USA Today* 19 Oct. C10/1 It might not
sound safe, but BASE jumpers — 4,000 worldwide — say
this is the second safest site, behind El Capitan in
California's Yosemite National Park. **1992** *Times* 22
May 3/8 The British Parachute Association..
dissociates itself from base jumping. *Ibid.*, He had
done a couple of other base jumps which were
successful. **1993** *Radio Times* 26 June 79/1 Both could

climb the Tower and Base jump from the top, 20,000
feet above sea level, onto the glacier below.

basehead ('beɪshɛd), *n. U. S. slang.* Also **basehead.** [f. FREE)BASE *n.* + HEAD *n.*¹] A person
who habitually takes freebase or crack (CRACK
*n.*¹ 20).

   1986 *MacNeil-Lehrer NewsHour* (TV programme
transcript) 21 Apr., Everybody into cocaine nowadays.
There's so many baseheads out here. **1989** 'DONALD
D' *F.B.I.* (*Free Base Institute*) (song) in L. A. Stanley
Rap: the Lyrics (1992) 95, I see baseheads in a state of
their own In the zone where the baseheads roam And
on the same block are the ones who sell to them. **1991**
P. J. O'ROURKE *Parliament of Whores* (1992) 131 Dirty,
skinny, disordered base-heads yelling at each other and
us and people who aren't there.

base pair (beɪs'pɛə(r)), *n. Biochem.* [f. BASE *n.*¹
+ PAIR *n.*¹] A pair of complementary bases held
together by hydrogen bonding and occurring in
sequences in the strands of DNA and RNA
molecules; such a pair as a unit in which to
express the size of a nucleic acid molecule.

   1956 *Proc. Nat. Acad. Sci.* XLII. 61 The base pairs
resulting from the above considerations are
listed. **1957** *Cold Spring Harbor Symp. Quant. Biol.*
XXI. 89/2 We know that the hydrogen bonds in DNA
can be readily broken by heating, but the value of the
activation energy of this process indicates that the bonds
reform unless they are broken in about 15 consecutive
base-pairs. **1975** *Nature* 12 June 530/1 More recent
work using nucleases has shown that the DNA in
chromatin exists in some regular fold which repeats
every 200 base pairs, the best value currently being
205 ± 15 base pairs. **1988** *Economist* 20 Feb. 83/1 'What
is man, that thou art mindful of him?' asked the
psalmist. To some molecular biologists,..the answer
is a list of 3 billion 'base pairs' of deoxyribonucleic
acid. **1993** *N. Y. Rev. Bks* 12 Aug. 52/1 A group of
my colleagues managed to recover nearly the entire
sequence — 1320 of 1431 base pairs — of a chloroplast
gene prominently involved in photosynthesis.
   So '**base pairing** *vbl. n.*, the combining of two
bases to form a base pair; an instance of this;
hence (as a back-formation) '**base-pair** *v. intr.*,
to pair in this way; also, '**base-paired** *ppl. a.*

   1956 *Proc. Nat. Acad. Sci.* XLII. 62 This base-
pairing scheme is shown in Figure 2, where it is seen
that N$_{base}$ — C$_{sugar}$ bonds are related by a twofold axis
parallel to the helical axis. **1959** *Brookhaven Symp.
Biol.* XII. 39 There is a second class of base, which
won't base pair, but these are not found in the RNA of
tobacco mosaic virus or in DNA. **1960** V. R. POTTER
Nucleic Acid Outl. I. iii. 83 These figures describe the
spatial relationships for the four possible base pairings
found in the double helix. **1970** *Proc. Nat. Acad. Sci.*
LXVII. 1473 Two shorter duplexes, each containing
one base-paired end and one protruding single-
stranded end were also studied. **1988** P. W. KUCHEL
et al. *Schaum's Outl. Theory & Probl. Biochem.* vii. 183
DNA is a duplex molecule in which two polynucleotide
chains (or strands) are linked to one another through
specific base pairing. **1988** *Nature* 24 Nov. 399/1 The
frequency of mismatches within the basepaired
region..will..influence..the effective life of the
mRNA. **1989** B. ALBERTS et al. *Molecular Biol. Cell*
(ed. 2) i. 7 (*caption*) By base-pairing to a coding RNA
molecule, these RNA molecules allow an RNA
sequence to act as a template for the synthesis of amino
acid polymers.

basho ('bæʃəʊ, ‖'bæʃo), *n.* Pl. unchanged. [Jap.,
f. *ba* place, occasion + *shŏ* place, locality (the
semantic repetition app. adding emphasis).
   Orig. a 'place of entertainment', the term now
specifically refers to a place or period (now 15 days) in
which a Sumo tournament is held.]
   A Sumo wrestling tournament.

1940 A. HANO *Sumo—Jap. Wrestling* iv. 77 The Grand Tournament in January is called the *Haru-basyo*, or Spring Event, and that of May as the *Natu-basyo*, or Summer Event. **1959** J. A. SARGEANT *Sumo* i. 8 The very first grand tournament, or *basho*, was held in a temple compound, and temple and shrine grounds continued to be one of the favorite sites for bouts through the centuries. **1978** *Britannica Bk. of Year* (U.S.) 255/2 Kitanoumi's growing dominance of the sport was strikingly evident when he won both the March and September *basho* with perfect 15-0 records. **1992** *Radio Times* 6 June 77/5 *Sumo* . . . Action from the final day of the Basho.

bass, *a.* and *n.*[5] Add: [B.] **6.** The low-frequency component of (esp. transmitted or reproduced) sound. Freq. *attrib..* Cf. *TREBLE *n.* 8.
   1930 *Wireless World* 26 Mar. 333/1 The tone control which emphasizes either treble or bass consists of a variable capacity between the input and output of the power valves.. **1936** *Wireless World* 28 Feb. 214 Bass and treble tone controls. **1957** *Practical Wireless* XXXIII. 706/1 Simple switched bass-boost and *top-cut compensation is provided by S_1 and S_2 respectively. **1975** G. J. KING *Audio Handbk.* iii. 66 For example, bass boost is secured by attenuation of the higher frequencies. **1988** V. CAPEL *Audio & Hi-Fi Engineer's Pocket Bk.* 42 To avoid loss of bass, a frequency-dependent phase-shifter progressively changes the relative phase until they [*sc.* the sounds] are in phase at the lowest frequency.

basuco (bəˈsuːkəʊ, bəˈzuːkəʊ), *n.* Also **basuko**, **bazuko**. [a. Colombian Sp. *basuco*, perh. related to Sp. *bazucar* to shake violently, or to *basura* waste, trash.
   An alternative derivation in Colombian Spanish is a borrowing of English *bazooka* rocket-launcher, presumably because of the drug's explosive effect.]
   A preparation of coca paste mixed with various other substances, containing an impure form of cocaine and highly addictive when smoked; also used of other low-grade forms of cocaine.
   1983 *Wall St. Jrnl.* 28 Nov. 35/2 Colombia has discovered a problem of drug abuse in its own backyard. A cigarette called *basuco* is appearing on the streets. **1983** *Times* 15 Dec. 10/4 'Bazuko', a cheap and extremely dangerous form of cocaine base variously mixed with marijuana and tobacco. **1985** C. NICHOLL *Fruit Palace* vii. 67 There's a big internal market: a lot of coke and basuko used by the street boys. **1986** *N.Y. Times* 20 Aug. I. 2/4 Because bazuco has not been purified into cocaine, it often carries residues of leaded gasoline, kerosene, sulphuric acid and potassium permanganate. **1987** *Times* 14 Sept. 10/6 While it takes two years of regular cocaine use to become addicted, it takes only a few weeks to become hooked on *bazuko*, a mind-blowing mix of coca base, marijuana and tobacco containing such impurities as petrol, ether and even sawdust. **1988** *Economist* 2 Apr. 65/1 Colombians themselves are taking to cocaine, especially in a form called 'basuko', a crude kind of crack. **1989** *Times* 4 Sept. 13/2 The lethal *basuco* which contains cocaine, lead and sulphuric acid.

basuko *n.*, var. *BASUCO *n.*

batch, *n.*[1] Sense 7 b in vol. 1 becomes 7 c. Add: [7.] **b.** *spec.* in *Computing*, in the sense 'pertaining to, intended for, or involving batch processing'.
   1967 *Technology Week* 23 Jan. 59/2 (Advt.), Design..language processors for various computer systems, including batch, remote-batch, and time-sharing configurations. **1976** *Scotsman* 25 Nov. 17/5 (Advt.), Experienced Systems Analyst/Programmer. We..require additional staff to join our existing team..in the development of a wide range of batch applications. **1985** *Personal Computer World* Feb. 189/2 Records retrieved in the above-mentioned way

may then be edited using the cursor controls, or you can carry out changes in a 'batch' mode.
   [c.] **batch job** *Computing*, a job scheduled to be executed by means of batch processing.
   1980 C. S. FRENCH *Computer Sci.* xxx. 261 With frequent changes a single source statement under time sharing may require all the control given to a whole *batch job. **1982** *Electronics* 10 Mar. 124/1 DJC allows the user of any work station to export a batch job to the NRM for remote execution. **1989** C. STOLL *Cuckoo's Egg* xxviii. 139 These were batch jobs, submitted during the day and postponed until evening.

bathometric (bæθəˈmɛtrɪk), *a.* [f. Gr. βάθο-ς depth + -METRIC.] = BATHYMETRIC *a.*
   1974 *Oceanology* XIV. 664 Salinity, oxidizability in particular, and the phosphorous content in the surface film were considerably greater than the corresponding results from the bathometric 'zero' depth. **1983** *Ibid.* XXIII. 378 An example of determination of a bathometric map of the sea bottom..is presented.

bathometry (bəˈθɒmɪtrɪ) *n.* [f. Gr. βάθο-ς depth + -METRY.] = BATHYMETRY *n.*
   1967 *Rep. Special Foreign Currency Sci. Information Program* (U.S. Nat. Sci. Found.) No. TT-67-56062. 1 Bathometry of lakes and seas enables ichthyologists to find and chart the fishing grounds. **1981** *Proc. 9th Ann. Conf. Remote Sensing Soc.* 179 (*heading*) Surface expressions of bathometry on synthetic aperture radar images.

*Bayesian, *a.* and *n.* (In *OED Additions* 1). Add: Hence ˈ**Bayesianism** *n.*, a Bayesian approach; advocacy of such an approach.
   1976 *Univ. W. Ontario Ser. Philos. Sci.* VI. II. 128 It is I believe not subject to the criticisms that are usually directed at other forms of Bayesianism. **1978** *Amer. Math. Monthly* LXXXV. 245 Subjective Bayesianism must face the challenge of scientific objectivity. **1987** *Nature* 25 June 663/1 Likelihood analysis has a long history, stretching back well before the recent resurgence of bayesianism which is sweeping through physics.

bazuco *n.*, var. *BASUCO *n.*

bazuko *n.*, var. *BASUCO *n.*

bean-counter (ˈbiːnkaʊntə(r)), *n. colloq.* (orig. and chiefly *U.S.*). Also **bean counter**, **beancounter**. [f. BEAN *n.* + COUNTER *n.*[2]] An accountant, *esp.* one who compiles statistical records or accounts; also applied *contempt.* to financial planners or statisticians. Hence, a person excessively concerned with accounts or figures.
   1975 *Interfaces* Feb. 74 (*title*) The measure of M.S./O.R. applications; or, Let's hear it for the bean counters. **1982** *N.Y. Times Mag.* 14 Nov. 86/2 Tension between engineers and marketing specialists..and financial experts, derided as 'bean counters,' are [*sic*] endemic in the automobile business. **1986** *Independent* 29 Nov. 17/1 The highly respected beancounters at Price Waterhouse have failed to recognise that times are changing in the City. **1991** *Observer* 7 July 20/8, I think they are all parsimonious, cheese-paring, gut-scrimping bean-counters. **1992** *Chicago Tribune* 22 Dec. I. 1/5 Bill Clinton..angrily derided as 'bean counters' leaders of national women's groups who complained that he has nominated too few women to his administration.

beardie, *n.* Sense 1 b in Dict. becomes 1 c. Add: [1.] **b.** *Austral.* A fish with a beard or barbel, *spec.* the red-brown gadoid fish *Lotella callarias* of south Australian coasts (also called *ling*).

1881 W. MACLEAY *Descr. Catal. Austral. Fishes* II. 114 *Lotella marginata, n. sp...* 'Beardy' of Fishermen...Port Jackson. Length twelve to twenty inches. **1906** D. G. STEAD *Fishes Austral.* 86 The Cod family..contains several species of economic value: the most important being the Beardie or Ling (*Lotella callarias*) and the Red Cod. **1951** T. C. ROUGHLEY *Fish & Fisheries Austral.* 25 The ling or beardie occurs round the southern half of the Australian coast. **1966** T. C. MARSHALL *Trop. Fishes Gt. Barrier Reef* 219 Beardie or tape-fish *Anacanthus barbatus*.

beast, *n.* Add: [II.] [5.] **c.** A sex offender. Cf. NONCE *n.*[2] *Prison slang*.

1989 J. MORTON *Lowspeak* 22/2 *Beast*,..a sex offender; the use is common amongst prisoners in Lancashire who do not know the term nonce. **1989** *Daily Tel.* 29 Nov. 8 The arrival of a police van at a prison might often be accompanied by comments such as 'a couple of beasts for you', with the result that the prisoners are immediately identified. **1990** *Guardian Weekly* 29 Apr. 21/1 It has not been an easy fortnight for nonces, monsters and beasts, the sexual offenders who are on the Rule. **1995** *Guardian* 28 Feb. II. 2/3 When I heard what happened I felt a bit rotten... Then I heard he was a beast, and I felt better...It might sound rotten, but I don't feel sorry for him. I would rather have a murderer on the loose than a child molester or a pervert.

beat-box ('biːtbɒks), *n.* (*a.*) *slang* (orig. *U.S.*). Also without hyphen and as one word. [f. BEAT *n.*[1] + BOX *n.*[2]] **1. a.** An electronic drum machine.

1983 *N.Y. Times* 7 Dec. C24/1 In several songs, electronic drum machines or 'beat boxes' augment or replace the band's drummer-percussionists. **1986** *Echoes* 27 Sept. 14/2 Raw, basic beatbox, heavy and hard raps, and a streetwise manner were carried off in such..style that the world just fell for it. **1987** *Daily Tel.* 6 Aug. 10/7 The 'human beat-box', Sipho,..makes drum- and percussion-like noises with his lips and throat. **1990** *Music Technol.* Apr. 5/1 Simon Trask investigates Roland's latest beat box and a selection of sound cards.

b. *attrib.* passing into *adj.* Esp. of music, rhythms, etc.: of, or characterized by the use of, an electronic drum machine.

1984 *N.Y. Times* 3 Aug. C5/5 The team performed them [*sc.* songs] in elaborate arrangements that interspersed seamless pop harmonies with the beat box rhythmic devices of contemporary dance music. **1985** *Ibid.* 9 Jan. C14/5 The sparse beat-box music and intensely engaging call-and-response served up by today's leading rap group, Run-D.M.C. **1987** *Q* Oct. 112/3 Westworld..are bent on marrying the Eddie Cochran book of guitar licks with beatbox rhythm patterns. **1993** *Music Technol.* May 90/1 [He] loves to improvise over an often programmed synth bass and beatbox groove.

2. = *ghetto blaster* s.v. GHETTO *n.* 3 b. See also *boom box* s.v. BOOM *n.*[1] 2.

1985 *Washington Post* 19 Mar. C1/1 Booming out of beat boxes on the street and bounced to in aerobics classes, the 'Big' beat sounds like the next equal-play anthem for American women. **1986** *Chicago Tribune* 16 May VII. 76/5 There are..hundreds of videos that are traveling ground that has been gone over before. If I see one more woman in a negligee dancing to a beat box, I'm gonna throw up. **1989** *Correspondent Mag.* 1 Oct. 34/2 If you hear a car with a beatbox booming at night, you know they're out looking for somebody. **1990** P. LEAR in *Quarterly* Summer 25 She hears rock music from a beat box. **1993** W. GIBSON *Virtual Light* 111 Sammy Sal swerved in beside her, bass pumping from his bikes's bone-conduction beatbox.

beaver, *n.*[1] Add: [2.] **d.** *Canad. Hist.* Pl. often unchanged. = *made beaver* s.v. *MADE ppl. a.* 5 b.

[**1708** in *Beaver* (1957) Winter 14/1, 10 [for] good skins; that is, Winter Beaver; 12 [for] skins of the biggest sort, 10 for the mean, and 8 for the smallest.] **1765** in A. HENRY *Trav.* (1809) II. i. 192 It is in Beaver that accounts are kept at Michilimackinac. **1851** J. RICHARDSON *Arctic Searching Exped.* I. xii. 391 To be accounted a chief among the Kutchin, a man must possess beads to the amount of 200 beavers. **1913** F. WILLIAMS *Wilderness Trail* xviii. 190 When the value [of the furs] is determined, the trader pushes over the counter as many 'beaver' (lead pellets), as the furs are worth. **1941** *Beaver* Sept. 14/2 The North-West Company, about 1820, issued beaver tokens, a form of coinage only a few pieces of which..have been saved.

becard ('beɪkɑːd), *n.* [ad. F. *bécarde*, f. *bec* beak; cf. earlier *bécard* male salmon, grilse.] Any of numerous tyrant flycatchers of the genus *Pachyramphus* (family *Tyrannidae*), of Central and South America.

1849 G. R. GRAY *Genera of Birds* I. 253 The fourth subfamily, Tityrinae or Becards, have the Bill generally short, and broad at the base. **1888** W. H. HUDSON *Argentine Ornithol.* I. 163 In the male of this species, as in many other Bécards, the second primary is abnormally shortened, being only about one inch in length. **1938** DICKEY & VAN ROSSEM *Birds of El Salvador* 341 Becards are ordinarily rather quiet, sedentary birds, usually to be found in pairs in thin, second growth and about the edges of clearings and open places such as trails and roads. **1989** *Encycl. Brit.* II. 27/2 The 15 species of becards (comprising the genera *Platypsaris* and *Pachyramphus*) are rather plain, small birds with thick bills hooked at the tip.

bench, *n.* Add: [4.] **d.** A worktop in a laboratory, etc.

Earlier with preceding adj. or attrib. n., as *work-bench* s.v. WORK *n.* 34 d, etc.

[**1866** A. W. HOFFMANN *Chem. Labs. Univs. Bonn & Berlin* 15 At these working benches, all ordinary chemical work and all operations, not requiring special arrangements provided in other parts of the institution, are carried on.] **1903** T. H. RUSSELL *Planning & Fitting-Up of Chem. & Physical Labs.* 39 The entire supply of gas and water to each bench should be controlled by stop-cocks at one end of the bench. **1921** A. E. MUNBY *Laboratories* ii. 44 Fume pipe for benches or lecture table. **1970** J. HUXLEY *Memories* v. 82 Between days of hard work at my bench I explored the exciting neighbourhood. **1977** 'E. CRISPIN' *Glimpses of Moon* ix. 169 Sir John went to a bench and swept a lot of chemical glassware to one side with a large hand.

benomyl ('benəmɪl), *n.* *Chem.* and *Agric.* [f. BEN(Z)O- + M(ETH)YL *n.*, elements of the systematic name.] A colourless, crystalline powder, $C_{14}H_{18}N_4O_3$, used primarily on fruit and vegetable crops as a broad-spectrum systemic fungicide.

1969 *B.S.I. News* Jan. 22/1 *Benomyl*, methyl *N*-benzimidazol-2-yl-*N*-(butylcarbamoyl)carbamate. **1969** *Jrnl. Agric. & Food Chem.* XVII. 267/1 This compound, formerly du Pont fungicide 1991, has the approved common name of benomyl and is the active chemical ingredient of Benlate benomyl fungicide. **1970** *New Scientist* 14 May 334/1 Roundworms (nematodes) can be killed off by the fungicides benomyl and thibendazole. **1977** *Jrnl. R. Soc. Arts* CXXV. 566/2 Benomyl..proved to be an outstanding wide spectrum fungicide. **1992** *Daily Mirror* 3 Oct. 22/2 Spray with benomyl mid-August and at the end of the month, to deal with brown rot.

Bergmann ('bɜːgmən), *n.* [The name of Carl *Bergmann* (1814–65), German biologist.] Used *attrib.* and in the possessive to designate an ecogeographical rule first formulated by Bergmann in 1847 (*Göttinger Studien* I. 707), according to which the average body size of a warm-blooded animal is larger in populations occupying the cooler parts of its geographical range. Cf. *ALLEN n.[2]

1929 R. MELL in *Lingnan Sci. Jrnl.* VIII. 187 The Bergmann law is not valid for cold-blooded animals. **1937** ALLEE & SCHMIDT ed. *Hesse's Ecol. Animal Geogr.* xxiv. 386 This principle has been called 'Bergmann's Rule' after its discoverer. *Ibid.* 502 The increase of size in the colder zones, in accordance with the Bergmann Rule, is a familiar phenomenon in the alpine zone. **1954** G. L. CLARKE *Elem. Ecol.* 158 These simple ecological relationships, in addition to underlying Bergmann's principle and Allen's rule, undoubtedly account in part at least for the fact that no extremely small mammals or birds exist, that is, as small as the majority of insects. **1955** *Evol.* IX. 24 There is no physiological evidence, in beast or man, that the minor and erratic subspecific trends expressed in Bergmann's and Allen's rules reflect phylogenetic pathways of heat-conserving adaptation. **1987** *New Scientist* 16 July 34/1 As the analysis moves from south to north, the tidy trend predicted by Bergmann's rule seems to hold good — at first.

berylliosis (bərɪlɪ'əʊsɪs), *n. Path.* [ad. It. *berilliosi* (coined by S. M. Fabroni 1935, in *Med. del Lavoro* XXVI. 302): cf. BERYLLIUM *n.*, -OSIS.] A lung disease caused by the inhalation of fumes or dust containing beryllium.

1943 *Bull. U.S. Nat. Inst. Health* No. 181. 8 Fabroni has coined the term 'berylliosis' for the type of lung damage caused by inhalation of the dust or fumes of beryllium compounds. **1968** *New England Jrnl. Med.* 22 Feb. 431/1 One might anticipate difficulty in differentiating hypercalcemic sarcoidosis from berylliosis. **1987** LOURENÇO & GARRARD in J. H. Stein *Internal Med.* (ed. 2) lxxv. 657/1 Inhalation of beryllium as the metal or one of its salts may cause an acute chemical pneumonia (acute berylliosis) or a chronic sarcoidlike granulomatous reaction (chronic berylliosis).

best, *a.* and *adv.* Add: [A.] [III.] [11.] [a.] *best-case.*

1975 *Aviation Week* 10 Nov. 23/2 Fuel saving ranged from a *best-case estimate of $120,911 per airplane per year to a worst-case estimate of $78,556. **1977** *Sci. Amer.* July 22/1 These and other possible outcomes are envisioned in 'best-case scenarios' for the future application of recombinant-DNA technology. **1991** J. MANDER *In Absence of Sacred* I. ii. 30 The information we are given describes the technologies solely in terms of their best-case use. This is so even when the inventors have significant knowledge of terrible downside possibilities.

beta, *n.* [2.] [i.] For *beta receptor* read *beta* (or β) *(adrenergic) receptor.* Add before *beta-blocker:* **beta-adrenergic** *a.*, pertaining to or affecting the beta receptors.

1959 *Pharmacol. Rev.* XI. 462 These data seem to provide verification of Ahlquist's division of α- and β-adrenergic receptors. **1964** *Brit. Med. Jrnl.* 19 Sept. 723/2 Beta-adrenergic blockade may be helpful in angina pectoris. **1994** *Sci. News* 22 Oct. 262/2 Volunteers received either a placebo pill or propanolol, a drug that lowers blood pressure by blocking beta-adrenergic stress hormones.

bhaji ('baːdʒiː), *n.* Also **bhajee, bhajji.** Pl. **bhajia** or **bhajis.** [Hindi. *bhájí* fried vegetables, f. Skr. *bhrajj-* to fry.] An Indian dish of fried vegetables. Also (esp. in *onion bhaji, spinach bhaji*), a deep-fried vegetable snack.

1832 J. SHARIF *Qanoon-e-Islam* iii. 27 They also cook *kheer, k'hinchree, bhajee,* according to their means. **1888** W. H. DAWE *Wife's Help to Indian Cookery* 85 Bhájís and Bhartás (vegetables fried and boiled). **1957** S. RANGARAO *Good Food from India* xiv.

153 A fair bhaji is best made with cucumbers, greens, peas, marrows, pumpkins, gourds, etc. **1967** L. DEIGHTON *London Dossier* 43 In these Hindu vegetarian restaurants you'll eat *bhajjis,* a curry of fried vegetables. There are hundreds of varieties. *Brinjal* is the word for aubergine (egg plant) and a *brinjal bhajji* is one of the most popular. **1986** G. SLOVO *Death by Analysis* iii. 33 The meal was almost very good — a delicious cauliflower bhajee on the same table as a bhindi dish which was obviously tinned. **1989** *Grocer* 29 Apr. 102/1 Anglo Oriental Foods . . is launching a range of chilled snack products . . . The initial range comprises onion bhajis, spinach bhajis, mild pakoras, spicy pakoras and vegetable samosas.

bhangra ('baːŋgrə, 'bæŋgrə), *n.* Also with capital initial. [a. Punjabi *bhangṛā.*] **1.** A traditional Punjabi male folk-dance; also, the music accompanying this dance.

1965 E. BHAYNANI *Dance in India* xiv. 183 A similar type of Bhangra is danced by men of the Dogra (warrior) community of Jammu. **1971** P. THOMAS *Festivals & Holidays of India* viii. 62/1 The first of Vaisakh or Baisakh (April–May) is the most important day of the year for the Sikhs . . . Village communities celebrate the occasion by many folk dances, of which the vigorous Bhangra is the most popular. **1980** *New Grove Dict. Mus.* XIV. 110 *Bolī* (improvised couplets) make up the principal dance-song for the men's *bhangra* and women's *giḍḍa* dance . . . Here the soloists accompany their recitative with mimetic gestures and the group dances in a circle while singing the refrain. **1985** N. SAHGAL *Rich like Us* xxi. 221 One youth, aged thirty-five or forty, *lungi* clad, straggly-haired, had his arms straight up in the air, his eyes rolling white, while his body twitched and lurched to the rhythm of the *bhangra* and a circle of loose-limbed dancers revolved around him. **1991** P. SWEENEY *Virgin Directory World Music* 144 Bhangra is traditionally danced by men, and its boisterous, hedonistic, slang lyrics make it an attractive entertainment even to non-Punjabis.

2. A type of popular music originating in the Asian community in Britain and incorporating elements of both Punjabi folk and Western dance music.

1987 *New Musical Express* 5 Sept. 46 Unheard on mainstream radio but selling in cart-loads, *Bhangra* — a mix of traditional Asian musics, disco and rock — is Britain's biggest musical underground. **1988** *Sunday Tel.* (Colour Suppl.) 22 May 36/2 It is getting big: so big that soon bhangra, like reggae before it, will break through the ethnic barrier. **1991** *Hammersmith, Fulham & Chiswick Guardian* 9 Aug. 5/5 The band's combination of a fresh and dynamic stage presence and explosive bhangra has made them the most sought-after bhangra band around. **1993** *Times* 10 July 20/6 Coming back from a jolly night out, slightly tanked up and woozy on the old pins, a quick blast of Bhangra would have me dancing exotic and erotic moves until I tripped over the cat.

biathlete (baɪ'æθliːt), *n.* [f. BIATHL(ON *n.* + ATHL)ETE *n.*, after PENTATHLETE *n.*, etc.] A competitor in a biathlon.

1972 *Times* 29 Jan. 16/7 Long journeys into the mountains in pursuit of skier, bobber, tobogganist and biathlete. **1984** *Marathon & Distance Runner* Oct. 62/1 Olympic biathlete Jim Woods was the 1983 short course winner [at a triathlon]. **1992** *N.Y. Times* 12 Feb. B10/6 A biathlete must squeeze off a shot while the heart rate has jumped to more than 170 beats a minute.

bicameral, *a.* Add: Hence **bi'cameralism** *n.*, advocacy or adoption of a bicameral system.

1917 J. A. R. MARRIOTT in *Edinb. Rev.* July 192 Mill was no fanatical believer in bicameralism, still less did he approve of a Second Chamber constituted like the House of Lords. **1931** F. G. CRAWFORD *State Govt.* vii. 115 When the national government was created in 1787, the principle of bicameralism was included. **1963** *Federal Suppl.* CCXIII. 584/2 The chief justification for bicameralism in State government now seems to be the thought that it insures against precipitate action—imposing greater deliberation—upon proposed legislation. **1987** *Summary of World Broadcasts: Far East* (B.B.C.) 4 July B11/3 We can't copy Western democracy with its bicameralism, multiparty system, and separation of power among legislative, executive and judicial branches.

bicycle, *n.* Add: [b.] **bicycle motocross** = BMX *n.*
1974 *Pop. Mech.* Mar. 192 (*heading*) *Bicycle motocross: new two-wheel sport. **1990** *Seattle Times* 24 Aug. C7/5 He has decided to retire, turning the bicycle-motocross track over to Mike Raich, a Seattle schoolteacher.

‖**biennale** (bien'naːle; anglicized biːɛ'naːleɪ, also (Fr.) bjɛnal) , *n.* [It.: cf. BIENNIAL *a.* and *n.*] Originally (with capital initial), an international art exhibition held every two years at Venice; hence, any biennial (esp. art) exhibition, festival, etc.
1931 *Creative Art* VIII. 411/1 It is always in an exceptionally expectant mood that one comes to the Biennale. **1951** *Ann. Reg. 1950* 400 In the field of contemporary painting Britain's representative at the Venice 'Biennale' was Matthew Smith. **1968** *Guardian* 23 Nov. 6/5 Britain's first print biennale opened last night in Bradford. Artists from 38 countries are exhibiting. **1990** *Mediamatic* Summer (Edge 90: Special Issue) 169 The theme of this year's biennale, *art and life in the Nineties*, has been chosen to express the collusion of many live and intermedia artworks with personal and architectural spaces normally associated with the everyday necessities of work, recreation, transport and so on.

biennial, *a.* and *n.* Add: [B.] **2.** Chiefly *U. S.* An event taking place biennially; *spec.* (*a*) an examination formerly held at Yale (and subsequently at other American universities); (*b*) any of various named art exhibitions, music festivals, etc. (cf. *BIENNALE *n.*); later extended to include similar events not held biennially.
1853 ROOT & LOMBARD *Songs of Yale* 4 The 'Biennial' is an Examination occurring twice during the course, —at the close of the Sophomore and of the Senior years, in all the studies pursued during the two years previous. It was established in 1850. **1928** *Art & Archaeol.* XXVI. 170/2 The Eleventh Corcoran Biennial is..the most significant and the broadest exhibit ever hung in Washington. **1946** *Britannica Bk. of Year* (U.S.) 555/1 The year 1945 was the year of the Corcoran Biennial in Washington. **1981** *Art News* May 25/1 These 'biennials'—a word used by rote now to indicate large juried, invitational survey shows—are actually descendants of the big annual painting salons of 19th-century Europe and the blockbuster Venice Biennale, which began in the 1890s.

big-headed, *a.* Add: Hence **big-'headedness** *n.*
1967 A. LASKI *Seven Other Years* xiii. 178 Without undue bigheadedness she could see at a glance that they weren't in the running. **1986** *Summary of World Broadcasts: Eastern Europe* (B.B.C.) 17 July B3 They must always keep in mind the duty never to separate words from deeds, and to show that they reject bigheadedness and conformism.

bi-media (baɪ'miːdɪə), *a.* Also **bimedia**. [f. BI-[2] + MEDIA *n. pl.*[2]] Involving or working in two of the mass communication media, esp. radio and television.
1985 *Time* 16 Sept. 65/1 Moviegoers made a bimedia star of *Family Ties'* Michael J. Fox, whose *Back to the Future* and *Teen Wolf* were the biggest box-office

winners of the past two weeks. **1989** *Sunday Tel.* 26 Nov. 43/4 The broadcasters will emerge from their temporary burrows in Bridge Street, in Central Hall and the Dean of Westminster's air raid shelter and install themselves in a grand 'bi-media' centre at Number 4 Millbank. **1990** *Times* 2 Feb. 14/3 Jones and his colleagues were the first truly 'bi-media' correspondents by virtue of their contributions to television news. **1993** *Sunday Times* 13 June IX. 15/5 Humphrys's contract specifies that he reads BBC1's Six O'Clock News for 30 days a year, and that of James Cox specifies he devote 184 days to BBC2's Newsnight and 20 to The World At One. That is the Birtist 'bi-media' revolution in action.

bin, *n.* Senses 7, 8 in Dict. become 9, 10. Add: **7.** Any receptacle for holding rubbish or waste, esp. waste paper; a waste-bin.
1972 T. STOPPARD *Jumpers* I. 23 Crouch enters from the Kitchen, carrying a bin of rubbish and several empty champagne bottles. **1977** P. BAILEY *Peter Smart's Confessions* ii. 20 A bin—I think—is what Mother puts the tea leaves in, and the outsides of potatoes, and shoes when they crack for good, and all the things we don't need any more. **1981** M. GEE *Dying* 151 He had spent hours at the back of the restaurant sorting out specially fresh specimens stupidly cast in the bins. **1985** *Times Lit. Suppl.* 12 July 770, I chuck the other pratts straight in the bin. **1990** *Pract. Health* Spring 9/3 Here's a clever idea.. —a three-compartment bin to help you separate recyclable waste in the kitchen.
8. Each of a series of ranges of numerical value into which data are sorted in statistical analysis.
1934 *Jrnl. Sedimentary Petrol.* IV. 68/2 In setting up a histogram, we are in effect setting up a series of separate 'bins', each of which contains a certain per cent of the grains. **1958** *IRE Trans. Nuclear Sci.* V. 156/1 Each distribution was normalized to the total detection efficiency of the crystal and divided into 'bins' whose centers were spaced at the above source-energy intervals. **1963** *Physical Rev.* CXXXII. 2253/1 In each figure the upper curve gives the result of the ½-MeV bin width unfolding while the bottom curve is a result of unfolding using one-MeV bin widths with two sets of interlacing points. **1971** *Nature* 11 June 372/1 To search for point sources above the atmospheric background a computer program was written which provided a contour output by summing over a 4×4 bin the centre of which was shifted in 1° and 0.02 steps. **1989** *New Scientist* 15 Apr. 42/1 In total we 'swept' through more than 600 000 frequency bins, each only 200 hertz wide.
[10.] binbag *n.* (*Brit.*), a large, strong (usu. plastic) bag designed to be used as a container for esp. household rubbish.
1986 D. CAUTE *News from Nowhere* xiii. 136 The debris, the litter, the overflowing *binbags and cardboard boxes outside the pub lifted his barmy spirits. **1988** *Yorks. Post* 27 Oct. 9/1 The body was dumped in bin bags with a carving knife blade still embedded in the neck.

bin, *v.* Add: [1.] **b.** *colloq.* To put in a waste-bin; to throw away; hence, by extension, to discard.
1940 *Times* 3 Feb. 7/5 My informant instanced the butter, served..in rounds half-an-inch or so thick...Something like two-thirds of the whole amount was often binned among the refuse after a meal. **1982** *Financial Times* 3 July 1. 13/1 'Blowpipe is the first thing to be binned after this' is the verdict of one of the brigade commanders. **1986** *City Limits* 16 Oct. 41 Buy the record, but bin the lyric sheet. **1990** *Independent on Sunday* 4 Nov. (Sunday Rev.) 33/2 Who remembers the kind of middle-class good behaviour, thrift and modesty that have been binned along with Bromo, the *Church Times* and meals for one?
2. To group together (data) in bins (*BIN *n.* 8).

1970 *Dissertation Abstr.* B. XXXI. 3611/1 The measured differential cross sections, binned in cos θ_{cm} intervals of 0.02, have statistical errors of about 10%. **1976** *Physical Rev. Lett.* XXXVI. 1238/1 These high-mass events are presented in Fig. 3 as $(d^2\sigma/dmdy)_{y=0}$..binned in 0.5-GeV intervals. **1992** S. P. MARAN *Astron. & Astrophysics Encycl.* 491/1 *(caption)* Both the data and predictions have been binned into time and energy bins.

binary *a.* and *n.* Add: [A.] [j.] *binary-coded decimal adj. phr.*, designating or expressed in a system of notation according to which each digit of a decimal number is expressed as its binary equivalent, with four binary digits for each decimal digit; also as *n.*, a number expressed in this notation.
1948 *Math. Tables & Other Aids to Computation* III. 286 Decimal numbers must also be..stored in the binary-coded decimal notation to a normal precision of 8 decimal digits. **1959** E. M. McCORMICK *Digital Computer Primer* iv. 47 As indicated previously, humans are trained to think decimally, but computers operate in a binary mode. This gap is bridged by the use of binary-coded decimal (bcd) systems. **1960** GREGORY & VAN HORN *Automatic Data-Processing Syst.* ii. 48 The conversion of a decimal number into a binary-coded decimal..is simpler than its conversion into binary. **1985** *Pract. Computing* July 35/4 The best cure for this sort of nonsense is to perform all arithmetic using the binary-coded decimal (BCD) notation of four bits per decimal unit.

binomial, *a.* and *n.* Add: Hence **bi'nomially** *adv.*, (*a*) *Biol.* (*rare*), in accordance with the binomial system of nomenclature; = *BINOMINALLY adv.*; (*b*) *Statistics*, in accordance with the binomial distribution.
1889 *Cent. Dict.*, *Binomially*, in a binomial manner; after the binomial method of nomenclature in zoölogy and botany. **1976** *Biometrika* LXIII. 441 A binomially distributed random variable.

binominal, *a.* Add: Hence **bi'nominally** *adv.* (*rare*), in accordance with the binominal (binominal) system of nomenclature.
1971 *Nature* 10 Dec. 360/1 The European stock [of the Atlantic salmon], binominally named by Linnaeus, must become the nominate subspecies.

bio-, *comb. form.* Add: '**bio-diesel**, a bio-fuel (see below) intended as a substitute for diesel; *spec.* rape methyl ester.
[**1982** *Chem. Engin.* 8 Feb. 104 Butanol-rich fuel...A newly discovered strain of bacteria produces a butanol-containing fuel that needs no distillation, from municipal, agricultural or food wastes...The developer, Bio-Diesel Fuels Ltd. (Toronto, Ont.), plans to build a demonstration plant by 1984.] **1986** *Ibid.* 27 Oct. 12 c/2 Bio Energy Philippines Inc..claims that it has developed a diesel fuel from copra that is better than regular diesel...Called *Biodiesel, it is said to also be better than Cocodiesel, a mixture of ordinary diesel fuel and coconut oil. **1991** *Daily Tel.* 17 June 5/8 In France the rape fuel is being used in trials to run a fleet of buses. Bio-diesel pumps are sited at a chain of filling stations in Austria. **1991** *South* Aug. 58/2 Bio-diesel is made by mixing rape seed oil (ESO) with Methyl Alcohol to produce Methyl RSO. Glycerol is then added to produce Rape Methyl Ester (RME)—Known as MRE in Germany and diester in France.

biodi'versity *Ecol.*, diversity of plant and animal life, as represented by the number of extant species.
1987 *Nature* 30 Apr. 871/1 Here *biodiversity increases with the introduction of understory vegetation. **1988** E. O. WILSON *Biodiversity* p. vi, The forum was conceived by Walter G. Rosen...Furthermore, he introduced the term

biodiversity [at a forum held on 21–5 September 1986 in Washington, D.C.]. **1988** *Conservation Biol.* II. 307 It's becoming a byword in both house and home, and a cause célèbre among rain forest researchers, but biodiversity has yet to receive the support it deserves from marine ecologists. **1989** *Times* 31 Mar. 5/4 The bio-diversity campaign is an attempt to bring the seriousness of the global situation to the attention of people in all walks of life. **1991** *Nature Conservancy* May-June 21/2 The idea of sustainable development—which acknowledges that human economies, human cultures and biodiversity are inextricably linked.

'**bio-fuel**, fuel derived immediately from living matter; = *biomass* (*b*) s.v. *BIO-*.
1970 *Physics Bull.* Sept. 401/1 The *biofuel cell uses the body's metabolism in the oxidation-reduction process. **1974** *Energy Primer* 106/2 Because wood is such an exploitable biofuel, we felt that reasonable space ought to be devoted to a discussion of its efficient use. **1985** *Fortune* 13 May 82/2 The use of biofuels in place of expensive oil naturally means big savings in energy costs. **1992** *Farmers Weekly* 14 Aug. 40/1 Within five years 600,000t of the new rape-based bio-fuel rape methyl ester (RME) will be produced on the Continent.

biochem (baɪə'kɛm), *n. colloq.* [Abbrev.] = BIOCHEMISTRY *n.*
1968 J. HUDSON *Case of Need* I. 10 A beautiful and efficient girl with a Ph.D. in biochem from Stanford. **1986** BENFORD & BRIN *Heart of Comet* (1987) I. 35 My biochem might screw up in some way the experts missed out on.

biocide, *n.* Add: Hence **bio'cidal** *a.*, having or designating the properties of a biocide.
1954 *Jrnl. Appl. Chem.* IV. 314 Possibilities for practical applications of organo-tin compounds as a consequence of their biocidal properties. **1964** *New Statesman* 20 Mar. 440/1 If biocidal chemicals bring our countryside nearer the American pattern,..then our grandchildren may well be grateful. **1991** *Discover* Mar. 10/3 Thiarubrine A, a potent biocidal agent that passes easily through the lining of the mouth but would be rendered ineffective by stomach acids if swallowed.

biomedicine ('baɪəʊmɛds(ə)n), *n.* orig. and chiefly *U. S.* [f. BIO- + MEDICINE *n.*[1]] Biology and medicine collectively; the biomedical sciences.
1923 DORLAND *Med. Dict.* (ed. 12) 172/2 *Biomedicine*, clinical medicine based on the principles of physiology and biochemistry. **1956** P. E. KLOPSTEG *Instrumentation in Bio-Med. Res.* (U.S. Nat. Res. Council: Biol. Council) 1 A secondary consideration is the enlistment into bio-medicine of those who are already trained in physics and engineering. **1966** *Ann. N.Y. Acad. Sci.* CXXVIII. 721, I believe that the applications of computers in biomedicine are going through a number of..stages. **1973** *Biomedicine* XVIII. 4/1 The new name of the journal, *Biomedicine*, is to underline once more that it is at the *crossroads* of biological and clinical investigation. **1986** *Social Sci. & Med.* XXII. 83/2 A woman who expects to attend college and wants to work in biomedicine selects training in pharmacy, nutrition or even dentistry.

bird, *n.* Add: [II.] [8.] [d.] *bird book.*
1900 *Nature* 1 Feb. 323/1 *(heading)* Three new *bird books. **1937** C'TESS OF WARWICK in S. V. Benson *Observer's Bk. Brit. Birds* 16, I have read many of these books, for I love birds.., but I do not remember seeing any bird book like this one before. **1965** *Jrnl. Lancs. Dial. Soc.* Jan. 5 They are listed in Wetmore Order, i.e. the system of classification which is generally accepted in modern bird books. **1989** I. FRAZIER *Great Plains* i. 14 Birds with long curved bills (Hudsonian godwits, the bird book said) flew just above us.

birr (bɪr), *n.*[2] Pl. **birr, birrs.** [ad. Amharic *bǝrr.* Earlier used of various foreign silver coins, esp. dollars.] The unit of currency in Ethiopia, consisting of 100 cents, which replaced the Ethiopian dollar in 1976; a note or coin of this value.

1976 *Times* 23 Sept. 6/1 Ethiopia is to introduce a new currency from October 14. The Ethiopian dollar will be replaced by the birr, with the same exchange rate in the international market. **1977** *Statesman's Year-Bk.* 1977–78 916 The Ethiopian *birr*..is based on 5.52 grains of fine gold. **1984** *Daily Tel.* 24 Nov. 16/4 The birr is linked to the dollar. **1991** R. WALDROP tr. *Borer's Rimbaud in Abyssinia* i. 22, I don't have any Ethiopian birrs yet, and charity seems suddenly an odious Western idea.

bisulphate (baɪˈsʌlfeɪt), *n. Chem.* [f. BI-[2] III + SULPHATE *n.*] A compound in which one of the two hydrogen atoms of sulphuric acid, H_2SO_4, has been replaced by another atom or group (as in potassium bisulphate, $KHSO_4$).

1818 W. HENRY *Elements Exper. Chem.* (ed. 8) I. xii. 346 The bi-sulphate or super-sulphate, it is probable, consists of one atom of base with two atoms of acid. **1845** E. A. PARNELL *Elements Chem. Anal.* (new ed.) iii. 96 Silver and palladium are the only noble metals which dissolve in melted bisulphate of potash. **1931** C. ELLIS *Hydrogenation Org. Substances* (ed. 3) lxi. 853 A method of utilizing the acid values of sodium acid sulphate or bisulphate is recommended by Becquevort and Deguide. **1966** *McGraw-Hill Encycl. Sci. & Technol.* XIII. 264/1 Sulfuric acid ionizes in water, forming hydrogen (H^+), bisulfate (HSO_4^-), and sulfate (SO_4^-) ions. **1980** M. ORCHIN et al. *Vocab. Org. Chem.* iv. 102 *Bisulfate Esters*, $ROSO_2OH$. Mono esters of sulfuric acid.

black, *a.* Add: [**19.**] **black caucus** *U.S.,* a political caucus composed of black people interested in advancing the concerns of blacks, *spec.* (with capital initial) that composed of black members of Congress.

1967 *N.Y. Times* 7 Sept. 42/4 When I tried to get into the *black caucus, they said, 'No peckerwoods allowed in here, Sonny.' **1971** *Washington Post* 20 May A13/1 The President's response to the congressional Black Caucus should stand as a comprehensive statement of 'where we are at this moment.' **1989** SPOCK & MORGAN *Spock on Spock* xiv. 173 The black caucus..absented themselves from the conference and effectively stalled it for two days while they formulated their 'nonnegotiable demands'. **1994** *Denver Post* 16 Jan. A11/5 The Congressional Black Congress..urged the United States to consider using force to dislodge the military leaders who overthrew Aristide.

black consciousness (freq. with capital initials), awareness of one's identity as a black person; *spec.* used *attrib.* and *absol.* to designate various political movements, esp. in the United States, seeking to unite black people in affirming their common identity.

1953 F. HENRIQUES *Family & Colour in Jamaica* iii. 62 The current expositors of *black consciousness in Jamaica are a group of people who call themselves Ras Tafarites. **1966** L. JONES *Home* 241 Malcolm X's great contribution..was to preach Black Consciousness to the Black Man...Malcolm talked about a black consciousness that took its form from religion. **1991** *Guardian* 13 May 1/6 Supporters of the black consciousness movement, Azapo.

blanket, *n.* [**4.**] For def. read: *Printing.* A layer of cloth or other soft material placed between the type and the impressing surface so as to deaden and equalize the pressure exerted; later also used in offset printing to designate the surface which receives the inked image from the plate. (Earlier and later examples.)

1683–4 J. MOXON *Mech. Exerc. Printing* II. 369 *Blankets.* Woollen Cloath, or White Bays, to lay between the *Tympans.* **1890** W. J. GORDON *Foundry* 221 (*Rotary Press*) It was customary to work entirely with soft packing—that is to say, with a thick blanket or cloth between the impression cylinder and the paper. **1894** *Amer. Dict. Printing & Bookmaking* 48/1 *Blanket,* any yielding substance used between the type and the impression plate or cylinder to soften or render the pressure even. It may be of paper, cloth or india-rubber. **1936** MENCKEN *Amer. Lang.* (ed. 4) vi. 261 In England, it appeared, stereotypers' blankets were called *packing.* **1963** KENNEISON & SPILMAN *Dict. Printing* 19 *Blanket,* the packing used on the impression cylinder of a printing machine. It may consist of cloth, rubber or paper used in various ways. The rubber covering to the printing cylinder of an offset machine is often referred to as the *blanket.* **1988** *Artist's & Illustrator's Mag.* Feb. 46/1 The edges of the plates must be filed in order that during printing they do not cut the paper or the press blankets.

blast, *n.*[1] Add: [**10.**] **blast-hole,** (*b*) *Mining,* a hole into which a charge of explosive is inserted.

1747 W. HOOSON *Miners Dict.* s.v. *Noger,* Their bigness is about an inch at least, for either *Blast-holes, or Clift-holes. **1944** *Mining Congress Jrnl.* June 77/3 The diamond drill is particularly adapted for blast holes. *Ibid.* 71/1 Blast hole drilling with diamond bits has been introduced recently..in the United States and Canada.

bleating, *ppl. a.* Add: Hence ˈ**bleatingly** *adv.,* in a manner suggestive of bleating.

1934 in WEBSTER. **1986** *Financial Times* 11 Mar. 1. 23/8 Matthew's function is unclarified...He occasionally bleatingly reminds us that the hero is English.

block, *n.* Add: [**V.**] [**23.**] **block party** *U.S.,* a party, usu. one held outdoors, given by and for all the residents of a block or neighbourhood.

1919 *Red Cross Mag.* Oct. 79/2 The *block party idea had just struck Waterbury in the middle of the summer but it seems to have struck hard. **1935** C. F. WARE *Greenwich Village 1920–1930* iv. 101 Such general forms of block organization..as the block parties which the political organizations used to stage had entirely disappeared by 1930. **1949** M. MEAD *Male & Female* xv. 307 The block-party for the only family that got into the new housing project. **1967** *Boston Sunday Globe* 21 May B60/7 (*caption*) An old fashion block party was held last week in penthouse apartment of Tremont-on-the-Common. **1992** *Buffalo* (N.Y.) *News* 23 Aug. C1/1 Mrs. Gates and a dozen or so neighbours decided to throw a block party on Saturday to thank the police and firefighters who serve them.

[**24.**] *c.* In the sense 'affecting a predefined block of text or data', esp. in *block delete, move.*

1962 *Gloss. Terms Automatic Data Processing* (*B.S.I.*) 25 *Block transfer,* the process of transferring a block of data as a single operation. **1981** *EDN* XXVI. 171/1 This word-processing package offers several features not found in similar products:..Column block moves, [etc.]. **1983** D. GOODMAN *Word Processing on IBM PC* xi. 155 This also gives you the option of changing the order of sections without doing repeated block moves. **1985** *Which Computer?* Apr. 8/2 The decision gives versatile editing commands such as block move, insert and delete. **1990** *Metals & Materials* July 437/1 Spreadsheets are available for processing and transformation of data using mathematical and block editing functions.

blonde, *a.* and *n.* Add: [**A.**] [**d.**] **blonde ray,** a pale brown ray, *Raja brachyura,* of south-west European waters.

1925 J. T. JENKINS *Fishes Brit. Isles* 333 A large *blonde Ray was caught by the trawl and placed alive in a tank. **1959** A. HARDY *Open Sea* II. ix. 186 The short-nosed species have their bodies of a typical diamond shape, due to the pointed wing-tips and short but well-defined snout; they are..the thornback ray..the blonde ray; [etc.]. **1976** *Southern Even. Echo* (Southampton) 12 Nov. 25/7 The blonde rays..put in the occasional appearance on the Shambles Bank.

blood, *n.* Add: [VI.] [20.] [a.] (In sense 1) *blood-sample*.
   1950 *Sci. News* XV. 106 In no case did the serum agglutinate the red cells which came from the same *blood sample. **1983** *Oxf. Textbk. Med.* I. ix. 5/1 It is better..if the GP immediately takes a blood sample for blood glucose estimation.

bloody-minded, *a.* Add: Hence **bloody-'mindedly** *adv.*
   1971 *Farmer & Stockbreeder* 23 Feb. 16/3 The way to get this altered is..to join the Union, and contribute to its debates as persistently and as bloody-mindedly as I did in my early days. **1991** *Economist* 26 Jan. 17 He must go on reassuring other parties—some of whom bloody-mindedly reject negotiation—that their views will be heard.

blot, *n.*[1] Add: [1.] f. *Biochem.* The distribution pattern of proteins, nucleic acids, etc., on a medium on which they have been blotted (*BLOT *v.* 7).
   1979 *Proc. Nat. Acad. Sci.* LXXVI. 860 (*caption*) Localization of the V and C regions in Ch603a6 by hybridization to Southern blots. *Ibid.* LXXVI. 4354/1 Enzymes separated on polyacrylamide gels could also be conveniently localized on blots by *in situ* assays. **1989** *Jrnl. Autoimmunity* II. 769 (*caption*) The blot was hybridized with a ^{32}P labeled IFN-α4-specific cDNA probe, and autoradiographed for 24 h.

blot, *v.* Add: 7. *Biochem.* To transfer (biochemical material under analysis) from a medium used for electrophoretic separation to an immobilizing medium on which specific target molecules can be identified.
   1979 *Proc. Nat. Acad. Sci.* LXXVI. 4350/2 The gel to be blotted was put on the nitrocellulose sheet and care was taken to remove all air bubbles. **1981** *Lancet* 21 Nov. 1126/1 After digestion, restricted DNA was run on 1 % agarose gels, in the presence of size markers, and 'blotted' onto nitrocellulose filters. **1986** *Sci. Amer.* Mar. 45/3 The DNA is unraveled into single strands and blotted onto special filter paper. **1989** *Jrnl. Autoimmunity* II. 769 RNA extracted from..peritoneal macrophages..was blotted at the indicated concentrations to a Zeta-Bind nylon membrane.

blotting, *vbl. n.* Sense 4 in Dict. becomes 5. Add: **4.** *Biochem.* The technique or process of blotting proteins or nucleic acids.
   1979 *Proc. Nat. Acad. Sci.* LXXVI. 4351/2 The blotting procedure removed all protein from the gel. **1983** J. R. S. FINCHAM *Genetics* vii. 186 This is a blotting procedure whereby a pattern of DNA bands in an agarose gel is transferred to a nitrocellulose sheet after first denaturing the DNA with alkali. **1989** *Molecular & Cellular Probes* III. 319 A new ultrasensitive bioluminescence-enhanced detection system for protein blotting has been developed.

Boat (bəʊt), *n.*[2] Also BOAT. [Acronym, f. the initial letters of *b*yway *o*pen to *a*ll *t*raffic.] In Britain, a public right of way open to all types of vehicle on the basis of historical evidence of vehicular use, although in the recent past used chiefly as a lane or path.
   [**1968** *Act Eliz. II (Countryside Act)* c.41 Sched. 3 §9(1) In the special review..the definitive map..shall show every road used as a public path by one of the three following descriptions—(*a*) a 'byway open to all traffic', (*b*) a 'bridleway', (*c*) a 'footpath'.] **1988** *Rights of Way Survey Manual* (Countryside Commission) 3/1

Byways open to all traffic (usually referred to just as 'byways' or abbreviated to BOAT). These can legally be used by all types of traffic, including motor and horse-drawn vehicles. **1989** *Daily Tel.* 17 Feb. 3/7 Councils are legally bound by the 1981 Wildlife and Countryside Act to re-classify such lanes as BOATs where there is past evidence of vehicular use. **1989** *Great Outdoors* Sept. 10/2 Vehicles can have a legal right to use some RUPPs (roads used as public paths) and BOATs (bridleways open to all traffic). **1990** *Times* 17 Mar. 11/3 Paths..are to be reclassified by the local authority into Boats.

bodacious, *a.* Add: **2.** *slang* (orig. and chiefly *U. S.*) **a.** Excellent, fabulous, great. **b.** Sexually attractive.
   1976 C. WHELTON *CB Baby* 168 A couple of days and you'll be doing a bodacious job again, for sure. **1979** *Farmington* (New Mexico) *Daily Times* 27 May (Comic Suppl.) 2 Thank goodness fer them bodacious child-proof caps. **1989** *California* Sept. 128/3 El Set, in the Conchas Chinas hotel south of town, serves bodacious grilled lobster. **1991-2** *Filmfax* Dec./Jan. 87 (Advt.), Curvaceous cuties and bodacious bouncing babes reveal the utmost in feminine beauty in these spicy peep shows and arcade loops. **1992** *Premiere* Jan. 97/4 Those bodacious dudes have an excellent time playing games with death. **1993** *Face* Sept. 110/1 The audience has a chance to check the baby oil dripping from the bodacious one's glistening torso.

bodice, *n.* Sense 3 becomes an ac block. Add: [3.] **bodice-ripper** *colloq.*, a sexually explicit romantic novel, *esp.* one in a historical setting with a plot involving the seduction of the heroine; also *transf.*, a film of a similar nature.
   1980 *N. Y. Times* (Nexis) 28 Dec. vii. 4/1 Women..too have their pornography: Harlequin romances, novels of 'sweet savagery,' *bodice-rippers. **1981** J. SUTHERLAND *Bestsellers* vii. 85 The most dramatic innovation in the field of popular women's fiction was the success of 'hot ones', 'bodice rippers', or 'sweet and savages' as they were called. **1984** E. JONG *Parachutes & Kisses* xii. 208 That scene in bodice-ripper romances where the vulnerable heroine meets the rakehell hero. **1987** *Times Lit. Suppl.* 17 Apr. 408/3 British cinema belatedly grew up—or so people thought at the time. Out, by and large, went the last traces of the Gainsborough bodice-rippers. **1989** C. D. GEIST in Wilson & Ferris *Encycl. Southern Culture* 863/2 Historic romances in an Old South setting were..similar to the traditional historical romance...By the 1970s the form was referred to as the 'bodice ripper' by critics. **1991** *Gay Times* Jan. 57/4 Replete with interesting details about gay life in the city at that time, this..novel is really a bodice-ripper constrained within a thriller corset.

body, *n.* Add: [VI.] [30.] **body double**, a stand-in for a film actor during nude scenes or action sequences.
   1981 *Washington Post* 22 June C1/4 She is too innocent, too sweet...She won't do the nude scenes, so we have to use a *body double. It is frustrating. **1983** *People* 26 Dec. 98/2 The footwork was done not by star Jennifer Beals, but by her body double, Jahan, 25. **1992** *N. Y. Times* 19 Jan. 11. 13/2 'Usually they'll put out a call for measurements,' says Shelley Michelle, who was Julia Roberts's body double in..'Pretty Woman'.
   body piercing, the piercing of parts of the body other than the ear, in order to insert rods, rings, and other objects either as a form of adornment or to enhance sexual pleasure; so **body-piercer**, a person who practises body piercing.
   1977 E. J. TRIMMER et al. *Visual Dict. Sex* (1978) 60/2 Infibulation is a form of *body-piercing that is found among a few primitive communities, and is usually intended to restrict sexual intercourse. *Ibid.*

60/3 Among Western *body-piercers, another form of infibulation is practised, in which partners put a padlock through the foreskin or the labia, and keep the keys with each other's consent, thus allowing for a variety of dominance situations. **1992** *Guardian* 4 Dec. II. 9/1 According to body piercer Teena Maree, 'The number and variety of people coming to be pierced has increased outrageously in the past year or so.' **1993** *Independent* 16 July 18/1 When the teen pin-up Howard Donald from the band Take That . . appears in prepubescent magazines such as *Smash Hits* or *Fast Forward* with a couple of inches of steel through his left nipple, you know that body piercing has become about as *risqué* as growing your hair long or having a tattoo on your buttock.

bodysuit, any (usu. close-fitting) garment which more or less covers the body, *esp.* a woman's one-piece stretch garment resembling a leotard.

1969 *Good Housekeeping* (N.Y.) July 130/1 The latest designs are the new improved bra slip and the never-before *body suit. Ibid.*, Body suits cling softly, to give a sleek, all-in-one look, control the figure gently. **1970** *Britannica Bk. of Year* (U.S.) 344/1 Warner's, the 'grandaddy of the bodysuit family', brought out 'You-Curve', a bodysuit in stretch tricot net. **1975** C. CALASIBETTA *Fairchild's Dict. Fashion* 45/1 *Body suit*, one-piece fitted garment without legs having a snap crotch. **1982** *Washington Post* 13 May C17/4 Before he changes into his tight red Spandex bodysuit with the plunging neckline, there is the quick hint of a tattoo lurking beneath the rolled-up sleeve on his right arm. **1990** *Observer* 25 Mar. 33/4 Bodysuits . . are usually made of skin-tight lycra and increasingly worn by girls as outerwear.

boggling, *ppl. a.* Add: **2.** [After *mind-boggling* adj. s.v. MIND *n.*[1] 21 b] That causes one to boggle or be overwhelmed; staggering, mind-boggling. Freq. as the second element in *comb.* with nouns.

1975 *Economist* 10 May 119/2 Merchant bankers Hill Samuel had unravelled a computer-boggling network of crossholdings. **1976** *National Observer* (U.S.) 31 Jan. 1/2 The press room . . is a bit boggling. It is really a complex of rooms, encompassing a Western Union setup, [etc.]. **1985** *N.Y. Times* 18 Aug. v. 9/2 Per-mile costs fell fractionally as a result of the additional travel, whose total was a boggling 1.526 trillion miles. **1990** *Which?* Mar. 144/1 Serious damage can mean even more boggling bills, but at least your insurance should cover it. **1993** *USA Weekend* 8 Aug. 14/2 The mouth-boggling 'Chatta-burger' is the stuff dreams are made of.

boho ('bəʊhəʊ), *n.* and *a. slang* (orig. and chiefly *U. S.*). Also (in sense 1) **bohoe**, and with capital initial. [Abbrev. of BOHEMIAN *a.* and *n.*: see -o[2].] **A.** *n.* **1.** A Czechoslovak, *spec.* one resident in the U.S. *Obs.* or *rare.* Cf. BOHUNK *n.*

1920 T. ČAPEK *Čechs in Amer.* x. 114 In some localities Bohemians are called 'Bohoes', in others 'Bohunks'; less familiar are the terms 'Cheskey' and 'Bootchkey'. **1936** MENCKEN *Amer. Lang.* (ed. 4) VI. vi. 295 For Czech: *bohoe, bohick, bohee, bohunk, bootchkey* and *cheskey.*

2. A person who has an unconventional or Bohemian way of life, *esp.* one with literary or artistic preoccupations; such a lifestyle, or the subculture associated with it. Cf. BOHEMIAN *n.* 3.

1958 J. DAVIS *College Vocab.* (term paper, Indiana Univ. Folklore Archive) 5 *Boho*, . . a nonconformist, usually an Art or Speech and Theater major. **1968** T. WOLFE *Electric Kool-Aid Acid Test* xxi. 316, 48-year-old bohos sucking up to young heads of the new generation of Hip. **1979** *Fanfare* (Toronto) 9 June 8/3 Following the New York example . . young professionals — architects, hairdressers, photographers — have decided that boho is chi-chi. **1988** *New Musical Express* 24 Dec. 37/6 *Neon Wilderness* is Algren at the very edge of things, tracing short story narratives from

the wild side, bohos, losers and night people surviving in inner city nightmare zones.

B. *adj.* Of or pertaining to such a person, lifestyle, or subculture; unconventional, decadent; artistic, fashionable. Cf. BOHEMIAN *a.* 3.

1958 J. DAVIS *College Vocab.* (term paper, Indiana Univ. Folklore Archive) 5 *Boho*, . . Bohemian. **1970** E. SEGAL *Love Story* i. 3 Her costume . . was a bit too Boho for my taste. I especially loathed that Indian thing she carried for a handbag. **1975** J. MITCHELL *The Boho Dance* (song) in *Hissing of Summer Lawns* (record), Down in the cellar in the Boho zone I went looking for some sweet inspiration. **1984** *Time* 29 Oct. 83/3 Sprouse had dropped out of the Rhode Island School of Design and done some apprentice work with Halston before taking up the boho life in Manhattan. **1993** *New Statesman & Society* 23 Apr. 40 She swandives gracefully into San Francisco's boho snakepit only to find, as one does, that beneath the alluring narratives of decadence 'it was chaos'.

bootable ('buːtəb(ə)l), *a. Computing.* [f. BOOT *v.*[4] + -ABLE.] Capable of being booted; containing the software required to boot a computer.

1982 *Computerworld* 31 May 47 Powertext is said to be a runtime bootable system requiring a minimum of 64K bytes of memory, two disk drives and a printer. **1984** *PC* 30 Oct. 142 You simply use . . the COPY command to move *Micro Trak* files onto a bootable disk. **1986** *Your Computer* Oct. 67/1 Prospell is on one disc which is not bootable with the main program on one side and the dictionary on the other. **1993** *Compute* Sept. 46/3, I backed up my hard disk . . . Then I created a DOS 6 bootable floppy and reformatted my hard disk . . to make the disk bootable.

Hence **boota'bility** *n.*

1984 *PC Week* 23 Oct. S10/4 The PC10 has a feature most other add-on systems lack — bootability.

bootleg, *n.* Sense 2 in Dict. becomes 3. Add: **2.** *Amer. Football.* A play in which the ball-carrier pretends to hand the ball to a team-mate but continues to carry it, concealing it from opposing players by holding it near his hip. Freq. *attrib.* Cf. *BOOTLEG v.*

[**1945** *Time* 3 Dec. 72/2 His favorite play is the 'bootlegger': Waterfield simply fakes to other backs, then pulls some fast sleight-of-hand and swings out around end, literally hiding the ball behind his back.] **1949** P. CUMMINGS *Dict. Sports* 44/1 *Bootleg play*, . . a play where the ball-carrier fakes giving it to a teammate, then conceals it behind his hip, and runs in a different direction from that indicated by the player who faked receiving it. **1958** *Sports Illustr.* 6 Oct. 51/2 I've never been able to run a bootleg against Andy Robustelli. **1960** BLAIK & COHANE *You have to pay Price* xix. 361 He also scored our other marker on a 24-yard bootleg run. **1990** *Pittsburgh Post-Gaz.* 1 Jan. 30/1 We were using that running play to set up a bootleg to the other side on the next play.

bootleg ('buːtlɛg), *v.* [f. the n.] **1.** (Formerly at BOOTLEG *n.* in Dict.).

2. *intr. Amer. Football.* To execute a 'bootleg'; to turn sharply in the course of this. Also *trans.*, with ball as obj.

1951 *Sport* (U.S.) Nov. 69/3 If Waterfield bootlegs around you this afternoon, it'll cost you 25 bucks. **1960** WENTWORTH & FLEXNER *Dict. Amer. Slang* 55/2 *Bootleg*, . . *v.t.* To carry the ball deceptively, as in football and other sports. **1969** BENGTSON & HUNT *Packer Dynasty* viii. 81 Starr masterfully faked the handoff, bootlegged, and then lofted the ball to Paul in the clear. **1989** *N.Y. Times* 3 Jan. B7/6 On third-and-goal from the 1, he bootlegged the ball on a fake sweep and then flipped a touchdown pass to Corwin Anthony.

born-again, *a*. Senses a, b in Dict. become 1 and 2. Add: **3.** Of objects: renovated, restored; 'new-look'.

1977 *Washington Post* 9 Apr. B2/6 The Old Post Office restoration will be a towering beginning for a born-again Pennsylvania Avenue. **1978** J. GROSS (*title*) The 30-day way to a born-again body. **1986** *Sunday Mail Mag.* (Brisbane) 27 Apr. 26/1 It has taken the Americans and the Swedes to turn Australians on to the latest home-improvement craze—'born again' wardrobes and storage cupboards. **1991** *Business* July (front cover), Born-again Berlin..Europe's new business capital.

4. More loosely: that has undergone a renewal of any kind; revitalized, transformed; given another opportunity to be (some specified kind of person).

1977 *Washington Post* 1 Jan. C3/5 Encouraging com[e]backs included Speedy Alka-Seltzer's resurrection..and a born-again Mister Peanut, whose daffily dancing reappearance can surely be linked to recent political history. **1980** *Chicago Tribune* 20 July VI. 1 The 'born-again' comic [*sc*. Rodney Dangerfield] gets respect from a new, young audience. **1986** *Los Angeles Times* 31 Aug. (Calendar) 75/2 In early May, he performed as Joe Clay for the first time in almost three decades...And when the year's unlikeliest born-again rocker finished his second encore, the chant started. **1988** *Pilot* Nov. 26/1 In March 1987 I was a born-again student, having got my PPL in 1954.., then having to let the licence go at the end of 1956 when marriage came along. **1990** *Sounds* 28 July 26/2 If it's not banal rhetoric celebrating born-again rockers it's eulogies to bands like U2 who're capitalising on the trend by paying homage to false idols.

Botswanan (bɒtˈswɑːnən), *n*. and *a*. Also (occas.) **-ian**. [f. the place-name *Botswana* + -AN.] **A.** *n*. A native or inhabitant of the republic of Botswana, which became an independent state in 1966. **B.** *adj*. Of or pertaining to Botswana.

In Botswana itself the standard terms amongst residents are *Motswana* (and pl. *Batswana*) for the noun, and *Tswana* (q.v.) for the adjective.

1967 *Britannica Bk. of Year* (U.S.) 176/2 The economy..remained overwhelmingly dependent on South Africa, both as a major market of exports and as an employer of Botswanan labour. **1967** *N.Y. Times* 26 Nov. 1. 150/3 The new industries are expected to create employment for a large number of Botswanans. **1970** *Times* 9 May 8/5 He hopes that the school's target of 250 pupils will eventually comprise a majority of Botswanans. **1977** *Facts on File* 23 Apr. 297/1 Two Botswanans who had been abducted into Rhodesia by security forces and charged with illegal arms possession. **1980** D. HUNT *Times Yearbk. World Affairs 1979–80* 56/1 On their way back to Rhodesia the force exchanged fire with an aircraft of the Botswanan air force. **1989** *Japan Times* 21 May 4/7 Botswanan Ambassador Joseph Legwaila is the front-runner for deputy head of the U.N. operation in Namibia.

bounce, *n*.[1] Add: **[3.] c.** orig. and chiefly *U.S.* (*a*) *Comm.*, a sudden increase in a price or rate; (*b*) *Pol.*, a sudden upward swing in the popularity of a candidate or party.

1975 *U.S. News & World Rep.* 2 June 55 The bounce in consumer prices followed another in the wholesale index that has not yet had time to be fully reflected in retail stores. **1980** *N.Y. Times* 20 Aug. B9/4 Jody Powell, Mr. Carter's press secretary, called the results enthusiastically 'the post-convention bounce we hoped for.' **1984** *Bond Buyer* 12 Mar. 16/2 Some bounce in bond prices should be almost a sure thing, but nobody late last week appeared likely to bet on it. **1986** *Washington Post* 26 Nov. A4/1 In the midterm election just passed, it [*sc*. Social Security] took what has by now become a familiar bounce, as Democratic candidates in state after state bashed their Republican opponents. **1989** *Money Observer* Jan. 5/3 The yen is

likely to be the best currency prospect for 1989, but I am also hopeful of a bounce in the dollar. **1992** *Time* 20 Apr. 38/2 It is rare enough for a candidate not to get a bounce in the polls after winning some major primaries; to lose ground is almost unheard of.

boundary, *n*. Add: [**1.**] [**b.**] **boundary condition** *Math.*, a condition required to be satisfied along part or all of the boundary of a region within which a given set of differential equations is to be solved.

1902 *Internat. Catal. Sci. Lit.* I. VII. A. 165/2 (*heading*) Dirichlet's problem and analogous problems, affected by *boundary conditions. **1927** E. L. INCE *Ordinary Differential Equations* ix. 206 Each boundary condition is equivalent to a linear difference equation connecting y_0, y_1, y_{s-1}, and y_s. **1972** M. KLINE *Math. Thought* xxviii. 688 These equations must be solved subject to appropriate boundary conditions.

boundary value *Math.*, a value specified by a boundary condition.

1898 *Proc. London Math. Soc.* XXIX. 373, R consists of terms involving the *boundary values of $f(x, y,...)$, $\psi(x, y,...)$ and their partial differential coefficients. **1957** L. FOX *Numerical Solution Two-Point Boundary Probl.* iii. 54 If the boundary condition is other than 'boundary value specified' the technique needs modification. **1968** E. T. COPSON *Metric Spaces* viii. 125 This boundary value problem has a continuously differentiable solution.

bovine, *a*. Add: **3.** Special collocation. **bovine spongiform encephalopathy**, spongiform encephalopathy of cattle, a fatal neurological disease characterized by behavioural disorders including unsteady gait and nervousness; abbrev. *BSE* s.v. B III. 1. Cf. *mad cow disease* s.v. *MAD a.* 9.

1987 G. A. H. WELLS et al. in *Vet. Rec.* 31 Oct. 420/2 Studies have been initiated but until further characterisation is achieved the authors suggest for this disorder the provisional appellation: *bovine spongiform encephalopathy. **1987** *New Scientist* 5 Nov. 30/1 Like scrapie..bovine spongiform encephalopathy is insidious and progressive. **1991** *Independent* 1 Nov. 7/1 'Mad cat' disease—the feline form of Bovine Spongiform Encephalopathy (BSE)—is likely to have been caused by contaminated cat food.

bowl, *n*.[1] Add: [**3.**] **e.** A sporting occasion, held in such a stadium, at which a football game is the main (orig. the only) event; later extended to include similar events held elsewhere. Also *spec.* = *bowl game*, sense *7 below. *U.S.*

1935 *Birmingham* (Alabama) *News* 31 Dec. 9/6 So that makes the Orange Bowl not so much of a test of the Warner vs Rockne systems. **1949** *Collier's* 31 Dec. 13/2 Only five bowls were played on college—or even on junior college athletic fields. *Ibid.*, The East-West game has been cited as a model for operations of its kind, but it is not a *bowl* in the accepted sense. **1969** *Eugene* (Oregon) *Register-Guard* 3 Dec. 1D/1 (*heading*) Bowls at a glance. **1988** *First Down* 19 Nov. 20/3 Our first consideration is a bowl that would give us the best chance at winning the national championship.

[7.] bowl game *Amer. Football*, an established post-season game, *spec.* one played at any of a number of named stadiums.

1935 *N.Y. Times* 29 Dec. v. 9/2 Dorais suggested that a committee be formed to investigate the *bowl games to determine whether they are 'healthy appendages or cancerous growths'. **1940** *Sun* (Baltimore) 3 Dec. 15/5 There also will be a bowl game New Year's Day on the Pacific Coast. **1982** S. B. FLEXNER *Listening to Amer.* 249 This 1917 game [in the Pasadena Rose Bowl] popularized the terms *Rose Bowl*, *bowl game*, and *postseason* game. **1991** *Rutgers Mag.* Fall 40/3 When was the last time Rutgers went to a bowl game? (The answer is 1978, when the Knights played in the late, unlamented Garden State Bowl.)

brachy-, *comb. form.* Add: **brachy'pellic** *a.* *Anat.* [Gr. πέλλα bowl, taken as = pelvis], having or designating a pelvis whose anteroposterior diameter is much greater than its transverse diameter.

1937 H. THOMS in *Surg., Gynecol. & Obstetr.* LXIV. 701/1 To these four types the following Greek derivatives lend themselves admirably..: (1) Dolichopellic type or anthropoid pelvis; (2) mesatipellic type or round pelvis; (3) brachypellic type or oval pelvis; (4) platypellic type or flat pelvis. *Ibid.*, I have introduced the term brachypellic, which Turner did not employ, in order to reserve the term platypellic for those pelves which show marked anteroposterior flattening, i.e., a transverse diameter greatly in excess of the anteroposterior diameter. **1980** *Gray's Anat.* (ed. 36) iii. 387/1 In one large series, children and males were found to be predominantly dolichopellic, females mostly mesati- and brachy-pellic.

brain, *n.* [6.] **brain-dead** *a.* Substitute for lemma: **brain-dead** *a.*, (*a*) having suffered brain death; (*b*) *slang* (orig. U.S.), lacking in (esp. intellectual) vigour; feeble-minded, stupid, vapid; also, enervated, moribund.

1976 *Time* 12 Apr. 50 Because Karen was not '*brain dead', few lawyers were surprised when Judge Robert Mair ruled against any 'pulling of the plug'. **1981** *Washington Post* 15 Jan. D15/1 Dickstein says he considers Brenner's success remarkable 'for a person who has been essentially brain-dead for years'. **1986** *Telegraph* (Brisbane) 12 June 5/5 A 17-day-old boy who last night was given the heart of a brain-dead infant.. gave no sign of rejecting the new organ. **1988** *Times* 26 Apr. 2/4 Mr Norman Tebbit, the former Conservative Party chairman, yesterday pronounced socialism as 'brain-dead' in Britain. **1990** *Daily Mirror* 3 Feb. 10, I squealed as.. Randy Ron.. dropped his G-string to have his way with brain-dead yomping freak Billy. **1993** *USA Weekend* 24 Jan. 20/1 They will invigorate brain-dead offices.. with a sense of mission.

brannigan ('brænɪgən), *n. N. Amer. slang.* Also **branigan.** [Origin unknown: prob. f. the proper name.] **1.** A state of intoxication; hence, a drinking bout; a spree or 'binge'. Also *transf.* Now *rare.*

1892 W. NORR *Stories of Chinatown* 31 The boxer was carrying.. what in Pell street parlance is termed a 'brannigan', a condition produced by two gallons of mixed ale to one quart of whiskey. **1903** ADE *People you Know* 210 By the time the Birds came along he had accumulated a very neat Brannigan. **1918** —— in *Cosmopolitan* July 102/2 Emerson truly says in his Essay on Compensation that those who would enjoy the wolfish Satisfaction of shoveling it in each Morning must forego the simple Delights of acquiring a Brannigan the Night before. **1927** E. WILSON *Amer. Earthquake* (1958) 91 One hears nowadays less often of people going on *sprees, toots, tears, jags, bats, brannigans* or *benders.* All these terms suggest, not merely extreme drunkenness, but also an exceptional occurrence, a breaking away by the drinker from the conditions of his normal life. **1928** *Amer. Mercury* May 100/1 He may seek escape by going on prolonged.. crossword puzzle brannigans. **1940** H. L. MENCKEN *Happy Days* 270 In the intervals of his washing and polishing Jim took out rigs to the homes of clients of the stable, and thereby sometimes acquired quiet brannigans, for it was the custom to reward him, not with money, but with drinks. **1978** in H. BERRY *Make Kaiser Dance* 312 Oh but we had a Branigan that night! So the next morning my mouth felt like the inside of a motorman's glove, and my gut wasn't any better.

2. A brawl or fracas; a violent argument.

1941 *Amer. Speech* XVI. 70 On a brannigan (I have seen this word used as meaning *in a fight*). **1955** *Star Weekly* (Toronto) 16 July 11. 12/2 It hadn't exactly been a brawl to rank with the most homeric barroom brannigans in which Simon had ever

participated. **1983** *Data Communications* Nov. 16 (*heading*) Another CATV/BOC brannigan.

brilliant, *a.* Add: [1.] **d.** *Brilliant Pebbles*: a defence strategy conceived as part of the U.S. Strategic Defence Initiative in which incoming enemy missiles are intercepted and destroyed by numerous small heat-seeking missiles; also (usu. in lower case), the intercepting missiles themselves.

1988 *Aviation Week* 21 Mar. 15 Lowell Wood, a directed energy advocate, last week suggested an alternative SDI architecture based on small, lightweight and inexpensive kinetic energy interceptors... 'Shrinking contemporary smart rocks into brilliant pebbles is an exercise in packaging engineering,' he told a symposium on SDI. *Ibid.* 22 Aug. 15 Edward Teller and Lowell Wood briefed President Reagan in secret in late July and.. early August on the Brilliant Pebbles interceptor. Brilliant pebbles are an alternative approach to the SDI's Space-Based Interceptor weapon. **1989** *Economist* 4 Feb. 44/3 'Brilliant pebbles'.. would be tiny heat-seeking missiles already lurking in orbit... Their brilliance would derive from single microchips frozen to superconducting temperatures, each with the power of a modern supercomputer. **1992** *Syracuse Herald Amer.* 8 Nov. C4/1 Clinton.. intends to scrap the massive space-based defense system known as Brilliant Pebbles.

bristlecone ('brɪs(ə)lkəʊn), *a.* [f. BRISTLE *n.* + CONE *n.*[1]] **bristlecone pine**, either of two long-lived species of pine, *Pinus aristata* and *P. longaeva*, native to south-western North America, having cone scales which terminate in bristle-like appendages. Also *ellipt.*

1908 G. B. SUDWORTH *Forest Trees Pacific Slope* 37 Bristle-cone pine.. is known in the field as 'fox-tail pine' and 'hickory pine'. **1917** *Bull. U.S. Dept. Agric.* No. 460. 23 An appropriate and distinctive name is bristle-cone pine, which is derived from the tree's specific name, aristata (bearded), referring to the bristlelike prickles of the cone scales. **1972** *Guinness Bk. Records* (ed. 19) ii. 49/2 The oldest recorded living tree is a bristlecone pine (*Pinus longaeva*).., growing.. in eastern Nevada. **1989** *Smithsonian* Dec. 20/3 As an admirer and longtime observer of the venerable bristlecone, I was honored to receive one of these tough and rugged pine bonsai trees as a gift.

bronchiole, *n.* Add: Hence **bronchi'olar** *a.*

1898 *Allbutt's Syst. Med.* V. 54 In its chronic form bronchiolar dilatation is relatively of small importance. **1976** *Lab. Investigation* XXXV. 246/1 The terminal bronchiolar epithelium may be damaged by oxidant gases. **1988** S. P. SOROKIN in L. Weiss *Cell & Tissue Biol.* (ed. 6) 777/1 The nonciliated bronchiolar cells give the epithelium its special character.

brown, *a.* Add: [7.] **brownfield(s)** orig. *U.S.*, used *attrib.* and *absol.* to designate an (urban) area, which is or has formerly been the site of commercial or industrial activity, *esp.* one now cleared and available for redevelopment; cf. *green field(s)* s.v. GREEN *a.* 2 a.

1977 *Fortune* Jan. 110/1 The new facility would be a *brownfield expansion (addition to existing plant), producing about 1.2 million tons of iron. **1984** *Science* 13 July 151/1 The report supports modernization of smokestack industries and urges that those that are relocated be kept in 'brownfield' areas where they will do less environmental damage and supply jobs in already industrialized regions. **1990** *R.I.B.A. Jrnl.* Oct. 25/4 A 'brown-field' site out of London, in say Leeds or Sheffield or York, could attract development grants, rates deferrals and provide jobs. **1994** *Buffalo News* 23 Oct. (Metro ed.) C-7/3 'Brown fields' redevelopment efforts were boosted by the state last week with the announcement of a new program that will limit liability. *Ibid.* Redeveloping existing brown fields makes economic and environmental sense.

buck, *n.*[1] Sense 1 e in Dict. becomes 1 f. Add: [1.] **e.** *Austral.* A male kangaroo.

1845 *Atlas* (Sydney) 26 Apr. 258/1 The large full-grown male is termed a Buck or Boomer, and attains a great size. **1866** *Cornh. Mag.* Dec. 762 Large flocks of kangaroo..the larger males..towered above the flying bucks, flying does and joeys, the half-grown bucks, does, and young ones. **1926** W. TURNBULL in Le Souef & Burrell *Wild Animals of Australasia* 177 The bucks grow fairly large, in rare cases almost equal to the Grey. **1968** K. WEATHERLY *Roo Shooter* 8 A number of roos were resting. The big buck was typical of the reds, standing on his tips about seven feet.

buckminsterfullerene (ˌbʌkmɪnstəˈfʊləriːn), *n.* *Chem.* [f. the name of Richard *Buckminster Fuller* (1895–1983), U.S. engineer and architect, who designed the geodesic dome + -ENE.] An extremely stable form of carbon whose molecule consists of 60 carbon atoms joined together as a truncated regular icosahedron of 12 pentagons and 20 hexagons, forming a symmetrical spheroidal structure suggestive of the geodesic dome.

1985 H. W. KROTO et al. in *Nature* 14 Nov. 162/1 (*title*) C_{60}: buckminsterfullerene. [*Ibid.* 163/1 We are disturbed at the number of letters and syllables in the rather fanciful but highly appropriate name we have chosen in the title to refer to this C_{60} species.] **1987** *Ibid.* 26 Feb. 760/1 One of the most aesthetically appealing molecules to be diagnosed in recent years is buckminsterfullerene.., a carbon cluster—more dispassionately called icosahedral C_{60}. **1991** *New Scientist* 27 Apr. 25/1 A soccer-ball-shaped molecule made of 60 carbon atoms, buckminsterfullerene, can become a superconductor if it is 'doped' with a small quantity of potassium atoms. **1992** *Jrnl. Physical Chem.* XCVI. 111 Estimates are presented for the enthalpy changes of Stone–Wales isomerization, of the excision of C_2, C_4, and C_6 groups from buckminsterfullerene (BF), and of the excision of C_2 from a closely related C_{62} molecule.

buckyball (ˈbʌkɪbɔːl), *n.* *Chem.* [f. *BUCK(MINSTERFULLERENE *n.* + -Y[6] + BALL *n.*[1]] A molecule of buckminsterfullerene, or more generally of any fullerene.

1989 *N.Y. Times* C9/2 The chemical bonds holding this molecule together are apparently arrayed in a geodesic soccer-ball pattern like the one often used by Buckminster Fuller in the buildings he designed. Investigators therefore dubbed the molecule 'buckminster-fullerene,' sometimes shortened to 'fullerene' or 'buckyball'. **1990** *Science* 12 Oct. 209/1 The object of all the excitement is the spherical molecule C_{60}, known as 'soccerene' or 'buckminsterfullerene' or 'buckyball'. **1991** *New Scientist* 6 July 26/1 An Australian scientist..says that fullerenes, more commonly known as 'buckyballs', are the key element of a medical imaging system he developed in 1984. **1991** *Industry Week* 2 Dec. 55/4 Researchers studying buckyballs, the soccer-ball shaped molecules of carbon, see promising potential in superconductivity and diamond films. **1992** *Sci. News* 8 Feb. 85/2 The sheet curves around to form a buckyball or one of its rounded fullerene cousins. **1993** *Observer* 30 May 64 'Buckyballs' are now one of the hottest topics in chemistry.

buckytube (ˈbʌkɪtjuːb), *n.* *Chem.* [f. *BUCKY(BALL *n.* + TUBE *n.*] A cylindrical molecule of carbon consisting of two or more concentric tubes each formed of sheets of carbon atoms arranged helically.

1991 *New Scientist* 16 Nov. 19/1 A Japanese scientist has discovered cylindrical carbon molecules, which he has dubbed 'buckytubes' because of their similarity to

fullerenes, or 'buckyballs'. **1992** *Ibid.* 29 Feb. 21/1 The molecules, known as buckytubes, are like sheets of graphite which have been rolled up into tubes about a micrometre long and up to 30 nanometres across. **1992** *Sci. Amer.* Oct. 92/3 Other buckytube variants should be insulators or semiconductors. But so far none has been shown to function as a superconductor. **1993** *Science* 9 Apr. 164/3 Buckyballs and buckytubes both form in an apparatus in which a carbon arc is enclosed in high-pressure helium gas.

buddy, *n.* Sense in Dict. becomes 1 a. Sense *2 in *OED Additions Vol. 1* becomes 3 b. Restrict *colloq.* (orig. *U.S.*) to sense 1 a and add: [1.] **b.** A person who befriends and provides support for someone suffering from an incapacitating disease, esp. Aids.

1984 *Esquire* Dec. 272/2 The patients..are a wreck…We act as their buddies. **1986** *Auckland Star* 6 Feb. A8 Now, to add insult to injury, some of them are posing as 'buddies' and 'counsellors' to men in domestic violence situations. **1987** *Observer* 10 May 45/2 Buddies start off as strangers yet often end up as the people closest to their PWAs. **1989** *Independent* 21 Mar. 15/5 When one of the members crossed the Rubicon from HIV to Aids, Helpline always appointed two or three buddies to 'see the person through'. **1991** *Advocate* 15 Jan. 33/1 Hearty congratulations and thanks are due to..the people delivering meals and working in 'buddy' programs.

2. A person's assigned or chosen working companion, esp. in the operation of a buddy system.

1917 U. SINCLAIR *King Coal* I. 30 A man might sink to sleep as he lay at work, and if his 'buddy', or helper, happened to be out of sight, and to delay a minute too long, it would be all over with the man. **1978** A. P. BALDER *Sport Diving* i. 4 Maintain contact with your buddy by sight and sound. **1990** *Alert Diver* May–June 17/2 The male, especially if he is a novice, may well delude himself that he is superior, and therefore knowledgeable about both his and his female buddy's problem—endangering both.

3. a. *attrib.* and *Comb.* **buddy film** = *buddy movie* below.

1977 *Gay News* 7–20 Apr. 30/1 Changing themes and trends (from the 'Woman's Pictures' of an earlier period to the '*Buddy Film' of the present). **1989** *Cineaste* Sept. 48/3 The mechanics of the buddy film whir into gear—the familiar tango between the avuncular pragmatist and the callow idealist.

buddy movie (also *occas.* **buddy-buddy movie**), a film in which camaraderie between two characters of the same sex (usu. men) is a central theme.

1978 *Washington Post* 26 Sept. C1/4 Weill denies that she was trying to make a female *buddy-buddy movie…The title, she says, refers to the many meanings of the term 'girl friends'. **1980** *Christian Sci. Monitor* 2 Jan. 13/3 The 'buddy movie' fashion of the 1960s gave way to films with strong and central female characters. In some cases these were mere 'female buddy' pictures. **1989** *Movie* Winter 2/1 Corday proposed that she and Avedon write a role reversal buddy movie featuring two women. **1993** *Mod. Rev.* Aug.–Sept. 19/2 When he's trying to persuade Jack Slater to accept him as his partner he says, 'Come on. I'm perfect buddy movie material'.

bugle-weed, *n.* Add: **2.** = BUGLE *n.*[2] 1.

1942 L. H. BAILEY *Stand. Cycl. Horticulture* (rev. ed.) I. 24L/1 Ajuga..Bugle-weed. **1969** *Plant Dis. Reporter* LIII. 295 The objectives of this experiment were:..to control *M. incognita* on creeping bugleweed by applying nematicidal drenches. **1975** *Daily Colonist* (Victoria, B.C.) 15 June 32/6 Ajuga reptans, commonly known as Bugleweed, grows to about six inches in height and spreads by rooting stems. **1988** *Jrnl. Environmental Horticulture* VI. 84 Bugleweed (*Ajuga reptans*) and variegated wintercreeper euonymus..grown under 64% light exclusion were of acceptable quality.

bully, *a.*[1] Add: [I.] [2.] [a.] **bully pulpit** *U. S. Pol.*, a public office or position of authority that provides its occupant with an outstanding opportunity to speak out on any issue.
App. orig. used by U.S. President Theodore Roosevelt to explain his personal view of the presidency.
1909 *Outlook* (N.Y.) 27 Feb. 430/1 He [*sc.* President Roosevelt].. swung round in his swivel chair, and said: 'I suppose my critics will call that preaching, but I have got such a bully pulpit!' **1977** *Newsweek* 14 Feb. 23/3 Carter took to what Theodore Roosevelt once called the bully pulpit of the White House. **1988** B. & E. DOLE *Doles* ix. 227, I have used the bully pulpit to wage my own war on drunk driving. **1993** *Coloradoan* (Fort Collins) 16 Jan. A12/1 What power the governor had comes from good will and the 'bully pulpit' of the office.

bungarotoxin (ˌbʌŋgərəʊˈtɒksɪn), *n. Biochem.* [f. mod.L. *Bungar-us* (see BUNGARUM *n.*) + -O[1] + TOXIN *n.*] Each of three neurotoxins isolated from the venom of the elapid snake *Bungarus multicinctus*; *spec.* α-*bungarotoxin*, which binds to acetylcholine receptors with a high degree of specificity.
1963 CHANG & LEE in *Arch. Internat. de Pharmacodynamie et de Thérapie* CXLIV. 245 For the sake of convenience, these neurotoxins will be henceforth designated as α-, β- and γ-Bungarotoxin respectively in the order of increasing electrophoretic mobility. *Ibid.* 255 It is concluded that α-Bungarotoxin blocks neuromuscular transmission by irreversible combination with the acetylcholine receptor in the motor end-plate whereas β- and γ-Bungarotoxins exhibit their action at pre-synaptic site(s). **1973** *New Scientist* 1 Mar. 471/3 Using radioactive bungarotoxin (which binds specifically to ACh receptor sites), Nirenberg is able to count the number of receptors in the clusters. **1982** *Acta Histochem. et Cytochem.* XV. 598 It is well known that crude bungarotoxin contains β-toxin which binds to the presynaptic site. **1989** B. ALBERTS et al. *Molecular Biol. Cell* (ed. 2) xix. 1085 A snake paralyzes its prey by injecting α-bungarotoxin to block the nicotinic acetylcholine receptor.

bungee, *n.*[2] Add: 2. (Usu. *attrib.*, as *bungee cord*, *rope*, etc.) an elasticated cord or cable, *spec.*: **a.** *Aeronaut.* (*a*) An elasticated cord used in launching a glider; (*b*) any of various springs or elasticated tension devices used in the control system of an aircraft to facilitate movement (esp. of landing gear) or absorb shock.
1938 W. HIRTH *Art of Soaring Flight* viii. 116 Bungy-launching, which brings out the team spirit among pilots, later became the standard method of taking-off. **1944** T. HORSLEY *Soaring Flight* xxi. 246 When the 'bunje' only is being used, the whole procedure will be slower and less effective. **1956** W. A. HEFLIN *U.S. Air Force Dict.* 95/2 A bungee is used.. in certain aircraft to assist in retracting landing gear. **1977** *New Yorker* 4 July 40/3 He built the new bungee-cord landing gear for his Champ. **1980** BENT & McKINLEY *Aircraft Maintenance & Repair* (ed. 4) xi. 341/1 When in the down-and-locked position and it is desired to retract the gear, the over-center links are released by the hydraulically actuated *bungee cylinder* to permit gear retraction. **1991** *Pilot* Nov. 41/2 Cubs are not the easiest of aeroplanes to land tidily. The un-damped bungee springing can lead to a bouncy arrival.
b. (*a*) A fabric-bound rubber strap with a hook on either end, used for binding and securing baggage, etc.; (*b*) the elasticated rope from which a jumper is suspended in bungee jumping (see sense *3 below): orig. *U. S.*
1962 J. GLENN in *Into Orbit* 150 We added a heavy bungee cord to the equipment in the capsule, and I planned to pull it as far as it would go at certain periods during the flight to see what effect a known amount of exercise would have on my heart. **1970** N. ARMSTRONG

et al. *First on Moon* iii. 56 He had to turn down an Apollo 10 recommendation that the 11 crew carry rubber cords called 'bungees' on their flight to hold down papers. **1982** *Boxwooder* No. 156. 2, I keep a set of bungee cords in the trunk of my car for fastening down suitcases on the luggage rack. **1986** *Daily Tel.* 19 Nov. 4/4 When he hit the ground he was still attached to the safety harness, and the bungee line was still attached to that. **1991** *OnSat* 17 Feb. 7/1 Bungie cords can be used as extra tie downs, if needed.
3. Special Combs. **bungee jumping**, the action of jumping from a height (as a bridge, precipice, etc.) while secured by an elasticated rope attached to the ankles or to a safety harness; a sport involving this (also as *bungee cording*, etc.). So **bungee jump** *n.* and *v. intr.*, **bungee jumper**.
1979 *N.Y. Times* 9 Oct. B17/2 Five Britons who call themselves the *'Bungee Jumpers' leaped from the Golden Gate Bridge today, their falls broken by thick rubber bands that stopped them short of the water. **1987** *Independent* 24 Jan. 3/1 His only experience of *bungee jumping was from a height of 40 feet. **1987** *Telegraph* (Brisbane) 26 June 11/5 A New Zealander bounced back from a headfirst leap from the Eiffel Tower today... He wanted to bring New Zealand's sport of 'bungy jumping' to Paris. **1989** *Forbes* (N.Y.) 30 Oct. 233/3 A. J. Hackett, who operates the two *bungy-jump sites around Queenstown, explains the bungy craze this way: 'It helps one's self-esteem.' **1991** *Times* 5 Oct. (Weekend Times) 4/3 Bungy jumping has its roots on the South Pacific island of Pentecost, where men jump from a wooden tower each April and May, attached only by a vine around the ankle, to encourage the yam harvest. The worldwide bungy cult is worth upwards of £500,000 a year. **1992** *Texas Monthly* Jan. 87/3 James Fedigan of Houston was charged with disorderly conduct for mooning Galveston beach users while bungee jumping from a construction crane platform.
Hence **'bungee** *v. trans.* and *intr.*
1988 *Sailplane & Gliding* Oct.–Nov. 241/2 Bungyed from there one could expect five or six seconds in the air. **1989** *Austin Amer.-Statesman* 29 Apr. F1/1 It's a long cord you tie to a fixed point... The other end you tie to your feet and then you jump off. You get bungeed up and down. **1992** *Daily Tel.* 9 Nov. 19/1 They bungee around the hall on elastic ropes. **1992** *Sky Mag.* (Delta Airlines) Dec. 79 (Advt.), They strapped it on wheels and then bungied accessories to the top of the whole affair.

buppie ('bʌpɪ), *n. colloq.* (orig. *U. S.*) Also **Buppie, buppy.** [Blend of BLACK *a.* and YUPPIE *n.* or acronym f. the initial letters of *b*lack *u*rban *p*rofessional + -IE.] A member of a socio-economic group comprising young black professional people working in cities. Freq. considered mildly *derog.*
1984 *People Weekly.* (U.S.) 9 Jan. 47/3 Bryant Gumbel and Vanessa Williams are both Buppies. Of course, it wouldn't be Yuppie to be Miss America unless you are the first black one. **1986** *Atlanta Jrnl. & Constitution* 3 Aug. G1/1 About 45 people.. braved an afternoon downpour last week to attend a wine-tasting given.. in honor of Fulton's top Buppie, Michael Lomax. **1987** *Blues & Soul* 3 Feb. 10/1 All of a sudden, I found that all kinds of people were buying this record—'buppies', 'yuppies', children, couples, singles, retireds. **1988** *Independent* 12 July 15/1 Derek Boland—the.. rap singer Derek B—was present as a representative of 'buppies' (black yuppies). **1990** *Sunday Correspondent* 8 Apr. 4/5 Three years ago I dealt to all sorts: women, estate agents, yuppies and buppies. **1992** *Washington City Paper* 21 Feb. 59/5 Wesley's trying to do too much—define principles of black economics, reconcile civil rights ideals with buppy avarice.

***bustier** ('bʌstɪeɪ, 'bʊst-; ‖bystje), *n.* (In *OED Additions Vol. 1*). Add: Also *attrib.* as **bustier**

dress, a dress having a bodice styled in this way.
1986 *N.Y. Times* 13 Nov. A6 (Advt.), The lustrous glow of your shoulders is half the glamour of our bustier dress. **1992** *Wedding & Home* June/July 78 (*caption*) White silk bustier dress and bolero jacket with lemon beads and embroidery by Allison Blake.

butt, *v.*¹ Add: [1.] **e.** *to butt out*: to stop taking part or interfering in (something); to leave off, to 'shut up'. Freq. *imp.* Sometimes const. *of.* (orig. and chiefly *N. Amer.*).

1906 T. BEYER *Amer. Battleship in Commission* vi. 209 Don't butt in wher' yer have ter butt out. **1930** J. Dos PASSOS *42nd Parallel* 400 He said it was about time for him to but out, and picked up his hat and coat and left. **1967** P. WELLES *Babyhip* (1968) xix. 126 'Drop dead', they said, 'butt out.' **1976** *Ottawa Citizen* 10 Dec. 6/3 If you do not read the Bible and are not a believer, then butt out—this is an Anglican family quarrel. **1988** R. RAYNER *Los Angeles without Map* E IV. 132 Barbara gave him a cool stare... 'Butt out, pal.' **1992** *Harper's Mag.* Oct. 72 If the score is high..word spreads quickly through the movie industry. The film will receive a generous ad budget, the studio will butt out of the editing process, and everyone is *thrilled.*

C

C. Add: [III.] [3.] [a.] **CD-I, CDI, CD-i,** compact disc interactive, a system that provides interactive access to sound, data, and visual images stored on compact discs and viewed through a television or similar monitor.

1986 *Library Jrnl.* 15 May 50/3 The *CD-I (compact disc-interactive) will enable compact discs to store a mixture of video, audio, and text. **1987** *New Scientist* 1 Oct. 35/1 Because viewers can interact with the system, Sony expects CDI to spark off a craze in very sophisticated computer games. **1990** MIRABITO & MORGENSTERN *New Communications Technol.* x. 207/1 The CD-I system would be..the 'ultimate computer' game that would not be repetitious and could be supported by an extensive database of pictures and sounds. **1991** *Bookseller* 6 Dec. 1672/3 Some 50 CD-I titles will be available in the US by Christmas. **1994** *Rolling Stone* 16 June 85/1 The CD-i library is broad and eclectic—games for adults and kids, music video and, most recently, movies.

CDTV [Commodore dynamic total vision or compact disc television], (U.S. proprietary name for) an interactive multimedia system developed to rival CD-I, until production ceased in 1994.

1990 *Daily Tel.* 13 Aug. 4/1 The *CDTV system involves a unit the same size as a video recorder which plugs into a standard television set. **1993** *Accountancy* Feb. 52/3 Developed by Commodore as a rival to CD-I, CDTV is now aimed at the educational/computer games market.

C-J *Path.*, Creutzfeldt-Jakob.

1972 *Nature* 8 Dec. 351/2 Rhesus monkeys inoculated with *C-J disease virus 42 months ago are still under observation. **1977** *Harper's Mag.* Jan. 29/1 Scrapie, Kuru, and C-J disease will all 'take' if inoculated into the brain of a chimpanzee.

CJD *Path.*, Creutzfeldt-Jakob disease.

1975 *Canad. Jrnl. Neurol. Sci.* Aug. 203/1 To our knowledge, these profiles have never been observed in *CJD. **1990** *Independent* 3 Apr. 19/3 Whereas the effects of Alzheimer's are primarily mental, with very slow physical degeneration, CJD has both mental and physical effects almost simultaneously. **1993** *Daily Tel.* 9 Mar. 4/3 Brain samples confirmed that he died from CJD. **1996** *Private Eye* 5 Apr. 12/2 The trigger of the current scare was the 10 new cases of CJD in persons under the age of 42, said to resemble the pattern of disease presented by BSE cows.

CoA *Biochem.*, coenzyme A.

1947 *Jrnl. Biol. Chem.* CLXXI. 833 Recently, a participation was reported of the pantothenic acid derivative, coenzyme A (*Co A), in enzymatic acetylation. **1965** *Canad. Jrnl. Biochem.* XLIII. 1605 CoA ligase (ADP)..catalyzes the formation of succinyl CoA. **1974** J. B. FINEAN et al. *Membranes & Cellular Functions* v. 75 The exit of mitochondrial citrate supplies acetyl-CoA for biosynthesis of fatty acids and sterols. **1990** *Lancet* 26 May 1288/2 Children with medium chain acyl-CoA dehydrogenase (MCAD) deficiency..develop normally until they are deprived of calories during an intercurrent infection.

crc, CRC *Printing*, camera-ready copy (see CAMERA n. 3 d).

1986 J. PEACOCK et al. *Print & Production Man.* IV. iii. 81 If the surface of the *CRC is uneven, or is rough cartridge, it is sometimes worthwhile to make up the display lines on to a separate piece of smooth artpaper or board. **1989** *Bookseller* 1 Dec. 1768/3 The paste-up of crc to make it up into page is eliminated, as the end product of dtp comes out as paged crc.

cabinet, *n.* Add: [11.] *cabinet wine* (also *ellipt.*), a designation for a special reserve of German wine; now *rare* (cf. *KABINETT *n.*).

1833 C. REDDING *Hist. & Descrip. Mod. Wines* vii. 205 That called the 'Cabinet', from the vintage of 1811, brought seventy pounds sterling the ahm. **1872** THUDICHUM & DUPRÉ *Treat. Origin Wine* xvii. 564 The so-called *Cabinet*, where the cabinet wines are kept..is a vault above ground. **1952** H. W. ALLEN *White Wines & Cognac* viii. 157 Those tremendous wines of Schloss Johannisberg and Steinberg, known everywhere, as Cabinet wines, belong to the world of pomp and ceremonial. **1965** A. SICHEL *Penguin Bk. Wines* iii. 178 In some cases *Cabinet* wines are further classified by individual owners by the use of different-coloured seals or capsules.

Cabinett *n.*, var. *KABINETT *n.*

cache, *v.* Add: 2. *Computing.* To store (data, files, images, etc.) in a cache or part of a memory used as a cache.

1983 *Electronics* 14 July 118/2 The Z80,000 may choose to cache only instructions, but caching data along with instructions typically improves performance by some 20%. **1986** *Personal Computer World* Nov. 171/3 Window images are normally cached in a form to allow fast screen redraw. **1988** *Computer Weekly* 29 Sept. 48 This is achieved by temporarily caching files on a system magnetic disc, and by emulating standard VMS file system on-disc structures.

-cain *suffix*, var. *-CAINE *suffix*.

-caine (kem), *suffix*. *Pharm.* Also -cain. [f. CO)CAINE *n.*, or G. *Co-caïn* (now *Kokain*).] Forming nouns denoting drugs, esp. ones with anaesthetic properties, as HOLOCAINE, NOVOCAIN, XYLOCAINE *ns.*, etc.

calamus, *n.* Add: 5. *Ornith.* The lower, unbarbed part of the shaft of a bird's feather.

1878 T. DUNMAN *Gloss. Biol., Anat., & Physiol. Terms* 18 *Calamus*, the quill of a bird's feather. **1940** *Physiol. Zoöl.* XIII. 155 In the formation of the calamus the same process..gives rise to a series of 'horny' partitions. **1974** D. & M. WEBSTER *Compar. Vertebr. Morphol.* viii. 168 The shaft of the pluma is composed of the calamus, which is embedded in the feather follicle and protrudes a short distance beyond it, and the rachis, which supports and is actually part of the feather's vane.

Callanetics (kælə'nɛtɪks), *n.* [f. the name of *Callan* Pinckney (b. 1939), U.S. inventor of the system + *-etics*, perh. after ATHLETICS *n.*] A proprietary name for a system of exercises designed to improve muscle tone by the performance of small repeated movements involving deeper-lying muscles.

1984 PINCKNEY & BATSON *(title)* Callanetics: ten years younger in ten hours. **1986** *Official Gaz.* (U.S. Patent Office) 19 Aug. TM106/1 *Callanetics*...First use 2-1-1974. **1989** *Times* 9 Mar. 15/1 We have the Duchess of York to thank for the current Callanetics craze. **1990** *Daily Tel.* 20 Mar. 17/2 Callanetics..is also boring, just like every other regime—more so in fact since the exercises are not done to music.

calmodulin (kæl'mɒdjʊlɪn), *n. Biochem.* [f. CAL(CIUM *n.* + MODUL(ATOR *n.* + -IN[1].] A calcium-binding protein in eukaryotic cells which when complexed with calcium regulates many intracellular functions, esp. the action of enzymes.

1978 W. Y. CHEUNG et al. in *Adv. Cyclic Nucleotide Res.* IX. 249 Within this context, the activator may serve as a Ca^{2+} mediator, or as a Ca^{2+}-dependent modulator. In view of the potential multiple and diverse functions, the activator protein may be designated calmodulin. **1979** *Science* 20 Apr. 306/2 Red blood cell activator and calmodulin are part of a family of Ca^{2+}-binding proteins that includes the Ca^{2+}-binding regulatory protein of skeletal muscle, troponin C. **1982** *Sci. Amer.* June 52/1 Calmodulin..is apparently a component of all eukaryotic (nucleated) cells. **1989** E. LAWRENCE *Guide Mod. Biol.* ix. 272 (*caption*) Each molecule of calmodulin has four Ca^{2+}-binding sites.

calyptra, *n.* Add: **2.** [ad. F. *calyptre* (used in this sense by Van Tieghem & Douliot 1888, in *Ann. des Sci. Nat.: Bot.* VIII. 11).] A thickened membrane of parenchymatous cells which protects the growing root of a vascular plant; a root-cap.

1898 H. C. PORTER tr. *Strasburger's Text-bk. Bot.* 15 A root may always be distinguished from a stem by the root-cap or calyptra sheathing its apex. **1914** M. DRUMMOND tr. *Haberlandt's Physiol. Plant Anat.* ii. 93 The inner apical envelope of the rootlet, or 'calyptra' is produced by the rootlet itself. **1960** C. R. METCALFE *Anat. Monocotyledons* I. 581 Montemontini..refers to the occurrence of a sclerotic calyptra (*Wurzelhaube*) on the roots when young.

cambazola *n.*, var. *CAMBOZOLA *n.*

cambozola (kambə'zəʊlə), *n.* Also **Cambazola**, **cambazola**, **Cambozola**. [Invented name, f. CAM(EMBERT *n.* + -*bo*- + GORGON)ZOLA *n.*] A proprietary name for a type of German blue soft cheese with a Camembert-like rind, and produced using Gorgonzola blue mould.

1984 *Trade Marks Jrnl.* 6 June 1437/1 *Cambozola*. **1987** *Canad. Heritage* (Ottawa, Ont.) Aug.-Sept. 21/3 Some of the finest, freshest fruit sold in the city, and a selection of groceries that runs from the plebian to gourmet fare—plump, boneless chicken breasts, Belgian endive, cambozola blue cheese, Haagen Dazs ice cream, and too many kinds of tea to count. **1989** R. MOON *Delicatessen* 69 Certainly the most successful of the 'modern' Bries has been Cambozola, a German cheese referred to as blue Brie. **1994** *Toronto Life* June 81/1 Juicy parmesan-crusted chicken breast is rolled around molten cambozola, over red pepper coulis; heavily buttered couscous seems too much of a good thing.

Campylobacter ('kæmpɪləʊˌbæktə(r), ˌkæmpɪləʊ'bæktə(r)), *n.* *Microbiol.* and *Med.* [mod.L. (coined in Fr. by Sebald & Véron 1963, in *Ann. Inst. Pasteur* CV. 907), f. Gr. καμπύλο-ς bent: see BACTER(IUM *n.*] A genus of microaerophilic bacteria including curved and spiral forms that frequently cause food poisoning in humans and abortion in some farm animals; (also **campylobacter**) a bacterium of this genus.

1971 *Ann. Rev. Microbiol.* XXV. 669 We believe that there are no close taxonomic affinities of campylobacters with bdellovibrios. **1977** *Brit. Med. Jrnl.* 2 July 10/2 The close association between the presence of campylobacters in faeces and the occurrence of a distinctive clinical enteritis alone suggests that these organisms are pathogens. **1986** *New Scientist* 10 Apr. 67/4 It is surprising not to find campylobacters listed alongside salmonellae as causes of food poisoning. **1989** *Daily Tel.* 7 Oct. 36/8 Salmonellosis, leptospirosis and campylobacter infection are among the commonest [zoonoses]. **1991** *Lancet* 2 Mar. 511/1

A sample of stool from every patient was cultured for bacterial pathogens (*Salmonells,..Campylobacter*).

Candida, *n.* Add: **2.** = *candidiasis* below.

1976 *Our Bodies, Ourselves* (Boston Women's Health Bk. Collective) (ed. 2) vi. 137/2 (*heading*) Yeast infections (also called Candida, Monilia, or Fungus). **1981** C. W. COOKE et al. *Good Health Guide for Women* xi. 289 You may contract candida while taking broad spectrum antibiotics to cure a streptococcal throat or urinary infection. **1985** *Jrnl. Alternative Med.* Apr. 20/4 New Theory about candida and its treatment has triggered the development of a new product to go with it. **1991** *New Yorker* 13 May 29/1 Where Adrian used to get wrapped up in galleries and theorists, his concerns now center on hairy leukoplakia and fulminant candida.

Caplet ('kæplɪt), *n.* *Pharm.* Also **caplet**. [Prob. f. CAP(SULE *n.* + TAB)LET *n.*] A proprietary name for a kind of coated capsule.

1937 *Official Gaz.* (U.S. Patent Office) 13 Apr. 249/1 *Caplets*...For medicinal products—namely, tablets composed of drugs, chemicals, and glandular material...Claims use since Feb. 18, 1936. **1955** *Trade Marks Jrnl.* 6 Apr. 361/2 *Caplet*... Pharmaceutical preparations and substances,..but not including preparations in tablet form for the treatment of headaches. **1979** *Forbes* (N.Y.) 24 Dec. 75/1 Raising the ad budget for Sterling's popular Midol Caplets..helped increase sales from $8 million to $10 million. **1986** *Times* 19 Feb. 9/2 Mr Burke urged users of Tylenol capsules to switch to coated, oval tablets known as 'caplets'. **1990** ANSEL & POPOVICH *Pharmaceutical Dosage Forms* (ed. 5) iii. 72/1 Capsules are prone to tampering by unscrupulous individuals. Thus, capsule-shaped and coated tablets, called 'caplets', are increasingly utilized. These are easily swallowed but their contents are sealed and protected from tampering like tablets.

car, *n.*[1] Add: [**6.**] **car lot**: see *LOT *n.* 6 c.

carbon, *n.* Add: [**3.**] [**a.**] **carbon tax**, a tax levied on fossil fuels with the aim of discouraging the production of harmful carbon dioxide by their being burnt.

1986 *Los Angeles Times* 1 Aug. II. 5/5 In the long run we should consider more aggressive actions, such as *carbon taxes, to discourage the excessive use of coal and shale. **1990** J. GOLDEMBERG in J. Leggett *Global Warming* viii. 176 The most common proposal is the creation of a general carbon tax designed to constitute a fund to curb further emissions of carbon dioxide into the atmosphere. **1990** *New Age* Dec. 14/1, 70 percent of US citizens now support a carbon tax, which would penalize all energy sources that produce the greenhouse gas carbon dioxide. **1993** *New Scientist* 1 May 11/1 Britain is the only member of the European Community blocking a carbon tax.

carboxylate (kɑː'bɒksɪleɪt), *v.* *Biochem.* [Back-formation from *CARBOXYLATION *n.*] *trans.* To introduce a carboxyl group into (a molecule or compound); to convert *into* by carboxylation.

1934 in WEBSTER. **1981** DUGAS & PENNEY *Bioorganic Chem.* vii. 469 The urea carboxylase component of ATP-amidolyase..reversibly carboxylates urea to form N-carboxyurea. **1988** L. STRYER *Biochem.* (ed. 3) xx. 484 ATP is used to carboxylate acetyl CoA to malonyl CoA.

Hence **car'boxylating** *ppl. a.*

1962 CALVIN & BASSHAM *Photosynthesis of Carbon Compounds* 51 (*table*) Carboxylating enzyme. **1982** M. J. DRING *Biol. Marine Plants* iii. 65 In red, brown and green seaweeds..RuBP-Case is the dominant carboxylating enzyme.

card, *n.*[2] Senses 12-14 in Dict. become 13-15. Add: [**III.**] **12.** *Electronics.* = *BOARD *n.* 2 h. *expansion card*: see EXPANSION *n.* 8.

1964 *Electronics* 31 Jan. 25/1 A plug-in card containing up to 250 individually replaceable microcircuits is shown in one of the photographs. **1974** *IEEE Spectrum* June 94/2 Among the cards available for these microprocessor systems are: the 8111, a central processing unit with clock, reset, data, address, memory, and input–output control; the 8112, a memory card which [etc.]. **1983** *Your Computer* (Austral.) Aug. 14/2 Standard features of the Fox-640 include a Forth programming system card, joystick port, [etc.] **1986** *What Micro?* Nov. 37/3 At the moment there are only two cards available to fit these expansion slots; an RS232 interface board..and a mouse interface/clock board are available for £69 each. **1989** *New Scientist* 21 Jan. 39/2 VideoFax comes as a pair of circuit boards, or 'cards', which plug into the back of the personal computer.

cariogenic, a. (In *OED Additions 1*.) Add: Hence **carioge'nicity** *n.*, the degree to which a substance is cariogenic; the property of being cariogenic.
    1950 *Jrnl. Nutrition* XL. 209 It is quite probable that the 6% of cereal in this diet..may have contributed to the cariogenicity of the diet. **1987** *Daily Tel.* 13 Oct. 15/3 Dentists measure the decay potential (cariogenicity) of foods in various ways.

carjacking (kɑːdʒækɪŋ), *n.* orig. and chiefly *U. S.* Also **car-jacking**. [f. CAR *n.*¹ + *hi)jacking* vbl.n. s.v. HIJACK *v.*] The stealing or commandeering of an occupied car by threatening the driver with violence; theft from or abduction of a driver by such means.
    1991 *Detroit News* 29 Aug. 1A/6 Most of the motorists victimized by carjacking..are city residents often attacked in their own neighborhood. **1992** *Independent* 13 Nov. 19/2 Carjacking has become such an epidemic that President George Bush has signed a law sentencing carjackers automatically to 15 years in jail for the crime, and life imprisonment if it involves death. **1993** *Premiere* Mar. 37/1 In L.A., car-jacking has surpassed drive-by shooting as the crime du jour. **1994** *Post* (Denver) 23 Jan. A14/1 [He] was shot in the head during a carjacking in southwest Denver.
    So (as a back-formation) **'carjack** *v. trans.* and *n.*; **'carjacker** *n.*
    1991 *Detroit News* 29 Aug. 1A/2 In a week ending Aug. 25, at least 40 people fell prey to carjackers, weapon wielding car thieves. **1991** *Economist* 14 Sept. 46/1 In the past six weeks more than 300 drivers have been carjacked in Detroit. **1992** *Washington Times* 6 Oct. B2/4 'If your car's being carjacked, give the car up,' Mr Schaefer said. 'Don't fight back.' **1992** *Daily Tel.* (Weekend Suppl.) 31 Oct. p.xxv/4 New York, Chicago, Los Angeles, Detroit and Washington have all reported significant rises in carjacks in the past 12 months. **1993** G. DONALDSON *Ville* 44 The victim of the carjack was beaten and stripped of his clothes. **1994** *Coloradoan* (Fort Collins) 23 Jan. F3/2 Some people have a negative association with their houses—people who have been attacked in their homes..or carjacked in their garages.

Carnian ('kɑːnɪən), *a.* [ad. L. *Carnicus* (see *CARNIC *a.*) + -IAN.] **1. *Carnian Alps* = *Carnic Alps* s.v. *CARNIC *a.* 1. *rare.*
    1802 J. PINKERTON *Mod. Geogr.* I. 377 The calcareous hills of Carinthia afford many singular scenes; which are however exceeded by those of the Carnian Alps, or Birnbaumer mountains, of Carniola. **1876** H. F. TOZER *Classical Geogr.* ix. 95 After this, the mountains that sweep round towards the Adriatic bear the name of Carnian or Julian Alps.
    2. *Geol.* Also **Karnian**. [After *CARNIC *a.* 2.] Of, pertaining to, or designating the first of the three stages constituting the Upper Triassic in Europe. Also *absol.*
    1948 R. L. SHERLOCK *Permo-Triassic Formations* I. 16 (*table*) Norian/Carnian. **1969** DUNBAR & WAAGE

Hist. Geol. (ed. 3) xiv. 321/2 Similar spread of the seas in other parts of the world apparently permitted much wider distribution of ammonoid faunas, for those of the Karnian and Norian stages of the Late Triassic..are worldwide. **1970** *Nature* 18 Apr. 255/2 An important halite of proved or probable Carnian age is found in Cheshire (the Upper Saliferous Beds). **1989** *Ibid.* 7 Sept. 16/2 The lithocolumn supplied by me has been changed without my knowledge to increase the thickness of the Triassic by about 30 m, possibly to accommodate the Carnian conodonts.

Carnic ('kɑːnɪk), *a.* [ad. L. *Carnicus*, f. *Carni*, name of a Celtic people of upper Italy: see -IC.] **1. *Carnic Alps* [tr. L. *alpes Carnicae*], a range of mountains extending along the border between Austria and Italy.
    1601 HOLLAND tr. *Pliny's Nat. Hist.* I. III. xxv. 71 These rivers of speciall name, and navigable, run into Danubius, Draus with more violence out of the Noricke Alpes; and Saus out of the Carnicke Alpes more gently. **1802** J. PINKERTON *Mod. Geogr.* I. 364 The Julian, or Carnic Alps, (now called Birnbaumer Wald,) which divide Carinthia from Italy. *a*1977 D. WHEATLEY *Time has Come* (1979) III. xxii. 213 Force the Ljubljana gap through the Carnic Alps. **1989** *Nature* 5 Jan. 39 A 330-metre core drilled through the marine Permian/Triassic boundary in the Carnic Alps of Austria allows closely correlated studies of geochemistry [etc.].
    2. *Geol.* Also **Karnic.** [ad. G. *karnisch* (coined by E. von Mojsisovics 1869, in *Verhandl. d. K. K. Geol. Reichsanstalt* (Vienna) IV. 65).] = *CARNIAN *a.* 2. Also *absol.* Now *rare.*
    1897 *Jrnl. Geol.* V. 510 The writer remembers once collecting numerous *Ceratites* in the Karnic limestone of the California Trias. **1948** R. L. SHERLOCK *Permo-Triassic Formations* II. 256 *Mytilus* (?) *problematicus* marks a very constant horizon about the middle of the Carnic in South Island.

carriage, *n.* Add: [V.] [35.] **carriage release**, the facility for allowing the carriage of a manual typewriter to move freely (as opposed to one space at a time); also, a lever which effects this.
    1904 *Typist's Rev.* Jan. 83/1 The marginal stops, the warning bell, the *carriage release..all is new. **1954** CROOKS & DAWSON *Dict. Typewriting* (ed. 6) 47 The carriage-release lever is useful when the machine is not fitted with a tabulator, for moving quickly from one column to another.

cartridge, *n.* Add: [1.] [d.] (*iv*) a small disposable container of ink, designed to fit into the barrel of a pen (usu. a fountain pen) and serve as a refill; cf. *ink cartridge* (*a*) s.v. *INK *n.*¹ 4 a.
    1945 *Business Week* 26 May 93/1 The radically new fountain pen with a ball-bearing point... The invention of a Hungarian by the name of Ladislav Biro..each full-sized pen will be equipped with a replaceable cartridge containing..a special, dry-writing, viscous ink. **1955** *Stationery Trade Rev.* Apr. 120/1 The first major change in design among English fountain pens for a number of years has now been announced officially, by the Waterman Pen Co. Ltd...Instead of a bulky..filling mechanism to draw fluid from an ink bottle, the ink is provided in a small plastic cartridge. The pen is unscrewed, the cartridge slipped into place and the instrument is ready to write. **1970** *Kay & Co.* (Worcester) *Catal.* 1970-71 Autumn/Winter 947/2, 14 ct. gold nib and a convertible filling system—with a Quink cartridge or an ink bottle refill. **1974** *Encycl. Brit. Macropædia* XIX. 1045/2 Later, successful fountain pens appeared that could be filled simply by inserting a filled ink capsule called a cartridge. The cartridge system is the most popular filling means in the U.S. today, but elsewhere filling from an ink bottle is preferred.

(*v*) Any of various disposable or refillable containers for ink, toner, etc., used in electronic printers and photocopiers.

1985 *Data Processing* Sept. 33/3 When the ink runs out, it is replenished by replacing an hermatically [*sic*] sealed drop-in cartridge. **1988** *Design Graphics World* Feb. 35/3 The printer displays an error message on the LCD panel when the toner cartridge needs to be refilled. **1991** *What Personal Computer* 126/1 PostScript isn't exactly fast, even on a dedicated laser printer, and it's postively tardy when it's cartridge-based.

[**4.**] **cartridge pen**, a fountain pen designed to take ink cartridges.

1955 *Stationery Trade Rev.* Aug. 67/1 What is claimed to be the 'first popular-priced cartridge fountain pen' has recently been introduced... Called the Sheaffer 'Fineline' *cartridge pen, it is filled by inserting an ink-loaded cartridge into the barrel. **1977** *Private Eye* 13 May 23/3 (Advt.), Refillable ballpens and cartridge pens that look good and feel good. **1990** *Amiga Computing* Dec. 166 (Advt.), The three pull-top pens in their presentation case consist of: One cartridge pen, One ballpoint pen, One fine liner.

cassette, *n.* Add: [**1.**] **e.** *Genetics*. A block of genetic material which can be readily inserted into a chromosome or moved between locations on a genome as a single unit, *esp.* one which is only expressed at a particular location.

1977 J. B. HICKS et al. in A. I. Bukhari et al. *DNA Insertion Elements, Plasmids, & Episomes* 457 Studies of mating-type interconversion in the yeast *Saccharomyces cerevisiae* have led us to propose a new mechanism of gene control involving mobile genes. In this hypothesis, the 'cassette model' of mating-type interconversion, cell type is determined by which of two blocs ('cassettes') of regulatory information is inserted into the mating-type locus. *Ibid.*, The cassettes themselves may be analogous to temperate prophages or transposable drug resistance elements, in which structural genes are flanked by sites governing their mobility. **1983** *Current Topics Developmental Biol.* XVIII. 5 We termed these genetic blocks 'cassettes' because they are expressed only when located at the mating type locus, which acts like the playback head of a tape recorder, and not expressed when the cassettes are located at storage loci *HML* and *HMR*. **1983** J. R. S. FINCHAM *Genetics* xvii. 486 The transposition or 'cassette' hypothesis was soon supported by impressive genetic evidence. **1987** *Nucleic Acids Res.* XV. 8115 Chimeric genes constructed with these cassettes can be used to transform plants. **1988** *New Scientist* 21 Apr. 40/2 The production of haemolysin is determined by a small cassette of genes (called *hly*).

[**2.**] **cassette deck** (see DECK *n.*¹ 3 f), a cassette player and recorder, usu. one designed to be connected to an external amplifier.

1972 *Gramophone* May 1953 (Advt.), This unit offers three sound sources—a stereo record turntable system, a VHF stereo/medium wave tuner and a stereo *cassette deck with simple front loading. **1984** *Which Micro?* Dec. 17/2, The Amstrad CPC464..comes with a colour monitor and cassette deck. **1990** N. WILLIAMS *Wimbledon Poisoner* xxxvii. 254 She..went towards the cassette deck by the bed.

cast, *n.* Add: [**IX.**] [**30.**] **d.** *Med.* = *PLASTER-CAST *n.* 2.

1934 in WEBSTER. **1949** E. BIRNEY *Turvey* iv. 29 The up-patients had gone about autographing all the casts with indelible pencils. **1965** P. DE VRIES *Let Me count Ways* xi. 140, I awaken with my leg in a hip-length cast. **1980** M. RICHLER *Joshua* I. i. 3 His right leg..was still held in a cast, multiple fractures healing slowly at his age.

casual, *a.* (*n.*) Add: [**A.**] **12.** Of a sexual relationship or (an instance of) sexual activity: conducted by individuals who are not regular or established sexual partners. Also used to designate a person's partner in such activity.

[*c* **1856** *Paul Pry* in C. Pearl *Girl with Swansdown Seat* (1955) vi. 256 French letters..prevent the spread of venereal contagion in casual intercourse between the sexes.] **1971** *Newsweek* 21 June 99/1 The way some..see it, the increasing number of American couples now participating in some form of group sex are actually attempting a radical redefinition of marriage that would make sex as casual and unemotional as a handshake or eating a steak. **1973** R. KEYES *We, the Lonely People* v. 99 The rise of swinging and casual sex generally. **1976** *Economist* 24 Apr. 50/3 It is..reported that [*sc.* in Cambodia] the rice ration in some areas has increased, and marriage is now permitted again—although casual sexual relationships still bring the death penalty. **1981** *Washington Post* 20 Jan. B11/2 The sexual relationship between casual lovers, or husband and wife, seems to me usually to be a fusion..of opposite poles. **1983** *Family* July 27/4 Many homosexuals get involved in gay clubs more to find friends than to get casual sex. **1985** *Los Angeles Times* 11 Apr. 1. 3/1 Men who father children as a result of casual relationships. **1992** L. TUTTLE *Lost Futures* 4 Even when everybody did it, casual sex had never been her scene.

[**B.**] **6.** In the U.K., a (male) youth who belongs to a peer group favouring a casual style of dress and conventional appearance, often characterized as aggressively nationalistic and freq. associated with football-related violence.

1980 *Daily Mirror* 10 Apr. 13/4 A Casual, 17-year-old printer, Jeff McNamara, lives in a skinhead stronghold in East London. Yet he dresses defiantly in smart slacks. **1985** *Guardian* 22 May 1/6 Muranyi and his army—called the Cambridge Casuals because of their Pringle sweaters and Nike training shoes—spent two months planning the attack. Chelsea fans were lured to an obscure pub.. and then set upon by a gang of 30. **1986** *Final Rep. Home Office Comm. Inquiry Crowd Safety & Control at Sports Grounds* (Cmnd. 9710) v. 57 One of the significant developments in Scottish football has been the emergence of the so-called 'Casuals'...They attach themselves to a club and adopt its name. They are bent on fighting the opposition fans in order to enhance their own prestige. **1988** *Arena* Autumn/Winter 29/3, I fail to see why people who see football aggro as infantile and pathetic should be regarded as ignorant and uneducated. Surely it is you soccer casuals who are uneducated, behaving like animals as you do. **1992** D. MCLEAN *Bucket of Tongues* 34 I'm a bit out of touch myself these days to be honest. When I was on the casual scene we were all into Fila sports gear and side shades and that. *Ibid.* 36 Football's a game, fighting's more than that. Football's something you just do, or just watch, but a casual, that's something you *are*.

cat, *n.*⁴ Add: **2.** *colloq.* A catalytic converter.

1988 *Performance Car* July 15/2 The VAG importers are deciding when, rather than if, the first 'cat' car will join their UK range. **1989** *Ibid.* May 24/2 In six months time, I have to work in Yugoslavia for five months and they do not have unleaded fuel. If I remove the cat, could I use leaded petrol or will it damage the engine? **1990** *Autocar & Motor* 19 Sept. 45/3 Ferrari continues to build the 348 in both cat and non-cat versions, the UK being one of the last markets to get the 'dirty' engine. **1991** *Internat. H&E* Spring Q. 70/3 Vauxhall have announced that they are to progressively fit 'cats' to all of their cars from now on.

catalytic, *a.* Add: *catalytic converter*, a device fitted to the exhaust system of some internal-combustion engines which catalyses the oxidation of some of the exhaust gases, rendering them less harmful as pollutants.

1955 *Sci. News Let.* 22 Jan. 54/1 The best way to remove carbon monoxide from auto fumes appears to be the use of nonleaded gasoline and a catalytic converter, Dr. W. L. Faith, chief engineer of the

Southern California Air Pollution Foundation, said. **1984** *Sydney Morning Herald* 10 Nov. 3/3 Imported cars will begin arriving fitted with expensive catalytic converters in anticipation of the introduction of lead-free petrol from January 1, 1986. **1989** J. BUTTON *How to be Green* 190 In the USA the compulsory fitting of catalytic converters has cut carbon monoxide emission by 90 per cent.

catastrophe, *n.* Add: **5.** Special Comb. **catastrophe theory** *Math.*, the topological description of systems which display abrupt discontinuous change.
[**1969** R. THOM in *Topology* VIII. 319 It is not too difficult a task to find all possible singularities $V(x)$ of finite codimension not exceeding four. These singularities are important, because they may appear on our space-time in a structurally stable way. They give rise to what we call the 'elementary catastrophes', when we interpret them as describing dynamical fields on our space-time.] **1971** *Times Lit. Suppl.* 10 Dec. 1557/3 Another interesting feature of *catastrophe theory is called the divergence effect. **1973** *Internat. Jrnl. Neurosci.* VI. 39/1 We can *explicitly* use catastrophe theory to explain and predict psychological phenomena. **1987** *Brit. Jrnl. Sociol.* XXXVIII. 503 Catastrophe theory is itself said to be in a catastrophic state. **1992** S. P. MARAN *Astron. & Astrophysics Encycl.* 294/1 Gravitational optics has an important connection with the branch of mathematics known as catastrophe theory.

catecholamine, *n.* (In *OED Additions 1*). Add: Hence **cate‚cholami'nergic** *a.* [after ADRENERGIC, CHOLINERGIC *adjs.*], liberating or stimulated by a catecholamine.
1970 *European Jrnl. Pharmacol.* X. 178 (*heading*) Disposition of newly synthesized amines in cell bodies and terminals of central catecholaminergic neurons. **1990** *Jrnl. Neuroendocrinol.* II. 830/2, 2-Hydroxyestradiol..is known to bind to catecholaminergic receptors.

category, *n.* Add: **3.** *Math.* A generalized mathematical entity consisting of a class of abstract objects sharing some property together with a class of morphisms, associative under composition and including an identity morphism, which preserve that property.
1945 EILENBERG & MACLANE in *Trans. Amer. Math. Soc.* LVIII. 237 We introduce a notion of 'category' which will embody the common formal properties of such aggregates. From the examples 'groups plus homomorphisms' or 'spaces plus continuous mappings' we are led to the following definition. A category ʊ = {*A*,α} is an aggregate of abstract elements *A* (for example, groups), the objects of the category, and abstract elements α (for example, homomorphisms), called mappings of the category. **1966** *Math. Rev.* XXXI. 41/1 If *A* is a semi-simplicial set and ʊ the category of its simplices, then $H(ʊ^{op}; F)$ becomes ordinary homology with local coefficients *F*. **1979** *Proc. London Math. Soc.* XXXVIII. 237 Let 𝒮 denote the category of sets and functions and 𝒯 the category of topological spaces and continuous maps.

Cauchy ('kəʊʃɪ), *n. Math.* [The name of Augustin-Louis *Cauchy* (1789–1857), French mathematician.] Used *attrib.* and in the possessive to denote concepts introduced by Cauchy or arising from his work, as **Cauchy distribution**, a probability distribution whose probability density is of the form $a/[1+b(x−λ)^2]$, where λ is the median of the distribution and *a* and *b* are constants; **Cauchy's integral (formula)**, a formula expressing the value of a function $f(z)$ at a point *a* in terms of an integral around a closed curve enclosing it, which may be written $\int[f(z)/(z−a)]dz =$

$2\pi i f(a)k$, where *k* has the value 1 if *a* is inside the curve, o if outside, and ½ if *a* lies on it; **Cauchy sequence**, any sequence of numbers a_n such that for any positive number ϵ, a value of *n* can be chosen so that any two members of the sequence after a_n differ by a quantity whose magnitude is less than ϵ; **Cauchy's theorem**, *spec.* the theorem that the integral of any analytical function of a complex variable around a closed curve which encloses no singularities is zero.
1878 *Encycl. Brit.* VIII. 503/1 Cauchy's theorem contains really the proof of the fundamental theorem that a numerical equation of the *n*th order..has precisely *n* roots. **1889** *Cent. Dict.* s.v. *Formula, Abel's, Cauchy's..formulæ*, certain formulæ relating to definite integrals. **1893** HARKNESS & MORLEY *Treat. Theory of Functions* v. 164 (*heading*) Cauchy's theorem. *Ibid.* 167 Cauchy's theorem can be extended to functions which are holomorphic within a region bounded by more than one closed contour. **1898** HARKNESS & MORLEY *Introd. Theory Analytic Functions* xvi. 222 The integral..$(1/2\pi i)\int x dx/(Ax−c)$, taken over a circuit *A* in Γ, may be called Cauchy's integral, for it plays an essential part in the development of the theory of functions along Cauchy's lines. **1910** *Encycl. Brit.* XI. 314/1 The theory of the integration of a monogenic function, and Cauchy's theorem, that $\int f(z)dz = o$ over a closed path, are at once deducible from the corresponding results applied to a single power series for the interior of its circle of convergence. **1932** E. C. TITCHMARSH *Theory of Functions* ii. 81 This is Cauchy's integral formula. **1948** *Ann. Math. Statistics* XIX. 428 R_0 is determined by integration over the upper tail of the Cauchy distribution. **1955** L. F. BORON tr. *Natanson's Theory of Functions of Real Variable* I. vii. 171 The Bolzano-Cauchy property: every Cauchy sequence $\{x_n\}$ has a finite limit. **1962** *Ann. Math. Statistics* XXXIII. 1258 Given a symmetric bivariate Cauchy distribution and knowledge of its marginal distributions in several directions, one would like to know what possibilities are available for the marginal distributions in a few other directions. **1982** W. S. HATCHER *Logical Found. Math.* v. 181 Completeness means that all Cauchy sequences converge or (equivalently for totally ordered fields) that every bounded nonempty set of elements of the field has a least upper bound. **1984** G. B. PRICE *Multivariable Anal.* x. 521 This section uses Theorem 67.2, Goursat's form of Cauchy's integral theorem, to prove Cauchy's integral formula. *Ibid.* 526 This formula is easy to remember because it can be derived from Cauchy's integral formula..by differentiating under the integral sign *n* times with respect to *z*. **1987** JONES & SINGERMAN *Complex Functions* 318 The basic theorem of complex integration is Cauchy's theorem.

Cauchy–Riemann (ˌkəʊʃɪ'riːmən), *n. Math.* [The names of Augustin-Louis *Cauchy* (see *CAUCHY *n.*) and G. F. Bernhard *Riemann* (see RIEMANN *n.*).] **Cauchy–Riemann equations**, the partial differential equations which must be satisfied if a function $f(x, y)$ of two variables, separable into a real part *u* and an imaginary part *v*, is to be analytic, namely the two equations
$$\frac{\partial u}{\partial x} = \frac{\partial v}{\partial y} \text{ and } \frac{\partial u}{\partial y} = -\frac{\partial v}{\partial x}.$$
1914 S. E. RASOR tr. *Burkhardt's Theory of Functions of Complex Variable* iv. 181 Prove by passing directly to the limit that in polar coördinates the Cauchy-Riemann differential equations take the form:
$$\frac{\partial u}{\partial r} = \frac{1}{r}\frac{\partial v}{\partial \phi}, \quad \frac{\partial v}{\partial r} = -\frac{1}{r}\frac{\partial u}{\partial \phi}.$$
1929 *Encycl. Brit.* IX. 919/2 The Cauchy-Riemann equations and Laplace's equation are of central importance in the theory of maps and in various problems of mathematical physics. **1968** C. G. KUPER *Introd. Theory Superconductivity* v. 82 Equations..have

the form of Cauchy–Riemann equations for the function $h = dw/dz$.

Cauchy–Schwarz (kəʊʃɪˈʃvɑːts), *n. Math.* [The names of Augustin-Louis *Cauchy* (see *CAUCHY *n.*) and Hermann Amadeus *Schwarz* (see SCHWARZ *n.*).] *Cauchy-Schwarz inequality*, the statement that for any two sets of *n* numbers, the sum of the *n* pairwise sums, squared, is no greater than the sum of the two sums formed by adding the squared magnitudes of the numbers in each set.
  1956 B. FRIEDMAN *Princ. & Techniques Appl. Math.* i. 6 $|<x, y>| \leq |x| \cdot |y|$. This result is known as the Cauchy–Schwartz inequality. **1957** T. M. APOSTOL *Math. Analysis* i. 6 We shall now derive a very useful result known as the Cauchy–Schwarz inequality. **1988** *Nature* 24 Mar. 329/1 Another interesting relation among these quantities is obtained by applying the Cauchy–Schwarz inequality to equations (1) to (3).

cell, *n.*[1] Add: [II.] [9.] **h.** The local area covered by one of the short-range radio stations in a cellular telephone system.
  1977 *Wireless World* June 40/1 The cellular system uses a number of low power stations, each covering a limited area. 'The area to be covered is divided into a number of cells, each cell having at its centre a fixed transmitter receiver installation, usually but not necessarily having a multichannel capability.' **1984** *Miami Herald* 27 Mar. 9D/2 (Advt.), Conversations are automatically switched from one cell to the next. **1988** *Independent* 23 Aug. 21 Cellular radio gets its name from the structure of the network—calls are made in one area or 'cell' through the cell's base station into the public network.

Cencibel (θɛnθɪˈbɛl, sɛnsɪˈbɛl), *n.* [a. Sp. *Cencibel*, of unknown origin: cf. *cencivera*, name of another early-ripening Sp. grape.] In central and southern Spain, esp. the Valdepeñas region: the Tempranillo grape. Cf. *TEMPRANILLO *n.*
  1966 G. RAINBIRD *Sherry & Wines Spain* v. 91 The black grapes, which make the *tintos*, are the Cencibel, in the Valdepeñas district, and the Garnacha in other districts. **1991** *Washington Post* 13 Mar. E1 Made from Tempranillo, called cencibel in Almansa.

cephalo-, *comb. form.* Add: [b.] **cephalo'metric** *a.*, pertaining to or obtained by cephalometry; also = *craniometric* adj. s.v. CRANIO-.
  1935 HUXLEY & HADDON *We Europeans* ii. 41 Spiegel introduced '*cephalometric lines'. He drew four lines in certain directions, within the skull, and if these lines were equal to each other he regarded the skull as regularly proportioned. **1977** *Proc. R. Soc. Med.* LXX. 432/1 Many assessments of relapse have been based upon cephalometric measurements and values for mean relapse, and standard error, standard deviation and probability for the samples are given. **1989** *Brit. Jrnl. Orthodontics* XVI. 121/1 A retrospective cephalometric study was carried out investigating vertical skeletal and dental changes in 30 patients treated with the Andresen appliance. **1991** *Daily Tel.* 24 Aug. 13/5 He..helped develop a computerised system for assessing cephalometric X-rays..which is now standard.
  cephalo'metrical *a. rare* = *cephalometric adj. above.
  1895 *Amer. Jrnl. Insanity* LII. 77 The two systems of measurement—the craniometrical and *cephalometrical—differ but slightly from each other, the former, of course, being the more exact, since every portion of the naked skull is attainable.
  cepha'lometry *n.* [cf. earlier Fr. *céphalométrie*.] measurement of the head, esp. of the foetal head; also = *craniometry* s.v. CRANIO-.
  1881 *Index-Catal. Library Surg.-General's Office, U.S. Army* II. 812/2 *Cephalometry. *See*

Craniometry. **1895** *Amer. Jrnl. Insanity* LII. 73 (*heading*) Craniometry and cephalometry in relation to idiocy and imbecility. **1977** *Lancet* 3 Dec. 1170/2 Ultrasound cephalometry should be a routine investigation early in pregnancy, but in reaching this conclusion we have assumed that ultrasound examination is harmless.

cephaloridine (sɛfəˈlɔːrɪdiːn), *n. Pharm.* [Blend of CEPHALOSPORIN *n.* (see def.) and PYRIDINE *n.*] An antibiotic, $C_{19}H_{17}N_3O_4S_2$, derived from cephalosporin which has been given (usu. by injection) in the treatment of some bacterial infections.
  1964 *Jrnl. Amer. Med. Assoc.* 26 Oct. 289/2 Cephaloridine. **1964** *New Scientist* 12 Nov. 430/1 Two members of a new family of antibiotics, the cephalosporins, have recently been introduced...One, named cephalothin, is made in the USA; the other, cephaloridine, is produced in Britain. **1976** *Lancet* 25 Dec. 1380/2 Cloxacillin and cephaloridine were relatively inactive against a large inoculum of penicillinase-producing bacteria. **1986** C. W. THORNBER in C. A. Heaton *Chem. Industry* iv. 199 Cephaloridine..is particularly effective against gram-positive organisms.

cephalothin (ˈsɛfələʊθɪn), *n. Pharm.* [Blend of CEPHALOSPORIN and THIO-.] An antibiotic, $C_{16}H_{16}N_2O_6S_2$, derived from cephalosporin, given (usu. by injection as the sodium salt) in the treatment of some bacterial infections.
  1962 *Jrnl. Amer. Chem. Soc.* LXXXIV. 3402/1 The sodium salt of 7-(thiophene-2-acetamido)-cephalosporanic acid, which has been given the generic name cephalothin, has received extensive clinical evaluation as a broad spectrum antibiotic. **1976** *Lancet* 13 Nov. 1040/2 She was febrile (39°C) and complained of locked jaw; she was given cephalothin (12 g/day) and gentamicin (120 mg/day). **1981** *Sci. Amer.* June 72/2 The first two semisynthetic cephalosporins, cephalothin from Lilly and cephaloridine from the Glaxo laboratories in Britain, were also active against the penicillin-resistant staphylococcus. **1987** *Oxf. Textbk. Med.* (ed. 2) II. XVIII. 111/2 Cephalothin causes acute renal failure only occasionally, and this is less clearly dose related.

ceratitic (sɛrəˈtɪtɪk), *a. Palaeont.* [f. CERATIT(E *n.* + -IC i.] Pertaining to or characteristic of a ceratite or ceratites; *spec.* designating the lobed suture line typical of fossil ceratites.
  1900 C. R. EASTMAN tr. *K. A. von Zittel's Text-bk. Palæont.* I. VI. 559 Saddles and lobes have the typical ceratitic outlines, as a rule. **1920** A. M. DAVIES *Introd. Palæont.* iv. 163 In the Jurassic period the ceratitic type is absent, and the highly complex (ammonitic) suture is alone found. **1976** *Geol. Mag.* CXIII. 40 The only internal evidence for age assignment of the Greville Formation is the collection of ceratitic ammonoids. **1986** G. CULVERWELL tr. *Arduini & Teruzzi's Macdonald Encycl. Fossils* No. 91, The simple 'ceratitic' suture line has broad, rounded entire saddles and no denticulation.

cerclage (sɜːˈklɑːʒ, ‖sɛrklaʒ), *n. Med.* Also in anglicized form **circlage**. [a. F. *cerclage*, lit. 'encirclement'.] The use of a ring or loop to bind together the ends of an obliquely fractured bone or encircle the os of an incompetent cervix.
  1920 in STEDMAN *Med. Dict.* (ed. 6). **1961** *Amer. Jrnl. Obstet. & Gynecol.* LXXXI. 469/1 Planned circlage operations and prophylactic procedures, particularly when based on a history only, raise the question as to whether hazards to the mother and the pregnancy justify such procedures. **1965** *Obstet. & Gynecol.* XXV. 145/2 Cerclage should be delayed until the second trimester, to be done preferably after the fourteenth week. **1981** *Lancet* 13 June 1320/1 The operation of cerclage for pregnant women with a history

of 'cervical incompetence' has been in use for a quarter of a century, yet there is no general agreement as to the appropriate indications.

cercus, *n.* Add: Hence 'cercal *a.*
1889 in *Cent. Dict.* **1977** *New Scientist* 7 Apr. 20/1 S. G. Matsumo and R. K. Murphy immobilised the cercal hairs with Clinique facial cleansing cream.

cereologist (sɪərɪˈɒlədʒɪst), *n.* Also **cerealogist**. [f. the name of the goddess *Ceres* (see CEREAL *n.*) + -OLOGIST.] One who studies or investigates crop circles.
1990 *Fortean Times* LIII. 42 He is a pioneer and leading theorist of the strictly meteorological school of crop circle investigators (or cereologist, from Ceres the goddess of corn). **1990** *Daily Tel.* 27 July 17/5 The news that the latest rash of giant acne in the Wiltshire cornfields is a hoax has done nothing to dispirit some devoted circle spotters who are about to bring out the first edition of the Cereologist. **1993** *Observer* 11 July 64/3 Pity the humble cerealogist. Saddled with the Herculean task of explaining the existence of crop circles.
So **cere'ology** *n.*
1990 *New Scientist* 1 Dec. 61/1 The array of experts who have collaborated to found the Centre for Crop Circle Studies and co-author *The Crop Circle Enigma*, the parents of cereology. **1993** *Sunday Times* 6 June VI. 6/4 In the early days of cereology, a principal attraction of this field of research..was publishers' appetites for sensationalist speculations about the mystery crop formations.

cestode ('sɛstəʊd), *n.* and *a.* *Zool.* [f. mod.L. *Cestoda*, class name (formerly *Cestoidea*): see CESTOID *a.* and *n.*, -ODE[1].] **A.** *n.* A parasitic worm of the class Cestoda, having a flat, ribbon-like body; a tapeworm. **B.** *adj.* Of, pertaining to, or designating this class; = CESTOID *a.*
1864 T. S. COBBOLD *Entozoa* viii. 105 Every cestode passes through several distinct phases during its life-history. *Ibid.* 107 It is..difficult to estimate the number of true cestode species at present in existence. **1870** H. D. ROLLESTON *Forms Animal Life* 137 The cestode many-jointed tapeworms. **1919** *Parasitology* XI. 405 (*heading*) On two species of the cestode genus *Oochoristica* from lizards. *Ibid.*, The cestodes of lizards have received little recent attention from systematic zoologists. **1959** A. HARDY *Open Sea* II. xii. 244 We come now to the cestodes or tapeworms, those animals which are apt to fill us with disgust because one of their kind..may come to reside in our own inside. **1977** T. I. STORER et al. *Elem. Zool.* (ed. 4) xvii. 290/1 The cestodes..are all internal parasites of vertebrates.

chalco-, *comb. form.* Add: **chalcophil(e)** *a.* *Geol.* and *Chem.* [ad. G. *chalkophil* (V. M. Goldschmidt 1923, in *Skrifter utgit av Videnskapsselsk.* I: *Mat.-nat. Kl.* III. 7); see -PHIL], applied to elements which are commonly found as sulphides or native and are supposed to have become concentrated in the mantle when the earth was molten; also as *n.*, (a naturally occurring form of) such an element.
1923 *Mineral. Abstr.* II. 159 The chemical elements are divided into..: (1) Siderophil elements.. (2) *Chalcophil elements of sulphide fusions, represented in meteorites by the troilite phase (S, Se, Te, Fe, Cu, Zn, Pb, As, Sb, Bi, Ag, Au, Hg, Pd, &c.); (3) Lithophil elements of silicate fusions. **1979** A. H. BROWNLOW *Geochem.* i. 31 The electrons of lithophile and chalcophile elements are more available; thus these elements tend to form ions. **1981** J. W. BUTTLE et al. *Chemistry* (ed. 4) viii. 190 Metallic sulphides (chalcophils) would dissolve in the iron sulphide phase. **1984** GREENWOOD & EARNSHAW *Chem. of Elements* (1986) xv. 760 The chalcophiles..are associated with copper, specifically as sulfides.

challah ('xɒlə, 'xalə), *n.* Also **challa**, **halla**, and varr. Pl. **challas**, **chalot(h)**. [ad. Heb. *ḥallāh* a form of bread, prob. f. Heb. *ḥll* hollow, pierce (perh. a reference to its original form).] A loaf of white leavened bread, often plaited in form, traditionally baked to celebrate the Jewish Sabbath.
[*c* **1782** D. LEVI *Succinct Acct. Rites, & Ceremonies, of Jews* 9 They must also spread on the table, a clean tablecloath, and set two loaves upon it; which loaves are baked on the Friday, and are called in Hebrew..*Cholith*.] **1937** 'BALABUSTA' *Prize Kosher Recipe Bk.* 2 (*caption*) Challah. **1951** L. W. LEONARD *Jewish Cookery* v. 26 It is customary to place two *challas* under a special napkin... The two loaves are symbolic of the 'two portions of manna' which fell for the Sabbath. **1988** *Jerusalem Post* 7 Oct. ('In Jerusalem' Suppl.) 2/2 Both bombs were hidden in halla loaves. One of the owners of the store in the Jewish Quarter removed the bread from the store after a worker remarked that it seemed unusually heavy. **1992** *Jewish Chron.* 7 Feb. 11/3 The shop is stocking a range of pre-packed kosher foods, as well as bagels and chalot.

chalot(h) *n. pl.*: pl. of *CHALLAH *n.*

chaology, *n.* Restrict *rare*-0 to sense in Dict. Add: **2.** = *chaos theory* (*b*) s.v. *CHAOS *n.* 6.
1987 *Nature* 19 Nov. 293/2 The concepts and methods of chaology have penetrated into virtually all branches of science. **1989** *Independent* 14 Oct. 31/5 Then he told me about chaology, which he called the new buzz thing.
Hence **cha'ologist** *n.*, an expert in or student of chaology.
1987 J. GLEICK *Chaos* ii. 38 The chaoticists or chaologists (such coinages could be heard) turned up with disproportionate frequency on the yearly lists of important fellowships and prizes. **1987** *Newsweek* 21 Dec. 55/1 'Chaologists' find that, although it may never be possible to precisely predict the weather or the stock market.., one can see the patterns of their behavior. **1989** *Daily Tel.* (Colour Suppl.) 12 Aug. 24 (*caption*) The 'strange attractor' has become the chaologist's favourite motif.

chaos, *n.* Add: [**3.**] **c.** *Math.* Behaviour of a system which is governed by deterministic laws but is so unpredictable as to appear random, owing to its extreme sensitivity to changes in parameters or its dependence on a large number of independent variables; a state characterized by such behaviour.
The quotations before quot. 1974[2] do not represent precisely this sense.
1960 *Jrnl. Chem. Physics* XXXIII. 1342/1 The chaos condition becomes more accurately satisfied as *n* becomes large. **1969** *Proc. Japan Acad.* XLV. 450 Kac's propagation of chaos should hold for a wide class of Markov processes. **1974** *Proc. Nat. Acad. Sci.* LXXI. 2618/1 Equation 1.1 is based on the 'molecular chaos assumption'. **1974** *Science* 15 Nov. 646/2 Li and Yorke's general theorem for cycles of period 3 may be extended..to show that equations of the generic form of 1 and 2 will enter a regime of chaos, with an uncountable number of cycles of integral period along with an uncountable number of aperiodic solutions. **1975** *Jrnl. Theoret. Biol.* LI. 514 The equation $N_{t+1} = \lambda[1 + aN_t]^{-b}N_t$ has been used..to provide a two-parameter fit to a wide range of field and laboratory data on single-species population growth:..relatively large values of both *b* and *λ* leads [*sic*] to chaos. **1975** LI & YORKE in *Amer. Math. Monthly* LXXXII. 985 (*title*) Period three implies chaos. **1978** *Jrnl. Math. Anal. & Applic.* LXIII. 200 Although chaos was originally observed in the context of a hydrodynamical system, this phenomenon has spurred the interest primarily of mathematical biologists, particularly those in the field of population dynamics. **1988** I. PETERSON *Math. Tourist* vi. 144 The technical definition of chaos..carries with

it an image of order in the midst of disorder. **1989** I. STEWART *Does God play Dice?* i. 21 One of the characteristic features of chaos is that tiny errors propagate and grow. **1990** *Times* 29 Oct. 2/1 The extraordinary thing about chaos is that you can get some mind-bogglingly complex behaviour from simple equations.
   [6.] chaos theory, (*a*) *nonce-wd.*, a theory based on the concept of chaos; (*b*) the mathematical study of chaotic systems and their behaviour.
   1924 R. M. OGDEN tr. *Koffka's Growth of Mind* iii. 134 According to the *chaos-theory the phenomena corresponding to a human face can be nothing but a confused mass of the most varied light-, dark-, and colour-sensations. [**1986** *Nonlinear Analysis* X. 541 (*heading*) On the existence of Li-Yorke points in the theory of chaos.] **1987** *Nature* 23 Apr. 753/2 A survey of how determinism fares in various branches of physics, including classical mechanics, relativity theory.., probabilistic theories, modern chaos theory and the quantum theory. **1988** *Jrnl. Monetary Econ.* July 73 Chaos theory deals with deterministic processes which look random but whose dimension is finite.

chaotic, *a.* Add: **3.** *Math.* Pertaining to, characteristic of or characterized by chaos (*CHAOS *n.* 3 c); pertaining to systems which exhibit chaos.
   [**1974** *Science* 15 Nov. 646/2 Episodes of apparently chaotic behavior.] **1975** R. M. MAY in *Jrnl. Theoret. Biol.* LI. 512 A regime which can only be described as 'chaotic' (an apt term coined by Li & Yorke, 1974). **1975** LI & YORKE in *Amer. Math. Monthly* LXXXII. 986 In this paper we analyze a situation in which the sequence $\{F^n(x)\}$ is non-periodic and might be called 'chaotic'. Theorem 1 shows that chaotic behavior for (1.1) will result in any situation in which [etc.]. **1977** *Lect. Notes Physics* LXXI. 337 A good example of such a 'chaotic' signal.. is provided by the time dependence of the magnetic field of earth. **1978** *Progress Theoret. Physics* LIX. 1029/1 Dynamic systems that are 'chaotic' in the physicists' intuitive sense. **1990** *Scope* Summer 11/2 Populations of birds, insects and other animals fluctuate in apparently chaotic ways. **1990** *Times* 9 Aug. 13/5 One of the tasks facing students of complex chaotic systems, meteorological or social, is to investigate fully the range of predictability in each case. **1992** *New Scientist* 14 Mar. 56/2 Jim Lesurf describes a seemingly neat idea, namely using a chaotic function to generate pseudo random numbers for use in cryptosystems. **1994** *Nature* 6 Jan. 33/2 The Earth-crossing asteroids include rocky and metallic objects derived from main-belt asteroids through collisional fragmentation and chaotic dynamics.

chaotically, *adv.* Add: (examples corresponding to *CHAOS *n.* 3 c, *CHAOTIC *a.* 3).
   1978 *Jrnl. Math. Anal. & Applic.* LXIII. 202 The question remains then under what conditions will the general problem (1.2) behave chaotically. **1988** *Times Lit. Suppl.* 22 July 800/3 Chaotically fluctuating flow patterns.. have long been studied under the name of turbulence. **1994** *New Scientist* 15 Oct. 16/1 The suspicion that three bodies can move chaotically predates the recognition of chaos in mathematics.

charioteer, *n.* Add: **2.** *Astron.* (With capital initial.) The constellation Auriga; = WAGONER *n.*[1] 3 a.
   [**1810** J. GREIG *Astrography* vi. 125 He was Mirtilus, ..charioteer to Aenomaus..; his name is famous for his great address in the management of horses;.. he was..made a constellation after his death.] **1885** R. HILL *Stars & Constellations* 24 The constellation *Auriga*, called also, *the Charioteer*, and *the Wagoner*. **1930** A. C. DE LA CROMMELIN *Story of Stars* i. 21 On the opposite side of the Pole to Vega we find another bright star, Capella, in the Charioteer. **1965** ZIM & BAKER *Stars: Guide to Astron.* 87 Auriga, the Charioteer is the last of the autumn constellations,

heralding the coming winter. **1994** *Daily Tel.* 31 Dec. 22/7 The star Capella in the constellation of Auriga the Charioteer is shown prominently in the centre of the chart.

charm, *n.*[1] Add: **[7.] charm offensive,** the adoption of a plausible manner or cooperative approach as an expedient strategy for achieving a goal (esp. in *Pol.*).
   1979 *Summary of World Broadcasts: Far East* (B.B.C.) 18 Apr. A3/12 Sihanouk, 'who has launched a veritable "*charm offensive" towards the Philippines since he retired here [*sc.* Peking] from political activity, increased his public attentions to the country.' **1993** *U.S. News & World Rep.* 11 Jan. 18/3 Instead of taking a hard line, the official expects Hussein to emphasize a new 'reasonableness'...If the 'charm offensive' fails, U.S. officials fear a resumption of military probing and acts of terrorism.

charophyte ('kærəʊfaɪt), *n. Bot.* [f. mod.L. *Charophyta,* former name of the Characeae, f. *chara* (see CHARA *n.*[1]): see -O[1], -PHYTE.] A member of the Characeae (formerly called the Charophyta), a group of macroscopic mainly freshwater algae marked by whorls of short branches arising from a main axis, often partly encrusted with calcium carbonate; = STONEWORT *n.* 3.
   1920 GROVES & BULLOCK-WEBSTER *Brit. Charophyta* I. 1 For a while teaching botanists were wont to select some species of Charophyte as one of their plant-types. **1950** G. O. ALLEN *Brit. Stoneworts* 9 Charophytes do normally grow in mud though in clean water only, and they are often smothered in debris or coated with algae. **1968** H. J. M. BOWEN *Flora Berks.* ii. 22 The aquatic flora includes *Potamogeton coloratus*..together with the charophytes *Chara contraria* and *C. hispida.* The latter are believed to be characteristic of waters which are low in phosphate. **1988** *Nature* 14 Apr. 639/2 The ostracodes and charophytes from the same beds suggest close affinities to taxa from the late Cretaceous Nemegt Basin of Mongolia.
   So **charo'phytic** (kærəʊ'fɪtɪk), *a.*
   1920 GROVES & BULLOCK-WEBSTER *Brit. Charophyta* I. 12 Certain parts of Switzerland, where the Charophytic deposits are collected from pools and lakes, left to dry in heaps, and then spread upon the land as manure. **1950** G. O. ALLEN *Brit. Stoneworts* 12 An American geologist considers some fruits from the Devonian to show definite charophytic affinities.

charter, *n.* Add: **[5.] Charter Mark:** in the U.K., an award granted to institutions for exceptional public service under the terms of the Citizen's Charter (see *CITIZEN *n.* 5).
   1991 *Economist* 27 July 23/2 All public bodies taking part in the charter programme will be candidates to receive a '*Chartermark' where their services are deemed to be up to scratch...But in the public sector, without competition, name badges and chartermarks could soon be empty gimmicks. **1992** *Observer* 2 Feb. 16/1 (Advt.), The Citizen's Charter sets a new Standard for public services. The Charter Mark recognises this Standard. If you think your organisation meets the Standard, why not apply for a Charter Mark? **1992** *Private Eye* 8 May 13/1 Such sound management has lead [*sic*] Dr John Roylance, chief executive of the United Bristol Healthcare Trust (UBHT), to apply for a 'charter mark', the department of health's new gold standard of service provision.

chayote, *n.* Substitute for entry: **chayote** (tʃaɪˈəʊtɪ, ‖tʃaˈjote), *n.* Chiefly *U.S.* Also †chayota, †cheyote. [a. Sp. *chayote,* ad. Nahuatl *chayotli.*] = CHOCHO *n.*
   1884 tr. *A. de Candolle's Orig. Cultivated Plants* 274 The *chayote* was not cultivated in Cayenne ten years

ago. **1884** *Health Exhib. Catal.* 159/1 Farinaceous Roots and Fruits.—Red Batata, Fruits of Chayota. **1889** in *Cent. Dict.*, Cheyote. **1975** E. L. ORTIZ *Caribbean Cooking* (1977) 217 Many islands make a mock applesauce from papaya..or from chayote (christophene). **1986** B. FUSSELL *I hear Amer. Cooking* II. 97 The products of the land are..plants like..mirlitons, which others call 'chayotes'.

chemo-, *comb. form.* Add: ˌchemoautoˈtrophic *a*. *Bot.* [after G. *Chemoautotrophie* n. (E. G. Pringsheim 1932, in *Naturwiss.* XX. 479/1)], (of micro-organisms or their environment) obtaining the energy needed to sustain autotrophism by chemical means; deriving energy from the oxidation of inorganic compounds.
1941 *Adv. Enzymol.* I. 265 Pfeffer later coined the name chemosynthesis for this group of processes for which Pringsheim, more recently, has proposed the term *chemo-autotrophic. **1981** *Sci. Amer.* Oct. 109/1 Like the free-living bacteria at the vents, the symbiotic ones are chemoautotrophic: they sustain themselves on inorganic substances, and thereby they sustain the worm.
so **chemoˈautotroph**, a chemoautotrophic organism.
1943 *Physiol. Rev.* XXIII. 347 Instead of carrying out a photosynthetic metabolism they now behave as *chemo-autotrophs. **1982** M. J. DRING *Biol. Marine Plants* ix. 174 The H₂S which is released may support a small population of chemoautotrophs throughout the upper part of the sediments.
ˌchemoautoˈtrophically *adv.*, by means of chemoautotrophy, in a chemoautotrophic manner.
1961 WEBSTER, *Chemoautotrophically. **1979** *Nature* 27 Sept. 256/1 *Thiocapsa* can be grown chemoautotrophically in the dark under oxygen.
ˌchemoautoˈtrophism = *chemoautotrophy below.
1943 *Physiol. Rev.* XXIII. 340 It would, of course, be possible to re-define *chemo-autotrophism in such a manner that the above difficulty could be avoided.
chemoˈautotrophy, chemoautotrophic nutrition.
1951 J. W. FOSTER in Werkman & Wilson *Bacterial Physiol.* 385 (*heading*) Energetics of *chemoautotrophy. **1987** *Sci. Amer.* Apr. 89/2 A high ratio of surface area to volume is ideal for the feeding strategies known as photoautotrophy and chemoautotrophy.
ˌchemoprophyˈlaxis, the prevention of disease by the administration of drugs (esp. antibiotics).
1949 *New Gould Med. Dict.* 205/2 *Chemoprophylaxis, prevention of disease by the administration of chemical drugs, as sulfanilamide. **1961** *Lancet* 9 Sept. 589/2 For operative chemoprophylaxis surgeons commonly rely on streptomycin. **1989** *Brit. Med. Jrnl.* 27 May 1422/1 The two babies with reflux were receiving chemoprophylaxis, and neither had a urinary tract infection.
hence ˌchemoprophyˈlactic *a*.
1961 WEBSTER, *Chemoprophylactic. **1975** *Nature* 20 Mar. 169/1 Two trials have also been carried out in India using sulphones for their protective or chemoprophylactic effect by giving them to healthy people.

chemotaxis, *n.* Add: **chemoˈtactically** *adv.*
1910 *Ann. Bot.* XXIV. 654 Strasburger's suggestion that the chromosomes are chemotactically sensible seems rather unlikely. **1946** *Physiol. Rev.* XXVI. 324 Such accumulations of lymphocytes suggest that they may have been attracted chemotactically. **1989** B. ALBERTS et al. *Molecular Biol. Cell* (ed. 2) xi. 672 The cells could migrate and respond chemotactically to a source of cyclic AMP.

chemotherapy, *n.* Add: ˌchemotheraˈpeutically *adv.*
1955 *Pharmacol. Rev.* VII. 279 In this review an attempt is made to give a general account of the drugs which are chemotherapeutically active against filarial infections. **1986** M. KOGUT tr. *Schlegel's Gen. Microbiol.* vi. 206 Chloramphenicol..is used chemotherapeutically as a highly effective bacteriostatic agent.

chemotropism, *n.* Add: **chemoˈtropically** *adv.*
1895 *Ann. Bot.* IX. 344 The other possible explanation is that the hypha seeks the nucleus in virtue of its chemotropism, the chemotropically active substances being manufactured or accumulated in greatest quantities nearest the nucleus of the infected cell. **1979** *Nature* 14 June 635/1 The mature seed of *Orobanche*, stimulated chemotropically by diffusion of compounds from the host, germinates and its extending radicle establishes contact with the host.

Chenin (ʃənɛ̃), *n.* [Fr., perh. f. the name of the manor of Mont-*Chenin*, Touraine, where it was first imported from Anjou. The place-name may ult. derive from OF. *chenin* 'dog-like'; cf. CANINE *a*.
In *Gargantua & Pantagruel* (1534) I. xxv., Rabelais mentions *raisins chenins*; there is some confusion as to whether this refers to the red or the white grape (see quots. 1611 at sense 1, 1928 at sense 2 below).]
1. *rare*. Usu. in full as **Chenin Noir**. A variety of black grape native to the Loire region, more commonly known as *Pineau d'Aunis* (see quot. 1994).
[**1611** R. COTGRAVE *Dict. Fr. & English* sig. Qvi/2 *Raisins chenins*, a kind of great red grapes, fitter for medicines than for meat.] **1896** *Rep. Viticultural Wk.* (U.C. College Agric.) I. 364 *Chenin noir*..this is one of the chief red-wine grapes of the department of Maine-et-Loire. **1994** J. ROBINSON *Oxf. Comp. Wine* 733/2 *Pineau d'Aunis*, sometimes called Chenin Noir, is a variety that is neither a Pinot nor a Chenin according to Galet, but a distinct black-berried Loire vine variety associated since the Middle Ages with the Preuré d'Aunis near Saumur.
2. Usu. in full as **Chenin Blanc**. A variety of white grape, native to the Loire valley but now also widely cultivated elsewhere (esp. in the Americas and in South Africa), and used to make wine with a distinctive flowery taste; also, the vine producing this grape, or the wine made from it.
1928 P. M. SHAND *Bk. of French Wines* iii. 111 In *Gargantua*, Rabelais classifies the Touraine wines into 'Pineaultz, Fiers, Muscadeaulz, Bécanes, Foyards, Francs Aubiers, and Chenins' for the white, and 'Verrons' for the red. **1913** A. L. SIMON *In Vino Veritas* iii. 95 At Saumur, the Chenin Blanc is the vine chiefly cultivated for white wines. **1952** A. LICHINE *Wines of France* xv. 197 Saumur..is made of two-thirds white Chenin and one-third Cabernet. **1984** J. DENTINGER *First Hit of Season* v. 35 She..poured a glass of Chenin Blanc. **1990** *Good Food* Jan.-Feb. 68/1 The Chenin also produces flowery wines, apparently honeyed even when they are dry. **1994** J. ROBINSON *Oxf. Comp. Wine* 224/2 Chenin..is probably the world's most versatile grape variety, capable of producing some of the finest, longest-living sweet wines although more usually harnessed to the yoke of basic New World table wine production.

‖**chen shu** (dʒən ʃuː), *n.* Also **Chêng-Shu**, †**Chincù**. [Chinese *zhēnshū*, f. *zhēn* true, genuine + *shū* script, writing.] = *KʻAI SHU *n.*
1655 tr. *Semedo's China* vi. 33 The second [type of letters] is called *Chincu*, and is the most current. **1938** CHIANG YEE *Chinese Calligraphy* iii. 67 In *Kʻai Shu* there was an inflexible regularity of design that earned for it the additional name of *Chêng-Shu*..or Regular. **1958** W. WILLETS *Chinese Art* II. vii. 572

There is no mistaking the stylistic similarities between *li shu* and *k'ai shu*, 'Official Writing', otherwise known as *chên shu* or 'Regular Writing'. **1974** *Encycl. Brit. Macropædia* III. 667/2 In *chen shu*, or regular style, each stroke, even each dot, suggests the form of a natural object.

chernozem, *n.* Add: Hence **cherno'zemic** *a.*, constituting or characteristic of a chernozem.

1965 B. T. BUNTING *Geogr. Soil* xiii. 157 Invasions of *populus* on to chernozemic soils in Canada have caused degradation to gray wooded soils. **1972** J. G. CRUICKSHANK *Soil Geogr.* v. 158 In Glinka's later work..he recognised five major pedogenic processes (lateritic, podsolic, chernozemic, solonetzic, and swampy) on which he based his soil classification.

chiasmate (kaɪ'æzmeɪt), *a. Biol.* [f. CHIASM(A *n.* + -ATE².] = *CHIASMATIC *a.*

1950 *Chromosoma* IV. 13 The chiasmate structure of most of the bivalents is shown by the constancy of the open cross formation during the stretch stage. **1968** *Canad. Jrnl. Genetics & Cytol.* X. 898 The sex multiple to be described..seems to be the only known naturally occurring, mechanically and genetically competent chiasmate sex quadrivalent. **1992** *Heredity* LXVIII. 232/2 The frequency of chiasmate association *a* and *b* of the two average arms of the chromosomes may also be estimated.

chiasmatic (kaɪæz'mætɪk), *a.* [f. CHIASMA *n.*: see -ATIC.] **1.** *Anat.* Of or pertaining to the optic chiasma.

1912 T. L. STEDMAN *Med. Dict.* (ed. 2) 169/2 *Chiasmatic*.., relating to the optic chiasm. **1930** *Arch. Ophthalm.* III. 507 These tumors, as previously pointed out, have their point of dural attachment over the chiasmatic sulcus. **1968** *Amer. Jrnl. Ophthalm.* LXV. 432/2 Chiasmatic arachnoiditis most commonly follows basal meningitis or head injury. **1990** *Brain* CXIII. 577 Chapters on the sylvian fissure, the carotid cistern, the chiasmatic cistern, [etc.].

2. *Cytol.* Exhibiting or involving the formation of chiasmata.

1965 *Chromosoma* XVI. 296 Male meiosis is chiasmatic and several of the larger bivalents usually form 3 chiasmata. **1992** *Brain Res.* DLXXVI. 332 The distribution of the neuropeptide Y (NPY) was studied in geniculate and peri-chiasmatic regions in the lesser hedgehog-tenrec.

chill, *v.* Senses II. 4-8 in Dict. become II. 5-9. Add: [I.] **4.** *fig.* **a.** Freq. with *out.* To calm down, relax, take it easy. Also as *int. phr. slang.* (orig. *U.S.*).

1979 S. ROBINSON et al. *Rapper's Delight* (song) in L. A. Stanley *Rap: The Lyrics* (1992) 325 There's a time to laugh, a time to cry A time to live, and a time to die A time to break and a time to chill To act civilized or act real ill. **1983** *Time* 7 Nov. 94 It'd be nice to just chill out all the time and hunt and fish. **1988** J. McINERNEY *Story of my Life* x. 156, I kneed Trent in the balls and said, fuck off, I'm going to tell Rebecca if you don't chill out. **1991** *Time Out* 20 Nov. 57/2 Guest DJs choose the upfront, fonky tunes while upstairs there are board games, a film room and the comfortable balcony bar to chill-out in. **1992** *N. Y. Times Mag.* 12 Apr. 14/4 Jerry, chill out!.. Cool off a little. **1993** LOWE & SHAW *Travellers* IV. 171 We'd been to Lechlade, played there, done a party in Stroud, went and chilled out in Wales for a bit and then went looking for the Avon Free Festival.

b. To pass time idly; to hang around, esp. *with* other members of a group. *U. S. slang.*

1985 J. SIMMONS et al. *My Adidas* (song) in L. A. Stanley *Rap: The Lyrics* (1992) 274 Now the Adidas I possess for one man is rare Myself, homeboy, got fifty pair Got blue and black 'cause I like to chill And yellow and green when it's time to get ill. **1988** *New Musical Express* 24 Dec. 87 The perfect Xmas prezo would be

to spend it at home 'chilling out'..with the Schoolly family. **1991** *Essence* Dec. 42/1 She always seems to be just chillin' with friends. **1991** 'D. J. QUIK' *Born & Raised in Compton* (song) in L. A. Stanley *Rap: The Lyrics* (1992) 91 Compton is the place where the homeboys chill. **1992** *Vibe* Fall (Preview Issue) 90/1 Carmen is recounting a recent Friday night excursion. 'The guys we were chillin' with tried to herb this guy,' she says. To 'herb' means to rob.

chill-, *comb. form.* Add: [2.] **b.** **chill-out** *adj. phr. slang* [see *CHILL *v.* 4 a, b], designed to induce or enhance a relaxed mood, esp. in *chill-out music*; **chill-out room**, an area in a nightclub, usu. with air-conditioning and seating, where quiet or ambient music (*AMBIENT *n.* 3 c) is played.

1990 *Rave!* 6 Mar. 30/4 The Cavern Club..plays Sunday night host to Spice, a regular 6.30pm-10.30pm 'chill out' session. **1990** *Independent* 23 May 31/2 All four rooms are open and the club is firing; the Jam MCs, the main DJs; Spice, ambient DJs, provide a chill-out room. **1991** *Time Out* 20 Nov. 57/3 A jazz/flamenco guitarist in the chill-out room and happy hour prices at the bar before midnight. **1992** *Daily Tel.* 12 Sept. (Weekend Suppl.) p. xv/5 The vogue for chill-out music in all its forms—the ambient house of the Orb, the laboratory experiments of Brian Eno, the quiet bits of Mike Oldfield's hypnotic bells—mean that it has never been more fashionable to sound as though you are heavily sedated. **1992** *Face* Dec. 45 The only RPG [*sc.* role-playing game] that you won't get too embarrassed buying is Toe Jam and Earl, an ideal chill-out kind of game about two alien rappers who strut the screen looking for the missing parts of their spaceship. **1994** *Hypno* I. 69/1 Dress for cities, hotels, and think tanks is casual, comfortable meta-chic chill-out wear.

chilli, *n.* Add: [2.] chilli (usu. **chili**) **powder**, a spice made from dried powdered red chillies.

1898 *Thomas' Amer. Grocery Trades' Ref. Bk. 1899* 218 San Antonio...Gebhart *Chili Powd[er] Co[mpany]. **1981** B. CLEARY *Ramona Quimby* v. 98 The girls studied the spice shelf, unscrewed jar lids and sniffed. Nutmeg? No. Cloves? Terrible. Cinnamon. Uh-uh. Chili powder? Well....

chlordiazepoxide (ˌklɔːdaɪˌeɪzɪˈpɒksaɪd), *n. Pharm.* [f. CHLOR-² + *diazep*- after BENZODIAZEPINE *n.* + OXIDE *n.*] A benzodiazepine, $C_{16}H_{14}ClN_3O$, given in tablet form and by injection in the treatment of anxiety and as a hypnotic.

Among the proprietary names for this drug is LIBRIUM.

1960 *Jrnl. Amer. Med. Assoc.* 10 Sept. 198/2 The makers of the new drug, chlordiazepoxide hydrochloride,..seriously warn that it should be taken only on a physician's advice. **1961** *Lancet* 5 Aug. 323/1 This case confirms that chlordiazepoxide is a comparatively safe drug. **1965** J. POLLITT *Depression & its Treatment* iv. 48 When tension is more prominent than depression, chlordiazepoxide, meprobamate or even amylobarbitone in average doses will help tide the patient over difficult phases. **1980** *Brit. Med. Jrnl.* 29 Mar. 910/1 'Long'-acting benzodiazepines, whose half-life exceeds 10 hours—for example..chlordiazepoxide, and medazepam.

chlorinity (klɔː'rɪnɪtɪ), *n. Oceanogr.* [f. CHLORINE *n.* + -ITY, after SALINITY *n.* Cf. Ger. *Chlormenge* (S. P. L. Sørensen 1902, in *Kongel. Danske Vidensk. Selsk. Skr., Naturvidensk. og Math. Afd.* XII. 97).] The proportion by mass of dissolved chloride ions in water.

1930 *Rep. Internat. Fisheries Comm.* III. 5 The chlorinity is defined as the number of grams of chlorine contained in one kilogram of sea water, assuming the small quantities of bromine and iodine are replaced by chlorine. **1942** H. U. SVERDRUP *Oceanogr. for Meteorologists* ii. 9 The chlorinity that appears in this equation is also a *defined* quantity and does not represent the actual amount of chlorine in a sample of sea water. **1957** G. E. HUTCHINSON *Treat. Limnol.* I. vii. 484 The basin contains dilute sea water of chlorinity 15.2 to 15.7 per cent. **1973** *Nature* 23 Feb. 503/2 The chlorinity of 16 per cent is quite similar to that of Atlantis II Deep.

chlorophyte ('klɔːrəʊfaɪt), *n. Bot.* [f. mod.L. *Chlorophyta* (H.G.L. Reichenbach *Conspectus Regni Vegetabilis* (1828) 23): see CHLORO-[1], -PHYTE.] †**1.** (See quot.) *Obs. rare*–[0].
1882 *Syd. Soc. Lex.*, *Chlorophyte*,..applied to all plants having a successive evolution, and green parts or expansions.
2. [The mod.L. *Chlorophyta* was reassigned to a division of the algae by A. Pascher 1921, in *Ber. d. Deutschen Bot. Gesellsch.* XXXIX. 247.] An alga of the division Chlorophyta, typically having two kinds of chlorophyll, cellulose cell walls, and starch grains, as in land plants; a green alga.
1937 E. E. STANFORD *Gen. & Econ. Bot.* xiii. 346 Spirogyra..is so abundant, so characteristic, and so readily studied that it commonly passes as a 'characteristic' chlorophyte, which decidedly it is not. **1967** *Jrnl. Gen. Microbiol.* XLVIII. 379 Light caused up to a 20-fold increase in the rate of nitrate and nitrite assimilation by the marine chlorophyte *Dunaliella tertiolecta.* **1979** *Nature* 29 Mar. 447/2 Freshwater turtles may bear branched filamentous chlorophytes in the genus *Basicladia.*

-chore (kɔə(r)), *suffix. Bot.* [f. Gr. χωρεῖν to go, be spread abroad.] Used to form words denoting plants whose seeds are dispersed in a particular way, such as *hydro-chore* s.v. HYDRO-, *MYRMECOCHORE *n., *zoochore* s.v. ZOO-.

chorismate (kə'rɪzmeɪt), *n. Biochem.* [f. *CHORISM(IC *a. + -ATE[1].] A salt or ester, or the anion, of chorismic acid.
1965 *Austral. Jrnl. Chem.* XVIII. 1238 The solution (50 ml) of ammonium chorismate obtained from chromatography was acidified with IN HCl to pH 1.5. **1975** *Nature* 24 Apr. 667/2 The biosynthetic pathway for aromatic amino acids begins with the condensation of erythrose-4-phosphate and phosphoenolpyruvate, the first of seven enzyme reactions that culminate with the formation of chorismate. **1992** *Jrnl. Org. Chem.* LVII. 182/1 Several bicyclic chorismate analogues have been synthesized as mutase inhibitors.

chorismic (kə'rɪzmɪk), *a. Biochem.* [f. Gr. χωρισμός separation + -IC.] **chorismic acid**, a hydro-aromatic acid, $C_6H_5(OH)(COOH)\cdot O\cdot C(CH_2)COOH$, which is formed from shikimic acid in bacteria, fungi, and higher plants as a precursor of aromatic amino acids.
1964 M. I. & F. GIBSON in *Biochem. Jrnl.* XC. 249/1 As a result of this work a substance with the properties expected..was isolated, identified and named 'chorismic acid'. **1968** A. WHITE et al. *Princ. Biochem.* (ed. 4) xxiv. 573 As indicated in the figure, chorismic acid..is a branch point in the synthesis of the aromatic amino acids; conversion to anthranilic acid leads to tryptophan synthesis, while transformation to prephenic acid provides a precursor of phenylalanine and tyrosine. **1992** *Jrnl. Org. Chem.* LVII. 178 The mechanism of chorismate mutase, the enzyme which catalyzes the Claisen arrangement of chorismic to prephenic acid, remains a fascinating area for bioorganic research.

chrome, *v.* Add: **2.** *trans.* To add chromium-plated accessories to (a vehicle). Cf. *CHROMED *ppl. a.* 2.

1954 *Amer. Speech* XXIX. 94 'If it won't go, chrome it,' i.e. if the car isn't fast, make it look pretty.

chromed (krəʊmd), *ppl. a.* (Formerly s.v. CHROME *v.* in Dict.: quots moved here from former Dict. entry.) [f. CHROME *n.*, CHROME *v.* + -ED[2], -ED[1].] **1.** *Dyeing.* Treated with a solution of a chromium-containing salt (see CHROME *n.* 2 b) such as potassium dichromate.
1876 *Textile Colourist* II. 318 Chromed logwood colours have a tendency to become green. **1892** *Dyer* 20 Jan. 3/2 Chrome Violet may be used in wool dyeing on a chromed wool. **1906** *Ibid.* 20 Feb. 25/1 On chromed material it yields considerably darker shades.
2. = *chromium-plated* ppl. adj. s.v. CHROMIUM *n.* 2; also (of a car), having chromium-plated fittings.
1951 *Hot Rods* iv. 55 (*caption*) Note the special shackles used for the mounting of the tubular shock absorbers and the dropped, chromed and filled axle. **1957** *Life* 29 Apr. 137/1 (*caption*) A dream boat for hot-rodders is a chromed roadster like this one. **1969** *Jane's Freight Containers* 1968–69 540/3 Hard chromed steel. **1991** *Bicycling* Feb. 106/2 Nice touches such as chromed chainstays and dropouts.

chromosome, *n.* Add: **chromo'somally** *adv.*, as regards chromosomal properties; by means of chromosomes.
1921 *Proc. R. Physical Soc. Edin.* XX. 256 The question naturally arises as to whether these individuals are chromosomally females which become converted into males, or chromosomally males with an initial deficiency of the male-determining substance. **1965** *Times Lit. Suppl.* 27 May 483/4 Within this representation.. are encoded, chromosomally, the directives by which daughter cells behave like their mother. **1970** *Watsonia* VIII. 47 With no possibility of analysing these plants chromosomally. **1981** D. J. MERRELL *Ecol. Genetics* ix. 201 In chromosomally monomorphic species such as *D. simulans, D. virilis,* and *D. repleta,* inversion polymorphism is absent.

chromyl ('krəʊmaɪl, -mɪl), *n. Chem.* [f. CHROM(IUM *n.* + -YL.] **1.** The divalent radical $=CrO_2$. Usu. *attrib.*
1868 *Jrnl. Chem. Soc.* XXI. 514 In the course of an investigation.. I had occasion to prepare a considerable quantity of pure chromyl dichloride. **1950** N. V. SIDGWICK *Chem. Elements* II. 1004 All attempts to make chromyl bromide or iodide have failed.
2. Special Comb. **chromyl chloride**, a fuming red liquid, Cl_2CrO_2, used as an oxident and chlorinating agent.
1869 H. E. ROSCOE *Lessons Elem. Chem.* (new ed.) xxiii. 231 (*heading*) Chromium oxychloride, or chromyl chloride. **1979** *Sci. Amer.* May 110/3 On absorption of the infrared photons the chromyl chloride strongly emits a broad spectrum of visible light, predominantly orange in hue.

chronobiology (ˌkrəʊnəʊbaɪ'ɒlədʒɪ, also ˌkrɒnəʊbaɪ'ɒlədʒɪ), *n.* [f. Gr. χρόνο-ς time + BIOLOGY *n.*] The scientific study of temporal or periodic phenomena in biology.
1969 F. HALBERG in *Ann. Rev. Physiol.* XXXI. 677 'Chronobiology' is the study of the temporal characteristics of biologic phenomena, leading to an objective description of biologic time structure. **1976** *Nature* 22 Apr. 718/2 Recent reviews have suggested that melatonin has an endocrine role, particularly in relation to chronobiology, pituitary function and cerebral physiology. **1990** *N.Y. Times* 2 Oct. C1/4 A leader in the new field of human chronobiology, the study of how people are affected by internal and external rhythms.
Hence ˌchronobi'ologist *n.*, an expert in or student of chronobiology.

1976 *Sci. News* 10 Apr. 233 Chronobiologists are not completely sure why humans have seasonal or 'circannual' rhythms. **1987** *Times* 19 May 17/1 Time.. is the concern of chronobiologists testing jet-lag pills to help both travellers and shift-workers.

chronostratigraphy (ˌkrɒnəʊstrəˈtɪɡrəfɪ, ˌkrɒnəʊstrəˈtɪɡrəfɪ), *n. Geol.* [f. Gr. χρόνο-ς time + STRATIGRAPHY *n.*] The branch of stratigraphy concerned with the age of strata on an absolute scale (i.e. in terms of years).
1961 *Rep. 21st Internat. Geol. Congr. 1960* xxv. 12 A major goal of chronostratigraphy is the regional and.. world-wide assignment of the rocks of the earth's crust to their proper position with respect to the passage of geologic time. **1970** *Earth-Sci. Rev.* VI. 267 Stratigraphy comprises three major aspects: lithostratigraphy, biostratigraphy and chrono-stratigraphy. **1989** *Nature* 27 July 296/1 The Specmap project has defined the timing of δ18O variations in the ocean of the past 800 kyr, providing the basic chronostratigraphy for late Pleistocene palaeoclimatology.
So ˌchronostratiˈgraphic, ˌchronostratiˈgraphical *adjs.*
1954 *Compt. Rend. XIX Congrès Géol. Internat. 1952* XIII. 205 Time-stratigraphic (chrono-stratigraphic) units are often used incorrectly with the connotation of a certain lithology or a certain fossil content. **1966** *Earth-Sci. Rev.* I. 5 A three-fold stratigraphical classification—lithostratigraphical, bio-stratigraphical and chronostratigraphical—seems to have been accepted by a majority of stratigraphers. **1969** *Proc. Geol. Soc.* Aug. 158 'Chronostratigraphic zones' or 'Chronozones' are regarded as informal units. **1979** *Nature* 18 Jan. 190/1 It is also clear that glaciers reached Poland only during parts of the corresponding chronostratigraphical unit, the Weichselian Stage. **1992** A. G. DAWSON *Ice Age Earth* iv. 45 A major difficulty in the Late Quaternary literature of Canada and the USA is the different chronostratigraphic terminology used in both countries.

ciabatta (tʃəˈbɑːtə, tʃəˈbætə), *n.* Pl. ciabattas, ciabatte. [It. dial. *ciabatta* an old, down-at-heel shoe, a slipper, with reference to the shape of the loaf.] A type of moist, open-textured Italian bread made with olive oil; a loaf of this bread.
1985 C. FIELD *Italian Baker* 106 Slice an entire *ciabatta* horizontally and stuff it with salami and cheese. **1987** *N.Y. Times* 14 Jan. c3/1 What motivates the people of the Lake Como area.. to persist in making their beloved ciabatta?.. Ciabatta, which begins innocently enough with a little yeast, flour and warm milk, soon becomes brave and billowy. **1989** *Wine* Nov. 75/1 Ciabattas alone, the favourite slipper-shaped loaves with a feathery light texture and delicious flavour, account for a staggering 30,000 per day. **1993** *Independent on Sunday* 24 Oct. (Sunday Rev.) 65/2 The British high street ciabatta, oozing with oil, soft of crumb and supple of crust, is actually a modern invention.

circlage *n.*, var. *CERCLAGE *n.*

circle, *n.* Senses 16–25 in Dict. become 17–26. Add: [II.] **16.** A crop circle (see *CROP *n.* 22).
1980 *Now!* 29 Aug. 21/3, I have never seen marks cut as deeply as these recent circles. The spiral effect is important. **1982** G. T. MEADEN in *Jrnl. Meteorol.* VII. LXVI. 47 As with the Westbury 'circles'.., the circles are all clockwise spirals. **1987** *Flying Saucer Rev.* XXXII. VI. 12/2 While we continue to use the term '*circles*' in general, very few of them are actually perfectly round. **1993** J. SCHNABEL *Round in Circles* vi. 65 [He] began to assert in his confident, somewhat headmasterish manner that the circles were definitely caused by whirlwinds, and that any other theory was foolish and misguided and unscientific.

cisterna (sɪˈstɜːnə), *n.* Pl. cisternae. [a. L. *cisterna*: see CISTERN *n.*] **1.** *Anat.* A fluid-filled cavity, *esp.* a reservoir of cerebrospinal fluid in the subarachnoid spaces; = CISTERN *n.* 4. Freq. with postmodifying mod.L. adj.
1894 D. J. CUNNINGHAM *Man. Pract. Anat.* II. 482 Certain of the cisternae require special mention. *Ibid.* 483 Leading out from the cisterna basalis there are certain wide subarachnoid channels. **1921** *Johns Hopkins Hosp. Bull.* XXXII. 70/1 The most frequent location for an obstruction in communicating hydrocephalus is in the cisternæ. **1967** *Canad. Med. Assoc. Jrnl.* 2 Sept. 493/2 It was.. injected into the CSF.. by suboccipital puncture into the cisterna magna with the patient sitting. **1987** *Oxf. Textbk. Med.* (ed. 2) II. xv. 23/2 Lymph, draining from the cisterna chyli in the abdomen, passes up through the thoracic duct in front of the dorsal spine to the left subclavian vein.
2. *Cytol.* A saccular vesicle in some intracellular structures, esp. in the endoplasmic reticulum and Golgi apparatus.
1962 *Sci. Survey* III. 166 At this magnification these sacs—or, as they are called, cisternae—can be seen to be covered on the outside with attached particles making them look 'rough'-surfaced. **1979** *Jrnl. Compar. Path.* LXXXIX. 522 The most commonly encountered forms of linear membrane structure consisted of several fused or closely apposed cisternae. **1984** HOLTZMAN & NOVIKOFF *Cells & Organelles* (ed. 3) II. iv. 137 From the polysomes where the proteins are manufactured, they enter the cisternae of the ER and move toward the Golgi apparatus. **1988** *Sci. Amer.* Sept. 57/1 The Golgi cisternae themselves contain no insulin.

citizen, *n.* Add: [**5.**] **Citizen's Charter** (also **Citizens' Charter**) *Pol.*, a name given to various documents which concern the rights of citizens; *spec.* a British government document produced in 1991, designed to guarantee that public services meet certain standards of performance, and to give the public rights of redress when such standards are not upheld.
1913 C. E. INNES (*title*) The *Citizens' Charter. A scheme of national organisation. [*Ibid.* 5 This Scheme constitutes, in the making, a Charter of Citizenship, emphasizing and recording the rights and obligations of the citizen.] **1938** C. L. NORDON *State of Emergency* 11 (*heading*) The Citizens' Charter and the People's Pledge. **1991** J. MAJOR *Speech* 23 Mar. in *Citizen's Charter* (House of Commons Libr. Ref. Sheet 92/8) (1992) (cover), What we now aim to do is to put in place a comprehensive Citizen's Charter. It will work for quality across the whole range of public services. **1991** *Economist* 3 Aug. 27/1 In the 'citizen's charter', unveiled on July 22nd, the government confirmed its plans to deregulate the capital's buses. **1992** *Observer* 2 Feb. 16/1 (Advt.), The Citizen's Charter sets a new Standard for public services.

city, *n.* Add: [**II.**] [**9.**] **city farm**, (*a*) *U.S.*, any of various kinds of penal institution which also function as a farm.
1910 B. FLEXNER in H. H. Hart *Preventive Treatm. Neglected Children* xviii. 289 The probation officer keeps in touch with boys paroled from the *City Farm School and Boys' Industrial School and girls released from the Convent of the Good Shepherd. **1912** in *Jrnl. Amer. Inst. Crim. Law & Criminol.* (1927) XVII. 636 (*title*) First City farm for inebriates. **1977** *Washington Post* 8 Jan. E4/3 Martin escaped from a minimum security city farm in Martinsville, Va., in 1973, two days after pleading guilty to two charges of possession of marijuana with intent to sell.
(*b*) a farm established within an urban area for educational purposes, as a museum, etc.
1981 *N.Y. Times* 27 Aug. C12/1 Since 1976 one such group.. has maintained a thriving city farm called El Sol Brillante Community Garden. **1990** *Times* 15 Feb. 35/1 Salford has a city farm and part of the county

arboretum within its borders, and 27 miles of rural footpaths through its urban heartland.

cladogram ('klædəʊgræm, 'kleɪdəʊ-), *n. Taxon.* [f. CLADO- + -GRAM.] A dendrogram illustrating the supposed evolutionary relationships between clades; a diagram showing cladistic relationships.

1965 CAMIN & SOKAL in *Evolution* XIX. 312/2 We suggest the term *cladogram* to distinguish a cladistic dendrogram from a phenetic one which might be called a *phenogram*. **1965** E. MAYR in *Systematic Zool.* XIV. 81/2 In a cladogram..the ordinate gives estimated time. **1978** *Systematic Zool.* XXVII. 84/2 Mayr and Camin and Sokal, unknown to each other, proposed on December 29, 1964 the terms cladogram and phenogram at the same meeting of the Society of Systematic Zoology, Knoxville, Tenn. **1987** *Amer. Anthropol.* LXXIX. 973/2 Using features of the cranial base, Dean constructs alternative cladograms for the relationships of *Australopithecus, Paranthropus,* and *Homo.* **1988** *Nature* 22 Sept. 310/1 A matrix of taxa and their characters is constructed, and that information is used to infer a branching diagram (cladogram) specifying all the clades supported by the data. **1993** *Times Lit. Suppl.* 26 Mar. 11/4 Wilson and his colleagues looked for the most parsimonious cladogram of human mitochondria.

clan, *n.* Sense 4 in Dict. becomes 5. Add: **4.** *Petrogr.* A group of igneous rocks of very similar chemical composition.

1914 R. A. DALY *Igneous Rocks & their Origin* ii. 40 Field and laboratory observations..have already simplified the problem by showing that the many types [of igneous rocks] can be grouped in chemical series of relatively small number. For temporary, convenient use in this book, these series may be called 'clans'. **1932** F. F. GROUT *Petrogr. & Petrol.* II. 52 If a mineral is listed in the 'formula' of any clan it must be present in notable amount (though occult in the glasses), say about 10 per cent. **1936** H. L. ALLING *Interpretative Petrol. Igneous Rocks* xxiii. 278 The term kindreds was introduced by Tyrrell; this can be subdivided into series, suites, tribes, and clans. **1973** *Jrnl. Geol. Soc. India* XIV. 411 The common association of large bodies of Precambrian anorthosites with charnockites has led to the recognition of these rocks as forming a distinct clan. **1983** *Meteoritics* XVIII. 293 The Qinzhen enstatite chondrite, a recent fall in the People's Republic of China, is the first highly unequilibrated member (E3) of the enstatite chondrite clan.

clastogen ('klæstədʒɛn), *n. Genetics.* [f. Gr. κλαστός broken in pieces + -OGEN.] An agent that causes breaks in chromosomes.

1970 M. W. SHAW in *Ann. Rev. Med.* XXI. 409 A term was needed for the cumbersome phrase 'chromosome-breaking agent'...The word 'chromosomoclastogen' is suggested...In this article the more euphonious form 'clastogen' will be used. *Ibid.,* Certain genes, viruses, and protozoa are examples of biological clastogens. **1975** *Poultry Sci.* LIV. 310 Failure to detect chromosomal aberrations in either group indicated that Aroclor 1242..is not an effective clastogen. **1988** *Human Genetics* LXXX. 135 Spontaneous and clastogen-induced damage was analyzed in cultures of peripheral blood lymphocytes. So **clasto'genic** *a.,* causing breaks in chromosomes; **clastoge'nicity** *n.*

1970 M. W. SHAW in *Ann. Rev. Med.* XXI. 410 Some chemicals which are clastogenic may also be mutagenic. *Ibid.* 411 Among the DNA inhibitors, azascrine, mitomycin C, phleomycin, and streptonigrin have been tested for clastogenicity. **1977** *Mutation Res.* XLVII. 183 Most of the in vitro studies performed on the clastogenicity of LSD indicate either suppression of mitosis or enhanced chromosome damage. **1990** *Mutagenesis* V. 588/1 α-Ni₃S₂..presented a significant clastogenic activity which could be made evident *in vitro* by cytogenetic analysis of cultured human lymphocytes.

claustrophobe ('klɒstrəfəʊb), *n.* and *a.* [Back-formation f. CLAUSTROPHOBIA *n.*: see -PHOBE.] **A.** *n.* A person who suffers from claustrophobia.

1911 C. A. MERCIER *Conduct & its Disorders* vii. 111 Like the sufferer from agoraphobia, the claustrophobe experiences the revival of an instinct that has been dormant for untold generations. **1954** ENGLISH & FINCH *Introd. Psychiatry* ix. 195 Such a patient, like the claustrophobe, fears his own inner, childish impulses. The agoraphobe fears his exhibitionistic and other sexual impulses. **1974** K. MILLETT *Flying* I. 12 Nell showed me a volume of prison memoirs, thought I'd be pleased...Showing it to me, a claustrophobe, a coward. **1977** *Fortune* Nov. 217/2 Many of the single rooms are very small, and claustrophobes will probably be bothered. **1987** *New Scientist* 3 Dec. 83/4 While driving through the Fréjus tunnel between France and Italy I discovered that I'm a claustrophobe. **B.** *adj.* Claustrophobic; stifling. *rare.*

1954 W. FAULKNER *Fable* 410 A smell subterrene and claustrophobe and doomed to darkness.

clean, *n.* Add: **2.** *Weight-lifting.* The action of lifting a bar-bell from the floor to shoulder height in a single movement: usu. the first part of an overhead lift, followed by a jerk or press. Freq. in phrs. *clean and jerk, clean and press.* Cf. *JERK *n.*[1] 2 e, PRESS *n.*[1] 7 c.

1913 *Health & Strength* 6 Dec. 632/2 L.h. clean and jerk. **1928** *Health & Strength Ann.* 77 'Two Hands Clean and Military Press with Barbell'..and the 'Two Hands Clean and Jerk with Barbell'. **1947** *Brit. Amateur Weight-Lifter* Jan. 12/2 He also set up a new American Clean and Jerk record. **1961** *Muscle Power* Nov. 18 If you had only one exercise to do, what would it be? I asked this question of a number of prominent bodybuilders. About 60% of them agreed that they would favor the Two-hands Clean and Press. *Ibid.,* The Clean to chest requires great leg and lower back strength. **1975** *Oxf. Compan. Sports & Games* 1099/1 At the 1924 Olympic Games the lifts were one hand snatch, opposite one hand jerk, two hands clean and press, two hands snatch, and two hands clean and jerk. **1991** *Longevity* Jan. 60/2 The riskiest moves for your back are the clean-and-jerk, the snatch, the squat and the dead-lift.

clean, *v.* Add: **7.** *trans. Weight-lifting.* To lift (a weight attached to a bar-bell) from the floor to shoulder height in a single movement: usu. the first part of an overhead lift. Freq. in phrs. *to clean and jerk* (or *press*). Cf. *CLEAN *n.* 2.

1936 *Health & Strength* 26 Sept. 455/3, I can jerk 180 lb to arms' length from the shoulders but cannot 'clean' more than 154 lb. **1956** *Muscle Power* Mar. 46/3 To equal Eder's press Paul would have to clean and press 482 pounds. **1956** *Strength & Health* Nov. 17/2 The Russian is here seen cleaning a formidable 391-lb. weight. **1957** *Muscle Power* Jan. 48/3 In a meet in which most of Russia's famous lifters took part against an Egyptian team, he pressed 248, snatched 270 and cleaned and jerked 319½. **1988** *Strength Athlete* Oct./Nov. 7/1 After someone had been trying to bench press 260lbs Louis strode over and clean and pressed the weight (on an exercise bar) with ease. **1990** D. ACKERMAN *Nat. Hist. of Senses* ii. 102 The human body is miraculous and beautiful, whether it can 'clean and jerk' three hundred pounds, swim the English Channel, or survive a year riding the subway.

cleaning, *vbl. n.* Add: **[1.] d.** *Weight-lifting.* The action or technique of lifting a bar-bell from the floor to shoulder height.

1949 *Brit. Amateur Weight-Lifter* Apr. 18/1 Improving 'Cleaning' ability. **1950** J. HALLIDAY *Olympic Weight-Lifting* i. 22 Most lifters using this method of cleaning..are comparatively poor jerkers. **1986** *Weight Lifting* ('Know the Game' Ser.) (ed. 2) 27/3 These are exercises.. for the development of power and technique such as all pulling movements, power cleaning and power snatch, [etc.].

clean-up, *n*. Add: **e.** *Baseball*. Also **cleanup**. The fourth position in a team's batting order, usu. reserved for a strong batter whose hits are likely to enable any runner who is on base to score, thus clearing the bases. Freq. *attrib.*, esp. as *clean-up hitter* or *man*.

[**1907** *N. Y. Even. Jrnl.* 16 Apr. 10/2 He has a splendid arm, and he can surely play the ball. He is the cleaner-up hitter of the team.] **1909** *Baseball Mag.* Nov. 5/2 They are both batters of the 'clean-up' kind, that is, they are likely to break up a game at any moment. **1922** *N. Y. Times* 3 June 10/1 He shifted.. Meusel and Ross Young in the order of facing opposing pitchers, the former going to the clean-up position. **1955** E. BURKHOLDER *Baseball Immortals* App. 133 Frank Delahanty, that old time slugger in clean up. **1984** *Gainesville* (Florida) *Sun* 26 Mar. 1B/5 UF chose to pitch to cleanup man Clark, who popped to UF catcher Tim Owen. **1991** D. LAMB *Stolen Season* iii. 40 Then L.A.'s clean-up hitter Clarence Maddern smacked a fastball.. that soared over the left-field fence.

Cleifden *n.*, obs. var. *CLIFDEN *n*.

cleptoparasite *n.*, var. *kleptoparasite* n. s.v. *KLEPTOPARASITISM *n*.

cleptoparasitism *n.*, var. KLEPTOPARASITISM *n*.

click, *n*. var. *KLICK *n*.

Clifden ('klɪfdən), *n. Ent.* Also †**Cleifden**. [A former spelling of the name of Cliveden, a village in Buckinghamshire, where the moth was first observed.] **Clifden nonpareil** ('nɒnpərel), a large Eurasian noctuid moth, *Catocala fraxini*, with grey forewings and a bluish band across each black hindwing.

1749 B. WILKES *Eng. Moths & Butterflies* 45 The Cleifden Nonpareil, a Moth. This curious Fly was found by Mr Davenport, sticking against the Body of an Ash Tree, near Cleifden, in Buckinghamshire. **1766** M. HARRIS *Aurelian* 65 (*heading*) The Clifden Nonpareile. **1863** J. G. WOOD *Illustr. Nat. Hist.* (new ed.) III. 539 The caterpillar of the Clifden Nonpareil is very scarce in this country, and when found is almost invariably in one of the southern counties. **1913** W. F. KIRBY *Butterflies & Moths, in Romance & Reality* 125 The largest species [of *Catocalidae*], the Clifden Nonpareil.. is widely distributed in Britain, but is always very scarce. **1937** P. B. M. ALLAN *Moth-hunter's Gossip* iii. 84, I verily believe that the sight of a Clifden Nonpareil flying round my bedroom would make me leap from my death-bed. **1955** E. B. FORD *Moths* x. 147 The Clifden Nonpareil has recently become abundant in Denmark. **1984** B. SKINNER *Colour Identification Guide Moths Brit. Isles* 151/2 *Clifden Nonpareil*,.. resident in aspen woodland near Hamstreet, Kent, from 1935 to 1964, and in the Norfolk Broads from the early to mid 1930s.

Clintonite ('klɪntənaɪt), *n.* (and *a.*) *U.S. Pol.* [f. the name of William J. D. *Clinton* (b. 1946), American Democratic politician, Governor of Arkansas 1979–81 and 1983–92, and President of the United States 1993– + -ITE[1].] A supporter or adherent of President Clinton or his policies. Also *attrib.* or as *adj.*

1992 *Seattle Times* 5 Mar. A6/2 The sole Clinton supporter in Precinct 37-001 was warned that.. her vote would not count. 'Well, that's our political system for you,' the die-hard Clintonite responded good-naturedly. **1992** *Sunday Tel.* 25 Oct. 1. 25/4 'Regardless of what happens to Bill, the nation will be exposed to Hillary Clinton,' intoned a close female friend in the Clintonite Magazine, Vanity Fair. **1993** *Times* 7 Jan. 15/2 The Clintonites of the new Labour party will be no better at winning elections than the prophets of Clause Four.

So '**Clintonism** *n*.

1992 *Nation* (N.Y.) 3 Feb. 116/2 P.P.I. [*sc.* Progressive Policy Institute] heavies and adherents have converged on Op-Ed pages all over the United States in a deliberate drive to legitamize Clinton and the ideology of Clintonism that the institute has created.

Clintonize ('klɪntənaɪz), *v. U. S. Pol. colloq.* Also with lower-case initial. [f. *Clinton* (see *CLINTONITE *n.*) + -IZE.] *trans.* (and *intr.* for *refl.*) To modify in accordance with or as a result of the policies of President Clinton. So **Clintoni'zation** *n.*; '**Clintonized** *ppl. a.*

1992 *Chicago Tribune* 31 June 23/4 (*heading*) Brace yourselves: Our culture is about to be clintonized. *Ibid.*, The Candidate's press secretary.. was quoted in The New York Times—that sure guide to clintonization—as saying that The Candidate makes it a point to re-read the meditations of Marcus Aurelius every couple of years. *Ibid.*, The clintonized style will not be limited to the campaign and its hangers-on. **1992** *U.S. News & World Rep.* 2 Nov. 92/1 That's why investors really don't need to 'Clintonize' their portfolios. **1993** *Times* 12 Jan. 21/4 The government should study US experience… It could Clintonise: recovery now, financed by bigger defence cuts, and deficit reduction later. **1993** *Observer* 24 Jan. 19/8 A Clintonised wing of the Labour Party wants to import his language of political renewal on the cheap.

Clintonomics (klɪntə'nɒmɪks), *n. pl. U. S. Pol. colloq.* [Blend of *Clinton* (see *CLINTONIZE *v.*) and *economics* (ECONOMIC *n.* 2 c), after *Nixonomics* (see NIXONIAN *a.*), *REAGANOMICS *n. pl.*] The economic policies of President Clinton.

1992 *Investor's Business Daily* 24 Apr. 1/4 Are his positions as a candidate and his overall record accurate guides to what has been called 'Clintonomics'—Clinton's agenda for America's economic future? **1993** *Newsweek* 25 Jan. 27 (*caption*) A favorite of business for tax breaks he backed in the Senate, this consummate insider will try to sell Clintonomics to Congress from his new post at the Treasury.

clonazepam (kləʊ'neɪzɪpæm, -'næz-), *n. Pharm.* [f. *clon-* (prob. f. C(H)LO(RO-[2] + N(ITRO-) + *-AZEPAM.] A benzodiazepine, $C_{15}H_{10}N_3O_3Cl$, with anticonvulsant properties, given orally (as the hydrochloride) and by injection in the treatment of epilepsy and other conditions involving seizures.

1970 *Pharmacologist* XII. 219/1 Application of methods developed to study clonazepam, 5-(2-chloro-phenyl)-1,3-dihydro-7-nitro-2H-1,4-benzodiazepin-2-one, in the presence of minor motor seizures has produced evidence of anticonvulsant activity. **1977** *Lancet* 16 July 143/1 Post-anoxic intention myoclonus can be controlled with clonazepam or L-5-hydroxytryptophan plus carbidopa. **1989** *Arch. Neurol. & Psychiatry* (Chicago) XLVI. 699/1 The behavioral changes coincided with a clonazepam serum level of zero and did not abate until clonazepam treatment was restarted.

Cnidaria (nɪ'dɛːrɪə, naɪ'dɛːrɪə, kn-), *n. Zool.* [mod.L. (coined in Fr. in Milne-Edwards & Haime *Hist. Nat. des Coralliaires* (1857) I. ii. 94), f. Gr. κνίδη nettle + L. -*āria*, pl. of -*ārium* -ARY[1].] A phylum of aquatic invertebrates (cnidarians) typically having a simple tube-shaped or cup-shaped body, which includes sea anemones, hydras, jellyfish, and corals; the Coelenterata (as now understood). **1884** SEDGWICK & HEATHCOTE tr. C. Claus *Elem. Text-bk. Zool.* vii. 222 The Cnidaria represent the Cœlenterata in a more restricted sense. **1910** *Encycl. Brit.* XIV. 172/2 In this way is formed a ring of tentacles, the most characteristic feature of the Cnidaria. **1940** L. H. HYMAN *Invertebrates* I. v. 252 The three lowest metazoan phyla, the Porifera, the Cnidaria, and the Ctenophora, are commonly stated to have remained at the gastrular level of construction. **1987** LAVERACK & DANDO *Lect. Notes Invertebr. Zool.* (ed. 3) iv. 30/1 Cnidaria..possess nematocysts, special cell organelles used for offence and defence, located in cnidoblast cells of epidermis and gastrodermis.

cnidarian (nɪ'dɛːrɪən, naɪ'dɛːrɪən, kn-), *n.* and *a. Zool.* [f. *CNIDARIA *n.* + -AN.] **A.** *n.* An animal of the invertebrate phylum Cnidaria (see *CNIDARIA *n.*); a coelenterate (as now understood). **B.** *adj.* Of, relating to, or designating the phylum Cnidaria.

1934 in WEBSTER. **1967** *Oceanogr. & Marine Biol.* XII. 292 As advanced cnidarians, sea anemones are essentially sedentary predators. *Ibid.* 314 The behavioural implications of cnidarian symbioses..are all virtually unsolved at present. **1977** T. I. STORER et al. *Elem. Zool.* (ed. 4) xvi. 273/1 The lowest animals with cells definitely forming tissues are the cnidarians. **1987** LAVERBACK & DANDO *Lect. Notes Invertebr. Zool.* (ed. 3) iv. 33/1 Cnidarians are generally carnivorous. **1988** R. S. K. BARNES et al. *Invertebrates* iii. 56/1 Two basically different forms can occur in cnidarian life cycles: a relatively mobile medusa that carries gonads, and a sedentary polyp that primitively probably did not.

coach, *n.* Add: [6.] **coach bolt**, a large bolt for fastening wood, having a square collar below the head to prevent it from turning as the nut is tightened on it.

1869 *Bradshaw's Railway Man.* XXI. p. xxiii, Patent Nut & Bolt Co...*Coach bolts...Coach screws. **1991** *Woodturning* Winter 18/1 The bearers are bolted on on either side with two 10mm ⅜″ diameter coach bolts, ..sandwiching the tongue of the centre post between the bearers.

hence **coach-bolted** *a.*, fastened or held by means of coach bolts.

1957 *Archit. Rev.* CXXII. 256/1 The whole platform is surrounded by a deep softwood trimmer, *coach-bolted to the platform. **1991** *Pract. Householder* Apr. 11/2 The panels are all coach bolted together.

co-enzyme, *n.* Add: **2.** Special Comb. **coenzyme A** [f. A(CETYLATION *n.*], a coenzyme mononucleotide which acts as a carrier of acyl (esp. acetyl) groups, and which is synthesized from pantothenic acid.

1947 NOVELLI & LIPMAN in *Arch. Biochem.* XIV. 23 More recently this coenzyme was recognized as a pantothenic acid derivative..for which the term *coenzyme A was introduced. **1977** *Ann. Internal Med.* LXXXVI. 338/1 Brain acetylcholine is synthesized by combining molecules of choline and of acetyl coenzyme A, a process catalyzed by the enzyme choline acetyltransferase. **1988** *Biofactors* I. 267/1 Coenzyme A esters are the substrates and regulators of many enzymatic reactions, among them condensations, ..acylations, isomerizations and epimerizations.

cold, *a.* Add: [19.] **cold dark matter** *Astron.*, dark matter consisting of weakly interacting particles whose random motion soon after the big bang was negligible.

[**1984** PRIMACK & BLUMENTHAL in *NATO ASI Ser.* C CXVII. 166 We will consider here the physical and astrophysical implications of three classes of elementary particle D[ark] M[atter] candidates, which we will call hot, warm, and cold. (We are grateful to Dick Bond for proposing this apt terminology.).. Cold DM consists of particles for which free streaming is of no cosmological importance.] **1984** *Astrophysical Jrnl.* CCLXXXV. L39 (*title*) Fine-scale anisotropy of the cosmic microwave background in a universe dominated by *cold dark matter. **1986** *Sci. Amer.* Dec. 57/3 The cold-dark-matter hypothesis has forged a strong link between particle physics and cosmology. **1993** *Time* 18 Jan. 49/3 Both [axions and WIMPS] are known..as cold dark matter (cold refers not just to their temperature but also to the fact that they move slowly..).

cold fusion, nuclear fusion taking place at temperature lower than ordinarily required, *spec.* at or near room temperature.

[**1981** *Acta Physica Polonica* B. XII. 230 The realization of the idea of the cold nuclear fusion catalysis with the help of heavy stable particles requires either creation of new generation methods, or discovery of such particles in a 'ready state' in Nature.] **1982** G. MÜNZENBERG in N. M. Edelstein *Actinides in Perspective* 241 The nuclei formed in the chosen target projectile combinations need no extra energy above the Coulomb barrier to undergo fusion. So we have a new hope, to reach the island of superheavy nuclei by *cold fusion of 48Ca and 248Cm. **1989** *Los Angeles Times* 24 Mar. 1. 20/1 More recently, Jones has concentrated his research in the 'cold fusion' process like that announced Thursday by his colleagues at the University of Utah. **1991** *Chron. Higher Educ.* 20 Feb. A10/4 A group that initially reported confirmation of cold fusion and then retracted its report when the scientists realized their neutron counter was giving erroneous measurements. **1992** *Wilson Q.* Spring 59 Many supposed 'breakthroughs' are only beginnings, and some have little more substance than cold fusion.

coley ('kəʊlɪ), *n.* [Perh. a contraction of COAL-FISH *n.* (see -Y6), or f. COALSEY *n.*] = COAL-FISH *n.*

1969 A. WHEELER *Fishes Brit. Isles & N.-W. Europe* 274 (*heading*) Saithe (Coalfish; Coley) *Pollachius virens* (Linnaeus, 1758) (*Gadus virens*). **1972** *Which?* May 135/1 Saithe..may be called coal fish, coley, and a whole host of local names from cooth to prinkle. **1982** S. B. FLEXNER *Listening to Amer.* 210 Many Americans wouldn't know..that a coalfish or a coley fillet is black cod. **1987** *Financial Times* 22 Dec. 5/8 The ships..will fish for cod, haddock and coley off Rockall.

colobine ('kɒləbaɪn, -iːn), *a.* and *n. Zool.* [f. mod.L. *Colobinae*, f. generic name *Colobus* (see COLOBUS *n.*): see -INE1.] **A.** *adj.* Of, pertaining to, or characteristic of the subfamily Colobinae (family Cercopithecidae) of mainly leaf-eating Old World monkeys, characterized by a complex sacculated stomach and the absence of cheek pouches. **B.** *n.* A monkey of the subfamily Colobinae; a leaf-monkey.

1958 W. C. O. HILL in H. Hofer et al. *Primatologia* III. 155 The peculiar features of the colobine stomach are adumbrated at a very early period in prenatal life. **1967** J. R. & P. H. NAPIER *Handbk. Living Primates* I. v. 24 (*in figure*) Colobines. **1968** *Nature* 16 Nov. 658/2 Compared with cercopithecines, the colobines have high, sharp cusps and interconnecting lophs. **1970** J. R. NAPIER in J. R. & P. H. Napier *Old World Monkeys* 79 Colobines are essentially arboreally adapted in locomotion and diet. **1984** *Encycl. Mammals* I. 399 The greatest concentrations of colobine species are in Borneo with six species..; and in northeastern Indochina and West and Central Africa, each with three species. **1988** *Sci. Amer.* Feb. 14/3 The same digestive specializations arose independently in the leaf-eating colobine monkeys.

colonic, *a.* and *n.* Add: **B.** *n.* (*pl.* sometimes const. as *sing.*). The use of colonic irrigation for therapeutic purposes. Also, an instance of this (esp. in *high colonic*).

1948 *Sat. Even. Post* 24 Apr. 27/2 She stressed the necessity of using the genuine Arden product. If it fails, she suggests 'a little enema' and in stubborn cases, ' a high colonic'. **1981** V. KULVINSKAS et al. *Life in 21st Cent.* IV. iv. 312 The topic of colonic irrigations is surrounded by much argument and controversy. There are some who claim that the colonics have great therapeutic value, and as might be suspected, others avoid its use and decry its value. **1990** S. KING *Stand* (rev. ed.) I. xxxvii. 341 Western Man needs an occasional high colonic, a purging... And in this case, we've been given a super-enema. **1990** *Daily Tel.* 14 Aug. 13/4 Practitioner D'Ann Coburn, who came to colonics after doctors gave her three months to live, says: 'Colonics enhances the immune system.'

colorectal (kəʊləʊ'rɛktəl), *a. Med.* [f. COLO- + RECTAL *a.*] Pertaining to or (esp. of cancer) affecting the colon and rectum.

1959 P. A. ROSI in R. Turell *Dis. Colon & Anorectum* I. xxi. 452 The colorectal anastomosis is carried out in two layers. **1965** *Surg. Clinics N. Amer.* XLV. 1083 Chemotherapy for patients with colorectal cancer is undergoing extensive study and development. **1986** *Jrnl.* (Fairfax Co., Va.) 28 May B20/1 Testing for high blood pressure, colorectal cancer and diabetes. **1993** *Daily Tel.* 13 Jan. 4/5 Mr Lyndon will perform colorectal and stomach surgery.

colour, *n.*[1] Add: [IV.] [18.] [b.] *colour graphics* [GRAPHIC *a.* and *n.* B. 1 b.]

1975 *Papers IEEE Cement Industry Techn. Conf.* v. ii. 1 The computer system embodies *color graphics and alphanumeric displays for all man/computer interface. **1985** *Personal Computer World* Feb. 41 (Advt.), Its colour graphics and new Bitstik make it welcome in design studios.

coloured, *ppl. a.* Add: **4.** *Particle Physics.* Possessing the quantum property of colour (COLOUR *n.*[1] 17).

1972 *Acta Physica Austriaca* Suppl. IX. 738 We are then faced with two alternatives: one is that there are three quarks, fictitious and obeying funny statistics; the other is that there are actually three triplets of real quarks... In the latter case we would replace the singlet restriction with the assumption that the low lying states are singlets and one has to pay a large price in energy to get the colored SU_3 excited. **1975** *Sci. Amer.* June 60/3 One of a class of proposed interpretations of the psi particles suggests that they may be the first observed states of colored matter. **1977** *Dædalus* Fall 33 The colored particles include the gluons themselves, which is presumably why gluons have never been observed as real particles. **1981** D. WILKINSON in J. H. Mulvey *Nature of Matter* i. 26 The gluons that flit between the coloured quarks must also carry colour.

combination, *n.* Add: [11.] **combination therapy**, a form of treatment in which a patient is given two or more drugs (or other therapeutic agents) for a single disease, esp. cancer.

[**1952** *Cancer Res.* XII. 713 (*heading*) Combination chemotherapy..on a mouse mammary carcinoma.] **1957** *Ibid.* XVII. 646/1 The principal criterion employed for judging the merits of *combination therapy was that the drugs in combination elicit greater antitumor effect. **1990** *Sci. Amer.* May 38/3 We began her combination therapy with LAK cells and interleukin-2. **1993** *Guardian* 19 June 11. 11/2 The new buzz word in [AIDS] treatment is combination therapy. The hope is that by giving three or four drugs together, the virus will not be able to mutate fast enough to become resistant to all of them.

comfort, *n.* Add: [11.] **comfort food**, food that comforts or affords solace; hence, any food (freq. with a high sugar or carbohydrate content) that is associated with childhood or with home cooking. orig. *N. Amer.*

1977 *Washington Post Mag.* 25 Dec. 30/4 Along with grits, one of the *comfort foods of the South is black-eyed peas. **1984** *Bon Appétit* Feb. 56/1 Split Pea Soup with Smoked Ham, although it has become an international 'comfort food', is traced to French-Canadian cooks in Quebec. **1989** *N. Y. Woman* Oct. 136/2 After being dumped by her boyfriend, the heroine..goes to d'Agostino's to buy comfort food. **1990** *Courier-Mail* (Brisbane) 16 Jan. 15/6 Even at fairly formal dinner parties, 'comfort foods' have starred—corn soup, meat loaf, cold black bean soup. **1992** *Independent* 15 Sept. 3/2 Single people..also tend to eat more 'comfort foods' such as cakes, biscuits and jam, though they balance this by spending a greater amount on fresh fruit.

Comice ('kɒmɪs, ‖kɔmis), *n.* [a. F. *comice* association, co-operative, *spec.* the *Comice Horticole* of Angers where the variety was developed.] A kind of dessert pear: = *Doyenne du Comice* s.v. DOYENNE *n.*[1] Also *Comice pear.*

1866 R. HOGG *Fruit Man.* (ed. 3) 276 Comice. See *Doyenné du Comice.* **1935** *Nature* 19 Jan. 84/1 Cox may be the perfect apple and Comice the perfect pear, but each has its short season and other drawbacks. **1957** E. HYAMS *Speaking Garden* iii. 29 When grown in England it is no good at all unless it is either trained against a south wall and pampered like a peach or *Comices* [*sic*] pear. **1976** *Evening Post* (Nottingham) 16 Dec. 11/2 Still lots of good pears about with Conference selling at 10p to 12p and some excellent Comice, the pear with the distinctive flavour, at 14p to 16p lb. **1988** *Times* 29 Jan. 7/1 Other fruits in good supply are conference pears 22p-25p and comice pears 30p-45p.

common, *a.* Add: [21.] **commonhold** *n.* (freq. *attrib.*): in the U.K., a scheme of flat ownership under which tenants own their flat on a freehold basis, but share certain responsibilities and pay for certain services in common; so **commonholder**.

1987 *Law Comm. Commonhold* II. 5 in *Parl. Papers* (Cmnd. 179), *Commonhold*, property which is divided into freehold units, possibly but not necessarily with some collectively used property as well, managed as a whole under the proposed Commonhold Act. **1990** *Independent* 24 Feb. 38/1 The Law Commission proposals would enable commonholders collectively to share the benefits and responsibilities of owning the freehold of a block of flats. **1991** *Which?* Oct. 581/2 A commonhold association, in which all the flat-owners have a vote, will have certain legal obligations, such as managing a reserve fund for major repairs, and keeping proper accounts.

compand (kɒm'pænd), *v. Telecommunications* and *Electronics.* [Back-formation from *COMPANDER *n.*] *trans.* To subject (a signal) to the action of a compander, usu. in order to reduce the dynamic range and noise.

1951 [implied in *companding* vbl. n. below]. **1969** *Bell Syst. Techn. Jrnl.* XLVIII. 1459 We compand a one-bit coder by increasing its step size when a string of equal bits is detected in the transmitted code. **1988** *Internat. Broadcasting* XI. 16/2 The largest sample in the block then determines the amount by which the block will be companded.

So **companded** *ppl. a.*, **companding** *vbl. n.*

1951 *Bell Syst. Techn. Jrnl.* XXX. 719 The general principles used in determining the noise advantage of instantaneous companding..may be applied with equal convenience to other systems. **1962** *Ibid.* XLI. 215 As the companded coder system comprises the major portion of the PCM system, only over-all system measurements were taken. **1982** *IEEE Trans. Communications* XXX. 1774/2 The companded two-loop coder is better than the flat spectrum coder. **1989**

Sound Choice Autumn 25/3 High frequencies are boosted within the tape recorder as part of the pre-emphasis/de-emphasis network designed to reduce noise without the use of companding techniques.

compander (kɒmˈpændə(r)), *n.* Also **compandor**. *Telecommunications* and *Electronics*. [Blend of COMPRESSOR *n.* and EXPANDER *n.*] A device that improves the signal-to-noise ratio of reproduced or transmitted sound by compressing the range of amplitudes of the signal before transmission, and then expanding it on reproduction or reception.

1934 *Bell Syst. Techn. Jrnl.* XIII. 321 The transmitting device is called the compressor; the receiving device, the expandor; and the complete system, the compandor. **1959** K. HENNEY *Radio Engin. Handbk.* (ed. 5) xxviii. 40 A circuit diagram of one type P carrier-system terminal is shown in fig. 35. It includes .. a compandor for each channel which compresses the volume range of the speech after it passes the modulator. **1975** *Official Gaz.* (U.S. Patent Office) 11 Nov. TM178/2 DBX Inc., Waltham, Mass... *dbx* for companders and parts thereof for recording systems. **1988** V. CAPEL *Audio & Hi-Fi Engineer's Pocket Bk.* 88 Though seemingly an ideal solution, simple companders suffer from several disadvantages.

compandor *n.*, var. *COMPANDER *n.*

complementary, *a.* and *n.* Add: [A.] [1.] **g.** Designating or pertaining to medicine seen by its practitioners as complementary to traditional or orthodox medicine but not based on modern scientific knowledge and not recognized by the majority of medical practitioners. Cf. *alternative medicine* S.V. ALTERNATIVE *a.* 7.

1981 *Which?* Aug. 473/3 Many alternative practitioners prefer the terms *complementary* or *supplementary* therapies for their work. **1982** FULDER & MONRO *Status Complementary Med. in U.K.* i. 1 After extensive consideration of titles such as 'alternative medicine', 'fringe medicine' or 'natural therapeutics' we have decided to use the term '*complementary medicine*' to describe systems .. which stand apart from but are in some ways complementary to conventional scientific medicine. **1986** *Here's Health* Apr. 128/1 Alternative, or complementary, medicine .. stands for systems of medicine which treat people rather than disease. **1986** *Guardian* 18 May 3/1 Treatments ranging from acupuncture to Bach flower remedies were condemned as divisive and negative by the two leading organisations for complementary medicine. **1987** *Daily Tel.* 3 Mar. 11/1 About one in seven of us visit some form of 'natural', 'alternative', 'unorthodox' or 'complementary' therapist each year. **1988** *Natural Choice* I. 15/1, I would advise you to see a doctor or a complementary practitioner. **1989** S. FULDER *Handbk. Complementary Med.* (rev. ed.) ii. 31 Some doctors of the author's acquaintance assume that complementary therapy patients are either neurotic or hypochondriacal. **1989** *Brit. Med. Jrnl.* 6 May 1200/2 Conventional and complementary treatment for cancer.

complementation, *n.* Sense in Dict. becomes 1 b. Restrict *Linguistics* to sense in Dict. and add: [1.] **a.** Completion by the addition of a complement or of complementary matter; also, the fact or condition of constituting such completion, complementarity (esp. in phr. *in complementation*).

1931 *Economist* 30 May 1151/1 The Commonwealth and State Savings Banks have already announced a 1 per cent reduction in their interest rates, conditional upon the completion of the scheme. **1958** *Southern Reporter* (U.S.) CII. 508/2 Such documentary evidence may be received in complementation of the pleadings to determine in limine whether plaintiff's cause of action is well founded.

2. a. The combining of complementary colours (see COMPLEMENTARY *a.* 1 c). *rare.*
1934 in WEBSTER.

b. *Genetics.* The phenomenon by which a phenotypic character affected by two or more different mutations is displayed normally in a hybrid or heterokaryon containing both of them (taken as indicating that the mutations are on different, non-allelic, genes).

1958 *Cold Spring Harbor Symp. Quant. Biol.* XXIII. 137/1 Two cases have been described recently.. in which mutants, each lacking a particular function, show partial manifestation of the function when combined in a heterocaryon... Each set of mutants is divisible into three groups, A, B, and C, on the basis of heterocaryon complementation. **1964** D. MICHIE in G. H. Haggis et al. *Introd. Molecular Biol.* x. 269 The result of mixed infection is italicized in the table to emphasize that complementation does not here occur. **1984** M. J. TAUSSIG *Processes in Path. & Microbiol.* (ed. 2) vi. 733 The approach is to look for gene complementation, i.e. a situation in which fusion of two cancer cells produces a non-malignant hybrid. **1990** *EMBO Jrnl.* IX. 3876/1 By genetic complementation analysis, we had previously shown that four genes .. are necessary for normal production of the toxin.

c. The complementary action of two or more commercial enterprises, *spec.* an accord between a company and two or more governments to lower or eliminate duties mutually on items produced by that manufacturer in one or more of the signatory states, thus inducing further local investment by the company.

1979 *Facts on File* 23 Feb. 133/2 Under the government's new 'complementation scheme', vehicle manufacturers would be allowed .. to use export credits to meet 5% of the local content requirement. **1979** *Financial Rev.* (Austral.) 1 May 34 The recently announced government plans to permit import complementation by Australian car manufacturers. **1990** *Automotive News* 23 Apr. (Insight section) 11 1/5 Renault has 10-liter engines we can use for our lower-horsepower ratings... This is where complementation between Renault and Mack starts to take effect.

3. *Math.* and *Computing*. [Prob. ad. F. *complémentation* (A. Tarski 1931, in *Fundamenta Mathematicae* XVII. 225).] The operation of finding the complement of a set, number, etc.

1946 A. W. BURKS in *Moore School Lect.* (1985) 92 By contrast, complementation in the nines system is easy, since every digit (except the sign digit) is treated the same, and since no carry-overs can occur. **1968** E. T. COPSON *Metric Spaces* i. 9 Let *A, B, C* be subsets of a given set *E*. Then the operations of union, intersection and complementation have the following properties: (*a*) $A \cup A' = E$, $A \cap A' = \phi$. [Etc.]. **1982** W. S. HATCHER *Logical Found. Math.* iii. 81 These are the usual laws governing the operations of union, intersection, and complementation.

complete, *a.* Add: [8.] *Math.* **a.** Of a metric space: such that every Cauchy sequence in the space is convergent within it.

1934 C. C. KRIEGER tr. Sierpiński's *Introd. Gen. Topol.* vii. 120 Fréchet calls a space complete when a metric can be established for it such that Cauchy's Theorem is true. **1946** *Trans. Amer. Math. Soc.* LX. 529 A topological linear space, being a topological group, has a natural uniform structure... Hence one may speak of .. whether or not it is complete. **1964** A. P. & W. ROBERTSON *Topological Vector Spaces* iii. 63 If *S* is a separated compact or locally compact space, the space $\mathscr{C}(S)$, under the topology of compact convergence .., is complete.

b. Of a graph: such that every pair of points is joined by just one edge.

1935 *Compositio Mathematica* II. 466 If the number of points is N⩾m(k,l) then there exists in our graph a complete graph of order *l*. *Ibid.* [*Note*] A complete graph is one in which every pair of points is connected. **1972** R. J. WILSON *Introd. Graph Theory* ii. 16 The complete graph on *n* vertices is usually denoted by K_n... The reader should check that K_n has exactly $\frac{1}{2}n(n-1)$ edges. **1980** *Sci. Amer.* Mar. 18/2 No matter how the arrowheads are placed on a complete digraph, there will always be a directed path that visits each point just once. **1989** *VNR Conc. Encycl. Math.* (ed. 2) xxxvi. 689 A complete graph is connected.

completist (kəm'pliːtɪst), *n.* and *a.* [f. COMPLET(E *a.* + -IST.] **A.** *n.* An obsessive (and often indiscriminate) collector.

1955 *N.Y. Times Bk. Rev.* 6 Feb. 25/2 Perhaps the one point of interest here, even for the Holmesian completist, is the effort in the introduction to identify Watson as Doyle's secretary, Maj. Alfred Wood. **1967** *New Yorker* 16 Sept. 38 Among the veteran collectors [of science fiction].. was Gerry de la Ree, who identified himself as a forty-three-year-old 'completist'. 'That means I buy everything that comes out in the field, and never throw anything away.' **1987** *Q* Oct. 99/1 This compilation of singles, B-sides and radio sessions.. has its usefulness for Colenso completists, but it is difficult to divine any other reason for the LP's existence. **1993** *Bookseller* 7 May 17/2, I list 281 twentieth century authors.., 115 of whom are.. regularly producing new offerings which the hopelessly dedicated completists are obliged to add to their earlier rarities [*sic*].

B. *attrib.* passing into *adj.* Intent on completeness or comprehensiveness.

1968 *Sat. Rev.* (U.S.) 28 Sept. 59/2 The 'completist attitude', which has governed several projects, finds the company [*sc.* Columbia Records] in the position of either having finished or nearing the end of the complete recorded works of Stravinsky, Varèse, Webern, Schönberg, and Copland. **1990** *Marxism Today* June 27 The linked trends in the quality Sundays towards physical bulk and internal diversity is most developed in a market leader like *The Sunday Times* which seeks to 'cover' everything (and every angle) through a 'completist' strategy designed to overwhelm both the competition and the reader.

complex, *a.* Add: [**2.**] **e.** *Math.* Of a problem or a problem-solving algorithm: having high computational complexity (*COMPLEXITY *n.* 2 c). Hence of a system: such that the task of describing it is complex in these terms.

1965 *Trans. Amer. Math. Soc.* CXVII. 304 The subset of Turing machines which are T-recognizers is recursively enumerable and therefore there are arbitrarily complex recognition problems. **1982** J. CAMPBELL *Grammatical Man* II. ix. 102 Complexity.. turns out to be a special property in its own right, and it makes complex systems different in kind from simple ones. **1989** *Nature* 14 Sept. 100/2 If a structure can, in principle, be described completely, it is not complex.

complexant (kɒmˈplɛksənt), *n. Chem.* [a. F. *complexant* adj. (coined by Chapron & Condom 1967, in *Compt. Rend.* CCLXV. 914): see COMPLEX *v.*, -ANT[1].] A substance which readily forms complexes with an ion or molecule (usually one of a specified kind).

1969 *Acta Chim. Acad. Sci. Hungaricae* LXII. 244 As eluent chloride and as complexant nickel (II) ions were chosen. **1972** *Soil Sci.* CXIV. 416/2 A general method for calculating the maximum complexing ability of water-soluble complexants forming anionic or zero-charge metal complexes is discussed. **1977** *Analytical Biochem.* LXXXII. 167 Calex ranks among the strongest calcium complexants known to date, at least in the physiological pH range of 5–8. **1987** *Sci. Amer.* Sept. 61/1 The complexant and the alkali metal are placed in separate containers under high vacuum.

complexity, *n.* Add: [**2.**] **c.** *Math.* More fully *computational complexity*. A measure of the difficulty of solving a class of problem, as measured by the expected number of computational steps required to do so using an algorithm; the branch of computational theory concerned with this property.

1963 *Israel Jrnl. Math.* I. 211 Hartmanis, J. and Stearns, R. E., On the computational complexity of algorithms, *Trans. Amer. Math. Soc.* **1965** HARTMANIS & STEARNS in *Trans. Amer. Math. Soc.* CXVII. 285 The computational complexity of a sequence is to be measured by how fast a multitape Turing machine can print out the terms of the sequence. **1967** *Jrnl. Assoc. Computing Machinery* XIV. 322 The complexity theory offered here is machine-independent. **1979** PAGE & WILSON *Introd. Computational Combinatorics* vi. 155 The problems which have so far attracted most study by theorists working in complexity fall into two classes. **1982** J. CAMPBELL *Grammatical Man* II. ix. 105 The power of a small number of fixed rules to produce an *unpredictable* amount of complexity. **1989** *Encycl. Brit.* XVI. 632/2 The prominent research in this field concerns the theory of computational complexity. *Ibid.* 633/1 The complexity of the best available algorithm for the solution of a problem is compared with the complexity of the problem to decide whether a better algorithm can be devised.

compress, *v.* Add: [**3.**] **c.** *Electronics* and *Telecommunications.* To reduce the amplitude variation or the bandwidth of (a signal). Cf. *COMPRESSION *n.* 1 f.

1943 F. E. TERMAN *Radio Engineers' Handbk.* v. 412 Here the signal to be compressed (or expanded) is amplified. **1951** *Bell Syst. Techn. Jrnl.* XXX. 709 If the samples are compressed in accordance with an arbitrary but known law.. the wanted information can be recovered. **1961** G. MILLERSON *Technique Television Production* iii. 48 A low gamma device accepts a wide range, but compresses it to fit reproduction limits. **1991** *Pop. Sci.* May 107 The sampling cuts the amount of information to be transmitted and compresses the rest into a narrower bandwidth.

d. *Computing.* To reduce the size of (a file, digitized signal, etc.) by compression (*COMPRESSION *n.* 1 g).

1966 *Datamation* Apr. 39/1 If the data is compressed first and then logged, the volume of data.. is greatly reduced. **1989** *PC Resource* Sept. 102/3 Other function keys let you compress files to save disk space. **1992** *N.Y. Times* 21 Jan. C5/3 Another option is to use a program.. that compresses regular programs into a fraction of their normal space.

compression, *n.* Add: [**1.**] **f.** *Electronics* and *Telecommunications.* The reduction of the variability of a signal; *spec.* the introduction of a variable gain factor in such a way as to reduce the range over which the signal amplitude varies.

1938 G. E. STERLING *Radio Manual* (ed. 3) iv. 124 Even weak speech-sounds can be made to over-ride noise.. without overloading the transmitter on the sounds which are (before compression) strong. **1943** F. E. TERMAN *Radio Engineers' Handbk.* v. 412 Expanders are used to counteract the compression of volume range that is necessary in sound recording. **1986** W. SINNEMA *Digital, Analog, & Data Communication* (ed. 2) iii. 139 Compression is applied to the signal to slightly reduce the maximum signal amplitudes and significantly raise the minimum signal amplitudes.

g. *Computing.* [tr. Russ. *svertyvanie*; first used in Russ. in this sense by L. N. Korolev 1957, in *Doklady Akad. Nauk SSSR* CXIII. 746.]

The process of reducing the amount of space occupied by data that is being stored or transmitted, by minimizing redundant information.

1957 tr. L. N. Korolev in *Doklady Acad. Sci. U.S.S.R.* CXIII. 724 (*title*) Coding and compression of codes. **1966** *Datamation* Apr. 39/1 Data compression eliminates redundant data and retains useful data. **1987** S. BRAND *Media Lab* i. v. 81 Analogy is a wonderful way to think of semantic data compression: this signal is like that signal, and you got that signal already. **1991** *Personal Computer World* Feb. 20/2 The MNP level-5 error correction and compression offers up to 80% additional throughput.

compute, *v.* Add: **computed** *ppl. a.*: esp. in *computed tomography* (cf. *CT* s.v. C III. 3), = *computed axial tomography* s.v. CAT *n.*[5]
1974 *Radiology* CXIII. 351/1 Recently developed equipment for performing computer-analyzed axial tomography (computed tomography) has been employed at the Cleveland Clinic in the detection of orbital lesions. **1991** *Lancet* 9 Mar. 605/2 The ward doctor thought subarachnoid haemorrhage more likely than meningitis and he arranged for a computed tomography (CT) scan.

computer, *n.* Add: [**3.**] **computer crime**, (an instance of) crime involving illegal access to or manipulation of electronic data.
1972 *New Scientist* 2 Mar. 497/3 A growth business indeed, with the highest growth in the unspectacular areas: fraud, credit-card cheating, *computer crimes. **1990** *Sun* (Baltimore) 7 Mar. c3/4 That seat-of-the-pants approach to cracking computer crime isn't taught in the police academy.

computer dating, the use of a computer to match potential partners, according to prespecified criteria of compatibility, desirability, etc.; matchmaking by computer.
1966 *Look* 22 Feb. 35/1 With all the joys and ploys of *computer dating, social life at sexually segregated schools in the Ivy League remains plenty anxiety-laden. **1968** *Economist* 3 Feb. 18/1 The present fad for computer-dating—matching people with people. **1990** P. WESTCOTT *Finding Someone to Love* vii. 86 There are other computer dating agencies, but, there's little doubt that Dateline is the biggest and most successful.

computer-friendly *adj.*, (*a*) suitable for use with computers, compatible with computers; (*b*) (of a person) well-disposed towards computers; computer-literate: cf. *-FRIENDLY, *FRIENDLY *a.* 5 c.
1982 *Christian Science Monitor* 30 Apr. B16/2 The challenge of making the microcomputer revolution '*computer friendly'..was also a primary concern. **1983** *U.S. Banker* July 36 The new computer-friendly VISA Electron card 'speaks' three computer languages. **1983** *National Jrnl.* (U.S.) 24 Sept. 4/4 We did not become more computer-friendly. They [*sc.* computers] became more people-friendly. **1989** *Guardian* 10 Aug. 19/4 Headmasters become factory managers, chosen because they are accountants or computer-friendly. **1991** *S.W. Sampler* (U.S.) Summer 11. 27/1 Siggins even offers computer-friendly desks with built-in keyboard trays.

computer game, a game played on a computer, *esp.* one involving graphics and operating in real time; also, a software package for such a game.
1965 *Times Educ. Suppl.* 14 May 1480/1 We have found that it is very instructive to use what we call the *computer game in this respect. **1966** *Jrnl. Canad. Operational Res. Soc.* 115 *Game, computer*, a simulation of a competitive situation carried out completely on a computer in which the only human intervention is by the players themselves issuing orders. **1972** A. M. PARKS *Computerized Games & Simulations for Speech Communication* 3 As far as could be determined, there have been no computer games designed specifically for the speech communication classes. **1988** D. LODGE *Nice Work* III. ii. 120 Sandra and Gary squabbled over the TV, Sandra wanting to watch the *Eastenders* omnibus and Gary wanting to play a computer game. **1993** *Wired* (Premiere issue) 1. 66 Zero's life revolves around computer games. He only ventures out of his six-mat in Kawagoe to acquire new gameboards.

computer graphic, (*a*) *pl.*, the use of a computer linked to a VDU to generate and manipulate visual images; (*b*) a visual image produced or modified by means of a computer; usu. in *pl.*
1965 *Proc. AFIPS Conf.* XXVII. 883/2 Only with the most recent advances in computer speed and scope performance has a real-time on-line *computer graphics system become practicable. **1986** *Master Photogr.* Oct. 42/3 More and more labs are also becoming involved in computer graphics—enabling highly complex graphic presentations to be quickly converted to a photographic form without the need for expensive and time consuming artwork. **1991** H. RHEINGOLD *Virtual Reality* II. v. 119 By this method, the computer graphics were converted to video format. **1992** *Industry Week* 7 Dec. 62/4 The inventor is in front of a computer graphic which gains depth through the technique. **1993** *N.Y. Times* 24 Oct. v. 15/1 Inside the visitor center, the interactive exhibits use computer graphics, touch screens and speakers to offer information.

computer science, the branch of knowledge that deals with the construction, operation, programming, and applications of computers.
1961 *IRE Trans. Electronic Computers* X. 759 The author describes his discussions with several important Soviet personalities in the *computer sciences. **1964** *New Scientist* 30 Apr. 327/3 (Advt.), Successful completion of the course leads to a Diploma in Computer Science. **1982** S. BELLOW *Dean's December* iii. 32 For a while he had taken special courses in computer science. **1991** MORNINGSTAR & FARMER in M. Benedikt *Cyberspace* (1993) 298 Cyberspace architects will benefit from study of the principles of sociology and economics as much as from the principles of computer science.

computer scientist, a specialist in computer science.
1968 *Brit. Jrnl. Psychiatry* CXIV. 1497/1 Psychiatry may perhaps be able to learn something from the *computer-scientists; but it is just as likely that the computer-scientists will be able to learn from the psychiatrists. **1992** *Personal Computer World* Jan. 366/1 Neural networks are now an established and important part of the computer scientist's toolkit.

computerize, *v.* For etym. read: [Back-formation from *COMPUTERIZED *ppl. a.*]

computerized (kəmˈpjuːtəraɪzd), *ppl. a.* (Formerly at COMPUTERIZE *v.* Quots 1960[2], 1963 moved from COMPUTERIZE *v.*) [f. COMPUTER *n.* + -IZE + -ED[1].] **1.** Performed or carried out by, or with the assistance of, a computer.
1960 *Times* 4 Aug. 13/5 The initial paperwork for each computerized job is therefore often formidable. **1963** *Publishers' Weekly* 5 Aug. 83/1 (*caption*) Computerized typesetting via communications satellite. **1966** *Lancet* 24 Dec. 1409/2 They were suspicious that the evaluator might produce..some computerised prestidigitation. **1987** A. FIECHTER et al. in Rose & Harrison *Yeasts* (ed. 2) II. v. 126 Currently, major efforts are being made to develop suitable hardware and software for computerized process control.

2. Adapted or designed for computer operation; *spec.* machine-readable.
1962 *Sunday News* (N.Y.) 15 Apr. 69/3 The command..consists of four computerized 'words'. **1964** *New Statesman* 6 Mar. 373/1 This chosen-brethren approach..looks pretty antisocial on a giant computerised organisation that seems to have bought

up half England. **1971** M. SPARK *Not to Disturb* iii. 82 We're all computerised these days, Reverend. The personal touch is gone. We simply programme the meals. **1977** *Time* 21 Nov. 78/1 Near by, cashiers match bingo winners against a computerized list of more than 4,000 cards. **1985** P. LAURIE *Databases* ii. 40 The first advantage to a computerized database over a paper system is that you can ask it far more varied questions. **1988** *Lit. & Ling. Computing* III. 94/1 It is this text that is presupposed, or, rather, the computerised version of it as it is distributed by the NAVF computer center for the humanities in Bergen.

3. Incorporating or making use of a computer or computers.

1964 *Science* 29 May 1113 The Systems Development Corporation (SDC) was 'spun off' by RAND in 1956 to help specifically with design and programming for the first computerized air defense system. **1976** C. BONNINGTON *Everest Hard Way* v. 63 Keith..owns one of those tiny computerised watches, on which, if you press the right button the time and date lights up in red lettering. **1985** G. PALEY *Later Same Day* 95 It soon became the people's knowledge, outwitting the computerized devices.

4. Produced by, or with the assistance of, a computer; computer-generated.

1969 J. REICHARDT *Cybernetic Serendipity* 54 (*title*) Computerized Japanese haiku. **1979** *Tucson* (Arizona) *Citizen* 20 Sept. 5A/3 The Pallottines' local mission office had mailed out 1.6 million computerized letters, greeting cards and 'sweepstakes' flyers. **1984** 'TIRESIAS' *Notes from Overground* 154 All we have to show is a computerised payslip.., a tupperware sandwich-box. **1989** *Brit. Med. Jrnl.* 10 June 1563/1 A random sample of 1824 principals in general practice was selected by using a computerised list from a mailing company.

5. Special collocation: **computerized (axial) tomography** = CAT $n.^5$

1973 *Brit. Jrnl. Radiol.* XLVI. 148/1 *Computerized transverse axial tomography is a new approach to the use of diagnostic X rays. **1973** *Surg. Neurol.* I. 217 (*heading*) Computerized axial tomography of the heads. **1984** A. SMITH *Mind* IV. xiv. 277 Computerized axial tomography (CT scanning) has revolutionized investigation of brain tumour suspects. **1991** *New Scientist* 9 Feb. 27/1 Neuroscientists say computerised catalogues would provide 'a common language' for new specialties emerging from neuroscience, especially imaging techniques such as..computerised tomography (CT).

concordance, *v.* Add: **con'cordancing** *vbl. n.*
1976 *Bull. Board Celtic Stud.* Nov. 45 (*heading*) Automated concordancing of Welsh dialects with output in the IPA. **1982** *Papers Dict. Soc. N. Amer. 1979* 142 The application of computer concordancing techniques to dictionary definitions promises to be a useful technique. **1989** *Lit. & Ling. Computing* IV. 106/1 The move towards combining database management systems and concordancing programs was..a logical one.

con'cordanced *ppl. a.*
1986 *ICAME News* May 22 A larger corpus, of twenty to twenty-five million words, again in concordanced format, could be transferred to compact disk, and distributed with accompanying software. **1992** *English Today* July 28/1 The value of concordanced information is..[that] the grammatical patterning which is typical of a lexical item emerges very clearly when there are plentiful examples.

conference, *n.* Sense 9 in Dict. becomes 10. Add: **9.** Usu. with capital initial. A late-ripening variety of pear, somewhat elongated in shape, with a russet-flecked dark green skin and sweet, juicy flesh. Also *Conference pear*.
App. named after the 1885 National Pear Conference.
1885 *Jrnl. Hort.* 17 Dec. 536/1 Of new varieties, the Conference Pear exhibited by Messrs. Rivers and Son (season, October) was awarded a first class

certificate. **1925** J. W. MORTON *Pract. Fruit-growing* xiv. 110 In Conference we have a large pear which is ready to be marketed in October and November. **1976** *Eastern Daily Press* (Norwich) 19 Nov. 19/4 Pears, Conference, best 9p to 11p, Dutch Conference 8p to 12p lb. **1988** *Times* 29 Jan. 7/1 Other fruits in good supply are conference pears 22p-25p and comice pears 30p-45p.

Connect (kə'nɛkt), *n.* [f. the vb.] A proprietary name for a debit card issued in the U.K. by Barclays Bank.
1987 *Daily Tel.* 14 May 21/5 Connect is a debit card..due to be launched in three weeks. **1988** *Banking World* Mar. 29/2 Barclays will presumably be using Connect as its EFTPOS debit card. **1990** *Which?* June 318/1 These proposed new rules will apply to all bank and building society cashpoint cards, and the recently introduced debit cards such as Switch and Connect. **1994** *Daily Mail* 21 Dec. 43/5 Barclays is offering its 4.6 million Connect card holders a set of travel and leisure discounts.

conspiracy, *n.* Add: **4.** Special Combs. **conspiracy theory**, the theory that an event or phenomenon occurs as a result of a conspiracy between interested parties; *spec.* a belief that some covert but influential agency (typically political in motivation and oppressive in intent) is responsible for an unexplained event; so **conspiracy theorist**.
1909 *Amer. Hist. Rev.* XIV. 836 The claim that Atchison was the originator of the repeal may be termed a recrudescence of the *conspiracy theory first asserted by Colonel John A. Parker of Virginia. **1952** K. R. POPPER *Open Society* (ed. 2) II. xiv. 94, I call it the '*conspiracy theory of society*'. It is the view that an explanation of a social phenomenon consists in the discovery of the men or groups who are interested in the occurrence of this phenomenon. **1964** *New Statesman* 1 May 694/2 *Conspiracy theorists will be disappointed by the absence of a dogmatic introduction. **1975** *N.Y. Times* 12 May 10/4 Conspiracy theorists contend that two of the men have strong resemblances to E. Howard Hunt Jr. and Frank A. Sturgis, convicted in the Watergate break-in. **1987** W. GREIDER *Secrets of Temple* I. ii. 52 From the beginning, the Federal Reserve was implicated in nativist conspiracy theories. **1990** *Times Educ. Suppl.* 7 Dec. 5/1 Conspiracy theorists see the invisible hand of the Department of Education and Science behind the emergence of Walter Ulrich as secretary of the National Association of Governors and Managers.

contragestion (kɒntrə'dʒɛstʃən), *n. Med.* [f. CONTRA- + GEST(AT)ION *n.*, after CONTRACEPTION *n.*] Birth control effected after fertilization has occurred, either by preventing the implantation of the ovum in the uterine wall or by disrupting gestation at an early stage, causing abortion.
[**1971** *Rep. Family Planning* July 20/1 Once-a-month contraprogestational pill. **1973** SEGAL & ATKINSON in H.J. & J.D. Osofsky *Abortion Experience* xix. 403 The possibility exists..that the contragestational activity of estrogenic compounds may be independent of their general estrogenicity.] **1985** E.-E. BAULIEU in Baulieu & Segal *Antiprogestin Steroid RU486 & Human Fertility Control* 2 The term *contragestion* (for contragestation) is proposed to cover all aspects of fertility control interfering with the establishment or continuation of early pregnancy. **1987** *Contraception* XXXV. 426 The dose was lowered in this contragestion study. **1989** *Daily Mail* 24 Oct. 13/1 Its fundamental action is similar to that of..the IUD or coil, both of which make it impossible for the pregnancy to be sustained. Doctors call this method of fertility control, contragestion.

contragestive (kɒntrə'dʒɛstɪv), *a.* and *n. Med.* [f. *CONTRAGEST(ION *n.* + -IVE.] **A.** *adj.*

Pertaining to or effecting contragestion. **B.** *n.* A contragestive agent, *esp.* a drug.

1985 E.-E. BAULIEU in Baulieu & Segal *Antiprogestin Steroid RU486 & Human Fertility Control* 1 (*heading*) RU486: an antiprogestin steroid with contragestive activity in women. **1987** *Contraception* XXXV. 424 Antiprogestins are new compounds used as postcoital contragestives. **1991** K. M. NORRIE *Family Planning Pract. & Law* iv. 52 (*heading*) Particular contragestive methods. **1992** *Utne Reader* May-June 19/1 Even the most ardent pro-choice advocates have to ask whether there isn't a critical distinction between a contraceptive and a 'contragestive'.

control, *n.* Add: [**5.**] *control algorithm.*

1966 *ISA Jrnl.* Sept. 43/1 The basic *control algorithm of a direct digital control (DDC) system. **1984** *Computerworld* 17 Dec. 57/3 The user can create or edit one control algorithm while displaying another.

control centre.

1941 *Sun* (Baltimore) 19 Dec. 14/7 Directors of civilian defense air-raid *control centers will alone be responsible for..alerting..their..districts. **1951** A. M. PRENTISS *Civil Defense in Mod. War* xvi. 293 The local civil defense control centers will function as the command posts of local civil defense. **1960** *Aviation Week* 14 Nov. 27/3 Under Army plans, Zeus control centers are to be scattered across the country, with each center controlling a number of missile batteries. **1983** *Chem. Week* 24 Aug. 22/3 The key to high purity..is a computerized control center.

control equipment.

1957 *Railway Mag.* Mar. 159/2 A cubicle containing the majority of the low-tension *control equipment is housed in a van compartment in the motor coach. **1968** *Electrical Communication* XLIII. 329/1 The system uses new ITT miniaturized components, and a large amount of electronics in the control equipment. **1985** *Discover* Aug. 34/1 A tiny microchip-filled box inside the weapon prevents it from firing unless the authorized codes from the President are punched in on control equipment outside.

control structure.

1968 *Internat. Encycl. Soc. Sci.* III. 51 The hard-core noncommissioned officers constituted a cadre of 'opinion leaders' who supported the *control structure. **1973** C. W. GEAR *Introd. Computer Sci.* i. 5 The first element of a problem is the control structure. **1983** *Dict. Computing* 78/2 *Control structure*, a syntactic form in a language, used to specify flow of control in a program, e.g. repeat <statements> until <condition>.

control engineering, the study and design of control systems.

1954 (*title of periodical*) *Control engineering. **1958** *Times Rev. Industry* June 9/2 The Engineering Faculty of McGill University is to institute a chair in Control Engineering. **1981** *Acad. Amer. Encycl.* XI. 174/1 It [*sc.* information theory] has strong associations with control engineering, theories of learning, and the physiology of the nervous system.

control theory, the quantitative study of control systems.

[**1948** N. WIENER *Cybernetics* 19 We have decided to call the entire field of control and communication theory, whether in the machine or in the animal, by the name Cybernetics.] **1962** *Listener* 6 Dec. 953/1 Economists are now starting to study seriously the implications of *control theory for their problems. **1974** *Encycl. Brit. Micropædia* III. 117/2 Control theory has applications in the physical and life sciences, in technology and economics, and in any area in which the system under consideration can well be described in quantitative terms. **1978** *Nature* 28 Sept. 347/3 We can understand and predict the hunting behaviour of a system incorporating negative feedback only in terms of control theory and not in terms of previously existing physical concepts.

core, *n.*[1] Add: [**16.**] **core dump** *Computing* [so called orig. because the main memory was a core memory: see sense 10 b above], a dump of the contents of main memory at the time of a crash, usu. as an aid to debugging.

1967 D. H. STABLEY *System 360 Assembler Lang.* (ed. 2) 107 Hexadecimal *core dumps may appear to be an unwieldy means of program debugging and analysis. **1978** J. McNEIL *Consultant* xxi. 188 It was bad enough getting the bank's permission to bring a core dump out of the Data Centre. **1988** *Byte* June 176/2 Another bug resulted in several aborts with core dumps when I pressed PageUp.

corn, *n.*[1] Add: [**IV.**] [**11.**] **corn circle** = *crop circle* s.v. *CROP n. 22.

[**1987** *Flying Saucer Rev.* XXXII. vi. 12/2 The surface plants..were laid out along the same veining contours that we had already come to associate with all the cornfield circles.] **1989** in J. Schnabel *Round in Circles* (1993) 80, I have been meaning to write to you for some time on the subject of *corn circles...About six or seven years ago I was fortunate enough to see one of these form in a field at Westbury. **1990** *New Scientist* 11 Aug. 23/3 Dozens of flattened rings in wheat have been reported recently in Australia...The rings resemble the corn circles found in southern Britain. **1991** *Independent* 5 Jan. (Mag.) 9/3 In this respect the shroud controversy is reminiscent of that of the corn circles, about which feverish debate continues.

corpus, *n.* Add: [**2.**] **b.** *Bot.* [Introduced in this sense (in Ger.) by A. Schmidt 1924, in *Bot. Archiv* (Berlin) VIII. 352.] The inner mass of cells in an apical meristem, which are enclosed by the tunica and whose division contributes to the increase in volume of a plant.

1939 *Bot. Rev.* V. 460 The growth of the central core or corpus, by contrast, consists in an increase in mass. **1958** *Jrnl. Faculty Sci. Univ. Tokyo* VII. 368 Two tissue zones occur in the apical meristem, that is, the tunica, consisting of one or more periclinal layers of cells, and the corpus, a mass of cells enclosed by the tunica. **1965** K. ESAU *Plant Anat.* (ed. 2) v. 94 Although the epidermis usually arises from the outermost tunica layer.., the underlying tissues may have their origin in the tunica or the corpus or both. **1984** L. W. BROWDER *Developmental Biol.* (ed. 2) xiii. 647 The tunica and corpus are thought to be maintained by division of the initial cells contained within them.

correct, *a.* Add: **4.** Conforming to a dominant political or ideological orthodoxy: **a.** *spec.* in Communist China, according with or adhering to Maoist doctrine (now chiefly *hist.*).

1932 M. SHACTMAN tr. L. Trotsky *Probl. Chinese Revol.* 198 The party will utilize quite differently the discontentment of the masses, if it considers it by reckoning with a correct political perspective. **1950** tr. Liu Shao-Chi *On the Party* 52 Our Party's correct political line cannot be separated from its correct organisational line. **1951** *Ann. Amer. Acad. Pol. & Social Sci.* CCLXXVII. 80/2 Another essential idea is the Marxist dogma that there is only one 'correct' line of thought and action... The central authorities define what is correct, and..the entire mass membership of any organization is expected to think and act 'correctly'. **1953** tr. Mao Tse-Tung *On Rectification of Incorrect Ideas in Party* 1 The failure of the Party's leading bodies..to educate the members along the correct line is also an important cause of the existence and growth of such incorrect ideas. **1960** T. CHEN *Thought Reform of Chinese Intellectuals* ii. 9 An ideologically correct person..is likely to overcome old habits of thought and action. **1966** TUNG CHI-PING & H. EVANS *Thought Revolution* iii. 47 Despite his 'correct' political attitude, the teachers singled him out for criticism.

b. In recent (chiefly *N. Amer.*) use, ellipt. for *politically correct* s.v. **POLITICALLY adv.* 3 b; hence, with other defining terms, as *eco-correct*, *environmentally correct*, *gender-correct*, *socially correct*, etc.

1973 S. DAVIDSON in *Esquire* July 74/1 The mood of the original feminists changed utterly... People recount the rise and fall of groups, the setting up and toppling of 'correct political lines', the purges and counter-purges. **1973** A. WALKER in J. O'Brien *Interviews with Black Writers* 207 To be 'correct' she should consider it her duty to let ugliness reign. The most 'incorrect' thing about Sammy Lou is that she loves flowers... Whenever you hear a black person talking about the beauties of nature, that person is not a black person at all. **1986** H. J. MARONEY in Mitchell & Oakley *What is Feminism?* 113 Unable to agree upon a 'correct' and effective programme of action, they have dwindled into theoreticism, split, or been reduced to passivity. **1990** *Taxation & Environmental Policy* (Inst. Fiscal Stud. Commentary No. 19) 3 Ideally, the economically correct procedure in introducing an environmental tax would be to value the economic costs of activities which take place outside of any market, and to calculate a tax level per unit output to reflect these costs. **1991** *Raritan* Summer 41 Are we..in the business of granting degrees that mean: 'Your son or daughter has turned out correct. Politically, morally, socially correct; at least, by this year's standards. **1991** *New Yorker* 16 Dec. 120/2 Not only the merchandise but all the materials used in the construction of the store are about as environmentally correct as is possible these days. **1992** J. & M. STERN *Encycl. Pop Culture* 398/1 Potato chips are not exactly in style—they are too fatty and too salty to be N.C. ('nutritionally correct', as determined by health-food killjoys). **1993** *Albuquerque* (New Mexico) *Jrnl.* 6 Jan. B2/4 For the most part, message toys are geared to parents, not to children, and most environmental- and gender-correct toys haven't made much of a dent. **1994** *USA Weekend* 9 Jan. 28/2 How do you pack the car for an eco-correct family vacation?

correctness, *n.* Add: **2.** Conformation to a dominant political or ideological orthodoxy: **a.** *spec.* in Communist China, adherence to Maoist doctrine (now chiefly *hist.*). **b.** In recent (chiefly *N. Amer.*) use, ellipt. for *political correctness* s.v. **POLITICAL a.* 6; hence with other defining terms, as *eco-correctness*, *environmental correctness*, etc.

1955 F. T. C. YU *Strategy & Tactics of Chinese Communist Propaganda* vi. 59 When professors and scholars praise the 'correctness'..of Marxism-Leninism, the communists hope that the common people will be more inclined to accept the new ideology. **1957** *New Republic* 13 May 24/1 The group is also fortified by..an absolute doctrinal authority for the 'correctness' of all of its solutions. **1960** T. CHEN *Thought Reform of Chinese Intellectuals* ii. 9 There is another and more important reason for Communist insistence on ideological correctness. **1977** P. FULLER *Jrnl.* 29 Mar. in *Marches Past* (1986) 117 The jostling for rarefied, nuanced, over-tuned theoretical [Marxist] 'positions' heats up. As one might expect of 7 Carlisle Street [*sc.* office of the *New Left Review*]..everyone vies with each other for the most perverse and punishing 'correctness'. **1992** *N.Y. Times* 12 Feb. C1/1 The brilliant new vehicle for environmental correctness, health consciousness and graphic self-expression: toothpaste. **1993** *Fort Collins* (Colorado) *Triangle Rev.* 21 Oct. 4/3 The elementary school fanfare is the last hurrah before social correctness cuts them off at the right brain. **1993** *USA Weekend* 24 Oct. 2/2 He has a broad agenda for eco-correctness.

cosmic *a.* Add: [**3.**] **d.** *cosmic string*: see **STRING n.* 33.

cottage ('kɔtɪdʒ), *v.* [f. COTTAGE *n.* 3 b.] *intr.* To use or frequent public toilets for homosexual sex. So **cottaging** *vbl. n.* and *ppl. a.*

1972 *Come Together* XII. 4/2 This straightaway undermines any obsession with sex for sex's sake, and collapses the secondary sexist structures of cruising, cottaging etc. **1976** J. SEABROOK *Lasting Relationship* 179, I go cottaging because there's nothing to be ashamed of and because I think you ought to get rid of your fears about the police. **1983** *Gay News* 31 Mar. 4/4 The 'agent provocateur' system which brings so many gay men to court on cottaging offences. **1984** *Times Lit. Suppl.* 24 Feb. 192/4 Another character we never see is Chateau Charles, a cottaging queen with a penchant for young boys. **1984** A. MAUPIN *Baby-Cakes* xxiv. 105 'I was busted for cottaging.'.. 'You know..doin' it in a cottage.'.. 'A cottage', Wilfred repeated. 'A *public loo.*' **1986** Q Oct. 14/1 According to some sources, early deals never got off the ground because a number of film moguls didn't want to be associated with a character like Orton whose idea of fun was cottaging in the Holloway Road. **1990** *Gay Times* Dec. (Centre Section) 2/2 Is there a man in this town who is not on the rebound, does not cottage and is not sleeping with someone else?

council, *n.* Add: [**17.**] **council tax**: in the U.K., a tax levied on householders by local authorities, calculated according to whichever of several bands the estimated capital value of a property falls into, and introduced in 1993 to replace the community charge (see **COMMUNITY n.* 11 a).

1991 *Daily Tel.* 19 Apr. 2/3 Mr Major secured full Cabinet backing yesterday for a new local tax—expected to be called the *Council Tax—which will be based on a two-person household, with a discount for a single person living alone. **1992** *Daily Mail* 17 Aug. 12/1 The new council tax, designed to replace the community charge, is expected to be based on the 1990 value of properties.

crack *n.* Add: **IV. 21.** *attrib.* and *Comb.* (in sense 20), as **crackhead** *slang* (orig. *U.S.*) [HEAD *n.*[1] 7 e], a person who habitually takes or is addicted to crack cocaine.

1986 *Time* 2 June 17/1 A recent survey..indicates that..more than half the nation's so-called *crackheads are black. **1988** *Observer* 24 July 15/1 Charlie and two fellow 'crackheads' took me to a vast concrete housing estate in south London where crack is on sale for between £20 and £25 a deal. **1991** P. J. O'ROURKE *Parliament of Whores* (1992) 139 The crack-heads had their pockets emptied; their drugs, pipes, needles and paraphenalia given the bootheel and their money torn up in front of their faces.

crack house chiefly *U.S.*, a place where crack is bought and sold.

1985 *San Francisco Chron.* 6 Dec. 3/6 In New York and Los Angeles drug dealers have opened up drug galleries called '*crack houses'. **1989** *Times* 7 Sept. 16/6 Will they still be behind the campaign when in their electoral districts..drug-pushing single mothers..are thrown out of their crack-houses on to the streets? **1993** *Globe & Mail* (Toronto) 17 June A1/6 [He] was hauled out of his car outside a suspected crack house on Nov. 5. There was an argument over what he was holding.

craton ('krætɒn), *n. Geol.* Also †kraton. [f. KRATO(GE)N *n.* with alteration of initial letter, perh. after CRATER *n.*, etc.] A large stable block of the earth's crust that has resisted deformation over a (geologically) long period of time; = KRATOGEN *n.*

1935 tr. H. Stille in *Res. & Progress* I. 10 In the Asiatic portion of the latter [*sc.* continental Eurasia] we observe the same process of continental growth as in Europe. Here too we have primordial craters [*corrected* (Ibid. 94) *to* cratons], such as 'Angaraland' in the centre of Northern Siberia..and also a 'Paleo-Asia'. **1942** *Bull. Geol. Soc. Amer.* LIII. 1640 The Michigan basin..is a geosyncline defined by causes within its area; the latter [*sc.* the Allegheny belt] was depressed in complement to uplift near by...Both are within the craton or 'shield'. **1970** *Cambr. Anc. Hist.* (ed. 3) I. i. i. 5 For these platforms incorporating remnants of past orogenic belts Stille invented the term 'kraton', of obscure etymology but considerable convenience. **1979** *Sci. Amer.* Jan. 70/2 Together the shields and platforms constitute the cratons, the stable blocks that are the nuclei of present-day continental masses. **1986** *New Yorker* 24 Feb. 39/3 Had this been a May morning a hundred million years ago,..we would have been many fathoms underwater, in a broad arm of the sea, which covered the continental platform—reached across the North American craton, the Stable Interior Craton—from the Gulf of Mexico to the Arctic Ocean.

Hence cra'tonic *a.*, of, pertaining to, or designating a craton.

1935 tr. H. Stille in *Res. & Progress* I. 10 And so there arose at last the great craterous [*corrected (Ibid.* 94) *to* cratonic] ring 'Peri-Arctis'. **1944** *Science* 9 June 462/2 The cratonal flexure of the Lower Pennsylvanian miogeosyncline lies west of the Adirondack line. **1971** I. G. GASS et al. *Understanding Earth* xxii. 320/2 All of these areas lie within the older cratonic regions of Africa. **1976** A. & L. RITTMANN *Volcanoes* 120/1 Deposits of mercury, silver, gold, uranium and lead are derived from orogenic volcanism, and iron, copper, nickel, manganese and titanium from cratonic volcanism. **1991** *Sci. Amer.* May 54/1 Simultaneously, another type of ore deposit began to form in cratonal regions, the growth centers of continents. **1992** *Earth Surface Processes & Landforms* XVII. 339 This contradicts Fairbridge and Fiukl's suggestion that cratonic denudation rates are several orders of magnitude less than those of other areas.

crazy, *a.* Add: [6.] **crazy ant**, substitute for def.: any of several ants that exhibit very fast or erratic movement, esp. *Prenolepsis longicornis*, native to tropical regions. (Later examples.)

1905 *Bull. Amer. Mus. Nat. Hist.* XXI. 111 Prenolepsis longicornis..This tropicopolitan species which is common in New Providence..but very sporadic on the eastern coast of Andros.., occurs in houses and is known as the 'crazy ant' on account of its singular erratic movements. **1915** C. A. EALAND *Insects & Man* vi. 245 The Argentine ant, *Iridomyrmex humilis*...The ant has received its popular name from the fact that Argentina is believed to be one, at least, of the countries in which it is native. At first it was called the 'New Orleans' ant'..; other names which have been suggested and dropped..are the 'crazy ant', the 'tropical ant', and the 'pernicious ant'. **1971** E. O. WILSON *Insect Societies* xxi. 447/2 *Paratrechina longicornis*, the swift-running *hormiga loca* (crazy ant) found in tropical cities around the world, is an example of a class of species I have come to call 'opportunists'. **1983** *Listener* 27 Oct. 16/3 Another new import is the long-legged ant, which is also called the Crazy Ant, which has appropriately turned up in a psychiatric hospital.

cred (krɛd), *n.* and *a. slang.* [Abbrev. of CREDIBILITY *n.* or CREDIBLE *a.*, earliest in *street cred* s.v. STREET *n.* 4 f.] **A.** *n.* Credibility; reputation or status among one's peers. **B.** *adj.* Credible; fashionable, trendy.

1981 *Guardian Weekly* 6 Sept. 4/5 A couple of expressions have only come my way in the last month or so. One is 'street wise' and the other 'street cred'. **1985** *Internat. Musician* June 9/4, I know that walking down main street with an oboe in hand does nothing for the street cred. **1986** B. GELDOF *Is that It?* ix. 125 'Cred' was achieved by your rhetorical stance and no one had more credibility than the Clash. **1988** *New Scientist* 7 Jan. 74/3 But 'lab cred' has somehow eluded this most lucid way of thinking about our planet. **1990** *Sydney*

Morning Herald 1 Feb. 28/11 'They've got to have total cred,' Boxall insisted, when listing the special qualities he is looking for. **1991** *Hot Air* Oct.-Nov. 19/1 Annie Nightingale's got the most cred show in the air...Tune in and groove.

Creutzfeldt–Jakob (ˌkrɔɪtsfɛltˈjækɒb), *n. Path.* Also (*misspelt*) Creutzfeld–Jakob. [The names of Hans G. *Creutzfeldt* (1885-1964) and Alfons M. *Jakob* (1882-1927), German neurologists. Cf. earlier Ger. *Creutzfeldt-Jakobsche Krankheit.*] Used *attrib.* and in the possessive, usu. in *Creutzfeldt-Jakob disease*, to designate a communicable progressive disease of the human brain, caused by a prion, in which the degeneration and loss of neurones result in dementia and loss of mobility, and which is accompanied by histological changes characteristic of other spongiform encephalopathies.

1939 *Q. Cumulative Index Medicus* XXIV. 1047/1 (*title*) Creutzfeldt-Jakob's disease (spastic pseudosclerosis). **1957** *Jrnl. Neuropath. & Exper. Neurol.* XVI. 134 Several years ago I had the opportunity of studying the microscopical sections of a Norwegian case of Creutzfeld-Jakob disease. **1963** *Jrnl. Neuropath. & Exper. Neurol.* XXII. 381 Creutzfeldt-Jakob's disease..shares the following clinical features with Alzheimer's and Pick's diseases. **1985** *Times* 8 Nov. 13/7 A suspicion that the hormone..might be a source of the virus which causes Creutzfeldt-Jakob disease. **1987** *Economist* 14 Nov. 94/1 Others [*sc.* examples of slow-virus diseases] include Creutzfelt-Jakob [*sic*] syndrome and Gerstmann-Straussler syndrome, both mercifully rare. **1993** *Guardian* 30 Oct. 8/8 He argues that, if man is susceptible to BSE, then at least 8 million adults are likely to have eaten enough to get Creutzfeldt-Jakob Disease (the human form) unless they die first from other causes. **1996** *Daily Tel.* 25 Mar. 1 Douglas Hogg, the Agriculture Minister, confirmed his department was actively considering several slaughter options to combat the renewed threat of BSE in the wake of the announcement last week of a possible link with Creutzfeld-Jakob Disease in humans.

crop, *n.* Add: [V.] [22.] **crop circle**, a circular area in a field of standing crops (esp. wheat or other cereal), in which the stalks have been flattened, usu. in concentric rings; also called a *corn circle* (see *CORN *n.*[1] 11).

1988 *Jrnl. Meteorol.* XIII. 290 (*heading*) The mystery of the *crop-circles: a B.B.C. film. **1989** *New Scientist* 2 Sept. 30 (*heading*) Ionised whirlwinds could create crop circles. **1992** *Science News* 1 Feb. 76/1 The study of these mysterious crop circles has itself grown into a thriving cottage industry. **1993** *Guardian* 30 July 1. 20/3 A glorious chapter in the annals of British summertime lunacy appears to be drawing to a close. Only 45 crop circles have been found this year, compared with more than 400 in each of the last two years.

cruelty, *n.* Add: **5.** **cruelty-free** *a.*, involving minimal cruelty to animals; *spec.* (of consumer goods) produced without involving any cruelty to animals in the development or manufacturing process.

1986 *Campaigner* Jan. 7/1 An animal rights march with a difference took place in November. Each participant was asked to bring along a *cruelty-free product. **1988** *Vegetarian* Mar./Apr. 42/3 Mary Bonner showed over 50 people how enjoyable a cruelty-free Christmas can be with her celebration roast, mushroom stuffing and red wine sauce, vegan Christmas Cake and mince pies. **1990** *Green Mag.* Apr. 72/3 A relatively harmless alternative to the plastic biro might be a quill pen—though it could hardly be described as cruelty-free. **1992** *Looks* July 33/2 The natural girl is a barefaced beauty and she's determined to stick to her principles—it's only the cruelty-free beauty products for her.

crusty, *a.* and *n.* Senses in Dict. become **A.** *adj.* 1 and 2. Add: **B.** *n.* (Also **crustie**.) One of a group of homeless or vagrant young people, generally living by begging in cities, and characterized by rough clothes, matted, often dreadlocked hair, and an unkempt appearance; also, the name given to this subculture as a whole.

1990 *Guardian* 30 Apr. 36/6 This covers a whole range of styles, from the leather jackets and DMs of more or less unreconstructed punks to the rags of the 'crusties', who 'never wash at all and look like it'. **1991** *Twenty Twenty* Spring 52 A familiar sight on every city's streets—look for the matted hair, donkey jacket and the dog on a string lead—Crusties are the cult that got away. **1991** *Independent* 26 Oct. (Mag.) 67/1 Crusty was born out of punk, nurtured by hippy foster-parents on the free festival scene, and has now come of age. *Ibid.* 68/1 In the mid-Eighties, Bristol punks started behaving in more and more extreme ways. Spiky hair and ripped jeans were no longer shocking anybody, so they started vomiting on themselves, rolling in filth, and never, ever washing—Crusty originated as a descriptive term. **1992** *i-D* July 29/2 They attract a huge following of young 'Deadheads' decked out in a mixture of '69 and crusty styles. **1993** LOWE & SHAW *Travellers* IV. 151, I've been moved on quite a lot begging in London, but begging there's horrible anyway...I've been beaten up just for looking like a crustie.

cryo-, *comb. form.* Add: ,**cryopre'cipitate** *Med.*, a substance precipitated by controlled freezing; *spec.* a precipitate rich in a clotting factor obtained when rapidly frozen blood plasma is thawed at 4°C.

1965 *New England Jrnl. Med.* 30 Dec. 1443/2 (*heading*) Preparation of *cryoprecipitates rich in antihemophilic globulin. **1967** *Brit. Med. Jrnl.* 8 Apr. 91/1 Cryoprecipitate is an extremely valuable therapeutic material for the treatment of haemophilia. **1977** *Lancet* 24 Sept. 641/1 Cryoprecipitate therapy is still widely used for treatment in hæmophilia A, especially in developing countries. **1985** *Brit. Med. Jrnl.* 14 Sept. 695/2 Concentrates became freely available in the early 1970s, when their many advantages over fresh frozen plasma and cryoprecipitate were recognised.

,**cryoprecipi'tation** *Med.* and *Biol.*, the low-temperature production or formation of a precipitate, esp. a cryoprecipitate.

1965 *Biol. Abstr.* XLVI. 4233/1 (*heading*) *Cryoprecipitation in the neuro-psychiatric milieu. **1966** *Ibid.* XLVII. 1983/1 The phenomenon of cryoprecipitation takes place not only in extracts but also in the cytoplasmic fluids of some seeds. **1969** *Britannica Bk. of Year* (U.S.) 498 Cryoprecipitation, so-called because it is effected at low temperature, enables the antihemophilic factor from a pint of blood to be concentrated in a volume of only 10 ml. **1985** *Molecular Immunol.* XXII. 717/2 A hapten-induced conformational change can accompany the cryoprecipitation of the immunoglobulin.

'**cryoprobe**, (*a*) *rare*, a nose section of a rocket cooled to a very low temperature for collecting samples of air from the upper atmosphere; (*b*) *Med.*, an instrument with a tip cooled to a very low temperature, used in cryosurgery for destroying tissue.

1965 *Aviation Week* 11 Jan. 44/2 The Nesco cryogenic probe, designated *cryoprobe, is a streamlined nose section which is fitted to the Genie booster. **1965** *N.Y. Times* 25 Dec. 21/4 Dr. Armao intends his cryoprobe for such operations as the knifeless removal of a diseased prostate. **1967** *Time* 21 July 44/2 Faced with cases that seemed beyond help, Dr. Bellows decided to try a cryoprobe chilled to a temperature of −65°C. **1981**

Brit. Med. Jrnl. 10 Oct. 945/1 Intercostal nerves frozen with a cryoprobe.

'**cryosphere**, the part of the earth's surface that is permanently frozen; also, the entire region of the earth (atmospheric and lithospheric) that is below 0°C.

1957 *Gloss. Geol.* (Amer. Geol. Inst.) 69/2 *Cryosphere, all of the earth's surface that is permanently frozen. **1968** R. W. FAIRBRIDGE *Encycl. Geomorphol.* 227 In some regions of permafrost, the cryosphere penetrates the lithosphere as deep as 600 meters. **1975** *Nature* 28 Aug. 689/3 An improved understanding of the workings and interactions of the five physical elements of the total climatic system—atmosphere, hydrosphere, cryosphere, lithosphere and biosphere—is badly needed. **1982** BARRY & CHORLEY *Atmosphere, Weather & Climate* (ed. 4) viii. 332 Two categories of causal factors affecting the earth's climate system can be distinguished...This second category, especially, involves complex feedback effects between atmosphere, ocean and cryosphere.

hence **cryos'pheric** *a.*

1975 *Nature* 28 Aug. 717/1 These results..seem capable of providing accurate estimates of the lag times involved in the change of the oceanic and *cryospheric systems from glacial to interglacial modes. **1986** *Internat. Jrnl. Remote Sensing* VII. 1359 The well-established effect of orographic shadowing is particularly important for cryospheric surfaces.

cryo'therapy *Med.* [ad. F. *cryothérapie* (F. Bordas 1913, in *Compt. Rend.* CLVI. 84)], the use of very low temperatures for therapeutic purposes, esp. the treatment of skin cancer.

1939 *Arch. Dermatol. & Syphilol.* XXXIX. 997 *Cryotherapy should be guardedly administered when there is atrophy of the skin. **1969** *New Scientist* 30 Jan. 230/2 In advanced ano-rectal neoplasms and bladder tumours palliative cryotherapy provides worthwhile symptomatic relief by surface destruction of the tumour and by its ability to reduce local haemorrhage and mucoid discharge. **1985** E. H. HART *German Shepherd Dog* xxii. 296 Cryotherapy, the freezing of tissues by agents such as liquid nitrogen and freon via a probe, is being used successfully by many veterinarians.

cryonics (kraɪ'ɒnɪks), *n. pl.* (const. as *sing.*). [f. CRY(O- + -*onics* (after BIONICS *n. pl.*, etc.).] The practice or technique of deep-freezing the bodies of people who have died, usu. of an incurable disease, with the aim of reviving them once a cure has been found.

1965 *Christian Cent.* 27 Oct. 1313/2 At this writing there exist at least three nonprofit organizations formed to promote cryogenic internment:..Cryonic [*sic*] Society of New York. **1967** *N.Y. Times* 20 Jan. 44/2 The experiment is being conducted by the Cryonics Society of California. *Ibid.* 29 Jan. 1. 58/1 Most cryonics enthusiasts..concede that present methods of freezing a body offer no guarantee that the harm done by the freezing process can be repaired. **1977** C. D. SIMAK *Heritage of Stars* 183 You read what was written about going to the stars centuries before there was any possibility of going to the stars...You read about cryonics: freezing the passengers and then reviving them. **1990** *Sunday Tel.* 3 June 16/2 It also promises to put under the legal microscope the burgeoning cryonics industry—the controversial experimental procedure in which all or part of a person's body is frozen and preserved in the expectation of bringing it back to life sometime in the future.

Hence **cry'onic** *a.*, of, pertaining to, or involving cryonics; **cry'onically** *adv.*; **cry'onicist** *n.*, one who advocates or practises cryonics.

1968 *Courier-Mail* (Brisbane) 3 Aug. 4/2 Steven Jay Mendell..who died last Sunday will have a so-called cryonic interment. **1968** *Newsweek* 12 Aug. 29/3 Cryonicists hope that..somebody may be brought back to life. **1976** M. APPLE *Oranging of Amer.* (1986) 18 The man who..already kept one freezer in his car merely ordered another, this one designed according to cryonic specifications. **1982** *Time* 26 July 45/1 Parton plays Mona as if Mae West had been cryonically preserved but someone didn't quite finish the job of unfreezing her. **1988** *L.A. Times* 17 Jan. 1. 3/1 The cryonicists, who say that the coroner's tests would harm the head beyond hope of resurrection, will not say where it is. **1990** *Daily Tel.* 3 May 12/8 In his lawsuit..he is asking that the state should be barred from stopping him from undergoing cyronic suspension before he is declared legally dead.

cryoprotectant (ˌkraɪəʊprəʊˈtɛktənt), *n.* and *a.* [f. CRYO- + PROTECTANT *a.* and *n.*] **A.** *n.* A cryoprotective agent.

1968 *Jrnl. Protozool.* XV. 723/2 The best cryoprotectants were ethylene glycol, glycerol, and DMSO. **1982** *High Technol.* Jan.-Feb. 85/1 Researchers..study ways to prevent freeze-thaw damage by using chemical cryoprotectants that pre-condition seeds prior to freezing by cold-hardening. **1984** HOLTZMAN & NOVIKOFF *Cells & Organelles* (ed. 3) III. xi. 470 Cells can be stored, apparently indefinitely, in liquid nitrogen at −196°C. When frozen carefully, in order to limit the formation of ice crystals (sometimes 'cryoprotectants' such as glycerol or dimethylsulfoxide (DMSO) are added), and then carefully thawed, cells..will resume growth and division. **1994** *Interzone* July 44/3 Even with the use of glycol as a cryoprotectant, White will suffer freezing damage which must be repaired before he can live.

B. *adj.* = *CRYOPROTECTIVE *a.*

1969 *Surg., Gynecol. & Obstetr.* CCXXVIII. 571 (*heading*) Effects of cryoprotectant compounds on mammalian heart muscle. **1972** *Sci. News* 19 Aug. 125 Offerijns has actually frozen them [*sc.* the 'pacemaker' cells of the heart], using a cryoprotectant agent called dimethyl sulfoxide (DMSO), and revived 80 percent of them successfully. **1986** *Cryo-Lett.* VII. 355 The cryoprotectant solution utilized in this study was Dimethyl Sulphoxide.

cryoprotection (ˌkraɪəʊprəˈtɛkʃən), *n.* [f. CRYO- + PROTECTION *n.*] Protection against damage when the temperature, esp. of biological material, falls below freezing; the action of a cryoprotectant.

1967 *Cryobiology* III. 336/2 The mechanism of cryoprotection afforded by chemical agents is still to be fully elucidated. **1986** *Cryo-Lett.* VII. 208 The overwintering success of some cold hardy trees can now be explained by the natural cryoprotection obtained from intracellular vitrification.

So **cryopro'tect** *v. trans.*, to protect against damage caused by freezing temperatures; **cryopro'tected**, **cryopro'tecting** *ppl. adjs.*

1974 *Cryobiology* XI. 70/1 Such an approach may bear fruit in trying to cryoprotect platelets or neutrophiles. **1976** *Ibid.* XIII. 31 (*heading*) Enzyme activity of cryoprotected myocardium. **1977** *Planta* CXXXVII. 195/1 Production of cryoprotecting compounds was suggested by a significant higher stability against NaCl observed with class C chloroplasts isolated from frost hardened needles as compared to that of plastids from frost labile material. **1980** *Nature* 3 Jan. 14/1 Freeze-fracture replicas of eggs fixed with glutaraldehyde and cryoprotected with glycerol before freezing.

cryoprotective (ˌkraɪəʊprəˈtɛktɪv), *a.* [f. CRYO- + PROTECTIVE *a.*] Giving protection against damage, esp. to biological material, caused by freezing temperatures.

1967 *Cryobiology* III. 337/1 Cryoprotective agents could stabilize macromolecules during freezing. **1971** *McGraw-Hill Yearbk. Sci. & Technol.* 106 Glycerol and some other cryoprotective agents allow long frozen storage of bull's sperm for artificial insemination and tissues like cornea for surgical repair of damaged eyes. **1973** *Nature* 15 June 371/1 The eggs were then

frozen to −196°C with dimethylsulphoxide, a cryoprotective (antifreeze) agent, replacing some of the water in the embryo cells to prevent ice forming within them. **1980** *N.Y. Times* 20 July VI. 52/4 At room temperature, a cryoprotective agent is added to the 8- or 16-cell embryo, in its vial of culture medium.

cryptand ('krɪptænd), *n. Chem.* [f. CRYPT(O- + -AND², after *CRYPTATE *n.*] An organic bicyclic compound whose molecule contains a cavity capable of holding metal cations.

1975 Y. M. CAHEN et al. in *Jrnl. Physical Chem.* LXXIX. 1289/1 Lehn introduced a new class of complexing agents of hexaoxadiamine macrobicyclic type called 'cryptands'. *Ibid.* 1291/2 Following the suggestion of Lehn (personal communication) we designate the ligands as *cryptands* and the corresponding complexes as *cryptates*. **1977** *Sci. Amer.* July 100/2 In pure ethylamine..sodium is virtually insoluble; when 2,2,2-cryptand is present, several grams of sodium per liter of solvent can be dissolved. **1980** *Tetrahedron* XXXVI. 493 Cryptands..have also been referred to as 'lanterns' (the name originally proposed by Pedersen). **1988** P. D. BEER in T. E. Edmonds *Chem. Sensors* ii. 32 Because the cryptand host cavity is three-dimensional and spheroidal in shape, it is well adapted for a 'ball-like' guest metal cation.

cryptate ('krɪpteɪt), *n. Chem.* [a. F. *cryptate* (coined by B. Dietrich et al. 1969, in *Tetrahedron Lett.* 2892), f. Gr. κρυπτός hidden or L. *crypta* cave, crypt: see -ATE¹.] An organometallic complex in which a hydrogen or metal cation is trapped within a cryptand.

1969 *Tetrahedron Lett.*: *Subject/Author Index Nos.1-60* p. ix/2 Cryptates, metal cation inclusion complexes, into molecular cavity of bicyclic ligands, 2889. **1970** J. M. LEHN in *Angewandte Chemie* (Internat. ed.) IX. 175/2 Since the cation is 'hidden' in the center of the molecule, the name 'cryptates' is proposed for these compounds. **1975** Y. M. CAHEN et al. in *Jrnl. Physical Chem.* LXXIX. 1291/2 Following the suggestion of Lehn (personal communication) we designate the ligands as *cryptands* and the corresponding complexes as cryptates. **1978** *Accounts Chem. Res.* XI. 54/1 Cryptate formation may become a powerful criterion of mechanism for ionic reactions involving complexable metal cations. **1984** GREENWOOD & EARNSHAW *Chem. of Elements* (1986) v. 137 Cryptates..are also known and usually follow the stability sequence Mg<Ca<Sr<Ba. **1988** *Nature* 18 Feb. 564/3 Electron-pair trapping sites in the large cavities of the cryptate at the intersection of the various channels.

Cumberland, *n.* Sense 2 in Dict. becomes 3. Add: **2.** Used *attrib.* and *absol.* to designate a lop-eared pork and bacon pig of a breed now extinct.

1811 R. HENDERSON *Breeding Swine* I. i. 14 The Berkshire pig..generally of a brown, or rather reddish colour..; the ears bending forward, but not hanging down so much as those of the large Cumberland kind. **1860** S. SIDNEY *Youatt's Pig* (ed. 2) I. ii. 17 At the Carlisle show of the Royal Agricultural Society, the Cumberland pigs shown in the large classes were roach-backed brutes. *Ibid.* 21 The small Cumberland is a great deal larger than the small Yorkshire. **1861** I. M. BEETON *Bk. Household Managem.* 365 Varieties of the Domesticated Hog...Native—Berkshire, Essex, York, and Cumberland. **1949** J. E. NICHOLS in F. Gerrard *Bk. Meat Trade* I. ii. 31 The Cumberland breed is..all white in colour, and compared with the Large White is shorter, wider and more thickly fleshed. **1985** *Times* 5 Dec. 14/5 At least 20 breeds of farm animal have become extinct this century. They include..the Cumberland pig,..as recently as 1963. **1989** HALL & CLUTTON-BROCK *Two Hundred Yrs. Brit. Farm Livestock* xvii. 221 It is at least possible that the genetic make-up of this breed includes contributions from the

Lincolnshire Curly Coat, the Cumberland, and the forerunners of the Large White.

cummingtonite ('kʌmɪŋtənaɪt), *n. Min.* [f. the name of *Cummington*, a town in Massachusetts, U.S.A., where it was first found: see -ITE[1].] A basic silicate of magnesium and ferrous iron, $(Mg, Fe)_7Si_8O_{22}(OH)_2$, that is an amphibole mineral similar to anthophyllite but monoclinic and with more iron, and that occurs as fibres and lamellae in metamorphic rocks.

1824 C. DEWEY in *Amer. Jrnl. Sci. & Arts* VIII. 59 *Cummingtonite*, I have given this name to a mineral found by Dr. J. Porter in Cummington. **1966** *McGraw-Hill Encycl. Sci. & Technol.* III. 623/1 The observed ranges of composition of cummingtonite and anthophyllite overlap considerably...Cummingtonite is optically positive and thus distinct from the other monoclinic amphiboles. **1977** *Lancet* 9 July 80/2 The Duluth water supply contained mineral fibres resembling asbestos, which were shown to be an asbestos amphibole, cummingtonite-grunerite. **1989** *Jrnl. Petrol.* XXX. 42 The occurrence of cummingtonite instead of garnet in the amphibolite is also consistent with low-pressure hornblende-granulite grade metomorphic conditions.

curd, *n.* Add: [3.] **curd cheese** (orig. *U.S.*), any soft cheese made from unfermented curds.

[**1909** VAN SLYKE & PUBLOW *Sci. & Pract. Cheesemaking* viii. 87 Stiff, corky or curdy cheese is hard, tough, overfirm; it does not crush down readily when pressed in the hand.] **1941** H. KURATH *Ling. Atlas New Eng.* II. 1. Map 299 The map shows the terms *cottage cheese, Dutch ch.,..*curd ch*[eese] or *curd* (*cheese curd*). *Ibid.*, *Curd ch*[*eese*], heard from one old woman. **1946** *Publ. Amer. Dial. Soc.* V. 18 *Curds, curd cheese..*, cheese made of the drained curd of sour milk, especially that fed to turkeys or chickens; mostly in the Tidewater area. **1973** S. SKIPWORTH *Eat Russian* i. 16 Cottage cheese and curd cheese are the nearest equivalent to the Russian Tvorog which is dry but not 'cheesy'. **1992** *Financial Times* 11 Apr. II. 9/7 As for containers, try the little plastic tubs with snap-on lids used by delis and supermarkets for weighing and potting such things as curd cheese.

cusk, *n.* Add: **2.** Special Comb. **cusk-eel**, any of a number of mostly small deep-sea fishes of the family Ophidiidae, having modified whisker-like fins under the throat.

1905 D. S. JORDAN *Guide Study of Fishes* II. 520 The more important family of *Ophidiidae*, or *cusk-eels*, is characterized by the extremely anterior position of the ventral fins.., each one appearing as a long forked barbel. **1961** E. S. HERALD *Living Fishes of World* 241/1 The slender cusk eels are similar in appearance to some of the common tide-pool eel-like blennies. **1989** *New Scientist* 25 Feb. 53/1 Male rattails and cusk eels of the continental slope use the swimbladder as a drum operated by large drumming muscles.

cyanelle (saɪə'nɛl), *n. Bot.* Also **cyanella** (pl. **cyanellæ**). [a. G. *Cyanelle* (coined by A. Pascher 1929, in *Jahrb. f. wissensch. Bot.* LXXI. 387), f. CYAN- + -*elle*, -*ella*, after *zoochlorella*, etc.: see -EL[2].] A cyanobacterium living symbiotically inside the cell of a protozoan or the like.

1952 *Physiol. Rev.* XXXII. 415 The most interesting associations occur when the cyanelle (Pascher's term for a cyanophytic endosymbiont) is regulated by the host. **1971** M. ALEXANDER *Microbial Ecol.* xi. 262 These algae are subdivided on the basis of their color, and one speaks of..cyanellae to designate the algae that are..blue-green. **1983** *Nature* 28 July 373/1 The intracellular photosynthetic entities (cyanelles) of the protozoan *Cyanophora paradoxa*..have long been regarded as endosymbiotic cyanobacteria.

cyano-, *comb. form.* Add: **cya'nophilous** *a. Biol.* [ad. G. *cyanophil* (coined by A. Schönemann 1892, in *Arch. f. path. Anat. u. Physiol.* CXXIX. 317): see -PHIL], readily stained by blue and green dyes.

1895 *Jrnl. R. Microsc. Soc.* 159 'Oxychromatin' and 'cyanophilous granulation' are independent structural parts of the chromatin network. **1959** W. ANDREW *Textbk. Compar. Histol.* iii. 74 They consist in Turbellaria of two main types: (1) the cyanophilous glands, which are basophilic, and (2) the eosinophilous glands, which are acidophilic. **1984** *Mycotaxon* XX. 607 *P*[*ulvinula*] *ascoboloides* n. sp., with a cyanophilous sheath surrounding the ascospores.

cyanoacrylate (saɪənəʊ'ækrɪleɪt), *n.* [f. CYANO- + ACRYLATE *n.*] A chemical compound containing the substituted acrylate group $CH_2\cdot C(CN)\cdot COO-$; any of various exceptionally strong adhesives based on such a compound.

1957 *Chem. & Engin. News* 21 Oct. 56/2 Adhesive action results from the polymerization of a cyanoacrylate monomer. **1957** *Technol.* Nov. 328/3 Eastman Kodak report a new fast drying adhesive of considerable strength. A liquid cyanoacrylate compound, it will bond glass to glass, wood to wood, or steel to steel. **1969** *Mil. Med.* CXXXIV. 247/1 Changes in the length and isomeric configuration of the alkyl side chain alter the physical and chemical properties of cyanoacrylate molecules. **1974** *Encycl. Brit. Macropædia* I. 89/2 The cyanoacrylates, monomers that polymerize spontaneously in place, form excellent bonds almost instantly to a variety of surfaces. **1977** *Sci. Amer.* Nov. 38/3 Alkyl cyanoacrylates have wide applications in surgery, mainly as supplements to sutures. **1982** *diytrade* May/June 18/1 Cyanoacrylates, or superglues, are a natural diy line, now worth £7m.

cyanobacterium (ˌsaɪənəʊbæk'tɪərɪəm), *n. Biol.* Also **Cyanobacterium**. Pl. **cyanobacteria**. [mod.L., f. CYANO- + BACTERIUM *n.*] Any of a division of prokaryotic micro-organisms that contain chlorophyll (green) and phycocyanin (blue), produce free oxygen in photosynthesis, and occur widely in unicellular, filamentous, and colonial forms; also called *blue-green alga.* Usu. in *pl.*

1973 *Proc. Nat. Acad. Sci.* LXX. 3133/1 Allophycocyanin appears to be the most efficient light-harvesting pigment in all the cyanobacteria that we have examined. **1975** *Nature* 9 Oct. 489/2 Profound differences in structure and function separate the prokaryotic cyanobacteria (blue-green algae) from eukaryotic algae and plants. **1977** *Sci. Amer.* Mar. 71/1 Another symbiosis involves a small aquatic fern, *Azolla*, and a cyanobacterium that is capable of both photosynthesis and nitrogen fixation. Occupying cavities in the fern leaves, the cyanobacterium supplies nutrients that enable the fern to propagate in waters deficient in fixed nitrogen. **1981** D. J. & T. J. BELLAMY *Bellamy's Backyard Safari* 13 The Cyanobacteria, or blue-green algae as they used to be called are far commoner members of the garden scene than plastic gnomes. **1984** *Times Lit. Suppl.* 10 Aug. 903/3 Atmospheric oxygen was produced by cyanobacteria, a kind of bacteria which used to be called 'blue green algae'. **1987** SINGLETON & SAINSBURY *Dict. Microbiol. & Molecular Biol.* (ed. 2) 244/1 The taxonomy of the cyanobacteria is confused. Until quite recently they were regarded as algae and were therefore subject to the Botanical Code of nomenclature. **1989** B. ALBERTS et al. *Molecular Biol. Cell* (ed. 2) vii. 366 The evolution of cyanobacteria from more primitive photosynthetic bacteria first made possible the development of aerobic life forms.

Hence ˌcyanobac'terial *a.*, of or pertaining to a cyanobacterium or cyanobacteria.

1974 R. Y. STANIER in Carlile & Skehel *Evol. in Microbial World* 236 Although the cryptophytes also use phycobiliproteins as light-harvesting pigments, their chloroplasts differ in many structural and functional respects from those of rhodophytes..and cannot plausibly be ascribed a cyanobacterial derivation. **1989** B. ALBERTS et al. *Molecular Biol. Cell* (ed. 2) vii. 386 (*caption*) Oxygen respiration..seems to have evolved independently in the green, purple, and blue-green (cyanobacterial) lines of photosynthetic bacteria.

cyanophycean (saɪənəʊˈfaɪsɪən), *a. Bot.* Also **Cyanophycean.** [f. mod.L. *Cyanophyceae*, f. CYANO- + PHYCO- + -ACEA: see -AN.] Of or pertaining to the class Cyanophyceae, which comprises the blue-green algae (cyanobacteria) and is coextensive with the division Cyanophyta.

1902 *Encycl. Brit.* XXXI. 409/1 The sheaths of a Cyanophycean Alga. **1922** *New Phytologist* XXI. 87 The minute internal structure of the Cyanophycean cell. **1935** J. E. TILDEN *Algae* iii. 27 A long time must have elapsed between the Cyanophycean and Rhodophycean periods, in which the blue-green and the red algae in turn constituted the dominant flora of the sea. **1957** G. E. HUTCHINSON *Treat. Limnol.* I. xii. 745 The development of cyanophycean water blooms in some lakes in late July and early August. **1980** R. E. LEE *Phycology* ii. 53 The warm conditions demanded by the rice, the availability of nutrients, the reducing conditions in the soil, and the cynaophycean ability to withstand desiccation all favor growth of blue-greens. **1983** S. HOLMES *Outl. Plant Classif.* (1986) iv. 22 Food reserves include a special starch, cyanophycean or myxophycean starch and a protein, cyanophycin.

Also **cyano'phyceous** *a.*

1898 A. C. SEWARD *Fossil Plants* I. vii. 125 It is conceivable that in some of the tubular structures referred to *Girvanella* we have the mineralised sheaths of a fossil Cyanophyceous genus. **1934** *Q. Rev. Biol.* IX. 442/1 Geitler (1925) holds that all cyanophyceous cell walls consist of pectins, but contain neither chitin nor cellulose.

cyanophyte ('saɪənəʊfaɪt), *n. Bot.* [f. CYANO- + -PHYTE.] A member of the division Cyanophyta, which comprises the blue-green algae and is coextensive with the class Cyanophyceae; = *CYANOBACTERIUM n.

1952 *Physiol. Rev.* XXXII. 415 Cyanophyte (blue green algae) endosymbionts have repeatedly been interpreted as intracellular organelles. **1979** D. ATTENBOROUGH *Life on Earth* (1981) i. 22 The organisms that did this used to be called blue-green algae because they appeared to be close relatives of the green algae but, because they are common in ponds, but now that their very primitive character is recognised, they are referred to as cyanophytes or simply, blue-greens. **1984** A. C. & A. DUXBURY *Introd. World's Oceans* xiv. 432 Kingdom Monera: includes bacteria and cyanophytes.

Hence **cyano'phytic** *a.*

1952 *Physiol. Rev.* XXXII. 415 The cyanelle (Pascher's term for a cyanophytic endosymbiont). **1972** *Science* 27 Oct. 405/1 The evidence previously used to indicate a cyanophytic origin for these stromatolites.

cyberpunk ('saɪbə,pʌŋk), *n.* Also **cyber-punk.** [f. CYBER(NETICS *n.* + PUNK *n.*[3]] **1. a.** A subgenre of science fiction typified by a bleak, high-tech setting in which a lawless subculture exists within an oppressive society dominated by computer technology. **b.** An author of, or protagonist in, such writing.

1983 B. BETHKE (*title*) in *Amazing Stories* Nov. 94 Cyberpunk. **1984** *Washington Post* 30 Dec. (Book World section) 9/1 About the closest thing here to a self-willed esthetic 'school' would be the purveyors

of bizarre hard-edged, high-tech stuff, who have on occasion been referred to as 'cyberpunks'—Sterling, Gibson, Shiner, Cadigan, Bear. **1988** *Times Lit. Suppl.* 21 Oct. 1180/3 The subgenre of science fiction now widely known as Cyberpunk, in which life in the computerized jungle of the near future can only be survived by young street-wise masters of software interfaces and the arts of combat. **1989** *Adbusters Q.* Winter 30/1 Cyberspace is inhabited by Cyberpunks. **1992** *Independent* 19 May 12/4 Cyberpunk protagonists are electronic cowboys in a battle for the control of information.

2. *transf.* A person who accesses computer networks illegally, esp. with malicious intent. Cf. HACKER *n.* 3 b.

1989 C. STOLL *Cuckoo's Egg* xlvi. 245 This was a sensitive medical device, not a plaything for some cyberpunk. Some poor computer geek, indeed. **1989** *Daily Tel.* 4 Nov. 2/3 A 'stinky Sperry computer' caught fire after a cyber-punk sent an instruction to its printer to overwrite the same line of text 1,000 times. **1991** HAFNER & MARKOFF *Cyberpunk* I. 123 In the ten years Reid had taught at Stanford, he had been involved in network security, had met several such 'cyberpunks' and had sparred with dozens of them inside the Stanford computers. **1993** *Wired* Sept./Oct. 90/2 Cyberpunks are setting the stage for a coming digital counterculture that will turn the '90s zeitgeist utterly on its head.

cyberspace ('saɪbəspeɪs), *n.* [f. *cyber-* after CYBERNETICS *n.* + SPACE *n.*[1]] The notional environment within which electronic communication occurs, esp. when represented as the inside of a computer system; space perceived as such by an observer but generated by a computer system and having no real existence; the space of virtual reality. Cf. *virtual reality* s.v. *VIRTUAL *a.* 4 g.

1982 W. GIBSON in *Omni* July 72/2, I knew every chip in Bobby's simulator by heart; it looked like your workaday Ono-Sendai VII, the 'Cyberspace Seven', but I'd rebuilt it so many times that [etc.]. **1984** —*Neuromancer* II. iii. 52 Molly was gone when he took the trodes off, and the loft was dark. He checked the time. He'd been in cyberspace for five hours. **1991** H. RHEINGOLD *Virtual Reality* (1992) i. 17 Although I stayed in cyberspace for just a few minutes, that first brief flight through a computer-created universe launched me on my own odyssey to the outposts of a new scientific frontier. **1993** *Guardian* 18 Oct. I. 8/7 The search for a kidnapped girl from a small town in California has leapt into cyberspace as her picture criss-crosses the world's computer networks, databases and electronic mail systems.

cyclin ('saɪklɪn), *n. Biochem.* [f. CYCL(E *n.* or *v.* + -IN[1].] **1.** A protein found in cell nuclei, in amounts which fluctuate during the cell cycle, being greatest during DNA replication. Now called *proliferating cell nuclear antigen* (*PCNA*).

1981 R. BRAVO et al. in *Exper. Cell Res.* CXXXVI. 319/1 To avoid confusion between the different numbering systems we have termed the nuclear acidic polypeptide 'cyclin'. **1984** *Nature* 24 May 376/1 We suggest that the name PCNA be used in future, as it is the earlier nomenclature and the term cyclin has recently become ambiguous. **1989** *Proc. Nat. Acad. Sci.* LXXXVI. 3189/1 Proliferating-cell nuclear antigen (PCNA; also called cyclin) was originally described in proliferating mammalian cells as a nuclear protein.

2. Any of a class of structurally similar proteins that are synthesized and destroyed at different points in the cell cycle and are instrumental in the control of DNA replication and division in eukaryotes.

1983 T. EVANS et al. in *Cell* XXXIII. 389/1 Oocytes of the surf clam Spisula solidissima also contain proteins that only start to be made after fertilization and are destroyed at certain points in the cell division cycle.

We propose to call these proteins the cyclins. **1985** *Biol. Bull.* CLXIX. 545 The Cyclin A protein which is encoded by a maternally stored mRNA was also studied. **1986** *Cell* XLVII. 870/1 What is the relationship between cyclin A and cyclin B, a related but distinctly different protein whose levels also oscillate in phase with the mitotic cell cycle? **1991** *EMBO Jrnl.* IX. 2865/2 Cyclin B has been isolated from a wide variety of organisms that include yeast, sea urchin, starfish, clam, frog, fly and man. **1992** *Trends Cell Biol.* II. 77/1 Cyclins have come to occupy a central position in our understanding of the regulatory processes that coordinate the cell cycle.

cynodont ('saɪnəʊdɒnt), *n.* and *a.* [f. CYNO- + Gr. ὀδούς, ὀδοντ- tooth. Cf. earlier DICYNODONT *n.* and *a.*] **A.** *n.* An extinct mammal-like reptile of Triassic times with well-developed teeth specialized for chewing. **B.** *adj.* Of, pertaining to, or designating this reptile.

1896 *Phil. Trans. R. Soc.* B. CLXXXVI. 59 The Theriodontia include the Cynodontia, because the Cynodont genera were grouped in this way by Sir R. Owen. *Ibid.* 60 The specimen makes known the essential parts of the largest skeleton of a Cynodont, a group previously known only from small skulls allied to *Galesaurus*. **1907** *Trans. S. Afr. Philos. Soc.* XVI. 376 *Ælurosuchus browni*...The only previously described Cynodont which bears much resemblance to it is the type of *Microgomphodon oligocynus*. **1933** A. S. ROMER *Vertebr. Paleont.* xi. 235 The posterior, or cheek, teeth of cynodonts varied widely. **1966** E. PALMER *Plains of Camdeboo* vi. 105 A number of small Cynodonts or 'Dog-Tooths' with mammal-like jaws and teeth. **1977** A. HALLAM *Planet Earth* 278/1 Some large Triassic cynodonts developed wide, peg-like cheek teeth. **1985** D. NORMAN *Illustr. Encycl. Dinosaurs* 36/2 In the early part of the Triassic, the thecodontians..lived alongside a very diverse fauna of herbivorous (dicynodont) and carnivorous (cynodont) mammal-like reptiles. *Ibid.* 186/3 The subsequent evolution of herbivorous dinosaurs to fill the niche vacated by the herbivorous cynodonts and dicynodonts.

D

D. Add: [III.] [3.] [a.] **DCC** = *digital compact cassette* s.v. *DIGITAL *a.* 5 d.

1990 *Sunday Times* 11 Nov. IV. 11/3 The Philips system is called Digital Compact Cassette (*DCC). It will use the current cassette format, with a shield to protect the tape, as with videos and DAT cassettes. **1993** *Q* May 114/2 DAT is like a tiny videotape, DCC is the same size and shape as an ordinary music cassette—but the basic difference in the systems is in the recording and playback head.

ddC, DDC *Pharm.*, dideoxycytidine.

1987 *Daily Tel.* 17 Feb. 2/8 Animal trials indicate that dideoxycytidine (*DDC), is less toxic to man than Retrovir. **1990** *AIDS Res. & Human Retroviruses* VI. 695 ddC is one of the most potent anti-HIV agents. **1992** *Sun* (Baltimore) 23 June A3/6 The studies showed that ddC, used in combination with AZT, tended to cause an increase in the number of CD4 cells in the immune systems of HIV patients.

ddI, DDI *Pharm.* = *DIDEOXYINOSINE.

1989 *Science* 28 July 412/3, 2′,3′-Dideoxyinosine (*ddI)..is a purine dideoxynucleoside with potent activity against HIV in vitro. **1990** *Lancet* 10 Mar. 596/2 The UK trial of ddI will be accompanied by a similar trial in France. **1992** *N.Y. Times Mag.* 5 Jan. 12/3 Now that drugs like AZT and DDI can slow the progress of the disease, I could be relatively healthy for years.

DTP, dtp = *desk-top publishing* s.v. DESK-TOP *n.* 2.

1986 *Nation's Business* (U.S.) Mar. 57/1 Aldus created software that enables *DTP systems to combine text and graphics on the screen. **1991** *Computing* 10 Jan. 20/1 In the past, the first question the would-be desktop publishing user asked was: is my word processor compatible with the dtp package I want?

dahoma (dəˈhəʊmə), *n.* *Bot.* Also **danhoma**. [f. DAHOMAN *n.* and *a.* or *Dahomey*, former name of Benin in West Africa.] A tropical tree, *Piptadeniastrum africanum*, of the family Leguminosae (Mimosoideae), which is native chiefly to central and western Africa, and is harvested for its yellowish-brown timber; the wood of this tree.

1955 *Nomencl. Commerc. Timbers* (*B.S.I.*) 62 Dahoma. **1956** *Handbk. Hardwoods* (Forest Products Res. Lab.) 80 Dahoma reaches a height of 120 ft. or more with a diameter of 3–4 ft above buttresses. **1957** *Archit. Rev.* CXXII. 388 The veneer to the booths, externally and internally, is agba: the floor is dahoma. **1990** D. K. ABBIW *Useful Plants of Ghana* iv. 78 Heavy construction demands timbers which are very durable, hard, and heavy..*Piptadeniastrum africanum* (Danhoma)..and..Red Ironwood (Kaku) are examples.

daisy-chain (ˈdeɪzɪtʃeɪn), *v.* Also **daisychain** and as two words. [f. the n.] **1. a.** *intr.* To form a 'daisy chain' of people (in a dance, etc.). Also *transf.*

1968 *Punch* 9 Oct. 519/1 The cast leap, stamp, rock and daisychain about the stage to the exhilarating beat of Galt MacDermot's music. **1980** *Outdoor Life* (U.S.) (Northeast ed.) Oct. 110/2 Tarpon often 'daisy chain' or swim in rough circles, with one fish's nose almost touching the tail of the fish in front of it.

b. *spec.* in *Comm.* (*trans.* and *intr.*) To inflate (the price of a commodity, esp. oil) artificially by means of a daisy chain (see sense *2 c of the noun).

1979 *Washington Post* 31 May A11/4 They have been buying crude from resellers who illegally inflated the prices and supplying products to brokers whose only function was to 'daisy chain' the prices [i.e., raise them through a series of transactions] while the fuel was being shipped directly to the utilities. **1979** *Oil & Gas Jrnl.* 11 June 3 This use of middlemen has no function but to daisy-chain prices...The major companies have been able to raise the general price of fuel to its present artificially high level. **1984** *Fortune* 23 Jan. 49/2 The Arco lawyer emphatically denies that the company was 'daisy-chaining with Rich, or anyone else.'

2. *Electronics* and *Computing.* **a.** *trans.* To join (components or devices) so as to form a single sequence, usu. with the output from one member of the sequence forming the input to the next; to connect (one component or device) *to* another as part of such a sequence.

1972 [implied in *daisy-chaining* vbl. n. below]. **1980** D. LEWIN *Theory & Design Digital Computers* (ed. 2) ix. 399 When the Bus Controller receives a request it acknowledges on the bus available line which is linked through to each device (daisy chained). **1981** *Electronics* (Internat. ed.) 10 Feb. 166/3 No. 1 card slot of an RTP7400-series subsystem..and as many as seven other equally complex subsystems can be daisy-chained to the host via the one DIOC. *Ibid.* 28 July 217/2 Up to eight drives..can be daisy-chained together from the TC 110. **1987** *Production Engin.* Mar. 48/2 Microcomputer-based controllers daisy-chained to a host were employed to control the robotic subsystem. **1989** *Times* 2 Mar. 36/5 Up to 256 jukeboxes could be daisy-chained to create one gigantic data store.

b. *intr.* To be capable of being daisy-chained.

1984 *Austral. Personal Computer* Apr. 30/3 The keypad..comes as an optional extra that daisychains onto the Macintosh keyboard. **1994** *CD-ROM World* Apr. 7/2 (Advt.), 18 discs that daisy chain to quickly access a whopping 126 CD-ROM discs.

So (chiefly in sense *2 above) **daisy-chained** *ppl. a.*; **daisy-chainer** *n.* (*rare*), a participant in a 'daisy chain'; **daisy-chaining** *vbl. n.*

1941 G. LEGMAN in G. W. Henry *Sex Variants* II. 1162 *Daisy-chain*, a spintry; a group of more than two persons—heterosexual, homosexual, or both—linked together in simultaneous sexual intercourse of any kind or combination of kinds...A person participating in a spintry is termed a *daisy-chainer*. **1972** *Proc. AFIPS Conf.* XLI. 721/2 Centralized Daisy Chaining is illustrated in Figure 7. **1981** *Electronics* (Internat. ed.) 27 Jan. 139/2 The circuit can be connected between daisy-chained disk drives and the disk controller. **1985** *Pract. Computing* May 94/2 These signals are located on the same pins at all points on the bus, with no daisy-chaining or physical positioning required for any purpose. **1989** *UNIX World* Sept. 140/2 Up to eight daisy-chained write-once, read-many (WORMs) can be supported for large archival requirements.

daisy chain, *n.* Add: [2.] **c.** *Comm.* A group of dealers who agree to buy and sell a particular commodity (orig. crude oil, esp. in a single shipment) amongst themselves, thereby inflating the price at which it is eventually sold to an outside buyer.

1982 J. M. ROSENBERG *Dict. Banking & Finance* 155/1 *Daisy chains*, oil sale overcharges through transactions designed primarily to increase the price of crude oil. **1984** *Fortune* 23 Jan. 46/1 Arco..allegedly fed oil into a Texas 'daisy chain' that further enriched Rich's trading company. **1986** *Times* 19 Feb. 17/3 Can..order be brought to the daisy chain market? The daisy chain takes its name from the string of traders who sell or buy from each other on paper a cargo of Brent crude. **1990** *Independent on Sunday* 11 Feb. (Business Suppl.) 3/5 Lincoln traded the bonds with other members of the daisy chain at artificial and escalating prices which enabled both sides of the deal to realise unreal and improper profits, the prosecution said.

dark, *a.* Add: [14.] [c.] **dark matter** *Astron.*, *(a)* (now *rare*) non-luminous matter; *(b) spec.* matter which has not been directly detected but whose existence is postulated to account for the dynamical behaviour of galaxies or the universe; cf. *cold dark matter* s.v. *COLD *a.* 19, *hot dark matter* s.v. *HOT *a.* (*n.*[1])
    1922 *Astrophysical Jrnl.* LV. 314 Suppose that in a volume of space containing *l* luminous stars there be *dark matter with an aggregate mass equal to *Kl* average luminous stars. *Ibid.*, The means of estimating the mass of dark matter in the universe. **1950** *Irish Astron. Jrnl.* I. 8 At Alpha Scorpii the belt suddenly ceases...The stream has been blacked-out by nearby dark matter. **1954** *Ibid.* III. 61 By reason of the inevitable encounters with galaxies and clusters of galaxies..some dark matter will be dislodged into outer space. **1979** *Ann. Rev. Astrophysics* XVII. 165 The binary data seem to imply the existence of dark matter. **1989** J. SILK *Big Bang* (rev. ed.) viii. 154 We expect that most plausible candidates for the dark-matter particles will eventually annihilate. **1993** *Time* 18 Jan. 48/1 The dark matter could be made up of giant planets, failed stars, black holes, clouds of unknown particles, or even, so far as the laws of physics are concerned, bowling balls.

date, *n.*[2] Add: [8.] **date rape** orig. and chiefly *U.S.*, rape of a woman by a man she is dating or with whom she is on a date; hence as *v. trans.*
    1975 S. BROWNMILLER *Against our Will* 257 *Date rapes and rapes by men who have had prior relationships with their victims also contain elements of coercive authority that militates against decisive resistance. **1980** *Mademoiselle* Nov. 211/3 He could be prosecuted if only the legal system would accept that 'date rape' is possible. **1984** M. AMIS *Money* (1985) 22 She just came out of a two-year analysis. Then she was date-raped in Bridgehampton by her weekend therapist. *Ibid.*, With a regular rape, lust plays no part in it... But with a date rape, lust features. **1991** *N.Y. Times* 8 Dec. IV. 5/5 Most date rape cases come down in the end to Her versus Him.

datum, *n.* Add: [3.] **dataglove, DataGlove**, a device worn like a glove and containing sensors linked to a representation of a hand in a computer display, allowing the manual manipulation of images in virtual reality.
    1987 S. S. FISHER in D. P. Casasent *Intelligent Robots & Computer Vision* (Proc. SPIE DCCXXVI) 396 The *DataGlove is a lightweight, glove-like device that electronically records and transmits data-records of hand and finger shape and dynamics to a host computer by measuring the amount of joint bend, finger abduction, and thumb circumduction. **1989** *Technol. Rev.* Apr. 10/1 Someday, headset users might even 'touch' a remote patient with a 'dataglove' that receives sensations from a robot surgeon on the space station. **1993** *Whole Earth Rev.* 22 June 30/1 A live improvisation on musical instruments that exist only in virtual reality. The piece is performed by a single hand in a DataGlove.

deboost (diːˈbuːst), *n.* and *v. Astronaut.* [f. DE- II + BOOST *n.*[2]] **A.** *n.* The slowing down of

a spacecraft by the firing of a retro-rocket; a manoeuvre involving such deceleration.
    1966 *Pop. Sci. Monthly* Apr. 118 In an Apollo lunar-landing mission, these critical events will include: ..Deboost (slowing by retrofire) into lunar orbit. **1979** *Aviation Week* 1 Jan. 19/1 NASA some time earlier had..determined that no manned or unmanned Soviet hardware had the basic capability for even minimal deboost requirements. **1988** *Aerospace Amer.* Nov. 26/1 Deboost of payloads up to 75,000 lb could start from a 160-n.mi. orbit.
    B. *v. intr.* and *trans.* To decelerate as a result of or by means of a deboost.
    1967 *Time* 10 Nov. 25/1 This combination would prevent anti-ballistic missile radar..from ascertaining the point of impact until the rocket 'deboosts'—about three minutes and 500 miles from target. **1978** *Aviation Week* 19 June 31/1 Until Skylab reenters the atmosphere on its own or is reboosted or deboosted by the second space shuttle mission.

decision, *n.* Add: [5.] **decision tree**, a tree diagram representing a sequence of decisions to be taken as a means of selecting one course of action out of many.
    1964 P. C. FISHBURN *Decision & Value Theory* ii. 26 A *decision tree is a graphical representation of the alternative actions available to the decision maker and the 'alternative actions available to nature'. **1976** *Path. Ann.* XI. 145 The decision tree depicts a sequence of binary, yes or no, decisions which progress until a conclusion is reached. **1991** *Processing* June 56/2 Also included are decision trees for determining the best approach in particular applications.

denet (diːˈnɛt), *v.* Also **de-net**. [f. DE- + NET *a.* 3 b.] *trans.* To sell or permit the sale of (a book) at a price lower than that fixed under the terms of the Net Book Agreement. Hence **de'netted** *ppl. a.*; **de'netting** *vbl. n.*
    1962 *Guardian* 31 Oct. 4/7 A publisher could..'de-net' a book if he wished. **1988** *Bookseller* 13 May 1881/2 We would de-net most of the autumn list if that were the case. **1991** *Ibid.* 15 Feb. 397/1 The rumours point to a series of campaigns involving non-net or denetted books. **1991** *Daily Tel.* 2 Oct. 17/2 Tom Rosenthal at Andre Deutsch describes himself as a believer in the NBA 'both as a reader and a publisher', yet he is experimenting with denetting one of his likely bigger sellers. **1992** *Accountancy* Nov. 29 Denetting is simply a form of price promotion.

denial, *n.* Add: 7. *Psychoanal.* The suppression (usu. at an unconscious level) of a painful or unacceptable wish or of experiences of which one is ashamed. Now also in more general use, esp. in phr. *in denial* (orig. and chiefly *U.S.*). Cf. RESISTANCE *n.* 2 b.
    1914 A. A. BRILL tr. *Freud's Psychopathol. Everyday Life* vii. 149 Certain *denials* which we encounter in medical practice can probably be ascribed to *forgetting*. **1927** O. RANK in *Mental Hygiene* XI. 187 Freud is obliged to refer to special mechanisms, in particular the 'procedure of making a thing as if it had not happened'—a circumlocution by which he avoids using the simpler and more natural terms proposed by others. (For a long time I have used the term '*Verleugnung*', denial.) **1930** W. HEALY et al. *Struct. & Meaning Psychoanalysis* VII. 457 On the basis of his theory of 'denial', Rank demands that there be an emotional reproduction rather than intellectual recollection...The fact that denial has occurred is, he says, often more important than the content of the corresponding memory. **1950** R. P. BISSELL *Stretch on River* xxi. 207 It's a transferral of intent. It's a result of childhood trauma. It's Oedipus denial. **1959** *Jrnl. Personality* XXVII. 364 The opposite syndrome, composed of high Admission, low Denial, and high Anxiety scores describes the other end of the repression continuum. **1979** H. SEGAL *Klein* x. 127 The denial

of his mourning is also apparent in his running away. **1992** *Village Voice* (N.Y.) 8 Apr. 25/1 'You're living in denial. Abortion is killing your baby.' He sounds the prolifers' warning of never-ending guilt, as if morality were mere avoidance of pain.

dental, *a.* and *n.* Add: [A.] [1.] [c.] **dental hygiene**, the preservation or improvement of the health of the teeth and gums, esp. by care on the part of the individual concerned, such as regular brushing.
   1884 *Brit. Jrnl. Dental Sci.* XXVII. 649 Without straining a term we may include alike the criterion of health among dental practioners and the health condition of the dentists' rooms, under the heading Dental Hygiene. **1921** C. E. TURNER *Hygiene, Dental & General* viii. 155 The recent and rapid development of dental hygiene work among school children has created an opening for dental hygienists. **1992** T. F. WALSH et al. *Clin. Dental Hygiene* iv. 38 The most significant influence on dental hygiene will be the efforts that the patient makes at removing dental plaque deposits.
   dental hygienist, an ancillary dental worker specializing in dental hygiene, scaling and polishing of teeth, etc.
   1916 A. C. FONES (*title*) Mouth hygiene, a course of instruction for dental hygienists. **1920** *N.Y. Med. Jrnl.* 12 June 1025/2 Since the legalizing of dental hygienists by..the State of New York in 1916, Connecticut, Massachusetts, Iowa,..[etc.] have passed similar laws. **1943** *Evening News* 21 May 3/7 A new trade for the W.A.A.F.s is that of dental hygienist... Treatment by the hygienists includes scaling, polishing and cleaning of teeth. **1987** *N.Y. Times* 14 June VII. 14/3 Bartle..falls deeply in love with a young Jewish dental hygienist made pregnant by her employer.

derivative, *a.* and *n.* Add: [A.] **5.** *Engin.* Of, pertaining to, or designating a control element whose output is a linear function of the derivative (the rate of change) of its input.
   1944 E. S. SMITH *Automatic Control Engin.* v. 83 A rate, or derivative, component..is required for stability with some classes of systems in which the plant lags are consecutively compounded. **1946** *Mech. Engin.* LXVIII. 136/2 Derivative Action is that in which there is a predetermined relation between a derivative function of the controlled variable and position of a final control element. **1957** E. B. JONES *Instrument Technol.* III. II. 99 Derivative action may be added to proportional action or to proportional plus integral action by introducing a second restriction known as the 'derivative restriction' into the line connecting the nozzle to the proportioning bellows. **1981** P. W. MURRILL *Fund. Process Control Theory* v. 58 By adding derivative action to the controller, lead is added in the controller to compensate for lag around the loop.

desk-top, *n.* Add: [A.] **3.** *Computing.* The working area of a computer screen regarded as a representation of a notional desktop and containing icons representing items such as files and a waste bin, used analogously to the items they symbolize.
   1982 *Byte* Apr. 256/1 Every user's initial view of Star is the 'Desktop', which resembles the top of an office desk. *Ibid.* 256/3 You can move the icons around to arrange your Desktop as you wish. **1986** *PC Mag.* 25 Feb. 110/1 A shell that turns your display into a menu-oriented 'desktop' for selecting and running PC applications. **1990** *MacWeek* 24 Apr. 51/1 It lets you organize files by arranging icons inside windows or on the desktop, sorting alphabetically or chronologically. **1991** *Personal Computer World* Feb. 237/1 Windows on screen could not be overlapped, effectively removing the advantage of displaying several windows on the desktop.

destain, *v.*[1] (In *OED Additions Vol. 1*). Add: de'stained *ppl. a.*
   1930 *Stain Technol.* V. 137 In a perfectly destained slide, the cytoplasm should not show a bluish color. **1990** *Acta Cytologica* XXXIV. 670/1 Follow-up immunoperoxidase staining for Leu-M 1 was performed on a destained smear.

detritus, *n.* Add: **4.** *spec.* in *Ecol.* Non-living organic material, esp. as a source of nourishment. Freq. *attrib.*, esp. in *detritus-feeding*.
   1925 O. D. HUNT in *Jrnl. Marine Biol. Assoc.* XIII. 567 Those which feed by selecting from the surrounding water the suspended micro-organisms and detritus,..for want of a better term, may be termed Suspension-feeders. **1949** *New Biol.* VI. 17 The appearance of reeds..leads to large increases in the numbers of algæ and in the amount of organic detritus. **1959** *Ibid.* XXIX. 99 Others have used tubs containing water in which algae and small herbivorous and detritus-feeding animals succeeded one another. **1984** A. C. & A. DUXBURY *Introd. World's Oceans* xv. 481 (*caption*) The sea cucumbers feed on detritus suspended in the water. **1990** *Compl. Angler's Guide* Spring 6/1 Nymphs mostly live in or among the silt and bottom detritus.

deuteride ('dju:təraid), *n. Chem.* Also †deutride. [f. DEUTER(IUM *n.* + -IDE.] A binary compound of deuterium and a metal or radical.
   1934 *Nature* 31 Mar. 496/2 Investigations of the band spectra of other deutrides (BiD, HgD, etc.) now in progress in this laboratory. **1935** *Physical Rev.* XLVII. 27/1 The spectrum of calcium deuteride has been photographed at high dispersion with a Ca arc in an atmosphere of heavy hydrogen as a source. **1949** *Proc. Leeds Philos. & Lit. Soc.* (*Sci. Section*) V. 252 BD has zero valency, and must be excited before it can combine at all. This may possibly be associated with some anomalies connected with boron hydrides and deuterides. **1975** *Sci. Amer.* Oct. 111/1 The notion of substituting easy-to-handle lithium deuteride for the hard-to-handle liquid deuterium. **1989** *Nature* 12 Oct. 492/1 Titanium chips of technical purity were tested in conjunction with heavy water, deuterated polypropilenium..and lithium deuteride.

device, *n.* Add: [7.] **c.** orig., a detonating mechanism for an explosive; in extended use, any explosive or incendiary apparatus; *spec.* a nuclear bomb (in full, and more usually, *nuclear device*: see NUCLEAR *a.* 3 b.).
   1931 MUNRO & TIFFANY *Physical Testing Explosives* 2 Manufacturers' samples of permissible explosives or blasting devices... The manufacturer is required to proceed according to the schedule governing application for tests of a new explosion or a new blasting device. **1945** *Newsweek* 4 June 90 British fighter pilots ran into a new German weapon..a small glider with a bomb for a body. Directed by remote control from a launching plane, the device assumed attack position and hurtled itself at the target, where it exploded. **1954** *Life* 19 Apr. 21/1 Instead of a black and white shadow of the explosion, viewers saw in glaring redness the bulging fireball of the hydrogen device which vaporized Elugelab Island at Eniwetok on Nov. 1, 1952. **1957** *Wall St. Jrnl.* 25 Jan. 1/3 Only low-yield nuclear tests will be conducted at the Frenchman's Flat Proving Ground... The announcement added high-yield devices (hydrogen bombs) are never tested in Nevada. **1969** *N.Y. Times* 11 Nov. 1/7 The explosives, described by the Fire Department as devices 'that could cause extensive damage', injured at least one person. **1972** *Sci. Amer.* Dec. 13/3 China exploded a fission device in 1964 and a fusion device in 1967, and it has tested several hydrogen bombs since that date. **1973** *New Yorker* 13 Dec. 58/3 The word 'bomb' was almost never used [at Los Alamos]. A bomb was a 'device' or a 'gadget'. **1978** KOBETZ & COOPER *Target Terrorism* 97 Car bombings can be very spectacular and

especially frightening. The device is often constructed so as to explode when certain action‥is taken. **1981** *Washington Post* 3 Jan. A1/2 After sprinkling them with an unidentified liquid, an explosive charge was put on top of the human pile. The device detonated as planned. **1990** A. BEEVOR *Inside Brit. Army* (1991) xxiii. 377 The British sappers alone had dealt with over 600,000 mines, unexploded ordnance and other devices by mid-March.

dex ('dɛks), *n. slang* (orig. *U. S.*). [f. DEX(EDRINE *n.*] The drug Dexedrine; also, a Dexedrine tablet. Cf. *DEXIE *n.*

1961 T. I. RUBIN *In the Life* xv. 50 'Doc, do you think‥you could maybe give me something? You know, to kind of give me a lift?' 'Well, maybe a dex or something.' **1968** *Guardian* 21 Nov. 20/3 The pushers passing out bombers, meths, dexes, and blues. **1971** *Harper's* Sept. 63 Pops a dex or a bennie occasionally, especially during exam week. **1984** W. GIBSON *Neuromancer* I. i. 7 It was a flat pink octagon, a potent species of Brazilian dex he bought from one of Zone's girls.

dexie ('dɛksɪ), *n. slang* (orig. *U. S.*). Also **dexy**, and with cap. initial. [f. DEX(EDRINE *n.* + -IE.] A tablet of the drug Dexedrine (usu. in *pl.*); also, the drug itself. Cf. *DEX *n.*

1956 S. LONGSTREET *Real Jazz* xviii. 146 Of course, you can take bennies (Benzedrine) or dexies (Dexedrine), but they make me too nervous. **1960** WENTWORTH & FLEXNER *Dict. Amer. Slang* 145/2 *Dexie, dexy,*‥Dexedrine; Dexedrine tablets. *a***1969** J. KEROUAC *Visions of Cody* (1972) 106 Now I'm in Danny's music store, in a booth, just took dexy‥. Have fifty-five dollars‥and fifteen dexies. **1970** L. SANDERS *Anderson Tapes* xxvii. 79, I think he's on something. I'd guess Dexies. **1972** *N. Y. Times Bk. Rev.* 7 May 11. 1/1 Death (perhaps murder, possibly self-induced) after several months of taking 'Dexie', marijuana, 'copilots', LSD, heroin, everything. **1984** *Sounds* 29 Dec. 24/4 Contrary to what he tells us, he sounds like he's gobbled 100 Dexys in one go.

dialogue, *n.* Add: [4.] **dialogue box** *Computing*, a window produced by a system to elicit a response by the user, such as the choice of an option.

1984 *Electronics* 26 Jan. 149/2 Toolkit/32 is a generic application that shares the features of Lisa's user interface, including windows, menus, scrolling, printing, *dialog boxes, mouse, graphics, and cut-and-paste integration. **1992** *Personal Computer World* Mar. 255/2 The typestyle and point size are specified when text is typed into the text dialogue box.

diamond, *n.* Add: [III.] [12.] **diamond willow** *N. Amer.*, any of various willows, esp. *Salix bebbiana*, which have diamond-shaped depressions on the trunk as a result of fungal attack; the wood of any of these trees.

1884 C. S. SARGENT *Rep. Forests N. Amer.* (10th Census IX) 170 *Salix cordata*‥*Diamond willow. **1930** J. E. KIRKWOOD *N. Rocky Mt. Trees & Shrubs* 69 The Diamond Willow is reported on stream banks and wet places from Wyoming to the British possessions and west to California and Nevada. **1953** D. CUSHMAN *Stay away, Joe* iv. 49 Grandpere standing with his hands crossed over the knob of his diamond willow stick. **1971** *Islander* (Victoria, B.C.) 29 Aug. 12/1 The diamond willow‥is widely used on the prairies since it makes excellent material for fence posts.

didanosine (dɪ'dænəʊsiːn), *n. Pharm.* [f. *DIDE(OXY)NOSINE *n.*, with phonetic alteration.] = *2′,3′-dideoxyinosine* s.v. *DIDEOXYINOSINE *n.*

1990 *Rev. Infectious Dis.* XII. S523/1 A purine dideoxynucleoside, 2′,3′-dideoxyinosine (didanosine;

ddI)‥was observed to possess a number of‥properties that made it a suitable candidate for clinical testing. **1991** *New Scientist* 19 Oct. 15/1 The US and Canadian health authorities jointly approved a second AIDS drug, ddI or didanosine, last week. **1993** *Lancet* 2 Jan. 31/2 The commonest serious toxicity of didanosine is peripheral neuropathy.

didemnid (daɪ'dɛmnɪd), *n.* and *a. Zool.* [f. mod.L. family name *Didemnidae*, f. DI-² + Gr. δέμνιον bed: see -ID³.] **A.** *n.* An ascidian (sea squirt) of the family Didemnidae. **B.** *adj.* Of, pertaining to, or designating the family Didemnidae.

1893 *Funk's Stand. Dict.*, Didemnid, *n.* **1931** A. B. HASTINGS in *Sci. Rep. Gt. Barrier Reef Exped.* (Brit. Mus. (Nat. Hist.) IV. 94 The shore Didemnids of similar type have burr-like spicules. **1950** N. J. BERRILL *Tunicata* I. 115 Didemnid zooids are constricted by a narrow oesophageal neck into a thorax and abdomen. **1967** *Oceanogr. & Marine Biol.* V. 471 Among these one may mention‥the small didemnid ascidian *Diplosoma gelatinosum*. **1976** *Nature* 24 June 697/2 Algal cells found living inside the colonies of other didemnid ascidians at Enewetak Atoll, Marshall Islands, [etc.].

dideoxycytidine (ˌdaɪdɪɒksɪˈsaɪtɪdiːn), *n. Pharm.* [f. DI-² + DEOXY- + CYTIDINE *n.*] Either of two isomeric pyrimidine nucleoside analogues having the formula $C_9H_{13}N_3O_3$; *spec.* (in full *2′, 3′-dideoxycytidine*) a compound which inhibits the replication of certain viruses (including HIV) and has been used experimentally in the treatment of HIV infection. Abbrev. *ddc.*

1965 *Jrnl. Org. Chem.* XXX. 3068/1 Hydrogenation‥gave the desired 2′,5′-dideoxycytidine as the hydriodide salt. *Ibid.* 3069/1 A desirable derivative of 2′-deoxycytidine of potential biological significance is 2′,3′-dideoxycytidine. **1980** *Jrnl. Biol. Chem.* CCLV. 11850/2 Dideoxycytidine triphosphate‥is a potent inhibitor of DNA polymerases β and γ. **1988** *New Scientist* 21 Jan. 28/1 A preliminary trial of dideoxycytidine (ddC) in 20 patients with AIDS or severe disease caused by HIV infection. **1992** *Independent* 1 Feb. 6/4 There is a third anti-retroviral, DDC (dideoxycytidine), and now large-scale trials into combination therapy‥are under way.

dideoxyinosine (ˌdaɪdiːɒksɪˈɪnəʊsiːn), *n. Pharm.* [f. DI-² + DEOXY- + *INOSINE *n.*] Any of several isomeric purine nucleoside analogues which inhibit the replication of certain viruses; *spec.* (in full *2′,3′-dideoxyinosine*), one which has been used in the treatment of HIV infection.

1975 *Cancer Res.* XXXV. 1548/1, 2′,3′-Dideoxyinosine had absorbance maxima at 248nm (pH 2) and 254nm (pH 12). **1980** *Biochemistry* XIX. 105/1 Similar substrate activation occurred at high concentrations of the sugar-modified analogues 5′-deoxy- and 2′,5′-dideoxyinosine. **1989** *New England Jrnl. Med.* 23 Nov. 1478/1 Dideoxyinosine should be considered for development as an alternative to AZT in patients with impaired hematopoiesis. **1990** *New Scientist* 26 May 32 The start of Britain's trials of the AIDS drug dideoxyinosine (DDI) this week comes shortly after the publication‥of initial studies on the drug's safety. **1992** *Boston Globe* 26 July 6/3 Some newly approved drugs like dideoxyinosine, or DDI, work better in combination with the original standby, zidovudine, or AZT.

die, *v.* Add: [I.] [3.] **d.** *to die for*: (as if) worth dying for; superlatively good or highly desirable; extraordinary. Also *to die*, fabulous, astonishing. *colloq.* (orig. and chiefly *U. S.*).

1898 E. N. WESTCOTT *David Harum* xxiii. 209 Oh! and to 'top off' with, a mince-pie to die for. **1980** G. B. TRUDEAU (*title*) A tad overweight, but violet eyes to die for. **1982** A. MAUPIN *Further Tales of City* 96 The guy had this incredible loft..with neon tubing over the bed and high-tech everything..to die, right? **1986** *Philadelphia Inquirer* 11 July E3/2 The dark chocolate is to die for—it actually tastes dark. **1992** M. RIVA *Marlene Dietrich* 645 The things he said about Olivier..to die! **1993** *Face* Apr. 73/2 Lacroix and Lagerfeld remained the to-die-for labels.

digenean (daɪdʒə'niːən), *n.* and *a.* [f. mod.L. order name *Digenea* (coined by Gerstaecker & Carus, 1863, in *W. C. H. Peters' Handbuch d. Zool.* II. 478), f. Gr. δɩγενής (see DIGENEOUS *a.*): see -AN. Cf. F. *digenèse* (P.-J. Van Beneden 1858, in *Bull. de l'Acad. R. de Belgique* V. 581).] **A.** *n.* A trematode of the order Digenea, which comprises endoparasitic forms whose life cycle involves two or more host species (usually vertebrate and molluscan). **B.** *adj.* Of, pertaining to, or designating the order Digenea.
1963 *Jrnl. Marine Biol. Assoc.* XLIII. 119 The progressive decrease in numbers of introduced digeneans which survive is probably not due to the acquisition of an immunity by the host. **1966** *Parasitology* LVI. 753 Just investigations of the ultrastructure of digenean germinal sacs. **1972** D. A. ERASMUS *Biol. Trematodes* i. 13 The..information which is now available seems to support the basic divergence in life-histories evident between the monogeneans and the digeneans. **1987** LAVERACK & DANDO *Lect. Notes Invertebr. Zool.* (ed. 3) vi. 51/2 Haemoglobin has been reported in some digenean species but its role is not known. **1988** R. S. K. BARNES et al. *Invertebrates* iii. 86/1 The Schistosomatidae is a family of digeneans.

digital, *a.* and *n.* Add: [A.] [5.] c. *digital compression* (more fully *digital signal compression*), the compression of digitized audio or video signals so as to increase the amount of information that can be transmitted over a given route in a given time. Cf. *COMPRESSION *n.* 1 f.
1984 *Aviation Week* 24 Sept. 79/2 Driving such traffic volume through the available 500 MHz. of bandwidth each for broadcast and other more common transmission types such as telephony or data will be possible using digital signal compression, higher frequency bands, monolithic microwave integrated circuits and spacecraft technology. **1991** *Computerworld* 17 July 73/5 By the end of the '90s, digital signal compression will offer a great enough advantage, and cable and satellite transmission will be affordable enough that it will become cost-effective to transmit and locally decompress. **1990** *What Satellite* July 41/2 They're looking at the possibilities of getting a number of channels out of one transponder, by digital compression and splitting frequencies. **1993** *Coloradoan* (Fort Collins) 10 Jan. F5/1 Digital compression, the technology that makes the brave new world of television possible, increases the available number of channels by squeezing more information through the same conduit.
d. *digital compact cassette*, a format for tape cassettes similar to ordinary audio cassettes but with digital rather than analogue recording; a cassette in this format, abbrev. *DCC*.
1985 *Chicago Tribune* 6 Jan. XIII. 26/3 This state-of-the-art PCM/VCR combination may be supplanted in a year's time by digital compact cassettes. **1990** *Dallas Times Herald* 9 Oct. BI/5 Tandy is one of several companies teaming with Philips Consumer Electronics of Knoxvill, Tenn., to produce a 'Digital Compact Cassette' system that could play both specially designed digital tapes and standard cassette tapes. **1992** *Economist* 30 May 97/1 Sony is out to position the Mini Disc as a direct rival to the tape-based Digital Compact Cassette (DCC) recently announced by Matsushita and Philips.

digitization (ˌdɪdʒɪtaɪ'zeɪʃən), *n.* [f. DIGITIZE *v.* + -ATION.] = *DIGITALIZATION *n.*[2]
1961 *Proc. Internat. Conf. Instrumentation High-Energy Physics* 245 (*caption*) Digitization of a minimum track. **1975** *Proc. Conf. Computer Graphics* 21/1 Experience with this scan system has also led to strong interest in the advantages for interactive graphics..of the digitization and efficient storage of scanned pictures. **1987** *Electronics & Wireless World* Jan. 54/2 Data is exchanged between the digitization unit and computer memory via the 1MHz bus.

Dilantin (daɪ'læntɪn), *n. Pharm.* [f. DI-[2] + -l- + *hyd*)*ant*(*o*)*ïn* n. s.v. HYDANTOIC *a.*] A proprietary name in the U.S. for phenytoin.
1938 *Official Gaz.* (U.S. Patent Office) 24 May 741/1 *Dilantin.* For preparation intended for the treatment of spasmodic and convulsive conditions. **1952** *Brit. Jrnl. Psychol.* XLIII. 85 Phenytoin sodium or sodium diphenylhydantoinate; also known, in the U.S.A., as dilantin sodium or dilantin. **1977** F. SOYKA *Ion Effect* ii. 14 Doctors control these aberrant brain waves with the drug dilantin or DPH. **1979** R. JAFFE *Class Reunion* I. ix. 95 Time to get to the pharmacy.., fill her prescriptions for Dilantin and Tridione.

dino ('daɪnəʊ), *n. colloq.* Pl. **dinos**, (rarely) **dinoes**. [Abbrev.] A dinosaur. Freq. used *attrib.*
1936 F. CLUNE *Roaming round Darling* xxiv. 250 Hanging near a window..was the petrified rib of a rhoetosaurus dinosaur...Mrs Finn told us that dinoes used to patronize the mud baths of Central Australia, but that this particular one hadn't touched water for thousands of years. **1981** *Washington Post* 4 Dec. (Weekend section) 5/3 Clips from 'One Million Years, B.C.', 'The Land Time Forgot', and other dino classics show how Hollywood brought beast and man together, despite the 60-million-year gap between the former's extinction and the latter's evolution. **1987** *Courier-Mail* (Brisbane) 21 Feb. 24/3 They have also used the hysterically bad footage from the film *Caveman*, which shows Ringo Starr saving Shelley Long from the jaws of a vile dino by feeding it an intoxicating herb. **1990** *Sci. Amer.* Dec. 100/1 Illustrated chapters recount dino classification and dino biology, summarize museums and finds worldwide, and present a long list of dinosaurologists by name and accomplishment. **1994** K. KELLY *Out of Control* xvi. 312 The absolutely neat thing about the dinosaurs in the movie *Jurassic Park* is that they possess enough artificial life so that they can be reused as cartoon dinos in a Flintstones movie.

dino- ('daɪnəʊ), *comb. form.* [Shortened form of DINOSAUR *n.*: cf. *DINO *n.*] **a.** Prefixed to nouns forming chiefly nonce-words relating to dinosaurs, as *dinomania* (also *-maniac*).
1986 *Times* 19 May 5/4 It [*sc.* a mechanical replica of a pterodactyl] plummeted to earth, much as the flying lizards are thought to have done 65 million years ago...Onlookers quickly called [it] the 'dinoflop'. **1987** *St. Petersburg* (Florida) *Times* 23 May 1B/4 To some extent, the museum has been hit with Dino-mania. In one viewing room is Dinosaurs—The Video. Near the regular gift shop is the Dino-store. **1990** *Times* 3 July 13/6 Homo consumerus took to the cuddly dinosaur with a vengeance, leaving a deposit of inflatable stegosaurs, dinosaur soap, lunch boxes, dino-burgers and robotic dino-roadshows. **1991** *New Scientist* 30 Nov. 50/4 Illustrations [of dinosaurs] are of a good standard...Dinomaniacs can have fun trying to identify the various sources of inspiration. **1991** *Discover* (U.S.) Mar. 2/2 (*caption*) New fossil evidence suggests that 130 million years ago Earth was ruled not by thundering stegosaurs and tree-munching brontosaurs but by curious dino-midgets, some no bigger than a pigeon. **1993** *Daily Tel.* 10 June 19/2 Dinosaurs are being offered stuffed, painted on lip balm or charging around in Nintendo video games. McDonald's is dishing up dinofries and brontosaurus burgers.

b. Special Comb. **dinoturbation** *Palaeont.* and *Geol.* [*-turbation* after *BIOTURBATION *n.*, *cryoturbation* s.v CRYO-], the disturbance of layers of sediment by dinosaur trampling; the effects of this process on the formation of sedimentary rock.

1980 P. DODSON et al. in *Paleobiol.* VI. 229/1 We believe that trampling by large dinosaurs ('*dinoturbation') may have had an impact on both the sediments and remains of the small biota. **1986** *Nature* 19 June 732/3 A brontosaur trampled across a collection of living unionid clams in shallow water and preserved them for posterity in the base of the huge footprints, a sedimentological phenomenon termed dinoturbation. **1989** *Sci. Amer.* Sept. 133/2 Many sites show dinosaur trampling that is dense enough to disturb the sedimentary layers themselves. There is a name for this process: dinoturbation.

diode, *a.* and *n.* Add: [B.] **c.** Special Comb. **diode-transistor logic** *n. Electronics*, logic in which diodes rather than resistors form the coupling elements between transistors.

[**1957** *Wescon Convention Rec. IRE* II. 3 Both of these designs can be derived . . by the substitution of diode-transistor logical equivalents for the series and parallel combinations of transistors of DCTL. **1959** *Ann. Computation Lab. Harvard Univ.* XXX. 170 A type of transistor-diode logic circuit design.] **1960** *IRE Trans. Electronic Computers* IX. 16/2 Resistor-transistor logic, though simple and reliable in a component sense, is slower than *diode-transistor logic. **1987** MILLMAN & GRABEL *Microelectronics* (ed. 2) vi. 219 This gate realization is called diode-transistor logic (DTL) and was one of the early semiconductor logic families developed.

disc, *n.* Add: [8.] [f.] **disc camera**, a camera in which the image is formed on a disc rather than a roll of film.

1973 D. A. SPENCER *Focal Dict. Photogr. Technol.* 168 *Disc camera, high speed camera making records from cathode ray tubes as concentric traces on a disc of film rotating at up to 12,000 revs/sec. **1983** *Wall St. Jrnl.* 5 Jan. 4/1 Despite gratifying sales of Kodak disk camera products and sharp increases in copier product revenue, overall Kodak results continue to be inhibited. **1991** *Photographer* Aug. 10/2 Today's ISO 200 colour negative films were devised *originally* for disc cameras with a fixed exposure.

disconnect, *v.* Add: Hence **disco'nnectable** *a.*, capable of being disconnected.

1967 W. OLIVER in J. D. Lenk *Applications Handbk. Electr. Connectors* (Introd. for Eng. readers), Detachable or disconnectable connectors. **1978** *Nature* 6 Apr. 519/2 The electrical demand for space and water heating could be met by wind power generation by providing a form of heat store on the consumers' premises . . and making the storage heating load disconnectable from the electricity supply system. **1987** *Offshore* Feb. 43/2 The disconnectable articulated riser turret (DART) mooring concept also incorporates a rigid extension integrated into the bow or stern of the vessel.

dish, *n.* Add: [I.] [4.] [b.] *spec.* one used as a receiving aerial for the domestic reception of satellite television; a satellite dish. (Later examples.)

1980 *New Scientist* 28 Feb. 645/1 Even a dish of just under a metre in diameter, as proposed for domestic receiving installations, has such a tight beam that the dish must be aimed at the satellite to an accuracy of within half a degree. **1982** *Ibid.* 2 Sept. 633/1 The satellite will be one of the first in the world to offer TV to viewers equipped with the necessary 'dishes'.

[10.] **dish aerial** = sense *4 b above.

1962 *Listener* 19 July 112/1 A *dish aerial at Goonhilly Down. **1982** *New Scientist* 24 June 840/2 Many

proponents of satellite broadcasting put about the story that, in the future, people will have satellite dish aerials in their gardens, balanced on their roofs or attached to a wall. **1991** *Computing* 10 Jan. 76/1 A dirty great 100 ft. radio mast, replete with large dish aerials, on top of Trundle Hill.

division, *n.* Add: [III.] [12.] **division sign** *Math.*, the symbol ÷, placed between two quantities to indicate that the former is to be divided by the latter.

[**1845** *Encycl. Metrop.* I. 483/1, ÷ *by*, the sign of division.] **1934** WEBSTER s.v. *Division*, The sign ÷, *division sign or mark, placed between numerical expressions indicates [etc.]. **1957** *Encycl. Brit.* XV. 76/1 The division sign (÷) used in Great Britain and in the United States comes from an algebra written by Johann H. Rahn.

DNA, *n.* Add: [2.] [a.] **DNA fingerprint**, a genetic fingerprint involving the characterization of DNA; *spec.* one obtained by DNA fingerprinting.

1969 *Jrnl. Molecular Biol.* XLIII. 611 In the *DNA fingerprints, however, every spot consisted of a mixture of several isomers. **1978** *Chromosoma* LXVI. 9 That they were related but not identical was deduced from DNA 'fingerprint' studies. **1988** *Mouse News Let.* Nov. 124 Inbred strains of mice have less complex DNA fingerprints than wild mice. **1995** *Daily Express* 17 Mar. 17/3 Each suspect's sample will be checked against 'DNA fingerprints' left behind during every outstanding crime in the country.

DNA profile, a distinctive pattern obtained by analysis of the DNA of an individual or organism; *spec.* = *DNA fingerprint above.

1971 *Arch. für Mikrobiol.* LXXVIII. 252 (*title*) *DNA profile of the spore of *Blastocladiella emersonii*. **1976** *Acta Path. et Microbiol. Scand.* A. LXXXIV. 461/2 In all cases of malignant tumour, the DNA profile was abnormal. **1988** *Daily Tel.* 31 Dec. 4/8 Mr Gale says that it would not be difficult for everyone's DNA profile to be put on their medical record. **1992** *Police Rev.* 17 Jan. 100/2 Mr Williams was eliminated from the inquiry, but his DNA profile was stored on a database.

DNA profiling = **DNA fingerprinting*.

1988 *Evidence: Blood Group Tests, DNA Tests & related matters* (Scottish Law Commission Discussion paper no. 80) iii. 32 The court should have power to order samples of blood or other matter to be taken from a person's body for the purpose of blood group tests, *DNA profiling or other procedures. **1990** *Sci. Amer.* May 18/3 DNA profiling, a recent technique that in theory can identify an individual from his or her DNA with a high degree of certainty.

doctor, *n.* Add: [6.] **e.** *Doctor Feelgood* (usu. written as *Dr.*), a physician who readily prescribes mood-enhancing drugs, such as amphetamines, esp. for non-medicinal use; hence, any doctor who provides short-term palliatives rather than a more effective treatment or cure; also *transf.* and *attrib.*

The term seems to have been first used as a simple self-designation (without any of the later negative connotations) by the blues pianist 'Piano Red' (William Perryman) who broadcast, and subsequently recorded, under this sobriquet. The words of the 1967 hit song which popularized the phrase do, however, suggest awareness of the sense described above.

[**1962** 'PIANO RED' (*title of record*) Dr. Feelgood and the Interns.] **1967** A. FRANKLIN & T. WHITE in *Doctor Feelgood* (song) Don't send me no doctor Filling me up with all those pills Got a man named Dr. Feelgood That man takes care of all of my pains and my ills. **1967** J. KRAMER *Instant Replay* (1968) 40 Ever since then, we've called him 'Doctor Feelgood'. **1973** *Oui* Apr. 55 Dr. Feelgood used to shoot Duke What's-His-Name in the ass every week or so with a nice mixture of speed

and vitamins. **1975** *Business Week* (Industr. ed.) 24
Nov. 12/2 [There are those] who treat the famous, and
those who are famous because they treat disease better
than other doctors. Among the former, you might find
the Dr. Feelgoods and the Marcus Welby types who
offer concern and gentle bedside manners at very high
prices. **1978** *Time* 9 Oct. 45/1 The Carter
Administration has responded with a Dr. Feelgood
litany that the dollar's health is sound . . . But the world's
money traders are not buying that happy talk. **1981**
Washington Post 14 Aug. A29/5 We have here a problem
that Ronald Reagan is peculiarly suited to address. He
is no phony Dr. Feelgood. He is the Real Stuff. **1986**
S. CHURCHER *N.Y. Confidential* xii. 288 What you need
is a Dr. Feelgood. Most of the physicians who provide
rejuvenating blasts of dope to rich New Yorkers use
amphetamines. **1992** M. LEYNER *Et Tu, Babe* (1993)
v. 100 Wachtel was one of the White House 'Dr.
Feelgoods' who pumped JFK full of speed every day.

Donau ('dɒnaʊ), *n. Geol.* [The German name
of the river Danube, adopted in this sense by
B. Eberl 1928, in *Zeitschr. der deutschen geol.
Gesellschaft B: Monatsber.* LXXX. 112.] Used
attrib. to designate an early Pleistocene
glaciation of the Alps (preceding the Günz),
and the corresponding stratigraphic stage. Also
absol.

1957 *Geol. en Mijnbouw* XIX. 243/1 The phases
Donau II, Günz I and Günz III are likely to represent
glacials. **1965** A. HOLMES *Princ. Physical Geol.* (ed. 2)
xxi. 681 A fifth glacial stage, older than the Gunz,
has since been discovered and is called the Donau or
Danube. **1983** T. NILSSON *Pleistocene* v. 75 There
seems to be no record of a clear fossil soil corresponding
to the Biber/Donau interval. According to Graul, the
most sizable palaeosols observed disconnect the Donau
and Günz deposits.

dyad, *n.* Add: [**2.**] **e.** *Anat.* A structure found
in vertebrate cardiac muscle and some insect
muscle, consisting of a transverse tubule in
contact with a terminal cisterna of the
sarcoplasmic reticulum.

1957 PORTER & PALADE in *Jrnl. Biophysical &
Biochem. Cytol.* III. 286 Within the area enclosed by
the arms of the U there may be an additional circular
or oval profile which in some instances is continuous
with the inner surface of the U-shaped element . . . This
unit of two components will be referred to as a
dyad. **1964** *Jrnl. Cell Biol.* XXII. 694/1 In cardiac
muscle and in certain insect muscles the homologue of
the triad is to be found in the dyad. **1984** J. F. LAMB
et al. *Essent. Physiol.* (ed. 2) iii. 59 The T system opens
to the extracellular space and is related to the SR
[*sc.* sarcoplasmic reticulum] via a series of flattened
membranous sacs (dyads).

E

eco-, *comb. form.* Add: **eco-'terrorism**, violence carried out to further environmentalist ends; also, politically motivated damage to the natural environment.

1990 A. TOFFLER *Powershift* v. 377 A second wing [of an environmental pressure group] .. might well step up from eco-vandalism to full-scale *eco-terrorism to enforce its demands. **1991** *Time* 27 May 50/2 Saddam's eco-terrorism raised the amount of carbon dioxide that humans are pumping into the atmosphere by up to 2%. **1992** *New Scientist* 25 Apr. 8/1 (*caption*) The Earth Observation Satellite Corporation, which operates the Landsat satellites, has released these infrared images showing the extent of the world's worst act of ecoterrorism.

eco-'terrorist, one who participates in or supports eco-terrorism.

1988 *Arena* Autumn/Winter 35 He came up with the idea for *Tourist Season*, the story of *eco-terrorists taking on the grossness of the tourist trade. **1993** *Coloradoan* (Fort Collins) 16 Jan. A9/5 Hagar's group flooded the local media with ads deriding the wolf supporters as 'eco-terrorists' who are pouring into this frigid subarctic settlement from 'the outside'.

‖**e contra** (eɪ 'kɒntrɑ:), *adv. phr.* [Late L. (also as one word, *econtra*).] **a.** Conversely; vice versa.

?**1550** tr. *Vigo's Lytell Practyce* sig. Biiiv, Take powdre of Osmonde, and of the roote of Pyeny for the man the male, & for the woman E contra, and the powdre of Mortegon. **1621** R. BURTON *Anat. Melancholy* III. ii. 653 He loves her most impotently, shee loues not him, and so *è contra*. *a*1680 T. GOODWIN *Wks.* (1681) I. 201 All Salvation hath a Life supposed to be saved, but not *è contrà*; the Angels live, yet are not said to be saved. **1727** *Cowell's Interpr.* sig. Ggi/1 Where the Men hock the Women on Monday, and e contra on Tuesday.

b. In the opposite direction; from the opposite side.

1782 J. ADAMS *Diary* 18 Oct. (1961) III. 29 Doors through which Men pass from the Canal, under the Street into the Cellars of the Houses and e contra from the Cellars to the Canal.

c. *Logic* and (esp. *U. S.*) *Law.* On the contrary, on the other hand; in return.

1843 J. S. MILL *Syst. Logic* II. III. xx. 100 If .. every resemblance proved between B and A, in any point not known to be immaterial with respect to *m*, forms some additional reason for presuming that B has the attribute *m*; it is clear, *è contra*, that every dissimilarity which can be proved between them, furnishes a counter-probability of the same nature on the other side. **1936** *Atlantic Reporter* CLXXXI. 320/1 When the factual issues, real or claimed, are submitted to a jury for determination, such an assignment does not point to a reviewable judicial ruling in a matter of law; e contra, it does when the trial judge determines the issues without a jury. **1947** *U.S. Tax Court Rep.* IX. 502 This fact reduced petitioner's costs. E contra, had adequate recognition been given to this fact, petitioner's proper costs would have been greater.

‖**e contrario** (eɪ kɒn'trɑ:rɪəʊ), *adv. phr.* Chiefly *Logic* and *Law.* Also **a contrario**. [L.] **a.** From a contrary position (esp. in argument); in opposition; by dint of opposition or antagonism.

1602 W. WATSON *Decacordon* 164 We were never made acquainted therewith, hauing *è contrario* formerly imparted our minds vnto them, &c. vnlawfully

confirmed. **1957** H. F. JOLOWICZ *Roman Found. Mod. Law* ii. 18 It is also subject to the argument *e contrario*. Words expressly applying a rule to one case may be held impliedly to exclude it in others. **1970** B. BREWSTER tr. *Althusser & Balibar's Reading Capital* II. i. 76 We can convince ourselves that this double reading is indispensable *a contrario* too, by the difficulties and misconstructions that simple immediate readings of *Capital* have produced in the past. **1989** C. BERNHEIMER *Figures of Ill Repute* vii. 209 Proudhon is responsible *a contrario* for giving the feminist movement in France .. a new lease on life. His misogynist rantings stimulated in response some of the strongest feminist writing to be published in the early 1860's.

b. Conversely; vice versa. Cf. *E CONTRA *adv. phr.* a.

1895 *U.S. Supreme Court Rep.* XXXIX. 368/1 Upon their answer he will say, then it is for the defendant, though they find for the plaintiff, or *e contrario*, and thereupon they rectify their verdict. **1934** WEBSTER *Add.*, A contrario. **1947** *Federal Suppl.* LXXI. 992/1 Just as a magazine meant for sale as an independent publication cannot acquire the status of a newspaper part simply by being folded with the news section of a newspaper, so e contrario, a comic supplement is not deprived of its character as part of a newspaper simply because it is not yet placed in physical contiguity with the rest of its fellow parts. **1980** *Sci. Amer.* May 8/3 It is based on no a priori assumption whatsoever since it is constructed as a theorem, more precisely as a proof *a contrario*.

edutainment (ɛdjuːˈteɪnmənt), *n.* orig. and chiefly *U. S.* [f. EDU(CATION *n.* + ENTER)TAINMENT *n.*, after *DOCUTAINMENT *n.*, *INFOTAINMENT *n.*] An activity or product (esp. in the electronic media) intended to be educational as well as enjoyable; informative entertainment. Freq. *attrib.*

1983 *Fortune* 2 May 164/3 Software specialists believe that the greatest growth may come from so-called 'edutainment' games that attempt to make learning fun. **1985** *Ibid.* 28 Dec. 75/3 A former Long Island, New York, schoolteacher, Tessler calls his stores 'edutainment' centers. They are profit centers too. He charges $2.75 an hour for the baby-sitting. **1990** *New Scientist* 20 Jan. 66/3 A video loop .. had been so cleverly put together that it caught the attention of both mother and son ... Thanks to bang-up-to-date electronic wizardry, this [museum] promises to break new grounds in hands-on edutainment. **1991** L. PARKER *House Niggas* (song) in L. A. Stanley *Rap: the Lyrics* (1992) 40 In the face of intelligence, ignorance dies Dear, it's simple edutainment Rap needed a teacher, so I became it. **1991** H. RHEINGOLD *Virtual Reality* (1992) xiii. 288 The unlikely but actual Nintendo-Media Lab partnership will pop up again in the realm of VR 'edutainment', a critically important cousin of cyberspace amusements. **1992** *N. Y. Times* 15 Dec. C15/2 Everbright recently became a label of Epyx, the longtime computer game developer. Bible Builder is described as the alliance's first 'edutainment' title.

eight hundred number (eɪt 'hʌndrəd nʌmbə(r)), *n. U. S.* Usu. written **800 number**. [f. EIGHT *a.* & *n.* + HUNDRED *n.* & *a.* + NUMBER *n.*] A U.S. telephone number with the prefix *800* which allows customers to call a business or information service without charge to themselves. Cf. *0800 number* s.v. *O n.*[1] 4; TOLL-FREE *a.* b.

1976 *Harvard Business Rev.* Sept.–Oct. 72/2 With the availability of Wide Area Telephone Service (WATS lines), FX calls, 800-numbers (inbound WATS), and declining long-distance telephone charges, telephone selling that is organized with production-line rationality has become a major means for the industrialization of various kinds of selling and sales-related communications. **1980** *N.Y. Times* 28 Dec. III. 1/3 Comdata, for example, would not have been possible before the advent of toll-free, long-distance calls through an 800 number, and before computers could instantaneously pluck one individual's checking account or credit line from millions of others. **1991** *OnSat* 24 Mar. 8/2 In the spring of 1991, Toshiba will begin shipping an upgraded version of the TRX-2000 IRD that will feature built-in impulse pay-per-view (PPV) with Super Video outputs and will gain this PPV capability through the addition of a modem-on-module (MOM) thereby eliminating the necessity of calling an 800 number to order a PPV event. **1992** *Newsweek* (Election Issue) Nov./Dec. 36/2 Clinton bought two 30-minute segments of TV time for electronic town meetings, answering questions from callers. He also set up an 800 number manned and womaned by friends from Arkansas who explained him to doubters.

electro-, *comb. form.* Add: [a.] **e‚lectrony'stagmogram** *n.*, an image obtained by electronystagmography.

  1967 *Acta Oto-Laryngol.* Suppl. CCXXIV. 391 We were unable to show that enucleation of one eye produced any significant changes in the *electronystagmo*gram. **1993** *Clin. Electroencephalogr.* XXIV. 151/1 For many years the main clinical test of vestibular function has been the electronystagmogram.

  e‚lectronystag'mography *n.* *Med.*, the electroencephalographic recording of eye movement, as a diagnostic and evaluative tool.

  1929 I. L. MEYERS in *Arch. Neurol. & Psychiatry* XXI. 901 (*heading*) *Electronystagmography. A graphic study of the action currents in nystagmus. **1964** *Trans. Ophthalm. Soc.* LXXXIII. 531 (*heading*) Electronystagmography and its uses in the study of spontaneous nystagmus. **1975** *Year Bk. Ear, Nose & Throat* 22 Eye movements were recorded by electronystagmography. **1989** *Clin. Otolaryngol.* XIV. 343/1 Electronystagmography (ENG), the method differing considerably between laboratories, has been widely used in the examination of dizzy patients since the 1950s.

  hence **e‚lectronystagmo'graphic** *a.*; **e‚lectronystagmo'graphically** *adv.*

  1964 *Trans. Ophthalm. Soc.* LXXXIII. 555 *Electronystagmographic findings. **1975** *Year Bk. Ear, Nose & Throat* 21 Nystagmus was recorded *electronystagmographically with the patient supine and in both lateral positions.

Elster ('ɛlstə(r)), *n.* *Geol.* [The name of a tributary of the River Elbe in Germany.] Used *attrib.* to designate a Pleistocene glaciation in northern Europe preceding the Saale, and the corresponding stratigraphic stage. Also *absol.*

  1934 R. A. DALY *Changing World of Ice Age* i. 29 Recently four Glacial stages have been traced in Germany. Figure 19 shows the nested moraines of three, named in order of decreasing age, Elster, Saale, and Weichsel. **1937** W. B. WRIGHT *Quaternary Ice Age* (ed. 2) x. 134 The Elster Glaciation is recognised to have been the most extensive except around Görlitz in Silesia, where the Saale Glaciation probably overstepped its margin. **1950** *Nature* 24 June 1002/1 Between the Elster and the Saale glaciation there is intercalated the transgression of the so-called 'Holstein Sea'. **1965** A. HOLMES *Princ. Physical Geol.* (ed. 2) xxi. 690 (*caption*) The Elster front was overrun by the Saale in the Netherlands. **1983** T. NILSSON *Pleistocene* x. 138 A potential 'Interglacial IV' has been added to

the Dutch system of warm stages predating the classical Elster Glacial Stage.

  Hence **El'sterian** *a.*

  1969 BENNISON & WRIGHT *Geol. Hist. Brit. Isles* xvi. 355 It was not until Elsterian times that ice from centres spread outwards into the lowlands of Scotland, northern England . . and East Anglia. **1975** *Nature* 10 Jan. 96/1 The faunas of the Calcareous Group and the Rodent Earth correlate well with the European sites at Mosbach, Mauer, Hundsheim and Tarkö, which are usually considered to be between Cromerian (*sensu stricto*) and Elsterian in age.

e-mail ('iːmeɪl), *v.* *Computing.* Also **E-mail**, **email**. [f. EMAIL *n.*[2]] *trans.* To send by electronic mail; to communicate with (a person) by electronic mail. Also *intr.*, to establish contact by electronic mail.

  1987 *Whole Earth Rev.* Spring 124/1 Articles . . become files, which are then transferred . . to my Ohio office via electronic mail on the GEnie computer network (this article, however, was e-mailed through The WELL). **1990** *Pract. Computing* Sept. 35 (*caption*) Written or typed comments can be added, and the document then processed via Freestyle's icon-based desktop . . and emailed to other network users. **1993** *Unix Rev.* Mar. 28/3 (*Advt.*), Call, fax or email for a free demo. **1994** *Loaded* Sept. 111/1 For Sonic Youth we would first e-mail them at SERV@CORNELL.EDU. **1995** T. CLANCY *Op-Center* xx. 93 The ex-FBI agent went to the computer on the other side of the room and began E-mailing his sources in Asia and Europe.

emalangeni *n. pl.*: pl. of *LILANGENI *n.*

environmental, *a.* Add: [2.] **environmental audit**, an assessment of business activity as regards its observance of practices which seek to minimize harm to the environment (cf. *green audit* s.v. *GREEN *a.* 13 a).

  1971 *College & Univ. Business* Oct. 49 (*heading*) *Environmental audit uncovered pollution no one knew was there. **1981** *Chem. Engin.* 15 June 101/1 Many corporations are demanding environmental audits as a prerequisite to real estate transactions. **1990** *Managing Environment* (Business International Ltd.) vii. 96 The essential purpose of an environmental audit . . is the systematic scrutiny of environmental performance *throughout* a company's existing operations.

erub *n.*, var. *ERUV *n.*

eruv ('ɛrʊv), *n.* Also 8 **eyeruv**, 9- **erub**. Pl. **eruvin**, **erubim**, **eruvs**, and varr. [ad. Heb. *'ērūb.* f. root *'rb* mixture (because the concept implies the mixing of public and private).] Any of various symbolic arrangements which extend the private domain of Jewish households into public areas, thereby permitting activities in them that are normally forbidden in public on the Sabbath; *spec.* an urban area within which such an arrangement obtains, and which is symbolically enclosed by a wire boundary.

  1718 W. WOTTON *Eruvin* in *Misc. Discourses* II. 159 The name of this *Title* is *Eruvin*, in *English Mixtures*; and it treats of those *Mixtures* which are directed to be made upon the *Eve of the Sabbath*, by means of which several Families that inhabit in the same common Passages . . may lawfully carry into each others Houses, such things as may lawfully be removed upon the Sabbath-Day. *c*1782 D. LEVI *Succinct Acct. Rites, & Ceremonies, of Jews* 288 *Eyeruvin*, i.e. mixtures or associations, this treats of the mixing for courts and entries, which are called associatious [*sic*]; because thereby *all* the inhabitants of the court, or entry where the mixture is made, are accounted as belonging to one family; and, are therefore allowed to carry victuals from one house to the other. It also treats of the mixtures of a Sabbatic journey. **1843** DE SOLA & RAPHALL tr. *Mishna* XIII. ix. 92 R. Jehudah further said, 'It is lawful to combine, by [means of] erub, an alley that is open at both ends.' **1903** *Jewish Encycl.* V. 204/1 To modify the inconvenient consequences of the Law the 'erub was introduced, which..converted an open space into an enclosed one...Such completion may be noticed in some ancient towns and villages in which there is a Jewish congregation, at the ends of streets leading out of the place; and it is known by the name of "erub'. **1963** S. STEIMAN *Custom & Survival* viii. 86 An annual *Eruv* was established on the eve of Passover, but the Maharil meticulously set up an *Eruv* for the city of Mainz every Friday. **1971** *Encycl. Judaica* VI. 849 The accepted practice among Jewish communities for generations has been to erect..an *eruv* by connecting poles..with iron wires. **1993** *Independent on Sunday* 21 Feb. 4/2 Planning consent is crucial to the 'gaps' in the *eruv*, mainly roads that must be spanned by 'gateways'. Hence the poles and wires.

escape, *n.*[1] Add: [8.] **escape sequence** *Computing*, an escape code consisting of a sequence of characters.
1975 *Code Extension Techniques 7-Bit Coded Character Set* (Amer. Nat. Stand. Inst.) 11/2 *Escape sequences provide single or sets of control functions other than for transmission control. Escape sequences are also used to designate sets of graphics, different uses of some or all of the 7-bit code combinations, and coded character sets. **1982** *Byte* Apr. 298/2 Searching for a metacharacter itself requires using an 'escape sequence' (pressing a series of keys to escape from one mode of operation to another), a concept beginners find hard to grasp.

Essex, *n.* Add: **2. Special Combs. Essex girl** *Brit. derog.* [after *Essex man* below], a contemptuous term applied (usu. *joc.*) to a type of young woman, supposedly to be found in and around Essex, and variously characterized as unintelligent, promiscuous, and materialistic.
1991 'R. LEIGH' & 'B. WOOD' *Essex Girl Joke Bk.* Foreword, *Essex girls have been with us since Roman times. Perhaps the most famous was Boadicea...This *meisterwork* [*sic*], drawing on both legend and contemporary reality, faithfully records the language, philosophy and iconography of Essex girl. **1991** *Independent* 1 Nov. 3/1 How does an Essex Girl turn on the light afterwards? She kicks open the car door...Essex Girl jokes are told on the radio; they are faxed around between offices. **1992** *Pract. Fishkeeping* Apr. 142 It was soon obvious I had a blue-green algae problem. The stuff spreads faster than an Essex girl joke in a bar full of salesmen. **1993** *Independent* 26 Mar. 22/6 You can parade in shiny and pricey skin-tight leggings. The look can be jazzed up with Essex-girl gold jewellery for weekends.
Essex man *Brit. derog.*, a term used to denote a supposed new type of Conservative voter, to be found esp. in London and the south-east of England in the late 1980s, typically (esp. contemptuously) characterized as a brash, self-made young businessman who benefited from the entrepreneurial wealth created by Thatcherite policies: cf. SELSDON MAN *n.*
1990 *Sunday Tel.* 7 Oct. 23/1 The mass of the tribe has changed: the life and soul of the new Conservative Party, and the bedrock of its support, is *Essex man. *Ibid.*, Essex man does not exclusively live in Essex; for spiritual purposes, Essex is to be found all over the newly affluent parts of the outer London suburbs. **1991** *Times* 23 Nov. (Sat. Rev.) 52/2 He belongs to the Thatcher era, Essex Man without the boorishness or conspicuous displays of self-earned money. **1992** *New Statesman & Society* 17 Apr. 22/3 The race is on to see which party adopts that credo as its own. Don't worry. Enough Essex men and women will vote for it when it's on offer. **1994** *Guardian* 11

Jan. 1. 16/8 Essex Man has returned to his two-up two-down in Billericay and loadsamoney has been silenced under loadsadebts.

estuary *n.* Add: **6. Special Comb. Estuary English**, a term applied (with reference to the estuary of the River Thames) to a type of accent identified as spreading outwards from London, mainly into the south-east of England, and containing features of both received pronunciation and such regional accents as Cockney.
1984 D. ROSEWARNE in *Times Educ. Suppl.* 19 Oct. 29/1 What I have chosen to term *Estuary English* may now and for the forseeable future, be the strongest native influence upon RP. 'Estuary English' is a variety of modified regional speech...'Estuary English' is a mixture of 'London' and General RP forms. **1993** *Sunday Times* 14 Mar. 1/8 It is the classless dialect sweeping southern Britain. Estuary English, the 'high cockney' diction typified by Ken Livingstone, Nigel Kennedy and Lord Tebbit, has taken such a hold on the way millions speak that it could become the standard spoken English of the future. **1993** *New Musical Express* 8 May 24/1 With his hangdog expression and deadpan Estuary English patter, rock telly's most unlikely host not only presents *Later* but..arranges many ground-breaking musical collaborations.

ethosuximide (eθəʊˈsʌksɪmaɪd), *n. Pharm.* [f. ETH- + -O[1] + *suximide* (phonetically altered and shortened form of SUCCINIMIDE *n.*).] An anticonvulsant drug, 3,3-ethylsuccinimide, $C_7H_{11}NO_2$, which is given orally to suppress petit mal and other seizures.
1962 *Drugs of Choice 1962–1963* xvi. 269/2 The latest succinimide compound available, ethosuximide, is also said to have a high therapeutic index in petit mal seizures. **1977** *Lancet* 3 Sept. 509/2 We gave propoxyphene hydrochloride capsules 65 mg three times a day to seven outpatients, six with epilepsy and one with trigeminal neuralgia who had been treated with carbamazepine alone or in combination with phenobarbitone, clonazepam or ethosuximide. **1982** *Chemical Week* 15 Sept. 43/2 The Washington University group claims that the new anticonvulsants work differently than ethosuximides and pentylenetetrazoles, two classes of drugs now used to prevent seizures.

Euro-, *comb. form.* Add: [2.] [a.] **Eurobabble** *n. colloq.*, pretentious jargon or meaningless talk relating to or emanating from the European Union.
1986 *N.Y. Times* 9 Nov. VII. 11/2 Acts of terrorism or Soviet duplicity occasion from our Atlantic partners outbursts of oily *Eurobabble. **1987** *Economist* 18 July 20/1 In the European Parliament, Eurobabble can turn to EuroBabel. **1990** *Times* 27 Apr. 13/2 No matter that the Kohl-Mitterand accords might amount to no more than Eurobabble.
Euro-sceptic, a person, esp. a politician, who is sceptical about the supposed benefits to Britain of increasing cooperation with the fellow members of the European Union, *esp.* one who strongly opposes greater political or economic integration; occas. *transf.*; also *attrib.* or as *adj.*
1986 *Times* 30 June 9/1 Mrs Thatcher is seen in most of the EEC as a *Euro-sceptic at best. **1990** *Daily Tel.* 29 Nov. 23/2 It would be very regrettable if anyone sought to divert the party down a Euro-sceptic path. **1991** *Washington Times* 8 Dec. A17/2 Denmark: Nation of Euro-sceptics that nevertheless has come round to integration. **1992** *Independent* 31 Oct. 29/6 I'm not a Euroceptic. I'm a Europragmatist...I would support the treaty if we could get a proper definition of subsidiarity, but I won't support a motion that says, 'We are going to ratify Maastricht. Have a nice day!' hence **Euro-sceptical** *a.*

1990 *Guardian* 17 July 6/1 'It's the old money versus the garageistes,' a *Euro-Sceptical Tory MP said yesterday. **1991** *Economist* 22 June 34/3 Mr Major entrusted much of the sensitive work on his 'hard ecu' alternative to monetary union to the Euro-sceptical Mr Maude.

Euro-scepticism.

1992 *Economist* 26 Dec. 49/2 The great German beer row has, it is generally thought, done more for *Euro-scepticism in Germany than any incident since the creation of the Community. **1996** *Independent* 16 Jan. 14/6 Two sentences in Baroness Thatcher's Keith Joseph Memorial lecture reveal the self-delusion at the heart of Euroscepticism.

excludable (εks'klu:dəb(ə)l), *a.* Chiefly *U.S. Law.* [f. EXCLUDE *v.* + -ABLE.] That may or should be excluded.

1916 *Federal Reporter* (U.S.) CCXXVIII. 932 If an excludable alien so presenting himself actually secures admission, either by the deception or mistake or connivance of the officials, or if he enters at such a place of entry without presenting himself for admission.., his entry is in violation of the act and his presence in this country is unlawful. **1933** *U.S. Board Tax Appeals Rep.* XXVI. 130 Such percentage of the construction costs each year is excludable from gross income or sales. **1952** *Federal Reporter* (U.S.) CXCII. 494/1 If DeMeyer was a supervisor, his repetition of Jones' threat was not excludable as hearsay. **1972** *N. Y. Law Jrnl.* 14 Nov. 6/5 An excludable adjournment. **1986** *N.Y. Times* 13 Nov. A30/2 Last month Patricia Lara, a distinguished Colombian journalist, was declared excludable and deported. **1991** *Nuclear Energy* June 174/2 In the post-operational phase, the radionuclides.. might reach the biosphere via the water path as a result of transport processes not completely excludable.

exo-, *prefix.* Add: 'exodermis *n.* Bot. [cf. earlier F. *exoderme* (coined by P. Vuillemin in *De la Valeur des Caractères Anatomiques.. Tiges des Composées* (1884) iii. 52)], a protective outer layer formed beneath root epidermis, as it breaks down, from the outermost cortex.

1889 D. H. SCOTT in *Ann. Bot.* IV. 149 What we generally term epidermis is here an absorptive structure, but this is only the case in *young* roots. The older roots cease to be absorptive and require, like sub-aërial organs, a protective dermal structure... This epidermoidal layer, or better *exodermis, is especially evident in monocotyledonous roots, which have a persistent cortex, and often no periderm, so that the exodermis here has to form a permanent protective structure. **1919** F. O. BOWER *Bot. Living Plant* v. 72 The outermost layer, lying directly below the piliferous layer, and with its cells alternating with these, is called the exodermis. **1976** BELL & COOMBE tr. *Strasburger's Textbk. Bot.* (rev. ed.) 172 The rhizodermis dies with the root hairs, and its place is taken by a typical secondary boundary tissue, the exodermis.

export, *n.* Add: [3.] c. *Comb.* **export-led** adj.

1963 *Economist* 18 May p. xxxi/1 It was on the basis of this *export-led expansion that the economic miracle of General de Gaulle was founded. **1990** S. GEORGE in J. Leggett *Global Warming* xviii. 454 Export-led growth as a development strategy is a recipe for resource depletion.

exuviae, *n. pl.* Add: c. Also in *sing.* in the form *exuvium* (the reconstructed L. fem. sing. *exuvia*

being reinterpreted as neut. pl.), and in pl. as *exuvia.*

1678 SIR T. BROWNE *Let.* 6 July (1946) 97 You may observe how the *exuvium* of the little snake showes in a microscope. **1893** *Funk's Stand. Dict.*, Exuvium, *n.* [*-vi-a*, pl.]. **1965** B. E. FREEMAN tr. *Vandel's Biospeleol.* xix. 326 These animals eat the mucous layer impregnated with bacteria, diatoms and algae, which covers their bodies and detaches itself at intervals, rather like an exuvium. **1978** *Environmental Sci. Res.* XII. 207 Generally, exuvia from second ecdysis were lighter in dry weight and had less calcium than exuvia from the first ecdysis. **1987** *Jrnl. Animal Morphol. & Physiol.* XXXIV. 46 Head perpendicular to the body, legs out of the exuvium.

eye, *n.*[1] Add: [28.] **eyephone**, (*a*) *pl.*, an audio headset which provides the wearer with synchronized visual signals and images as well as sound (a proprietary name, with capital initial, in the U.S.); (*b*) (freq. as **EyePhone**) a headset used in virtual reality, providing audio and visual feedback about a virtual environment.

1981 *Washington Post* 19 July G3/2 *Eyephones, which effectively shut out outside light sources, consist of interchangeable color chip slides and tiny flashing lights that are activated by plugging into a stereo sound source. **1989** *Time* 1 May 66/1 VPL, which.. has developed its own EyePhones goggles and full-body DataSuit. **1993** *Guardian* 14 June (Educ. Suppl.) 14/3 The key to immersive VR is the use of a headset, or 'eyephone', which projects a small image of the virtual world on to each eye.

eyedness ('aɪdnəs), *n.* [f. EYED *ppl. a.* + -NESS; cf. HANDEDNESS *n.*] **1.** As the second element of combs., as *blear-eyedness* (BLEAR-EYED *a.*), *cock-eyedness* (COCK-EYED *a.*), *cross-eyedness*, *one-eyedness* (ONE-EYED *a.* 26), etc.

c **1440** *Promp. Parv.* 39 Blerydnesse. **1591** R. PERCIVALL *Spanish Dict.*, *Entordatura*, .. squinteidnes, crookedness. **1904** *Science* 8 Apr. 593/2 It may be better for the oculist to leave a person right-eyed rather than to give such lenses as suddenly compel left-eyedness. **1921** G. B. SHAW *Back to Methuselah* p. li, There is no reason to suspect Weismann of Sadism... It was a mere piece of one-eyedness; and it was Darwin who put out Weismann's humane and sensible eye. **1941** A. KOESTLER *Scum* 78 And yet in this apparent cock-eyedness there was the same administrative logic. **1992** *Independent* 4 Aug. 13/5 Brain-damaged left-handers.. are much more likely than right-handers to suffer a range of problems: insomnia.., cross-eyedness.., [etc.].

2. The dominance of, or preference for the use of, either the right or the left eye.

1934 in WEBSTER. **1937** S. T. ORTON *Reading, Writing, & Speech Probl. in Children* i. 48 We have no guide.. as to which is the dominant hemisphere except the 'laterality' of the individual, that is, his handedness, eyedness, and footedness. **1964** M. CRITCHLEY *Developmental Dyslexia* viii. 51 The inadequacies of most accepted tests of eyedness. **1982** *Sci. Amer.* July 32/2 Of course, we are not really one-handed at all. The two hands work in mutual aid; handedness refers to the active partner in many two-handed forms of behaviour. Similarly, eyedness is by no means simple.

eyeruv *n.*, var. *ERUV *n.*

F

face, *n.* Add: [**5.**] **e.** *to get out of* (someone's) *face*, to leave (someone) alone, to stop harassing or annoying (a person). Freq. *imp.* Chiefly *U. S. slang* (orig. *Blacks'*).

1931 *PMLA* XLVI. 1307 Git out o' my face, or I'll slap ye into the middle of next week. **1946** MEZZROW & WOLFE *Really the Blues* I. i. 4 Jim Crow just wouldn't get out of my face. **1964** C. COLTER in *Chicago Rev.* XVII. LV/LVI. 169 'You git outa my face,' the newsman whispered. 'You little bastard, you.' **1981** *N. Y. Times* 28 June II. 1/5 Guys come up to me with their arms outstretched, I say: 'What's that for?' And they say, '1947, Chicago, remember? We got high together.' I say: 'No. Get out of my face.' **1987** *Chicago Tribune* 2 Sept. I. 3/1 Didn't we ask Iraq to kind of cool it, to stay out of the ayatollah's face for a while? **1991** P. J. O'ROURKE *Parl. of Whores* (1992) 4 It's democracy that doesn't understand its rightful place in the operation of us—to shut up and get out of our faces.

f. *in your face slang* (orig. *U. S.*), (*a*) as *int. phr.*, an exclamation of scorn or derision; (*b*) as *adj. phr.* (freq. hyphenated) bold or aggressive; blatant, provocative, brash.

1976 C. ROSEN *Mile Above Rim* xv. 159 'Stuffed!' shouted the taller boy. 'Doobie got himself stuffed!.. In yo' face, Doobie!' **1977** *Washington Post* 25 Feb. (Nexis) D1 Pipkin was the epitome of the 'hot dog', interested only in a personal, in-your-face confrontation with the defender of the moment. **1979** *Verbatim* Summer 6/2 The expression 'Face!' Apparently, it is an abbreviation of 'In your face, Ace!' **1990** MIZELL & BROWN *Faces* (song) in L. A. Stanley *Rap: the Lyrics* (1992) 268 In your face all the time All in your face when I'm kickin' my rhyme. **1990** *Chicago Sun-Times* 30 Nov. I. 90/1 Ismail is unusual in that he's not you prototypical chest-out, in-your-face, strut-your-stuff star. **1992** *N.Y. Times* 6 June 23/1 The voters are saying, 'In your face, Bush!' They are saying, 'In your face, Clinton!' That's because the voters are stressed out. **1993** *Face* Sept. 109/1 Testosterone-fuelled in your face and on your case macho is not his bag.

fag, *n.*[5] Retain *slang* label before etym, but restrict *U. S.* label to a. Add: **b. fag hag** orig. *U. S.*, a heterosexual woman who prefers or seeks out the company of homosexual men. Usu. *derog.*

1969 *Screw* 18 Aug. 16/1 I'd hazard a guess that you're simply a Faggot's Moll, Fag hag, or Fruit Fly...A girl who enjoys the company and attention of males-who-go-to-bed-with-males is generally quite hung up about sex. **1972** B. RODGERS *Queens' Vernacular* 78 Fag-hags fall into no single category: some are plain janes who prefer the honest affection of homoerotic boy friends. **1978** J. KRANTZ *Scruples* vii. 206 Was she a fag hag, condemned to feel emotion only for men who didn't want women? **1983** E. PIZZEY *Watershed* III. xlii. 334 If they're single, they're gay. I don't fancy being a fag hag, though plenty of my friends do it. **1993** *Guardian* 22 July II. 14/5 The fag hag of yore could best be described as a woman who took on the more extreme mannerisms of gay men, such as campness and theatricality—a straight woman masquerading as a drag queen.

‖**Fatah** ('fætə), *n. Islam.* Also with def. article prefixed **Al Fatah.** [Arab. reverse vocalized acronym of the initial letters of *ḥarakat taḥrīr Filasṭīn* movement for the liberation of Palestine.

The reverse form of the acronym, vocalized to give the sense 'victory' and echoing Koranic references to the victory of the faithful (*al-*)*fatḥ*, was preferred to the vocalized acronym *ḥtf* death.]

A Palestinian political organization, founded in Cairo in 1957 by Yasir Arafat (b. 1929) and fellow Palestinians, which defined its goal as the liberation of Palestine by armed struggle; latterly, the dominant faction of the P.L.O., of which Arafat became Chairman in 1969.

1966 *Observer* 16 Oct. 2/8 All now depends on the attitude of the Syrian Government and whether or not it is willing, or indeed able, to halt the operations of the Palestinian terrorist organisation, Al-Fatah, whose latest series of raids is the cause of all the trouble. **1969** *New Yorker* 29 Nov. 153/1 Arabs..have been threatened by the Fatah and are afraid. **1972** *Times* 6 Sept. 7/3 The Black September organization, the secret cell of Al Fatah, has links with Germany's revolutionary underground movement. **1981** *Christian Science Monitor* 21 Apr. 2/5 The Palestinian parliament-in-exile has ended a nine-day session, electing a new executive committee of the Palestine Liberation Organization which appeared to strengthen still further the leading position of the moderate commando group Al-Fatah. Fatah advanced from 2 to 3 seats. **1984** A. HART *Arafat* 471 From 1957 to 1965 it was a network of secret and underground units...Fatah became a functioning organization with a Central Committee in 1963, but did not emerge from the underground until 1965. Fatah took control of the P.L.O. in 1969. **1991** A. M. DERSHOWITZ *Chutzpah* vii. 220 Various Palestinian groups—beginning with Yasir Arafat's Fatah and the PLO—have resorted to the most vicious forms of terrorism.

feel-good ('fiːlgʊd), *n.* and *a.* orig. *U. S.* Also **feel good, feelgood,** and with capital initial(s). [f. the vbl. phr. *to feel good*: see FEEL *v.* and GOOD *a.*] **A.** *n.* **1.** *ellipt.* for *Doctor Feelgood* s.v. *DOCTOR *n.* 6 e. *rare.*

1972 *Newsweek* 25 Dec. 29/3 The best way to guard against Feelgoods and charlatans is for the medical profession to keep its own house in order.

2. a. [f. sense *B below.] A feeling of well-being, confidence, or ease; contentment; euphoria. **b.** A person or thing that induces such a feeling.

1977 *N. Y. Times Mag.* 15 May (Late City ed.) 12/2 The chief exponents of psychic feelgood tend to come from Asia, California and the psychological sciences, no one of which has an impressive record at making people feel good. **1987** *Washington Post* 31 Mar. (Final ed.) C2/2 The era of fitness and feelgood has left a clear imprint on the unrelenting euphoria of these dances. **1992** *Financial Post* 30 Sept. I. 17 Without it, real recovery may be two years off. Even with electoral change in Washington, though, feelgood may take a year to seep north. **1993** *Coloradoan* (Fort Collins) 11 July E2/3 Boomer politicians..love fuzzy feelgoods.

B. *attrib.* or as *adj.* That induces or seeks to induce (often unwarranted) feelings of well-being, confidence, or ease.

1972 'F. STURGEON' (*title of comic book*) Feelgood funnies. **1977** *N.Y. Times Mag.* 15 May (Late City ed.) 12/2 The latest aberration in the American pursuit of happiness is the feelgood movement. **1977** *Washington Post* 24 May A11/2 (*heading*) Test of Carter's 'Feel Good' Foreign Policy is Workability. **1990** R. BLOUNT *First Hubby* 21, I am not one of these feel-good shrinks...I am usually stern. **1991** *Rolling Stone*

14 Nov. 80/2 A feel-good New Agey spiel tailored to make yuppies feel better about themselves. **1995** *Independent on Sunday* 1 Jan. 22/4 Retailers and holiday tour operators have reported a surge of business in the week since Christmas, suggesting that the elusive feelgood factor may at last be breaking through.

So 'feelgoodism *n.*; 'feelgoodist *n.*

1977 *N. Y. Times Mag.* 15 May (Late City ed.) 12/4 Tom Wolfe observes that feelgoodism rests on an obsessive passion. *Ibid.*, The feelgoodists are heretics. **1990** *Nation* 22 Oct. 437/2 The day looked ripe, all in all, for a little Democratic feelgoodism. **1993** *Guardian* 13 Aug. 11. 6/1 Soft drugs have lately predominated on the dance scene, coinciding with the rise of eco-friendly feel-goodists such as the Stereos and Jamiroquai.

female, *a.* and *n.* Add: [B.] [3.] **female condom,** a contraceptive sheath worn inside the vagina.

1988 *Independent* 21 Apr. 6/1 The *female condom..consists of a polyurethane bag with a thin ring of plastic at the open end. **1993** *Chicago Tribune* 28 Apr. 1. 5/3 The Food and Drug Administration moved closer Tuesday to approving the first female condom for sale in the U.S., saying the device offers limited protection against sexually transmitted diseases.

Femidom ('fɛmɪdɒm), *n.* [f. FEMI(NINE *a.* & *n.* + CON)DOM *n.*] A proprietary name for a female condom.

1989 *Trade Marks Jrnl.* 4 Oct. 5447/1 Femidom...Date claimed under International Convention. 5 November 1987 (Denmark). Contraceptives and hygienic articles, all included in Class 10...Medic Group of Scandanavia A/S...Copenhagen V, Denmark. **1990** *Independent* 16 July 14/1 They were anything but a joke: Femidom, which was invented by a Danish nurse and tested by volunteers, is still undergoing worldwide trials and should be available in Britain next year. **1991** *Observer* 24 Feb. 42/8 Femidom, the female condom, is almost here and three London agencies are lining up to advertise the Chartex product. **1992** *Guardian* 7 July 37/7 The Margaret Pyke Centre's research findings on Femidom's efficacy and acceptability are due out next month, but signs are that it should be as reliable as the male condom.

finite, *a.* and *n.* Add: [A.] [3.] *finite automaton,* a finite-state automaton.

1956 S. C. KLEENE in Shannon & McCarthy *Automata Stud.* 4 In showing that each regular event is representable in the state of a finite automaton, the automaton we use is a McCullough-Pitts nerve net. Thus their neurons are one example of a kind of 'universal elements' for finite automata. **1966** *Math. Rev.* Jan. 10/1 Markov's result entails the unsolvability of certain mass problems of finite-automata theory. **1985** *Sci. Amer.* Nov. 16/1 Each flib is equipped with the simplest decision-making apparatus possible. This is the biological equivalent of what computer scientists call a finite automaton.

Fleming's left-hand rule *n. phr.*: see *left-hand rule* s.v. *LEFT HAND *n.*[3]

flip, *v.* Add: [9.] **b.** *to flip out intr.*, to lose control (orig. under the influence of drugs); to go wild or crazy. Also *trans.*, to induce anger or a sudden loss of control in (someone); to astound.

1964 N. MAILER in *Esquire* June 116/2, I came to the conclusion I'd flip out so far I'd not come back if I stayed in Vegas too long. **1974** *News & Press* (Darlington, S. Carolina) 25 Apr. 9/2, I could see something in their lives that 'flipped me out!' I thought, 'what's wrong with these people?' **1984** L. ALTHER *Other Women* (1985) III. iii. 285 She asked me not to sleep with Brian Stone at our house, so I flipped

out. **1988** J. McINERNEY *Story of my Life* iii. 43 What really flips him out is the meat counter. He looks at all this red meat under plastic and he goes to his cousin—*who for is all this meat?* **1991** J. PHILLIPS *You'll never eat Lunch in this Town Again* (1992) 192 Jeremy..disappears in my car for fourteen hours, in search, he explains when he returns, of Steven's wallet. I flip out. More about the car than anything. **1993** *Empire* Aug. 95/2 Heston's captive astronaut recovering his voice to insult the apes who've resnared him, totally flipping them out.

fly, *a.* Sense 3 in Dict. becomes 5. Add: **3.** *U. S.* **a.** Stylish, sophisticated; fashionable. **b.** Chiefly *Black English*, attractive, good-looking; hence, excellent, fabulous (cf. **fly boy, *-guy* below; *FLY GIRL *n.*).

1879 *Nat. Police Gazette* (U.S.) 20 Sept. 15/2, I am speaking now of the young..men about town who think it is awfully 'fly' to know tow-headed actresses, and that to sip crab-apple champagne with the gaudy, vulgar thing in pink tights is just the nobbiest thing on earth. **1896** G. ADE *Artie* xviii. 169 They get in with a lot o' cheap skates and chase around at nights and think they're the real thing...They think they're fly, but they ain't. **1946** MEZZROW & WOLFE *Really Blues* ii. 23 Marcelle must have figured me for a fly cat too, and her curiousity was aroused. **1954** L. ARMSTRONG *Satchmo* (1955) iii. 42 They were playing *At the Animals' Ball*...When the break came I made it a real good one and a fly one at that. **1970** *Current Slang* (Univ. S. Dakota) V. II. 7 Fly, *adj.*, well dressed. **1980** E. MORRIS et al. *Superrappin'* (song) in L. A. Stanley *Rap: the Lyrics* (1992) 145 M.C.s, disc jockeys to all the fly kids and the young ladies Introducin' the crew ya got to see to believe. **1991** *Source* Dec. 48/2 In the elite world of Hip-Hop money makers, boys believe there are two kinds of women. The first are the sistas who have a 'man' or are considered both fly and virtuous enough to be a brotha's 'girl'. **1992** *Vibe* Fall (Preview Issue) 100/3 To work with him? That would be the most exciting thing to ever happen to me. That shit would be fly.

4. *U. S.* Unrestrained or rebellious in one's behaviour: *spec.* **a.** (esp. of a woman) flirtatious or sexually promiscuous; wanton.

1880 C. L. MARTIN *Sam Bass* iv. 18 The woman who made the least secret about the color of her garters, and who was the 'flyest of all the mob', was the belle of the place. **1888** in Farmer & Henley *Slang* (1893) III. 42/1 I'm just gettin' sick'n tired o' the way't them fly dames go on, 'n the way't the fellahs hang round 'em 'n dance with 'em. **1931** F. HURST *Back Street* i. 3 You're one of those cheating girls who act fly, but aren't. You'll lead a man on, but you won't go all the way. **1948** Z. N. HURSTON *Seraph on Suwanee* xi. 113 That Corregio woman was 'fly' and doing her level best to bait Jim Meserve in.

b. Wild, audacious, impertinent; brash.

1884 in Miller & Snell *Why West was Wild* (1963) 515 A pair of very 'fly' Chicago drummers came down last week bent on doing the 'boys' up and painting the town red...Denhollem's..safe was broken open during the night while these 'fly ones' were peacefully reposing in their beds. **1896** G. ADE *Artie* iv. 34 Artie stopped short, slowly rubbed his chin and looked at the intruder. 'You won't think I'm too fly if I ask you a question, will you?' **1919** F. HURST *Humoresque* 135 You won't forget to nag me even then for duds to go automobiling with fly men that can't bring you no good. **1970** C. MAJOR *Dict. Afro-Amer. Slang* 54 Fly, fast, and ecstatic; brash. **1992** *Newsweek* (Canad. ed.) 4 May 64/1 People make the circle when they think you have the flavor and you're gonna do something fly...But my life's not *about* bein' large, ya know?

[5.] fly boy orig. and chiefly *U. S.*, (*a*) a sharp or shrewd young man; (*b*) (esp. in *Black English*) a stylish or sophisticated young man.

1888 in *Random House Hist. Dict. Amer. Slang* (1994) I. 791/1 Jim Blake lived in the country, and though a pretty *fly boy among the rustics was not up in the ways of the outside world. **1896** G. ADE *Artie* vi. 57 Here comes a whole crowd o' people—a lot o' swell girls and their fly boys. The car was nearly full. **1950** A. LOMAX *Mr. Jelly Roll* 182 Here were the fly boys of the burgeoning entertainment industry. **1980** L. CODY *Dupe* ii. 13 Bit of a fly-boy, anyway, I shouldn't wonder. **1993** *Independent* 18 Feb. 22/6 The rapper Butterfly..tries to push the hip vernacular to implosion-point, unleashing a stream of all-purpose, timeless hepcat babble that would be just as easily understood by Fifties beats as Nineties fly-boys.

fly guy = *fly boy* above.

1906 in *Random House Hist. Dict. Amer. Slang* (1994) I. 792/1 They're *fly guys there all right... But the flyer they are the easier it is to trim them. **1979** S. ROBINSON et al. *Rapper's Delight* (song) in L. A. Stanley *Rap: the Lyrics* (1992) 322 So I rocked some vicious rhymes like I never did before She said, 'Damn, fly guy, I'm in love with you The Casanova legend must have been true.'

fly girl ('flaɪˌgɜːl), *n. U.S. slang.* Also **fly-girl.** [f. FLY *a.* + GIRL *n.*] **1.** A lewd or sexually promiscuous young woman, *esp.* a prostitute.

1893 FARMER & HENLEY *Slang* III. 41 *Fly-girl,..a* prostitute. **1986** 'ICE T' *Six in the Morning* (song) in B. Cross *It's not about Salary* (1993) 25 Posse'd to the corner where the fly girls chill, Threw some action at some freaks 'til one bitch got ill... As we walked over to her, hoe continued to speak So we beat the bitch down in the goddamn street. **1994** *People Weekly* (U.S.) 8 Aug. 19/1 Shanice is Gidget goes Fly Girl, bumping, grinding and cooing her way through a string of sex-kitten manifestos... Yet for all of the do-me posturing, Shanice is still a romantic.

2. An attractive or stylish young woman (orig. and chiefly *Black English*).

1979 S. ROBINSON et al. *Rapper's Delight* (song) in L. A. Stanley *Rap: the Lyrics* (1992) 319 'Cause I'm 'a get a fly girl Gonna get some spank 'n' Drive off in a def OJ. **1980** G. JACKSON *Spoonin' Rap* (song) in L. A. Stanley *Rap: the Lyrics* (1992) 304 'Cause I'm the baby-maker, I'm the woman taker I'm the cold crushin' lover, the heartbreaker So come on fly girls, please don't stop. **1993** *Courier-Mail* (Brisbane) 23 Dec. 3/4 The grunge look introduced into the mainstream earlier this year is already old-hat in the United States. This summer look out for 'fly girls' in 'slammin' threads' and 'stud muffins' who are 'cool like dat'.

footballene ('futbɔːliːn), *n. Chem.* [f. FOOTBALL *n.* + -ENE.] = *BUCKMINSTERFULLERENE n.*

1986 A. D. J. HAYMET in *Jrnl. Amer. Chem. Soc.* CVIII. 319/2 Any structure of 12 pentagonal rings and 20 hexagonal rings..constitutes a roughly spherical molecule... For convenience this molecule is called here 'footballene' ('soccerballene' in the US). **1992** *Jrnl. Physical Chem.* XCVI. 23/1 The NIS spectrum of footballene is shown divided into two parts.

forex ('fɔrɛks), *n. Comm.* Also **Forex.** [f. FOR(EIGN *a.* + EX(CHANGE *n.*] = *foreign exchange* s.v. FOREIGN *a.* 9. Cf. also EXCHANGE *n.* 4.

1947 (*title of periodical*) Forex service. **1965** *Economist* 20 Nov. (Internat. Banking Suppl.) p.xxxvi/2 The London branch of Forex, the foreign exchange dealers' association, has about 540 members. **1968** *Ibid.* 2 Nov. 90/3 An Association of International Bond dealers (to be called Inbond, on the lines of the foreign exchange dealers' Forex?) is to be formed. **1979** *Daily Tel.* 21 July 17/5 (*headline*) Forex markets unimpressed. **1985** *Sunday Mail* (Brisbane) 14 July 30 (Advt.), Do you need instant share and commodity prices, interest rates, forex and futures plus expert commentaries? **1992** *Times of India* 30 July 8/4 In the current system, where the government buys forex..at the low official rate, the government's cost-saving is achieved by shifting the cost on to the exporters.

free, *a., n.,* and *adv.* Add: [D.] [2.] **freeware** *Computing*, software which is available free of

charge (sometimes with the suggestion of a donation to the provider); cf. *shareware* s.v. *SHARE v.*[2] 8.

[**1982** *Computerworld* 6 Dec. 2 Freeware, a software company that depends entirely on voluntary contributions for revenue.] **1983** *Christian Science Monitor* 22 Mar. 17 A number of electronic bulletin boards offer '*freeware*' of various sorts for the cost of copying the program. **1989** *MacWeek* 4 Apr. 32/4 Disinfectant, the latest virus-fighting utility, is a freeware program. **1992** B. STERLING *Hacker Crackdown* 82 Many computer games are 'freeware', not copyrighted—invented simply for the love of it and given away to the public; some of these games are quite good.

free, *v.* Add: [3.] **e.** *to free up*, to release; to make available (esp. a valuable or restricted resource, as time, space, or money). orig. *U.S.*

1955 *Surgery* XXXVIII. 63 The abdominal aorta was freed up for a distance of 5 cm. from the trifurcation. **1972** *N.Y. Law Jrnl.* 22 Aug. 2/7 (Advt.), Para-legals..are used by an ever-increasing number of prominent attorneys to reduce their unwanted load of paralegal matters and free up their time to render legal advice more efficiently. **1978** J. UPDIKE *Coup* (1979) vii. 271 Make him a Donald X. Gibbs Travelling Fellow... We can free up a grant somewhere. **1982** *Times* 25 Aug. 13/4 Dome has attempted a number of manoeuvres to free up cash. **1984** *Sears Catal.* 1985 Spring/Summer 849 Free up valuable counter space with a Microwave Cart. **1988** *New Scientist* 26 May 48/2 The department is currently freeing up the 49 MHz frequency for this type of low frequency device, it says. **1992** *Economist* 22 Feb. 16/2 A less *dirigiste* space programme could free up the extraordinary technical enthusiasm there is for the task.

fullerene ('fʊləriːn), *n. Chem.* [f. *BUCKMINSTER)FULLERENE n.*] Any of several forms of carbon consisting of atoms joined together as a hollow structure, as in buckminsterfullerene.

1987 H. W. KROTO in *Nature* 8 Oct. 529/2 It is convenient to retain this name for C_{60} and use the name fullerene generically for the class of all closed carbon cages. **1990** *New Scientist* 13 Oct. 18/3 The chemists' work on C_{70} provides important evidence that there exists a whole sequence of closed-cage structures—the 'fullerenes'. **1991** *Ibid.* 6 July 25/1 Fullerene chemistry has taken another step forward with the discovery by chemists..that they can add fluorine atoms to buckminsterfullerene. **1993** *Nature* 11 Nov. 123/2 Mass spectra of material sublimed from the recovered soot showed normal fullerenes.

fund, *n.* Add: [8.] **fund-holder**, (*b*) *Brit.*, a general practitioner who is provided with and controls his or her own budget; also *transf.* of a medical practice.

1991 *Brit. Med. Jrnl.* 9 Mar. 581/1 He is also anxious that his block contracts—which specify six quality measures for each specialty, such as waiting times and communication with general practitioners—should not be used to subsidise purchasers at the margin, particularly general practitioner fundholders. *Ibid.* 16 Mar. 638/1 The hope is..that as non-fundholders watch the fundholders—many of whom are among the best practices—get good deals for their patients they will want them too. **1992** *Economist* 29 Feb. 35/1 GP fundholders and opted-out hospitals are determined to defend their new-found privileges. **1993** *Guardian* 26 Oct. I. 2/5 She rejected criticisms that GP fundholders were creating a two-tier system of care, saying their ability to purchase services directly had instead 'gingered up' health authorities into improving services for all patients.

so **fund-holding** *n.* and *adj.*

1989 *Independent* 23 Nov. 3/3 As with self-governing hospitals, which the Bill firmly describes as 'NHS Trusts', ministers have changed the name from 'practice budgets' to '*fund-holding practices' to remove the word budget from the title. **1991** *Pulse* 6 Apr. 84/6 GP fundholding is largely credited to a personal initiative by former Health Secretary Kenneth Clarke who introduced it into the NHS reforms after the original concept of the new NHS internal market..had been agreed. **1993** *Private Eye* 4 June 10/2 Hertfordshire now has so many fundholding GPs competing and bickering over contracts that cash-strapped hospitals are unable to cope with their excessive demands. **1993** *Guardian* 20 Oct. 1. 2/8 The royal colleges are anxious for action to curb what they call the gross inequalities of care produced by fund-holding, and the growing practice of hospitals refusing elective (non-emergency) treatment for patients of other doctors once contracts are fulfilled. **1995** *Nursing Times* 22 Mar. 148/1 (Advt.), Associate Nurse required to work with..a busy 20,000 patient, fundholding, computerised general practice.

G

G. Add: [III.] [f.]   **G7** (also **G-7**), Group of Seven (see *GROUP *n*. 3 h).

1986 *Courier-Mail* (Brisbane) 29 Sept. 23/2 Finance ministers.., meeting as the group of seven (G-7), said in a joint statement they agreed to 'close and continuous coordination of economic policy during the period ahead.' **1986** *Ibid.* 30 Sept. 23/2 Buying support from West Germany's central bank was believed to have arrested the US dollar's decline in Asia following the G7 meeting in Washington over the weekend. **1989** *U.S. News & World Rep.* 26 June 54/1 Secretary James Baker.. got the *G-7 nations — Japan, West Germany, Britain, France, Italy, Canada and the U.S. — to agree to act in unison to weaken the dollar's value. **1993** *Times* 7 July 11/1 America and Japan yesterday failed to reach a deal on a bilateral trading agreement in one of the early setbacks on the eve of the G7 summit in Tokyo.

g.   G-spot = *Gräfenberg spot* s.v. *GRÄFENBERG *n*. Freq. *fig*.

1982 A. K. LADAS et al. *G Spot* i. 21 As a result of stimulation of the G spot, women often have a series of orgasms. **1983** S. KITZINGER *Woman's Experience of Sex* ii. 56 The fanfare about the G-spot.. was the claim that women, too, could ejaculate in orgasm. **1988** *New Republic* 25 Apr. 42/3 This is what happens when you get carried away in massaging the great American g-spot ('g', in this case, for greed). **1991** *Independent* 5 Jan. 22/3 The first act was a disaster orchestrally, with any number of musical G-spots whizzing by unnoticed by conductor Michael Lloyd.

gaijin (gaɪˈdzɪn), *n*. and *a*. Pl. unchanged. [a. Jap. *gaijin*, contraction of *gaikoku-jin*, f. gai foreign country + *jin* person.] **A.** *n.* A Japanese term for a foreigner or alien; a non-Japanese person. **B.** *attrib.* or as *adj.* Of or relating to a gaijin; foreign, alien.

1964 I. FLEMING *You only live Twice* (1965) xiii. 121 Bond would be explained away to the elders as a famous *gaijin* anthropologist. **1968** *Sat. Rev.* (U.S.) 20 Jan. 40/2, I also learned that, according to visiting *gaijin*.. Japanese bath water is inhumanly hot and impossible to endure. **1980** 'J. MELVILLE' *Chrysanthemum Chain* (1981) 27, I can't imagine what those two *gaijin* thought of the sort of organisation I run. *Ibid.* 34 'All his friends were men.' '*Gaijin* as well as Japanese?' **1985** S. SUCHARITIKUL *Alien Swordmaster* III. xvi. 122 They came for the *gaijin* martial arts master... They said he was hiding in the institute. **1989** *Japan Times* 21 May 18/7 My, what a lovely little 'half' girl. Your husband must be a gaijin. **1992** *Sunday Times* 18 Oct. v. 7/3 Stories of *gaijin* crime abound in the headlines, as Korean thieves and Nigerian credit card fraudsters head to this previously crime-free country.

Game Boy ('geɪmbɔɪ), *n*. Also **Gameboy**. [f. GAME *n*. + BOY *n.*[1]] A proprietary name for a hand-held, electronic device, incorporating a small screen, which is used to play computer games loaded in the form of cartridges.

1989 *USA Today* 6 June 2B/4 Last weekend.. Nintendo unveiled Game Boy, a hand-held portable version of its popular video game. **1990** *Omni* Nov. 137/2, I bought a Game Boy for my brother.. The problem is, his boss has a Game Boy, too, and he's constantly going to my brother's office and taking his cartridges. **1991** J. ROVIN *How to win at Game Boy Games* p. vii, In addition to portability, Game Boy features wonderfully fluid graphics and terrific sound. **1991** *New Scientist* 24 Aug. 51/2

Walkmans are the ultimate shut-out. Gameboys are not far behind. **1992** *New Musical Express* 14 Nov. 23/1 So, come on. Put down that Gameboy and your copy of Madonna's *Sex*,.. and mull over the year that's drawing to a close. **1995** J. MILLER *voXpop* x. 155, I still go to games arcades occasionally, see what new games they've got, but I've got a Gameboy at home.

Gan (gæn), *n.*[2] (and *a.*) Also **Kan**. [a. Chinese *Gàn*, another name for the Jiangxi province in S.E. China.] The Chinese dialect spoken in the Jiangxi province and in south-eastern areas of Hubei province. Also *attrib.* or as *adj.*

1943 *China Handbk.* i. 30 The Kan-Hakka group is spoken mainly in Kiangsi and Kwangtung... The Northern or Kan group has the tendency to pronounce all aspirated surds as voiced in connected speech. **1961** CHANG-TU HU et al. *China* v. 100 Kan, spoken by eight million people in northern Kiangsi. **1974** *Encycl. Brit. Macropædia* XVI. 801/1 The Northern languages (or Mandarin dialects) are closer to each other than the Southern ones (Wu, Hsiang, Kan, Yüeh, Min). **1987** M. RUHLEN *Guide to World's Langs.* I. iv. 143 Some 927 million total Chinese speakers.. with a distribution roughly as follows: Mandarin (680), Wu (69),.. Gan (21), [etc.].

‖**ganbei** (ganˈbeɪ), *int*., *n*., and *v*. Also **kan-pei**, **kaanpei**. [Chinese *gānbēi*, f. *gān* empty, dry + *bēi* cup.] A Chinese drinking-toast, a call to drain one's glass. Also as *v. intr.* and *trans.*, to drink (as) a toast.

1940 V. CRESSY-MARCKS *Journey into China* VII. i. 257 We 'Kaanpei-ed' frequently, raising the small wine cups, and drinking the warm wine. They use the word *Kaanpei*, raising the glass to the guest, rather like our saying 'Good health'. **1962** E. SNOW *Other Side of River* (1963) vii. 59 '*Kan-pei!*' (Bottoms up!) we all said. **1976** *Courier-Mail* (Brisbane) 7 July 4/2 One of the cordial customs in China is to ganbei a Mao-tai — to down in one dash a glass of the country's famous colourless wheat-based liquor. **1977** O. SCHELL *China* (1978) I. 131 He arrives at our table with several other merrymakers, all holding wineglasses, and proposes a *kan-pei* (bottoms up). **1987** *Time* 13 Apr. 85/1 Many *ganbei*, or toasts, drunk with.. mao-tai whisky, cloyingly sweet orange soda or cool, refreshing Chinese beer were raised.

‖**ganbu** ('ganbuː), *n*. Also **kanpu**, **kan-pu**. Pl. **ganbu**, **ganbus**. [Chinese *gànbù* cadre.] In the People's Republic of China, an office-holder in an (esp. Party or military) organization; a cadre.

1956 *Contemp. China 1955* I. (Index), Cadres (*kanpu*). **1960** CHANG-TU HU et al. *China* vii. 151 A cadre, *kan-pu*, is a Communist agent or activist entrusted with the task of carrying out party policies on all levels. **1962** E. SNOW tr. *China Youth* in *Other Side of River* (1963) xxx. 232 All *kanpu* hereafter must do physical labor. **1965** M. MICHAEL tr. *J. Myrdal's Report from Chinese Village* (1967) I. 45 We let ganbus from the town come out and work it on Sundays. **1971** A. D. BARNETT in S. E. Fraser *Educ. & Communism in China* VI. 282 The new elite of the country — the students, *kanpu*, government workers, and Party members. **1980** *Washington Post* 4 Nov. A13/2 The only fat people in China are ganbu... At least that's the favorite joke.

garam masala ('gʌrəm məˈsɑːlə, 'gɑːrəm məˈsɑːlə), *n*. [f. Urdu *garam* hot, burning +

*MASALA *n.*] A mixture of ground spices used in Indian cookery. Cf. *MASALA *n.*

[**1832** G. A. HERKLOTS *Jaffur Shurreef's Qanoon-e-Islam* App. p. lxv, *Chukoleean* alias *Sootreean*..a dish consisting of wheat flour made into paste, formed into small cakes, and boiled in water..with meat, *gurm* and t'*hunda mussala*, and salt.] **1954** S. CHOWDHARY *Indian Cooking* 91 Add garam-masāla and lemon juice a few minutes before removing from the heat. **1969** *Femina* (Bombay) 26 Dec. 57/3 When potatoes are done, add fried fish. Simmer for a few minutes. Add ghee and *garam masala* powder. **1977** *Sunday Times* (Colour Suppl.) 27 Nov. 30/1 Although you will not find curry powder on the shelf in most Indian kitchens, you *will* find garam masala, a spicy mixture used to give an aromatic lift to many plain and simple dishes. **1986** *Options* Apr. 80/3 Add the garam masala, yoghurt, red chilli powder..and ½ teaspoon salt. **1990** *Health Now* Apr. 9/1 Serve them hot with chappati or rice sprinkled with garam masala.

gay, *a.*, *adv.*, and *n.* Add: [**A.**] [**9.**] **gay-bashing** *slang* (orig. and chiefly *U. S.*) = *queer-bashing* s.v. QUEER *n.*[2]; hence (as a back-formation) **gay-bash** *v. intr.* and *trans.*; also **gay-basher** = *queer-basher* s.v. QUEER *n.*[2]

1989 *Chicago Tribune* 16 Feb. II. 1/3 A newspaper which is clearly denigrating not only to me, but clearly an attempt to create hostility to those males who may have feminine attributes and clearly an attempt to *gay bash. **1992** *Nation* (N.Y.) 15 June 825/2 Let Dannemeyer gay-bash and yell about the fetus. **1986** *Los Angeles Times* 10 Apr. 1. 32/5 The San Francisco group is also reaching out to potential *gay bashers. **1990** *Pink Paper* 10 Feb. 3/6 A gay-basher was sentenced to 10 years in prison. **1984** *Washington Post* 18 May A21/2 It's hard to understand Nunzio's incredibly light sentence as anything other than a statement that *gay-bashing isn't really all that terrible. **1993** R. HUGHES *Culture of Complaint* i. 44 The same putrid stew of gay-bashing, thinly veiled racial prejudice, black Irish paranoia and authoritarian populism continued to bubble beneath the commonfellow surface.

ge *n.*, var. *KO *n.*[3]

gel, *n.* Add: **3.** Special Comb. **gel electrophoresis** *Biochem.*, electrophoresis in which a gel of an organic polymer such as polyacrylamide or agarose is used as a medium for the separation of macromolecules.

1955 *Biochem. Jrnl.* LXI. 635/1 a₁-Globulin does not appear as a definite band between a₂-globulin and albumin in starch *gel electrophoresis. **1982** T. M. DEVLIN *Textbk. Biochem.* iii. 114/1 The hyperlipoproteinemias are classified..according to the abnormal pattern observed in plasma lipoprotein gel electrophoresis. **1991** *Saudi Med. Jrnl.* XII. 287/2 Karyotyping..is carried out using pulsed field or field inversion gel electrophoresis.

glass, *n.*[1] Add: [**IV.**] [**16.**] **glass ceiling** orig *U. S.*, an unofficial or unacknowledged barrier to personal advancement, esp. of a woman or a member of an ethnic minority in employment. Also *transf.*

1984 *Adweek* 15 Mar. (Magazine World 1984) 39/2 Women have reached a certain point—I call it the *glass ceiling. They're in the top of middle management and they're stopping and getting stuck. **1988** *New Scientist* 8 Oct. 62/3 Sadly, astronomers from all countries report a 'glass ceiling'. The proportion of women is highest for the lower grades. **1991** *Newsweek* 11 Mar. 57/1 In the Army, where three in 10 enlistees are African-American, 11 percent of the officers are black. Advances in the ranks are obstructed by 'glass ceilings', where networking and old-boyism still speed the advance of mediocre whites. **1994** *Daily Tel.* 25 Aug. 25/1 After several spirited assaults, the FT-SE's 3200 glass ceiling

finally gave way yesterday, allowing the index to close sharply higher after a day of drifting. **1995** *Economist* 7 Jan. 5/3 For most top amateurs there is a glass ceiling on the professional circuit, and it does not take them long to hit it.

-glossia ('glɒsɪə), *suffix.* [f. Gr. γλῶσσα tongue, language + -IA[1].] A word-forming element used (*a*) in *Path.*, in terms denoting congenital abnormalities of the tongue, as in *ankyloglossia* (1848), *macroglossia* (1862); (*b*) in *Philol.*, in the sense 'language(s)', as in *idioglossia* (1891), *diglossia* (1959).

glucan ('glu:kæn), *n. Biochem.* [f. GLUC(O- + -AN.] A polysaccharide consisting entirely or chiefly of glucose residues, such as cellulose and starch; = GLUCOSAN *n.* b.

1943 BARRY & DILLON in *Proc. R. Irish Acad.* XLIX. B 177 In 1894 Salkowski isolated from yeast a polysaccharide which he called 'yeast cellulose'...Zechmeister and Tóth..refer to the substance as 'yeast polyose'. In this paper it will be called yeast glucan—a more definite term. **1950** *Jrnl. Chem. Soc.* II. 1944 Barry and Dillon..deduced a chain-length of 28 glucose radicals for the yeast glucan. **1978** *Sci. Amer.* Jan. 89 Glucosyltransferase.. polymerizes the glucose into a long polysaccharide called a glucan. **1986** M. KOGUT tr. *Schlegel's Gen. Microbiol.* xiv. 412 Plant starch is composed of two glucans: amylose and amylopectin.

glue, *n.* Add: [**6.**] **glue ear**, a condition in which a viscous fluid blocks the Eustachian tube and impairs hearing, occurring chiefly in children as a result of infection of the middle ear; secretory otitis media.

1960 B. H. SENTURIA et al. in *Trans. Amer. Acad. Ophthalmol. & Otolaryngol.* LXIV. 61 (*table*) Chronic Otitis Media...*Glue Ear...Secretory Otitis Media. **1989** *Brit. Med. Jrnl.* 10 June 1549/1 Middle ear effusion (glue ear) is the commonest reason for admitting young children for an operation. **1991** *Times Educ. Suppl.* 18 Jan. 12/5 Children with glue ear..should be put at the front of the class, so they can hear better. Some have even inadvertently taught themselves to lip-read.

Gräfenberg ('grɛːfənbɛəg), *n.* [The name of Ernst *Gräfenberg* (1881–1957), German-born U.S. gynaecologist.] **Gräfenberg ring** now *Hist.*, an intrauterine contraceptive device consisting of a flexible ring of silver wire, described by Gräfenberg in 1929 (in K. Bendix *Geburtenregelung: Vorträge u. Verhandlungen des Ärztekurses vom 28–30 Dezember 1928*, 50). **Gräfenberg spot**, a sensitive area of the anterior wall of the vagina believed by some to be highly erogenous and capable of ejaculation (first described by Gräfenberg & Dickinson 1944, in *Western Jrnl. Surg.* LII. 338); abbrev. *G.-spot.*

1930 *Internat. Med. Group Investigation Contraception* (3rd issue) Sept. 3 For Great Britain the event of outstanding importance this year has been the popularisation of the method of the Gräfenberg ring. **1964** *Guardian* 8 Dec. 8/4 Five years ago experiments with stainless steel and plastic variants on the Gräfenberg ring were reported in medical journals. **1981** F. ADDIEGO et al. in *Jrnl. Sex Res.* XVII. 15 The subject identified an erotically sensitive spot, palpable through the anterior wall of her vagina. We subsequently named this area the 'Grafenberg spot' in recognition of the person who wrote of its existence and relationship to female ejaculation. **1990** *Arch. Sexual Behavior* XIX. 608 As to the existence of a discrete anatomical structure..which swells upon being tactilely stimulated (Grafenberg spot), the evidence for it..is so far inconclusive.

gravad lax *n.*, var. *GRAVLAX *n.*

gravlax ('grævlæks), *n.* Also **gravlaks, gravad lax**. [Sw. *gravlax* (Norw. *gravlaks*), f. *grav* grave, trench (f. *grava* (Norw. *grave*) to dig, bury) + *lax* (Norw. *laks*) salmon (see LAX *n.*[1]); so called because the salmon was originally marinated and fermented in a hole in the ground.

The variant element *gravad*, pa. pple. of *grava* and the only form of the vb. extant in mod. Sw., has evolved the meaning 'raw and spiced', and now occurs in the names of similar dishes, such as *gravad makrel*.]

A Scandinavian dish consisting of dry-cured salmon marinated in a mixture containing salt, spices, and dill.

1935 I. NORBERG *Good Food from Sweden* 56 *Gravlax* is a Swedish 'Gentleman's relish' and much appreciated by Scandinavian *gourmets*. It may, or it may not appeal to the British palate, but no harm in trying it. **1958** *Times Lit. Suppl.* 24 Jan. 47/2 The taste of Swedish *Gravlax* (jellied raw salmon). **1975** *Daily Colonist* (Victoria, B.C.) 7 Oct. 19/1 The increasing appeal for Americans of raw fish delicacies such as..gravlax. **1986** *Sunday Tel.* (Colour Suppl.) 21 Sept. 50/3 Country people took to burying their perishables, particularly fish...Modern *gravlaks* is prepared with less risk. **1990** *Daily Tel.* 26 May 23/7 Sweeting's, the City fish restaurant and oyster bar, yesterday hosted the first international gravadlax tasting finals.

green, *a.* and *n.* Add: [A.] [III.] [13.] [a.] **green audit** = *environmental audit* s.v. *ENVIRONMENTAL *a.* 2.

1989 *Accountant* Dec. 9/1 *Green Audits to be comprehensive should cover: – use of Resources, and – the pollution and other effects of the business on the environment. **1992** *Independent* 3 Apr. 12/4 All of government will be subject to exactly the same kind of green audit as the Treasury now gives to public expenditure.

green marketing, the marketing of products on the strength of their (supposed) environmental friendliness.

1989 *Daily Tel.* 7 June 17/4 On the *green marketing front, Heinz..has been named the Green Manufacturer of the Year. **1991** *N.Y. Times* 26 Jan. A50/3 Their new approach is called 'green marketing' and in their efforts to portray themselves as environmentally concerned, some companies are making claims that do not stand up under close examination.

green shoots *pl.*, signs of growth or renewal, *spec.* indications of economic recovery following a period of recession.

[**1985** P. KOME *Women of Influence* i. 21 When feminism regained public attention in the Western world, during the 1960s and 1970s, Canada still had a deep-root system across the country that needed only a few thunderstorms for it to send up green shoots, and blossom, and spread like dandelions.] **1989** *Independent* 24 Nov. 10/4 In the greenhouse political atmosphere of this Prague November, all manner of dead wood is sprouting *green shoots. **1992** *New Republic* 13 Apr. 19/1 Every week in the last four months of 1991 was marked by predictions from one minister or another that the recession was about to end. The 'green shoots' of recovery were now showing. **1993**

Computing 21 July 23/1 The government is in even worse trouble than before, leading to further economic uncertainty. So are the green shoots real this time, or are we in for more hard times?

grief, *n.* Add: [8.] **c.** *colloq.* (orig. *U.S.*). Trouble, unpleasantness, 'hassle'; unstinting criticism or disparagement. Freq. in phr. *to give* (*make, have,* etc.) *grief.*

1891 *Sportsman* 28 Feb. in P. Beale *Partridge's Dict. Slang* (1984) 503/1 The flag had scarcely fallen than [*sic*] the grief commenced. **1929** D. HAMMETT *Dain Curse* xii. 121 'You could have got me in on it,' he had complained before our soup was in front of us...'I had', I said, 'enough grief with the one guy I did let in on it – Eric Collinson.' **1940** R. CHANDLER *Farewell, my Lovely* xviii. 141 There's not much money in it. There's a lot of grief. But there's a lot of fun too. **1974** A. LURIE *War between Tates* (1977) viii. 160, I thought how I was making all this grief for you and Danielle, and what I ought to do is..take the next bus to New York. **1986** C. HOPE *Hottentot Room* xiv. 203 Say you'll come home, Caleb. It will save a lot of grief. **1989** *Face* Jan. 66/2 Mann has had grief from snobby film critics and from the censorship lobby. **1990** D. PETERSON *Dress Gray* i. 10 One female several doors down kept her curling iron. She got caught trying to use it one weekend and really took some grief from the cadre.

group, *n.* Add: [3.] **h.** *Group of Seven*, an association of the seven major industrialized nations (excluding the former Soviet Union); abbrev. *G7* (G III. f).

1977 *Economist* 26 Nov. 92/1 The Group of 5 is made up of the largest economies (United States, Japan, West Germany, France, Britain). But by this year's London summit the top economies' club had become the Group of 7. **1986** *Courier-Mail* (Brisbane) 30 Sept. 23/2 Failure of the Group of Seven industrialised nations to agree on exchange and interest rate policies left foreign exchange markets in limbo yesterday. **1992** *Harper's Mag.* Mar. 59/3 The Soviet prime minister..tried to push the national panic button when Gorbachev came away empty-handed from his London meeting with the leaders of the Group of Seven.

guest, *n.* Add: [6.] [b.] **guest beer**, (*a*) in a free house, a beer which is available only temporarily; (*b*) in a tied public house, a beer (usu. an independent real ale) offered in addition to those produced by the brewery.

1977 *Good Beer Guide* (CAMRA) 51, 15th-century inn in small village. Occasional *guest beers. [**1987** *Financial Times* 25 Sept. 10/5 Britain's brewers should allow tenants in their public houses to stock a 'guest' draught beer in addition to their own beers according to a report to the Monopolies Commission by the Consumers' Association.] **1989** *Oxf. Today* I. II. 33/1 Free house, with seven real ales (Burtonbridge, Wethereds, Morlands, Flowers, Wadworths 6X, Youngers No. 3 and Brakspears) plus a visiting guest beer every month. **1991** *Purchasing & Supply Managem.* Apr. 17/2 Another threat being used by some brewers..was that tenants' rents would be reviewed in the light of their purchase of guest beers. **1993** *Guardian* 5 Nov. 1. 5/8 Two-thirds of tied houses now have guest beers, with some buying direct from small breweries, compared with one in five before.

H

hack, $n.^3$ Add: [4.] [**a.**] (*b*) *slang*, a journalist or reporter, *esp.* a staff newspaper writer (orig. disparaging, now chiefly jocular).

1810 *Irish Mag.* III. 427/1 Let them hire a newspaper hack, a shameless, trading defamer, a master of Babylonish dialect. **1894** E. L. SHUTMAN *Steps into Journalism* 65 One of the most prolific newspaper hacks in Chicago once remarked that he did not consider a man..a reporter unless he could make good reading out of anything. **1958** *Punch* 27 Aug. 265/3 No pools investor of quality would seek advice from hacks who write: Wolves have banker look. **1973** *Guardian* 30 June 11/3 'He wasn't up to much as a sub-editor,' said one of the older hacks, sniffily. **1985** S. LOWRY *Young Fogey Handbk.* i. 10 The most noticeable Young Fogeys are hacks (never journalists, please). **1990** *Village Voice* (N.Y.) 30 Jan. 59/1 A narrator..recounted an episode more or less lifted from the novelist's life, the supposedly hilarious courtship and marriage of a young radio station hack and his aunt.

hackette (ˌhæk'ɛt), *n. slang.* [f. HACK $n.^3$ + -ETTE.] A jocular or disparaging term for a female journalist. Cf. *HACK $n.^3$ 4 a (b).

1976 *Private Eye* 5 Mar. 5/1 Also on this holiday was petite hackette Ms ——. **1983** *Financial Times* 2 Apr. 15/3 It is a..wise child who knows how to deflect the hostile questioning of Mummy's fellow hacks and hakettes. **1985** *Listener* 16 May 37/1 Perhaps Mr Cameron was misquoted, or plied with drink and led on by a *Sunday Times* hackette. **1990** *Sunday Times* 18 Feb. H8/3, I, innocent hackette on my first foreign assignment, passed up the chance of becoming part of the action of Frederick Forsyth's life.

halla *n.*, var. of *CHALLAH *n.*

halo- ('hæləʊ), *comb. form*[2]. Chem. [Shortened f. HALOGEN *n.*] Used to form names of compounds, radicals, etc., containing one or more halogen atoms, as *haloacyl, halohydrocarbon, halomethane,* HALOTHANE *n.*

First used in *haloform below.

1951 *Chem. Abstr.* XLV. 1951/2 The C-halogen bonds in *halomethane. **1955** *Jrnl. Chem. Physics* XXIII. 1960/2 The collision lifetimes of molecular vibrations for fourteen halo-methanes at 300°K. **1966** *Jrnl. Org. Chem.* XXXI. 908 The behaviors of trialkylaluminums, alkyl Grignards, and alkyllithiums toward *halohydrocarbons are compared. **1970** *Proc. Nat. Sci. Acad.* LXVII. 1688, X is a chemically reactive group, such as diazonium or *haloacyl. **1975** *Nature* 17 July 193/1 Measurements of methyl chloride and other halomethanes in the air and coastal waters of southern England between December 1974 and April 1975. **1984** GREENWOOD & EARNSHAW *Chem. of Elements* (1986) xvii. 959 Such nucleophilic reagents may replace other halogens in halohydrocarbons by F but rarely substitute F for H.

'halocarbon *n.*, any compound in which the hydrogen of a hydrocarbon is replaced by halogens (wholly or in part).

1953 F. J. HONN in Kirk & Othmer *Encycl. Chem. Technol.* XI. 691 The oils are also available..under the name *Halocarbon. **1958** W. A. PENNINGTON in Clark & Hawley *Encycl. Chem. Suppl.* 148/1 Strictly speaking, the term halocarbon applies to compounds containing only halogen and carbon atoms. **1986** *Age* (Melbourne) 6 Sept. 1/8 Dr Forgan said the Cape Grim station had monitored marked increases in the incidence of halocarbons and carbon dioxide levels over the past few years. **1991** BARNES & MANN *Fund. Aquatic Ecol.* (ed. 2) vi. 112/2 Other synthetic halocarbons show similar properties.., including carbon tetrachloride, methyl chloroform and various exotic solvents.

'haloform *n.* [after CHLOROFORM *n.*], any compound in which three of the four hydrogen atoms of methane are replaced by halogens.

1931 *Jrnl. Amer. Chem. Soc.* LIII. 3494 (*title*) The *haloform reaction. **1934** *Chem. Rev.* XV. 275 The haloform reaction comprises those processes whereby the haloforms are derived from organic compounds by the action of hypohalites. **1972** R. A. JACKSON *Mechanism* iv. 67 Carbenes can be generated in several ways, for example by photolysis of diazo-alkanes, or by treatment of haloforms with strong base.

halo'phosphate *n.*, any of a group of ionic compounds containing a mixture of halide and phosphate anions, some of which are used as phosphors.

1946 *Brit. Patent 578,192* 1/1 The term *halophosphate will be used to denote any compound of the form $3M_3(PO_4)_2.1M^1L_2$, where M and M^1 are bivalent metals, which may be the same, and L is a halogen (F, Cl, Br, I). **1966** P. JOHNSON in P. Goldberg *Luminescence of Inorg. Solids* v. 288 The halophosphates, which have the chemical composition $M_5(PO_4)_3X$ and the structure of the mineral apatite. **1972** *Physics Bull.* Mar. 151/3 The most important advance in the phosphor field was the application of halophosphate phosphors to the fluorescent lamp around 1946.

halon ('heɪlɒn), *n. Chem.* [f. *HAL(O-[2] + -ON[2].] Any of a class of compounds in which the hydrogen atoms of a hydrocarbon (usually methane or ethane) are replaced by bromine and other halogens, many of which are gases noted for their lack of reactivity and useful in firefighting. Also *halon gas.*

1960 *Nat. Fire Protection Assoc. Q.* Oct. 173/2 One agent, bromotrifluoromethane (Halon 1301), was the most effective of the agents evaluated...Bromotrifluoromethane (referred to frequently by its Halon designation 1301) is a liquified compressed gas. **1975** *Halogenated Fire Suppressants* (ACS Symposium Ser. No. 16) Pref. p. ix, Halon is an abbreviation devised by the Army Corps of Engineers to designate halogenated hydrocarbon. If the compound under discussion has the formula $C_aF_bCl_cBr_dI_e$, it is designated as halon abcde. Terminal zeros are dropped. **1983** *Jrnl. Soc. Archivists* VII. 168 An automatic release halon system may be installed. **1986** *Daily Tel.* 27 May 8/8 Firefighters who put on breathing masks and entered the small compartment around the hatch to switch on the halon gas fire suppression system. **1991** *Earth Matters* Winter 9/3 Friends of the Earth has caught out ICI who have been aggressively marketing ozone-depleting halons for fire extinguishers to developing countries such as India and Argentina.

happy-clappy ('hæpɪ'klæpɪ) *n.* and *a. colloq.* (*joc.* or mildly *derog.*). Also **happyclappy.** [Rhyming combination f. HAPPY *a.* + CLAP $n.^1$ + -Y[1].] **A.** *n.* A member of a Christian charismatic group. **B.** *attrib.* passing into *adj.* Of or pertaining to such a group.

1990 R. MALAN *My Traitor's Heart* II. 100 Both were members of the Apostolic Church, happyclappies in South African slang—into the laying on of hands, faith healing, and speaking in tongues. **1991** *Daily Tel.* 15 Apr. 16/2 Did Archbishop Temple actually say that the

Church *purely* exists for the benefit of non-members? In that case.. we might as well all pack up, Happy Clappies and Traditionalists as well. **1992** *Sunday Times* 8 Mar 11. 5/3 He's one of the happy-clappy lot. They're always speaking in tongues, casting out demons and frightening the old ladies. **1993** *Times* 7 Oct. 37/7 Is the man at the helm of the church an intelligent astute leader or a happy-clappy simpleton who will plunge his church into disestablishment. **1994** *Guardian* 20 May 11. 18/5 Now Asian families have to live not only in fear of BNP attacks but with the threat of muddled happy-clappies patronising them every week.

her, *pron.* Add: [4.] b. **her indoors** (also **'er indoors**) *Brit. colloq.*, one's wife or girlfriend; in extended use, applied to any woman occupying a position of authority who is regarded as domineering.

The phrase was popularized by the Thames Television series *Minder* (1979–93), in which the leading character Arthur Daley habitually referred to his wife as 'her indoors'. The series' original writer, Leon Griffiths, app. first heard it used by 'a taxi-driver drinking companion of his' (*Independent* (1992) 16 June 13/6).

1979 L. GRIFFITHS *Smaller they Are* in *Minder* (television script, second draft) 10 May 2 That's what her indoors doesn't understand Terry. A young bird keep [*sic*] you feeling young. **1984** *Guardian* 17 Oct. 12/2 These days, her indoors (and Mr Walker too) are said to be seldom off the phone with words of wisdom for Mr MacGregor. **1986** R. SPROAT *Stunning Punters* 156, I was taking Her Indoors out for a day at the Zoo. **1988** *Times* 2 Nov. 21/1 She [*sc.* the mistress of a Great Artist] is immortalized in oils, while 'Er Indoors cleans up the mess afterwards. **1992** *Pilot* July 36/1, I began to consider buying a single-seat kitplane, a microlight, or even a taildragger. But there were howls of disagreement from Her Indoors and the rest of the tribe.

hit, *v.* Add: [IV.] [23.] g. *to hit off the line*: see *LINE *n.*[2] 26 d (b).

hole, *n.* Add: [II.] [7.] [b.] (*b*) **hole-in-the-wall** (*colloq.*, chiefly *Brit.*), an automatic teller machine installed in the (outside) wall of a bank or other building.

1985 *Guardian* 9 Feb. 24 (*heading*) Just ask at the hole in the wall. **1987** *Today* 18 Feb. 23/3 Three [banks], along with Bank of Scotland.. are set to unveil their joint hole-in-the-wall cash machine network. **1989** *Times* 30 Aug. 23/2 'Phantom' cash withdrawals from hole-in-the-wall dispensers are the biggest grievance. **1992** *Independent* 23 Apr. 2/1 They believe the men may be responsible for several early-morning 'hole-in-the-wall' raids in London and Kent.

homeboy, *n.* Senses a, b, c in *Dict.* become 1, 2, 3. [3.] For def. read: *slang* (chiefly *Black English*). **a.** orig. *U.S.* and *S. Afr.* [In S. Afr. Eng., tr. *umkhaya* person from home, family, f. *khaya* home.] A person from one's home town, region, or neighbourhood; hence, a male friend or associate, *esp.* one who has a similar background. **b.** orig. *U.S.* (esp. among young urban blacks). A member of one's peer group or gang. Sometimes used as a term of address. Also *attrib.*

Since the early 1980s the term has become particularly strongly associated in the U.S. and the U.K. with the hip-hop subculture.

1946 in V. Randolph *Pissing in Snow* (1977) 80 The home boys all laughed like hell when they heard that [joke about incest in Arkansas families], but.. a big farmer from Arkansas.. got mad. **1953** P. LANHAM *Blanket Boy's Moon* 1. vi. 40 Ntoane.. also came from

Lesotho... 'Welcome, home-boy. What work are you to do? *Ibid.* 56 Monare now made Koto known to Ntoane, and for a time the three home-boys sat and exchanged news about the home country. **1961** J. CAREW *Last Barbarian* 7 'It's like an ice-box in here, Alice.' 'All right home-boy, take it slow, man.' **1963** WILSON & MAFEJE *Langa* 55 In the barracks every man questioned could define his home-boy group. **1972** *Drum* (S. Afr.) 22 Oct. 18 When I came to Johannesburg in 1949.. I stayed with the homeboys in Sophiatown who also got me a job with a garage. **1982** ROBINSON & CHASE *On the Radio* (song) in L. A. Stanley *Rap: The Lyrics* (1992) 57, I asked him to explain what I was talking about My man was too excited, he begin to shout I finally figured out what homeboy was saying You never guess what the radio's playing. **1992** *Face* Feb. 46/2 Those guys are my homeboys, if they're in trouble then I'm in trouble. **1992** *Time* 16 Mar. 15/1 Gangs are like families. Little kids get disciplined in gangs. When a little kid drifts into a gang, he doesn't just get a gun thrust into his hands. He's gonna get homeboy love, which is pretty potent.

homegirl ('həʊmˌgɜːl), *n.* slang (orig. and chiefly *U. S.*, esp. *Black English*). Also **home-girl**, **home girl**. [f. HOME *n.*[1] + GIRL *n.*; cf. HOMEBOY *n.*] **a.** A woman or girl from one's home town, region, or neighbourhood; hence, a friend or associate, *esp.* one who has a similar background; a member of one's peer group. Sometimes used as a form of address. Also *attrib.*

Since the early 1980s the term has been strongly associated in the U.S. and the U.K. with the hip-hop subculture.

1934 T. WILDER *Heaven's my Destination* iii. 53 And *this* is Mississippi, the sweetest and snappiest little home-girl in Oklahoma, if I do say it. **1968** *Amer. Speech* 1967 XLII. 238 *Home boy* and .. *home girl* and *home people*, denote individuals who come from the same hometown as the speaker. **1980** J. COCK *Maids & Madams* 62 In Johannesburg it was found that the networks of most domestic workers were both socially and spatially closed. They tended to interact with persons similarly employed in the same locality. 'Homegirls' played no particular part in these networks. **1990** G. JACOBS *Doowutchyalike* (song) in L. A. Stanley *Rap: The Lyrics* (1992) 77 Homegirls, for once forget you got class See a guy you like, just grab him in the biscuits And doowutchyalike. **1991** *Allure* June 71/2 With his frayed denim, quilted baseball caps, and oversize gold necklaces.. Kaiser Karl was obviously evoking homegirl chic.

b. A young woman or girl who likes to stay at home; a domesticated, shy, or unworldly young woman or girl.

[**1961** R. B. LONG *Sentence & its Parts* ii. 54 She isn't a *home girl*.] **1980** E. A. FOLB *Runnin' down some Lines* iii. 77 The expressions homeboy or homegirl, when used in a pejorative sense, often refer to someone who sticks close to home (close to his or her mother) and has little feel for life on the streets. **1992** *Voice* 22 Dec. 18/1 She said we want you to go to college so you don't turn out to be so much of a homegirl.

hospital, *n.* Add: [7.] **hospital trust**: in the U.K., a self-governing administrative body within the National Health Service, comprising a hospital (or often a group of neighbouring hospitals) which has withdrawn from local health authority control.

1989 *Independent* 4 Nov. 3/1 Mr Clarke has still knocked some district bids off the list. The St George's teaching *hospital trust—which was virtually the whole of the Wandsworth health authority's services—is currently excluded, for example. **1993** *Private Eye* 4 June 10/3 At St Clements hospital in Bow, part of the Royal London hospital trust.

hot, *a.* Add: [12.] [c.] **hot dark matter** *Astron.*, dark matter consisting of particles whose motion soon after the big bang was very energetic.

[**1984** PRIMACK & BLUMENTHAL in *NATO ASI Ser. C* CXVII. 166 We will consider here the physical and astrophysical implications of three classes of elementary particle D[ark] M[atter] candidates, which we will call hot, warm, and cold. (We are grateful to Dick bond for proposing this apt terminology.) Hot DM refers to particles, such as neutrinos, which were still in thermal equilibrium after the most recent phase transition in hot early universe.] **1985** *Astrophysical Jrnl.* CCXCIX. 583 We consider the Einstein–de Sitter universe dominated by two kinds of collisionless relics: neutrinos as *hot dark matter, and X particles having negligible thermal velocity as cold dark matter. **1990** GRIBBIN & REES *Cosmic Coincidences* (1992) iii. 79 Most of these difficulties would be resolved if the dominant dark matter consisted of particles that were 'cold' in the sense that they had low random speeds and therefore did not disperse and homogenise on galactic scales, as would neutrinos (which are, by contrast, described as 'hot' dark matter).

hotter ('hɒtə(r)), *n.*[2] *Brit. slang.* [Back-formation, f. *HOTT(ING *vbl. n.* + -ER[1]] A person, esp. a youth, who engages in 'hotting'; a joyrider.

1991 *Independent* 3 Sept. 3/1 The 'hotters' of Blackbird Leys prepared for another night of violence yesterday as they boasted of their terrifying exploits behind the wheels of stolen high-performance cars. **1991** *Guardian* 4 Sept. 2/3 They can do handbrake turns at 40-60 mph. The smoke from the burning tyres and exhausts is everywhere. You should see the way the hotters dodge between the police vans. **1992** *Today* 2 Mar. 13/3 If lucky and given enough wellie (acceleration), the hotter (he who is doing the hotting) will dust or dazzle (leave behind) the filth (police).

hotting ('hɒtɪŋ), *vbl. n. Brit. slang.* [f. HOT *a.* (see senses 7 e and 7 f), perh. reinforced by *hot-wire* s.v. HOT *a.* 12 c.] Joyriding in stolen, high-performance cars, esp. dangerously and for display.

1991 *Independent* 3 Sept. 7/2 Some residents have claimed that the 'hotting'—so called because the cars are 'hot', or stolen—has led to an increase in street violence. **1991** *Times* 12 Sept. 2 The drivers took part in a 15-minute display of 'hotting', in which young men steal performance cars and take part in high-speed manoeuvres in front of cheering crowds. **1992** *Today* 18 Feb. A joyriding handbook targeted at teenagers and detailing a list of 'hotting' techniques is on sale openly in many cities. The book shows how to ram roadblocks, escape a chase and shoot at cars in pursuit. **1993** *Scotsman* 22 Feb. 1/6 Recent incidents, including the spread of 'hotting' or 'joyriding' by youngsters in stolen cars, have taken juvenile crime to the top of the political agenda.

hypercard ('haɪpəkɑːd), *n.* [f. HYPER- + CARD *n.*[2]] **1.** A three-dimensional shape, used to perform certain card tricks, which may be formed by making three transverse cuts halfway into a playing card from alternate sides and then rotating one end of the card through 180°, creasing along a line joining the ends of the cuts so as to allow a central area of the card to stand at right angles to the plane of the remainder. *rare.*

1975 *Pallbearers Rev.* X. 1042/2 (*heading*) Hyper Card. **1978** *Sci. Amer.* Nov. 20/2 The form has come to be called a hypercard. Magicians have learned of it and have made it the basis for a number of magic tricks.

2. *Computing.* Also **Hypercard, HyperCard.** A proprietary name for a programming system which uses symbols resembling index cards to represent the content and structure of an on-screen database, and permits the creation of hypertextual links.

1987 *InfoWorld* 22 June 78/4 A combination database and AI tool (the program is said to have been named Hypercard, having incorporated hypertext searching techniques). **1989** *Byte* Aug. 205/3 The classes of objects in HyperCard are assigned a definite hierarchy. **1990** *Managem. Computing* Nov. 44/2 Plus 2 is an extension to Apple's Hypercard, and can actually run many Hypercard stacks. **1993** *N. Y. Times* 13 Apr. c8/4 Voyager used Apple's Hypercard and its own multimedia development tools to link the text and the video segments.

I

I. Add: [III.] ISDN = *integrated services digital network* s.v. *INTEGRATED *a.* b.
1974 *Internat. Conf. Communications* (Inst. Electr. & Electronic Engineers) 33E-1 An integrated services digital network (*ISDN) is a network in which the various services such as telephony, data and telex use the same switching and transmission facilities. **1986** E. L. SCACE in T. C. Bartee *Digital Communications* iii. 87 One part evolution, one part revolution, and one part philosophy, ISDNs represent a unique historical development. **1993** *Daily Tel.* 24 Feb. 30/7 Now..network operators worldwide have in place national ISDN services..which are simple to use, simple to install and simple to run. *Ibid.* 30/8 Britain's ISDN network is already connected to 12 other countries.

image, *n.* Add: [10.] **image processing**, the electronic analysis and manipulation of an image, esp. in order to improve its quality; freq. *attrib.*
1959 *RCA Rev.* XX. 739 The incorporation of intra-panel logic provides a powerful *image-processing tool. **1968** *Jrnl. Optical Soc. Amer.* LVIII. 1272 It has been traditional to constrain image processing to linear operations upon the image. **1989** C. STOLL *Cuckoo's Egg* xlviii. 260 We've got a dedicated artificial intelligence group, active robotics researchers, and our image-processing lab really cooks.
   hence **image processor** *n.*, a device or system for performing image processing.
1968 *IEEE Trans. Computers* XVII. 635/1 A need for a special-purpose electronic computer to process visual images arose... For these and other reasons, a special-purpose computer, the Visual *Image Processor (VIP), was built. **1969** *Med. & Biol. Engin.* VII. 393/1 These conclusions..yield guides for the future design of circuits to improve the performance of image processors. **1989** B. ALBERTS et al. *Molecular Biol. Cell* (ed. 2) iv. 142 By using video systems linked to image processors, contrast can be greatly enhanced so that the eye's limitations in detecting small differences are overcome.

Imax ('aımæks), *n. Cinematogr.* Also IMAX. [f. I(MAGE *n.* + MAX(IMUM *n.*] A proprietary name for a technique of wide-screen cinematography in which 70mm film is shot and projected in such a way as to produce an image approximately ten times larger than that normally obtained from standard 35mm film. Freq. *attrib.*
1969 *Hamilton* (Ontario) *Spectator* 7 Nov. 24/3 The world's largest movie projector was unveiled at McMaster University yesterday. Known as IMAX, it's big in every way. **1970** *N. Y. Times* 14 Feb. 33/6 The key component in what is described as the world's largest movie projector..was patented this week...The invention..is a 'rolling loop' mechanism for advancing the film. The projector, called the Imax..was built by the Multiscreen Corporation, Ltd., of Galt, Ontario. **1977** *Washington Post* 10 July H6/2 There's the Candidan [*sc.* Canadian] Imax system that they use for the flight movie at the Air and Space Museum. **1988** *New Scientist* 24/31 Dec. 54/2 The largest Imax screen in Britain is 16 metres deep by 20 metres long and is housed at the National Museum of Photography, Film and Television at Bradford. **1991** *Amer. Cinematographer* Sept. 10/3 We have built a 'print-down' machine designed to produce 35mm frames from 65mm camera negatives for IMAX editing.

inculturation (ɪnkʌltʃəˈreɪʃən), *n.* [f. IN-² + CULTURATION *n.*]   **a.** The acquisition of the behavioural characteristics of a particular culture or group by a person, another culture, etc.; = ENCULTURATION *n.* Cf. SOCIALIZATION *n.*
1968 W. J. SAMARIN in J. A. Fishman *Readings Sociol. of Lang.* 661 By *natural language* is meant any language acquired by the normal processes of inculturation. **1993** *Guardian* 22 June 11. 6/4 They found that a chimpanzee can learn to communicate if it is raised as though it were a child. Dr. Savage-Rumbaugh calls that..inculturation.
   b. *spec.* The adaptation of Christian liturgy so as to accommodate the beliefs and practices of non-Christian cultures.
1970 *Liturgical Arts* XXXIX. 31/1 Can Christian liturgy use the readings from Buddha & Confucius? One group affirms this is praisworthy inculturation. **1986** *Tablet* 1 Nov. 1182/2 Engelbert Zeitler..was instrumental in establishing several institutes for the study of Indian art and culture to put into effect the directives of the second Vatican Council in inculturation. **1989** *Church Times* 28 July 4/3 Within China there is little or no effort towards inculturation. **1992** *New Republic* 11 May 20/2 An especially heartening development is black parishes' response to the Second Vatican Council's call for 'liturgical inculturation', which aims to make the liturgy reflect the shared culture of the parishioners.

Indianapolis (ˌɪndɪəˈnæpəlɪs), *n.* [The name of the state capital of Indiana.] Used *attrib.* (esp. in *Indianapolis 500*) and *absol.* to denote a 500-mile circuit race for rear-engined racing cars held annually since 1909 at the Indianapolis Motor Speedway.
[**1909** *Automobile* Dec. 16 (*heading*) Indianapolis Speedway is Ready 1909. **1911** *Ibid.* June 1 (*heading*), 500-mile Sweepstakes Run off at the Indianapolis Speedway.] **1914** *Ibid.* June 4 65/1 The victors of the Indianapolis 500-mile automobile race. **1939** *Motor Sport* June 181/1 Last year..Indianapolis was run under the Grand Prix formula laid down by the A.I.A.C.R., specifying engine limits of 3-litres supercharged and 4½ litres unsupercharged. **1946** F. CLYMER (*title*) Indianapolis Race History. A complete detailed History of Every Indianapolis Race Since 1909. **1986** *Daily Mirror* (Sydney) 30 May 62/2 For Indianapolis 500 fans, the bad news was that the race had to be abandoned because of rain for three consecutive days this week. **1991** *Sports Illustr.* 3 June 3/2 Rick Mears bided his time until the late going, then hammered his way to a fourth Indianapolis 500 victory.

Indy ('ɪndɪ), *n.*² [Abbrev. of *INDIANAPOLIS *n.*] **1.** Used *attrib.* and *absol.* to denote the annual Indianapolis 500 motor race or any of a series of similar high-speed circuit races; also, this style of motor racing.
1956 B. W. YATES *Indianapolis 500* I. 5 The early engines used at Indy differed from present designs. **1964** WILSON & LOVE *Fun, Fun, Fun* (song) in *Beach Boys Complete* (1973) 56 She makes the 'Indy' five hundred look like a Roman chariot race now. **1982** *Harper's Mag.* Aug. 54 In *Time*, Tom Callahan deplored the whole Indy enterprise. **1987** *Autosport* 28 May 26/2 He's now a four-time Indy 500 winner..and he finished fifth, second, third and fourth respectively in each Indianapolis 500 from 1982 to '85. **1988** P. FUSSELL *Indy* in *Thank God for Atom*

Bomb (1990) 241 No wonder..that the rituals of the Indy world are so strenuously male, macho as all get-out. **1991** *Courier-Mail* (Brisbane) 16 Mar. 25/1 The Gold Coast is locked into Indy fever this weekend with the running of the first Indy race outside North America.

2. *Comb.* **Indy car** (freq. in form **IndyCar**), a rear-engined, turbocharged racing car designed to compete in such an event; also used *transf.* and *attrib.* to denote the sport of competitive Indy car racing.

1975 *N.Y. Times* 1 Apr. v. 10/3 Miss Murphy is the only woman to have been allowed to drive an *Indy car on the race track. **1979** *Arizona Daily Star* 1 Apr. C12/2 The first on-the-track action by the U.S. Auto Club's Indy-car division and the rival Championship Auto Racing Teams has been completed and nobody is winning. **1993** *Toronto Sun* 17 June 97/1 Bourbonnais and Villeneuve drive for Forsythe-Green Racing, a crew with IndyCar experience and IndyCar aspirations.

ink, *n.*[1] Add: [4.] [a.] **ink cartridge**, (*a*) = *CARTRIDGE *n.* 1 d iv; (*b*) any of various similar containers used in electronic typewriters, computer printers, etc.

1955 *Stationery Trade Rev.* June 82/3 The Waterman C/F Pen...Ink always fresh. Each ink cartridge hermetically sealed with fresh Instant-Flo real ink. **1978** *Oil & Gas Jrnl.* 26 June 173/3 New Speedomax 165/250 Series one-pen and two-pen recorders are now available with either disposable ink cartridge or thermal inking system. **1983** *Money* May 194/1 Disdaining modern ink cartridges, the Diplomat has a manual plunger that siphons ink from a bottle into the reservoir. **1983** *InfoWorld* 21 Nov. 79/1 Atari's 1027 uses an ink cartridge instead of a ribbon. **1992** *R S Components: Electronic & Electr. Products* July–Oct. 115/1 A replacement ink cartridge, containing a specially formulated free flowing non-clogging ink, for the Epson SQ-2500 ink jet printer.

insulin, *n.* Add: [2.] **insulin-dependent** *a.* *Path.*, designating or pertaining to a form of diabetes caused by autoimmune destruction of insulin-secreting cells, which is characterized by low or absent production of insulin and usually develops in childhood or youth.

1961 DUNLOP & DUNCAN in D. Dunlop et al. *Textbk. Med. Treatment* (ed. 8) 355 All diabetic children have *insulin-dependent juvenile-type diabetes. **1983** ALBERTI & HOCKADAY in *Oxf. Textbk. Med.* I. ix. 6/1 It is probably preferable to use the type I, type II scheme, in that considerable confusion arises from the term 'insulin-dependent', which is often equated in practice with insulin-*treated*, which will depend on clinical practice and the state of the patient at a particular time. **1991** *Lancet* 3 Aug. 310/1 In December, 1989, a letter was published in *The Lancet* describing the results of administration of a microemulsion-derived formulation of oral insulin to three insulin-dependent diabetic patients.

integrated, *ppl. a.* Add: [b.] **integrated services digital network**, a telecommunications network through which sound, images, and data can all be transmitted as digitized signals; abbrev. **ISDN**.

1974 *Internat. Conf. Communications* (Inst. Electr. & Electronic Engineers) 33E-1 An integrated services digital network (ISDN) is a network in which the various services such as telephony, data and telex use the same switching and transmission facilities. **1981** *Electronics* 6 Oct. 176/2 This capability lets manufacturers and operators interconnect equipment at different hierarchical levels to form..an integrated services digital network. **1991** H. RHEINGOLD *Virtual Reality* III. xi. 244 The central idea of an Integrated Services Digital Network..is simple: all forms of signals..now can be reduced to digital form and sent as bits..over very wide networks. **1993** *Computer*

Weekly 25 Mar. 21/3 The Post Office is to provide Integrated Services Digital Network (ISDN) services to its internal business users.

internal, *a.* and *n.* Add: [A.] [5.] **internal market** *Econ.*, commercial operations within a given area or group; *spec.* (*a*) = *single* (*European*) *market* s.v. *SINGLE *a.* III. 17 a; (*b*) in the U.K., a system of decentralized funding within the National Health Service whereby each hospital department is allocated a budget with which to provide patient care or support and to purchase specialist or ancillary services contractually from other health authority departments or private companies.

1960 *U.S. Treaties & Other Internat. Agreements* (U.S. Dept. State) XI. II. 1546 Stabilizing the *internal markets for this commodity in India. **1963** *Times* 29 May 15/2 Most of these countries have tiny internal markets—'mini-markets' Mr. Gates calls them. **1975** *Economist* 1 Feb. 54/1 The EEC commissioner for the internal market, Mr Finn Olav Gundelach, advised his fellow-commissioners this week against intervention. **1986** McGOWAN & TRENGROVE *European Aviation* (Inst. Fiscal Stud.) i. 18 Its proposals..effectively contradict..the Community's broader objectives, in particular that of reaching a free internal market by the early 1990s. **1989** *Brit. Med. Jrnl.* 22 July 263/1 For resources to follow patients across NHS boundaries..hospitals had to be adequately funded in proportion to the work they did. It did not require an administrative nightmare of contracts and an internal market. **1991** *Pulse* 6 Apr. 11/1, Only days before he was expected to compete in the NHS's new so-called internal market, north-east Thames region accepted.. Dr David Keene's claim for a budget of £50 per patient to cover hospital referrals.

intertext ('ɪntətɛkst), *n.* [f. INTER- + TEXT *n.*[1]] **1.** *Lit. Theory.* [Back-formation f. *INTERTEXTUALITY *n.*] A text considered in the light of its relation (esp. in terms of allusion) to other texts; a body of such texts considered together.

1974 *Romanic Rev.* LXV. 280 A text can realize the poetic model either in conformity with or contrary to the expectations raised. Such expectations are the awareness of an intertext. **1981** M. RIFFATERRE in *New Lit. Hist.* XII. 228 The text refers not to objects outside of itself, but to an intertext. The words of the text signify not by referring to things, but by presupposing other texts. **1988** *Times Lit. Suppl.* 16 Dec. 1401/2 At the other extreme, texts may be cut loose altogether from their historical moorings and considered synchronically as forming one vast intertext, irrespective of such considerations as authorship, date, or audience. **1992** *Times* 13 May II. 1/3 For the deconstructionists, the proposition has nothing but a fragment of a larger polysemic text, part of the global intertext that encompassed everything and everyone.

2. *Linguistics* and *Lit. Theory.* Language or text which is either intermediate, as between different language forms (cf. *INTERLANGUAGE *n.* 2), or an intermediary (between the reader and the text) such as a commentary or exegesis.

1986 *Austral. Rev. Applied Linguistics* IX. II. 130 The mixed pieces could be understood as a form of 'interlanguage'.., not merely as deviations from the target, but as transitional approximations of text...I have called these forms 'intertext'. **1988** *Times Lit. Suppl.* 4 Nov. 1227/3 Laforgue is using an intertext he expects his contemporary readers to recognize. **1989** *Whole Earth Rev.* Summer 80/2 I'm thinking of writing an intertext for *Neuromancer* for *Foundation*..a little annotated bit saying this came from that.

intertextual (ɪntə'tɛkstjuːəl), *a.* *Lit. Theory.* [Back-formation f. *INTERTEXTUALITY *n.*, after Fr. *intertextuelle* (coined in J. Kristeva

Semeiotike (1969) 115).] Denoting literary criticism which considers a text in the light of its relation to other texts; also used of texts so considered.

1973 *Lang. & Lang. Behavior Abstr*. VII. 856 Because certain texts make use of other texts, the problem of inter-textual and intra-textual relations is considered. **1974** *Romanic Rev*. Nov. LXV. 280 The poem negativizes this intertextual definition of a poem in yet another way: even a prose poem is supposed..to be polished and complete..whereas this poem is made to look like a preparatory sketch. **1982** J. CULLER *On Deconstruction* (ed. 2) i. 32 A structuralist pursuit of codes leads critics to treat the work as an intertextual construct—a product of various cultural discourses on which it relies for its intelligibility—and thus consolidates the central role of the reader as a centering role. **1985** *Times Lit. Suppl*. 15 Nov. 1279/4 Such a method gives the author abundant opportunity for intertextual slides... He illuminates Webster by Oscar Wilde. **1991** *Greece & Rome* 82 A reviewer familiar with the methods of Hellenistic poets will be more sympathetic than most to the idea of inter-textual allusion; but all too often G. appears to be striving too hard to create order out of verbal echoes from distant parts of the Homeric poems.

Hence **inter'textually** *adv.*

1985 *N.Y. Times* 17 Mar. VII. 19/1 They proclaim the existence of a black literature connected not so strongly by a common black culture or struggle as by images and techniques found from book to book ('intertextually'). **1987** *Nation* 15 Aug. 136/3 These later images—vertical, even square—have become more intertextually implicated in webworks of art-historical allusion. **1991** *Oxf. Art Jrnl*. XIV. 106/2 The issue here isn't whether..statements which emerge in one discourse function intertextually across a range of other enunciations and knowledges.

intertextuality (ɪntətɛkstjuːˈælɪtɪ), *n. Lit. Theory*. [ad. F. *intertextualité* (coined by J. Kristeva 1967, in *Critique* XXIII. 444): see INTER- and TEXTUALITY *n.*] The need for one text to be read in the light of its allusions to and differences from the content or structure of other texts; the (allusive) relationship between esp. literary texts.

1973 *Sociol. Abstr*. XXI. 960/1 2 hyp's [*sc.* hypotheses] have been extracted which seem appropriate in characterizing this text: the idea of constant reversibility between lanuage & reality; & the idea of 'intertextuality', of a dialogue between this and other texts. **1976** *Mod. Lang. Notes* Dec. 1382 The notion of intertextuality emphasizes that to read is to place a work in a discursive space, relating it to other texts and to the codes of that space. **1979** S. STEWART *Nonsense: Aspects of Intertextuality in Folklore & Lit*. ii. 48 Intertextuality is..a relationship between universes of discourse. **1984** S. GOLDHILL *Lang., Sexuality, Narrative: Oresteia* ii. 195 The intertextuality of the *Oresteia* and the *Odyssey*, which is so often ignored, is constitutive of the 'dynamics of misogyny' in the *Oresteia*. **1989** G. STEINER *Real Presences* II. iv. 85 Are all theories of hermeneutics and 'intertextuality'—a characteristic piece of current jargon which signals the obvious truth that, in Western literature, most serious writing incorporates, cites, denies, refers to previous writing—a waste product? **1995** *Extrapolation* Spring 60 Given the intertextuality of the *Star Trek* universe, it is likely that the miners Kamala meets in Ten Forward are an homage to 'Mudd's Women'.

J

J. [III.] Add: JIT, JiT *Comm.* = *JUST-IN-TIME.*
1984 E. P. DeGarmo et al. *Materials & Processes in Manuf.* (ed. 6) i. 9 They have a *Just-in-Time* (*JIT) production objective, in which they try to operate their production in very small batches. **1991** *Professional Engin.* July/Aug. 34/1 One of the fundamental principles of JIT manufacturing is the use of daily rates to regulate the flow of material through the factory.

jajoba *n.*, var. *JOJOBA *n.*

jemmy ('dʒɛmɪ), *v. colloq.* Also 9– **jimmy** (see JIMMY *n.*¹). [f. JEMMY *n.* 6.] *trans.* To force open (a lock, window, etc.) with a jemmy or similar implement. Also *fig.*
1893 J. Hawthorne *Confessions of Convict* iii. 49 We took the safe..and carried it..to the basement...We jimmied it open in no time. *Ibid.* xi. 172, I have drilled holes in large safes so accurately that the bolts could be 'jimmied' without leaving a mark. **1905** *N.Y. Even. Post* 22 Dec. 3 The thieves jimmied the front door. **1922** R. Parrish *Case & Girl* xxxii. 247 Finally we jimmied open the back door of this garage. **1933** J. V. Turner *Homicide Haven* xvii. 206 Ripple had demonstrated that even with a garden pick a window can be easily jemmied. **1973** *Islander* (Victoria, B.C.) 8 Apr. 5/2 Not a footprint, not a gate left open or a lock jemmied. **1973** *Sat. Rev. Society* (U.S.) May 42/2 Any attempt to jimmy the doors, hood, or trunk will cause the horn to begin sounding. **1973** *Times Lit. Suppl.* 29 June 741/3 Her stable of talented students..would have had a harder row to hoe if Mary Quant had not jemmied open the door for young designers. **1980** *Amat. Gardening* 4 Oct. 31/1 A garden spade is just about the best tool there is for jemmying a door or window. **1991** D. Coupland *Generation X* II. xv. 86 Give parents the tiniest of confidences and they'll use them as crowbars to jimmy you open and rearrange your life.

jerk, *n.*¹ Senses 2 e and f in Dict. become 2 f and g. Add: [2.] e. *Weight-lifting.* A lift in which a bar-bell held at shoulder level is raised above the head in a sudden movement by straightening the arms and legs; usu. as the second part of a *clean and jerk* (see *CLEAN *n.* 2). Cf. SNATCH *n.* 3 e.
1913 *Health & Strength* 6 Dec. 632/2 L.h. clean and jerk. **1928** *Health & Strength Ann.* 77 Two Hands Clean and Jerk with Barbell. **1956** *Muscle Power* Mar. 28/1 He just failed with an attempt for a new world Jerk record of 292 [lbs]. **1974** *Rules of Game* ii. 43/1 In a competition, weights must be lifted using one of two methods: the snatch and the jerk (or clean and jerk). **1986** *Weight Lifting* ('Know the Game' Ser.) (ed. 2) 13 The feet should then be stepped in to hip-width prior to the jerk.

jerk, *v.*¹ Add: [2.] c. *Weight-lifting.* To lift (a weight attached to a bar-bell) from shoulder level to above the head by straightening the arms and legs in a sudden movement. Freq. in phr. *to clean and jerk* (see *CLEAN *v.* 7). Cf. *JERK *n.*¹ 2 e.
1936 *Health & Strength* 26 Sept. 455/3, I can jerk 180 lb to arms' length from the shoulders but cannot 'clean' more than 154 lb. **1956** *Strength & Health* Nov. 18/2 A lifter should, by these means, be able to Jerk 5-10 kilos more than he can Clean. **1960** *Muscle Power* Feb.-Mar. 32/3 Chao Ching-Kuei succeeded in Jerking 392 pounds. **1986** *Weight Lifting* ('Know the Game' Ser.) (ed. 2) 17/2 To develop the skill and timing in jerking weights overhead and to develop power in this movement.

jet, *n.*³ Add: [IV.] [11.] **jet-lagged** *a.*, suffering from jet lag (freq. *predic.*); also *fig.*
1976 *Nature* 29 Apr. 737/1 Businessmen at Heathrow..couldn't know whether they were *jet lagged until they had found out whether their internal clocks were waking them up at the witching hour of 3 AM the following morning. **1985** *N. & Q.* Sept. 406/1 The reader leaves rather jet-lagged, yet might have flown further and reached a more satisfying destination. **1991** H. Gold *Best Nightmare on Earth* viii. 118 Thirty years later in Paris, criminally jetlagged, I was walking at three A.M. in St.-Germain-des-Prés.
  jet-lagging *a.*, that induces jet lag.
1982 *Life* Apr. 8/1 Right from the *jet-lagging start, I was knocked out by the place.

jeu, *n.* Add: **2.** Phrase. *les jeux sont faits* (lɛ ʒø sɔ̃ fɛ) [Fr., lit. 'the games are made']: the stakes are set; in roulette, the call made by the croupier as the wheel is set in motion. Also occas. in *sing.* Freq. followed by *RIEN NE VA PLUS *int. phr.*
1871 *Catal. Exhib. R. Acad. Arts* CIII. 12 The Salon d'Or, Homburg...W. P. Frith, R.A. 'Le jeu est fait—rien ne va plus.' **1922** Joyce *Ulysses* 496 Sieurs et dames, faites vos jeux! (..Tiny roulette planets fly from his hands.) Les jeux sont faits! (The planets rush together, uttering crepitant cracks.) Rien n'va plus. **1982** *Financial Times* 21 July 14/5 Discreet murmurs of 'Les jeux sont faits. Rien ne va plus.'

ježekite ('jeʒɪkaɪt, 'dʒɛzɪkaɪt), *n. Min.* (now *rare*). Also jezekite. [a. F. *ježekite* (coined by F. Slavik 1914, in *Bull. Soc. Française de Min.* XXXVII. 153), f. the name of Bohuslav *Ježek*, 20th-century Czech mineralogist.] A fluophosphate of sodium, calcium, and aluminium now recognized as identical with morinite.
1916 *Mineral. Mag.* XVII. 352 Ježekite. **1954** *Ann. Acad. Sci. Fennicæ* A. III. xxxix. 86 This work gives a description of the zoning in the lithiumpegmatite of Viitaniemi, Eräjärvi, Central-Finland, including the order of crystallization of 43 Pegmatite minerals. Phosphates—Triplite,.. Morinite, Jezekite, Hureaulite and a new mineral..are described. **1958** *Amer. Mineralogist* XLIII. 594 The presence of 1.1 ion of Li in the ježekite unit cell seems very doubtful; more probably there was some amblygonite contamination. **1962** *Ibid.* XLVII. 398 (*heading*) Ježekite is morinite. *Ibid.*, It is stated by Frondel (1947) that x-ray and optical study of morinite..showed it to be identical with ježekite. This was confirmed by Fisher and Runner (1958), who however considered that the name ježekite should be dropped, since morinite has priority. **1993** A. M. Clark *Hey's Mineral Index* 471/1 Morinite...At one time regarded as the same as jezekite, but the former name has priority.

jicama ('hiːkəmə), *n.* Chiefly *U.S.* Also 7 xiquima. [Mexican Sp. *jícama*, ad. Nahuatl *xicama.*] The white, fleshy tuberous root of the yam bean as a vegetable that is eaten raw or cooked, esp. in salads. Also, the plant itself, a tropical leguminous vine, *Pachyrhizus erosus*, cultivated esp. in Central America.
1604 E. Grimstone tr. *J. d'Acosta's Hist. Indies* IV. xviii. 260 There is *Ocas, Yanococas, Camotes, Vatas,*

Xiquimas,.. and an infinite number of other kindes [of roots]. [**1884** F. A. OBER *Mexican Resources* 9 (*table*) The fruits of Mexico... *Mexican name*. Jícama... *English*. Farinaceous root.] **1909** in *Cent. Dict.* Suppl. **1977** C. McFADDEN *Serial* iii. 13/2 Poking kumquats and wondering if Harvey would eat jicama, Kate ran down the list of men she knew. **1983** M. YAMAGUCHI *World Vegetables* xiv. 164 Jicama can be found wild in Mexico and northern Central America. **1988** *Independent* 15 Aug. 24/2 Warm lobster taco with.. jicama salad. **1991** *Sun* (Baltimore) 18 Aug. G4/4 Perhaps some chopped red bell peppers and jicama with salsa while she's fixing dinner.

jigger, *v.*[1] Add: **3.** *trans*. To rearrange or adjust (statistics, procedures, etc.), esp. to produce the desired result; to manipulate, tamper with. Chiefly *U.S.*
1961 F. LEIBER *Big Time* (1965) 57 It's sweet to jigger reality, to twist the whole course of a man's life or a culture's, to ink out his or its past and scribble in a new one. **1976** *Forbes* (N.Y.) 15 Nov. 129 Conventional price indexes.. often jigger the market basket's content in an effort to minimize social changes that don't reflect changes in the quantity of money. **1980** *N.Y. Times* 18 Dec. B5/4 To the extent that we keep jiggering it to meet special needs, this whole thing can fall down around our ears. **1992** P. J. PLAUGER *Standard C Libr.* 199 Where it's possible, the linker can be jiggered to avoid the possibility.

Jimmy, *n.*[2] Add: **11.** Chiefly *Sc*. or in representation of Scottish speech: used as a form of address to a man, esp. a stranger. Cf. JOCK *n.*[1] 1 a, JOHN *n.* 1 b. *colloq.*
1981 A. GRAY *Lanark* (1982) xlii. 524 'It means, Jimmy, that you'd better come quietly with us,' said a policeman... He said feebly, 'My name is Lanark.' 'Don't let it worry you, Jimmy.' **1982** S. BAXTER *Parliamo Glasgow* xi. 84 Glasgow girl enters. *Girl*: Hey Jimmy. *Basil*: How dare you interrupt me in the middle of a rehearsal! **1983** P. TURNBULL *Fair Friday* ii. 30 In Edinburgh the law students.. had starched white collars.. and called their clients 'the Jimmies'. **1986** R. SPROAT *Stunning the Punters* 127 'Oh, aye, ah, you're no offended then, Jimmy?' says one of the Scotch boys.

job, *n.*[2] Add: [**1.**] **e.** *Computing*. An item of work (to be) performed by a computer; a set of programs and the data that they will operate on stored, forwarded, or executed as a unit.
1964 T. W. McRAE *Impact of Computers on Accounting* vii. 209 By far the most interesting development.. has been the introduction of multi-programme machines, which can process a number of jobs at the same time. **1973** C. W. GEAR *Introd. Computer Sci.* iv. 168 When a job is terminated, the scheduler uses the space for another job and puts the output on a work list for the output processor. **1989** *PC World* Oct. 239/2 To prevent a printing traffic jam, the spooler stacks the print jobs in one or more queues and sends the files to one or more printers.
f. An operation involving cosmetic surgery, or the result of such an operation: as the second element in Combs., as *breast job, nose job* (see NOSE *n.* 18), etc. *colloq*. (orig. *U.S.*).
1963 T. PYNCHON *V* iv. 95 Chapter four. In which Esther gets a nose job. **1978** *Washington Post* 7 Dec. B1/3, I thought of this recently because of the flap over Betty Ford and her face job. She.. had some of the creases ironed out of her neck. **1986** *Economist* 20 Dec. 57 The faddish plastic surgery of the moment is the breast-job. **1989** *What Diet & Lifestyle* Dec. 12/1 Lip-jobs are overtaking nose-jobs in the cosmetic surgery stakes in America, with some surgeons reporting doing between 25 and 80 lip jobs a month. **1990** *Sun* 23 May 11/6 [The nurse], who had a boob job to boost her part-time modelling, has been sacked.

[**7.**] **job club**, in the U.K.: an organization set up either by a local community or by a Job Centre which aims to help the long-term unemployed find work, by offering encouragement and material support such as free postage and use of a telephone.
1985 *Financial Times* 1 Oct. 9/1 A chain of 200 '*jobclubs*' is to be established by the end of next year to help the long-term unemployed. **1989** *Independent* 17 Nov. 6/6 At the area's 'job club'—set up in Accrington by local industry at the height of the recession to help long-term unemployed find jobs—only two of the 26 members are from Clitheroe. **1991** *Economist* 5-11 Jan. 26/2 The government is getting much value for its money, he claims, from Jobclubs which offer the unemployed services such as free telephones and confidence-boosting sessions, but which eschew training.

job control language *Computing*, a language in which instructions may be written to control the running of jobs (sense *[1] e).
1967 E. R. LANNON in Cox & Grose *Organiz. Bibliogr. Rec. by Computer* IV. 82 The function of these programs is to determine which additional programs are required.. and to insert into the Job Stream the required *Job Control Language to operate the same. **1972** BARRON & JACKSON *Software* II. 173 The user of a sophisticated operating system is faced with.. the necessity of learning a job control language or a command language in which to talk to the operating system. **1992** *Macworld* Dec. 164/2 If you grew up with the mainframe world's Job Control Language (JCL), you might think of the Rosanne-AppleScript combination as a friendlier and more powerful JCL.

job stream *Computing*, a series of jobs awaiting processing.
1967 E. R. LANNON in Cox & Grose *Organiz. Bibliogr. Rec. by Computer* IV. 82 The function of these programs is to determine which additional programs are required.. and to insert into the *Job Stream the required Job Control Language to operate the same. **1989** *DEC Professional* Nov. 172/2 Target-Batch is used to submit production jobs and job streams at pre-established dates and times with error.. reports.

Joe, *n.*[2] Add: [**5.**] **e. Joe Public**. (A member of) an audience; hence, (a member of) the general public. Freq. mildly *derog. slang* (orig. *U.S. Theatr.*).
1942 BERREY & VAN DEN BARK *Amer. Thes. Slang* §584/4 *Audience*,.. Joe Public. **1953** *Commercial & Financial Chron.* 14 May 13 (*heading*) Paging Joe Public. **1972** *Bankers Mag.* (Boston, Mass.) Winter 102/2 Some very powerful bankers and brokers leaked.. news of the downturn in the affairs of Douglas Aircraft. This permitted those who were privy to the information to get out from under before 'Joe Public'. **1978** D. NORDEN in Muir & Norden *Take my Word for It* 80 We've really got to provide Joe Public with some sort of ongoing visual reference-point. **1991** *Model Railways* Mar. 111/1 The East Midlands Model Railway Exhibition.. is actually aimed at the railway modeller and the enthusiast, rather than 'Joe Public'.

Johnny, *n.* Sense 5 in Dict. becomes 6. Add: **5.** Also with lower-case initial. A condom; = *rubber johnny* s.v. RUBBER *n.*[1] 14. Also *johnny bag*. Cf. JOHN *n.* 1 g. *slang*.
1963 (in list of teenage slang vocabulary given to M. Laski) J. B.: Johnny Bag: durex. **1965** *New Society* 14 Jan. 16/1 As regards birth control they all said it was easy to get 'Johnny bags' at the barbers. **1970** *Times Educ. Suppl.* 4 Dec. 23/3 At 50.. things became much warmer, and went up by a carefully graded system to 100, which, my informant wrote, 'is rightly reserved for full intercourse without a johnny'. **1986** *Observer* 23 Nov. 64/3 The contraceptive sheaths that three generations of British males have known variously as Durex, rubbers, Johnnies and French Letters. **1991**

Rage 13 Feb. (Sex Suppl.) 17/1 *Johnnies*. Otherwise known as condoms, rubber love is back in pop with the advent of Aids.

jojoba (həˈhəʊbə), *n. Bot.* Formerly also jajoba, jojobe, jojove. [a. Sp. *jojoba*, ad. native Indian *hohohwi*.] **a.** A desert shrub, *Simmondsia chinensis* (family Simmondsiaceae), native to northern Mexico and the south-western U.S., that is used for the oil it yields. Also, = **jojoba oil* below.

  1900 E. J. WICKSON *California Fruits* (ed. 3) 43 The 'jajoba' (*Simmondsia californica*) is a low shrub, the fresh fruits of which..are eaten like almonds. **1933** *Bot. Gaz.* LXXXXIV. 826 *Simmondsia californica*, commonly known in the southwest as 'jojobe' or 'jojove', is an evergreen shrub. **1958** *Econ. Bot.* XII. 261 Jojoba, the gray box bush, is a drought-resistant, long-lived, evergreen, desert shrub bearing fruit like an acorn set in sepals. **1983** *Houston* (Texas) *Chron.* 21 Aug. 1. 19/5 The August harvest of jojoba looks good so far, raising the spirits of manufacturers of just about everything from food to floor wax. **1989** *Times* 31 Aug. 25/6 Jojoba is hardly absorbed in the gut—an attractive feature if you are trying to make low-calorie foods. **1989** *Sunday Tel.* 10 Dec. 43/4 Brown paper wrapped grapefruit and jojoba soap, £2.25.
  b. jojoba oil, oil extracted from the fruit of the jojoba, used in cosmetics and as a substitute for sperm oil.
  1975 *Nature* 22 May 272/3 Chemical analysis of jojoba oil has confirmed that it is strikingly similar in composition to sperm oil. **1986** *Look Now* Oct. 68/2 The Renewer Lotion contains collagen, jojoba oil and a special firming ingredient to smooth and soften the skin.

joke, *v.* Add: [2.] **b.** To utter as a joke, or in a joking manner. Freq. with direct speech or clause as obj.
  1863 TROLLOPE *Rachel Ray* III. xiv. 281 The farmer had come in and had joked his joke, and Mrs Sturt had clacked over them as though they were a brood of chickens of her own hatching. *a*1911 D. G. PHILLIPS *Susan Lenox* II. vi. 155 'I've been a lot of things in my day,' said Max with pride. 'So I've heard,' joked Maud. **1917** R. FROST *Let.* 13 Nov. (1972) 17, I wish I thought Miss Waite was joking the joke I joke when she said 'You have some hope of yourself then?' **1962** N. FREELING *Love in Amsterdam* I. 15 ' Who's dead?' he joked. **1972** *Fairbanks* (Alaska) *Daily News-Miner* 3 Nov. 1/5 The candidate's national political director..joked that the remark had been rather natural for a Democratic nominee. **1986** J. NAGENDA *Seasons of T. Tebo* I. vi. 33 Baby and Jane had often joked, romantically, that if anything happened to them they would go to the coast.

joky, *a.* Add: Hence 'jokily *adv.*, in a joky manner.
  1976 *Star* (Sheffield) 29 Oct. 2/5 Jokily-named Baudines regret helping wounded man in Shanklin. **1988** *Observer* 30 Oct. 15/4 He claims this practice is a joke, but who wants to be stabbed jokily?

journo ('dʒɜːnəʊ), *n.* (and *a.*) *colloq.* (orig. *Austral.*). [Abbrev. of JOURN(ALIST *n.* + -o².] A journalist, esp. a newspaper journalist. Also *attrib.* or as *adj.*
  1967 *Kings Cross Whisper* (Sydney) xxxv. 6/3 *Journo*, journalist. **1973** *Nation Rev.* (Melbourne) 31 Aug. 1444/5 He will be reinstated at the level of an A grade journo, and *not* as executive producer of *TDT*. **1981** C. WALLACE-CRABBE *Splinters* 50 Smashed out of his mind he was when some creeping journo got onto him. **1984** *Listener* 10 May 23/3 Rupert Murdoch once said, if the journos don't like it they can always get out; there are plenty more journos on the street. **1984** M. DELAHAYE *Third Day* 27 He was being set up by Matzliah and his 'journo' friends. **1987** *Daily Tel.* 11

Apr. 9/6 Women reporters have exposed the secrets of the changing rooms...One lady journo tells us that women players shower in the nude. **1994** *Guardian* 27 June 11. 12/3 Stan was put on this Earth to reassure those people who think all journos are alcos, defiantly churning out copy while two and a half sheets to the wind.

Jovian, *a.* and *n.* Add: [B.] **2.** An (imagined) inhabitant of the planet Jupiter.
  1929 S. LESLIE *Anglo-Catholic* xv. 209 Mary and Julius emerged with the supreme British condescension of Jovians or Neptunians visiting a minor planet. **1943** R. BRADBURY in *Thrilling Wonder Stories* Feb. 90/1 The blue-skinned Jovian..said nothing. **1953** A. C. CLARKE in *If* May 15/1 We have never found any trace of what might be called a religion among the Jovians. **1976** *Sci. Amer.* May 108/2 They would make for Jovians the same changes of shape that the moon makes for us Terrestrials. **1987** *Times Lit. Suppl.* 23 Jan. 76/1 Christian Wolff calculated that the height of Jovians must be 13$\frac{819}{1440}$ Paris feet.

judicial, *a.* and *n.* Add: [A.] [2.] **d. judicial review** orig. *U. S.*, a process whereby a judicial body re-examines and rules upon a matter previously decided in another (esp. subordinate) court or assembly; *spec.* in the U.S., a procedure by which the Supreme Court may pronounce on the constitutional validity of a legislative act; an instance of this. Hence, any process by which a judicial body rules upon the legal validity of some action, condition, etc., referred to it for assessment.
  1851 *Federal Cases* (U.S.) (1895) IX. 793/1 The propriety of the reissue in the case before us can hardly claim a judicial review. **1882** *Supreme Court Reporter* (U.S.) I. 346 The District Court, in correcting the order of distribution made by the trustees, acted within its powers, and..that order has passed beyond judicial review. **1923** *Central Law Jrnl.* XCVI. 277/2 It is also generally known that it is proposed by constitutional amendment to take from the Supreme Court the power of judicial review of legislative enactment. **1959** S. A. DE SMITH *Judicial Rev. Admin Action* i. 16 In England judicial review is a function of the ordinary courts and has developed empirically from the fundamental principles that the courts are competent to pass on the *vires* of administrative action and that it is for the superior courts to contain inferior tribunals within their allotted jurisdiction. **1966** *Texas Law Rev.* XLIV. 939 When one looks at the problems which judicial review of law enforcement activities presents to police departments, [etc.]. **1982** *Financial Times* 5 Feb. 27/4 The Commodity Futures Trading Commission..has said 'no'..to the courts who want judicial review of CFTC emergency powers. **1991** *Industrial Law Jrnl.* XX. 294 Once the revised statutes are in place, an academic who is dismissed will have three possible causes of action: for unfair dismissal, wrongful dismissal or judicial review. **1996** *Daily Mail* 19 Mar. 51/4 Judicial review is a relatively recent way by which an administrative decision, such as that made by a civil servant or minister, or a quasi-judicial or judicial decision, such as that made by a tribunal, may be reviewed by the High Court.

jug, *n.*² Add: [2.] **c.** *slang.* A woman's breast. Usu. in *pl.*
  1957 F. KOHNER *Gidget* v. 54 Someone would sit up and point at some sex display, 'Look at those boobs!' The whole gang came to life. 'Ahhhh—the Ekberg!'..'Some jugs!' **1971** E. E. LANDY *Underground Dict.* 39 *Breast*.., jug, knocker, marshmallow, ninny jug. **1987** T. WOLFE *Bonfire of Vanities* (1988) iii. 70 She must allow him the precious currency he had earned, which is youth and beauty and juicy jugs and loamy loins. **1989** 'C. ROMAN' *Foreplay* ix. 109 Nancy Nipples balances popcorn boxes on her jugs. **1991** *Independent* (Mag.) 26 Oct. 67/1 Her reverie

is interrupted by a ribald cry, delivered in a strong West Country accent: 'Get your jugs out for the lads!'

juggle, v. Add: [**2.**] **b.** *spec.* To toss and catch several objects continuously, keeping at least one of them in the air while handling the others. Also, to toss an object, etc., from hand to hand with dexterity; (of two or more persons) to toss an object, etc., back and forth between them. Freq. const. *with*.

1892 *Routledge's Bk. of Circus* 56 All acrobats can juggle. *Ibid.* 58 It is very difficult to juggle with articles of various..weights at the same time. **1901** *Playgoer* Oct. 15/2 Before he left the cradle, he juggled with his feeding bottle. **1921** J. E. T. CLARK *Juggling* 98 Learning to juggle is like learning to walk on stilts. **1930** H. S. WALPOLE *Rogue Herries* I. 131 A company of Chinese people travelling with the Fair..juggled with gold balls and swallowed silver swords. **1938** N. STREATFIELD *Circus is Coming* vii. 117 The first Risley who had the idea of juggling with a real boy. **1975** R. DAVIES *World of Wonders* (1977) II. iii. 185 He can't juggle and he can't walk rope.

c. *transf.* Const. *with.* To manipulate something (or several often conflicting things simultaneously), esp. with ingenuity or skill.

1897 *Strand* XIV. 95/2 The Burmese are born jugglers; they juggle with everything..even their finances. **1902** KIPLING in *Windsor Mag.* Dec. 13/2 Kysh's hands juggling with the levers behind the discreet backward sloping dash. **1927** E. BOWEN *Hotel* ix. 96 Happiness, she said to herself, is not to be solicited, but coming, for however short a time, comes with an appearance of finality, to be juggled with offhand. **1935** D. L. SAYERS *Gaudy Night* xviii. 382 How *dared* he pick up her word 'sleep' and use it four times in as many lines, and each time in a different foot, as though juggling with the accent-shift were child's play? **1964** *Mod. Law Rev.* XXVII. 264 To juggle with the language of the forms of action and say that the plaintiff's action sounds in tort not contract, cannot alter the fact. **1982** A. PRICE *Old 'Vengeful'* vi. 87 The child juggled with her burdens the better to display the garment.

[**4.**] **c.** *Baseball.* Of a fielder: to mishandle (a ball) without dropping it, thereby failing to prevent a runner reaching a base.

1873 *N. Y. Herald* 13 Sept. 5/3 Fulmer tried Pearce with a scorching hot grounder, but Dickey juggled it and Devlin went to second. **1889** *Century Mag.* Oct. 833/1 A short-stop or third baseman finds that he has no time to 'juggle' the ball and then throw the man out. **1911** Z. GREY *Young Pitcher* vi. 63 Raymond..pounced upon the ball...Nothing got past him, but he juggled the ball. **1993** *Chicago Tribune* 29 June IV. 3/4 He scored when Tony Gwynn doubled and Sosa juggled that ball.

d. To toss and catch (a number of objects) continously, keeping at least one of them in the air while handling the others. Also, to toss (an object, etc.) from hand to hand with dexterity; (of two or more persons) to toss (an object, etc.) back and forth between them.

1897 *Strand Mag.* XIII. 94/2 He juggles a heavy knife, a fork, and a turnip. **1909** H. R. CORT *Donakin Circus* 10 They could juggle balls while dancing a waltz. **1921** J. E. T. CLARK *Juggling* 98 It is advisable for the novice to acquire skill in..juggling various and diverse articles. **1959** F. ASTAIRE *Steps in Time* iv. 26 The older Japanese would lie on their backs..and juggle my pal back and forth with their feet. **1981** W. SOYINKA *Aké* iii. 37 The man in the lead juggled an enormous mace. **1984** J. UPDIKE *Witches of Eastwick* iii. 240 Van Horne juggled first three, then four, then five tangerines.

e. *trans.* To handle or combine (something or several things) adroitly; to balance (one thing) *with* another.

1935 G. GREENE in *Spectator* 9 Aug. 222/2 What matters is the witty dialogue, the quick intelligent acting

of Mr. Tone and Miss Merkel, who juggle death so expertly and amusingly between them. **1985** G. EHRLICH *Solace of Open Spaces* 98 They have to know how to do many things—from juggling the futures market to overhauling a tractor or curing viral scours..in calves. **1990** *OnSat* 17-23 June 9/1 Bachelor dads have juggled leading their own lives with being a good influence on their dependents.

juggler, n. Add: [**2.**] **b.** *spec.* A person who practises juggling (sense *c).

This sense separated gradually from sense 2 a as the specific skill gained recognition as a form of entertainment distinct from conjuring, etc.

*a***1807** W. WORDSWORTH *Poems in Two Vols.* I. 119 A Juggler's Balls old Time about him toss'd. **1816** *Handbill* 3 Sept., The Chinese Jugglers...Three large knives are thrown up and caught together with..dexterity. **1821** W. HAZLITT *Table Talk* IX. 181 The chief of the Indian Jugglers begins with tossing up two brass balls. *c***1894** in *Entertainment Soc.* 8 Juggler, suitable for garden party or school treats, &c. **1931** H. S. WALPOLE *Judith Paris* II. vii. 383 The sky tossed cloud after cloud as though there were some giant juggler over the hill. **1937** F. FOSTER *Clowning Through* 100 One is apt to think of a juggler as a person who throws up and catches a number of balls. **1963** A. FARRER in F. F. Bruce *Promise & Fulfilment* 104 Keeping (like jugglers) half a dozen balls in the air at once. **1987** *Telford Jrnl.* 4 June 11/3 The..circus acts..will include jugglers.

juggling, *vbl. n.* Add: **c.** The art of tossing and catching a number of objects continuously, keeping at least one of them in the air while handling the others, esp. as a form of entertainment. Also *transf.* (cf. *JUGGLE v. 2 c).

1836 *Handbill* (Vauxhall Gardens) July, Great Attractions of this Fête..include..Double Juggling. **1874** L. CARR *Judith Gwynne* I. vii. 202 Dinner being got through, not unaccompanied by some terrible feats of knife-juggling. **1879** C. KEITH *Circus Life & Amusements* iii. 23 We armed ourselves with some juggling knives. **1921** J. E. T. CLARK *Juggling* 98, I ask the keen aspirant to practice diligently simple juggling. **1947** J. J. MILLS *How to do Juggling* 5 There is an unusual interest in juggling at the present time. **1976** F. HOWERD *On the Way I lost It* ii. 31 Acts that demanded any degree of physical dexterity, such as conjuring, juggling [etc.]. **1989** C. TRILLIN *Couple of Eccentric Guys* in *Amer. Stories* (1991) 115 He spent only most of his time practicing juggling, leaving some time to practice the unicycle.

jugum, n. Restrict *Bot.* to sense 1 and add: **3.** *Anat.* A ridge or furrow connecting certain structures, esp. on bone. Chiefly in specific applications with (modern) Latin epithet, as *juga alveolaria, jugum sphenoidale*, etc.

1887 L. HEITZMANN tr. *C. Heitzmann's Anat.* I. 23 Right superior maxillary bone...The alveolar process contains 8 alveoli for the reception of the teeth; its outer plate shows eminences, *Juga alveolaria*. **1893** J. B. SUTTON in H. Morris *Treat. Human Anat.* I. 37 In the course of the first year the orbito-sphenoids fuse in the middle line to form the *jugum sphenoidale*, which excludes the anterior part of the pre-sphenoid from the cranial cavity. **1962** *Gray's Anat.* (ed. 33) 314 Anteriorly the jugum articulates with the posterior margin of the cribriform plate.

juice, v. Sense 2 in Dict. becomes 3. Add: **2. a.** To extract the juice from (a fruit, vegetable, etc.).

[**1629** J. PARKINSON *Parad.* II. vi. 478 [Sage] being beaten and iuyced (rather than minced as manie doe) is put to a rosted Pigges braines.] **1950** *Publ. Amer. Dial. Soc.* XIV. 42 [S. Carolina word-list] Juice me these lemons. **1977** *New Yorker* 18 July 61/2 (Advt.), These individual grapes together make up one sample which our field man 'juices' on the spot. **1982** *Observer* 31 Oct. 31/4 Lance Loud juices two pounds of spinach and two pounds of carrots daily. **1986** *N.Y. Times* 2 Mar. (Connecticut Weekly section) 18/2 Always grate the rind before juicing the fruit, not the other way round.

b. *transf.* and *fig.* Cf. MILK *v.* 4.

1915 *Dialect Notes* IV. 227 *Juice,..* to milk. Formerly very common, this verb is now chiefly used facetiously (as '*Juice* the heifer'). **1961** *New Left Rev.* May–June 47/1 The actors..juiced the improvisational tendency in the play... Some of the minor characters were even playing for laughs. **1975** *Business Week* 17 Feb. 54/2 As was the case during last year's decline, some stocks have been juiced by tender offers.

juiced, *a.* Add: **3.** Of a fruit, vegetable, etc.: that has had the juice extracted. Also *fig.*

1965 *Economist* 28 Aug. 785/2 California—where on over 100,000 acres grow two-thirds of all the tomatoes tinned, juiced and ketchupped in the United States. **1981** *Guardian Weekly* 29 Mar. 20/3 Albeit 'juiced, tired, lonesome and run down', Waits is now in a position to be more selective about his activities. **1988** *Boston Globe* 21 Nov. 39/1 For the vinaigrette: 1 small sweet pomegranate, juiced to yield ⅓ cup liquid.

juke, *n.* Add: [**2.**] **juke-box**, (*b*) *Computing*, a device which stores a number of disks in such a way as to enable data to be read from any of them as required.

1979 *Proc. Soc. Photo-Optical Instrumentation Engin.* CC. 69, 10 of the jukebox reader units are grouped together through a common read controller to provide a 10^{14} bit system with a 3 second access time to any data record. **1985** *Which Computer?* Apr. 125/3 The amount of storage is extended by the use of a disc exchanger (called a 'juke box'). **1991** *Offshore Engineer* Sept. 137/4 IDL and Rank Xerox..will supply the new Windows 3-based document management software, a jukebox and a full drawing and editing facility.

Julia (ˈdʒuːlɪə), *n. Math.* [The name of Gaston Maurice *Julia* (1893–1978), Algerian-born French mathematician.] **Julia set**, the set of complex numbers z which do not stay within a bounded region of the complex plane when a given mapping, esp. one of the form $z \to z^2 + c$ (where c is a constant complex number), is repeatedly applied to them. Also, the boundary of such a set; a diagrammatic representation of such a set.

1976 *Canad. Jrnl. Math.* XXVIII. 1211 We consider now those Julia sets which are sets of non-uniqueness and hence are very far from being Weierstrass sets. **1983** *Jrnl. Statistical Physics* XXXIII. 560 The Julia set of a renormalization transformation is nothing but the limiting set of all the zeros in the complex plane of the partition function. **1986** *Nature* 16 Oct. 590/2 For some values of the added constant, the Julia set is a connected fractal. **1990** *Sci. Amer.* Apr. 15/1 He began using a computer to map out Julia sets, which are generated by plugging complex numbers into iterative functions.

junk, *n.*[2] Add: [**5.**] **junk bond** *Finance* (orig. *U.S.*), a stock with a high rate of interest and substantial risk, issued esp. to finance a corporate take-over or a buy-out.

1974 *Business Week* 28 Sept. 77/1 A more daring way to play converts is to sift among what people call '*junk' bonds, whose yields have become spectacular. **1988** *Sunday Tel.* 30 Oct. 35/2 The event was the withdrawing..of a $1.15 billion issue of high-interest bearing (and high risk—hence 'junk') bonds. **1991** *Economist* 5 Oct. 103/1 With the economy weak and financial markets still hurt by a credit crunch and the collapse of the junk-bond market, this is not a good

time for the cold-shower business of repaying, rolling over or replacing corporate debt.

just-in-time (ˌdʒʌstɪnˈtaɪm), *adj. phr.* and *n. phr. Comm.* Also unhyphenated. [f. the phr. *just in time*: see JUST *adv.*, *in time* s.v. TIME *n.* IV. 46.] **A.** *adj. phr.* Designating or relating to a manufacturing system in which components are delivered at the time required for assembly in order to minimize storage costs; = *KANBAN *n.* 2. Abbrev. *JIT* s.v. *J III.

1977 *Internat. Jrnl. Production Res.* XV. 559 A production control system for just-in-time production and making full use of workers' capabilities is the Kanban System. **1984** *Internat. Managem.* (Asia/Pacific ed.) Mar. 13/1 In addition to just-in-time systems, which are based on Toyota Motor Co.'s famed *kanban* (a recorder authorization card) method..a rash of new computer simulation programs is sweeping the manufacturing world. **1988** *Design Graphics World* Feb. 40/2 The publication presents major concepts for integrating management information and plant floor information. 'A just-in-time information system can result in dramatic quality improvements.' **1991** *Purchasing & Supply Managem.* Apr. 40/1 Just In Time supplies were observed being delivered to the assembly line by a fleet of fast moving forklift trucks. **1992** *Economist* 15 Feb. 80/2 In a sample of 20 firms that Ms Milkman studied more closely, a mere four had the vaunted 'just-in-time' stock-control system.

B. *ellipt.* as *n. phr.* The just-in-time system.

1984 *Fortune* 2 Apr. 13/1 The essence of just-in-time is that the manufacturer does not keep much inventory on hand—he relies on suppliers to furnish parts just in time for them to be assembled. **1989** *Accountancy* May 153/1 Just-in-time demands spot on planning systems or a very stable order board. **1991** D. LODGE *Paradise News* III. iii. 266 'It sounds like what we call just-in-time in industry,' said Brian Everthorpe. 'Each operation on the assembly line is buffered by a card that instructs the operative to supply the next operation precisely when needed. Eliminates bottlenecks.'

juvenile, *a.* and *n.* Add: [**4.**] **juvenile-onset** *adj. Path.*, *spec.* designating or pertaining to forms of diabetes that develop in children or young adults; *esp.* insulin-dependent diabetes.

1975 *Diabetes* XXIV. 44/2 There do appear to be two relatively polar forms of diabetes in children, adolescents and young adults. The classical, and more common form (here called classical *juvenile-onset type diabetes, or classical JOD) is usually characterized by an abrupt clinical onset, severe symptoms, and a tendency to ketoacidosis. **1977** *Ann. Internat Med.* LXXXVI. 56/1 Thirteen juvenile-onset diabetics with azotemic diabetic neuropathy..being evaluated for renal transplantation underwent cardiac catheterization with angiography. **1990** *Sci. Amer.* July 42/2 The autoimmune process that causes insulin-dependent diabetes is highly selective and frequently begins before adulthood (which is why the disease was formerly called juvenile-onset diabetes).

juvenilize (ˈdʒuːvɪnɪlaɪz), *v. rare.* [f. JUVENILE *a.* and *n.* + -IZE.] *trans.* To render juvenile; to make or keep young or youthful; to arrest the development of. Also *fig.*

1833 *Blackw. Mag.* XXXIII. 848/1 Our system is juvenilized by all matin rural influences. **1989** *Forbes* (N.Y.) 23 Oct. 94/1 His mother juvenilized him by keeping him dependent on her.

juvenilized (ˈdʒuːvɪnɪlaɪzd), *ppl. a. Ent.* [f. as *JUVENILIZE *v.* + -ED[1].] Of an insect or a feature of its anatomy: rendered juvenile in appearance or physiological characteristics; displaying immaturity as a result of arrested or reversed development.

1975 *Entomologia Experimentalis et Applicata* XVIII. 87 (*title*) Ovarian development in juvenilised adult

Dysdercus cingulatus affected by some plant extracts. **1985** *Genetics* CXI. 805 The abnormal abdomen syndrome in *Drosophila mercatorum* is characterized by the persistence of juvenilized cuticle on the adult abdomen. **1985** *Acta Entomologica Bohemoslovaca* LXXXII. 81 Juvenilized larvae differed from controls mainly in their very intensive metabolism, higher water and fat content and lower glycogen content.

juvenilizing ('dʒuːvɪnɪlaɪzɪŋ), *ppl. a.* [f. as *JUVENILIZE *v.* + -ING².] Rendering young or youthful; that preserves youth, rejuvenating; chiefly *Ent.*, producing or pertaining to the arrest or reversal of the maturation of an insect or its organs.

1959 *Punch* 19 Aug. 52/1 To keep that lovely youthful contour pat in the deeply nourishing, juvenilizing cream for half an hour each morning and evening. **1969** *Life Sciences* VIII. 831 Their failure to induce a juvenilizing effect was puzzling since the larvae readily react to tiny amounts of Cecropia juvenile hormone. **1973** *Acta Entomologica Bohemoslovaca* LXX. 293 It is important to note that low doses of juvenilizing substances which affected older larvae had no effect on younger larvae. **1981** *Toxicology* XIX. 268 The possible juvenilizing effects of Dimilin and Altosid against larvae of *Culex pipiens* .. were studied. **1989** *Compar. Biochem. & Physiol.* A. XCII. 163 At 18°C the last instar *Galleria mellonella* larvae respond to juvenilizing treatment — chilling stress or juvenile hormone analogue — with a very low percentage or no supernumerary moults, respectively.

K

K. Add: [4.] [c.] **K.C.M.G.** (examples).

1842 *Royal Kalendar* sig. a*, *K.C.M.G.*, Knight Commander of St. Michael and St. George. **1880** *Foreign Office List* 172/2 Rose, Sir John,.. was made a K.C.M.G., January 15, 1870...Was made a G.C.M.G., October 29, 1878. **1907** W. S. CHURCHILL *Let.* 6 Nov. in R. S. Churchill *Winston S. Churchill* (1969) II. Compan. II. 695 Delighted Governor who is just made KCMG. **1986** *Independent* 31 Dec. 4/3 CMG is known by juniors as 'Call Me God' and KCMG as 'Kindly Call Me God'.

kaanpei, *n.*, var. of *GANBEI *int.* and *n.*

Kabinett (kabɪˈnɛt), *n.* Also †Cabinett. [a. G. *Kabinett(wein)* lit. 'cabinet or chamber wine', from its orig. being kept in a special cellar. Perh. originally from the name given to such a cellar at the monastery of Eberbach in southern Germany.]

A superior grade of wine, esp. German or Austrian wine, made from fully ripe grapes that ferment without added sugar; a wine of this grade, *spec.* a light wine of controlled quality under the German wine-classification system introduced in 1971 or the similar system effective in Austria since 1973. Also *Kabinett wine*.

1929 P. M. SHAND *Bk. Other Wines than French* iii. 42 In cases where the wine is a selected one.. the inscription should terminate with the word *Auslese*, *Goldbeerenauslese*,.. *Edelgewächs*, *Grosse Spitze*, or, in a very few isolated instances, *Cabinett*. **1957** L. W. MARRISON *Wines & Spirits* viii. 159 A *Kabinett* wine is one of these 'extra-special' wines, the inference being that it is equal to that put aside for the proprietor's own 'Kabinett'. **1971** H. MEINHARD *German Wines* iv. 35 The new German wine-law.. was effective from July, 1971...'Predicates', or quality designations.. begin at the bottom with 'Cabinet' (or 'Kabinett'), and rise.. to the pinnacle of 'Trockenbeerenauslese'. **1974** H. J. GROSSMAN *Guide to Wines, Spirits & Beers* (ed. 5) vii. 114 Kabinett wines must be made from fully ripe grapes..; the minimum must weight of 75 (or 72 in certain cold areas like the Mosel). **1991** *Sun* (Baltimore) 18 Aug. G6/4 There were relatively few wines made in the traditional, off-dry kabinett style that matches so well with food.

‖**kahu** (ˈkɑːhuː), *n.* N.Z. [Maori.] The Pacific marsh harrier, *Circus approximans*.

1843 E. DIEFFENBACH *Trav. N.Z.* II. III. ix. 365/2 *Kahu*, name of the hawk. **1882** W. D. HAY *Brighter Britain!* II. vi. 220 The Kahu (*Circus Gouldi*) is chief among several of the hawk tribe. **1946** *Jrnl. Polynesian Soc.* June 151 *Kāhu*, a bird (*Circus gouldi*), hawk, harrier. **1966** R. A. FALLA et al. *Field Guide Birds N.Z.* 98 Harrier. *Circus approximans*. Other names: Hawk, Swamp Harrier, Gould's Harrier, Kahu.

kainic (ˈkaɪnɪk), *a.* Pharm. [f. Jap. *kain(in* (f. *kainin-sō*, the name of the alga *Digenea simplex*) + -IC.] **kainic acid**, a neurotoxic organic acid, $C_{10}H_{15}NO_4$, which is obtained from the red alga *Digenea simplex* and is used as an anthelmintic.

1954 S. MURAKAMI et al. in *Jrnl. Pharmaceutical Soc. Japan* LXXIV. 560 (*heading*) Proposed change of the name 'Digenic Acid' to 'Kainic Acid'. **1961** *Jrnl. Formosan Med. Assoc.* LX. 341 The present study was carried out to assess the efficacy and practicability of use of a single dose of two kinds of ascaris drugs,

Piperazine derivatives and [a] combination of Santonin and Kainic acid, for mass treatment. **1974** *Nature* 26 Apr. 804/1 Kainic acid, a pyrrolidine derivative isolated from the seaweed *Digenea simplex*. **1988** *New Scientist* 21 Apr. 22/1 Researchers injected kainic acid—an algal extract normally used to kill intestinal worms—into rat brains to simulate the effects of Huntington's disease. **1992** P. G. STRANGE *Brain Biochem. & Brain Disorders* xi. 194 Kainic acid injection into the striatum of rats replicates many of the neurochemical alterations seen in Huntingdon's disease.

kairomone (ˈkaɪrəʊməʊn), *n. Biol.* [f. Gr. καιρό-ς opportunity, advantage + -*mone* after PHEROMONE *n.*] A chemical secreted and released by an organism which, when detected by an organism of another species, evokes a response which adaptively favours the latter.

1970 W. L. BROWN et al. in *Bioscience* XX. 21/1 Organisms also produce a wide range of substances that act as stimulants, inhibitors, or behavioral cues for species other than their own. Among these substances, we propose to designate two major functional groupings by the terms *allomone* and *kairomone*, chosen as intentional parallels to the term *pheromone*. *Ibid.* 21/2 A kairomone is here defined as a transspecific chemical messenger the adaptive benefit of which falls on the recipient rather than on the emitter. **1971** *Nature* 13 Aug. 484/1 Work is in progress.. making use of the parasites' ovipositional response as a bioassay for the kairomone. **1978** *Nature* 27 Apr. 817/2 I[*ps*] *avulsus*.. aggregates in response to ipsdienol and (*S*)-(−)-ipsenol, apparently the combination of a pheromone and a kairomone. **1989** *Ann. Entomol. Soc. Amer.* LXXXII. 656/1 In most parasitoid species investigated to date, host-emitted kairomones figure prominently in the foraging process.

Kaiser, *n.* Restrict *Hist.* to sense 1 in Dict. and add: **2.** *N. Amer.* [perh. directly ad. G. *Kaisersemmel*.] Ellipt. for *Kaiser roll* below.

1927 J. P. BRYANT *Commercial Exhib. & Fancy Breads* 106 The beginner will find it difficult at first to make nicely shaped Kaisers. **1986** *Waterloo* (Ontario) *Chron.* 12 Mar. 7/4 Sliced ham on a kaiser. **1993** *Canad. Living* Feb. 39/1 Breaded Veal on Kaisers... This hearty meal will satisfy even the most voracious appetite.

3. Kaiser (also **kaiser**) **roll** *N. Amer.* [tr. G. *Kaisersemmel*], a round roll made from unsweetened dough with several edges pulled and folded in at the centre to form a radial pattern.

[**1968** SINGER & GOTTLIEB tr. I. B. Singer *Manor* II. xx. 268 There was bread left over from breakfast, but Mrs Frankel sent a girl to the bakery to buy a fresh loaf and some Kaiser buns.] **1978** *Washington Post* 2 Feb. DC10/2 A ham sandwich.. made with canned ham, sliced and piled on a fresh *Kaiser roll. **1984** S. BELLOW *Him with his Foot in his Mouth* 262 A small work-force of Polish bakers, had supplied.. immigrant grocery stores with bread and kaiser rolls.

‖**k'ai shu** (kaɪ ʃuː), *n.* Also kai shu, †keae shoo. [Chinese *kǎishū*, f. *kǎi* model + *shū* script, writing.] The standard calligraphic script used for the Chinese language, developed during the Later Han dynasty (A.D. 23-220) as a simplified form of the official *li-shu* script. Also as *CHEN SHU *n.* Cf. *LI SHU *n.*

1876 *Encycl. Brit.* V. 655/2 The *Keae shoo* or 'model character'. **1910** *Ibid.* VI. 220/2 The final standardization of Chinese writing was due to the great calligraphist Wang Hsi-chih of the 4th century, who gave currency to the graceful style of character known as..*k'ai shu*, sometimes referred to as the 'clerkly hand'. **1958** W. WILLETTS *Chinese Art* II. vii. 572 There is no mistaking the stylistic similarities between *li shu* and *k'ai shu*, 'Official Writing', otherwise known as *chên shu* or 'Regular Writing'. **1973** D. HAWKES tr. *Cao Xueqin's Story of Stone* I. 444 After that everyone made up a riddle about some object of their choice, wrote it out in the best *kai-shu* on a slip of paper, [etc.]. **1974** JIU-FONG L. CHANG in T. C. Lai *Chinese Calligraphy* (1975) p. xiii, K'ai Shu or Regular Script..reached its apex during the T'ang dynasty.

‖**kaizen** ('kaɪzen), *n.* [Jap., lit. 'a change for the better', '(an) improvement', f. *kai* revision, change + *zen* (the) good.] A Japanese business philosophy of continuous improvement in working practices, personal efficiency, etc.; hence, an improvement in performance or productivity.
   1985 *Chicago Tribune* 10 Nov. II. 4/1 It features an obsession with daily improvement (kaizen in Japanese), practices such as rotating tasks to lessen boredom and giving employees real influence over the manufacturing process. **1989** *Business Week* 14 Aug. 80/1 They use the kaizen concept that calls for assemblers to make continuous improvements in performing their tasks. **1991** *Times* 19 Oct. (Rev. Suppl.) 12/5 Individuals are encouraged to achieve *kaizen*. **1992** *Engineering News* Sept. 16/3 Intoxicated by the liberating whiff of Kaizen..British management.. flocked to hear their own kind enthuse about the miracles they had witnessed at the foot of Mount Fuji. **1993** *Business Week* 25 Oct. 134/2 Particularly in the auto and electronics industries, lean-manufacturing teams are swarming over America's factories. Their aim is to boost productivity by bringing about what the Japanese call *Kaizen*..to the shop floor.

kakaki (ka'kaki), *n.* [Hausa.] In West Africa, a long metal trumpet used on ceremonial occasions.
   1932 P. G. HARRIS in *Jrnl. R. Anthrop. Inst.* LXII. 119 The *kakaki* is roughly six feet long and is made in three sections...Like the *tambari* drum, the kakaki is reserved for special public occasions, but it may be heard on Thursday evenings being blown in the residence of the chief. **1938** J. CARY *Castle Corner* vii. 350 Loud trumpets, the kakaka [*sic*] of a great chief were heard. **1976** J. MONTAGU in *Early Mus.* July 355/3 The mouthpiece of the kakaki is not unsuitable due to its conicity but because of its size as well as its shape. **1984** *New Grove Dict. Mus. Instruments* II. 347/2 The *kakaki* may..be blown as a solo instrument..but is normally used in groups of four or more.

kalkoentjie (kal'kuiŋki, -intʃi), *n. S. Afr.* Also -tje, †calcoon. [a. Afrikaans *kalkoentjie*, f. *kalkoen* turkey + *-tjie*, dim. suff.] **1.** Any of several African pipits of the genus *Macronyx*; *esp.* the Cape longclaw, *Macronyx capensis*, which has a distinctive red throat and yellow breast.
   1835 T. H. BOWKER *Jrnl.* 11 June in *Voorloper* (1976) 448 Shot three Calcoons this morning. **1867** E. L. LAYARD *Birds S. Afr.* 120 *Macronyx Capensis...Kalkoentje* of Colonists, lit. Little Turkey... This handsome lark is common throughout all the open country. **1936** E. L. GILL *First Guide S. Afr. Birds* 78 Cape Longclaw, kalkoentjie, cutthroat lark...A well-known bird; the name Kalkoentjie (little turkey) presumably referring to its red throat. **1937** M. ALSTON *Wanderings of Bird-Lover in Afr.* i. 21 Mouse-birds I saw too, and Cape bulbuls, and several 'Kalkoentjes' or orange-throated long-claws..rose up from the grass as I walked along, and besides, there were chats and warblers.

2. Any of various plants of the family Iridaceae with flowers resembling a turkey's wattles, *esp.* the gladiolus *Gladiolus alatus*, native to the Cape, which bears brick-red and yellow flowers.
   1906 B. STONEMAN *Plants S. Afr.* xix. 198 *Gladiolus*...Painted Ladies and 'Kalkoentjes' belong here. Eighty-one species of this large genus are found in South Africa. **1949** *Cape Times* 13 Sept. 14/2 A colleague who drove to his farm..on Sunday reports seeing fields of gousblom, baby blue flax, lemon and mauve cineraria, lachenalias, blue bobbejantjies, kalkoentjies, scarlet sundew and other veld flowers. **1971** *Ibid.* 28 Aug. 1/7 The display of cinerarias, forget-me-nots, daisies, vygies, gousblomme and kalkoentjies would not be a mass of colour till mid-September.

Kan *n.*, var. of *GAN *n.*[2]

‖**kanban** ('kænbæn), *n. Comm.* [Jap. *kanban*, *kamban* sign, poster.] **1.** In Japanese industry: a card or sheet displaying a set of manufacturing specifications and requirements which is circulated to suppliers and sent along a production line to regulate the supply of components.
   1977 *Internat. Jrnl. Production Res.* XV. 561 When content of a container begins to be used, conveyance Kanban is removed from the container. A worker takes this conveyance Kanban and goes to the stock point of the preceding process to pick up this part. He then attaches this conveyance Kanban to the container holding this part. **1981** *Industrial Engin.* May 29/2 A withdrawal Kanban specifies the kind and quality of product which the subsequent process should withdraw from the preceding process. **1983** RIGGS & FELIX *Productivity by Objectives* vii. 135 A Kanban is actually a small card on which directions are given to produce or deliver a certain item. A Kanban is thus a tool that triggers production or delivery of necessary products in the appropriate quantities at the precise time. The simplicity of Kanban is refreshing—no elaborate computer programs or multisheet ordering forms.
   2. Usu. *attrib.*, *esp.* as *kanban system.* The coordinated manufacturing system employing kanbans, which ensures that components arrive from suppliers at the time they are required for assembly, thus minimizing factory storage and surplus. Cf. *JUST-IN-TIME adj. phr.* and *n. phr.*
   1977 *Internat. Jrnl. Production Res.* XV. 559 A production control system for just-in-time production and making full use of workers' capabilities is the Kanban System. **1982** *Sci. Amer.* Oct. J12 (Advt.), Much of the increased efficiency is credited to the *Kanban* system of 'just-in-time' production and inventory delivery. **1984** *Fortune* 2 Apr. 54/1 Taiichi Ohno, a Toyota vice president,..named the system *kanban*, after the cards that production workers find in their parts bin and use to call for a fresh supply. **1986** *New Yorker* 10 Nov. 58/3 It also allows the company to maintain almost no inventory, and to produce mainly to order, in a European version of the Japanese kanban system. **1989** *Accountancy* May 153/1 In its machine shops Cummins makes use of Japanese *kanban* techniques to help workers decide when to manufacture more of a component.

Kango ('kæŋgəʊ), *n.* Pl. **Kangos.** [Invented name, perh. suggested by Austral. slang *kanga* pneumatic drill (from KANGAROO *n.*).] A proprietary name for power tools, esp. a mechanical hammer.
   1925 *Trade Marks Jrnl.* 1 Apr. 708 *Kango*..Electrical percussion machine tools. **1947** CROWTHER & WHIDDINGTON *Science at War* iv. 174 In order to discover which road-drill was most suitable for..exploding the [acoustic] mines, a sub-lieutenant was sent to buy specimens of each that was available. The most effective was the Kango. **1971** *New Society*

1 July 30/2 The North London Ladder Hire Company hires out Kango Hammers...Where else but on the Balls Pond Road can one hire a Kango Hammer? **1977** *Belfast Tel.* 14 Feb. 17/8 (Advt.), Generators, Kangos, Drills, Grinders, Saws, Sanders, Nibblers and many others. **1993** LOWE & SHAW *Travellers* 50 She spent the morning working on a Kango breaking up concrete.

kan-pei *n.*, var. *GANBEI *int.* and *n.*

kanpu *n.*, var. *GANBU *n.*

Kansan, *n.* and *a.* Add: [B.] **2.** *gen.* Of, pertaining to, or belonging to the State of Kansas. Somewhat *rare*.
1909 *Cent. Dict.* (Suppl.) 678/1 *Kansan*,..of or pertaining to the State of Kansas. **1915** *Lit. Digest* 10 Apr. 830/3 'Kansas Language.' This is the phrase coined by William Allen White in 1908 to signify the kind of speech that rings with true Kansan loyalty and idealism. **1936** F. PALMER *This Man Landon* i. 5 Sharing the eastern view of Kansan ardor for any son or cause adopted by Kansas I was surprised to find how relatively restrained Kansans I met in the east were about Landon. **1987** R. BERTHOULD *Henry Moore* xi. 224 George Ablah, the Kansan collector, tried unsuccessfully to buy the Stevenage cast.

‖**karanga** ('karaŋa), *n.* N.Z. [Maori.] A Maori ritual chant of welcome. Cf. HAEREMAI *n.*
1905 W. BAUCKE *Where White Man Treads* 253 It was part of his festal ceremonies to chant a 'Karanga'.., when he brought food to set before the stranger guests. **1974** *N.Z. Listener* 20 July 10/4 The karanga, the shrill haeremai, haeremai coming down the marae. **1986** *Auckland Metro* Feb. 107 Although perhaps only half those gathered..to see the comeback concert of rocking grandmother Tina Turner understand the words of the karanga, it still reaches into the souls of most.

Karnian *a.*, var. *CARNIAN *a.* 2.

Karnic *a.*, var. *CARNIC *a.* 2.

Katangese (ˌkætæŋˈgiːz), *n.* and *a.* [f. *Katanga*, former name of Shaba, a province of S.E. Zaire + -ESE.] **A.** *n.* A native or inhabitant of Katanga, *esp.* (*Hist.*) a member of an Angola-based rebel force opposing the integration of Katanga into the Congo Republic (now Zaire). Chiefly *collect.* **B.** *adj.* Of, pertaining to, or belonging to Katanga. Cf. CONGOLESE *a.* and *n.*
1962 C. C. O'BRIEN *To Katanga & Back* 104 Most of the people who talked about 'the Katangese nation' had their tongues in their cheeks. *Ibid.* 133 The Katangese overestimated their military importance. **1967** *Times* 9 Nov. 6/7 They tried to recruit former Katangese gendarmes. **1972** J. C. WILLAME *Patrimonialism & Polit. Change in Congo* iv. 68 The numerical strength of the Katangese Army has been estimated at 5,000 men..in February 1961. **1980** *Summary of World Broadcasts: Middle East & Afr.* (B.B.C.) 1 Nov. B4 The demonstrations were held in the wake of President Kaunda's revelations that an insurgent army of former Katangese rebels attempted to overthrow the Zambian Government two weeks ago. **1986** *Los Angeles Times* 24 Aug. v. 2/2 A nephew of the late Katangese leader Moise Tshombe, he was educated in Belgium.

Kensitite, *n.* Add: Hence 'Kensitism *n.*, the doctrine or beliefs of the Kensitites.
1898 *Church Times* 7 Oct. 375/4 Last week we asked Dr. Moule to take note of this curious alliance between Kensitism and Popery. **1936** *Irish News* 17 Nov. 2/4 Orator of Kensitism.

keto-, *comb. form.* Add: **keto'pentose** *n.*, a ketose with five carbon atoms.

1914 *Jrnl. Biol. Chem.* XVIII. 321 All the present evidence seems to support the view that the urine pentose analyzed in this work is a *ketopentose corresponding to *l*-xylose or *d*-xylose. **1985** *Appl. & Environmental Microbiol.* XL. 158 Washed cell suspensions of either mutant incubated with 0.5% pentitol would oxidize 60–65% of the pentitol to the corresponding ketopentose.

Kevlar ('kɛvlɑː(r)), *n.* Also kevlar. [Cf. MYLAR *n.*] A proprietary name for a synthetic fibre of high stiffness and tensile strength, used mainly as a reinforcing agent in composite materials and as a constituent of ropes and cables; also, any of various materials made from or strengthened with this fibre.
1974 *Official Gaz.* (U.S. Patent Office) 12 Feb. TM54/1 *Kevlar*...For man-made fibers for generalized use in the industrial arts...First use Apr. 6, 1973. **1976** J. E. GORDON *New Sci. Strong Materials* (ed. 2) viii. 201 Weight for weight, the stiffness of Kevlar is not quite as good as that of boron or carbon. **1978** A. WELCH *Bk. of Airsports* i. 23/2 (*caption*) The Swiss C-FL Canard, designed for high performance, and built of kevlar and epoxy. **1981** *Daily Tel.* 12 July 21/2 Battledress made from kevlar (a synthetic material that is waterproof, fireproof—and protects against blows). **1987** *On Board* Mar. 65/1 Prestretched rope is used rather than kevlar to tightly fix the boom to the mast, since it has little give if overtightened.

key, *n.*[1] Sense 6 d in Dict. becomes 6 e. Add: [II.] [6.] **d.** *Bot.* and *Zool.* [tr. L. *clāvis* key (e.g. Linnaeus *Systema Natura* (ed. 6, 1748) 78).] A set of descriptive statements designed so that selecting those which apply to a particular specimen leads to its identification or its attribution to a particular taxon.
1836 G. BENTHAM *Labiatarum Genera et Species* p. xi, The same object may, perhaps, be better answered by an Analysis, or *Conspectus Specierum*, prefixed to each genus. This I have endeavoured to do, both as a key to the species and as a test of the validity of species. **1856** A. GRAY *Man. Bot. Northern U.S.* p. xi, By means of an *Analytical Artificial Key to the Natural Orders*..I enable the student very readily to refer any of our plants to its proper Family. This Key is entirely remodelled in the present edition. **1872** E. COUES *Key to N. Amer. Birds* 53 The key conducts to a genus, by presenting in succession, certain alternatives. **1928** *Forestry* II. 63 Considerable experience is necessary in recognizing structural differences between woods and in the preparation of keys as an aid to identification. **1946** J. HUTCHINSON *Common Wild Flowers* (rev. ed.) p. vi, We should be fairly well qualified to use the simple type of key beginning on page xi. **1987** N. J. W. KREGER-VAN RIJ in Rose & Harrison *Yeasts* (ed. 2) I. ii. 19 The characteristics in the key which lead to a species name do not give a complete description of the species. **1989** C. A. STACE *Plant Taxon. & Biosystematics* (ed. 2) ix. 207 Multi-access keys are usually produced not on pages in a book, but on separate punched cards.

key, *v.* Senses 6–8 in Dict. become 7–9. Add: **6.** Chiefly *Bot.* **a.** *trans.* To arrange or set out in a key (*KEY *n.*[1] 6 d) for the purposes of identification; to devise a key for. Also, to cause (a species, etc.) to be reached when a key is used. Usu. const. *out.*
1925 A. S. HITCHCOCK *Methods Descr. Systematic Bot.* v. 25 Out of the numerous characters pertaining to the several species to be keyed out, an author, in devising a key, strives to select constant characters, and, as a rule, relatively conspicuous ones. **1954** *Proc. Bot. Soc. Brit. Isles* I. 202 Two species and one variety are recognised in Belgium, keyed as follows: **1967** *Adv. Appl. Microbiol.* IX. 245 Very short rods ought to be 'keyed-out' both as cocci and rods before final classification. **1972** *Watsonia* IX. 197 Plants with an

overall superficial similarity do not necessarily belong to the same species..and may be easily confused. In our experience this confusion often arises..because specimens are carelessly keyed and compared with descriptions. **1981** WIGGINTON & GRAHAM *Guide to Identification Difficult Plant Species* (Nature Conservancy Council) 90 It was found necessary to key out several species (whose characters widely overlap) at more than one place in the key. **1989** C. A. STACE *Plant Taxon. & Biosystematics* (ed. 2) ix. 206 In practice it is often better to key out very distinctive taxa first (e.g. the banana in Fig. 9.3).

b. *intr.* To be identified by a key. Usu. const. *out.*

1961 *Watsonia* IV. 277 *A*[*maranthus*] *clementii,* although it keys out near *A. quitensis* H.B.K. on account of the leafless apical part of its inflorescence.., is probably not at all closely related to *A. quitensis.* **1965** *Proc. Bot. Soc. Brit. Isles* VI. 50 In most British floras *B*[*runnera*] *macrophylla* keys down to *Omphalodes verna*! **1979** *Bot. Soc. Brit. Isles News* Oct. 16 *V. hirsuta* (beware now this Br. species tends to key out as *V. vicioides* in the Flora Europaea 2 key).

keyboarder ('kiːbɔːdə(r)), *n.* [f. KEYBOARD *v.* + -ER[1].] A person who operates a (computer) keyboard; *spec.* a person who sets copy or enters data into a computer by keyboarding.

1961 in WEBSTER. **1971** J. W. SEYBOLD *Primer for Computer Composition* xx. 191 Suppose we assume lower wage costs for the input keyboarder than for the linotype journeyman. **1984** S. LANDAU *Dictionaries* vii. 279 The computer keyboarders could not be expected to make this kind of decision. **1990** *Rev. Eng. Stud.* Feb. 77 The standard of accuracy achieved by the keyboarders is outstanding.

keyboardist ('kiːbɔːdɪst), *n.* [f. KEYBOARD *n.* + -IST.] One who plays a keyboard instrument, esp. an electronic one.

1976 *New Musical Express* 17 Apr. 11/4 The line up is Roy Estrada, Napolean Murphy-Brock, keyboardist Andre Lewis, and drummer Terry Bozzio. **1978** *Gramophone* Apr. 1749/1 The Trio Sonatas are in all senses of the word beautifully balanced performances, given with an expressive, conversational freedom hardly available to [a] single keyboardist having to watch his p's and q's. **1984** *Tampa* (Florida) *Tribune* 28 Mar. 2D/1 Everytime a shot of keyboardist Nick Rhodes or bassist John Taylor flashed, an ear-piercing din rang out. **1990** *Sphere* (Sabena Airlines) July 38/2 Liège-born composer and keyboardist César Franck died 100 years ago this year.

Khanty ('kænti), *n.* Also **Khanti.** [a. Russ. *Khantȳ,* f. Khanty *Xanti.*] **a.** A Finno-Ugric people living in the Ob River basin in western Siberia (= OSTYAK *n.*). **b.** The Ob-Ugrian language of this people.

1947 G. B. D. GRAY *Soviet Land* II. v. 81 On either side of the Northern Urals there are the *Nyentsi*..; the *Khanti* (or *Ostyak*); and the *Komi.* **1965** C. SIMPSON *This is Russia* i. 7 In Siberia..there were hunting-and-fishing peoples in the north called Nentsi, Khanty, Evenki, Chukchi and Koryaks. **1972** E. G. LEWIS *Multilingualism in Soviet Union* ii. 38 There are several indigenous Ugrian languages in the Soviet Union, some of which like Ostyak (Khanti) and Vogul (Mansi) spoken around Omsk in Western Siberia are the languages of fishing, herding, and hunting tribesmen. **1980** *Amer. N. & Q.* Oct. 29/1 Marianne Sz. Bakró-Nagy..has pulled together some 500 terms..on the bear as a tabu animal in the Urals among the Ostyak (Khanti) and Vogul (Mansi) speaking peoples. **1983** L. SYMONS *Soviet Union* vi. 91/2 To the east of the Urals, the west Siberian lowland..is thinly occupied by the *Khanty* (21000), *Mansi* (7700) and other small Finno-Ugrian tribes. **1985** *Canad. Jrnl. Linguistics* XXX. 107 Research on Khanty, a Ural-Altaic language also called Ostyak..spoken along the

Ob river in north-western Siberia, has had a long history.

khoum ('kuːm), *n.* [ad. F. *khoums* (typically taken in Eng. for a pl.), ad. Arab. *ḵums* one-fifth.] A unit of currency in Mauritania (introduced in 1973) equal to one-fifth of an ouguiya.

1974 *Ann. Reg. 1973* VI. 274 At the end of June, on the same day as a total eclipse of the sun brought hundreds of visitors to Mauritania, the new currency was launched. The denominations were the ouguiya (worth 5 CFA francs) and the Khoum (worth one CFA franc). **1981** A. G. GERTEINY *Hist. Dict. Mauritania* 44 The ouguiya is divided into 5 *khoums.* There are 1-khoum coins. **1989** *Statesman's Yearbk.* 856 The monetary unit is the *ouguiya* which is divided into 5 *khoums.*

Kiangsi ('kjæŋsɪ, ‖'gjɑŋsɪ), *n.* Now *Hist.* Also **Kiang-si.** [ad. Chinese *Jiāngxī* the name of a province in S.E. China, f. *jiāng* river, *spec.* the Yangtze river of central China + *xī* west.] *attrib.* Designating or pertaining to the period of communist rule in this province from 1929 to 1934, *esp.* the independent soviet republic established by Mao Zedong in 1931.

1937 E. SNOW *Red Star over China* XI. v. 389 Two great errors committed in the last days of the Kiangsi Red Republic. **1966** F. SCHURMANN *Ideol. & Organization in Communist China* ii. 131 Party strength during the Kiangsi soviet period is a controversial problem. *Ibid.* vii. 426 The Kiangsi period marked the beginning of large-scale Communist organization in China. **1977** 'S. LEYS' *Chinese Shadows* (1978) i. 33 All the changes of direction in the party line..since Yenan or even since the Kiang-si soviet, have been only *tactical* changes. **1989** *Encycl. Brit.* VI. 849/2 When Chiang Kai-shek launched his fifth military campaign against the Kiangsi Soviet in 1933, the new leadership resorted to a strategy of fixed positional warfare, and the Soviet was overwhelmed.

kibble ('kɪb(ə)l), *n.*[5] [f. KIBBLE *v.*[1]] **a.** That which is produced by kibbling, *esp.* (a small piece of) coarsely ground cereal or grain.

1905 *Eng. Dial. Dict.* III. 430/2 *Kibble,*..crushed oats; split beans; lumps of coal about the size of swans' eggs. **1973** *Philadelphia Inquirer* 7 Oct. (Today Suppl.) 54 Alpo..was marketed as a mixer; the label said to mix it half-and-half with cereal or kibble. **1980** *Washington Post* 7 Aug. EI/1 After the ripened and partly dried pods of certain edible varieties [of carob] are harvested, they are broken into small pieces called kibbles.

b. *spec.* A type of dry pet-food consisting of small pellets of processed food; *pl.,* pieces of this. Chiefly *N. Amer.*

Kibbles is a proprietary name in the U.S.

1965 *Official Gaz.* (U.S. Patent Office) TM119/2 Millers Dog Food Company...*Kibbles*...For dog food. First use February 1931. **1967** *Field & Stream* Aug. 62/2 One way to liven up chow time without going overboard is to use the water drained from cooked or canned vegetables to moisten and flavor your dog's kibbles. **1972** 'L. EGAN' *Paper Chase* ii. 26 Jesse heaped a large bowl with kibbled meal..stewing beef...Sally [*sc.* a dog] began to eat kibble and stewing beef. **1980** M. F. K. FISHER in Michaels & Ricks *State of Language* 275 Perhaps it is assumed that most people who buy Kibbles do not bother to read the printed information. **1985** A. TYLER *Accidental Tourist* iv. 47 Dogs ate mammoth amounts of food, too; Edward's kibble had to be lugged home from the supermarket. **1993** *Dog World* Nov. 52/2 (Advt.), Small kibble shapes for easy chewing.

kick, *v.*[1] Add: [I.] [4.] [a.] **to kick ass** (*slang,* orig. and chiefly *U.S.*), to act roughly or aggressively; to be powerful or assertive.

1977 *Rolling Stone* 7 Apr. 83/2 Carter plays an adventurous brand of chamber jazz that even kicks ass on occasions such as 'One Bass Rag'. **1981** T. MORRISON *Tar Baby* vii. 222 Kicking ass at Con Edison offices, barking orders in the record companies. **1989** *Spin* Oct. 10/1 Your August issue kicks ass. Great story on Tom Petty, a tear-jerker on China, all you ever needed to know on rap. **1990** *N.Y. Woman* June–July 40/1, I think it's great fun to kick ass,.. but women are taught not to fight. **1993** *Albuquerque Jrnl.* 10 Nov. c3/1, I didn't just exist in government. I prevailed. I kicked ass.

[III.] [**14.**] **kick-ass**, *a. U.S. slang* (see sense *4 a above), rough, aggressive, powerful (also *ellipt.* as *n.*).

1977 *Rolling Stone* 16 June 60/3 Jan Hammer's cranked-up Moog and Beck's raving guitar, given even a taste of fusion's structure, turned especially *kickass. **1987** *New Musical Express* 14 Feb. 33/2 Whatever Etta grabs, be it blues, ballad, or R&B kick-ass, she handles in the same emotive way that's kept her bill-topping since her days with the Otis Revue. **1991** *Times* 16 Feb. 10/2 His point is that 'the old, kick-ass way of managing' is counter-productive. **1994** *M.E.A.T.* Sept. 9/2 This mind-blowing, mind-stoning release has been worthy of *several* repeat listens in the to-be-heard Masters' kick ass car stereo.

kicking, *ppl. a.* Sense b in Dict. becomes c. Add: **b.** Exciting, lively; great, excellent. *slang*.

1989 *Just Seventeen* 20 Dec. 19/3 Her latest song is really kickin' and we think she's probably the best female newcomer. **1991** *Esquire* Jan. 57/2 'You were really kickin', girl!' 'Brilliant!' They whoop and cheer. **1991** *Sun* 13 June 23/6 The joint was kicking. **1993** *Entertainment Weekly* (U.S.) 23 Apr. 26/1 Check out Joey, adopting a finger-pointing, in-yo'-face rap stance in his customary quasi-grunge ensemble of T-shirt, artfully ripped jeans.., plaid flannel shirt, and kickin' motorcycle boots. Yum!

kid, *n.¹* Add: [**6.**] **kidflick** *slang* (orig. *U.S.*) [FLICK *n.¹* 1 e], a cinematographic or video film for children; = *kidvid* below.

1977 *Time* 22 Aug. 43/3 Even the Disney studios are joining the sci-fi follies with a new *kid flick titled *The Cat from Outer Space*. **1980** *N.Y. Times* 1 Oct. C19/1 It's never.. embarrassingly moving in the schmaltzy way of such slick Hollywood kidflicks as 'Paper Moon'. **1987** *Sunday Mail* (Brisbane) 7 June 33/1 One of the latest kidflicks to hit town, this joust in the ongoing war between teenagers and grown-ups takes place amid the prejudices of a small country town.

kidvid *slang* (orig. and chiefly *U.S.*) [*vid*, abbrev. of VIDEO *n.*], a television programme or video made for children; also *collect.*, children's broadcasting or programming generally.

1955 M. REIFER *Dict. New Words* 116/2 *Kidvid,.. a children's television broadcast. **1969** *TV Guide* (U.S.) 29 Nov. 10/1 What kinds of programs *would* satisfy the social scientists.. who are unhappy about the current state of 'kidvid' in the United States? **1971** *Variety* 3 Feb. 31/5 The CBS-TV o&os would have little choice but to carry the projected weekday afternoon kidvid. **1985** *Fortune* 15 Apr. 130/3 She's bringing a new, nonviolent, Disney-created cartoon series.. to NBC's kidvid schedule. **1991** J. MENICK *Lingo* v. 77 He continually dipped into everything else, from soap operas to nature shows, from kidvid to live operas.

kideo ('kɪdɪəʊ), *n. slang* (orig. *U.S.*). [Blend of KID *n.¹* and VIDEO *n.*] = *kidvid* s.v. *KID *n.¹*

Kideos is a proprietary name in the U.S. for a children's television series.

1983 *InfoWorld* 5 Dec. 33/1 Send a stamped, self-addressed envelope to The Kraft Kideo Game Contest, [etc.]. **1984** *Daily Tel.* 11 Feb. 3/2 'Kideo' and 'Kidvid' should be used when one is writing about Children's TV. **1986** *Daily Express* 20 Aug. 21/1 With the summer holidays in full swing there are plenty of 'kideo' videos available. **1989** *Adweek* (N.Y.) 31 July (Eastern ed.) 49/3 'Kideo', is how Mark Goldston, senior vice president/director of marketing for Reebok, describes the first TV campaign for children's shoes.

†**kidsman** ('kɪdzmən), *n. slang. Obs.* [f. KID *n.¹* 5 b + MAN *n.¹*] A person who trains children to become thieves, esp. one who also provides them with board and lodging. Cf. FAGIN *n.*

1839 H. BRANDON *Poverty, Mendicity & Crime* 163/2 *Kidsman*, one who boards and lodges boys, training them to become thieves. **1859** G. W. MATSELL *Vocabulum* 48 The kidsman accompanies the kid, and though committing no depradations himself, he controls and directs the motions of the others. **1870** D. J. KIRWAN *Palace & Hovel* xliv. 620 'Ye'll not find a man or woman 'ere as would 'crack a case'.. and the 'Kidsmen' are.. as perlite as young Sweks.'

kidult ('kɪdʌlt), *n.* and *a. slang* (orig. and chiefly *U.S.*). Freq. *derog.* [f. KID *n.¹* + AD)ULT *a.* and *n.*] **A.** *n.* **a.** A television programme, film, or other entertainment intended to appeal to both children and adults. **b.** A habitual viewer of this, *spec.* an adult with juvenile tastes. **B.** *adj.* Designating or pertaining to entertainment of this kind.

1960 *Britannica Bk. of Year* (U.S.) 752/2 Kidult, a television adventure series that attracts both young people and adults. (1958). **1967** *TV Times* (Austral.) 5 Apr. 17/3 For shows like Flipper and The Flintstones (supposedly appealing equally to adults and children) the channels have coined a new, ghastly adjective—kidult. **1973** *Ibid.* 3 Feb. 20/1 The format is simple, maybe old-fashioned, but we'll be making half-hour programs for the kidult market, both here and in America. **1987** *Broadcasting* 2 Nov. 48/2 Such 'kidult' off-network fare as *The Brady Bunch* and *I Dream of Jeannie*. **1988** *N.Y. Times* 31 July H20/5 It's a movie designed for, and best appreciated by, the kidult, the amalgamated child-adult whose capacities and interests are fixed at an early age.

Kikongo (kɪ'kɒŋgəʊ), *n.* [Kikongo, f. *ki-* (cf. KISWAHILI *n.*) + *KONGO *n.*] = *KONGO *n.* b, used as a lingua franca in Zaire, Congo, and adjacent areas (see also quot. 1988).

[**1884** H. H. JOHNSTON *River Congo* xvi. 400 The Bakongo group is split up into several separate tribes, all of which, however, speak more or less the same tongue, which is sometimes called Fiote (meaning 'the common people'), and more correctly Ki-shi-kongo.] **1890** H. WARD *Five Years with Congo Cannibals* iii. 32 By hard study I had become proficient in the Kikongo language. *Ibid.* v. 52 They call this people the Avumbi, from 'vumbi', the Kikongo for 'corpse'. **1951** tr. *Traveller's Guide to Belgian Congo & Ruanda-Urundi* ii. 60 *Kikongo* or *Fiote*, spoken in Bas-Congo, part of Kwango and even in Angola and French West Africa. **1988** *Canad. Jrnl. Linguistics* XXXIII. 157 Pidginized Kikongo, the language that has come to be known as Kituba or vehicular Kikongo.

kill, *n.¹* Add: [**4.**] **kill zone** = *killing zone* (a), (b) s.v. *KILLING *vbl. n.* 1 b.

1981 *Defense & Foreign Affairs* Dec. 29/3 Producers are looking for higher speeds which mean getting the vehicle away from the *kill-zone more quickly. **1983** *Washington Post* 4 Oct. B4/4 Repeatedly, the agents practice trying to hit the 'kill zone'—the torso or head. **1991** T. DUPUY *How to defeat Saddam Hussein* vi. 77 The Iraqis lay out their minefields so as to require the attacker to concentrate his armor into an open 'kill zone'.

killing, *vbl. n.* Add: [**1.**] [**b.**] **killing zone**, (*a*) chiefly *Mil.* (orig. *U.S.*), a sector of a military engagement with a high concentration of fatalities; an area bombarded with heavy artillery fire, etc.; also *transf.* and *fig.* (*b*) orig. *U.S.*, an area of the human body where entry of a projectile would cause fatal injury, esp. as indicated on a practice target.

1970 W. C. Woods (*title*) The *killing zone. **1974** W. Garner *Big enough Wreath* i. 7 'Five in K5 again...' K5 was the killing zone. The marksman laid the cards alongside the rest. **1981** *Time* 9 Nov. 116/2 Harrison scores well on the firing range: his humor usually strikes in the killing zone. **1985** *Washington Post* 10 Aug. D3/2 In describing a U.S. rocket and bomb attack on the North Vietnamese base camp or rangers caught in the killing zone of a flawlessly executed NVA ambush, Scott puts the reader in the middle of the violence and confusion, the pain, the horror. **1990** *Match Fishing* Feb./Mar. 14/2 The bait will get down to the 'killing zone' within two to three seconds.

kina ('kiːnə), *n.*[1] *N.Z.* [Maori.] An edible sea urchin, *Evechinus chloroticus*.

1960 N. Hilliard *Maori Girl* II. xiii. 153 Netta took the tongues from the *kinas* and put them into a dish with vinegar. **1968** *Landfall* XXII. 19 Green *kina* shells looking coppery. **1978** P. Grace *Mutuwhenua* ix. 59 Then diving, and pulling the kina from the bottom of the lagoon, turning and kicking for the surface.

‖**kina** ('kiːnə), *n.*[2] Also **Kina**. Plural unchanged. [a. Tolai, lit. 'clam, oyster, mussel' (sometimes used as currency).] A monetary unit of Papua New Guinea, equal to one hundred *toea*, introduced in 1975.

[**1971** F. Mihalic *Jacaranda Dict. Melanesian Pidgin* 110 *Kina*,.. the goldlip or large mother-of-pearl shell, which in the Highlands is the 'bullion' representing the price of brides, pigs, etc.] **1974** *Pacific Islands Monthly* Apr. 1/2 Papua New Guinea's new currency will be known as Kina and Toea. Kina is a word from the pidgin languages spoken mainly by New Guineans. Toea is from Motu, the common language of Papua. Both designations refer to types of shell money used before the arrival of Europeans in PNG. **1975** *Telegraph* (Brisbane) 29 Apr. 23 It's getting hard to convince some Papua New Guineans that the country's new dollar equivalent, the kina, is only money after all. **1978** *Daily Tel.* 29 Aug. 15 (Advt.), Salary (payable in Kina) will be negotiated in a range equivalent to £12,000–£14,000. **1987** *Sunday Mail Mag.* (Brisbane) 4 Jan. 46/2 Because the PNG kina is worth more than the Australian dollar, the four stamps will cost Australian collectors $2.82.

kinaesthesiometer (ˌkɪnɪsθiːzɪˈɒmɪtə(r)), *n.* Also **kinesthesiometer**. [a. G. *Kinaesthesiometer* (now *Kinästhesiometer*); cf. KINÆSTHESIS *n.* and -OMETER.] An instrument for measuring the kinaesthetic sensitivity of an individual.

1890 Billings *Med. Dict.* II. 10/2 *Kinæsthesiometer*, apparatus for testing the muscular sense. **1900** C. S. Sherrington in E. A. Schäfer *Text-bk. Physiol.* II. 1022 Hitzig's kinæsthesiometer has been frequently employed; it is a set of balls outwardly alike, but individually loaded so as to be of different weights. **1985** *Developmental Med. & Child Neurol.* XXVII. 223/2 The task used in this study involved the passive rotation of the child's arm which was placed on a trough of a standard kinesthesiometer instrument.

kinesis, *n.* Add: **3.** *Zool.* [Adopted in this sense in Ger. by T. Lakjer 1927, in *Zool. Jahrb.* (*Abt. f. Anat. u. Ontogenie*) XLIX. 250.] Mobility between seprate parts of the skull, esp. in birds and certain reptiles. Cf. PROKINESIS *n.*, RHYNCHOKINESIS *n.*

1960 *Biol. Abstr.* XXXV. 1871/1 The possibility of a close connection between the various types of kinesis of the skull and the variations in the morphology of the middle ear is discussed. **1962** *Jrnl. Morphol.* CXI. 287/1 In more recent times, the term 'kinesis' has been more loosely interpreted and applied to various types of skulls. **1969** A. Bellairs *Life of Reptiles* I. iv. 154 Various types of kinesis occur among other vertebrates, in sharks for instance, in some carnivorous dinosaurs and in birds. **1986** A. S. Romer & T. S. Parsons

Vertebr. Body (ed. 6) viii. 244 Many groups have kinetic skulls, but the number and positions of the functional components varies greatly; thus, kinesis has clearly evolved (or re-evolved) numerous times.

king, *n.* Add: [**7.**] **d.** Of a commodity or currency. Cf. sense 6 b above. orig. *U.S.*

1855 D. Christy (*title*) Cotton is king or, The culture of cotton, and its relation to agriculture, manufactures and commerce, [etc.]. **1862** R. H. Newell *Orpheus C. Kerr Papers* 1st Ser. 202 When economy can be thus artistically blended with plentitude.. money ceases to be king, and butcher-bills dwindle. **1884** W. Shepherd *Prairie Experiences* 121 The dollar is king here as elsewhere. **1929** Moberly & Cameron (*title*) When fur was king. **1943** E. K. Brown *On Canad. Poetry* I. v. 20 Canada is a nation where the best-seller is king. **1984** *Times* 8 Aug. 26/7 Traditionally, Durham was very much a moderate area, producing redoubtable right-wing leaders such as Sam Watson... That was when coal was still king hereabouts.

kinky, *a.* and *n.* Add: Hence 'kinkily *adv.*, in a kinky manner; eccentrically, bizarrely, pervertedly.

1934 in Webster. **1964** in *Hamblett & Deverson Generation X* 146 [The Tonups] have always been an untouchable group on their own, kinkily keen on their bikes. **1979** *Washington Post* 1 May B12 A spaced-out, self-centered imbecile, she finds this strange new suitor kinkily irresistible. **1987** *Guardian Weekly* 4 Jan. 21/5 Some of the stage pictures.. were kinkily strange (such as a topless lady in a black-swan tutu trapped in a plastic tunnel).

‖**kippah** (kɪˈpaː), *n.* Also **kipa(h, kipoh, kippa**. [ad. Heb. *kippāh*.] A skullcap worn by Orthodox male Jews. Cf. KOPPEL *n.*, YARMULKE *n.*

1964 H. Kemelman *Friday Rabbi slept Late* xxi. 163 'What do you call that thing you're wearing?' The rabbi touched his black silk skullcap. 'This? A *kipoh*.' **1973** *Jewish Chron.* 14 Sept. 22/2 Jerusalemites.. are getting to be more religious by the year. One proof of this is the kipah-count. **1975** *Ibid.* 3 Jan. 16/2, I have little against the skull-cap (or *kippa* as I prefer to call it), but what I can't stand are the brethren who feel that the kippa does not represent the full measure of their piety, and who therefore cap their cap with a hat. **1978** *Church Times* 16 June 11/2 Orthodox Jewish boys, all wearing the regulation *kipa*, played outside. **1981** *Christian Science Monitor* 27 Mar. 22/2 Young Jews in Paris had stopped wearing the kipah (skullcap) when walking on the streets or riding the metro. **1988** *Times* 22 Jan. 6/2 A red-haired young infantryman in a khaki *kippa* chimed in. **1991** A. M. Dershowitz *Chutzpah* v. 157 Joe Lipner.. wears a Kippah, keeps kosher, and observes the Sabbath.

kiss, *n.* Add: [**1.**] **b.** Forming part of an expression of affection written at the close of a letter, etc. (conventionally represented by the letter x); = X 6.

1882 W. S. Churchill *Let.* 3 Dec. in R. S. Churchill *Winston S. Churchill* (1966) I. iii. 48 With love and kisses I remain your loving son. Winston. kisses. **1894** — *Let.* 14 Mar. in *Ibid.* (1967) I. Compan. i. vii. 456 Please excuse bad writing as I am in an awful hurry. (Many kisses.) xxx WSC. **1898** *Daily News* 25 Jan. 7/3 There were hieroglyphics in the form of crosses for kisses. **1976** D. Storey *Saville* III. xii. 165 There'd been a row of kisses at the foot of each. **1985** *Women's Wear Daily* 11 Mar. 23/1 The flowery, first-name signature of the 19-year-old model and actress, complete with two love-and-kisses XXs.

kitschy, *a.* (Formerly at KITSCH *n.*) Add: Hence 'kitschily *adv.*; 'kitschiness *n.*

1977 *Washington Post* 10 Oct. C1/2 A more harmless butt of his.. kitschiness than many subjects. **1987** *Times* 12 Sept. 19/4 The Old Vienna [a restaurant].. is bound to . . conform to and confirm British ideas of the country it kitschily represents. **1994** *This Mag.* Nov. 10/3 She's playing with a look that is so out it's in, revelling in the kitschiness of the way some people, *other* people, dress. This isn't a case of fashion nostalgia. This is fashion slumming.

klepto- ('klɛptəʊ), *comb. form.* [a. Gr. κλεπτο-, combining form of κλέπτης thief, κλέπτειν to steal: see -o[1].] Forming words in which it has the sense 'theft, thieving', as *kleptocracy, kleptomania*.

kleptoparasitism (klɛptəʊ'pærəsɪtɪz(ə)m), *n. Zool.* Also **clepto-**. [f. *KLEPTO- + PARASITISM n.*] A form of parasitism in which a bird, insect, or other animal habitually steals prey or food-stores from members of another species.

1952 ROTHSCHILD & CLAY *Fleas, Flukes & Cuckoos* i. 10 Some birds, of which the skuas . . are good examples, live by a curious form of food robbing known as clepto-parasitism. **1960** H. OLDROYD tr. *Jeannel's Introd. Entomol.* vii. 182 All degrees of kleptoparasitism have been observed, sometimes with remarkable habits. **1963** *Bull. Mus. Compar. Zool. Harvard* CXXVIII. 384 Cleptoparasitism is known to occur in various aculeates, including *Nysson* and some Pompilidae, but not in groups closer to *Stizoides*. **1975** *Nature* 25 Dec. 710/1, I report here the kleptoparasitism of the prey of web-building spiders by scorpionflies of the genus *Panorpa*. **1978** J. B. NELSON *Sulidae* viii. 721 The significance of the sex differences in frigate kleptoparasitism is completely obscure. **1994** *Nature* 24 Feb. 638/2 At sea, skuas obtain food mainly by 'kleptoparasitism', meaning that they search for smaller seabirds that have caught food, chase them, and force them to drop or regurgitate the food.

Also **klepto'parasite** *n.*, an animal that engages in kleptoparasitism; ˌ**kleptopara'sitic** *a.*; **klepto'parasitize** *v. trans.*, to subject to kleptoparasitism.

1952 ROTHSCHILD & CLAY *Fleas, Flukes & Cuckoos* xv. 253 The only real British bird clepto-parasites are the skuas. *Ibid.* 254 The frigate-birds . . never settle on the water and this particular aversion may well be one of the factors contributing to the development of the clepto-parasitic habit. **1974** *Nature* 5 Apr. 476/1 Often, the kleptoparasites were seen to rush in and start feeding while *Nephila* was actually subduing or wrapping its prey. **1978** J. B. NELSON *Sulidae* viii. 722 Frigate-birds are often found breeding alongside or among red-footed boobies, which they klepto-parasitise. **1984** F. VOLLRATH in C. J. Barnard *Producers & Scroungers* iii. 68 A highly mobile host like a fly can only be kleptoparasitised by either an equally mobile klepto or conversely by an 'ecto'-kleptoparasite, i.e. a parasite which . . clings to the outside of the host. **1989** *Jrnl. Exper. Biol.* CXLVII. 322 We predict that warm-up rates in kleptoparasitic bees . . will be lower than those in related bees of similar mass.

klick (klɪk), *n. slang* (orig. *U.S. Army*). Also **click, klik.** [Origin obscure. Orig. used amongst American servicemen during the Vietnam War.] A kilometre. Also *pl.* (*Austral.*), *ellipt.* for 'kilometres per hour'.

In Australia usu. spelt *click*.

1967 WENTWORTH & FLEXNER *Dict. Amer. Slang* Suppl. 678/1 *Click*, a kilometer. **1968** *New Yorker* 16 Mar. 86/3 'There's one hootch down there about a klik south of us . . ,' the ground commander said. **1969** *Newsweek* 28 Apr. 46/2 We went a few clicks into the fields. **1970** *Time* 6 July 24/1 Sipping lemonade or good Russian vodka, they trade experiences. Nothing to the north for 20 klicks (kilometers). **1982** J. SAVARIN *Water Hole* 95 They've gone sixty miles by now. Nearly a hundred klicks, if you prefer. **1984** *Truckin' Life* Feb. 55/1 You can't roll a smoke with one hand and scratch your ear with the other, at 90 clicks. **1988** *Arena* Autumn/Winter 59/2, I counted off 20 kliks on the car's speedo and stopped.

klutz, *n.* Add: ˈ**klutziness** *n.*, clumsiness, awkwardness.

1976 *Globe & Mail* (Toronto) 10 Dec. 17/5 Tom, a grade-school boy of normal klutziness, spunk, bravado and pranks, solves the murder of a gorgeous but nasty blonde while riding a Pullman across the Prairies. **1985** *New Yorker* 25 Feb. 82/2 Coen's style is deadpan and klutzy, and he uses the klutziness as his trump card.

knob, *n.* Add: [1.] f. The penis. *slang.*

1961 PARTRIDGE *Dict. Slang* Suppl. 1160/2. **1971** B. W. ALDISS *Soldier Erect* iii. 272 Probably every man-jack in the Mendips had his hand on his knob that night, giving thanks for survival. **1973** M. AMIS *Rachel Papers* 158 My knob was knee-high to a grasshopper, the size of a toothpick, as I skipped across the room and fell to a crouch by the side of the bed. **1987** *Melody Maker* 15 Aug. 7 *No* pictures of pop stars' knobs this week due to a bit of 'Spycatcher' type censorship round these parts.

knock, *n.*[1] Sense 6 in *Dict.* becomes 7. Add: [3.] Also, the batsman's score during an innings, *esp.* a good score rapidly achieved.

1976 *Milton Keynes Express* 30 July 41/1 Arnold Mann was top scorer with a patient knock of 24. **1986** *Club Cricketer* May 21/1 He . . averaged 36.75 in four innings for the county, thanks largely to a knock of 72.

6. *Angling colloq.* A pull on the line by a fish. Cf. BITE *n.* 3.

1969 in P. Beale *Partridge's Dict. Slang* (1984) 654/1. **1987** *Coarse Angler* Feb. 29/2 Up to darkness I did have a modicum of success with two small chub and a few knocks which did not materialise and which I put down to small chub or dace.

‖**ko** (gəʊ, kəʊ), *n.*[3] *Chinese Antiq.* Also **ge.** [Chinese *gē* (Wade-Giles *ko*) spear, lance.] A weapon that can be used as both a dagger and an axe; a halberd.

1923 *Bull. Geol. Survey China* v. 8 A favourite weapon in the Chinese Bronze age . . is called *ko* . . in Chinese, and ordinary dictionaries define it as being a kind of spear. **1929** W. P. YETTS *George Eumorfopoulos Coll. Catal.* I. 66 Andersson's conclusion that the *ko* is a *hache-poignard* or dagger-axe, comparable with a weapon used in the early Bronze Age of Europe, leaves more to be said. **1940** J. C. FERGUSON *Survey Chinese Art* i. 8 Military implements . . made of bronze . . in ancient China . . may be roughly divided into a few general classes: (a) those used for striking, such as the ko, chi, fu and tsih . . (b) those used for thrusting [etc.]. **1978** *New Archaeol. Finds in China* II. 29 The 60 or so burial objects in the tomb included . . the weapons *mao* (spear), *ko* (dagger-axe) and *fu* (axe). **1978** *Nagel's Encycl.-Guide: China* 107 The characteristic weapon was the *ge*, a sort of hook mounted on a handle.

komatiite (kəʊ'mætɪaɪt), *n. Petrogr.* [f. the name of the *Komati* river, Transvaal, South Africa, site of the first occurrence to be so designated + -ITE[1].] An ultramafic extrusive rock notably rich in magnesium, often with a characteristic spinifex texture.

1969 M. J. & R. P. VILJOEN in *Geol. Soc. S. Afr. Special Publ.* II. iv. 60 All of these peridotitic rocks have a distinctive and unusual chemical composition. They are unlike any class of peridotitic or picritic rock known and a new name, peridotitic komatiite, . . has been proposed. *Ibid.* v. 89 It is suggested that these rocks, which have chemical affinities with the associated ultramafics, might well constitute a new class of basaltic rock and the name basaltic komatiite is proposed. **1977** *Jrnl. Petrol.* XVIII. 321 Three types of komatiites are recognized: peridotitic, pyroxenitic, and basaltic komatiites. **1979** *Nature* 5 Apr. 545/1 Gorgona is one of the rare places in the world where young pyroxenitic komatiites exhibiting typical quenched spinifex textures..occur. **1992** S. P. MARAN *Astron. & Astrophysics Encycl.* 547/1 A minor constituent of these ancient volcanic rocks..is..komatiite, which indicates that the early Earth had a hotter mantle and greater magma production than it does now.

Hence **komati'itic** *a.*, of the nature of, containing, or resembling komatiite.

1975 *Nature* 4 Dec. 413/2 Included in the DAT category are komatiitic tholeiites. **1989** *Jrnl. Petrol.* XXX. 179 The komatiitic series will be hereafter divided into peridotitic.., pyroxenitic.., and basaltic. **1993** P. KEAREY *Encycl. Solid Earth Sci.* 355/1 The association of komatiites and komatiitic basalts is termed the komatiite suite or series.

Kondratieff (kɒnˈdrɑːtɪˌɛf), *n. Econ.* Also **Kondratiev.** [The name of Nikolai Dmitrievich *Kondratieff*, Russian economist (1892–*c* 1935).] Used *attrib.* and *absol.* to designate any one of a series of cycles or 'waves' of economic contraction and expansion each lasting about fifty years, postulated by Kondratieff in the 1920s.

1935 *Jrnl. Amer. Statistical Assoc.* XXX. 167 The year 1897..can be shown to have been comparatively 'normal'. From it arises the third of the three Kondratieff waves which we are able to follow up statistically. **1939** J. A. SCHUMPETER *Business Cycles* I. iv. 169 We decide now to content ourselves, for the rough purposes of this volume, with three classes of cycles, to which we shall refer simply as Kondratieffs, Juglars and Kitchins. **1965** *McGraw-Hill Dict. Mod. Econ.* 286 Kondratieff cycles consist of waves in prices, production, and trade lasting from fifty to sixty years. **1979** *Dædalus* Winter 51 An exceptional historical phase that will not be repeated..before fifty years have elapsed on the would-be Kondratieff-cycle calendar. **1988** *Brit. Med. Jrnl.* 20 Feb. 562/2 The crash occurred within days of the Soviet Union's rehabilitation of Nikolai Kondratiev, the legendary Russian economist who explained the changes in prices and interest rates in the Western world in terms of 60 to 70 year cycles—the Kondratiev waves. **1990** *Business* Apr. 111/3 The prophets of the 'Kondratiev cycle' hold that industrial economies move in technologically propelled 50-year waves.

Kongo (ˈkɒŋɡəʊ), *n.* and *a.* Pl. unchanged. [Kikongo; cf. CONGO *n.*] **A.** *n.* **a.** A member of a group of peoples indigenous to the region of the Zaire (formerly Congo) river, in south-western Africa. **b.** The Bantu language of these people; = *KIKONGO n.* **B.** *adj.* Of or pertaining to the Kongo or their language.

1862 W. H. I. BLEEK *Comp. Gram. S. Afr. Langs.* ii. 22 Kongo *bhobha* (to speak, talk) is Hereró *pópa* (to warn, persuade). **1910** *Encycl. Brit.* III. 359/2 In the south the Kongo dialects melt imperceptibly into the closely-allied Angola language...The river Loje to some extent serves as a frontier between the *Kongo* and *Mbundu* tongues. **1936** *Discovery* June 172/1 The area of the Western Bantu includes..in the west [the home of] such renowned cannibals as the Fang; it also includes the territory of considerable and highly organised kingdoms, such as the medieval kingdoms of the Kongo and the Balunda, and the later Bushongo Empire. **1974** *Encycl. Brit. Macropædia* I. 273/1 (*caption*) Kongo nail fetish, coastal region, Lower Congo cultural area. *Ibid.* IV. 1121/1 After converting to Christianity, the kings of the Kongo became allied with the Portuguese. **1988** *English World-Wide* IX. 150 The suprasegmentals cannot be derived from Twi, Yoruba or Kongo.

korma (ˈkɔːmə, ‖ˈkɔrmɑː), *n.* Also 9- **Quoorma, 20 khorrma, koormah, Quormah.** [a. Urdu *ḳormā, ḳormah,* f. Turk. *ḳavurma* lit. 'cooked meat'.] A mildly spiced Indian curry dish of meat or fish

marinaded in yoghurt or curds. Freq. with qualifying word, as *lamb, mutton korma.*

1832 G. A. HERKLOTS tr. *J. Shurreef's Qanoon-e-Islam* (1863) App. p. xxx, *Qoorma Polaoo,*..the meat is cut into very thin slices. *Ibid.* p. xxxix, *Saloon of Qoormā,* ..chopped meat, add some water, all *gurm* and *thunda mussalas,* tamarind and *ghee.* **1883** 'WYVERN' *Culinary Jottings* (ed. 4) xxix. 302 The 'Quoorma', if well made, is undoubtedly an excellent curry. **1902** 'KETAB' *Indian Dishes for Eng. Tables* 14 (*heading*) Koormah or Quormah curry. *Ibid.* 15 Koormah should be of a rich golden brown colour, with no gravy. **1932** M. R. ANAND *Curries* 46 Add a little, very little, warm water if the kormah is in danger of drying. There should, however, be no gravy. **1954** S. CHOWDHARY *Indian Cooking* 54 When ready, khōrrma should be quite dry and of an attractive colour. **1960** R. P. JHABVALA *Householder* iii. 189 'You owl! How many times must I tell you for korma the meat must be soaked in curds!' **1976** *Telegraph* (Brisbane) 15 July 21/2 Lamb Korma curry is a case in point. Traditionally from Punjab, Korma is an Indian curry containing lamb, spices and yoghurt. It is one of the house specialities. **1988** A. GHOSH *Shadow Lines* (1989) 120 In her mounting excitement, she began to make mistakes. There's a nice Gujarati mutton korma for you, she said.

†**kraton** *n.*, obs. var. *CRATON n.*

kratonic *a.*, var. *cratonic* adj. s.v. *CRATON n.*

krytron (ˈkraɪtrɒn), *n. Electronics.* [f. *kry-* of uncertain origin + -TRON.] A high-speed solid-state switching device which is triggered by a pulse of coherent light.

1970 *Proc. Inst. Electr. Engin.* CXVII. 1060/2 A subnanosecond voltage step is generated by short-circuiting a charged transmission line with a krytron. This 4-element valve, comprising an anode, radioactive cathode, ignition grid and keep-alive electrode, is designed to work in an arc-discharge mode. **1975** *Rev. Sci. Instruments* XLVI. 1333/1 The new krytron-switched Blumlein circuit has demonstrated a significant improvement in performance over the spark gap circuit. **1985** *Science* 14 June 1293/1 High-speed electronic switches known as krytrons. **1990** *Daily Tel.* 4 Apr. 3/7 In a [nuclear] bomb, a capacitor would be used to dump a large pulse of electricity through a high-speed switch like a krytron to set off the conventional explosives used to detonate the weapon.

kundalini (ˈkʊndəlɪniː), *n. Yoga.* [a. Skr. *kuṇḍalinī,* fem. of *kuṇḍalin* coiled, circular, f. *kuṇḍala* ring.] **a.** The latent (female) energy said to lie coiled at the base of the spine. **b.** In full, **kundalini yoga.** A system of meditation which aims to direct and release this energy.

1897 *Open Court* XI. 256 The pithecanthropic mummery, colloquially called monkey-business, connected with closing one nostril and breathing through the other and then of closing both till the compressed columnar air-current is imagined to bump against the triangular fundament of Kundalini. **1915** C. R. JAIN *Key of Knowl.* ix. 666 Withdrawing his senses, mind, and intellect from the outside, he turns the full concentrated current of will on itself, sets the *ahankara* ablaze with the fire of *Kundalini* (the serpent force, or Will). **1927** V. G. RELE *Mysterious Kundalini* 39 Normally, this kundalini is in Yoga-nidra or sleeping the sleep of trance. **1960** J. HEWITT *Teach Yourself Yoga* 16 The mysterious *Kundalini* Yoga..sets out to awaken what is symbolically described as Kundalini, 'the coiled serpent' said to sleep at the base of the spine. **1962** A. HUXLEY *Island* v. 52 She would secretly retire to do breathing exercises, practice concentration and raise Kundalini. **1977** *Time Out* 17–23 June 76/3 (*Advt.*), Kundalini Yoga is a highly evolved science of revitalising the physical body, developing the powers of the mind and awakening the highest spiritual consciousness that man can realise. **1988** *Yoga &*

Health Apr. 23/3 Asanas are practised. . to stimulate the nervous system which can in turn tone up all the body organs and raise kundalini. **1994** G. NICHOLSON *Everything & More* (1995) xiv. 112 She tried yoga, but she soon realized she was looking for something far more concrete and earthbound than any kundalini.

Kurukh ('kʊrʊx), *n.* Also **Khurñkh.** Pl. unchanged. [Kurukh.] **a.** A member of a people inhabiting northern areas of the Indian subcontinent, esp. the state of Bihar. **b.** The Dravidian language of this people.
Also called ORAON *n.*
1872 E. T. DALTON *Descriptive Ethnol. Bengal* VIII. i. 245 The Khurñkh or Oráons of Chútiá Nágpúr are the people best known in many parts of India as 'Dhángars', a word that from its apparent derivation (*dang* or *dhang*, a hill) may mean any hillmen. **1900** F. HAHN *Kurukh Gramm.* Introd. p. i, For ascertaining the position Kurukh takes up among the members of the Dravidian family, I am greatly indebted to Bishop. . Caldwell's 'Comparative Grammar of the Dravidian languages'. **1906** G. A. GRIERSON *Linguistic Survey India* IV. 447 Malto does not possess a literature of its own . . . The Malto language very closely agrees with Kurukh. **1955** T. BURROW *Sanskrit Lang.* viii. 387 The Dravidian languages Kurukh and Malto are preserved even now in Northern India, and may be regarded as islands surviving from a once extensive Dravidian territory. **1989** *Encycl. Brit.* VII. 44/3 Without a written tradition, Kurukh is documented only since the European colonization of India and in many areas is being displaced by Hindi.

‖**kwanza** ('kwanzɔ), *n.* Pl. unchanged or **kwanzas.** [Prob. f. the name of the River *Kwanza* (now *Cuanza*), in Angola.] The basic monetary unit of Angola, equal to 100 lweis, introduced in 1977; also, a note or coin of this value.
1977 *Washington Post* 10 Aug. A18/4 An escort guarding the new Angolan currency, called kwanzas, which were exchanged for the old Portuguese escudo bills in early January. **1980** *Summary World Broadcasts: Middle East & Afr.* (B.B.C.) 9 Apr. B2 Damage caused by. . bombing raids on 26th September 1979 on the industrial area of Lubango town has been valued at approximately 139,000,000 kwanzas. **1985** *Statesman's Year-Bk. 1985-86* 80 The 1981 budget balanced at 10,874m. kwanza. **1990** *Financial Times* 2 Oct. (Final London ed.) 4/2 The Angolan government has. . embarked on an economic reform programme, including last week's introduction of a new currency and devaluation, with the official rate of exchange falling from 30 kwanza to 60 kwanza to the US dollar.

L

L. Add: [III.] [8.] [a.] **L** *Physics*, lambert.

1915 *Trans. Illuminating Engin. Soc.* X. 648 (*table*) Photometric Units and Abbreviations... Brightness...Lambert. *L = dF/dS*. **1929** *Recueil et Compt. Rend. Commission Internat. de l'Éclairage: Septième Session* 254 Apparent total brightnesses of background from 1 mL to 400 mL. **1971** S. DRESNER *Units of Measurement* i. 62, 1 L = $\frac{1}{\pi}$ cd/cm² = $\frac{1}{\pi}$ stilb... The use of this unit, although common in the US, is deprecated: the stilb should be used in its place.

Linguistics, language, esp. in *L1*, first language, *L2* second language.

1959 J. C. CATFORD in Quirk & Smith *Teaching of English* vi. 188 Conscious preverbalization in *L1, and translation into L2, may be entirely suppressed, but errors due to interference from L1 still keep breaking through. **1964** M. A. K. HALLIDAY et al. *Ling. Sci.* iv. 78 This distinction, between an L1 and an L2, a native and a non-native or learnt language, is of course not clearcut. **1987** *ELT Jrnl.* XLI. 63/1 Even L1 literacy is perceived as more of a problem than an asset.

L or **l**, large.

1942 PARTRIDGE *Dict. Abbrev.* 55/1, l., large. **1987** *Damart Stately Homes Collection* Autumn/Winter 8/1 Golf glove...Sizes S, M, L. *Ibid.* 30/3 Wraparound skirt...Size M 12-16, L 18-22.

litre(s).

1872 S. P. SANFORD *Common School Arithmetic* 372, 10 decilitres = 1 litre, *L. **1881** E. M. AVERY *Elements of Chem.* 316 The cubic centimeter (cu. cm.) is .0001 of a liter (*l*). **1957** *Amer. Jrnl. Med.* XXIII. 567/2 His daily urinary output increased to 2 L. after dialysis. **1978** *BSI News* Oct. 14/3 A number of countries (including the USA) have already decided to use 'L'. **1991** *Lancet* 5 Jan. 56/1 Platelet count below 50 000/μl.

LATS (also with pronunc. læts) *Med.*, long-acting thyroid stimulator.

1961 *Jrnl. Clin. Endocrinol.* XXI. 799 A thyroid-stimulating agent which differs from thyrotropin..is present in the serum of thyrotoxic patients...In the past, this agent has been called, variously, 'an abnormal thyroid-stimulating hormone'..'the thyroid activator'..and 'the abnormal thyroid stimulator'...It is now called 'long-acting thyroid stimulator', abbreviated as *L.A.T.S. **1974** J. D. MAYNARD in R. M. Kirk et al. *Surgery* xii. 248/1 It is generally accepted that the disease is the result of the presence of a humoral..substance known as long-acting thyroid stimulator (LATS). **1981** R. N. HARDY *Endocrine Physiol.* viii. 102 LATS is one of a group of IgG immunoglobulins which affect the thyroid.

LAV *Med.*, lymphadenopathy-associated virus (a former name for the virus now called *HIV-3*).

1983 *Jrnl. Amer. Med. Assoc.* 26 Aug. 1010/1 Antibodies to *LAV proteins have been demonstrated in all six patients. **1985** *New Statesman* 27 Sept. 14/1 HTLV-III, or ARV in the United States and LAV in France, is now known to have infected hundreds of thousands of people across the world, mostly within the last ten years. **1991** *Lancet* 9 Mar. 568/2 The LAV strain of HIV-1 grown in CEM cells.

LBC, London Broadcasting Company.

1973 *Times* 10 Dec. 4/8 An emergency resolution..calls for rigorous investigation..of the conduct of *LBC's board and management in running the station. **1983** *Listener* 27 Jan. 15/1, I was asked recently by LBC to take part in a phone-in programme.

LDL *Biochem.*, low-density lipoprotein.

1962 *Canad. Jrnl. Biochem. & Physiol.* XL. 1300 The low-density lipoproteins (*LDL). **1978** *Detroit Free Press* 2 Apr. (Parade Suppl.) 7/1 LDL seems to be involved in transporting cholesterol to—and depositing it in—tissues, including blood vessel walls. **1990** *Medical Observer* (Sydney) 27 Apr. 2/2 (*heading*) Decaf coffee linked to higher LDL.

LDP, Liberal Democratic Party (in Japan).

1964 *Pacific Affairs* XXXVII. 277 Rank and file *LDP Diet members. **1987** S. H. NOLTE *Liberalism in Mod. Japan* viii. 322 The Liberal Democratic party (Jiyū Minshutō, or LDP, formed when the Liberals merged with the Democrats in 1955). **1991** *N. Y. Rev. Bks.* 25 Apr. 39/1 Ishihara Sintaro, LDP politician, novelist, hawk-about-town,..coined the famous phrase that Japan must say No-No to Big Brother USA.

Lf *Med.* [notionally f. *limit of flocculation*], that quantity of a specified toxin which flocculates most rapidly when mixed with one unit of antitoxin; freq. *attrib.* in *Lf dose*, *Lf value*.

1924 GLENNY & OKELL in *Jrnl. Path. & Bacteriol.* XXVII. 189 We think it useful to employ the symbol *Lf for the amount of a toxin equivalent to 1 unit of a standard antitoxin as established by flocculation...The Lf value may therefore be added to the Lo, L+ and Lr values in defining the combining properties of individual toxins. **1949** *Jrnl. Hygiene* XLVII. 107/1 The potency of toxins and toxoids, as measured by the Lf dose, may constitute some rough measure of antigenic efficiency. **1981** *Lancet* 1 Aug. 219/2 Single doses (100 Lf or 250 Lf) of a potent tetanus toxoid were given to such individuals with naturally acquired antitoxin.

LGV *Med.*, lymphogranuloma venereum.

1949 *New Gould Med. Dict.* 564/1 *L.G.V. **1964** KING & NICOL *Venereal Dis.* xix. 193 (*heading*) Lymphogranuloma venereum (LGV). **1979** D. BARLOW *Sexually Transmitted Dis.* iii. 24 Only treatment for the recognized venereal diseases would be free, i.e. gonorrhoea, syphilis, chancroid, and LGV. **1991** *Traveller* Spring 11/3 In tropical countries, more exotic diseases also occur, such as chancroid and LGV.

LIBOR, **libor** (pronunc. ˈlaɪbɔː(r)) *Comm.*, London inter-bank offered rate, the basic rate of interest used in lending between banks on the London inter-bank market.

1974 *Times* 5 Mar. (Europa Suppl.) p. ii/2 The loan will be for seven years...The rate will be fixed according to *LIBOR (London inter-banking offered rate). **1986** *Daily Tel.* 2 Sept. 17 Both will pay eight basis points over their Libor rate. **1988** *Mortgage Mag.* May 9/3 We intend to make the initial lower interest rate a continuing feature of the LIBOR linked mortgage.

LIFFE, **Liffe** (also with pronunc. laɪf), London International Financial Futures Exchange.

1982 *Times* 30 Sept. 16 *LIFFE. **1983** *Times* 10 June 19/6 The day's business brings Liffe's total volume since its inception to more than 750,000 contracts. **1996** *Financial Times* 11 Jan. 32/2 On Liffe the March 10-year bund future reached 100.15 but slipped in the afternoon.

LJ (pl. **LJJ**), Lord Justice.

1866 *Law Rep. Chancery Appeal Cases* (Council of Law Reporting) I. 45 (*heading*) *L.JJ. *Ibid.*, Sir G. J. Turner, L.J. **1987** *Daily Tel.* 30 Mar. 19/3 Slade LJ delivered a concurring judgment.

LL.B., *Legum Baccalaureus*, Bachelor of Laws (see B III. 1).

1796 *Cambr. Univ. Calendar* 20 Trinity Hall... Members, *L.L.B. Ds. Allan [etc.]. **1888** T. E.

KEBBEL *Life Geo. Crabbe* iii. 49 As a degree was necessary to enable him to hold his new preferment, he obtained an LL.B. at once from the Archbishop of Canterbury, Dr. Moore. **1987** *Oxf. Univ. Pocket Diary 1987–1988* 156 Oriental Institute... *Secretary* Miss J. M. Noon, MA status, LLB.

LL.D., *Legum Doctor*, Doctor of Laws (see D III. 3).

1763 J. BELL *Trav. from St. Petersburg* I. Sig. a4ᵛ, T. Llewellin, *L.L.D. **1830** F. WITTS *Diary* 10 May (1978) 89 My neighbour at Adlestrop has proceeded to the degree of LLD as he tells us. **1987** *Who's Who*, Denning, Baron... Hon LLD: Ottawa, 1955.

LL.M., *Legum Magister*, Master of Laws (see M III. 6 b (*b*)).

1874 *N. & Q.* 21 Feb. 149/2 *LL.M. Degree.—I have just taken this comparatively new degree at Cambridge. **1986** *Cambr. Univ. Handbk. 1986–87* 37 Except with the approval of the Vice-Chancellor, no degree other than those of B.A., LL.M., Mus.B., Vet. M.B., and B.Ed. may be conferred on a day of General Admission.

LME *Stock Market*, London Metal Exchange.

1957 *Metal Bull.* 2 July 23/1 The behaviour of the market recently has left the R.S.T. fixed price above *L.M.E. quotations most of the time. **1986** *Times* 28 May 24/2 The LME's members.. did what they could to defend sanctity of contract.

LMG, light machine-gun.

1922 H. WILSON *Jrnl.* 1 Mar. in M. Gilbert *Winston S. Churchill* (1977) IV. Compan. III. 1792 Collins was very much alarmed at the theft.. of 300 rifles, much ammⁿ & *LMGs by Valera's from the RIC. **1964** T. WHITE tr. P. *Leulliette's St. Michael* 164 It was.. hopeless to try to give covering fire with L.M.G.s or ordinary machine-guns aimed at the entries to the caves. **1990** C. ALLEN *Savage Wars of Peace* (1991) 60 Each troop also had its Bren light machine gun. 'The youngest member of the troop will always be lumbered with the LMG,' remembers Lillico.

LMH, Lady Margaret Hall (Oxford).

1890 *Daisy* 8 Feb. 2/2 A meeting of the *L.M.H. Guild was held on Jan. 23rd. **1986** A. LEJEUNE *Strange & Private War* ii. 25 Diana's voice.. spoke of Benenden and LMH.

LMS, local management of schools (in the U.K.) (the Education Reform Act of 1988 largely devolved responsibility for financial and other aspects of school management from local education authorities to individual state schools).

1988 Q. THOMPSON et al. *Local Managem. of Schools* (Coopers & Lybrand Rep.) 5/1 The changes require a new culture and philosophy of the organization of education at the school level. They are more than purely financial; they need a general shift in management. We use the term 'Local Management of Schools' (*LMS). **1990** *Independent* 24 May 17 Changes have included GCSE, profiling.. and now local management of schools (LMS).

LMT, local mean time.

1909 WEBSTER, *L.M.T. **1951** *Gloss. Aeronaut. Terms* (*B.S.I.*) III. 9 Local mean time *abbr.* L.M.T. **1982** *Giant Bk. Electronics Projects* xi. 494 All one needs to know is one's approximate longitude.. and the local mean time (LMT).

LO *Electronics* = *local oscillator* s.v. LOCAL *a.* 4 b; freq. *attrib.*

1946 *Radar: Summary Rep. & Harp Project* (U.S. Nat. Defense Res. Comm., Div. 14) 142/1 *LO, Local oscillator... The LO signal is mixed with the echo to give a 'beat' at intermediate frequency. **1982** *Giant Bk. Electronics Projects* v. 182 To stop this LO feedthrough, the converter output is filtered.

LP, low pressure.

1899 A. F. RAVENSHEAR *Man. Locomotive Engin.* iii. 67 (*caption*) *L.P. cylinder 26″ × 24″. **1975** *Petroleum Rev.* XXIX. 359/2 One tank contained 300 tons of material and the other 775 tons, and both were fitted with LP steam coils.

lpm, LPM *Computing*, lines per minute.

1966 C. J. SIPPL *Computer Dict. & Handbk.* 106/2 *LPM. **1979** *Personal Computerworld* July 4 (Advt.), New low-cost printer.. 112 cps - 84 lpm bi-directional. **1984** *Australian* 6 Nov. 25/1 (Advt.), C. Itoh's new.. printer is a high speed performer, prints out with a throughput of 100 LPM.

LPN *N. Amer.*, licensed practical nurse.

1948 *Amer. Jrnl. Nursing* May 316/3 South Carolina... The title of *Practical Nurse* and the letters *L.P.N.* are protected by the law. **1958** *Hospitals* (Chicago) 16 Aug. 52 (*table*) LPN. **1976** *Islander* (Victoria, B.C.) 13 June 2/2 I'm sure she's a nurse's aide, or more properly, an L.P.N.—Licenced practical nurse. **1986** *Cambr.* (Mass.) *Chron.* 6 Mar. 9A/4 (Advt.), Addiction Treatment Center of New England.. seeks LPN to facilitate groups, counsel individual clients and dispense Methadone.

LPO, London Philharmonic Orchestra.

1932 *Gramophone* Dec. 268/2 The *L.P.O. sounds heaviest. **1958** *Spectator* 6 June 732/3 The string tone of the LPO. **1988** *Financial Times* 20 Jan. 21/8 To keep the festival spirit going orchestras, like the LPO, have been prepared to change their schedule to play works like Mahler's 9th Symphony.

LPTB (*obs. exc. hist.*), London Passenger Transport Board.

1933 *Times* 3 July 11/1 The new letters indicating the change of control, '*L.P.T.B.', will not begin to appear until next week. **1959** *Britain: Official Handbk.* (H.M.S.O.) 357 In that year [*sc.* 1933] these were all vested in a single public corporation, the London Passenger Transport Board. In 1948, with the establishment of the British Transport Commission, the London Transport Executive took over control. **1983** *Buses Extra* No. 26. 7/3 The fleet of motorbuses never in fact increased in size very much beyond that originally acquired by the LPTB in 1933.

LSO, London Symphony Orchestra.

1920 *Mus. Times* 1 Dec. 820/2 At this first L.S.O. concert M. Cortôt played Rachmaninov's Pianoforte Concerto. **1973** *Times* 27 July 15/4 Mr Previn drew the right pliable phrasing from the LSO.

LTA, Lawn Tennis Association.

1896 *Lawn Tennis* 17 June 4/2 Another change is the abolition of the entrance fee for all members of the A.E.L.T.C. and players nominated in writing by a club belonging to the *L.T.A. or an affiliated association. **1988** *Today* 4 Feb. 39/4 The semi-finals of the LTA men's indoor event.

LU, lu *Austral.*, (of a building) lock-up.

1969 *Sydney Morning Herald* 24 May 37/2 (Advt.), Kitchen, laundry and a *L.U. Garage. **1986** *Courier-Mail* (Brisbane) 9 Aug. 55/3 (Advt.), New Markets.., 120 stalls, l.u. premises.

LWR, light-water reactor.

1974 *Times* 7 Oct. 13/7 Far from reflecting on the safety of *LWRs.. I submit that the facts demonstrate the stringent safety controls built into the United States programme. **1991** *Nuclear Energy* June 165/1 Light Water Reactor (LWR) fuel rod irradiations are conducted using irradiation capsules specially designed to simulate Pressurized Water Reactor (PWR) and Boiling Water Reactor (BWR) operational conditions.

LZ, landing zone.

1956 W. A. HEFLIN *U.S. Air Force Dict.* 310/2 *LZ, .. landing zone. **1969** I. KEMP *Brit. G.I. in Vietnam* ii. 29 The L.Z.s (landing zones) where we were to drop were clear. **1987** D. A. DYE *Platoon* ii. 13 Second Lieutenant Wolfe had mentioned that when Chris and Gardner had met him at an LZ hacked out of the bush.

Lab (læb), *n.*³ *Brit. Pol.* [Written abbrev. of LABOUR *n.* 2 c.] = LABOUR *n.* 2 c. (Cf. LIB-LAB *a.*)

1892 *Daily News* 4 July 4/1 L means Liberal; D.L. Dissentient Liberal; C, Conservative; Lab., Labour. **1923** *Daily Tel.* 21 Nov. 6/3 Maj. C. R. Attlee.. (Lab.). **1947** *Whitaker's Almanack* 333/2 Parliamentary Constituencies... Oxford City.. Hon.

Quintin Hogg, *C.* 14,314; F. Pakenham, *Lab.* 11,451. **1988** *Daily Tel.* 2 Feb. 11/1 Mr Tony Benn (Lab, Chesterfield) also failed to get an emergency debate.

Lab (læb), *n.*[4] *colloq.* (orig. *N. Amer.*). Also **lab.** [Abbrev. of LABRADOR *n.*] A Labrador dog.
   1950 *Dog World* June 73/3 (Advt.), Five choice bitch puppies by.. Canada's great sire of field-trial winning Labs. **1954** W. H. IVENS in F. Griscom *Labrador Retriever* 44 The shining beauty of the coat is one of the vanities of the Lab owner. **1963** *Globe & Mail* (Toronto) 13 Mar. 2/1 They were just about as nervous of the Labs as the hunters were of the mean-looking animals tied to the stakes in the Indian camp. **1976** *Billings* (Montana) *Gaz.* 16 June 12-c/7 (Advt.), 4 puppies... ½ Golden Retriever/½ Black Lab. **1986** R. RENDELL *Live Flesh* x. 141 She wasn't a puppy when I had her... They don't usually live past eleven, those labs.

‖**là-bas** (laba), *adv.* [Fr.] Over there, down there.
   Chiefly in literary use, perh. sometimes echoing the title of J.-K. Huysmans' novel (1891).
   1881 H. JAMES *Portrait of Lady* II. iii. 35 'And do you go back to Rome to-night?' her father asked. 'Yes, we take the train again. We have so much to do là-bas.' **1910** E. WHARTON *Let.* 25 Oct. in R. & N. Lewis *Lett. Edith Wharton* (1988) 224 Take whatever turns up in the way of provisional work là-bas. **1922** 'K. MANSFIELD' *Let.* 27 Oct. (1977) 281 I've learnt more in a week than in years là-bas. **1941** W. STEVENS *Let.* 30 Jan. (1967) 386, I hope that you and Mrs. Church will be happy *la-bas*. **1946** A. HUXLEY *Let.* 12 Dec. (1969) 558, I gather from your telegram that you will not be coming this way before proceeding là-bas.

label, *n.*[1] Senses 7 c, d-f in Dict. become 7 d, f-h. Add: [**7.**] **c.** The name by which a manufacturing or retail company or its products are generally known; a brand-name. Also, the company trading under this name.
   1902 *Westm. Gaz.* 13 June 10/1, If there was an amalgamation of six or seven houses whose names were household words, the outsider would at once go to the wall. Mr. Dewar thought the public suffered from this fondness for certain 'labels'. **1926** P. M. SHAND *Bk. Wine* v. 66 Montbazillac.. is a label still met, which prepares one for a rich, sweet white wine. **1968** *Times* 29 Nov. p. iv/4 Since they are still price-maintained it is not possible for retailers to cut prices, though in recent years budget labels have emerged. **1971** *Sunday Nation* (Nairobi) 11 Apr. 22/2 The suits come from the Highlight label and sell for 198/-. **1987** *N.Y. Times* 4 June D5/2 Mr Klein.. bought the Klein men's-wear label back.
   e. *Lexicography.* In a dictionary entry, a word or phrase used (often in italics) to specify the geographical area, register, etc., to which the term being defined belongs.
   1911 H. W. & F. G. FOWLER *Conc. Oxf. Dict.* Pref. p. v, We admit colloquial, facetious, slang, and vulgar expressions with freedom, merely attaching a cautionary label. **1962** A. W. READ in Householder & Saporta *Probl. Lexicogr.* 221 The average Englishman, accustomed to the labels *Americanism, Scotticism, provincialism,* etc. for designating locutions to be avoided, [etc.]. **1988** R. W. BURCHFIELD in T. L. & J. Burton *Lexicogr. & Ling. Stud.* 186 It has been customary for English lexicographers to make free use of regional labels like *U.S., Brit.* (or *U.K.*), *Austral., N.Z.,* and so on.

labetalol (lə'bi:tələl), *n. Pharm.* [f. *la-* (perh. an inversion of AL(PHA *n.*) + BETA *n.* + *-o)LOL.] An α- and β-adrenoceptor blocking agent used in the treatment of hypertension, and occurring as four stereoisomers with different degrees of interaction;   2-hydroxy-5-[1-hydroxy-2-[(1-methyl-3-phenylpropyl) amino]ethyl]benzamide, $C_{19}H_{24}N_2O_3$.
   1975 *Approved Names 1973* (Brit. Pharmacopœia Comm.) Suppl. v, Labetalol. **1977** *Lancet* 23 Apr. 890/2 If the alpha-blocking potency of labetalol is sufficient to enhance blood-pressure control substantially, it may also be sufficient to cause disabling symptoms. **1985** *Brit. Med. Jrnl.* 10 Aug. 366/1 In one study babies born to women taking labetalol were up to 500 g heavier than those from women taking atenolol. **1987** *Oxf. Textbk. Med.* (ed. 2) II. XIII. 374/2 Although the α-blocking potency is relatively mild labetalol appears to be significantly better in hypotensive potency than a β-blocker alone.

labile, *a.* Add: [**3.**] **b.** *Psychol.* Emotionally or behaviourally unstable. Cf. VOLATILE *a.* 4.
   1934 in WEBSTER. **1953** E. JONES *Sigmund Freud* I. ix. 188 His moods were certainly labile and when things were going well they could be markedly euphoric. **1984** S. BELLOW *Him with his Foot in his Mouth* 127 He seemed to her unstable, off center. The term often used in *Psychology Today* was 'labile'.

laboratory, *n.* Add: [**4.**] *laboratory assistant.*
   1889 *Phil. Mag.* XXVIII. 51 This curve was given to the *laboratory assistant, Mr. Davies, who cut out a pair of wooden templates to the pattern. **1989** *Gamut* Summer 40/1 The idea of a conniving laboratory assistant involving his superior in fraud smacks of class bias.
   laboratory bench.
   1962 M. M. SOLOMON in H. F. Lewis *Laboratory Planning* vi. 67/1 Although an improvement over unprotected steel, the lead-coated steel *laboratory bench had certain weaknesses. **1985** R. DAVIES *What's bred in Bone* (1986) v. 291 A laboratory bench whose water supply came from visible, ugly piping.
   laboratory-bred a.
   1938 *Ann. Trop. Med. & Parasitol.* XXXII. 231 A fungal infection on the surface of *laboratory-bred [mosquito] larvae was also noted. **1970** *Jrnl. Gen. Psychol.* LXXXII. 28 Fertig & Layne emphasize the differences in data gathered from laboratory bred and field collected animals.
   laboratory coat.
   c **1936** *Catal. Chem. Apparatus* (F. E. Becker & Co.) (ed. 25) 54 *Laboratory coats, Men's.* Strongly made, with step collar, outside breast pocket and two side pockets. **1977** *Daily Tel.* 28 Jan. 1/4 Nuclear workers reporting for work in radioactive areas are handed white laboratory coats and protective overshoes.
   laboratory worker.
   1892 W. JAMES in *Philos. Rev.* I. II. 149 A psychology so understood might be safely handed over to the keeping of the men of facts, of the *laboratory workers and biologists. **1988** J. C. BELL et al. *Zoonoses* 172 Formol inactivated vaccine has been used for veterinarians and laboratory workers in enzootic areas.

laboratory school *U.S.*, a school attached to a college or university and used for educational research and in the training of student teachers and the demonstration of teaching methods; a demonstration school (see DEMONSTRATION *n.* 8).
   1902 J. DEWEY in *Elementary School Teacher* Nov. 203 It is proposed.. to publish from time to time discussions.. derived from the actual work of both the *Laboratory and Elementary Schools. **1929** *Junior-Senior High School Clearinghouse* Nov. 168/1 At the outset the laboratory school was an essential.. feature of the teacher-training institution. **1981** *Childhood Educ.* Nov./Dec. 99/1 John Dewey served as Director of the laboratory school of the University of Chicago, known as the Dewey School.

labour, *n.* Add: [**2.**] **e.** *Pol. Econ.* (esp. *Marxism*). **labour theory of value**, the theory that the value of a commodity is influenced or determined by the amount of human labour expended in the course of its production; cf. *value theory* (a) s.v. VALUE *n.* 8.

1904 *Stud. in Hist., Econ. & Publ. Law* (Columbia Univ.) XIX. II. i. 9 The following history of the labor theory of value begins with Adam Smith. **1925** A. D. LINDSAY *Karl Marx's Capital* ii. 50 The labour theory of value..is common ground with Marx and the individualist economists. **1950** THEIMER & CAMPBELL *Encycl. World Politics* 282/1 Marx adopted the labour theory of value from Ricardo. **1971** I. DEUTSCHER *Marxism in our Time* (1972) i. 18 In the classical economy..Marx saw the main elements out of which he developed his own theory, especially the labor theory of value. **1987** F. VIANELLO in J. Eatwell et al. *New Palgrave Dict. Econ.* III. 110/2 A major difference between the Ricardian version of the labour theory of value and its Marxian version..lies precisely here: that the former can be regarded as an approximation, whereas the latter cannot.

[**8.**] **labour brigade**, a band or unit of workers, *esp.* one organized by the authorities.

1951 G. B. SHAW *Farfetched Fables* III, in *Buoyant Billions* 112 Youll be enlisted in the military police or kept under tutelage in a *Labor Brigade. **1965** M. MICHAEL tr. *J. Myrdal's Rep. from Chinese Village* (1967) I. 44 Every member of the labour brigade is given a private plot. **1978** *Detroit Free Press* 16 Apr. (Record) 7/5 It is assumed that the Jews..will either be thrown into the streets or put into ghettos and concentration camps, or impressed into labor brigades and put to work for the Third Reich.

Labour Day, (*b*) (with lower-case initials) [tr. Russ. *trudoden'*, f. *trud* labour + *den'* day], in the former Soviet Union and China: the notional unit of labour on the basis of which collective-farm workers were paid, derived from the level and quantity of work completed.

1930 *Economist* (Russ. Suppl.) 1 Nov. 17/2 In general, work is organised and paid for on a five-grade tariff, the basis of which is a 10-hour 'labour day'. **1975** A. WATSON *Living in China* iii. 76 Once a peasant's work-points have been settled, they are added up and converted into labour days at the rate of 10 points per day... The peasants are then paid according to the number of labour days they have worked during the year.

labour hero, in the People's Republic of China: a title awarded to a worker who produces an exceptionally high output.

1945 G. STEIN *Challenge of Red China* IV. xvi. 159 We wanted to know how Wu Men-yu had become a *Labor Hero. **1979** *China Now* Jan.-Feb. 11/1 Several Chinese have reportedly received awards as labour heroes.

similarly **labour heroine**.

1952 *China Reconstructs* I. 34/1 Women are doing everything nowadays. We already have *labour and combat heroines, women government leaders and workers...And now women tram drivers in Peking. **1976** D. DAVIN *Woman-Work* iv. 135 Finally as a national labour heroine she saw Chairman Mao in Peking.

labour secretary *U.S.*, the U.S. cabinet member in charge of the Department of Labor, who has responsibility for employment, labour relations, and related matters (see SECRETARY *n.*[1] 3 a).

1913 *N.Y. Times* 27 Feb. 1/4 E.H. Farr may be Attorney General and Congressman Wilson new *Labor Secretary. **1961** *Newark Even. News* 14 Mar. 24/1 Treasury Secretary Dillon and Labor Secretary Goldberg fell into line..though there has been some reluctance to do so at the White House. **1992** *Time* 20 Jan. 25/1 Labor Secretary Lynn Martin gave North

Carolina 90 days to strengthen its laggard factory-inspection program.

labour spy *U.S.*, a person engaged in covert observation of the activities of fellow workers, esp. union members.

1907 M. FRIEDMAN *Pinkerton Labor Spy* i. 7 The appelation 'secret operative' is but another name for 'labor operative' or '*labor spy'. **1959** CLARENCE & BONNETT *Labor-Managem. Relations* vii. 130 So long as there are strikes, detectives (labor spies and union spies) will continue to operate in some form or manner, legally or illegally. **1978** HAGBURG & LEVINE *Labor Relations* ii. 17 The La Follette Committee, investigating industrial espionage, reported as late as 1937 that its census of working labor spies from 1933-1937 totaled 3871 for the entire period.

labour turnover = TURN-OVER *n.* 6 c.

1915 *Ann. Amer. Acad. Pol. & Social Sci.* LXI. 128 By *labor turn-over is meant the number of hirings and firings in a plant and the relation which that bears in a year to the total number employed. **1989** *Appl. Econ.* XXI. 1465 This paper examines the determinants of labour turnover within an industry.

Labour weekend *N.Z.*, the bank holiday weekend preceding and including Labour Day.

[**1947** *Evening Post* (Wellington, N.Z.) 28 Oct. 8 The Labour Day weekend is traditionally the time when tomato plants may first be planted.] **1948** *Ibid.* 22 Oct. 6 If the tradition of wet *Labour weekends is not maintained in Wellington this year sportsmen..should..enjoy themselves. **1976-7** *Sea Spray* (N.Z.) Dec.-Jan. 98/1 Opening of the season at Labour Weekend featured a mystery cruise in the Marlborough Sounds.

labour, *v.* [II.] [**14.**] [**a.**] Delete 'Now *rare*' and add later examples.

1934 H. ROTH *Call it Sleep* III. v. 319 She shuffled toward a nearby house and labored slowly up the stoop. **1970** J. DICKEY *Deliverance* 124 We hauled and laboured away from the creek between the big water oak trunks. **1985** W. MCILVANNEY *Big Man* iii. 71 Frankie was on his bike and going. Dan had no option but to labour after him.

[**16.**] Delete †*Obs.* and add: Revived in *lit.* sense: To go through the process of giving birth.

1974 PASSMORE & ROBSON *Compan. Med. Stud.* II. xl. 16/1 In Scandinavia many women labour without any analgesia. **1986** *Times* 31 Jan. 11/2 A large majority of women labour successfully and have a normal delivery.

[**17.**] **b.** Of an engine of a motor vehicle, etc.: to work noisily and with difficulty, esp. while climbing a steep gradient.

1961 *Scots Mag.* Mar. 487/1 The engine laboured to a standstill. **1969** M. PUGH *Last Place Left* xv. 108 He was in third on the flat and labouring in top when we crested the hill. **1983** J. COETZEE *Life & Times Michael K* I. 56 The engine began to labour as they entered the mountains. **1985** R. L. HARRISON *Aviation Lore in Faulkner* 114 At the onset of the stall, the controls go slack and the engine labors vainly to keep the machine climbing.

labouring, *ppl. a.* Add: [**1.**] [**a.**] Also *labouring class(es)*.

1807 *Deb. Congress U.S.* (1852) 13 Jan. 303 The laboring classes of the community receive but a very small portion of relief from a total abolition of the salt tax. **1979** P. MORTIMER *About Time* iv. 44 It was therefore unthinkable (to her) to send him to the village school, to learn his three Rs with the labouring classes.

[**2.**] Delete †*Obs.* and add: In mod. use, undergoing the process of giving birth.

1972 S. KITZINGER *Experience of Childbirth* (ed. 3) v. 111 The labouring woman need not worry about getting enough oxygen.

Labourism, *n.* Add: Chiefly with lower-case initial, (*U.S.*) **laborism**, in general use. More widely, an outlook emphasizing working-class solidarity rather than ideology.

1909 in WEBSTER. **1976** ARMSTRONG & NICHOLS *Workers Divided* 19 But rather than neatly categorizing these [*sc.* foremen] as having 'false consciousness',.. it may be necessary to take account of the pervasive ideology of 'labourism'; an ideology which.. informs a lot of trade union activity.

Labourist, *n.* and *a.* Add: Also labo(u)rist. B. *adj.* Of or pertaining to the interests of Labour; emphasizing working-class solidarity through the trade-union movement rather than ideological socialism.

1920 H. H. HENSON *Jrnl.* 26 July in *Retrospect* (1943) II. i. 14 The Report and resolutions were, of course, strongly 'Labourist'. **1976** T. EAGLETON *Crit. & Ideology* i. 25 Both Romantic and labourist ideologies are in partial conflict with bourgeois hegemony. **1985** *New Statesman* 27 Sept. 12/2 It is not only organisations with a Labourist tradition and manual background that have gladdened hearts at Walworth Road.

Hence **labou'ristic** *a.* (*rare*).

1932 H. R. SPENCER *Govt. & Politics Italy* xxiii. 261 This Chamber of Deputies.. had turned out to be.. much more Fascist than laboristic.

Labourite, *n.* Add: Also (*U. S.*) **laborite**. (Earlier and later examples.) orig. *U. S.*

1889 *Denver Press* 9 Aug. 4/2 The democrats were for the saloons and.. only two of the laborites were for prohibition. **1913** V. G. SIMKHOVITCH *Marxism versus Socialism* 292 Whether they call themselves revisionists, reformers, laborites or plain socialists.. the overwhelming majority of the socialists of today are tending to be reformers. **1949** *Time* 14 Mar. 64/2 At least one powerful group of Catholic laborites, the Association of Catholic Trade Unionists, last week took sharp issue with His Eminence. **1973** J. SPEIGHT *Thoughts of Chairman Alf* 56 That's your bloody Labourites for you.

Labrador, *n.* Add: **Labrador current** *Geogr.*, a cold surface current running south between Greenland and Baffin Island and continuing along the Newfoundland coast until it meets the warm Gulf Stream.

1837 W. C. REDFIELD in E. M. Blunt *Amer. Coast Pilot* (ed. 13) 666, The current in question is neither more nor less than a direct continuation of the polar or *Labrador current, which bears southward the great stream of drift ice from Davis' Strait. **1910** *Encycl. Brit.* II. 857/1 At this point the Gulf Stream water mixes with that from the Labrador current.. and a drift current eastwards is set up. **1965** F. RUSSELL *Secret Islands* (1966) vii. 116, I imagined the island.. naked as a statue against the silent hiss of mist coming out of the Labrador Current. **1984** A. C. & A. DUXBURY *Introd. World's Oceans* iv. 140 When the warm, moist air over the Gulf Stream flows over the cold water of the Labrador Current, the famous fogs of the Grand Banks result.

labrish ('læbrɪʃ), *n.* and *a.* Jamaica. [Perh. f. *laba* or *labber* 'to blab, let out secrets' (Cassidy & Le Page *Dict. Jamaican Eng.*: cf. LAB *v.* and *Eng. Dial. Dict.* s.v. *lab*) + -ISH¹.]

The different parts of speech are not always distinguishable in context, and several of the examples below are open to alternative analysis. **A.** *n.* Gossip; rumour, idle talk.

1942 L. BENNETT *Jamaica Dial. Verses* 2 Me 'ave lot a labrish fe tell yuh. *Ibid.* 4 Gimme Dela, all De labrish from yuh yard. **1959** A. SALKEY *Quality of Violence* vi. 89 You really believe that idle labrish, eh? Well.. there's no truth in it. **1981** *Westindian World* 11 Sept. 5/1 Contrary to me little labrish de adda day bout him was a sell up fe go to America tings have never looked so good in town.

B. *adj.* Garrulous, given to gossiping.

c **1948** in Cassidy & Le Page *Dict. Jamaican Eng.* (1967) 269/1 Woman wa mek you labrish so Shut up you mouth an' gwan. **1961** F. G. CASSIDY *Jamaica Talk* viii. 185 As an adjective *labrish* would.. mean wordy,.. gossiping.

Hence '**labrish** *v. intr.*, to gossip idly; to chatter.

1943 in Cassidy & Le Page *Dict. Jamaican Eng.* (1967) 269/1 *Labbrish, Labris*, to chat plenty a story; to give plenty news; to talk much. **1976** J. BERRY *Bluefoot Traveller* (1977) 26 Things harness me here. I long For we labrish bad.

labrusca (lə'bruskə), *n.* (and *a.*). Also **Labrusca**. [a. L. *lābrusca* n. and adj., (designating) a wild vine; adopted as a specific epithet by Linnaeus.] **A.** *n.* A wild vine, *Vitis labrusca*, of the eastern U.S. from which many cultivated varieties have been derived; the grape of this vine (also called *fox grape*). **B.** *attrib.* or as *adj.* Designating this vine and its grape, and wine made from it.

1885 T. V. MUNSON *Address on Native Grapes U.S.* 9 To call the musky flavor of Labrusca 'foxy' is a misnomer, as no fox smells or tastes like that; but the under side of many Labrusca and Caribbea leaves have a true foxy appearance, while no other species has. **1908** U. P. HEDRICK *Grapes N.Y.* iv. 151 Labrusca is indigenous to the eastern part of North America. *Ibid.*, In its wild state Labrusca is probably the most attractive to the eye of any of our American grapes. **1977** *Westworld* (Vancouver, B.C.) May–June 49/1 The villain was the hardy labrusca grape. **1977** *Time* 21 Nov. 57/3 Made basically of labrusca, many of these wines were watered, sugared and tarted out with as much as 25% California wine. **1984** *N.Y. Times Mag.* 4 Nov. 82/2 Labruscas can withstand tough Eastern winters, but they produce a harsh-tasting wine. **1988** *N.Y. Times* 2 Mar. c12/5 Made from classical vinifera and native American labrusca wines, Wagner Vineyards varietal wines have been widely acclaimed.

labyrinth, *n.* Add: [5.] **labyrinth fish**, any fish of the perciform suborder Anabantidae, most members of which possess an accessory breathing organ above the gill chambers, and which includes many aquarium fishes (e.g. gouramis, Siamese fighting fish, and paradise fish).

1950 WEBSTER Add., *Labyrinth fish*, any fish of the order Labyrinthici. **1961** E. S. HERALD *Living Fishes of World* 243/2 Because of the special labyrinthine breathing apparatus located in a cavity above each gill chamber.., the members of this family [*sc.* Anabantidae] are called labyrinth fishes. **1985** BANISTER & CAMPBELL *Encycl. Underwater Life* 120/1 The anabantids include the climbing perch, the Kissing gourami and the genus of Siamese fighting fish. They are also called labyrinth fishes.

Lacatan (lækə'tæn), *n.* Also **lacatan**. [Tagalog.] A variety of banana, orig. from the Philippines but now widely cultivated elsewhere.

1908 *Philippine Agric. Rev.* I. 317 The varieties of bananas are discussed... The chief ones listed are.. Lacatan, the apex obtuse, and not angular. Bungulan, smaller than the lacatan. **1928** *Trop. Agric.* V. 23/2 The most promising substitute for Gros Michel is thought to be the Lacatan banana from the Philippines. **1949** *Caribbean Q.* I. III. 43 Bananas resistant to Panama disease (e.g. Lacatan), are being grown commercially. **1962** *Queensland Fruit & Veg. News* 11 Oct. 338/1 Bodles Altafort has good qualities, which are superior to those of Lacatan and Gros Michel. **1971** E. JONES in D. G. Wilson *Anthol. West Indian Poems* 30, I have ten acres of mountain side And a dainty foot donkey that I ride Four Gros Michel and four Lacatan.

lace, *n*. Add: [8.] [a.] *lacework* (*fig*. examples).
1763 W. STUKELEY *Palæogr. Sacra* i. 18 The mullion'd lacework of the windows. **1859** C. KINGSLEY *Misc.* (1860) I. 144 Its lace-work of interwoven light and shade. **1984** J. HELLER *God Knows* VI. 129 Reports that I was a man of war and a valiant man are but the lacework of hero worship.

lace, *v*. Add: [2.] [a.] Freq. with *up* (also *absol.*).
1851 *Ann. Reg.* 38/1 He was lacing up his high-lows in the washhouse. **1921** E. O'NEILL *Emperor Jones* ii. 170 He sits down and begins to lace up his shoes in great haste. **1985** G. KEILLOR *Lake Wobegon Days* (1986) 222 You lace up and teeter down the plywood ramp and take your first glide of the season.
[7.] *colloq*. **b.** *intr*. With *into*. Also *transf.*, to attack verbally. orig. and chiefly *U. S.*
1922 H. C. WITWER in *Collier's* 2 Dec. 7 When the sport writers find out I am not kidding, why, they laced into me with a gusto! *a* **1961** *Time* in WEBSTER S.V., Reviewers laced into the play. **1976** *Sunday Mail* (Brisbane) 7 Nov. 47/11 The teenage savages who push their victims into their apartments.. and then lace into them. **1988** N. BISSOONDATH *Casual Brutality* x. 194 A couple o' years before you come back, the *Casaquemada Times* had a columnist... He lace into the government, this fella, twice a week. Inside information. Language like a knife.

Lachryma Christi, *n*. Substitute for def.: A white, red, or pink Italian wine, either still or sparkling, orig. made from grapes grown on the slopes of Mt. Vesuvius but now produced in other regions of Italy. (Earlier and later examples.)
1653 T. URQUHART tr. *Rabelais's Works* (1664) I. v. 29 O *lachryma Christi*, it is of the best grape;.. O the fine white wine. **1877** E. S. DALLAS *Kettner's Bk. of Table* 452 Some of the Italian white wines—as white Capri or white Lachryma Christi. **1959** W. JAMES *Word-bk. Wine* 107 Lacryma Cristi.. is grown in the Naples area.. and may be red, white, or rosé; in northern Italy they make a sparkling Lacryma Cristi which is on the sweet side. **1975** P. V. PRICE *Taste of Wine* v. 68/2 The Greco grape that makes white Lacrima Christi is capable of producing wines of good acidity and more bouquet than might be expected so far south. **1980** — *Dict. Wines & Spirits* 193 Lacrima (*Lachryma*) *Christi*... The wine gets its name because of a legend that Christ, looking down on the beautiful Bay of Naples, wept at the sins of the inhabitants.

lacis, *n*. Add: **2.** *Anat.* [Adopted in this sense in Ger. by Oberling & Hatt 1960, in *Ann. d'Anat. Path.* V. 448.] A network of cytoplasm occupying the space between the juxtaglomerular apparatus and the macula densa of a renal corpuscle. Usu. *attrib.*, esp. in **lacis cell**, one of the cells whose cytoplasmic extensions form the lacis, and which differs from other juxtaglomerular cells in having no cytoplasmic granules.
1962 *Jrnl. Ultrastructure Res.* VI. 548 The cells of the cellulo-conjunctive lace-work or 'lacis' of Oberling and Hatt. *Ibid.* 562 Intercapillary or mesangial cells in the centrolobular region of renal glomeruli of rats are similar to and continuous with 'lacis' (pseudo-meissnerian) cells of the juxtaglomerular apparatus. **1968** E. L. BECKER *Struct. Basis Renal Dis.* i. 34 The juxtaglomerular apparatus.. is considered to consist of four portions: the specialized portion of the afferent arteriole containing characteristic granules; the first portion of the distal convoluted tubule, or macula densa; the cushion of cells at the vascular pole, continuous with the mesangium, termed the polkissen 'lacis' cells; and the efferent arteriole. **1974** *Jrnl. Cell Biol.* LXIII. 349/1 We report here an additional morphological specialization of mesangial as well as lacis cells which consists of the presence of gap junctions in both cell types. **1979** *Amer. Jrnl. Vet. Res.* XL.

802/1 These modified cells were indistinguishable from the juxtaglomerular cells of the lacis region (extraglomerular mesangium). **1985** C. R. LEESON et al. *Textbk. Histol.* (ed. 5) xiii. 421/1 Associated with the granulated JG cells are some lightly staining cells called Lacis or extraglomerular mesangial cells. **1987** *Amer. Jrnl. Path.* CXXVII. 149/2 It is concluded that.. there is a pathway in the mesangium for these cells to shift from the capillary to the extraglomerular area by way of the vascular pole and lacis area.

lacking, *ppl. a.* Add: [2.] Freq. const. *in*. (Later examples.)
1902 G. B. SHAW *Mrs. Warren's Profession* Pref. p. xxi, Critics.. revile me as lacking in passion, in feeling, in manhood. **1927** S. T. WARNER *Mr. Fortune's Maggot* 30 He would not like to think him lacking in natural affection. **1983** R. SUTCLIFF *Blue Remembered Hills* (1984) ix. 69 Though not usually lacking in imagination, I never realized what marvels could have been wrought with a lick of prettier paint.

lacquer, *n*. Senses 2 c, 4 in Dict. become 2 d, 5. Add: [2.] **c.** A coating material consisting of organic polymers dissolved in a solvent which is applied to a surface as a liquid and dries to give a hard glossy finish (differing from a paint in that the solvent simply evaporates and no chemical change is involved in the drying).
1861 BARNWELL & ROLLASON *Combining Pyroxylene with Other Substances* (*Provisional Brit. Pat. Specification 2249*) 3 Our invention consists in dissolving pyroxylene in any of its known solvents, and adding thereto oils.. gums or resins... In a state of solution its uses would be as.. a lacquer or wash for gilded and plated wares. **1904** A. H. SABIN *Industr. & Artistic Technol. Paint & Varnish* xi. 112 The commercial use of pyroxylin lacquers for adorning and protecting manufactured articles is a subject of interest and importance. **1911** E. C. WORDEN *Nitrocellulose Industry* I. x. 297 The same year [*sc.*1856], Parkes devised a waterproofing lacquer prepared by dissolving 'guncotton' in 'a mixture of wood spirit or naphtha distilled from chloride of lime and sulphuric acid'. **1930** *Motor Body Building* LI. 105/2 *Cellulose Lacquer*, a finishing material containing nitro-cellulose. **1935** *Discovery* Nov. 326/2 Cellulose lacquers, paints, distempers, etc. **1958** *Economist* 20 Dec. 1051/1 Cellulose Acetate makes tough, water-resistant wire and cable coatings. Cellulose Acetate Butyrate produces lacquers, adhesives, airplane dopes and melt and peelable coatings possessing high strength, flexibility and excellent weathering properties. **1971** *Nature* 3 Dec. 254/1 Thermosetting acrylic finishes which should prove to be more durable than thermoplastic acrylic lacquers now widely used as car finishes. **1984** E. P. DEGARMO et al. *Materials & Processes in Manuf.* (ed. 6) viii. 194 Adequate corrosion resistance can usually be provided by enamel or lacquer finishes. **1992** *Independent* 22 Feb. 33/3 Most fitted kitchens are basically chipboard.. with spray-on lacquer, fibre or veneer skin on top.
4. *ellipt.* = *lacquer disc*, sense *5 below.
1946 *Electronic Industries* Nov. 65/1 Although a stylus that is used to cut wax masters does not require a burnishing facet, this feature is indispensable on a stylus designed for lacquers. **1976** *Audio* June 40/2 From the remix studio the tape goes to the mastering studio where a mastering engineer cuts a 'reference lacquer'. **1987** *Music Week* 28 Feb. (Studio Week Suppl.) 1/3 Capitol Magnetics halts productions as demand for lacquers plummets.
[5.] **lacquer disc**, a disc coated with lacquer that is the first in the series of discs involved in the manufacture of a gramophone record, being cut from a tape or (formerly) directly during the recording process.
1945 *Proc. IRE* XXXIII. 761/1 *Lacquer disks*, disks, usually of metal, glass, or paper, which are coated with a lacquer compound.. and used either for 'instantaneous' recordings or for lacquer masters. **1968** *Times* 29 Nov.

(Leisure Suppl.) p.iv/6, The programme matter on the tape is transferred to a lacquer disc by means of a cutting machine.

lacrosse, *n*. Add: [b.] *lacrosse association*.
   1868 M. H. ROBINSON *La Crosse* p. iii, The rules of the game, as settled by the *La Crosse Association [of Canada] are now *published for the first time*. **1898** *Outing* XXXII. 10/1 The Columbia University Union..is composed of the Rowing Club..the Gun Club, the Hockey Club, the Lacrosse Association, the Golf Club and the Fencing Club. **1950** *Oxf. Jun. Encycl.* IX. 306/1 In 1867 the National Lacrosse Association was founded.
   lacrosse ball.
   1899 T. *Eaton & Co. Catal.* Summer Needs 9 *Lacrosse balls..030 [cents each].
   lacrosse boot.
   1926-7 *Army & Navy Stores Catal.* 650/9 *La Crosse boots..from 10/9. **1984** B. REID *So much Love* vi. 82 There was an extraordinary conglomeration of things: a string vest, one lacrosse boot, a sun hat, [etc.].
   lacrosse match.
   1892 *Photogr. Ann.* II. 51 We remember at a *lacrosse match taking a shot at the moment a goal was scored. **1986** A. SEBBA *Enid Bagnold* ii. 20 Although mostly concerned with clothes, lacrosse matches and the teachers, she evidently already had a talent for telling a good story.
   lacrosse player.
   1877 *Canad. Monthly* XI. 396/1 To urge upon *Lacrosse players, both here and in England, the adoption for it of its original Indian appellation of 'Baggatiway'. **1994** *Madison* (New Jersey) *Eagle* 21 July 7/1 Reilly is the seventh women's lacrosse player at Drew to be named an All-American, and the first defender ever.
   lacrosse team.
   1921 *Daily Colonist* (Victoria, B.C.) 15 Mar. 10/4 Orangeville's *lacrosse team is anxious to go to the coast to play for the Mann Cup. **1948** *Daily Ardmoreite* (Ardmore, Okla.) 12 Apr. 8/3 Dick expects to..join the lacrosse team for the second quarter.
   lacrosse stick (examples).
   1884 *Echo of Niagara* (Niagara-on-the-Lake, Ont.) 17 May 6/4 Capt. Bill's *lacrosse sticks are on hand. **1989** C. HARKNESS *Time of Grace* i. 32, I could not understand why it was considered sociable to hit one another over the head with lacrosse sticks every afternoon.

lactation, *n*. Add: [2.] Also, a continuous period during which this process takes place, beginning with birth and ending with weaning. (Earlier and later examples.)
   1847 H. OLDHAM in *Guy's Hosp. Rep.* V. 109 A female carries a child in the womb to the full period of gestation; but the process of labour is literally missed, and lactation follows on completion of gestation. **1900** DORLAND *Med. Dict.* 343/2 *Lactation*, ..the period of the secretion of milk. **1928** W. C. MILLER *Black's Vet. Dict.* 540/2 A cow may produce on an average 800 to 1000 gallons, distributed over from 35 to 45 weeks, in a single lactation. **1947** DAVIDSON & ANDERSON *Text Bk. Dietetics* (ed. 2) ix. 214 The diet during lactation should contain at least 100 milligrams of vitamin C per day. **1960** VANSTONE & DOUGALL *Princ. Dairy Sci.* iii. 30 Under natural conditions the animal supports its offspring throughout the lactation and supplies its different requirements as it grows. **1979** *Irish Times* 28 Sept. 15/8 There will also be a 1/2p a gallon increase for milk which is also welcome, though it will do little good this year as the lactations are nearly finished. **1987** *Jrnl. Dairy Sci.* LXX. 2168/1 Observed frequencies of clinical mastitis were calculated in 7240 Holstein and Jersey lactations.

lactic, *a*. Restrict *Chem.* to sense in Dict. and add: **2.** Of dairy products, wine, etc.: containing an unusually high proportion of lactic acid,

through having been inoculated with lactobacilli. Of bacteria: producing lactic acid.
   1910 *Health & Strength* 7 May 505/1 (Advt.), Lactic St. Ivel Cheese contains the pure Bulgarian bacilli in great abundance. **1912** *Bull. Bureau Animal Industry, U.S. Dept. Agric.* No. 150. 12 In certain cases the plates thickly seeded show colonies of but a single organism, usually the ordinary lactic organism, *Bacterium lactis acidi*. **1950** J. G. DAVIS *Dict. Dairying* 123 *Lactic*, a general name for sour milk cheese from whole or skim milk. *Ibid.* 401 Lactic cheese. **1973** *Which?* Feb. 49/2 Lactic butter is made by leaving cream to ripen after inoculating it with bacteria, so that its lactic acid level rises, before churning. **1985** *Cincinnati Enquirer* 18 Oct. D6/2 Fraud investigators say lactic culture farming was a huge, well-organized and highly sophisticated Ponzi scheme.

lacto-, *comb. form*. Add: [1.] ˌlacto-ˌovo-veˈgeˈtarian *a*. and *n*., (*a*) *adj*., (of a diet) consisting only of dairy products, eggs, and vegetables; (*b*) *n*., a person who eats such a diet.
   1940 *Jrnl. Amer. Dietetic Assoc.* XVI. 222/1 Meat was not served, and the diets were essentially *lacto-ovo vegetarian*. **1975** *New Yorker* 17 Mar. 32/3 Technically, I'm a lacto-ovo-vegetarian, which means that I eat milk products and eggs as well as vegetables. **1977** *Washington Post* 23 June E1/5 The low-calorie, low-sodium, low-cholesterol diet at the 40-acre ranch is lacto-ovo-vegetarian, made up of lots of whole grains, fresh fruits and vegetables with some eggs and milk products. **1987** *Times* 6 Feb. 11/6 Even people who are lacto-ovo vegetarians fail to meet normal dietary goals.
   lactopeˈroxidase *n*. *Biochem*., a peroxidase occurring in milk and saliva.
   1943 THEORELL & ÅKESON in *Arkiv för Kemi, Mineral. och Geol.* XVII. B. VII. 1 Agner's peroxidase, that occurs in cells belonging to the myeloic system, should be referred to as 'myelo-peroxidase', while the milk peroxidase should be called '*lacto-peroxidase*'. **1970** *Biochem. Jrnl.* CXVII. 779 Lactoperoxidase.., an enzyme present in various mammalian glands and in their secretions, catalyses the oxidation of thiocyanate by hydrogen peroxide. **1987** *Ibid.* CCXLVII. 147 The haem prosthetic group of lactoperoxidase can be prepared from the enzyme in high yield by reductive cleavage with mercaptoethanol in 8M urea.
   ˌlacto-veˈgeˈtarian *a*.: also as *n*., a person who eats only dairy products and vegetables; also, †a lacto-ovo-vegetarian.
   1912 STEDMAN *Med. Dict.* (ed. 2) 475/2 *Lactovegetarian*, one who lives on a mixed diet of milk and milk products, eggs and vegetables, but eschews meat. **1977** C. MCFADDEN *Serial* xv. 37/1 Marsha Wilson had become a lacto-vegetarian since Kate had last seen her. **1987** *Bodybuilding* Oct. 85/2 There's the lacto vegetarian who includes all dairy products in his/her diet except eggs.

lactoferrin (ˌlæktəʊˈfɛrɪn), *n*. *Biochem*. [ad. F. *lactoferrine* (Blanc & Isliker 1961, in *Helvetica Physiol. Pharmacol. Acta* XIX. C13): see LACTO-, FERRO-, -IN[1].] A protein found in milk and other secretions, whose iron-binding properties have a bactericidal effect.
   1965 *Experientia* XXI. 604/1 A specific iron-binding protein, different from serum transferrin, has been isolated from bovine and human milk...Among the various names given to this protein, e.g. red milk protein, lactoferrin, lactotransferrin, and lactosiderophilin, the two latter are particularly ill-chosen...The name lactoferrin..will be used in the present publication. **1972** *Brit. Med. Jrnl.* 8 Jan. 69/1 Human milk contains large quantities of iron-binding protein, of which the greater proportion is lactoferrin. **1977** *Lancet* 26 Nov. 1113/2 The artificial feeds would also have lacked maternal antibody and lactoferrin. **1988** G. PALMER *Politics of Breastfeeding*

iii. 42 The protein lactoferrin binds with iron to prevent too much being utilized.

lactulose ('læktjʊləʊz), *n. Biochem.* and *Pharm.* [f. LACT(O- + -*ul*- + -OSE², perh. after CELLULOSE *a.* and *n.*] A synthetic disaccharide of fructose and galactose that is given as a laxative; 4-*O*-β-D-galactopyranosyl-D-fructose, $C_{12}H_{22}O_{11}$.
  Orig. (*Science* (1929) 24 May 556/2) called *lactoketose.*

  1930 MONTGOMERY & HUDSON in *Jrnl. Amer. Chem. Soc.* LII. 2101 The name lactoketose was.. used for the sugar but it has been decided subsequently to name it lactulose. **1938** M. L. WOLFRAM in H. Gilman *Org. Chem.* I. xvi. 1442 The Lobry de Bruyn dilute alkali interconversion reaction was used.. in obtaining the crystalline ketose of lactose (lactulose). **1983** *Oxf. Textbk. Med.* I. XII. 14/2 Lactulose.. is useful in patients whose colons are full of hard scybala as it softens the stool partly by an osmotic effect and partly by the production of lactic acid and other organic acids. **1989** *Martindale's Extra Pharmacopoeia* (ed. 29) 1093 Lactulose is a synthetic disaccharide which is used in the treatment of.. hepatic encephalopathy. **1991** *Lancet* 7 Sept. 633/1 For three weeks before admission she had been taking terodiline 25mg twice daily plus lactulose and 'Fybogel'.

lacunate (lə'kjuːneɪt), *a. Biol.* [f. LACUN(A *n.* + -ATE².] Of, pertaining to, or characterized by the presence of lacunae.

  1957 in J. H. KENNETH *Henderson's Dict. Sci. Terms* (ed. 6) 252/1. **1981** *Amer. Jrnl. Bot.* LXVIII. 154 The exodermis, fibrous layer, lacunate cortex and endodermis appear to present a formidable barrier to radial ion movement in the mature portions of the root. **1987** *Jrnl. Invertebr. Pathol.* L. 184 A single, dense lacunate inclusion develops within the nuclei of these cells, ranging from 20 to 30 μm in midgut epithelial cells, and averaging 18μm in fat body cells.

lacy, *a.* Add: Hence 'lacily *adv. rare.*
  1934 in WEBSTER. **1981** *N. Y. Times* 5 May C11/3 It was a marvelously complex, lacily ornamented kind of music. **1990** P. GOSLING in T. Heald *Classic Eng. Crime* (1991) 176 A plain sponge.. lacily covered with swirls.. of.. icing.

lad, *n.*¹ Add: [2.] **d.** *pl.* (usu. with *the*). Men of any age belonging to a group sharing common working, recreational, or other interests, esp. with the implication of comradeship and equality; *spec.* the rank-and-file members of a trade union. Cf. BOY *n.*¹ 6 d.

  1888 'J. S. WINTER' *Bootle's Childr.* ii, All the 'lads'.. had gone home for the night, with the exception of the under-coachman. **1961** *Times* 7 June 18/4 Through the mullioned windows of the bar one can see a group of the 'lads'—a broad appellation, for their ages range from 17 to 70. **1974** P. WRIGHT *Lang. Brit. Industry* ix. 75, I don't know whether that offer'll get the lads back. **1979** *Daily Tel.* 25 Sept. 18/2 The schoolchildren [in the Irish Republic] play at 'the lads' versus 'Brit soldiers'. **1989** *Times* 29 June 29/1 The vote indicates the lads are absolutely solid.

ladder, *n.* Add: [1.] **d.** *fig.* A route leading to benefit or advantage, as in the children's board-game snakes and ladders.

  1933 N. STREATFEILD *Tops & Bottoms* xii. 146 Felicity thought that bringing up Beaty was rather like playing Snakes and Ladders, through no fault of your own stepping on the head of a snake and sliding to the bottom again; in this case, with no ladder in view up which to shoot to regain lost ground. **1971** 'D. HALLIDAY' *Dolly & Doctor Bird* xii. 166 With him.. was my friend Wallace Brady: up one ladder and down two possible snakes. **1985** A. PRICE *Here be Monsters* i. 22 Here was a *snake* or a *ladder*, and she could choose whether to go up or down.

laddered, *a.* Add: **2.** Of a piece of knitted fabric, stocking, etc.: that has developed a ladder (sense 3 b).

  1924 W. DEEPING *Three Rooms* xii. 101 Two pairs white stockings. Laddered. **1932** AUDEN in *Rev. Eng. Stud.* (1978) Aug. 282, I was.. Lost among waterproofs and laddered hose. **1985** *Company* Dec. 160/3, I too collect used plastic bags, obsolete magazines and laddered tights.

laddertron ('lædətrɒn), *n. Physics.* [f. LADDER *n.* + -TRON.] A device used to carry charge to the terminals of some electrostatic accelerators, consisting of a series of metal bars joined at each end by pivoted non-conducting links forming a closed loop (like a rope ladder with its two ends joined together).

  1972 *Nature* 26 May 192/3 The laddertron.. has a much greater current carrying capacity than either the conventional belt or the pelletron and has the advantage of greater mechanical rigidity. **1973** *Physics Bull.* Mar. 161/1 A new type of high current inductive charging system for electrostatic accelerators, with the unpronounceable name 'laddertron', has been developed by the *Daresbury Nuclear Physics Laboratory* (Stand 57) jointly with the University of Reading. **1974** *Nuclear Instruments & Methods* CXXII. 242/2 The accelerator will be charged using a specially developed high current inductive charging system known as the laddertron. **1981** *Nature* 16 Apr. 538/2 Dust.. caused a short circuit across the laddertron—the aluminium and plastic belt which carries charge up the 40-m column to terminals.

laddu ('lʌduː), *n.* Also **laddoo**, **ladoo**, **ladu**, etc. Pl. **laddus**. [Hindi *laḍḍū.*] A type of Indian sweetmeat, usu. made from a dough of flour, sugar, shortening, etc., which is fried and then shaped into balls; a ball of this. Cf. *JALEBI *n.

  1868 B. H. POWELL *Handbk. Econ. Products Punjab* I. III. 309/1 *Laddú*, of two kinds. **1873** E. BALFOUR *Cycl. India* (ed. 2) III. 371/1 Laddu, Hind. A sweetmeat in balls. Laddu is of two kinds, one called, 'bundi ka', the other is 'sada, plain, or maida ka'. **1954** S. CHOWDHARY *Indian Cooking* 145 Laddoo Sūji, Semolina laddoo... For 12 to 14 laddoos. **1960** R. P. JHABVALA *Householder* ii. 103 Indu.. was just pushing the remnant of a crumbly ladoo into her mouth. **1971** *Illustr. Weekly India* 25 Apr. 55/2 One was an enormous.. creature, used to winning bets about who could eat the largest number of laddus or jallebis. **1975** *Daily Colonist* (Victoria, B.C.) 11 May 4/2 LPC is mixed with maize, green gram (chick pea), jaggery (brown sugar), and peanuts to make laddu, which is formed into a soft, sweet ball. **1986** S. DUTTA tr. S. Gangopadhyay in Anand & Balurao *Panorama* 55, I too want some laddus like Sadhan dada.

lady, *n.* Add: [I.] [4.] [e.] **lady of the evening** (or **night**) (see also **17 b** below), a prostitute (*euphem.*). **lady of** (or **with**) **the lamp**, a popular name for Florence Nightingale (1820–1910), the hospital reformer and founder of modern nursing; also *transf.*

  [**1858** LONGFELLOW *Santa Filomena* in *Courtship M. Standish* 193 A Lady with a Lamp shall stand In the great history of the land, A noble type of good, Heroic womanhood.] **1898** *Corn. Mag.* Dec. 721 (*heading*) The Lady with the Lamp. **1911** D. A. REID *Mem. Crimean War* vi. 44 We now find that Queen Alexandra's Imperial Military Nursing Service is an integral part of the British Army... What better monument could be erected to the 'Lady of the Lamp'. **1919** W. T. GRENFELL *Labrador Doctor* (1920) xxiv. 398 The main impression on my mind was the extraordinary developments since the days of the Lady of the Lamp. *c*1925 M. H. GROPPER (*title of play*) Ladies of the evening. **1950** S. J. PERELMAN *Swiss Family Perelman* (1951) ii. 20 A peccadillo which involved a lady of the evening being sawed into stove lengths. **1969** *Listener* 10 Apr. 482/3 Not for nothing has the indefatigable Miss Jennie Lee earned for herself a Lady-with-the-Lamp reputation as Minister for the Arts. **1981** H. RAWSON *Dict. Euphemisms* (1983) 161 *Lady of the night*, *lady of pleasure* and *lady of easy virtue*..are euphemisms for prostitute. **1990** M. VAN DUYN *Near Changes* ii. 28 Even the starriest eye sees a fistfight raging over some hennaed lady of the night.

[6.] f. **Lady Baltimore cake** *U. S.* [the name of Lady *Baltimore*, wife of Lord Baltimore (d. 1632), founder of Maryland], a light-textured white layer cake, traditionally iced and with a filling containing pecans, dried fruit, etc. Also *ellipt.* as *Lady Baltimore*.

1906 O. WESTER *Lady Baltimore* vii. 89, I'll have to-day, if you please, another slice of that Lady Baltimore. **1912** M. DAWSON *Bk. Parties & Pastimes* 233 For this purpose a chocolate layer cake or a Lady Baltimore cake leads. **1948** *Chicago Tribune* 15 Jan. 4/6 (Advt.), Lady Baltimore Cakes, 85c–$1.10. 4 white, fine-grained layers, filled and iced with butter cream. **1970** *New Yorker* 5 Sept. 36/3 My mother stayed out of the kitchen..except for making..an occasional cake, like the monument for Father's birthday called a Lady Baltimore. **1986** *Ibid.* 17 Nov. 53/1 As the cook served dessert—a Lady Baltimore cake that must have cost her half a day—Laurance stood up.

[II.] [8.] Restrict †*Obs.* to sense in Dict. and add: **b.** A queen in a pack of playing-cards; *find the lady* = *three-card trick* s.v. THREE *a.* and *n.* B. III. 2.

1900 *Dialect Notes* II. 44 *Lady*,..queen at cards. **1938** F. D. SHARPE *Sharpe of Flying Squad* xviii. 194 If they are travelling to the R.A.F. Pageant 'the lady' is disguised as an airman, *en route* to the Cup Final the photograph of a footballer is pasted over the face of the queen. **1950** *Landfall* June 127 The poker game is in full swing . . He lays down a pair of bullets to my three ladies. **1961** J. HUGARD *Encycl. Card Tricks* 181 *Find the Lady*. Remove two K's and a Q, reversing the Q [etc.]. **1971** R. J. WHITE *Second-Hand Tomb* v. 52 People keep on disappearing and popping up again, as if the whole show were disintegrating into an endless game of Find-the-lady. **1977** *Irish Press* 29 Sept. 10/5 South..cashed the top hearts hoping the lady would drop.

[III.] [17.] [a.] **lady-beetle** (*a*) *nonce-use*, a female beetle; (*b*) chiefly *U. S.* = LADY-BIRD *n.* 1; cf. LADY-BUG *n.*

1832 W. IRVING *Alhambra* II. 33 The very beetle woos its *lady-beetle in the dust. **1869** J. GAGE *Jrnl.* 17 July in *Ann. Rep. Michigan Board Agric.* (?1869) VII. 175 Quite a number of lady-beetles have been noticed on the vines. **1891** C. M. WEED *Insects & Insecticides* 9 Predacious insects are those which attack other insects from the outside . . . The handsome little lady-beetles..furnish good examples of this class. **1930** *Times Lit. Suppl.* 18 Dec. 1078/3 The saving of the copra industry is as complete an example of what is now called 'biological control', the subduing of a living pest by the introduction of a living enemy of the pest, as the saving of the citrus industry of California by the introduction of a lady-beetle from Australia. **1972** SWAN & PAPP *Common Insects N. Amer.* xx. 403 The lady beetles or coccinellids are easily distinguished by their shape, and the three-segmented tarsi. **1991** *Amer. Horticulturalist* July 16/1 Tansy repels flies and attracts lady beetles.

[18.] [a.] **ladies' college**, a college established for the education of girls or young women (freq. in the name of such establishments).

1849 *Fraser's Mag.* July 104/1 We are able to announce that another *Ladies' College will be opened in October next in Bedford Square. **1895** C. M. YONGE *Long Vacation* xxi. 223 She had received from her father permission to enter a ladies' college, and the wherewithal. **1991** *Times Educ. Suppl.* 8 Mar. 5/3 Enid Castle, president of the Girls' Schools Association and

head of Cheltenham Ladies College, believes the recession has not yet fully set in.

ladies' compartment (now *rare*): on public transport, a compartment reserved for women.

1876 GEO. ELIOT *Dan. Der.* I. I. ii. 30 She persisted in refusing..companionship. She would be put into the *ladies' compartment and go right on. She could rest..in the train. **1931** D. L. SAYERS *Five Red Herrings* vii. 84 We made for a nice, old-fashioned Ladies' Compartment, not being great smokers in confined spaces. **1992** *Sunday Observer* (New Delhi ed.) 6-12 Sept. 7/7 The police was also successful in establishing the involvement of the Ganpathi group in the burning of the ladies compartment of the Kakatiya Express in late 1990.

Ladies' Mile = ROTTEN ROW *n.* 1.

1866 M. E. BRADDON *Lady's Mile* I. i. 1 The mighty tide of fashion's wonderful sea, surging westward, under the dusty elms and lindens of the *Lady's Mile. **1975** M. CRICHTON *Great Train Robbery* xvi. 82 The spongy, muddy pathway in Hyde Park called the Ladies' Mile, or Rotten Row.

c. The genitive *lady's*, *ladies'* is also used to designate items of clothing, accessories, and other goods designed or intended (with varying degrees of specificity) to be worn or used by women; freq. characterized as being smaller, daintier, or less robust than the equivalent item for men.

1692 W. CONGREVE *Let.* 21 Aug. (1964) 8, I am forced to Borrow Ladies paper but I think it will contain all that I can tell you. **1726** J. HOBSON *Diary* 8 Oct. in *Yorks. Diaries* (Surtees) 258 Out of all..came pyramidicall streams of light,..forming such a figure as a ladies' umbrella. **1793** *Cabinet-Makers' London Bk. of Prices* (ed. 2) 161 *A Rudd, or Lady's Dressing Table*..Three feet four inches long, two feet wide, three drawers in front, a glass frame hing'd to each end drawer, and supported by quadrants, a moulding on the edge of the top, plain Marlbro' legs, and an astragal round the bottom of the frame. **1840** R. H. DANA *Two Yrs. before Mast* iii. 20 A ship is like a lady's watch, always out of repair. **1895** *Army & Navy Co-op Soc. Price List* 1059 Ladies' knickerbockers. For walking, golf, tennis, riding and cycling. **1913** W. OWEN *Let.* 27 Dec. (1967) 224 A delightful silver Precision Watch, small (but not 'Ladies'). **1944** C. DREPPERD *Primer of Amer. Antiques* 233/1 Ladies' Twist, a dainty roll of flavored tobacco favored by ladies who chewed it as the most genteel manner of using tobacco. **1984** *New Yorker* 12 Nov. 134/2 It probably wasn't called a snubby but a..lady's gun.

Laennec (laɛ'nɛk), *n. Path.* Also **Laënnec**. [The name of R. T. H. *Laënnec* (1781-1826), French physician, who described the condition in 1819 (*De l' Auscultation Médiate* I. 368).] **Laennec's cirrhosis**, a type of cirrhosis of the liver characterized by a nodular appearance of the liver surface and associated with alcoholism.

1839-47 R. B. TODD *Cycl. Anat.* III. 188/2 The form of atrophy of the liver..named by Laennec *cirrhosis*. **1888** in *Syd. Soc. Lex.* **1934** *Arch. Path.* XVIII. 381 The name 'portal cirrhosis' is recommended as synonymous with 'Laënnec's cirrhosis'...The term 'Laënnec's cirrhosis' is not objectionable. It has historic significance and is seldom misunderstood. **1957** POPPER & SCHAFFNER *Liver* xxviii. 279/2 The contrast between the more common types of human cirrhosis, especially Laennec's cirrhosis, and experimental cirrhosis is probably related to differences in blood supply. **1981** D. W. GOODWIN *Alcoholism* ii. 7 People who develop a particular type of liver disease called Laennec's cirrhosis usually *are* heavy drinkers.

Laffer ('læfə(r)), *n. Econ.* [The name of Arthur *Laffer* (b. 1942), U.S. economist.] **Laffer curve**, a supposed relationship between the rate of taxation and the revenue received, under which

maximum revenue is attained at a particular tax rate beyond which higher tax rates reduce the yield by discouraging the activity taxed.
1978 J. WANNISKI in *Public Interest* Winter 3 (*title*) Taxes, revenues, and the 'Laffer curve'. **1978** — *Way World Works* p. xii, I came to see these political figures pushing against what I have come to call the Laffer curve, an exceedingly simple but powerful analytical tool for almost any form of human social or political interaction . . . The Laffer Curve merely posits that in any political economy, there are always two tax rates that will produce the same revenues. **1981** *Sci. Amer.* Dec. 17/1 Now, as a result of the upsurge of interest in 'supply side' economics, the curve of the hour is a brand-new one called, with strangely resonant overtones, the Laffer curve. **1986** *Economist* 14 June 13/2 Some countries could even discover the wild fancies of the Laffer curve: an extra dollar raised through higher taxes driving more than a dollar away. **1995** *N. Y. Rev. Bks.* 12 Jan. 5/1 This is the old supply-side hypothesis of the Laffer curve and the Reagan years, but Republicans now call it 'dynamic scoring' of budget effects.

lag, *n.²* Add: [3.] **lag bolt** *N. Amer.*, (*a*) a coach screw; (*b*) a coach bolt.
1893 *Funk's Stand. Dict.*, *Lag-bolt. **1963** J. T. ROWLAND *North to Adventure* ix. 135 The longer lag bolts with which he had fastened it had got a strong grip in the wood. **1975** *Sci. Amer.* July 123/2 Lag bolts screwed into the plug and through the two-by-six boards of the well anchor the pier to the bed of the trailer. **1994** *Canad. Workshop* Sept. 62 Other options, good for heavy-duty applications, are a lag bolt with a shield . . or a steel sleeve bolt.

‖**lagar** (læˈgɑː(r), ‖laˈgar), *n. Wine-making.* Pl. **lagares**. [Sp., f. L. *lacus* vat holding freshly pressed grape juice. Cf. LAKE *n.*⁴ 4.] In Spain and Portugal: a large (usu. stone) trough in which grapes are trodden.
1845 tr. *J. J. Forrester's Wine Trade of Portugal* (ed. 2) 15 The system of pressing the grapes half by night and half by day . . cannot fail to be injurious to the wine, by . . rendering it necessary that it should remain a longer time in the 'Lagar' than would otherwise be required. **1880** H. VIZETELLY *Facts about Port* iii. 51 The casa dos lagares is a long building with a low pointed roof, lighted with square openings along one side, and contains four lagares, in the largest of which sufficient grapes can be trodden at one time to produce thirty pipes of wine. **1975** P. V. PRICE *Taste of Wine* iii. 29/1 (*caption*) The grapes are previously dried on mats; in the old days they were trodden in wooden *lagares* and then pressed again in a sandwich device. *Ibid.* 29/4 (*caption*) The grapes used to be trodden in the *lagar* by barefoot workmen. **1987** *Sunday Express Mag.* 4 Jan. 40/4 At least one family — the Newmans . . — believe that the best port is produced by teams of men trampling down the grapes underfoot in what is known as a lagar. Great fun, the lagar.

‖**Lag b'Omer** (lag ˈbəʊmə(r)), *n.* Also **le-Omer**, **be-ʿOmer**, **Baomer** (baˈəʊmə(r)). [Heb., f. *lāḡ*, pronunc. of the letters LG (*lamed, gimel*) symbolizing 33 + *bā* in the + *ʿōmer* OMER *n.*] A Jewish festival held on the 33rd day of the Omer, traditionally regarded as celebrating the end of a plague in the 2nd cent. A.D.
1874 A. EDERSHEIM *Temple: its Ministry & Services* x. 175 Iyar . . . 18. Lag-le-Omer, or the 33rd day in Omer, *i.e.*, from the presentation of the first ripe sheaf offered on the 2nd day of the Passover, or the 15th of Nisan. **1905** *Jewish Encycl.* IX. 400/1 The cabalists attach a peculiar importance to Lag be-ʿOmer. **1923** E. E. LEVINGER *Jewish Holidays* 24 A dreadful plague that raged during the Sephira days suddenly ceased on Lag Baomer. **1975** *Jewish Chron.* 25 Apr. 26/4 During Lag b'Omer you will hear about the students of Rabbi Akiba who died in a dreadful plague. **1986** *Ibid.* 24 Jan. 25/1 Lag b'Omer 1986 Tues May 27.

lagena (ləˈdʒiːnə), *n. Zool.* [a. L. *lagēna* flagon.] An extension of the saccule of the ear in some vertebrates, corresponding to the cochlear duct in mammals.
1878 F. J. BELL tr. *Gegenbaur's Elem. Compar. Anat.* ix. 536 The portion of the labyrinth . . known in Mammals as the cochlea . . is . . differentiated in the Reptilia and Aves, where the diverticulum which forms it . . is a short conical piece . . . Its end is somewhat bent, and it forms the 'lagena'. **1888** ROLLESTON & JACKSON *Forms Animal Life* (ed. 2) 420 The connection between the vestibule and saccule is closed in *Batoidei*, bony *Ganoidei*, and some *Teleostei*; and in the latter the cochlear outgrowth (= lagena) is large. **1962** K. F. LAGLER et al. *Ichthyol.* xi. 387 The sacculus and the lagena are more broadly joined to one another in the sharks . . than in bony fishes. **1987** *Nature* 14 May 153/2 The posterior eighth nerve branch sends one ramus to the posterior canal, one to the lagena, and several rami to the sacculus.
Hence **laˈgenar** *a.*, of or pertaining to the lagena.
1946 *Jrnl. Laryngol. & Otol.* LXI. 207 Ross . . studied the electrical reactions from the saccular and lagenar nerves in the sucker (Catastomus). **1962** K. F. LAGLER et al. *Ichthyol.* xi. 386 The lagenar otolith, and the underlying sensory tissue are, to a small degree, also involved in gravistatic or righting reflexes. **1987** *Nature* 14 May 153/2 A separate lagenar recess including the lagenar epithelium was found in *Latimeria*.

lager (ˈlaːgə(r)) *n.* (Formerly at LAGER BEER in Dict.) orig. *U.S.* [Shortening of LAGER BEER *n.*] **a.** = LAGER BEER *n.* Also, a drink of this.
Lager has long been more usual than *lager beer.*
1855 J. E. COOKE *Ellie* I. i. 13 He was rotund, red and solemn — 'lager' was written in his eyes. **1858** in Bartlett *Dict. Amer.* (1860) 235 The German drinks his lager, and drinks it apparently in indefinite quantities. **1867** SIMMONDS *Dict. Trade* Suppl., *Bock-beer*, a favourite Bavarian . . beverage, of the best lager description. **1883** 'MARK TWAIN' *Life on Mississippi* xxiii. 260 Give an Irishman lager for a month and he's a dead man. **1891** *Daily News* 27 Apr. 3/2 'Large lagers', . . which were over half a pint. **1922** E. O'NEILL *Anna Christie* (1923) I. 6 Johnny draws the lager and porter and sets the big, foaming schooners before them. **1943** H. TAUBER *Enzyme Technol.* i. 28 Ale yeast does not contain melibiase, whereas lager yeast does. **1984** *Listener* 27 Sept. 22/1 A club with one of the worst records for drunken yobbery . . makes a deal with the makers of Holstein lager.
b. Special Comb. **lager lout** *colloq.*, a young man who behaves in an aggressive, boorish manner as a result of drinking (typically lager) excessively.
1987 C. THOMPSON *Beware Barmaid's Smile!* 8 When the *lager lout says that beer is an old man's drink, the reply is to ask if they have ever thought of growing up. **1989** *Q* Mar. 10/1 There's more to football supporters than Stanley knife-waving lager louts. **1993** *Independent* 4 Jan. 5/1 The recession is having one good effect — keeping lager louts away from foreign holiday resorts.

lagerphone (ˈlɑːgəfəʊn), *n. Austral.* [f. *LAGER *n.* (from the beer-bottle tops used) + -PHONE.] A percussion instrument consisting of a long pole with a cross-piece near the top, to which numerous beer-bottle tops are loosely nailed, producing a jingling noise when shaken or struck. Cf. *Chinese pavilion* s.v. PAVILION *n.* 13.
1956 *People* (Austral.) 11 Jan. 26/3 A lagerphone is a musical (?!) instrument based on Turkish cut crescent or jingle. **1967** MEREDITH & ANDERSON *Folk Songs Austral.* 17, I played the bush accordion . . Brian the

lagerphone. **1973** *Nation Rev.* (Melbourne) 24–30 Aug. 1421/2 Their percussion comes from Jan Wozitsky..and Bert Kahnoff (lagerphone). **1983** *New Oxf. Compan. Mus.* I. 119/1 The lagerphone, a kind of Turkish jingling johnny..made by loosely nailing numerous beer-bottle tops to a pole and pounding it on the ground.

laggardly ('lægədlɪ), *a.* [f. LAGGARD *a.* and *n.* + -LY¹.] Having the character or spirit of a laggard; hesitant, slow, sluggish.
1826 *Blackw. Mag.* XIX. 335 Some laggardly editorless..periodical. **1939** C. S. FORESTER *Captain Hornblower, R.N.* i. i. 14 Some laggardly or unlucky sailor. **1959** R. E. CAMPBELL *I would do it Again* xii. 85 Needless to say the men were not laggardly. **1975** *Economist* 3 May 123/3 To improve the laggardly money market. **1988** *Daily Tel.* 15 Mar. 40/1 [Crossword clue] What the laggardly dressmaker should do to a hem (5, 2).

lagger ('lægə(r)), *n.*³ [f. LAG *v.*⁴ + -ER¹.] One who installs and maintains insulation for pipes, boilers, etc.
1915 *Census of England & Wales, 1911* X. 85 in *Parl. Papers 1914–16* (Cd. 7660) LXXXI. 1 Boiler maker...Lagger. **1924** *Classif. of Occupations* (Registrar-General) 140/1 (Index), Lagger (boiler). **1971** *Brit. Med. Bull.* XXVII. 73/2 A marked excess of deaths from lung cancer in laggers..were discovered from a study of union records and a follow-up of union members. **1980** *Times* 27 May 2/1 On one side is the GMWU, who represent 27 laggers, and thermal insulation engineers, with 33 ancillary workers.

Lagosian (leɪ'ɡɒsɪən), *a.* and *n.* [f. *Lagos* (see below) + -IAN.] **A.** *adj.* Of, belonging to, or characteristic of Lagos, the federal capital of Nigeria, or its inhabitants. **B.** *n.* A native or inhabitant of Lagos.
1895 *Lagos Standard* 6 Feb. 2/2 (*heading*) Lagosian on dits. **1897** *Ibid.* 20 Oct. 3/3 The unity and oneness of purpose of the Lagosians. **1926** P. A. TALBOT *Peoples S. Nigeria* I. ii. 113 The vessels did not reach Egenie market till the 20th ultimo—which, according to a freed Lagosian, was only three days before Kosoko had arranged to start. **1967** A. DJOLETO *Strange Man* xviii. 271, I don't know of any Lagosian policeman in Ghana. **1976** *Sunday Times* (Lagos) 1 Aug. 9/3 It was a resort for affluent Lagosians who built houses there where they and their families could go for holidays. **1982** R. NIVEN *Nigerian Kaleidoscope* i. 16 The 'bar beach', as the Lagosians called it.

Lagrangian, *a.* and *n.* Add: [A.] **b.** *Astron.* **Lagrangian point**: each of the five points in the orbital plane of two bodies at which a third body of negligible mass will remain stationary relative to them.
1962 STRUVE & ZEBERGS *Astron. 20th Cent.* ii. 46 Particles of very small mass..which tend to linger near the Lagrangian point that lies about 70,000 mi. beyond the apex of the earth's shadow. **1975** *Physics Bull.* Nov. 485/2 Gravity vanishes at all Lagrangian points. **1985** *Sci. Amer.* Sept. 43/1 An excellent position for a satellite equipped to measure the small-scale distribution of velocities over the surface of the sun would be an orbit around the inner Lagrangian point, a point of gravitational equilibrium between the earth and the sun.

‖lah (lɑː), *int.* [Chinese (southern dial.).] In Singaporean English, a particle used with various kinds of pitch to convey the mood and attitude of the speaker.
1972 *New Nation* (Singapore) 25 Nov. 8/4 'Come and see lah,' he urged with a grin. **1982** TOH PAIK CHOO *Eh, Goondu!* 2 Don't act tough lah. *Ibid.* 90 You must have heard (or said it yourself) when answering a wrong number..with a 'Sala, sala, wrong number lah.' **1984** J. PLATT et al. *New Englishes* viii. 142 *Persuasion. lah* with a fall in pitch. Come with us lah! *Annoyance. lah* with a rise in pitch. Wrong lah! Tsch! Write again here! *Strong objection. lah* with a sharper fall in pitch. A: Shall we discuss this now? B: No lah! So late already. *Ibid.* 143 A: Have you been to the H (restaurant)? B: Yes, the food there not bad what—can try lah. **1992** *World Monitor* Jan. 52/1 'This one is how much, *lah*?' a passerby demands in the coarse pidgin English known here as Singlish.

Lahu (lɑː'huː), *n.* Also **La Hu, La-hu.** Pl. unchanged or **Lahus.** [Lahu.] **a.** (A member of) a minority people of the Lolo group in S.W. China, esp. Yunnan. **b.** The Tibeto-Burman language of this people.
1900 *Geogr. Jrnl.* XV. 503 The inhabitants of Nan Ma-chai are 'La Hu', a Lolo tribe known to the Chinese as the Lo Hei of Lo Hei-shan. They are akin to the Hsiang Tan, and are to be found spread over a wide area, from the Mekong to the Salwin. **1909** H. R. DAVIES *Yün-nan* 307 In the south-west, between the Salween and the Mekong, are the La-hus, who with their cross-bows and poisoned arrows proved formidable foes to the Chinese troops. *Ibid.* 351 Amongst the Lo-lo I have classed the La-hu, the Li-so and the Wo-ni, all three of which are scarcely to be considered as more than dialects of some original Lo-lo tongue. **1955** *Word* XI. 103 Burmic Division... Lolo Branch...Southern Unit:...Lahu. **1964** E. A. NIDA *Toward Sci. Transl.* ix. 195 When one translates from a highly inflected language, such as Greek, into a more or less isolating language, such as Chinese or Lahu, a gain in the number of words involved is inevitable. **1978** *Language* LIV. 484 In Chapter 5, G discusses and illustrates complementation and relativization in several languages (Bambara, Japanese, Lahu, Navaho, Uto-Aztecan, and English).

Laïs ('laɪɪs), *n.* Now *rare.* Pl. **Laïdes** ('laɪdiːz). [The name of either of two celebrated Greek courtesans of the 5th and 4th centuries B.C.] Used allusively of a beautiful and accomplished temptress.
1576 GASCOIGNE *Steele Glas* sig. Cii, Lais leades a Ladies life alofte, And Lucrece lurkes, with sobre bashful grace. **1600** THYNNE *Emblems* xiii, Dame Lais is a puritane. **1605** J. SYLVESTER *Du Bartas's Devine Weekes* 39 Like a Lais, whose unconstant Loue Doth euery day a thousand times remoue. **1665** T. HERBERT *Trav.* 317 The Amorosa's, or those of the order of Lais..be more sociable, have most freedome, and in this Region are not worst esteemed of. **1859** G. A. SALA *Twice round Clock* 200 She on the bay, yonder, is Lais. Yonder goes Aspasia...Some of those dashing delightful creatures have covered themselves with shame, and their mothers with grief. **1967** M. WARD *Du Barry Inheritance* xi. 174 The 'revolutionary jury'..was asked to decide the fate of this Laïs, for whose shameful pleasures a despot had sacrificed the blood and treasures of his people.

‖laissez vibrer (lese vibre), *imp. v. phr. Mus.* [Fr., lit. 'allow to vibrate'.] A musical instruction used to indicate that a note played by striking (esp. cymbals) or plucking should be allowed to fade away without damping.
[**1856** M. C. CLARKE tr. *Berlioz' Treat. Mod. Instrumentation* 229/1 The composer should always be careful to determine the length that he wishes his cymbal notes to last, followed by a rest; in case he wish to have the sound prolonged, he must write long and sustained notes..with this indication:—'let them vibrate' [tr. *laissez vibrer*].] **1907** T. S. WOTTON *Dict. Foreign Mus. Terms* 116 *Laisser vibrer*, allow to vibrate. **1931** G. JACOB *Orchestral Technique* vii. 70 The direction 'laissez vibrer' is given here to indicate that the cymbals are to be allowed to vibrate freely—to ring on until their vibration dies away naturally. **1983** *New Oxf. Compan. Mus.* I. 524/1 The sound is either

damped against the player's clothing..or the cymbals are raised for them to ring on (*laissez vibrer*).

lake, *n.*[2] For †*Obs.* read '*Obs. exc. north. dial.*' and add: **3.** Comb. **lake-lass**, a female companion or playmate.
1849 C. BRONTË *Shirley* III. xiv. 316, I can remember the old mill being built..; and then, I can remember it being pulled down, and going with my *lake-lasses (companions) to see the foundation-stone of the new one laid. **1875** J. FOTHERGILL *Healey* I. viii. 118 Hoo went wi' two o' her lake-lasses..for a walk.

lake, *n.*[4] Add: **[2.]** For †*Obs.* read '*Obs. exc. U. S.*' and add later examples.
1784 J. FILSON *Discovery of Kentucke* 31 Near the head of Salt river a subterranean lake, or large pond, has lately been discovered. **1835** C. P. BRADLEY *Jrnl.* 17 June in *Ohio Archaeol. & Hist. Q.* (1906) XV. 258 They call here every little pond a lake. **1917** S. LEACOCK *Frenzied Fiction* (1918) v. 59, I write this..down by the pond—they call it the lake—at the foot of Beverly-Jones's estate. **1988** *Chapel Hill* (N. Carolina) *Newspaper* 21 Feb. 6D/5 (Advt.), In this lovely, new 5-bedroom home, enjoy the private lake right outside the back door.

[5.] [a.] *lake-port.*
1837 H. MARTINEAU *Society in Amer.* I. II. 261 It [*sc.* Chicago] will be like all the other new and thriving *lake and river ports of America. **1872** *Atlantic Monthly* Apr. 455/1 There is no difficulty in determining the number who landed at our sea-ports and the lake-ports since October 1, 1819. **1986** *New Yorker* 29 Sept. 33/1 The Yavari..has not stirred from the dock at the lake port of Puno for a number of years.

[c.] *lake-dwelling a.*
1949 M. MEAD *Male & Female* iii. 54 (*heading*) The *lake-dwelling Tchambuli. **1989** *N. Y. Times* 20 Aug. VIII. 5/3 The fish is the seeforellen, a lake-dwelling form of the brown trout.

lakes (leɪks), *a.* (and *n.*) *slang.* [Shortened from *Lakes of Killarney*, rhyming slang for 'barmy': see LAKE *n.*[4]] (Also used in full form, *Lakes of Killarney*). Mad, crazy. Occas. as *n.*, a mad person.
1934 P. ALLINGHAM *Cheapjack* iv. 40 Thirty years on the road with a mug-faker and I come to Southend and graft to a bunch of grinnin' Lakes o' Killarneys. *Ibid.* 319 Lakes (Lakes of Killarney: Stone Lakes) (*RS*), a lunatic. **1955** M. ALLINGHAM *Beckoning Lady* xi. 164 Which is not like a bloke who's done a killing unless he's lakes. **1963** H. SLESAR *Bridge of Lions* (1964) iii. 52 'He's lakes' had come to mean 'he's barmy' (from Lakes of Killarney).

Lakota (ləˈkəʊtə), *n.* and *a.* Pl. unchanged or **Lakotas**. [a. Dakota (Teton dialect) *lakhóta*: see DAKOTA *n.* and *a.*] **A.** *n.* **1.** (A member of) a Sioux Indian people of western South Dakota; = TETON *n. a.*
[**1852** S. R. RIGGS *Gram. & Dict. Dakota Language* 135/1 *La-kó-ta, n.* Dakota.] **1918** F. DENSMORE *Teton Sioux Music* (U.S. Bureau Amer. Ethnol. Bull. No. 61) 2 The tribal name, which is pronounced Dakota by the Santee and by the Yankton group, and Lakota by the Teton. **1939** E. BUECHEL *Gram. Lakota* i. 2 The Teton Sioux Indian..or Lakota. **1979** J. HALIFAX *Shamanic Voices* (1980) iii. 70 John Fire Lame Deer, a full-blooded Lakota born on the Rosebud Reservation in South Dakota. **1992** *Native Peoples* Winter 70/2 (Advt.), **1991** American Indian Film Festival... Hundreds of Lakota riding horseback in 70° below zero weather commemorating the victims of The Wounded Knee Massacre.
2. The Sioux dialect of this people; = TETON *n.* b.
1939 E. BUECHEL *Gram. Lakota* i. 2 When the student masters Lakota, he may omit these marks and write as

the Indian does. **1990** *World Mag.* No. 46. 26/2 If we were caught speaking our language..the teacher would bend a ruler back and then let it go against our mouths. Another girl and I went on speaking Lakota anyway.
B. *adj.* Of or pertaining to this people or their language.
[?**1870** S. R. RIGGS (*title*) Lakota ABC wowapi.] **1971** E. SHORRIS *Death of Great Spirit* iii. 24 She, as a woman, a dreamer and wailer of her Lakota songs, must stop, disappear. **1989** M. DORRIS *Broken Cord* iv. 58 She..revealed that not only did she have a Lakota name to give to Adam but that she would bestow one on me as well.

Lakshmi (ˈlækʃmɪ), *n. Hinduism.* Also 8 **Lacshmí**, **Lakshmee**, 9 **Laksmi**. [Skr. *lakṣmī* wealth, beauty.] The name of the Hindu goddess of fortune and beauty, the wife and consort of Vishnu. Also called *Sri*.
[**1734** tr. A. Roger in B. Picart *Relig. Ceremonies* III. 384 Pagods..are usually plac'd round those of Eswara and Vistnou. Those of the latter have generally those of Lastemi his wife, of Garrouda and Annemonta near them.] **1788** *Asiatick Res.* I. 137 *Vànwā*, of celestial birth, was his consort, with whom neither the fickle Làkshmēē, nor Sātēē..constant to her lord, were to be compared. *Ibid.* 240 The Hindus also have their Goddess of Abundance, whom they usually call Lacshmí...Lacshmí may be figuratively called the Ceres of Hindustan. **1832** *Ibid.* XVII. 210 The personified *Sakti* is termed *Lakshmi*, or *Mahá Lakshmi*. **1895** *Brewer's Dict. Phr. & Fable* (new ed.) 724/1 *Laksmi* or *Lakshmi*, one of the consorts of Vishnu; she is goddess of beauty, wealth, and pleasure. **1961** V. S. NAIPAUL *House for Mr Biswas* II. ii. 346 The evening worship of Lakshmi stopped. **1993** *Capilano Rev.* Spring 104 During *Diwali*, everyone leaves doors, shutters and windows wide open because on this auspicious night, goddess Lakshmi visits homes.

laldy (ˈlældɪ), *n. Sc. colloq.* Also **laldie**. [Of uncertain origin: prob. imitative, but perhaps ult. f. OE. *lǣl* whip, weal, bruise.] A beating, a thrashing; punishment. Freq. in phr. *to gie* (or *give*) (someone) *laldy* and *to get laldy*. Now chiefly *fig.*, esp. in phr. *to gie* (or *give*) *it laldy*, to do something with the utmost vigour or enthusiasm. Cf. STICK *n.*[1] 4 c.
1889 H. JOHNSTON *Chron. Glenbuckie* 226 If it had come to the maister's ears I'm thinking ye would have got laldie. **1912** G. CUNNINGHAM *Verse* 118 Ye'll get laldie owre the bum. **1935** W. D. COCKER *Further Poems* 28 He focht alane for Israel against the Philistine, An' fairly gied them laldie wi' the jaw-bane o' a cuddie. **1974** *Sunday Post* (Glasgow) 28 Apr. 8/3 Some bairns were giving it laldy with ball and stick. **1981** A. GRAY *Lanark* xxxvi. 416 'Give him laldy, Gow!' yelled a voice behind the pillar. **1986** W. KAY *Scots* (1988) 58 The author of *The Complaynt of Scotland*..is nowhere more articulate than when he is giein the English laldy. **1992** I. PATTISON *More Rab C. Nesbitt Scripts* 38 *Jamesie*: Brilliant this isn't it boys! American fitba! *Andra*: Yi can get right mowed in and give it laldy.

Lamaze (laˈmaz), *n.* Chiefly *U. S.* [The name of Fernand *Lamaze* (1891–1957), French physician.] Used *attrib.* with reference to the use of psychoprophylaxis in childbirth, as advocated by Lamaze.
1959 M. KARMEL (*title*) Babies without tears: a mother's experiences of the Lamaze method of painless childbirth. **1965** *N. Y. Times* 25 Mar. 40/6 The birth of a baby by natural childbirth using the Lamaze technique. **1974** PASSMORE & ROBSON *Compan. Med. Stud.* III. II. xl. 18/1 It..is currently known as psychoprophylaxis or the Lamaze Method, after a French enthusiast. **1979** R. JAFFE *Class Reunion* III. iv. 246 The Lamaze method of natural childbirth was the new in-thing and everybody was doing it. **1986**

Courier-Mail (Brisbane) 9 Dec. 22 (*caption*) Tell him we're not interested in starting a Lamaze class!

lamb, *n*.[1] Add: [7.] [b.] **lamb's ears** (also **lamb's ear**), any of several plants whose leaves are covered with soft white hairs; *esp.* the labiate *Stachys byzantina*, often grown in gardens.

 *a*1876 E. LEIGH *Gloss. Dial. Cheshire* (1877) 119 **Lamb's Ears*, the Rose Campion. 1884 W. MILLER *Dict. Eng. Names Plants* 252 *Stachys..germanica*, Common Wound-wort, Lamb's-ear. 1900 DICKINSON & PREVOST *Gloss. Dial. Cumberland* (rev. ed.) 192/1 *Lamb's ear*,..Hoary Plantain—*Plantago media*. 1905 *Eng. Dial. Dict.* III. 510/2 *Lamb's-ears*,..the premorse scabious. 1944 T. C. MANSFIELD *Border in Colour* 221 S[tachys] lanata..has white woolly leaves and is commonly called Lamb's Ears. 1988 *Los Angeles Times* 19 Mar. v. 4/1 Stachys, or lamb's ears, is the darling of the perennial bed.

Lamb (læm), *n*.[2] *Physics*. (*Lamb shift*: formerly a main entry.) [The name of Willis E. *Lamb* (b. 1913), U.S. physicist.] Used *attrib.* to designate phenomena described, predicted, or demonstrated by Lamb, as **Lamb dip**, a drop in the output from a laser spectrometer at a particular frequency, as a result of atoms simultaneously absorbing two photons travelling in opposite directions; **Lamb shift** *Physics* [demonstrated by Lamb and R. C. Retherford in 1947], a displacement of energy levels in hydrogen and hydrogen-like atoms such that those with the same values of the quantum numbers *n* and *j* but different values of *l* are not coincident, as predicted by Dirac's theory, but separated by a very small amount (the level with the lower value of *l* being the higher).

 1948 *Physical Rev.* LXXIV. 1157 The effects treated are the Lamb shift, the correction of the *g*-factor..and the correction of the Compton scattering cross section. 1950 *Ibid.* LXXVII. 745 (*heading*) Departure of the Lamb shift from the n^{-3} law in He+. 1958 CONDON & ODISHAW *Handbk. Physics* VII. iv. 63/1 The Lamb shift has been interpreted..as resulting from changes in the electron self-energy which results from its interactions with the electromagnetic and electron-positron fields. 1964 E. A. POWER *Introd. Quantum Electrodynamics* i. 7 The modern versions of quantum electrodynamics have enabled a very accurate comparison to be made between theory and experiment. Well-known examples are the Lamb shift energy splitting of the $2S\frac{1}{2}$ and $2P\frac{1}{2}$ levels in hydrogen and the radiative corrections to the magnetic moment of the electron. 1965 *IEEE Jrnl. Quantum Electronics* I. 351/1 When the amplitude of the second harmonic is zero, the Lamb dip just vanishes, and the second derivative of the turning curve at line center is zero. 1967 *Appl. Physics Lett.* X. 304/1 A drop in saturated absorption, analogous to the Lamb dip, occurs when light is absorbed by atoms of the zero velocity class in the Doppler distribution of the low pressure neon. 1973 *McGraw-Hill Yearbk. Sci. & Technol.* 111/1 Experimental programs to measure heavy-ion Lamb shifts are now in progress. 1974 *Physics Bull.* Mar. 91/1 Lasers with frequencies locked to features such as the Lamb dip are routinely used in interferometry. 1989 H. M. GEORGI in P. Davies *New Physics* xvi. 449/2 Theorists used renormalisation to do finite calculations of quantum corrections to the first order results (such as..the Lamb shift).

lambada (læm'bɑːdə, ‖lam'bada), *n*. [a. Pg., lit. 'beating, lashing', f. *lambar* to beat, whip.] A fast, rhythmical, and erotic dance of Brazilian origin, danced by couples in close physical contact; also, the music to which it is danced. Occas. *fig.*

 1988 *Financial Times* 15 Sept. IV. p. viii/1 Sao Paulo's current cultural explosion is the lambada—a lithe, lascivious Caribbean dance that first arrived in the 1930s and was banned by the then-government as obscene. 1989 *Los Angeles Times* 18 Nov. FI/2 *Lambada* brings couple dancing back with a vengeance. 1990 *Times* 2 Apr. 8/3 The catchy lambada song now has Latin America and the seaboard cities of the US in its grip. 1991 C. HIAASEN *Native Tongue* (1992) xxi. 229 The authentic Green Corn Dance..was politely discarded as too solemn and repetitious; instead Golden Sun danced the *lambada*. 1993 *Coloradoan* Fort Collins 28 Mar. B1/2 I'm trying to act and sound calm..but my nerves are doing the lambada.

lambda, *n*. Add: 6. *Microbiol.* A temperate bacteriophage originally isolated from *Escherichia coli* and much used in genetic research; also denoted by λ. Freq. *attrib.*

 1952 J. LEDERBERG et al. in *Cold Spring Harbor Symp. Quant. Biol.* XVI. 436/1 The exposure of sensitive cells to suspensions of the free phage, which we named 'λ', by analogy to a killer factor in *Paramecium*, results in the lysis of a variable proportion of cells. 1953 *Ibid.* XVIII. 95/1 Two *lambda* mutants have been used in our experiments. 1963 *Jrnl. Bacteriol.* LXXXV. 1202 (*heading*) Mutant of lambda bacteriophage producing a thermolabile endolysin. 1973 R. G. KRUEGER et al. *Introd. Microbiol.* xiv. 405/1 When bacteriophage λ infects a nonlysogenic host cell, the infection results in lysis in about 70% of the cases and lysogeny the other 30% of the time. 1976 *Sci. Amer.* Jan. 65/2 The repressor we have studied is a protein molecule manufactured by bacteriophage lambda, a virus that infects the common colon bacterium *Escherichia coli*. 1983 J. R. S. FINCHAM *Genetics* xi. 300 Lambda is but one of a large family of closely related phages which..have their genomes integrated into the host DNA in the lysogenic state.

lambdoid, *a*. Add: 2. *Microbiol.* Relating to or mutated from bacteriophage lambda. Also *ellipt.*

 1958 *Adv. Virus Res.* V. 157 Several other phages (lambdoids) which can be considered to belong to the same species as λ have been isolated by Jacob and Wollman. 1968 *Ann. Rev. Genetics* II. 305 The lambdoid phages provide a set of natural variants of a single species. 1973 R. G. KRUEGER et al. *Introd. Microbiol.* xiv. 404/2 Other temperate phages related to λ (the 'lambdoid' phages) have very similar properties. 1987 *Nature* 11 June 465/1 The structural basis of operator binding by the repressor protein of the lambdoid phage 434.

lambliasis (læm'blaɪəsɪs), *n. Med.* [f. mod.L. *Lamblia*, former genus name of *Giardia*, f. the name of Wilhelm *Lambl* (1824–95), Czech physician + -IA[1]: see -IASIS.] = *GIARDIASIS n.

 1916 *Lancet* 10 June 1167/1 Most of the lambliasis patients had received a number of injections of emetine before they reached England. 1926 *Arch. Dis. Childhood* I. 97 It has to be remembered in connection with all claims to cure lambliasis that the flagellate will spontaneously disappear for a time from the stools. 1943 *Q. Cumulative Index Medicus* XXXIII. 465/1 Intestinal lambliasis in occupied Poland. 1974 J. CAMERON *Indian Summer* vi. 127 The guts-ache came in so many sneaking shapes: amoebiasis, bacillary dysentery, lambliasis. 1983 *Helvetica Paediatrica Acta* XXXVIII. 87 (*heading*) Salicylazosulfapyridine therapy in a child with chronic lambliasis due to acquired hypogammaglobulinemia.

Lambrusco (læm'broskəʊ, ‖lam'brusko), *n*. [a. It. *lambrusco*, lit. 'grape of the wild vine', f. *lambruscare* to allow (a vine) to grow wild.] A sparkling red wine produced in both dry and sweet varieties throughout the Emilia-Romagna region of N. Italy; the grape from which this wine is made. Also applied *transf.* to red or white wines of similar character produced elsewhere. **1934** SCHOONMAKER & MARTEL *Compl. Wine Bk.* vi. 142 The one internationally celebrated Emilian wine..is Lambrusco. *Ibid.* 143 Lambrusco is made from the grape of the same name (which should not be confused with the American Labrusca) and the best of it is supposed to come from the neighborhood of Modena. **1958** A. L. SIMON *Dict. Wines* 98/2 *Lambrusco*, one of the best red wines of the Province of Emilia (Italy). **1965** *House & Garden* Jan. 63/1 The most lighthearted of all red wines: Lambrusco. **1977** *Times* 15 Nov. (Italian Wine Suppl.) p. iii/3 Lambrusco, the famous wine of Modena..is a varietal, the Lambrusco being the grape from which it is vinified. **1986** *Courier-Mail* (Brisbane) 29 Oct. 22/5 The Italian Lambrusco was originally a dry red. *Ibid.* 22/6 Australian Lambrusco is usually sweet and red. **1988** *Sunday Tel.* (Colour Suppl.) 21 Feb. 56/2 'Real' Lambrusco is..herby, spicy, gloriously refreshing and, above all, bone dry.

lamb's tongue, *n. phr.* Add: **3.** = *lamb's ears* s.v. **LAMB n.*[1] 7 b. Also *lamb's tongue plant.*
1882 H. FRIEND *Gloss. Devonshire Plant Names* 33 Lamb's-tongue, *Stachys lanata* L. **1956** *Dict. Gardening* (R. Hort. Soc.) (ed. 2) IV. 2011/1 *S*[*tachys*] *lanata*. Lamb's Tongue. Whole plant densely and persistently white-woolly...Often used for summer-bedding. **1974** F. A. BODDY *Ground Cover* xi. 105 The lamb's-tongue plant, *Stachys olympica* (*S. lanata*), is making a name for itself as a ground coverer. **1987** *Woman & Home* July 16/3 From the mountains of the Caucasus comes the Lamb's Tongue — *Stachys lanata* — a carpeting perennial whose leaves and 18 in stems are clothed with a silvery-grey wool, soft to the touch.

lamburger ('læmbɜːgə(r)), *n.* orig. *U.S.* [Blend of LAMB *n.* + HAMBURGER *n.*] A meat patty made from minced lamb.
1939 *Amer. Speech* XIV. 154/2 *Lamburger*, ground lamb. **1969** D. SCHULTZ *Busy Cook's Look-It-Up Bk.* 42 Neck or shank meat is good for grinding into 'lamburgers'. **1984** *Auckland Star* 2 Mar. A1/6 (*caption*) Meet the lamburger — New Zealand's answer to the hamburger and hot dog. **1990** *Courier-Jrnl.* (Louisville, Kentucky) 18 Apr. c8/3 Make lamburgers with ground lamb instead of beef and top with imported mustard or creamy goat cheese.

lame, *a.* Add: **[2.] d.** Of a person: inept, naive, easily fooled; *spec.* unskilled in the fashionable behaviour of a particular group, socially inept. Cf. LAME *n.*[2] 2. *slang* (orig. and chiefly *U.S.*).
1942 BERREY & VAN DEN BARK *Amer. Thes. Slang* §491/9 *Easy to take, lame, soft,*..easily victimized. **1955** *Amer. Speech* XXX. 303 *Lame.* Used to describe an oaf. 'That cat is a real lame stud'... Lame is the opposite of solid. **1961** *N.Y. Times Mag.* 25 June 39 *Lame*, square, but not beyond redemption. If you're lame, man, you can learn. **1967** *Time* 2 June 26 Anyone who does not know that is obviously lame..or perhaps just over 25 and into the twilight of life. **1972** W. LABOV *Language in Inner City* vii. 258 To be *lame* means to be outside of the central group and its culture. **1990** *New Statesman* 16 Feb. 12/1 With his top lip curled to signify contempt, he goaded an imaginary hapless friend: 'You a *lame* chief, *well* lame, *serious* lame!' **1991** *Sun* 13 June 23/6 This DJ is lame. **1994** D. CASSIDY & C. DEFFAA *C'mon, Get Happy* vi. 61, I don't want to be associated with people I think are lame.

lamellipodium (ləˌmɛlɪ'pəʊdɪəm), *n. Cytol.* Pl. -podia. [f. LAMELL(A *n.* + -*i*- + **FILO*)PODIUM *n.*] A thin flattened extension of a cell by which it moves over or adheres to a surface.
1970 M. ABERCROMBIE et al. in *Exper. Cell Res.* LX. 443/2 We have therefore three kinds of structures..the thin anterior tip of the cell which..may protrude or withdraw..the ruffle formed by the bending upwards of this anterior tip..and the vertical ruffles that appear directly on the dorsal surface behind the anterior edge. We propose for future discussion to introduce the term *lamellipodium*, on the analogy of filopodium, for such thin, sheet-like, mobile, commonly transitory projections from the cell. **1973** *Developmental Biol.* XXX. 75/1 A lamellipodium is a large, flattened cell extension... This strictly morphological usage differs from that of Abercrombie et al...but has, I believe, wider application. **1978** *Sci. Amer.* Apr. 74/1 When a 3T3 cell comes into contact with another 3T3 cell or with a nonmigrating cell, the sheetlike lamellipodium at the front end of the cell ceases its ruffling movement. **1987** *Developmental Biol.* CXIX. 45/2 Lamellipodia..are responsible for firm adhesion of the neuron to its substratum.
Hence **laˌmelli'podial** *a.*, of the nature of or involving lamellipodia.
1989 *Nature* 28 Sept. 328/2 The lamellipodial projections of migrating Dictyostelium amoebae. **1989** B. ALBERTS et al. *Molecular Biol. Cell* (ed. 2) xiii. 757 Lamellipodial movement.

‖**lamento** (la'mento), *n. Mus.* Pl. -enti. [It., = LAMENT *n.* 2.] An elegiac or mourning song; in Italian opera, a tragic aria, esp. one preceding the climax.
[**1934** C. LAMBERT *Music Ho!* v. 315 The *Lamento e Trionfo*, the idea of the artist as hero winning through adversity to a glorious apotheosis,..lies behind so much of nineteenth-century romanticism.] **1944** W. APEL *Harvard Dict. Mus.* 393/1 In 17th-century opera the Lamento is a scene expressing utter despair, usually placed shortly before the unexpected 'turn to the happy end'. **1979** *Early Mus.* Jan. 29/2 The title of the *Lamento* suggests a slow tempo. **1983** *Nat. Geographic* Apr. 516/1 The notes fade, but the bittersweet words of the 1930s *lamento*..for the island..seem to hang in the night air.

laminaran ('læmɪnəræn), *n. Biochem.* [f. **LAMINAR(IN *n.* + -AN I. 2.] A polysaccharide that consists chiefly of glucose residues and occurs in seaweeds of the genus *Laminaria* and other brown algae.
Earlier called *laminarin*.
1961 *Nature* 16 Dec. 1078/2 In 1939 Nisizawa isolated a soluble laminaran from the fronds of the brown alga, *Eisenia bicyclis*. **1967** PERCIVAL & MCDOWELL *Chem. & Enzymol. Marine Algal Polysaccharides* iii. 53 Laminaran, earlier named laminarin, a water-soluble β-glucan, is the food reserve material of the Phaeophyceae. **1983** KENNEDY & WHITE *Bioactive Carbohydrates* viii. 179 The major polysaccharides elaborated by fungi include..a number of storage products of the laminaran type.

laminaranase (lə'mɪnərəneɪz, læmɪ'nærəneɪz), *n. Biochem.* [f. **LAMINARAN *n.* + -ASE.] Any enzyme which catalyses the hydrolysis of laminaran.
1974 HAUG & LARSEN in J. B. Pridham *Plant Carbohydrate Biochem.* xiv. 211 The polysaccharide was also degraded by a laminaranase isolated from the same plant. **1978** *Appl. & Environmental Microbiol.* XXXVI. 594 All lytic strains produced laminaranase and α-mannanase.

laminaribiose (ˌlæmɪnərɪ'baɪəʊz), *n. Biochem.* [f. **LAMINARI(N *n.* + BIOSE *n.*] The disaccharide derived from laminaran; 3-β-D-glucosyl-D-glucose.
[**1939** *Sci. Proc. R. Dublin Soc.* XXII. 63 It should be possible to isolate from it [*sc.* laminarin] a disaccharide (laminariose) having the structure shown.] **1941** V. C. BARRY in *Ibid.* 423 By partial acid hydrolysis of laminarin, the disaccharide was isolated...It is proposed to name this sugar laminaribiose. **1952** *Jrnl. Chem. Soc.* 1243 (*heading*) The synthesis of

laminaribiose (3-β-D-glucosyl D-glucose) and proof of its identity with laminaribiose isolated from laminarin. **1966** *Biochem. Jrnl.* XCVIII. 19C/1 A branched glucan containing both β-(1→3)- and β-(1→2)-linkages should, on partial hydrolysis, yield laminaribiose and sophorose. **1974** R. J. STURGEON in J. B. Pridham *Plant Carbohydrate Biochem.* XV. 227 Hydrolysis of the glucan by a bacterial laminarinase released glucose, laminaribiose, laminaritriose and a water-soluble 'limit dextrin'.

laminarin ('læmɪnərɪn), *n. Biochem.* [a. G. *Laminarin* (P. Schmiedeberg 1885, in *Tageblatt 58. Versammlung Deutsch. Naturforscher u. Aertzte Strassburg* 427), f. mod.L. *Laminaria*: see LAMINARIAN *a.*, -IN[1].] = *LAMINARAN *n.*
1934 in WEBSTER. **1938** *Sci. Proc. R. Dublin Soc.* XXI. 615 Laminarin . . is a polysaccharide occurring plentifully in the fronds of marine algae during the autumn months. **1952** *Ann. Reg. 1951* 420 The Secretary of State for Scotland was shown the only known sample of laminarin, a new substance which it was hoped to develop as a substitute for blood plasma. **1967** *Biochem. Jrnl.* CIV. 32P/2 Incubation of laminarin with a bacterial laminarinase preparation . . resulted in slow random degradation with the production initially of glucose . . and other sugars. **1984** A. C. & A. DUXBURY *Introd. World's Oceans* XV. 473 Storage products [of seaweeds] include the carbohydrates laminarin and mannitol.

laminarinase (lə'mɪnərɪneɪz, læmɪ'nærɪneɪz), *n. Biochem.* [f. *LAMINARIN *n.* + -ASE.] = *LAMINARANASE *n.*
1966 *Biochem. Jrnl.* XCVIII. 20C/1 Incubation of glucan A with a bacterial laminarinase preparation . . gave glucose, laminaribiose and laminaritriose. **1967** PERCIVAL & McDOWELL *Chem. & Enzymol. Marine Algal Polysaccharides* II. 65 The enzymes which hydrolyse laminaran are termed laminarases (= laminarinases). **1974** R. J. STURGEON in J. B. Pridham *Plant Carbohydrate Biochem.* XV. 227 Hydrolysis of the glucan by a bacterial laminarinase released glucose, laminaribiose, laminaritriose and a water-soluble 'limit dextrin'. **1987** *Jrnl. Phycol.* XXIII. 494/1 This glucan had a median molecular weight of 4600 . . and could be hydrolyzed by laminarinase.

laminator, *n.* Add: Also occas. **laminater**. **2.** A machine for making laminates, *esp.* one for bonding paper or the like to plastic film.
1958 *Plastics Technol.* Dec. 1126/1 In conjunction with the modern extruder-laminater, servo feed-back controls on the machine cut rejects and save material. **1967** *Mod. Office Executive Buyers' Guide* (ed. 5) 95/1 Ply-on laminator. Automatically seals anything written, printed, photographed, typewritten or drawn in thin clear plastic. **1975** *Language for Life* (Dept. Educ. & Sci.) xxii. 320 It would be unrealistic of us to make a simple recommendation that *every* school should have . . a punch-binding machine and an electric laminator. **1980** *Nature* 3 Jan. p. x/1 (Advt.), Pelling & Cross Ltd announce the availability of a neat, low-cost, desk-top laminator. **1987** *Graphics World* Nov./Dec. 80/4 The document is inserted into a plastic pouch which is then fed directly through the laminator.

laminin ('læmɪnɪn), *n. Biochem.* [f. LAMIN(A *n.* + -IN[1].] An adhesive glycoprotein in the basement membrane and the ground substance of connective tissue.
1979 R. TIMPL et al. in *Jrnl. Biol. Chem.* CCLIV. 9933/1 We have isolated a large noncollagenous glycoprotein, laminin, from a mouse tumor that produces basement membrane. *Ibid.* 9936/2 This protein, which we have named laminin, is a high molecular-weight protein joined with disulphide bonds. **1985** *Sci. News* 20 July 39/3 Laminin receptors

have been correlated with invasiveness in tumor cells. **1988** *Nature* 1 Dec. 487/1 Fibronectin, collagen and laminin are three major components of the subendothelial matrix which support platelet adhesion.

Lamium ('leɪmɪəm), *n.* [a. L. *lāmium* dead-nettle (adopted as a genus name by Linnaeus), f. Gr. λάμια gaping mouth (with reference to the shape of the flowers).] A genus of labiate plants which includes several kinds of dead-nettle; (also **lamium**) a plant of this genus.
1682 N. GREW *Anat. Flowers* App. §11 The Top is . . Poynted, or at least, Roundish, as in Lamium, Ironwort. **1736** *Compl. Family-Piece* II. iii. 307 Perennial shrubby Lamium or base Hore-hound. **1880** A. GRAY *Struct. Biol.* vi. 247 A corolla the upper petal or part of which is arched . . as in Aconite and Lamium. **1903** *Jrnl. Bot.* XLI. 150 (*heading*) Some entire-leaved forms of Lamium. **1974** *Country Life* 21 Mar. 627/3 The backstops of the tennis court have been successfully masked by alternating green and gold hops . . growing in a border of lamium at the base. **1990** *House & Garden* Nov. 111 A selection of ground-cover plants and perennials with blue, pale pink and soft yellow flowers like lamiums.

lamp, *n.*[1] Add: [2.] **c.** *pl.* (With capital initial.) A nickname for a person responsible for looking after lamps, esp. on board ship. ?*Obs.*
1866 DICKENS *Mugby Junction* in *All Year Round* Extra Christmas No. 10 Dec. 6/1 The answer to his inquiry, 'Where's Lamps?' was . . that it was his off-time. **1900** F. T. BULLEN *Men of Merchant Service* 152 How can a sailor be expected to show due deference to a man, who, after all, is only 'Lamps'. **1919** E. O'NEILL *Moon of Caribbees* 18 Fetch a light, Lamps, that's a good boy. **1933** M. LOWRY *Ultramarine* ii. 62 Both Lamps and Chips have been up for ten minutes.

[5.] **lamp-worker**: hence **lamp-working** *n.*
1925 HODKIN & COUSEN *Textbk. Glass Technol.* xxxvi. 483 For *lamp-working and general purposes a soft soda-lime glass is preferred. **1976** *Canad. Collector* (Toronto) Mar.–Apr. 38/3 Lampworking for him was both profitable work and an absorbing hobby.

lamp, *v.*[1] Add: **5.** *trans.* and *intr.* To hunt by lamping (sense *2).
1988 *Shooting News & Weekly* 26 Aug.–1 Sept. 9/2 Rabbits that have been unsuccessfully lamped become lamp-shy. **1991** *Working Terrier* Feb. 18/1 My best ever dog . . was in his prime and I was lamping every chance I got.

lamp (læmp), *v.*[3] *dial.* (chiefly *north.*) and *slang.* [Of uncertain origin; perh. alteration of LAM *v.*] To beat, strike; to thrash. Also *fig.*
1808 in JAMIESON. **1895** T. PINNOCK *Tom Brown's Black Country Ann.* (E.D.D.), I'll lamp his hide when I catch him. **1902** in *Eng. Dial. Dict.* III. 513/2 Ye thought ye wad lamp us, did ye? I was fairly lampet at that game. **1969** D. GRIFFITHS *Talk of my Town* 21 *Lamp it*, kick it (e.g., a football) hard. **1985** M. MUNRO *Patter* 42 Lamp that oot the windy.

lamper, *n.* Restrict *U. S. colloq.* to sense in Dict. Add: **2.** One who engages in lamping (sense *2).
1985 *BBC Wildlife* July 326/2 The lampers had split up, though still within contact distance (working two men and a dog to a beam) . . . A lamper well to my rear caught her [*sc.* a vixen] in his light. **1991** *Working Terrier* Feb. 4/2 The *Mansfield & Ashfield Recorder* . . printed a front page editorial . . which again carried a police officer being quoted as saying 'diggers and lampers should not be approached as they are just as likely to hit you over the head with a spade as hit an animal'.

lamping, *vbl. n.* Add: **2.** A method of hunting by night using a bright light to illuminate or dazzle the hunted animal; the practice of this. Cf. *pit-lamping* vbl. n. s.v. PIT *n.*[1] 15.

1984 *Times* 10 Jan. 3/4 Two deer had been taken by a method known as 'lamping' — using a lamp to light up animals which were then chased by lurcher dogs. **1985** *BBC Wildlife* July 326/1 Another way of hunting for foxes, rabbits or whatever comes is by 'lamping', waiting in a field for some nocturnal creature to make a rustle, dazzling it with a powerful spotlight, then shooting it. **1991** *Working Terrier* Feb. 20/2 Ferreting is a lot less taxing on a dog's strength than either hares or lamping.

Lancashire, *n.* Add: **Lancashire hot-pot** [HOT-POT *n.*], a dish of meat, onion, and potato, resembling Irish stew.

1898 'P. BROWNE' *Year's Cookery* 126 *Lancashire Hot Pot. — Take the best end of the neck of mutton, the sheep's kidneys, a moderate-sized onion, and the tinned oysters. **1939** *Radiation Cookery Bk.* (ed. 21) 291 Menu 16. — Lancashire hot-pot, butter beans, jam sponge. **1978** G. GREENE *Human Factor* VI. i. 308 It's best to go English and I would suggest the Lancashire hot pot.

lance, *n.*[1] Senses 9, 10 in Dict. become 10, 11. Add: **9.** (With capital initial.) A short-range U.S. surface-to-surface ballistic missile system designed to be used chiefly with nuclear warheads; a missile of this system.

1964 *Guide Subject Indexes for Sci. & Techn. Aerospace Rep.* Apr. A-122/1 (*heading*) Lance missile. **1975** R. PRETTY *Jane's Pocket Bk. Missiles* 119/1 Development of Lance started in 1962-3... The first production model was delivered for US Army testing in April 1971. **1981** P. GUDGIN *Brit. Army Equipment* 37 (*caption*) The US-designed and built Lance nuclear surface-to-surface (SSM) tactical missile.. replaced the American-produced Honest John in British service. **1987** *Armed Forces* Sept. 408/1 The Lance has a range of 100km, a warhead with a variable yield of 1-100 kilotons, and a CEP of 150-400m. **1989** *New Yorker* 23 Oct. 102/3 The issue was short-range nuclear weapons — whether.. to create a new and vastly improved version of a short-range American system called Lance.

[**10.**] [**a.**] †*lance-staff* (pl. *-staves*) (*obs. exc. Hist.*).

1489 in *Sanctuarium Beverlacense* (Surtees Soc. V) (1837) V. 154 Cognovit se commisisse homicidium, viz., quemdam ignotum servientem Edwardi Barnaby, gentilman, cum baculo vocato a *launce stafe. **1920** J. MASEFIELD *Enslaved* 22 They struck us with their lance-staves to make them room to ride.

lancet, *n.* Add: [**4.**] [**a.**] **lancet clock**, a bracket clock having a case shaped like a lancet arch.

[**1899** F. J. BRITTEN *Old Clocks & Watches* 333 The 'lancet' case, in the form of a pointed Norman or Gothic arch, and named from its resemblance to the well-known cutting instrument used by surgeons.] **1922** *Ibid.* (ed. 5) 815/2 (Index), *Lancet clocks. **1973** A. BIRD *Eng. House Clocks: 1600-1850* xi. 219 The antique trade name for this style is 'lancet clock', and they appear nearly always to have been black.

land, *n.*[1] Add: [**I.**] [**2.**] **c. the land**, the (cultivable) earth viewed as a repository of natural resources and the chief source of human sustenance or livelihood. Freq. in phrases: see BACK TO THE LAND, *the fat of the land* s.v. FAT *n.*[2] 2 c, *to live off the land* s.v. LIVE *v.*[1] 2.

c **1382** BIBLE (Wycliffe) *Gen.* xlv. 18, I shall ȝyue to ȝow al þe goodis of Egipte, þat ȝe eeten þe mary of the loond. **1766** BLACKSTONE *Comm.* II. II. v. 67 The king used to take.. the *first fruits*, that is to say, one year's profits of the land. **1954** W. FAULKNER *Fable* 399 Work is the only anesthetic to which grief is vulnerable... Restoring the land would.. palliate the grief. **1990** *EastWest* Dec. 52/2 The industrial eater

is.. one who does not know that eating is an agricultural act, who no longer imagines the connections between eating and the land.

d. on the land (*Austral.*), in or into a rural (esp. agricultural) occupation or way of life.

1902 *Advocate* (Burnie, Tasmania) 20 Feb. 4/1 Go on the Land! **1930** BILLIS & KENYON *Pastures New* iii. 50 Charles Bonney.. not caring for the shackles of the Sydney Government routine, went on the land. **1984** *Bulletin* (Sydney) 24 Apr. 68/1, I was born on the land... I've farmed my own properties since 1948. **1989** J. CONWAY *Road from Coorain* (1990) iii. 6 The contingent of country boys in the school.. expected to go back home to a cheerfully horsey life on the land.

[**3.**] [**b.**] **Land of (the) Little Sticks** (*Canad.*), a sub-arctic region of northern Canada, whose vegetation includes stunted and dwarf trees. *land of the free*: see *FREE *a.*, *n.*, and *adv.* B. 1 b.

1896 C. WHITNEY *On Snow-Shoes to Barren Grounds* xvi. 187 No man may consider himself an expert until he has driven dogs and handled a sledge over such country as that approaching the Land of the Little Sticks. **1930** R. W. SERVICE *Coll. Verse* 301 Why do you linger all alone in the splendid emptiness, Scouring the Land of the Little Sticks on the trail of the caribou? **1965** F. SYMINGTON *Tuktu* 9 Urged by the high suns of May, the snow retreats through the land of the Little Sticks and the caribou pour out on the tundra. **1993** *Up Here* Aug.-Sept. 39/1 East of the North Arm, you're in the Land of Little Sticks, the Dene name for the rugged granite and uncountable lakes of the Canadian Shield where stunted birches, pine and spruce somehow cling to the rock.

[**c.**] **land of opportunity** (applied esp. to the United States of America).

1948 MENCKEN *Amer. Lang.* Suppl. II. 636 New Mexico.. has also been called.. the *Land of Opportunity.* **1965** J. VON STERNBERG *Fun in Chinese Laundry* (1966) i. 11 Had the land of opportunity been good to him, he might have taken time out to reflect. **1991** D. RIEFF *Los Angeles* II. vi. 100 It was said that criminals from South Central L.A. referred to the Westside and the Valley as the 'lands' for lands of opportunity.

[**II.**] [**10.**] [**b.**] **land developer**.

1961 *Providence Jrnl.* 3 Feb. 21/7 While *land developers tell them when, where, and in what manner the community shall grow. **1984** S. BELLOW *Him with his Foot in his Mouth* 33 Numerous failed entrepreneurs had preceded him in this private park, the oilmen and land developers who had caused this monument to be built.

land management.

1944 E. H. GRAHAM *National Princ. Land Use* xiv. 230 To many people, ecology and *land management are very general terms. **1988** *National Trust Thames & Chilterns News* Spring 1 Balance is fundamental to the Trust's policy and is vital to good rural land management.

land manager.

1909 *Westm. Gaz.* 16 June 1/3 A skilful *land-manager undoubtedly confers a benefit on the public. **1986** *Farmers Weekly* 3 Jan. 9/4 Land managers should meet the market demand for food.

land settlement.

1924 S. H. ROBERTS *Hist. Austral. Land Settlement* p. xiii, I conceived the idea of surveying the whole field of *land settlement. **1987** *N. Y. Times* 5 Aug. A26/2 A merging of Sri Lanka's northern and eastern provinces into a single united province with its own legislature and control of law enforcement and land settlement.

[**c.**] *land-bound a.*

1972 F. RAPHAEL *April, June & Nov.* 382 Sometimes their captains become *landbound and turn into shopkeepers. **1983** G. PRIESTLAND *At Large* 124 We seem to have become a landbound people who no longer do business in great waters. **1993** *Sci. Amer.* Jan. 90/2 For land-bound latecomers such as primates.., the only possible means of access to Madagascar was by 'rafting'.

[11.] [b.] *land terrapin* (also *transf.*).

1709 J. LAWSON *New Voy. Carolina* 133 The *Land-Terebin is of several Sizes, but generally Round-Mouth'd and not Hawks-Bill'd, as some are. **1896** LYDEKKER *Royal Nat. Hist.* V. 65 The spinose land-terrapin (*Geoëmyda spinosa*). **1939** *Florida* (Federal Writers' Project) I. 28 Turtles found in Florida are . . the mud turtles, and a land terrapin which is peculiar to the State. **1952** B. HARWIN *Home is Upriver* i.9 Kip did not know these people, except that they were river folk, and therefore not strangers like the land terrapins.

[12.] **landnam** *Archaeol.* [a. Da. *landnam* occupation of land (J. Iversen 1941, in *Danmarks Geol. Undersøgelse* 2nd Ser. LXVI); cf. *landnám* above.], the clearance of forested land for (usu. short-term) agricultural purposes; esp. such an event as evidenced by sudden changes in pollen spectra.

1950 F. E. ZEUNER *Dating Past* (ed. 2) iv. 78 Iversen holds that these changes indicate the arrival of farmers, the phase of landnam or land occupation, that the charcoal comes from clearance fires. **1973** P. A. COLINVAUX *Introd. Ecol.* vii. 108 A landnam event has been found in many parts of Europe, everywhere first dated at about 5000 years ago and suggesting that men quickly learnt the new ways from each other throughout the whole continent. **1980** K. RANDSBORG *Viking Age in Denmark* iv. 53 The first stage is the Neolithic landnam, which, for example, is earlier on the Danish islands than in, say, southern Norway. **1991** *Antiquity* LXV. 997/2 One can more easily envisage the strategy of midslope settlement and radial *remuages* as a late rationalization of a *landnam*.

land-wash. (b) orig. and chiefly *N. Amer.*, the part of a beach which is washed by the sea.

1770 G. CARTWRIGHT *Jrnl.* 26 Oct. (1792) I. 49 They had tailed a trap on the land-wash at the head of Niger Sound. **1969** F. MOWAT *Boat who wouldn't Float* iii. 22 Two-score . . houses . . clambered up the slope from the landwash. **1991** *Newfoundland Lifestyle* Aug.–Oct. 19/3 Sail out of it she did, to the applause and wonder of about a thousand people on the wharf, along the landwash, and on the low hill across the road.

land, *v.* Add: [II.] [8.] e. *fig. to land on one's feet* = *to fall on one's feet* s.v. FALL *v.* 65 h. Cf. *to light on one's feet* (or *legs*) s.v. LIGHT *v.*[1] 9. *colloq.*

1958 P. BRANCH *Murder's Little Sister* iii. 32 Landing slap on your feet like a ruddy cat! Well, eight lives to go. **1979** J. C. OATES *Unholy Loves* iii. 207 He's in California . . being interviewed by one of the state universities . . . At least he'll land on his feet. **1990** E. BLAIR *Maggie Jordan* iii. 67 You've certainly landed on your feet getting a job at Templeton's.

Landau ('lændaʊ), *n.*[2] *Physics.* [The name of Lev Davidovich *Landau* (1908–68), Russian theoretical physicist.] Used *attrib.* to designate concepts introduced by Landau or arising out of his work, as **Landau damping**, the damping of a plasma oscillation through conversion of some of its kinetic energy into the potential energy of plasma particles, rather than through loss of momentum in collisions between particles; **Landau level**, each of a series of discrete energy levels into which a magnetic field splits the continuous energy distribution of the conduction electrons of a metal at very low temperatures.

1960 G. FRANCIS *Ionization Phenomena in Gases* vii. 260 A physical picture of Landau damping, i.e. without collisions, now emerges. **1963** *Bull. Amer. Physical Soc.* VIII. 309/1 These oscillations can be explained by the scattering of electrons from the 1st to the 2nd or 3rd Landau levels through the absorption of optical phonons. **1968** *Jrnl. Physics C* I. 1711 In the magnetophonon effect an oscillatory variation of resistance with magnetic field is caused by resonant scattering of electrons between Landau levels by longitudinal optical phonons. **1973** *Appl. Physics Lett.* XXIII. 41/1 Because of the quantizing longitudinal magnetic field, the conduction band is split into Landau levels. **1987** *Nature* 9 Apr. 563/2 As a result . . the paradox arises of the disappearance of Landau damping in the magnetic field.

landed, *a.* Add: [1.] [a.] Freq. in colloc. *landed gentry.*

1752 HUME *Ess. & Treat* (1777) I. 221 It consists chiefly of nobles and landed gentry. **1860** W. COLLINS *Woman in White* III. 368 Do you talk in that familiar manner of one of the landed gentry of England? **1974** M. FIDO *R. Kipling* 28/1 He was of the landed gentry, and could teach his friends about the different bores of guns. **1992** *Spy* (N.Y.) May 52 Americans don't share the English landed gentry's time-honoured—and by now pretty vestigial—disdain for 'trade money'.

4. *Engin.* Having a land (LAND *n.*[1] 9 a, b); esp. in **landed plunger**, a plunger which when mated with a corresponding mould forms an accurate seal.

1942 J. SASSO *Plastics for Industr. Use* iii. 34 (*caption*) Accuracy of alignment of mold members makes the landed plunger mold especially suitable for parts with very thin sections. **1971** *Exper. Mech.* XI. 171/2 A method for correcting stress-concentration factors at fillets in landed structures has been presented and confirmed by strain measurements. **1984** E. P. DEGARMO et al. *Materials & Processes in Manuf.* (ed. 6) ix. 211 The landed-plunger type mold is most commonly used, providing good pressure and a definite cutoff to assure accurate dimensions.

landfill ('lændfɪl), *n.*, *a.*, and *v.* (Formerly at LAND *n.* 12.) orig. *U.S.* [f. LAND *n.*[1] + FILL *n.*[1]]
A. *n.* 1. A site where refuse is disposed of by burial under layers of earth.

1903 *Scribner's Mag.* Oct. 395/2 Before 1902 the ashes and rubbish of the city of New York were disposed of upon landfills . . . The landfills were those of private contractors, who bought marsh lands on speculation and filled them with city material. **1931** *Ann. Rep. N.Y. City Dept. Sanitation 1931* 76 Ten new 'Bulldozer' caterpillar tractors were purchased for 'leveling off' at the land fills. **1968** *Proc. Amer. Soc. Civil Engineers* XCIV. SA2 Apr. (*title*) Water movement in an unsaturated sanitary landfill. **1970** *Wall St. Jrnl.* 23 June 1/6 The garbage would be kept out of incinerators and landfills. **1985** *Sci. Amer.* July 50A/2 In the process PCB's have . . been disposed of in open landfills. **1990** *Green Mag.* Apr. 24/3 There is . . increased concern for the health of people living near landfills and incinerators.

2. The action or system of disposing of refuse by burial at such a site.

1938 *Engineering News-Record* 1 Sept. 270/2 The origin of the present technique of land fill goes back to the time, two years ago, when William F. Casey took over the duties of Commissioner of Sanitation. **1942** A. WOLMAN et al. *Rep. to Comm. on City Plan City of Baltimore* iv. 38/1 Certain American cities, notably New York, have had marked success in the use of the so-called sanitary or land fill for rubbish disposal. **1971** *Guardian* 11 Oct. 3/6 Land-fill is considered one of the most economical ways to dispose of refuse. **1973** *Bulletin* (Sydney) 25 Aug. 9/2 (Advt.), A carefully-engineered program called sanitary landfill. **1984** J. UPDIKE *Witches of Eastwick* ii. 137 She wants you put in jail . . for unauthorized landfill.

3. Material disposed of at such a site; material used to level an excavated site, etc. Also *fig.*

1969 *New Yorker* 17 May 131/2 We intend to put a lot of landfill in the Credibility Gap. **1970** *Nat. Hist.* Feb. 18/3 Philadelphia is now packaging its trash, . . shipping the material back to the strip mines as land fill. **1984** A. C. & A. DUXBURY *Introd. World's Oceans*

ii. 62 Sand and gravel used in cement and concrete for..landfill. **1991** *Flight Internat.* 9 Oct. 42/3 The..tiny island of Chek Lap Kok will be levelled, and the rock used as landfill to create a platform for the airport.
B. *adj.* (only *attrib.*). Of, pertaining to, or resulting from the disposal of refuse at a landfill; freq. in *landfill site.*
1938 *Engineering News-Record* 1 Sept. 273/2 The low cost of the land fill method is the chief argument for its use. **1942** in *Sun* (Baltimore) (1944) 10 Feb. 8/1 The so-called sanitary or land fill system. **1953** *Richmond* (Va.) *News-Leader* 2 Sept. 21 A bulldozer struck water in the landfill dump area. **1967** *Boston Sunday Globe* 23 Apr. 20/3 By 1970, it is expected that the majority of the area's dumps and landfill sites will be filled to capacity. **1971** *Pollution* (Greater London Council) 8 The Greater London Council..operates a code of practice for good management of landfill sites under its own control. **1978** *Detroit Free Press* 14 Apr. B6/2 Airports are particularly vulnerable to bird strikes because so many of them are located..adjacent to landfill sites and dumps. **1988** *Independent* 15 Aug. 3/2 Britain's worst explosion caused by landfill methane. **1990** *Environment* 59/1 There are some 5,000 landfill sites into which about 18 million tonnes of waste is disposed each year.
C. *v. trans.* **a.** to dispose of (refuse) by burial at a landfill site. **b.** to fill (something) with landfill.
1988 ELKINGTON & HAILES *Green Consumer Guide* (1989) 129 Japan only landfills 1 per cent of its scrap tyres. **1988** *New Yorker* 22 Feb. 54/1 Lava..had..extended the island..landfilling completely some twenty-five fathoms of sea. **1991** *Public Works* Oct. 67/3 By late 1986 LAWPCA had landfilled 10.6 acres with sludge and used an additional 6 acres for a borrow pit. **1992** *Earth Matters* Autumn 10/1 Sewage sludge heavily contaminated with toxic metals is unsuitable for use as a fertilizer. Instead, it has to be landfilled, creating a pollution threat to water.
Hence '**landfilling** *vbl. n.* = *LANDFILL *n.* 1.
1983 *Current Affairs Bull.* (Sydney) Dec. 25/1 Landfilling is the most widely used of all methods. **1990** *Times* 23 Oct. 5/5 Local authorities clamp down on the landfilling of tyres.

landing, *vbl. n.* Add: [III.] [8.] *landing mat.*
1941 *Sci. Amer.* Dec. 350/3 Three materials found suitable for use as an emergency *landing mat were steel plank, Irving grid with slip-ring connectors, and rod-and-bar grid with wedge connectors. **1973** *Times* 12 Jan. 14/2 The standard specifies all the commonly used types of [gymnasium] equipment, from landing mats..to boxing rings. **1987** A. MILLER *Timebends* (1988) ii. 127 Buddy joined the Seabees during the war and welded landing mats for aircraft on Pacific Islands.
landing zone.
1956 W. A. HEFLIN *U.S. Air Force Dict.* 292/2 *Landing zone*, a zone designated for the landing of aircraft in an airborne assault. **1976** *New Yorker* 15 Mar. 80/3 Two white-phosphorus rounds were exploded over the landing zone to indicate the 'all clear'. **1990** A. BEEVOR *Inside Brit. Army* (1991) xvi. 241 The non-para infantry..follow once the units dropped have secured a landing zone for their Hercules.
landing run *Aeronaut.*, the distance that an aircraft travels in contact with the ground during landing; also, that part of an aircraft journey during which the pilot prepares to land.
1920 E. B. WILSON *Aeronautics* 264/1 (Index), *Landing run, 37. **1931** *Jrnl. R. Aeronaut. Soc.* XXXV. 747 (*heading*) Shortening starting and landing runs. **1946** *Happy Landings* (Air Ministry) July 1/2 A type of failure which..can have disastrous effects on the next landing run. **1986** *Aircraft Illustr.* July 347/2 The landing gear gets its going over during..the take-off and landing runs.

landman, *n.* Add: **5.** *U.S. Oil Industry.* An agent employed by an oil company who researches property titles and negotiates with landowners for leases of mineral rights, land for drilling, etc.; = *leaseman* s.v. *LEASE *n.*[3] 4 b.
[**1923** *Federal Reporter* (U.S.) CCLXXXIX. 829 The plaintiff, through its vice president, Mr. Williams, and its lease and land man, Mr. Ford, agreed to withdraw from the association with the Allied Oil Corporation.] **1937** *Ibid.* 2nd Ser. XCIII. 640/1 They went to a hotel room of Mr. Davis, land man for Stearns-Streeter Company. **1962** H. SPENCE *Portrait in Oil* ii. 22 Another landman made an oral agreement to buy for $5,000, the lease on a farm adjacent to a drilling operation. **1978** *Oil & Gas Jrnl.* 9 Jan. 124/1 Douglas E. Masten, petroleum geologist, and P. D. Masten, landman, have opened consulting offices at Midland, Tex. **1990** *Nation's Business* Mar. 6/2 Since I had only a rudimentary education in the oil business, I decided to learn the industry from the bottom, with a job as a landman.

landmark, *n.* Add: [3.] *fig.* **b.** *attrib.* Of an event, action, statement, etc.: historically significant as marking a period or turning-point; epoch-making; *spec.* in *Law*, of a legal case or decision. orig. *U.S.*
1937 *N.Y. Suppl.* CCXCII. 615 All of the cases subsequent to that landmark decision by Chief Justices Marshall lean heavily thereon. **1959** *PMLA* Dec. 593/1 Mr. Chapman has already quoted the landmark statement about relative stress made by Otto Jespersen. **1972** *Tuscaloosa* (Alabama) *News* 22 Feb. 1 The current federal lawsuit against Partlow State School and Hospital may become a landmark decision in America. **1975** *New Yorker* 10 Feb. 105/1 Majority Leader Cuite rose to praise the Council's previous year as 'one of the busiest work sessions in history', noting that this 'landmark body' had held twenty-two meetings..during the year. **1986** *City Limits* 16 Oct. 97 The fourth of October saw the 50th anniversary of the battle of Cable Street, a landmark victory for the left. **1990** *Sky Mag.* Apr. 45/2 *Glory* joins *Roots* as a landmark film for both the use of black actors and sensitive retelling of a moment from black American history.

Landry ('lɑːndrɪ, ‖lɑ̃dri), *n. Path.* [The name of J. B. O. *Landry* (1826–65), French physician, who described the condition in 1859 (*Gaz. hebd. de Méd. et de Chir.* VI. 472).] **Landry's paralysis** (or *disease*), any acute ascending paralysis, *spec.* = *Guillain-Barré syndrome* s.v. *GUILLAIN-BARRÉ *n.*
1882 *Dublin Jrnl. Med. Sci.* LXXIV. 341 (*heading*) Acute ascending paralysis; Landry's paralysis. **1962** GORDON & LAVOIPIERRE *Entomol. for Students of Med.* xliii. 260 In some parts of the world..several species of ticks..produce a type of ascending motor paralysis..which is sometimes mistaken for..acute ascending paralysis (Landry's disease). **1985** *European Neurol.* XXIV. 162/1 Paralytic rabies..should be suspected in all cases of atypical landry's paralysis.
Also **Landry–Guillain–Barré syndrome** = *Guillain–Barré syndrome* s.v. *GUILLAIN-BARRÉ *n.*
1957 *Brit. Med. Jrnl.* 2 Mar. 484/1 The Landry–Guillain-Barré syndrome appears..to belong to a spectrum of diseases of the nervous system. **1966** WRIGHT & SYMMERS *Systemic Path.* II. xxxv. 1328/1 Corticotrophin and cortisone, which inhibit the development of the experimental autoimmune diseases, seem to have at most only a minor effect upon the progress of cases of the Landry-Guillain-Barré syndrome. **1967** *Brain* XC. 330 Humans who have recovered from polyneuritis of Landry-Guillain-Barré type (synonym acute 'infective' polyneuritis).

‖**landsman** ('lɒntsmɒn), *n.*[2] [Yiddish, f. MHG. *lantsman, lantman* a native. Cf. LANDMAN *n.*[1]]

In Jewish use: a Jewish person who immigrated, or whose family immigrated, from the same country as another (esp. oneself or one's family); a compatriot.

1933 *Amer. Mercury* Aug. 476/2 A friend who is rooming with a *landsman*, a man who has been in this country for twenty-five years, told me this illuminating story. **1950** B. MALAMUD in *Partisan Rev.* Sept.–Oct. 664 With, after all, a *landsman*, he would have less to fear than with a complete stranger. **1973** *Listener* 20 Sept. 377/1 You put on your Shabbat suit..and descended on a nearby relative or *landsman*. **1975** R. H. RIMMER *Premar Experiments* (1976) i. 94 Every last Jew is a *landsman*, and hence he's related to every other Jew. **1987** A. WISEMAN *Lucky Mom* in *Mem. Bk. Molesting Childhood* 164 Dr. Joe Greenberg, whose parents came from the same district in the Ukraine as mine, which makes him a landsman, practically a relative.

‖**Landsting** ('lantstiŋ), *n.* Now *Hist.* Also **Landsthing**, and hyphened. [Da., f. *lands*, gen. of *land* country, + *ting* assembly (see THING *n.*²).] Formerly (until 1953), the upper house of the Danish Parliament (cf. RIGSDAG *n.*).

1862 *Chambers's Encycl.* III. 493/1 Although the Landsthing bears some analogy to the English House of Lords in respect to..its position in regard to the Lower House, or Folksthing, its members do not of necessity belong to the aristocratic class. **1938** J. H. S. BIRCH *Denmark in Hist.* xx. 337 The Constitution provided for two Assemblies, the Folketing and the Landsting. **1972** S. OAKLEY *Story of Denmark* xiii. 178 As a concession to the Right, the *Landsting* was to be selected indirectly.

Langevin ('lãʒəvæ̃), *n. Math.* and *Physics.* [The name of Paul *Langevin* (1872–1946), French physicist.] Used *attrib.* and in the possessive to designate concepts invented by Langevin or arising out of his work, as **Langevin('s) equation**, **formula**, (*a*) the general differential equation governing the Brownian motion of a free particle; (*b*) any of several expressions for magnetic susceptibility formulated by Langevin; **Langevin function**, the function coth $x - 1/x$, usu. denoted by $\mathcal{L}(x)$.

[**1937** F. BITTER *Introd. Ferromagnetism* ii. 31 The function (coth $a - 1/a$) is sometimes written $L(a)$, after Langevin, who first performed the derivation that led to it.] **1943** *Rev. Mod. Physics* XV. 20 The modern theory of the Brownian motion of a free particle (i.e. in the absence of an external field of force) generally starts with Langevin's equation $du/dt = -\beta u + A(t)$, where u denotes the velocity of the particle. **1951** R. M. BOZORTH *Ferromagnetism* x. 458 The foregoing equation, known as Langevin's equation of diamagnetism, is applicable to all atoms. **1960** REITZ & MILFORD *Found. Electromagn. Theory* v. 100 Equation (5-19) then yields: $<p_0 \cos \eta> = p_0 \,[\coth y - 1/y]$, which is known as the Langevin formula. *Ibid.* xi. 222 For a material composed entirely of one molecular species, each molecule having magnetic moment m_0, the fractional orientation is given approximately by the Langevin function. **1962** CORSON & LORRAIN *Introd. Electromagn. Fields* iii. 109 The Langevin equation..was first derived by Langevin in 1905 for magnetic dipoles. **1974** *Jrnl. Chem. Physics* LXI. 4242/2 To reduce the atom-chain scattering to a two-body collision process involving the incident atom and an effective single harmonic oscillator..we first develop a generalized Langevin equation governing the motion of the effective oscillator. **1985** J. J. BECKER in R. M. Besançon *Encycl. Physics* (ed. 3) 684/1 In the classical theory of paramagnetism, the orientations of the moments are considered to be initially thermally randomized in space. An applied field produces a net magnetic moment in its direction, as described by the classical Langevin function. **1988** *Nature* 9 June 496/3 'Langevin' equations..model the fluctuations of the

polarization..and the laser electric field about their mean values.

Langmuir ('læŋmjʊə(r)), *n.* [The name of Irving *Langmuir* (1881–1957), U.S. physicist and chemist.] Used *attrib.* and in the possessive to designate various concepts introduced by Langmuir or arising out of his work, as **Langmuir('s) adsorption isotherm** *Physics,* (the equation of) a curve showing the relationship between the proportion of a surface covered by molecules of an adsorbed gas and the gas pressure; **Langmuir cell** *Oceanogr.*, each of the cells within which water circulates in Langmuir circulation; **Langmuir circulation** *Oceanogr.*, the large-scale organized motion, due to convection currents, observed near the surface of large bodies of water; **Langmuir isotherm** *Physics* = *Langmuir adsorption isotherm above; **Langmuir probe** *Physics*, an instrument for studying the density and other properties of plasma by measuring the current through a small electrode of known potential.

[**1924** *Physical Rev.* XXIX. 597 Potential distribution and ion concentration were investigated by Langmuir's modified probe method.] **1931** S. GLASSTONE *Recent Adv. Physical Chem.* vii. 300 The presence of the constant k may be attributed to the formation of a very stable complete layer of gas, upon which a subsequent unimolecular layer, satisfying the requirements of the Langmuir isotherm..is adsorbed. **1932** K. K. DARROW *Electr. Phenomena in Gases* 489/2 (Index), Langmuir probe-method. **1940** S. GLASSTONE *Textbk. Physical Chem.* xiv. 1177 $x/m = k_1k_2p/(1 + k_1p)$, where k_1 and k_2 are constants for the given system and p is the gas pressure..is known as Langmuir's adsorption isotherm. **1941** J. D. COBINE *Gaseous Conductors* 601/1 (Index), Langmuir probe. **1958** H. J. GRAY *Dict. Physics* 290/1 The Langmuir probe..is connected to a point of variable potential and the current drawn is studied against the current. **1963** *Deep-Sea Res.* X. 233 In Langmuir circulation the surface layers of two adjacent masses of water flow toward each other. **1964** G. I. BROWN *Introd. Physical Chem.* xlv. 498 The Langmuir adsorption isotherm gives a satisfactory theoretical interpretation of many experimental results. **1970** *Jrnl. Geophysical Res.* LXXV. 4177/1 Such circulation patterns are now generally known as Langmuir cells. **1978** P. W. ATKINS *Physical Chem.* xxviii. 946 Deviations from the Langmuir isotherm are widely observed. **1979** *Nature* 14 June 615/2 The data reported here are from three instruments on Pioneer Venus—the electric field detector, the magnetometer, and the Langmuir probe. *Ibid.* 26 July 273/3 Pollard then pointed to processes believed to be relevant in the mixed layer: the generation of Kelvin-Helmholtz billows, with subsequent mixing, surface wave breaking and Langmuir circulation due to interactions between surface waves and shear in the water. **1992** S. P. MARAN *Astron. & Astrophysics Encycl.* 191/2 The instrumentation carried for charged particle studies evolved from the original simple GM tubes to..Faraday cages, Langmuir probes, and channel electron multipliers.

Lango ('læŋəʊ), *n.* and *a.* Pl. **Lango**, or unchanged. [Nilotic.] **A.** *n.* **a.** A member of a village-dwelling people inhabiting the Nile region of Uganda. **b.** The Nilotic language of this people. **B.** *attrib.* and as *adj.* Also **Langi**. Of or pertaining to the Lango or their language.

1902 H. JOHNSTON *Uganda Protectorate* II. xx. 887 There is an obvious relationship between the Masai and the Nilotic tongues—*Dinka, Shiluk..Dyur, Shangala, Acholi, Aluru..Lango,* and *Ja-luo. Ibid.* xv. 600 The land of Bukedi was then, as now..peopled by a warlike race of Nilotic Negroes, the modern Acholi, Lango, Umiro, etc. **1902** C. W. HOBLEY *Eastern Uganda* i. 7

Elgumi or Wamia (Lango stock?). **1923** J. H. DRIBERG *Lango* 10, I..have noticed that several Nilotic words used by the Akum, which do not occur in Lango, are nevertheless heard in Alur and Acholi. **1946** *Uganda Jrnl.* X. 16 The Lango are not Lwo, but instead are allied to the Karimojong. **1973** *Reader's Digest* Feb. 186/1 The enlisted men of Uganda's army—angry because he had been packing it with men from his own Langi tribe—rose up and seized the government. **1976** D. TOPOLSKI *Muzungu* vi. 107 We were now crossing Langi country. **1984** *Times* 1 Sept. 9/5 Brigadier Smith Opon-Acak is a Lango but not a 'cousin' or any relation of President Milton Obote.

langosta (læŋ'gɒstə), *n. U.S.* [a. Sp. *langosta* locust, lobster, f. pop.L. alteration of L. *locusta* LOCUST *n.* Cf. LANGOUSTE *n.*] **1.** = LOCUST *n.* 1. Now *rare* or *Obs.*

1881 *Encycl. Brit.* XII. 131/1 The insect most dreaded is the 'langosta' or 'chapulin', which at intervals afflicts the entire country, vast columns passing from one end to the other, darkening the air, and destroying every green thing in their course. **1909** *Cent. Dict.* Suppl., *Langosta*, any injurious locust or grasshopper: so called in Spanish America and, to some extent, in the southwestern United States.

2. A lobster, *esp.* the spiny lobster, *Palinurus vulgaris* (= CRAYFISH *n.* 3 b).

1924 *Blackw. Mag.* June 807/1 A friend of his had a wonderful aquarium full of langostas. **1970** J. MCPHEE *Crofter & Laird* 22, I don't know what I expected to see come out of there—perhaps a snapping turtle,..or possibly a clawless Spanish *langosta*. **1977** *Washington Post* 10 July D3/3 Manuel brought up langosta, clawless lobster, for three of our dinners. **1987** *Los Angeles Times* 30 Aug. 30/2 Spiny lobsters, such as rock lobsters, crawfish and langosta.

language, *n.*[1] Add: **[1.] [a.]** (*b*) **foreign-language**: used *attrib.* to designate esp. films produced in a foreign language. Hence with other defining adjs., designating films, newspapers, translations, etc., in which the specified language is used.

1940 *N.Y. Times* 30 Dec. 20/2 'The Baker's Wife' was voted the best foreign-language production. **1950** *Britannica Bk. of Year* 173/1 The New York film critics made the following selections for 1949: best picture of the year, *All the King's Men*; best foreign-language picture, *The Bicycle Thieves* (Italian); [etc.]. **1962** *Maclean's Mag.* 17 Nov. 4/1 Editors of French language newspapers who had wailed about [etc.]. **1972** *Korea Herald* 17 Nov. 4/7 (Advt.), The Korea Herald is one of the liveliest English language papers in the Far East. **1974** *Listener* 14 Feb. 196/2 The Russian-language version which has now appeared in the West contains only the first two of seven parts. **1989** *N.Y. Times* 26 Dec. 25/1 Nestled among the samovars..is a stack of the Russian-language edition of Monopoly.

[6.] [a.] *language behaviour.*

1946 F. P. CHISHOLM in W. S. Knickerbocker *20th Cent. English* 178 Every observer of *language-behavior can call up examples of such 'misunderstandings' of language-fact relationships. **1986** R. CAMERON *Portage* v. 81 The expanded sequence incorporates language behaviours from all areas of the checklist and adds new behaviours to provide a profile of development.

language school.

1937 *Middlebury Coll.* (U.S.) *Bull. 1937–38* 28 (*heading*) *Language schools. **1943** *School & Society* 3 Apr. 370/1 After nine weeks of intensive instruction in the language school at Laramie, Wyoming, one graduate was sent on a mission to South America. **1974** D. MACKENZIE *Zaleski's Percentage* i. 22 After three weeks at a language-school he'd given up the struggle with syntax and cancelled the rest of the course. **1987** R. INGALLS *End of Tragedy* 82 Mr Murdoch recommended a language school he'd gone to for French.

[b.] language arts chiefly *Educ.* (orig. *U.S.*), skills such as reading, writing, spelling, etc.,

taught in order to develop proficiency in the use of language.

1939 *Recent Trends in Reading* (Conf. on Reading, Univ. Chicago) v. 87 By *language arts we mean all uses of language to convey or to receive the conceptions of the mind. **1953** J. B. CARROLL *Stud. of Lang.* i. 4 The psychometrician..tries to make tests of 'verbal intelligence' or tests of achievement in various language arts. **1981** *Amer. Speech* LVI. 167 The focus is on problems of language-arts education.

language death *Linguistics*, the process whereby a language, esp. that of a cultural minority, falls into disuse or becomes extinct.

1972 W. DRESSLER in *Papers 8th Regional Meeting Chicago Ling. Soc.* 448 *Language death has been viewed as an extreme case of language contact. The victorious language slowly replaces the dying language. **1987** *Cambr. Encycl. Language* lx. 360/2 As shown by the history of the Celtic languages.., the contact can lead to a language being completely eliminated (language death).

language loyalty *Linguistics*, the continued use of or preference for a language, esp. within a culture where another language is dominant.

1953 U. WEINREICH *Languages in Contact* (Publ. Linguistic Circle of N.Y. No. 1) iv. 99 The sociolinguistic study of language contact needs a term to describe a phenomenon which corresponds to language approximately as nationalism corresponds to nationality. The term *language loyalty has been proposed for this purpose. **1985** J. RICHARDS et al. *Longman Dict. Appl. Linguistics* 158 Some immigrant groups in the USA, such as Estonians, have shown a high degree of language loyalty.

language maintenance *Linguistics*, the (degree of) preservation of a language by users who are in contact with another language or languages; also loosely, = *language loyalty above.

1964 J. A. FISHMAN in *Linguistics* ix. 32 The study of *language maintenance and language shift is concerned with the relationship between change or stability in habitual language use,..and ongoing psychological, social or cultural processes. *Ibid.* 33 Although somewhat more cumbersome than previously proposed terms, 'language maintenance and language shift' may have the advantage of more clearly indicating that a continuum of processes and outcomes exists. **1980** *English World-Wide* I. 1. 14 Laws themselves are insufficient to either support or undercut language maintenance.

language planning *Linguistics*, the preparation or implementation of a formal policy on language use; *spec.* the codifying and standardization of the language(s) to be used in a nation having many local languages or dialects.

1959 E. HAUGEN in J. A. Fishman *Readings Sociol. of Lang.* (1968) 673 By *language planning I understand the activity of preparing a normative orthography, grammar and dictionary for the guidance of writers and speakers in a non-homogeneous speech community. **1971** RUBIN & JERNUDD *Can Language be Planned?* p. xv, Practitioners of actual language planning often attempt to solve language problems in purely linguistic terms. **1983** G. LEWIS in Cobarrubias & Fishman *Progress in Language Planning* 309 Language planning is an aspect of social change. **1994** *Lang. in Society* XXIII. 459 A significant body of data on language planning, language change, and the dissemination of literacy in the Uzbek-speaking area of Central Asia.

So **language planner**.

1959 E. HAUGEN in J. A. Fishman *Readings Sociol. of Lang.* (1968) 674 The *language planners have sought deliberately to upset the status quo by rejecting the linguistic models of their social élite. **1980** *Word 1979* XXX. 30 A 'language planner'..is not necessarily a professional linguist, grammarian, or lexicographer.

language shift *Linguistics*, the move from the habitual use of one language to the use of another (often culturally dominant) language by an individual or speech community.

1953 U. WEINREICH *Languages in Contact* (Publ. Linguistic Circle of N.Y. No. 1) ii. 68 A *language shift may be defined as the change from the habitual use of one language to that of another. **1964** J. A. FISHMAN in *Linguistics* IX. 32 The study of language maintenance and language shift is concerned with the relationship between change or stability in habitual language use, ..and ongoing psychological, social or cultural processes. **1980** *Word 1979* XXX. 43 It cannot be stated with certainty that whenever such conditions as prestige or advantage obtain, language shift inevitably occurs.

language universal *Linguistics* = UNIVERSAL *n.* 6.

1948 B. W. & E. G. AGINSKY in *Word* IV. 169 There is a double interest in the study of *language universals, due to the twofold nature of language itself. **1981** FERGUSON & HEATH *Language in U.S.A.* iv. 72 The language universals theory overcomes problems inherent in both the monogenetic and polygenetic theories.

Lanital ('lænɪtæl), *n.* [a. It., f. *lan-a* wool + *Ital-ia* Italy.] A casein-based man-made fibre.

1936 *Amer. Dyestuff Reporter* XXV. 552/1 The recently boomed Italian casein fibers or Lanital. **1937** *Nature* 75 Dec. 1090/1 The manufacture of artificial wool from milk has been successfully started in Italy, and the product known as Lanital has been shown to possess properties suitable for the textile industry. **1954** R. W. MONCRIEFF *Artificial Fibres* (ed. 2) xv. 204 The original Fibrolane, known as Fibrolane A, was very similar to Lanital.

lanky, *a.* (and *n.*) Add: Hence ˈ**lankiness** *n.*

1893 in *Funk's Stand. Dict.* **1972** *Daily Tel.* 14 Oct. 8/3 Between herbaceous plants whose rising growths will take some of the lankiness from the tulips. **1981** *Economist* 28 Feb. 92/2 His lankiness was notorious, as were his exaggerated and mannered gestures.

Lanson (lãsɔ̃), *n.* [The name of the firm which ships the champagne, *Lanson*, Père et Fils, A Rheims.] The proprietary name for a brand of champagne.

[**1888** *Trade Marks Jrnl.* 1 Feb. 150 (*in figure*) Lanson père & fils à Rheims.] **1891** in C. Ray *Compleat Imbiber* (1967) IX. 122 All Brands of Champagne in stock... G. H. Mumm, Ayala, Lanson. **1962** *Trade Marks Jrnl.* 6 June 729/1 *Lanson*...Champagne wines. **1964** A. LAUNAY *Caviare & After* xv. 106 Unlike other wines, Champagne is known under the name of the shipper... The best known are: Bollinger, Heidsieck, ..Lanson [etc.]. **1969** L. MEYNELL *Of Malicious Intent* iv. 45 The .. hall .. looked already pretty full; the Lanson Black Label was flowing; talk was loud... The Festival was under way. **1980** M. BROADBENT *Gt. Vintage Wine Bk.* 345 Charles Heidsieck was excellent, rich, soft yet firm in 1971, and Lanson was tired, flat but vinous in 1974.

lap, *n.*[1] Add: [2.] c. A breast of lamb, esp. when cut deep as in Scotland, Ireland, and parts of northern England; also, flank of beef.

1922 JOYCE *Ulysses* 154 Remember when we got home raking up the fire and frying up those pieces of lap of mutton for her supper with the Chutney sauce she liked. **1979** *Lore & Lang.* Jan. 27 Lap [of beef]. *Ibid.* 29 Lap of lamb.

[7.] **lap desk** orig. and chiefly *N. Amer.*, a portable writing-case or writing surface, *esp.* one designed to be used on the lap.

1937 E. D. & F. ANDREWS *Shaker Furnit.* 92 The frames of Shaker *lap-desks are pine. **1971** J. G. SHEA *Amer. Shakers & their Furnit.* vii. 159 The slant-lid lap desk, which was made at New Lebanon around 1850, is believed to have been used by Eldress Emma Neale. **1984** *New Yorker* 12 Nov. 150/1 (Advt.), Keep

your desk close at hand with this updated version of the classic lap desk.

lap portable *n.*, a lap-top computer.

1983 *Pract. Computing* Dec. 88/2 Ian Stobie visited Olivetti's U.K. headquarters to get the feel of its new Japanese-built *lap portable. **1984** *Listener* 9 Aug. 35/3 The 'lap portable' is a computer the size of a home micro, but incorporating its own small screen and a memory that will retain data even when the machine is switched off. **1986** *Pract. Computing* Oct. 63/1 The Z-181 and Convertible are aimed at the real lap-portable market of journalists, academics, travelling salespersons and suchlike.

lap, *n.*[3] Add: [5.] [b.] **lap of honour**, an additional, celebratory circuit of the track, completed by the victor after a race. Also *fig.*

1952 *Cycling* 7 Aug. 132/2 He took his bouquet and lap of honour. **1955** *J. B. Wadley's 'Coureur'* Winter 39/3, I saw Andre Lemoine ride two laps of honour on that day. **1968** J. LOCK *Lady Policeman* xvii. 147, I trailed after her on her lap of honour like Little Orphan Annie behind the 'It' girl. **1987** *Guardian* 31 Aug. 17/2 The Canadian raced into his lap of honour. **1989** *Times* 30 Sept. 11/1 Their candidate .. would have been accorded a lap of honour at next week's party conference.

c. *transf.* A part of a journey or other endeavour. *last lap:* see LAST *a.* 5 a.

1932 *Discovery* Dec. 393/1 We learned that weather conditions there had improved and that, for the last lap, we might expect better flying conditions. **1957** P. WHITE *Voss* v. 100 This ship .. would carry the party on the first and gentle lap of their immense journey. **1987** R. INGALLS *End of Tragedy* 180 The next lap was a good deal harder. **1988** *Washington Post* 17 Mar. D1/1 The company comes to us on the first lap of an extended tour.

[6.] (sense 2) *lap-weld* n. and v.: so *lap-welded a.*

1848 *Mechanics' Mag.* XLVIII. 287 (Advt.), *Lap-welded iron tubes. **1950** *Jrnl. Iron & Steel Inst.* CLXIV. 493/1 The manufacture of lap-welded pipe is described.

lap-dissolve *v.*: hence **lap-dissolve** *n.*

1927 H. C. McKAY *Handbk. Motion Picture Photogr.* xiv. 219 The first scene appears to melt and flow together and from the wreck arises the new scene. This was the original conception of the lap dissolve. **1979** *Farmington* (New Mexico) *Daily Times* 27 May (Entertainment Suppl.) 17/5 David and Margaret.. make love in quaint little country inns in scenes of lap-dissolve close-ups. **1986** *N.Y. Times* 4 May II. 19/3 She [*sc.* Elizabeth Taylor] is a lap-dissolve of dozens of contradictory images.

Laphroaig (lǝˈfrɔɪg), *n.* [The name of a distillery on Islay in the Inner Hebrides.] A proprietary name for a type of whisky made from a single malt and having a pungent smoky flavour.

1890 *Wine Trade Rev.* 15 Jan. 31/2 Laphroaig..6/3. **1916** *Trade Marks Jrnl.* 8 Mar. 242 *Laphroaig Islay*...The said Trade Mark has been used..since 16 years before the 13th August 1875. **1969** J. F. ADAMS *Two plus Two* iii. 23 This place did have a good bar—Laphroaig Scotch, as a matter of fact. **1972** 'M. DELVING' *Shadow of Himself* vii. 85, I hope you like single malt. This is Laphroaig. **1987** *Business Week* 9 Mar. 124/2 From the near-medicinal Laphroaig to the mellow Glendronach, each single-malt has a distinctive character.

Lapita (lǝˈpiːtǝ), *a.* and *n. Archaeol.* [The name of a site in New Caledonia.] **A.** *adj.* Designating, of, or characterized by a type of pottery found in Melanesia and western Polynesia, which dates from the second and first millennia B.C. and is characterized by elaborate geometric decorations with dentate markers; also, pertaining to the culture associated with this pottery. **B.** *n.* **a.** The Lapita ceramic style. **b.** The Lapita culture.

1966 *Jrnl. Polynesian Soc.* LXXV. 373 Known variously as Lapita, *roulette* or *pointillé*, these distinctive sherds with their diversity of delicately impressed geometrical patterns, are now taken to be an indication of a very early settlement horizon wherever they are found. **1971** *Ibid.* LXXX. 282 The Lapita-potters.. were undoubtedly the ancestors of the modern Tongans. **1971** J. GOLSON *Lapita Ware in Stud. Oceanic Culture Hist.* II. 73 The differences in the archaeological expression of the early cultures of Tonga and Samoa have been misread and their significance misinterpreted. My case is that the latter, no less than the former, is of Lapita inspiration. If this is so, then Lapita is the immediate source for the Polynesian cultures as a whole. **1972** *Times* 9 May 16/6 The pottery samples which they have recovered are of the type known as Lapita ware, which previous archaeological work has revealed across the south-west Pacific from Watom Island.. to Tonga. **1979** R. C. GREEN in *Prehist. of Polynesia* ii. 30/1 The Lapita villages.. often show evidence of permanent habitation. *Ibid.* 34/1 Lapita has been referred to as both a cultural horizon and a cultural tradition. **1993** *Amer. Anthrop.* XCV. iii. 613 Scholars.. argue that the origin of Lapita lies in Asian Near Oceania, with a migration of 'Lapita peoples' into Melanesian Near Oceania.

Lapland, *n.* Add: [2.] **Lapland longspur** *N. Amer.* = **Lapland bunting** above.

1828 C. L. BONAPARTE *Amer. Ornith.* II. 53 *Lapland Longspur, *Emberiza Lapponica*,.. long since known to inhabit the desolate Arctic regions of both continents, is now for the first time introduced into the Fauna of the United States. **1972** S. BURNFORD *One Woman's Arctic* ii. 56 Apart from the ever-present Lapland longspurs, there were few birds yet. **1993** *Uphere* Oct.-Nov. 62/1 As we pass, horned larks and Lapland longspurs frantically attempt to lure us away from their nests on the ground.

Laporte (læ'pɔːt), *n. Physics.* [The name of Otto *Laporte* (1902–71), German-born U.S. physicist.] Used *attrib.* with reference to the rule propounded by Laporte in 1924 (*Zeitschr. f. Physik* XXIII. 135), that electron transitions occur only between atomic states whose *l* quantum numbers differ by ±1 or (alternatively) between states of opposite parity (a rule which holds for electric dipole transitions).

1930 PAULING & GOUDSMIT *Struct. Line Spectra* vi. 94 The empirical rule that transitions will occur only from a state for which the l_i sum.. is odd to one for which it is even, or *vice versa*, is called the 'Laporte rule'. **1945** J. W. T. SPINKS tr. *Herzberg's Atomic Spectra* (ed. 2) iv. 154 For the particular case of two electrons *i* and *k*, the Laporte rule may be formulated: when $\Delta l_i = \pm 1$, Δl_k must be 0 or +2 or −2, and vice versa. **1966** *McGraw-Hill Encycl. Sci. & Technol.* IX. 566/1 The Laporte rule of atomic spectroscopy.. depends on the fact that the electric dipole radiation field has odd parity. **1966** PHILLIPS & WILLIAMS *Inorg. Chem.* II. xxi. 120 The most common type of transition giving rise to lanthanide spectra is that associated with a rearrangement of electrons inside the 4*f* sub-shell... Such transitions are Laporte forbidden (i.e. forbidden by first-order wave-mechanical treatment) so that the intensity of absorption is weak. **1977** I. M. CAMPBELL *Energy & Atmosphere* viii. 220 The Laporte rule precludes transitions between states which are derived from the same electronic configuration. **1989** A. SALZER tr. *Elschenbroich & Salzer's Organometallics* xiv. 243 Direct generation of an LF state (*d–d* transition) would be Laporte-forbidden.

lappery ('læpərɪ), *n. Motor-racing colloq.* [f. LAP *n.*[3]: see -ERY 2 a.] The action of driving round

a motor-racing track; hence, motor-racing in general.

1937 *Motor Sport* July 287/2 Preliminary rapid lappery showed that for Brooklands tight shock-absorbers were essential. **1949** *Ibid.* June 211/2 The E-type E.R.A. broke a piston after rapid practice lappery. **1957** S. MOSS *In Track of Speed* xiii. 173 The new track is a bit bumpy and dodgy and, after a little lappery on it, we put in some fast work on the old track. **1987** *Classic Racer* Summer 64/1 With two machines to test.. he made a snap decision, encouraged by the dry sunny morning, to start his season's lappery.

lappet, *n.* Sense 7 in Dict. becomes 8. Add: **7.** *Ceramics.* A decorative motif, usu. found as part of a repeating border, and taking various forms, most often that of a stylized petal or of the head of a sceptre. Freq. on Chinese porcelain.

1915 R. L. HOBSON *Chinese Pott. & Porc.* II. ix. 130 Formal designs.. consisted now of bands of ju-i shaped lappets filled with arabesque foliage, forming an upper and lower border. **1923** —— *Wares of Ming Dynasty* 32 The subsidiary ornament includes a band of foliate lappets enclosing lotus sprays on the shoulder. **1969** J. AYERS *Baur Collection* II. A136 Linked lappet panels containing lotus sprays appear above, and lotus-petal panels form a border below. **1972** *Trans. Oriental Ceramic Soc. 1969–71* XXXVIII. 99 Round the bottom.. a band of petal panels.. and round the shoulder large and small lappets alternate, the large ones enclosing flower scrolls and the small ones emblems. **1980** *Catal. Fine Chinese Ceramics* (Sotheby, Hong Kong) 44 Borders of petal lappets around the foot and florettes surrounded by an undulating line of scrolls at the rim.

lapping, *vbl. n.*[2] Add: **4.** *Commerce.* A method of embezzlement in which credit for money received is entered in an account but the money itself is withheld, the discrepancy being covered by not issuing receipts for money subsequently paid in to the account. Cf. *teeming and lading* s.v. TEEMING *vbl. n.*[2] 2.

1950 J. K. LASSER *How to run Small Business* iii. 40 Make certain that lapping (the holding back of funds despite entry in the receipt records) is not possible. **1952** J. J. W. NEUNER in J. K. Lasser *Executive Course in Business Managem.* XVII. 625 The use of an accounts-receivable ledger control account.. acts as a means of safeguarding cash received from customers and reduces the possibility of 'lapping'. **1970** R. LEWIS *Wolf by Ears* iii. 137 The technical terms are.. 'kiting' and 'lapping'. Money is transferred between two accounts, recording the receipt prior to the balancing date and the payment after the balancing date. **1977** *Washington Post* 4 Jan. A8/5 According to the Agriculture Department, most of the at least $294,000 in owed funds in which no criminal charges are pending involves 'lapping'. **1990** L. H. BRINE *Rock & Hard Place* ix. 171 Collins Transport had fallen victim to a common fraud scheme known as lapping.

lapsed, *ppl. a.* Add: [2.] **b.** *transf.* No longer an adherent to or practitioner of a particular (secular) principle, doctrine, etc. Freq. *joc.*

1959 *Times* 13 Feb. 13/4 Egon Wellesz, a lapsed Schönbergian. **1974** 'G. BLACK' *Golden Cockatrice* iii. 58, I have to meet a lapsed Maoist. **1978** P. FULLER *Jrnl.* 28 Mar. in *Marches Past* (1986) 21 If I were to.. look out of the windows behind me on either side of 'Reveries of a Lapsed Narcissist', I would see a lake surrounded by weeping willows. **1979** A. J. P. TAYLOR in *Observer* 29 July 9/3, I am a lapsed crank. I no longer have the enthusiasm for crankiness I had when I was young. **1992** *Washington City Paper* 21–27 Feb. 65/1 With the guidance of a lapsed psychiatrist.. the couple come to suspect that they are the reincarnated Strausses.

‖**laquais de place** (lakε də plas), *n. phr. Obs.* [Fr., lit. 'place-servant': see LACKEY *n.*] A manservant temporarily hired during a visit to a foreign city.

1789 P. THICKNESSE *Year's Journey* (ed. 3) I. xv. 120 Some *laquais de place*, who is paid for it, gives the earliest notice to one of the confederacy. **1805** P. BECKFORD *Familiar Lett. from Italy* I. 259 Boxes are always to be hired..for a few pauls, unless you send your *Lacquais de Place* who will always cheat you when he can. **1862** THACKERAY *Philip* II. ii. 40 Mugford would never consent to have a *laquais de place*, being firmly convinced to the day of his death that he knew the French language quite sufficiently for all purposes of conversation. **1889** W. FRASER *Words on Wellington* 125 His laquais de place told him..that Marshal Ney was to be shot in the Gardens of the Luxembourg.

Laramide ('lærəmaɪd), *a. Geol.* [f. *Laramie*, name of a city and mountain range in the Rocky Mountains, after *LAURENTIDE *a.*] Of, pertaining to, or designating the orogeny during which the mountain ranges in the west of the Americas, or the Rocky Mountains in particular, were formed (see quot. 1972). Also *absol.*

1895 J. D. DANA *Man. Geol.* (ed. 4) III. 359 The Laramide system of mountain ranges extends along the summit of the Rocky Mountains far northward into British America, and southward into Mexico. **1915** F. L. RANSOME in W. N. Rice et al. *Probl. Amer. Geol.* vi. 364 It has..been believed by many that the Laramide System is essentially Pacific in origin. **1924** J. JOLY *Radioactivity & Surface Hist. Earth* 30 The Tethys, which was greatly reduced at the close of the Laramide Revolution, has again increased and extends to the Pacific. **1972** *Gloss. Geol.* (Amer. Geol. Inst.) 397/1 Geologists differ as to whether to restrict the Laramide closely in time and space, as to a single event near the end of the Cretaceous, or to deformations near the type area—or whether to apply it broadly to all orogenies from early in the Cretaceous through the Eocene or later, and to deformations in the whole Cordilleran belt of western North America. **1974** *Nature* 8 Feb. 349/1 It has been traditional to apply the term Laramide to the period of deformation of the northern Rocky Mountains in Montana and Canada. **1993** D. V. AGER *Nature of Stratigr. Record* (ed. 3) viii. 136 The widespread regression at the end of Cretaceous times may be related to..the Laramide orogeny along the western edge of the American plate.

larch, *n.* Add: [**3.**] **larch sawfly**, a sawfly, *Pristiphora erichsonii*, whose larvae feed on the leaves of larch trees.

1883 *Rep. Comm. Agric.* (U.S. Dept. Agric.) 138 (*heading*) The *larch saw-fly worm. *Ibid.* 142 The eggs are described by Ratzeburg...The following is a free translation of his description of the saw-fly, which he calls the large larch saw-fly. **1890** *Country Gentleman* 18 Nov. 905/4 The juniper or larch..is being devastated of its leaves, and presents a withered, decayed appearance through the action of the larch saw-fly. **1975** M. C. DAVIS *Near Woods* vi. 102 Tamaracks are apt to fall prey to the larvae of a wasp, the larch sawfly.

lard, *n.* Add: [**3.**] **lard-ass** *slang* (orig. *N. Amer.*), (a term of abuse for) a person who has large buttocks or is fat (especially when attributed to laziness); freq. *attrib.*

[**1959** R. A. HILL *First Mate of 'Henry Glass'* iii. 40 All they do is eat and sit on their lard asses around the guns.] **1962** M. RICHLER in R. Weaver *Canad. Short Stories* (1968) 2nd. Ser. 169 Hey, big writer. *Lard-ass. How many periods in a bottle of ink? **1969** R. JESSUP *Sailor* 256 Let them find a way of getting out from under lard-ass bastards like yourself. **1986** *Weekend Austral.* (Brisbane) 21/22 June 8/5 The happy-go-lucky young 'lard-ass' had become a very serious Henry

Ford. **1993** R. SHILTS *Conduct Unbecoming* III. xxvii. 270 Airmen had come back from Vietnam with a serious attitude problem towards any REMFs or stateside lard-ass officers who had not seen any tough action overseas.

so **lard-assed** *a.*

1946 T. HEGGEN *Mister Roberts* p. xv, He is bow-legged and broad-beamed (for which the crew would substitute '*lard-assed*'). **1984** A. MAUPIN *Baby Cakes* xxxviii. 183 How can you just..surrender Easley [House] to that lard-assed bitch down there.

large, *a., adv.,* and *n.* Add: [**A.**] [**IV.**] [**15.**] [**c.**] **large-minded**: also *large-mindedly adv.*; *large-mindedness n.*

1885 *Harper's Mag.* July 863/2, I know that your largemindedness will receive it very differently from most people. **1895** T. HARDY *Jude the Obscure* IV. v. 298, I do feel I like his large-mindedness and respect him more than ever. **1907** *Daily Chron.* 19 Mar. 6/7 The matter ought to be dealt with, broadly and *large-mindedly, by a body representing both travellers and carriers. **1977** 'E. CRISPIN' *Glimpses of Moon* vii. 115 'So it's fair enough, really,' said Ling large-mindedly.

large print, a larger typeface than is usual, *esp.* one designed to enhance readability for partially-sighted people; freq. *attrib.*

1923 C. MATSON (*title*) Books for tired eyes: a list of books in *large print. **1968** *ALA Bull.* LXII. 738/1 Reader reponse..would seem to indicate strong interest in large-print book library service. **1988** *English for Ages 5 to 11* (Dept. Educ. & Sci.) 60/1 They may need special large-print books.

large-yield *a.* = *high-yield* s.v. HIGH *a.* 21.

1958 *N.Y. Times* 25 Oct. 4/6 The Atomic Energy Commission announced today that the Soviet Union had set off another '*large yield' nuclear test detonation. **1987** *Sci. Amer.* Jan. 24/2 Because of the TTBT [*sc.* Threshold Test Ban Treaty], neither country has been able to test these large-yield warheads at full yield for more than 11 years.

lari, *n.* (Formerly at LARIN *n.*) Restrict ‖ to sense in Dict. and add: Pronunc. ('lɑːri). **2.** Also **laari**. In the Maldives, a monetary unit equal to one hundredth of a rufiyaa.

1978 *Whitaker's Almanack* 1979 985 (*table*) Maldive Islands...Rupee of 100 Laris. **1982** *N.Y. Times* 14 Feb. II. 37/2 A 5-Laree stamp shows 'Self Portrait with a Palette'. **1985** *Statesman's Year-Bk. 1985–86* 830 The *rufiyaa* (Maldivian rupee) is divided into 100 *laaris.*

†**larixin** ('læriksin), *n. Chem. Obs.* Also -ine (-iːn). [f. LARIX *n.* + -IN[1].] = MALTOL *n.* Also called *larixinic acid* (lærik'sinik).

1863 J. STENHOUSE in *Phil. Trans. R. Soc.* CLII. 53 (*heading*) On larixinic acid, a crystallizable volatile principle found in the bark of the larch tree. *Ibid.* 57 Perhaps the name *Larixine* would be more appropriate. **1874** GARROD & BAXTER *Essent. Materia Medica* (ed. 4) 366 Larch bark...Contains larixin or larixinic acid. **1904** *Jrnl. Chem. Soc.* LXXXVI. 1. 61 The compound obtained by Stenhouse..from the bark of larches, and described as larixinic acid..is now shown to be identical with..maltol.

Larkinite ('lɑːkɪnaɪt), *n.* and *a.* [f. the name of James *Larkin* (1876–1947), Irish labour leader and founder of the Irish Transport and General Workers' Union + -ITE[1].] **A.** *n.* A follower or supporter of Larkin's labour principles. **B.** *adj.* Of, pertaining to, or characteristic of Larkin or Larkinites.

1913 *Times* 30 Sept. 6/4 One will find, outside the ranks of the workers, a very few thoroughgoing 'Larkinites'. **1913** *Daily Express* (Dublin) 28 Oct. 5/1 (*heading*) Nationalist M.P. and the Larkinite Policy. **1925** J. O'CONNOR *Hist. Ireland 1798–1924* II.

xxi. 271 Some of the other leaders, especially of the Larkinite section, were not satisfied. **1975** *Irish Times* 24 May 5/2 He is a Larkinite. 'My father was active in the foundation of the Workers' Union of Ireland and was closely associated with Big Jim Larkin.'

So '**Larkinism** *n.*, the principles or policies of Larkin and Larkinites.

1913 *Times* 30 Sept. 6/4 Whatever 'Larkinism' may be, it is no recognizable form of Socialism or of Syndicalism. **1964** W. P. RYAN in *1913: Jim Larkin & Dublin Lock-Out* (Workers' Union of Ireland) 14 The commission gave T. M. Healy.. an opportunity of denouncing in 'Larkinism' what in his younger days he had applauded in farmers who struggled to bring landlords to reason.

Larnian (ˈlɑːnɪən), *a.* (*n.*) *Archaeol.* [f. the name of the type site at *Larne*, Co. Antrim, + -IAN.] Of, pertaining to, or designating a culture which flourished mainly in Northern Ireland in the late mesolithic period. Also *absol.*, the Larnian culture.

1940 H. L. MOVIUS in *Proc. R. Irish Acad.* XLVI. c. 75 Since the Irish Mesolithic forms a distinct cultural complex, and since it is best known from the classic site at Larne, it is proposed to refer to it henceforth as the Larnian. **1954** A. D. LACAILLE *Stone Age in Scotl.* vii. 245 It may be surmised that this littoral culture of the North Sea basin evolved on the equivalents of the Hiberno-Scottish Larnian. **1963** E. S. WOOD *Collins Field Guide Archaeol.* I. iv. 52 Another hybrid culture .. is found in Galloway and Northern Ireland (the Larnian). **1975** J. G. EVANS *Environment Early Man Brit. Isles* v. 103 'Strandloopers', who subsisted to a considerable extent on shellfish, are represented by the Larnian and Obanian industries. **1986** BARRY & TILLING *Eng. Dialects of Ulster* 2 Archaeologists have called this earliest Irish culture 'Larnian' after the first sites to be identified near Larne.

larvi-, *comb. form.* Add: '**larviciding** *vbl. n.*, the action or practice of treating with larvicides.

1945 *Public Health Rep.* (U.S.) LX. 1274 Methods of control, such as *larviciding and drainage, are usually not applicable because of the high per capita cost. **1976** *Kingston* (Ontario) *Whig-Standard* 6 Apr. 6/2 The department of the environment estimates that larviciding costs annually $23 an acre (including start-up, training and license expenses).

'**larviposition** *n.* *Ent.*, the deposition of a larva (rather than an egg) by a female insect.

1913 *Rep. R. Soc. Sleeping Sickness Comm.* XIV. 11 There is an inverse relation between relative humidity and rate of *larviposition. **1956** *Ann. Trop. Med. & Parasitol.* L. 66 Larviposition occurred while the female was resting on the soil surface. **1989** *Jrnl. Heredity* LXXX. 73/2 Flies from the F_{50} generation were reared from larviposition to adult eclosion at 15°C.

lar'vivorous *a.*, feeding on larvae.

1889 *Cent. Dict.*, *Larvivorous. **1915** *Trans. Soc. Trop. Med. & Hygiene* VIII. 78 Willcocks, of Cairo, was the first to draw attention to the larvivorous habits of these useful insects. **1971** P. C. C. GARNHAM *Progress in Parasitol.* vii. 124 Desultory attention has been paid to biological control of mosquitoes, which started many years ago with the use of larvivorous fish.

laryngectomee (ˌlærɪndʒɛktəˈmiː, lærɪnˈdʒɛktəmɪ), *n.* [f. LARYNGECTOM(Y *n.* + -EE[1].] A person who has undergone a laryngectomy.

1956 *A.M.A. Arch. Otolaryngol.* LXIV. 2/1 The spirit [of] optimism and comradeship that prevails among laryngectomees is marvelous. **1976** SMYTHIES & CORBETT *Psychiatry* viii. 167 Group therapy with other laryngectomees has helped many patients. **1985** *Brit. Med. Jrnl.* 24 Aug. 514/2 Five laryngectomees reported having tried smoking through their stoma.

laser, *n.*[2] Add: [**2.**] **laser gun**, (*a*) (now *rare*) = sense 1 above; (*b*) orig. *Science Fiction*, a weapon incorporating a laser; a toy intended to resemble this; (*c*) any of various devices which use a laser to read or record information.

1961 *Business Week* 30 Dec. 46/2 (*heading*) *Laser gun shoots light rays. **1972** *New Republic* 8 Apr. 10/1 Several times a day, scientists pull the trigger of a gigantic 60,000-watt 'gas dynamic' laser gun, sending up puffs of light grey smoke followed by a muffled two-second roar. Two miles away, a wooden target bursts into flames. **1981** *Encycl. Sci. Suppl. 1982* (Grolier) 349/1 The laser gun moves slowly across the surface, leaving a special track. **1990** A. LURIE *Don't tell Grown-Ups* ii. 25 Jack doesn't zap the giant with a laser gun, because in real life when you meet a bully or an armed mugger or a boss who wants to push you around you probably won't have a laser gun. **1992** *Times Educ. Suppl.* 31 Jan. 47/6 Once the barcode is printed it needs to be read or scanned. Again a range of readers/scanners, such as hand-held wands, laser guns and touch scanners, are described.

Laservision (ˈleɪzəvɪʒən), *n.* Also **LaserVision**, **laservision**. [f. LASER *n.*[2] + VISION *n.*, after TELEVISION *n.*] A system for the reproduction of video signals recorded on a laser disc. A proprietary name in the U.S.

1981 *New Scientist* 19 Mar. 745/2 Philips's optical disc system, now known as Laservision, was firmly scheduled for its launch this spring. **1983** *Listener* 17 Mar. 34/1 In August 1972, Philips showed the press a prototype of what is now on sale as LaserVision. **1984** *Official Gaz.* (U.S. Patent Office) 30 Oct. TM906/2 *LaserVision... For reflective laser optical video discs, players and components. First use Apr. 1981; in commerce Apr. 1981. **1985** *Pract. Computing* Sept. 65/3 As soon as someone produces a cheap laservision disc which any television camera and computer can write to as well as read from, the real potentiality of the Microtext authoring system will be realised. **1987** *Which Video?* Jan. 15/2 No picture reproduced through a domestic VCR can approach the quality standards of 'live' broadcast TV (only Laservision amongst home equipment can do this). **1991** *Computing* 10 Jan. 22/4 A card allows analogue video from a LaserVision disc to be overlaid with computer text and graphics.

lash, *v.*[1] Add: [**I.**] [**3.**] **b.** *S. Afr. Mining.* To shovel and load (broken ore, rock, etc.) on to a truck; to fill (a truck) in this way.

1932 WATERMEYER & HOFFENBERG *Witwatersrand Mining Pract.* vi. 348 The snatch-block is moved nearer the face.., the object being to lash the rock directly from the pile into the truck. **1949** *Nat. Inst. Personnel Res. Aptitude Tests Native Labour Witwatersrand Gold Mines* (Pretoria) I. vi. 35 Figures 1 and 2 show the lashing efficiency of these groups, average number of cars lashed being plotted against total time on lashing duty.

lashing, *vbl. n.*[1] Senses a, b in Dict. become 1a, 2. Add: [**1.**] **b.** *spec.* in *S. Afr. Mining.* The action of shovelling broken ore, rock, etc., and loading it into a truck (from sense *3 b of the vb.).

1932 WATERMEYER & HOFFENBERG *Witwatersrand Mining Pract.* vi. 347 Lashing or shovelling. Except where advantage can be taken of the angle at which an end dips, all the ore is usually loaded into trucks by shovel. **1946** C. B. JEPPE *Gold Mining on Witwatersrand* I. ix. 688 Such cleaning out was largely done on night shift, some 4 to 6 natives being allocated to each end for lashing and tramming, depending on the distance to be trammed and the supply of cars. **1974** *S. Afr. Jrnl. Econ.* XLII. 293 The National Institute for Personnel Research has also demonstrated that even on a simple manual task like lashing (shovelling or loading broken rock) output can be appreciably increased by continuous practice.

‖**lassi** ('lʌsɪ), *n*. [Hindi *lassī*.] An Indian drink, traditionally based on diluted buttermilk or yoghurt, and usually served chilled.

1894 *Gazetteer Lahore District* (Punjab Govt.) (ed. 2) iii. 74 With their morning cakes they take *lassi* or butter milk and *ság* of rape or gram leaves. **1932** M. R. ANAND *Curries* 107 Lassi (whey).. may be drunk with all meals as a substitute for water in the hot weather... When made of milk it is sweetened with sugar; when made by beating curds it should be salted. **1954** S. CHOWDHARY *Indian Cooking* 18 A traditional cool and refreshing drink called lassi can be made by whisking and diluting the curd and adding a little salt or sugar to it. **1969** *Femina* (Bombay) 26 Dec. 27/1 You can.. have your choice of *lassi* or sugarcane juice to wash it down with. **1992** *Sunday Times of India* 19 Apr. (Review section) 2/1 Now, with not much effort, he pours in the curd, water, sugar, sets the machine churning, and in minutes has 37 glasses of *lassi* ready for his customers.

last, *a*., *adv*., and *n*.[6] Add: [A.] [2.] [a.] †**last change**, the passing over from life into death.

1670 EVELYN *Sylva* (ed. 2) ix. 61 The top-leaves and oldest would be gathered last of all, as being most proper to repast the worms with towards their last change. **1863** S. DOBELL in E. Arnold et al. *A Welcome* 92 Love shall be Love: in that transcendent whole Clear Nature from the swift euthanasy Of her last change, transfigured shall arise.

e. last hurrah (orig. *U.S.*) [the title of E. O'Connor's novel *The Last Hurrah* (1956), which was filmed in 1958], the final act in a politician's career; hence, any final performance or effort, a swansong.

1967 *National Observer* (U.S.) 9 Jan. 1/2 Mr. Rockefeller insists his recovery from Presidential fever is complete... Presumably, this campaign is Nelson Rockefeller's last hurrah. **1976** *Times Lit. Suppl.* 16 Apr. 456/5 A new era of American party politics which endured without much change until its last hurrah with Hubert Humphrey's abortive campaign for the presidency in 1968. **1991** *Star-Ledger* (Newark, New Jersey) 22 Sept. v. 6/3 There's no question this is probably the last hurrah for this club.

[3.] **e. last ship** *Naut. slang*, the ship on which a sailor previously served (recalled with nostalgia and typically viewed as superior in some or all respects to the present one).

1883 MELTON & OLIPHANT *Cruise of U.S.S. Galena* 70 Seated on the spar-deck,.. they would tell.. of the times they had, when, on the 'last ship', or in the 'Tidalyatalay', they sailed around the world. **1932** S. G. S. MCNEIL *In Great Waters* iii. 50 The real sailor always had everything of the best in his last ship! **1947** *Seafarers' Log* 26 Dec. 13/4 This is the old familiar case of the 'good old last ship' where everything was so much better and so much cleaner. **1956** E. N. ROGERS *Queenie's Brood* 10 Your last ship and your next ship are always the best.

[5.] [a.] *every last*: see EVERY *a*. 1 f.

[8.] †**last music**, the overture to a theatrical performance, formerly so called (esp. as a call to performers backstage) when this was the last of several pieces of music played by the orchestra.

1780 G. COLMAN *Manager in Distress* 16, I was just going to ring-in the *last musick*. **1849** *Theatrical Programme* 23 July 60/2 At the call of 'last music', *i.e.* the commencement of the overture, the first peeper through the curtain announced [etc.].

[B.] [2.] **c. last in, first out**: (*a*) *Accounting*, (designating) a method of accounting in which all goods of the same kind are valued at the price paid for those most recently acquired. See *LIFO n. (a.).

1934 *NACA Yearbk.* (Nat. Assoc. Cost Accountants, U.S.) 100 This inventory system is called the 'Last In, First Out' system... It provides for charging current

costs against current sales. **1945** *Ibid*. 81 A number of companies are using the last-in, first-out, or lifo method of valuing inventories. **1979** *Daily Tel*. 30 Nov. 21/2 The amount by which third quarter earnings would be reduced under that last-in first-out (LIFO) basis would have been £350 million and £675 million for the nine months. **1985** *Times* 11 July 13/2 The Revenue inserted a clause changing the calculation of gains on the sale of a part holding of shares from last-in-first-out (lifo) to assuming that the first holding of shares acquired was the one being sold.

(*b*) *Computing*, (pertaining to, using, or designating) a procedure in which the item removed from a buffer, queue, etc., is the one that has been most recently added to it.

1963 *IEEE Trans. Electronic Computers* XII. 872 A 'push-down' list is one that is manipulated in a last-in, first-out manner. **1968** D. E. KNUTH *Art of Computer Programming* I. ii. 236 Stacks have been called.. last-in-first-out ('LIFO') lists. **1973** C. W. GEAR *Introd. Computer Sci*. vii. 291 Thus the last item to be put into a stack is the first item to be removed. (For this reason, it is also called a Last In First Out queue or a LIFO queue.)

[C.] [1.] *last-born* (also *absol*.).

1837 CARLYLE *Fr. Rev*. II. v. i. 170 Pet son (her *last born?) of the Scarlet Woman. **1952** J. STEINBECK *East of Eden* xvii. 171 It was a criminal thing to leave your last-born.. sitting there by a hole in the ground with no one to care for him. **1972** S. FISHER *Female Orgasm* (1973) i. 37 Female firstborns had less liberal ideas about sex than lastborns. However, onlyborns and middleborns were very similar in their sexual attitudes.

lat (læt), *n*.[4] *slang* (orig. *Body-building*). [Abbrev.] = *LATISSIMUS DORSI *n*. Freq. in *pl*. Also *attrib*., esp. in **lat spread**, a body-building pose in which the latissimus dorsi muscles are stretched.

1939 *Health & Strength* 12 Aug. 234/2 'What is the meaning of the expression "contract the Lats." in connection with pose photography?' It is a slang expression, which would greatly shock the author of Gray's 'Anatomy', meaning 'contract the Latissimus dorsi'. **1949** *Ibid*. 11 Aug. 10/1 That loose back.. completely covers those permanently expanded 'lats' and the previously much envied wasp waist. **1956** *Muscle Power* Mar. 46/1 The reason I put so much stress on lat development is that when you acquire wide and thick lats you have no need to ever attempt to spread them. **1977** *Time* 24 Jan. 79/1 A small group of dedicated people.. have found happiness in the camaraderie of the gyms where they devote themselves to sculpting their lats and pects and stuff to preposterous perfection. **1982** A. MAUPIN *Further Tales of City* 66 My lats were great in the hayfork scene. **1986** *Flex* Feb. 80/2 Make.. the space ample enough for each contestant to do a double-biceps or a lat spread without blocking someone else. **1991** *Blitz* Sept. 85/2 I'll admit that the overall winner had good lats and abs. I am fair, like.

lata, *n*. Substitute for entry: ‖**latah** ('lɑːtə), *n*. and *a*. Also **lata**. [Malay.] **A.** *n*. **1.** *Path*. A state of extreme suggestibility and imitative behaviour occurring among Malays; a disorder characterized by this.

1884 *Western Daily Press* (Bristol) 25 June 7/5 This disease has been met with in Java, where it is known as 'Lata'. **1897** W. G. ELLIS in *Jrnl. Mental Sci*. XLII. 32 (*heading*) Latah. A mental malady of the Malays. *Ibid*. 33 Under the name 'Latah' the Malays describe a variety of peculiar nervous conditions of a transitory character. **1947** R. O. WINSTEDT *Malays* 18 There is the closest resemblance between the hysteria of the Samoyed and the *latah* of the Malay and Dayak. **1956** R. LINTON *Culture & Mental Disorders* iii. 115 *Latah* is like Arctic hysteria in its manifestations, and involves the same compulsive imitation. *Ibid*., Another interesting trait shared by both arctic hysteria

and *latah* is that the same individuals are subject to repeated attacks. **1987** *Culture, Medicine & Psychiatry* XI. 11 Reference has already been made to *latah* as a syndrome often precipitated by a startle stimulus and characterized by some or all of: echolalia, echopraxia, coprolalia and automatic obedience. We here use *latah* as a generic label to include similar phenomena in many cultures which often employ their own designations.
2. A person in a state of *latah*.
1912 *Brit. Med. Jrnl.* 24 Feb. 438/2 The lâtah in a state of lâtah is wholly unconscious of what he is doing. **1966** D. Forbes *Heart of Malaya* v. 60 Another type of *latah*, or madman, amongst these unstable people could be jerked into paroxysms of action by the use of a single word.
B. *adj.* Affected with *latah*.
1928 A. Gibson *Malay Peninsula* ii. 29 More interesting than the *amok* condition..is the predisposition in many Malays to become *latah* (hypnotised, entranced) on being spoken to sharply. **1966** D. Skirrow *It won't get you Anywhere* xiv. 63 'Not berserk,' I said, 'latah...All Malayans go latah from time to time.'

latch, *n.*[1] Add: [5.] **latch hook**, a hand-tool used chiefly in rug-making to draw the yarn through the canvas.
1900 J. K. Mumford *Oriental Rugs* xii. 235 One division of these Turkoman carpets, which avoids on the one hand close adherence to the Bokhara device, and on the other the *latch-hook style of the Yomuds, is called Beshir. **1937** *Textile Mercury & Argus* 16 July 63/2 *Latch-hook design*. This design motif..is the characteristic mark of Caucasian rugs and carpets since it is rarely absent from either field or border. It is not seen in Persian rugs. **1981** *Handtools of Arts & Crafts* (Diagram Group) xv. 256/4 Latch hooks for knotted rugs; these hooks take the yarn through the canvas and bring it back to the surface.

late, *a.*[1] (*n.*[2]) Add: [A.] [3.] [a.] *late-day* attrib. *phr.*: designating semi-formal clothing suitable for late afternoon or early evening wear.
1968 *Guardian* 26 July 1/3 Late-day clothes were topless, with the bare bosom showing through just one thin layer of ultra-sheer black mousseline. **1978** *Detroit Free Press* 5 Mar. (Spring Fashion Suppl.) 4/4 Spring flowers..are worth looking into—in the form of a shirt or a skirt or a late-day dress—to pick up a flagging, winter-worn spirit.
c. Of or pertaining to the sale of alcohol to the public after normal licensing hours; *spec.* as *late licence*.
[**1816** N. Conant in *Min. Evid. Sel. Comm. Commons Police* 25 If such houses are kept open at late hours..the present laws would reach them.] **1924** M. Arlen *Green Hat* iv. 115 It was a 'late night' at the Loyalty, which meant that you could drink wine until they took it from you. **1972** M. Gilbert *Body of Girl* xix. 170 There's two pubs and one drink shop with a late licence. **1990** *Face* June 101/2 British pubs and clubs usually face great difficulty securing a late licence on anything approaching a regular basis because of fears that longer hours will mean increased drunken mayhem.
[**4.**] **b.** *Archaeol.* and *Geol.* Usu. with capital initial. Designating a final phase or stage of a specified period, culture, etc.
1880, etc. [see *LATE-GLACIAL *a.*]. **1905** R. Munro *Archæol. & False Antiquities* i. 13 We have positive evidence of the existence of objects of the 'Late Celtic' civilisation in the lake village of Glastonbury. **1930** V. G. Childe *Bronze Age* vi. 192 The Late Bronze Age was an epoch of turmoil and migration. **1977** G. Clark *World Prehist.* (ed. 3) x. 439 The final emergence of urban as distinct from ceremonial centres defined the Late Intermediate phase of Andean prehistory. **1985** *Antiquaries Jrnl.* LXV. 286 The interior of the enclosure was sealed beneath alluvial clay in Late Iron Age times. **1993** *Playboy* Jan. 140/3 The inequality of

women and men in this poor world goes back at least to the late Neolithic Period.
c. Of a writer, composer, etc., or his or her works: (produced) relatively near the end of his or her career. Also *late-period*.
1879 F. J. Furnivall *Chaucer's Minor Poetry* 419 This late poem [*Envoy to Scogan*] composed of two Terns and an Envoy. **1928** H. H. Furness *Tragedie of Coriolanus* p.vii, *The Tragedie of Coriolanus* is classed among the late plays. **1951** *Music Rev.* XII. 52 The division of his work by Fétis, Lenz, and many later critics into three periods has led to a regrettable tendency to speak of early, middle and late Beethoven as though they were practically three different composers. **1970** 'R. Crawford' *Kiss Boss Goodbye* i. iv. 28 A late-period Gaugin..is presumably recorded somewhere. **1988** *Sunday Express Mag.* 3 Apr. 13/3 You venture into 'late Strauss', Janacek and Britten.

latecomer, *n.* (Formerly s.v. LATE *a.*[1] 2 d.) Add: **2.** *transf.* One who or that which arrives late; also, a recent arrival, a newcomer.
1872 'G. Eliot' *Middlemarch* II. iii. xxvii. 81 'What a late comer you are!' she said, as they shook hands. 'Mamma had given you up a little while ago.' **1892** J. S. Fletcher *When Chas. I was King* I. ii. 35 Then did late-comers, hearing the solitary bell, hurry their movements. **1912** T. Hardy *Far from Madding Crowd* (rev. ed.) xxxii. 247 In her topographical ignorance as a latecomer to the place, she misreckoned the distance. **1923** *Observer* 4 Mar. 11/5 Latecomers will not be admitted until the curtain has fallen after the first act. **1942** *R.A.F. Jrnl.* 13 June 14 There are no late-comers on parade. **1968** J. B. Priestley *Festival at Farbridge* III. ii. 453 An anxious latecomer making the quietest possible entrance. **1978** *Jrnl. R. Soc. Arts* CXXVI. 701/2 The drawing collection of the Chicago Art Institute was a late-comer amongst the rich art collections of the 'windy city'. **1991** *Bicycle Guide* Sept. 54/1 If Herbold sounds convinced, it could be because he is no latecomer to the suspension scene.

late-glacial (leıt 'gleıʃɪəl, leıt 'gleıʃəl), *a.* *Geol.* Also **late glacial**, **lateglacial**, and with capital initial(s). [f. LATE *a.*[1] + GLACIAL *a.*] Designating or pertaining to the latter part of a Quaternary ice age, *spec.* the time at the end of the Devensian immediately preceding the current post-glacial (Flandrian) period. Also *absol.* Cf. *LATE *a.*[1] 4 b.
1880 J. Geikie *Prehistoric Europe* xvi. 390 The red and parti-coloured brick-clays of the late glacial series. **1890** —— in *Rep. Brit. Assoc. Adv. Sci.* 1889 560 The löss..is not of postglacial age—even much of what one may call the 'remodified löss' being of Late Glacial or Pleistocene age. **1927** Peake & Fleure *Hunters & Artists* i. 11 (caption) Chart showing the correlation of the late glacial stages. **1957** *Encycl. Brit.* V. 826/2 Much information as to late-glacial and post-glacial climates is provided by the vegetation, especially of peat-bogs. **1968** R. G. West *Pleistocene Geol. & Biol.* xiii. 305 Compared with the succeeding interglacials the Cromerian vegetational history is distinct in the absence or scarcity of *Hippophaë* in the late-glacial zone. **1975** J. G. Evans *Environment Early Man Brit. Isles* ii. 46 A characteristic plant of the Late-glacial. *Ibid.* 48 The Late-glacial sequence on the Chalk can be tied in to the record of vegetational and other environmental changes. **1984** Lowe & Walker *Reconstructing Quaternary Environments* i. 9 Opinions differ over the extent to which the 'Lateglacial' period can be subdivided.

later, *a.* Add: **b.** Of creative artists or their work: = *LATE *a.*[1] 4 c.
1885 *Manch. Examiner* 22 July 3/2 The inventive grotesquerie of his [*sc.* Gustave Doré's] later work. **1918** *Cornh. Mag.* June 562 From Carlyle's later works chapter and verse for the whole doctrine of force could warrantably be quoted. **1934** C. Lambert *Mus.*

Ho! III. 175 This lack of rapport between the tune and harmony is particularly noticeable in some of the later works of Bartók. **1958** *Listener* 28 Aug. 310/3 His paintings are at present too close to the later Picasso to be taken quite seriously. **1991** P. OTTO (*title*) Constructive vision and visionary deconstruction. Loss, eternity, and the productions of time in the later poetry of William Blake.

lathe, *n.*[2] Add: [**3.**] *lathe operator*.
[**1921** *Dict. Occup. Terms* (1927) §200 Turret *lathe operator*; a turner..who sets-up and operates turret lathe.] **1974** *Times* 18 Feb. 14/7 We've got a nice job for you as a lathe operator. **1986** W. GIBSON *Winter Market* in *Burning Chrome* 141 My father was an audio engineer...He was a lathe operator, basically. People brought him audio recordings and he burned their sounds into grooves on a disk of lacquer.

lathyrogen ('læθɪrədʒən), *n.* *Med.* [f. LATHYR(ISM *n.* + -OGEN.] A substance which causes lathyrism.
1962 *Laboratory Investigation* XI. 697/1 It has not been proven whether the lesions result from the direct action of the lathyrogen on the cartilage or from the action of some metabolic product of the lathyrogenic agent. **1972** *Science* 5 May 512/2 Most common among toxic substances are the enzyme inhibitors... Physiological irritants might be the next most common category. These include..the lathyrogens, which disrupt collagen structure and occur in peas. **1978** *Nature* 11 May 151/2 Direct evidence that the structure of collagen influences morphogenetic events is provided by studies in vivo with lathyrogens such as β-amino-propionitrile, which interfere with the crosslinking of collagen by inhibiting the action of the enzyme lysyl oxidase.
So **lathyro'genic** *a*.
1958 *Proc. Soc. Exper. Biol. & Med.* XCVII. 114/1 Methyleneaminoacetonitrile has also been reported to be strongly lathyrogenic. **1983** *Exper. Neurol.* LXXIX. 102 The first question..is whether the fibrogenic components of the peripheral nerve will be exposed to the lathyrogenic effects of β-APN when it is topically applied.

Latin, *a.* and *n.* Sense A. 4 b: *Latin American:* now a new main entry. [**A.**] [**4.**] Add: **c.** Of or pertaining to those countries of Central, North, and South America in which Spanish or Portuguese is the dominant language, *spec.* as *Latin America*. Cf. *LATIN AMERICAN adj. a*.
1890 *Reciprocity Treaties with Latin Amer.* (U.S. State Dept.) 6 More than 87 per cent of our imports from Latin America are admitted free. **1900** *Jrnl. Soc. Arts* 17 Aug. 744/1 Everywhere in Latin America the [panama] hat is known under the name of 'Jipijapa' in honour of the city where its manufacture was first started. **1912** *Chambers's Jrnl.* June 358/2 The amount of British capital invested in the countries of Latin-America is very great. **1953** *Time* 19 Oct. 28/1 Latin America is in the midst of a 'population explosion'. Its people are multiplying 2½ times as fast as the populations in the rest of the world. **1991** M. HART in Hampson & Maule *Canada among Nations After Cold War* 91 From an economic perspective, the remarkable 'apertura' in Mexico marked a high point in this transformation of Latin America.
d. Designating the characteristics of temperament or behaviour popularly attributed to European or American peoples speaking languages developed from Latin: proud, passionate, impetuous, showy in appearance, etc. Sometimes somewhat *dismissive*.
1914 WYNDHAM LEWIS in *New Weekly* 20 June 13/2 For everything that is rubbishy puerile in the Latin temperament machinery has come as an immense toy. **1956** A. WILSON *Anglo-Saxon Attitudes* II. ii. 278 Sensual and elegant though Gerald was, he detested the flashy smartness of such Latin womanizers. **1970**

Times 19 Aug. 6/4 The weakness of every Yorkshireman is his Latin temperament, doubly dangerous when it has so often to be suppressed, as in..cricket. **1981** V. GLENDINNING *Edith Sitwell* iv. 61 He was extrovert, physical, unstable, and very Latin. **1989** *Sunday Tel.* 8 Jan. 17/1 His first language was Spanish and, not surprisingly, he describes his temperament as Latin. A proud man, he likes to be seen to succeed.
e. *ellipt.* for *LATIN AMERICAN adj. a*.
1954 M. WALDO *Compl. Round-the-World Cookbk.* 361 The wonderful soup-stew of the Latin countries, *sancocho*, is undoubtedly the [Dominican Republic] people's choice for a national dish. **1977** *Time* 22 Aug. 11/3 Carter's early forcefulness..drove six Latin countries..to reject U.S. military assistance rather than agree to prepare 'report cards' for Washington on human rights. **1994** *Wall St. Jrnl.* 25 Feb. C19/3 Sharp price drops of U.S. Treasurys sparked a sell-off among the government bonds of Latin nations, including Mexico, Argentina, and Venezuela.
f. Of, pertaining to, or characteristic of Latin American music or dance (see sense *B*. 5 below). Cf. also *LATIN AMERICAN adj. b*.
1962 'K. ORVIS' *Damned & Destroyed* iv. 30 The pianos segued smoothly into Latin rhythms. **1965** *Crescendo* Dec. 14/3 The arrangements are all in the Latin idiom and all of well-known tunes, getting off to a really swinging start with a L-A 'Peter Gunn' you *must* hear. **1969** *Sunday Times* 19 Jan. 58 This quintet..could begin a rush to what's been called Latin rock—a striking compound of bossa nova, rock and jazz. **1973** D. ROBINSON *Rotten with Honour* 8 He stood for a moment in the sunshine, snapping his fingers to a Latin beat. **1980** *Musicians Only* 26 Apr. 13/6 There's a Sonor drumkit, syndrums, and a whole range of Latin percussion. **1990** *Ballroom Dancing Times* Nov. 55/2 In the Latin championship for this age group Frank and Lily Aerts very easily retained their title.
[**B.**] **5.** A style of popular music, originating in Latin America (esp. among Afro-Americans of Cuba and Brazil), characterized by its dance rhythms and by extensive use of indigenous percussive intruments such as the cowbell and conga drum.
1983 R. L. SINGER in *Latin Amer. Mus. Rev.* IV. II. 196 The factors that define a style as Latin jazz as opposed to other types of Latin. **1989** *Q* Dec. 199/1 Take the coverage of the Springfields...O'Brien suggests their peppy brand of folk, Latin and supper-club swing prefigured today's world music. **1991** *Straight no Chaser* Winter 58/1 Check..The Drum and Monkey Sats for eclectic jazz through Latin into soulful grooves. **1994** *Keyboard Player* Sept. 29/1 The KN1200 provides 100 on-board styles, covering a territory from simple 8-beat rock, country rock, to standard issue Latin, and jazz.

Latin American ('lætɪn ə'mɛrɪkən), *a.* and *n.* Also hyphened. [f. LATIN *a.* + AMERICAN *a.* and *n.*] **A.** *adj.* **a.** Of or pertaining to Latin America or its peoples.
Until the early 20th cent. *Spanish American* was the preferred term.
1890 B. HARRISON in *Reciprocity Treaties with Latin America* 3 Our tariff laws offered an insurmountable barrier to a large exchange of products with the Latin American nations. **1892** C. R. MARKHAM (*title*) Latin-American republics. A history of Peru. **1903** *Westm. Gaz.* 22 June 11/1 Mexico..the richest district in the richest of the Latin-American countries. **1947** *Life* 17 Nov. 14/2 The tourist is not yet a creature existing only to be fleeced as he is in some Latin-American countries where *tourismo* has become big business. **1973** 'D. JORDAN' *Nile Green* xxxi. 145 It's oil sheiks and Latin American generals and Lebanese rentiers who are going to buy your bonds. **1991** N. MAILER *Harlot's Ghost* VI. xxxiv. 1233 For years and years, American policy has supported the Latin American oligarchies.
b. Designating a rhythm or style of music characteristic of Latin America; *spec.*

designating a type of ballroom dancing including dances of Latin American origin or inspiration, such as the rumba, samba, cha-cha, etc.

1937 *Mod. Lang. Forum* XXII. 24 Latin-American music is immediately appealing because its beauties are compatible with our own musical taste. **1948** F. BORROWS *Lat.-Amer. Dancing* i. 19 The profession has not been able..to cope with the public demand for instruction in the Latin-American dances. **1955** L. FEATHER *Encycl. Jazz* 30 The wedding of jazz with Latin-American rhythms. **1983** *N. Y. Times* 6 Mar. II. 1/6 The two men have been friends — tennis pals, fellow devotees of Latin American ballroom dancing — for 40 years.

  B. *n.* A native or inhabitant of Latin America; a person of Latin American origin or descent.

1912 *Chambers's Jrnl.* Nov. 720/2 An Englishman..soon wishes himself well rid of the..Latin-American. **1960** *Business Week* 3 Dec. 87 'Fidelism', or 'Fidelismo', as the Latin Americans call it..is the Castro-style revolution that's followed by a left-wing, Communist-influenced, perhaps Communist-controlled, government. **1973** A. MANN *Tiara* i. 4 In the Philippines, some crazy Latin American got near enough to Paul VI to attack him with a knife. **1992** *Christian Science Monitor* 9 Jan. 4/2 Spain refuses to require visas of Latin Americans visiting Spain, and maintains double-nationality accords with some countries.

‖**Latinxua** ('ladiŋxua), *n. Obs. exc. Hist.* Also **Latin-hua.** [Chinese *lādīnghuà*, f. *lādīng* Latin + *huà* '-ize', '-ify'.] A system of romanization for Chinese characters introduced in China in 1931 and widely popularized until superseded by Pinyin. Also in fuller form *Latinxua Sin Wenz* (lit. 'latinized new script').

1937 E. SNOW *Red Star over China* VI. v. 243 Part of the paper *Hung Ssu Chung Hua* (*Red China*) was published in *Latin-hua.* **1950** J. DE FRANCIS *Nationalism & Lang. Reform in China* v. 101 The Committee on the New Alphabet had brought literacy in Latinxua to some 2000 Chinese. **1951** R. PAYNE *Mao Tse-tung* vii. 160 Mao..immersed himself in the study of..Latinxua...Latinxua..consisted of romanized Chinese, and resembled the romanized languages introduced by the French into Indo-China and by the Russians into Siberia. **1958** M. A. K. HALLIDAY in *Proc. 8th. Internat. Congress Linguistics* 766 After much discussion,..the version [of a new script for Chinese] based on Latinxua Sinwenz and using only the letters of the Roman alphabet, was adopted by the Committee on a majority vote. **1968** P. KRATOCHVIL *Chinese Lang. Today* v. 169 Intellectuals of the extreme left..started propagating the rival scheme of *lādīnghuà* 'Latinization' (also known as Latinxua, first published..in 1929). **1974** *Encycl. Brit. Macropaedia* XVI. 804/2 In 1929 a National Romanization..was adopted...A rival Communist effort known as *Latinxua*, or Latinization of 1930, fared no better.

latissimus dorsi (laː'tɪsɪməs 'dɔːsiː, -saɪ), *n. Anat.* [mod.L., ellipt. for *musculus latissimus dorsi*, lit. 'broadest muscle of the back'.] Each of a pair of large, roughly triangular muscles covering the lower part of the back, extending from the sacral, lumbar, and lower thoracic vertebrae to the armpits and attached to the upper end of the humerus; the corresponding muscle in other vertebrates. Also *ellipt.* as *latissimus.* Cf. *LAT n.*[4]

1616 A. READ Σωματογραφία Ανθρωπίνη *or Descr. Body of Man* 75 The third muscle of the arme called *Latissimus.* **1684** T. GIBSON *Anat. Humane Bodies Epitomized* (ed. 2) v. xvii. 486 [The] Obliquè descendens..is said also to spring from the transverse processes of the lumbar vertebræ: but Dr. Croone thinks that to be a mistake, because those processes

are so covered with other muscles, especially with the Latissimus dorsi, that this can by no means spring therefrom. **1722** W. CHESELDEN *Anat. Humane Body* (ed. 2) II. iii. 93 Serratus Inferior Posticus, arises with a broad Tendon (inseparable from that of the *Latissimus Dorsi*) from the Spinal Processes of the Three superior Vertebrae of the Loyns, and Two inferior of the Thorax. **1889** J. LEIDY *Elem. Treat. Human Anat.* (ed. 2) v. 295 The greater teres..contributes with the latissimus to form the posterior border of the axilla. **1956** *Muscle Power* Mar. 22 This first article describes his latissimus exercises with the super sets method. **1986** ROMER & PARSONS *Vertebr. Body* (ed. 6) ix. 293 Both reptile and mammal have prominent fan-shaped dorsal muscles of this sort, the latissimus dorsi and the deltoideus. **1989** COLLIER & LONGMORE *Oxf. Handbk. Clin. Specialties* (ed. 2) ix. 610 The muscles used for movement at the shoulder joint...Extension: deltoid (latissimus dorsi, pectoralis major and teres major begin the extension if the shoulder starts out flexed).

latrine, *n.* Add: [2.] *latrine pit.*

1971 *Community* (E. Afr. Community) Apr. 8/1 The main breeding places were numerous flooded latrine pits which allow prolific mosquito breeding. **1990** *Independent on Sunday* 27 May (Sunday Rev. Suppl.) 15/2 They dig latrine pits.

laugh, *n.* Add: [3.] *to raise a laugh*: see RAISE *v.*[1] 14 d. *good for a laugh*, guaranteed to amuse or entertain.

1963 *New Statesman* 18 Oct. 537/1 The police..accuse the public of a lack of civic responsibility — a phrase that's good for a laugh over a bevy. **1965** *Telegraph* (Brisbane) 30 Apr. 37 His ways often seem strange — 'good for a laugh'. **1976** *New Yorker* 17 May 35/1 A pair of Bass Weejuns is always good for a laugh. **1987** *Newsweek* 18 May 51 It's good for a few laughs.

  [4.] **c.** (A source of) entertainment or amusement; a lark; esp. in phrs. *for a laugh* or *for laughs*, just for fun, for the hell of it. Sometimes used *iron.* See also *barrel of fun* (*laughs*, etc.) s.v. *BARREL n.* 2 b.

1936 WODEHOUSE *Laughing Gas* x. 107 Anything for a laugh is your motto. Well, good night, old cut-up. **1945** H. BROWN *Artie Greengroin* 182 Some day that mess sergeant is going to fill the Spam full of arsenic and knock off the whole company for a laugh. **1957** F. HOYLE *Black Cloud* xi. 218 Graft everywhere, executions just for the laughs. *a*1961 *Newsweek* in WEBSTER s.v., Girl mobsters beating up other girls simply for laughs. **1970** J. DIDION *Play it as it Lays* vii. 35 You're a lot of laughs this afternoon, Maria. **1986** *Times* 27 Jan. 9/7 Going out to work isn't a load of laughs. **1992** *New Yorker* 20 Jan. 8/2 The first one we caught was Iron Prostate, who play hardcore for laughs, including songs such as 'Bring Me the Head of Jerry Garcia', and one about 'Gilligan's Island'.

  [5.] **laugh meter** (also **laugh-o-meter**), a device for monitoring the volume of an audience's laughter.

1960 *Spectator* 28 Oct. 655/3 Carefully concocted from our favourite ingredients by managers whose henchmen have sat through countless performances..with stop-watches and *laugh-meters*. **1985** *Chicago Tribune* 18 Sept. C7 The giant Laugh-O-Meter, high in the tower in The Tribune's state-of-the-art sitcom-testing laboratory, rates 'Stir Crazy'..as 'funny'. **1977** *Washington Post* 1 May L2/1 'Right now it's so subtle I'm afraid it won't register,' he told his actor. 'It's about 2.8 on the laugh meter.' **1992** *Gazette* (Montreal) 11 June B11/3 Her latest movie, Sister Act, may not earn her an Oscar, like her role in Ghost, but it will earn her a high spot on the laugh-o-meter.

laugh, *v.* Add: [1.] [b.] *he laughs best* (or *longest*) *who laughs last* and varr. (cf. *to have the last laugh* s.v. LAUGH *n.* 3).

c **1608** *Christmas Prince* (1923) 109 Hee laugheth best that laugheth to the end. **1823** SCOTT *Peveril* IV. iii. 49 Your Grace knows the French proverb, 'He laughs best who laughs last'. **1923** D. H. LAWRENCE *Birds, Beasts & Flowers* 39 He laughs longest who laughs last; Nay, Leonardo only bungled the pure Etruscan smile. **1984** W. RUSHTON *W. G. Grace's Last Case* xviii. 233 'I dare, sir', I said, 'I dare'. I have the courage of my convictions—and he who laughs longest laughs last! **1994** *Spy* (N.Y.) Aug. 5 He laughs best that laughs last, so we're right now enjoying a good solid thigh-slapper.

to laugh till one cries: to laugh until tears run down one's face.

1838 E. EDEN *Jrnl.* 20 Oct. in *Up the Country* (1866) I. xxiii. 252 R. was never seen to laugh till he cried before. **1900** CONRAD *Ld. Jim* xiii. 139 He made us laugh till we cried, and.. would tiptoe amongst us and say, 'It's all very well for you beggars to laugh.' **1954** N. COWARD *Future Indefinite* I. 17 Two of my inquisitors laughed until they cried. **1990** *She* Aug. 74/1 How many times have you laughed until you cried? That's the release mechanism coming into play.

[2.] **c.** To say with a laugh. (Usu. with direct speech as obj.)

1843 DICKENS *Christmas Carol* iii. 105 'Ha, ha!' laughed Scrooge's nephew. 'Ha, ha, ha.' **1881** J. H. RIDDEL *Senior Partner* II. i. 15 'What a flatterer ladies must have found you', laughed Miss Pousnett. **1903** J. LONDON *People of Abyss* iv. 31 'Lor' lumme!' she laughed. **1945** E. WILSON *I am Gazing into my 8-ball* xx. 106 'That fluff from my office.' 'Fluff?' laughed Miss Lawrence. **1986** J. BARNES *Staring at Sun* II. 126 'Can you lend me a nightdress?' Rachel laughed that she didn't own one. **1991** *Vanity Fair* (N.Y.) Apr. 146/1 'I watch a lot of kitsch television,' she laughs.

6. *to laugh oneself sick* (or *silly*): to laugh uncontrollably and at length (freq. *iron.* or *fig.*).

1773 F. BURNEY *Diary* 29 Aug. (1889) I. 246 Mrs. Rishton and I laughed ourselves sick. **1921** H. C. WITWER *Leather Pushers* xii. 325 I'll wager she's laughing herself sick right now. **1933** A. MERRITT *Burn Witch Burn!* (1934) v. 68 They'll laugh themselves sick an' fry us at Sing Sing. **1954** 'M. COLES' *Not for Export* xii. 142 The attempt.. to divide Berlin must be one of the silliest efforts in history. Our grandchildren will laugh themselves sick when they read about it. **1986** *Philadelphia Inquirer* 11 July E11/2 (Advt.), The audience was laughing themselves sick and so was I. **1995** *Sugar* June 6 (*heading*) Laugh yourself silly at other readers' awesomely awful slip-ups.

7. *to laugh one's head off*: to laugh heartily or uncontrollably, esp. *at* a person or thing.

1974 R. JEFFRIES *Mistakenly in Mallorca* v. 44 Laugh your head off, thought Mayans sourly. **1987** *New Yorker* 26 Jan. 25/3, I don't think he should show up.. wearing.. a.. swimdress... The other kids would laugh their heads off. **1990** *Sun* 20 Oct. 13/1 When I said I'd started a strict diet the crew cracked up and just couldn't stop laughing their heads off at me.

laugher, *n.* Add: **3.** *U. S. slang.* **a.** *Sport* (esp. *Baseball*). A game so easily won as to be absurd; a 'walkover'. Also *transf.*

1964 *N. Y. Post* 27 May 88/2 The score was 4–0 in the first innings and Ron Kanehl sat in the daylight near the bullpen. 'A laugher?' 'Not yet,' said Kanehl. **1965** M. ALLEN *Now wait a Minute, Casey!* xviii. 151 A 'laugher' is baseball slang for sure thing. **1972** D. DELMAN *Sudden Death* (1973) iv. 101 We had gathered three [tennis] victories each.. Ann, two hard-fought wins and a laugher. **1990** J. LEAVY *Squeeze Play* I. 18 The Senators lost, 19–0. It was the ultimate laugher. **1992** *N. Y. Times* 9 Aug. VIII. 3/6 Rosen put Johnson where he could do the most good, and this race turned into a laugher quickly.

b. A highly amusing or laughably absurd statement, situation, etc.; a joke.

1973 *Pennsylvania Voice* 10 Oct. 8/1 There is a clause in the policy to the effect that '.. no pet shall cause damage to University property or grounds...' This

one is a laugher. **1977** *Washington Post* 17 July F1/3 The voice belongs to.. the engineer-producer for this laugher of a recording session. **1988** *Ibid.* 29 Feb. D16/1 Pick a put-down, any put-down, and you could make it a laugher.

laughing, *ppl. a.* Add: **laughingly** *adv.*: (*b*) with laughable inappropriateness; ludicrously.

1954 WYNDHAM LEWIS *Self Condemned* xi. 181 If you were a 'wine-hound' you could have what in Canada is laughingly called wine. **1967** P. SHAFFER *Black Comedy* 51 Then we can buy a super Georgian house and live what's laughingly known as happily ever after. **1990** *Industry Week* 5 Nov. 56/3 He has upped the ante so that fines are no longer laughingly small.

launch, *n.*[1] Add: [4.] **d.** The placing of a new product on the market; the publicity event at which this takes place.

1969 J. ARGENTI *Managem. Techniques* v. 25 Anxiety that the launch date [of a product] will be missed. **1969** *Punch* 15 Jan. 96/2 The Ford Capri, a sort of shrunken Mustang, is being built in Britain and Germany and will be launched later this month. But, of course, 'the launch', as the trade calls it, is not as simple as that. **1971** *Sunday Express* (Johannesburg) 28 Mar. 5/1 Mr. Uys.. vetoed the display of the same model's nipple when the launch advertisement was submitted. **1983** WILLIS & LEE *Captain's Diary* x. 168 The afternoon was hectic—a book launch for Glenn Turner,.. and then a store appearance. **1986** *Linlithgowshire Jrnl. & Gaz.* 17 July 13/3 Since its launch in 1980 'The Face' magazine has reached a worldwide readership. **1991** *R.A.F. News* 1 Nov. 7/1 Some of them were at the launch, at the Imperial War Museum.

[7.] **launch pad**: also *fig.*

1980 *Encounter* May 75/1 Even more dubious than the writer's obvious failure to ascertain simple facts is his tendency to use his impressions as a launch-pad for daring sociological speculation. **1989** *Franchise Mag.* Spring 80/2 The company sees the deal with Mansfield as a launchpad for its plans to penetrate the European market. **1995** *Nursing Times* 22 Mar. 98/2 (Advt.), The D grade staff nurse posts are excellent launch pads for career minded nurses.

launch, *v.* [2.] [c.] Delete *Obs.* For def read: To throw (a person); *refl.*, to hurl oneself; dart, rush. Also *fig.* (Later examples.)

1762 STERNE *Tr. Shandy* V. xxix. 104 Gymnast.. launched himself aloft into the air. **1851** H. MELVILLE *Moby Dick* III. xlviii. 287 The first uprising momentum of the whale.. involuntarily launched him along it [*sc.* the boat]; to a little distance from the centre of the destruction he had made. **1872** 'M. TWAIN' *Roughing It* li. 362 He then launched himself lovingly into his work. **1915** L. M. MONTGOMERY *Anne of Island* xvi. 166 Rusty.. launched himself at the Sarah-cat. The stately animal had stopped washing her face and was looking at him curiously. *a* **1961** P. ROONEY in *Webster* II. 1278/1 Suddenly launched himself from between his guards.. and vanished into the rocks and heather, still handcuffed. **1992** *Boston Globe* 31 July 68/4 She thundered down the runway, launched herself skyward and struck her first vault for a 9.975.

[5.] **b.** *fig.* Of a product, enterprise, etc.: to begin operation or trading; to be made publicly available.

1968 *Campaign* 1 Nov. 1/5 Since Campaign launched on September 12, [etc.]. **1984** *Broadcast* 7 Dec. 8/1 Called *Beeb*, it launches on 29 January with an initial print run of 400,000 and is clearly aimed to rival ITV's paper. **1987** *Times* 2 Apr. 19/3 When the new publishing house of Bloomsbury launches, its fictional first-born will be *Trust* by Mary Flanagan. **1991** *Campaign* 16 Aug. 10/5 With.. *Black Briton* launching shortly.

11. *Mil.* To mount (an assault or offensive); to open (an engagement, hostilities, etc.). Also *fig.*

1916 *Times* 18 May 6/3 In the Lagarina Valley..the enemy yesterday launched five violent attacks..on the slopes north of Zugna Torta. **1922** *Encycl. Brit.* XXXI. 601/1 A week later the Austrian offensive was launched. **1940** J. COLVILLE *Diary* 13 Jan. in *Fringes of Power* (1985) 70 The Cabinet has received information that an attack may be launched by the Germans against Holland and Belgium. **1961** G. F. KENNAN *Russia & West* xii. 168 He launched an offensive which carried Polish forces in a fortnight all the way to the Dnepr River. **1981** S. CHITTY *Gwen John* vi. 87 She launched a campaign of which a general might have been proud. **1988** *Financial Times* 24 Mar. 46/5 A British advertising agency..has launched a bitter legal attack against six senior..executives.

launder, *v.* Sense 1 b in Dict. becomes 1 c. Add: [**1.**] **b.** *fig.* To treat or process (something) so as to make it acceptable; to make expedient (and often unscrupulous) alterations or improvements to; *spec.* to lower (a mileometer reading) when selling a second-hand car.

*a***1961** H. R. WARFEL in WEBSTER s.v., Succeeded pretty well in laundering the grammar. **1976** *N.Y. Times* 3 May 35/7 Unscrupulous dealers.. 'launder' the mileage of cars. **1978** *Radio Times* 28 Jan. 15/4 Its followers believe the working class has been bamboozled out of its legitimate rights by a capitalist conspiracy that 'appropriated' trade unionism and socialism, then 'laundered' and returned them as harmless institutions. **1981** H. RAWSON *Dict. Euphemisms* (1983) 163 When dealers in used..cars turn back odometers..it is correct to say that the mileage on the vehicles has been laundered. **1985** *Toronto Sun* 10 Oct. 12/2 There is nothing we can do to launder the rhetoric of Soviet leaders. **1991** N. MAILER *Harlot's Ghost* II. iv. 290 He had also managed to expunge any paper trace of Herrick Hubbard's presence in the Snake Pit... My immediate past had been effectively laundered.

laundermat ('lɔːndəˌmæt), *n.* Chiefly *N. Amer.* [f. LAUNDER *v.* + -MAT, after LAUNDROMAT *n.*] A launderette. Also used *fig.*

1951 *Amer. Speech* XXVI. 166 There are.. 'Laundromats'—often called 'Laundermats' and 'Laundrymats'—open for public patronage. **1969** *Newsweek* 15 Dec. 90/3 Wall Street crime involves the use of secret foreign bank accounts..to provide a convenient 'laundermat' for organized crime in 'bleaching' illegal profits from narcotics and gambling. **1972** J. METCALF *Going down Slow* vi. 112 We were drinking Cokes and reading the magazines in a laundermat. **1987** *N.Y. Times* 26 Apr. VII. 26/5 Nothing can make you consider running a laundermat more than training a barn full of slow horses.

laundry, *n.* Add: [**2.**] **c.** *transf.* and *fig.* An establishment where articles are modified to meet specific requirements, *esp.* one that launders (illegal) funds.

1965 *New Scientist* 11 Nov. 406/3 Computer bureaux already exist which give the 'laundry' service to customers whose data is taken in by hand for processing. **1974** *National Rev.* (U.S.) 18 Jan. 100/2 It will resort to the Mexican laundries and to other roundabout routes, preferably within the law. **1978** *N.Y. Times Mag.* 26 Feb. 22/4 His Canadian and Bahamian companies provided a convenient 'laundry' for illegitimate mob money looking for a way to reach legitimate usage within the United States. **1982** *Times* 2 Aug. 3/3 The union-funded Labour Research Department..accuses British United Industrialists.. of acting as a 'laundry' for companies unhappy about contributing directly to Conservative funds. **1991** *Metalworking Production* Sept. 31 This complete metal laundry can meet customers requirements with a comprehensive range of decorative and industrial paint finishes.

Laura Ashley ('lɔːrə 'æʃlɪ), *n.* [The name of *Laura Ashley* (1925-85), founder of the British textile and clothing company bearing her name.] A proprietary name for clothing, fabric, interior decoration, etc., produced by the Laura Ashley company or typical of its style, often characterized by a small floral pattern. Freq. used *attrib.* Also *fig.* Hence, ˌLaura 'Ashleyish *a.*

[**1972** *Daily Tel.* 5 Apr. 13/5 Susannah York..wore an Ashley blouse and long skirt..to Elizabeth Taylor's lavish..party recently in Budapest.] **1974** *Trade Marks Jrnl.* 7 Aug. 1483/1 *Laura Ashley*...Dresses, smocks, slacks, blouses, shirts, skirts, aprons (for wear), sleeping garments, capes, jackets, coats and hats, all for women and girls...Ashley Mountney Limited. **1979** *Jrnl. R. Soc. Arts* CXXVII. 211/1 The females in our family are draped from head to toe in Laura Ashley. **1984** A. LURIE *Foreign Affairs* vii. 177 She is wearing..an olive-green densely flowered Laura Ashley cotton. *Ibid.* 178 In the bathroom she shakes out her sticky Laura Ashley and lays it in the tub. **1985** J. RABAN *Foreign Land* (1986) i. 16 A lady with large bones clad in something Laura Ashleyish. **1987** J. GREEN *Dict. Jargon* 323/2 *Laura Ashley* (*Music*), replacing 'schmaltz' as a word indicating excessively flowery, sugary or weedy music. **1989** *Independent* 21 Oct. 49/5 Visiting the prettified villages..full of gift shoppes selling Crabtree and Evelyn, English bone china and Beatrix Potter figurines I felt trapped in a Laura Ashley theme park. **1991** M. ATWOOD *Hairball* in *Wilderness Tips* 40 Her mind was room-by-room Laura Ashley wallpaper: tiny, unopened pastel buds arranged in straight rows.

Laurence, *n.*² Add: **2.** [perh. from the assoc. of St. Laurence with heat; see note above.] The shimmering effect that can sometimes be seen over a road, beach, etc., on a hot day. *U.S. colloq.*

1907 W. M. COCKRUM *Pioneer Hist. Indiana* viii. 189 When the older people thought their children were a little slack in their work, they would remind them that they were in danger of being caught by the Laurences, meaning the little heat waves caused by the heat from the earth on a very hot day. **1961** *Amer. Speech* XXXVI. 300 The shimmer of a Laurence is called a 'mirage' by riflemen; it may be seen clearly through a telescope. **1981** *Verbatim* Autumn 6/2 *Laurence*, blackish, shimmering reflection seen at the surface of a paved road on a hot summer's day.

Laurent (lɒ'rɑ̃), *n. Math.* [The name of P. A. *Laurent* (1813-54), French mathematician.] Used *attrib.* and in the possessive in **Laurent('s) expansion**, **series**, the expression of a function of a complex variable z as a power series in $(z - a)$, where a is a fixed point; **Laurent's theorem**, the theorem that a single-valued monogenic analytic function may be expressed as a Laurent series in $(z - a)$ at all points of any annular region centred on a and lying entirely within the domain of existence of the function.

1893 A. R. FORSYTH *Theory Functions Complex Variable* iii. 47 (*heading*) Laurent's expansion of a function. *Ibid.*, Laurent's theorem is as follows:—A function, which is holomorphic in a part of the plane bounded by two concentric circles with centre a and finite radii, can be expanded in the form of a double series of integral powers, positive and negative, of z − a, the series converging uniformly and unconditionally in the part of the plane between the circles. **1898** HARKNESS & MORLEY *Introd. Theory Analytic Functions* x. 125 We shall have to consider series in both ascending and descending powers, such as $a_0 + a_1(x - c) + a_2(x - c) + .. + a_{-1}(x - c)^{-1} + a_{-2}(x - c)^{-2} + ...$ These need no new notation, as they can be expressed by $P(x - c) + P(1/(x - c))$. The two constitute a Laurent series. **1932** E. C. TITCHMARSH *Theory of*

Functions xiii. 401 There is a close formal connexion between a Fourier series and a Laurent series. **1968** P. A. P. MORAN *Introd. Probability Theory* x. 479 We expand this in a Laurent series convergent in a ring $0 < \alpha < |z| < \beta$. *Ibid.*, The Laurent expansion of (10.70) is therefore $g_0(z, s) = $ [etc.]. **1974** P. HENRICI *Appl. & Computational Complex Analysis* I. iv. 211 Laurent's theorem contains the Taylor expansion as a special case, and a remarkable conclusion may be drawn from it. **1990** *Proc. London Math. Soc.* LXI. III. 546 We shall get the finiteness of the Laurent expansion in λ of the based extended solution Φλ for a pluriharmonic map from a compact complex manifold.

Laurentide ('lɒrəntaɪd, 'lɔ:-) *a. Geol.* [f. *Laurentides*, name of a range of hills in Canada parallel to the St. Laurence River on its north-west side, a. F. *Laurentides* (F. X. Garneau *Histoire du Canada* (1845) I. II. 180), f. *St.-Laurent* St. Lawrence.] Pertaining to or designating the ice sheet which covered the eastern part of northern North America during the most recent (Wisconsin) glaciation.
   1890 G. M. DAWSON in *Amer. Geologist* VI. 162 The writer ventures to propose that the eastern *mer de glace* may appropriately be named the great *Laurentide glacier*, while its western fellow is known as the *Cordilleran glacier*. **1897** W. B. SCOTT *Geol.* xxxii. 526 This is called the Laurentide Ice-sheet or Glacier. **1957** *Encycl. Brit.* X. 374/2 The Laurentide ice sheet overtopped the White mountains in New Hampshire and so was at least 5,000 ft. thick in that region. **1975** *Canad. Jrnl. Earth Sci.* XII. 1499/2 Laboratory analysis of Laurentide and Cordilleran tills. **1987** *Geology* XV. 537 (*heading*) Restricted regional extent of the Laurentide Ice Sheet in the Great Lakes basins during early Wisconsin glaciation.

lauroyl ('lɒr-, 'lɔ:rəʊɪl, -əʊaɪl), *n. Chem.* [f. LAUR(IC *a.* + -OYL.] The radical $CH_3(CH_2)_{10}CO-$ of lauric acid. Usu. *attrib.*
   1939 *Jrnl. Amer. Chem. Soc.* LXI. 1019/1 Lauroyl, myristoyl, palmitoyl and stearoyl chlorides react smoothly at the boiling point of ether to give the corresponding diesters of the unsaturated diols in substantial yields. **1946** *Industr. & Engin. Chem.* (Analytical Ed.) July 444 Several derivatives of lauroyl chloride were prepared which might lend themselves to quantitative recovery. **1955** *Jrnl. Soc. Cosmetic Chemists* VI. 412 One of the most important performance characteristics of a shampoo is its lather. Lauroyl sarcosine, with relatively minor manipulation, performs satisfactorily in this respect. **1973** *Biochim. & Biophys. Acta* CCXCIX. 222 Crystals of cadmium lauroyl sarkosidase were later found to be equally satisfactory for fractionating bacterial lysates, and have the advantage of forming at room temperature.

Lausitz ('laʊzɪts), *n. Archaeol.* [The German name of Lusatia: see LUSATIAN *n.* and *a.*] Used *attrib.* to designate a culture which flourished mainly in Saxony and Bohemia during the Late Bronze Age (Urnfield period).
   1928 V. G. CHILDE in *Antiquity* II. 37 On the continent as in Britain the later phases of the Bronze Age are marked by the spread of large cremation cemeteries generally termed urnfields. One of the several groups of urnfield cultures in Central Europe occupies such a pre-eminent position that it may even claim to be the parent of all the rest. It is known as the Lausitz or Lusatian culture. **1950** H. L. LORIMER *Homer & Monuments* i. 36 Then came the intrusion from Europe of a new population, who brought with them a culture of the Lausitz type with its characteristic *Buckelkeramik*. **1977** G. CLARK *World Prehist.* (ed. 3) iv. 189 Elements of Hallstatt culture appeared in several distinct Urnfield groups, among them the Lausitz culture, regarded by Polish prehistorians as the basis of the Slav people.

lautenclavicymbel ('laʊtənklavɪˌsɪmbəl), *n. Mus. Obs.* exc. *Hist.* Also **lauten-clavicymbel**, lautenklavizimbel. [ad. G. *Lautenklavizimbel*, f. *Laute* lute + *Klavizimbel* harpsichord: see CLAVICYMBAL *n.*] A type of harpsichord with gut rather than metal strings.
   1884 BELL & FULLER-MAITLAND tr. *Spitta's J. S. Bach* II. IV. ii. 46 In the year 1740 (or thereabout) he devised a 'Lauten-clavicymbel' (Lute-harpsichord). **1906** *Grove's Dict. Mus.* (ed. 2) II. 653/2 *Lautenclavicymbel*, 'lute-harpsichord', invented by J. S. Bach in 1740. **1959** *Collins Mus. Encycl.* 382/1 *Lautenclavicymbel*, lute-harpsichord . . harpsichord with gut strings instead of metal strings. The instrument existed in the sixteenth century, and Bach had one made in 1740. **1978** *Early Music* Apr. 253/1 No lautenklavizymbel are preserved, yet no one denies they existed. **1979** *Ibid.* Jan. 71/1 The two lute pieces that Bach himself transcribed for harpsichord (or, possibly, the strange hybrid *Lautenclavicymbel*).

||**lauter** ('laʊtə(r)), *a. Brewing.* [G. *läuter* vbl. stem of *läutern* to purify, refine, strain.] Involved with, used in, or resulting from the refining process, esp. in *Comb.* as *lauter tub*, *tun*; **lautermash** (see MASH *n.*[1] 1), refined liquid, wort. Hence '**lautering** *vbl. n.*, filtration.
   1901 WAHL & HENIUS *Amer. Handy-Bk. Brewing* 717 Draw off the liquid portion [of the wort]—'lautermash'. **1933** ARNOLD & PENMAN *Hist. Brewing Industry & Brewing Sci. in Amer.* 89 Effective pumps for water, 'lauter' mash or thin mash, thick mash and wort and even the raw grain mash. **1940** H. L. HIND *Brewing* II. xxiv. 588 The essential function of the lauter tun is that of a strainer. **1957** *Encycl. Brit.* IV. 103/2 Lautering, or filtration, may be carried out either in a combination mash-lauter tub, . . or in a separate lauter tub. **1976** *Milton Keynes Express* 28 May 21/3 (*Advt.*), In the lauter tun the spent grain is strained off and pumped into grain storage silos at the side of the brewhouse. **1980** W. L. DOWNARD *Dict. Hist. Amer. Brewing & Distilling Industries* 107 *Lautering*, in the lautering process, wort . . is strained or removed from solid and 'spent' grains. **1995** *Mother Earth News* Dec.–Jan. 60/2 The advantage of the cooler is its insulation; mashing, lautering, and sparging can be carried out all in one vessel.

lava, *n.* Add: [4.] [a.] **lava tube**, a tubular cave occurring naturally in some solidified lava flows.
   1927 H. S. PALMER *Geol. Honolulu Artesian Syst.* 29 Many lava flows develop hard crusts by the cooling and solidification of the upper surface. Later the supply of lava for the particular flow may cease and the liquid lava stream may drain out leaving a long tubular opening under the crust. *Lava tubes formed in this way would be as good as artificial pipes for carrying water. **1931** *Bull. Geol. Soc. Amer.* XLII. 310 Small stalactites of opal occur in a lava tube 20 miles northeast of Red Bluff, California. **1965** *Oregon State Dept. Geol. & Mineral Industry Bull.* LVIII. 9 This large lava tube . . is a mile long (1.6 km), and it can be easily entered where the roof has collapsed. **1979** *United States 1980/81* (Penguin Travel Guides) 510 There's good diving in the Pine Trees area (lava-tube caves big enough to drive a Volkswagen through, [etc.]). **1993** K. S. ROBINSON *Green Mars* 439 She stepped into an observation gallery cut into the side of the lava tube.
   lava tunnel = *lava tube* above.
   1905 *Bull. U.S. Geol. Survey* No. 252. 70 Access can be gained to a subterranean chamber of the ordinary type of *lava tunnels, formed by the outflow of molten lava from beneath the thick, rigid crust of a sheet of basalt. **1976** P. FRANCIS *Volcanoes* iv. 143 Lava tunnels result from the rapid cooling of the surface and the side of a flow. **1991** H. A. SUMMERFIELD *Global Geomorphol.* xix. 485/2 The Hadley Rille itself is thought to be a massive collapsed lava tunnel, smaller versions of which are known from lava fields on Earth.

lavage, *n.* Add: Hence as *v. trans.*, to cleanse or irrigate (an organ).

1961 W. PERCY *Moviegoer* IV. i. 173 Dr. Mink lavaged her stomach and gave her a stimulant. **1974** *Nature* 16 Aug. 595/2 After killing the peritoneal cavity was lavaged with 6 ml of Fischer's medium. **1988** *Amer. Jrnl. Respiratory Dis.* CXXXVII. 75/2 Such suspended bodies [of asbestos] represent roughly 2% of all the bodies stored in the portion of lung lavaged.

‖**lavaret** (lavarε, 'lævərət), *n.* [Fr.] The houting, *Coregonus lavaretus*, as it occurs in some European lakes.

1864 in WEBSTER. **1925** *Blackw. Mag.* Jan. 53/2 Better than trout was *lavaret* from the Lac du Bourget. **1966** P. V. PRICE *France: Food & Wine* 307 The mountain lakes and streams yield fine fish, of which three..are unlikely to be found elsewhere—the *féra*, *lavaret* and *omble chevalier*; all are types of salmon, but the last looks more like a trout.

lavatory, *n.* Add: [8.] *lavatory bowl.*

1974 V. CANNING *Mask of Memory* v. 88 He walked down the corridor to the toilet, burnt the letter over the *lavatory bowl and flushed the ashes away. **1980** Q. SKINNER in Michaels & Ricks *State of Language* 567 Recall the way in which Marcel Duchamp liked to designate certain familiar objects (coat-pegs, lavatory bowls) as works of art.

lavender, *n.*[2] and *a.* Add: [A.] [1.] d. *fig.* Effeminacy; homosexuality or homosexual tendencies; esp. in *dash*, *streak of lavender.*

1929 C. PORTER *I'm a Gigolo* (song) I'm a famous gigolo, And of lavender, my nature's got just a dash in it. **1931** G. FOWLER *Great Mouthpiece* ix. 99 (*heading*) An allegation in lavender. **1935** A. J. POLLOCK *Underworld Speaks* 115/2 *Streak of lavender*, an effeminate man; a sissy. **1941** G. LEGMAN in G. W. Henry *Sex Variants* II. App. VII. 1170 There are said to be 'seven recognized stages of homosexuality, from ga-ga to the "deeper tones" of lavender'. **1972** B. RODGERS *Queens' Vernacular* 124 Your trip to Tijuana certainly brought out your deeper tones of lavender. **1992** *New Republic* 4 May 26/3 Rick is so hard-boiled that any touch of lavender is wiped away.

[5.] **lavender oil**, a scented oil distilled from lavender flowers.

1868 WATTS *Dict. Chem.* V. 399 According to Gastell, spike-oil is obtained from the leaves and stalks, true *lavender-oil from the flowers, of several species of *Lavendula.* **1990** P. MELVILLE *Shape-Shifter* (1991) 64 'Lavender oil,' interrupted Pistol-Man loudly from behind Vera's shoulder. 'Give she lavender oil.' **1991** *Artist* Nov. 14/2 A drop of oil of spike (lavendar oil) should be added to preserve the egg.

[B.] **3.** [freq. as attrib. use of sense *1 d of the n.] *fig.* Refined, genteel, sentimental; hence (esp. of a man) effeminate, homosexual.

1928 S. O'CASEY *Let.* 15 June (1975) I. 280, I am very sorry..that I have hurt the refined sentimentalities of C. W. Allen by neglecting to use the lavender..language of the 18th and 19th centuries. **1973** C. WILLIAMS *Man on Leash* i. 9 He had no flowers to deposit on the grave and would have felt too uncomfortable and self-conscious in such a lavender-gesture anyway. **1974** *Times Lit. Suppl.* 1 Feb. 112/2 Susan Ferrier..can at least be credited with a certain lavender charm. **1979** *Guardian* 26 June 7/8 The effect of Lavender Power is worth examining... Gay achievements are impressive. **1986** *Times* 22 Feb. 8/6 An opinion often encountered..among Americans and Australians—that Britain is crawling with the lavender mob. **1991** *Village Voice* (N.Y.) 5 Feb. 67/3 Gone are the days when all that was visible of lavender sci fi were those long, lustful glances between Kirk and Spock.

lavish, *a.* Add: [2.] c. Of food, clothing, decoration, etc.: sumptuous, rich, luxurious, extravagant. Also *transf.*

1882 E. O'DONOVAN *Merv Oasis* I. iv. 62 He wore a silk tunic..with lavish gold embroidery. **1936** G. GREENE in *Spectator* 26 June 1171/2 For two hours we too had lived on the 'Queen Mary'..in an atmosphere of immense expenditure, of boat deck sentiment, of decorations lavish if not in the best of taste. **1972** *Daily Tel.* 5 Apr. 13/5 Susannah York..wore an Ashley blouse and long skirt..to Elizabeth Taylor's lavish..party recently in Budapest. **1974** P. CAREY *Fat Man in Hist.* (1980) 155 We..prepared ourselves lavish midnight snacks. **1992** *Antique Dealer* Jan. 17/1 The high-ceilinged reception room lined with 85 square yards of amber panelling carved in low relief..and encrusted with rubies and emeralds, was the lavish gift of Frederick I of Prussia to Peter the Great.

law, *n.*[1] Add: [III.] [17.] [b.] **law of averages**, *strictly* = *law of large numbers* s.v. LARGE *a.* 8 i; *popularly*, the (false) belief that future events are likely to be such as to reduce any overall deviation from an average represented by past events (= *Monte Carlo fallacy* s.v. MONTE CARLO *n.* 1 c).

[**1857** H. T. BUCKLE *Hist. Civilization in Eng.* I. i. 22 The great advance made by the statisticians consists in applying to these inquiries [into crime] the doctrine of averages, which no one thought of doing before the eighteenth century.] **1875** F. ARNOLD *Our Bishops & Deans* I. vi. 323 Here is the briefest and most complete refutation of Mr. Buckle's 'Law of Averages' with which we are acquainted. **1915** *Illustr. World* Oct. 222 All business of today takes cognizance of the law of averages. **1927** *Pop. Mechanics* Mar. 405/1 To get a working understanding of the law of averages for your own purposes..you begin by keeping records. **1941** W. J. CASH *Mind of South* II. ii. 155 If, under the law of averages for human nature, the majority of even the better sort did inevitably compromise, then they compromised by iotas and jots. **1968** R. KYLE *Love Lab.* (1969) viii. 109 Prescott knew, from the Kinsey material and the law of averages, that the Prosecutor himself was not without guilt. **1986** *Times* 5 June 39 The law of averages dictated that there would eventually be a line of dialogue that did not sound as if it came from a B-movie. **1993** M. ATWOOD *Robber Bride* li. 404 Tony is betting on the law of averages. Sooner or later..Zenia will appear.

[c.] (*f*) *Logic.* **law of Clavius** [see quot. 1951], the law of logic, sometimes used as an axiom, that if a proposition is implied by its negation then that proposition is true.

1951 J. ŁUKASIEWICZ *Aristotle's Syllogistic* iv. 80 The second axiom, which reads in words 'If (if not-*p*, then *p*), then *p*', was applied by Euclid to the proof of a mathematical theorem. I call it the law of Clavius, as Clavius (a learned Jesuit living in the second half of the sixteenth century, one of the constructors of the Gregorian calendar) first drew attention to this law in his commentary on Euclid. **1965** B. MATES *Elem. Logic* vi. 99, (-P→P)→P (Law of Clavius).

d. Hence in numerous jocular names for observations or guiding principles which humorously or ironically encapsulate some aspect of human experience; usu. preceded by the name of its supposed originator. *Murphy's law*: see MURPHY *n.*[2] 3. *Parkinson's law*: see PARKINSON *n.*[2] *Sod's law*: see SOD *n.*[3] 2 e.

1961 *Amer. Speech* XXXVI. 149 *Gumperson's Law*, the humorous theory that whatever can go wrong probably will. **1963** H. A. SMITH *Short Hist. Fingers* i. 7 *Fetridge's Law*,..states that important things that are supposed to happen don't happen, especially when people are looking. **1968** *N.Y. Times Mag.* 17 Mar. 116/3 The first law for officeholders is majestically short, simple and unassailable: 'Get re-elected'. **1969** *N.Y. Times* 20 Aug. 46/6 What Yugoslav wits call 'Meyers' law'..stipulates that: 'If the facts don't fit the theory, discard the facts'. **1973** H. McCLOY *Change of Heart* ix. 105, I call this Julian's Law: a great man's intimates are never as great as he is. **1983** *Truck &*

Bus Transportation June 30/2 Law No 3.0 (*Lowry*): If it jams—force it. **1995** *Guardian* 26 Jan. (OnLine section) 7/1 Software development, by contrast, is governed by the rule known as Hofstadter's law: 'It always takes longer than you expect, even when you take into account Hofstadter's law.'

[V.] [23.] **law centre**, in the U.K., a publicly-funded institution offering free legal advice and assistance.

1970 *Solicitors' Jrnl.* 24 July 557/1 It will not be possible to assess the significance of the opening of this country's first neighbourhood *law centre..for some time to come. **1985** R. C. A. WHITE *Admin. of Justice* IV. xv. 255 The law centre is located in shop-front premises...It is funded primarily by grants. **1991** *Parl. Affairs* XLIV. 543, I would also tip out the commercial lawyers of the City and Temple to work in High Street general practices and Law Centres, many of which are opting out of Legal Aid right now.

Law Commission, in England and Wales, and in Scotland, a body of legal advisers responsible for reviewing the law and proposing reforms; since 1965, permanently established under the Law Commissions Act 1965.

[**1833** *Hansard Lords* 30 Apr. 756 Law Commissions. The Lord Chancellor moved for a copy of the fourth Report of the Commissioners appointed to inquire into the state of the Common Law.] **1833** *Ibid.* 28 June 1285 (*heading*) *Law Commission (Scotland). **1965** *Mod. Law Rev.* XXVIII. 675 The [Law Commissions] Act provides for the appointment of a body of Commissioners, to be known as the Law Commission, consisting of a Chairman and four other Commissioners appointed by the Lord Chancellor. **1995** *Independent* 6 Mar. 3/1 The BMA is opposed to legalising living wills, although the Law Commission wants the position tidied up.

hence **Law Commissioner**.

1835 *Hansard Lords* 4 Sept. 1329 *Law Commissioners. Lord Brougham..alluded to the Commissioners of Law Inquiry..appointed.. in..1833..who had furnished two most valuable reports. **1963** GARDINER & MARTIN *Law Reform Now* i. 8 The setting up within the Lord Chancellor's Office of a strong unit concerned exclusively with law reform...The head of the proposed unit..should preside over a committee of..lawyers..; in the following we will call them *Law Commissioners. **1987** *Financial Times* 19 May 6/7 A former law commissioner..is to be the first building society ombudsman.

law society, a society for lawyers or law students; *spec.* (with capital initials) each of the national bodies established in England and Wales, and in Scotland to further the interests of solicitors and to regulate their professional conduct.

1821 (*title*) *Law Society. Rules and regulations of the Society of Practitioners, in the several courts of Law and Equity, resident in and near the Metropolis, established in the year 1739. **1838** H. MARTINEAU *Retrospect Western Trav.* II. 26 The students of this school have instituted a Law Society, at whose meetings the Professor presides, and where the business of every branch of the profession is rehearsed. **1974** M. GILBERT *Flash Point* i. 7, I joined the Law Society, as an assistant solicitor. **1993** *Independent on Sunday* 8 Aug. (Business section) 22/6 If overcharged by a solicitor, the Law Society makes an effort to lend a hand, although it is somewhat limp-wristed.

Lawford ('lɔːfəd), *n.* Tennis. [The name of Herbert F. *Lawford* (1851–1925), British tennis player.] Used *attrib.* to designate a powerful forehand stroke or drive considered characteristic of Lawford's play.

[**1890** C. G. HEATHCOTE *Lawn Tennis* x. 230 The invention of this [horizontal] stroke is attributed to Mr. Lawford, and forms a most valuable addition to

the power of attack.] **1893** J. DWIGHT *Pract. Lawn-Tennis* ii. 35 It has been the fashion in America to call any hard underhand stroke..the 'Lawford' stroke. **1914** *Outing* LXIV. 424/1 To the fellow who can play a Lawford underhand as well as side wheel, the low, bounding chop stroke is meat and drink! **1936** E. C. POTTER *Kings of Court* ii. 20 This forehand became so well known and so feared that some years later it was christened the 'Lawford stroke'. *Ibid.*, Long after Lawford retired novices cried, 'I've got it! The Lawford stroke!' **1977** *New Yorker* 25 July 60/2 Few players could cope with this fearsome forehand — 'the Lawford stroke', as it came to be called.

lawn, *n.*² Add: [4.] **lawn chair** *N. Amer.*, a garden chair, *esp.* a reclining garden chair.

1895 *Montgomery Ward Catal.* Spring & Summer 617/1 *Lawn Chair, high back, comfortable and durable; will stand outdoor use. **1987** J. WILCOX *Miss Undine's Living Room* viii. 113 Pulling up one of the webbed lawn chairs, the young man settled into it.

lawn edger, a cutting device for trimming the turf on the edges of a lawn.

1960 J. J. ROWLANDS *Spindrift* 177 Why pay twenty dollars or more for an electric *lawn-edger when you can..make one for little or nothing? **1988** *Independent* 9 July 18 There should be none of the wavy-edged beds that look as if they have been cut out by a man drunk in charge of a lawn edger.

lawned (lɔːnd), *ppl. a.*² [f. LAWN *n.*² + -ED².] Of a garden or other tract of land: laid to lawn; consisting of or containing lawns.

1960 *Sunday Express* 3 July 5/1 Wilderness House is a red-brick 22-roomed Wren building with a small lawned garden. **1978** *Cornish Guardian* 27 Apr. 17 (Advt.), Semi detached 1950's house...Pleasant lawned garden. Garage. **1979** *Church Times* 23 Mar. 1/2 Litter is the biggest problem to cathedrals with a lawned close. **1983** *Daily Tel.* 30 Apr. 12/4 A widow who put wreaths and vases of flowers on her husband's grave in a lawned cemetery. **1994** *Guardian* 2 July 26/7 It was they who inspired a London estate agent to describe a local property as 'beautifully lawned'.

Lawrentian, *a.* and *n.* Add: Also **Lawrencean**. **B.** *n.* **1.** An admirer of T. E. Lawrence or his writings. *rare.*

?**1957** L. DURRELL *Spirit of Place* (1969) 139 The fury of Lawrentians everywhere.

2. An admirer of D. H. Lawrence or his writings. *rare.*

1959 H. T. MOORE *D. H. Lawrence Misc.* p. xxv, Raymond Williams, whose comparison of Lawrence and Carlyle may flutter some of the Lawrenceans. **1973** *Times Lit. Suppl.* 9 Nov. 1369/1 Both the Lawrentians and the anti-Lawrentians have been exaggerating ever since. **1992** *Studies in Eng. Lit.: English Number* (Tokyo) 110 After he has reread *Women in Love*, he realizes that there is a distinction, though blurred, between the author and characters in their points of view and admits that he has converted into a true Lawrentian.

lawyer, *n.* Add: [6.] **lawyer's wig** = *shaggy ink-cap* s.v. SHAGGY *a.* 3.

?**1950** WAKEFIELD & DENNIS *Common Brit. Fungi* 205 *Coprinus comatus*. Shaggy Caps or *Lawyer's wig. **1972** *Times* 23 Sept. 14/7 Some fungi, like the 'Lawyers' Wigs'..sprout in their hundreds from roadside verges. **1987** M. BON *Mushrooms & Toadstools Brit. & N.-W. Europe* 270 *Lawyer's wig, ..a good edible fungus in the young state when quite white.

lax, *v.* Restrict †*Obs.* to sense in Dict. and add: **b.** *spec.* in *Phonetics*, to produce (a vowel sound) with the speech organs relaxed.

1968 CHOMSKY & HALLE *Sound Pattern Eng.* 333 Both of these rules decreased by one the number of consonants that must follow the vowel to be laxed. **1975** *Language* LI. 889 A special, morphologically conditioned rule laxes the vowels *in the nouns.* **1989** *Canad. Jrnl. Ling.* XXXIV. 455 They tend to use standard variants: their high vowels are not laxed as often.

Laxfordian (læks'fɔːdiən), *a. Geol.* [f. *Laxford,* name of a loch and river in the north of Scotland + -IAN.] Of, pertaining to, or designating the later metamorphism undergone by the Lewisian rocks of the Precambrian in north-west Scotland, the rocks formed by this metamorphism, and the structures to which they belong. Also *absol.,* these rocks and structures.

1950 SUTTON & WATSON in *Q. Jrnl. Geol. Soc.* CVI. 243 In the following pages the Lewisian is..regarded as belonging to two metamorphic complexes, the first, or Scourian, being older and the second, or Laxfordian, younger than the dolerite dykes. These names are taken from localities in Sutherland where the relations of the two complexes are particularly clearly displayed. **1959** *Nature* 5 Dec. 1793/1 Three samples came from the Outer Hebrides, three from the Laxfordian, and two from the Scourian. **1969** BENNISON & WRIGHT *Geol. Hist. Brit. Isles* iii. 44 On the Outer Isles the Laxfordian orogeny is dominant, much of Harris and Lewis being composed of a migmatite complex of Laxfordian age. **1973** *Nature* 6 July 10/2 The whole rock date of 1,670 ± 24 m.y. and that on hornblende at 1,566 ± 33 m.y. indicate a Laxfordian age for the material. **1991** R. G. PARK in G. Y. Craig *Geol. Scotl.* (ed. 3) 26 The main Laxfordian event is dated at *c*.1,800 Ma.

lay, *n.*[7] Add: [**8.**] **b.** *N. Amer.* In *Placer Mining,* a lease to work a claim for a percentage of the proceeds. Freq. const. *on.* Now *Hist.*

1898 *Yukon Midnight Sun* (Dawson, Yukon Territory) 11 June 1/2 Some of these lay holders say they have not made wages. **1908** I. BEEBE *True Life Story Sweetwater Bill Gales* viii. 74 Sweetwater..took a lay on a claim on Dexter Creek and cleaned up. *Ibid.* ix. 81 He took the money that he made from the lay on Dexter Creek and spent it gambling. **1927** H. YOUNG *Hall Young of Alaska* 352 Hundreds of *chechacos* had taken 'lays' along that creek and were putting down holes here and there in hope of finding a pay streak. The royalty on these lays received by the owners varied from thirty to seventy-five per cent of the gross output, according to the prospects of the claim. **1943** W. H. CHASE *Sourdough Pot* xii. 72 [They] endeavored to get lays on claims already located. That is, to work a part of a claim on shares, or a percentage basis. **1965** S. G. LAWRENCE *40 Yrs. on Yukon Telegraph* iii. 19 Lays on claims vary according to the owners. In this deal I keep seventy per cent of the gold I take out and the owner gets thirty per cent.

[**9.**] *point-of-lay*: see POINT *n.*[1] D. 16.

lay, *a.* (and *n.*[1]) Add: [**3.**] [**b.**] Also with reference to trade unions. (Later examples.)

1980 *Times* 10 Apr. 1/3 Lay delegates on the Transport and General Workers' Union national bus committee, representing about 140,000 busmen. **1986** *ASTMS Industry News* Spring 1/3 We have sent delegations from our Parliamentary Committee, together with lay representatives from Westland, to the Ministry of Defence.

lay, *v.*[1] Senses 50–61 in Dict. become 51–62. Add: [**VII.**] [**43.**] **c. to lay dead** *U. S. colloq.* (esp. in *Black English*), to be inconspicuous through inactivity; = *to lay low,* sense 43 *a* above; also, to do nothing in particular, to loiter, 'hang about'.

1947 *Amer. Speech* XXII. 122/1 The boys say, 'Lay dead and you'll get ahead'. **1955** *Publ. Amer. Dial. Soc.* XXIV. 55 Now we can cool off and lay dead for a week or two. *Ibid.* 178 Milwaukee is noted for being the toughest city in the Midwest to..lay dead in. **1967**

Trans-Action Apr. 6/1 The dudes could be found when they were 'laying dead'—hanging on the corner, or shooting pool and 'jiving' ('goofing' or kidding around) in a local community project. **1972** T. KOCHMAN *Rappin' & Stylin' Out* 165 Nonactivity on the street corner is 'laying dead', besides the more conventional 'hanging'. **1990** *Los Angeles Times* 22 May (Ventura County ed.) B1/3 According to transcripts of the conversation,..he was 'laying dead for Holmes' in the Courthouse parking lot, armed with a gun.

[**VIII.**] **50. lay back.** *intr.* To lean back, recline; freq. *fig.,* to do nothing, relax (in some later quots. prob. a back-formation f. *laid-back* s.v. LAID *ppl. a.* c). Cf. *lie back* s.v. LIE *v.*[1] 20.

1860 W. COLLINS *Woman in White* I. 67/1 He lay back in the chair, the whole time I was speaking, with his eyes closed. When I had done he opened them indolently. **1884** *Virginia* (Nevada) *Chron.* 1 Oct. 3/3 Old Bill..just lays back until there is a good jack-pot of trout in hand, and then he makes a bold bluff and walks off with it. **1920** E. POUND *Let.* 11 Sept. (1971) 157 You lay back, you let me have the whole stinking sweat of providing the mechanical means for letting through the new movement... Then you punk out, cursing me for not being in two places at once. **1956** M. DICKENS *Angel in Corner* x. 198 'Good girl.' He lay back on the pillow. 'That's my girl,' he murmured. **1977** *Rolling Stone* 13 Jan. 51/3 On her second album, Patti Smith lays back, refusing to assert herself. **1984** *Sears Catal. 1985* Spring/Summer 276 When it's time to lay back, recline seat and a flip of the handle changes it to a carriage.

[**52.**] **u.** To record (esp. popular music). *colloq.*

1967 *Melody Maker* 14 Jan. 7 They both have tremendous records out..and they are both laying down some great stuff. **1975** *New Yorker* 21 Apr. 34/1 He just spent six weeks in L.A. laying down the tracks for eight new cuts on an as yet untitled album. **1985** *Internat. Musician* June 79/1 In fact, while laying down four bass parts all requiring different tones I kept the bass DI'd and the results were very pleasing. **1986** *Keyboard Player* Apr. 2/2 He..intends to demonstrate multi-track recording techniques by laying down eight different tracks 'in public'. **1995** *Mojo* Feb. 104/3 They went to it with a collective will and lay down a very energetic, likeable collection of funk tracks.

[**54.**] **o.** *Basketball.* To bounce (the ball) off the backboard into the basket. Cf. *LAY-IN n.

1976 J. SCOTT *Bill Walton* iii. 111 Silas grabs the ball and lays it in, making it 4–0 Denver. **1987** *New Yorker* 19 Jan. 28 Twice, she stole the ball beneath her own basket and raced coast-to-coast to lay it in.

[**55.**] **k.** *Football, Hockey,* etc. To pass (the ball) a short distance, esp. into open space for a team-mate to collect.

1965 *Daily Express* 13 Aug. 15/5 *Laying off,* playing the ball at one of your team-mates—almost bouncing it off him to get the ball back again. **1966** J. GREAVES *Soccer Techniques* vi. 46 More and more we find that the ball must be passed straight to the feet of team-mates. Of course, if a man who receives such a pass lays the ball off first-time in an imaginative way it may be that he will be able to play it into an open space and let someone sprint on to it. **1970** *Observer* 19 Apr. 23/2 England were laying it off well but too slowly and the linkmen failed to break through often enough. **1976** *Northumberland Gaz.* 26 Nov. 19/4 Ross Mathie.. rounded the 'keeper and laid the ball off for the waiting Laing. **1986** *Open Rugby* Sept. 16/3 Both are deceptively fast, difficult to tackle and lay the ball off well.

[**56.**] **m.** *Angling.* To lower (a weight or shot) into the water until it rests on the bottom with the hook and bait. Freq. *absol.*

1934 E. MARSHALL-HARDY *Angling Ways* xiv. 105 The illustration shows two methods of adjusting the tackle for stret-pegging or laying-on. **1959** *Times* 7 Feb. 9/3, I do not suggest that coarse fishermen should 'lay on' with small roach to catch bigger fish. **1975** *Coarse Fishing* ('Know the Game' Ser.) 29/1 If they [*sc.* the fish] are feeding confidently,..the shot can be laid on. **1991** *Coarse Fishing* Feb. 10/3 My set up was a bristle pole float, overshotted, so I could lay on and hold it perfectly still.

[**58.**] **d.** *intr.* = *lie over* s.v. LIE *v.*[1] 28 d. *U. S. colloq.*

1817 *Indiana Hist. Soc. Publ.* (1918) VI. 296 We concluded to put up for the night and to lay over the Sabbath. **1872** 'MARK TWAIN' *Roughing It* ii. 28 You git out at Cottonwood..and lay over a couple o' days. **1922** R. LARDNER in *Cosmopolitan* July 59/2 Our train laid over in Washington two hours till another train come along to pick us up and I got out and strolled up the platform and into the Union Station. **1956** B. HOLIDAY *Lady sings Blues* (1973) xvii. 140 The Treasury agent fixed it so I'd arrive at the Philly jail on Friday night and have to lay over in that hellhole until Monday. **1986** *New Yorker* 26 May 62/3 One pilot..clipped part of a wingtip, and had to lay over while it was fixed.

[**IX.**] [**62.**] **lay-down**, (*c*) (as *n.*) an act of lying down, a rest; = *lie-down* s.v. LIE *n.*[2] 6; also *iron.*, a short stay in custody.

1897 *National Police Gaz.* (U.S.) 26 May 6/3 Nothing but 'dub' fights by novices, with now and then a deliberate 'lay down'. **1909** E. WYRALL *Spike* vi. 44 In tramp language, it was at least a decent 'lay down' — *i.e.*, bed. **1937** D. L. SAYERS *Busman's Honeymoon* vi. 137 What you want is a nice lay-down and a cupper tea. **1938** F. D. SHARPE *Sharpe of Flying Squad* 331 *A lay down*, a remand in custody. **1941** V. DAVIS *Phenomena in Crime* xix. 249 Joe..is remanded in Brixton Prison. A remand is called the 'lay-down'. **1984** *Police Rev.* 23 Mar. 584/1 Time spent in prison often begins with a 'laydown', a short spell on remand.

lay-away, *n.* Add: [**2.**] **b.** *concr.* (An item of) merchandise that has been reserved for a customer who has paid a deposit.

1974 *State* (Columbia, S. Carolina) 15 Feb. 11-B/2 (Advt.), Unclaimed layaway...Includes 2pc. black vinyl tuxedo sofa and chair. **1976** *National Observer* (U.S.) 23 Oct. 10/5 Under a headline of 'False Advertising is Stealing', the ads advise consumers to be chary of familiar phrases such as 'Unclaimed layaway', 'Going out of business', [etc.]. **1977** *Washington Post* 1 July D9/5 Only supervisory personnel was on hand to take care of layaways and alterations. **1988** *N.Y. Times* 21 Feb. XI. 21/1 Layaways can be held for two weeks, but with no exchanges or credits.

laybacking ('leɪbækɪŋ), *vbl. n. Mountaineering.* [f. LAY-BACK *n.* + -ING[1].] The climbing of a crack by means of a lay-back.

1955 R. W. CLARK *Come climbing with Me* vi. 84 Peter had his first practice at lay-backing, but a short while at it was enough to tire his wrists. **1965** A. BLACKSHAW *Mountaineering* vi. 178 Many of the best climbers nowadays jam where laybacking was formerly thought to be essential. **1972** D. HASTON *In High Places* ii. 20 The crux involves lay-backing and right hand pulling. Laybacking is hard work even with two good arms — it involves going up a corner crack with hands pulling against the edge of the crack and feet braced against the main wall. **1987** *Climber* Mar. 15/2 Our last contribution was a shorter fall left of Umbrella Fall..capped by a wind-twisted ice hood which was passed by laybacking and jamming between icicles.

Hence (as a back-formation) '**layback** *v. intr.*

1972 D. HASTON *In High Places* v. 67 We decided to climb on the extreme right,..laybacking up the edge. **1974** J. CURRAN *K2* (1989) I. vi. 82 The previous day Aid had reclimbed the fixed ropes to the high point, often laybacking on them to pull them clear, and had managed to fix one more rope-length to 7400 metres.

laybarge ('leɪbɑːdʒ), *n. Oil Industry.* Also as two words. [f. LAY *v.*[1] + BARGE *n.*[1]] A specialized barge used for laying underwater pipelines, such as those used in the oil and gas industries; a pipe-laying barge.

1956 *Pipe Line Industry* Dec. 20/1 Submarine pipe lines of the future may be given a quick, 'one-course', application of a combination weight-and-protective coating — applied continuously aboard the lay barge, in an on-line application. **1966** *Pipes & Pipelines Internat.* July 30/2 These measured stresses could be fed to a computerised controller on the laybarge to indicate quickly which corrective action should be taken to ensure proper laying of the pipeline. **1975** *Offshore Progress — Technol. & Costs* (Shell Briefing Service) 15 Huge semi-submersible laybarges have been built to permit continuous pipelaying operations, even in bad weather. **1985** A. C. PALMER in R. F. de la Mare *Adv. Offshore Oil & Gas Pipeline Technol.* vii. 87 If the pipeline is constructed by the laybarge method,..the pipe joints are loaded onto supply vessels and shipped to the barge, where they are unloaded by cranes onto racks. **1992** *Marine Engineers Rev.* Nov. 57/1 The deepwater section of the line was installed by laybarge *DLB-423*.

lay-day, *n.* Add: **2.** *Sailing.* A day in which a boat is delayed in port (usu. because of bad weather, or so that the crew may rest).

1934 WEBSTER, *Lay day*,..a day of delay in port. **1958** STONE & TAYLOR *America's Cup Races* xviii. 215 The committee declared the next day a lay day..to give both crews a needed rest. **1962** *Times* 15 Sept. 3/3 Either skipper..may ask for a lay-day before the next start. **1976** *Yachts & Yachting* 20 Aug. 374/2 The weather even obliged on Thursday's lay-day with a flat, oily calm. **1988** *Seahorse* Sept-Oct. 21/1 The seven race series is held over nine days with two laydays in mid regatta to give sailors some extra breathing space.

layer, *n.* Add: [**III.**] [**5.**] **layer cut** *v. trans.*, to cut (hair) in overlapping layers; hence as *n.*, a haircut done in this way.

1964 *Hairdo* June 65 (*caption*) The hair is one length except for the nape, which is *layer-cut. **1966** J. S. COX *Illustr. Dict. Hairdressing* 89/1 *Layer cut*,..hair cut in layers so that they overlap like roof shingles or fish scales. **1980** *Hair* Autumn 7 Rather than one length hair, he expects to see it layer cut as well. **1987** *New Yorker* 23 Mar. 96/3 His blond hair growing naturally in a thick layer cut.

layer dressing *Fashion*, the wearing of layers of clothes of varying lengths such that one layer shows beneath the next.

1975 *Times* 7 Oct. 11/1 The whole idea of *layer dressing was invented by America's Bonnie Cashin.

layer, *v.* Add: **4.** To cut (hair) in layers. Also *absol.*

1963 *Amer. Hairdresser* Jan. 40/1 Hair should be cut in one-inch lengths. Next, layer one or two inches longer up to the crown. **1974** G. MOFFAT *Corpse Road* v. 74 Chestnut hair which..looked as if it had been layered by Steiner. **1984** J. UPDIKE *Witches of Eastwick* ii. 188 'Wet hair is really the problem, this time of year.'.. 'I'm thinking of getting mine layered.' **1988** *Hairflair* Feb. 28 (*caption*) This versatile style has been layered throughout and dressed away from the face in a quiff shape. **1995** *Hair* Apr.-May 76/1 (*caption*) Above: Gamine crop has been softly layered and gelled over to one side.

layered, *ppl. a.* Add: **2.** *Fashion.* **a.** Applied to the look achieved by layer dressing (see *LAYER *n.* 5), and later also to clothes worn in this way. **b.** Of hair: cut in layers (see *LAYER *v.* 4).

1962 *Fashion Digest* Fall/Winter 9 The look is layered... Skirt or pants, heavy shirt, bulky sleeved or sleeveless sweater, fishermen's sweaters, to mix or match liberally. **1963** *Glamour* Feb. 129 This is an ideal style for naturally curly or wavy hair...Though it's layered, it still looks very soft. **1968** *N.Y. Times* 21 June 26/4 Overwhelming enthusiasm was registered by the judges for the award to Miss Cashin..who designs for Sills & Co...for..her enduring affection for the concept of layered clothing. **1974** *Country Life* 23 May 1316/1 A shirt over a high-necked sweater, an idea..now called 'layered' dressing. **1978** *Detroit Free Press* 5 Mar. (Spring Fashion Suppl.) (*caption*) A layered skirt. **1984** M. PIERCY *Fly away Home* xii. 160 She made fun of Annette's new layered hairdo. **1991** *Hair Styling* Feb. 26/2 (*caption*) A soft silhouette of curl is created with a gently layered crown and the fingers to fluff hair into place.

layering, *vbl. n.* Sense in Dict. becomes 2. Add: **1.** *Gardening.* The method or activity of propagation by layers (see LAYER *v.* 1).
   1703 tr. H. *van Oosten's Dutch Gardener* IV. i. 201 The right way of layring is done with a small Knife...Make a cut in the middle of a Joint, as close to the Plant as you can possibly. **1796** W. H. MARSHALL *Planting* I. 22 The time of layering is generally autumn. **1842** J. C. LOUDON *Suburban Horticulturist* II. iii. 273 The state of the plant most favourable for layering is the same as that most suitable for propagation by cuttings. **1934** W. BRETT *Pictorial Gardening* xx. 132/2 Practically all kinds of shrubs..can be propagated by layering. **1982** G. DAISLEY *Illustr. Bk. Herbs* 96/1 They [*sc.* lemon-scented geraniums] can also be rooted successfully by layering.
   3. *Fashion.* The cutting of hair in layers (see *LAYER *v.* 4). Also, = *layer dressing* s.v. *LAYER *n.* 5.
   1966 S. Cox *Illustr. Dict. Hairdressing* 89/1 *Layering*, see layer cut. **1971** *Sunday Times* 15 Aug. 23/1 Layerings won her [*sc.* Bonnie Cashin] a Nieman-Marcus Award in 1950, the year of her first collection in New York. **1975** *N.Y. Times* 16 Sept. 36 What makes the layering plausible is that clothes are increasingly unstructured and pliable. **1980** *Hair* Autumn 9 Concave and convex cutting, layering and precise razoring are being incorporated to add softness and body in new styles. **1993** *Guardian* 14 Oct. II. 3/1 Layering is a fine idea if artfully down, but Lacroix's heavily constructed and decorated garments don't lend themselves to the device.

layflat ('leiflæt), *a.* (*n.*) Also with hyphen and as two words. [f. LAY *v.*[1] + FLAT *a.*, *adv.*, and *n.*[3]] That lies flat, or can be laid flat; flattened, not cylindrical in cross-section; esp. designating tubing of this kind. Also as *n.*, something which can be laid flat.
   1957 *Farm & Home Sci.* Sept. 68/1 Tests with lay-flat tubing for conveying and distributing water were begun at Logan about ten years ago. **1967** *Gloss. Terms Plastics Industry* (*B.S.I.*) I. 17 *Layflat tube*, tubular film flattened in the process of manufacture, commonly supplied in roll form. **1976** B. GIBSON *Birmingham Bombs* vii. 56 Some pieces of 'layflat' flex. **1977** *Jrnl. R. Soc. Arts* CXXV. 565/2 Many ways of applying water and nutrients have been developed...Trickle and spaghetti drips, layflat, rigid and ooze tubes, all have their places. **1982** *Diytrade* May/June 36/1 InHome Ltd..has launched its first major product, Cassette Hose..a lay flat hose which, like a fireman's hose can be rolled up flat (the water being squeezed out in the process). **1986** *Short Wave Mag.* Dec. 394/1 Radio amateurs..love nothing more than taking things to bits—not easy nowadays with layflat components and integrated circuits. **1989** *Plastics World* Aug. 59/2 NDC markets a gamma backscatter nuclear gauge that can be mounted on either the collapsing frame or at the edge of the layflat.

laygear ('leigiə(r)), *n. Engin.* [f. LAY(SHAFT *n.* + GEAR *n.*] The set of gearwheels on a layshaft. Also *laygear cluster.*
   1947 *Brit. Repair Man.* II (Austin section) 27/2 To remove third motion shaft it will first be necessary to free it from the laygear. **1952** A. W. JUDGE *Mod. Motor Engineer* (ed. 5) II. xi. 440 Before the end cover can be removed from the gearbox, complete with the third motion shaft..and its gears, the laygear must be

dropped out of mesh. *Ibid.*, The laygear cluster and the thrust washers can be retained in their correct positions by following the layshaft through with a thin rod. **1962** *Engineering* 23 Feb. 285/2 To prepare Austin motor laygears for gear cutting. **1972** K. BALL *Fiat 1300, 1500 Autobook* 150 The laygear is driven by the first motion shaft and drives the third motion shaft according to the gear selected. **1979** *Motorcycling Manual* (Motorcycling Monthly) 53 (*caption*) Next comes the laygear cluster.

lay-in ('leiin), *n. Basketball.* [f. *to lay in*: see *LAY *v.*[1] 54 0.] A shot made at the top of a jump, usu. by bouncing the ball off the backboard into the basket.
   1951 *Oregonian* 17 Jan. III. 2/1 Strader..dribbled at break-neck speed..to flip in a nifty lay-in shot. **1961** J. GARDNER *Championship Basketball* v. 79 Players should not always expect to get a lay-in on the fast break. **1970** *San Francisco Chron.* 12 Mar. 51/8 Both teams..fighting nose to nose through the second half and two extras before two driving layins by Jeff Mullins. **1976** W. W. BRADLEY *Life on Run* vi. 82 After the lay-ins, the team starts individual warm-up shots. **1978** *Detroit Free Press* 5 Mar. C4/2 Giddings scored on two driving lay-ins by Giddings and backdoor lay-ups by Paxson. **1992** *N.Y. Times* B7/5 The Nets were up by only 122-120 when Johnson drove in for what looked like an easy lay-in to tie the score.

Laysan (lei'zɑ:n, -'zæn), *n. Ornith.* [Place name.] Used *attrib.* in the name of various birds found on Laysan, an island in the Hawaiian archipelago, as **Laysan albatross**, the albatross *Diomedea immutabilis* of the northern Pacific; **Laysan duck** = *Laysan teal* below; **Laysan finch**, the Hawaiian honeycreeper *Telespyza cantans*, a large finch-like bird noted for its song; **Laysan rail**, the extinct rail *Porzanula palmeri*; **Laysan teal**, a mallard of the subspecies *Anas platyrhynchos laysanensis.*
   1893 W. ROTHSCHILD *Avifauna of Laysan* I. 7 *Telespiza flavissima*, *Rothsch.* Yellow Laysan finch. *Ibid.* 19 *Anas laysanensis*, *Rothsch.* Laysan teal. [**1902** H. W. HENSHAW *Birds Hawaiian Islands* 98 Porzanula palmeri...Laysan crake. This little rail is very abundant on..Laysan.] **1903** *Auk* XX. 386 The Bonin Petrels..may be mentioned as exceeding even the Laysan Albatross in numbers. *Ibid.* 392 The Laysan Rail is a wide-awake, inquisitive little creature. **1945** *Audubon Mag.* XLVII. 343/2 The Laysan rail, has now suffered a fate from which there is no return. **1961** R. T. PETERSON *Field Guide Western Birds* (ed. 2) 276 Laysan Finch..was introduced on Midway but disappeared about 1944. **1962** R. S. PALMER *Handbk. N. Amer. Birds* I. 130 The world population of the Laysan Albatross, in 1957-58 season, was estimated at 1,500,000. **1973** *Sci. Amer.* June 40/1 The birds are..the Laysan duck, the Hawaiian duck, [etc.]. **1992** *Buzzworm* Nov.-Dec. 61/1 The burr is displacing the native bunchgrass, which is the preferred nesting habitat of the Laysan teal, one of the world's rarest birds.

lazy, *a.* Add: **[4.]** **lazy eight**, an aerobatic manoeuvre in which an aircraft executes an S-shaped path which, when viewed laterally, resembles a figure 8 lying on its side.
   1930 R. DUNCAN *Stunt Flying* 138 *Lazy 8's.* **1943** D. J. BRIMM *Air Acrobatics are Easy* iii. 66 There should be no approach to a stall in the lazy eight, and in the recovery or second half of the loop there is much less of the diving turn than in the recovery from the wingover. **1986** *New Yorker* 26 May 51/3 The instructor..taught him more advanced maneuvers—chandelles,..and lazy-eights.
   lazy eye (*a*) (see sense 2 b above); (*b*) the condition of having a lazy eye, amblyopia.
   1960 D. VAUGHAN et al. *Gen. Ophthalm.* (ed. 2) xxi. 333 (*heading*) Amblyopia ex anopsia (*lazy eye). **1975**

H. JOLLY *Bk. Child Care* xxxiv. 432 Because squint can be so dangerous I dislike the expression 'lazy eye' which is commonly used to describe it. **1987** *Oxf. Times* 15 May 2/4 His work is essential for the treatment of Amblyopia—commonly known as lazy eye—which affects more than one in 20 of the population.

lazy-jack, (*b*) *Naut.*, each of several light ropes on either side of a sail, placed so as to allow it to be gathered in easily.
1901 T. F. DAY *On Yachts* 167 *Lazy jacks are useful on cruising boats, especially if you are sailing short-handed, but they are a nuisance when reefing. **1984** *Pract. Boat Owner* Feb. 42/3 Notably efficient are the lazy jacks, which not only hold the boom steady on the moorings, but catch the sail and gaff—when you lower peak and throat halyards—as it slides down the mast. **1994** *Canad. Yachting* Summer 20/1 Full-length battens are helpful if you intend to instal lazy jacks.

leachable, *a.* Add: Hence **leacha'bility** *n.*, susceptibility to leaching.
1960 tr. *Wks. V. G. Khlopin Radium Inst.* (U.S. Atomic Energy Comm.) VI. 123 It was established by experiments set up to study the leachability of radioelements from minerals that the isotopes of thorium (Th, RdTh) and radium (ThX) behave differently. **1962** *Geochim. et Cosmochim. Acta* XXVI. 1137 In an effort to determine the possible sites of thorium and uranium in the samples, a study of their leachability in hot 2N hydrochloric acid was undertaken. **1983** *Current Affairs Bull.* Dec. 30/1 The significant geochemical advantage of Synroc over the major alternative, glass, is its lower leachability rate under realistic geological conditions. **1994** *Northern Miner* 3 Oct. 2/4 Gold mineralization is fine-grained (less than 150 mesh), and bottle-roll cyanide leachability analyses returned recoveries of more than 90% within two to six hours.

lead, *n.*[1] Add: [II.] [12.] [b.] *lead chromate*.
1866 H. E. ROSCOE *Lessons Elem. Chem.* xxiv. 214 Lead chromate is a yellow insoluble salt. **1962** J. R. PARTINGTON *Hist. Chem.* III. iii. 105 Collet-Descotils examined a lead ore . . in which del Río claimed to have discovered a new metal . . which was really vanadium . . , but Collet-Descotils reported that it was only basic lead chromate.

lead, *n.*[2] Senses 2 b–d in Dict. become 2 c–e. Add: [2.] **b.** The extent to which something or someone is leading (in a race or other contest); an advantage or 'edge' *on* or *over* an opponent, rival, etc.
1868 H. WOODRUFF *Trotting Horse Amer.* xxiv. 207, I passed first one and then the other, and came on the home-stretch with a clear lead. **1894** *Outing* XXIV. 36/2 The 'Una' turned the weather-mark with a lead of nearly half an hour. **1926** *Westm. Gaz.* 20 July 1/4 The Whip . . continues to hold a strong lead in Naps over the selections of the other racing critics. **1949** 'G. ORWELL' *Nineteen Eighty-Four* II. ix. 195 None of the three super-states ever gains a significant lead on the others. **1967** *Boston Herald* 1 Apr. 17/7 Harris built up an early lead over the baffled 29-year-old veteran. **1976** LD. HOME *Way Wind Blows* xii. 168 Today's superiority of the Warsaw Pact is in personnel roughly 3–1, and Russia's lead in numbers of tanks and aircraft is such that the allies are on the margin of safety. **1991** *Cycling Weekly* 27 July 3/2 Yellow jersey Miguel Indurain still held the three minutes lead which he took by finishing second in last Friday's epic Pyrenean stage.

[10.] **g.** *Railways.* The distance from the tip of the blade of a set of points to the point where one rail crosses another, usu. measured along the straight track; the section of track so measured.
1871 W. DONALDSON *Switches & Crossings* v. 131 The value of the circular measure of the angle of a crossing is expressed by a fraction whose numerator is unity. The value of the denominator will be sufficiently exact if it be put equal to the nearest integer if the lead of the crossing is long, or to the nearest half integer if

the lead is short. **1890** W. H. COLE *Notes on Permanent-Way Material* iii. 69 Some platelayers have an idea that they can make a crossing easier by lengthening the lead. **1908** W. G. RAYMOND *Elem. Railroad Engin.* II. vii. 82 The distance from head-block to the point of frog, measured by some makers along the straight rail and by others along the curved rail, is called the lead. Probably, technically, the distance along the curved rail is the lead, and the distance along the straight rail would better be known as the frog distance. **1920** PERROTT & BADGER *Pract. Railway Surveying* xii. 212 The length of a 'lead' is usually understood to be the length from the toe of the points to the splice of the V-crossing. **1953** W. W. HAY *Railroad Engin.* I. xxvii. 438 Turnouts are designed on the basis of the frog angle (or number), the length of point, and the degree of turnout curve. These, in turn, give rise to an overall dimension, the lead. **1971** D. H. COOMBS *Brit. Railway Track* (ed. 4) iii. 132 Switches and common crossings may be combined to give turnouts of varying leads and radii. With the introduction of curved switches, the range of available leads is much increased.

h. *Mech.* The axial distance travelled by a screw thread in one revolution. Cf. PITCH *n.*[2] 25 b.
1905 J. HORNER *Engineers' Turning* xiv. 266 A problem which arises more frequently now than formerly is that of cutting threads of steep pitch, or lead, for multiple-threaded worms. **1913** E. PULL *Screw Cutting for Engineers* i. 4 Lead is a term generally used when referring to multiple threads, and is the distance a nut would travel in one revolution, or the distance between the centre of one thread and the centre of the same thread allowing for one complete turn. **1936** COLVIN & STANLEY *Turning & Boring Pract.* v. 55 A double thread has a lead twice the pitch, a triple screw three times, and so on. **1967** J. H. POTTER *Handbk. Engin. Sci.* II. xiii. 1043 For a multiple-threaded screw, the lead is $l = np$, where n is the number of threads [and p = pitch]. **1991** *What's New in Design* Sept. 50/1 SX screws are available in lead precision classes G5, G6, G7 and G9 and with leads of 5, 10 or 20 to give ten diameter/lead combinations.

lead, *v.*[1] Sense 2 h in Dict. becomes 2 i. Add: [I.] [2.] **h.** *Boxing.* To make an attacking punch; to make the first of a series of punches. Freq. const. *with.* Cf. LEAD *n.*[2] 5 c.
1895 T. ROOSEVELT *Works* (1926) XIV. 205 If you are going to 'lead freely' you have got to 'take punishment', if you will allow me to speak in the language of those who box. **1927** D. HAMMETT in *Black Mask* Feb. 28/1 A paluka who leads with his right. **1935** *Encycl. Sports* 105/1 When a beginner is directed by his instructor to lead to the body, it is no use his aiming a blow at his antagonist's chest. **1952** *Amat. Boxing* ('Know the Game' Ser.) 16/1 As he leads, parry his right towards your right with the left and then lead with a right swing to head or body.

[5.] **b.** *Law.* To ask (a witness) leading questions. Cf. sense 20 a below. Chiefly *U. S.*
1833 A. ALISON *Practice Criminal Law Scotl.* xiii. 545 Witnesses are to be examined without being led. **1899** *Southwestern Reporter* (U.S.) L. 124/1 It . . enables the examiner to lead even an honest witness in such manner as to give to the testimony a false color. **1973** *Times* 17 Oct. 20/3 The police sergeant . . was . . slapped down by the clerk of the court for leading his witnesses. **1983** *Southern Reporter* (U.S.) CDXXXVI. 479/1 Ordinarily, leading questions are permitted on cross-examination, and the rule against leading one's own witness is relaxed.

[III.] [13.] **c.** *trans. Sport.* To be ahead of (another team or player) in terms of points, goals, etc. Usu. const. *by.* Also *transf.*, to exceed or outnumber *by* a specified margin.
1877 *Spirit of Times* 24 Nov. 449/2 At 800 yards the Massachusetts men held steadily, Wemyss leading with 71, Jackson and Law 70. **1907** C. E. MULFORD *Bar-20* xi. 120 In this contest Hopalong Cassidy led his

nearest rival.. by twenty cut-outs. **1946** *Times* 26 June 2/3 The Dutch pair, after missing a set point when leading by six games to five, finally secured the first set at 9-7. **1979** *Amer. Speech* LIV. 73 In another study.. *will* led *shall* in frequency of occurrence by only 59 percent to 41 percent. **1989** *Daily Tel.* 6 July 35 (*heading*) Northants, with seven wickets standing, lead Kent by 90 runs.

d. *intr.* Of a newspaper or other journalistic media: to use a particular item as the main story. Const. †*upon, with.*

1907 *Daily Chron.* 5 Mar. 6/7 The case was of an entrancing subtlety;.. and every newspaper 'led' upon the result. **1986** *Times* 23 July 16/6 For Princess Margaret's wedding *The Times*, under a notoriously uncourtierly editor, did not even lead with the story. **1990** A. GORDON *Safe at Home* iii. 14 There was nothing about the latest murder, which had been discovered after the morning edition deadline, but the 7:00 CBC Radio news led with it.

leader, *n.*[1] Add: [**II.**] [**8.**] **d.** *Comm.* A share that is leading the movement of prices on a stock exchange; more generally, a leading economic indicator.

1938 *New Statesman* 30 Apr. 750/1 Oil shares were banged in the 'Street' on Tuesday night, the leaders falling by about 5s. **1965** *Financial Times* 2 Jan. 1 (*in figure*) Leaders and Laggards. Percentage Change in 1964. **1971** WEBSTER *Add.*, Leader,.. an economic indicator.. that more often than not shows a change in direction before a corresponding change in the state of the economy. **1976** *Liverpool Echo* 7 Dec. 18/1 Leaders edged forward, but most had to struggle to hold the higher positions. **1990** *European Investor* May 35/1 For the moment, we believe it is safe to stay with the leaders with high earnings visibility such as AIB, CRH and FII-Fyffes.

leaderene (ˌliːdəˈriːn), *n.* Also **leaderine.** [f. LEADER *n.*[1] + *-ene,* perh. by analogy with F. *speakerine.* For spelling cf. the fem. names *Irene, Marlene,* etc.] Orig., a jocular or ironic name for Margaret Thatcher (see THATCHERITE *n.* and *a.*) while Leader of the Opposition and Prime Minister; hence *gen.,* any female leader, *esp.* a formidable one.

1980 *Times* 20 Aug. 12/6 The conchology expedition led by Mrs Smythe yielded 41 species in 90 minutes. The anonymous author of the field report.. respectfully supplies the leaderene with an 'Ms' for the occasion. **1980** *Private Eye* 26 Sept. 5/1 The Leaderene is devastatingly impressed by her new recruit, we were told. **1982** M. STOCKWOOD *Chanctonbury Ring* iii. 47 The leaderene of the Grandmothers' Union. **1985** *Daily Tel.* 19 Jan. 10/6 A new leaderene selected to add glamour to the management. **1987** *Private Eye* 29 May 8/3 In Finchley Central, part of the glorious leaderene's own constituency, there is only one policeman on patrol during the wee small hours. **1990** *Times Educ. Suppl.* 28 Dec. 5/4 Most shocking of all, at least for the sophisticated dons of Rouen University, was the demise of our great leaderene, Margaret Thatcher.

leaf, *n.*[1] Senses 17, 18 in Dict. become 18, 19. Add: [**II.**] [**10.**] **d.** *Building.* A continuous upright structure forming one layer of a cavity wall (or a wall in its own right).

1938 R. FITZMAURICE *Princ. Mod. Building* I. iii. 160 The weakness of cavity construction lies in the possibility that carelessness or accident may result in material being dropped into the cavity which may form a bridge across which water is transmitted to the inner leaf. **1949** D. NIELD *Walls & Wall Facings* II. iii. 145 Cavity walls.. are being increasingly built with hollow blocks or other material in place of bricks for the internal leaf. **1958** *House & Garden* Feb. 69/1 The cavity walls have an outer leaf of yellow-buff bricks. **1983** J. S. FOSTER *Struct. & Fabric* (rev. ed.) I. iii. 86/2 Without

bridging of any kind capable of transferring moisture to the inner leaf. **1986** *Do It Yourself* June 22/1 The walls are built with two 4in. solid concrete block leaves, 6in. apart, and the cavity is filled with 1:2:4 concrete. **1991** *New Civil Engineer* 3 Oct. 68/3 (Advt.), Single leaf wall with vertical and lateral load.

17. *Math.* and *Computing.* = *leaf node,* sense 19 below.

1968 D. E. KNUTH *Art of Computer Programming* I. ii. 305 A node of degree zero is called a terminal node or sometimes a 'leaf'. **1970** O. DOPPING *Computers & Data Processing* xxii. 359 Our decision tree.. has four branches... At the third level, each branch splits in two, and at the fourth level, where the 'leaves' are, there is no ramification at all. **1973** C. W. GEAR *Introd. Computer Sci.* vii. 282 The pointers from one node to another are called branches, while the nodes with no pointers leaving them are called terminal nodes (or leaves). **1979** PAGE & WILSON *Introd. Computational Combinatorics* vi. 133 In a general problem there could be different numbers of branches emerging from each node as well as different numbers of levels before the terminal nodes (the 'leaves') are reached which correspond to the possible complete vectors. **1992** *Dr. Dobb's Jrnl.* Jan. 44/1 Unlike a binary tree, a B-tree is a balanced tree structure. Every leaf is at the same distance from the root.

[**III.**] [**18.**] [**a.**] *leaf-area.*

1966 *Proc. 16th Alaska Sci. Conf., 1965* 26 (*heading*) A photoelectric device for measuring *leaf area.* **1981** *Southern Horticulture* (N.Z.) Spring 26/1 Root number and leaf number, and root length and leaf area, are related. **1991** *New Scientist* 21 Sept. 42/1 A rainforest's leaf area index—the total area of leaves above each square metre of forest floor—can reach 8.

leaf-wrapping.

[**1918** J. LONDON *Red One* 10 A roasted pig that steamed its essence deliciously through its green-leaf wrappings.] **1954** J. R. R. TOLKIEN *Fellowship of Ring* II. viii. 386 The cakes will keep sweet.. if they are.. left in their *leaf-wrappings.* **1992** M. MARGETTS *Classic Crafts* 110/1 There is *Banon* from Provence, a festive-looking cheese, with its sweet-chestnut leaf wrapping and tie.

[**c.**] *leaf-wrapped.*

1972 K. LO *Chinese Food* I. 59 In China in the summer.. Lotus *Leaf-wrapped Rice is a popular snack everywhere. **1985** *N.Y. Times* 14 Apr. x. 17/2 Fortified by a snack of crackers and queso de oja—leaf-wrapped mild, white cheese—the group walks toward the central plaza.

[**19.**] **leaf beet** *Hort.,* any of several varieties of beet cultivated for their leaves, *esp.* the spinach-beet.

1842 J. C. LOUDON *Suburban Horticulturist* 658 The spinach beet, *leaf beet, or white beet, Bèta cicla,.. a native of the sea-shores of Spain and Portugal. **1890** *Jrnl. R. Hort. Soc.* XII. 97 Of these Leaf Beets.. the Chilian is a very ornamental plant, producing broad fleshy leaf stalks... The Green, or Spinach Beet is quite a different plant. **1985** *Gardening from 'Which?'* Dec. 401/4 Members found.. leaf beet (perpetual spinach) easiest to grow.

leaf freak *U.S. colloq.,* an enthusiastic 'leaf peeper' (see below).

1974 *Time* 11 Nov. 92/1 The traffic is so bad along the Mohawk Trail that they had to bring out Indians to entertain all the *leaf freaks sitting in their cars with nothing to do. **1980** *N.Y. Times* 2 Nov. xxi. 22/3 Travel agencies have, no doubt, established tours to Craftsbury Common, Vt., [etc.].. to help those citybound 'leaf freaks' find their ultimate dream.

leaf-hopper, substitute for def.: any insect of the family Cicadellidae, which comprises small leaping homopterous insects that suck liquid from leaves and often spread plant diseases.

1841 T. W. HARRIS *Rep. Insects of Mass. Injurious to Vegetation* 183 The Tettigonians, or leaf-hoppers, have the head and thorax somewhat like those of frog-hoppers, but their bodies are, in general, proportionately longer. **1920** *Edin. Rev.* Oct. 338 The homopterous hosts are leaf-hoppers and other small insects (allied to cicads). **1972** SWAN & PAPP *Common Insects N. Amer.* xiii. 137 The Cicadellidae, or leafhoppers, comprise a large family of small, slender insects with short bristle-like antennae, and usually two ocelli. **1989** *Antenna* XIII. 134/2 Biological control now faces a new wave of challenges—western flower thrips, serpentine leaf-miner, and insecticide-resistant strains of aphids, leaf-hoppers and mealybug. **1989** *Sun* (Brisbane) 6 Jan. 27/4 The disease is spread by a small leafhopper.

leaf-litter *Bot.* and *Hort.*, litter (*LITTER *n.* 4 b) consisting primarily of leaf fragments.
1870 A. MONGREDIEN *Trees & Shrubs Eng. Plantations* viii. 316 Some leaf-litter or strawy manure placed over the stool of the plant will easily maintain its vitality during frosty weather. **1987** *Jrnl. Environmental Managem.* July 67/1 With its characteristically high tree density and possibly its relatively high foliage cover in its first 5-15 years, a high production of leaf litter is encouraged. **1989** *Landscape Design* June 27/1 Tons of leaf litter and road sweepings.. are delivered each Autumn.

leaf node *Math.* and *Computing*, a node or vertex of a tree which has only one connection to another node; a terminal node.
1980 *Information Processing Lett.* XI. 126/1 Now p must lie in the interior of a six-dimensional convex region defined by some *leaf node of the linear decision tree. **1986** D. DEUTSCH in T. C. Bartee *Digital Communications* v. 215 The object to be named is represented by a leaf node. **1990** WALL & SCHWARTZ *Programming Perl* ii. 55 Note that a recursive subroutine must have some means of distinguishing when it has reached a so-called 'leaf-node'.

leaf peeper *U.S. colloq.*, a person, esp. a tourist, who indulges in 'leaf peeping'.
1979 *United States 1980/81* (Penguin Travel Guides) 576 It's also popular with hikers, 'leaf peepers' hooked on the fall foliage. **1987** *Economist* 3 Oct. 43/1 Each autumn, northern New England draws thousands of 'leaf-peepers' to gape at the ravishing colours of the changing trees. **1991** *Sunday Times* 8 Sept. III. 7/2 Active leaf peepers could follow the fall all the way from Maine to Georgia.

leaf peeping *U.S. colloq.*, the popular activity of observing the spectacular colours of autumn foliage, esp. that of New England.
1979 *United States 1980/81* (Penguin Travel Guides) 632 The four weeks from mid-September to mid-October are leaf-peeping season, a magic time to be here. **1987** *Los Angeles Times* 9 Oct. I. 32/1 'Leaf peeping' season is about over in northern New Hampshire, and the mountains' spectacular palette of red, yellow and orange has begun to fade.

leaf shutter *Photogr.*, a shutter in which the exposure is controlled by an iris (IRIS *n.* 4 c).
1962 G. G. BATES *35 mm. Cameras* i. 14/1 The leaf or diaphragm shutter, consisting of a number of wafer-thin leaves or blades which overlap to form an opaque barrier to the rays of light. **1979** *Amat. Photogr.* 10 Jan. 61/1 The leaf shutter is incorporated into the camera because of requests from professional photographers who wanted flash sync at all speeds. **1991** *Photo Answers* Aug. 67/3 Leaf shutters.. are mounted between the lens elements and consist of a series of overlapping blades which open and close like an aperture.

leakage, *n.* Add: [**1.**] Also, the passage of radiation, flux, or the like through an intended barrier.
1928 *Science* 23 Nov. 516/2 The leakage of helium through Pyrex glass at elevated temperatures has been noted by various observers. **1938** *S.A.E. Jrnl.* May 36/1 Another method of magnetic testing.. involves the use of Magnaflux in which the parts to be inspected are first longitudinally or circularly magnetized... When properly magnetized, defects result in local flux leakage. Magnaflux powder, being of high magnetic

permeability.. adheres along the lines of flux leakage. **1958** O. R. FRISCH *Nucl. Handbk.* XVI. 32 Certain types of magnet have leakage factors which vary within fairly narrow limits. **1987** *Which?* July 302/1 We check all ovens we test for microwave leakage and have never found one which failed the current British Standard requirements.

leaker ('li:kə(r)), *n.* [f. LEAK *v.* + -ER.] One who discloses secret information or allows it to be disclosed.
1969 *Punch* 12 Feb. 227/3 Guilty leakers have been known to get the sack, but strenuous efforts are usually made to keep this out of the papers. *a***1974** R. CROSSMAN *Diaries* (1976) II. 367 But now I was obviously Harold's suspect as the chief leaker when he called on the Lord Chancellor to put into operation the procedure for leak detection. **1988** *Economist* 12 Mar. 39/2 Lie-detectors.. have also been much used in the Reagan administration to find leakers of information. **1993** D. C. REECE *Rich Broth* vi. 45 This would surely stimulate my unmasking as a master leaker before my thunderstruck boss. In any case the revelations.. would be easily traceable to me.

lean, *a.* and *n.²* Add: [**A.**] [**1.**] f. *Comm.* Of a business, sector of the economy, etc.: rendered more efficient or competitive through the reduction of unnecessary costs or expenditure. Freq. in comparative, esp. in phr. *leaner (and) fitter.*
1983 *Observer* 6 Feb. 20/6 Industry was now leaner and fitter and in a much better position to compete. **1984** *Times* 19 Apr. 20/6 The British Printing & Communications Corporation has.. emerged a stronger yet leaner enterprise. **1986** RICHARDS & MACKENZIE *Railway Station* 32 The use of new materials and new geometric shapes.. implied a lean, fit, up-to-date industry. **1989** *Independent* 30 Oct. 23/3 In 1988, a leaner, fitter Thomson boasted profits of FFr.2.37bn and a pre-eminence in the field of defence systems manufacture and consumer electronics. **1991** *N.Y. Rev. Bks.* 7 Mar. 46/1 In a similar vein, leaner-and-meaner companies tell us they are avidly cutting costs.

[**7.**] **lean-burn** *a.*, designating, pertaining to, or having an engine designed to run on a lean mixture (see sense 4 f above) and so to cause less pollution.
1975 *Chem. Week* 9 Apr. 30/3 Chrysler plans to convert its largest cars to 'lean-burn' engines that don't require catalysts. **1984** *Daily Tel.* 7 Sept. 9/1 In future motor car engines should be based upon 'lean burn' technology. **1985** *Sunday Tel.* 16 June 33/3 Ford has an engine that is lean-burn to a certain degree in the new Granada 1800. **1986** *Autocar* 26 Nov. 78/4 The only truly lean-burn car on sale. **1990** C. ROSE *Dirty Man of Europe* (1991) vi. 172 While lean burn engines produce lower quantities of hydrocarbons and carbon monoxide, they reduce NOx by only about 50 per cent.

lean, *v.¹* Add: [**4.**] [**a.**] *lean to one side*: also used *spec.* (freq. *attrib.*) with reference to Mao Zedong's policy of favouring the Soviet Union over the West in his establishment of diplomatic relations after the Chinese Communist Revolution of 1949.
[**1950** tr. *Mao Tse-Tung's People's Democratic Dictatorship* 11 'You incline to one side.' That is right. The forty years' experience of Sun Yat-sen and the twenty-eight years' experience of the Chinese Communist Party have convinced us that in order to attain victory and consolidate it we must incline to one side... The Chinese people must either incline toward the side of imperialism or toward that of socialism.] **1956** H. WEI tr. Mao-Tse-tung in *China & Soviet Russia* xiii. 264 'You lean to one side.' Exactly. To lean to one side is the lesson taught us by.. the twenty-eight years of experience of the Communist Party. **1960** Z.

K. BREZEZINSKI *Soviet Bloc* vi. 129 Mao Tse-
tung..repeatedly stressed his belief that Chinese
Communists..must pursue a 'lean-to-one-side
policy'. **1971** H. TREVELYAN *Worlds Apart* x. 125
Mao's proclaimed policy was to 'lean to one side',
though he was careful to maintain his balance. **1984**
J. GREEN *Newspeak* 141/1 Prior to 1960 China traded
almost exclusively with socialist countries, a process
known as *leaning to one side.*

learn, *v.* Add: [I.] [1.] **e.** *learn-to-(read, ski,
swim,* etc.): *attrib. phr.* used of a course of
lessons or step-by-step introduction to a skill,
sport, subject, etc. orig. and chiefly *U. S.*
  1963 *N.Y. Times* 1 Dec. x. 28/3 (Advt.), 'Learn-to-
ski' Weekends. **1965** J. STURM in C. K. Stead *N.Z.
Short Stories* (1966) 216, I..found an easy learn-to-
read little book. **1967** U. SEDGWICK *(title)* My learn-
to-cook book. **1976** *Milton Keynes Express* 11 June
40/7 Newport Pagnell Swimming Club commence
operations..on Tuesday..with learn to swim classes
for youngsters. **1983** *Money* Jan. 78/1 Learn-to-sail
and learn-to-cruise vacations are..offered by boat
chartering concerns. **1990** *Angling Times* 29 Aug. 14/4
The chances of anybody making a success of learn-to-
beachcast weekends and courses is [*sic*] a foregone
conclusion.

learner, *n.* Add: **5.** One who is learning a foreign
language; esp. in **learner's dictionary**, a
dictionary (esp. a monolingual one) designed
for the use of foreign students.
  1948 A. S. HORNBY et al. *(title)* A learner's dictionary
of current English. **1963** —— *Advanced Learner's Dict.
Current Eng.* Pref. p. v, These two books are designed
for learners in the earlier stages of study. **1974** *Times*
27 Mar. 10/1 He [*sc.* Hornby].. started to work on a
new sort of dictionary that would put words into
their context..and..lead the learner gently through
the labyrinthine idiosyncrasies of the English
language. **1984** *EURALEX Bull.* Dec. 8 A working
party..met at the Survey of English Usage, University
College London on 13 June, 1984 to discuss current
research into how learners' dictionaries are used. **1992**
Appl. Linguistics XIII. 25 One of the tasks of second
language researchers and teachers is to discover what
a learner needs to know in order to communicate in
actual social contexts in the setting of the new culture.

learning, *vbl. n.* Add: [4.] **learning set** *Psychol.*,
an ability to solve problems of a particular type
which is acquired through experience of solving
such problems.
  1949 H. F. HARLOW in *Psychol. Rev.* LVI. 51/2 The
learning of primary importance to the primates, at least,
is the formation of *learning sets; it is the learning how
to learn efficiently. *Ibid.* 53/1 It is this learning how
to learn a kind of problem that we designated by the
term *learning set.* **1975** *Lang. for Life* (Dept. Educ. &
Sci.) xxvi. 523 Before starting on a reading scheme
children should have had a wide range of preparatory
reading experiences and acquired certain 'learning
sets'. **1986** F. J. BRUNO *Dict. Key Words in Psychol.*
126 Experience with groups of similar problems results
in the gradual formation of a learning set.

lease, *n.*³ Add: [4.] **b.** Special Combs. *U. S. Oil
Industry.* lease-**broker,** -**grafter,** -**hound,** -**man**:
cf. *LANDMAN *n.* 5.
  1922 R. H. JOHNSON et al. *Business of Oil Production*
vii. 59 The general speculation in leases and
royalties..has brought into play a parasitic type of
trader who is usually called a 'lease grafter'...Narrowly
speaking, a 'lease grafter' is one who resorts to deceit
in his operations. [**1923** *Federal Reporter* (U.S.)
CCLXXXIX. 829 The plaintiff, through its vice
president, Mr. Williams, and its lease and land man,
Mr. Ford, agreed to withdraw from the association with
the Allied Oil Corporation.] **1926** E. R. LILLEY *Oil
Industry* iv. 66 The 'lease hound', a man of wide

acquaintance and a 'good mixer', is called upon to
trace the ownership of the lease. **1933** *Federal Reporter*
(U.S.) LXVI. 865/2 In February, 1926, the Roxana
Corporation..was acquiring a block of oil and gas leases
in the vicinity of the Russell land. Kirkbride, its
leaseman, understood that Benjamin owned the south
half and Nathan the north half of the quarter
section. **1943** *Tax Court Memorandum* (U.S.) II. 941/2
The lease brokers and lease hounds, as they are called,
would descend upon them, and the first thing they knew
the negroes had sold out and had nothing left. **1963** J.
P. GETTY *My Life & Fortunes* i. 19 The lobby, which
was perpetually jammed with lease-brokers,
wildcatters..and others directly or indirectly engaged
in the hunt for oil, was the best oil-business information
centre in Oklahoma. **1981** *Oil & Gas Jrnl.* 22 June
104/3 Farris..was an independent oil and gas leaseman
during 1950-57, when he joined Graham-Michaelis
Corp. as general manager of Sierra Petroleum Co.
Inc. **1985** *Washington Post* 11 Jan. D10/2 Oil industry
interest in exploring the rift remains intense. 'Lease-
hounds' have been nailing down mineral rights across
the region.

leather, *n.* Add: [I.] [2.] **f.** Clothing made
wholly or partly of leather, esp. when worn as
part of a style of dressing intended to suggest
strong masculinity (orig. associated with bikers,
and later with homosexuals); often with erotic
or fetishistic overtones, and hence also used
euphem. of sado-masochistic desires or practices.
See also sense *7 below.
  1966 *Realist* May 19/3 Remember the S-M ads: 'seeks
discipline', 'seeks uniforms', 'seeks leather and
rubber'. **1972** B. RODGERS *Queens' Vernacular* 124
When he takes his leather off he also removes his
masculinity. **1985** J. EPSTEIN in D. J. Enright *Fair of
Speech* 69, I take it to be indisputably a
euphemism..when it is said of a homosexual man who
takes part in sado-masochistic activity that he is 'into
leather'. **1991** *Pink Paper* 30 Mar. 18/2 (Advt.),
Attractive, passive, slim, exhibitionist guy, 30, likes
minimal clothing, leather, toys.
  [II.] **7.** Applied *attrib.* to people who
frequently wear leather clothing, esp. (orig.)
bikers and (in later use) homosexuals, and to
their subculture, meeting-places, etc.; esp. in
leather bar, boy, man. Cf. sense *2 f above.
  1961 'E. GEORGE' *(title)* The leather boys. **1966**
Listener 3 Mar. 308/1 Flesh-eating 'leather-boys' (on
their motor-bicycles)..wear a uniform; encased from
head to foot in black leather, they may be
individually..anonymous. **1977** *Gay News* 7 Apr.
20/2, I know leathermen are supposed to have fantasies,
but I don't. **1978** *Washington Post* 4 Sept. B3/1 The
Eagle, a 'leather' gay bar on Washington's Ninth Street
NW. **1982** E. GREGERSEN *Sexual Pract.* xix. 292/3
Leather bars, now commonplace in large metropolitan
centers in the United States, England and Germany,
were unknown before the 1950s. **1986** P. THEROUX
O-Zone xxvii. 316 She saw someone being screamed
at—another gang of leather boys howling at a cornered
Asian. **1990** *Gay Times* Dec. (Centre Section) 11/1
Leather biker seeks active, dominant type,..straight
looking mates..for raunchy times. **1991** *Advocate* 15
Jan. 10/3 A threatened picket by outraged leathermen
and leather dykes.

leathery, *a.* Add: Hence 'leatheriness *n.*
  1920 A. HUXLEY *Leda* 70 The buttered leatheriness
of a Jew's face. **1982** *N.Y. Times* 9 July C22/4 This
was replaced by a mushroom and scallion omelet of a
leatheriness fit to rival Charlie Chaplin's famous boot.

leave, *v.*¹ Add: [14.] [c.] **leave off.** (*d*) As *imp.
phr.* (*colloq.*): stop it! leave me alone! Cf. LAY *v.*¹
54 h.
  1915 CONRAD *Victory* II. viii. 160 'What's she like?
It's the girl you—' 'Leave off!' muttered Schomberg,
utterly pitiful behind his stiff military front. **1959** A.

Wesker *Chicken Soup with Barley* II. i, in *New Eng. Dramatists* I. 206 Leave off! That's all he can say—leave off, leave me alone. **1974** B. Bainbridge *Bottle Factory Outing* iv. 60 Leave off... I'm not an invalid. **1985** J. Winterson *Oranges are not only Fruit* 73 'Leave off Bill,' my auntie pushed him away.

(*e*) *trans.* To set (a person or thing) down (from a vehicle, etc.); to drop (someone) off (see *DROP *v.* 28 f).

1957 J. Kerouac *On Road* I. xiii. 98 They left me off a quarter-mile away and drove to the door. **1986** R. Ford *Sportswriter* viii. 202 You can see the UPS truck on our street every day still, leaving off hammocks and smokers and God knows what all.

[**d.**] **leave out.** (*b*) In imp. phr. *leave it out!*: stop it! esp. stop talking nonsense! come off it! *U.K. slang.*

1969 *Daily Mirror* 10 Oct. 18/3 *Leave it out*, I don't believe you, or pull the other leg. **1986** P. Theroux *O-Zone* xxxiii. 393 No—leave it out! He had been wrong. **1990** C. Brayfield *Prince* xx. 436 'It's like a nuclear disaster out there—no cars, no one on the streets...' 'Leave it out, Baz. You two have never been on time for a rehearsal yet.'

Lebesgue (lə'bɛg), *n. Math.* [The name of Henri *Lebesgue* (1875–1941), French mathematician.] Used *attrib.* to designate various concepts introduced by Lebesgue or arising out of his work, as **Lebesgue integral**, a definite integral of a bounded measurable function defined in a particular way, namely, that obtained by subdividing the range of the function, multiplying the lower (or upper) bound of each subdivision by the measure of its inverse image under the function, summing the products so obtained, and taking the limit of the sum as the width of the subdivisions tends to zero; an analogous integral of an unbounded function; **Lebesgue measure**, the measure (*MEASURE *n.* 2 g) of a given set in *n*-dimensional space as defined by Lebesgue in 1902 (*Annali di Matematica* VII. 236), being (in the case of *n* = 1) the greatest lower bound of the sum of the lengths of a countable collection of intervals containing the set, taken over all possible such collections.

1905 W. H. Young in *Phil. Trans. R. Soc.* A. CCIV. 244 Lebesgue gives two definitions of his generalised integral, which I shall, for convenience, allude to as the Lebesgue integral. **1912** *Bull. Amer. Math. Soc.* XVIII. 237 Suppose the function *f*(*p*) to be defined and limited and to have a double Lebesgue integral on the surface of a unit sphere. **1929** *Encycl. Brit.* XVII. 117/2 The Lebesgue measure of a set of points may not exist, but it does exist for all ordinary point sets. **1957** *Ibid.* XIII. 855/1 Lebesgue formulated, in brilliant memoirs of 1901 and 1902, a new definition of the definite integral... This 'Lebesgue integral' is one of the great achievements of modern real analysis. **1971** *Sci. Amer.* Aug. 95/2 Since each point *x* belonging to the set *I* is considered to be an interval of length 0, the Lebesgue measure *m* of each point *x* is 0. **1980** A. J. Jones *Game Theory* ii. 110 This function..is continuous everywhere, and differentiable except on an uncountable set of Lebesgue measure zero.

lechuguilla (lɛtʃə'giː(j)ə), *n. U.S.* Also **lechugilla, lecheguilla, †letchugia.** Pl. **-guilla.** [a. Mexican Sp. *lechuguilla*: cf. Sp. *lechuguilla* wild lettuce, dim. of *lechuga* lettuce.] A fibrous plant of the agave family, *Agave lecheguilla*, found in Mexico and the south-western United States, and used for various purposes including the extraction of istle from its leaves. Also, any of various similar plants of the same genus.

1834 B. Lundy *Jrnl.* 3 Feb. in *Life B. Lundy* (1847) xiii. 96 The men set themselves to work, in making ropes out of 'iste' [*sic*], a kind of stuff much used in this country, for ropes and bagging. It consists of the fibres of a plant called 'letchugia'. **1844** J. Gregg *Commerce Prairies* II. iv. 78 One of the most useful plants to the people of El Paso is the *lechuguilla*, which abounds on the hills and mountain sides of that vicinity. **1893** H. H. Bancroft *Resources & Devel. Mexico* v. 186 The lechuguilla grows in soil of fair quality. **1963** O. Breland *Animal Life & Lore* i. 43 They [*sc.* peccaries] also consume lechuguilla, an undesirable range plant. **1966** Mrs. L. B. Johnson *White House Diary* 3 Apr. (1970) 381 The desert was full of all kinds of cactus, Spanish dagger, agave, lechuguilla, so tall. **1972** H. S. Gentry *Agave Family in Sonora* (U.S. Dept. Agric.) 105 The people called *A. palmeri* 'lechuguilla' and said it was collected for eating and for making mescal. It was much used for food, fiber, and beverage by the Indians. **1987** D. J. Mabberley *Plant-bk.* 14 *A. lecheguilla* Torrey (lecheguilla, tula ixtle, Texas & N Mex.). **1993** C. McCarthy *All Pretty Horses* i. 61 They were down out of the mountains by midmorning and riding on a great plain..dotted with lechuguilla.

'lectric ('lɛktrɪk), *a.* and *n. colloq.* Also **lectric.** [Aphetic form of ELECTRIC *a.* and *n.*] = ELECTRIC *a.* and *n.*

1955 *Sci. Amer.* Aug. 80/3 Forms not yet admitted to the dictionaries are to be heard on every corner: for example, lectric (electric), pologize (apologize). **1973** *Amer. Speech* 1970 XLV. 77 It's made by General 'Lectric. **1977** *Hot Car* Oct. 15/2 Another problem with fitting 'lectric windys to English cars is their narrow door design. **1986** *Lancashire Life* Jan. 29/3 Since gas and 'lectric took the place Of cinders, wood and coal, My fuel bills are now so high They drive me up the wall. **1992** *Folk Roots* Sept. 46/2 If there's nothing here to quite match Johnnie Allan's *Promised Land*, Rod Bernard runs it close with a hymn to Merseybeat in Chuck Berry style, hook line: 'Recorded in England wid yo' 'lectric guitar!'

lectrice, *n.* Add: **2.** (With pronunc. lɛktris.) A female native speaker of a foreign language employed in a university to give practical instruction in that language.

1937 *Univ. Sheffield Calendar 1937-38* 103 Professors, Lecturers, etc. The Faculty of Arts...French...Lectrice—Yvonne Orhand, L. ès L. **1961** *Times* 20 May 10/6 Mlle. Monique Sengel..to be lectrice in French. **1975** M. Bradbury *Hist. Man* v. 82 A German lectrice in a see-through blouse is being encouraged to take it off. **1980** *Daily Tel.* 17 Sept. 8/3 Newnham College: Lectrice in French for 1980-1981.

led, *ppl. a.* Add: **5.** As the second element in instrumental *Combs.*: see the first element. **a.** In literary writing from the late 16th cent., as *star-led* (STAR *n.*[1] 15 c), PIXY-LED *a.*, *fancy-led* (FANCY *n.* and *a.* B. 1 c), etc. **b.** More commonly from the mid 20th cent. in *Pol.* and esp. in *Econ.* contexts, as *communist-led* (COMMUNIST *n.* 3 b), *export-led* (*EXPORT *n.* 3 a), etc.

1596 W. Smith *Chloris* xiii. sig. B2, A lust-led Satyre hauing hir in chace. **1852** M. Arnold *Empedocles on Etna* II. ii. 136 Be neither saint nor sophist-led, but be a man! **1968** *Punch* 29 May 761/1 She insists that the boom must be 'export-led' and not 'consumer-led'. **1984** *Dance Theatre Jrnl.* May 17/4 We..publish a features-led, rather than reviews-led arts page. **1990** J. Park *Brit. Cinema* vi. 111 Hammer was too much a market-led company to encourage fresh approaches to the monstrous.

ledge, *v.*[2] Add: **3.** To place or rest (an object) on a ledge, or in a position offering only narrow or slight support.

1926 A. Bennett *Lord Raingo* II. lxxxvi. 403 She ledged a large photograph of Delphine against the foot of the bed. **1960** T. Hughes *Lupercal* 37, I could lean over The upper edge of the high half door, My left foot ledged on the hinge.

ledger, *v.* Add: Hence 'ledgered *ppl. a.*, used as ledger-bait.

1959 *Times* 7 Feb. 9/4 Chub..can be caught with ledgered dead baits. **1976** *Southern Even. Echo* (Southampton) 1 Nov. 7/1 At Milford the other day I saw one angler reel in four good-sized dogfish within 45 minutes. They all took legered herring on double-hook gear. **1986** *Coarse Fishing* June 44/1 When I first began to fish the legered meat all those years ago, I realised very quickly that it was a method that could only win when the rivers were in flood. **1992** *Angling Times* 22 Apr. 7/3 There are plenty of..skimmers now being taken from pegs in the wides on legered maggot.

lee, *n.*[1] Add: [II.] [5.] **lee wave** *Meteorol.*, a standing wave generated on the leeward side of an obstacle by an airflow passing over or round it.

1955 *Tellus* VII. 367 The stationary lee-waves produced by a big mountain often break up into turbulent..whirls or 'rotors' in the lower layers of the air flow. **1966** *McGraw-Hill Encycl. Sci. & Technol.* XIV. 417/2 Internal waves have been found in the atmosphere as lee waves (waves in the wind stream down-wind from a mountain) and as waves propagated along an inversion layer. **1982** BARRY & CHORLEY *Atmosphere, Weather & Climate* (ed. 4) ii. 94 A series of lee waves developed in the tropospheric airflow.

Leech (liːtʃ), *n.*[5] *Math.* [The name of John *Leech* (1926–92), British mathematician, who described the concept in *Canad. Jrnl. Math.* (1967) XIX. 251.] **Leech lattice**, a set of points in 24-dimensional Euclidean space regularly arranged such that each point has exactly 196,560 nearest neighbours.

1968 J. H. CONWAY in *Proc. Nat. Acad. Sci.* LXI. 398 The Leech lattice *Λ* is the union of the sets [*C, m*] over all *C* ∈ *C* and all integers *m*. **1974** *Nature* 8 Feb. (Advt. facing p. 402), In the final chapter Steiner systems and sphere packings are related via the famous Leech lattice. **1982** D. GORENSTEIN *Finite Simple Groups* ii. 120 Conway constructed his three simple groups from the automorphism group of the remarkable 24-dimensional Leech lattice. **1986** *Nature* 20 Feb. 621/3 The Leech lattice (an economical way to pack spheres in 24-dimensional space).

leech, *v.*[2] Add: **2.** *intr.* Const. *on* (*to*). To attach oneself like a leech; to be parasitic *on*. Also const. *off*.

1937 R. NARAYAN *Bachelor of Arts* xiv. 201 It was nearly two years since he left college, and he was still leeching on his father. **1983** *Listener* 23 June 14/2 A silver-tongued mountebank leeching on to suffering, pitilessly fleecing the gullible. **1986** *Philadelphia Inquirer* 6 Nov. 4D/5 As you might imagine, the greedy and the tasteless are wanting to leech onto him, to cash in on The Farewell Tour. **1988** *People Weekly* 23 May 11/1 They exist to leech on our fears and desires for revenge and to use the suffering of victims to boost ratings. **1990** *Sunday Mail Mag.* (Brisbane) 25 Mar. 22 To leech off the American people!

3. *fig.* To drain (someone or something) of energy, money, etc.; to drain (something) *away* or *from* something.

There appears to be some confusion with LEACH *v.*[2] 4.

*a*1961 in WEBSTER s.v., Bankers who had always leeched them white. [**1964** *Listener* 13 Aug. 225/2 It [*sc.* a modern office block] has neither virtues nor vices; it just sits there like a graceless woman, leeching away a bit more of the city's vitality.] **1974** *Times Lit. Suppl.* 1 Mar. 211/4 The invading Englishman..leeching the land with his reservoirs and his crass afforestations. **1981** R. DAVIES *Rebel Angels* iii. 98 'What's he been up to?' 'Leeching and bumming and

sornering.' **1988** *Times* 17 Feb. 12/1, I see no reason why the London cabbie should not..leech his heritage..for mutual gain. **1990** *Times* 5 Apr. 1/3 The brain-drain..leeched 45,000 people from the territory.

leery, *a.*[2] Add: **'leeriness** *n.*

1961 in WEBSTER. **1976** *Aviation Week* 16 Aug. 35/1 The present leeriness of lenders toward the airlines would be accentuated by..deregulation. **1991** R. BROOKHISER *Way of WASP* iii. 32 The English..are also suspicious of ambition, but the social origin of their leeriness is rather different.

left, *a.*, *adv.*, and *n.* Add: [A.] [3.] **d.** *Math.* Designating an entity whose definition involves two elements in a conventionally defined order, opposite to that denoted by 'right' (RIGHT *a.* 18 b).

[**1933** *Ann. Math.* XXXIV. 483 When $F(x) = D_1(x)D_2(x)$ we shall call $D_2(x)$ a right-hand and $D_1(x)$ a left-hand divisor of $F(x)$.] **1938** F. D. MURNAGHAN *Theory of Group Representations* iv. 91 The set Hs^{-1} (which consists of the inverses of the elements of the left coset *sH*) has no element in common with *H*. We term it the right coset of *H* determined by s^{-1}. **1965** J. J. ROTMAN *Theory of Groups* i. 7 Let *G* be a group and let *a* ∈ *G*. Define a function $T_a : G \to G$ by $T_a(x) = a \cdot x$; (T_a is called left translation by *a*). **1972** A. G. HOWSON *Handbk. Terms Algebra & Anal.* ii. 17 An element *e* is said to be a left identity (unit) for ∗ if *e* ∗ *x* = *x* for all *x*. *Ibid.* v. 28 We..denote E_s by x^s and refer to it as a left coset of *S* in *G*. **1990** *Q. Jrnl. Math.* XLI. 22 The biggest problem is to show that a left order in a regular ω-semigroup must have a stratified semigroup of left quotients.

[C.] **6.** A left turn. Chiefly *U. S.* Cf. *to hang a left* s.v. *HANG *v.* 4 e.

1973 G. SIMS *Hunters Point* i. 7 Straight on is Fort Mason... We make a left on to Lombard. **1973** R. L. SIMON *Big Fix* (1974) v. 37, I turned off the freeway..and made a left up the hill into the canyon. **1976** *Billings* (Montana) *Gaz.* 20 June (Advt.), ¾ mile past the single bridge over the Yellowstone, take a left. **1991** R. BANKS *Sweet Hereafter* i. 19 At Route 73 by the old mill, I banged a left and headed north along the Ausable River.

left hand, *n.* Add: [3.] **(Fleming's) left-hand rule** *Physics*, a mnemonic (proposed by J. A. Fleming (1849-1945), English electrical engineer, concerning the behaviour of a current-carrying conductor in a magnetic field, according to which the directions of the magnetic field, the current, and the force exerted on the conductor are indicated respectively by the first finger, second finger, and thumb of the left hand when these are held out perpendicular to each other.

1923 H. MOORE *Textbk. Intermediate Physics* lxx. 713 The field is then represented by the forefinger, and the current by the second finger, while the thumb points along the direction of the force acting on the conductor. This is known as Fleming's Left-hand Rule. **1934** I. M. FREEMAN tr. *Joos's Theoret. Physics* xv. 296 The current in the segment, the magnetic field, and the ponderomotive force must form a right-handed orthogonal system in this order (Fleming's left-hand rule). **1947** *Sci. News* IV. 117 If cosmic rays are influenced by a magnetic field, they must have a charge. Is it positive or negative? We apply the well-known Left Hand rule. **1980** J. W. HILL *Intermediate Physics* xx. 193 The motion can be worked out using the left-hand rule when the direction of the magnetic field and the current are known.

leftward, *adv.* and *a.* Add: [B.] (Of welding) executed from right to left.

1941 A. C. DAVIES *Sci. & Pract. Welding* iii. 143 Leftward or Forward Welding..is used nowadays for welding steel plate under ⅛in. thick and for welding non-ferrous metals. **1951** FUCHS & BRADLEY *Welding Pract.* I. i. 8 As generally practised, oxy-acetylene welding is carried out by the 'leftward' technique. When welding downhand the flame in this technique points along the welding seam towards the unwelded portion and travel is from right to left. **1989** L. GOURD *Welding* II. x. 144 Rightward welding is faster than leftward and consumes less gas.

leg, *n*. Add: [I.] [2.] **h**. In various expressions with reference to sexual intercourse, esp. *to get one's leg over*, (of a man) to copulate or achieve sexual intercourse (with). See also **leg-over*, sense 17 *a* below. *Brit. slang*.

1719 T. D'URFEY *Wit & Mirth* V. 45 No sneaking Rebel shall lift a Leg o'er me. **1975** J. PIDGEON *Flame* i. 21 Still quite a one for the birds is our Jack. He'll be getting his leg over in the pension queue. **1980** D. MORRIS *Tribal Words* (typescript) 391 It is sometimes said of a player that 'he played so well today, he must have got his leg over last night'. **1987** D. KARTUN *Megiddo* xxviii. 264 Daft, spending like that on a tart like her. Half the garrison have had their leg over. **1991** R. DOYLE *Van* (1992) 256 Maybe just the once he'd like to get the leg over one of these kind of women, only the once, in a hotel room or in her apartment, and then he'd be satisfied. **1995** *Independent* 25 May 26/7 Everyone dicking around chasing tail and trying to get their leg over.

i. *pl*. The potential (in a book, film, play, etc.) for popularity; the ability to 'run' (RUN *v*. B. 27 c). Esp. in phr. *to have legs*. *colloq*. (orig. and chiefly *U. S.*).

1930 R. R. CLARK *Let.* in *Texas Folk-lore Soc. Publ.* VIII. 153 His stuff was much copied and when he wrote something that went the rounds he would say that 'it had legs'. **1978** *N. Y. Times Mag.* 23 July 22/2 Books that used to be called pageturners but are now referred to as books with legs, presumably because they seem to walk off the shelves. **1985** *Time* 4 Feb. 85 Sometimes.. movies can elude their death warrants and flourish into cult objects through doggedness and word of mouth. They acquire 'legs'. **1991** *Spy* (N.Y.) Mar. 19/2 The Tracking Study can be used to assess a film's potential 'legs'. **1993** *Globe & Mail* (Toronto) 31 July C13/2 A TV endorsement by a smitten Oprah Winfrey in May certainly helped boost sales, but *The Bridges of Madison County* had shown its legs long before that.

[5.] **b**. A woman, considered as a source of sexual satisfaction; sexual intercourse. *U. S. slang*.

[**1942** BERREY & VAN DEN BARK *Amer. Thes. Slang* §427/2 *Well-formed young woman*,.. legs.] **1968-70** *Current Slang* (Univ. S. Dakota) III-IV. 78 *Leg*, *n*. A girl. **1977** *Amer. Speech* 1975 L. 62 *Leg n*, promiscuous female, one who readily engages in sexual intercourse. **1977** *Maledicta* 1977 I. 227 Some free *leg* (sex). **1988** M. MUSTAPHA *Playboy of W. Indies* II. 45 *Mama Benin*: Well he musta been a good looking fella, going after de women and erm, eh. *Mac*: Woman wat. If he see a piece a leg coming gross de field he'd run hide in de ole shed.

[11.] **c**. *Oil Industry*. Each of the steel columns extending below the main deck of an oil rig, used to float and stabilize the vessel or to rest it on the seabed.

1957 *Oil & Gas Jrnl.* 1 Apr. 77/1 The tripod platform.. has legs 4 ft. in diameter and 129 ft. long. **1967** *Rep. Inquiry Causes Accident to Sea Gem* (Cmnd. 3409) 1. 6 in *Parl. Papers* 1966-7 XXI. 169 Every contact of a floating object having a dead weight of several hundred tons with the supporting legs of an oil rig is a potential source of danger. **1969** *Punch* 26 Feb. 313/2 The control room man can flood or pump out the legs just by squeezing small levers—four thousand tons of water in each leg, and she sinks to rest on the sea bottom. A bit less and she floats. **1973** C. CALLOW *Power from Sea* vi. 126 Once the legs were driven into the sea-bed no one could see or could know exactly what there was in the lowermost nine feet of

the leg. **1992** D. McLEAN *Bucket of Tongues* 38 There was a couple of divers doing maintenance on the outside of the leg.

[III.] [17.] [a.] **leg-over** *Brit. slang*, (an act of) sexual intercourse.

1975 *Time Out* 7 Mar. 25/4 Alan Price showing those M'mselles ('Oooh, Alfee!') what a British *leg over is all about. **1986** *City Limits* 16 Oct. 41 Whether it's snogging, leg-over or bedroom, this is a form of soul that is continuously in demand. **1992** *Daily Star* 2 July 9/2 Imagine how much easier life would be if every time they indulged in an extra-marital legover they got away with it by saying they'd done it to save the world.

legal, *a*. Add: [3.] **b**. *gen*. Allowed by or in accordance with a particular set of rules; acceptable, permissible. *colloq*.

1850 *Morning Chron.* 11 Feb. 5/6 Having thus given the characteristics and conditions of the 'legal', or honourable trade, I next turn my inquiry to the state of the labouring men. **1973** *Times* 24 May 13/7 Cans of 'legal' spaghetti (yes, allowed on the diets in limited quantities). **1983** *Your Business Computer* Aug. 21/2 A couple of funnies occurred on my system: once, the system locked up.. and refused to accept any character as legal. **1992** *Dr. Dobb's Jrnl.* Sept. 34/2 In the beginning, I enabled one interrupt at a time and started up Windows to see what exception conditions were 'legal'.

legalist, *n*. Add: **lega'listically** *adv*.

1934 in WEBSTER. **1939** *Federal Reporter* (U.S.) 2nd Ser. CVI. 721/2 Section 8 of the National Labor Relations Act, relating to company-controlled unions, must not be construed so strictly or so legalistically so as to destroy its purpose or the legislative intent. **1971** LD. GEORGE-BROWN *In My Way* vii. 136 All of this was legalistically true. **1994** *N. Y. Times* 22 Nov. C6/1, I find it totally absurd to conclude legalistically that the endangered species act did not mean to include habitat.

legalitarian (ˌliːgælɪˈtɛərɪən), *a*. [Blend of LEGALITY *n*. and EGALITARIAN *a*. and *n*.] Favouring legislation as the best means of bringing about greater social equality.

1967 C. SETON-WATSON *Italy from Liberalism to Fascism* v. 189 For ten months he preached insurrection and campaigned vigorously against the Socialist party's legalitarian degeneration. **1970** A. M. BICKEL *Supreme Court & Idea of Progress* iv. 108 Another of the principal themes of the Warren Court, related to the egalitarian, legalitarian, and centralizing themes, was majoritarianism. **1973** *Times Lit. Suppl.* 2 Mar. 226/1 Spitting upon the conservative, legalitarian aspirations of the former nationalist leaders in the [Italian Fascist] party. **1975** A. M. BICKEL *Morality of Consent* i. 8 His vision was of a legalitarian society. He was a judicial activist, quick to regulate what seemed disordered and unruly.

Hence **legali'tarianism** *n*.

1969 C. DAVIDSON in Cockburn & Blackburn *Student Power* 352 We should avoid getting bogged down in 'legalitarianism'. We cannot count on this society's legal apparatus to guarantee our civil liberties. **1987** *Forbes* (N.Y.) 1 June 112/2 Liberal politics and a willingness to judicialize them—the heady brew once described by.. Professor Alexander Bickel as 'legalitarianism' or legal egalitarianism.

legend, *n*. Sense 8 in Dict. becomes 9. Add: **8**. A person of such fame or distinction as to become the subject of popularly repeated (true or fictitious) stories; esp. in phr. *a legend in one's (own) lifetime*.

1918 L. STRACHEY *Eminent Victorians* 168 She was a legend in her lifetime, and she knew it. **1940** W. FAULKNER *Hamlet* I. ii. 28 They all knew Stamper. He was a legend, even though still alive. **1948** *Time* 19 July 34/3 Klondike Mike, the greatest of the mushers, the sourdough who struck it rich and kept his poke, is a living legend. **1978** *Lancashire Life* Sept. 51/1 During the last war he became something of a legend. **1987** *Hairdo Ideas* July 20 Reminiscent of the styles worn by the glamour girls of the 40's, this long, thick mass of loose waves will make you a legend in your own time!

legendary, *a.* Add: Hence 'le**g**endarily *adv.*, according to legend or popular report; famously. *a*1961 in WEBSTER s.v., Legendarily successful personality. **1978** *Economist* 22 Apr. 16/1 Neither he nor his legendarily chaotic staff has strong contacts with the various interests in the Democratic party. **1994** *Daily Tel.* 1 Aug. 13/6 Whooping cough, the legendarily awful disease of children's imaginations.

leggy, *a.* Add: **c.** *slang* (orig. *U. S.*). Of a woman: having long, slender legs; hence, more loosely, attractive in a provocative manner; 'sexy'.
1927 C. WOOLRICH *Children of Ritz* i. 17 Angela reappeared in an enormous broad-brimmed hat that made her look like one of the Gish sisters... And she was leggier than ever. **1942** BERREY & VAN DEN BARK *Amer. Thes. Slang* §427/2 *Well-formed young woman*, ..leggy femme. **1976** *Southern Even. Echo* (Southampton) 13 Nov. 8/5 (*caption*) They missed the chance of a close-up of three leggy lovelies who called in at a city supermarket. **1984** *Listener* 12 Jan. 30/1 The celebrity is invariably male, assisted inevitably by a couple of leggy dollybirds. **1992** *N.Y. Times* 23 Aug. II. 27/5 Saturday night after Saturday night.. he went through his shtik, bellowing 'How sweet it is!' and 'And away we go!', sipping his 200-proof coffee, ogling leggy women.

leghaemoglobin (ˌlɛghiːməʊˈɡləʊbɪn), *n.* *Biochem.* Also (*U. S.*) **leghemoglobin**. [f. LEG(UME *n.* + HÆMOGLOBIN *n.*] A red pigment in the root nodules of legumes whose haemoglobin-like component enables nitrogen-fixing bacteria to function.
1945 A. I. VIRTANEN et al. in *Suomen Kemistilehti* B. XVIII. 50 To avoid the long terms as e.g. 'haemoglobin of the leguminous root nodules' we have begun to use the terms: leghaemoglobin and legmethaemoglobin. **1974** *Nature* 6 Sept. 74/2 Leghaemoglobin (Lb), a myoglobin protein, is found in large quantities in the root nodules which result from the symbiotic association between the bacterium *Rhizobium* and plants of the family Leguminosae. **1984** HOLTZMAN & NOVIKOFF *Cells & Organelles* (ed. 3) III. iii. 359 A protein related to hemoglobin (leghemoglobin) is synthesized by the host.

legitimate, *a.* Add: [**2.**] **e.** In extended use: valid or acceptable; justifiable, reasonable.
1847 *Sporting Life* 28 Aug. 16/2 The system of adopting leggism as a legitimate part and parcel of horse-racing is one that must soon explode. **1864** *Sat. Rev.* XVIII. 445/2 Objurgating impotence has always been a legitimate subject for ridicule. **1894** *Daily News* 17 Jan. 3/1 The most nosey visitor has no legitimate ground for offence from organic causes. **1934** G. GREENE *It's a Battlefield* ii. 103 They were careful never to give him reason for legitimate complaints; they sprang to his orders as they would never have sprung to the orders of a man they liked. **1958** P. GIBBS *Curtains of Yesterday* xvii. 143, I have a perfectly legitimate reason for coming.., but what's yours, old boy? **1995** *Daily Tel.* 14 Mar. 17/7 It is legitimate to abridge a classic, so long as it is done with tact and sympathy,.. just as it is legitimate to novelise an original screenplay.

legitimate, *v.* Add: **legitimating** *ppl. a.* and *vbl. n.*
1970 *Internat. & Compar. Law Q.* XIX. 330 A person whose father was domiciled both at the time of the

child's birth and at the time of the legitimating event in a country by the law of which he became legitimated. **1973** *Listener* 27 Dec. 891/1 The great legitimating myths which—sociologists suppose—once gave shape, order and coherence to our lives. **1981** *Times Lit. Suppl.* 13 Feb. 163/1 The legitimating of art as a set of professions and industries maintains a caste system in contemporary society. **1991** *Jrnl. S. Afr. Stud.* XVII. 408 A legitimating marriage became possible only if proof could be produced that the first wife's behaviour would have warranted a divorce or legal separation.

Lego ('lɛɡəʊ), *n.* Also **lego**. [a. Da. *Lego*, a respelling of *leg godt* 'play well', f. *lege* to play.] A proprietary name for a constructional toy consisting principally of small interlocking plastic blocks; such blocks collectively. Freq. *attrib.*
1957 *Trade Marks Jrnl.* 5 June 598/2 *Lego*... Toy models and sets of parts for constructing such toys, all made of rigid plastics. **1969** *Sunday Oregonian* 14 Dec. I. 38/1 (Advt.), Jumbo lego, larger scale pieces of framed lego design. **1971** *Habitat Catal.* 108 No self-respecting toy box.. should be without Lego. **1974** J. WILSON *Snap* vi. 85 'I want to make a submarine..' said Max irritably, holding out an unwieldy cluster of Lego bricks... Ginnie sighed and joined up various pieces of Lego. **1986** *Listener* 6 Feb. 32/1 My feet ankle-deep in Lego models and Cindy dolls. **1991** DORRIS & ERDRICH *Crown of Columbus* ii. 29 He constructed labyrinthine Lego cities, but refused to tie his own shoes.

‖**lei** (leɪ), *n.*[2] *Archaeol.* Pl. **lei**. [Chinese *léi*.] An urn-shaped Chinese bronze wine-vessel of the Shang to Middle Chou period (*c* 1500-249 B.C.).
1929 W. P. YETTS *Catal. George Eumorfopoulos Coll.* I. 47 The lei are large vessels from which wine or water was poured into smaller. **1946** L. BACHHOFER *Short Hist. Chinese Art* 33 The lei was a large *p'ou*. **1958** W. WILLETTS *Chinese Art* I. iv. 192 Nowadays the wealthy go in for [lacquer vessels with] silver rims and gilt handles, gold *lei*, and bells of jade. **1978** *New Archaeol. Finds in China* II. 20 The bronzes *tsun* (wine containers), *lei* (wine containers) and *pien chung* (a chime of bells) were shaped like those in the Central Plains.

Leibniz, *n.* Also **Leibnitz**. Add: **Leibniz('s) theorem** *Math.*, the theorem that the *n*th derivative of a product of two functions may be expressed as a sum of products of the derivatives of the individual functions, the coefficients being the same as those occurring in the binomial theorem.
1852 B. PRICE *Treat. Infinitesimal Calculus* I. iii. 85 The following theorem, due to Leibnitz, and commonly called *Leibnitz's Theorem, may be conveniently employed to find the general (the *r*th) derived-function of a product of two functions of *x*. **1965** *Math. Gaz.* XLIX. 49 The derivation involved a generalized form of Leibniz's theorem. **1967** *Math. Rev.* XXXIII. 675/1 The Leibniz theorem referred to in the title is Wilson's theorem in the form $(p - 2)! \equiv 1 \pmod p$.

Leidenfrost ('laɪdənfrɒst), *n.* *Physics.* [The name of J. G. *Leidenfrost* (1715-94), German physicist.] Used *attrib.* and in the possessive with reference to a phenomenon observed by Leidenfrost, in which liquid, when placed in contact with a surface whose temperature exceeds some critical value (the *Leidenfrost point*), forms a layer of vapour which insulates it from the surface.
1863 E. ATKINSON tr. *Ganot's Elem. Treat. Physics* VI. 258 Leidenfrost's phenomena... When liquids are thrown upon incandescent metallic surfaces they present remarkable phenomena, which were first

observed by Leidenfrost a century ago. **1878** *Encycl. Brit.* VIII. 728/2 This condition of the liquid is called the spheroidal state, and is often referred to as Leidenfrost's phenomenon. **1977** *Sci. Amer.* Aug. 126/3 The temperature at which the drops last longest is the Leidenfrost point. **1981** *Daily Tel.* 3 June 16 The phenomenon which aids fire-walkers is called the Leidenfrost effect. **1986** *Nature* 13 Mar. 119/3 The Leidenfrost effect created by an insulating layer of water or sweat may also reduce energy transfer to the surface of the body.

Leighton Buzzard ('leɪtən 'bʌzəd), *n.* [The name of a town in Buckinghamshire.] Used *attrib.* to designate a light-coloured sand quarried in Leighton Buzzard and used esp. in refractory moulding and as a standard in cement testing.

1916 P. G. H. BOSWELL *Sands Suitable for Glass-Making* vi. 49 'Leighton Buzzard' sand...The available resources are at least 500 million tons. **1923** A. B. SEARLE *Sands & Crushed Rocks* I. iii. 119 The Leighton Buzzard Sands vary from nearly pure white to pale yellow sands associated with carbonaceous matter to highly ferruginous deposits. **1950** E. LUCAS *Newbold's Mod. Pract. Building* (ed. 3) I. xiii. 337 Sands of light colour, such as Leighton Buzzard sand, are also used to make pointing mortar. **1965** J. KOLBUSZEWSKI *Sand Particles & their Density* 53 The effect of particle shape was studied using two sands—Leighton Buzzard sand (rounded) and Biddulph Medium sand (angular).

Leinster House ('lɛnstə(r) 'haʊs), *n.* [The name of the former Dublin home of the Dukes of Leinster.] Used to designate the Irish parliament since it began meeting at Leinster House in 1922.

[**1922** *Times* 9 Sept. 8/2 The first Session of the Provisional Parliament will be opened to-morrow at 11 o'clock in the lecture theatre of Leinster House, the headquarters of the Royal Dublin Society.] **1949** ST. J. ERVINE *Craigavon Ulsterman* III. x. 418 Some very queer fish have been elected to Stormont,..but Stormont, at its worst, has never declined to the depths of Leinster House. **1979** *An Phoblacht* 29 Sept. 10/4 People can be held for up to forty-eight hours merely on suspicion and the power to intern remains on the Leinster House statute book today. **1987** *Whitaker's Almanack* 1988 858/2 Members of Dáil Éireann are..granted free telephone and postal facilities from Leinster House.

leio-, *comb. form.* Add: **leiomyosar'coma** *Path.*, a malignant sarcoma arising from smooth muscle.

1914 F. B. MALLORY *Princ. Pathologic Histol.* I. 307 Leiomyoblastomas grow at various rates...They are commonly called leiomyomas, or fibroids...The term *leiomyosarcoma has been used. **1976** *Path. Ann.* XI. 330 Malignant glandular epithelial cells, as a rule, are not present unless the tumor is a mixed mesodermal tumor rather than pure leiomyosarcoma. **1984** TIGHE & DAVIES *Pathology* (ed. 4) xvi. 149 Neoplasms of the small intestine are rare and include.. leiomyosarcoma.

‖**lei wên** (leɪ wɛn), *n. Ceramics.* Also **lei-wan**, **leiwen**. [Chinese *léi wén*, lit. 'thunder symbol'.] A spiral fret motif often used to form a background or decorative filler on ancient Chinese bronze or ceramic wares.

1922 A. L. HETHERINGTON *Early Ceramic Wares of China* ix. 59 The old hieroglyphic for thunder was a simple spiral; but, as a series of circular signs is more difficult to engrave than a series of square ones, it was changed into a 'quadrangular spiral' and two of these combined make the design known as *lei wên* or 'thunder pattern'. **1958** W. WILLETTS *Chinese Art* I. iii. 165 The spiral appears in a variety of forms...It is the device called by the Sung cataloguers *lei wên* or 'thunder pattern'. **1971** *Ashmolean Mus. Rep. Visitors 1970* 61 Small bronze *Chüeh*, single band of *lei-wan* around the waist. **1974** *Encycl. Brit. Macropædia* XIV. 918/2 The *lei-wen*,..which resembles the Greek key fret..and is sometimes used on the later ceramic wares, appears on bronzes as early as the Shang and Chou dynasties. **1980** *Catal. Fine Chinese Ceramics* (Sotheby, Hong Kong) 204 Carved with a central band of *taotie* (*t'ao t'ieh*) reserved on a *leiwen* ground. **1990** *Antique Collector* May 106/3 Pieces tended to be decorated throughout, the background with a *leiwen* motif setting off *taotie* masks or zoomorphic ornaments such as dragons or cicadas.

Lelantine (lɪ'læntaɪn), *a.* [f. L. (*flumen*) *Lelantum* a river in this region, mentioned by Pliny (*Nat. Hist.* IV. 64), ad. Gr. Λήλαντον πεδίον the name of this plain + -INE[1].] Pertaining to or designating a coastal plain in Euboea mentioned by Herodotus; *spec.* designating the war between the ancient cities of Chalcis and Eretria in the late 8th cent. B.C., fought mainly over the possession of the plain.

1900 J. B. BURY *Hist. Greece* iii. 151 An exhausting war for the Lelantine plain. **1913** H. R. HALL *Anc. Hist. Near East* xi. 532 The Lelantine War..ended disastrously for Eretria. **1934** A. TOYNBEE *Study of Hist.* II. ii. 42 The Chalcidian farmers..sailing out into the Aegean..took to the land again wherever they found another Lelantine Plain awaiting the Chalcidian plough. **1945** A. W. GOMME *Hist. Commentary Thucydides* I. 126 The Lelantine war was primarily a land war between neighbours, though the fact that the allies on either side were mostly sea-powers suggests that it was a phase in a commercial and colonial struggle. **1968** V. EHRENBERG *From Solon to Socrates* i. 15 We hear of a number of such disputes..; the most famous was the Lelantine war between Chalcis and Eretria in Euboea.

Le Mans (lə mɑ̃), *n.* [The name of a city in the département of Sarthe in north-west France.] Used *colloq.* to designate the 24-hour long touring and sports car race held annually at Le Mans since 1923. Also freq. used *attrib.* to designate a type of race start, originated there, in which the competitors are stationed at a distance from their cars (also *transf.*).

1928 *Autocar* 6 Jan. 17 (*heading*) Twenty-six entries for Le Mans. **1930** *Ibid.* 26 Dec. 1297/2 Le Mans looks like being exceptionally good, for to the three Bugattis already announced have been added a team of twelve-cylinder Loraines. **1957** *Motor Sport* ('Know the Game' Ser.) 6/2 Jaguars have again made Le Mans a British province. **1962** *Times* 31 July 7/3 All is not speed, noise, and Le Mans-type starts. **1966** *Publ. Amer. Dial. Soc. 1964* XLII. 6 *Le Mans start*,..a type of racing start that originated at Le Mans, where the cars are lined up on one side of the starting *grid*, with the drivers standing some distance away. **1974** *Country Life* 17 Oct. 1079/2 Crosby's..oil, *Carrying On*, ..shows the battered No 3 Bentley..in the 1927 Le Mans. **1977** *West Briton* 25 Aug. 11/2 The handicap event began 'Le Mans' style, with boats starting from the beach with sails at the ready. **1989** *Independent* 2 Dec. 64/3 The West German team which won Le Mans in 1984 and 1985 and now has the responsibility of running the works Porsches.

lemma, *n.*[1] Add: [**2.**] **c.** *Lexicography.* [Used earlier in this sense in Ger. and It.] A lexical item as it is presented, usu. in a standardized form, in a dictionary entry; a definiendum.

1951 tr. *Busa's Sancti Thomae Aquinatis Hymnorum Ritualium Varia Specimina Concordantiarum* Introd. 20 Five stages..of compiling a concordance:..3—indicating on each card the respective entry (lemma); 4—the selection and placing in alphabetical order of all the cards according to the lemma and its purely material quality. **1967** *Computers & Humanities* II. 79 Punched cards: one word per occurrence, abstract sentences limited to 10 lines: main entry word, run-on entry, inflected form, reference and dating in print; lemma, text code number and dating punched. **1974** R. W. BURCHFIELD in *Trans. Philol. Soc. 1973* 18 Dictionary editors in this country probably cannot be required to move lower-case lemmata, or to delete literary examples showing a trade mark used more or less generically, provided that the entry accurately reflects usage. **1979** *Amer. Speech 1976* LI. 138 The pages are pleasingly uncluttered.., with just enough contrast between the boldface lemmas and the lightface commentaries. **1983** R. R. K. HARTMANN *Lexicogr.* i. 7 The 'lemma'.. a distillation of the word from which all non-essential features have been eliminated. **1992** *Appl. Linguistics* XIII. 4 In the lemma, the lexical entry's meaning and syntax are represented.

lemmatic (lɛ'mætɪk), *a.* [f. Gr. λῆμμα, λῆμματ- (see LEMMA *n.*¹) + -IC.] = LEMMATICAL *a.*
 1955 *Trans. Philol. Soc. 1954* 116, I begin with a lemmatic discussion on certain case-forms. **1982** *Papers Dict. Soc. N. Amer. 1979* 135 Alinei's 1974 study of lemmatic types in the *Dizionario Garzanti*. **1986** *Times Lit. Suppl.* 8 Aug. 867/1 The book offers far more than new texts and lemmatic commentaries.

lemniscus, *n.* Delete ‖ and add: **3.** *Anat.* A band or bundle of fibres in the central nervous system, *esp.* one of those connecting sensory nuclei to the thalamus. Also (now *arch.*) with mod.L. adjs.
 1857 DUNGLISON *Dict. Med. Sci.* (rev. ed.) 527/1 *Laqueus*, a prominent band in the brain, *Lemniscus*, behind the brachium posterius of the corpora quadrigemina, which marks the course of the superior division of the fasciculus olivaris. **1884** *Med. Rec.* (N.Y.) XXVI. 394/1, I have intended to pave the way for the understanding of the lemniscus: a nerve tract of at least equal importance with that of the pyramids. **1913** *Cunningham's Text-bk. Anat.* (ed. 4) 563 After decussating in the median plane, all the internal arcuate fibres which arise from these nuclei do not enter the lemniscus medialis. **1955** *Sci. Amer.* Oct. 81 When the body is touched or stimulated in some way, nerve impulses go from the site of stimulation by pathways called the lemnisci to the thalamus in the center of the brain. **1961** *Lancet* 26 Aug. 446/2 In the lower brain-stem degeneration was.. moderate in the right medial lemniscus. **1974** D. & M. WEBSTER *Compar. Vertebr. Morphol.* xii. 278 Like the ventral spinothalamic tract, with which it is confluent, the lateral spinothalamic tract joins the medial lemniscus in the brainstem. **1980** *Gray's Anat.* (ed. 36) VII. 911/1 The fibres of the trapezoid body turn upwards to contribute to the lateral lemniscus, as the ascending part of the auditory pathway. **1990** *Sci. Amer.* June 36/2 From the cochlea, signals are processed sequentially, beginning at the cochlear nucleus and proceeding to the lateral lemniscus.

lemon, *n.*¹ Add: **[1.] [c.]** *esp.* a substandard or defective car. (Later examples.)
 1978 J. WAMBAUGH *Black Marble* ix. 162 This lousy lemon we took in trade on a Buick. **1987** *Times* 5 May 10/4 Plagued by component failures, mainly in their electrics, Jaguars became the 'lemons' of luxury cars in the United States in the 1970s. **1993** *Dr. Dobb's Jrnl.* Jan. 121/1 Just as youth is wasted on the young, new-car smell is wasted on a pile of metal just out of the factory, that may or may not be a lemon and self-destruct in your driveway.

 [7.] [a.] lemon law *U.S. colloq.*, a law designed to provide redress for buyers of faulty or substandard cars (cf. sense *1 c above).
 1981 *Washington Post* 2 Mar. 25/4 The slick pamphlet touts the *Lemon Law Litigation Conference, an unusual gathering sponsored by the Center for Auto Safety. **1983** *N.Y. Times* 21 June B1/6 Governor Kean today signed a 'lemon law' to protect buyers of defective

new automobiles. **1990** *Daily Tel.* 26 Jan. 19/5 Automobile 'lemon laws' vary, but in most states a motorist whose car has spent as much time in the repair shop as on the road in its first year stands a reasonable chance of getting a new replacement.

lempira (lɛm'piːrə), *n.* Pl. **lempiras.** [The name of *Lempira* (1497–1537), an Indian chieftain killed at Cerquín when leading an army of 30,000 against the conquistadors under Alonso de Cáceres.] The principal monetary unit of Honduras, equivalent to 100 centavos; a coin of this value. Also called *peso.*
 [**1930** *N.Y. Times* 30 Mar. 4/5 The money will be used to stabilize the new Honduran currency, called the empira.] **1931** *Bull. Pan Amer. Union* June 644 By virtue of a decree passed by Congress on March 9, 1931, and signed by the President of the Republic on the following day, the lempira has been adopted as the new monetary unit of Honduras. Its value is fixed at 50 cents, United States currency. **1946** *Whitaker's Almanack 1947* 916/2 [Honduras] Revenue (*Budget*) Lempiras 14,582,493. **1962** R. A. G. CARSON *Coins* 434 The coinage degree [*sic*] of 1926 instituted a new unit—the lempira—which, together with the 50 and 20 centavo values, was struck in silver. **1979** *Internat. Jrnl. Sociol. of Law* VII. 138 United Brands sold Honduras 190 miles of railroad track together with two wharves for the token sum of 2 lempira. **1986** *Times* 28 May 16/2 A refugee from Nicaragua with only 300 lempiras in his pocket.

lender, *n.* Add: **b.** An institution, as a bank, building society, etc., that lends money at interest.
 1873 W. BAGEHOT *Lombard St.* vii. 172 In the worst part of the crisis of 1866, 50,000l. 'fresh money' could not be borrowed even on the best security.. except at the Bank of England. There was no other lender to new borrowers. **1892** *Daily News* 21 Dec. 7/3 Trust shares received a smart shock. Banks are reported unwilling lenders on some trust securities. **1951** R. W. JONES *Thomson's Dict. Banking* (ed. 10) 124/1 If.. there is a limitation on the borrowing powers and the company exceeds such limit, the result may be serious for the lender. **1955** *Times* 10 May 19/2 Some of the big banks called in money, in addition to non-clearing lenders. **1967** *Wall St. Jrnl.* 24 Apr. 32/1 Unregulated lenders have financed.. the capital needed by persons engaging in these activities. **1988** *Daily Tel.* 9 June 2/1 The mortgage war has led building societies, banks and other lenders to mislead borrowers about how much they will have to pay for their home loans.
 c. lender of last resort, a financial institution that will lend to a borrower who cannot obtain funds elsewhere; *esp.* a central bank that will lend to other banks, etc., when they experience heavy withdrawals.
 1932 R. G. HAWTREY *Art of Central Banking* iv. 116 The Central Bank is the *lender of last resort.* **1953** J. L. HANSON *Textbk. Econ.* xxiv. 422 When the other banks are unwilling to lend, the central bank should be prepared to assist eligible borrowers—that is, it should act as a 'lender of last resort'. **1979** F. E. PERRY *Dict. Banking* 137/1 The Bank of England acts as lender of last resort for the London discount houses. **1981** *N.Y. Times Mag.* 29 Mar. 9/2 There would be an international lender of last resort that would serve as a safety net for third-world loans in the event of international turmoil. **1991** *Economist* 13 July 93/2 Unusually, BCCI had no lender of last resort; since 1988 its operations have been supervised, with mixed success, by a 'college' of regulators from seven countries.

length, *n.* Add: **[2.] d.** *Math.* In graph theory, the number of edges in an edge sequence; also more generally, the number of components in any connected sequence.

1959 *Sociometry* XXII. 143 The matrix *M* contains all these paths and also a path of length *l* from each point to itself. **1962** O. ORE *Theory of Graphs* ii. 23 When *S* has both an initial vertex a_0 and a terminal vertex a_n we can write $S = S(a_0, a_n)$ and call a_0 and a_n the endpoints of *S*. We also say that *S* is an edge sequence of length *n* connecting a_0 and a_n. **1965** J. J. ROTMAN *Theory of Groups* iii. 32 α is an *r*-cycle. We also say that α is a cycle of length *r*. **1969** F. HARARY *Graph Theory* ii. 13 A walk of a graph G is an alternating sequence of points and lines.. beginning and ending with points... The length of a walk.. is.. the number of occurrences of lines in it. **1979** *Proc. London Math. Soc.* XXXVIII. 445 A path in a graph is to be regarded as a subgraph with a distinguished end (the initial vertex) rather than a sequence of vertices; it has at least one vertex, and no 'repeated' vertices. Its length is the number of edges in it. **1990** *Glasgow Math. Jrnl.* XXXII. 267 Thus there is a series of finite length in *G* whose infinite factors are either cyclic or quasicyclic.

lens, *n.* Add: [**1.**] **c.** *spec.* Either of the two pieces of glass or other transparent material which are enclosed by the frames of a pair of spectacles, sunglasses, goggles, etc.; the corresponding piece of glass, etc., in a monocle.

*a*1877 E. H. KNIGHT *Dict. Mech.* I. 899 *Folder*, a form of spectacles in which the lenses fold together for the pocket. **1927** F. B. YOUNG *Portrait of Clare* 26 She brushed the dust from her skirt.. her grey eyes swimming behind the lenses of her pincenez. **1965** T. CAPOTE *In Cold Blood* (1966) iv. 237 Mrs. Hickock removed the spectacles she was wearing, polished the smeared lenses and resettled them on her pudgy, agreeable face. **1976** *Verbatim* Sept. 10/2 Both lens [*sic*] of my safety glasses were so scratched up they had to give me new ones. **1987** B. MOORE *Colour of Blood* xviii. 137 He stared at this man, at the.. angry eyes behind thick lenses.

d. = *contact lens* s.v. CONTACT *n.* 6 a. Freq. in *pl.*

1888 C. H. MAY tr. A. E. Fick in *Arch. Ophthalm.* xvii. 226 If the lens fits well, the patient does not complain, has no flow of tears, and either has no injection of the ocular conjunctiva, or very little. **1938** *Trans. Ophthalm. Soc.* LVIII. 120 The question of tolerance was early recognized as important when it was found that some patients could wear a lens and others not. **1962** L. & R. K. DAILY in M. B. Raiford *Contact Lens Managem.* 155 After many weeks or months of wearing the lens, the patient may complain that vision is poor. **1987** *New Yorker* 16 Feb. 36/2 My lenses dry up, and I take them out. **1990** C. BRAYFIELD *Prince* xxii. 487 Her eyes were tired and she had taken out her lenses, so she rummaged at the back of a drawer for her old spectacles to look at them properly.

[**3.**] Also, a similarly-shaped body of other material.

1975 J. G. EVANS *Environment Early Man Brit. Isles* iii. 57 Differential melting of a glacier sometimes results in isolated lenses of ice remaining in rock debris or till long after the bulk of ice has gone. **1984** A. C. & A. DUXBURY *Introd. World's Oceans* vi. 188 Above this water a lens of very salty.. but very warm.. surface water remains. **1990** *Independent* 5 Nov. 15 The coconut palms and breadfruit trees.. depend on a lens of fresh groundwater.

lens, *v.* Restrict *Geol.* to existing sense and add: **2.** *trans.* = FILM *v.* **3.** Also *absol. slang* (orig. and chiefly *U.S.*).

1942 *Variety* 28 Oct. 4 (*heading*) U.S. Signal Corps turning out army of ultra pix technicians for combat lensing. **1950** *Variety* 22 Mar. 20/1 While the pic was lensed as a locationer in Havana, little use has been made of the Cuban capital's natural surroundings. **1981** *Gossip* (Holiday Special) 7/2 To get the look and feel — that gritty realism so necessary for the film — the movie was lensed in the midst of the real *Ft. Apache.* **1983** *Fortune* 7 Mar. 47/3 Twenty Cheshire clerics have thumbed down homevid cameras

lensing during wedding services. **1986** *What Video?* Dec. 46/1 Structures are clearly given extraordinary impact when lensed from a low-angle. **1990** *Rolling Stone* 22 Mar. 29/1 (*heading*) Prince to lens 'Purple Rain' sequel.

So **'lenser** *n.* (now *rare*), a cameraman.

1941 *Variety* 31 Dec. 15/3 (*heading*) Lensers' row threatens to stall prod[uction]. **1943** *Ibid.* 31 Mar. 8/1 A number of the lensers are said to have been killed in the shooting of the footage.

lensed (lɛnzd), *a.* [f. LENS *n.*, LENS *v.*: see -ED[1], -ED[2].] **1.** Having a lens or lenses.

1859 G. A. SALA *Twice round Clock* 255 If you eye him narrowly through the many-lensed lorgnette. **1892** *Illustr. London News* 1 Oct. 431/3 An eye lensed like a microscope, though also lensed like yours and mine. **1976** *Gramophone* Sept. 505/1 A concrete land-based lighthouse uses a lensed array of sixty 100-watt high pressure loudspeaker units. **1987** *Daily Tel.* 13 Oct. 3/1 A slightly-built man with thick-lensed glasses.

2. *Astron.* Of a celestial object or its image: having an appearance affected by a (usu. gravitational) lens situated between it and the observer.

1980 *Astrophysical Jrnl.* CCXLII. L138/2 It appears quite likely that the apparently most luminous quasars will be heavily contaminated by lensed objects. **1985** *Astron. & Astrophysics* CXLVIII. 369 (*heading*) Mutual coherence of gravitationally lensed images. **1988** *Nature* 17 Mar. 235/2 The emission features.. provide evidence that some of the lensed sources are accretion disks around black holes. **1992** *Astronomy* May 26/1 By studying lensed images closely, astronomers can infer something about the intervening material between the quasar and Earth.

lensing, *vbl. n.*[1]: see LENSE *v.*

lensing ('lɛnzɪŋ), *vbl. n.*[2] [f. LENS *v.* + -ING[1].] **1.** *Geol.* The fact or manner of lensing out (LENS *v.* 1).

1923 F. H. LAHEE *Field Geol.* (ed. 2) v. 88 (*heading*) Pinching or lensing of strata. **1953** *Bull. Amer. Assoc. Petroleum Geologists* XXXVII. 1048 The lensing is not cumulative; the following beds tend to smooth off the effect of a pinch-out.

2. The making of a film; the taking of a photograph or photographs. *slang* (orig. *U.S.*).

1942 *Variety* 28 Oct. 4 (*heading*) U.S. Signal Corps turning out army of ultra pix technicians for combat lensing. **1983** *Listener* 4 Aug. 33/4 Your correspondent was fortunate enough to secure an interview with the delightful Miss Bergen.. during the lensing of this masterpiece. **1990** *Bop* Oct. 34/1 England's capital city, London, was home to the hazel-eyed actor during the lensing of the flick!

3. *Physics* and *Astron.* Effects resembling those produced by a lens or lenses, *esp.* a bending or focusing of light or other radiation by a strong gravitational field (cf. *gravitational lens* s.v. *GRAVITATIONAL adj.* b) or by inhomogeneities in refractive index caused by non-uniform heating.

1970 *Appl. Optics* IX. 1727 (*heading*) Simple measurement of thermal lensing effects in laser rods. **1977** *Jrnl. Chem. Physics* LXVI. 667/2 It is hoped that in the near future the spectral range of the highly sensitive thermal lensing spectroscopy will be greatly extended. **1981** *Nature* 12 Feb. 533/1 The differences in redshift [of the quasars] rule out any kind of gravitational lensing of a single object. **1988** *Ibid.* 17 Mar. 234/1 (*heading*) Gravitational radiation and gravitational lensing as a source of electromagnetic bursts. **1992** *New Scientist* 29 Feb. 21/2 Although each image will look like a normal star that is not being lensed by the black hole, the researchers think there could be a way of telling whether gravitational lensing is really taking place.

lensing ('lɛnzɪŋ), *ppl. a. Astron.* [f. **LENSING vbl. n.²*: see -ING².] That causes lensing of light or other radiation.

1984 *Science* 10 Feb. 574/3 None of the lensing galaxies lie in a straight line with their quaser images. **1988** *Nature* 24 Nov. 358/1 From the enhancement of the quaser surface density in the vicinity of the galaxies we are able to draw some general conclusions about the distribution of the lensing matter. **1989** C. WILL in P. Davies *New Physics* ii. 13/1 The number and characteristics of the images.. can be used as a probe of the mass distribution of the lensing galaxy or cluster of galaxies.

lenslet ('lɛnzlɪt), *n.* [f. LENS *n.* + -LET.] A small lens, *esp.* one of many in a compound eye or a lenticular film.

1956 J. S. COURTNEY-PRATT in Naslin & Vivie *Actes du 2ème Congrès Internat. de Photogr. et Cinématogr. Ultra-Rapides* 153/1 A plate embossed with a large number of small lenslets. **1961** *New Scientist* 30 Nov. 570/3 Adjacent lenslets of an insect eye are coherently illuminated by a small source. **1962** W. G. HYZER *Engin. & Sci. High-speed Photogr.* i. 42 A lenticular plate, comprised of an array of spherical lenslets, is employed to produce a corresponding array of spots on the photo-sensitive film. **1978** *Sci. Amer.* Dec. 98/1 *(caption)* Hexagonal array of lenslets in the refracting compound eye of the diamondback moth (family Plutellidae) is clearly visible in a scanning electron micrograph. **1984** L. W. WALLIS *Electronic Typesetting* i. 6 Lenslets associated with each character diverted the images to a common optical path. **1992** *N.Y. Times* 17 Mar. C8/3 Light from the telescope's mirror will be split up among many tiny lenses arranged in an array pattern. Each 'lenslet'.. will focus its own little image of the star on its own light detector.

lenticular, *a.* and *n.* Add: [A.] [1.] [b.] **lenticular cloud** *Meteorol.*, a lens- or lentil-shaped cloud with sharp, sometimes iridescent outlines, which usually occurs in association with lee waves.

[**1894** W. C. LEY *Cloudland* iv. 49 When a patch of cloud has an approximately circular periphery, and a somewhat greater vertical thickness at or near its centre than at its edge, towards which it shelves off, being, in fact, a flat spheroid, its largest diameter lying parallel to the earth's surface, we call the cloud Lenticular.] *Ibid.* 50 Rather rarely, I have seen very perfect *Lenticular clouds during a frosty afternoon in winter lying above the summits of low hills. **1926** W. J. HUMPHREYS *Fogs & Clouds* iii. 58 The lenticular cloud.. often is only the cloud cap to a stationary.. air billow produced as a rule by the flow of the wind over an uneven surface. **1978** A. WELCH *Bk. Airsports* vii. 122/2 *(caption)* Wave systems are often characterized by smooth-edged lenticular clouds which remain almost stationary in the sky. **1985** *Nat. Geographic* May 673/1 Wave, or lenticular, clouds.., partly created by strong winds blowing perpendicular to a mountain range.

lenticular galaxy *Astron.*, a galaxy having the flattened shape and dense centre characteristic of spiral galaxies, but without discernable spiral arms.

1953 E. E. SMITH *Second Stage Lensmen* xvii. 231 But the *Dauntless* was not within any *lenticular galaxy—nowhere was there any sign of a Milky Way! **1977** J. NARLIKAR *Struct. Universe* iii. 68 Apart from this there are lenticular galaxies So, which resemble the spirals in many respects but which are very much dominated by the bulge. **1992** M. J. WEST in S. P. Maran *Astron. & Astrophysics Encycl.* 95/2 The galaxy populations of rich regular clusters tend to be composed primarily of elliptical and So (lenticular) galaxies, with only a small fraction of spirals.

lentigo, *n.* Add: In mod. use, a small brown hyperpigmented patch of skin usually occurring on the face or hands, particularly in elderly

people; **lentigo maligna** [mod.L., tr. F. *lentigo malin* (coined by W. Dubreuilh 1894, in *Annales de Dermatol. & Syphiligr.* V. 1092)], a darker lentigo in which there are epidermal changes and which in time may become malignant. Freq. without article.

1894 *Arch. Surg.* V. 253 *(heading)* Lentigo-melanosis. **1934** *Amer. Jrnl. Cancer* XXII. 24 Lentigo is a brownish non-elevated lesion appearing in normal skin. It is usually dark brown, much darker than ephelids, which are more commonly known as freckles. **1936** *Arch. Dermatol. & Syphilol.* XXXIII. 125 Greater uniformity in the use of the term 'lentigo' is needed, and the term should not be used synonymously with 'ephelis'. *Ibid.* 109 The subject of lentigo has received scant attention in the American literature, and the term has usually been employed synonymously with 'ephelis' or 'freckle'. **1940** BECKER & OBERMAYER *Mod. Dermatol. & Syphilol.* xviii. 292/1 Lentigo (in contrast to ephelis, which is the common freckle) is a localized dark brownish macular discoloration, appearing all the way from early adult life to old age, varying in size from a few millimeters in diameter to a centimeter or more. The lesions are distinguished from freckles by the later age of appearance, the darker color, and the tendency to increase in size. **1954** *Jrnl. Investigative Dermatol.* XXII. 219 Lentigo maligna has been classed as melanoma *in situ* or as a premelanomatous lesion. **1955** V. NABOKOV *Lolita* I. xxvii. 148 Her cheeks looked hollowed and too much lentigo camouflaged her rosy rustic features. **1967** *Med. Jrnl. Austral.* 21 Jan. 125/1 *Lentigo*, a pigmented lesion composed of proliferated melanocytes, but there are no distinct nests of nævus cells. The epidermal rete ridges are often elongated. **1987** *Oxf. Textbk. Med.* (ed. 2) II. xx. 45/2 Spreading pigmented actinic keratoses show slight verrucous changes and can merge into a squamous cell carcinoma or into a lentigo maligna. **1988** *Brit. Med. Jrnl.* 5 Mar. 704/4 The even flat brown lentigo on the face of elderly patients grows slowly over the years. However, a nodular raised portion indicates the development of more rapidly growing invasive melanoma.

lentivirus ('lɛntɪvaɪrəs), *n. Biol.* and *Med.* [f. L. *lent-us* slow + -I- + VIRUS *n.*] Any retrovirus of the subfamily Lentivirinae, infection by which is characterized by a delay in the appearance of any symptoms.

1979 *Vet. Rec.* 8 Sept. 220/2 The maedi/visna group of viruses are classified as lentiviruses in the family Retroviridae. **1985** *Jrnl. R. Soc. Med.* LXXVIII. 613/2 The AIDS virus is a retrovirus of the subfamily Lentivirinae.. of which only three other species are known: the lentiviruses causing maedi-visna in sheep, infectious anaemia in horses, and encephalitis-arthritis in goats. **1986** *N.Y. Rev. Bks.* 16 Jan. 44/4 Some researchers have argued that it should be classified as one of the lentiviruses, which cause brain disorders in sheep and other animals. **1987** *Nature* 16 Apr. 636/1 Recognition that AIDS (acquired immune deficiency syndrome) is caused by a lentivirus has been slow in coming.

Hence **lenti'viral** *a.*

1985 *Rev. Infectious Dis.* VII. 75 *(title)* Experimental visna in Icelandic sheep: the prototype lentiviral infection.

lentoid, *a.* and *n.* Add: **B.** *n. Embryol.* A lens-shaped or spherical structure composed of retinal cells adhering together.

1940 *Jrnl. Exper. Zool.* LXXXIII. 115 Description of injuries to the optic cup and the relation of lenses and lentoids to the edges of the iris are given.. to show the improbability of considering such cases as examples of lenses arising from the iris. **1956** *Acta Morphol. Neerlando-Scand.* I. 88 Next to the depressed ectoderm there is an extensive placode area. The lentoid is localized at the exact edge of the thickened ectoderm plate. **1979** *Nature* 6 Dec. 628/2 Lentoids (structures composed of lens fibre cells) have the highest proportions of σ-crystallins when derived from retinas of earlier embryonic stages.

leontiasis, *n.* Add: **2.** *Path.* In full **leontiasis ossea** ('ɒsɪə) [coined in Ger. (R. Virchow *Die krankhaften Geschwülste* (1865) II. 23), f. L. *osseus* bony]. A condition of overgrowth of facial and other cranial bones, giving the head a supposedly lion-like appearance.

1885 *Trans. Acad. Med. in Ireland* III. 316 Every bone in the body..was very heavy, unduly bulky, and exemplified the condition named by Virchow 'leontiasis'. **1891** *Internat. Clinics* I. 17 In *leontiasis ossea* there is a growth of true bony tumors of the face and cranium, instead of the uniformly distributed hyperostosis of this disease [*sc.* acromegaly]. **1900** DORLAND *Med. Dict.* 351/1 *Leontiasis,*..1. A bilateral and symmetric hypertrophy of the bones of the face and skull, leading to a lion-like facial expression. Called also *L. ossea* or *L. ossium.* **1914** *Med. Chron.* (Manchester) May 86 Some of the records again suggest examples of diffuse osteoma or sarcoma rather than a true leontiasis. **1957** *Encycl. Brit.* XIII. 941/1 *Leontiasis ossea,* a rare disease characterized by an overgrowth of the facial and cranial bones. **1991** *Nephron* LVIII. 475/1 Facial leontiasis is an extremely rare form of renal osteodystrophy.

leopon ('lɛpən), *n. Zool.* [f. LEOP(ARD *n.* + LI)ON *n.*] An animal born of a mating between a leopard and a lion. Cf. LIGER *n.*, TIGON *n.*

1960 *Internat. Zoo Yearbk.* I. 44 (*heading*) Leopons born at Koshien Zoo-Botanical Gardens. **1976** *Observer* (Colour Suppl.) 5 Sept. 42/2 Two leopons were born at a zoo in Japan in 1959. **1985** *Sunday Tel.* 21 July 2/4 The last of the 'Leopons', a cross between a leopard and a lion, has died at a zoo in western Japan.

lepidoptery (lɛpɪ'dɒptərɪ), *n.* [f. LEPIDOPTER(A *n. pl.* + -Y[3].] = LEPIDOPTEROLOGY *n.*

1959 *Times* 31 Jan. 10/4 He is becoming something of a specialist in lepidoptery. **1972** *Times Lit. Suppl.* 25 Aug. 984/3 Even the lepidoptery brings lovely evanescence and hard, abstract taxonomy together. **1982** B. TRAPIDO *Brother of More Famous Jack* xvii. 62, I wore the butterfly pinned to my book-bag which caused Jacob..to remark innocently that the young these days seemed curiously disposed to lepidoptery. **1991** *New Scientist* 21/28 Dec. 72/4, I needed to know more of the major figures of lepidoptery and ornithology.

Lepontian (lɪ'pɒntɪən), *n.* and *a.* [f. L. *Lēponti-i* a people of Cisalpine Gaul + -AN.] **A.** *n.* A native or inhabitant of the Lepontine Alps. **B.** *adj.* = *LEPONTINE a.*

1565 A. GOLDING tr. *Cæsar's Gallic War* IV. f. 89, Now the Rhyne ryseth among the Lepontians who inhabit the Alpes. **1857** E. H. BUNBURY in W. Smith *Dict. Greek & Roman Geogr.* II. 161/1 The name of *Alpes Lepontiae,* or Lepontian Alps, is generally given by modern geographers to the part of this chain extending from *Monte Rosa* to the *St. Gothard*; but there is no ancient authority for this use. **1921** *Philologica* I. 38 (*heading*) The Lepontian personal names in -alo-s and some remarks on the Lydian inscriptions.

Lepontic (lɪ'pɒntɪk), *n.* and *a.* [ad. L. *Lēponticus:* see *LEPONTIAN n.* and *a.,* -IC.] **A.** *n.* The Celtic dialect anciently spoken in the region of the Lepontine Alps. **B.** *adj.* Of or pertaining to this dialect.

1926 R. S. CONWAY in *Cambr. Anc. Hist.* IV. xiii. 435What differences existed between Ligurian and other dialects farther north and east, Lepontic and Raetic, it is difficult to say. **1933** C. D. BUCK *Compar. Gram. Greek & Latin* 24 'Lepontic' inscriptions, from the region of the North Italian lakes, which probably

represent a form of Ligurian. **1948** D. DIRINGER *Alphabet* II. ix. 500 The inscriptions of Lugano, termed Lepontic, or else Ligurian-Celtic. **1989** J. P. MALLORY *In Search of Indo-Europeans* iii. 95 There is also Lepontic, a Celtic language known from about 70 inscriptions which derives from the Alpine region to the north of Milan.

Lepontine (lɪ'pɒntaɪn), *a.* [ad. late L. *Lepontinus:* see *LEPONTIAN n.* and *a.,* -INE[1].] **a.** Pertaining to or designating a mountain range in southern Switzerland and northern Italy, which encompasses the valley of the River Ticino. **b.** Denoting an ancient language of this region. Cf. *LEPONTIC n.* and *a.*

c **1802** REES *Cycl.* s.v. *Alps,* The eastern part of this ridge was denominated the Lepontine Alps, from the appellation of a people who inhabit the country. **1853** *Encycl. Brit.* II. 623/2 *Lepontine Alps,* also named Alps of Switzerland..extend from Monte Rosa..separating Lombardy from Switzerland. **1939** L. H. GRAY *Foundations of Lang.* 335 In the extreme north of Italy..some seventy-two inscriptions..have been discovered. These are conventionally called Lepontine. **1989** *Encycl. Brit.* X. 385/3 *San Bernadino Pass,*..mountain pass..in the Lepontine Alps of Graubünden canton, southeastern Switzerland.

lepto-, *comb. form.* Add: **leptomeninx** (-'mɛnɪŋks) *Anat.* [MENINX *n.*], pl. **-meninges** (-mɪ'nɪndʒiːz), the arachnoid and pia mater considered together; usu. in *pl.* in same sense.

1889 *Cent. Dict.,* *Leptomeninges.* **1893** *Funk's Stand. Dict., Leptomeninx.* **1899** *Allbutt's Syst. Med.* VII. 712 The leptomeninges stripping, on the contrary, with undue ease. **1934** R. R. GRINKER *Neurology* iii. 62 Recent experiments have been interpreted to suggest that the primitive leptomeninx is of ectodermal origin. *Ibid.,* The external layer of the leptomeninx lies underneath the dura mater. **1959** ROIZIN & KOLB in Kies & Alvord '*Allergic*' *Encephalomyelitis* i. 6 The lesions..were generally irregular in form and size, involving the gray and white matter of the cerebral cortex, and extending into the surrounding areas, including the periventricular regions, subarachnoid spaces and leptomeninges. **1977** *Lancet* 9 July 90/1 Foci of round-cell infiltration were found in the leptomeninges and in the wall of small vessels intracerebrally. **1985** C. R. LEESON et al. *Textbk. Histol.* (ed. 5) vii. 228/2 Pia and arachnoid have a similar structure and sometimes are regarded as a single layer called the leptomeninx or leptomeninges.

leptonema (lɛptəʊ'niːmə), *n. Cytol.* [a. F. *leptonema* (coined by V. Grégoire 1907, in *La Cellule* XXIV. 371): see LEPTO-, *-NEMA.*] = LEPTOTENE *n.*

1911 *Q. Jrnl. Microsc. Sci.* LVII. 8 For the various stages of the prophase I have used the nomenclature now generally adopted, based on that proposed by von Winiwarter in his work on mammalian oögenesis. The stages run: leptonema, zygonema, pachynema, strepsinema or diplonema (adjectives leptotene, zygotene, etc.), and diakinesis. **1924** L. DONCASTER *Introd. Study Cytol.* v. 67 The early stage of the primary spermatocyte, when the nucleus contains a network of thin threads, is called leptonema. **1971** *Chromosoma* XXXV. 11 Nuclei of cells in leptonema fixed within one half hour after being placed into culture characteristically contained condensed chromatin attached to a less dense fibrous core. **1984** *Cytologia* XLIX. 88 Sporocytes in a single anther were in meiotic stages from leptonema to pollen development.

leptoquark ('lɛptəʊkwɑːk), *n. Particle Physics.* [f. LEPTO(N *n.*[2] + QUARK *n.*] Any of several hypothetical subatomic particles supposed to have some lepton-like and some quark-like properties.

1974 GREENBERG & NELSON in *Physical Rev. D.* X. 2568/2 We suggest that the word 'quark' be reserved for a real or fictitious fundamental field or particle for hadron physics, and suggest the word 'leptoquark' as the leptonic analog of quark. **1978** *Nature* 5 Jan. 22/2 Form factors arising from a composite nature (a pair of quarks, heavy leptons, leptoquarks?) or a hidden strong interaction of W± could save the day. **1979** *Ibid.* 19 Apr. 688/1 An outcome of such a unification is that in addition to the photon and the coloured gluons of QED and QCD, there will exist a new ultraweak force whose quanta carry and couple both to electrical and to colour charge. These quanta have been called 'leptoquarks'. **1982** *Sci. Amer.* Apr. 95/1 To account for such a disintegration novel particles called leptoquarks are introduced to change quarks..into leptons... The leptoquarks would be extremely heavy, perhaps 10¹⁴ times as heavy as the proton. **1992** *Ibid.* Aug. 15/1 The accelerator will truly deserve a place on Mount Olympus if it produces an exotic particle known as a leptoquark.

lesion ('liːʒən), *v.* Chiefly *Med.* and *Zool.* [f. LESION *n.*] *trans.* To cause a lesion in (an animal, organ, etc.). Usu. in *pass.* Also *fig.*

1926 J. DEVANNY *Butcher Shop* xxiii. 280 How could she blame that dear mother, who had married young herself, and had been fortunate enough to meet no other man to lesion the content of her domestic life? **1961** *Amer. Jrnl. Physiol.* CCI. 426/2 In the final group of animals lesioned in the pallido-hypothalamic tract immediately dorsal to the fornix columns..there developed a sudden hyperphagic tendency 2 days later. **1973** *New Scientist* 15 Mar. 604/1 He recalled that he had lesioned in cats the 'brake' that prevents them from moving while they dream. **1974** *Nature* 13 Dec. 587/2 There was no significant difference between rats lesioned with 6-OH-dopamine and those lesioned with 5,6-HT. **1987** *Ann. Neurol.* XXII. 735 In some of the monkeys the BNM [*sc.* basal nucleus of Meynert] was lesioned only partly with some surrounding tissue affected as well.

So **'lesioned** *ppl. a.,* **'lesioning** *vbl. n.*

1961 *Amer. Jrnl. Physiol.* CCI. 424/1 No evidence of adipsic or aphagic 'escape'..was seen in any of the far-laterally lesioned animals. *Ibid.* 428/2 These findings indicate a complex organization of the hypothalamic 'feeding center', with 'motivational' and 'metabolic' elements running in separate circuits.., and thus dissociable by lesioning and stimulation methods. **1966** *Jap. Jrnl. Pharmacol.* XVI. 276 (*title*) Effects of some centrally acting drugs on food intake of normal and hypothalamus-lesioned rats. **1972** *Sci. Amer.* Dec. 75/3 They found that immediately after a unilateral lesion had been made the animals were completely unable to follow objects in the visual field contralateral to the lesioned colliculus. **1987** *Jrnl. Exper. Biol.* CXXXII. 59 Glial regeneration in insect central nervous connectives, following selective chemical lesioning, involves both exogenous and endogenous elements. **1991** M. AMIS *Time's Arrow* iii. 100 In the mouth the buccal mucosa are lesioned, the oropharynx inflamed. **1991** M. BENEDIKT *Cyberspace* (1993) i. 23 With mature cyberspaces and virtual reality technology, this kind of warpage, tunneling, and lesioning of the fabric of reality will become a perceptual, phenomenal fact at hundreds of thousands of locations.

less, *a.* (*n., adv.,* and *conj.*) Add: [B.] [1.] c. Special collocation: **less developed,** *spec.* applied to a country in which economic growth, income per capita, the literacy level, etc. are low compared with some other group of countries. Cf. DEVELOPING *ppl. a.*

1940 G. CROWTHER *Outl. Money* ii. 76 The more highly developed banking systems are more prone to suffer from such a 'liquidity preference' than the *less developed countries. **1962** *U.N. Econ. & Social Council Resolution* XXXIV. cmxvii, in *Unctad—Basic Documents* (1966) i. 1 Both the developed and the less developed countries are to intensify their efforts in

order to ensure a self-sustaining growth. **1979** *Dædalus* Winter 85 War and famine might not immediately break out again; but their banishment would depend to a greater extent on.. the strength of the less-developed world. **1992** *Economist* 29 Feb. 77/2 Portugal will be helped in its fiscal consolidation effort by the agreement reached at Maastricht to create an economic cohesion or catch-up fund to help the less developed member states prepare for EMU.

lestobiosis (ˌlɛstəʊbaɪ'əʊsɪs), *n. Zool.* [ad. F. *lestobiose* (A. Forel 1901, in *Ann. de la Soc. entomol. de Belgique* XLV. 394), f. Gr. λῃστής robber + βίωσις way of life, after SYMBIOSIS *n.,* etc.] A form of symbiosis found among certain social insects in which a small species inhabits the nest of a larger one and feeds on the food stored there, or on the brood of the larger species. Cf. KLEPTOBIOSIS *n.*

1903 *Biol. Bull.* IV. 147 This mode of life has been the recently called 'lestobiosis' by Forel. **1927** H. ST. J. K. DONISTHORPE *Guests of Brit. Ants* iii. 78 Ants exhibit a variety of associations, symbiotic, mutualistic, and parasitic... Such associations consist of—Cleptobiosis (originally used to denote thievery, now applied to brigandage by Wheeler); Lestobiosis [etc.]. **1967** J. H. SUDD *Introd. Behaviour Ants* v. 78 Forel coined the name lestobiosis for the supposed life of brigandage which *S. fugax* leads. **1975** E. O. WILSON *Sociobiol.* 588 *Lestobiosis,* the relationship in which colonies of a small species of social insect nest in the walls of a larger species and enter the chambers of the larger species to prey on brood or to rob the food stores.

Hence **lestobiotic** (-baɪ'ɒtɪk) *a.,* exhibiting or pertaining to lestobiosis.

1913 W. M. WHEELER *Ants* xxiii. 427 The lestobiotic species, most of which belong to the Myrmicine tribe Solenopsidii, comprise the following. **1967** J. H. SUDD *Introd. Behaviour Ants* v. 78 Most of the other ants which are said to be lestobiotic are found well away from the nests of other ants too.

let, *v.¹* Add: [8.] c. *trans.* To assign or grant (work, a contract, etc.) *to* an applicant. Also const. *out:* cf. sense 37 f below.

1850 C. KINGSLEY *Alton Locke* I. x. 147 Were not the army clothes..furnished by contractors and sweaters, who hired the work at low prices, and let it out again to journeymen at still lower ones? *a* **1852** H. MAYHEW *London Labour* (1861) II. 330/1 The first man who agrees to the job takes it in the lump, and he again lets it to others in the piece. **1881** GOLDW. SMITH *Lett. & Ess.* 164 He [Mr. Brassey] favoured the butty-gang system, of letting work to a gang of a dozen men, who divide the pay, allowing something extra to the head of the gang. **1901** *Daily News* 18 Feb. 5/6 Imagine a great city letting out its lines of communication to concessionnaire contractors with dividends to make. **1952** E. J. PRATT *Towards Last Spike* v. 20 In 1880 Tupper lets contract to Onderdonk for survey and construction through the Pacific Section of the mountains. **1975** *Economist* 18 Jan. 76/1 In early 1972 the American air force let contracts for 'lightweight fighter' prototypes, primarily to develop technology. **1991** *South* Aug. 60/1 Schemes, long promised, finally came out to tender and contracts were let.

letchugia *n.,* obs. var. *LECHUGUILLA *n.*

lethal, *a.* and *n.* Add: [A.] [4.] In weakened sense: highly damaging or injurious, devastating. Cf. DEADLY *a.* 8 b, DEVASTATING *ppl. a.*

1942 BERREY & VAN DEN BARK *Amer. Thes. Slang* §702/2 *Hard blow.* Baby,..lethal left *or* right, lethal potion, lil, [etc.]. *a* **1961** in *Webster* s.v., Showed a lethal skill in his dissection of the..book. **1978** V.

BROME *Jung* xii. 119 One particularly lethal champagne-party. **1989** *Guardian* 3 July 14/3 A lethal drop shot, and a determination to hunt down every ball. **1989** *Independent* 19 Dec. 24/3 He devised..desserts of a baroque and lethal richness. **1991** *Ace* Feb. 111/1 While a bit slow and irritating running from floppies due to all the swapping, a hard disc shows the game to be far faster and more lethal than normal Chess.

letter, *n.*[1] Add: [I.] [1.] [a.] Also *transf.*, the smallest meaningful unit of a code, esp. the genetic code.

1954 *Nature* 13 Feb. 318/2 The enzymes..are long peptide chains formed by about twenty different kinds of amino-acids, and can be considered as long 'words' based on a 20-letter alphabet. **1957** *Proc. Nat. Acad. Sci.* XLIII. 417 Gamow's code was also 'degenerate' — that is, several sets of three letters (picked in a special way) stood for a particular amino acid. **1962** *New Scientist* 4 Jan. 33/3 Thus the two most important questions have been answered. The code is made up of three-letter words and has to be read consecutively from one end. **1977** *Time* 4 Apr. 39/2 There are certain constraints on the way that the nucleotides, or 'letters' of the genetic message are arranged. **1992** *U.S. News & World Rep.* 4 Nov. 69/1 Sickle cell anemia..is the tragic result of a single incorrect letter in the 60,000-letter gene for hemoglobin.

[II.] [8.] [b.] *letter-sorting*.

1897 *Patents for Inventions: Abridgments of Specifications* 1884–88: *Class* 52 57/2 Dickson, W...*Tables.*—Relates to postal or *letter-sorting tables. **1963** *Hansard Commons: Written Answers* 2 Aug. 203 Mr. Mawby: Current contracts are as follows...One contract..covering three items — a high-speed letter sorting machine, a single position letter sorting machine and a letter coding desk. **1993** H. PETROSKI *Evolution of Useful Things* 35 Rabinow holds 225 patents for devices ranging from self-regulators for watches and clocks to the automatic letter-sorting machines used by the Post Office.

[9.] **letter-drop**, (*b*) = DROP *n.* 17 d; also, the act or practice of placing a letter, information, etc., in a letter-drop.

1971 'A. HALL' *Warsaw Document* iii. 32 He delivers the goods by letter-drop and he's caught doing it because he's meant to be. **1975** *Forbes* (N.Y.) 1 July 70/1 We've got a letter drop in Nassau, but who doesn't? We do have an equity investment in a European bank, but we're not in any consortia. **1978** *Washington Post* 5 July A16/6 One of the men said that their 'Suite 6' does not receive much mail for the Club, that they serve several other clients as a letter drop, [etc.]. **1989** *N.Y. Times* 17 Sept. VI. 82 He also admitted making dead letter drops to the Russians but it is now conceded that any information he did pass was to dupe the Russians.

letter jacket *N. Amer.*, a blouson-style jacket in school or college colours with an embroidered or sewn-on letter, orig. indicating achievement in sport (see sense 1 e above).

1974 J. IRVING *158-Pound Marriage* ii. 35 He wore a blatant college *letter-jacket, black with leather sleeves and a thick, oversized gold 'I' on the breast. **1985** *New Yorker* 28 Jan. 66/2 In Bydalek's classroom sat twenty gangly examples of the modern yeoman class, wearing letter jackets, their hair teased and blow-dried, their faces happily expectant.

letter sweater *N. Amer.* = *letter jacket* above.

1959 *Times Lit. Suppl.* 18 Dec. 737/1 Football is God, a letter sweater the height of ambition for the boys (for the girls it is to be chosen as cheer leader..). **1989** *Washington Post* 22 July C1/2 Archie, the eternal teen, has graduated from saddle shoes and letter sweaters to jeans and sneakers.

Letterer–Siwe (ˌlɛtərəˈsiːvə), *n. Path.* [The names of Erich *Letterer* (b. 1895) and Sture August *Siwe* (b. 1897), German physicians.] Used *attrib.* and in the possessive to designate

a usually fatal histiocytosis of soft tissues, occurring in early childhood.

1936 ABT & DENENBERG in *Amer. Jrnl. Dis. Children* LI. 499 (*heading*) Letterer-Siwe's disease. **1949** *Amer. Jrnl. Path.* XXV. 49 These cases fulfill the requirements for Letterer-Siwe's disease as formulated by Abt and Denenberg. **1953** L. LICHTENSTEIN in *A.M.A. Arch. Path.* LV. 102 The conditions previously designated eosinophilic granuloma of bone, 'Letter-Siwe disease' and 'Schüller-Christian disease' are interrelated manifestations of a single malady. The name 'histiocytosis X' is suggested as a provisional broad general description for this nosologic entity. **1961** R. D. BAKER *Essent. Path.* xviii. 489 Reticuloendotheliosis (Letterer-Siwe disease) is either a hyperplasia or a true neoplasm of the macrophage system of infants, with enlargement of the liver and spleen. **1986** *Times* 13 June 13/2 Doctors have to be on the look-out for..the very rare hystiocytosis [*sic*] X (Letterer-Siwe disease).

leuco-, *comb. form.* Add: **leuko·dystrophy** *Path.* [f. mod.L. *leukodystrophia*, coined in Ger. (Bielschowsky and Hennenberg 1928, in *Jrnl. f. Psychol. und Neurol.* XXXVI. 180)], any of several disorders of the white matter of the central nervous system (sometimes also affecting peripheral nerves), characterized by defective formation or breakdown of myelin; cf. *leucoencephalitis* below.

1960 *Jrnl. Neuropath. & Exper. Neurol.* XIX. 334 A survey of the literature shows that there are apparently only 10 reported instances of pathologically verified cases of infantile metachromatic *leukodystrophy. **1984** TIGHE & DAVIES *Pathology* (ed. 4) xxv. 245 The leucodystrophies are abnormalities of myelin leading to deficient myelination. **1991** *Lancet* 21–8 Dec. 1603/1 We report here on our experience with this drug in the symptomatic treatment of spasticity due to metabolic diseases with leukodystrophy in six children.

leucoencepha·litis, (*a*) *Vet. Sci.*, softening of the white matter of the brain in horses following a diet of mouldy corn; (*b*) *Path.*, inflammation of the white matter of the brain in humans.

1909 *Cent. Dict.* Suppl., *Leucoencephalitis*, same as *forage-poisoning*. **1917** D. S. WHITE *Text-bk. Princ. & Pract. Vet. Med.* iii. 125 Mycotic gastro-enteritis (Silage poisoning. Forage poisoning...Falsely called 'Cerebrospinal meningitis'. Leuko-encephalitis). **1928** *Arch. Neurol. & Psychiatry* XIX. 263 Leuko-encephalitis periaxalis concentrica means a disease in the course of which the white matter of the brain is destroyed in concentric layers. **1950** J. G. GREENFIELD in *Brain* LXXIII. 150 The name *subacute sclerosing encephalitis* therefore appears fully justified. Dr. van Bogaert's term 'leuco-encephalitis' emphasizes the characteristic damage to the white matter, but leaves out of account the cortical changes which are also important. Perhaps the term 'Panencephalitis' already adopted by Pette (1942) for forms which attack both grey and white matter could be usefully employed here, i.e. 'Subacute sclerosing panencephalitis'. **1961** *Lancet* 16 Sept. 656/1 He illustrated also the biopsy findings in two instances of subacute sclerosing leucoencephalitis. **1977** *Ibid.* 7 May 1001/1 One had a severe chronic leucoencephalitis. **1989** *Jrnl. Royal Soc. Med.* LXXXII. 307/1 Opportunistic infection in this series included toxoplasmosis, cytomegalovirus.. encephalitis and progressive multifocal leuko-encephalitis.

leuco·tactic *a. Physiol.*, of, pertaining to, encouraging, or resembling leucotaxis.

1963 *Biol. Abstr.* XLIV. 514/2 Isolation of a basic polypeptide with a *leukotactic and permeation-promoting action. **1977** *Lancet* 15 Oct. 799/2 Leucocytes migrate in response to an increasing leucotactic (chemotactic) gradient in vitro and, most probably, in vivo.

leuco'taxis *n. Physiol.* [see *leuco-taxin* above], the migration of leucocytes in a particular direction.

1949 *Amer. Jrnl. Path.* XXV. 5 There was no leukotaxis, in that none of the lesions showed significant numbers of polymorphonuclear leukocytes or other elements of suppurative inflammation. **1969** WARD & SCHLEGAL in *Lancet* 16 Aug. 344/2 We describe here a different type of leucocyte defect that involves chemotactic function (leucotaxis) of neutrophils. **1985** *Agents & Actions* XVI. 48/1 Amplification and perpetuation of the primary inflammatory response depends on leukocyte recruitment by leukotaxis.

leucosin ('l(j)uːkə(ʊ)sɪn), *n. Biochem.* Also **leukosin.** [f. Gr. λευκός white + -IN¹, after G. *Leucosin, Leukosin.*] **1.** An albumin found in some cereal grains.

1894 OSBORNE & VOORHEES in *Jrnl. Amer. Chem. Soc.* XVI. 528 Leucosin, an albumin, .. was found to form between 0.3 and 0.4 per cent of the wheat kernel. **1907** T. B. OSBORNE *Proteins of Wheat Kernel* 114 Leucosin resembles the animal proteins in ultimate composition. **1963** E. G. YOUNG in Florkin & Stotz *Comprehensive Biochem.* VII. I. i. 6 The albumins which have been most carefully characterized are ovalbumin and conalbumin of egg white .. leucosin of cereals, myoalbumin and the myogens of muscle. **2.** A polysaccharide occurring in food storage vesicles in some of the golden algae, now regarded as related to laminaran.

1914 *Archiv für Protistenkunde* XXXII. 251 In solutions containing sugar the leukosin body is conspicuously large... Owing to its ready solubility leukosin is often not present in fixed and stained material. It seems possible that it is a form of sugar. **1928** *Funk's Stand. Dict.,* Leucosin. **1955** G. M. SMITH *Cryptogamic Bot.* (ed. 2) v. 168 Oil is the chief food reserve accumulated in protoplasts of Xanthophyceae, but leucosin, an insoluble white substance, is also a rather widely distributed food reserve. **1965** *Jrnl. Chem. Soc.* 7036 The food reserve polysaccharide of the *Chrysophyta* .. has been given different names in the different classes, but it appears that leucosin, volutin, and chromatin are the same substance. **1983** *Plant Physiol.* LXXIII. 418 Leucosin is a polysaccharide composed of β-(1→3)-linked D-glucose residues.

leucotriene *n.,* var. *LEUKOTRIENE *n.*

leukotriene (l(j)uːkəʊ'traiiːn), *n. Biochem.* Also **leuco-.** [f. LEUCO- + TRIENE *n.*] Any of a group of biologically active metabolites of arachidonic acid, originally isolated from leucocytes, which contain three conjugated double bonds.

1979 B. SAMUELSSON et al. in *Prostaglandins* XVII. 785 The term *leukotriene* is introduced for compounds which like SRS [*sc.* slow reacting substance] are non-cyclized C_{20} carboxylic acids with one or two oxygen substituents and three conjugated double bonds. **1983** *Oxf. Textbk. Med.* II. xv. 60 Humoral mediators producing bronchoconstriction .. include histamine, the leucotrienes, and bradykinin. **1984** TIGHE & DAVIES *Pathology* (ed. 4) iii. 15 The leukotrienes .. have been shown to be responsible for the activity attributed to slow-reacting substance (SRS) in the earlier literature. **1989** *Nature* 9 Feb. 555/1 Arachidonic acid is converted to prostaglandins by cyclooxygenase and to leukotrienes by 5-lipoxygenase.

levallorphan (ˌliːvə'lɔːfæn), *n. Pharm.* [f. LEV(O- + ALL(YL *n.* + M)ORPH(INE *n.* + -AN, elements of the systematic name.] A morphine analogue and opioid antagonist, $C_{19}H_{25}NO$, given intravenously (usu. as the tartrate) to counteract some of the depressant effects of certain narcotics.

1953 *Anesthesiology* XIV. 550 Levallorphan is the generic name of 3-hydroxy-N-allylmorphan and was originally designated as R_0 1-7700. **1977** *Drug Metabolism & Disposition* V. 273 Narcotic antagonists, naloxone, nalorphine, levallorphan, and naltrexone, specifically inhibited morphine glucuronidation. **1988** *Biol. Abstr.* LXXXV. XI. AB929/1 Neuroleptanalgesia was performed by intravenous injection of fentanyl and levallorphan 5 minutes before local anesthesia. **1989** *Martindale's Extra Pharmacopoeia* (ed. 29) 84 2/2 Levallorphan reverses severe opioid-induced respiratory depression but may exacerbate respiratory depression such as that induced by alcohol or other non-opioid central depressants.

levamisole (lɪ'væmɪsəʊl), *n. Pharm.* [f. LEV(O- + *tetr*)amisole s.v. TETRA- 2 a.] The laevorotatory isomer of tetramisole, an anthelminthic drug which has also been used in the treatment of some cancers on account of its immuno-stimulatory properties.

1969 *Brit. Med. Jrnl.* 8 Nov. 340/1 Levamisole (the laevorotatory isomer of tetramisole) is a new synthetic anthelmintic. **1974** *Nature* 7 June 567/2 Levamisole (2,3,5,6-tetrahydro-6-phenylimidazo(2,1-b)thiazole) a compound known to be active against a wide range of nematodes, has been reported to enhance the humoral and cellular immune responses of animals and to reduce the incidence of both primary tumours and lung metastases in the Lewis lung (3a) tumour system in C_5 7BL mice. **1978** *Ibid.* 22 June 629/1 Tetramisole and/or its levorotatory isomer levamisole is used in many countries against a broad range of nematodal infections in birds, pigs, ruminants and man. **1987** *Stock & Land* (Melbourne) 2 July 24/1 (Advt.), Oxfendazole is a third generation benzimidazole that kills levamisole-resistant roundworms in an adult or immature state.

leveed (lə'viːd), *ppl. a.* Chiefly *U. S.* [f. LEVEE *v.*¹ + -ED¹.] Of a district: surrounded by or provided with levees. Of a channel, river, etc.: having natural levees.

1958 *New Scientist* 2 Oct. 947 Tracings of echograms of some leveed channels found off the California coast. **1964** *Bull. Amer. Assoc. Petroleum Geologists* XLVIII. 1126 Where the survey was discontinued, in depths of 2,200 fathoms, the leveed canyon was still a prominent feature. **1983** *Oil & Gas Jrnl.* 7 Feb. 91/2 Each of the upper fan facies is characterized by a single, sinuous, leveed channel. *Ibid.* 6 June 33/3 The material will be deposited inside leveed areas to be built onshore at the port. **1987** *New Yorker* 23 Feb. 88/2 The towboat Mississippi is more than halfway down the Atchafalaya now—beyond the leveed farmland of the upper basin and into the storied swamp.

level, *n.* Add: [I.] [1.] **d.** *Astron.* **the Level,** the constellation Norma.

1899 R. H. ALLEN *Star-Names* 293 (*heading*) Norma et Regula, the Level and Square. **1964** D. H. MENZEL *Field Guide Stars & Planets* iv. 114 Since they are currently recognized groups, I must include them in the list of 88 constellations .. Norma (et Regula), the Level (and Ruler). **1976** I. RIDPATH *Illustr. Encycl. Astron. & Space* 143/2 Norma (*the level*), a small, faint constellation .. introduced by Nicolas Louis de Lacaille.

[3.] **h.** A storey, floor, or other horizontal subdivision in a building or other structure; used esp. in relation to split-level buildings, rooms, etc.

1968 *Globe & Mail* (Toronto) 13 Jan. 42/1 (Advt.), Lower level features striking walk-out family room and sauna. **1973** 'A. BLAISDELL' *Crime by Chance* (1974) ii. 33 It was a big and beautiful store with impressive 'levels' instead of floors. **1984** R. RENDELL *Tree of Hands* II. xi. 132 They slept in different rooms that night, he on the .. lower level of the first floor. **1987** *New Yorker* 23 Feb. 23/2 Hasbro occupies three levels of a six-story white building. **1990** *Apollo* July 43/3 At present the Musée de la Mode occupies the top five floors of the pavilion, with the visit beginning on the sixth level and continuing on the floors above.

level, *a.* and *adv.* Add: [A.] [1.] c. Of a quantity, esp. a spoonful, of a dry substance or ingredient: even with the brim of the container or measure; not heaped (see HEAPED *ppl. a.* 2).

1907 *Mrs. Beeton's All about Cookery* (new ed.) 216/2, 3 level cupfuls of flour. **1936** E. CRAIG *Cookery & Housek. Managem.* 8 When measuring ingredients which are not liquid..a heaped spoonful equals 2 level or liquid spoonfuls. **1965** *Observer* (Colour Suppl.) 28 Mar. 34/1 One could be pedantic and write back: I mean 'a rounded tablespoon' unless you want a thinner soup, sauce or stew, in which case I mean 'a level tablespoon'. **1982** *N.Y. Times* 17 Mar. C7/1 Subtract two level tablespoons of flour for each cup of cake flour that the recipe calls for.

lever, *n.*[1] Add: [2.] b. Also, by extension, used of any projecting arm or handle (usu. in the form of a straight rigid bar) by which a mechanism is operated or adjusted, whether or not the main object is to do mechanical work.

1862 *Illustr. Catal. Internat. Exhib., Industr. Dept., Brit. Div.* II. No. 2256, The upper ladders unship by means of shifting levers. **1904** A. B. F. YOUNG *Compl. Motorist* iii. 64 All that is necessary in changing gear is to move the lever which tightens a band on one of the friction drums and locks it. **1954** J. MASTERS *Bhowani Junction* vii. 62 There was a lever on one handlebar to work the front brake. **1971** P. TOYNBEE *Working Life* iv. 60 You slip your card into the slot and pull down the lever which punches the time on it. **1988** *Toronto Sun* 13 Apr. 159 (*caption*) According to the instructions, a simple flip of a lever will enable the bike to be folded.

c. *fig., spec.* in *phr.* **to pull the lever** and varr., to activate, experiment with, or facilitate the means or agency of making something happen.

1903 *Contemp. Rev.* Mar. 410 The papal nuntius presses every lever and turns every screw. **1974** *Times* 4 Apr. 14 Job satisfaction might be found by moving to a new job that gave him or her the chance to 'pull levers and see what happens' rather than advising other people before they pull the levers. **1976** *National Observer* (U.S.) 30 Oct. 3/3 Jane Henry, wife of a community-college professor and mother of two, is concerned about the environment, so she will pull a lever for Carter. **1985** *Christian Science Monitor* 8 Feb. 26/3 There have been times when the Fed pulled the normal levers to coax the economy to zig, when instead that led the economy to zag.

leverage, *n.* Add: [2.] c. *Comm.* (chiefly *U.S.*). The increase in earning potential of shares in a company which results from its making only a relatively small proportion of its capitalization available as ordinary shares; the ratio of a company's capitalization to the value of its ordinary shares (cf. GEARING *vbl. n.* 3 b); also, the use of credit or borrowed capital to increase the earning potential of shares, the action of leveraging.

1931 CHAMBERLAIN & HAY *Investment & Speculation* xi. 125 The common stock..has a leverage that gives him [*sc.* the speculator] the full equitable benefit..of any good management of the companies the common stocks of which are in his trust. **1938** J. B. WILLIAMS *Theory of Investment Value* xii. 151 If growth is attended by a change in leverage, so that the ratio of bonds to stocks is altered, then the dividends to be paid by a company will increase at a different rate from its assets. **1974** 'E. LATHEN' *Sweet & Low* xvii. 164 People who'll talk you to death about the leverage they get in commodities. *a*1976 in WEBSTER *Suppl.* s.v., Buying stocks on margin is a simple example of leverage. **1987** *Economist* 21 Mar. 90/3 The reason for dealing in futures..is that the gains (and the losses) are potentially much greater because of the leverage that these markets allow. **1995** *Times* 9 June 23/2 He will

also contain the expansion of BAe [*sc.* British Aerospace] and improve the leverage to achieve his ultimate ambition..: a merger of GEC's defence businesses with those of BAe.

Levied ('liːvaɪd), *a.* Also **Levi'd**, and with lower-case initial. [f. LEVI's *n. pl.* + -ED[2].] Clad in Levi jeans; wearing Levi's.

1966 *Listener* 30 June 955/1 The mini-skirted or levied young. **1976** *Soho Weekly News* 13 May 15/2 He sat on a stool in a diner, his levied-legs spread wide. **1984** L. ALTHER *Other Women* (1985) II. ii. 150 Caroline released her grip on the sofa and stretched out her Levi'd legs.

Lévi-Straussian (ˌleɪvɪ'straʊsɪən), *a.* and *n.* *Anthropol.* [f. the name of Claude *Lévi-Strauss* (b. 1908), French anthropologist + -IAN.] **A.** *adj.* Of or pertaining to Lévi-Strauss or his work; similar in kind to his arguments or ideas, esp. his theories of structuralism (q.v.). **B.** *n.* A follower of Lévi-Strauss; an exponent of his theories.

1967 E. LEACH *Struct. Study Myth & Totemism* p. xix, We can choose how we are related..even to that enigmatic Lévi-Straussian cat. **1977** *Brit. Jrnl. Sociol.* XXVIII. 110b Levi-Straussian structuralism can be explained psychoanalytically. **1980** *Economist* 9 Aug. 92/2 Watson or Crick could demonstrate the validity of their double helix model of genes... A Freudian (or Jungian, or Marxist, or Lévi-Straussian) cannot do the same for their models of humanity. **1981** P. JORION in J. Wintle *Makers of Mod. Culture* 306/1 Foucault's 'épistème'..functions much like a Lévi-Straussian 'group of transformations'. **1987** *Amer. Ethnologist* XIV. 735 The three structuralisms, functionalist, Lévi-Straussian, or Marxist.

levonorgestrel (ˌliːvəʊnɔː'dʒestrəl), *n.* *Pharm.* [f. LEVO- + NORGESTREL *n.*] The laevorotatory isomer of norgestrel, with similar uses.

1977 *Approved Names 1973* (Brit. Pharmacopœia Comm.) Suppl. VII, *Levonorgestrel*, (−)-13β-ethyl-17β-hydroxy-18,19-dinor-17α-pregn-4-en-20-yn-3-one. Progestational steroid. **1980** *Brit. Med. Jrnl.* 29 Mar. 940/3 The combination of levonorgestrel (D-norgestrel) with 30μg of ethinyloestradiol or 1mg norethisterone acetate with 50μg of ethinyloestradiol would appear to be appropriate choices. **1990** *New Scientist* 29 Sept. 21/1 The ring..releases low doses of a progestogen called levonorgestrel, the same hormone as that contained in the 'mini Pill'.

levorphanol (liː'vɔːfənɒl), *n.* *Pharm.* [f. LEV(O- + M)ORPH(INE *n.* + -AN(E + -OL.] A narcotic analgesic drug more potent and longer-lasting than morphine, usually administered as the hydrogen tartrate; (−)-3-hydroxy-*N*-methyl-morphinan.

1960 *National Formulary* (Amer. Pharmaceut. Assoc.) (ed. 11) 188/2 Levorphanol Tartrate occurs as a practically white, odorless, crystalline powder. **1974** M. C. GERALD *Pharmacol.* xiii. 256 Unlike levorphanol (Levo-Dromoran), a narcotic analgesic agent, dextromethorphan, its methylated dextro-isomer, possesses no analgesic activity..and is not a respiratory depressant. **1977** *Sci. Amer.* Mar. 46/2 Potent opiates such as levorphanol and morphine have a much greater affinity for the receptor than weak ones such as meperidine and propoxyphene (Darvon).

Lexan ('leksæn), *n.* Also **lexan**. [Invented name.] A proprietary name for a polycarbonate thermoplastic of high impact strength, produced by the reaction of bisphenol A with phosgene.

1956 *Official Gaz.* (U.S. Patent Office) 28 Aug. TM125/2 *Lexan.* For synthetic resinous compositions useful in molding applications and other industrial arts.

First use Nov. 10, 1955. **1969** *New Yorker* 12 Apr. 127/1 The astronauts.. will have to close the hatch and build up the oxygen pressure in the cabin, so that they can take off their Lexan bubble helmets. **1975** *New Yorker* 29 Sept. 28/1 The painting and frame would be completely surrounded by a bullet-resistant box of Lexan plastic. **1975** *Nature* 2 Oct. 361/3 The evidence is the track of a particle passing through a balloon-borne stack of Cerenkov film, nuclear emulsion and lexan sheets. **1985** *Survival Weaponry* Dec. 43/1 Space age materials such as Lexan (which is bullet proof!) as used by Blackie Collins on some of his boot knives. **1995** T. CLANCY *Op-Center* xvii. 69 After passing through the keycard and keypad entry and greeting the somber armed guards behind the Lexan, she replaced her own evening team counterpart.

lexigram ('lɛksɪgræm), *n. Linguistics.* [f. Gr. λέξις word + -GRAM.] Any of a set of symbols representing words; *spec.* one of those used in the investigation of language learning by chimpanzees.

1973 *Times-Herald-Rec.* (Middletown, N.Y.) 30 Apr. 24/1 Scientists are teaching a young chimpanzee named Lana to punch out 'sentences'...The keyboard uses symbols instead of words. Lana knows between 35 and 40 of the 45 symbols—called lexigrams. **1978** *Amer. Speech* LIII. 272 For Rumbaugh's program, von Glasersfeld designed one [*sc.* language-like system] in which the unit signals are visual configurations of uniform size, dubbed 'lexigrams'. **1980** *Nature* 24 Apr. 685/1 Their chimpanzees seem to have the ability to use a lexigram or geometric design such as the design for 'key', in a highly specific context, but become bewildered upon its application to a wider array of contexts. **1985** *Amer. Jrnl. Mental Deficiency* XC. 185/2 Smith and White found that their four severely retarded subjects, who had extensive experience..with lexigrams, responded as accurately to English words as they did to lexigrams. **1991** *Discover* Mar. 20/2 Kanzi [*sc.* a chimpanzee].. pointed to the lexigram for 'chase', and scampered playfully away.

lexon ('lɛksɒn), *n. Linguistics.* [f. LEX(ICON *n.* + -ON1.] In stratificational grammar, an element of lexicon, one or more of which combined may constitute a lexeme. Cf. MORPHON *n.*, PHONON *n.*, SEMON *n.*

1964 S. M. LAMB in Romney & Andrade *Transcultural Stud. in Cognition* (Amer. Anthropologist: special publication) The elementary units of which the phoneme, the morpheme, the lexeme, and the sememe are composed may be called the *phonon*, the *morphon*, the *lexon*, and the *semon* respectively. **1966** S. M. LAMB *Outl. Stratificational Gram.* 58 A lexon may be symbolized by the same symbol (except for the brackets) as is used for its morphemic realization. **1968** P. M. POSTAL *Aspects Phonol. Theory* viii. 200 On the next or lexemic stratum there is one lexeme which is of maximally simple structure, i.e. consists of a single lexon..which, it must be emphasized, is a single unanalyzable symbol. **1976** *Language* LII. 238 A lexemic idiom..contains lexons which are themselves lexemes in other environments.

Hence **le'xonic** *a.*

1966 S. M. LAMB *Outl. Stratif. Gram.* ii. 23 When a lexonic ordering is of elements belonging to different morphotactic classes, e.g. verb stem and verb suffix, it is up to the morphotactics to determine their relative order.

lexotactics (lɛksəʊ'tæktɪks), *n. pl.* (const. as *sing.*) *Linguistics.* [f. LEX(ICON *n.* + -o + TACTICS *n. pl.*] The study of the ordering of lexemes in a language.

1966 S. M. LAMB *Outl. Stratificational Gram.* 14 A nominal in English lexotactics may function as a predicate nominative, as object of a verb, as subject of a clause, or in construction with 's.

So **lexo'tactic** *a.*; **lexo'tactically** *adv.*

1966 S. M. LAMB *Outl. Stratificational Gram.* 14 Occasional upward ANDS are also found in lexotactic patterns. **1972** A. MAKKAI *Idiom Struct.* 85 Lexotactically it is bad, because it [*sc.* the sentence] follows the German word order. **1979** *Amer. Speech* LIV. 135 The semotactic and lexotactic levels are generative devices that specify which combinations of individual emic elements are well-formed.

ley, *n.* Add: Also *ley line*; hence **ley-liner**, a believer in ley lines. (Further examples.)

1972 N. SAUNDERS *Alternative London* (ed. 3) xv. 140 *The* magazine about ley lines, plus lots of information about megalithic sites etc. in Britain. **1981** A. BURL *Rites of Gods* 3 Before concluding that this was a Golden Age in these islands, as ley-liners would have us believe. *Ibid.* 8 The illusory ley-lines that entice their believers farther and farther from the realities of prehistoric existence. **1991** *Here's Health* Jan. 65/3 (Advt.), Lighthouse on Ley Lines offers unique setting for Relaxation, Floating & B&B.

∥**li** (liː), *n.*4 [Chinese *lì.*] An ancient Chinese cooking vessel of bronze or pottery with usu. three hollow legs.

1945 W. B. HONEY *Ceramic Art China* ii. 26 The well-known tripod cooking-vessel after the bronze *li.* **1958** W. WILLETTS *Chinese Art* I. i. 19 That curious emblem of Chinese culture, the *li* tripod. **1965** T. R. TREGEAR *Geogr. China* ii. 47 The *li*, a very efficient tripod cooking vessel with hollow legs, shaped rather like a goat's udders, sometimes large enough to cook, say, a goose in one leg, an antelope in another and vegetables in a third. **1977** G. CLARK *World Prehist.* (ed. 3) vii. 299 Classical Lungshan ware..included a series of novel forms. These included cooking vessels with solid feet (*ting*), cauldrons with hollow feet (*li*), sometimes with necks, spouts and handles (*kuei*).

liability, *n.* Add: [3.] **b.** *fig.* An attribute or trait which sets one at a disadvantage; hence, a burdensome or disadvantageous person or thing, a handicap. Freq. opp. ASSETS *n. pl.* 4.

1938 C. CONNOLLY *Enemies of Promise* vi. 55 Cleverness seemed a liability rather than an asset. **1949** *Jrnl. R. Aeronaut. Soc.* III. 903/1 Large grass areas on runwayed aerodromes are a liability in upkeep, except insofar as grass drying is a revenue-earning aspect. **1964** E. HUXLEY *Back Street New Worlds* x. 101 Since Muslim customs rigidly preclude his wife's going out to work, she's bound to be an economic liability, not an asset as Jamaican wives are. **1977** *Time* 19 Sept. 25/1 The financial razzle-dazzle that later was to become such a liability. **1985** 'J. HIGGINS' *Confessional* (1986) ix. 147 To his masters he was not only expendable. He was now a liability.

Lib (lɪb), *n.*3 *Pol. colloq.* (orig. *Brit.*) Also **lib.** [Abbrev. of LIBERAL *a.* and *n.* B.] = LIBERAL *a.* and *n.* B, in various senses. Freq. in *Comb.* with the name of another political party: see also LIB-LAB *a.*

1885 *Punch* 8 Aug. 61/1 'Tory-demmycrat' sounds nice and harmless, but *if* it means simply cold scran From the Rad's broken-wittel bag, drat it! far better the Libs' Grand Old Man. **1910** D. LLOYD GEORGE *Let.* 15 Dec. in *Family Lett.* (1973) 154 One Lib gain on balance today—so we are now one ahead. **1959** *Punch* 28 Oct. 360/3 Are you now in favour of a Lab-Lib hook-up? **1966** *Listener* 24 Nov. 781/3 His plots are banal, his views a wishy-washy lib-con pink. **1973** *Washington Post* 5 Jan. B1/1 He seems to think the senatorial libs just couldn't get it through their thick heads that in reality the Family Assistance Plan was another three banana jackpot for bureaucratic liberalism. **1986** *Sun* (Melbourne) 10 Jan. 8 (*heading*) Libs create an albatross for their electoral necks.

libero ('lɪbərəʊ, ∥libɛro), *n. Assoc. Football.* [a. It., abbrev. of *battitore libero*, f. *battitore* lit.

'beater', (in this sense) 'defender' + *libero* free.]
A player who ranges across the field as a last
line of defence behind the full-backs; = SWEEPER
n. 1 e.

1969 E. BATTY *Soccer Coaching* ii. 33 The creation of
the *libero* (free-back). **1978** D. MILLER *World Cup*
i. 12 Passarella, the dynamic *libero* (the free man or
'sweeper' as he is known in Britain). **1979** *Guardian* 19
Nov. 22/7 Ondrus, their [*sc.* Czechoslovakia's] captain,
and libero, still mixes destructive tackles with
marvellously creative moments. **1982** *Ibid.* 11 June
22/2 Stielike is a libero of defensive strength and
attacking vision. **1987** *World Soccer* Mar. 33/1 If the
tournament was to start today, we would put
Schumacher in goal, Berthold at right full-back, then
Hörster, Augenthaler or Herget as 'libero'. **1990** *New
African* June 62/2 The libero can organise his full-
backs to take attacking responsibilities and threaten to
move into vacant midfield space himself.

libidinal, *a.* Add: Hence **li'bidinally** *adv.*, as
regards libido.

1923 *Internat. Jrnl. Psycho-Analysis* IV. 280 Our
patient had of course actually - not only libidinally -
lost her father. **1967** *Jrnl. Amer. Psychoanal. Assoc.*
XV. 258 Mechanically, there is an ego split with the
fantasy of the 'bad' (which includes the aggressive)
portion of the self being isolated, externalized,
observed, and the 'good' self being libidinally attached
to the maternal love object. **1988** N. SYMINGTON
Analytic Experience xiv. 150 Initially the young boy is
libidinally attached to his mother.

lick, *n.* Add: [4.] **c.** *pl.* Adverse comments;
criticism, censure, condemnation. Cf. KNOCK *n.*[1]
1 b. *U. S. colloq.*

1971 *Torch* 18 Dec. 4/2 Someone thought they should
set him up to get his share of licks and so eliminate
him or level off his chances in the ministerial
stakes. **1977** *Time* 24 Jan. 4/1 Barbra Streisand's A
Star is Born does not deserve the licks it has got from Jay
Cocks. **1987** *Time* 11 May 12/1 He and his.. Socialist
Movement have been taking their licks.

lick, *v.* Add: [3.] [b.] Also *intr.* with *adv.* or
advb. phr. indicating direction (esp. with *at*).
(Later examples.)

1909 *Chambers's Jrnl.* Sept. 572/2 The swish of the
water licking sloppily against the yacht's side. *a*1961
in WEBSTER s.v., The surf licked at the seawall. **1979**
N. WALLINGTON *Fireman!* i. 19 High over a roof leaping
flames were now clearly visible, licking skyward. **1987**
New Yorker 26 Jan. 28/1 Abe looked out their bedroom
window.. and saw a small flame licking at the edge of
the ashes.

[6.] **c.** *transf.* To solve (a problem or puzzle);
to overcome, transcend (a difficulty). Chiefly
U. S.

1946 E. O'NEILL *Iceman Cometh* IV. 225 You've finally
got the game of life licked. **1957** A. STEVENSON *New
Amer.* III. iv. 151 We have never yet in this country
met a problem we couldn't lick, and we have come
through every crisis stronger than we went in. **1974**
E. BOWEN *Henry & Other Heroes* ii. 30 She had me
licked before we started. **1985** YEAGER & JANOS *Yeager*
(1986) 161 We had licked the elevator problem.

lie, *n.*[1] Sense 3 in Dict. becomes 4. Add: **3.** In
weakened or non-pejorative sense: an anecdote,
tale, 'tall story'. **lie and story**, gossip. orig. and
chiefly *Black English.*

1934 Z. N. HURSTON *Jonah's Gourd Vine* vi. 105 Y'all
wanta heah some lies? **1935** Z. N. HURSTON *Mules &
Men* i. ii. 37 'Zora,.. you come to the right place if lies
is what you want. Ah'm gointer lie up a nation.'... It
was a hilarious night with a pinch of everything social
mixed with the story-telling. **1943** CASSIDY & LE PAGE
Dict. Jamaican Eng. (1967) 274/2 *Lie an story*,
gossip. **1950** L. BENNETT et al. *Anancy Stories & Dial.
Verse* 33 Him start fe carry lie and story between dem

and start big kas-kas. **1960** P. OLIVER *Blues fell this
Morning* vi. 152 When there is nothing else to do he
joins his fellows to tell 'lies'. **1966** D. J. CROWLEY *I
could talk Old-Story Good* ii. 14 The narrators
themselves refer to a tale as 'a wonderful lie', but they
mean to indicate a work of the imagination rather than
an untruth. **1977** in J. L. Dillard *Lexicon Black Eng.*
viii. 139 Sometimes the joke, or the lie told, makes up
the better part of the occasion.

lie, *v.*[1] Add: [B.] [IV.] [20.] [a.] Also, to assume
or resume a recumbent posture (earlier and later
examples).

1862 'C. BEDE' *College Life* 74 Mr. Percival Wylde
was lying back upon his pillows, apparently engaged in
sipping the gruellous compound. **1920** E. O'NEILL
Beyond Horizon III. i. 153 He lies back and closes his
eyes, breathing pantingly. **1979** W. GOLDING *Darkness
Visible* xiii. 216 She lay back again and shut her
eyes. **1986** A. BROOKNER *Misalliance* x. 154 Alone,
Blanche lay back thankfully, but again sleep did not
come.

b. *spec.* with reference to unwanted but
inevitable sexual intercourse (also sometimes
humorously *fig.*) in phrs. *lie back and think of
England*, *lie back and enjoy it*, and varr.

[**1912** LADY HILLINGDON *Jrnl.* in J. Gathorne-Hardy
Rise & Fall of Brit. Nanny (1972) iii. 71 When I hear
his steps outside my door I lie down on my bed, open
my legs and think of England.] **1969** S. HYLAND
TopBloody Secret ii. 113 He relaxed on the principle of rape-impossible-lie-back-and-enjoy. **1974** L.
DEIGHTON *Spy Story* viii. 82 Reunification is
inevitable—lie back and enjoy it. **1977** PARTRIDGE
Dict. Catch Phrases 138/2 Lie back and enjoy it! 'A c.p.
allegedly used as advice to a girl when escape from rape
is impossible' (Barry Prentice, 15 December 1974):
since *c*. 1950. **1987** *Daily Tel.* 4 Apr. 9/1 From then
until the end of the play's three-hour traffic, I lay back
and thought of England, letting Trevor Nunn have his
way with me and with Heywood's mundane piece of
early 17th-century drama.

lie, *v.*[2] Add: [1.] **d.** To talk, gossip; to tell 'tall'
stories or exchange lies. orig. and chiefly
Black English.

1935 Z. N. HURSTON *Mules & Men* I. iv. 92 Cliffert
Ulmer told me that I'd get a great deal more [stories]
by going out with the swamp-gang. He said they lied
a plenty while they worked. **1953** *Amer. Speech*
XXVIII. 117 *Lie*, to talk. 'Let's sit down and lie to one
another'.

‖**Liederabend** ('liːdərabənt), *n. Mus.* Pl. -abende.
[Ger., lit. 'evening of songs'.] An evening recital
of lieder.

1958 *Times* 10 Nov. 14/3 The recital given at the
Festival Hall.. by Mme. Irmgard Seegfried was more
like a *Liederabend* at home than a public concert. **1974**
Times 4 Mar. 9/7 Nowadays, as his schedule tells you,
Liederabende have to take their place alongside
appearances at the Metropolitan, La Scala, Vienna,
Salzburg and Covent Garden.

Liederkranz ('liːdəkrænts), *n. U. S.* [a. G.
Liederkranz, lit. 'garland of songs'.
A name given in the 19th cent. to German-American
men's choral societies; adopted as the name of the
cheese in 1892 in honour of such societies.]

A proprietary term for a type of soft white
cheese, creamy in texture and with a strong
flavour and smell.

1909 *Official Gaz.* (U.S. Patent Office) 21 Sept. 799/2
Liederkranz...Cream-Cheese. **1927** *Good Housekeeping* (N.Y.) Apr. 102/3 Limburger is slightly harder
than Camembert...Liederkranz, Brick, and Muenster
are similar types. **1962** *N. Y. Herald Tribune* 6 Aug.
8/7 Not only is Van Wert, Ohio, the site of the world's
largest cheese plant,.. but from this same giant factory
comes every ounce of Liederkranz made in the

world. **1966** MARQUIS & HASKELL *Chéese Bk.* iii. 197 Strong cheeses like Limburger and Liederkranz are not for cocktail parties because after an hour or so at warm temperatures they will all but clear the room. **1979** CUNNINGHAM & LABER *Fannie Farmer Cookbook* 350 Try buttery Camembert, rich blue-veined Stilton.. or combine tangy chèvre.., stolid Edam, and pungent Limburger or Liedercranz [*sic*].

‖ **Liégeois** (ljeʒwa), *n.* (and *a.*) Also †Liegois, Liègeois, and without accent. Pl. same. [Fr.] A native or inhabitant of the Belgian city or province of Liège. Also (with lower-case initial) as *adj.*, of, pertaining to, or characteristic of Liège or its inhabitants.

1596 T. DANETT tr. *P. de Commines's Historie* 51 A few of the Liegeois after they were put to flight relied themselves togither at their cariage. **1699** M. LISTER *Journey to Paris* 208 To furnish all this Water, there is a most stupendious [*sic*] *Machine*, which was invented by 2 Liegois. **1769** 'CORIAT, JUNIOR' *Another Trav.* (ed. 2) I. i. v. 37 All the officers, French and Liegois, of any distinction, were there. **1823** SCOTT *Quentin D.* II. ix. 221 Well were the Liegeois then assured, that.. this Charles.. would have given their town up to spoil. **1961** T. HENROT *Belgium* 68 Liège.. remains most independent in its ways and rather disdainful of what is not '*liégeois*'. **1989** *Daily Tel.* 25 Oct. 17 Bertrand blames the folie de grandeur of the socialist administration.. and the bizarre financial optimism of the Liègeois.

lieutenant, *n.* Add: [**2.**] **d.** A police officer next in rank below a captain; also, a senior prison officer. Chiefly *U. S.*

1907 *Daily Chron.* 11 Apr. 3/5 [In Glasgow] when a prisoner was brought into a police station the lieutenant on duty would not accept the charge.. unless [etc.]. **1909** L. F. FULD *Police Admin.* ii. 58 In Boston, St. Louis, Baltimore, and a few other cities,.. provision has been made for a lieutenant of police. Such lieutenants of police exercise all the powers and discharge all of the duties of captains, in the event of the sickness or absence of the latter. **1940** B. SMITH *Police Syst. in U.S.* vii. 256 In the small force.. which consists of one lieutenant, one sergeant, and nine patrolmen, subdivision by levels of activities has not been carrried far. **1942** *Handbk. Amer. Prisons & Reformatories* (ed. 5) II. 8 Promotion to the rank of lieutenant is made only from the senior officer's group. **1965** G. JACKSON *Let.* June in *Soledad Brother* (1970) 63, I talk to fewer convicts every day. Just one lieutenant here has tried to do anything for me. **1985** E. KUZWAYO *Call me Woman* II. xiv. 207, I asked the prison lieutenant to phone a woman doctor friend of mine.

e. The title, until 1966, of an assistant to the captain of a company of Girl Guides (subsequently officially called an Assistant Guide Leader).

1909 R. BADEN-POWELL *Girl Guides: Suggestion for Character Training* (Pamphlet A) 6 The unit for work or play is the 'Patrol' of eight girls, of whom one is 'Patrol Leader', another the 'Corporal'. Three or more Patrols form a Company under a 'Captain' and a 'Lieutenant'. **1932** R. KERR *Story of Girl Guides* vi. 92 There is not much objection to 'captain', which is not exclusively military..; but there was at one time a great agitation against the term 'lieutenant'. Suggestions were invited from the Movement, but no better name was sent in. **1966** *Tomorrow's Guide* (Girl Guides Assoc.) iii. 21 Guide Leader [and] Assistant Guide Leader.. should be used instead of Captain and Lieutenant. We believe that the time has come to drop the terms Captain and Lieutenant which, when used in conjunction with each other, have a military sound. **1976** *Norwich Mercury* 10 Dec. 2/1 She is retiring from her post of Captain.. and handing over to Mrs. Dianne Perrott—who.. is her present lieutenant.

life, *n.* Add: [**III.**] [**12.**] **f.** *the life* (*U. S. slang*): (*a*) prostitution (cf. GAME *n.* 5 f); usu. in phr. *in the life*; (*b*) any unorthodox lifestyle.

1960 R. G. REISNER *Jazz Titans* 160 *Life, the*, the world of prostitution. **1961** T. I. RUBIN *In the Life* Preface p. i, Through Jennie's eyes we learn about Jennie herself and 'the life': prostitution... There is nothing gentle, pretty or nice about 'the life'. **1973** C. & R. MILNER *Black Players* i. 10 Players will ask a new acquaintance: 'How long have you been in The Life? '—meaning, at what age did you leave the 'square' or 'straight' world. **1976** M. MACHLIN *Pipeline* viii. 97 They say I'm too nice a girl to be in the life. **1983** *Maledicta 1982* VI. 135 Gay women are far less promiscuous and in the life than gay men. **1986** T. McGUANE *To Skin Cat* (1989) 184 Say, is that the young lady—is she in the life? **1988** D. FRENCH *Working* 6 All of the prostitutes' names, the madams' names, the agents' names, and the clients' names have been changed... Even so, in essence, my life and my account of The Life are intact.

[**VI.**] [**17.**] **life list** *Ornith.*, a list of the different kinds of bird recorded by an observer during his or her life.

1959 *Audubon Mag.* LXI. 201/2 (*caption*) His '*life*' list of birds seen was well over 3,000 species. **1987** *Nat. World* Winter 27/1 The park.. is mainly renowned for its birds, and even if you are a keen birdwatcher you could almost certainly add several species to your life-list here. **1990** *Birder's World* Aug. 64/2 A Slaty-backed Gull sent birders trekking to Delta, British Columbia, while at Sandy Hook, New Jersey, life lists were extended after the sighting of a Little Gull.

life scientist, an expert in or student of a life science.

1969 *Sci. Res.* (N.Y.) 3 Feb. 24/2 When statisticians are working with *life scientists in basic research areas, too many assume that the purpose of this kind of experimentation is to produce statistically valid tests for something. **1976** SOUCEK & CARLSON *Computers in Neurobiol. & Behavior* i. 3 Behavioral biologists, neurophysiologists, and other life scientists. **1984** *Peptide & Protein Rev.* IV. p. iv, This volume should.. be of the utmost interest to all scientists working in the area of protein structure.. as well as in general medical and life scientists. **1990** S. MAITLAND *Three Times Table* (1991) I. ii. 17 'Real scientists,' said Simon tauntingly, 'not life scientists like you.'

lifestyle, *n.* Add: Also **life-style.** **c.** *attrib.* Of or relating to a particular way of living; *spec.* in *Marketing*, designed to appeal to a consumer by depicting a product in the context of a particular lifestyle.

1976 *Carn* Feb. 20/2 In the more important lifestyle area, big changes have to be made in people conditioned from the cradle to consume more. **1977** *Washington Post* 7 Oct. E2/4 Instead of showing women's clothes with other women's clothes, the new gift catalog uses what Penney's calls 'life style merchandising', like scenes of families having fun outdoors in which everything but the snow can be ordered from Penney's. **1981** *Event* 9 Oct. 28/4 *Lifestyle merchandising*,.. clothing departments arranged by life image rather than product groups. **1987** *Fulham Times* 2 Oct. 9/4 The first floor will comprise 'lifestyle' goods such as lighting, glassware, china and soft furnishings. **1988** *Creative Rev.* Jan. 3/2 Where will creatives go for an idea beyond lifestyle marketing? **1990** *M & M* Sept. 51 (Advt.), Al Fares is the only serious upmarket lifestyle magazine in the Middle East. **1992** *New Age Jrnl.* Feb. 70/3 This information may well lead to some lifestyle decisions or result in our becoming involved in the EMF issue.

LIFO ('laɪfəʊ), *n.* (*a.*) orig. *U. S.* Also **Lifo, lifo.** [Acronym f. the initial letters of *last in, first out.*] **a.** *Accounting.* = *last in, first out* (a) s.v. *LAST adv.* 2 c. Opp. FIFO *n.* a.

1945 *N.A.C.A. Yearbk.* (Nat. Assoc. Cost Accounting, U.S.) II. 81 Because of the possible ramifications involved in the use of the lifo method, any attempt..to set forth an outline of operating procedure..would probably end..in confusion. **1972** *Bookseller* 25 Mar. 1714/2 It indicates a guiding redundancy principle of lifo (last in, first out—as opposed to filo, lilo and fifo). **1980** *Oil Majors in 1979* (Shell Internat. Petroleum Co.) 2 In general, companies which apply the LIFO method of inventory accounting will report lower inventory values during a period of rising prices than companies using FIFO. **1990** *EuroBusiness* June 33/3 If the prices of inputs and outputs are constant Lifo and Fifo give the same results.

b. *Computing.* = *last in, first out* (b) s.v. *LAST adv.* 2 c. Opp. FIFO *n.* b.

1968 D. E. KNUTH *Art of Computer Programming* I. ii. 236 Stacks have been called..last-in-first-out ('LIFO') lists... Queues are sometimes called..first-in-first-out ('FIFO') lists. The terms LIFO and FIFO have been used for many years by accountants as names of methods for pricing inventories. **1969** P. B. JORDAIN *Condensed Computer Encycl.* 406 It is possible to organize lists with neither LIFO nor FIFO. **1973** C. W. GEAR *Introd. Computer Sci.* vii. 291 Thus the last item to be put into a stack is the first item to be removed. (For this reason, it is also called a Last In First Out queue or a LIFO queue). **1986** *Austral. Personal Computer* Aug. 101/1 A stack is also called a LIFO..stack and various other names.

lift, *n.*[2] Sense 18 in *Dict.* becomes 19. Add: [I.] [5.] [e.] (*iii*) Upwardly-moving air which provides sufficient upward force to support a glider, etc., or to carry it higher. Freq. in the phr. *in lift.*

1938 N. HERON-MAXWELL tr. *Hirth's Art of Soaring Flight* 49 Karl Bauer was towed up in a Grunau Baby, and..found sufficient lift to enable him to make a good soaring flight. **1947** A. C. DOUGLAS *Gliding & Advanced Soaring* ii. 44 By means of kiting to a height of 1800-2800', the glider..obtains enough height to circle in lift without risk. **1978** A. WELCH *Bk. Airsports* ii. 27/1 Very slowly the needle moves upwards; it is still showing sink, but not so much. Then, quite suddenly you are in the lift. **1986** *Sailplane & Gliding* Oct./Nov. 213/3 Flying in lift I reached the club and checked my watch. **1987** *Pilot* Apr. 16/1 Other gliders nearby are giving away useful information by..their changes in attitude [*sic*] as they dive to speed up through sinking air and pull up in any lift.

j. *Sport.* Any of the set movements by which a weight-lifter lifts a weight or a wrestler lifts an opponent.

1908 *Health & Strength Ann.* 93 Continental lifts differ considerably from those in practice in this country. **1928** *Ibid.* 77 Lifters are urged to maintain themselves in a state of readiness on the three Olympic lifts. **1939** R. C. HOFFMAN *Weight Lifting* i. 17 Three lifts known as the Olympic lifts had been selected. For a time there were five lifts—the one hand snatch, the one hand jerk, the two hands press, the two hands snatch and the two hands clean and jerk. **1954** J. MURRAY *Weight Lifting* iii. 54 Each competitor has three trials in each of the three lifts. **1958** C. P. KEEN et al. *Championship Wrestling* xiv. 170 A, to counter the lift, kicks backward to a prone position, changing the angle of lift. If B persists in attempting the lift, A keeps pushing backward, remaining prone. **1968** B. DOUGLAS *Wrestling* 153 The wrestler from Arizona State..prepares for a lift and a sweep. **1980** S. COMBS *Winning Wrestling* ii. 25 Practice actual body lifts with a partner, using each other as dead weight. **1992** *Olympics 92* 138/2 In Seoul Britain's leading heavyweight, Welshman Andrew Davies, failed to record a lift at all.

k. *Audio.* A relative amplification of signals within a particular part of the audible range, esp. the bass.

1962 A. NISBETT *Technique Sound Studio* 243 *Boomy,* subjective description of a sound quality which has resonances in the low frequencies, or a broad band of bass lift. **1970** J. EARL *Tuners & Amplifiers* iv. 95 With the two controls set to 'zero'..there could be a little bass or treble lift or cut. **1975** G. J. KING *Audio Handbk.* iii. 71 Bass lift occurs because C2 in the feedback path reduces the gain at high frequencies.

[III.] [8.] [a.] Also, an extra layer added to the heel or sole of a shoe or a device worn in a shoe to make the wearer appear taller.

1862 *Illustr. Catal. Internat. Exhib., Industr. Dept., Brit. Div.* II. No. 3557 A lift for a short leg, and shell for boot: also a boot for a wooden leg. **1964** G. VIDAL *Julian* iv. 46 Like the emperor Augustus he wore lifts in his shoes to make himself appear tall. **1977** J. D. MACDONALD *Condominium* iii. 27 He was a short plump man in his forty-third year. The lifts in his shoes brought him up to five foot six and a fraction. **1986** *Runner* Mar. 12/2 If you have a leg shortage and it has not been accommodated with a lift, I suggest that you have someone measure and prescribe one for you.

[IV.] 18. *U.S. Criminol.* A fingerprint, *esp.* an impression of a fingerprint taken from an object as part of a criminal investigation. See sense 11 j of the vb.

1951 W. R. SCOTT *Fingerprint Mechanics* 182 It sometimes happens that a lift is lost or damaged. *Ibid.* 183 A second lift..reveals better ridge detail. **1957** *Sci. of Fingerprints* (U.S. Fed. Bureau of Investigation) xii. 176 Lifts, negatives and photographs are readily enclosed with letters. **1977** J. WAMBAUGH *Black Marble* (1978) ix. 182 It's very hard to get good lifts unless a surface is hard, smooth and clean. **1992** *Police Chief* (U.S.) Feb. 33/2 Fingerprint images are taken from a tenprint card or latent lift with a forensic-quality camera.

lift, *v.* Add: [3.] [a.] (*iv*) To be or become visible above or against the surrounding landscape. Now *rare* or *poet.*

[**1590** SPENSER *F.Q.* II. ix. 45 That Turrets frame most admirable was..And lifted high aboue this earthly masse, Which it suruewd, as hils doen lower ground.] **1912** BELLOC *This & That* 125 The chestnuts made a dark belt from which the tall graces of the birches lifted. **1930** W. FAULKNER *As I lay Dying* 221 Against the sky ahead the massed telephone lines run, and the clock on the courthouse lifts among the trees.

8. b. *transf.* To take and use in one's writing (another person's words, subject, idea, etc.). Also *absol.*

1885 *Spectator* 10 Jan. 51/2 In painting-in his background, he is, therefore, reasonably entitled to 'lift' his materials wherever he finds them. **1892** *Nation* (N.Y.) 15 Dec. 456/3 All that is vitally concerned with Lincoln, is lifted bodily from Herndon's book. **1921** G. B. SHAW *Back to Methuselah* Pref. p. viii, The surest way to produce an effect of..originality was..to lift characters bodily out of the pages of Charles Dickens. **1951** E. B. WHITE *Let.* ?Oct. (1976) 342 Here's a college president lifting from another college president, for his maiden speech. **1963** L. MACNEICE *Varieties of Parable* (1965) iii. 67 Coleridge had lifted some tricks from Percy's *Reliques* but it does not read like pastiche or parody. **1979** C. JAMES *At Pillars of Hercules* I. ii. 47 The lines about Leonidas are lifted straight from the *Imitations* version of Rilke's 'Die Tauben'. **1986** *Listener* 4 Dec. 25/1 *Life is Elsewhere*, a title Kundera lifts from the end of André Breton's first Surrealist manifesto.

c. *Sport.* To win, to carry off (a trophy or title).

1901 *Outing* (U.S.) June 320/1 Another challenge has now been received from them..and a second attempt to 'lift' the Davis Cup will be made this season. **1940** N. MONKS *Squadrons Up!* vi. 162 The boys were certainly proud of their aircraft, but they made up their minds to lift that gold cup for the crazy-flying event, and their two crack flyers went into training. **1969** *Femina* (Bombay) 26 Dec. 45/1 The versatile collegians of Bombay lifted the Inter-Varsity table tennis, kabaddi and swimming titles. **1977** *Belfast Tel.* 28 Feb. 20/1 Wolves, bidding to become the third Second Division side in five years to lift the FA cup. **1991** *Highways & Transportation* Sept. 24/3 Extremely heavy showers did not deter the golfers and especially Neil Balmer who lifted the trophy with an excellent score of 40 points.

[**11.**] **j.** *U. S. Criminol.* To take up an impression of (a fingerprint or fingerprints) from an object, usu. by means of adhesive tape.

1931 H. BATTLEY *Single Finger Prints* vi. 75 Latent impressions may be transferred or lifted after development by means of Folien,..a dark surface to which an adhesive preparation has been applied. **1942** B. C. BRIDGES *Pract. Fingerprinting* xiii. 257 Despite its usefulness in lifting latents, Scotch tape..has some disadvantages. **1951** W. R. SCOTT *Fingerprint Mechanics* 182 Prints in some cases can be lifted more than once. **1978** S. BRILL *Teamsters* vi. 225 They were able to lift a fingerprint off the title. **1986** *Jrnl.* (Fairfax County, Virginia) 28 May A3/2 Arlington County police have talked to witnesses and lifted fingerprints from the stolen convertible.

lifting, *vbl. n.* Add: [**1.**] **d.** *pl. Comm.* The amount of a product, usu. mineral oil, transported through or out of a particular place, or by a particular means.

1973 *Oil & Gas Jrnl.* 29 Oct. 51/3 Exxon Corp.. listed gross production of 2.59 million b/d and liftings of another 411,000 b/d. **1983** *Austral. Transport* Aug. 11/3 Liftings have increased dramatically since we concluded this agreement. We are increasing our capacity at a time when other lines are cutting back. **1988** *Financial Times* 22 Mar. 30/5 MISC said that, although the current levels of liftings in the liner container trade and freight and charter hire rates should hold for the first half of this year, long-term prospects are still uncertain.

[**2.**] [**b.**] **lifting tape** *Criminol.*, a kind of adhesive tape used for lifting fingerprints.

1942 B. C. BRIDGES *Pract. Fingerprinting* xiii. 258 With this type of *lifting tape there is provided celluloid or acetate cover material to which the tape may be affixed after the latent impression has been lifted. *Ibid.*, The technique of using this transparent lifting tape is easy. **1983** J. F. COWGER *Friction Ridge Skin* iv. 87 After making the lift, lifting tape is adhered to *lift cards*.

Lifu ('liːfuː), *n.* and *a.* [The name of the largest of the Loyalty Islands in the South Pacific.] (Designating, of, or pertaining to) a Melanesian language spoken on Lifu Island.

1852 A. CHEYNE *Descr. Islands W. Pacific Ocean* 179 (*heading*) Vocabulary of the Lifu language. **1855** V. LUSH *Jrnl.* 27 July (1971) 161 This little child, Lizzie, talks a little Nengone—a little Maori—a little Lifu—and a little English, and so is called the Polyglot Baby. **1858** J. C. PATTESON *Let.* in C. M. Yonge *Life J. C. Patteson* (1874) I. viii. 346, I am.. printing..translations in Nengonè, Bauro, and Lifu. **1917** *Jrnl. R. Anthrop. Inst.* XLVII. 271 The first Lifu primer had a lesson: 'Don't go out during public worship to.. pick out and eat fleas'. **1952** *Word* VIII. 252 Every word in Lifu is stressed on the first syllable. **1971** A. G. HAUDRICOURT in T. A. Sebeok *Current Trends in Linguistics* VIII. 380 In 1967 Tryon treated the syntax of Lifu in his thesis.

Lifuan ('liːfuən), *n.* and *a.* [f. the name of *Lifu* Island (see *LIFU n.*) + -AN.] **A.** *n.* A native or inhabitant of Lifu. **B.** *adj.* Of or pertaining to Lifu, its people, or its language.

1873 S. MACFARLANE *Story of Lifu Mission* 7 There seems to have been amongst the Lifuans a most extraordinary propensity for human flesh, and an utter disregard for human life. **1917** *Jrnl. R. Anthrop. Inst.* XLVII. 240 Lifuan ethnography. *Ibid.* 247 There is

no information.. as to whether the Lifuans possess the distinctive body odour attributed to the New Caledonian natives. *Ibid.* 291 It does not appear that the words in the chiefs' language which differ from the common speech are other than Lifuan. **1977** K. R. HOWE *Loyalty Islands* i. 8 Uveans and Lifuans sent shell trinkets as well as chiefs' daughters to the north and central east coast of New Caledonia.

ligand, *n.* Add: [**1.**] **a.** (Earlier examples.)

1938 *Bull. Chem. Soc. Japan* XIII. 388 In more special cases, selective absorption bands due to ligands themselves may superpose on those proper to the co-ordination combination. [*Note*] Throughout this article, the word ligand will be used in its original German sense, i.e., an ion or a molecule co-ordinated in a complex radical. **1948** *Nature* 6 Nov. 746/1 It is seen that the stability of complexes increases steadily to reach a maximum at copper whether the ligands be ammonia, ethylene diammine, propylene diammine or salicylaldehyde.

b. *Immunol.* A molecule or group which binds to another molecule (usu. a macromolecule) with a high degree of specificity.

1968 B. BELLEAU in E. J. Ariëns *Physico-Chem. Aspects Drug Action* 207 A fundamental study of the interaction mechanisms of ligands (or small molecules) with macromolecules. **1971** *Proc. Nat. Acad. Sci.* LXVIII. 1047/1 Acting on the hypothesis that *in vitro*, ACh receptor retains its affinity for cholinergic ligands and binds them reversibly and competitively, we searched for such macromolecules in different excitable tissues. **1978** *Res. in Reproduction* May 2/1 Increasing quantities of serum in particular tubes yields dose-related inhibition of binding of the ligand to the antibody or receptor. **1989** B. ALBERTS et al. *Molecular Biol. Cell* (ed. 2) vi. 325 Mast cells secrete histamine.. when triggered by specific ligands that bind to receptors on their surface.

light, *n.* Add: [**12.**] **b.** *Hairdressing.* = HIGH LIGHT *n.* 1 b.

1963 'N. DUNN' *Up Junction* 22 We go into the chemist. 'I want a black rinse, please, with blue lights in it.' **1967** N. FREELING *Strike Out* 27 Brown hair with blonde lights. **1979** J. RATHBONE *Joseph* I. xiii. 130 Her darkish hair had coppery lights in it. **1995** *Hair* Apr.–May 24/1 (*caption*) Be bold with colour…Choose a full head application or ask about high, low or slicing techniques that give reflective lights to natural colourings.

[**16.**] **light-emitting diode** *Electronics* = LED *n.*

1968 *Electronics World* Jan. 36 (*heading*) *Light-emitting diode. **1978** PASACHOFF & KUTNER *University Astron.* ix. 271 Gallium production.. is used in many solid state devices including the light-emitting diodes (LED's) that form the digits on most pocket calculators and digital watches. **1986** *Sci. Amer.* Oct. 52/2 The light source is a semiconductor laser or a light-emitting diode.

light, *a.[1]* Add: [**1.**] **c.** *Stock Market.* Of trading: low in quantity, sparse. Also *transf.*, characterized by sparse trading.

1875 *Chicago Tribune* 8 July 6/3 Few buyers were present and the 'mail order' business also was light. **1882** *Daily News* 27 July 4/7 The settlement was commenced on the Stock Exchange yesterday, and contangoes proved light. **1930** *Daily Express* 6 Sept. 2/6 The turnover..remained light, the upturn reflecting an extreme scarcity of sellers rather than any considerable number of buyers. **1981** *Times* 11 Aug. 14/2 Selling pressure was described as light. **1989** *Independent* 10 Oct. 1 Trading was comparitively light in both currency and equity markets.

d. Of traffic: not abundant, sparse.

[**1909** *Westm. Gaz.* 30 Aug. 2/1 On lightly trafficked roads.] **1935** C. G. BURGE *Compl. Bk. Aviation* 136/1 The cheaper way at intermediate towns or where traffic is light, is to assemble the passengers at a central point. **1940** *Maryland* (Writers' Program) III. 313 This route..has relatively light traffic and few billboards to obstruct pleasant views. **1957** *Encycl. Brit.* I. 233/2 Airports with light and limited traffic. **1973** D. BARNES *See the Woman* (1974) I. 111 Traffic on Western Avenue was light. **1985** *Interavia Aerospace Rev.* Feb. 163/1 Intercontinental airline routes with relatively light traffic.

e. *Finance* and *Stock Market.* Of a currency or share: relatively low in value or price.

1958 *Times* 29 Dec. 6/4 For a time next year both the old franc and the new, the 'light' and the 'heavy', will probably be in circulation. **1963** *Rep. Comm. Inquiry Decimal Currency* iii. 19 in *Parl. Papers 1962–3* (Cmnd. 2145) XI. 195 The halfpenny systems give either a 'light' main unit, or a mil system. **1977** *Daily Tel.* 13 Apr. 19 The lira is certainly the lightest currency, with nearly 900 units to the dollar. **1981** *Times* 30 Apr. 26/4 Royal Bank of Scotland slipped 4p to 184p with its predators Hongkong & Shanghai 1p lighter at 130p.

[10.] Also (of beer), containing fewer calories than ordinary beer. Cf. *LITE *a.* 2.

1971 *Advertising Age* 1 Feb. 6/5 'The appeals are almost uniformly stereotyped,' Mr. Brown said. 'Coors is "America's fine light beer".' **1974** S. TERKEL *Working* IX. 526 'Light beer'—that's the ad phrase for watered and thin beer. So the schmucky kid thinks he's a stud fighting for the babe by consuming all that alcohol. **1981** *Bon Appétit* Mar. 32/2 Light beer is the fastest growing segment of the malt beverage market. **1986** *Marketing Week* 29 Aug. 16/3 Its idea of what makes a light beer light is that it contains 100 calories or less in a 12-oz serving. **1991** *Washington Post* 6 Nov. A1/6 The rules state..that 'light' or 'lite'..may be used only on foods that have one-third fewer calories than comparable products.

[13.] e. In superl. phr., as *lightest wish, word.* Prob. after quot. 1602.

1602 SHAKES. *Ham.* I. v. 16, I could a Tale vnfold, whose lightest word Would harrow vp thy soule. **1869** 'MARK TWAIN' *Innoc. Abr.* xxxvii. 394 The Autocrat of Russia, whose lightest word is law to seventy millions of human beings. **1936** *Punch* 9 Sept. 287/2 My lightest wish..is eagerly served. *Ibid.* 30 Dec. 755 The millions that hang upon your lightest word. **1956** I. MURDOCH *Flight from Enchanter* viii. 100 This kindly body was indeed ready to provide staff of any description in response to a department's lightest wish. **1987** *Financial Times* 29 Aug. (Weekend Suppl.) p. i/3 There are still a few operators whose lightest word can move individual stocks.

f. *Bridge.* Low; short of points for a traditional bid. *to come in* (or *open*) *light*, to begin or come into the bidding with less strength than is conventional.

1899 A. DUNN *Bridge* 29 As the dealer's hand is not worth a single trick, a light 'no-trumper' means absolute ruin. **1906** W. DALTON '*Saturday' Bridge* ii. 46 A light No Trump, however anæmic it may be, is always preferable to a light red suit declaration, but a strong red suit declaration..is far better than an average No Trump call. **1935** E. CULBERTSON *Encycl. Bridge* 265/1 A light bid is based on nearly the strength which it implies. **1959** *Listener* 13 Aug. 262/3 Some players do not like to open light when they have a part score. **1971** *Daily Tel.* 21 Aug. 8/3 A fine contract to reach on light values. **1976** *Bridge Mag.* July 40/1 A good partnership must..console itself with the..gains which are brought in by one partner coming in light and the other not crucifying him for doing so.

[18.] c. Slight in amount or extent (and therefore not demanding).

1969 *Internat. Herald Tribune* (Paris) 6 Nov. 14/4 (Advt.), Light knowledge of French. **1969** in Halpert & Story *Christmas Mumming in Newfoundland* 109 A boy will be expected to do a 'light bit' of drinking. **1977** *Chicago Tribune* 2 Oct. XII. 59/1 The diversified nature of this position is based in a southwest suburb of Chicago and requires light travel. **1987** P. LIVELY *Moon Tiger* ii. 21 What she was retreating from

was..any commitment more intense than light church attendance and an interest in roses.

light, *a.*² Add: **[2.] c.** *light ale,* pale-coloured bottled ale; also *absol.* in phr. *light and bitter,* a drink consisting of light ale and draught bitter in equal measures; similarly *light and mild.*

1893 *Army & Navy Co-op. Soc. Rules & Price List* 15 Mar. 77 Allsopp's Light Dinner Ale. **1903** *Civil Service Supply Assoc. Ltd. Price List* 1 May 181 Bull Dog, Light Ale. **1914** *N.E.D.* s.v. *Treacle* sb., *Treacle ale, beer,* a light ale or beer brewed from treacle and water. **1953** *Word for Word* (Whitbread & Co.) 24/2 *Light ale,* pale ale...*Light and mild,* a mixture, pale ale and mild, half-and-half. **1979** M. LEIGH *Abigail's Party* I. 34 Tone, have a light ale, 'cos he got them specially for you. **1982** L. CODY *Bad Company* xv. 111 Bernie..went to the bar to order a pint of light and bitter. **1986** J. MILNE *Dead Birds* xiv. 113, I wanted a light and bitter and no, I couldn't have one. Would I like a Schlitz instead? **1992** *New Musical Express* 12 Aug. 45 He actually resembles the working class hero he's always strived to be, the 'Armchair Anarchist' with a bottle of light ale in one hand and an incendiary device in the other.

lighten, *v.*² Add: **[5.] c.** To become gradually lighter; also (of a colour, or something coloured) to become paler. Also *fig.*

1841 EMERSON *Ess.* 1st Ser. ix. 224 If we consider what happens in conversation, in reveries, we shall catch many hints that will broaden and lighten into knowledge of the secret of nature. **1893** *Funk's Stand. Dict.* I. 1030/1 The fabric lightened in the wash. **1931** E. LINKLATER *Juan in Amer.* 162 But presently the sky began to lighten, and a cock crew. **1958** A. WILSON *Middle Age of Mrs Eliot* I. 104 Everywhere a great rocky plateau stretched—grey, pinkish, brown, lightening to a lemon yellow, paling to a deathly chalk. **1980** *Catal. Fine Chinese Ceramics* (Sotheby, Hong Kong) 96 Covered in a translucent glaze streaked predominantly in purple changing to lavender and lightening on either side of each lobe. **1991** *Mirabella* May 60/2 The shock of carrot-colored hair..had lightened to a soft strawberry blond.

ligno-, *comb. form.* Add: **lignocellulose** *n.*: hence **lignocellu'losic** *a.,* of the nature of or containing lignocellulose; also as *n.,* lignocellulosic material.

1944 *Pulp & Paper Mag. Canada* XLV. 752 The amount and types of *lignocellulosic wastes from forest and agricultural sources are examined in the light of present industrial uses. **1974** *Sci. Amer.* Apr. 58/3 The International Paper Company built a 9,000-pound bridge solely from high-yield lignocellulosic papers (such as kraft liner board) and adhesive to demonstrate the merits of strong paper in structural engineering. **1990** *Review* (Dept. of Energy) Summer 13/1 Energy recovery from the organic fraction..is limited by the restricted ability of anaerobic bacteria to degrade lignocellulosics—paper, cardboard, wood, etc.

like, *v.*¹ Add: **[6.] [a.]** Also with vbl. n. as obj. (Further examples.)

1824 M. M. SHERWOOD *Waste Not* II. 5 How do you like being boxed up with the old lady? **1898** G. B. SHAW *You never can Tell* I. 233 Oh, if you like being hurt, all right. **1914** D. H. LAWRENCE *Prussian Officer* 104 He sang in the choir because he liked singing. **1945** E. WAUGH *Brideshead Revisited* II. i. 198, I had chosen to do what I could do well,..and liked doing. **1980** *Observer* 22 June 12, I don't like being recognised in the street. **1995** *Mixmag* May 100 I'm serious about my music, but I like having a laugh.

likelihood, *n.* Add: **[2.] d.** *Statistics.* A function of a (variable) hypothesis which, given some observations, is proportional to the probability of getting those observations given the hypothesis; a function of the variable parameters of a family of probability distributions that depends on a fixed set of data and is equal to the probability of the data, if these are assumed to relate to a population whose distribution has the given parameters. **1922** R. A. FISHER in *Phil. Trans. R. Soc.* A. CCXXII. 326, I suggest that we may speak..of the *likelihood* of one value of *p* being thrice the likelihood of another, bearing always in mind that likelihood is not here used loosely as a synonym of probability, but simply to express the relative frequencies with which such values of the hypothetical quantity *p* would in fact yield the observed sample. *Ibid.* 367 It is proposed to use the term *likelihood* to designate the state of our information with respect to the parameters of hypothetical populations. **1933** *Med. Res. Council Special Rep. Ser.* No. 183. 39 The conception of likelihood was introduced by Fisher in 1921, but..its properties are not yet universally known. **1972** A. W. F. EDWARDS (*title*) Likelihood. **1974** — in *Nature* 6 Dec. 509/3 Since *P* is the probability of what was observed, given *N*, it is the likelihood of the hypothesis *N* given what was observed. **1987** *Nature* 25 June 663/1 My complaint about..estimating the probability of a future nuclear accident was that they had ignored the distinction between probability and likelihood, thereby committing a logical error which had led them to estimate the probability with unjustified precision.

5. *attrib.* and *Comb.* (in sense *2 d) *likelihood function.*

1932 *Biometrika* XXIV. 476 For a specified sample (i) *F*, (ii) *F*ₐ and (iii) *F*ₘ may be considered as functions of population parameters, and will be called *likelihood functions or simply L-functions of (i) the sample, (ii) the variances and covariances, and (iii) the means. **1962** J. RIORDAN *Stochastic Service Syst.* vi. 126 It turns out that the formulation of a likelihood function for the stationary case is excessively complicated. **1972** A. W. F. EDWARDS *Likelihood* ii. 13 Although the likelihood function, and hence the curve, has the mathematical form of a beta-distribution, it does not represent a statistical distribution in any sense. **1987** *European Jrnl. Operational Res.* XXXII. 291 The posterior measure under a partial prior information, which is constructed on the maximized likelihood function, is compatible with the Bayesian properties of the likelihood sets.

likelihood ratio, the ratio of two likelihoods based on alternative hypotheses about the parameters of a distribution, used in testing these hypotheses.

1938 *Ann. Math. Statistics* ix. 60 (*title*) The large-sample distribution of the *likelihood ratio for testing composite hypotheses. **1972** A. W. F. EDWARDS *Likelihood* ix. 176 Neyman and Pearson were attracted to the likelihood ratio on intuitive grounds in advance of their realization that their theory of testing led necessarily to it. **1987** *IEEE Trans. Aerospace & Electronic Syst.* XXIII. 789/1 Optimization of a distributed detection network using the minimum global cost criterion results in local processors that individually form the likelihood ratio when the input observation vectors are statistically independent.

Likert ('laɪkət), *n. Psychol.* [The name of Rensis *Likert* (1903-81), U.S. psychologist.] Used *attrib.* (esp. in **Likert scale**) with reference to a scale devised by Likert (and described in his doctoral thesis at Columbia University in 1932) for the measurement of the directionality and intensity of individuals' attitudes to a topic. Also in *Comb.*, as *Likert-type.*

1946 *Jrnl. Appl. Psychol.* XXX. 76 We found..that construction of the Thurstone scales required about twice as much time..as did the Likert scale. **1972** *Jrnl. Social Psychol.* LXXXVII. 45 For each item in the Scale of Beliefs, five Likert-type response alternatives are provided: strongly agree, agree,

irresolute, disagree, and strongly disagree. **1983** F. G. BROWN *Princ. Educ. Psychol. Testing* (ed. 3) xvii. 436 In the behavioral sciences Likert scales are used most frequently because they are easier to construct and generally are as reliable and valid as the more complex types of attitude scales. **1991** *Internat. Jrnl. Law & Family* V. 301 Satisfaction scores were developed for housing and neighbourhood, and quality of life satisfaction for each of the subjects based on a 5 point Likert scale and calculation of a 100 point total score.

‖**lilangeni** (liːlɑːŋ'geɪniː), *n.* Pl. **emalangeni.** (ˌɛmɑːlɑːŋ'geɪniː) [f. Swazi *lilangeni* member of Swazi royal family (pl. *emalangeni*).] The basic monetary unit of Swaziland, equal to 100 cents; also, a coin or note of this value.

1974 *Times of Swaziland* 29 Mar. 1/2 Swaziland gets its own currency in September. On Somhlolo Day (September 6), marking independence, the new money (Emalangeni) becomes legal tender...One Lilangeni..equals R 1. *Ibid.* 6 Sept. 7/2 Our new Emalangeni money becomes legal currency today..the Emalangeni is equal with the Rand in all respects...In note form there will be one lilangeni, two, five and ten Emalangeni. One lilangeni is divided into 100 cents. **1977** *Britannica Bk. of Year* 638 The Umbuluzi dam scheme, which would irrigate 8,000 ha, was allotted a further 3 million emalangeni. **1985** *Statesman's Year-bk. 1985-86* 1130 The currency in circulation in Swaziland is the *emalangeni*, but remains in the rand monetary area. **1992** *Daily Tel.* 12 May 17/6 The lilangeni, which is worth about 20p, turned up in its thousands in British slot-machines.

Limacol ('laɪməkɒl, 'lɪm-), *n.* Also **limacol.** [Origin unknown.] The proprietary name for a skin lotion popular in the West Indies.

1936 *Trade Marks Jrnl.* 25 Nov. 1478/1 Limacol...Toilet lotions (not medicated). **1960** *Tamarack Rev.* XIV. 29 Nature seemed monstrous from his greenest years. Prone to malaria, sweating inherent sin, Absolved through limacol and evening prayers, The separate child..Watched. **1974** R. A. K. HEATH *Man come Home* xxv. 155 He had broken the jar of limacol...All day the place smelt like a sick room. **1981** F. CHARLES *Signposts of Jumbie* xiv. 92 When he comes to, he is lying on the bed and the Obeah-man is rubbing his face with red lavender mixed with limacol and asafoetida. **1982** *Official Gaz.* (U.S. Patent Office) 11 May TM 168/1 Guyana Pharmaceutical Corporation Limited...Limacol...For Perfumes, Hair tonic, face cream, face powder and body lotions...First use Dec. 31, 1933.

limacology (lɪmə'kɒlədʒɪ, liː-), *n.* [f. L. *līmāc-, līmāx* slug, snail + -OLOGY.] The branch of zoology which deals with slugs.

1981 *Daily Tel.* 9 Feb. 17/5 The group..say limacology may soon rival bird spotting. **1981** *Observer* 15 Feb. 6/2 Limacology or slug-watching is similar to bird-watching with the added convenience that slugs don't fly away before you've got a good look at them.

So **limaˈcologist** *n.*, an expert in or student of limacology.

1974 *Daily Tel.* 3 Jan. 10/6 Wider field-work on slugs is expected by limacologists this year. **1981** D. J. & T. J. BELLAMY *Bellamy's Backyard Safari* 75 It didn't take too much arm twisting to persuade him with the help of a fellow limacologist, Noel Jackson, to produce a brand new key to the slugs of Britain.

limb, *n.*¹ [4.] [b.] Add: The upper or lower half of a long-bow (also *fig.*, of a rainbow). (Earlier and later examples.)

1801 T. ROBERTS *Eng. Bowman* IV. v. 142 The English bow-makers have, generally, placed the *upper* part of the handle..*above* the exact *center* of the bow; which..makes the lower limb so much longer. The reason..is..in order to make *both* limbs act *equally.* **1823** W. SCORESBY *Jrnl. Voy. Northern Whale Fishery* 23 A little before sunset, a weather-gall (or the limb of a rain-bow), of extraordinary brilliancy, appeared. **1939** P. H. GORDON *New Archery* I. ii. 10 Here the bows were long and angular in the top limb, short and rigid in the lower. **1972** T. FOY *Beginner's Guide to Archery* iii. 26 Determine which limb of the bow should be at the top, which can be done by looking at the handle. **1991** *Peterson's Bowhunting* Dec. 14/3 In the evolution of the longbow, bowyers concentrated on limb design to improve cast.

limber, *a.* Add: [4.] **limber pine**, a North American mountain pine, *Pinus flexilis*, with a short, stout trunk and short, flexible branches.

1901 A. REHDER in L. H. Bailey *Cycl. Amer. Hort.* III. 1351/1 [Pinus] flexilis, James. *Limber Pine...Seems to be best adapted for ornamental planting on rocky slopes. **1961** R. M. PATTERSON *Buffalo Head* iv. 138 Away out on this point stood a very old limber pine. **1991** *Montana* June 79/3 The drama is heightened by the bizarre shapes of gale-battered limberpine and whitebark pine clinging tenaciously to exposed slopes and ridges.

limit, *n.* Add: [5.] **limit cycle** *Math.* [tr. Fr. *cycle limite* (coined by H. Poincaré 1880, in *Compt. Rend.* XC. 674).] A closed path in phase space representing a limit, *esp.* one that is an attractor.

1948 *Mat. Japonicae* I. 130 Thus a closed curve across which the integral curve cuts inward always, and there exists a *limit cycle between a closed curve about (o,o) and the now obtained closed curve. **1978** *Bull. Math. Biol.* XL. 31 In the theory of ordinary differential equations a *limit cycle attractor* is a periodic solution to a differential equation which has the property that the trajectory through every point in phase space sufficiently close to the closed curve defined by the periodic solution approaches that closed curve asymptotically as $t \to \infty$. **1979** *Nature* 23 Aug. 677/2 A two-dimensional limit-cycle model..predicts the behaviour in darkness of..the *Drosophila pseudoobscura* circadian eclosion rhythm. **1986** *Sci. Amer.* Dec. 42/1 Another familiar system with a limit-cycle attractor is the heart. **1988** I. PETERSON *Math. Tourist* vi. 146 The same principle applies to metronomes and the human heart: they repeat the same motion over and over again. In phase space, such a motion corresponds to a cycle or a periodic orbit. Such attractors are called *limit cycles.*

limiting, *ppl. a.* Add: **1.** That constitutes a limit; *spec.* constituting a value or case that is approached but never surpassed or never reached.

1647 SANDERSON *Serm.* II. 221 Such kind of limiting and diminuent terms. **1799** J. WOOD *Elements Optics* iv. 56 The limiting ratio of an evanescent arc to its sine is a ratio of equality. **1884** F. KROHN tr. *Glaser de Cew's Magneto- & Dynamo-Electr. Machines* 161 The slightest current then started in one or the other direction..will rapidly increase to a limiting value. **1895** N. STORY-MASKELYNE *Crystallogr.* 291 The trigonal proto-pyramid may be regarded..as being a limiting case of the ditrigonal proto-pyramid. **1914** C. D. BROAD *Perception* i. 7 Qualities which vary continuously as we move about and which, in some limiting case, coincide with those of what exists whether we perceive it or not. **1989** *Brit. Jrnl. Philos. Soc.* XL. 507 The overall entropy change is zero only in the limiting case of a reversible process.

limonene ('lɪməniːn), *n. Chem.* [ad. G. *Limonen* (J. Liebig 1885, in *Ann. der Chemie* CCXXVII. 301): see LIMONIN *n.*, -ENE.] = *citrene* s.v. CITR-.

1901 *Chem. News* 15 Mar. 131/1 Limonene, under the action of peroxide of nitrogen, gives an alcohol having totally different properties from limonene. **1927** ARNALL & HODGES *Theoret. Org.*

Chem. II. vi. 59 Pinene and limonene undergo racemisation on simple heating. **1969** B. P. MOORE in Krishna & Weesner *Biol. Termites* I. xiii. 427 The scent consists almost entirely of the monoterpenoid hydrocarbon, limonene. **1989** J. BUTTON *How to be Green* 32 The lemon smell in your cleaning liquid is usually created with limonene, a possible carcinogen.

linch-pin, *n.* Add: Also 20- linchpin, lynchpin. **2.** *fig.* A person or thing vital to an enterprise; a key component or governing principle.

1954 M. MUGGERIDGE *Diary* 5 Jan. in *Like it Was* (1981) 457 Tony Powell agreed with me that the death of Duff Cooper removed linchpin in particular social set. **1974** *Nature* 27 Sept. 363/2 He follows Holmes..in treating the Earth as a machine and making this, not the stratigraphical record, the linch-pin of his arguments. **1978** *Detroit Free Press* 16 Apr. 1C/2 The shuttle is the linchpin of Uganda's economic relationship with the west. **1981** *N. & Q.* June 221/1 He is really the linchpin of a criminal empire. **1988** *New Scientist* 19 Nov. 42/1 The lynchpin of the debate is whether the characteristics that lungfishes and amphibians share are specialised characters of real evolutionary significance. **1994** *Washington Post* 23 Aug. A1/1 DNA fingerprinting is likely to be the linchpin of the prosecution's case.

line, *n.*[2] Senses 19 b, c, and d in Dict. become c, d, and e. [II.] [7.] [f.] For def. read: (Usu. as *the line*). In various sports and games, a mark limiting an area of play on a court or pitch; *spec.* a mark that must be crossed in order to score; in a race, a mark on the track (actual or notional) that must be crossed in order to win; in *Rugby Football*, etc. = *line of scrimmage* s.v. SCRIMMAGE *n.* 4 c; contextually = *bye-line* s.v. BYE *n.* 1 c, *goal-line* s.v. GOAL *n.* 6, TOUCH-LINE *n.* 3. Also *fig.* in phr. (taken from American football, but influenced by sense 20 b) *to hold the line*, to maintain or support a position, viewpoint, etc. (Further examples.)

1892 *Football Calendar 1892–93* 63 Not more than 25 yards behind the goal line, and parallel thereto, shall be lines, which shall be called the Dead-Ball Lines. **1902** W. CAMP *How to play Football* Introd. 10 If he elects to continue his running attempts, and eventually carries the ball across the line, he secures a touchdown at the spot where the ball is finally held, after being carried over. **1935** *Encycl. Sports* Pl. 30 (*caption*) A throw-in from the line. **1965** *Austral. Encycl.* VII. 535/2 Prizes are awarded both for the handicap and for the first yacht across the line. **1976** J. ARCHER *Not Penny More* xiv. 162 They're neck and neck—one hundred yards to go—it's anybody's race and on the line it's a photo finish. **1978** *Rugby World* Apr. 40/3 They played commendably open and entertaining Rugby, scoring a total of 30 tries and failing on only one occasion to cross their opponents' line. **1987** *Greyhound Star* Sept. 7/5 The other semi went to Rogley Avalong who led from trap to line in 34.49.

[13.] **h.** *U.S. Betting.* The odds quoted by a bookmaker, esp. on a non-racing event (cf. *morning line* s.v. MORNING *n.* 9); also, the point-spread predicted in a football game, from which such odds are calculated.

1964 *Maclean's Mag.* 7 Mar. 14/2 A line of 'Ottawa eight' for an Ottawa-Edmonton football game means that Ottawa must win by eight points or more or its backers lose. **1976** *N.Y. Times* 15 Dec. A18 He is an amateur oddsmaker and has access to 'the Las Vegas line', the gambling underworld's football point spread. **1979** *Maclean's Mag.* 22 Jan. 35 The line, published in many daily newspapers, establishes for bookmakers and bettors across the continent the team favored to win each game and by how many points. **1992** *Esquire* Feb. 63/1 It was his line out of Las Vegas upon which all the bets across the country on college and pro games were based.

[III.] [19.] **b.** In certain team games, a strategic formation of players in a row, as for a throw-in; *spec.* in *Rugby Football* = *three-quarter line* s.v. THREE-QUARTER *n.* D; in *Rugby Union* = LINE-OUT *n.*

1891 *Football News* 12 Sept. 1/4 The Newark Committee were very desirous to see the line of forwards opposed to some really good backs. **1896** B. F. ROBINSON *Rugby Football* xii. 209 Away it flies, fair and true, about half-way down the long line. **1929** *Daily Express* 15 Apr. 16/2 The line never moved with a swing that looked like bringing a goal. **1968** *Globe & Mail* (Toronto) 13 Jan. 39/5 Doug Acomb and Frank Hamill scored two goals each as their line turned in one of its best performances of the season. **1976** *Leicester Mercury* 14 Oct. 46/1 When the ball did come down the line it inevitably went to John Reeve. **1991** *Don Heinrich's Pro Preview 91* 28/2 Right tackle Howard..Ballard has come a long way since quarterback Jim Kelly fingered him two years ago as the line's weak link.

f. A dose of a powdered narcotic, esp. cocaine, laid out in a thin line for inhalation. *slang.*

1971 *Black Scholar* Sept. 36/1 He..rolled a ten dollar bill up into a quill and gave the coke and quill to Christine, who snorted half of the line on the card. **1980** *Observer* 30 Mar. 1/6 Everybody I know takes heroin...Every party I go to has smack available, lines and lines of it. **1988** J. McINERNEY *Story of My Life* iv. 59 Didi's just bought her stash for the night and she wants to come over. God, I don't know. A couple of lines would be nice, but I've got class in the morning. *Ibid.* 61 She rolls her own bill, [and] does a couple of monster lines—what Didi calls lines other people call grams. **1990** K. WOZENCRAFT *Rush* iv. 49, I snuffed up the lines and passed the tooter back to him. **1992** *Guardian* 28 Mar. (Weekend Suppl.) 9 Some Krug, a couple of Es, a few lines and, nowadays, it shows. I suppose it's called getting old. I'm 26.

[22.] **b.** *spec.* = AIR-LINE *n.* 2.

1920 *Aerial Year Bk.* 261/2 Many commercial lines have been established for carrying passangers. **1935** C. G. BURGE *Compl. Bk. Aviation* 217/1 Where there is competition with other lines on the London-Paris route, this comfort is found to attract custom. **1960** C. H. GIBBS-SMITH *Aeroplane* xiii. 99 The world's first daily commercial scheduled air service opened on August 25th [1919]...The line was operated.. by..Aircraft Transport and Travel Ltd. **1965** M. SPARK *Mandelbaum Gate* v. 134 'There's a Dutch line from Amman...' 'Well, Joanna, there's no record of the name Vaughan on any of the airlines.' **1977** *Rolling Stone* 30 June 81/1 After a mere forty-minute lay-over we were to connect with that line's nine-hour-plus direct flight to Honolulu.

[IV.] [24.] **e.** *Biol.* = *LINEAGE *n.* 3.

1951 G. S. CARTER *Animal Evolution* i. 30 This conception is very different from that generally held a few years ago. A population was then thought of as consisting of many lines or lineages, each evolving more or less independently and replacing each other as the result of natural selection. **1973** J. BRONOWSKI *Ascent of Man* i. 38 *Australopithecus robustus* is manlike and his line does not lead elsewhere; it has simply become extinct. **1979** D. ATTENBOROUGH *Life on Earth* (1981) ii. 35 To trace the invertebrate lines back to their origins, we must find another site where rocks were not only deposited continuously throughout this critical period, but have survived in a relatively undistorted condition. **1992** *Nat. Hist.* Feb. 70/3 Falk also notes common features in the brain venous sinuses of gracile australopithecines and hominids,..and she constructs the lineage accordingly. *A. gracilis* led to the hominid line in which brain size increased so dramatically.

[25.] **b.** *spec.* A breed or variety of plant or animal universally characterized by a feature or trait whose strength is the criterion for continued selection by breeders. Cf. *line-bred* adj., *line-breeding*, sense 32 below.

1805 R. W. DICKSON *Pract. Agric.* II. xiii. 1103 It would appear that..the most certain method..is to breed in the same line, perhaps in the same family; as, by a careful procedure in this way, the expert breeder may not only have the greatest security for attaining that improvement which he is anxious to produce, but run the least risk of deterioration. **1909** R. H. LOCK *Recent Progress Study Variation, Heredity & Evolution* (ed. 2) xi. 318 In a single pure line genetic variability is sensibly absent. The members of such a pure line exhibit, however, very considerable acquired variability, so that in this way each line shows a normal variability of its own. **1974** A. HUXLEY *Plant & Planet* xiii. 123 Continuously self-pollinated plants of one species in limited habitats may produce such pure-breeding 'lines' as to create virtually new species. **1985** E. H. HART *German Shepherd Dog* iv. 66 It is..not that these lines have disappeared; it is just that they have not been so seriously bred upon as they once have been.

[26.] [d.] (*b*) The scent that the hounds have of the quarry; esp. in phr. *to hit off the line*, to pick up the scent after a check.

1898 *St. James's Gaz.* 15 Nov. 6/1 Hounds drove along after their fox in rare style,..the line was worked out to Houghton. **1900** LD. COVENTRY in A. E. T. Watson *Young Sportsman* 352 An old hound drops his nose; he shows a line; his companions follow his lead. **1930** I. BELL in C. Frederick et al. *Fox-Hunting* v. 59 They will try hard all day on a poor scent, yet at the first improvement..will quicken on the line. **1930** C. ALDIN in *Ibid.* xxvi. 257 The huntsman hits off the line again with hardly a check. **1977** *Abingdon Herald* 17 Mar. 6/6 They were lifted back towards Besselsleigh, hit off the line again, and killed on the plough near the woods. **1991** *Sports Illustr.* 14 Jan. 5/3 The lead hound gives tongue, and the pack takes off, following the line of scent.

h. For def. read: In *Golf*, the direction of the hole from the position of a player's ball. In *Cricket*, the direction of flight of the ball from the bowler's hand; freq. in phr. *to play* (*hit*, etc.) *across the line*. (Further examples.)

1961 *Times* 18 Aug. 3/3 At 18 Pullar was bowled by Davidson, playing across the line. **1969** *Times* 25 Aug. 9/2 Harris, eventually, was leg-before, hitting enthusiastically across the line.

[VI.] [32.] **line switch** *Teleph.*, orig., any switch for connecting a subscriber's line; now, a preselector.

1898 BELL & WILSON *Pract. Telephony* xii. 157 Suppose No. 5 wishes to speak to No. 3, he turns the handle of the *line-switch until the pointer is opposite 3, presses the ringing button, takes the receiver off the hook, and, after finishing conversation, replaces the receiver, which causes the pointer to return automatically to zero. **1909** *Trans. Amer. Inst. Electr. Engin. 1908* XXVII. 509 For the benefit of those not familiar with automatic switchboards, the writer will state that each line terminates in what is generally called a line switch. **1924** H. H. HARRISON *Introd. Strowger Syst. Autom. Telephony* i. 26 The preselector or line switch..hunts to find one of ten or more idle group selectors. **1938** C. W. WILMAN *Automatic Telephony* (ed. 2) iii. 20 Each subscriber's line is now connected to the wipers of a single-motion, non-numerical selector, known as a lineswitch. **1982** G. LANGLEY *Telephony's Dict.* 115/1 *Lineswitch*, a switch in a dial office which connects a subscriber's line with the first available idle trunk in the next switching stage.

line, *v.*[1] [1.] [a.] Add to def.: *spec.* in *Cookery*, to cover the inside of (a dish, tin, or other vessel) *with* pastry, paper, etc., esp. before baking. (Earlier and later examples.)

1846 A. SOYER *Gastronomic Regenerator* 696 A round-bottomed basin..which line with two thirds of the paste. **1861** *Mrs. Beeton's Bk. Househ. Managem.* 854 Having lined a hoop with buttered paper, fill it with the [cake] mixture. **1908** F. A. GEORGE *Vegetarian Cookery* v. 56 Butter a pie-dish and line it with half the lentil paste. **1948** *Good Housek. Cookery Bk.* 552 For sponge sandwiches line the bottom of the tins with a round of greaseproof paper. **1978** C. CONRAN *Brit.*

Cooking 195/2 Summer pudding...Take a 1-litre..
pudding basin and line it with slices of bread. **1992**
Food Entertaining Summer 88/3 Line a baking tray
with baking parchment (not greaseproof paper) and
smooth on the meringue mixture.

lineage, *n.* Add: **3.** *Biol.* A sequence of species
each of which is considered to have evolved
from its predecessor.
   1940 J. S. L. GILMOUR in J. S. Huxley *New
Systematics* 469 The palaeobiologist..working with
fossil material, expresses his phylogenetic judgments
in terms of lineages. For example, Arkell and Moy
Thomas..describe parallel lineages in the evolution of
the Ammonites in Devonian rocks. **1951** G. S. CARTER
Animal Evolution i. 30 This conception is very different
from that generally held a few years ago. A population
was then thought of as consisting of many lines or
lineages, each evolving more or less independently and
replacing each other as the result of natural
selection. **1983** E. C. MINKOFF *Evolutionary Biol.* xvii.
278/2 A lineage is defined as a succession of species
arranged in a continuous ancestor-to-descendant
sequence. **1992** *Discover* May 30/2 Anthropologists..had assumed that all modern humans
descended from *Homo erectus*, a hominid lineage that
left Africa a million years ago.

linear, *a.* and *n.* Add: **[A.] [3.] c.** Of causation,
evolution, time, etc.: progressing in a single
direction by regular steps or stages, sequential.
   1948 E. WHITTAKER *Space & Spirit* xxxix. 126 In
the argument as usually presented..all chains of
causation are simple linear sequences. **1954** A. P.
USHER *Hist. Mech. Inventions* (ed. 2) ii. 30 The cultures
of antiquity do not fit the patterns of the linear
sequences of social and economic evolution developed
by the German Historical Schools. **1972** R. D.
WALSHE in G. W. Turner *Good Austral. Eng.* xi. 228
The McLuhan thesis that..'linear thinking'..had been
rendered obsolete by the new 'in-depth', 'all-at-once'
thinking of the electronic media. **1979** P.
MATTHIESSEN *Snow Leopard* i. 60 The Australian
aborigines..distinguish between linear time and a
'Great Time' of dreams, myths, and heroes, in which
all is present in this moment. **1983** P. LIVELY *Perfect
Happiness* viii. 112 Time, that should be linear, had
become formless. **1992** *Forum Mod. Lang. Stud.* Jan.
22 It is impossible to over-emphasise the importance
of the poet's decision to keep the inexorable linear flow
of time intact on each occasion when a-temporality is
alluded to.
   d.   *Linguistics.*   Of   phonological,
morphological, or syntactic elements or their
ordering: consisting of a series arranged
sequentially; *spec.* (in *Generative Grammar*) of
a surface structure.
   1955 N. CHOMSKY *Theory of Linguistic Struct.*
(microfilm, Mass. Inst. Technol.) vi. 235 The linear
grammar is a sequence of conversion statements S_1,..
S_n where each S_i is of the form '$X_i \rightarrow Y_i$'. **1959** W.
BASKIN tr. *F. de Saussure's Course in Gen. Linguistics*
II. v. 123 In discourse..words acquire relations based
on the linear nature of language because they are
chained together. **1968** J. LYONS *Introd. Theoret.
Linguistics* vi. 209 We..adopted the view that all
sentences had a simple linear structure. **1969** *Canad.
Jrnl. Ling.* XV. 25 It was speculated..that the reason
that languages had embedding transformations..was
to 'linearize' or spread out in linear form the deeply
embedded concoctions which the human mind can
produce. **1982** *Ibid.* XXVII. 74 Werth observes that
it is possible to eliminate linear order in the base...If
there is no linear order in the base, then grammatical
relations must be marked in the base. **1991** *Applied
Linguistics* XII. 189 It is based ultimately on a pre-
Chomskyan linear model of language production.
   [7.] linear algebra *Math.*, a finite-dimensional
vector space, with multiplication defined and
distributive over addition, in which $(\lambda a)b =
\lambda(ab) = a(\lambda b)$ for any scalar λ of the associated

field and any vectors **a** and **b**; also, the branch
of algebra which deals with the properties of
these entities, esp. of vector spaces over the real
or complex numbers.
   1870 B. PEIRCE in *Amer. Jrnl. Math.* (1881) IV. 107
An algebra in which every expression is reducible to
the form of an algebraic sum of terms, each of which
consists of a single letter with a quantitative coefficient,
is called a *linear algebra. **1945** E. T. BELL *Devel.
Math.* (ed. 2) x. 231 The introduction of general
methods into linear algebra, beginning in the first
decade of the twentieth century, prepared that vast
field of mathematics..for partial arithmetization in the
second and third decades. **1965** PATTERSON &
RUTHERFORD *Elem. Abstr. Algebra* v. 187 The set of all
$m \times m$ matrices over a field F forms a linear algebra of
dimension m^2. **1975** I. STEWART *Concepts Mod. Math.*
xv. 227 A proper understanding of linear algebra
requires a synthesis of three points of view: (i) the
underlying geometrical motivation, (ii) the abstract
algebraic formulation, (iii) the matrix-theoretic
technique. **1986** C. W. NORMAN *Undergraduate
Algebra* p. vii, Many of the problems which linear
algebra sets out to solve are dealt with in a practical
way by the row-reduction algorithm in Chapter 8.
   linear search *Computing*, a search in which
items stored in a file are examined sequentially.
   1968 *Communications Assoc. Computing Machinery*
XI. 36/1 It has been noticed..that the *linear search
process itself produces clustering and is therefore
intrinsically slow. **1970** *Ibid.* XIII. 103/2 The simplest
search is the linear search in which the search progresses
by a multiple of an increment m, e.g. $k + 1m, k + 2m$,
.., etc. **1987** *Austral. Personal Computer* Aug. 224/1
Linear search takes, on average, $N/2$ operations to find
an item and N operations to discover that an item is
not on the list.

linearity, *n.* Add: **c.** *Linguistics.* The property
of being linear (in sense *3 e of the adj.).
   1959 W. BASKIN tr. *F. de Saussure's Course in Gen.
Linguistics* II. v. 123 Words acquire relations based on
the linear nature of language...Combinations
supported by linearity are *syntagms*. **1964** N.
CHOMSKY *Current Issues in Linguistic Theory* iv. 78 The
linearity condition..requires that each occurrence of a
phoneme..be associated with a particular succession
of (one or more) consecutive phones. **1975** —— *Logical
Struct. Linguistic Theory* viii. 267 Even if we drop the
requirement of proper linearity for grammars, we are
not able to present a satisfactory description of the
system of phrase structure in question. **1979** *Amer.
Speech 1978* LIII. 275 Linearity means that single
devices must serve multiple functions. *Ibid.* 282 It is
linearity..that has led linguists to the concept of surface
and deep structure. **1988** *Appl. Linguistics* IX. 351
One should note that simultaneity and linearity are not
absolute characteristics of sign languages and spoken
languages respectively.

lineation, *n.* Add: **3.** *Geol.* A line-like or linear
feature in rock, landscapes, etc.
   1938 KNOPF & INGERSON *Struct. Petrol.* 69 An axial
control of movement can be recognized in the hand
specimen by a parallel linear arrangement, a
lineation. **1969** BENNISON & WRIGHT *Geol. Hist. Brit.
Isles* iii. 44 The dykes are quite unfoliated at their
centres, but at their margins they have a steep lineation
corresponding to structures formed during a later fold
episode. **1971** I. G. GASS et al. *Understanding Earth*
xx. 297/2 Axial structures such as lineations and
folds. **1976** *Physics Bull.* Oct. 450/3 This..revealed
that the anomalies are remarkably linear, the lineations
extending for thousands of kilometres. **1990** C.
PELLANT *Rocks, Minerals & Fossils* 25 Stress, directed
pressure produced by folding and other movements in
the Earth's crust, creates new fabrics such as lineation
and cleavage which replace original structure like
sedimentary bedding.

linefeed ('laɪnfiːd), *n.* Also **line-feed, line feed.** [f.
LINE *n.*[2] + FEED *n.*] The action of causing paper

to be advanced through a printer by the height of one line; an instance of this. Hence, in *Computing*, a similar action involving material displayed on-screen, either by downward movement of the cursor or by scrolling the displayed material up by one line; a character or code denoting such an action.

1966 *Proc. AFIPS Conf.* XXIX. 399/2 The most elementary keyboard printer terminal uses such functions as idle, carriage return and line feed. **1966** C. J. SIPPL *Computer Dict. & Handbk.* (1967) 174/1 *Line-feed code*, a function code that causes page teleprinters or similar devices to rotate the platen up one line. **1979** *Pract. Computing* May 53/3 Other features include..automatic carriage return and line-feed, underlining, [etc.]. **1983** *Austral. Microcomputer Mag.* Oct. 108/3 Down linefeeds, software formfeed, parallel or serial interface, backspacing, either by special code or two pass can be set from PRINTGEN. **1986** D. DEUTSCH in T. C. Bartee *Digital Communications* v. 192 Each header-content..is terminated with a carriage-return character followed by a linefeed character. **1991** *Lit. & Linguistic Computing* VI. 35/2 The ASCII-only approach — not in fact markup-free but effectively a restriction to procedural markup readily executed by a teletype machine (tabs, carriage returns, line feeds, backspaces, and punctuation) — represents a misguided and inadequate theory of texts.

liner, *n.*[1] Add: [2.] **d.** *Packaging.* (*a*) Any paper or board intended as the outer surface of a composite board, esp. corrugated cardboard. See also LINERBOARD *n.* orig. *U. S.*

1921 *Paper* 5 Jan. 12/3 You are experiencing trouble trying to water-proof container liner with a furnish of kraft pulp. **1940** J. LEEMING *Mod. Export Packing* 87 The different strengths of the liners or facing sheets used in corrugated fiberboard. **1951** W. H. DE MONTMORENCY in J. N. Stephenson *Pulp & Paper Manuf.* II. 103 Two liners are separated by the corrugated medium and held to it by an adhesive applied at the points of contact. **1960** FRIEDMAN & KIPNEES *Indust. Packaging* ii. 71 *Facings* or *liners* as they are more commonly called, are relatively heavy, coarse paperboard usually of kraft or jute material. **1983** F. A. & H. Y. PAINE *Handbk. Food Packaging* v. 147 Different grades and types of board can be produced by varying the materials, the thickness and weight of the liners and the fluting medium. **1990** S. SONSINO *Packaging Design* iii. 107/1 The multi-ply boards known as duplex boards are made from wood pulp surfaced with a bleached kraft liner.

(*b*) An inner container, of impermeable material, separating a container from its contents.

1921 C. C. MARTIN *Export Packing* xx. 552 The shoes..are packed in a waterproof liner made of two layers of heavy paper with a thin coating of waterproof substance between the layers. **1948** *Packaging & Display Encycl.* 119 All screw closures require liners to form a leak-resistant seal between the..closure and the..glass. **1950** *Ibid.* (ed. 2) 382/1 (*caption*) A case returned by the War Office..after nine months on the Normandy Beaches. The contents were found to be in perfect condition due to the use of the war-type double impermeable case liner. **1974** *Encycl. Brit. Macropædia* XIII. 856/1 More than half the polythene is used in film form and much is converted into shrink film, liners, sacks, and bags. **1981** in W. Stern *Handbk. Package Design Res.* xxxi. 337/2 A system design that would automatically form a lightweight thermoformable plastic barrier liner inside a folding carton.

e. Any removable lining, *esp.* one designed to protect a container from its contents or to allow their easy removal. Usu. with function explained or implied by the context: cf. *bin liner* s.v. BIN *n.* 8, *nappy liner* s.v. *NAPPY *n.*[3] b.

1959 *Sears, Roebuck Catal.* Spring/Summer 409/3 Diaper liners...Disposable paper liner...Protects diapers and reduces laundry problems. **1966** *Amer. City* June 100/2 Each resident received three plastic liners and wire twists. *Ibid.*, The instructions told them how to place the liners in their cans, how to gather them at the top when full..and how to remove secured liners..and carry them to the street on collection day. **1974** P. DE VRIES *Glory of Hummingbird* (1975) iii. 36 A garbage bag, one of those polyethylene liners for refuse cans. **1977** P. LEACH *Baby & Child* ii. 85/1 A liner is only effective if you put it next to the baby's skin. **1984** *Gainesville* (Florida *Sun* 27 Mar. 7A/4 (Advt.), Kotex Lightday pantyliners. **1988** *Washington Post* 21 Feb. 10/2 A manufacturer will insert the liners with the patented wetness indicators into a production run of otherwise normal disposable diapers. **1990** M. DIBDIN *Vendetta* (1991) 209 There was the washbasin, the rack for glasses below the mirror and the dud bulb above, the metal rubbish bin with its plastic liner, the barred window lying open into the room.

liner, *n.*[2] Sense 13 in Dict. becomes 14. Add: [II.] [9.] **b.** A ferret attached to a line, used in rabbiting.

1902 A. NIBLETT in W. Carnegie et al. *Ferrets & Ferreting* (ed. 3) vi. 46 One of your ferrets should always be a good liner, and a good line ferret possesses qualifications which are actually detrimental in the others. **1946** W. THOMAS *Rabbit Shooting to Ferrets* iii. 19 Let us assume that you have purchased a strong, steady hob as liner and a couple of carefully selected jills in whelp. **1966** *Punch* 13 July 82/2 This 'liner' disappeared into the same hole, spaced knots on the string recording his descent. **1979** *Shooting Times & Country Mag.* 10–16 May 19/3 A good liner will home in on a rabbit and either bolt it or kill it.

13. Orig., an advertisement occupying a line of print; hence more generally, with preceding numeral: something occupying a specified number of lines (of print, etc.). See also *one-liner* (*a*) s.v. ONE B. 35.

1901 *Daily Colonist* (Victoria, B.C.) 24 Oct. 5/2 A valuable fur collar, which was advertised in yesterday's Colonist, was restored to its owner before noon, thus showing the prompt returns received from the use of Colonist 'liners'. **1904** 'MARK TWAIN' in *Harper's Weekly* 2 Jan. 18/1 There were headings — one-liners and two-liners. **1974** P. DE VRIES *Glory of Hummingbird* (1975) v. 65 Those two-liners in down-home newspapers. **1983** *Austral. Personal Computer* Oct. 114/1 This short two liner lists a cassette file to the screen on an Atari.

‖**ling chih** (lɪŋ dʒə), *n.* Also **lingzhi.** [Chinese *língzhī*, f. *líng* divine + *zhī* fungus.] The fungus *Ganoderma lucidum*, believed in China to confer longevity and used as a symbol of this on Chinese ceramic ware.

1904 S. W. BUSHELL *Chinese Art* I. vii. 148 The *ju-i* sceptre..derives its peculiar form from the sacred fungus called *ling-chih*, the *Polyporus lucidus* of botanists, one of the many Taoist emblems of longevity. **1915** R. L. HOBSON *Chinese Pott. & Porc.* II. iv. 38 Branches of *ling chih* rings supporting the Eight Precious Symbols. **1958** W. WILLETTS *Chinese Art* I. iv. 290 The *ling chih*, 'fungus of immortality', is cultivated and harvested by the Immortals as ordinary people grow rice. **1974** *Country Life* 26 Sept. 826/1 The saucer dish..painted with..the fungus the Chinese call *ling chih* which is a symbol of longevity. **1980** *Catal. Fine Chinese Ceramics* (Sotheby, Hong Kong) 46 A rare early Ming blue and white Ewer,..the shoulders [encircled] by an undulating *lingzhi* (*ling chih*) scroll amidst foliage.

Linguet ('lɪŋgwɛt), *n. Pharm.* and *Med.* Also **linguet.** [f. L. *lingu-a* tongue + -ET[1].] A tablet intended to be retained in the mouth (esp. under the tongue) for its active ingredients to be absorbed through the oral tissues.

A proprietary name in the U.S.

1943 *Official Gaz.* (U.S. Patent Office) 16 Mar. 421/1 Linguets. **1951** *Brit. Med. Jrnl.* 8 Sept. 570/2 The D.C.A. linguets had been discontinued, as she had had an implant of 200 mg. on October 3. **1970** PASSMORE & ROBSON *Compan. Med. Stud.* II. xii. 11/2, 17a-Methyltestosterone is active by oral administration; it is usually given in the form of linguets for buccal absorption. **1987** *Oxf. Textbk. Med.* (ed. 2) II. xx. 62/2 Methyltestosterone 10 mg as linguets after breakfast and another when there is a suspicion of developing oedema often aborts attacks.

linish ('lɪnɪʃ), *v. Manuf.* [Blend of LINEN *n.* and FINISH *v.*] *trans.* To polish or remove excess material from (an object) by holding it in contact with a moving continuous belt coated with abrasive material. Usu. as the vbl. n. (see below).

1971 W. F. WALLER *Electronics Design Materials* 223/1 *Linish*, to remove material by means of an abrasive belt. **1976** *Product Finishing* June 16/1 After the bumper has been pressed and rolled the metal surface has become stretched, marked and generally mutilated . . . It therefore has to be linished and polished prior to its coatings of copper, nickel and chrome. **1990** *Mountain Biking UK* Aug. 103/2 After mitring, the tube is cleaned, de-greased and then 'linished', this is a process which puts a grain on the surface of the metal which helps the brazing and makes for a stronger join.

So '**linisher** *n.*, a machine used for linishing; '**linishing** *vbl. n.*

1943 A. H. SANDY *Dict. Engin. & Machine Shop Terms* 89 *Linisher*, a shop term for a power-driven endless emery cloth band used to remove rough surfaces, burrs, etc. **1945** A. T. BIRKBY *Phenolic Plastics* x. 103 The removal of flash is performed in different ways . . . On flat surfaces a linishing machine is used. *Ibid.* 105 (*caption*) Band linishing. **1976** *Product Finishing* June 16/1 The linishing and polishing process provides a smooth and level surface upon which other metals can be deposited. **1990** *Woodworker* July 671/3 There are three main types of narrow belt sanding machine; horizontal belt (pad) sanders, small horizontal belt sanders (linishers) and vertical belt sanders.

link, *n.*[2] Add: [3.] **i.** *Computing.* An instruction or code which serves as a connection between two parts of a program, or between consecutive elements of a list. Cf. *linked list* s.v. *LINKED ppl. a.* 2.

1951 M. V. WILKES et al. *Preparation of Programs for Electronic Digital Computer* iii. 22 Any order may be punched on the tape for the last order of the subroutine, since it is overwritten by the link order. **1962** *Gloss. Terms Automatic Data Processing* (B.S.I.) 39 *Link*, an instruction or address for leaving a closed subroutine on its completion in order to return to some desired point in the routine from which the subroutine was entered. **1967** D. G. HAYS *Introd. Computational Linguistics* ii. 30 In the block of storage set aside for the list, let the first cell be a link. **1980** C. S. FRENCH *Computer Sci.* x. 57 Pointers may also be called links. **1991** *Personal Computer World* Feb. 190/3 The program includes a script link option that allows one script to call another.

[7.] **link house** [cf. Sw. *kedjehus*], a house joined to its neighbour by only a single room, garage, or the like.

[**1967** E. ROCKWELL tr. H. Hoffmann (*title*) One-family housing. Solutions to an urban dilemma. Terrace houses. Patio houses. Linked houses.] **1968** *Svensk-Engelsk Ordbok* (Svenska Bokförlaget) 358/2 *Kedjehus*, *link house. **1976** *Cumberland News* 3 Dec. 37/1 (Advt.), A three bedroomed centrally heated link house with brick garage and easily manageable gardens in first class order throughout. **1977** *Grimsby Even. Tel.* 27 May 17/9 (Advt.), Spacious link house now being built in Hawerby Road, Laceby.

link, *v.*[1] Add: [1.] **f.** To associate in speech, thought, writing, etc., *with* or *to*.

1851 H. MELVILLE *Moby Dick* I. xl. 288 One of the wild suggestings referred to, as at last coming to be linked with the White Whale in the minds of the superstitiously inclined, was the unearthly conceit that Moby Dick was ubiquitous. **1921** J. MOFFATT *Approach to New Testament* i. 60 In the so called Zadokite document of Jewish piety . . the idea of a new covenant . . began to be linked to the expectation of a Messiah. **1938** *Time* 28 Feb. 63/3 His saccharine cinema roles and cream-puff publicity have all too closely linked the word 'beauty' with the name 'Taylor'. **1950** J. A. MASON in J. H. Steward *Handbk. S. Amer. Indians* VI. 265 *Sacuya* . . is generally linked with *Remo* and probably is a subgroup. **1975** E. L. DOCTOROW *Ragtime* (1976) vii. 39 Her name was linked with dozens of men around town. **1993** M. ATWOOD *Robber Bride* xlvii. 370 She made a brief traverse through the gossip columns when her name was linked with that of a cabinet minister.

linkage, *n.* Sense a in Dict. becomes 1 a; sense b in Dict. becomes 2. Add: [1.] **b.** *spec.* in *Pol.*, the linking together of different political issues as a strategy for negotiations between countries, esp. by stipulating that progress on one front is necessary for progress on any other.

1969 *Washington Post* 9 Feb. 2/1 President Nixon now seeks to develop a linkage between the most discussed subject of future U.S.-Soviet negotiations, the control and cutback of nuclear missilery, and basic East-West political tensions . . . His associates, now are trying to clarify the 'linkage' concept. **1973** *New Yorker* 19 May 112/3 Diplomatic circles recorded that Moscow was unhappy about linkages. **1976** *U.S. News & World Rep.* 29 Mar. 17/3 In the Angola operation, Kremlin leaders ignored 'linkage' and also violated the agreement to steer clear of such tension-building actions. **1979** *Time* 8 Jan. 34/1 The real stumbling block is 'linkage'—the relationship between an Egyptian-Israeli treaty and a wider Middle East settlement. **1986** *N.Y. Times* 13 Nov. A30/1 You can't talk about arms control when Soviet behavior in other areas is unacceptable, Mr. Reagan said. 'In other words, I believe in linkage.' **1991** *Independent* 15 Jan. 19/1 To support linkage would be to dilute the original demand of the UN and encourage President Saddam to believe that he could stay in Kuwait without a war. Linkage became a code-word for political softness.

linked, *ppl. a.* Add: **1. d.** *Genetics.* Of genes: occurring on the same chromosome. Of genetic characters or factors: associated with linked genes. Cf. LINKAGE *n.* b. See also SEX-LINKED *a.*, *cross-linked ppl. a.* s.v. CROSS- B.

1912 *Biol. Bull.* XXIII. 174 Two factors that have been found to be linked are here described. These are the yellow factor in the absence of which the flies are black, and a factor . . in the absence of which the fly is wingless. **1919** *Jrnl. Genetics* VIII. 299 (*title*) The combination of linkage values, and the calculation of distances between the loci of linked factors. **1955** *Virology* I. 190 (*title*) Transduction of linked genetic characters of the host by bacteriophage P1. **1973** J. BRONOWSKI *Ascent of Man* xii. 386 You could not test for eight different characters without getting two of the genes lying on the same chromosome, and therefore being at least partially linked. **1989** B. ALBERTS et al. *Molecular Biol. Cell* (ed. 2) xviii. 1041 Two linked clusters of genes . . together comprise the major histocompatibility complex.

2. Special collocations: **linked list** *Computing*, an ordered set of data elements, each of which contains a pointer or link to its successor (and sometimes its predecessor); cf. CHAIN *n.* 5 i.

1971 I. H. GOULD *IFIP Guide Concepts & Terms Data Processing* 29 *Linked list*, a list in which each element contains one pointer to its successor, and none to other elements of the list. **1985** *Pract. Computing*

June 118/3 The chain or linked list is a common data structure used to provide pathways through a data set.

linksland ('lɪŋkslænd), *n.* [f. links (LINK *n.*¹ c) + LAND *n.*¹] Land with the characteristics of Scottish links (see LINK *n.*¹ b) and suitable for or used as golf-links.

1926 R. HUNTER *Links* 11 Such golf is much more frequently seen inland than by the sea. Place these Titans on links-land and what a difference when the wind blows! **1952** G. CAMPBELL *Links & Courses* in B. Darwin et al. *Hist. Golf in Brit.* v. 108 The results [of landscaping], especially on links land, met with a measure of success. **1964** *New Yorker* 6 June 96/3 The British championships have always been held exclusively on linksland courses. **1968** *Sunday Times* 7 July 24/7 Carnoustie.. like so many seaside links.. is nothing much to the eye, being on a comparatively flat expanse of reclaimed linksland. **1979** *United States 1980/81* (Penguin Travel Guides) 501 Part of the premier resort.. is built on lava flows that have somehow solidified to give the course a linksland character. **1987** *Golfer's Compan.* June 19/1 He took a lovely piece of linksland that was designed in heaven for the use of golfers. **1991** *N.Y. Times Mag.* 1 Dec. (Advt. Suppl.) 6A/1, One can reasonably conclude that golf began where it has always been played most avidly, the sandy, breezy linksland of coastal Scotland.

linkspan ('lɪŋkspæn), *n.* Also **link span**. [f. LINK *n.*² + SPAN *n.*¹] In full *linkspan bridge*. In a port or at a ferry terminal, a kind of hinged bridge that can be adjusted so as to link on to the stern ramp of a vessel to form a bridge for loading or unloading.

1964 *Ports & Terminals* Dec. 20/3 For the Gothenburg service, there will be link spans for heavy vehicles and containers. *Ibid.*, A stern link span for vehicles. **1969** *Jane's Freight Containers 1968-69* 187/2 Photograph shows cars being loaded by a linkspan bridge. **1981** E. CORLETT *Revolution in Merchant Shipping* 34/1 The linkspan or bridge hinged at one end and resting on the ship at the other. **1984** *Cargo Syst.* Apr. 28/1 It is now often necessary for a linkspan to handle two lane, double decked or road and rail traffic over twin stern ramps. **1991** *Ships Monthly* Nov. 29/3 Externally, *Sterna Invicta* looks good in the Sealink livery, although appearance at the bow has hardly been improved by substantial additional steelwork to fit the linkspans at Calais.

linuron ('lɪnjʊərɒn), *n. Agric.* [f. *lin-* (perh. after LINDANE *n.*) + UR(EA *n.* + *-on* (of unknown origin).] A selective herbicide used esp. to control weeds among root crops; 3-(3,4-dichlorophenyl)-1-methoxy-1-methylurea, $C_9H_{10}Cl_2N_2O_2$.

1962 *B.S.I. News* Sept. 34 Linuron. **1971** *Arable Farmer* Feb. 12/3 Triazine herbicides such as simazine, substituted phenylureas such as linuron, and uracils such as lenacil. **1981** *Southern Horticulture* (N.Z.) Spring 6/1 Metribuzin, linuron, aziprotryne and methabenzthiazuron caused 15 per cent depression in asparagus growth when applied as post-emergence treatments. **1982** FLETCHER & KIRKWOOD *Herbicides & Plant Growth Regulators* v. 236 Repeated application of linuron reduces the germination ability of barley grains, promoting protease activity and reducing protein contents. **1989** *Green Mag.* Dec. 44/1 'It's very hard to assess the exact risks and I'm not a medical expert...' Our informant.. is talking about pesticide and herbicide residues and four in particular, Atrazine, Simazine, Dimethoate and Linuron.

lion, *n.* Add: [4.] **e.** *pl.* Members of a Lions Club (see sense *11 c below); also (const. as *sing.*) = **Lions Club.*

1949 CASEY & DOUGLAS *World's Biggest Doers* iv. 32 The last mentioned of these qualities, Fidelity, has a deep and peculiar significance for all Lions. **1964** MRS.

L. B. JOHNSON *White House Diary* 5 Jan. (1970) 30 We drove to the little house in Johnson City.. where, hopefully,.. Kiwanis, or Lions, or ladies' groups, or whatever can hold their meetings. **1972** *Stand. Encycl. S. Afr.* VI. 652/1 Lions is a non-political organisation for service to the under-privileged. **1986** *Horse & Rider* Sept. 8/4 The Watford Lions' 10th annual sponsored horse ride.

[5.] **d.** *pl.* (With capital initial.) Also *British Lions.* The name of the British Isles rugby union team or squad, composed of members selected from the 'home' international teams, when touring abroad. Also in *sing.*, a member of the British Lions.

1938 *Star* (Johannesburg) 16 Sept. 30/5 There will be a big crowd to watch the game between the 'Lions' and the representatives of Capetown [*sic*] and Stellenbosch Universities. The British victory in the Test last week has stimulated booking. **1955** *Times* 13 Sept. 9/4 All followers of Rugby football will have been greatly heartened by the outstanding success of the 'Lions' in South Africa. **1973** *Stand. Encycl. S. Afr.* IX. 432/1 The ordering off of a Lion at Springs. **1974** *Country Life* 9 May 1134/1 The British Lions, representing the best players from the four home countries... The most recent Lions tours have been in 1968 to South Africa and in 1971 to New Zealand. **1986** *Open Rugby* Sept. 33/2 The 'Lions' moved next to South Australia and Victoria. **1990** *Daily Star* 23 Oct. 34/1 England have axed British Lions Brian Moore and Mike Teague for the clash against Argentina.

[11.] **c.** **Lions Club**, any of numerous associated clubs devoted to social and international service, the first of which was founded in Chicago in 1917. orig. *U.S.*

1922 *Collier's* 29 Apr. 5/2 It had a civic association, and Rotary, Kiwanis, and *Lions Clubs. **1971** 'E. LATHEN' *Longer the Thread* iii. 28 A member of the Real Estate Department attended the Lions Club luncheon at the Caribe Hilton. **1976** M. APPLE *Oranging of Amer.* 100 Cut flowers bloomed from the carcasses of dried-out batteries. The Lions Club glass and the March of Dimes cup twinkled in their fullness. **1988** *Oxf. Times* 29 Apr. 13/3 The Lions Club of Oxford is helping to organise a special diabetes information day. **1992** *Times of India* 30 July 14/2 The Children's Education Trust of India.. has invited Applications from eligible students, studying any where in the country, directly or through schools or Lions Clubs for selection to the Country's Most Prestigious A.I.T.S. Award-92.

lips (lɪps), *n. Computing.* Also **LIPs, Lips.** [Acronym, f. the initial letters of *logical inferences per second.*] A unit of computing power used to measure the rate at which a machine can execute logical inferences.

1982 *Computerworld* 14 June p. 1D/13, 1 Lips is equivalent to 100 to 1,000 instructions per second. Present-generation computers are capable of 10^4 to 10^5 Lips. **1984** *Listener* 1 Nov. 38/4 The machine of the future, ICOT says, will be capable of one billion of those Logical Inferences Per Second (LIPS). **1988** *New Scientist* 26 Nov. 45/1 PIM is expected to operate at between 100 million logical inferences per second (lips).

liquefied ('lɪkwɪfaɪd), *ppl. a.* (Sense 1 formerly at LIQUEFY *v.*) Also **liquified.** [f. LIQUEFY *v.* + -ED.] **1.** Transformed into a liquid state; *spec.* (of a solid) molten; (of a gas) made liquid by cooling or compression (now freq. in *liquefied natural gas*, *liquefied petroleum gas*).

1598 FLORIO *Worlde of Wordes* 108/3 *Disquagliato*, melted, vnthawed, liquified. **1599** A. M. tr. *Gabelhouer's Bk. Physicke* 243/1 Which foresaye.. paper balle, ye muste winde in liquefyede waxe. **1731** *Hist. Litteraria* III. 252 Iron melted into a liquified Matter. **1795** R. KIRWAN *Elem. Mineral.*

(ed. 2) I. 400 Any matter that has issued out of a volcano in a liquified state . . is in general, styled a lava. **1825** J. NICHOLSON *Operative Mechanic* 741 Liquefied amber . . separated from the oily portions which alter its consistence. **1860** J. TYNDALL *Glaciers of Alps* I. xi. 83 After we had divided the liquefied snow . . amongst us we had nothing to drink. **1910** *Encycl. Brit.* I. 137/1 Liquefied acetylene was far too dangerous for general introduction for domestic purposes. **1930** *Engineering* 4 July 28/2 'Bottled' gas, in the form of liquefied propane and butane. **1938** *Trade Marks Jrnl.* 8 June 699/1 Liquefied fuel gas. **1940** *Gas Age* 24 Oct. 47/1 The liquefied natural gas would be stored in special insulated tanks, to be withdrawn . . and regasified when need arose. **1943** in *Chambers's Techn. Dict.* Suppl. 963/2, Liquefied petroleum gases. **1977** *Ann. Internal Med.* LXXXVI. 189/2 A huge sterile retroperitoneal hematoma of approximately 1200 ml of clots and old liquified blood was evacuated. **1989** *Green Mag.* Dec. 74/1 Petrol cars have had one economical unleaded option for many years — *LPG or Liquified Petroleum Gas.*

2. *joc.* Intoxicated by drink.

1939 JOYCE *Finnegans Wake* 430 And oft, when liquefied, (vil!) he murmoaned abasourdly in his Dutchener's native, visibly unmoved, over his treasure trove for the crown: *Dotter dead bedstead mean diggy smuggy flasky!* **1981** R. A. SPEARS *Slang & Euphemism* 233/2 *Liquefied*, intoxicated with alcohol . . . (U.S. slang, early 1900s — pres [ent].).

liquid, *a.* and *n.* Add: [A.] [6.] **b.** Of a corporation, etc.: characterized by a high proportion or substantial quantity of assets in liquid form.

1930 *Economist* 24 May 1178/2 Marks and Spencer, being a 'cash and carry' concern, is liquid in every respect. The turnover is large and stock in trade represents only 115 percent of the net profit. **1947** J. W. KEARNS in *Amer. Bar. Assoc. Proc., Section of Corporation, Banking & Mercantile Law* 46/1 The origin of the 'lease-back deal' is probably traced back to high taxes, high taxes coupled with the desire of almost any corporate manager to see a liquid balance sheet with very few fixed assets on it. **1962** L. NAMIER *Crossroads of Power* xvi. 182 Even a surplus will not, as a rule, render the position of the farmer more liquid. **1976** J. ARCHER *Not Penny More* x. 96 His bank now held very few shares as he . . had suspected that the Dow Jones Index would collapse and had therefore gone almost entirely liquid. **1982** *Financial Times* 21 Jan. 30/1 Panic spread like wildfire, and investors in even the most liquid companies fell into the rush. **1988** *Ibid.* 18 Apr. (Survey section) p. vii/3 Most big Italian companies are highly liquid.

[7.] **Liquid Paper**, a proprietary name in the U.S. for a type of correction fluid; more generally (also with lower-case initials), any correction fluid.

1968 *Trade Marks Jrnl.* 23 Oct. 1810/1 *(figure)* *Liquid Paper correction fluid. *Ibid.*, Registration of this Trade Mark shall give no right to the exclusive use of the words 'Liquid Paper'. **1969** *Official Gaz.* (U.S. Patent Office) 25 Mar. TM146/1 *Liquid Paper*. . For liquid correction fluid . . . First use May 18, 1967. **1981** *N.Y. Times* 8 Feb. (Long Island Weekly Section) 18/2 At the entrance, the visitor is invited to pick up a wire mesh fragment on which liquid paper has been allowed to dry. **1990** *Daily Tel.* 22 Feb. 17/1 Since neither liquid paper nor crossings out are appropriate on such documents, the Crown Office had to draw up a second document.

liquor, *n.* Restrict ‖ to sense 6 a. Add pronunc. ('laɪkə(r)) to sense 6. Add: [6.] **b.** *Obstetr.* = *liquor amnii*, sense 6 a above.

1902 H. J. GARRIGUES *Textbk. Sci. & Art Obstetr.* xvii. 68 The liquor amnii takes up the urine occasionally voided by the fœtus and protects the fœtus against injury. The liquor prevents parts of the fœtus from coalescing and favors the free development of the

limbs. **1962** G. G. LENNON *Diagnosis in Clin. Obstetr.* xxv. 154 The exact origin and fate of the liquor is obscure. **1977** *Lancet* 25 June 1352/2 Babies delivered with 'smelly' liquor in one hospital received prophylactic ampicillin + cloxacillin for 7 days. **1979** G. BOURNE *Pregnancy* (rev. ed.) iv. 84 Throughout its whole development and growth the baby is surrounded by the amniotic fluid, otherwise known as the liquor amnii or just simply liquor. **1990** *Parents* Mar. 73/2 Liquor . . comes away during labour as 'the waters'.

‖**lis** (lɪs), *n.*[3] *Law.* [L. *līs* quarrel, dispute. Cf. LITIGATE *v.*] A lawsuit; an action; a dispute. Usu. in one of the following phrs.: **lis pendens** ('pɛndɛnz), a pending legal action; also, a formal notice of pending litigation; in *abl.* as **lite pendente** ('laɪtɪ pɛn'dɛntɪ): see PENDENTE LITE *advb. phr.*; **lis alibi pendens** ('ælɪbaɪ), an action pending elsewhere (i.e., between the same parties in another court); **lis mota** ('məʊtə), a legal action that has been initiated.

1601 A. COPLEY *Answere to Let. of Jesuited Gentleman* 27 To decree against him *lite pendente*, was vnjust dealing. **1742** T. BARNADISTON *Rep. Cases Chancery* 454 A Bill that is not to be brought to Hearing is not such a Bill as can properly create a *Lis Pendens* so as to affect a Purchaser claiming under one of the Parties after the filing of the Bill. **1848** WHARTON *Law Lex.* 388/1 The statement of facts . . on which the claim was founded, was . . was to be deemed the commencement of the *lis mota*. *Ibid.*, No *lis pendens* shall bind a purchaser or mortgagee without express notice thereof. **1872** *Law Jrnl. Rep. Queen's Bench* XLI. 170/1 A *lis pendens* does not bind purchasers or mortgagees in the absence of express notice. **1932** *Law Rep. King's Bench* II. 386 There can be no *lis* until the rights and duties are ascertained and thereafter questioned by litigation. **1959** JOWITT *Dict. Eng. Law* II. 1100/2 *Lis alibi pendens*, a suit pending elsewhere. **1987** *Times* 13 Mar. 31/8 It was the duty of counsel and solicitors . . , whenever an event occurred which arguably disposed of the *lis*, . . to bring the facts promptly to the attention of the appellate court.

lisente *n.*, pl. of *SENTE *n.*

‖**li shu** (liː ʃuː), *n.* Also 9 le(e) shoo. [Chinese *lishū*, f. *li* government servant in charge of records + *shū* script, writing.] An ancient Chinese calligraphic script developed during the Han dynasty (206 B.C.–A.D. 200) and widely adopted for official and educational purposes. Cf. *K'AI SHU *n.*

1824 *Encycl. Brit.* Suppl. III. 85/1 The first attempt at a regular system of classification of the characters . . is stated to have been that of dividing them into nine classes, called the *Lee-shoo*. **1876** *Ibid.* V. 655/2 The *Le shoo* or 'official character'. **1910** *Ibid.* VI. 220/2 The *li shu* is perfectly legible to one acquainted only with the modern character, from which indeed it differs but in minor details. **1958** W. WILLETTS *Chinese Art* II. vii. 570 The 'modern script', in which the text of *Shuo wên* was originally written, was that properly known as *li shu*, or 'Clerical Writing'. **1978** *New Archaeol. Finds in China* II. 67 When the Chin rulers unified the script, they . . adopted the *li shu* (clerical writing), which had been created by the masses, for ordinary use throughout the country.

list, *n.*[6] Senses a–c, d in Dict. become 1 a–c, 2 respectively. Add: **1. d.** *Computing.* A formalized representation of a list, used as a data structure (see also *linked list* s.v. *LINKED *ppl. a.* 2) or in list processing (see below, sense 2).

1956 NEWELL & SIMON in *IRE Trans. Information Theory* II. 64/1 The storage memories consist of lists. A list holds either a whole logic expression or some set of elements generated during a process, such as a set of elements having certain properties. **1973** C. W.

GEAR *Introd. Computer Sci.* vii. 272 Even if the list is ordered, however, we cannot use a binary search since it is scattered through memory and we cannot access its midpoint directly. **1980** C. S. FRENCH *Computer Sci.* x. 53 Lists provide a flexible way of handling data items in order. **1986** *Pract. Computing* Oct. 106/1 The Card Index File module can contain up to 36 different databases, which are known as lists.

list, *v.*⁴ Add: [**1.**] **f.** *intr.* Of goods: to be catalogued or advertised for sale *at* or *for* a price. orig. *U.S.*

[**1935** *Industr. Equipment News* Apr. 34/2 Polishing machine...Prices list from $91 to $191.] **1952** *Automobile Topics* Jan. 1 Aero Wing, Super deluxe two-door sedan, lists at $1,903.50. *a***1961** *Industr. Equipment News* in *Webster* s.v., The wrench alone lists at $3. **1974** *Cleveland* (Ohio) *Plain Dealer* 19 Oct. 3-D (Advt.), They list for $300 to $500 less than comparable '75's. **1987** *Stamps* Feb. 23/2 The item..lists in Stanley Gibbons at £8,500 in used condition and is unpriced as unused. **1994** J. BARTH *Once upon Time* 32 Maryland waterfront real-estate values have so escalated that those homely, often cheek-by-jowl stock items may list for half a million.

g. *trans. Computing.* To display or print out (a program, the contents of a file, etc.); to produce a listing of. Also, to transmit (a program or file) *to* a peripheral where it can be displayed or printed.

1958 [implied in *LISTING *vbl. n.*² 5]. **1962** *Gloss. Terms Automatic Data Processing (B.S.I.)* 93 *List*,..to print every relevant item of input data on the general basis of one line of print per card. **1979** P. J. BROWN *Writing Interactive Compilers & Interpreters* ii. 46 A further feature of interactive working that differentiates it from batch working is that a typical user will frequently want to list all or part of his program, especially if he has been doing a lot of editing. **1984** *Creative Computing* June 182/2 Now we have a resource of 167 article citations, dealing with various aspects of computer crime that we can list. **1986** *ZX Computing Monthly* Oct. 74/3 In LISTing the program to its network port, the Spectrum collects 256 bytes in a buffer first; only when the buffer is full is the data sent down the line.

list, *v.*⁵ Add: Also *transf.* and *fig.* (of an object or animal, or *joc.* of a person).

1929 E. BOWEN *Shoes* in *Joining Charles* 40 The female shoes, uncertainly balanced because of their high heels, listed towards the strong shoes of Edward timidly and lackadaisically. **1943** *Horizon* VIII. 156 The crazy dunikins, outside w.c.s listing away from the prevailing wind. **1969** M. BRAGG *Hired Man* I. vii. 70 The weaker horse listed over to the stronger at the slightest relaxation of the biased hold. **1985** M. GORDON *Men & Angels* v. 79 She listed like a heavy ship.

listen, *v.* Add: [**2.**] **g.** *slang* (orig. *U.S. Armed Forces*). *to listen up*, to listen carefully, pay attention. Usu. in *imp.*

1970 W. C. WOODS *Killing Zone* (1971) ii. 23 Now you men knock off the goddam chatter in there and listen up. **1973** T. O'BRIEN *If I die in Combat Zone* vii. 68, I got me two purple hearts, so listen up good. **1980** W. SAFIRE in *N.Y. Times Mag.* 28 Sept. 16/2 'I'm only going to say this once, so listen up.' A Washington Star sportswriter put that now-hear-this command in the mouth of an imaginary pro-football star. **1986** T. CLANCY *Red Storm Rising* (1988) xix. 244 Listen up, asshole! The guy who knows how to work this damned radio is dead, and I'm all you got. **1988** U. HOLDEN *Unicorn Sisters* xi. 119 Listen up, that's Captain now. **1992** *Metro* (San Jose, Calif.) 7–13 May 37/1, I was struck by the feeling that the violence in L.A. was a graphic and chilling realization of the rage and frustration expressed by rappers..for a long time. Maybe now the suits in Washington will listen up.

listing, *vbl. n.*² Add: **4.** *Comm.* Inclusion on an official register of securities accepted for trading and quotation on a stock exchange.

1909 *N.Y. Times* 17 June 2/5 At time of listing companies should state how much stock was issued for cash and how much in exchange for property. **1919** H. S. MARTIN *N.Y. Stock Exchange* 257 The placing of a stock on the Exchange is called 'listing'. **1922** J. E. MEEKER *Work of Stock Exchange* xvi. 446 Applicants for listing must comply with these requirements. **1955** M. MAYER *Wall St.* vi. 104 The other side of the listing war is keeping on the A.S.E. corporations large enough to qualify for the big board. **1965** *McGraw-Hill Dict. Mod. Econ.* 300 The New York Stock Exchange has the most stringent listing requirements...Only large corporations..are eligible for listing. **1978** *Penguin Dict. Econ.* (ed. 2) 279 Companies with an equity share capital valued at less than £500,000 are not eligible for listing on the London Stock Exchange. **1990** *New Europe* 13 Sept. 5/3 Nadir now says he intends to seek non-UK listings for some of the company's subsidiaries.

5. *Computing.* A printed or displayed copy of a program or the contents of a file.

1958 *Jrnl. Assoc. Computing Machinery* V. 57 Figure 1 is an illustration of a typical computer program listing. It is the list of the commands that the computer is to execute in solving a fractional part of a problem. It shows where the commands are stored, what they are to do, and contains some descriptive comments. **1965** SWALLOW & PRICE *Elem. Computer Programming* ix. 148 Figure 9-9 is the source listing of a program that will perform the required function. In this listing, note that the page and line numbers have been printed and separated. **1977** B. J. BURIAN *Simplified Approach to S/370 Assembly Lang. Programming* xviii. 302 The listing returned to the programmer contains job control statements, operating system messages, the source listing, information from the linkage editor, and a printout (dump) of computer storage. The source listing contains both the user-submitted source code, and the generated machine code. **1984** *Which Micro?* Dec. 12/1 Listings are only as good as the printer used to generate them. **1987** *Byte* Nov. 58/2 He does not provide full program listings but uses his book as a vehicle for demonstrating the process from concept through validated simulation.

7. *pl.* Lists providing details of forthcoming concert, film, or theatre performances, television schedules, etc., often printed as part of a newspaper or magazine.

1971 *Time Out* 7 May 3/1 *Time Out* is published every Thursday. Listings run from Friday to Thursday each week. **1979** *United States 1980/81* (Penguin Travel Guides) 269 For up-to-date listings and performance times, check local listings. **1985** *New Yorker* 23 Sept. 40/1 She poked me and pointed to the *TV Guide*...I gave her the guide and then watched her look up listings. **1987** E. LEONARD *Bandits* iv. 53 He remembered from the TV listings that both movies first came out in 1957. **1989** *Which?* Sept. 449/2 The BBC and ITV/Channel 4 teletext listings of today's or tomorrow's programmes can be used to help you programme your video. **1991** *History Workshop* Spring 73 London listings magazines have a regular section for the tours on offer, with daily summer choice of up to seven.

Lisu ('liːˌsuː), *n.* and *a.* Also Lissoo, Lissu, Li su, and varr. Pl. unchanged or **Lisus.** [Lisu self-designation.] **A.** *n.* **a.** A member of a people indigenous to the mountainous south-western region of China; an ethnic sub-group of the Yi. **b.** The Tibeto-Burman language of this people. **B.** *adj.* Of, pertaining to, or concerned with the Lisu or their language.

1896 *Geogr. Jrnl.* VII. 301 The Lissus and Lamajen on the Mekong are very timid...[*Note*] Generally the travellers were well received; sometimes the Lissu bards..sang impromptu songs in honour of the 'great men' come from afar. **1908** *Ibid.* XXXII. 260 The Lissoo race..is undoubtedly an offshoot from the south-east of Tibet...None of the Lissoo..show the least trace of Buddhist influence. **1909** H. R. DAVIES *Yün-nan* 351 Amongst the Lo-lo I have classed the Lahu, the Li-so and the Wo-ni, all three of which can scarcely be considered as more than dialects of some original Lo-lo tongue. *Ibid.* 391 The name by which these people call themselves is *Li-su.* This the Chinese have corrupted into *Li-so.* **1909** *Geogr. Jrnl.* XXXIV. 610 The travellers' first experience was in the territory of the 'white' or tame Liso, whose country extends as far north as..lat. 26°25'..., whilst beyond this point lie the villages of the 'black' or wild Liso. **1923** C. M. ENRIQUEZ *Burmese Arcady* ix. 137 The various Lisu dialects vary considerably and are not mutually intelligible. **1948** G. H. JOHNSON *Death takes Small Bites* i. 26 A moon-faced Lisu began again to pluck spasmodically at the strings of a guitar. **1977** YIN MING *United & Equal* 4 There is hardly any place along China's long border without its communities of minority nationalities. Among them are..the Lisu, Tulung, Nu, Chingpo, Wa, Tai and Yi in Yunnan. **1983** *Word* XXXIV. 63 There are sentences in Lisu that are synonyms with different surface forms. **1992** *Cultural Survival Q.* Fall 25/2 Patrilineal groups such as Akha, Hmong, and Lisu, place great emphasis on male children.

litany, *n.* Insert sense number a after *transf.* label. Add: [**2.**] **b.** A succession or catalogue *of* phenomena, esp. unfortunate events. Cf. CHAPTER *n.* 10 d.

1961 M. SPARK *Curtain Blown by Breeze* in *Voices at Play* 72, I lay on my bed listening to a litany of tennis noises from where my two brothers played. **1963** P. LARKIN *Let.* in A. Thwaite *Sel. Lett. Philip Larkin* (1992) 357, I ought to have written at once..and can only repeat the usual litany of excuses to say why I didn't. **1978** J. CARROLL *Mortal Friends* III. ii. 269 She had taken her place by accident..among Brady's shuffling litany of ghosts. **1985** *Globe & Mail* (Toronto) 10 Oct. B3/4 Mercantile has been..looking around for a merger partner..after a litany of troubles, including serious exposure to bad loans. **1987** *Times* 6 Feb. 9/7 Many operations were a litany of disasters. **1990** *Guardian* 28 May 20/7 The Bank Holiday weekend..brought the usual litany of traffic jams and queues at air and sea ports.

lite (laɪt), *n.*[5] [Phonetic respelling of LIGHT *n.* Cf. NITE *n.*[2]] = LIGHT *n.* in various senses, esp. in commercial use; *spec.*, a lamp, spotlight, etc. Cf. SCOTCHLITE *n.*

1955 M. REIFER *Dict. New Words* 122 *Lite-lift*.., a..forwarding arm device which permits immediate raising and lowering of a spotlight. **1970** *Globe & Mail* (Toronto) 28 Sept. 27/7 (Advt.), Vinyl roof, hidden lites. **1973** *Black World* June 63 Strobe lites flickering all over the place. **1990** *Gus Home Shopping Catal.* No. B726. 16 (*caption*) Magnetic lite.

lite (laɪt), *a.*[2] and *n.*[6] [Phonetic respelling of LIGHT *a.*[1]] **A.** *adj.* **1.** Occas. in advertisements: = LIGHT *a.*[1] 18 a.

1954 *Los Angeles Times* 21 Mar. 3/2 (Advt.), Clerk-lite steno..$200 start.

2. *Comm.* Designating a manufactured product that is lighter (in weight, calorie content, etc.) than the ordinary variety, esp. (with capital initial) low-calorie beer. Freq. used postpositively. Cf.*LIGHT *a.*[1] 10.

1962 L. S. SASIENI *Optical Dispensing* i. 17 On light-weight spectacles a small joint known as the 'Lite-Elete' is sometimes used. **1967** *N.Y. Times* 14 Sept. 65/3 The leotards match the packaging and labeling of Meister Brau Lite, a no-carbohydrate beer to be introduced this week. **1971** *Official Gaz.* (U.S. Patent Office) 30 Nov. TM283 *Lite*...For beer with no available carbohydrates...First use May 15,

1967. **1975** *Business Week* 13 Oct. 116/1 Lite beer, the low-calorie brew introduced by Miller Brewing Co...last February. **1984** M. AMIS *Money* 304, I sit in a bar drinking lite beer. **1990** T. ROBBINS *Skinny Legs & All* 391 He was sipping from a can of Miller Lite. **1991** *Public Works* Nov. 32/1 (Advt.), Efficiency Production Ultra-Lite Aluminum Trench Boxes let you use small backhoe/loaders to lift, swing, and place them in the ditch easily. **1992** *Men's Health* May-June 44/1, It does little good to switch to the 'lite' versions of bologna made from turkey or chicken.

3. *fig.* Designating a simplified or moderated version of something; so (*dismissively*), lacking in substance; over-simplified, facile. Freq. used postpositively, in humorous imitation of brand names (see sense *2 above). *U.S. colloq.*

1989 *Spy* (N.Y.) Mar. 96/1 Whereas camp *during* the fifties and sixties emerged from the more passionate, fabled art forms of ballet, opera and Joan Crawford vehicles, Camp Lite is almost purely the spawn of fifties and sixties television, with its bland sitcom chuckles. **1990** *Omni* Dec. 92/3 Blum's view that the government knows little more than we do about UFOs is a decidedly 'lite' version of the cover-up. **1991** *Creem* Apr.-May 78 With substantial songs inspired by real-life situations, Breathe are quickly putting behind them the notion that they're merely the lite fodder for teenaged dreams. **1992** *Newsweek* 27 Apr. 58/3 USA Today is still dogged by the perception among many would-be advertisers and the media elite that it remains News Lite, a triumph of marketing over substance. **1992** *Playboy* Sept. 37/2, I am the happy feminist, the feminist who likes men, the feminist lite. **1995** *Internet World* Feb. 14/3 InternetWorks has a suggested retail price of $129 and includes and electronic version of New Rider's Internet Yellow Pages. A lite version is available via FTP.

B. *n.* Low-calorie beer. orig. *U.S.*

1975 *Business Week* 13 Oct. 118/2 Lite actually tastes like beer. **1978** *Esquire* 18 July 76/3 Lite also has less alcohol than regular beer.

literate, *a.* and *n.* Add: Hence 'literately *adv.*

1958 *Misc. Rep.* (N. Y.) 2nd Ser. VIII. 307 The apellation 'strip-tease' in common vernacular, more literately known as 'ecdysis'. **1978** *Washington Post* 3 Dec. F7/4 Lucid description, classical commentary, ..all literately written to make serious archeology joyful and easy to read. **1989** *N. Y. Times* 30 July VII. 16/1 The book..smoothly and literately translated by Anselm Hollo.

lith (lɪθ), *n.*[5] [Abbrev. of LITHOGRAPHY *n.*] A photographic film that is thinly coated with emulsion for producing images of extremely high contrast and density, used in lithographic printing. Usu. *attrib.*, esp. in *lith film*.

1955 *Jrnl. Photogr. Sci.* III. 98/1 The modern 'lith' type of dry plate emulsion. **1959** E. JAFFE et al. *Color Separation Photogr.* 167 Lith-type developers refer to the high-contrast, formaldehyde developers. **1967** E. CHAMBERS *Photolitho-Offset* ix. 123 A 'lith' film must have a gamma above 10 which is necessary to build up screen dots having an extremely steep density gradient. *Ibid.* 124 With 'lith' developer blackening starts in the areas of maximum action of light, spreading gradually until the areas of minimum light action are developed. **1977** *Transatlantic Rev.* LX. 196 The Gorilla story had to be entirely re-set when the lith-film had gone through the plate-makers' department totally blank. **1979** *Amat. Photogr.* 10 Jan. 74/2 If you want to do any ortho film work (like lith films) you can work under safelight conditions, but check on the correct ortho safelight filter before you buy. **1991** *Photo Answers* Mar. 38 (*caption*) Lith is great for many subjects but here it has been used to create a really eye-catching portrait.

lithostatic (lɪθəʊ'stætɪk), *a. Geol.* [f. LITHO- + STATIC *a.*] Designating pressure exerted by overlying rock.

1950 *Econ. Geol.* XLV. 542 Under a depth cover of two miles the pressure may range from hydrostatic, the weight of a two mile column of water to lithostatic, the weight of a two mile column of rock, or to something greater than lithostatic. **1960** *New Scientist* 21 Apr. 997/1 Some lava..was forced outward into the innermost collapse pit by the lithostatic pressure being applied around the periphery of the main collapse area. **1975** *Nature* 10 Apr. 486/1 Granitic liquid would have a low magma density of about 2.3, and an analysis is made of the relationships between hydrostatic (magma) pressures and lithostatic (load) pressures in the vicinity of such diapirs. **1987** *Trans. Amer. Nucl. Soc.* LV. 134/1 We assume a far-field lithostatic pressure of 16.3 MPa.

lithotomy, *n.* Add: **3.** Special Comb. **lithotomy position** *Obstetr.*, a position of the body similar to that required for lithotomy, in which a person lies supine with the legs raised in stirrups, flexed and apart.
1879 *St. George's Hospital Rep.* IX. 271 The patient was placed in the lithotomy position. **1958** J. BARTH *End of Road* xii. 220 Rennie's legs were drawn up and spread wide in the lithotomy position. **1967** *Amer. Jrnl. Obstetr. & Gynecol.* XCVII. 871/1 *(heading)* Femoral neuropathy from the lithotomy position: case report and new leg holder for prevention. **1984** *Sunday Tel.* 19 Feb. 11/1 The Princess will be sent screeds of literature about the new fashions in giving birth—the lithotomy (lying down) position is now *out*, the squatting position and the 'borning chair' are now *in*.

lithotripsy, *n.* Restrict variant **lithotripsis** to sense in Dict. Label sense in Dict. *Surg.* and add: **2.** *Med.* The disintegration of calculi (usu. in the renal tract or the gall bladder) by the administration of ultrasonic shocks, without the need for surgery. [After G. *Ultraschall-Lithotripsie* (K. H. Gasteyer 1971, in *Der Urologe A.* X. 30).]
1980 *Lancet* 13 Dec. 1265/2 Physical methods, such as ultrasound lithotrypsy [*sic*] or administration of electrohydraulic waves, are applicable only in the lower urinary tract. **1983** *Jrnl. Med. Engin. & Technol.* VII. 3/2 The Dornier Company of FR Germany, in conjunction with workers at the University of Munich, have produced a..method..called 'extracorporeal lithotripsy'. **1985** *Brit. Med. Jrnl.* 14 Sept. 691/2 Ultrasonic lithotripsy entails inserting a percutaneous guide wire into the renal collecting system under *x* ray control. **1987** *Ibid.* 10 Oct. 893/2 This report..reiterates the experience of others that extracorporeal shockwave lithotripsy is a safe, effective, and economic method of treating renal and ureteric calculi. **1992** *Day* (New London, Connecticut) 27 July A7/3 Recently concerns have been raised about fragments of stones left behind by the ultrasound technique, called lithotripsy.

lithotripter ('lɪθəʊ̩trɪptə(r)), *n. Med.* [a. G. *Lithotripter* (B. Terhorst et al. 1972, in *Urologia Internat.* XXVII. 458): cf. LITHOTRIPTOR *n.*, -ER[1].] A machine used for ultrasound lithotripsy which generates ultrasonic waves and focuses them on a chosen site in the body. Cf. LITHOTRIPTOR *n.*
[**1972** *Urologia Internat.* XXVII. 458 A new ultrasound lithotriptor in the treatment of bladder calculi is presented.] **1982** *Lancet* 4 Dec. 1256/1 Renal stones can now be pulverised by externally applied shock waves. The apparatus, known as the lithotriptor, was developed by the Dornier Company. **1984** *Economist* 28 July 70/2 The lithotripter creates loud shock waves which pass through the body and shatter kidney stones into fragments that can pass cleanly out of the kidney in the urine. **1986** *Age* (Melbourne) 22 Feb. 3/1 The lithotripter, also known as 'the big banger', will be located at a major public hospital. **1990** *N. Y. Times* 14 Aug. C2/2 Some medical centers have shut down their gallstone lithotripters because of high costs and a far more limited number of candidates than projected.

lithotype, *n.* Add: **4.** *Petrogr.* A macroscopically visible constituent of coal distinguished by its physical characterisitics; a macroscopically distinguishable variety of coal. Cf. MACERAL *n.*
1957 VAN KREVELEN & SCHUYER *Coal Sci.* iii. 52 The Heerlen nomenclature distinguishes between the rock types (lithotypes) and their more or less homogeneous microscopic constituents, which are called macerals. **1961** D. W. VAN KREVELEN *Coal* iv. 58 Charcoal inclusions..can be noted between the coal bands. These macroscopic ingredients are the rock types (lithotypes) occurring in coal. **1984** C. R. WARD *Coal Geol. & Coal Technol.* iii. 74/2 The material [*sc.* durain] is relatively hard compared to other lithotypes, and tends to break into large, blocky fragments. **1987** P. J. MCCABE in A. C. Scott *Coal & Coal-Bearing Strata* 53 Lithotypes of coal are normally defined on both the maceral composition and the overall texture of the coal.

‖ **li ting** (liː dɪŋ), *n.* Also **liding, li-ting.** [Chinese *lí dǐng.*] An ancient (usu. tripodal) Chinese bronze or pottery cooking vessel with solid legs; = TING *n.*[4]
1958 W. WILLETTS *Chinese Art* I. iii. 138 There is an intermediate pottery form, also rendered in bronze, that Karlgren calls *li-ting.* **1974** *Times* 26 June 20/4 An early bronze *li-ting* and domed cover. **1980** *Catal. Fine Chinese Ceramics* (Sotheby, Hong Kong) 226 *(caption)* An archaic bronze tripod cauldron, *liding* (*li ting*), standing on three cylindrical feet.

litter, *n.* Add: [**3.**] **d.** Decomposing but still recognizable vegetable debris that has fallen from trees and other plants and forms a distinct layer above the soil, esp. on the floor of a forest. See also *leaf-litter* s.v. *LEAF *n.* 19.
1905 *Terms Forestry & Logging* (U.S. Dept. Agric. Bureau Forestry) 14 *Litter*, that portion of the forest floor which is not in an advanced state of decomposition. **1938** WEAVER & CLEMENTS *Plant Ecol.* (ed. 2) viii. 184 Litter comprises the upper portion of the forest floor, slightly or not at all decomposed. The more or less decomposed organic matter just beneath the litter constitutes a layer of duff. **1947** R. F. DAUBENMIRE *Plants & Environment* ii. 25 Just beneath the fresh litter may be found a layer derived from the preceding seasons' litter in which the processes of disintegration seem actively at work. **1974** *Nature* 4 Jan. 3/2 If stress is low, then grasslands become dominated by species of high physical competitive ability, that is species which grow rapidly, are robust and produce dense litter. **1990** *Forest Resources Arizona* (U.S. Dept. Agric. Forest Service) 31 Descriptive locational observations on litter depth..were made at each field location to get an idea of the general condition and stability of the woodland soil resource in the State.
[**6.**] **litter case,** a person too ill or badly injured to walk, who is carried on a litter (sense 2 b above): cf. *stretcher case* s.v. STRETCHER *n.* 12.
1944 *Sun* (Baltimore) 9 June 2/3 First to be unloaded on the pier were the *litter cases*—seriously injured and dying. **1966** MRS. L. B. JOHNSON *White House Diary* 24 Dec. (1970) 464 A litter case came down the steps [of the ambulance plane] and a young man raised his head.

litterfall ('lɪtəfɔːl), *n. Ecol.* Also **litter fall.** [f. LITTER *n.* + FALL *n.*[1]] **a.** The fall of leaves and other vegetable matter from plants to form litter (sense *3 d). **b.** = *LITTER *n.* 3 d.
1967 P. J. NEWBOULD *Methods estimating Primary Product of Forests* iv. 22 Regular measurements of litter fall..will give an indication of the total number of leaves shed. *Ibid.* vi. 32 It is important that the litter

fall should drop into the trap. **1969** *Jap. Jrnl. Ecol.* XIX. 243/1 Efforts have been made to find appropriate methods for. . assessing the rate of litterfall. **1975** *Ecol.* LVI. 1193/2 The type and composition of the litterfall and forest floor vary markedly from spot to spot. **1987** *Canad. Jrnl. Forest Res.* XVII. 1435/2 Litterfall was collected in conifer-hardwood plots.

little, *a.,* *adv.,* and *n.* Add: [A.] [I.] [1.] [c.] (*b*) Also used in combination with place-names to denote somewhere which resembles or is reminiscent of the place mentioned, or which constitutes a 'colony' or microcosm of it (as a community of expatriates, immigrant quarter, etc.). See also **little England, little Venice,* sense 13 below.
1749 J. CLELAND *Mem. Woman Pleasure* I. 134 But had it been a dungeon. . his presence would have made it a little Versailles. **1822** *Weekly Reg.* (York, Ontario) 20 June 92/3 We know of no place labled 'Little York', in Canada, and beg that he [*sc.* Mr. W. Patton] will bear that little circumstance in his recollection. **1909** WEBSTER s.v., *L*[*ittle*] *Hungary, Italy,* etc., the Hungarian, Italian, etc., quarter in a city;—so called in various cities of the United States. *colloq.* **1929** H. MILES tr. *Morand's Black Magic* I. 46 The Negro quarter, 'Little Africa', as it is called. **1947** H. A. SMITH *Lo, Former Egyptian* i. 13 If you take a map of Illinois and draw a line east and west from Vincennes, Indiana, to St. Louis, Missouri, all that part of the state to the south of the line. . is called Egypt or, sometimes, Little Egypt. **1971** R. A. CARTER *Manhattan Primitive* (1972) i. 14 Monroe Street, deep in Little Italy. **1989** WILSON & FERRIS *Encycl. Southern Culture* 439/1, Many of the migrants settled in separate neighborhoods called 'little Oklahomas', where they set up their own. . churches.

[3.] **b.** Used as an (ironic) intensifier in various constructions intended to emphasize the following noun, as *quite a little* (. .), *a nice little* (. .), etc.; *this little lot:* see LOT *n.* 9.
1861 *Sporting Rev.* Oct. 249 Kettledrum's walk-over was quite a little tit-bit for the Yorkshiremen. **1891** N. GOULD *Double Event* xvi. 112 A nice little swindle you worked off on me that time. **1951** J. D. SALINGER *Catcher in Rye* xv. 127 'Who is this?' she said. She was quite a little phoney. I'd already told her father who it was. **1984** S. T. WARNER *One Thing* 8 He. . made a nice little profit on the transaction, having bought them off a white-elephant stall for eighteenpence apiece. **1992** *Daily Tel.* 24 July 14/8 The Mercury Prize is worth £20,000 to the winner. A nice little earner for Bheki Mseleku, Jah Wobble or even Primal Scream, no doubt, but small change to Mick Hucknall or Bono.

[8.] **c.** Applied, sometimes with connotations of social inferiority, to tradespeople, usu. ones who do work (esp. dressmaking) on commission. See also LITTLE MAN *n.* 2 a, *little woman* (b), sense 13 below.
1780 SHERIDAN *Sch. Scand.* IV. iii. 54 'Tis a little French Milliner, who calls upon me sometimes. **1850** 'L. LIMNER' *Christmas Comes* 9 He seeks refuge in his organ, much to the annoyance of a little tailor in the attic who has no soul in him. **1857** MRS. GASKELL *Let.* 28 Sept. (1966) 476 Only last week a letter to a little dressmaker, living not a mile off. . was returned to me by the Post Office. **1930** E. H. YOUNG *Miss Mole* xxvii. 239 Ethel's Chinese silk had been made up hastily by an obliging little dressmaker. **1957** 'P. PORTOBELLO' *Deb's Mum* 58 'I know a splendid little woman in Beauchamp Place'. . 'There are two little men in Mavies Street, right up on the fourth floor'. . . Perhaps in a few more years the diminutive will be acknowledged in dictionaries to imply that, although the person so described may be six feet tall or weigh fourteen stone, he or she can clothe you at short notice and at a reasonable price. **1975** P. HARCOURT *Fair Exchange* I. 16 A little Italian dressmaker who ran up copies of dresses for next to nothing.

[III.] **13. little England,** (*a*) in full, *little England beyond Wales:* the English-speaking area of Pembrokeshire (Dyfed); (*b*) a microcosm or 'colony' of England; (*c*) Barbados; (*d*) a derogatory term for the insular state supposedly advocated by Little Englanders.
1586 W. CAMDEN *Brit.* 373 (*margin*), *Little England beyond Wales. **1610** P. HOLLAND tr. *Camden's Brit.* I. 652 This tract was inhabited by Flemings. . [and] is tearmed by the Britains Little England beyond Wales. **1802** C. WILMOT *Let.* 30 July in *Irish Peer* (1920) 77 At present Paris is become a little England, 5000 is the calculation this last week. **1888** E. LAWS *Hist. Little Eng. beyond Wales* iii. 34 The English-speaking inhabitants of Pembrokeshire have for generations called their home 'Little England beyond Wales'. **1890** FARMER *Slang* I. 199/1 The island of Barbadoes. . is also sometimes jeeringly called *Little England.* **1895** J. CHAMBERLAIN *Speech at Walsall* 15 July in *Times* 16 July 10/2 Men who. . were 'Little England' men, who took every opportunity of. . criticizing those brave Englishmen who have made for us homes across the sea. **1925** *Observer* 31 May 9/4 Pembrokeshire, the county which some call 'Little England beyond Wales'. **1953** G. LAMMING *In Castle of my Skin* ii. 25 Barbados or Little England as it was called in the local school texts. **1963** J. Mander (*title*) Great Britain or Little England? **1973** 'D. JORDAN' *Nile Green* xiii. 56 An elderly bill-broker spoke up wearily for the cause of scepticism and Little England. **1989** *Independent* 23 Dec. 52 Little England views about 1992 [were] being expressed by the proprietor. . . 'English people don't like being told what to do, especially by the Frogs.'

little ice age *Meteorol.,* a period of comparatively cold climate occurring between major glaciations; *spec.* (freq. with capital initials) the period of this kind which reached its peak during the 17th cent.; cf. NEOGLACIATION *n.*
1939 F. E. MATTHES in *Trans. Amer. Geophysical Union* XX. 520 All of the glaciers of the latter class, however,. . now have far greater extent and volume than they had during the middle third of the Post-Pleistocene interval, and accordingly it may well be said that we are living in an epoch of renewed but moderate glaciation—a 'little ice age', that already has lasted about 4000 years. **1957** *Science* 1 Feb. 183/3 Matthes introduced the term Little Ice Age for an episode of renewed glaciation that began sometime after the driest part of postglacial time and culminated in or shortly before the 18th century A.D. **1975** *Nature* 1 May 26/2 The cold period from 1450 to 1700, often called 'the little ice age', was not particularly cold at Crete or in Iceland. **1978** *Daily Tel.* 8 May 11/6 Very cold periods, or 'little ice ages', seem to happen when the Sun is relatively quiet. **1988** *New Scientist* 7 Apr. 55/1 Increased volcanic activity in the 1780s produced dust veils in the upper atmosphere which prolonged the Little Ice Age for decades.

littoral, *a.* and *n.* Add: [A.] **2.** *Histol.* [After G. *Uferzelle,* lit. 'shore cell' (H. Siegmund 1923, in *Münch. med. Wochenschr.* LXX. 5/2).] Designating a cell of the macrophage system which occurs temporarily attached to the walls of the sinuses in lymphoid tissue.
1930 MAXIMOW & BLOOM *Text-bk. Histol.* v. 103 The cells which line the walls of the sinuses, and which are attached to the fibers passing through the cavity of these spaces, often have a decidedly flattened form and are somewhat similar to endothelial cells. . . Their biological properties, especially the storing of vital dyes and the transformation into phagocytosing, free, ameboid macrophages are identical with those of the reticular cells of the lymphoid tissue. . . Their flattened form is merely an adaptation to their peculiar position on the wall of channels through which the lymph flows. They may be called conveniently the littoral cells of the histiocytic system. **1938** *Jrnl. Path. & Bacteriol.* XLVII. 459 The subcapsular lymph sinus and its

continuations are lined with specialised endothelial cells or littoral cells..which lie on their margins and on the loose network of reticulin fibrils which cross their cavity. **1985** C. R. LEESON et al. *Textbk. Histol.* (ed. 5) v. 166/2 The sinuses present within lymphoid tissue are lined by littoral cells of the macrophage system.

live, *a.* Add: [**2.**] **e.** Of a recording, film, etc.: taken from or made at a live performance rather than in a studio.
   1947 *Audio Engin.* Dec. 27/2 There are definite advantages to the live performance method of recording. It would be interesting to hear how a wide range live recording might sound. **1959** W. S. SHARPS *Dict. Cinematogr.* 107/1 *Live recording*, a recording of sound made at the same time as it originates. **1977** *Washington Post* 16 Jan. E5/3 His live album, recorded at the Montreux Jazz Festival in 1974. **1979** MARSH & SWENSON *Rolling Stone Record Guide* (1980) 440/2 [B. B.] King's best records..are the live sets, where the electricity of audience/performer interaction spurred King on to elaborate vocal and instrumental histrionics. **1985** *Sounds* 27 July 2/1 The Sex Pistols have another live album coming out next week. **1990** *Opera Now* May 78/2 Live recording or not, muddled enthusiasm cannot rescue the Corale Amerina from some approximate tuning and lack of ensemble.
   [**4.**] **b.** Of electrical apparatus: switched on and functional; (esp. of a microphone) receptive to sound.
   1936 *P. O. Electr. Engineers' Jrnl.* Apr. 10/2 Until the valves in the loudspeaking set have heated up and the set is 'live'. **1937** *Printers' Ink Monthly* apr. 54/2 *Hot mike*, a microphone in which the current is flowing. A live microphone. **1984** *Washington Post* 3 July D2/1 In a studio like this, a live microphone propped before them, they must..give precisely timed noises to the movements on film. **1991** *Electronic Musician* Nov. 71/2 *Hypercardioid* microphones are highly sensitive in front and less sensitive at the sides. This pattern diminishes the potential for feedback in live situations.

live-in, *a.* and *n.* Add: [**A.**] **2.** That may be lived in; applied to clothing designed to be comfortable or practical enough for continuous wear; also applied *occas.* to property not usually expected to afford living accommodation.
   1978 J. IRVING *World according to Garp* xix. 428 Roberta went to..Duncan's live-in studio. **1984** *Sears Catal. 1985* Spring/Summer 103 This jumpsuit is..destined to be your 'live-in' item for spring and summer. **1986** *Sunday Express Mag.* 11 May 45/3 This is that kind of 'live-in' dress that everyone loves. Comfortable..but capable of looking very chic too.
   B. *n.* A person who lives in (in various senses) or shares living accomodation.
   1974 T. KENRICK *Two for Price of One* vii. 71 We have about twenty live-ins and the rest come up to see the shrink a couple of times a week. **1977** *Guardian Weekly* 6 Mar. 19/2 She devotes her time to writing, pottery, Ben, her live-in (American for permanent boyfriend..), friends, cats and plants. **1979** *Arizona Daily Star* 5 Aug. (Advt. Section) 6/6 Reliable Person wanted as live-in for elderly gentleman. **1985** K. GOVIER in Atwood & Weaver *Oxf. Bk. Canad. Short Stories* (1988) 402 One couple had a live-in already, and about half the women were going back to work. **1987** H. MURPHY *Murder takes Partner* xiii. 115 Neither Reuben nor Cynthia could tell whether they were simply friends or if Francisca was a 'live-in'. **1992** *Chicago Tribune* 22 Nov. XVI. 1N/4, I counseled a gentleman, an amputee who couldn't get out of his house. He had two live-ins and he didn't want to leave the community.

livery, *n.* Add: [**9.**] **b.** *Horse-riding colloq.* (*a*) A horse from a livery-stable, or one for which livery is needed; (*b*) a place for a horse at a

livery-stable; (*c*) an owner of a horse kept at livery.
   1896 *Dialect Notes* I. 420 *Livery*, a turn-out from a livery stable. **1948** *Horse & Hound* 3 Jan. 14/3 (Advt.), Liveries. Ye Olde Felbridge Livery Stables...Horses taken at livery. *Ibid.* 14 Feb. 15/4 (Advt.), A unique opportunity! Two liveries, good stables, exercise, every care. **1950** *Ibid.* 23 Sept. 22/4 (Advt.), Accommodation available for 2 or 3 good hunting liveries. **1982** *Daily Tel.* 15 Dec. 10/8 (Advt.), McLeod liveries. Full Hunter Horse liveries available. Take the worry out of hunting. **1986** *Horse & Rider* Sept. 35/1 Livery yards could be more helpful..by putting a notice somewhere prominent where all liveries will see it.

living, *ppl. a.* Add: [**3.**] **living will**: orig. *U. S.*, a written request that, if the signatory suffers severe disablement or terminal illness, he or she should not be kept alive by artificial means (such as a life-support system).
   1969 L. KUTNER in *Indiana Law Jrnl.* XL. 551 The document indicating..consent may be referred to as 'a *living will*'. **1973** *Britannica Bk. of Year* (U.S.) 732/2 *Living will*, a written declaration in which a person requests that if he becomes disabled beyond reasonable expectation of recovery he be allowed to die in dignity rather than be kept alive by artificial means. **1976** *National Observer* (U.S.) 24 Jan. 9/1 The 'living will', which is available free from the nonprofit Euthanasia Educational Council. **1984** *Sci. Amer.* Dec. 62/1 Living wills have been recognized by 21 states and the District of Columbia. **1988** P. MONETTE *Borrowed Time* xii. 340 That is the point of the living will he'd signed, that we couldn't take him to intensive care and put a tube down his throat. **1995** *Independent* 6 Mar. 3/1 The BMA is opposed to legalising living wills, although the Law Commission wants the position tidied up.

load, *n.* Restrict †Obs. to sense 1a and add: [**1.**] **b.** *Computing.* [f. the vb.] The action of loading a program, etc., into memory; an instance of this. Usu. *attrib.*
   1962 *Gloss. Terms Automatic Data Processing* (B.S.I.) 42 *Load program*,..An input routine for reading programs. **1967** E. R. LANNON in Cox & Grose *Organiz. Bibliogr. Rec. by Computer* IV. 87 The Load which actually updates the system files. **1969** J. HELLWIG *Introd. Computers & Programming* (ed. 2) vi. 172 What does a linkage editor do? It prepares your program for execution, by creating what may be called a load module. **1977** W. S. DAVIS *Operating Syst.* ii. 22 Another program, a linkage editor or loader.., performs a number of functions needed to prepare the program for execution on the computer and produces a load module. *Ibid.* vii. 103 The asterisk indicates that the phase is to be loaded at the first available location in the partition. This load address can be specified in a number of different ways. **1986** *ZX Computing Monthly* Oct. 12/1 In one load, the game gives you access to any of the 12 world championship tracks, including Silverstone.
   [**2.**] **d.** A quantity of items washed or to be washed in a washing machine or dishwasher at one time.
   1926 *People's Home Jrnl.* Feb. 22/1 (Advt.), In fifteen minutes or less, the entire load, of 10-1/2 pounds of dry clothes, is immaculately washed and blued. **1935** D. MYERSON *Homemaker's Handbk.* v. 46 In the first load, place sheets, pillowcases, and other garments which are not being boiled or hand-rubbed. **1946** *Consumers' Res. Bull.* Feb. 10/3 The maximum load for the machine is 9 pounds of clothes. **1959** *Sears, Roebuck Catal.* Spring/Summer 907/1 Kick-out switch..signals when load is unbalanced. **1972** *Which?* Jan. 16/1 We based our loads on the size of the wash drum. **1991** *Consumers Digest* Dec. 111/2 You won't need a liquid-fabric-softener dispenser, of course, if you only plan to use fabric-softener sheets in dryer loads.

[3.] h. **under load** *Mech.*, subjected to a load (esp. in senses 3 a, c, and d above).

1893 B. WILLIS in *13th Ann. Rep. U.S. Geol. Survey* II. 250 In strata under load an anticline arises along a line of initial dip, when a thrust, sufficiently powerful to raise the load, is transmitted by a competent stratum. **1928** E. BUCKINGHAM *Spur Gears* xii. 444 Hardened gears are sometimes run together under load with some form of abrasive introduced with the lubricant to smooth the surfaces and correct some of the errors. **1946** W. H. CROUSE *Automotive Mech.* xviii. 413 The gears that are under load when the noise is produced should be examined. **1983** J. S. FOSTER *Structure & Fabric* (rev. ed.) I. iii. 14/1 The overall behaviour of structures under load. **1988** *Pract. Motorist* Mar. 24/4 Whine is the noise.. associated with rear axles, whether under load or on the over-run.

load, *v.* Senses 5b, c become 5c, d. Add: [5.] b. *to be loaded for bear(s)*, to be well prepared for an anticipated confrontation, opponent, emergency, etc.; to be ready for anything; also (*joc.*) drunk; hence *to be loaded (for)*, to be well prepared (for).

1888 *World* (N.Y.) 19 Oct. 3/5 Ewing was loaded for bear and was just spoiling for a chance to catch somebody on the bases. **1890** BARRÈRE & LELAND *Dict. Slang* II. 22/2 *Loaded for bears* (American), .. signifies that a man is slightly intoxicated, enough to feel ready to confront danger. **1896** *Dialect Notes* I. 420 *Loaded for bear*, .. 3. Said of one who has a big supply of anything... 4. Full of indignation which is likely to be vented upon its object. **1904** F. CRISSEY *Tattlings of Retired Politician* 423, I caught a gleam in the tail of the President's eye that showed he had been loaded for his caller and had given him this shot with malice aforethought. **1937** *San Francisco Examiner* 1 Dec. 22/3 (*heading*) Texans 'loaded' for Don contest. **1948** *San Francisco News* 20 Sept. 15/6 Loyola, supposedly loaded, .. was plagued by poor field generalship. **1957** M. SHULMAN *Rally round Flag, Boys!* (1958) iv. 55 The O'Sheel woman is coming in loaded for bear this time. She's got some brand-new gimmick, and she's also got a lot of people on her side. **1982** *Verbatim* Autumn 14/2 Don't we also know bright-eyed and bushy-tailed tigers who are always loaded for bear? **1989** T. CLANCY *Clear & Present Danger* x. 199 *Christ, but they're loaded for bear*, the colonel thought. Not wearing standard-issue uniforms.... Obviously a covert insertion.. but they were clearly planning to stay awhile.

e. *Computing.* To transfer (a program or data) into memory, or into the central processor from a more remote part of memory.

1953 *Proc. IRE* XLI. 1274/1 The last section showed how a new program may be loaded from tape, drums, or cards. **1965** *IBM Systems Jrnl.* IV. 66 A file loader program is needed to load the test record system. **1973** C. W. GEAR *Introd. Computer Sci.* ii. 37 The CPU can be told to load a number into its accumulator from a specific cell in the memory. **1981** D. FRANCIS *Twice Shy* xviii. 210 She nodded, not lifting her eyes from the.. job of loading Grantley Basic into a machine that would accept it. **1991** *Personal Computer World* Feb. 100/2 If you load the program onto a naked machine, it looks for 'spare' memory high in the address map and leaves only 5k of itself in the normal address space.

f. To take up a quantity of paint, etc., on (a brush).

1978 C. HAYES *Compl. Guide Paint & Draw. Techn.* viii. 132 (*caption*) Fully load the brush. **1984** W. WHARTON *Scumbler* (1986) xi.101, I squeeze the usual pigments, load my brush. **1986** *Do it Yourself* June 10/2 To load the brush, dip about one third of the bristles into the paint. **1990** M. ROBERTS *In Red Kitchen* (1991) 54, I cut lengths of lining paper, loaded my brush with paste, worked it to and fro until each long sheet was well coated.

12. *Comb.* **load-and-go** *Computing*, an operating technique in which the loading and execution of a program form one continuous process; usu. *attrib.*

1964 *Gloss. Data Processing & Communications Terms* (Honeywell Inc.) 35/2 **Load-and-go..*, an operating technique in which there are no stops between the loading and execution phase of a program, and which may include assembly or compilation. **1976** A. RALSTON *Encycl. Computer Sci.* 804/1 The load and go compiler compiles and executes these programs one at a time. **1983** T. S. FRANK *Introd. PDP-11 & its Assembly Lang.* ix. 208 The linker might even begin program execution of the load module, since it knows the program's transfer address. This is the so-called load-and-go mode of loading, editing and linking, which would be accomplished simply by MOVing the program's transfer address into the PC. **1991** *Nature* 24 Jan. p. xx (Advt.), It features an Apple Macintosh II CX computer plus powerful 'load and go' software.

loaded, *ppl. a.* Add: [4.] b. Of a car (or occas. other item) for sale: equipped with optional extras, de luxe; containing more than the standard equipment. *N. Amer. colloq.*

1968 *Globe & Mail* (Toronto) 3 Feb. 38/5 (Advt.), **1965** *Buick Wildcat*. Loaded, immaculate. **1976** *Washington Post* 19 Apr. c23/1 (Advt.), Loaded car, very sharp. **1976** *Billings* (Montana) *Gaz.* 30 June 5-D/7 (Advt.), Luxury living on modest budget 2 bdrm's & loaded! **1991** *Times* (Florence, Alabama) *Daily* 16 Apr. B10/5 (Advt.), 1983 Honda Accord. 4-door, automatic, loaded.

loader, *n.*[1] Add: [1.] d. *Computing.* A program which controls the loading of other programs.

1959 M. H. WRUBEL *Primer of Programming for Digital Computers* viii. 193 A simple way to load a program is to punch the instructions, one to a card, in the form of 'single-word loaders'. There are load cards containing not only information to be stored, but also a short program for moving it to an arbitrary location and provision for reading in the next card. **1966** C. J. SIPPL *Computer Dict. & Handbk.* 175/2 The loader alters all necessary addresses in the object program to allow loading at an address of main storage assigned by the control program. **1972** *Computer Jrnl.* XV. 195/1 Binary code.. requires packing up into words before it is supplied to the loader. **1980** C. S. FRENCH *Computer Sci.* xxiv. 183 A loader will take a program written in machine code and in some suitable input form such as paper tape, and input the instruction from the paper tape into.. specified storage locations. **1985** *Personal Computer World* Feb. 162/2 A small implementation requirement is the inclusion of the SEG loader directive in definition modules.

loading, *vbl. n.* Senses 6, 7 in *Dict.* become 7, 8. Add: [1.] h. *Med.* The administration of a large amount of a (usu. biologically active) substance, esp. a loading dose of it. Freq. preceded by the name of the substance being administered.

1965 *Jrnl. Neurochem.* XII. 491 No 5-hydroxytryptophan was detected in the brain after tryptophan loading, although it appeared in measurable amounts in the plasma. **1975** *Nature* 20 Nov. 227/1 Four hours after salt loading, vagotomised rats still drank less. **1985** *Bodypower* Oct. 12/1 (Advt.), This product is also used for carbohydrate loading prior to an athletic event or body-building contest. **1990** *Ironman* Oct. 32/1 You'll learn how your body reacts to carb or protein 'loading' or depletion and how specific foods make you feel and look.

[3.] b. *Austral.* An amount or percentage awarded in addition to a wage or salary; = WEIGHTING *vbl. n.* 4. See also *holiday loading* s.v. *HOLIDAY *n.* 4 c.

1937 *Sydney Morning Herald* 24 June 6/3 The [Arbitration] Court formed the opinion that the highest loading should be made for New South Wales, Victoria, and Queensland. **1941** *Commonwealth Arbitration Rep.* XLIV. 456 In addition to amounts otherwise payable a special loading at the rate of 3s. per week shall be payable to occupants of any of the callings specified. **1965** *Austral. Encycl.* I. 447/2 All courts award 'margins' or 'loadings', for skill, overtime, week-end work, danger, and dirt. **1972** *Age* (Melbourne) 14 Dec. 1/7 Victorian painters will receive a 17½ per cent. loading of their three-weeks holiday pay as a Christmas bonus. **1984** *Austral. Financial Rev.* 9 Nov. 17/4 (Advt.), The Company provides an outstanding benefits package including immediate superannuation, 4 weeks' annual leave with loading and a comprehensive health benefits plan. **1991** *Chron. Higher Educ.* (U.S.) 20 Feb. B6 (Advt.), Salary will be at the rate of $A67,812 p.a., plus a clinical loading of $A12,058. Additional allowances may be payable by the Central Sydney Area Health Service.

[4.] c. The number of passengers carried by a vehicle or vessel.

1957 *Buses Illustr.* VII. 200/1 First impressions [of driving a bus in a holiday resort] are of abnormally heavy loading, which is spread fairly evenly throughout the day. **1976** *Southern Even. Echo* (Southampton) 13 Nov. 6/1 Loadings are higher on Saturday through the day with football enthusiasts and shoppers. **1987** *Ships Monthly* July 20/2 With some fully booked sailings and generally high loadings, the Easter and May Day Bank Holiday period suggested no obvious public reaction to Zeebrugge. **1987** *Railway World* Nov. 650/1 Apart from poor loadings on 6 September, patronage has been good, with 480 passengers on the 11.05 ex-Swansea of 12 September. **1992** *Mod. Railways* Mar. 145/2 Times change; today's loadings are well within the capacity of at most a couple of buses or coaches.

6. The concentration or amount of one substance in another. Used esp. with reference to the impregnation of solid materials, as wood, leather, etc.

1931 WILSON & MERRILL *Anal. of Leather* ii. 33 Users of sole leather are interested in the 'loading' which the leather has undergone—that is, in the quantity of material (glucose, Epsom salt, tannin, or non-tannin) deposited in the leather by impregnating it with a strong solution and drying out or in the quantity of material that will be leached out of the soles in actual wear. **1948** *N.Z. Jrnl. Sci. & Technol.* B. XXX. 20 From the weight of treating solution absorbed and its concentration the amount of preservative in the block is calculated. This amount is expressed as a percentage of the calculated oven-dry weight of the block and is then termed 'loading'. **1952** *Rev. Appl. Entomol.* A. XL. 185 The concentration of the solution used was such that it would produce an average loading of 0.2 per cent. boric acid with treatment at pressures rising to 200 lb. per sq. in. **1968** *Gloss. Terms Timber Preservation* (B.S.I.) 18 *Impregnation*, strictly the saturation of wood with a preservative. Generally used to describe treatments giving a high loading of preservative in the wood, e.g. pressure treatments. **1978** *Nature* 19 Oct. 631/1 The decrease in atmospheric transmission in 1928 was caused by an increase in the stratospheric dust loading.

loading, *ppl. a.* Add: [4.] **loading dose** *Med.,* a large dose of a drug administered at the beginning of a course of treatment in order to achieve a therapeutic concentration in the body quickly.

1961 *Lancet* 19 Aug. 400/2 Cortisone 250 mg. by intramuscular injection was given as a loading dose. **1976** *Ibid.* 20 Nov. 1143/2 Treatment with intravenous metronidazole was resumed with a loading dose of 1 g and was continued with 500 mg 8 hourly. **1988** *Neurol.* XXXVIII. 399/2 We found that a loading dose of barbiturate led to a very prompt, reproducible, and effective cessation of seizure activity.

Lobachevskian (lɒbə'tʃɛvskɪən), *a. Math.* Also **Lobatchevskian,** etc. [f. the name of Nikolai Ivanovich *Lobachevsky* (1793–1856), Russian mathematician + -IAN.] Of, pertaining to, or designating a kind of non-Euclidean geometry

(also called *hyperbolic geometry*) postulated by Lobachevsky in 1826, in which space is everywhere negatively curved. Cf. RIEMANNIAN *a.*

1896 G. B. HALSTED in *In Memoriam N. I. Lobatchevskii* (1897) 24 Considered as subjective systems, the Lobachevskian, Euclidean, and Riemannian geometries are equally true. **1908** *Trans. Amer. Math. Soc.* IX. 182 In Riemannian or Lobatchewskian space, conformal and equilong transformations are identical. **1937** *Mind* XLVI. 173 Einstein's law of composition of velocities can be represented on a Lobatchevskian plane. **1961** E. NAGEL *Struct. of Sci.* ix. 237 In the Lobachewskian geometry, the angle sum of a triangle is not constant for all triangles. **1976** *Sci. Amer.* Aug. 98/1 The antinomy of space persisted, however, because the new Lobachevskian space (as it is often called) had the same overall topological structure as Euclidean space. **1989** R. PENROSE *Emperor's New Mind* v. 156 In Lobachevskian geometry, this sum [of the angles of a triangle] is always *less* than 180°.

lobby, *n.* Sense 4 in Dict. becomes 5. Add: **4.** [Prob. f. the vb.] An organized event at which people go to a house of legislature to lobby its members.

1939 W. I. JENNINGS *Parliament* vii. 228 As part of its agitation against the Incitement to Disaffection Bill, 1934, members of the National Council for Civil Liberties 'called out' their representatives by means of a 'mass lobby'. **1969** *Oz* Apr. 25/1 There will be a lobby of Parliament which far from pleading with MPs will probably take Whitehall apart. **1987** *NATFHE Jrnl.* Mar. 4/3 NATFHE representatives supported the Parliamentary lobby organised by the National Union of Students on 4 March.

lobe, *n.* Add: [2.] **lobe-fin,** a crossopterygian fish.

1941 A. S. ROMER *Man & Vertebr.* (ed. 3) i. 33 Typical *lobefins were fresh-water fishes which.. early became extinct. **1962** K. F. LAGLER et al. *Ichthyol.* iv. 115 Cosmoid scales are found both in the living (Latimeria) and extinct lobefins. **1979** D. L. DINELEY *Fossils* v. 120 Not long ago the lobe-fins were thought to have become extinct... Then in 1938 a living lobe-fin was dredged up. **1994** *Nature* 7 Apr. 507/1 For much of the middle of this century, there was general agreement that most of the Tetrapoda had arisen from osteolepiform lobefins.

lobe-finned *a.,* (of a fish) crossopterygian.

1933 A. S. ROMER *Man & Vertebr.* i. 41 The ray-finned forms are the most important fish as fish. But far more important in an evolutionary sense have been the crossopterygians, the lobe-finned fishes. **1970** R. M. BLACK *Elements Palaeont.* xvii. 249 The lobe-finned fish have, since the Devonian, remained numerically restricted. **1991** N. ELDREDGE *Fossils* iv. 92 Coelacanths are lobe-finned fishes. Their closest relatives are the extinct rhipidistians.

lobopod ('ləubəupɒd), *a.* and *n. Zool.* [f. *LOBOPODIUM n.*] **A.** *adj.* Of a worm or worm-like animal: possessing a lobopodium.

1938 R. E. SNODGRASS in *Smithsonian Misc. Coll.* XCVII. No. 6. 134 The members of the other group developed segmental pairs of lobelike outgrowths of the body wall containing extensions of the somatic muscles, which served as primitive legs... The lobopod forms were the ancestors of the walking Onychophora and Arthropoda. **1965** *Zoologichesky Zhurnal* XLIV. 817 Lobopod annelids were the central group from which other groups.. of higher taxonomic rank originated. **1979** A. P. GUPTA in M. Camatini *Myriapod Biol.* xxxv. 373 Although it is debatable whether the Myriapoda, as a group, are mono- or polyphyletic.. their origin from either a lobopod ancestor or from Onychophora has been suggested. **1989** S. J. GOULD *Wonderful Life* (1991) 331 The lobopod animal *Aysheaia pedunculata.*

B. *n.* = *LOBOPODIUM *n.* 2.

1967 H. W. & L. R. LEVI tr. *Kaestner's Invertebr. Zool.* I. xviii. 442 Many articulates also have paired appendages. In some, probably old groups, these appendages are unsegmented lobopods and are used primarily for locomotion. **1974** *Biol. Abstr.* LVIII. 5388/1 (*heading*) Percentage of sexes and variations in the number of lobopods in a sampling of several hundred individuals. **1986** *Revista de Biol. Tropical* (San José, Costa Rica) XXXIV. 277 Fourth creeping pad of fourth and fifth lobopods is slender and curves itself around the nephridial tubercle. **1993** *New Scientist* 21 Aug. 15/2 Living lobopods include the land-dwelling *Peripatus*, which has legs and a number of characteristics reminiscent of arthropods.

lobopodium (ləʊbə'pəʊdɪəm), *n. Zool.* Pl. -ia. [a. G. *Lobopodium* (coined in A. Lang *Lehrbuch d. vergleichenden Anat.* (ed. 2, 1901) II. ix. 108): see LOBE *n.*, -O, PODIUM *n.* 2.] **1.** A blunt or lobe-like pseudopodium of a protozoan.

1906 M. HARTOG in *Cambr. Nat. Hist.* I. ii. 47 Lang distinguishes 'lobopodia', 'filopodia', and 'pseudopodia' according to their form,—blunt, thread-like, or anastomosing. **1910** G. N. CALKINS *Protozool.* i. 35 The motile organs of these low types are in constant, endlessly changing centres of protoplasmic energy... They appear and disappear again with an ever-fascinating, inexplicable regularity. These are the so-called lobose, 'lobopodia', or finger-form pseudopodia. **1975** *Jrnl. Cell Sci.* XIX. 169 The process of circus movement involves blebbing of a hyaline pseudopodium, spreading of the bleb, and thus propagating of the lobopodium around the cell circumference. **1976** *Nature* 3 June 413/1 Some blebs extend to form lobopodia. **1987** LAVERACK & DANDO *Lect. Notes Invertebr. Zool.* (ed. 3) ii. 19/1 Pseudopodia are temporary protoplasmic extensions of the cell. If broad and lobose as in naked amoebae they are called lobopodia; if slender and tapered as in shelled amoebae, filopodia [etc.].

2. A blunt limb or limb-like organ on some worms and worm-like animals, esp. ancestral ones.

1966 A. CROZY tr. *Sharov's Basic Arthropodan Stock* i. 11 The lobopodia of *Spinther*..still retain the character of tentacles although they have acquired annulation and are armed with well-developed claws. *Ibid.* 14 In the annelids later passing from a creeping to a burrowing or swimming way of life, the locomotor organs—lobopodia—became the ventral parts of the parapodia, i.e. neuropodia. **1967** *Jrnl. Nat. Hist.* I. 11 We have no ancestral lobopod worm on which to study the structure and mode of action of a lobopodium. **1978** S. M. MANTON *Arthropoda* i. 26 The only lobopodium we can study alive is a leg of an onychophoran. This uniramous limb is worked by antagonistic muscles and by the flow and resistance of haemolymph.

Hence **lobo'podial** *a.*, of the nature of or possessing a lobopodium.

1967 *Jrnl. Nat. Hist.* I. 13 (*caption*) Diagrams..to show features associated with the mode of action of the lobopodial limb. **1974** *Jrnl. Zool.* CLXXI. 124 We have little evidence of the existence of soft bodied lobopodial animals living alongside the armoured arthropods. **1978** S. M. MANTON *Arthropoda* ix. 399 These joints..could only have evolved from a soft-bodied lobopodial leg. **1982** *Cancer Res.* XLII. 2804/1 TPA also induced circumferential rotations of lobopodial blebs in blastula cells cultured on plastic.

lobotomy, *n.* Add: **lo,botomi'zation** *n.*, the performance of a lobotomy.

1974 E. BRAWLEY *Rap* x. 133 Through persuasion, intimidation.. and through torture, lobotomization and even murder, the Man has definitely made some large and painful slashes in our ranks. **1977** *Transatlantic Rev.* LX. 63 Both of us have enjoyed the benefits of lobotomization for many years.

lobster, *n.*[1] Add: [**1.**] **e.** *Austral.* and *N.Z.* = CRAYFISH *n.* 3 a; also, any similar crustacean.

1826 J. ATKINSON *Acct. Agric. & Grazing N.S.W.* ii. 25 Lobsters, crayfish, and prawns, are also found in many places. **1834** G. BENNETT *Wanderings N.S.W.* I. xi. 214 In this colony, cray-fish abound in the sea, and lobsters in the river. **1909** G. SMITH *Naturalist in Tasmania* iv. 108 In Tasmania the term Crayfish is applied to the marine Rock Lobster (*Panulirus* [sic]), the term Lobster to the Freshwater Crayfish (*Astacopsis*). **1972** L. IRISH *Time of Dolphins* viii. 109 She rescued the lobsters—why *do* we call them lobsters when they're crays. **1983** *Austral. Women's Weekly* Aug. 20/3 In NSW and Queensland any large, edible, stalk-eyed member of the marine crustacean family, except a crab, is a lobster.

local, *a.* and *n.* Add: [**B.**] [**1.**] **c.** *Finance* (orig. *U.S.*). An independent trader in options or futures who acts on his or her own account.

1969 R. J. TEWELES et al. *Commodity Futures Trading Guide* ii. 25 Floor traders trading for their own accounts are sometimes referred to as 'locals'. **1975** G. GOLD *Mod. Commodity Futures* (rev. ed.) vii. 58 Floor traders who trade for their own account are known as 'scalpers' or 'locals'. **1984** *Times* 19 May 23/3 Liffe needs more 'locals'—private investors—to give it a more speculative flavour. **1986** *Times* 14 Jan. 17/7 For a maximum fee of £10,000 individuals could become trading members of the market [*sc.* the London Commodity Exchange], opening the way to locals on the American pattern. *Ibid.* 18 Dec. 24/4 Some 60 locals do business on the London International Financial Futures Exchange. **1995** *Independent* 6 Mar. 17/2 For seven years her husband, Fergus, was a 'local' on the Liffe exchange, trading on his own account, which means *with his own money.*

[**2.**] **i.** Short for 'local anaesthetic' (see sense 4 a of the adj.).

1961 in WEBSTER. **1970** 'J. HERRIOT' *If only they could Talk* xxv. 153 A few c.c.'s of local in there and I could twist it off easily with the spoons. **1971** D. FRANCIS *Bonecrack* vii. 93 He..shot the freezing local in Indigo's near fore. **1978** *Rugby World* Apr. 21 A player with severe toothache had to be given a 'local' before the match. **1988** J. McINERNEY *Story of my Life* xii. 181 I've heard they give you Demerol.., but the doctor says for outpatients all they recommend is a local.

localist, *n.* and *a.* Add: **B.** *adj.* Confined to or concentrated upon matters of local interest; parochial, provincial.

1934 in WEBSTER. **1963** *Ann. Reg. 1962* 200 'Localist' tendencies within the regional economic councils. **1988** *New Statesman* 17 June 46/1 There's a real commitment to a cultural policy which is simultaneously 'localist' and internationalist.

localize, *v.* Add: **4.** *intr.* **a.** In *Path.*, (of a symptom, infective agent, etc.) to be or become restricted to a particular part or parts of the body; in *Ecol.*, (of a species) to adopt a geographically restricted area as its territory.

1957 R. W. RAVEN *Cancer* I. viii. 270 The viruses of West Nile, Ilheus and Bunyamwera localized preferentially in the tumours of some patients. **1972** A. L. SMITH *Microbiol. & Path.* (ed. 10) x. 78/2 Meningococci localize in the leptomeninges. **1988** *Zool. Jrnl. Linn. Soc.* XCII. 45 At the pond '*P*[*rocordulia*]' *grayi* usually localized on, and patrolled, an area of pond. *Ibid.* 46 Male *H*[*emicordulia*] *australiae*, whether on ponds or lakeshores, localized in a small area or near some geographical feature and defended this territory aggressively.

b. Of a person: to adapt oneself to a place and settle there.

1930 H. MORRIS *Barrister* iii. 49 A decision.. whether to practise in London or to localise in some provincial town. **1941** K. TENNANT *Battlers* xxvi. 285 'You won't think he'd localise?' The Apostle shook his head. 'I don't think he ever would. He's been on the track so long, it's in his blood.'

location, *n.* Add: [3.] **b.** *spec.* in *Computing*. A position or address in computer memory; also, a unit of memory occupying a given position.
1946 J. W. MAUCHLY in Campbell-Kelly & Williams *Moore School Lect.* (1985) 455 The question is how many locations or addresses in the internal memory are to be included in the standard instruction? **1948** GOLDSTINE & VON NEUMANN in J. Von Neumann *Coll. Wks.* (1963) V. 197 An accommodation for a sequence of length *n* + *m*, consisting of (*n* + *m*)(*p* + 1) consecutive memory locations, is available. **1969** P. B. JORDAIN *Condensed Computer Encycl.* 15 Location 1001 contains the instruction PLACE MQ CONTENTS IN LOCATION 15000; the computer thus stores zeros in location 15000, and..goes to the next instruction in sequence, that is, to location 1002. **1973** C. W. GEAR *Introd. Computer Sci.* ii. 74 If we are not going to want to reference an instruction, we do not need to give a location address. **1980** C. S. FRENCH *Computer Sci.* vi. 23 Once data is stored in a location in main storage it remains there until it is replaced by other data. **1984** *Which Micro?* Dec. 36/3 The Lynx has.. graphics chars stored from location FC00. **1992** *Dr. Dobb's Jrnl.* Sept. 86/2 An executable file contains a header structure whose fields contain the location of the symbol table, the location of the string table, and the number of symbols.

loci *n.*, var. *LOCIE *n.*

locie ('ləʊki), *n.* Also loci, lokey, etc. *N. Amer.* and *N.Z. colloq.* [f. LOC(OMOTIVE *a.* and *n.* + -IE. Cf. LOCO *n.*[3]] A locomotive.
1942 BERREY & VAN DEN BARK *Amer. Thes. Slang* §774/18 *Locomotive*,..lokey. **1943** R. E. SWANSON *Rhymes of Lumberjack* 80 A weird type of locomotive developed... This *locie*, due to its climbing ability, was called a *Climax*. **1947** A. P. GASKELL in D. M. Davin *N.Z. Short Stories* (1953) 287 She often saw wisps of smoke rising against the bush on the hills at the back... Sometimes she heard a lokey puffing. **1950** *Landfall* June 125 The gang of chamberhands who usually dawdle along behind me are already crossing the loci tracks up in front. **1962** *Amer. Speech* XXXVII. 134 *Lokie, locie, lockie, loky,* a locomotive. **1975** *Islander* (Victoria, B.C.) 31 Aug. 5/3, I came back to Nairobi on the overnight train which is a steam locie on a narrow gauge railway. **1993** *Westcoast Logger* Feb.-Mar. 20/2 Daddy Lamb railroad logged into Menzies Bay during tough times when his equipment and locies were being held together with scrap iron and haywire.

lock, *n.*[2] Add: [V.] [20.] **lock-washer**, (*a*) *Engin.*, a washer, usu. consisting of one complete turn of a helical spring, for placing between a nut and bolt to prevent the nut from coming loose; (*b*) *Biol.*, a protein sub-unit resembling a lock-washer in shape.
1903 *Official Gaz.* (U.S. Patent Office) 23 June 1973/1 A *lock-washer comprising in its construction a body portion of helical shape and constructed of spring material, said body portion being tapered in cross-section. **1941** *Motor Commerce* July 25/3 Adjust the pinion assembly to the correct bearing pre-load..and lock the adjusting nuts in position by a lock-washer. **1971** A. C. H. DURHAM et al. in *Nature New Biol.* 13 Jan. 42/1 The results show that the helical rods can be formed by direct end to end aggregation of single disks, into which a dislocation has been introduced... We call this converted disk a 'lock-washer'. **1984** *Jrnl. Gen. Virol.* LXV. 256 While there had previously been doubt as to whether the short proto-helix (or 'lockwasher') would exist free in solution, the change in sedimentation coefficient from 19S at pH 7.0 to 20S.. has now been shown to correlate with measurable proton binding. **1987** *Ham Radio*

Today Jan. 22/3 After checking that there are no protruding wires on the underside of the PCB, fit it into place and secure with a lockwasher and nut.

lock, *v.*[1] Sense 12 in Dict. becomes 13. Add: **12.** *Electronics.* **a.** *trans.* To cause (an oscillator, etc.) to keep *to* a particular frequency, e.g. by driving it with a signal from an external source; to stabilize (an oscillator's frequency).
1933 R. A. W. WATT et al. *Applic. Cathode Ray Oscillograph* i. 42 Use a linear time-base which is 'locked' in its rate of recurrence to that of the signal pulse. **1959** K. HENNEY *Radio Engin. Handbk.* (ed. 5) xvi. 65 Any of the *RC* oscillators previously described is capable of being locked to a control frequency signal. **1975** D. G. FINK *Electronics Engineers' Handbk.* XIII. 42 It is often desirable to lock the oscillator frequency to an input reference. Usually this is done by injecting sufficient energy at the reference frequency into the oscillator circuit. **1990** *Sci. Amer.* June 13/1 The frequency of the oscillator can be locked to an atomic standard.
b. *intr.* Of an oscillator, etc.: to become locked.
1943 E. E. ZEPLER *Technique Radio Design* iv. 129 Locking occurs when a strong signal of approximately oscillator frequency is applied across the oscillator, forcing it to oscillate at this frequency. The tendency to lock is the larger the smaller the frequency difference. **1953** F. LANGFORD-SMITH *Radio-Designer's Handbk.* (ed. 4) xxxvi. 1293 The locked oscillator circuit may produce severe distortion as the signal crosses the locking threshold in the side tuning positions, or stations may tune with a definite 'plop' as the oscillator locks. **1982** *Giant Bk. Electronics Projects* vi. 260 Check to see that the synthesizer locks over the same frequency range. **1986** *Photogr.* May 26/2 This is not always possible with some recorders which lock to a particular channel when in record to prevent accidental changing.

locus, *n.*[1] Add: [4.] **locus coeruleus** (also **caeruleus, ceruleus**) *Anat.* [mod.L. *locus caeruleus* (J. & C. Wenzel *De Penitiori Structura Cerebri* (1812) xvii. 168)], a bluish-grey area on the floor of the fourth ventricle of the brain.
1858 GRAY *Anat.* 472 Opposite the crus cerebelli, on the outer side of the fasciculi teretes, is a small eminence of dark grey substance, which presents a blueish tint through the thin stratum covering it; this is called the *locus cœruleus. **1874** DUNGLISON *Dict. Med. Sci.* (new ed.) 607/1 *Locus caeruleus*, a small eminence of dark gray substance, opposite the crus cerebelli, which presents a bluish tint through the thin stratum covering it. **1957** E. G. WALSH *Physiol. Nervous Syst.* xii. 458 One anatomical point is worth considering at this point, the extremely rich blood supply to the hypothalamus... The supraoptic nucleus is the most vascular region, but the paraventricular nucleus also is richly supplied with blood, as is also the locus caeruleus in the brain stem. **1972** *Exper. Neurol.* XXXV. 1 (*heading*) Nuclear size variations in cells of the locus ceruleus during sleep, arousal and stress. **1987** *Daily Tel.* 22 Apr. 5/2 The changes in the brain after 40 are seen in the locus coeruleus, a tiny area in the brain-stem that is a key centre for anxiety and fear.

lod (lɒd), *n.* Chiefly *Genetics.* [Acronym f. the initial letters of *logarithmic odds*.] The logarithm of the odds in favour of or against a given event; also, the logarithm of the ratio of two odds. Usu. in *pl.* exc. when *attrib.* Freq. in *lod score.*
1949 G. A. BARNARD in *Jrnl. R. Statistical Soc.* B. XI. 116 There are great advantages in working in terms of odds rather than in terms of probabilities — and greater advantages still in working in terms of logarithms of odds... This suggested the adoption of log odds (or, as they are called below, lods) as the fundamental idea in the theory, in place of probabilities. **1955** *Amer. Jrnl. Human Genetics* VII.

292 The scores in a sequential test are 'lods', or logarithms of the probability ratio...Tables 4–8 give the possible certain matings and the lod scores appropriate to them. **1974** *Nature* 7 June 595/2 The evidence can be evaluated in the conventional currency used in human linkage studies, the lod, or logarithm of the odds ratio. **1977** *Lancet* 24/31 Dec. 1311/1 The lod-score analysis for genetic linkage between HLA and C.A.H. for families 1, 2, 3, 4, and 5 demonstrated that HLA and the C.A.H. trait are very closely linked. **1988** *Nature* 26 May 308/3 The publication of another paper in *Nature* which uses 'Lod scores' to describe the analysis of human linkage data prompts me to wonder whether it might not be an opportune moment for linkage workers to abandon their idiosyncratic statistical terminology so that others can better follow their analyses. **1990** *Ann. Human Genetics* LIV. 254 An average liklihood is meaningful, an average lod is not.

lofter ('lɒftə(r)), *n.*[1] (Formerly at LOFT *v.* in Dict.) *Golf.* [f. LOFT *v.* + -ER[1].] A golf club, esp. a number 8 or 9 iron, for lofting the ball. Cf *lofting-iron* s.v. LOFTING *vbl. n.* 4. Now *rare*.
   1889 in P. Davies *Dict. Golfing Terms* (1980) 106/2 It was announced that young Willie Park had at length succeeded in fashioning a lofter that will do all that is desired. **1892** *Pall Mall Gaz.* 15 Mar. 3/1 A ridge of snow..necessitated in many cases the use of a 'lofter' instead of the regulation 'putter'. **1993** H. PENICK *If you play Golf you're my Friend* 122 His bag had five clubs in it—driver, a midiron, a niblick, a lofter, and a putter. In modern terms this would be like carrying a driver, 2-iron, 5-iron, 9-iron, and putter.

lofter ('lɒftə(r)), *n.*[2] [f. LOFT *n.* + -ER[1].] A decoy placed in a tree, etc., to attract pigeons.
   1972 *Shooting Times & Country Mag.* 4 Mar. 21/2 If ever the value of 'lofters' was demonstrated this was it. **1984** G. HAMMOND *Sauce for Pigeon* i. 15 It's a decoy, a 'lofter', put in the tree to complete the realistic pattern.

lofting, *vbl. n.* Add: [4.] **lofting pole**, in pigeon-shooting, a pole used for placing decoys in trees, etc. (cf. *LOFTER *n.*[2]).
   1964 C. L. COLES *Shooting Pigeons* viii. 60 A rubber pigeon mounted on the top of wooden *lofting poles. **1987** *Shooting Mag.* Mar. 34/3 The kit takes its name from an ingeniously designed set of light alloy tubes which, using the metal collars supplied, can be fitted together to make a lofting pole tall enough to place a decoy some 25 ft. up in a tree.

lofty, *a.* and *n.* Add: [A.] [4.] **b.** Of wool and woollen or piled fabrics: bulky and springy; resilient.
   [**1889** J. BURNLEY *Hist. Wool & Woolcombing* xii. 321 The same curl or crochet, the same softness and loftiness, and the same high spinning qualities as the best handcombed wool of the old days.] **1909** WEBSTER, *Lofty*, full-bodied;—said of wool. **1974** *Anderson* (S. Carolina) *Independent* 18 Apr. (Sears Advt. Suppl.) 7 Luxurious towels with a thick and lofty feel. 100% cotton-looped on one side for absorbency and sheared on the other for velvety softness. **1976** *National Observer* (U.S.) 2 Oct. 3/3 (Advt.), A warm, lofty blend of Dacron and worsted wool for good looks, wrinkle resistance and long wear.
   B. *n. colloq.* (A nickname for) a very tall person or (*iron.*) a short person.
   1933 M. LOWRY *Ultramarine* ii. 101 Lofty, you come, will you? Pateman, you too. **1949** P. NEWTON *High Country Days* vii. 69 Lofty, in happy mood,..delighted young Wallace with tall stories of 'down south'. **1959** I. & P. OPIE *Lore & Lang. Schoolch.* ix. 169 In the following [terms] the chief emphasis is in height, 'Lofty' being the most popular nickname, followed by 'Longshanks'. **1962** J. FRANKLYN *Dict. Nicknames* 63/2 *Lofty*, nickname for a tall man. Of naval origin,

its use has spread to other Services and into civilian life. Via the mechanism of humour by inversion it is very frequently bestowed upon a particularly small man. **1975** L. RYAN *Shearers* 97 'All set?' Lofty asked. 'Set!' Sandy said. 'Come in, Spinner!'

log, *n.*[1] Add: [II.] [7.] [d.] (*d*) *Austral.* A list or summary of claims for a wage increase, or other employee benefits. Freq. more fully, *log of claims*.
   1911 *Commonwealth Arbitration Rep.* V. 181 The claims of the employees have been framed into a log of wages and conditions. **1925** *Round Table* June 587 Delay on the part of various Government departments of Western Australia in dealing with a log lodged by such [harbour] employees. **1948** G. FARWELL *Down Argent St.* 102 When the unions submitted their log of claims for the 1925 Agreement, they asked for increased wages and yet shorter hours. **1969** *Age* (Melbourne) 24 May 3/2 Negotiations over the log of claims. **1984** *Austral. Financial Rev.* 9 Nov. 7/3 Workers at the Rosella factory..are on strike over a log of claims, including a 5 per cent wage claim.

log cabin, *n.* Add: 2. A pattern in patchwork, quilting, etc., in which overlapping strips or squares of material are arranged in adjoining squares suggestive of the patterning of wood in a log cabin.
   1887 *Harper's Mag.* Dec. 36/1 Reluctantly she slipped her book under the log-cabin quilt and said 'Come in'. **1907** 'E. C. HALL' *Aunt Jane of Kentucky* 57 There seemed to be every pattern that the ingenuity of woman could devise..'four patches', 'nine patches', 'log cabins', [etc.]. **1943** R. PEATTIE *Great Smokies & Blue Ridge* 129 The old coverlet patterns had life running through them; Log Cabin, Castle City, [etc.]. **1965** A. COLBY *Patchwork Quilts* 78 Log cabin quilts were popular in England and America from about the middle of the nineteenth century, and were so called because the square blocks were composed of a square centre patch surrounded by strips of material or 'logs'..overlapped..in much the same fashion as the log cabins were built. **1978** N. JONES *Embroidery* 62/3 The usual arrangement of colours in log cabin is dark on two adjacent sides, light on the two sides opposite. **1991** DORRIS & ERDRICH *Crown of Columbus* x. 170 He was sprawled on my favorite log cabin quilt and had not removed his shoes.

loggia, *n.* Add: **b.** Also, an open-sided extension to a house, typically of stone or brick construction.
   1927 *Homes & Gardens* Feb. 319/1 The loggia is the true middle world between house and garden...Mr. Robert Atkinson..has given to column and balustrade in the loggia of his own house at Sheen..that refinement of detail which..is as needful and satisfying without as within. **1951** *Good Housek. Home Encycl.* 237/1 Good rush mats are useful for a veranda or loggia. **1977** *S. Wales Echo* 18 Jan. (Advt.), Ground floor..door to sun loggia overlooking rear garden. **1978** *N.Y. Times* 30 Mar. C1/6 The loggia of Tiffany's own home..will be incorporated into the south court wall of the new American wing..of the museum. **1984** R. FRAME *Winter Journey* (1986) i. 13 He keeps indoors, or—if the night is especially warm—he sits out on his loggia.

log-in ('lɒgɪn, lɒ'gɪn), *n. Computing.* Also **login**. [f. vbl. phr. *to log in*: see LOG *v.*[1] 5 d.] The action or an act of logging in; = *LOG-ON *n.* Also *attrib.*, esp. designating a procedure which is carried out every time a user logs in.
   1965 *IEEE Spectrum* II. 61/2 The total number of user-hours between logins and logouts turns out to be approximately 17 times the number of computer hours used. **1974** *Communications Assoc. Computing Machinery* XVII. 442/2 (*heading*) A high security log-in procedure. **1985** *Computerworld* 8 Apr. 83/2 Automatic dial-up and login procedures that allow the

micro user to set up job parameters and I/O files for VIP applications running on the host Cyber 205. **1986** D. DEUTSCH in T. C. Bartee *Digital Communications* v. 220 The user may be identified by a log-in identifier.

logit ('lɒgɪt), *n. Statistics.* [Acronym f. *log*arithmic un*it*.] The natural logarithm of the quotient of a probability and its complement. Usu. *attrib.*, esp. in *logit analysis*, a form of regression analysis which makes use of this function.
   1944 J. BERKSON in *Jrnl. Amer. Statistical Assoc.* XXXIX. 361 Instead of the observations q_i we deal with their logits $l_i = ln(p_i/q_i)$. [*Note*] I use this term for ln p/q following Bliss, who called the analogous function which is linear on x for the normal curve 'probit'. **1965** *Biometrics* XXI. 731 (*heading*) Examples of fitting the generalised logit-normal distribution. **1967** *Biometrika* LIV. 181 The use of logits in the quantal bioassay problem is briefly explored with particular reference to the asymptotic results of Hitchcock regarding the bias of the estimators. **1977** *Lancet* 15 Jan. 107/2 The statistical significance levels of the rate trends were assessed by a logit analysis. **1988** *Amer. Jrnl. Obstetr. & Gynecol.* CLVIII. 470/2 Logit analysis, a maximum-likelihood technique..permits the measurement of variations in the probability of an event occurring according to the characteristics possessed by the mother.

logocentric, *a.* Substitute for etymology: [f. Gr. λόγο-ς word, reason (see LOGOS *n.*) + -CENTRIC.] and add: **2.** Centred on language; regarding language as a fundamental source of meaning. Cf. *LOGOCENTRISM n.
   1971 S. HEATH in J. Kristeva et al. *Signs of Times* 24 That logocentric tradition which refuses to think itself in its adherence to a point of rest that veils the distribution of its own discourse. **1975** H. BLOOM *Map of Misreading* III. vii. 176 A mode that *is* intra-textual, but that stubbornly remains logocentric, and that still follows Emerson in valorizing eloquence, the inspired voice, *over* the scene of writing. **1979** M. CHÉNETIER *Lett. V. Lindsay* p. xxvi, Such a sentence gives an idea of the importance of Vachel Lindsay's theoretical and practical breakthrough..one that may well be the missing link between..the logocentric rule of nineteenth-century civilization and the media theories of Marshall McLuhan. **1981** *New Lit. Hist.* XII. 564 Is language (and therefore literature also) 'an absolutely reliable moral indicator of life, acting as an infallible witness to all that happens in the world, part of the preestablished and perhaps even mystical harmony between words and action'? (This is the traditional, the life-enhancing, the logocentric view.) **1985** *Rev. Eng. Stud.* May 303 It is not a logocentric vision (language is the outermost frame), but typocentric. **1990** R. KIMBALL *Tenured Radicals* Preface p. xii, With their criticism of the 'logocentric' and 'phallocentric' Western tradition, their insistence that language always refers only to itself, and their suspicion of logic and rationality, they exhibit a species of skepticism that is essentially nihilistic.

log-on ('lɒgɒn, lɒ'gɒn), *n. Computing.* Also logon. [f. vbl. phr. *to log on*: see LOG *v.*[1] 5 d.] The action or an act of logging on; = *LOG-IN n.* Also *attrib.*, esp. designating a procedure which is carried out every time a user logs on.
   1977 *Sci. Amer.* July 65/3 (Advt.), With 300 people authorized to use the terminals,..we now average over 400 'log-ons' a day. As many as 70 people may be online simultaneously. **1982** *Electronics* 10 Feb. 214/1 An entire log-on sequence can be programmed for automatic transmission. **1986** *Personal Computer World* Nov. 150/3 The communications module also allows you to automate the log-on sequence for different services. **1988** C. J. CHERRYH *Cyteen* 58 There was nothing he dared use: every log-on was recorded.

logophile ('lɒgəʊfaɪl), *n.* [f. Gr. λόγο-ς word (see LOGOS *n.*) + -PHILE. Cf. earlier F. *logophile* (1890).] A lover of words.
   1959 *Sunday Times* 1 Feb. 25 We are pretty sure that since all *Sunday Times* readers are natural and inveterate logophiles..he [*sc.* Mr. Burchfield] will get some invaluable assistance. **1972** *Sci. Amer.* Oct. 110/2 Who except a numerologist or logophile would see the letters *U, S, A* symmetrically placed in LOUISIANA. **1977** *Times Lit. Suppl.* 11 Feb. 145/1 A mortifyingly funny novella.. written by a logophile who has always been able to make prose mean precisely what he wants it to mean. **1983** *Observer* 29 May 31/6 When we turn to the 500 Adages of this first volume..we find more Erasmuses, including the scholar, the collector, the catalogue-maker, the serendipitist, the logophile. **1988** *English Today* Jan. 22/1 Her book is a treasure trove for..logophiles with a classical bent.
   Hence **logo'philia** *n.*, love of words.
   1980 C. R. LOVITT tr. M. Pierssens (*title*) The power of Babel: a study of logophilia. *Ibid.* p. x, We should..construct a model of a perhaps common experience that..gives birth to logophilia [*logophilie*]. **1980** *Times Lit. Suppl.* 22 Feb. 211/1 The market in logophilia is encouraged by large and eager colonies, who absorb the surplus product of rules and principles, providing raw material in exchange.

Loire (lwɑː(r)), *n.* [The name of a river in France, which rises in the Massif Central and flows 1,015 km (630 miles) north and west to the Atlantic at St.-Nazaire.] Used *attrib.* and *absol.* to designate wines of diverse types made from grapes grown in the valleys of the Loire and of its tributaries.
   1930 G. KNOWLES tr. *P. de Cassagnac's French Wines* viii. 204 Why are Loire wines, with a few exceptions, richer in alcohol and sugar as one goes down the river? **1951** R. POSTGATE *Plain Man's Guide to Wine* iv. 86 Loire wines: Vouvray, Saumur, Anjou. **1974** *Times* 10 Aug. 11/3 A very unusual white Loire in the 1973 Chinon Blanc, Château de Ligné. **1988** *Limited Edition* (Oxford Times Suppl.) June 32/1 Neither of the two Loire wines made much impact on the [wine-tasting] panel.

lokey *n.*, var. of *LOCIE n.*

lonely, *a.* Add: **[4.] [b.]** Also applied, freq. by hypallage, to places in which feelings of loneliness are experienced. Cf. sense 2 above.
   1635 F. QUARLES *Emblemes* IV. xii. 230 At length...She re-betakes her to her lonely bed. **1684** DRYDEN *Prol. to Southerne's Disappointment*. 46 He hires some lonely room, love's fruits to gather. **1761** F. SHERIDAN *Mem. Miss Sidney Bidulph* II. 308 She has no business to go into her own lonely house again; it would be enough to kill her. **1818** KEATS *Endymion* I. 121 The surgy murmurs of the lonely sea. **1852** P. J. BAILEY *Festus* (ed. 5) 127 A maiden sat in her lonely bower Sadly and lowly singing. **1927** A. CONAN DOYLE *Case-bk. Sherlock Holmes* ix. 233 My house is lonely. I, my old housekeeper, and my bees have the estate all to ourselves. **1982** J. SIMMS *Unsolicited Gift* viii. 149 Offstage, the soloist waited in her lonely dressing room.

long, *a.*[1] Add: **[A.] [I.] [1.] h.** Used as a trade term, freq. in conjunction with another measurement, to indicate that an item of clothing (such as a skirt or a pair of trousers) is longer than average for its specific chest or waist measurement; usu. opp. to *regular* (cf. REGULAR *a.* 3 e) or *short*.
   1908 W. H. BAKER *Dict. Men's Wear* 232 Sizes..are classified as regular, long,..short-stout, corpulent [etc.]. **1940** *Good Housek.* (N.Y.) July 98/2 When buying slacks: Be sure of waist measure and whether

the wearer is 'short' or 'long' type. **1980** *Freemans Catal.* Spring/Summer 393 Slightly flared jeans in fine cord... Regular inside leg 32 in... Long inside leg 34 in. **1990** *Washington Post* 6 Mar. A11/4 Stock sizes: regular, short, extra-short, long, extra-long, portly and portly-short.

[B.] [II.] [8.] c. A garment that is longer than average for its specific chest or waist measurement.

1908 W. H. BAKER *Dict. Men's Wear* 152 Longs, trade term for readymade garments designed to fit tall men. **1952** *Amer. Speech* XXVII. 266 With regard to sizes of suits there are three basic divisions: *regulars*—for men of average height and weight; *shorts*—for men of short stature; and *longs*—for tall men. **1986** *Jrnl.* (Fairfax Co., Va.) 27 May A3 (Advt.), Winfield Suits... In regulars, shorts and longs.

d. A long (formal) dress, skirt, etc. *colloq.*

1971 *Guardian* 17 Aug. 7/3 Summer 'longs' go on very happily into winter for theatres and parties. **1974** *State* (Columbia, S. Carolina) 28 Mar. 2A (Advt.), Young junior dresses and longs.

long, *adv.* Add: [7.] **b.** *Sport.* (*a*) To or for a considerable distance (across or along a field, course, etc.); (*b*) beyond the point aimed at; too far. Cf. SHORT *adv.* 7 a.

1839 in R. CLARK *Golf* (1875) 100 Come all you Golfers stout and strong Who putt so sure and drive so long. **1969** J. NICKLAUS *Greatest Game of All* xvii. 267 Compared to most golfers, I hit the ball quite long. *a***1973** in *Webster's New Collegiate Dict.* s.v., Faded back and threw the ball long. **1977** C. McCARTHY *Pleasures of Game* 73 One opponent hit short and into the trap, the other hit long. **1986** *Rebound* No. 1. 66/3 We had players who could shoot long but they were never given a chance to show this because the ball never came back out. **1990** *Guardian* 28 May 13/2 He still gets a twinge when he goes to kick the ball long.

Longshan *n.*, var. of *LUNG-SHAN *n.*

loonie ('luːniː), *n. Canad. colloq.* Also **looney, loony.** [f. LOON *n.*[2] + -IE, from the representation of a loon (or diver) on the reverse.] The Canadian one-dollar coin introduced in 1987; also, *transf.*, the Canadian dollar.

[**1987** *Vancouver Sun* 8 Jan. 1/1 The master dies of the new $1 coin have been lost in transit and the government has ordered a new design. The new design will be a loon, replacing the original voyageur depiction.] **1987** *Globe & Mail* (Toronto) 21 Jan. A7/5 Following the typical Canadian bureaucratic foul-up with the new dollar coin, I hereby name it the 'looney'. **1990** *Ottawa Citizen* 26 July E4/1 'The Canadian dollar is very strong,' said Berger, who added that the news could carry the loonie over 87 cents U.S. later this week. **1991** R. P. MACINTYRE *Yuletide Blues* v. 32 A loonie slides out of Boog's pocket, a loonie then twenty-five cents. **1994** *Outdoor Canada* Summer 23/1 Glue a small compass (no bigger than a Loonie) on top of the cap.

loop, *n.*[1] Add: [1.] **g.** *in the loop*, well-informed; privy to information not generally known; included; part of a process. Cf. *in the know* s.v. KNOW *n.*[2] Chiefly *U. S.*

1970 *Sunday Tel.* 22 Mar. 7/7 Fully automatic landing has now been perfected, though it will still be necessary to keep the pilot 'in the loop'. **1981** *N. Y. Times Mag.* 4 Jan. 10/3 The people at the power center have already adopted the White House favorites—'in the loop,' for those privileged to be 'copied' by receiving copies of memoranda. **1987** *Atlanta Jrnl. & Constitution* 9 Aug. c2/3 'We were not in the loop. When you don't know something,' he told me, 'it's hard to react.' **1993** *Coloradoan* (Fort Collins) 28 Mar. E2/2 A modem hookup to the office and a satellite to the world keeps Frank in the loop.

h. *out of the loop*, not privy to information; excluded; not part of a process. orig. and chiefly *U. S.*

1976 *Aviation Week* 12 Apr. 63/2 Automation technology can lead to complacency when it takes the controller 'out of the loop' by reducing the need for his interaction with a flightcrew and deemphasizing the cooperative aspects of the air traffic system. **1987** *Atlanta Jrnl. & Constitution* 19 Dec. A16/1 Bush tries to portray himself as the indispensable right-hand man in his boss' successful enterprises, but... out of the loop in Reagan's most deplorable foreign policy debacle. **1989** T. CLANCY *Clear & Present Danger* xi. 217 Moore almost replied that Admiral Greer was out of the loop because of his physical condition. **1990** *Sunday Tel.* 9 Sept. 21/7 There was a rumour that Secretary of State Baker was 'out of the loop'—that for some unspecified reason he had lost the President's confidence and was not being fully consulted. **1993** *Vanity Fair* (N.Y.) May 82/3 Clifford eventually accused Chellino of keeping a new, Clifford-picked agent out of the loop.

loop, *v.*[1] Add: [6.] **b.** *intr.* *Aeronaut.* Of a pilot, aircraft, etc.: to execute an aerobatic loop. Also *transf.* Hence *trans.*, to cause (an aircraft) to loop the loop.

1913 *Aeroplane* V. 641/1 The interest of the onlookers was centred in Mr. B. C. Hucks, who looped in the most engaging way. *Ibid.* 688/2 M. Chanteloup was the first pilot to loop on a biplane. **1914** *Flight* VI. 368/1 Perhaps on finishing a race every pilot will be required to loop on crossing the finishing line. **1918** H. BARBER *Aerobatics* 41 The pupil will have no difficulty in continuing to loop in increasingly finished style. **1927** C. A. LINDBERGH *We* ii. 32 Slowly pulling back on the stick I began to loop. **1935** C. G. BURGE *Compl. Bk. Aviation* 86/2 A.. single seater fighting aeroplane can be looped without any previous dive to gain speed, and an ordinary light aeroplane can be looped after a brief period of nose-down engine-on flying to gain momentum. **1953** C. A. LINDBERGH *Spirit of St. Louis* II. vi. 265, I stood on the top wing of an airplane while it looped. **1968** T. ROETHKE *Coll. Poems* 16 The bat.. Loops in crazy figures half the night Among the trees. **1988** *Air Display* Dec. 22/3 Westland's Lynx demonstrator looped for the benefit of the crowds.

loopy, *a.* Add: Hence **'loopiness** *n. colloq.*, craziness, insanity.

1939 WODEHOUSE *Uncle Fred in Springtime* xvi. 239 The Peke.. knew Sir Roderick Glossop well, her cousin Lionel having been treated by him for some form of loopiness. **1987** *Times* 16 May 18/2 Many regard his behaviour, at the least, as eccentricity tending to loopiness.

loose, *a.* and *adv.* Sense A. 1 l in *Dict.* becomes A. 1 m. Add: [A.] [1.] **l.** Active, agile. *Newfoundland dial.*

1907 J. G. MILLAIS *Newfoundland* ii. 40 A' was a 'loose' (active) little kid, and used to help de men. *Ibid.* 41 You're bound to fall in the cracks [in the floe ice] least once a night, however 'loose' you may be. **1982** in G. M. Story et al. *Dict. Newfoundland Eng.* 314/2 [She] was complimented on her agility by an elderly gentleman who said to her, 'My, miss, you'm a loose woman.' *Ibid.*, [He's a] loose man on ice.

loosener, *n.* Add: **3. a.** *Cricket.* A ball delivered early in a spell, while the bowler is 'loosening up' before settling into a regular rhythm. **b.** *transf.* A deliberately easy round, question, etc., occurring early on in a contest; a warm-up.

'**1962** *Times* 24 May 4/3 Graveney was caught off the first ball after tea. It was a loosener from Platt before he took the new ball. **1982** M. BREARLEY *Phoenix from Ashes* v. 61/1 Botham, with his third ball, which was little more than a loosener, had Wood LBW. **1986** *Sports Illustr.* 27 Oct. 90/3 First balls from fast bowlers tend to be just looseners. **1987** *Shooting Life* Spring 5/1 Few ardent game shooters bother with the clays..other than as a pre-season loosener. **1992** *Independent* 24 Feb. 8/6 The early stages were deceptively simple, a few looseners about classic films and novels which all of us got right.

loperamide (ləʊˈpɛrəmaɪd), *n. Pharm.* [Prob. f. CH)LO(RO-[2] + PI)PER(IDINE *n.* + AMIDE *n.*] An opiate drug, $C_{29}H_{33}N_2O_2Cl$, which inhibits peristalsis and is given orally as the hydrochloride in the treatment of diarrhoea.

1971 *WHO Chron.* XXV. 425 Loperamide. **1976** *Gastroenterology* LXX. 1026/1 Loperamide specifically inhibits peristaltic activity by its direct effect on the gastrointestinal wall. **1980** *Lancet* 26 Jan. 209/1 A further argument against the use of loperamide is that it may induce ileus in children. **1987** *Brit. Med. Jrnl.* 28 Feb. 555/1 The regular use of loperamide would be advisable since it is often effective in reducing frequency of defecation. **1994** L. A. GRAF *Traitor Winds* xvii. 236 Trazadone hydrochloride, dextromethorphan, loperamide, sodium salicylate... Vial after vial sported labels.

lopho-, *comb. form.* Add: **loˈphotrichous** *a.* [TRICHO-[1]], designating or characteristic of a bacterium in which several flagella occur as a crest or bundle at one end of the cell.

1900 A. C. JONES tr. *Fischer's Struct. & Functions Bacteria* ii. 15 The lophotrichous bacteria have in place of the single flagellum a brush or tuft of cilia. **1973** R. G. KRUEGER et al. *Introd. Microbiol.* iii. 33/1 Three general patterns occur: polar (one polar flagellum), lophotrichous (several polar flagella), and peritrichous (lateral flagella) distribution. **1988** MYRVIK & WEISER *Fund. Med. Bacteriol. & Mycol.* (ed. 2) ii. 37 Polar flagella exist either as a tuft of flagella (lophotrichous) or a single flagellum (monotrichous).

lophophorate (ləʊˈfɒfəreɪt), *n.* and *a. Zool.* [f. mod.L. *Lophophorata*: see LOPHOPHORE *n.*, -ATE[1].] **A.** *n.* An invertebrate organism possessing a lophophore; *spec.* a phoronid, brachiopod, bryozoan, or (in some classifications) entoproct. **B.** *adj.* Designating a lophophorate; of or pertaining to lophophorates.

1959 L. H. HYMAN *Invertebr.* V. xix. 229 Three groups of coelomates—Phoronida, Ectoprocta, and Brachiopoda..have in common the possession of a lophophore. A relationship..was first surmised by Caldwell (1882), but it remained for Hatschek (1888) to express this..by making them classes of a phylum Tentaculata... The name Lophophorata would have been far more appropriate, and here the three groups in question will be referred to as the lophophorate phyla, or lophophorates. **1962** D. NICHOLS *Echinoderms* xiv. 173 There is some evidence that the lophophorate body is subdivided into three regions. **1972** P. A. MEGLITSCH *Invertebr. Zool.* (ed. 2) 672/1 The preponderance of evidence points to the lophophorates as deuterostomes. **1979** *Nature* 8 Nov. 135/2 H. and G. Termier..envisaged the evolution of coelomates as involving an early separation of echinoderms from lophophorates and chordates. **1983** E. C. MINKOFF *Evolutionary Biol.* xxvi. 465/2 All lophophorate phyla have a simple digestive tract, complete with mouth and anus.

loq., *v.* Now *rare.* [Written abbrev.] *intr.* = *LOQUITUR v.*

1853 *Punch* XXIV. 107 Fortunate digger (loq.) 'Half a hogshead of Port, waiter.' **1903** G. BELL *Let.* 30 June (1927) I. viii. 165 G. B. loq.: 'I think you'll have to pay some of the piper if you want to call so much of the tune.' Waiter, loq.: 'I guess that's so.' **1917** J. LEE *Work-a-day Warriors* 35 Orderly Corporal, *loq.* Fall in the lazy, the lousy, and the lame, [etc.].

‖**loquitur** (ˈlɒkwɪtə(r)), *v.* [L., 3rd sing. pres. of *loqu-ī* to speak.] *intr.* (Used following the speaker's name, as a note to the reader) '..speaks'. Abbrev. *LOQ *v.*

1855 W. BAGEHOT in *National Rev.* Oct. 274 'Remember my joke against you' (Sydney Smith *loquitur*) 'about the moon.' **1909** E. POUND *Personae* 25 Such an one picking a ragged Backless copy from the stall,.. Loquitur, 'Ah-eh! the strange rare name.' **1915** V. WOOLF *Voyage Out* iii. 54 R. D. *loquitur*: Clarice has omitted to tell you that she looked exceedingly pretty at dinner.

lorazepam (lɔːˈreɪzɪpæm, -ˈræz-), *n. Pharm.* [f. CH)LOR(O-[2] + *-AZEPAM.] A benzodiazepine, $C_{15}H_{10}Cl_2N_2O_2$, which is used as a tranquillizer and hypnotic.

1969 *Jrnl. Amer. Med. Assoc.* 25 Aug. 1213/1 (*table*) Lorazepam. **1975** FELTON & FOWLER *Best, Worst, & Most Unusual* 155 Lorazepam deadens sensation locally while the patient remains awake. However, it also induces postoperative amnesia, permanently blocking the patient from ever remembering the process. **1986** C. W. THORNBER in C. A. Heaton *Chem. Industry* iv. 187 Lorazepam..is a close relative of temazepam but is used mostly as an anxiolytic and an injectable sedative.

Lorentz, *n.* Add: **Lorentz force**, the force exerted on a charged particle by a magnetic field (or a magnetic and an electric field). **Lorentz group**, the group (GROUP *n.* 5 a) of Lorentz transformations.

1931 H. P. ROBERTSON tr. *H. Weyl's Theory of Groups & Quantum Mech.* iii. 147 Lorentz transformations constitute a group, the 'complete Lorentz group', and this group describes the homogeneity of the 4-dimensional world. **1935** J. DOUGALL tr. *M. Born's Atomic Physics* ii. 26 The Lorentz force $e(v/c)H$ is directed towards the centre of the circle. **1940** *Nature* 31 Aug. 283/2 Special attention has been given to the..Lorentz group and the concept of semi-vectors. **1951** M. HAMMERMESH tr. *Landau & Lifshitz's Classical Theory of Fields* iii. 45 The equation of motion of a charge in an electromagnetic field can now be written as $dp/dt = e\mathbf{E} + e\mathbf{v}/c \times \mathbf{H}$. The expression on the right is called the Lorentz force. **1967** CONDON & ODISHAW *Handbk. Physics* (ed. 2) II. vi. 41/1 The formulation of current quantum-mechanical field theory requires use of all transformations of the inhomogeneous Lorentz group. **1968** *Amer. Jrnl. Physics* XXXVI. 1102 Henri Poincaré was the first to introduce four-vectors, the Lorentz group and its variants. **1969** *New Scientist* 4 Sept. 487/2 Negative mass—inertial and gravitational—need not, however, predicate the abandonment of either principle provided we allow the Lorentz force on a particle to depend on the sign of its mass as well as that of its charge. **1986** A. PAIS *Inward Bound* vii. 132 It should be..remembered how innovative for their time were the applications of the Maxwell equations and the Lorentz force to the design of experiments on the deflection of charged particles.

Lorentzian (ləˈrɛntsɪən), *a.* and *n. Physics.* Also **lorentzian.** [f. LORENTZ *n.* + -IAN[1].] **A.** *adj.* Of, pertaining to, or characteristic of Lorentz (see LORENTZ *n.*), his theories, or the concepts arising out of his work; *spec.* designating a curve or function having the same form as that representing the intensity of a spectral emission line as a function of frequency in classical radiation theory.

1958 *Physical Rev.* CXII. 1940/2 Δ_v is the half-width of the atomic resonance at half-maximum intensity, assuming a Lorentzian line shape. **1967** CONDON & ODISHAW *Handbk. Physics* (ed. 2) VIII. ix. 119/2 Homogeneous broadening yields Lorentzian line shapes whereas Gaussian line shapes occur when inhomogeneous broadening is involved. **1978** *Nature*

31 Aug. 903/1 In all twitch and most slow fibre junctions at negative voltages the spectral density of the fluctuations could be adequately fitted with a Lorentzian function. **1988** *Ibid.* 16 June 609/3 In the curve-fitting module, up to three peaks of different height, position, width and shape (gaussian, lorentzian or mixed) can be studied with various levels of noise superimposed. **1992** S. P. MARAN *Astron. & Astrophysics Encycl.* 194/2 Fabry-Perot filters.. are stable within the dimensional stability of the plate spacing and refractive index of the cavity medium. The transmission function is approximately Lorentzian in shape.

B. *n.* A Lorentzian curve or function.

1973 *Physics Bull.* Jan. 51/1 It is intended.. to deal in particular with aspects of the interpretation of experimental data such as multiple scattering and the unfolding of lorentzians. **1988** *Nature* 14 Apr. 661/2 Fitting the haloes by a gaussian or a lorentzian, we estimate a coupling range.. which corresponds to the size of an insulin monomer or dimer.

Lorenz (lə'rɛnts), *n.*[1] *Econ.* [The name of Max Otto *Lorenz* (b. 1876), U.S. statistician, who devised the curve (*Q. Publ. Amer. Statistical Assoc.* (1905) IX. 217).] **Lorenz curve**, a graph in which the proportion of the total personal income of a country is plotted against the proportion of individuals who collectively receive that proportion; more widely, any similar graph relating proportion of a total to the proportion of recipients, etc., of it.

1909 *Q. Jrnl. Econ.* XXIV. 172 A small difference in method of compilation at this point will affect *every* part of the Lorenz curve. **1920** *Econ. Jrnl.* XXX. 353 Another interesting measure of inequality is based upon what some writers have called a Lorenz curve. [*Note*] Originally proposed by Mr. M. O. Lorenz. **1938** M. D. ANDERSON *Dynamic Theory Wealth Distrib.* x. 199 A Lorenz curve is a graph depicting the cumulative percentage of total income on one axis and the cumulative percentage of persons receiving the income on the other axis. **1965** *McGraw-Hill Dict. Mod. Econ.* 306 The greater the sag of the Lorenz curve, the greater the inequality of the income distribution. **1977** D. M. SMITH *Human Geogr.* vi. 135 The Lorenz curve can reveal a number of interesting properties of a distribution. **1980** *Sci. Amer.* Sept. 76/1 One procedure is to present the observed distribution of household income in a country in a Lorenz curve. **1988** C. PASS et al. *Collins Ref. Dict. Econ.* 85, 50% of market sales are accounted for by the largest 25% of total firms, as the Lorenz curve indicates.

Lorenz (lə'rɛnts), *n.*[3] *Physics.* [The name of Edward N. Lorenz (b. 1917), U.S. meteorologist.] **Lorenz attractor**, a strange attractor in the form of a two-lobed figure resembling a mask, formed by a trajectory spiralling round the mask's 'eyeholes' and alternating randomly between its two sides. Cf. *strange attractor* s.v. *STRANGE *a.* 17.

1976 *Lect. Notes Math.* DLXV. 147, I shall however turn now to the discussion of an object which has greater geometric simplicity, and intuitive appeal: the Lorenz attractor. **1989** I. STEWART *Does God play Dice?* vii. 138 (*caption*) The Lorenz attractor: trajectories cycle, apparently at random, round the two lobes. **1991** *Sci. Amer.* Aug. 13/2 (Advt.), This 63-minute video turns the Mandelbrot set and Lorenz attractor into visible objects as their discoverers discuss the details of their work.

lorilet ('lɒrilɛt, lɒri'lɛt), *n.* *Ornith.* [f. LORY *n.* + -LET.] Any of several very small, mainly green, short-tailed parrots of the genera *Opopsitta* and *Psittaculirostris*, native to the rainforests of north-east Australia and New Guinea. Also called *fig-parrot*.

1901 A. J. CAMPBELL *Nests & Eggs Austral. Birds* II. 600 During my own Cardwell camp-out (1885) we procured skins of the Blue-faced Lorilet. **1929** *Emu* 1 Oct. 81 Is there any genus of Australian birds, containing more than one species, so little known as the Lorilets or Fig-Parrots? **1966** EASTMAN & HUNT *Parrots Austral.* 46 The Lorilets are almost impossible to distinguish from each other in flight.

Los Angeleno (lɒs ændʒə'liːnəʊ), *n.* Fem. **Los Angelena.** Pl. **Los Angelenos.** [f. the name of *Los Angeles*: see ANGELENO *n.*] A native or inhabitant of Los Angeles; = ANGELENO *n.*

1960 *Guardian* 11 July 1/7 He protected Mr Khrushchev from the sulking Los Angelenos last Fall. **1975** *Time Out* 30 May 51/3 As a native Los Angeleno, I can vouch for the way his.. style captures that.. beautiful city. **1977** *N. Y. Rev. Bks.* 12 May 50/4 (Advt.), Vivacious, audacious, perspicacious, loquacious Los Angelena seeks droll nonchauvinist male, fortyish. **1988** *Jerusalem Post* 7 Oct. (In Jerusalem Suppl.) 6/5 'I would like to see Israel become more of a light unto the nations,' said former Los Angeleno Eva Katz. **1992** *Times* 28 Nov. (Sat. Rev.) 27/4 Los Angelenos seem almost proud of the amount of driving they do.

lose, *v.*[1] Add: [**3.**] **k.** To shed (weight, fatty tissue, etc.). Cf. *to lose weight* s.v. WEIGHT *n.*[1] 8 c.

1890 *Lancet* 27 Sept. 663/2 The patient will rapidly lose flesh. **1941** G. KERSH *They die with their Boots Clean* II. 85 The first weeks or two cracks up quite a few rookies... This here Spencer drops weight... Millions of stones that rook lost. **1956** J. BARTH *Floating Opera* xiv. 139, I had lost twenty pounds, countless prejudices, much provincialism, my chastity.., and my religion. **1976** W. BRECKON *You are what you Eat* viii. 138 The object of slimming is to lose fat.. to have a greater output of energy than input from food. **1992** *N.Y. Times* 31 May 37/1 Janet says she has lost about 10 pounds while mooning and pining over the man of her dreams.

[**9.**] **e.** To dispose of, eliminate, or remove (something perceived as inconvenient or unwanted); *occas.*, to kill. *colloq.*

1942 BERREY & VAN DEN BARK *Amer. Thes. Slang* §27/5 *Eliminate; discard; get rid of.* Axe, basket,.. lose, mop up, [etc.]. **1951** P. H. ABRAHAMS *Wild Conquest* II. i. i. 173 Another naked easterner... Lose him, my brave Rauwe! My brave soldiers! **1970** G. CHAPMAN et al. *Monty Python's Flying Circus* (1989) I. xxiii. 314 Whoever heard of a lion in the Antarctic. Right. Lose the lion. **1984** J. PARTRIDGE *One Touch Photogr.* 31 An untidy background can detract from your picture and a good rule is to 'use it or lose it'. **1987** *Which?* June 278/2 We're not convinced that losing the flex is much of an advantage—especially as the model we looked at couldn't do things like liquidise soup in a saucepan.

lot, *n.* Add: [**6.**] **c.** A plot of land used for parking cars, *spec.* (*a*) for sale or hire (esp. in (*used*) *car lot*); (*b*) = *parking lot* s.v. PARKING *vbl. n.* 3 b. Chiefly *N.Amer.*

1939 W. SAROYAN *Peace, it's Wonderful* 31 All I do now is hang around this used car lot and wait for people to come around and start asking questions about the jalopies we're showing. **1959** L. LIPTON *Holy Barbarians* 25, I didn't shuck the customers enough to please the crook who was running the car lot. **1968** J. IRVING *Setting Free Bears* (1979) II. 166 Grandfather—who's parked and locked the taxi in the lot at Karl's Church—walks Hilke and the cookie crock home. **1979** J. RABAN *Arabia through Looking Glass* iv. 144 Coming into Abu Dhabi we passed a huge desert lot filled with parked cars. **1985** *Weekly World News* (U.S.) 1 Jan. 3/1 She paid $20 000 for her new hot rod, and drove it off the lot.

[**10.**] (sense 6 c) *lot attendant.*

[**1974** S. TERKEL *Working* IV. 219 He is forty-nine and has been a parking lot attendant for about thirty years.] **1979** *Arizona Daily Star* 5 Aug. (Advt. Section) 2/6 *Lot Attendant for used car lot. Apply in person. **1986** *Jrnl.* (Fairfax Co., Va.) 23 May C10 (Advt.), Alamo Rent-a-Car is expanding...We are hiring: Rental Agents, Bus Drivers and Lot Attendants.

‖**loti** ('ləʊti, 'luːti), *n.* Pl. **maloti** (məˈləʊti, məˈluː ti). [Sesotho.

Maloti, the plural form (also written *Mulati*), is the name of a mountain range in northern Lesotho; in Lesotho itself the term is used to refer to the entire mountainous north and east of the country and simply means 'mountains'. The singular form, *loti*, is a recent derivative of the same word.]

Since 1980, the basic monetary unit of Lesotho, equal to 100 lisente; also, a note or coin of this value.

1980 *Sunday Times* 27 Jan. 59/5 The new coin collection minted on behalf of the African kingdom of Lesotho..includes..the gold Maloti..which contains one ounce of fine gold. **1981** *Britannica Bk. of Year 1980* 490/1 On Jan. 19, 1980, Lesotho issued its new currency, the loti (plural, maloti), backed by South Africa's rand, and launched the Lesotho Monetary Authority. **1986** *Christian Science Monitor* 27 Jan. 12/4 Depositors in Maseru banks started withdrawing deposits in South African currency—which alongside the Lesothan loti, is legal tender here. **1985** *Statesman's Year-bk. 1985-6* 789 The currency is the *Loti* (plural *Maloti*) divided into 100 *Lisente* which is at par with the South African *rand*.

Lotka–Volterra ('lɒtkəvɒl'tɛrə), *n. Ecol.* and *Math.* [The names of Alfred James *Lotka* (1880-1949), Austrian-born U.S. statistician, and Vito *Volterra* (1860-1940), Italian mathematician, who proposed the model.] Used *attrib.* with reference to a mathematical model of the variation with time in the populations of a predator species and a prey species, as governed by a pair of coupled differential equations (the *Lotka-Volterra equations*).

1959 E. P. ODUM *Fund. Ecol.* (ed. 2) vii. 232 Some of the most widely debated theoretical aspects of competition theory revolve around what have become known as the Lotka-Volterra equations. **1970** *Amer. Naturalist* CIV. 73 Theoretical community ecology frequently relies on a series of simplified models compounded to represent the behavior of a larger system. One simple system amenable to this approach is that represented by the Lotka-Volterra equations describing competition between species. **1973** P. A. COLINVAUX *Introd. Ecol.* xxx. 422 (*caption*) Coupled oscillations predicted by the Lotka-Volterra equations for predation. **1977** J. L. HARPER *Population Biol. of Plants* xxiii. 738 Many of the characteristics of the predator-prey oscillations that are predicted by the Lotka-Volterra model are very strongly dependent on the length of time involved in the feedback between predators and prey, [etc.]. **1988** *New Scientist* 2 June 60/4 Sharks and fish fight out their ecological battle on the toroidal planet of Wa-Tor, discretely simulating stochastic Lotka-Volterra cycles.

Lotto ('lɒtəʊ), *n.*[2] [The name of the Venetian painter Lorenzo *Lotto* (c 1480-1556).] Used *attrib.* and occas. *absol.* to designate Turkish (Ushak) rugs and carpets resembling those depicted in paintings by Lotto (see quot. 1983).

1931 A. U. DILLEY *Oriental Rugs & Carpets* vi. 147 Field color of the Lotto rugs is scarlet, the dominant pattern yellow. **1977** *Penguin Dict. Decorative Arts* 806/2 Two other types, essentially Turkish and made in W. Anatolia, are named Holbeins and Lottos after the C16 European painters in whose works they appear. **1983** J. MILLS *Carpets in Paintings* 28 Another type of Ushak rug..is the 'arabesque Ushak' or 'Lotto'

rug, the latter name arising from the appearance of one in the *Family Group* of 1547 by Lorenzo Lotto as well as another painting by the same artist, the *Sant' Antonino Elemosinario* in Venice. *Ibid.* 38 Both these border types appear..up till about 1680. After this other carpet types displace the 'Lottos'.

Lou Gehrig (luː 'gɛərɪg), *n.* [The name of Henry Louis '*Lou*' *Gehrig* (1903-41), U.S. baseball player, who died from the disease.] **Lou Gehrig('s) disease**, amyotrophic lateral sclerosis.

Not a term used formally in *Med.*

1941 *Evening Star* (Washington) 4 June PC-1/1 No virus has been found in cases of 'Gehrig's disease' as the affliction has become popularly termed. **1953** *Sci. News Let.* 19 Sept. 184/1 (*heading*) Lou Gehrig disease study started on Guam. **1958** *New Scientist* 17 July 430/1 Amyotrophic lateral sclerosis (Lou Gehrig's Disease). **1986** *New Yorker* 7 Apr. 37/2 This lady's only fifty, she's got Lou Gehrig's disease. **1990** DiMAGGIO & GILBERT *Real Grass, Real Heroes* ii. 24 It took a terminal disease to stop Lou Gehrig—amyotrophic lateral sclerosis—ALS, known ever since as 'Lou Gehrig's disease'.

louro ('luːrəʊ), *n.* [a. Pg. *louro*, orig. 'laurel'.] Any of various tropical American hardwood trees belonging to *Ocotea*, *Nectandra*, and related genera of the laurel family, *esp.* (in full *red louro*) the tree *O. rubra*; the dense wood of any of these trees. Also, any of several similar Brazilian trees of the genus *Cordia* of the borage family, or their wood.

1816 H. KOSTER *Trav. Brazil* xiv. 300 The *louro* is a large tree, and of it there are three species, all of which are used principally for the beams of houses, for the timber of them rots quickly under ground. **1914** J. F. WOODROFFE *Upper Reaches of Amazon* xx. 276 The following woods are especially used. Louro (of the family of *Lauraceas*), found in swampy lands in many qualities, such as the common yellow, black, white, grey, odoriferous cedar, beech and tachi. **1923** ZON & SPARHAWK *Forest Resources of World* vi. 723 The louros in general are the cheapest commercial woods of Brazil, and are widely used for construction, boxes, and cooperage. **1980** *Acta Amazonica* X. 409/2 Various types of locally available organic materials, such as cocoa pods, rice husks, brewery wastes, Pistia, water hyacinth..and sawdust from louro wood, were tested for their ability to produce biogas.

love, *n.*[1] Add: [**16.**] [**a.**] **love handle** (usu. in *pl.*) *slang* (orig. and chiefly *U.S.*), excess fat at the waist.

1970 *Current Slang* (Univ. S. Dakota) IV. III.-IV. 20 *Love handles*, n. The fat on one's sides. **1981** J. FONDA *Workout Bk.* (1982) 52 Something certainly happens to those saddle bags,..love handles and plain old lumps. **1989** T. CLANCY *Clear & Present Danger* xiii. 306 His picture was at her bedside, taken only a year before his death, working on his sailboat. No longer a young man when it had been taken, love handles at his waist, much of his hair gone, but the smile.

love, *v.*[1] Add: [**4.**] **d.** (With gerund or gerundive phrase as obj.) To enjoy, to take pleasure in (doing, being, etc.). Cf. *LIKE v.*[1] 6 h.

*a*1500 *Emare* viii. 78 The emperour..myche loued playnge. **1545** R. ASCHAM *Toxophilus* (Arb.) 45 The best learned and sagest men in this Realme..both loue shoting and vse shoting. **1623** *New & Merry Prognost.* sig. E2, Beggars loue brawling, And wretches loue wrawling. **1732** in T. Fuller *Gnomologia* 216 They love dancing well, that dance barefoot upon thorns. **1828** E. BULWER-LYTTON *Pelham* II. v. 46 For the rest, he loved trotting better than cantering. **1911** M. BEERBOHM *Let.* 6 Dec. (1964) 211 You who..love being behind the scenes among T-lights and properties. **1991** *N.Y.*

Times Mag. 17 Nov. 43/2 While she has a driver in the city, she loves taking the wheel in the country.

low, *a.* and *n.* Add: [**A.**] [**II.**] [**9.**] **f.** Of (a source of) light or radiant heat: not bright or intense; weak, dim, reduced (orig. with the implication of small physical extent, as of a flame, candle, wick, etc., which has burned down or been turned down (cf. sense 1 above). Also *fig.* Sometimes quasi-*adv.*: see sense *19 below.
  1811 SHELLEY *St. Irvyne* i. 17 'Twas dead of the night, when I sat in my dwelling; One glimmering lamp was expiring and low. **1882** M. ARNOLD *Poor Matthias* in *Poetical Wks.* (1950) 454 As age comes on, I know, Poet's fire gets faint and low. **1919** E. O'NEILL *In Zone* in *Moon of Caribbees* 85 A lantern in the middle of the floor, turned down very low, throws a dim light. **1932** W. FAULKNER *Light in August* v. 108 Four people sat about a card table, the white faces intent and sharp in the low light. **1963** *Times* 25 Feb. (Canada Suppl.) p. xv/1 Eskimo children.. huddled inside their sealskin *parkhas* and warmed by the low flame of a blubber lantern. **1990** D. M. THOMAS *Lying Together* i. 17 Victor concentrated; asked for the lamp to be turned down low.
  [**III.**] [**19.**] (Further examples.)
  1827 T. WILSON *Pitman's Pay* II. iii, The unsnuff'd lights are now burnt low. **1871** B. TAYLOR tr. Goethe *Faust* (1875) II. v. iv. 356 The fire sinks down and flickers low. **1915** *St. Nicholas* June 689/1 They continued to crawl slowly up, their candles flickering low in the impoverished air of the long-inclosed place. **1943** V. NABOKOV in *Atlantic* Jan. 70/1 The lamp burned low, and strange objects glimmered upon the writing desk. **1991** I. GOWER *Shoemaker's Daughter* (1992) vi. 87 The fire was burning low in the grate and the kettle was cold on the hob.
  [**IV.**] [**23.**] **low-end** *a. Comm.*, of, pertaining to, or associated with the cheaper end (END *n.* 5 d) of the market for a particular product or service.
  1961 WEBSTER, *Low-end.* **1977** *New Yorker* 6 June 96/3 It stands to reason that 'high end' means expensive,.. but why does 'promotional', as well as 'low end' mean cheap? **1986** *Courier-Mail* (Brisbane) 21 Oct. 26/6 Very high quality, high-cost systems and low-end limited function systems using personal computers and based on a page-by-page approach. **1992** N. STEPHENSON *Snow Crash* i. 8 Art the Barber.. runs the second-largest chain of low-end haircutting establishments in the world.

lowball ('ləʊbɔːl), *n.* (and *a.*) Also **low-ball** and as two words. [f. LOW *a.* + BALL *n.*[1]] **1.** *Baseball.* A ball pitched so as to pass over the plate below the level of the batter's knees. Also *transf.* in other sports. Freq. *attrib.* or as *adj.*
  1867 *N.Y. Herald* 3 July 8/3 Pabor knocked a low ball pretty 'warm' between short and second. **1911** Z. GREY *Young Pitcher* vi. 59 Drive that fellow away from the plate... give this one a low ball... now straight over the pan. **1940** L. H. FISCHER *How to play Winning Softball* ii. 22 Low balls should be aimed at the catcher's knee. **1955** P. RICHARDS *Mod. Baseball Strategy* iii. 41 It becomes a matter of whether the pitcher is a better low-ball *pitcher* than the hitter is a low-ball *batter.* **1964** L. WATTS *Fine Art Baseball* ii. 119 Generally speaking, low-ball pitching is the most effective. **1979** *Washington Post* 11 Apr. D5/4 Lowball hitters such as Lee Trevino. **1990** DiMAGGIO &GILBERT *Real Grass, Real Heroes* xii. 161 Mickey could handle low-ball pitchers like Higbe and Casey and still throw out base runners.
  2. *fig.* (in *Comm.*). The quotation of a deceptively or unrealistically low price or estimate, usu. in order to ensure a contract, etc.; also, the price so quoted or offered. Also *attrib.* or as *adj.* See also *LOWBALL.
  1961 *Time* 24 Mar. 80/2 The lowball: the salesman quotes a rock-bottom price for the new car to win the

customer, later hikes up the price. **1967** M. E. DOWD *How to save Money* iv. 54 '*Lowball*' offers are aimed at shoppers with no car to trade in. Here the 'lowball' cash price may be far below other offers. **1977** *Rolling Stone* 16 June 13/2 'Lowball' or 'cutthroat' retail outlets.. sell major new releases at slightly above, or sometimes actually below, cost. **1983** *Fortune* 2 May 160/3 Even scarier is the ultimate low-ball: a $50 program. **1993** *Rep. on Business* Feb. 36/3 Forsyth would launch a formal offer to buy back all of its outstanding shares at a low-ball price of $3 apiece.

lowball ('ləʊbɔːl), *v. Comm.* (chiefly *U. S.*). [f. *LOWBALL *n.* 2.] *trans.* **a.** To give a low estimate of (a cost or price) to a potential customer, esp. with the intention of raising it after a deal has been agreed; more generally, to underestimate or understate (an amount). Also *absol.* **b.** To deceive (a customer) by offering an unrealistically low price, estimate, etc.
  1978 *Business Week* 3 July 23/3 You can't lowball a price and expect to buy anything. **1983** in *Webster's Ninth New Collegiate Dict.* s.v., To give (a customer) a deceptively low price or cost estimate. **1987** *Forbes* (N.Y.) 18 May 144/2 The managers back in Tokyo have been lowballing bids and accepting dangerously thin margins. **1988** *Crain's Chicago Business* 11 Apr. 3/4 Anchor management lowballed on their estimates of increases in medical charges and health care utilization. **1991** *Connecticut* May 93 Are you being lowballed by someone who hopes to make money on extras later?
  So '**lowballing** *vbl. n.* and *ppl. a.*; '**lowballer** *n.*
  1977 *Rolling Stone* 16 June 13/5 Thus do the Jimmy's and Peaches of this world go on their lowballing ways, slowly but inevitably cutting into the rack jobbers' share of the market. **1978** S. BRILL *Teamsters* v. 198 'Lowballing' is a procedure whereby one trucking company takes away business from another company.. by underbidding that company for the work. *Ibid.* x. 198 Reputable department stores.. use the low-ballers for deliveries. **1987** *Drug Topics* 20 Apr. 13/1 Kirk R. Agthe.. said the profession is in this current mess due to lowballing of prices and services. **1992** *Independent* 16 Nov. 23/3 Desperation for work, particularly in the devastated commercial property market, has led to reports of the 'lowballing', or uneconomic tendering, that has supposedly become commonplace in auditing.

low-boy, *n.* Add: **3.** *U. S.* A low-slung trailer used esp. for transporting exceptionally tall or heavy loads. Freq. *attrib.*
  1953 *Western Trucking* June 50/1 Freesh Construction Company.. has a.. large White 200 diesel with a 36-foot-long semi-lowboy trailer for hauling company tractors. **1961** *Publ. Amer. Dial. Soc.* XXXVI. 29 *Lowboy*, a large semi-trailer whose bed is built especially low for ease of loading; used for hauling construction material and equipment. **1977** M. TAK *Truck Talk* 42 The gooseneck on a lowboy trailer is removable on certain models to make it easier to load the trailer. **1978** *Detroit Free Press* 16 Apr. F11 (Advt.), Trailers:.. Nelson Tri-axle 40-ton lowboy (1956); Fruehauf 25-ton tandem lowboy. **1985** *New Yorker* 22 Apr. 51/1 The auction business thrived:.. lowboy trailers.. lithographs—they were all for sale. **1991** *Construction Equipment* Oct. 20/3 The Roadrunner Mark -70SL is a 35-ton capacity lowboy with the patented self-lifting detachable gooseneck.

Löwenheim–Skolem ('lɜːvənhaɪm 'skɔːləm, 'skəʊləm), *n. Logic.* [The names of Leopold *Löwenheim* (1878-1957), German mathematician, and Thoralf Albert *Skolem* (1887-1963), Norwegian mathematician, who formulated the theorem.] *Löwenheim–Skolem theorem*, the theorem that any consistent set of sentences may be interpreted by some finite or countable model.

1952 S. C. KLEENE *Introd. Metamath.* xiv. 394 If a predicate letter formula F is satisfiable in some (non-empty) domain, then F is satisfiable in the domain of the natural numbers. (Löwenheim's theorem, 1915, also called the Löwenheim-Skolem theorem.) **1965** B. MATES *Elem. Logic* viii. 141 The question thus arises whether one could find a consistent set of sentences that is satisfiable only by interpretations having non-denumerably infinite domains. In view of the Löwenheim-Skolem theorem, the answer is negative. **1967** J. VAN HEIJENOORT *From Frege to Gödel* 582 His proof yields, besides completeness, the Löwenheim-Skolem theorem, which states that a satisfiable formula is $\aleph_0$-satisfiable. **1982** W. S. HATCHER *Logical Found. Math.* i. 38 Finally, we state (without proof) a modern form of the famous Löwenheim-Skolem theorem.

lower, *v.* Sense 1 f. in Dict. becomes 1 g. Add: [1.] **f.** To direct (one's eyes or gaze) downwards, as after looking at something in a higher position; to allow (one's head, eyelids, etc.) to droop, esp. as a gesture of humility, evasion, etc.

1826 J. F. COOPER *Last of Mohicans* I. viii. 116 'Go, generous young man,' Cora continued, lowering her eyes under the gaze of the Mohican, with an intuitive consciousness of her power. **1843** A. BETHUNE *Sc. Peasant's Fire-side* 134 The sudden jerk..brought the shaft horse, who was a powerful animal, still nearer to that side of the road, while it made both him and the tracer lower their heads. **1915** CONRAD *Victory* II. v. 114 Schomberg lowered his eyes, for the sight of these two men intimidated him. **1928** E. O'NEILL *Strange Interlude* IX. 350 *Nina.* [Finally lowering her eyes—confusedly]. **1960** C. DAY LEWIS *Buried Day* iii. 47 He would at the slightest provocation lower his eyelids rebukingly. **1987** D. WIGODER *Images of Destruction* vi. 229 She looked at me, and I tried not to lower my eyes.

[5.] [a.] Freq. *refl.*, esp. without const.

1816 J. AUSTEN *Emma* III. xiii. 238 She supposed she must say more before she were entitled to his clemency; but it was a hard case to be obliged still to lower herself in his opinion. **1849** C. BRONTË *Shirley* I. vi. 130, I never wish you to lower yourself. **1907** G. B. SHAW *John Bull's Other Island* IV. 103 God knows I dont grudge you me money! But to lower meself to the level of common people—. **1919** WODEHOUSE *Coming of Bill* (1920) I. iv. 40 He knew no artists, but he had..gathered a general impression that they were..shock-headed, unwashed persons of no social standing whatever... And his sister had lowered herself by association with one of these. **1937** R. NARAYAN *Bachelor of Arts* ix. 139 We have a status and a prestige to keep. We can't lower ourselves unduly. **1990** C. BRAYFIELD *Prince* xii. 252 She felt she would be lowering herself if she quizzed him about Lady Katriona, or Lady Annabel.

low-level, *a.* Add: [1.] **b.** *spec.* in *Nuclear Sci.*, designating mild radioactivity and mildly radioactive waste.

1949 *Analytical Chem.* XXI. 1588/1 (*heading*) Portable radioactivity indicator for low-level surveys. **1952** A. P. TALBOYS *Contamination of Plumbing by Low-Level Radioisotope Wastes* (Report, Johns Hopkins Univ.) 1 To determine the extent to which plumbing may become contaminated by low-level radioactive wastes, practical tests have been conducted at the Johns Hopkins University. **1977** *Offshore Engineer* May 28/2 Low level nuclear wastes can include everything from radiotherapy pellets to soiled technicians' clothing. **1986** *Economist* 22 Feb. 22/2 The company might have done better to emphasise that this was very low-level waste containing just half a curie of radiation. **1989** C. CAUFIELD *Multiple Exposures* (1990) xii. 127 From the mid-1950s on, the scientific debate in the United States about fallout and the effects of low-level radiation became ever more polarized.

lowlight ('ləʊlaɪt), *n.* and *a.* Also **low-light**. [f. LOW *a.* + LIGHT *n.*, after HIGHLIGHT *n.*] **A.** *n.* **a.** Chiefly *Hairdressing*. A dark streak in lighter hair, esp. one artificially introduced; *occas.* an area of relatively dark make-up.

1926 *Hairtinting & Beauty Culture* 1 Apr. 13/2 (*heading*) Painting in the low lights. To-day's 'make-up' trend. *Ibid.*, This season, paint in the 'low lights'. **1979** *Hair* Autumn 13/4, I also put a few low-lights through. **1985** *Ibid.* Summer 72/4, I suggest you have either fine highlights to make your hair look lighter, or lowlights to produce a warmer effect. **1991** *She* May 151/1 Lowlights, which last eight to 12 weeks, help improve the appearance of grey hair by diffusing rather than masking it.

b. *gen.* A poor performance, a low point; opp. HIGHLIGHT *n.*

1966 *Sunday Times* 18 Dec. 38/5 Company news continued to produce lowlights rather than highlights—with a few honourable exceptions. **1977** *Washington Post* 6 Oct. (District Weekly) DC6/1 Here's how we hit the lowlights for 40 cents apiece before lunching at a cafeteria called the Patent Pending. **1984** *Morning Herald* (Durham, N. Carolina) 13 Oct. 3C It was as pathetic [a] performance as the Blue Devils have had in some time. Duke's record book doesn't list the lowlights, but this certainly was one. **1990** *N.Y. Times Bk. Rev.* 30 Sept. 13/2 Discussions of the spectacular crash of Gary Hart, the Joseph Biden plagiarism scandal,..and several other high- and lowlights of the campaign.

B. *adj.* (Usu. as **low-light** and with pronunc. (ləʊ'laɪt)). Used *attrib.* (esp. in *Photogr.*) to designate devices designed for operation in low levels of illumination, activities carried out under such circumstances, etc.

[**1969** in A. Boni *Photogr. Lit.* 1960-70 (1972) 291/2 (*title*) Solving the light level lens selection problem.] **1977** *Which?* Dec. 648/3 ASA 400 film adjusts low-light warning only. **1984** J. PARTRIDGE *One Touch Photogr.* 11 It is advisable to support the camera in some low-light situations. **1989** T. CLANCY *Clear & Present Danger* viii. 133 The clear night made for surprisingly good visibility, even without the low-light goggles with which they were normally equipped. **1992** *Fly Rod & Reel* Jan.-Feb. 14/2 A Big Eye #22 has an eye like a #16 hook; the #16, an eye the size of a #10—a boon for low-light fishing or heavier tippets.

So **'lowlighting** *n.* (*Hairdressing*).

1972 J. R. RAYNES *Men's Hairdressing* III. 68 Lowlighting is effected by putting dark streaks into light hair. **1988** *Grocery Update* June 39/4 Poly is relaunching Poly Hi-lights in new packaging which complements the redesigned auburn lowlighting kit.

Lowry ('laʊərɪ), *n.*[2] [The name of Laurence S. *Lowry* (1887–1976), British painter.] Used *attrib.* or *absol.* to designate a figure, scene (esp. an urban industrial landscape), etc., which is reminiscent or characteristic of Lowry's work. Also in *comb.*, as *Lowry-like a.*

1945 M. AYRTON in *Spectator* 23 Feb. 171/2 The Lowry figure is a mindless, herded, seedy figment painted into an industrial landscape which is in a class by itself. **1951** M. COLLIS *Discovery of L. S. Lowry* 17, I saw that it was a Lowry house, not unlike the Georgian house in the centre of *An Island*. **1954** *Guardian* 31 Oct. 8/3, I look down on the Lowry landscape—asphalt and figures passing and repassing: the leaden sky, the walkers padded out against the cold. **1987** C. PHILLIPS *European Tribe* xiii. 108 Moving between, in and around them, were Lowry-like figures in black, shuffling their way to and from work. **1988** *Vogue* Aug. 20/1 Part of the pleasure of seeing the Lowrys in Salford lay in spotting Lowry figures next to the pictures.

So **Lowry'esque**, '**Lowryish**, *adjs.*, reminiscent of Lowry's landscapes or scenes.

1961 *Punch* 5 July 17/2 The difference between Yorkshire breadth of human nature and Lancashire Lowry-ish leanness is the difference between woollens and cottons. **1969** *Guardian* 8 Nov. 9/4 The urban landscapes are Lowryesque. **1973** *Ibid.* 18 Oct. 17 This Lowryesque scene is from Helen Bradley's 'Miss Carter Came With Us'. **1992** *Daily Tel.* 10 Feb. 4/7 It..shows Lowryesque children learning against a backcloth of smoking stacks and grimy cottages.

‖**lü** (ljuː), *n.* Also **liu**, **liuh**. [Chinese *lù*.] In ancient Chinese musical theory, a fundamental pitch; any of the twelve pitches in an untempered chromatic scale; also used *attrib.* to refer to (each of) a series of bamboo pipes used to produce these pitches.
    In Chinese, although known collectively as the twelve *lü*, there are two separate characters; *lü* for the odd-numbered pitches, and *lü* for the even-numbered.

1655 tr. *Semedo's China* I. xi. 54 They [*sc.* the Chinese] have twelve Tones, six to rise, which they call *Live*, and six to fall, which they call *Liu*. **1874** *Jrnl. N. China Branch R. Asiatic Soc.* VIII. 94 The *Lu* is a demi-note, of which twelve go to the Chinese octave. **1908** C. ENGEL *Mus. Instruments* (rev. ed.) v. 39 The tones of the *pien-ch'ing* are attuned according to the Chinese intervals called *lü*, of which there are twelve in the compass of an octave. **1954** *Grove's Dict. Mus.* (ed. 5) II. 221/2 *Period of Huang Ti* (from *c.* 2697 B.C.)...His system of the *Huang Chung* (foundation tone) and the 12 *lü* (cycle of fifths for transposing) has remained fundamental in Chinese music until the 20th century. **1957** *New Oxf. Hist. Mus.* I. ii. 95 The two 'whole-tone scales' of the male and female *liuh* (both *leu* and *liuh* are referred to collectively as the twelve *liuh*) were the result of a classification of the series into two groups by origin. **1974** *Encycl. Brit. Micropædia* VI. 394/3 *Lü pipes*, in Chinese music theory, 12 bamboo pipes closed at one end and cut in lengths mathematically proper to produce..the 12 tones of the untempered scale. **1980** *New Grove Dict. Mus.* IV. 261/1 The names of the 12 *lü* first appeared in *Kuo-yü* (4th century BC).

Luba ('luːbə), *n.* and *a.* Pl. **Balouba**, **Baluba**, **BaLuba**, **Luba**, or with -s. [Bantu. Forms with the *Ba-* plural class prefix are applied only to the people.]
    A. *n.* **a.** (A member of) a people inhabiting areas of southern Zaire, chiefly the Shaba province. **b.** Either of the two languages (distinguished as Ciluba and Kiluba) spoken by sections of this population. **B.** *attrib.* or as *adj.* Of or pertaining to the Luba or their languages.

[**1857** D. LIVINGSTONE *Missionary Trav. & Res. S. Afr.* xxiii. 458 Neither guns nor native traders are admitted into the country, the chief of Luba entertaining a dread of innovation.] **1883** R. N. CUST *Sketch Mod. Lang. Afr.* I. xi. 280 *Mittu*..is the name of a tribe whose language is spoken by a small group of independent tribes, Mittu, Madi, Abukeya, and Luba. **1919** H. H. JOHNSTON *Compar. Stud. Bantu & Semi-Bantu Lang.* I. ii. 25 Good-looking 'negroid' types may be encountered among the Zulus, the Becuana, the Hererw, the Alunda, Baluba, Manyuema, [etc.]. *Ibid.*, Bantu languages are spoken by..the Assyrian-like Baluba and Busoñgw [etc.]. **1922** *Ibid.* II. v. 109 The Luba-Lunda languages..must be regarded as associated with an ancient culture and a remarkable endemic civilization produced in South Central Congoland. **1957** V. W. TURNER *Schism & Continuity in Afr. Society* i. 5 Verhulpen mentions how the razzias of the Lunda and Luba states swept the Central African area for slaves. **1972** E. A. NIDA *Bk. 1000 Tongues* 400/1 KiSonge is a Luba language, spoken by about half a million people..in southeastern Congo-Kinshasa...The people are sometimes known as the Western Kalebwe BaLuba. Their Bantu language is related to the other Luba tongues. **1984** *Times* 10 Apr.

2/5 A Luba wood arrow rest in the form of a female figure with three incised projections springing from her head. **1992** A. BELL tr. M. Toussaint-Samat *Hist. Food* (1993) I. 10 The Baloubas of Zaire use the bark of trees for cooking *au plat*.

lubricated, *ppl. a.* Add: **b.** *slang.* Affected by drink; inebriated, drunk (freq. in *well-lubricated*). Cf. OILED *ppl. a.* 3.

1927 *New Republic* 9 Mar. 71/2 The following is a partial list of words denoting drunkenness now in common use in the United States..lubricated. **1983** NEAMAN & SILVER *Dict. Euphemisms* 99 Clearly, the human machine functions better when it is well oiled or lubricated. **1986** *National Jrnl.* (U. S.) 20 Sept. 2264/1 'For a man who doesn't drink,' said a well-lubricated observer, 'he's the most popular man in this bar.' **1990** A. TOFFLER *Powershift* IV. xv. 173 It is in the *dokikai* that men, lubricated with alcohol, speak to one another with *honto*—expressing their true feelings—rather than with *tatemae*—saying what is expected. **1993** *Q* Jan. 26/2 The audience—invariably a generously lubricated collective—bawl along to every word.

Lubyanka (lʊb'jænkə, ˌluːbi'ænkə), *n.* Also **Lubianka**. [Place name.] The name of a street in Moscow used *attrib.* and *absol.* to denote the headquarters of the Soviet secret police formerly sited there, and the detention centre for political dissidents within it. Also *transf.*

1938 E. AMBLER *Cause for Alarm* xiv. 221 When I thought of Russia I thought..of the Lubianka prison. **1963** *Listener* 24 Jan. 181/3 The Lubianka seemed to cast no more shadow over them all..than the Tower of London does over us. **1967** STEVENSON & HAYWARD tr. *Ginzburg's Journey into Whirlwind* I. xxv. 142 The drive was a long one. That meant we were going to the Butyrki prison: the Lubyanka was only a short way from the Kazan station. **1983** 'J. LE CARRÉ' *Little Drummer Girl* (1984) ii. 44 His greatest feat had been performed in the Lubyanka, where he had faked documents for fellow inmates from back numbers of *Pravda*, repulping them to press his own paper. **1990** F. KANGA *Trying to Grow* vii. 62 The Parsee old people's home being a cross between a loony house and the Lubyanka. **1991** *Climber & Hill Walker* Nov. 38/1, I met him first in the Lubyanka, that brick lump on Manchester's Oxford Road that serves as home to the BMC.

Lucchese (luː'kiːz, luː'keɪsɪ), *n.* and *a.* Also **Luquesse**. Pl. same or **Lucchesi**. [a. It. *Lucchese*, f. LUCCA + *-ese* -ESE.] **A.** *n.* †**a.** A dialect of Italian once spoken in the city or (former) province of Lucca in north-west Tuscany. *Obs. exc. hist.* **b.** A native or inhabitant of Lucca.

1642 J. HOWELL *Instructions for Forreine Travell* xi. 138 These varieties of Dialects in France and Spaine, are farre less in number to those of Italy...There is in Italy..the Toscan, the Roman, the Venetian, the Neapolitan, the Calabrese, the Genovese, the Luquesse..and others. **1660** E. WARCUPP tr. *Schottus' Italy* I. 135 In 1303 the *Lucchesi* colleagued with the Florentines against the *Pistoiesi*. **1886** W. D. HOWELLS *Tuscan Cities* 230 He might as well be a Lucchese. **1912** J. SULLY *Italian Trav. Sketches* x. 237 The Torre..rebuilt by the Lucchesi...During this spell of comparative calm..the Lucchesi took down the tower. **1965** E. WHELPTON *Florence & Tuscany* ix. 112 The Lucchese got rid of the Pisans when Castruccio Castracane became the absolute ruler of their city.
    B. *adj.* Of or pertaining to Lucca or the Lucchese.
1883 *Encycl. Brit.* XV. 38/2 The most precious of the Lucchese relics, a cedar-wood crucifix, carved, according to the legend, by Nicodemus, and miraculously conveyed to Lucca in 782. **1884** A. J. C. HARE *Cities Central Italy* I. iii. 63 A member of a noble Lucchese family. **1905** *Westm. Gaz.* 5 Sept. 2/1 The

sheep grazing around us belonged, the shepherd told me, to the Lucchese village of Montefegatesi. **1936** G. F.-H. & J. BERKELEY *Italy in Making* II. xvi. 243 He made money out of the Lucchese finances. **1959** *Chambers's Encycl.* VII. 792/2 Pascoli . . borrowed many words from the dialect of the Lucchese peasants. *Ibid.* XV. 629/1 (Index) Lucchese dialect. **1970** E. R. JOHNSON *God Keepers* (1971) xiv. 146 The choice between public opinion pressure and Lucchese string-pulling pressure.

lucky, *a.* Add: [**4.**] **b.** With connotations of improbability: (esp. of a person) unexpectedly or exceptionally fortunate. Usu. as an ironic or resigned comment on an aim or hope unlikely to be fulfilled, as in phrs. *I'll (you'll,* etc.) *be lucky* and *vars.* (often foll. by *if* with finite verb or *to* with infinitive); *I (you,* etc.) *should be so lucky* (cf. SHALL *v.* B. II. 18 d).
   1762 T. STERNE *Tristram Shandy* VI. xviii. 44 When he gets these breeches made, . . he'll look like a beast in 'em . . . And 'twill be lucky if thats the worst on't, added my father. It will be very lucky, answered my mother. **1888** *Times* 6 Sept. 3/2 He will be lucky if he escapes with six months, 'sharpened' by one fast day a month. **1919** G. B. SHAW *Heartbreak House* Pref. p. xliv, When he [*sc.* a millionaire] has paid his income tax and super tax, and insured his life for the amount of his death duties, he is lucky if his net income is £10, 000. **1937** 'G. ORWELL' *Road to Wigan Pier* vi. 100 If he were, say, an Indian or Japanese coolie, . . he wouldn't get fifteen shillings a week—he would be lucky if he got fifteen shillings a month. **1955** J. MORRISON *Black Cargo* 14 It will need only one shout of 'Sniper!' and Lamond will be lucky to get out without being knocked down. **1958** P. LARKIN *Let.* 16 Dec. in A. Thwaite *Sel. Lett. Philip Larkin* (1992) 296 [I am] being hessled by the record makers, who want £50 down. They'll be lucky. **1973** E. SCHUMACHER *Small is Beautiful* III. iv. 195 What proportion of national income . . can one reasonably expect to be available for . . job creation? I would say . . you are lucky if you can make it five per cent. **1986** *More* (N.Z.) Feb. 48/1, I said, 'And I want back pay.' And they said, 'Ooh, you'll be lucky.' **1989** *Guardian* 22 Nov. II. 42/8 Some men are very vulnerable when it comes to sex. They go around joking with friends: 'I should be so lucky.'

lug, *n.*[7] [**b.**] For def. read: *concr.* A thing which is or needs to be lugged, *spec.* a box or crate used for shipping fruit. Orig. as *lug box. N. Amer.*
   1916 B. S. BROWN *Mod. Fruit Marketing* i. 15 If they do not care to take the regular packing box into the field, they supply what is known as the 'lug' box holding about 50 pounds each. **1921** *U.S. Dept. Agric. Farmers' Bull.* No. 1196. 29 The lug box is used very extensively in the West for wine grapes. These lugs are . . designed to hold from 20 to 40 pounds of grapes. **1929** *Ibid.* No. 1579. 6 California avocadoes are shipped in three different sizes of crates known as the lug, the half lug, and the flat. The lug . . holds about 2 dozen medium to large fruits. **1949** *Los Angeles Times* 2 July 5/4 It takes an hour for a lug of grapes to pass through the [precooling] tunnel. **1952** J. STEINBECK *East of Eden* xxi. 246 You can buy fruit . . for two bits a lug. **1977** *Daily Colonist* (Victoria, B.C.) 17 July 9/2 A crate of lettuce and two lugs of tomatoes. **1992** D. MORGAN *Rising in West* I. iii. 58 There was a café across the street and outside it a truck piled high with wooden lugs of grapes.

luge, *n.* Add: **b.** The sport involving such toboggans, in which each competing individual or pair completes in turn a timed descent of the course.
   1966 H. BASS *Winter Sports* i. 5 International Luge Federation. **1976** *All about Games* (Com. Org. des Jeux Olympiques) 27 The Winter Games program includes . . luge, skating and skiing. **1980** C. JAMES in *Observer* 24 Feb. I. 20/8 The luge is pretty tricky . . since

you have to lie on your back standing to attention with your head pointing up the hill while you are travelling very rapidly down it. **1986** R. FORD *Sportswriter* ii. 50 Body building, sky-diving, the luge. **1994** *Time Out* 16 Feb. 144/5 Day five sees the finals of the women's luge, the freestyle moguls skiing and the men's 1,500m speed-skating.

luggable ('lʌgəb(ə)l), *a.* (*n.*) [f. LUG *v.* + -ABLE.] That can be lugged; barely portable; used *esp.* to designate a computer which is designed to be portable but requires considerable effort. Freq. as *n.* Cf. PORTABLE *a.* and *n.*
   1978 *Washington Post* 8 June (Virginia Weekly) 3/1 Reinke had . . set on making a book . . She asked herself, 'How can I do it,' without a luggable printing press that she could take to the center? **1983** *Money* May 154 (*heading*) Get ready for the lovable luggables. **1985** *Your Computer* May 23/3 IBM is expected to release a true 'lap' portable, rather than a luggable one, later in the year. **1988** *Daily Tel.* 1 Feb. 21/3 But it is not a great bulky luggable of 35 pounds, and is relatively easy to move about, especially as it has a nylon carrying case. **1991** *U.S. News & World Rep.* 27 May 67/1 At the heavyweight end lies Toshiba's . . T3200SXC, a luggable laptop with a spectacular colour screen. **1994** *Spy* (N.Y.) Sept./Oct. 90/2 Owning a luggable is like owning one of those small foreign convertibles.

luggage, *n.* Add: [**1.**] **d.** *spec.* Bags, suitcases, etc., designed to hold the belongings of a traveller.
   1915 *Trunks, Leather Goods & Umbrellas* Jan. 60/1 The only assumption to make in having luggage in your store is that the man or woman who comes in to buy a bag is going to travel. **1919** *Travel* Aug. 1/2 (Advt.), Correct luggage. Wardrobe, dress and steamer trunks [etc.]. **1948** H. G. KATES *Luggage & Leather Goods Manuf.* 83 Because of the small size of the skins, calf is rarely used for luggage. **1969** *Sears Catal.* Spring/Summer 293 Introducing our new economical semi-molded luggage. **1990** N. BISSOONDATH *Smoke* in *On Eve of Uncertain Tomorrows* (1991) 109 Althea Wilson and a friend would be going to Hawaii. She was going to have . . a set of new luggage to put her new designer wardrobe into.

lumber ('lʌmbə(r)), *n.*[4] *slang* (chiefly *Sc.*). [f. *LUMBER *v.*[4]] **a.** Amorous or sexual play. **b.** A person regarded as a prospective sexual partner; a casual pick-up, a date.
   1966 P. WILLMOTT *Adolescent Boys E. London* iii. 49 They would often try to move on from kissing to sexual play; as they put it, they . . 'had a bit of lumber'. **1973** 'J. PATRICK' *Glasgow Gang Observed* v. 56, I was roundly abused . . for walking a girl home. 'Yir lumber's a cow,' they informed me. **1985** M. MUNRO *Patter* 43 We were at the jiggin last night; couldny get a lumber, but. **1987** *Sunday Times* 30 Aug. 21/5 She and her four companions—all from Scotland—end the evening in a disco where they wait for a lumber. **1992** I. BANKS *Crow Road* (1993) ix. 222 Lost track of you at the Urvills' party, Prentice . . . You just slope off, or did you get a lumber?

lumber ('lʌmbə(r)), *v.*[4] *slang* (chiefly *Sc.*). [Of uncertain origin.] **a.** *intr.* and *trans.* To engage in amorous or sexual play (with); sometimes, to copulate (with). **b.** *trans.* To court, to chat up; to pick up.
   1938 G. KERSH *Night & City* iv. 53 All right, . . I'm a ponce; they marry money. Zoë lumbers for a fiver; them women lumber for a million. **1960** *Punch* 9 Mar. 345/1 Many of us are chatting or lumbering (courting!). **1960** *News Chron.* 5 Mar. 5/1 When we talked about 'lumbering' they thought we meant making love . . It means chatting, going steady. **1966** J. GASKELL *All Neat in Black Stockings* (1968) 96 The girl with fish-net stockings Tom brought back with him from Jersey and was still lumbering. **1981** A. GRAY

Lanark (1982) xvii. 173 'Last Friday I saw her being lumbered by a hardman up a close near the Denistoun Palais.' 'Lumbered?' 'Groped. Felt.' **1985** M. MUNRO *Patter* 43 Ma pal got lumbered by your big brother. **1991** J. KELMAN *Burn* (1992) 220 Derek slept with this woman a coupla years ago... He lumbered her from a pub up in London.

luminance, *n.* Restrict *Physics* to sense 2 a in Dict. and add: [**2.**] **b.** *Television.* The component of a television signal which carries information on the brightness of the image. Also *luminance signal.* Cf. CHROMINANCE *n.*

1953 *Electronics* Dec. 139/3 The term 'chrominance' refers to two signals which carry color information. These signals, when added to the luminance signal, provide the hue and saturation components of the color image. **1957** V. J. KEHOE *Technique Film & Television Make-up* viii. 95 As to.. the reception of a color telecast on a monochromatic receiver, only the luminance portion will be supplied to the single electron gun in the monochrome tube to produce a black-and-white version of the signal. **1973** *Sci. Amer.* May 118/2 Here there is an analogy with color television, in which the luminance—the three-color sum—is transmitted separately, along with two color-difference signals, rather than three color signals directly. **1983** E. TRUNDLE *Beginner's Guide Videocassette Recorders* ii. 21 If we regard the FM luminance spectrum as extending from 1 MHz to 6 MHz, it is now occupying less than three octaves. **1990** *OnSat* 29 July-4 Aug. 8/2 The luminance signal is markedly increased (from a low of 3.4 MHz to a high range of 5.4 to 7.0 MHz) and separated from the chrominance signal (color) through special Y/C input and output connectors.

luminescence, *n.* Add: **2.** Light, or a glow, emitted by a luminescent (cool) object or surface.

1908 *Westm. Gaz.* 13 Mar. 2/1 It is generally agreed that the auroral rays are a luminescence caused by the absorption of kathode rays in the atmosphere. **1955** *Sci. News Let.* 29 Oct. 288/3 The intensity of the luminescence that some rocks give off when heated is an indication of their geologic age. **1979** D. ATTENBOROUGH *Life on Earth* (1981) i. 32 At night they are particularly spectacular for they glow with a bright purple luminescence and if you touch them, ghostly waves of light pulsate along their slowly writhing arms. **1985** *Observer* 28 Apr. 9/6 This is just the luminescence on the belly of an old mackerel.

luminosity, *n.* Add: [**1.**] **d.** *Particle Physics.* A parameter of a colliding-beam accelerator, equal to the ratio of the rate of interactions to the reaction cross-section, and proportional to the product of the rates of arrival of particles in the two beams divided by the cross-sectional area of the intersecting region.

1964 F. AMMAN et al. in *Proc. Internat. Conf. High Energy Accelerators 1963* 250/2 The interaction rate per beam crossing region, $\dot{n}$ for an event whose cross section is σ.. is given by: $\dot{n} = .. = L\sigma$ (events/sec)..; the quantity L, measured in $cm^{-2}.s^{-1}$ or $cm^{-2}.h^{-1}$, includes all the ring parameters and is called luminosity. **1976** *Physics Bull.* Apr. 159/2 In general, colliding beam devices suffer in comparison with accelerators and conventional solid targets from a relatively low beam-beam interaction rate (or 'luminosity') at the intersection. **1980** *Nature* 7 Feb. 515/2 As the luminosity of storage rings increases rapidly with energy, it is hoped to raise the present 50 per day event rate by a factor of ten. **1985** *Sci. Amer.* June 64/2 The luminosity of each beam of the SSC is to be 10^{33} per second per square centimeter.

Lunda ('lʌndə), *n.* and *a.* Pl. **Balonda, Balunda, Lunda,** and with **-s.** [Bantu.

Forms with the *Ba-* plural class prefix are applied only to the people.]

A. *n.* **1.** A member of a people inhabiting areas of eastern Angola, south-eastern Zaire, and northern Zambia.

1857 D. LIVINGSTONE *Missionary Trav. & Res. S. Afr.* xv. 268 Two of the people called Balunda, or Balónda, came to see us in their little canoe. *Ibid.* 277 She thought that he would visit the Balonda more frequently afterwards, having the good excuse of going to see his wife. **1861** F. T. VALDEZ *Six Yrs. of Traveller's Life in W. Afr.* II. v. 148 The Jaga.. prevented the Lundas, or Cazembe people, from communicating with the Portuguese merchants. **1908** H. H. JOHNSTON *George Grenfell & Congo* I. xi. 194 Round him [*sc.* a person of Hima descent] a community would group itself... Thus.. the kingdoms.. of the Luba, Lunda, and other Bantu countries came into existence. **1936** *Discovery* June 172/1 The area of the Western Bantu.. includes the territory of considerable and highly organised kingdoms, such as the medieval kingdoms of the Kongo and the Balunda, and the later Bushongo Empire. **1960** I. CUNNISON tr. *Gamitto's King Kazembe* II. ii. 116 The pure descendants of the conquered chief are called Shila, and they live.. quite isolated, and without any intercourse with the Lunda. **1989** *Encycl. Brit. Micropædia* VII. 560/3 Most Lunda live in savanna country intersected by belts of forest along the river.

2. The Bantu language of this people.

1883 R. N. CUST *Sketch Mod. Lang. Afr.* II. xii. 399 *Lúnda*,.. is the central language of Africa South of the Equator, and is mentioned by travellers both from the East and West Coast. **1897** A. J. BUTLER tr. *Ratzel's Hist. Mankind* II. 404 Here, Lunda will be spoken; there, pehaps only half a mile away, Kioko. **1945** C. M. DOKE *Bantu* 106 *Lunda*,.. this is known as Ndembo or Lunda of Kalunda, and must be distinguished from Luunda of the Central zone. It is spoken to the southwest of the Luba region, on the eastern side of the Upper Kasai, mostly in Belgian Congo, but reaching into Angola and into Northern Rhodesia at the headwaters of the Kabompo River. **1977** C. F. & F. M. VOEGELIN *Classification & Index World's Lang.* 59 Zone L is subdivided into Kaonde.. Luba.. Lunda.. Nkoya .. Pende .. Songe. Altogether 3,500,000 speakers. Zaire, Zambia, extending into Angola.

B. *attrib.* passing into *adj.* Of or pertaining to this people or their language.

1911 *Encycl. Brit.* III. 362/2 There is a treatise on the Lunda language of the south-western part of the Belgian Congo, in Portuguese, by Henrique de Carvalho. **1930** C. G. SELIGMAN *Races of Afr.* xiii. 13 The Lunda Empire traditionally originates in a Baluba hunter from the north-east, who with a band of followers settled among the far more numerous Balunda whose home is the highlands constituting eastern Angola and the south-west portion of the Congo. **1957** V. W. TURNER *Schism & Continuity in Afr. Society* i. 2 Kanongecha's migration occurred at about the same time as the migrations of other Lunda leaders. **1973** G. M. D. HOWAT *Dict. World Hist.* 905/2 This Luba-Lunda political and economic system.. began to crumble in the mid-19th cent. when the pattern of trade was radically altered by the sudden growth of the ivory trade, which the Lunda were ill-equipped to master. **1989** *Encycl. Brit. Micropædia* VII. 561/2 Guerrilla warfare against the Congo Free State continued until 1909, when the Lunda leaders were captured and executed.

lunge, *n.²* Add: **3.** An exercise or gymnastic movement involving a sudden forward or sideways movement, *spec.* one in which one leg is thrust forward with the knee bent while the other is stretched-out behind the body.

1889 G. L. MÉLIO *Man. Swedish Drill* 24 In the Large Steps, or Lunges, as shewn in Diagrams 20-21, the foot is placed from 30 to 40 inches, according to the length of limb. *Ibid.* 73 (*in figure*) Pass, or outward lunge pos[ition]. **1910** *Health & Strength* 12 Mar. 268/2 The Lunge... The pupil takes a fairly long step forward, and simultaneously extends the arm that covers the leg which is put forward. **1957** T. BURNS *Tumbling Techniques Illustr.* 94 *Lunge*, an abrupt and forceful forward reach, as for a tuck during a forward somersault. **1963** E. HUGHES *Gymnastics for Girls* iii. 55 In the lunge, most of the body weight is on the right leg, which is directly in front of the body. **1971** C. ATWATER *Tap Dancing* ii. 40 You must learn to hold a Lunge while maintaining proper posture. **1981** J. FONDA *Jane Fonda's Workout Bk.* (1982) 148 Bring your right foot forward in a 'lunge' with your left leg stretched out behind you. **1988** *Flex* Dec. 104/2 Step ups is a variation of a lunge movement but when I do lunges in the conventional way I just don't seem to feel it as much in the muscle tissue.

lunge, *v.*[1] Add: **4.** In callisthenic exercises, to make a sudden forward or sideways movement, *spec.* in which one leg is thrust forward with the knee bent while the other is stretched out behind the body.
  1905 G. A. McMILLAN *Swedish Recreative Exercises* I. xxvi. 57 At 'hither', all lunge to the left, and recover, and at 'thither', all lunge to the right. **1917** L. CLARK *Physical Training for Elementary Schools* 269 Hands on hips—place! To the right—lunge! Foot—replace! **1971** N. A. KOUNOVSKY *Joy of Feeling Fit* 106 From a standing position, lunge forward with your right leg... Inhale as you lunge. **1981** J. FONDA *Jane Fonda's Workout Bk.* (1982) 165 Now lunge lower.

Lung-shan (ˌlʊŋˈʃɑːn), *n. Archaeol.* Also (Pinyin) **Longshan, Lung Shan, Lungshan.** [The name of a town in the Shandong province of eastern China.] Used *attrib.* and *absol.* to designate a Neolithic Chinese culture of *c* 3000–2500 B.C., and its artefacts (*spec.* a fine, burnished black pottery), evidence of which was first unearthed at Lung-shan in 1928.
  1938 G. D. WU *Prehistoric Pottery in China* iii. 59 The Ch'êng-tzŭ Yai site was discovered by myself in 1928... As this site is just opposite the town of Lungshan, it is often called the Lung-shan site, and the Black Pottery culture, the Lung-shan culture. **1948** A. L. KROEBER *Anthropol.* (rev. ed.) xvii. 735 The Black Pottery or Lung-shan culture, also called Ch'eng-tzu-yai, though perhaps overlapping with the Painted Pottery culture in time, is at least mainly later. **1961** W. WATSON *China before Han Dynasty* i. 50 The crescent knife is characteristic of Lung Shan culture. **1961** G. CLARK *World Prehist.* vii. 197 Technically the fine black Lung-shan ware was more advanced than the others because it was made on the potter's wheel. **1972** *Trans. Oriental Ceramics Soc.* 14 Rough bucket-shaped vases of grey clay were also made, and these.. mark a phase preceding the classical Lungshan. *Ibid.* 16 The fine black ware of Lungshan. **1987** *Amer. Anthropologist* LXXXIX. 811 Other developments seen by the time of the final Neolithic period, the Longshan, include permanent rulers, status differentiation, and craft specialization. **1989** J. P. MALLORY *In Search of Indo-Europeans* ii. 61 The archaeological evidence for the Tarim Basin becomes exceedingly dim until the Neolithic (4000–2000 BC), when we find evidence for the monochrome wares of the Longshan horizon.
  Hence **ˈLungshanoid** *a.*
  1963 K.-C. CHANG *Archaeol. Anc. China* iv. 89 A sufficient number of stratified sites have been found to show that the Lungshanoid assemblages invariably lie above the Yangshao remains. **1983** R. D. WHITEHOUSE *Macmillan Dict. Archaeol.* 291 The term lungshanoid embodies the assumptions of the nuclear theory and should probably be avoided.

lusophone (ˈluːsəfəʊn), *a.* Also **Lusophone.** [f. LUSO- + -PHONE.] Portuguese-speaking.
  1974 *Times* 2 Mar. 15/2 The idea of a 'Brazilian solution' for Portuguese Africa.. postulates multi-racial and lusophone, virtually sovereign governments

in Africa which would however cooperate with Portugal voluntarily. **1981** *Times Lit. Suppl.* 30 Jan. 102/2 It is only the dearth of good literature that has relegated the Lusophone countries to a back room. **1991** K. MAGUIRE *Pol. in S. Afr.* iii. 46 The fall of the Portuguese Lusophone countries led to an escalation of the guerrilla resistance. **1993** *Guardian* 12 May 11. 24/1 (Advt.), You should have at least 3 years' experience in development and relief work overseas, preferably in Lusophone Africa.

lutchet (ˈlʌtʃɪt), *n. Naut.* [Of uncertain origin, perh. f. LUTCH *v.* or an alteration of LATCHET *n.*] A fitting on the deck of a sailing vessel (esp. a barge or wherry) to which the foot of the mast is pivoted so that it may be lowered when passing under a bridge, etc. Cf. TABERNACLE *n.* 7. Now chiefly *dial.* (*Yorks.*).
  1825 *Proc. Comm. House of Commons on Liverpool & Manchester Railroad* 223, I want to know whether you have made inquiries as to the height of the lutchet of the vessel..? *Ibid.,* Do you not know when a vessel is loaded with cotton goods it is piled up some feet higher than the lutchet. **1948** R. DE KERCHOVE *Internat. Maritime Dict.* 438/2 *Lutchet*, a boxlike structure similar to a tabernacle, in which the mast heel does not go below deck. **1977** *Grimsby Even. Tel.* 14 May 2/5 (Advt.), Flag pole, 70ft., excellent condition, ground anchors, lutchet fittings and 2ft, turned apex. **1984** *Trans. Yorks. Dial. Soc.* LXXXIV. 14 Below deck the lutchet was solid and tapered down to the bottom of the boat, but above deck one of the four sides of the lutchet was open so that the 40-45ft mast could be raised or lowered.

lute, *n.*[1] Add: [**2.**] **lute harpsichord** = *LAUTENCLAVICYMBEL *n.*
  1884 BELL & FULLER-MAITLAND tr. *Spitta's J. S. Bach* II. iv. ii. 46 In the year 1740 (or thereabout) he devised a 'Lauten-clavicymbel' (*Lute-harpsichord). **1959** *Collins Mus. Encycl.* 382/1 *Lautenclavicymbel*, lute-harpsichord.. harpsichord with gut strings instead of metal strings. The instrument existed in the sixteenth century, and Bach had one made in 1740. **1989** E. M. RIPIN et al. *Early Keyboard Instr.* IV. vii. German makers in the first half of the 18th century seem to have been those most interested in the potentials of the lute-harpsichord and a number of different types were produced.

Lutetian, *a.* Add: **2.** *Geol.* [ad. F. *lutétien* (coined in A. de Lapparent *Traité de Géol.* (1883) II. 989).] Of, pertaining to, or designating the stage of the Eocene in western Europe which was followed by the Ypresian. Also *absol.,* the Lutetian stage or period.
  1895 J. D. DANA *Man. Geol.* (ed. 4) IV. 925 The *Calcaire grossier* of Paris (*Lutetian* of Lapparent). **1903** A. GEIKIE *Text-bk. Geol.* (ed. 4) II. 1236 Middle Eocene.—This division is so fully developed in the Paris basin that the name of Lutetian (from Lutetia, the old appellation of Paris) has been given to it. *Ibid.* 1237 The Lutetian stage of the Paris basin is regarded as the probable equivalent of the Lower Bagshot sands and the clays of Bracklesham and Bournemouth in the English Tertiary series. **1911** *Q. Jrnl. Geol. Soc.* LXVII. 649 The Lutetian formation and its fauna are so well known in North African countries, that it is needless to go into particulars respecting their history. **1921** *Brit. Mus. Return* 149 in *Parl. Papers 1921* XXVII. 495 A shell of *Fusus serratus* from the Lutetian (middle Eocene) of Seine-et-Oise. **1967** D. H. RAYNER *Stratigr. Brit. Isles* xi. 349 Sometimes the Lutetian has been termed Middle Eocene and the stages above and below, Upper and Lower Eocene. **1977** A. HALLAM *Planet Earth* 227 The most commonly accepted stages include (from oldest to youngest) the Ypresian, Lutetian and Bartonian. **1991** R. GOLDRING *Fossils in Field* viii. 156 (*caption*) The Middle Eocene, Lutetian and Bartonian, showing zonal schemes for various groups of fossils.

lutino (luːˈtiːnəʊ), *a.* and *n. Ornith.* Also **Lutino.**
[f. L. *lūt-eus* yellow + *-ino*, after ALBINO *n.*] **A.**
adj. Of a bird: having plumage that is yellower
than is usual for the species.
   1919 C. P. ARTHUR *Budgerigars & Cockateels* 9 The
father of my Lutino Budgerigars, pure yellow with pink
eyes, which I bred in 1887, never had any long flight
feathers for years. **1952** L. P. LUKE *Lovebirds &
Parrotlets* xvi. 83 At least two British breeders have
produced lutino Nyasas [*sc.* Nyasaland lovebirds].
1976 *Cumberland News* 3 Dec. 16/5 Best novice and
best adult was a lutino cock, benched by J. K. Ivor,
Longtown. **1986** *Los Angeles Times* 2 Sept. II. 5/1 The
Avian Husbandry Program, in which children select a
Lutino Cockatiel chick at birth and hand-feed and care
for it until it is ready to be taken home.
   B. *n.* A lutino bird (usu. a cage bird of the
parrot family).
   1935 N. W. CAYLEY *Budgerigars in Bush & Aviary*
115 There has been no recorded occurrence of Albinos
or Lutinos in Australia. **1945** *All Pets Mag.* Oct. 17/3
When the Lutino or Albino is used, it must be
remembered that these are genetically Green or Yellow
and Blue or White birds respectively. **1983** R. M.
MARTIN *Encycl. Aviculture* 122 The production of
unmarked (Clear) Lutinos is furthered by the use of
Dark Greens as outcrosses.

Lutyens (ˈlʌtʃənz), *n.* [The name of Sir Edwin
Landseer *Lutyens* (1869-1944), English
architect.] Used *attrib.* to denote (features of)
buildings designed by Lutyens, or those in a
similar neoclassical style.
   1921 L. WEAVER (*title*) Lutyens houses and
gardens. **1944** *Connoisseur* CXIII. 60/1 He.. built an
entirely new wing in brick with transomed windows,
panelled interior and a very promising classic corridor,
in fact the Lutyens detail fully developed. **1945** *Jrnl.
R. Inst. Brit. Architects* LII. 127/1 Living in a Lutyens
house may have its disadvantages, the offices are
sometimes queer, you can't always see out of the
windows, and there is an awful lot to dust and keep
clean. **1974** *Times* 20 May 14/5 The 1930s red brick
Lutyens building on Massachusetts Avenue. **1975** P.
SOMERVILLE-LARGE *Couch of Earth* iii. 43 The embassy
buildings, part functional modern, part Simla official,
part Lutyens domestic. **1988** M. STEWART-WILSON
Queen Mary's Dolls' House i. 16/2 The house has not
been lent out to a public exhibition since 1925, but
remains where it was designed to stand, the only
completely untouched Lutyens house in existence.
1992 *Accountancy* Nov. 37/2 The clubhouse, built in
the Lutyens style, includes two bars, a restaurant, and
a club room with snooker table.
   So **Lutyens′esque** *a.*
   1961 B. W. ALDISS *Primal Urge* in *Brian Aldiss
Omnibus* (1969) ii. 33 He could recall the look of the
house now; it crouched between two Lutyensesque
chimneys. **1982** *Financial Times* 22 June 15/7 Now
the British Pavillon is the most delightful of them all,
a Lutyensesque treat commanding the highest point
and principal vista of the gardens. **1994** *Independent
on Sunday* (Sunday Rev. Suppl.) 49/1 The house was
built in 1598, with creeper-covered stone walls, a broad
Lutyens-esque tiled porch over the door into the garden
[etc.].

luvvy (ˈlʌvɪ), *n. Brit. colloq.* Also **luvvie.**
[Respelling of LOVEY *n.*: see LUV *n.*] **a.** As a
term of address: = LOVEY *n.*
   1968 M. ALLWRIGHT *Roundabout* ix. 60 Albert, luvvy,
I didn't hate you. **1989** *Guardian* 11 Aug. 5/6 'Come
on, luvvy,' entices Sue, tugging as an excited crowd
creaks from its deckchairs. **1991** M. KILBY *Man at
Sharp End* xxi. 262 'Well, don't try too hard, luvvie, or
you'll burst a blood vessel,' she called above the noise
of the open tap.
   b. An actor or actress, *esp.* one who is
considered particularly effusive or affected;
hence, anyone actively involved with

entertainment or the arts. *joc.* and mildly *derog.*
   1990 *Guardian* 19 May (Weekend Suppl.) 21/3 The
43rd Cannes International Festival of Cinema...It's a
rough deal for the poor luvvies being paid to watch
movies and party. *Ibid.* 29 Sept. (Weekend Suppl.)
18/4 Perfectly at home in the glittering world of
'darlings' and 'luvvies'.. [they] can usually turn their
skills to any branch of showbiz. **1992** *Daily Tel.* 24
Mar. 16/4 Actors are always saying that the stage is the
loneliest place in the world and I'd always thought it
was hyperbolic luvvy talk. **1992** *Face* Sept. 16/2 Jane
Horrocks is not your usual 'luvvie dahling' type at
all. **1993** *Radio Times* 28 Aug. 98/3 I'm a fairly regular
theatre-goer...But I try not to surround myself with
actors or get sucked into the 'luvvy' scene.

‖**lwei** (ləˈweɪ), *n.* [Native name.] A monetary
unit of Angola, equal to one-hundredth of a
kwanza.
   1977 *Whitaker's Almanack 1978* 982 Angola..
[Monetary Unit] Kwanza of 100 Lweis. **1985**
Statesman's Year-Bk. 1985-86 80 Coins are of 50 *lwei*,
1 2, 5 and 10 *kwanza.* **1987** *Guardian Weekly* 4 Oct.
11/2 The monetary unit in use is no longer the highly
devalued official kwanza (100 lwei to the kwanza), but
a pack of 24 beers with which anything.. can be
bought. **1990** in *Summary World Broadcasts: Middle
East, Africa, Latin Amer.* (B.B.C.) 2 Oct. A2/1 The lwei
will be in the form of metal coins with denomination
value of 50 lwei.

lygaeid (laɪˈdʒiːɪd), *n.* and *a. Ent.* Also **Lygaeid.**
[f. mod.L. *Lygaeidae*, f. mod.L. *Lygaeus* (coined
in J. C. Fabricius *Entomologia Systematica*
(1794) IV. 133), ad. Gr. λυγαῖος shadowy, gloomy:
see -ID³.] **A.** *n.* An insect of the family Lygaeidae
of dark or brightly coloured mainly plant-
feeding bugs (heteropterans), some of which
(e.g. the chinch bug) are agricultural pests.
   1893 in *Funk's Stand. Dict.* **1902** L. O. HOWARD
Insect Bk. 310 The Lygæids are distinguished from
other bugs chiefly by the membrane of the front wing,
which has four or five simple veins, and by the antennæ,
which are inserted low down on the side of the
head. **1962** C. L. METCALF et al. *Destructive & Useful
Insects* (ed. 4) vi. 226 The Lygaeids are of moderate
size, ranging from about ⅛ to ⅜ inch long. **1981** D. J.
BORROR et al. *Introd. Study Insects* (ed. 5) xxii. 295/2
The big-eyed bugs.. are unusual among the lygaeids
in being at least partly predaceous.
   B. *adj.* Of, pertaining to, or designating the
family Lygaeidae.
   1893 in *Funk's Stand. Dict.* **1919** W. L. DISTANT in
Bull. Entomol. Res. X. 41 (*title*) A new Lygaeid bug
found among stored rice in Java. **1994** GULLAN &
CRANSTON *Insects* xiii. 361/2 Cardenolides are very
widespread, occurring notably in.. lygaeid bugs,
pyrgomorphid grasshoppers and even an aphid.

Lygus (ˈlaɪgəs), *n. Ent.* [mod.L. *Lygus* (coined
in Ger. in C. W. Hahn *Wanzenartigen Insecten*
(1831) I. 28), ad. Gr. λύγος chaste-tree, withy.]
A genus of plant-sucking heteropteran insects
(family Miridae or Lygaeidae), some of which
carry plant disease viruses; (also **lygus**) an insect
of this genus; also *lygus bug.*
   1926 W. S. BLATCHLEY *Heteroptera* 783 In addition
to the eastern species of *Lygus* above treated, there is
one described by Reuter which is at present
unknown. **1933** *Jrnl. Econ. Entomol.* XXVI. 1076
There appears to be some confusion as to the scientific
and common names which shall be applied to certain
of our western *Lygus.* **1936** *Ibid.* XXIX. 457 The
alfalfa.. was heavily infested with *Lygus* bugs. **1948**
Nature 6 Mar. 340/2 It is.. estimated that if the lygus
pest in Uganda were controlled, [cotton] output would
be increased by 50 per cent. **1959** SOUTHWOOD &
LESTON *Land & Water Bugs Brit. Isles* x. 272 Many
Lygus bugs are important crop pests in Europe and
U.S.A. **1974** E. C. STACEY *Peace Country Heritage* ii.

86 Pankiw begs the growers [of alfalfa] to check their fields for lygus, a tiny insect which sucks at the base of the flower and thus..greatly reduces seed set. **1991** *New Scientist* 2 Mar. 47/1 One of the main pests in cotton, the bollworm, could be kept in check by common mites. But California's farmers were wiping out these mites at the same time as they were ridding their fields of another pest, the lygus bug.

Lyme ('laɪm), *n. Path.* [The name of the town of *Lyme*, Connecticut, where an outbreak of the disease occurred in 1975.] Used *attrib.* (esp. in *Lyme arthritis* or *disease*) and *absol.* to designate an infectious disease caused by the spriochaete *Borrelia burgdorferi* and transmitted by tick bites, with clinical manifestations including an initial erythematous rash, arthritis, and often neurological and cardiac abnormalities.

[**1976** *Jrnl. Amer. Med. Assoc.* 19 July 241 A possible new form of arthritis has been found in a cluster of 51 patients. The people known to be involved so far are from three contiguous communities (Lyme, Old Lyme, and east Haddam).] **1976** *Valley Town Crier* (McAllen, Texas) 20 Oct. 5/2 The disease, called Lyme arthritis is marked by recurrent attacks of joint pain sometimes preceded by unusual rash. **1979** *Medicine* LVIII. 281 Lyme disease (erythema chronicum migrans, tick borne meningopolyneuritis, myocardial conduction abnormalities, and Lyme arthritis). **1985** P. A. DIEPPE et al. *Rheumatol. Med.* x. 204/1 Lyme arthritis will..be described as an example of a persistent arthritis resulting from a chronic spirochaete infection. **1986** *Daily Tel.* 8 Sept. 3/2 In spite of the fact that many people are bitten annually by ticks in the New Forest it is extremely rare for any of them to develop Lyme disease. **1990** *N.Y. Times* 3 July C9/1 Federal and state health officials are making Lyme a nationally reportable disease, effective next year.

Lymeswold ('laɪmzwəʊld), *n.* [Invented name (see quot. 1982² b), perh. an alteration of *Wymeswold*, the name of a town in Leicestershire.] A proprietary name for an English blue cheese, soft in texture and mild-tasting, introduced in 1982.

The cheese was withdrawn from sale in 1992.

1981 *Times* 19 Oct. 3/8 Lymeswold has the distinction of being the first English cheese to carry an invented name. **1982** *Daily Tel.* 28 Sept. 6/3 The first new English cheese for 200 years was launched yesterday with the blessing of Mr Walker, Agriculture Minister. Lymeswold is the first soft blue cheese to be produced commercially in Britain. **1982** *Ibid.* 12 Oct. 16/5 We looked for a word that was evocative of all that is familiar in the English countryside. Moreover, we found that, once heard, 'Lymeswold' is rarely forgotten. **1984** *Out of Town* Feb. 8/3 Evoking our rural past, most of our recently introduced cheeses have come out under English countrified names: Lymeswold.., Tendale.., and Melbury. **1988** *Guardian Weekly* 4 Sept. 24/2 While never personally threatening (the man is as mild as Lymeswold) his confrontations with authority and plain folk going about their business are..entirely unpredictable and demand reaction. **1992** *Economist* 2 May 103/1 On April 27th Lymeswold was ignominiously withdrawn from the market. The French must be cackling over their Camembert.

lymphadenectomy (ˌlɪmfædə'nɛktəmɪ), *n. Surg.* [f. LYMPH *n.* + ADEN- + -ECTOMY.] Surgical removal of lymph nodes; an instance of this.

1934 *Amer. Jrnl. Obstetr. & Gynecol.* XXVIII. 665 On Nov. 22, 1932, typical lymphadenectomy was performed. **1948** *Southern Med. Jrnl.* XLI. 896/1 The operative procedure was not the 'Wertheim operation.' It was the radical panhysterectomy with the added procedure of radical pelvic lymphadenectomy. **1961** *Lancet* 30 Sept. 761/2 It seemed logical..that the same dose of radiation which might be incapable of destroying cancer cells in glands on the lateral pelvic wall might be adequate to deal with isolated cells in the operative field after lymphadenectomy. **1989** *Brit. Med. Jrnl.* 4 Feb. 288/2 Radical hysterectomy with pelvic lymphadenectomy was the preferred treatment for stage Ib and IIa disease.

lymphangiosarcoma (lɪmˌfændʒɪəʊsɑː'kəʊmə), *n. Path.* [f. LYMPH *n.* + ANGIO- + SARCOMA *n.*] A sarcoma of the lymphatic vessels.

1900 DORLAND *Med. Dict.* 368/2 *Lymphangiosarcoma*, lymphangioma blended with sarcoma. **1901** *Boston Med. & Surg. Jrnl.* CXLIV. 280/1 Diagnosis: Lymphangiosarcoma, or perhaps better, lymphangio-endothelioma. **1962** SCHIRGER & HARRISON in D. I. Abramson *Blood Vessels & Lymphatics* xxiv. 745 A rare primary lymphangiosarcoma may arise in chronic lymphedema of various types. **1984** TIGHE & DAVIES *Pathology* (ed. 4) xiii. 117 Lymphangiosarcomas are found following chronic lymphatic obstruction.

lympho-, *comb. form.* Add: ˌlymphopro'liferative *a. Path.*, (of a disease or syndrome) tending to increase the rate of production and the quantity of lymphoid tissue (often with the implication of malignancy).

1964 *Lancet* 17 Oct. 843/2 Cultured peripheral blood lymphocytes from patients with sarcoidosis and *lymphoproliferative diseases behaved differently from those of normals. **1978** *Nature* 4 May 16/2 It is a matter of conjecture whether lymphocytes from special tissues or from subjects with lymphoproliferative disorders may have a surface morphology which is reflected in these *in vitro* changes. **1991** *Biotech Forum Europe* Sept. 517/2 Enzootic bovine leukosis, a chronic lymphoproliferative disease characterized by persistent lymphocytosis.

lymphocytotoxic (ˌlɪmfəʊsaɪtəʊ'tɒksɪk), *a. Med.* [f. *LYMPHOCYTOTOX(IN *n.* + -IC¹.] Toxic towards lymphocytes; pertaining to lymphocytotoxicity or its investigation.

1965 *Transplantation* III. 400 An understanding of the 'complement' activity of rabbit serum in the human lymphocytotoxic system will require separate and intensive study. **1966** *Vox Sanguinis* XI. 269 The association of the two methods, leucocyte agglutination in a sequestrene medium and the lymphocytotoxic technique, enabled Dausset and Ivanyi..to demonstrate 10 leucocyte antigens. **1977** *Lancet* 14 May 1063/2 Patients on chronic hæmodialysis may have in their serum lymphocytotoxic antibodies which react with their own lymphocytes. **1980** *Brit. Med. Jrnl.* 29 Mar. p.vi (Advt.), Lymphocytotoxic antibodies in systemic lupus erythematosus.

So ˌlymphocytoto'xicity *n.*, the property of being lymphocytotoxic; freq. *attrib.*, with reference to a method for establishing compatibility in organ and bone marrow transplantation by comparing the reactions of cells to various lymphocytotoxins.

1965 *Transplantation* III. 389 Titration of the lymphocytotoxicity of post-graft or post-injection serum. **1967** *Histocompatibility Testing* III. 357 (*heading*) Anticomplementary factors affecting the lymphocytotoxicity test. **1972** *Science* 20 Oct. 304/2 Two-way lymphocytotoxicity cross matches are routinely performed between leukemia patients and their parents and sibs. **1989** *Nature* 19 Jan. 220/3 Walford and colleagues discovered that rabbit complement allowed Gorer's lymphocytotoxicity test to be used with human reagents, thus providing a reliable test.

lymphocytotoxin (ˌlɪmfəʊsaɪtəʊ'tɒksɪn), *n. Med.* [f. LYMPHOCYTE *n.* + -O¹ + TOXIN *n.*] A lymphocytotoxic substance.

1904 GOULD *Dict. New Med. Terms* 345/2 *Lymphocytotoxin*,..a bacterial product having specific action on the lymphocytes. **1970** MOTTIRONI & TERASAKI in P. I. Terasaki *Histocompatibility Testing 1970* 301 (*heading*) Lymphocytotoxins in disease. **1970** *New Eng. Jrnl. Med.* 1 Oct. 724/1 The possible pathogenic importance of lymphocytotoxins becomes more interesting with the extension to systemic lupus erythematosus (SLE) and the finding that the antibodies were autocytotoxic as reported here. **1987** *Tissue Antigens* XXIX. 232 There were no significant differences between either pre-eclampsia group and controls in HLA antigen homozygosity, HLA antigen sharing or in lymphocytotoxin production.

lymphoreticular (ˌlɪmfəʊrɪˈtɪkjʊlə(r)) *a. Med.* [f. LYMPHO- + RETICULAR *a.*] = RETICULOENDO-THELIAL *a.*; (see also quots. 1942, 1958).

 1942 HADFIELD & GARROD *Recent Adv. Path.* (ed. 4) iv. 37 If the fixed and stable connective tissues such as..bone, cartilage and muscle be excluded, the remaining mesenchyme of the adult is composed of a cellular highly reactive tissue rich in fertile cells such as that found in the hæmopoietic marrow and spleen. In each of these situations the basic structure is a loose reticulum of cells richly supplied with capillary sinusoids. This tissue may, as was suggested by Maximow, be called the reticular or lympho-reticular system. Aschoff's reticulo-endothelial system of phagocytic cells thus forms only a part of Maximow's reticular system. **1958** W. ST. C. SYMMERS in R. W. Raven *Cancer* II. xxiv. 448 The lymphoid tissue and the so-called reticuloendothelial system are so intimately associated, anatomically, functionally, and in disease, that it is appropriate to consider them together as the lymphoreticular system (LRS). **1968** PASSMORE & ROBSON *Compan. Med. Stud.* I. xxvii. 2/2 The organs of the lymphoreticular system consist of the lymph nodes, spleen and bone marrow. **1970** WALTER & ISRAEL *Gen. Path.* (ed. 3) xxx. 649 Reticulo-endothelial organs..are also sometimes described as the lymphoreticular tissues because of their reticulin framework and the predominance of lymphocytes. **1974** R. M. KIRK et al. *Surgery* ii. 31 Reticuloses... The name signifies proliferation of the lymphoid and lymphoreticular tissue. **1984** J. F. LAMB et al. *Essent. Physiol.* (ed. 2) iv. 76 The fixed scavenger cells are found in a system of lymphoreticular organs which consist of thin-walled supporting tubes with the phagocyte cells in their walls.

lyonization (ˌlaɪənaɪˈzeɪʃən), *n. Genetics.* Also **Lyonization.** [f. the name of Mary Frances *Lyon* (b. 1925), English biologist, who proposed the idea (*Nature* (1961) 22 Apr. 372/1).] A process occurring in the very early stages of development of female mammalian embryos, in which one of the two X chromosomes is randomly inactivated in each of the existing cells.

 1963 *Lancet* 12 Oct. 769/1 Mary Lyon proposed her hypothesis..in 1961... A colloquium on chromosome anomalies and D.N.A., held in Oporto on Sept. 12–14, devoted a good part of its time to this subject... This 'Lyonisation' (a convenient word invented at the colloquium) occurs in man presumably about the 12th day. **1977** *Lancet* 13 Aug. 339/2 This first occurs early in the growth of the female embryo, when a random decision on which chromosome to inactivate is apparently taken by each of the small number of cells then present, setting a precedent which is thereafter faithfully followed in each cell line, a process known as lyonisation. **1987** C. A. CLARKE *Human Genetics & Med.* (ed. 3) viii. 59 Lyonization..explains why 15% of carrier females of the haemophilia gene have a normal concentration of factor VIII.

lyrical, *a.* Add: **3.** Excitedly effusive; highly enthusiastic, fervent. Freq. in phr. *to wax lyrical. colloq.* (orig. *U. S.*).

 1875 H. JAMES *Roderick Hudson* iv. in *Atlantic Monthly* XXXV. 426/2 He delivered himself of a lyrical greeting to the great church and to the city in general, in a tone of voice so irrepressibly elevated that it rang through the nave in rather a scandalous fashion. **1949** B. A. BOTKIN *Treas. S. Folklore* IV. i. 552 Marylanders grow lyrical over Brunswick stew..and Louisianians, over the superiorities of the Cajun and Creole cuisine. **1965** E. CURRENT-GARCIA *O. Henry* iv. 126 Once again O. Henry waxes lyrical about the gold and silver delights of New York. **1977** *Economist* 9 Apr. 54/2 The immigration minister of that time..issued lyrical messages of thanks for the vigour and vitality that all these newcomers..had brought to their adopted country. **1992** *Independent* 20 Jan. 16/1 Roxy Rifken waxes lyrical about the therapeutic value of blasting a clipful of .45 bullets into a torso-shaped target.

lysarden (ˈlɪzədən), *n. Early Mus.* Also **lyzarden, lyzardyne.** [f. *lysard*, obs. var. of LIZARD *n.*, on account of its shape: see -EN², -INE⁴.] A wind instrument of the cornett family, predating the serpent.

 a **1601** J. HOOKER *Descr. Citie Excester* (1919) III. 946 The shall trewlye & in salffitie redelyver at all tymes when the same shalbe required of theym such settes & noyses of Instrumente as they have of the Citie aswell Recordes as others bought at the Cities charges... A doble Curtall a Lyserden Too tenoᵣ hoyboyes [etc.]. *c* **1602** in F. W. Galpin *Old Eng. Instruments of Mus.* (1910) ix. 166 Three hoeboys with a curtall and a lysarden. **1910** F. W. GALPIN *Ibid.* xv. 280 A lysarden (probably a serpent). **1940** *Grove's Dict. Mus.* (ed. 4) Suppl. 409 The Lyzarden or Lyzardyne is named as a musical instrument in inventories of the 16th and 17th centuries. **1953** W. L. WOODFILL *Musicians in Eng. Soc.* iv. 85 The Norwich waits played..a lyzardyne (probably a great cornett in *S* form) by about 1585. **1976** D. MUNROW *Instruments Middle Ages & Renaissance* 70/4 The tenor cornett in C was so large that it necessitated two curves in the tube instead of one; hence an English name *lysarden* or lizard. **1980** *Early Mus.* Jan. 111 (Advt.), For details of Curved Cornetts, Mute Cornetts, Lysarden and Serpents write for new pricelist and brochure.

lysogen (ˈlaɪsədʒən), *n. Microbiol.* [Back-formation f. LYSOGENIC *a.*] A lysogenic bacterium, phage, or prophage.

 1958 *Virol.* V. 275 It is concluded that in lambda double lysogens both prophages establish and maintain a definite orientation with respect to one another. **1969** A. M. CAMPBELL *Episomes* i. 1 Each natural lysogen produces a single type, or a limited number of types, of phage particles. **1980** *Nature* 3 Jan. 104/2 This indicated that they were lysogens of λ*cam105* and the parental strains showed unimpaired growth at 42° C. **1987** *Ibid.* 11 June 465/1 Whether a phage multiplies and lyses an infected bacterium or integrates into its chromosome as a silent passenger (lysogen) is a decision that rests on differences..in the binding affinities of two proteins..for their operator sites.

lysopine (ˈlaɪsəʊpiːn), *n. Biochem.* [f. LYS(INE *n.* + *OCT)OPINE *n.*] An opine, $C_9H_{18}N_2O_4$, synthesized by plant cells infected by some tumour-inducing plasmids present in the crown gall pathogen *Agrobacterium tumefaciens.* Cf. *NOPALINE *n.*

 1960 K. BIEMANN et al. in *Biochim. & Biophys. Acta* XL. 370 We propose the name *lysopine* for the new amino acid..as it is the lysine analogue of octopine.., a characteristic component of octopus muscle. **1972** *Plant Physiol.* XLIX. 135/1 Nopaline-producing tumors induced by strain T-37 responded to lysopine and octopine as well as to nopaline. **1978** *Nature* 9 Feb. 570/2 Two other opines, lysopine and octopinic acid, which are synthesised concomitantly with octopine in crown-gall cells. **1988** *Ann. Bot.* LXII. 441 Lysopine and nopaline dehydrogenase were not detected in any of the selected protoclones.

M

M. Add: [III.] [6.] [a.] **MARC** (mɑːk) *Library Science* machine-readable cataloguing, a standard format for the encoding and representation of bibliographic information in machine-readable form.

1965 *Proc. 2nd Conf. Machine-Readable Catal. Copy* (U.S. Libr. Congress) 23 The eventual expansion of *MARC and its importance for foreign-area acquisitions and bibliographic control programs. **1968** *Library Assoc. Rec.* Aug. 198/2 The single objective of the MARC Project is to supply to any library catalogue data for current books in magnetic tape form so that the receiving library is not only relieved of the necessity of cataloguing and classification but can also reformat the data to suit its own purposes. **1987** *Ibid.* Aug. (Vacancies Suppl.) p. ccxxx/1 Experience of AACR2 and UK MARC are essential. **1991** *Lit. & Linguistic Computing.* VI. 4/2 The MARC formatting could.. facilitate the eventual uploading of the database from our office IBM PCXT to a mainframe library catalogue.

MDA *Pharm.* [f. 3,4-methylene*dioxy*-amphetamine], a synthetic hallucinogenic drug usually taken in capsules, which induces mild euphoria.

1959 G. A. ALLES in *Proc. 4th Conf. Neuropharmacol.* 195 Methylenedioxy-amphetamine (*MDA). **1967** A. T. SHULGIN et al. in D. H. Efron *Ethnopharmacologic Search for Psychoactive Drugs* 212 The base that corresponds to safrole.. is 3,4-methylenedioxyamphetamine, or MDA. **1974** M. C. GERALD *Pharmacol.* xvii. 328 DOM and MDA are more recent additions to the drug scene. **1987** R. SHILTS *And Band played On* (1988) II. iv. 38 In the middle of it was Michael, the perfect host, handing out tabs of the drug MDA to all comers.

MDMA *Pharm.* [f. 3,4-methylene*dioxy*-methamphetamine], the drug also known as *ecstasy* (*ECSTASY *n.* 5).

1978 A. T. SHULGIN in Stillman & Willette *Psychopharmacol. of Hallucinogens* vi. 77 A second compound to be described in this presentation is the N-methyl homolog of a well-studied psychotomimetic, 3,4-methylenedioxyphenylisopropylamine (MDA..). As with MDA, *MDMA.. has the aromatic substitution pattern of the essential oil safrole. **1982** *Biol. Psychiatry* XVII. 808 Monomethylation of the terminal amine of MDA results in MDMA. **1991** *Independent* 23 Dec. 5/1 Ecstasy was synthesised as MDMA in Germany in 1898, first marketed in 1914 as an appetite suppressor, dropped when its side effects were noticed, rediscovered by hippies in the 1960s and eventually banned in 1977.

MIRAS ('maɪərəs), mortgage interest relief at source, a scheme in the U.K. whereby the tax relief on mortgage repayments is paid direct to the lender by the Government.

1983 *Financial Times* 15 Jan. 1. 6/1 In April, *MIRAS appears on the house mortgage scene and its impact on millions of unsuspecting houseowners could well result in chaos and confusion for all concerned. **1983** *Scotsman* 24 Jan. 9/5 Those paying off their mortgages through the repayment method have the right not to change to the new MIRAS system but they must inform their building society. **1986** *House Buyer* Nov. 53/1 Now that the MIRAS system (mortgage interest relief at source) is operating, tax relief is deducted *before* your repayments are made. **1991** *Financial Times* 20 Mar. 28/8 Any allowance for relief at the higher rate in respect of interest on loans within MIRAS will be withdrawn.

MIS *Computing,* management information system.

1972 SCHMALZ & SIPPL *Computer Gloss. for Students & Teachers* 107/1 An *MIS gives the executive the capability of controlling the operation of a firm on a real-time basis. **1977** *Fortune* Feb. 81/2 The routine business and government transactions clustered under the acronym MIS (Management Information Systems). **1992** *UNIX World* Apr. 44/1 MIS departments *are* working on applications that will let users access corporate data, but each mainframe-connected network has its own unique combination of problems.

MLRS *Mil.* = *multiple launch rocket system* s.v. *MULTIPLE *a. and *n.* A. 4 c.

1979 *Aviation Week* 26 Feb. 64/1 The United Kingdom, France and West Germany.. [will become] partners with the U.S. in what will be called the multiple launch rocket system (*MLRS). **1987** D. ROBERTSON *Dict. Mod. Defence & Strategy* 207 The MLRS will become even more deadly in the near future, as the USA is co-operating with European NATO members to develop 'terminally guided' or Smart Bombs to be fitted to these rockets. **1991** *Independent* 22 Feb. 3/3 The MLRS has a range of between 8 and 30km. Each rocket drops 644 bomblets like grenades. The firepower of each launcher is said to equal an entire battalion of 24 guns of traditional 155mm artillery firing three rounds each — enough to take out an entire grid square.

MORI, Mori ('mɔːrɪ, 'mɒrɪ), Market & Opinion Research International (a proprietary name in the U.K.).

1969 *Internat. Managem.* Sept. 7/2 Robert Worcester, the author of this article, is managing director of Market and Opinion Research International (*MORI), a joint venture of Opinion Research Corporation of America and Britain's National Opinion Polls. **1973** TEER & SPENCE *Polit. Opinion Polls* v. 119 The MORI survey showed considerable support among chairmen and managing directors of the top 500 companies in Britain for Britain's entry. **1987** *Daily Tel.* 5 June 17/1 The elegant Georgian offices of Bob Worcester's Mori opinion poll organisation in.. Westminster. **1992** *Independent* 7 Apr. 1/3 With Labour requiring an 8 per cent swing from the Conservatives to win an overall majority on Thursday, a MORI poll for Yorkshire Television showed a 10 per cent swing.

MRI *Med.,* magnetic resonance imaging; also, a unit for producing images in this way.

1983 *Amer. Jrnl. Roentgenol.* CXLI. 1101 Information obtained by *MRI was compared to CT and/or sonographic studies. **1986** *Times* 13 June 31/1 In the basement of the Churchill Clinic, newly redecorated in fashionable shades of pink and grey, is the MRI or Magnetic Resonance Imaging unit. **1990** *Sun* (Baltimore) 7 Mar. C10/2 MRIs are like CAT scan machines, but they create images by a placing patient in a strong magnetic field. **1992** *N.Y. Times* 29 Dec. c3/4 Many people older than 45 have some arthritic changes on spinal X-rays, and on M.R.I. scans 25 percent of adults have ruptured disks.

MRL *Mil.* = *multiple rocket launcher* s.v. *MULTIPLE *a.* 4 c.

1970 *Army* Nov. 31/1 The Soviet Army and its Warsaw Pact allies use an entire family of *MRL systems. **1976** *Field Artillery Jrnl.* Nov.-Dec. 30/2 The Soviet Army has relied continuously on MRLs since.. the first combat volley was fired by a battery of BM-13 launchers.

MS-DOS (ɛmɛs'dɒs) *Computing* [f. Microsoft *disk *operating* *system:* cf. *DOS* s.v. D III. 3], a proprietary term in the U.S. for an operating system developed for a particular family of microprocessors and widely used in personal computers.

1982 *Byte* July 330/3 Microsoft's *MS-DOS (sold by IBM as PC-DOS and by Lifeboat Associates as SB-86)...MS-DOS is faster [than CP/M-86] primarily because it buffers more data in each gulp and because it keeps the File Allocation Table in memory rather than on disk. **1992** *PC World* Apr. 30/1, I upgraded to MS-DOS 5.0 so I wouldn't have to partition the disk.

MTV orig. *U.S.*, Music Television, a proprietary name for a cable and satellite television channel broadcasting popular music and promotional music videos.

1981 *N.Y. Times* 19 June D15/4 Warner Amex has *MTV: The Music Channel, 24 hours of that noise with pictures to match. **1985** *Music Week* 2 Feb. 1/1, 7m homes in Europe and Scandinavia are now connected to cable..although that represents only a third of MTV's audience. **1993** *Albuquerque* (New Mexico) *Jrnl.* 4 Apr. C3/3 Morally obtuse grunge rockers who spend their time eating junk food and watching MTV.

8. *Astron.* **M** (orig. with point), used with following (orig. †preceding) numeral to denote any of various indistinct non-stellar objects (orig. all classed as nebulae) listed in the catalogue of Charles Messier (see *MESSIER *n*.).

1868 J. N. LOCKYER *Elem. Lessons Astron.* i. 34 The finest ring-nebula is the 57th in Messier's catalogue (written 57 M. for short). *Ibid.* 34, 33/ M. Piscium, and 99/ M. Virginis, are other examples of this strange phenomenon. **1911** *Encycl. Brit.* XIX. 332/2 *Planetary nebulae*, examples: the 'owl' nebula (M. 97) in Ursa Major, M.1 in Taurus. **1929** J. H. JEANS *Universe around Us* i. 30 The most conspicuous of all the spiral nebulae is the Great Nebula (*M*31) in Andromeda. **1964** *Yearbk. Astron. 1965* 173 South, in the obscure group Vulpecula.., lies the Dumb-bell Nebula, M27. *Ibid.* 174 Sagitta..contains M71, a rather faint globular cluster between Gamma and Delta. **1992** S. P. MARAN *Astron. & Astrophysics Encycl.* 21/1 The Andromeda galaxy..is often referred to as M31 or Messier 31 because it is number 31 in the famous catalog of Messier (1730-1817).

ma, *n.* Add: **c.** *attrib.* and *Comb.* **ma-and-pa** (chiefly *U.S.*), used *attrib.* to denote a small business, esp. a shop, owned and operated by a couple or family, and *transf.* of other similarly small-scale commercial enterprises (cf. *mom-and-pop* s.v. MOM *n*.).

1973 J. GORES *Final Notice* i. 6 *Ma and Pa businesses alternated with the houses or occupied their ground floors. **1979** *New Yorker* 15 Jan. 6 Ali's Alley...Sort of a ma-and-pa jazz loft, owned and managed by drummer Kashied Ali. **1980** A. TYLER *Morgan's Passing* (1983) II. iii. 43 He slowly built this scene in his mind where she and he were the owners of a small-town Ma-and-pa hardware store. **1988** *Courier-Mail* (Brisbane) 18 July 9/1 A few years ago, there were at least 200 or more of them.., mostly 'Ma and Pa' operators with strong backs...One by one, they have been taken over by bigger competitors. **1994** *Chicago Tribune* 21 July III. 3/2 The boutique, or ma and pa, firms that once lined LaSalle Street and were the hallmarks of these exchanges are being supplanted rapidly by international financial behemoth.

Maalox ('meɪlɒks), *n. Pharm.* (chiefly *U.S.*). [Acronym, f. *ma*gnesium and *al*uminium hydr*ox*ide.] A proprietary name for a preparation containing dried aluminium hydroxide and magnesium hydroxide, taken (usu. in tablet form) as an antacid for the relief of indigestion; a tablet of this.

1951 *Official Gaz.* (U.S. Patent Office) 26 June 1030/1 *Maalox* for anatacid. Claims use since Aug. 4, 1949. **1976** *National Observer* (U.S.) 24 July 8/5, I was using six to eight Maalox a day. But then I began pouring this milk on my cereal every morning. **1977** *Rolling Stone* 16 June 43/2 His tubes run wild with Maalox. **1994** *Amer. Spectator* Jan. 65/3 Just finished reading P. J. O'Rourke's 'Collective Guilt'...Since the reading(s) were during lunch, I must confess to a dessert of double-strength Maalox.

Maastricht ('mɑːstrɪxt), *n.* [The name of a city in the south of the Netherlands, near the Belgian border.] Used *attrib.* (esp. as *Maastricht agreement* or *treaty*) or *absol.* to denote an agreement reached between European Community leaders at a summit meeting held at Maastricht in December 1991 concerning progress towards European economic, monetary, and political union, and also containing a protocol regarding social and employment policy in member states (see *social charter* s.v. *SOCIAL a.* 12).

1991 *Independent* 24 Oct. 1/3 The Prime Minister's office..suggested last night that such bumps were to be expected on the road to Maastricht. **1992** *Police Rev.* 17 Jan. 120/3 That is why the Maastricht agreement on a Europol police intelligence agency—with drugs intelligence as the first building block—is so welcome. **1992** *Time* 28 Sept. 42/2 Supporters of European unity could claim that the closer union envisaged in the Maastricht treaty would give everyone else a greater say over Germany's actions. **1993** *Evening Standard* 22 June 13/6 The minute Maastricht is ratified, the European Commission will start inflicting its directives again, and the question of closer European interference will return to the forefront of debate.

Macanese (mækə'niːz), *n.* and *a.* Also (formerly) **Macaoese** (mækaʊ'iːz), **Macaonese** (mækaʊ'niːz). Pl. unchanged. [f. the place-name *Macao* (ad. Jap. *Amakawa*) + *-n-* + *-ESE*: in Pg. *macaense* (see quot. 1902).] **A.** *n.* **a.** A native or inhabitant of Macao, a city and Portuguese dependency on the south-east coast of China, *esp.* one of mixed Chinese and Portuguese descent. **b.** The Portuguese-based creole language spoken in Macao. **B.** *adj.* Of or pertaining to Macao or the Macanese.

Under the terms of a Joint Statement issued by the Chinese and Portuguese governments in April 1987, China will resume sovereignty over Macao (*Aomen* in Mandarin Chinese) on 20 Dec. 1999.

[**1902** C. A. MONTALTO DE JESUS *Historic Macao* iv. 41 The Macanese patois..attests a predominant Malaccan element.] **1905** J. D. BALL *Macao* 57 The Macaoese patriotically used their best endeavours to prevent Spanish Governors from having rule over the city. **1932** *Nat. Geogr. Mag.* LXII. 344 (*caption*) Incense ranks third in Macao's industrial life; some 1, 300,000 Macanese dollars' worth is produced annually. **1948** C. R. BOXER *Fidalgos in Far East 1550-1770* xv. 258 Green Island was now about the only place left for the Macaoense to disport themselves *extra muros*. **1951** *New Yorker* 17 Nov. 114/3 Macao's Portuguese community..is fairly well cut off from the..Chinese and Macanese (Eurasians) of the city. **1962** *Listener* 22 Nov. 868/3 To this widespread [language] group belong..Jamaican Creole, Papiamento, Neo-Melanesian, Macanese. **1967** 'A. CORDELL' *Bright Cantonese* x. 110 'Are they all Chinese?' ' 'No. Some are Macanese.' **1974** 'G. BLACK' *Golden Cockatrice* iii. 49 The man..was mostly Portuguese but like so many Macanese had obviously escaped..into the larger world. **1977** *Times* 16 Apr. 11/3 The Macanese *pataca* is at par with the HongKong dollar. **1983** *Times* 20 Dec. 6/7 Local Macanese—Eurasians speaking Portuguese and Cantonese interchangeably—are annoyed at the influx of civil servants from Portugal.

Macaronesia (ˌmækərə(ʊ)'niːzjə, -ʒə), n. Chiefly *Bot.* [mod.L., f. Gr. μακάρων νῆσοι Islands of the Blessed (islands in the western ocean later identified with the Canaries, etc.) + -IA¹, after POLYNESIA n., etc.] A biogeographical region which embraces islands in the eastern North Atlantic, principally the Azores, Madeira, Canary Islands, and Cape Verde Islands.

1917 H. B. GUPPY *Plants, Seeds & Currents in W. Indies & Azores* xviii. 416 The parent stocks have since been driven from their European home, and the Laurel woods of Macaronesia are all that remains of a period when trees now characteristic of Asia and America formed the forests of our continent. **1947** R. GOOD *Geogr. Flowering Plants* viii. 143 *Erica arborea*..is distributed northward from tropical Africa well into the Mediterranean region and in Macaronesia. **1973** *Nature* 1 June 261/1 The term Macaronesia is a collective name for the Atlantic Islands including Madeira, the Azores, the Canary Islands and the *Cape Verde* Islands which have long been recognized by plant geographers as together forming a floristic region characterized by many common elements associated with high endemism.

So **Macaro'nesian** a., of or pertaining to this region.

1917 H. B. GUPPY *Plants, Seeds & Currents in W. Indies & Azores* xviii. 416 Their descendants now give character to the Laurel woods of all three Macaronesian groups. **1928** *Jrnl. Bot.* LXVI. 223 The degree of endemism of the group with relation to the Macaronesian floral region to which the Canaries belong. **1973** *Nature* 1 June 261/1 Some seventy-two botanists..participated and provided convincing evidence of the increasing international interest in the Macaronesian flora. **1980** J. MERCER *Canary Islanders* 9 The archipelago [of the Canaries] has 1600-1700 species, 470 being endemic and 110 limited to the immediate Atlantic islands (Macaronesian).

MacBride (mək'braɪd), n. [The name of Seán *MacBride* (1904-88), Irish statesman and promoter of human rights.] **MacBride principles**, the code of conduct, first advocated by MacBride in 1976, that U.S. firms or investors in Northern Ireland should pursue a policy of non-discrimination and ensure the employment of a balanced workforce.

1985 *Economist* 13 Apr. 78/3 The resolution will ask the companies to adopt the MacBride principles, which are similar to the civil rights laws that compel American companies at home to bar discrimination at work based on race, religion, colour or sex. **1987** *Listener* 24 Sept. 6/2 His officials, working with..the Irish National Caucus, came up with the MacBride principles, a code of conduct for US firms in Northern Ireland to ensure that they employed a 'balanced' workforce. **1994** *Irish Times* 9 July 3/2 The New York Comptroller, Mr Alan Hevesi, has urged the British government and unionist politicians to accept and apply the MacBride Principles on fair employment.

maccaph ('mækəf, mæ'kæf), n. Also makaf, makaph, maqqeph. [ad. Heb. *maqqāp*, lit. 'binder'.] A Hebrew diacritic, similar in form to a hyphen, indicating that words thus joined should be pronounced as if they were one.

1593 J. UDALL tr. P. Martinius *Key of Holy Tongue* II. x. 199 There is a mark of uniting words in the Hebrue very often, and it is called *Makaph*, beeing a lyne drawne a long from one woord to the other. **1668** J. WILKINS *Ess. towards Real Char. & Philos. Lang.* II. i. vi. 45 For uniting those words which are to be pronounced as one..HYPHEN, *Maccaph*. **1738** R. GREY *Meth. Hebrew* p. v, A long Vowel, before the Line of Union called *Maccaph*, is always pronounced short; as..*ben* for *bên*, *col*, for *côl*, *et* for *êt* & c. **1874** A. B. DAVIDSON *Introd. Hebrew Gram.* 22 Part of the accentual or rhythmical machinery is the Maqqeph or hyphen which binds two or more words together...All

the words joined by Maqqeph losing their accents except the last, their long vowels if changeable become short. **1993** I. ELDAR in L. Glinert *Hebrew in Ashkenaz* iii. 33 The treatise itself is in two parts. The first provides an impressive range of rules concerning the place of stress..and the juncture and phonological rhythm (as marked by the *meteg* and *makaf*).

MacDonaldism (mək'dɒnəldɪz(ə)m), n. *Pol. Hist.* [f. the name of James Ramsay *MacDonald* (1866-1937), British statesman and prime minister, leader of the first Labour governments (1924 and 1929-31) and a non-Labour coalition administration (1931-5) + -ISM.] The political and economic policies pursued by Ramsay MacDonald and his supporters, sometimes characterized as a moderate socialism. Freq. with negative connotations.

1924 *Labour Monthly* May 259 There is no doubt that MacDonaldism and all that it stands for is not only temporarily in the ascendant, but has achieved for a space a measure of insecure control over the whole movement. **1934** G. A. ALDRED *Socialism & Parliament* (ed. 2) I. xiv. 52 The I.L.P. has stressed how slight was the difference between Labourism and MacDonaldism at the time of the National Government rupture in 1931. **1950** R. CROSSMAN in Koestler et al. *God that Failed* 10 They saw that..Baldwinism and MacDonaldism in Britain..were lazy intellectual shams. **1962** *Listener* 25 Jan. 187/1 The same moderation ensured that the Party, in spite of its humiliating defeat in 1931, would remain on the path of constitutional parliamentary opposition, 'MacDonaldism without MacDonald'. **1982** *Guardian Weekly* 24 Oct. 21/4 Within the political game he [*sc.* Oswald Mosley] was inevitably an *enfant terrible*. This let him cut through the footling pathos of MacDonaldism.

MacDonaldite (mək'dɒnəldaɪt), a. and n. [f. the name of James Ramsay *MacDonald* (see *MACDONALDISM n.*) + -ITE¹.] **A.** n. A supporter of Ramsay MacDonald or his policies, esp. the moderate socialist policies associated with him, or such policies in general. **B.** adj. Of, pertaining to, or supporting Ramsay MacDonald or his policies.

1924 *Labour Monthly* May 266 While the workers are awakening to new attacks, the MacDonaldites are all pouring out the propaganda of Industrial Peace. **1938** J. STRACHEY *What are we to Do?* xix. 327 The real criticism of the MacDonaldite leadership..was not that the Labour Governments which it controlled did nothing more than enact reforms. **1961** *Economist* 17 June 1278/2 Two things followed from this lack of coherence on the part of the MacDonaldites. *a*1974 R. CROSSMAN *Diaries* (1975) I. 155 Callaghan is really representing the MacDonaldite attitude to the bankers in 1931. **1986** M. FOOT *Loyalists & Loners* 166 Labour, both the MacDonaldites and the Hendersonites, all the moderates of every breed and hue, did 'run away' in 1931, according to the gibe of time.

Macedonian, a.¹ Sense in Dict. becomes A 1. Add: [A.] 2. Special Comb. **Macedonian phalanx** *Hist.*, the characteristic formation of the Macedonian army, consisting of infantry armed with long two-handed pikes and marshalled sixteen-deep in close formation; introduced by Philip II, king of Macedonia 395-36 B.C., as an improvement on the earlier Greek hoplite infantry.

1585 T. WASHINGTON tr. *Nicholay's Voy.* III. iii. 73 Ianissaries..The order of which is nothing els then the following of the *Macedonian Phalangue with the which Alexander the great extended his domination. **1745** SWIFT *To Dr. Sheridan* 31 Thy words together ty'd in small hanks, Close as the

Macedonian phalanx. **1989** R. L. O'CONNELL *Arms & Men* iv. 61 Designed around a basic building block, or *syntagma*, of 256 men, lined 16 across and 16 deep, the Macedonian phalanx was not only uniformly thicker but projected a good deal farther ahead than its Greek counterparts.

maceration, *n*. Add: [1.] **d.** In full, *carbonic maceration*. In wine-making, a technique used to produce a fruitier, less tannic, and more palatable wine by inducing fermentation within uncrushed grapes in a carbon dioxide environment before crushing and pressing them, completing fermentation, and processing the wine in the usual way.

[**1971** J. JEFFS *Wines of Europe* ii. 45 The method..*maceration carbonique* was invented. A slow fermentation begins and after three or four days..the grapes are pressed and the must is fermented out of contact both of the stalks and skins.] **1977** H. JOHNSON *World Atlas Wine* (ed. 2) 125/3 A number of producers are using Beaujolais-style vinification (carbonic maceration) to make their wine full and fruity. **1988** K. LYNCH *Adventures on Wine Route* (1990) v. 152 In a word carbonic maceration wines are not considered macho. **1992** *Food Entertaining* Summer 126 (Advt.), The Rose is certainly not delicate, a full bodied Pinot Noir made by the maceration method.

e. *Obstetr.* The degenerative changes that take place in a foetus that has died in the uterus.

1873 A. S. TAYLOR *Princ. & Pract. Med. Jurisprudence* (ed. 2) II. lxxiv. 325 M. Sentex states..that the dead foetus retained in utero, with the membranes unruptured, undergoes one of three changes—maceration, putrefaction, or mummification. The first is the most common condition. **1981** H. JOLLY *Bk. Child Care* (new ed.) lii. 593 A baby who has died some hours or days before delivery develops 'maceration' of the skin. **1992** *Textbk. Neonatology* VII. xxxviii. 1160/1 Maceration is accelerated by oedema and amniotic fluid infection.

macfarlane (mək'fɑːlən), *n*. [The surname *Macfarlane*, prob. f. the name of the original designer or manufacturer of the coat, which was app. first popular in France, where the term is attested from 1859: see *Trésor*.] A type of overcoat incorporating a shoulder cape and with slits at the waist to allow access to pockets, etc., in clothing worn underneath.

1920 E. WHARTON *Age of Innocence* I. xvii. 156 The overcoats were in fact the very strangest he had ever seen under a polite roof...One was a shaggy yellow ulster of 'reach-me-down' cut, the other a very old and rusty cloak with a cape—something like what the French called a 'Macfarlane'. **1925** L. P. SMITH *Words & Idioms* ii. 39 France has acquired from England the *mackintosh*, the *macfarlane*. **1928** in *Funk's Stand. Dict.* **1939** JOYCE *Finnegans Wake* 180 A scrumptious cocked hat and..a coat macfarlane (the kerssest cut, you understand?). **1959** S. BECKETT *Embers* in *Evergreen Rev.* Nov.–Dec. 30 Hands behind his back holding up the tails of his old macfarlane.

Mach *n*. Add: **c.** **Mach's principle** *Physics* [tr. Ger. *Machsches Prinzip* (A. Einstein 1918, in *Ann. d. Physik* LV. 241)], the proposition that the inertia of a body depends on the distribution of matter in the universe.

1918 *Sci. Abstr.* A. XXI. 352 Mach's Principle by which the G-field is determined without residue by the masses of the bodies. **1930** L. SILBERSTEIN *Size of Universe* ii. 73 Einstein in his 'cosmological contemplations' of 1916 set out with the resolute plan of satisfying what he called 'Mach's principle' (relativity of inertia). **1951** *Ann. Math.* LIII. 472 In general relativity Mach's principle is interpreted as stating that the nature of space-time is determined by the matter present. **1965** J. D. NORTH *Measure of Universe* xiv.

306 Did Bondi think that 'Mach's Principle' was essential to any satisfactory physical theory? **1977** J. NARLIKAR *Struct. Universe* v. 169 Mach's principle, and its implication that inertia is not an intrinsic property of matter but is due to the background of distant stars, have received a mixed reception in the world of theoretical physics. **1987** *Nature* 6 Aug. 501/2 Ernst Mach advocated that..the vanishing cosmic rotation is part of the empirical basis of what is known as Mach's principle.

machinable, *a*. Add: **2.** Capable of being processed by a machine, esp. a computer; machine-readable.

1960 H. P. LUHN (*title*) General rules for creating machinable records for libraries and special reference files. **1984** *Sci. Amer.* Jan. 57/2 Letter sorting at the 211 major post offices that handle approximately 90 percent of all 'machinable mail'.

machine, *v*. Add: **6.** *intr.* To undergo machining; to be suited to shaping, etc., by machine.

1939 CARPENTER & ROBERTSON *Metals* I. x. 734 Forgings of the same steel are expected to machine under the same conditions. **1988** *Pract. Woodworking* Mar. 32/3 Some woods do machine better than others, and the direction of working in relation to the grain also effects [*sic*] the quality of the surface.

macho, *n*.[2] and *a*. Add: [B.] **2.** Special collocation: **macho man** *colloq.* (freq. *derog.*), a man characterized by (esp. exaggeratedly) assertive masculinity; (without article) this type of man; also *attrib.*

1976 *Soho Weekly News* (N.Y.) 13 May 15/2 Their baked red necks, their roughness, ruggedness made city man look parboiled. If I had to pick or choose, the trucker won. The trucker was *macho man. **1984** STEWARD & GARRATT *Signed, Sealed & Delivered* iii. 73/1 She claims that the stereotype of the neanderthal, macho-man roadie is now way off the mark. **1989** *Guardian* 21 July 8/4 Macho man spends Friday night in the pub, Saturday at the match, and thinks of his girlfriend or wife as 'her indoors'. **1991** *Newsweek* 9 Mar. (Canad. ed.) 33/1 Ironically, macho-man Bush is making a special play for middle-class Southern Republican women.

mackerel, *n*.[1] Add: [4.] **mackerel-snapper** *U.S. slang* (*derog.*, *rare*), a Roman Catholic (alluding to the Catholic tradition of eating fish on Fridays).

1960 WENTWORTH & FLEXNER *Dict. Amer. Slang* 330/1 *Mackerel-snapper. **1978** J. CARROLL *Mortal Friends* II. iv. 175 Who wouldn't be glum working for a mackerel-snapper who'd betray his people by coming out for a Protestant patrician over one of his own? **1990** T. ROBBINS *Skinny Legs & All* 161 Both Ellen Cherry and Buddy surveyed St. Patrick's...'Well, what *are* you doin' here? In front of the doors through which pass the richest mackerel-snappers in New York City?'

Mackinaw *a.* and *n*. Add: Hence 'mackinawed *a. rare*, wearing a Mackinaw coat.

1960 C. L. COOPER *Scene* vi. 159 The little cripple..pushed himself through the night...The tiny, twisted, childlike body..belied the wide mackinawed chest of a grown man.

Maclaurin (mə'klɒrɪn), *n. Math.* [The name of Colin *Maclaurin* (1698-1746), Scottish mathematician.] **Maclaurin('s) series**, a representation of a function $f(x)$ as a Taylor series about the origin; **Maclaurin's theorem**, Taylor's theorem applied to a function at the origin.

1820 G. Peacock *Coll. Examples Differential & Integral Calculus* I. 41 Examples given by our author of the application of Maclaurin's theorem to the developement of transcendental functions. **1902** J. W. Mellor *Higher Math.* v. 227 The series on the right-hand side is known as Maclaurin's Series. **1934** E. J. McShane tr. R. Courant *Differential & Integral Calculus* I. vi. 320 A special case of this [*sc.* Taylor's] theorem is often referred to..as Maclaurin's theorem. **1970** *Amer. Jrnl. Physics* XXXVIII. 1293/1 A series in positive integral powers of *t*—namely, a Taylor (or Maclaurin) series. **1989** *Numerische Math.* LV. 281 For the function arctan z, we give graphical contour maps of the number of significant digits in the approximations $f_n(z)$, $g_n(z)$ and $p_n(z)$, the nth partial sum of the Maclaurin series, for z in a key region of the complex plane.

Macoun (mə'ku:n), *n. Agric.* (chiefly *N. Amer.*). [The name of William Tyrrell *Macoun* (1869-1933), Canadian farmer.] A kind of dessert apple, originally grown in Canada.

1924 *Techn. Bull. N. Y. Agric. Exper. Station, Geneva* No. 106. 70 Jersey Black..was crossed with McIntosh in 1909 for the purpose of securing a variety equal to McIntosh in quality but later in ripening and superior in color. One such seedling has been produced and is now being distributed under the name Macoun. **1942** W. H. Chandler *Deciduous Orchards* xvi. 264 A considerable number of promising new varieties have recently been introduced by plant breeders. Among these are Seneca, Macoun, Sweet McIntosh..and others. **1975** P. Wynne *Apples* ii. 49 Macoun was introduced by the New York Agricultural Experiment Station in 1923...The original seed was produced by pollinating McIntosh with Jersey Black. Many people consider the Macoun the finest dessert apple grown in the Northeast. **1987** C. MacLeod *Recycled Citizen* xv. 122 Eating Brie and French bread and a crunchy Macoun apple.

Macoute (mə'ku:t), *n.* [Shortened from Tonton Macoute *n.*] In Haiti, a member of the Tonton Macoute; hence *gen.*, an intimidating villain, a criminal, a thug.

1971 *Guardian* 23 July 11/6 All abuses of power by the Macoutes would in future be severely punished. **1987** *New Republic* 21 Dec. 6/2 Bazin..was run out of the country by the Macoutes who controlled the Duvalier kleptocracy. **1989** *New Yorker* 11 Dec. 106/2 After the fall of Duvalier and the destruction of those who had served him—Macoutes, *houngans*, or, as was often the case, both—came the eruption of a deep-seated religious and cultural struggle. **1991** *N. Y. Times* 24 Nov. 1. 12/4 'Others feel that because you have a job, you must be some kind of Macoute, and they want to attack you.'.. The word Macoute long ago became generic for bad guy.

macro-, *comb. form.* Add: [**1.**] [**d.**] **macro'nodular** *a. Med.*, characterized by the presence of large nodules; freq. in *macronodular cirrhosis*; cf. *micronodular* s.v. *MICRO- 4.

1967 *Jrnl. Clin. Path.* XX. 748/1 In some livers..there was indeed a superficial resemblance to *macronodular cirrhosis of the incomplete septal type. **1976** Edington & Gilles *Path. in Tropics* (ed. 2) xi. 542 The terms portal and postnecrotic would probably be better expressed morphologically as micronodular and macronodular respectively. **1984** Tighe & Davies *Pathology* (ed. 4) xvii. 163 In macronodular cirrhosis it [*sc.* the liver] is usually small and coarsely scarred. **1987** *Oxf. Textbk. Med.* (ed. 2) I. x. 22/1 The rare syndrome of macronodular adrenocortical hyperplasia must be distinguished from adrenal adenomas.

[**e.**] **macro-engi'neering** *n.*, the design and construction of engineering projects on the largest scale possible.

1964 *New Scientist* 12 Mar. 685/1 The real cause of our attachment to *macroengineering is at once more subtle and more profound. **1978** *N. Y. Times* 19 Feb. IV. 7/1 A one-day discussion was held on 'macro-engineering' projects—the construction of things so big size alone makes them different from all other things. **1983** *Space Solar Power Rev.* IV. 65 Macro-engineering is nothing more than the study, preparation, and execution of the largest engineering works which mankind can accomplish at any particular period of time.

macro-evolution *n.*: hence ‚macro-evo'lutionary *a.*

1940 R. Goldschmidt *Material Basis of Evolution* v. 396 Species and the higher categories originate in single *macroevolutionary steps as completely new genetic systems. **1987** *Economist* 23 May 95/1 This notion is part of 'macro-evolution'. Here is another macro-evolutionary idea: if creatures get better adapted to their environments, they should..get better at avoiding extinction.

‚**macroso'cietal** *a.*, relating to or affecting wider society.

1966 F. Schurmann *Ideol. & Organization in Communist China* Introd. 3 Every civilized society has complex organizations, ranging from *macrosocietal political networks down to the smallest human groupings. **1977** *Lang.* LIII. 180 He misses the interplay between macro-societal factors and language choice in the individual interaction. **1992** *Guardian* 30 May 23/8 It was the Tories, though initially beleaguered by the new spirit, who learnt how to master it in its macro-societal form.

[**2.**] **d.** *Econ.* (*a*) [Freq. as abbrev. of *macro-economic* adj. s.v. MACRO-ECONOMICS *n. pl.*] Of or pertaining to macroeconomics; (*b*) taking into account the aggregate economic situation; total, overall.

1958 Henderson & Quandt *Microeconomic Theory* I. ii. 3 Prices are relevant in macro theories, but macro theorists usually..deal with aggregate price indices. **1961** G. Ackley *Macroecon. Theory* (1965) xx. 572 We can derive no..meaningful macro-functions. **1974** *Times Lit. Suppl.* 8 Mar. 242/5 The forms and methods of economic management, both micro and macro. **1979** E. Newman *Sunday Punch* iii. 24, I had recently written a stirring editorial coming down on the macro side and thought it only a matter of time before microeconomics gave up the unequal struggle. **1985** *Investors Chron.* 8 Nov. 20/2 The other important 'macro' influence is of course the growth of disposable income. **1991** *Financial Times* 20 Mar. 34/6 On the macro side, the action fortunately rests now far more with the Bank of England..than with the British Budget.

macrobenthos (mækrəʊ'benθɒs) *n.* [f. MACRO- + BENTHOS *n.*] The macrofauna of the benthos; *spec.* the organisms at or near the sea floor or a lake bed with a length of at least 1 mm.

1942 M. F. Mare in *Jrnl. Marine Biol. Assoc.* XXV. 519 A new terminology is needed, and these groups are here designated the macrobenthos, meiobenthos, and microbenthos. **1973** *Nature* 30 Mar. 324/1 Meiobenthos has a much wider dissemination than macrobenthos within the sediments. **1985** *Oceanogr. & Marine Biol.* XXIII. 586 The high productivity..resulted chiefly from the very high densities of meiofauna and..typical estuarine macrobenthos was restricted in both variety and density.

Hence **macro'benthic** *a.*

1967 *Oceanogr. & Marine Biol.* V. 477 The population of characteristic macrobenthic animals includes four species: *O. radiata*, *Nerine cirratulus*, the isopod *Eurydice affinis* and the small pelecypod *Mesodesma corneum*. **1988** *Nature* 6 Oct. 535/1 The two active vent fields..are all devoid of the luxuriant macrobenthic communities that have become the hallmark of analogous mid-oceanic ridge sites studied to date.

macro-economics, *n. pl.* Add: **macro-e'conomist** *n.*

1964 *Economist* 26 Dec. 1411/2 Efforts to maintain sterling in its prestigious role as a key international currency by deflating demand more frequently and sharply than many British and Hungarian macro-economists..consider to be desirable. **1979** *Amer. Banker* 12 July 4/1 Every macro-economist believes that government has been at least partly responsible for business cycle instability in the United States. **1993** *Business Week* 25 Oct. 48 How macroeconomics went astray...The 1970s. Keynesianism comes under attack when macroeconomists are surprised by the 'theoretically impossible' combination of slow growth and high inflation.

macrofauna (mækrəʊ'fɔːnə), *n. Biol.* [f. MACRO- + FAUNA *n.*] A fauna consisting of animals which are visible to the naked eye.

1918 *Trans. Wisconsin Acad. Sci., Arts & Lett.* XIX. 443 Insects compose about 60% of the macrofauna of the lake, excluding fish. **1942** *Jrnl. Marine Biol. Assoc.* XXV. 519 The macrobenthos is equivalent to the macrofauna of the bottom. **1989** *Times* 9 Aug. 16/6 The macrofauna—larger seabed animals such as crabs and shellfish which spend their young lives in the plankton at the surface of the sea.

macro level ('mækrəʊ ˌlɛvəl), *n.* Also **macrolevel**, **macro-level**. [f. MACRO- + LEVEL *n.*] The most general or abstract level of a concept, process, etc.; freq. *spec.* with reference to macroeconomics. Cf. *MICRO LEVEL *n.*

1961 G. H. ORCUTT et al. *Microanal. Socioecon. Syst.* p. xv, Given the possibility of experimentation at both micro- and macrolevels, it has been possible for the physical sciences to achieve great successes at both levels without the necessity of predicating aggregate behavior on the basis of knowledge about microbehavior. **1978** *Financial Rev.* (Austral.) 17 Aug. 2/4, I think it is safe to assume that at the macro level the effects of the change in the health insurance arrangements will be very small. **1992** *Unesco Courier* Mar. 41/2 Linking the experience of women at the level of their daily lives (the micro level) to economic trends and their global environmental impacts (the macro level).

macrolinguistics (mækrəʊlɪŋ'gwɪstɪks), *n. pl.* (const. as *sing.*). [f. MACRO- 1 e + LINGUISTIC *n.* b.] The branch of linguistics that deals with language and related extra-lingual phenomena as a whole; sometimes *spec.* the statistical analysis of large-scale linguistic phenomena. Cf. MICROLINGUISTICS *n. pl.*

1949 G. L. TRAGER in *Stud. in Ling.: Occasional Papers* I. 2 The whole of the field concerned with language..we shall call Macrolinguistics. The three subdivisions we shall call Prelinguistics, Microlinguistics, Metalinguistics. **1972** HARTMANN & STORK *Dict. Lang. & Linguistics* 135/2 Some linguists regard macrolinguistics as the study, by statistical means, of large-scale linguistic phenomena. **1983** *Lang. & Lang. Behavior Abstr.* XVII. 710/1 Linguistics may possess two dimensions: one studying the system in and by itself ('microlinguistics'), the other studying all aspects of linguistic events ('macrolinguistics'). **1992** W. BRIGHT *Internat. Encycl. Linguistics* IV. 75/1 A proposed new discipline of 'macrolinguistics'..was intended to bear the same relation to grammar (or 'microlinguistics') as thermodynamics bears to the mechanics of individual gas molecules.

Hence **macrolin'guistic** *a.*, of or pertaining to macrolinguistics.

1960 E. DELAVENAY *Introd. Machine Transl.* 93 Macrolinguistic analysis will be brought to bear on sign/meaning combinations and not on signs alone. **1985** *English World-Wide* VI. 322 Most of these [papers]..attempt to make macrolinguistic or

theoretical conclusions that are drawn on the basis of pitifully small populations.

macrophyte ('mækrəʊfaɪt), *n. Bot.* [ad. G. *Makrophyt* (coined in A. F. W. Schimper *Pflanzen-Geogr.* (1898) III. v. 848): see MACRO-, -PHYTE.] A (usu. aquatic) plant visible to the naked eye.

1903 W. R. FISHER tr. *Schimper's Plant-Geogr.* III. v. iii. 811 In contrast with their behaviour in salt-water seas the majority of macrophytes are rooted to the ground in fresh water. **1933** *Jrnl. Ecol.* XXI. 89 In a fast-flowing river macrophytes are not so plentiful, yet it is here that their presence is most valuable, especially because they act..as a shelter and an agent for stabilising the river bed. **1974** *Environmental Conservation* I. 54/1 It seems that, in turbid lake water, macrophytes develop dense canopies of leaves near the surface.

So **macro'phytic** *a.*

1900 in B. D. Jackson *Gloss. Bot. Terms* 151/1. **1903** W. R. FISHER tr. *Schimper's Plant-Geogr.* III. v. ii. 789 The macrophytic algae are almost exclusively denizens of the photic region, and the phanerogams are exclusively so. **1988** *Arch. für Hydrobiol.* CXI. 362 The emergent-life is highly productive, locking up 62.68% of the total macrophytic standing crop of the lake.

macropodid (mə'krɒpədɪd), *n.* and *a. Zool.* [f. mod.L. *Macropodidae* (coined by J. E. Gray 1821, in *London Med. Repository* XV. 308), f. mod.L. genus name *Macropus* (coined in G. Shaw *Nat. Miscell.* (1790) I. sig. O2), f. MACRO- + Gr. πούς, ποδ- foot: see -ID³.] A. *n.* A marsupial of the family Macropodidae, which includes kangaroos and wallabies.

1895 *Funk's Stand. Dict.*, Macropodid *n.* **1969** FRITH & CALABY *Kangaroos* 10 At the end of the period of his active interest in the Australian fauna, few species of macropodids remained to be discovered. **1977** *Sci. Amer.* Aug. 79/1 One of the most significant aspects of faunal change in Australia over the past 10 to 15 million years has been the increase in abundance and diversity of macropodids.

B. *adj.* Of, pertaining to, or designating a macropodid.

1948 *Bull. Amer. Mus. Nat. Hist.* XCI. 241/2 The macropodid mandible shows a further peculiarity that can be matched in no genus of the Phalangeridae. **1976** *Nature* 1-8 Jan. 42/1 To investigate whether one of these mechanisms could account for the behaviour of the newborn quokka (*Setonix brachyurus*) we have observed parturition in this macropodid marsupial.

mad, *a.* Sense 4 c in Dict. becomes 4 d. Add: [4.] c. Phr. *to go mad* (*about, for, over*, etc.): to allow oneself to be carried away by enthusiasm or excitement.

1850 R. W. EMERSON *Goethe* in *Representative Men* vii. 261 The ambitious and mercenary bring their last new mumbo-jumbo, whether tariff, Texas, railroad, Romanism, mesmerism, phrenology or California, and..a multitude go mad about it. **1876** W. BESANT & J. RICE *Golden Butterfly* xvi, Why should we not go mad for china? It is as sensible as going mad over rinking. **1936** G. B. SHAW *Millionairess* 27 The whole town went mad about the angry-eyed woman. It rained money in bucketsful. **1992** *Pract. Fishkeeping* July 98/3, I went mad and bought a 24″ glass tank with a crude external filter.

[9.] **mad cow disease** *colloq.* (chiefly *Brit.*) = *bovine spongiform encephalopathy* s.v. *BOVINE *a.* 3.

1989 *New Scientist* 4 Mar. 25/1 BSE, or '*mad cow disease*', is a neurological disorder that eventually destroys the nervous tissues. **1989** *Observer* 17 Sept. 4/8 Mad cow disease or bovine spongiform encephalopathy (BSE) has an incubation period of up to four years. **1990** *Australian* 17 Jan. 6/3 The British government yesterday denied United States military bases had banned British meat because of 'mad cow' disease. **1996** *Private Eye* 5 Apr. 12/1 In the West Country it is common knowledge that 'mad cow disease' was present at epidemic levels long before it was 'discovered' by Maffia [*sc.* Ministry of Agriculture, Fisheries, and Food] vets in Kent in 1985.

mad-dog *attrib. phr.*, (*a*) **mad-dog skullcap**, **weed** *U.S.*, the skullcap *Scutellaria lateriflora*, formerly reputed to cure hydrophobia.

1818 *Amer. Jrnl. Sci.* I. 371, July 17. *Mad dog weed (*Scutellaria lateriflora*), and purple vervain (*Verbena hastata*) in blossom. **1821** *Mass. Hist. Soc. Coll.* (1832) 2nd Ser. IX. 156 Scutellaria lateriflora, Mad dog scullcap. **1894** *Outing* Nov. 180/1 A delicate little herb with dainty, blue flowers is called mad-dog skull cap, from its imputed power of curing hydrophobia. **1968** PETERSON & MCKENNY *Field Guide Wildflowers Northeastern & North-Central N. America* 346 Mad-dog Skullcap... Easily recognized because the flowers are in slender 1-sided racemes in the leaf axils.

(*b*) orig. and chiefly *U.S.*, wild, reckless, or hare-brained, esp. dangerously so.

1904 *Collier's Mag.* 7 May 4/1 With the only successful trust curber a Republican and President, and the Democratic party full of mad-dog policies..it is impossible to draw this line. **1946** *Essays & Stud.* XXXI. 60 She knows..the divine patience of a Viola, the mad-dog fury of a Constance. **1962** S. E. FINER *Man on Horseback* x. 162 Mad-dog acts like..the Japanese February mutiny and the generals' revolt in France. **1987** R. R. MCCAMMON *Swan Song* I. i. 11 The arms brokers had fed..mad-dog leaders thirsting for power.

mad hatter [after one of the two eccentric hosts at the 'mad tea-party' in Lewis Carroll's *Alice's Adventures in Wonderland* (1865). As in the phrase *mad as a hatter* (see sense 10 below), Carroll's allusion is to the effects of mercury poisoning sometimes formerly suffered by hat-makers as a result of the use of mercurous nitrate in the manufacture of felt hats.], a highly eccentric or crazy character (freq. in *mad hatter's tea party*).

1909 *Westm. Gaz.* 28 Aug. 14/2 What possible interest can Spain have in a *mad-hatter attempt to subjugate the Riff district? **1955** *Times* 20 May 9/2, I shudder to think of the..consequences of this mad hatter's export subsidy scheme. **1974** *Times* 9 Nov. 12/6 The world of catering sometimes has the air of a mad hatter's tea party, as chefs and proprietors move from one place to the next. **1990** *Scuba Times* Mar.-Apr. 32/3, I watched the mad hatter of the sea, a large puffer fish, hovering over the top of our tiny world, flitting his tiny fins.

‖**Mädchen** ('mɛːtʃən), *n.* Also **mädchen**, **madchen**. [Ger.] In Germany and other German-speaking areas: a girl.

[**1827** M. WILMOT *Jrnl.* 28 June in *More Lett.* (1935) 264 We travel post in our close carriage, leaving Mrs Baynon to follow in the little green calash with Julia the stuben Mädchen and Nanny the Koechin.] **1854** C. M. YONGE *Heartsease* II. III. vii. 212 Is he not a hero, equal to his *hoch-beseeltes Mädchen?*...I cannot doubt who the *mädchen* is. **1892** E. DOWSON *Let. c13* Feb. (1967) 224 And for das Mädchen—she has never been more intimately charming. **1982** *N.Y. Times* 7 Nov. II. 5/2 Merely putting that idea in the mouth of a mindless blond madchen does not convey the horror of what Taylor attempted to portray. **1989** *Boston Globe* 13 Aug. Sports 68/1 Look out for the East German madchen to dominate this week's European swimming championships.

made, *ppl. a.* Sense in 5b in Dict. becomes 5c. Add: [**II.**] [**5.**] **b. made beaver** *Canad. Hist.*, a unit of exchange formerly used among fur traders, equivalent to the value of the prepared skin of one adult beaver in prime condition; a coin or token equivalent to this. Pl. often unchanged. Cf. *BEAVER n. 2 d.

1723 in K. G. Davies *Lett. from Hudson Bay* (1965) xx. 96, I understand their last year's trade did not exceed 12,000 skins everything made beaver. **1796** in A. M. JOHNSON *Saskatchewan Jrnls.* (1967) 25 Traded with three Indians that arrived at 3 a.m., brought ninety-two made beaver and a small quantity of provisions. **1843** in C. Wilson *Campbell of Yukon* (1970) vii. 63 Them you will engage for a summer's trip by boat to Fort Simpson and back..to be paid 50 Made Beaver each. **1928** L. R. FREEMAN *Nearing North* II. iv. 191 Accounts of white servants were kept in pounds, shillings and pence; those of the Indians in 'Made-Beavers'. *Ibid.*, Later brass discs were substituted for convenience, values as low as '¼ Made-Beaver' being issued. **1965** *North* (Ottawa) Nov./Dec. 29/2 Foxes were valued and an equivalent amount in 'Made Beaver' or shiny round HBC tokens was spread out on the counter. **1992** *Beaver* Aug. 32/1 This 'skin' or 'made beaver' is really of no special value except for the sake of book-keeping.

[**7.**] **d.** Used (esp. in *made man*) to designate a person who has been formally inducted as a full member of the Mafia. *slang* (orig. *U.S.*).

[**1950** H. E. GOLDIN *Dict. Amer. Underworld Lingo* 132/1 *Made*,...lifted out of mediocrity to a position of wealth or influence in the underworld. **1969** D. R. CRESSEY *Theft of Nation* x. 237 In the 1930's, members were 'made' in a rather elaborate oath-swearing ceremony which also was used by the Sicilian Mafia.] **1976** *Sunday Sun* (Brisbane) 13 June 54/5 The Mafia wouldn't..let them be 'made men' (official Mafiosi) because they thought they were too crazy. **1977** *Time* 16 May 28/2 The Mafia numbers about 5,000 'made men' or members. *Ibid.* 37/1 'Made' guys (Mafiosi) don't like their wives to mingle with the wives of other 'made' guys. **1983** *Daily Tel.* 1 Sept. 3 Not all are so-called 'made' members—those who have taken the Mafia oath of secrecy. **1987** C. SIFAKIS *Mafia Encycl.* 165/2 Jack Dragna..presided over the Weasel's initiation as a made man in the Los Angeles crime family. **1992** *Spy* (N.Y.) May 8/2 Having spent more than 15 years as a made member, I believe I am a good judge as to accuracy of mob-related stories.

[**II.**] [**9.**] [**a.**] **made-up**, (*h*) of a person or their face, features, etc.: wearing make-up (see MAKE-UP *n.* 2 b).

1773 O. GOLDSMITH *She stoops to Conquer* II. 45 You must allow her some beauty. *Tony*. Bandbox! She's all a made up thing, mun. **1792** M. WOLLSTONECRAFT *Vind. Rights Woman* xii. 392 Unless the understanding be cultivated, superficial and monotonous is every grace. Like the charms of a made up face, they only strike the senses in a crowd. **1815** F. BURNEY *Jrnl.* in *Jrnls. & Lett.* (1980) VIII. 539 M. de Talleyrand...The nearly imperturbable composure of his general—& certainly *made up* countenance. **1869** 'M. TWAIN' *Innocents Abroad* xxix. 311 They used to have a grand procession..once a year, to shave the head of a made-up Madonna—a stuffed and painted image, like a milliner's dummy—whose hair miraculously grew and restored itself every twelve months. **1915** W. S. MAUGHAM *Of Human Bondage* xxxv. 157 She was plain and old. His quick fancy showed her to him, wrinkled, haggard, made-up, in those frocks which were too showy for her position and too young for her years. **1937** A. CHRISTIE *Dumb Witness* xi. 121 She's a very queer-looking girl. Ultra modern, of course, and terribly made-up. **1969** ASHBERY & SCHUYLER *Nest of Ninnies* iv. 49 'What strangeness,' the woman said, opening her elaborately made-up eyes very wide. **1982** *Facts on File* 31 Dec. 993/1 Hair, soft with curls or chignons...and heavily made-up faces completed the 1982 fashion look.

b. **made-for-TV**, **made-for-television**, specially made for, or (occas.) ideally suited to, television. Similarly, **made-for-video**.

1973 *Chicago Sun-Times* 29 Dec. 25/1, I say Fred Astaire played a drunk in the made-for-TV movie 'The

Over-the-Hill Gang Rides Again'. **1985** *Music Week* 2 Feb. 16/4 There is a trend towards specific 'made-for-video' material. **1986** T. O'BRIEN *Nuclear Age* vi. 106 She closed her eyes during those made-for-TV combat clips. **1989** *Independent* 8 Nov. 36/8 You certainly don't get much [camaraderie] in snooker, that other great made-for-television sport. **1993** *Globe & Mail* (Toronto) 8 Jan. A9/5 The three Amy Fisher made-for-TV movies that aired last week.

Madeiran (mə'dɪərən), *a.* and *n.* Also (formerly) **Maderan**. [f. MADEIRA *n.*[1] + -AN.] **A.** *adj.* Of or pertaining to the island of Madeira or its people.
  1826 H. N. COLERIDGE *Six Months W. Indies* 27 The quintas or country residences of the English merchants are delightful, and it is a pretty thing to spend a Madeiran afternoon in riding about..from one to another. **1841** R. T. LOWE in *Trans. Zool. Soc. London* III. 174 This common Mediterranean and Maderan species appears occasionally to visit the coasts of Cornwall, following pieces of floating wreck or timber. **1883** *Encycl. Brit.* XV. 180/2 There are about a hundred plants which are peculiarly Madeiran. **1965** D. A. & W. M. BANNERMAN *Birds of Atlantic Islands* II. 89 The Madeiran chaffinch is a very handsome bird indeed. **1990** *Bull. Hispan. Stud.* LXVII. 343 Peninsular refers to the Spanish-speaking areas of the Peninsula; Portuguese to the continental Portuguese tradition as well as the Madeiran and Azoran versions.
  B. *n.* A native or inhabitant of Madeira.
  1885 J. Y. JOHNSON *Madeira* (ed. 3) v. 58 If the Azoreans and Madeirans would go in sufficient numbers, they would soon have 'Sandwich' to themselves, for the natives are rapidly dying off. **1900** A. J. D. BIDDLE *Madeira Islands* (rev. ed.) I. x. 238 Though they dislike the English, Madeirans are ardent admirers of the Americans. **1965** D. A. & W. M. BANNERMAN *Birds of Atlantic Islands* II. 55 A Madeiran with considerable..knowledge of the local birds. **1990** J. & S. FARROW *Madeira* (ed. 2) xii. 115 Like most Portuguese people, the Madeiran is very friendly and polite and, on occasions, very formal.

Madelung ('mæd(ə)lʊŋ), *n.*[1] *Path.* [The name of Otto Wilhelm *Madelung* (1846–1926), German surgeon, who described the condition in 1878 (*Verhandl. Deut. Ges. Chir.* VII. 259).] **Madelung's deformity**, a condition in which the hand is displaced in the direction of the radius owing to faulty development of the lower forearm, occurring mainly in girls.
  1905 BRADFORD & LOVETT *Treat. Orthopedic Surg.* (ed. 3) 663/1 (Index), Mahdelung's [*sic*] deformity of wrist. **1921** *Med. Jrnl. S. Afr.* XVI. 158/1 Dr. Dee showed a case of..spontaneous luxation of wrists—Madelung's deformity. **1944** S. BUNNELL *Surg. of Hand* xvi. 625/2 Madelung's deformity.. though first mentioned by Dupuytren in 1839, was described more completely in 1878 by Madelung. **1966** *McGraw-Hill Encycl. Sci. & Technol.* XII. 368/1 Rarer congenital defects include..deformities of growth of the bones of the lower arm (Madelung's deformity). **1979** *Hand* XI. 74 The radiological criteria in the report leave no doubt that this is a case of Madelung's deformity.

Madelung ('mæd(ə)lʊŋ), *n.*[2] *Physics.* [The name of Erwin *Madelung* (1881–1972), German physicist.] Used *attrib.* to designate concepts relating to crystal structure, as **Madelung constant**, a fixed number associated with a specified ionic crystalline solid, usually defined for materials with a halite-like crystal lattice as the product of potential energy per constituent ion and the inter-ionic distance divided by the square of the electronic charge, and similarly for materials with other crystal structures; **Madelung potential**, the potential at any point

in an ionic lattice due to the combined electric field of all the ions in the lattice.
  1932 J. SHERMAN in *Chem. Rev.* XI. 106 In the sodium chloride structure, the first for which the Madelung constant was evaluated (by Madelung himself), the positions of the ions are completely determined by the symmetry requirements of the structure. **1966** *Physical Rev.* CXLIV. 753/1 Crystals of the general types M_n and X_m do not have this property of a symmetric Madelung potential influence. **1978** H. M. ROSENBERG *Solid State* (ed. 2) i. 14 For the NaCl lattice the Madelung constant is almost exactly 1.75. **1987** *Jrnl. Chem. Physics* LXXXVI. 6959/2 The Mulliken charge approximation for the evaluation of the Madelung potential.

madison ('mædɪsən), *n.*[1] *Cycling.* Also **Madison**. [App. f. the name of *Madison* Square Garden, the sports and entertainment arena in New York City, where the first such race was held in 1892.] A relay race for teams of (usu.) two riders, traditionally lasting for six days, but freq. of much shorter duration. Also *attrib.* as **madison race**.
  The earliest six-day races (apparently referred to at the time as 'Six Days' and 'Grinds') were for individual competitors; the first team event was held in 1899.
  1951 *Cycling* 10 May 498/1 The professional sprinter may be seen in Madison and six-day races. **1977** B. GEORGE *Bicycle Track Racing* 38 The most prestigious, most demanding..of all the all-around track events is the Madison, or team race...A track race for teams of two or three riders each, the Madison can last six days or six hours. **1992** *Bicycle* Feb. 98/2 We're a very successful team together; we think along the same lines and are both technically similar in the way we race. So not having madisons put us at a disadvantage

Madisonian (mædɪ'səʊnɪən), *a.* [f. the name of James *Madison* (1751–1836), President of the United States 1809–17 + -IAN.] Of or pertaining to President Madison or his political doctrines, esp. his federalist views on democracy.
  1813 *Niles' Weekly Reg.* IV. Suppl. 65/1 This is true Jeffersonian, Madisonian, democratic economy. **1975** *Economist* 25 Oct. 32/2 America's multi-consensus Madisonian system is now causing the money spent on government to soar and yet be insufficient at the same time. **1991** *N. Y. Times Mag.* 1 Dec. 73/1 If the people are sovereign, they must be free to examine and criticize those whom they choose to govern from time to time. It is the Madisonian premise..of democracy.

Mad Max (mæd 'mæks), *n.* [The name of the eponymous hero of the film *Mad Max* (1979) and its sequels.] *attrib.* Denoting situations and objects (such as vehicles, clothing, etc.) similar to those portrayed in the Mad Max films, set in a futuristic world characterized by extreme and anarchic violence; also (freq. *absol.*) denoting people (both real and fictional) resembling Mad Max.
  1986 *Courier-Mail* (Brisbane) 26 June 10/2 To publicise its drive for more police, the association has produced a series of advertisements, to start this weekend, showing people in the type of Mad Max gear it predicts will be needed soon on Sydney streets. **1991** *Christian Science Monitor* 22 Oct. 5/2 He also operates six or seven workshops that convert four-wheel-drive trucks into 'Road Warriors' or 'Mad Max' vehicles mounted with 106mm antitank cannons and heavy machine guns. **1992** *City Limits* 2 July 28/3 Hauer plays Harley Stone, a kind of international Mad Max, out to avenge his pardner. **1995** *Empire* July 28/4 Set in a drought-stricken Mad Max futurescape..the film stars Petty as the gun-crazed heroine.

Madras, *n.* Add: **4.** A hot curry dish traditionally associated with Madras, containing chicken, meat, or fish in a vegetable sauce. In early use freq. *attrib.* as **Madras curry**; now also used postpositively.

1870 'P.O.P' *Nabob's Cookery Bk.* 10 (*heading*) A Madras currie. **1891** *Girl's Own Paper* 11 Apr. 440/1 Madras curry. Take three large onions, slice and fry them in butter. Then fry your meat in the same pan, first taking out the onions. Stir into a pint of well-seasoned gravy—two large spoonfuls of curry powder, a little sour apple, and a little salt. **1914** 'SAKI' *Beasts & Super-beasts* 117 Your great-aunt Adelaide..was a charming woman..but somehow she always reminded me of an English cook's idea of a Madras curry. **1959** *Good Food Guide* 316 Curried chicken Madras with poppadoms and Bombay duck. **1973** M. BENCE-JONES *Palaces of Raj* i. 25 Most curries are labelled Madras, even though they may bear scant resemblance to the magnificent dish found..at the Madras Club. **1982** BARR & YORK *Official Sloane Ranger Handbk.* 27/1 His macho-masochisms decree that he must order the hottest Vindaloo, Madras, or even Bangalore Phal.

‖**madre** ('madre, ∫p. maðrə), *n.* [It., Sp.] Mother. Chiefly in exclamatory phrases, as **Madre de Dios** (It. *di Dio*) [lit. 'mother of God'], **Madre mia!** [lit. 'mother mine'] (cf. **Mamma mia** s.v. MAMMA *n.*[1] d).

1815 F. BURNEY *Let.* 27 July in *Jrnls. & Lett.* (1980) VIII. 458 Dearest Madre, I came here yesterday [etc.]. **1964** J. MASTERS *Trial at Monomoy* ii. 49 *Madre mia*, why did people have to come when they were least wanted? **1971** H. MACINNES *Message from Malaga* (1972) xii. 181 'Oh, *Madre de Dios*,' she said impatiently. 'How should I know?' **1972** B. LILLIE *Every Other Inch a Lady* (1973) xii. 225 The future Duke of Edinburgh..used to call Cobina, Sr., '*madre*'. **1973** M. CATTO *Sam Casanova* vi. 126 *Madre di Dios*, what are we going to do? **1987** *Life* Dec. 133/2 Outside, American expatriates cheer the Sandinistas. Madre de Dios, what happens next?

madreporian (mædrɪ'pɔːrɪən), *a. & n. Zool. rare.* [f. MADREPOR(E *n.* + -IAN.] **A.** *adj.* = MADREPORIC *a.* **1.** **B.** *n.* = MADREPORE *n.*

In some instances prob. a mistake for MADREPORARIAN *a. & n.*

1890 WEBSTER, *Madreporian*, resembling, or pertaining to, the genus Madrepora. **1898** *N.E.D.* s.v. *Gemmipore*, A genus of madreporian corals. **1961** WEBSTER, *Madreporian*, madreporic..madrepore. **1984** *Bollettino Malacologico* (Milan) XX. 91 (*Abstr.*) We suppose that the relationship between the mollusk and the madreporian is both trophic (parasitism) and linked to spawning. **1991** *New Scientist* 30 Nov. 53/3 Each interconnected, flower-like madreporian polyp is impregnated with zooanthellae [*sic*].

‖**madrich** (ma'drix, 'madrɪx), *n.* Also **madrikh.** Pl. **madrichim.** [ad. Hebrew *maḏrīk* guide, leader, f. *dereḵ* path, route.] A group leader or supervisor (esp. on a kibbutz).

1944 N. BENTWICH *Jewish Youth comes Home* xi. 115 Parties of fifty to one hundred would travel together, accompanied by their Madrich, who taught them on the way. **1952** S. SPENDER *Learning Laughter* vii. 97 He should see a *madrichim* [*sic*] attached to each group of 20 or 30 children. **1968** P. DURST *Badge of Infamy* i. 3 There were two others in the picture; a man of twenty-five or so who was probably the *madrich* or supervisor, and another girl...It had been taken..at a..kibbutz. **1971** *Encycl. Judaica* XVI. 864/2 Each *ḥevrat no'ar* had a *madrikh* and a *metappelet* (house mother)...In the early years most of the *madrikhim* were temporary, coming from the kibbutzim for a spell of duty. **1973** *Jewish Observer* Nov. 28/3 Our *madrichim*, who expected us to be fatigued, were surprised at our heightened mood when we came home.

madrigalian, *a.* Add: Hence **madri'galianism** *n.* = *MADRIGALISM *n.*

1968 *Listener* 25 July 121/2 These melting dissonances..seem to be obvious madrigalianisms, word-painting of a kind conventional enough at this time. **1977** *Gramophone* Jan. 1167/2 The later sixteenth-century composers, with their madrigalianisms and the resources of *musica reservata*.

madrigalism ('mædrɪgəliz(ə)m), *n. Mus.* [f. MADRIGAL *n.* + -ISM 3. Cf. F. *madrigalisme*.] A musical feature characteristic of a madrigal, *spec.* a word or phrase set to music in a way which vividly illustrates its literal meaning.

1968 *New Oxf. Hist. Mus.* IV. iii. 122 Schein almost completely forsook the model of Regnart's *villanelle*.., crowding his work with imitations, word-repetition, madrigalisms, and passage-work. **1976** *Early Mus.* July 335/3 The renaissance masters were not above using the occasional madrigalism. **1979** *Ibid.* July 371/2 The madrigalisms for which Pevernage and Lassus both show a fondness. **1980** *New Grove Dict. Mus.* XX. 529/1 Word-painting..was one of the principal features defined by the word 'madrigalism'.

‖**madrina** (ma'ðrina; *anglicized* məd'riːnə), *n.* [Sp. *madrina* godmother; protectress; lead mare.] **1.** A mare of at least five years old which wears a bell and leads a troop of pack animals, esp. mules.

1835 C. DARWIN *Diary* 18 Mar. (1933) 288 The Madrina is a mare with a little bell round her neck...The affection of the mules for the Madrina saves an infinity of trouble. **1913** WEBSTER s.v., *Madrina*, an animal (usually an old mare), wearing a bell and acting as the leader of a troop of pack mules. **1928** *Funk's Stand. Dict.* s.v., *Madrina*, the leader of a train of pack-mules.

2. a. [The literal sense in Sp.] A godmother.

1971 J. H. KELLEY in R. Moisés et al. *Tall Candle* p. xlv, Rosalio's paternal grandmother was almost a professional *madrina*, so many times did she serve in that capacity. **1986** D. CHÁVEZ *Last of Menu Girls* 168 God help the ahijado, if he forgets who his madrina or padrino is. **1992** R. ANAYA *Alburquerque* viii. 91 In the faces of the padrino and madrina I saw and understood the godparents' role.

b. *transf. and fig.*

1979 *Washington Post* 27 May F5/6 The madrina (or godmother) gives you a bath with 1001 herbs and sings in African. **1991** *Internat. Jrnl. Refugee Law* III. 225 There are only officially about 1,500 federal judicial police.., but each of them has his own private paramilitary group working with him. These men, known as 'Madrinas', godmothers, number an estimated 5,000. **1994** *Town & Country Monthly* May 134/1 Donors are invited to become madrinas 'godmothers' to funded projects, helping with fundraising and public relations.

maenad, *n.* Add: '**maenadism** *n.*, wild or frenzied behaviour.

1909 WEBSTER, Mænadism. **1961** A. HUXLEY *Let.* 29 Oct. (1969) 925 Maenadism, the Dionysian orgies, ..represent methods for harmlessly expressing the dangerous feelings engendered by instinctive drives. **1977** *Times Lit. Suppl.* 29 July 924/4 The Greek mystery cult of Bacchus, which featured a considerable streak of maenadism,..spread rapidly through the peninsula. **1993** W. WEAVER tr. *U. Eco's Misreadings* 78 As if, in the grip of a kind of maenadism, they viewed the path to the sea as their only escape.

maestro, *n.* Senses a-b in Dict. become b-c. Delete quot. 1797 from sense a. Add: **a.** With capital initial. A title used to denote or address one who is a master of or who has achieved eminence in a skill or profession, esp. a musician.

1607 Sir H. Wotton *Let.* 13 Sept. (1907) I. 399 A very true picture..of Maestro Paulo the Servite. **1797** A. Radcliffe *Italian* p. vii, He might be a ghost, by his silence, for aught I know, Maestro. **1875** H. James *Roderick Hudson* in *Atlantic Monthly* Mar. 307/2 The marriage was most unhappy, and the Maestro Grandoni was suspected of using the fiddle-bow as an instrument of conjugal correction. **1991** *Piano Q.* Fall 24/2 Maestro, the tone is already better than at the beginning.

Maffei ('mæfeɪ), *n. Astron.* [The name of Paolo *Maffei* (b. 1926), Italian astronomer, who described the galaxies in 1968 (*Publ. Astron. Soc. Pacific* LXXX. 618).] *attrib.* and *absol.* Designating either of two galaxies discovered by Maffei near the galactic equator, which are visible only in red and infrared light. More fully in *Maffei 1* and *Maffei 2.*

1971 *Astrophysical Jrnl: Lett.* CLXIII. L25 Maffei 1 is a nearby elliptical galaxy, probably on the edge of the Local Group. **1983** *Monthly Notices R. Astron. Soc.* CCV. 150 Maffei 1 is probably not a member of the Local Group, but, instead, is a likely member of the nearby Ursa Major-Camelopardalis Cloud. **1985** *Astrophysical Jrnl.* CCXCVII. 566/1 This value of the column density was used in the flux determination for source 4 (which is probably associated with the Maffei galaxy). **1993** *Astron.* Oct. 58/2 Instead of producing thousands of nearly identical M 31 images each year, astro-imagers are now imaging Maffei I, NGC 520.., and NGC 2683. **1993** *Astrophysical Jrnl.* CDXIV. 122/2 The emission peaks in Maffei 2 and IC 342 are displaced 25–50 pc from the nuclei.

magalogue ('mægəlɒg), *n.* orig. *U.S.* Also **magalog.** [Blend of MAGAZINE *n.* and CATALOGUE *n.*] A (usu. free) promotional catalogue or sales brochure designed to resemble a high-quality magazine.

1978 *Business Week* 23 Oct. 148/3 One experiment that Texaco Inc. hopes will boost volume is a 'magalogue', a new kind of mailing to 200,000..credit-card customers. **1985** *Folio* (U.S.) June 19/2 Many catalogs and magalogs now have distribution and even publishing frequencies rivaling those of monthly magazines. **1986** *Observer* 19 Oct. 16/2 A 'magalogue'—the media jargon for the new wave of free magazines which, like catalogues, are designed primarily to part the well-off from their cash. **1990** *Atlantic* Apr. 43/1 Each of them comes sidling toward us dressed up as non-advertising, just as other kinds of ads now routinely come at us as 'magalogues' and 'advertorials'.

‖**magatama** ('mɑːgətɑːmə), *n.* Pl. **magatama, magatamas.** [Jap., lit. 'curved jewel', f. *magaru* to curve, bend + *tama* jewel.] A type of small, comma-shaped ornamental jewel, usu. made of green jade, worn as a pendant, earring, etc., esp. in Japan, where it also forms part of the imperial regalia.

1876 W. C. Borlase *Niphon & its Antiquities* 28 A *magatama* proper is in shape like a magnified comma, rounded at the larger end..and tapering to a point at the other. **1931** G. B. Sansom *Japan* I. i. 9 Most prominent among them are the 'curved jewels' (*magatama*), which are evidently derived from the claws or tusks of animals. **1970** J. W. Hall *Japan from Prehist. to Mod. Times* iii. 21 They decorated themselves with *magatama*, or curved jewels. **1977** G. Clark *World Prehist.* (ed. 3) vii. 330 Among personal ornaments it is interesting to note the popularity of perforated animal teeth and claws, prototypes of the imperial curved jewel (*magatama*). **1989** *Encycl. Brit.* VII. 667/2 In Korea, jade *magatamas* are also sporadically found at prehistoric sites, but they were in greatest vogue during the old Silla kingdom, the period corresponding to the Tumulus period in Japan.

magcon ('mægkɒn), *n. Astron.* [f. *magnetization concentration*, after MASCON *n.*] Any of several regions of the lunar surface where the magnetic field strength is anomalously high.

1971 A. Barnes et al. in *Science* 14 May 716/3 It is unlikely that such a region of permanent magnetism ('magcon') is unique. *Ibid.* 717/2 We expect that at some distance from the limb the presence of a magcon is manifested in a hydromagnetic shock wave. **1983** *Nature* 18 Aug. 589/2 The discovery of small regions of the [Moon's] surface with magnetic fields of 10nT coherent over many 10 km, termed 'magcons'. **1987** *Geophysical Res. Lett.* XIV. 846/2 From the observed angular extents of the magcons (several hundred km), field amplifications by factors of..300 may be expected.

Magdalen, *n.* Add: Hence '**Magdalenism** *n.*, prostitution.

1840 W. Tait (*title*) Magdalenism. An inquiry into the extent, causes, and consequences of prostitution in Edinburgh. **1951** E. Paul *Springtime in Paris* iv. 90 Non-professional competition..has gnawed away the foundations of Magdalenism.

Maghrebin (magrebɛ̃n), *n.* and *a.* Also (anglicized) **Maghrebine** (-bin) and with lower-case initial. [ad. Fr. *Maghrébin*, f. Arab. *maġribi* (see MAGHRIBI *n.* and *a.*) + *-in* masculine suffix (see -INE¹).] = MAGHRIBI *n.* and *a.*

1898 A. J. Butler tr. *Ratzel's Hist. Mankind* III. v. v. 196 The Islamite world witnessed a great struggle for supremacy between..the Maghrebin in the west, the Mashrikin in the east. **1911** D. S. Margoliouth *Mohammedanism* i. 20 At the battle of Las Navas de Tolosa in 1212 the Maghrebine power received a serious blow in Spain. **1976** *Brit. Jrnl. Sociol.* XXVII. 3 We cannot seek the model for the classical Maghrebin city either in Western Feudal society or in 'Asiatic' society. **1991** *Times Educ. Suppl.* 22 Feb. 29/2 In France being of Maghrebin origin..now 'equals Muslim fundamentalism equals an admirer of Saddam Hussein'.

magic, *a.* Add: [**2.**] [a.] **magic bullet** *colloq.* (chiefly *Med.*) [prob. tr. G. *Zauberkugel*, attributed to Paul Ehrlich (1854–1915), German medical scientist, in connection with his search for a cure for syphilis], a therapeutic agent that is highly specific for the organism or disorder concerned, *esp.* one not yet discovered or isolated; also *transf.*

[**1936** G. B. Shaw *Millionairess* Pref. 127 War is like the seven magic bullets which the devil has ready to sell for a human soul. Six of them may hit the glorymonger's mark very triumphantly; but the seventh plays some unexpected and unintended trick that upsets the gunman's apple cart.] **1940** *Life* 4 Mar. 74/3 In 1910 the little physician who said: 'We must learn to shoot microbes with *magic bullets, was acclaimed for 'the greatest single therapeutic agent known to medicine'. **1949** M. Marquardt *Paul Ehrlich* ix. 91 The antibodies..are Magic Bullets, which find their target by themselves. **1954** *Antibiotics & Chemotherapy* IV. 250 Paul Ehrlich..once said, 'We have to learn to make magic bullets, which, like those of the ancient fable, will not miss the mark and will destroy only those pathogenic agents they are aimed at.' **1976** *Jrnl. Amer. Med. Assoc.* 13 Sept. 1286/3 Laetrile, no longer claimed to be a 'magic bullet' that destroys cancer cells with cyanide. **1988** *Times* 24 Mar. 5/2 Monoclonal antibodies, popularly known as 'magic bullets', can be directed against cancer cells, bacteria and viruses. **1990** *Gay Times* May 10/4 Finding a 'magic bullet' against HIV is a daunting task; some experts believe it is impossible. **1992** *Jrnl.* (Milwaukee) 25 July A6/1 No one has yet found a magic bullet for quickly cutting Milwaukee's crime rate.

magic mushroom *colloq.* (orig. *U. S.*), any of several types of mushroom with hallucinogenic properties, *esp.* one containing psilocybin.

1966 *N. Y. Times* 21 Mar. 1/3 It damn near turned into a recipe-swapping session for peyote and the *magic mushrooms. **1982** *Sunday Times* 28 Nov. 14/7 The magic mushroom, *psilocybin* [*sic*] *semilanceata*, produces hallucinogenic effects comparable to LSD. It grows widely in Britain, but is particularly plentiful in west Wales. **1991** J. PHILLIPS *You'll never eat Lunch in this Town Again* 569 The next day we have the last of some magic mushrooms and Stuart gets so loose he takes off all his clothes.

magic realism *Art* and *Lit.* [tr. G. *magischer Realismus* (coined in 1924 by Franz Roh and used in 1925 in the subtitle of his book *Nach-Expressionismus*)], orig. a style of painting which depicts fantastic or bizarre images in a precise representationalist manner (first used in German to describe the work of members of the Neue Sachlichkeit movement); *transf.*, any artistic or esp. literary style in which realistic techniques such as naturalistic detail, narrative, etc., are similarly combined with surreal or dreamlike elements.

1933 J. LEFTWICH tr. *F. Werfel's Saverio's Secret* in *Yisroël* 526 You will find it in all the little shop windows in the rue de la Boëtie, that *magic realism which is the new word. **1963** B. S. MYERS *Expressionism* v. §29 229 In the hands of progressive Germans of the twenties (as with the Americans Charles Sheeler and Georgia O'Keefe, the Frenchman Pierre Roy, and others), Magic Realism is a meaningful and historically important movement. **1970** R. S. RUDDER tr. A Serrano-Plaja (*title*) 'Magic' realism in Cervantes. **1987** M. ATWOOD *Sunrise* in *Bluebeard's Egg* 246 People bought her paintings though not for ultra-top prices, especially after magic realism came back in. **1991** E. J. SMYTH *Postmodernism & Contemp. Fiction* i. 34 Fantasy also figures centrally in the work of Salman Rushdie, its interfusion with the more prosaic material demonstrating Rushdie's incorporation into the novel in English of the exuberant magic realism developed by South Americans such as Gabriel Garcia Marquez.

magic realist *n.* and *a.*

1943 MILLER & BARR *Amer. Realists & Magic Realists* 5 The subject, *Realists and *Magic Realists*, was chosen to demonstrate a widespread but not yet generally recognized trend in contemporary American art. **1959** *Times Lit. Suppl.* 6 Nov. p. xxix/2 For his intensity of vision he [*sc.* Charles Sheeler] may well be considered a forerunner of the Magic Realists. **1981** *N.Y. Times* 11 Oct. VII. 36/4 A number of Chicano writers admit what critics of contemporary Latin American fiction call 'magic realist' elements into their work. **1990** *Sunday Tel.* 18 Feb. 50/5 The magic realist mode frees him from any obligation to make the incidents he devises probable or in any way convincing.

b. Effecting or permitting change, development, success, etc., as if by magic; all-important, crucial, momentous.

1861 DICKENS *Great Expect.* II. xiv. 224, I requested a waiter..to show us to a private sitting room. Upon that, he pulled out a napkin, as if it were a magic clue without which he couldn't find the way up-stairs, and led us to the blackhole of the establishment. **1869** L. M. ALCOTT *Little Women* II. iv. 49 'I think the money is the best part of it. What *will* you do with such a fortune?' asked Amy, regarding the magic slip of paper with a reverential eye. **1916** JOYCE *Portrait of Artist* (1969) ii. 65 Weakness and timidity and inexperience would fall from him in that magic moment. **1938** I. KUHN *Assigned to Adventure* iii. 26 The thing I wanted most was a by-line — that magic inch of print above a story I had written which would identify me as the author of the gem. **1986** *Observer* 17 Aug. 29/1 The gold price has refused — as yet — to break through the 'magic' $400-an-ounce barrier that chartists (and gold-bugs) cherish. **1993** *Sci. News* 30 Oct. 280/2 The

magic ingredient? Polyacrylamide (PAM), a long-chain molecule commonly used to clean waste water.

magical, *a.* Add: **4.** Special collocations: **magical realism** = *magic realism* s.v. *MAGIC a.* 2 a.

1937 H. T. LOWE-PORTER tr. *F. Werfel's Twilight of World* 394 In all the little show-windows in the rue de La Boëtie you will see the *magical realism which is the last word today. **1980** *N.Y. Times* 29 June (Connecticut Weekly section) 16/1 'Mysterious and Magical Realism', the theme now at the Aldrich Museum through August, has more than 50 works by 40 artists to illustrate it. **1983** *Ibid.* 22 May II. 14/5 Masters of 'magical realism', like Gabriel Garcia Marquez and Miguel Angel Asturias.

magical realist *a.* and *n.* = *magic realist n.* and *a.* s.v. *MAGIC a.* 2 a.

1981 *N.Y. Times Bk. Rev.* 11 Oct. 36/5, I would like to think that a novelita like 'Tamazunchale' transcended the labels ethnic, Chicano, *magical realist, or fantasist. **1983** *Time* 7 Mar. 79/1 The man who once dreaded that he might become 'the third-rate Faulkner of the Third World' was hailed as its leading magical realist. **1986** *Atlantic Monthly* Mar. 104/2 The Latin-American novel has always been Quixotic — playful, self-conscious, 'magical realist'. **1990** N. WILLIAMS *Wimbledon Poisoner* xxii. 148 Henry disliked most species of fiction writer but of all of them considered magical realists to be the most suspect.

magma, *n.* Add: **mag'matically** *adv.*, as regards magma; from or by means of magma.

1947 *Jrnl. Geol.* LV. 330/1 A group of basic intrusions in the Baker quadrangle are all believed to be magmatically related and hence of a single intrusive cycle. **1977** A. HALLAM *Planet Earth* 112 Magmatically derived water, meteoric water.. sea water and water contained in deep sedimentary formations have all been found in the cores of porphyry copper deposits. **1988** *Nature* 28 Apr. 779/1 A cause of controversy is the hypothesis that this accretionary plate boundary is segmented into adjacent but separate spreading cells, each driven magmatically but possibly by different plumes.

magnaflux, *n.* Add: Hence as *v. trans.*, to test using the magnaflux method.

1959 *Manch. Guardian* 3 Jan. 5/4 'Magnaflux the elephant ears and run a test on the kill switch before checking out the tranquillisers.' This is not a code. A technician at the new American air base at Vandenberg, California, would understand it perfectly. **1987** *Dirt Wheels Mag.* Aug. 25/1 You can take the stock rod and have it magnafluxed for hidden flaws and then shot-peened for strength.

magnesiochromite (mæg,niːzɪəʊˈkrəʊmaɪt), *n. Min.* [f. *MAGNOCHROMITE n.* after MAGNESIOFERRITE *n.*] Orig., a mineral, (Mg, Fe)Cr_2O_4, analogous to chromite (FeCr_2O_4), with magnesium replacing much of the iron. Now usu., a spinel of the general formula (Mg, Fe)(Cr,Al)$_2O_4$, *spec.* the end-member picrochromite, MgCr_2O_4.

1892 E. S. DANA *Dana's Syst. Min.* (ed. 6) 228 The iron may be replaced by magnesium as in magnochromite (magnesiochromite) below. **1913** *Mineral. Mag.* XVI. 364 Magnesiochromite.., the same as magnochromite (G. M. Bock, 1868). A variety of chromite containing magnesium, (Fe,Mg)Cr_2O_4. **1929** *Amer. Mineralogist* XIV. 355 Chromite is usually a combination of the pure chromite molecule plus the so-called magnesiochromite of Bock, hercynite and spinel. Magnesiochromite represents a spinellid that stands between spinel and chromite. **1976** *Earth & Planetary Sci. Lett.* XXIX. 12/2 By far the most common type of spinels observed are magnesiochromites. *Ibid.*, Magnesiochromites have Cr as the dominant trivalent cation and

$Mg^{2+} > Fe^{2+}$. *Ibid.* 19/1 The three spinel groups closely reflect the gross chemical nature of the basalts: magnesiochromites are found in olivine-normative tholeiites, chromian spinels in Al_2O_3-rich picrite and titaniferous magnesiochromites in olivine basalt with pronounced alkaline affinities. **1992** W. A. DEAR et al. *Introd. Rock-Forming Minerals* (ed.2) 568 In general terms the magnesiochromites and the chromites (*sensu stricto*) have the same paragenesis, the commonest member of the series probably being ferroan magnesiochromite.

magnetic, *a.* and *n.* Sense A.5 in Dict becomes A.6. Add: [A.] **5.** *Naut.* and *Aeronaut.* Of a bearing: measured relative to magnetic north. Also *postpositive.* Cf. TRUE *a.* 4 i.
    1744 W. MOUNTAINE *Atkinson's Epitome Art Navigation* x. 257 In the Afternoon let the Sun's true Azimuth be 115 Degrees and the Magnetic Azimuth 101 Degrees. **1772** J. H. MOORE *Pract. Navigator* 179 The Magnetic Azimuth is an Arch of the Horizon contained between the Sun's Azimuth Circle and the Magnetic Meridian. **1850** J. GREENWOOD *Sailor's Sea-bk.* 1. 6 This last is called the true course; while E.S.E.½s. is the compass or magnetic course. **1896** V. J. ENGLISH *Navigation for Yachtsmen* ix. 81 The correct magnetic course is the angle between the direction of a ship's head and the magnetic meridian, or line passing through the place of the ship and the magnetic pole. **1930** F. CHICHESTER *Solo to Sydney* iii. 41, I went over them all [sc. strip-maps], first marking the magnetic variation every few hundred miles, next working out the magnetic bearing of each change in direction. **1958** 'N. SHUTE' *Rainbow & Rose* ii. 39, I . . laid out the course upon my map . . . It was about a hundred and fifteen miles, course 178 degrees magnetic, practically due south. **1983** *Boating* Apr. 100/1 Distances are nautical miles, bearings in degrees (magnetic or true), and time in hours and minutes.
    magnetic resonance imaging *Med.*, imaging of the internal structure of body tissue by the observation of magnetic resonances induced in them; abbrev. *MRI.*
    1977 *Jrnl. Magnetic Resonance* XXVIII. 133 (*heading*) 19F *magnetic resonance imaging. **1989** *Brit. Med. Jrnl.* 22 July 215/2 Measurement of the volume of prostate by magnetic resonance imaging showed a 28% reduction. **1992** *N.Y. Times Mag.* 18 Oct. 50/3 In the $9.5 million brain-imaging center located in the basement of the hospital, the Iowa team has already pushed magnetic resonance imaging to its limit.

magnetoid ('mægnɪtɔɪd), *n. Astron.* [ad. Russ. *magnitod* (coined by L.M. Ozernoï 1966, in *Astron. Zhurnal* XLIII. 301): see MAGNET *n.,* -OID.] A hypothetical supermassive rotating body of magnetized plasma, postulated to account for the huge energy output of quasars. Cf. SPINAR *n.*
    1966 tr. L. M. Ozernoï in *Astron. Zhurnal* XLIII. 301 A quasistationary configuration — magnetoid is considered for the construction of an idealized scheme of multivarious phenomena occurring in galactic nuclei and especially in the central parts of quasistellar radio sources. **1970** *Nature* 19 Dec. 1175/1 The most plausible hypothesis to explain the activity of QSOs and galactic nuclei seems to be the so-called 'magnetoid' hypothesis. **1977** *Astron. & Astrophysics* LVI. 166/2 We will consider the simplest realization of a magnetoid i.e. in the form of a supermassive oblique rotator . . having solid-body rotation and quasi-dipole magnetic field. **1984** *Q. Jrnl. R. Astron. Soc.* XXV. 28 We use the term 'spinar' even though the term 'magnetoid' would be equally well applicable.

magnificent, *a.* and *n.* Add: [A.] **7.** *attrib.* and *Comb.* in the names of animals, esp. birds, having an imposing or splendid appearance (cf. SUPERB *a.* 2 b), as *magnificent scallop.*

1990 *Scuba Times* Mar.-Apr. 30/3 Red-lipped batfish, 'yellow' black coral, *magnificent scallops, red-spotted barnacle blennies, Galapagos sharks and endangered green sea turtles are only a few of the other marine anomalies you will encounter. **1991** *Sea Frontiers* Mar.-Apr. 12/1 (*caption*) Bright blue eyes dot the mantle edges of a magnificent scallop (*Lyropecten magnificus*. .), found in the Galapagos.
    magnificent bird of paradise [tr. Fr.: see quot. 1776], the bird of paradise *Diphyllodes magnificus.*
    [**1776** P. SONNERAT *Voyage à la Nouvelle Guinée* xii. 163 Le cinquieme oiseau de Paradis, ou celui que je nommerai le Magnifique, est d'un tiers moins gros que le précédent.] **1782** J. LATHAM *Gen. Synopsis Birds* I. Plate XIX (*caption*) *Magnificent Bird of Paradise. **1931** L. S. CRANDALL *Paradise Quest* v. 100 Before the day was out we had received two more male six-plumes, as well as two or three of the species known as the magnificent bird of paradise. **1989** *Sci. Amer.* Dec. 71/3 The polygymous magnificent bird of paradise.
    magnificent frigate bird, the largest of the frigate birds, *Fregata magnificens,* found on the tropical and subtropical coasts of the Americas and on the Cape Verde Islands.
    1956 R. T. PETERSON & J. FISHER *Wild Amer.* xiii. 142 The *magnificent frigate-birds . . numbered about eighty. **1992** *From the Land* Fall 10/2 The presence of magnificent frigatebirds soaring overhead reminds us this is the tropics.
    magnificent fruit dove = *WOMPOO *n.*
    1976 E. S. GRUSON *Checklist Birds of World* 42 *Ptilinopus magnificus.* *Magnificent Fruit Dove.
    magnificent fruit pigeon = *WOMPOO *n.*
    1844 J. GOULD *Birds Austral.* (1848) V. Pl. 58 *Carpophaga magnifica.* *Magnificent Fruit Pigeon. **1940** B. O'REILLY *Green Mountains* 111 An occasional wampoo — that miracle of purple and green, to which the naturalist . . has given the vernacular name of magnificent fruit pigeon. **1966** N. W. CAYLEY *What Bird is That?* (ed. 4) 23 Wompoo Pigeon . . . Also called Magnificent Fruit-Pigeon.
    magnificent rifle bird, the rifle bird *Ptiloris magnificus,* of northern Queensland and New Guinea.
    1855 A. WHITE *Pop. Hist. Birds* 58 If gorgeous plumage confer kingship on birds, the truly *magnificent Rifle-bird (*Ptiloris magnifica*) . . may be regarded as a king of its family. **1890** *Ibis* II. 151 We came across the magnificent Rifle-bird (*Ptilorhis magnifica*) on Mount Kowald, as also on Mount Belford, at an altitude of 3000 feet and over. **1969** E. T. GILLIARD *Birds of Paradise & Bower Birds* vi. 118 The Magnificent Rifle Bird has the distinction of being one of the two species of birds of paradise which is shared by both New Guinea and Australia.
    magnificent spider, the spider *Dicrostichus magnificus* of eastern Australia, noted for making spindle-shaped egg sacs several inches long.
    1936 K. C. McKEOWN *Spider Wonders Austral.* vi. 94 These spiders whose unobtrusive habits conceal behaviour perhaps unparalleled in the spider-world are the *Magnificent Spider, her sister, the Hairy Imperial Spider, and the Orchard or Death's Head Spider. **1952** W. A. BEATTY *Unique to Austral.* 63 The Magnificent spider . . has a beautiful mosaic pattern with a finely sculptured royal crown upon its back . . . This spider comes out at night to feed upon night-flying moths. **1969** D. CLYNE *Guide Austral. Spiders* 74 *D. Magnificus . . the* Magnificent spider — is a rather lumpy-looking spider when at rest.
    B. *n.* An animal, esp. a bird, with a common name beginning 'magnificent'.
    1931 L. S. CRANDALL *Paradise Quest* v. 100 In the mountains, magnificents are the most abundant of the birds of paradise. **1931** *Times Lit. Suppl.* 5 Nov. 859/3 The first day's work produced three six-plumes (*Parotia lawesi lawesi*) and two or three magnificents (*Diphyllodes magnificus hunsterni*) — the latter, a lovely little bird

hardly as large as an American robin. **1989** *Sci. Amer.* Dec. 69 (*caption*) Male and female magnificents..are similar in size.

magnificently, *adv.* Add: **3.** More generally: extremely well, wonderfully, excellently. Cf. SPLENDIDLY *adv.* 3.

1869 L. M. ALCOTT *Little Women* I. xxii. 316 Jo frequently convulsed the family by proposing utterly impossible or magnificently absurd ceremonies, in honor of this unusually merry Christmas. **1897** J. F. INGRAM *Natalia* i. 11 With his magnificently organised armies he pitilessly swept the country. **1930** G. W. KNIGHT *Wheel of Fire* ix. 194 *Lear* gives one the impression of life's abundance magnificently compressed into one play. **1940** G. MARX *Let.* 5 Sept. (1967) 25 El Capitan..has done magnificently with the Coward one-acts. **1958** *Observer* 19 Jan. 11/2 Tweed car-coats will be lined in firm handknits, some in the 'bawneen' yarn which washes so magnificently. **1991** R. KEENE *Battle of Titans* 11 Kasparov's gaffe in the next game appeared to have cost him the title, but in game 24 he rose magnificently to the occasion.

†**magnochromite** (ˌmægnəʊˈkrəʊmaɪt), *n. Min. Obs.* [ad. G. *Magnochromit* (coined by G.M. Bock, 1868): see MAGNESIUM *n.*, CHROMITE *n.*] = *MAGNESIOCHROMITE *n.* Also, a magnesiochromite containing no iron, MgCr₂O₄.

1892 E. S. DANA *Dana's Syst. Min.* (ed. 6) 228 *Magnochromite*,..a magnesian variety of chromite from Grochau, Silesia. Analysis...Cr₂O₃ 40.78, Al₂O₃ 29.92, FeO 15.30, MgO 14.00 = 100. **1913** *Mineral. Mag.* XVI. 364 *Magnesiochromite*.., the same as magnochromite...A variety of chromite containing magnesium. **1929** *Amer. Mineralogist* XIV. 355 The study of the analyses indicates the probable presence of a pure magnesium chromite to which the name magnochromite might be given to differentiate it from the chromite sub-species, magnesiochromite.

magnum, *n.* Add: **3.** *Zool.* The section of a bird's oviduct which secretes albumen.

1935 WARREN & SCOTT in *Poultry Sci.* XIV. 196/2 Five major divisions have been recognized, the infundibulum (funnel), albumin-secreting section, isthmus, uterus and vagina. The second region 'albumin-secreting section' is apparently one portion which has remained unnamed except for the cumbersome descriptive phrase. We, therefore, propose the term 'magnum' which is somewhat descriptive of the region and much more concise. **1959** *New Biol.* XXX. 16 Within about 15 minutes the yolk has entered the more solid-looking albumen secreting region or magnum. **1970** *Sci. Amer.* Mar . 89/3 As the yolk passes along the oviduct, layers of albumen are laid down in the magnum. **1979** *Nature* 6 Dec. 567/2 Conalbumin (or ovotransferrin) is one of the major egg white proteins synthesised by the tubular gland cells of the magnum portion of hen oviduct.

magpie, *n.* Add: **[2.]** **b.** One who collects or hoards objects, information, etc., esp. indiscriminately; an acquisitive or eclectic person; also, a petty pilferer. Cf. sense 8 b.

1903 *Eng. Dial. Dict.* IV. 8/2 *Magpie*,..in Birmingham the word is used of collectors. 'What a magpie he is', he is enthusiastic in adding to his collection. **1944** J. H. FULLARTON *Troop Target* iv. 34 You bloody magpie, what have you done with my tobacco? **1956** A. WILSON *Anglo-Saxon Attitudes* II. i. 236 That must be a *mot* she's picked up second-hand, Gerald thought, she's a cultural magpie. **1963** *Daily Tel.* 24 Dec. 6/2 Some cherished beliefs about trading stamp collectors take a rude knock from a survey published in *Sales Director*. Apparently the keenest magpie is the London male. **1985** L. BLUE *Kitchen Blues* 79 There is a magpie in all of us, and..there is enough tucked away in our cupboards to supply church bazaars, tombolas and countless bring-and-buys. **1990** *Newsweek* 16 July 61/2 Screenwriter Bruce

Joel Rubin is a clever magpie: he's raided every genre to create this seductive, funny hybrid.

mailer, *n.*² Sense 4 in Dict. becomes **5**. Add: **4**. Chiefly *N. Amer.* **a.** A container (such as a cardboard tube) for the conveyance of items, esp. papers, by post.

1923 *Catal. Stationery* (Zellerbach Paper Co., U.S.) 268/2 We manufacture the National line of Photo Mailers. They are made with a gummed flap and single corrugated reinforcement. **1934** A. WOOLLCOTT *While Rome Burns* 13, I regained custody of it and, with the print still rolled in its cardboard mailer, hurried around to the nearest picture-framer. **1967** *Boston Sunday Herald Mag.* 26 Mar. 26/1 (Advt.), Free film mailers on request. **1986** *Master Photogr.* Oct. 47/2 Special stickers available from the Kodak Fulham location must be applied to the outside of the mailer.

b. A (usu. free) advertising pamphlet, brochure, or catalogue sent out by post; = self-mailer s.v. SELF-MAILING *a.*

1958 *Mass. Rep.* CCCXXXVII. 492 The plaintiff spent some $5,515,000 for advertising, including expenditure for space in magazines..and for catalogs, mailers, displays, mats supplied to retailers, booklets, and other printed advertising. **1970** R. K. KENT *Lang. Journalism* 84 *Mailer*,..an advertising leaflet to be sent out by direct mail. **1987** *Graphics World* Nov./Dec. 17 (Advt.), You will have already received our mailer, extolling the virtues of the White Knight. **1991** *Professional Heating* Sept. 59/1 At the end of the warranty period, customers are sent a mailer offering breakdown insurance.

Mailgram (ˈmeɪlgræm), *n. U. S.* Also **mailgram**. [f. MAIL *n.*³ + -GRAM 2.] A proprietary name for a system of sending messages whereby the text of a message is transmitted to a post office near its ultimate destination, printed out, and delivered by ordinary post; also, a message delivered by this or (more generally) a similar service.

1969 *N.Y. Times* 1 July 6/6 The mailgram is transmitted over Western Union lines, then written out at the Post Office in the town for which it is destined. It is then delivered in the regular mail. **1973** T. H. WHITE *Making of President* 1972 (1974) xii. 325 There would be in the last week eight million 'mailgrams' to the nine largest states..plus 9,000,000 letters to Republicans. **1976** *New Yorker* 1 Mar. 23/3 Two items..had come from U.P.I.'s City Hall reporter. All the rest had come from press releases: press releases via mail, telephone, telex, Mailgram. **1985** *New Yorker* 29 Apr. 44/3 He issued reports, sent Mailgrams, dictated his thoughts, made statements, [etc.].

mail-in (ˈmeɪlɪn), *n. (and a.)* orig. *U. S.* [f. vbl. phr. *to mail in* (MAIL *v.*⁴).] The act of sending something in by post; usu. *attrib.* or as *adj.*, esp. designating ballots, surveys, etc., in which results are collected by post. Hence also *concr.*, an item intended to be sent in by post.

[**1959** *Amer. Speech* XXXIV. 151 *Mail in*, a promise to mail in cash for tickets.] **1963** *Sunday Times* 17 Nov. 11/1 A premium..can be anything given away or sold cheap to persuade people..to buy..a product...The self-liquidator, the on-pack offer, the dealer-loader, the free mail-in, and the personality promotion. **1975** *Business Week* 3 Feb. 21/2 The manufacturers are..worked up over another.. proposal: a ban on matchbook mail-in coupons for home-study courses. **1979** *Tucson* (Arizona) *Citizen* 20 Sept. 9A/1 Mail-in ballots from traditionally conservative voters reversed the standings in Sweden's general election. **1984** *Gainesville* (Florida) *Sun* 28 Mar. 7A/2 (Advt.), 7.49 sale price −1.00 mail-in rebate. **1988** *Grocer* 22 Oct. 127/1 All three styles..will carry a collarette offering a free mail-in. The offer is a rose bush, available in red or white.

mailing, *vbl. n.*² Add: **b.** A batch of mail or a number of items posted at one time, esp. as part of a publicity campaign, survey, etc. Also, a letter, parcel, etc., sent by post.

1928 *Metered Postage Regulation* (U.S. Senate Comm. Post-Offices & Post Roads) 3 In the case of first-class matter..each mailing should consist of not less than 100 pieces. *a***1961** *Canada Year Bk.* in WEBSTER s.v., Over a million domestic postcards, circulars, parcels, and other mailings reached the Dead Letter Office. **1971** *Publishers' Weekly* 22 Mar. 14 Publishers for Peace..has just gotten out a mailing concerning the planned April 24 March On Washington. **1976** *National Observer* (U.S.) 7 Feb. 8/2 She sent the mailing off to Roberta Wieloszynski and the Syracuse Consumer Affairs Unit. **1983** H. G. LEWIS *Mail Order Advertising* viii. 187 The mailing may not make sense, and the sequence in which ideas are presented can be out of phase. **1991** *Precision Marketing* 16 Sept. 5/3 The mailings consist of 50-100,000-strong roll-outs several times a year.

MailMerge ('meɪlmɜːdʒ), *n. Computing.* Also **mail merge**, **mail-merge**, and with lower-case initials. [f. MAIL *n.*³ + MERGE *v.*] A proprietary name for a program that draws on a file of names and addresses and a text file to produce multiple copies of a letter each addressed to a different recipient; (also *MailMerge facility*) the facility for doing this.

1981 *Mag. Bank Admin.* (U.S.) Sept. 86/2 Currently available for the Apple are MailMerge, a powerful data and text merging tool that enables WordStar to produce personalized form letters, [etc.]. **1984** S. CURRAN *Word Processing for Beginners* ix. 108 Wordstar itself costs between £250 and £300, and you have to pay over £100 more for each of Mailmerge (the form letter package) and Spellstar, the spelling checker. **1984** *Daily Tel.* 3 Sept. 9/1 A word-processing program with mailmerge facility would enable you to compose letters from standard paragraphs quickly and accurately. **1986** *Brit. Jrnl. Aesthetics* Autumn 418 (Advt.), *Nota Bene* has..mailmerge, and automatic generation of tables and contents. **1993** *Computing* 9 Sept. 10/3 The new features include..conditional selection of records for mail-merge.

Hence '**mail-merge** *v. trans.*; also '**mail-merged** *ppl. a.*; '**mail-merging** *vbl. n.*

1983 *Computerworld* 18 July 70/4 Edit Pak System costs $3,995 including.. CP/M, word processing and mail-merging software. **1986** *PC Week* 4 Nov. 99/2 The more advanced applications software ranges from word processing and mail merging to sales forecasting and market research. **1991** *Which?* June 352/2 To send a letter to lots of people, you can 'mailmerge' it. **1992** *MacWorld* June 161/1 PAA need to keep a database of contributors, to whom the organization sends mail-merged letters.

mailout ('meɪlaʊt), *a.* and *n.* orig. *U.S.* Also **mail-out** and as two words. [f. vbl. phr. *to mail out* (MAIL *v.*⁴); cf. *MAIL-IN *n.* (and *a.*).] **A.** *adj.* Usu. **mail-out.** Applied *attrib.* to the distribution of a bulk mailing, esp. of unsolicited material such as promotional information, questionnaires, etc., and to items sent out in this way.

1967 *Jrnl. Amer. Statistical Assoc.* LXII. 734 (*title*) The 'mail-out/mail-back' census research program. **1976** *Times* 1 May (Food Marketing Suppl.) p. iii/3 Traders receive mail-out shots from the cash-and-carry stores. **1984** *Which Micro?* Dec. 30/4 'Skeleton documents' to permit mail-out operations (as used by many firms who specialise in unsolicited mail). **1988** *DM News* 1 Apr. 42/2 The embossed hologram..can easily be applied to mail-out pages or documents.

B. *n.* **a.** A mail-out campaign; an instance of mailing out, a mailshot. **b.** *concr.* A letter, form, brochure, etc., sent out by post in this way; a mailer.

1977 *Washington Post* 2 June (Virginia Weekly) 2/2 Scott said his campaign consists mostly of public speaking and mail-outs. **1978** D. A. DILLMAN *Mail & Telephone Surveys* v. 188 The effectiveness of the certified mailout is substantial. **1985** *Music Week* 2 Feb. 24/4 Taking on extra staff for quarterly mailouts. **1986** *What Micro?* Nov. 90/2 Word processors..really come into their own dealing with large mail-outs or standard letters. **1989** *Times* 15 Aug. 21/1 Lloyds will also have a role in the post-flotation mailouts of share certificates and refund cheques. **1995** *Artists & Illustr.* Apr. 15/3 Time your mailout to reach guests a week before the event; second class mail can save on costs.

Maine, *n.*² Add: Hence **Mainer** *n.*, a native or inhabitant of the State of Maine.

1879 *Harper's Mag.* LVIII. 799/2 An elder in his church was present, a way-down-East 'Mainer', as they are called in this region. [**1938** K. ROBERTS *Trending into Maine* vii. 147 The chef had made hash for which no State-of-Mainer would need to apologize.] **1977** *Washington Post* 11 Oct. B1 One did see the town constable and any number of old 'Mainers' in thermal hunting jackets, baseball caps, and Mr. L. L. Bean's famous Maine Hunting Shoe. **1990** *Yankee* Mar. 106/2 Like Down East Mainers who are suspicious of people and influences from 'away', many New England residents automatically give the benefit of the doubt to foods produced in the region.

mainstream ('meɪnstriːm), *v. U.S.* [f. MAIN STREAM *n.*] **a.** *trans. Educ.* To place (a child with a disability) in a school or class for those without special needs (for all or part of the school day); to educate in such an integrated environment. Also *absol.*

1974 *Today's Educ.* Mar.-Apr. 25/3 That children will be mainstreamed without backup services is always a danger in times of financial stress. **1974** *Exceptional Children* Nov. 152/2 Efforts to provide training and experiences for regular classroom teachers are not keeping pace with efforts to mainstream. **1977** *Time* 30 May 37/1 Education experts..fear that the money crunch will force schools to 'mainstream' ill-prepared students into regular classrooms rather than putting them in small special classes. **1988** *Washington Post* 10 Nov. DC3/1 Should the child be mainstreamed into public schools or attend a school for the deaf? **1991** *Governing* Dec. 40/1 She was placed in a classroom with 12 other handicapped children and a teacher specially trained to teach children with disabilities. Within a year, Jennifer was 'mainstreamed' for two periods a day—storytime and playtime.

b. *gen.* To incorporate *into* the mainstream. Also without const. orig and chiefly *U.S.*

1982 G. M. DALGISH *Dict. Africanisms* p. xiii, The editor has attempted to record the most well-known items [from the African languages]..in the belief that such items are most likely to become fully 'mainstreamed' into the English language. **1982** *Amer. Speech* LVII. 288 He would argue that the language of drugs has been mainstreamed for several years. **1993** *Body & Soul* Fall 65/1 Vegetarianism has been mainstreamed, due to increased interest in environmentalism and the green movement.

So '**mainstreaming** *vbl. n.*

1973 *School Managem.* Aug./Sept. 28/1 The new practice of mainstreaming recognizes that the individual child may have specific learning or behavior problems which can and should be dealt with only part of the time in an isolated class. **1982** *Amer. Speech* LVII. 216 Federal legislation and mainstreaming in public education have helped in dispelling some of these prejudices. **1991** *San Francisco Rev. Bks.* Fall 2/1 This issue's Special Feature surveys and explores black American writing, arts, and culture. However, the mainstreaming of these artists has not come about through the integration of the board room.

Majorana (mæjɔː'rɑːnə, maiɔː'rɑːnə), *n. Physics.* [The name of Ettore *Majorana* (1906–38), Italian physicist.] Used *attrib.* with reference to his ideas or to concepts arising out of his work, as **Majorana effect**, birefringence to light travelling in a direction at right angles to an applied magnetic field, observed in some liquids and some crystalline materials; **Majorana force**, the exchange force between two nucleons, in which charge and spin are both exchanged; **Majorana neutrino**, a neutrino which is a Majorana particle; **Majorana particle**, a particle of spin 1/2 which is its own antiparticle.

1938 *Proc. R. Soc.* A. CLXVI. 524 The interaction is therefore just of the required form consisting of Heisenberg and Majorana forces of the right sign so as to allow one to make the triplet state of the deuteron the lowest stable state. **1960** *McGraw-Hill Encycl. Sci. & Technol.* VIII. 68/1 Majorana effect. This deals with optical anisotropy of colloidal solutions. **1970** *Physical Rev. D* I. 571 The current operator is shown to be timelike even for the spacelike solutions, and it is shown to lead to a finite process of emission of light by charged Majorana particles. **1980** *Physics Lett.* B. XCIII. 390/2 A Majorana neutrino is its own antineutrino. Its mass is of course observable. **1984** *Nature* 1 Mar. 14/1 If neutrinos are their own antiparticles (that is, are Majorana rather than Dirac particles), the probability of neutrinoless double β decay is greatly enhanced. **1987** *Nuclear Physics* A. CDLXV. 26 It has now become possible to determine the strength of the Majorana force for the first time in a large number of nuclei. **1987** *Physics Lett.* B. CXCVI. 218 (*heading*) Magnetic moments of Dirac and Majorana neutrinos.

makaf *n.*, var. *MACCAPH *n.*

Makah (mə'kɑː), *n.* and *a.* Pl. unchanged or Makahs. [Clallam *màq́ á̓ a.*] A. *n.* **a.** A member of a North American Indian people, inhabiting Cape Flattery in northwest Washington State. **b.** The language of this people, a member of the Nootkan branch of the Wakashan group. B. *adj.* Of or pertaining to the Makah.

1855 *Rep. Indian Affairs 1854* (U.S.) 244 The Clallams as well as the Makahs . . carry on a considerable trade with Van Couver's island. **1855** *Treaty between U.S.A. & Makah Indians* (1859) 3 Articles of agreement and convention . . on the part of the United States, and the undersigned chiefs, headmen and delegates of the several villages of the Makah tribe of Indians. **1870** J. G. SWAN *Indians of Cape Flattery* 44 The shrub is from ten to fifteen feet high . . . The name in Makah is hul-li-á-ko-bupt. **1911** *Encycl. Brit.* XIV. 462/1 (*table*) Tribe . . Makah . . . Stock . . Wakashan . . . Situation, Population, &c., . . 400 on Makah, 25 on Ozette Reservation, Washington. **1931** *Travel* June 25 (*caption*) The older women among the Makah Indians of Neah Bay still carry on the art of weaving. *Ibid.* 73/2 The Quil-e-utes and the Makahs were separated by miles and miles of this rough Pacific coast. **1953** E. COLSON *Makah Indians* i. 3 On the reservation, the Makah approximate more and more to the whites in custom. *Ibid.* iii. 53 The rest use English at least as commonly as they do Makah. *Ibid.* iv. 18, I heard other Makah engaged in arguments with whites. **1975** *New Columbia Encycl.* 1667/3 Makah culture was fundamentally that of the Pacific Northwest Coast area. In 1855 they ceded all their lands to the United States except a small area on Cape Flattery . . . Today they live on Makah Reservation, where they number some 500. **1991** *Vis à Vis* May 54/1, I . . chatted with fellow passengers, including a Makah Indian from Neah Bay.

makai (mə'kai), *a.* and *adv. Hawaii.* [Hawaiian, f. *ma* beside, at, on, towards + *kai* sea.] Towards or beside the sea; seaward.

1945 L. MUMFORD *Rep. on Honolulu* in *City Devel.* iii. 80 No attempt has been made . . to preserve the approaches to the water to give vistas of the sea at the end of the makai-pointed streets. **1976** *Honolulu Star-Bull.* 21 Dec. D-1/2 The would-be kidnapper sped off in the makai direction, but not before the quick-thinking girl had memorized his license number. **1989** *Hawaii Business* Aug. 197/1 It was the last undeveloped property in the Hale Nani business tract on the *makai* end of Umi Street. **1991** *World Monitor* Oct. 76/1 An hour or so *makai* . . by car from Kilauea and you are at the ocean.

makaph *n.*, var. *MACCAPH *n.*

make, *n.*[2] Add: [8.] **b.** *to put the make on*, to make sexual advances to (a person); to pursue sexually. *U. S. slang.*

1967 *Trans-Action* Apr. 6/1 One needs to throw a lively rap when he is 'putting the make on a broad'. **1974** K. MILLETT *Flying* II. 202 The incorrigible satyr tried to put the make on her. **1986** V. SETH *Golden Gate* xi. 251 Tonight Bjorn tries to put the make on A dainty little . . lass. She . . fends off his pass. **1993** A. R. SIDDONS *Hill Towns* (1994) vii. 145 Put the make on you, did she, Joe? I should have warned you. Past a certain blood alcohol level Yolie gets snuggly.

make, *v.*[1] Sense 65 c in Dict. becomes 65 d and sense 51f becomes 51g. Add: [I.] [2.] **c.** *U. S.* To bring (a crop) to maturity; to raise (RAISE *v.*[1] 10 c). Also *absol.* for *pass.* Cf. senses 16 a below.

1714 *Boston News-Let.* 9–16 Aug. 2/2 We have had an extraordinary drought here last Spring and all of this Summer, which makes us apprehensive of a Scarcity of Corn, and little or no Tobacco to be made. **1763** G. WASHINGTON *Diary* 1 Sept. (1925) I. 187 My . . Corn was just beginning to show . . . Quere, has it time to make or Ripen? **1848** *Southern Lit. Messenger* XIV. 635/2 Some corn and some cotton are 'made', as the Virginians say. **1867** *Country Gentleman* XXIX. 388/1 Seventeen years ago it rained more or less for 27 days in the month of May . . . Enormous crops of hay were made that year. **1898** *Ibid.* LXIII. 418/1 Corn crop is now made, well-eared in most cases. **1938** M. K. RAWLINGS *Yearling* xiv. 140 Pa, the quail has hatched under the Scuppernog. And the grapes is makin'. *Ibid.* 143 There was no more corn and would not be until the summer's crop was made. **1972** F. KNEBEL *Dark Horse* (1973) vi. 83 Eddie, you don't want no old man like me around. I ain't even made a crop in ten years. **1989** MAHARIDGE & WILLIAMSON *Their Children After Them* IV. iv. 221 He had stopped planting Hobe's Hill, but was again hoping to make a crop on the bottomland to pay off his debt.

[5.] **e.** To create (a recording, film, etc.) *of* a musical or dramatic work; to produce (a filmed adaptation) *of* or *from* a literary work; also *occas.*, to represent (a literary work) cinematographically. Also without const. Cf. senses 1 a, 5 a above.

1914 J. B. RATHBUN *Motion Picture Making* ii. 29 (*heading*) Making the picture. **1918** C. SANDBURG *Cornhuskers* 51 There is drama in that point . . . Griffith would make a movie of it to fetch sobs. **1932** *Times Educ. Suppl.* 17 Dec. p. ii/2 The records made by the great tenor . . have been re-recorded by the Company. **1962** J. McCABE *Mr. Laurel & Mr. Hardy* iii. 76 For a while they worked as extras for a small company which was making L. Frank Baum's *Wizard of Oz* stories. **1976** *Gramophone* June 69/3 Trevor Pinnock's previous Rameau recording . . of the E minor and the later A minor Suites was made on a Rubio instrument after Tasquin. **1978** *Lancashire Life* Apr. 29/3 The two-disc album is from a recording made in Holland in 1951. **1987** C. SIMMONS *Belles Lettres Papers* vi. 97 He was promoting a movie that was being made from a best-seller.

[9.] **f.** To make available (the time necessary for a task, etc.) by careful scheduling of one's activities. Cf. FIND *v.* 10 b. See also sense 66.

1841 T. CARLYLE *Let.* 21 Sept. in H. J. Nicoll *T. Carlyle* (1884) iv. 112 If at anytime a definite service can be done by answering, doubt not I shall make time for it. **1853** C. BRONTË *Villette* II. xxiii. 129 '*You* write to *me!*—You'll not have time.' 'Oh! I will find or make time.' **1869** L. ALCOTT *Little Women* II. xi. 175 'I'm very proud of him and should like you to see him.'... 'I fear I shall not make the time for that.' **1984** K. WATERHOUSE *Thinks* xvi. 147, I could arrange to make some time and we could perhaps go out for a little drink or a meal. **1987** L. GOLDMAN *Part of Fortune* xxii. 99 Frequently her calendar was so full that she couldn't make time for him.

[30.] **[b.]** To create the opportunity for or 'set up' (a particular move, stroke, or manoeuvre) by means of skilful play. (Further examples.)

1923 *Daily Mail* 16 Apr. 11/5 Chambers really 'made' England's two goals and he was as good as any forward on the field. **1988** I. MORRISON *Billiards & Snooker* 28/2 Billiards is a scientific game and .. you will have to learn how to 'make' your shots; .. you need to know where the cue and object-balls are going to finish after every shot.

[III.] **[48.]** **[a.]** Freq. in parenthetical phrases *to make matters* (or *things*) *worse*, *to make it worse*, to cause an already awkward or distressing situation to deteriorate further; to encounter a specified circumstance as an additional difficulty, disadvantage, etc.

1722 D. DEFOE *Moll Flanders* 110, I was sorry I had gone so far, since I saw what disorder it put him in, but I desir'd him not to talk to me of Explanations, for that would but make things worse. **1816** SCOTT *Antiquary* III. xiii. 287 The man is doing his miserable duty, and you will only make matters worse by opposing him. **1861** DICKENS *Great Expectations* I. xiii. 105 In the minds of the whole company .. I was an excrescence on the entertainment. And to make it worse, they all asked me from time to time .. why I didn't enjoy myself. **1903** J. LONDON *Call of Wild* iv. 115 The dogs were tired, the drivers grumbling, and to make matters worse, it snowed every day. **1943** 'TAFFRAIL' *White Ensigns* ii. 32 To make matters worse the 'nozzers,' or novices, .. had their soap and water purloined. **1987** C. PHILLIPS *European Tribe* Introd. 8 My appetite for academic study was gone, and to make things worse it was the transitory season of autumn.

[III.] **[51.]** **f.** In *imp.*, with *it*: 'let it be' (what is denoted by the complement), esp. as a suggested modification to or clarification of a previous proposal; *spec.* with complement denoting (*a*) a drink requested by the speaker (also with *mine*, etc.); (*b*) the time or place of an appointment; (*c*) an amount, number, or price. *colloq.* (orig. *U. S.*).

1883 'MARK TWAIN' *Life on Mississippi* li. 507 'Have you got that drink yet?'.. He softened, and said make it a bottle of champagne. **1900** G. ADE *Fables in Slang* 96 He was ready to Weep for anyone who would hand him $8. Afterthought—make it $7.50. **1934** *Neuphilol. Mitt.* XXXV. 132 Euchre ... *To make it next,* 'to declare the trump suit changed to the opposite suit of the same colour'. **1940** W. FAULKNER *Hamlet* I. iii. 70 'Ten dollars,' Ratliff said ... 'Make it five.' 'No,' Ratliff said pleasantly. **1962** S. GORE *Down Golden Mile* vi. 120 Make mine a glass this time, seein' I have to go on the scoot with you booze artists to-night. **1973** M. RUSSELL *Double Hit* viii. 55 Make it an hour. I'll be twenty minutes loosening up ... I'm after the exercise. **1985** J. RABAN *Foreign Land* (1986) iii. 46 Tom thought: it could be worth three hundred pounds, no, make it four.

[V.] **[63.]** Also *intr.* for *pass.* (Further examples.)

1833 J. J. STRANG *Diary* 9 Feb. in M. M. Quaife *Kingdom of St. James* (1930) 214 Powerful exertions were making to delay until Congress could get upon facts to act upon. **1914** D. H. LAWRENCE *Prussian Officer* 12 He saw the young man's breast heaving as he made an effort for words. **1973** E. F. SCHUMACHER

Small is Beautiful III. iii. 182 Many people .. plead that the rich countries ought to make a much bigger financial effort.

[65.] **[b.]** Add before 'Freq.': Also, to 'manage' (an appointment, date, etc.). (Further example.)

1974 K. AMIS *Ending Up* x. 56 They can't make Boxing Day. They'll be down with us. **1993** *Beautiful British Columbia Mag.* Fall Insert 24–25 For those who can't make it for the big weekend (Sept. 9-12), the sandsculptures will be on display until October 11.

c. orig. and chiefly *U. S.* Of a pupil, student, etc.: to attain (a grade); to obtain (a mark or score). Cf. sense 30 b above. *to make the grade*: see also GRADE *n.* 10 e.

1870 B. P. PATRICK *Let.* 24 Oct. in M. Collie-Cooper *Lett. from Two Brothers* (1988) 49, I will be glad to hear of your making a diploma this session and one at Phil. [Philadelphia] next year. **1928** 'W. FABIAN' *Unforbidden Fruit* i. 12 She had 'made' a key in Junior year and was hot on the trail of other honors. **1954** W. FAULKNER *Fable* 249 He graduated not only at the top of the class but with the highest marks ever made at the Academy. **1976** *Laurel* (Montana) *Outlook* 9 June 8/4 Four students made 4.00 point averages. **1987** A. MILLER *Timebends* i. 51 They had looked up my .. academic record and laughingly reported that I had made all D's.

e. *colloq.* (orig. *Naval*). With ellipsis of article: to attain the rank of.

Cf. the earlier, related naval usage *to be made post* s.v. POST *n.[3]* 4 a.

1918 *Our Navy* May 11/1 In time of peace, in the regular Navy, they would probably go to sea .. as yeomen second class and make first class in a year. **1942** G. GACH *In Army Now* xxiv. 253 If Sayad can make Looey I betcha I can make General. **1951** D. & C. CHRISTIE *His Excellency* I. i. 16 She joined up in the war, made sergeant inside six months, and had the time of her life. **1987** *New Yorker* 29 June 67/2 O'Brien had made sergeant, and it is the policy of the New York Police Department to transfer a newly promoted sergeant to another unit.

f. To achieve a place in (a list).

1928 *Publishers' Weekly* 24 Nov. 2184/2 Two books that almost made the Best Seller List. **1979** R. JAFFE *Class Reunion* (1980) I. vi. 73 When she got two A's and two B's she couldn't believe it. She had made the Dean's List! **1984** *National Times* (Austral.) 2 Nov. 41/3 Companies like Revlon and Atari should never have made the list in the first place. **1987** S. QUINN *Mind of her Own* (1988) ii. 46 Fraulein Banning was the first woman to make Karen's list of real-life and literary heroes.

g. To receive prominent attention in (the news media, etc.), esp. in *make the front page(s)*. *to make* or *hit the headline*: see HEADLINE *n.* 2 c.

1938 *Life* 4 Apr. 30/1 This year, at the spring openings, publicity-wise Schiaparelli made headlines by showing circus print dresses. **1939** *Florida* (Federal Writers' Project) III. 311 If the storm is of dangerous intensity .. it 'makes' the front page. **1983** S. RUSHDIE *Shame* IV. x. 216 The murders barely made the newspapers; they were not reported on the radio. **1992** *New Republic* 25 May 22/2 Bradley made the front page with his announcement that he wanted to cut the .. police force by 7 percent.

[VII.] **[96.]** **[c.]** *[c]* Freq. in colloq. phr. *to make it up* to (someone), to compensate or atone to (someone) for a loss or wrong suffered. Cf. sense 96 l (c).

1860 W. COLLINS *Woman in White* II. vi. 142, I must make it up to you for having been afraid to speak out at a better time. **1879** H. JAMES *Confidence* (1880) xix. 201 He had wronged her. ... As he could not make it up to her, the only reasonable thing was to keep out of her way. **1915** W. CATHER *Song of Lark* 405 My own father died in Nebraska when Gunner was born .. and I was sorry, but the baby made it up to me. **1946** K. TENNANT *Lost Haven* (1947) xii. 188 You're a good girl ... Make it up to you some time. **1973** A.

MacVicar *Painted Doll Affair* xi. 130, I persuaded myself that it was justified. Tomorrow I would make it up to him. **1992** I. Pattison *More Rab C. Nesbitt Scripts* 16 *Rab*: Jaffa cakes on a Wednesday, Mary.. Pure decadence. *Mary*: I had to lash oot on them, din't I? To make it up to the wean!

o. *transf.* To promote to a higher rank. *colloq.* (orig. *Services'*).

1943 Hunt & Pringle *Service Slang* 45 *Made up*, promoted. (Applied to the stages from Corporal to Warrant Officer.) **1958** A. Hunter *Gently through Mill* viii. 97 'Then why was Blacker made foreman?'.. 'I made him up on his ability!' **1975** *Daily Tel.* 19 July 9/7 Jones is working-class made-up to lance-corporal. **1992** *Independent* 16 Nov. 23/3 Companies are narrowing the path that leads toward the holy grail of partnership. Slaughter and May.. 'made up' just one partner in the current financial year, compared with 10 in 1991–92.

make-over ('meikəʊvə(r)), *n.* orig. and chiefly *U.S.* [f. vbl. phr. *to make over*: see MAKE *v.*[1] 92 d.] A complete transformation or remodelling of something; *esp.* a thorough refashioning of a person's appearance by beauty treatment.

1966 *Punch* 17 Aug. 260/2 The sudden make-over of the Cabinet..did little or nothing to improve Mr. Wilson's standing in Fleet Street. **1969** *Hairdo* Feb. *(title on cover)* Make-up make-over for a busy homemaker. **1979** *Arizona Daily Star* 1 Apr. j1/3 Several home makeovers are featured in House and Garden's March issue. **1985** *Hair* Summer 17/3 Five Anglia TV viewers.. who had a 'before and after' make-over. **1986** *Fortune* 18 Aug. 9/3 In mid-July American Can completed its makeover by selling its packaging operations to Triangle Industries. **1990** *Catch* Feb. 55/1 Do you think she looks better before or after the make-over? **1991** *Time* 3 June 32/1 The Soviet President began by indirectly asking the West to help him plan an economic makeover.

maker, *n.* Add: [**2.**] [**a.**] Now freq. in phr. *to meet one's Maker*, to die; sometimes humorously, (of a thing) to be destroyed.

1933 D. L. Sayers *Murder must Advertise* xv. 261 The wretched man had gone to meet his Maker in Farley's Footwear. **1967** in R. D. Abrahams *Positively Black* (1970) ii. 26 'Nigger boy,' he said to me, 'how'd you like to meet your maker right now?' *a***1978** *TV Times* in A. P. Cowie et al. *Oxf. Dict. Current Idiomatic Eng.* (1983) II. 383/2 As these tired old notes meet their maker in Essex, a new load is on its way into our pockets. **1989** *Premiere* Dec. 42/4 Nat Maudlin almost met his maker thanks to a rafting expedition.

make-up, *n.* Add: [**5.**] **c.** *U.S. colloq.* A second examination for a student who has missed or failed the first one. Cf. RESIT *n.*

1934 in Webster. **1942** Berrey & Van den Bark *Amer. Thes. Slang* §835/1 *Make-up* (*exam*), a second examination to take the place of one omitted or in which a student has failed. **1958** *Barnard Coll. Announcement* 1958–59 161 Instructors are not required to give make-ups to those absent from previously announced quizzes. **1976** *National Observer* (U.S.) 13 Mar. 11/2 (Advt.), Separate subject courses for 8th grade math, history, English . . . Excellent for make-up, brush-up or enrichment. **1987** D. A. Dye *Platoon* iv. 65 Out here there are no make-ups for failed exams. **1992** R. M. Davis *Mid-Lands* x. 129 Every job was a test with no make-up.

[**6.**]   **make-up game** *Baseball*, a game previously postponed which is played to complete the number of scheduled league matches.

1976 *Laurel* (Montana) *Outlook* 30 June 18/1 A *make-up game was played with the Owl Cafe scoring 9 and Terry's Texaco, 4. **1986** *Toronto Star* 28 May E2/5 Bridge has played a dozen club matches in 30 days because of makeup games squeezed between regular-season weekend matches. **1992** B. Geist *Little League*

Confidential xv. 143 Perhaps they smelled blood in the water in our makeup game with Yo Norb's Stool Concepts squad.

making, *vbl. n.*[1] Add: [**8.**] [**a.**] Also *ellipt.* as *the makings.* See also sense b below.

*a***1953** E. O'Neill *Long Day's Journey* (1956) IV. 154 He hasn't even got the makings. **1977** *Rolling Stone* 13 Jan. 55/1 Phoebe Snow is not yet a mature artist. Though the makings are nowhere more evident than on her third album.

‖**makiwara** (maki'wara, anglicized mækɪ'wɑːrə), *n. Karate.* [Jap., lit. 'sheaved straw', f. *maki* a roll, something rolled up + *wara* straw.] An object (orig. a post or board covered with straw, hemp, etc.) intended to be struck during training in order to toughen the skin of the hands and feet.

1959 E. J. Harrison *Man. Karate* v. 32 The two types most frequently installed are the fixed and movable makiwara. **1962** H. D. Plée *Karate by Pictures* 12 Only time can strengthen certain bones through regular training with the Makiwara (post covered with straw). **1981** *Best of Karate '81* Spring 30/2 The makiwara they had was covered with plain heavy sisal rope and we woûld hit it until it tore the hide off our hands. **1990** *Martial Arts Illustr.* III. vii. 89/3, I had watched Takahashi kicking the dojo's Makiwara—one of those old fashioned car springs—full bare on to the toes.

malalignment (mælə'laɪnmənt), *n.* Chiefly *Path.* [f. MAL- + ALIGNMENT *n.*] Imperfect alignment or displacement, esp. of bones, joints, or teeth.

1939 *Jrnl. Exper. Podiatry* I. 19 Orthodigita may be defined as the amelioration or correction, by non-surgical   means,   of   toe   deformities   or malalignments. **1946** *Nature* 5 Oct. 468/2 The malalignment produces an upsetting couple about the mass centre and causes the rocket to deviate from its theoretical trajectory. **1982** *Brit. Med. Jrnl.* 24 Apr. 1224 *(title)* Malalignment of the shoulder after stroke. **1984** *Marathon & Distance Runner* Oct. 65/4 Abnormal   gait   because   of   a   malalignment problem. **1990** *Brit. Jrnl. Orthodontics* XVII. 161/1 Pericision is advocated in malalignment cases and not just for rotations.

malanga (mə'læŋgə), *n.* [a. Amer. Sp. *malanga*, f. Kikongo *melanga* taro.] Any of several plants of the arum family cultivated in the Caribbean and Central and South America for their edible tubers and medicinal value, esp. ones of the genus *Xanthosoma.*

1910 *Bull. Bureau Plant Industry, U.S. Dept. Agric.* No. 164. 11 Malanga is the Arawak name for taro, and is still current in Cuba for both yautias and taros. **1929** *Trav.* Jan. 21/2 Dim lights half reveal humble, dark-skinned folk gathered at their simple meal of malangas, rice and fish. **1948** *Amer. N. & Q.* VIII. 117/2 *Malanga*, tubercle similar to that of arum (Puerto Rico). **1962** *Spectator* 31 Aug. 297 We could grow..*malangas* (tubers with a more interesting flavour than either the potato or the sweet potato). **1972** J. W. Purseglove *Trop. Crops: Monocotyledons* I. 68 Eddoes in Spanish-speaking parts of the Caribbean are called 'malangas', but the term may also be used for other aroids, including *Xanthosoma*. **1973** E. L. Ortiz *Compl. Bk. Caribbean Cooking* 432 *Taro*..belongs to the arum family and is known in Jamaica, Barbados, and Trinidad as coco, eddo and baddo, the leaves being called callaloo. A closely related group, the malangas, cultivated in many of the islands, are found in markets as malanga, dasheen, tanier, tannia, and yautia. **1994** *Esquire* Aug. 31/3 Latin American cuisine that is full of flavors like boniato, sugarcane, and malanga.

Malanite (mə'lanaɪt), *n.* (and *a.*) *S. Afr. Hist.* [f. the name of Dr Daniel F. *Malan* (1874–1959), leader of the S. African Nationalist Party and Prime Minister 1948-54 + -ITE[1].] A supporter of D. F. Malan or his policies, esp. those of apartheid which were implemented under his leadership.

1933 *Rand Daily Mail* 15 Feb. 9/3 The feeling between the Prime Minister and the Malanites is strained. **1934** *Times* 20 Jan. 9/6 A manifesto expressing unshakable confidence in General Hertzog..and deprecating Malanite agitation. **1968** W. K. HANCOCK *Smuts* II. xiii. 253 In October 1933 at Bloemfontein the Malanites repudiated Hertzog. **1971** D. WORRALL *South Africa* v. 201 After the election the opposition of the Malanites stiffened as the trend towards fusion quickened. **1991** T. R. H. DAVENPORT *S. Afr.* 277 Dr N. J. van der Merwe, a prominent Free State Malanite.

malapportionment (mælə'pɔ:ʃənmənt), *n. U. S. Pol.* [f. MAL- + APPORTIONMENT *n.*] Bad or inequitable apportionment, *spec.* of representation in a political assembly, legislative body, or electoral constituency.

1962 *U.S. Supreme Court Rep.* (Lawyers' ed.) 2nd Ser. VII. 718/2 The totality of the malapportionment's effect..results in 'a distortion of the constitutional system'. **1964** D. M. BERMAN *In Congress Assembled* xiv. 387 In Congress, the malapportionment of the Senate is constitutionally ordained: the equality of all states in the Senate was part of the 'Great Compromise', under which the small states agreed to the creation of a strong National Government. **1981** *Christian Science Monitor* (Midwestern ed.) 2 Oct. 23/4 The Supreme Court's 'one man, one vote' decisions of the 1960s eliminated the worst form of gerrymandering malapportionment. **1993** *Newsday* (Nassau ed.) 7 June (Viewpoints) 34/3 Cuomo and the Legislature must find a way to end this grotesque malapportionment. The Second Department's 6,000-case backlog is an affront to justice.

Hence **mala'pportioned** *a.*, (of a legislative or electoral body) badly or inequitably apportioned: structured or constituted in such a way as to deprive sectors of the population of fair representation.

1964 D. M. BERMAN *In Congress Assembled* xiv. 388 The malapportioned Congressional districts have been laid out by rural-dominated state legislatures. **1966** *Economist* 19 Nov. 808/2 The lower house has been declared 'malapportioned' by the United States Supreme Court and it is under court order to redraw the boundaries of its districts by May. **1980** *N. Y Times* B4/1 A malapportioned convention, where the cities were denied their share of delegates,..told us they symbolized democracy. **1993** *St. Louis Post-Dispatch* 3 Jan. (Everyday Mag.) 5C The late Richard Bolling protested..that malapportioned constituencies.. constituted a major roadblock to enactment of the liberal agenda.

malapropism, *n.* Add: Hence **'malapropist** *n.*, a person who commits a malapropism, or is given to committing malapropisms; **malapro'pistic** *a.*, of the nature of a malapropism.

1906 *Daily Chron.* 18 Jan. 9/4 The prize 'malapropist' says:—'The "firstnamed"..was run out of it by the topweight, greatly to the chagrin of the rider, as well as the owner of the horse.' **1978** *Verbatim* Sept. 9/1 Vaguely related to spoonerisms are a number of instances of utterances connected by an unthemely common theme with some juncture, some assonance, a few malapropistic and apropostic features, foul wordplay, and untenable juxtapositions. **1989** *Ibid.* Spring 25/2 Small children are often malapropists. **1993** *Daily Tel.* 18 Dec. (Weekend Suppl.) 24/4 The upper classes are 'eccentric', their servants malapropistic.

Malaysianization (mə,leɪzɪənaɪ'zeɪʃən), *n.* [f. MALAYSIAN *a.* and *n.* + -IZATION. Cf. earlier MALAYANIZATION *n.*] The process or result of rendering (more) Malaysian in character or composition.

1970 G. P. MEANS *Malaysian Politics* xx. 390 An oblique reference to the Malaysianization issue. **1976** *Scotsman* 20 Nov. 3/2 The emigration is a result of the Malaysian Government's 'Malaysianisation' policy. **1981** *Times* 25 Aug. 15/1 Sime has so far skillfully [*sic*] negotiated the Malaysianization minefield. **1990** *Nat. Westm. Bank Q. Rev.* Feb. 20 The 'Malaysianisation' of foreign banks..was a hot topic in the early 1980s.

So **Ma'laysianize** *v. trans.*; **Ma'laysianized** *ppl. a.*; **Ma'laysianizing** *vbl. n.*

1972 *Sunday Times* (Kuala Lumpur) 25 June 4/2 The Straits Times has already been told to Malaysianise its staff. **1972** *Straits Times* (Malaysian ed.) 23 Nov. 13/3 The management had thought the costume would give a 'Malaysianised' atmosphere. **1982** *Times* 19 July 4/2 The attitude of the City of London towards the 'malaysianizing' of British plantations and firms only made matters worse. **1985** *Financial Times* 26 Mar. 34/4 The company was formerly Danish-owned but was Malaysianised in 1983.

maldeployment (mældɪ'plɔɪmənt), *n.* [f. MAL- + DEPLOYMENT *n.*] Inefficient deployment of manpower or resources; an instance of this.

1950 *Times* 14 Mar. 8/3 There was obviously a mal-deployment of labour. There were far too few houses and they were costing too much. **1978** *Sci. Amer.* May 50/2 Various maldeployments of forces could be corrected. **1990** *Independent* 2 Aug. 6/4 The Army has been plagued by 'maldeployment' since the end of the Second World War.

male, *a.* and *n.*[2] Add: [**B.**] [**4.**] **male-chauvi'nistic** *a.*, characterized by or exhibiting male chauvinism.

1968 *Ramparts* May 12/3 What disturbs me most is..the *male chauvinistic attitude toward all women's activity. **1989** R. WATERFIELD *Before Eureka* vii. 81 Unusually for the male-chauvinistic Greeks, Empedocles allowed that both the man and the woman contribute towards their offspring's nature.

Malecite *n.* and *a.*, var. *MALISEET *n.* and *a.*

Malekite *n.* (and *a.*), var. *MALIKITE *n.* (and *a.*)

†**malem** ('mæləm), *n. Obs.* Also malim, malum. [ad. Arab. *mu'allim* instructor, master (in any trade or craft).] **1.** In the Arabic-speaking world, a person responsible for the conduct or transportation of merchandise.

1609 W. BIDDULPH in T. Lavender *Trav.* 39 The Malims & Muckremen (as they call the Carriers) were not yet come down with their Cammels to carrie them vp. **1617** F. MORYSON *Itinerary* I. 242 They call him Malem, who conducts the Merchants goods.

2. *Naut.* A ship's pilot, master, or mate, *esp.* one of foreign nationality, as referred to by an Arabic-speaking crew. Freq. used as a title, as in comb. **malem sahib**.

1615 T. ROE *Jrnl.* 21 July in *Embassy to Great Mogul* (1899) I. 22 The pilott of the Iunke, Malim-Abrimme, spake Portigue. **1886** YULE & BURNELL *Hobson-Jobson* 418/2 *Malum*...In a ship with English officers and native crew, the mate is called *málum sahib*. The word..is properly applied to the pilot or sailing-master. **1894** *Nautical Mag.* Mar. 275 Loss owing to master continuing to stand on after sounding showed that he was in shoaling water. Certificate as malim recommended to be cancelled. **1907** M. ROBERTS *Flying Cloud* xxix. 275 You t'ink I tell the Malem Sahib, tell the mate?

malignancy, *n.* Add: **6.** *Path.* A malignant tumour or cancerous growth.

1934 in WEBSTER. **1935** IMPERATORI & BURMAN *Dis. Nose & Throat* xxx. 352 Operable malignancies are those which are limited to the soft palate, or uvula. **1974** *Anderson* (S. Carolina) *Independent* 24 Apr. 4A/3 She told me the doctor had just told Mr. Coffee he had a malignancy and she wanted me to know. **1988** P. GAY *Freud* xii. 634 Freud stopped work . . in early September, when there were alarming signs that his malignancy was active once again.

malignant, *a.* and *n.* Add: [A.] [2.] [a.] *malignant melanoma*: see *MELANOMA *n.*

Maliki ('mælɪkiː, 'mɑː-), *n.* and *a.* *Islam.* Also †**Malachee**, †**Malikee.** Pl. unchanged or with -s. [ad. Arab. *mālikī*, f. the name of *Mālik* ibn Anas (d. 796), Muslim jurist.] **A.** *n.* A member of one of the four Sunni schools of Islamic law, founded in the 8th century and based on the teachings of Mālik ibn Anas, and now prevalent mainly in western and northern Africa. **B.** *adj.* Of or pertaining to the Malikis.

1704 J. PITTS *Acct. Mahometans* vii. 93 The *Malachees* and *Shaffees* lift up their Hands in a sort of careless manner, and then let them fall down and hang by their sides. **1845** *Encycl. Metrop.* XXIV. 440/2 The Malekites or Málikís, named from the Imám Málik ibn 'Ans or 'Anas, who was born and died at Medínah . . . He was . . extremely diligent in collecting the traditions as to the Prophet's own determinations. **1875** *Encycl. Brit.* II. 250/1 In the eastern provinces, Hara, Katee, Bahreyn, and Katar, the Malikee sect is more common; as also, it is said, in Hadramaut, and in some parts of Yemen. **1932** *Times Lit. Suppl.* 1 Sept. 602/2 The preference of the Moslems of Barbary for the Maliki form of orthodox Sunni Islam. **1959** *Listener* 19 Nov. 858/2 The classical *Maliki* doctrine of the Islamic text-books. *Ibid.*, The *Maliki* definition of wilful homicide. **1980** *Oxf. Compan. Law* 651/1 Different schools, called 'rites' have been admitted, each constituting a particular interpretation of Islamic law. There are four orthodox rites, the Hanafi, the Maliki, Shafi'i, and the Hanbali, which generally prevail in different countries.

Malikite ('mælɪkaɪt, 'mɑː-), *n.* and *a.* *Islam.* Also **Malekit.** [f. the name *Mālik* (see *MALIKI *n.* and *a.*) + -ITE¹.] = *MALIKI *n.* and *a.*

1845 *Encycl. Metrop.* XXIV. 440/2 The Malekites or Málikís. **1874** J. H. BLOUNT *Dict. Sects* 283/1 Four sects, named, after their founders, Hanifites, Malekites, Shafeites, and Hanbalites, who differ in some unimportant points of ritual and Koranic interpretation. **1911** D. S. MARGOLIOUTH *Mohammedanism* v. 184 Though calling himself a Malikite, he introduced certain alterations in the prayer-ritual. **1957** M. BANTON *W. Afr. City* vii. 136 The Africans are of the Sunni Malikite school. **1975** *New Columbia Encycl.* 1372/1 The Malikite [Rite], founded by Malik ibn Anas . . followed [the Hanafite] in the western and northern parts of Africa. **1991** R. OLIVER *Afr. Experience* (1993) vii. 87 He stayed for a while in Kairouan, where he consulted a leading jurist of the Malikite school about how best to reform the lax and corrupt observance of Islam by his own people.

malintegration (mælɪntɪ'greɪʃən), *n.* Also **mal-integration.** [f. MAL- + INTEGRATION *n.*] Unsuccessful or defective assimilation into a whole of heterogeneous elements, as of communities within a society.

1951 PARSONS & SHILS *Toward Gen. Theory of Action* I. i. 22 The nature and sources of the mal-integration of cultural patterns are as important to the theory of action as the integration itself. **1970** D. GOLDRICH et al. in I. L. Horowitz *Masses in Lat. Amer.* v. 209 The next generation could greatly raise the costs to the nation of malintegration of the settlements, by venting their frustrations in either political opposition, across-the-board delinquency, or extreme privatization. **1977** R. HOLLAND *Self & Social Context* v. 178 The gradual, exploratory development of interdisciplinary work . . tends to be at the cost of administrative complexity and . . serious malintegration. **1986** *Sociol. Abstr.* Suppl. 140. 16/2 Their visible minority status results in malintegration of even third and subsequent generations.

Maliseet ('mæləsiːt), *n.* and *a.* Also **Malecite,** †**Melicete,** and other forms from Canad. Fr. Pl. unchanged or (occas.) with -s. [ad. Fr. *Malecite* (1722) or ad. its etymon Micmac *mali-sit,* lit. 'a person who speaks poorly or incomprehensibly'.] **A.** *n.* **a.** A member of a North American Indian people of Quebec, New Brunswick, and Maine, nearly identical in language and culture to the neighbouring Passamaquoddy. **b.** The Eastern Algonquian language of this people. **B.** *adj.* Of, pertaining to, or designating this people or their language.

1847 A. GESNER *New Brunswick* v. 108 The Melicetes, from being descended from the Delaware stock, speak a dialect of that people. **1855** J. STEPHENS (*title*) A primer for young children applicable to the Indian language, as spoken by the Mee-lee-ceet tribe in New Brunswick. **1863** (*title*) The ten commandments, the Lord's Prayer, etc., in the Maliseet language. **1884** *Encycl. Brit.* XVII. 603/1 There are 2125 Indians in Nova Scotia, principally Malicites and Micmacs. **1899** M. CHAMBERLAIN *Maliseet Vocab.* 6 That slurring and drawling of the syllables which lends a musical quality to the Maliseet speech. **1908** *Catholic Encycl.* III. 229/2 To the east are the Micmac, Malecite, Abnaki, Nascapi, and the Montagnais of Labrador. **1912** T. MICHELSON in *28th Ann. Rep. U.S. Bureau Amer. Ethnol.* 280 The existing dialects . . are Micmac, Malecite, Passamaquoddy, Penobscot, and Abnaki. **1979** I. GODDARD in Campbell & Mithun *Lang. Native Americas* 111, In Maliseet -*s*(*əpən*-) is suffixed after the central endings and before the peripheral endings. **1992** *Beaver* Aug. 59/3 Noel Lola is included . . partly for his life as a New Brunswick Malecite, but also for his later reputation as a restless ghost.

mallat *n.*, var. *MALLET *n.*³

mallet ('mælət), *n.*³ Also **9 mallat.** [ad. (probable) Aboriginal (Nyungar, W. Austral.) *malard*.] Any of several Western Australian eucalypts, having a bark rich in tannin. Also, the bark of such a tree; in full *mallet-bark, mallet wood.*

1837 G. F. MOORE *Evidences Inland Sea* 49 Here we saw another variety of the *Eucalyptus,* called 'Mallat'. **1897** L. LINDLEY-COWEN *W. Austral. Settler's Guide* II. ii. 215 Mallet, or fluted gum, or gimlet wood (*E. salubris,* F. von Mueller). **1905** *Chambers's Jrnl.* Aug. 622/1 The wattle-barks . ., which are used in large quantities in Australia for tanning sheepskins, are being replaced by a material called mallet-bark. **1919** *Jrnl. Amer. Leather Chemists' Assoc.* XIV. 311 The eucalypt tannins, especially mallet, may give much better results when they are used in a drum tannage, but at present they cannot be considered an important factor in the production of Australian leather. **1921** *Jrnl. Soc. Leather Trades' Chemists* V. 368 In West Australia several distinct species are classified locally as 'mallets' and are stripped and sold as 'mallet'. **1934** A. L. HOWARD *Timbers of World* (ed. 2) 308 *Malletwood, brown, Rhodamnia argentea* . ., Queensland. Also known as white myrtle, blackeye, or brush turpentine . . . The principal uses are for mallets, heads of mauls, etc. **1969** T. H. EVERETT *Living Trees of World* xxvii. 262/2 Because its bark has the highest tannin content of any commercial tanbark, the brown mallet . . is cultivated in Australia. **1973** G. M. CHIPPENDALE *Eucalypts W. Austral. Goldfields* viii. 91/2 The term 'mallet' was applied to several tall, smooth-barked trees.

malolactic (meɪləʊˈlæktɪk), *a.* and *n.* *Wine-making.* Also **malo-lactic**. [App. ad. F. *malolactique*: see MALIC *a.*, LACTIC *a.*] **A.** *adj.* Designating or pertaining to a secondary fermentation during which malic acid in wine is converted to lactic acid.

1908 *Jrnl. Chem. Soc.* XCIV. II. 723 The malic acid of grape-juice partly disappears during fermentation, but no lactic acid is formed, and the 'malo-lactic' fermentation of Rosenstiehl..does not exist. **1951** AMERINE & JOSLYN *Table Wines* vii. 100 Certain wines, particularly those of high acidity, are sometimes left on the lees in order to promote the malo-lactic fermentation. **1959** *Jrnl. Appl. Bacteriol.* XXII. 385 Knowledge of the systematic classification of the malolactic bacteria is now much improved. **1991** *Wine & Spirits* Apr. 46/2 The total aroma profile of the full malolactic wine..is huge.
B. *n.* Malolactic fermentation.
1989 *Daily Tel.* (Colour Suppl.) 16 Sept. 66/2 This involves..encouraging a second, softening fermentation called the 'malolactic'. **1991** *Wine Spectator* 31 Aug. 43/2 After about four to five days, nearly all the wine is transferred to French oak casts, where the fermentation and the malolactic occurs [*sic*].

Malorian (mæˈlɔːrɪən), *a.* Also **Maloryan**. [f. the name of Sir Thomas *Malory* (d. 1471), author of *Le Morte d'Arthur* + -AN.] Pertaining to or characteristic of Sir Thomas Malory or his writing.
1904 M. CORELLI *God's Good Man* i. 3 There was a certain 'man of worship'.. who found himself very well-disposed to 'flourish his heart' in the Maloryan manner prescribed. **1973** *Studies in Eng. Lit.: Eng. Number* (Tokyo) 152 His [*sc.* Professor Vinaver's] edition has..promoted Malorian works all over the world. **1976** *Times Lit. Suppl.* 23 July 930/1 To give a Malorian example of the more extreme kind: when Sir Gareth [etc.].

Maloryan *a.*, var. of *MALORIAN *a.*

‖**malossol** (malaˈsɒl, anglicized mæləˈsɒl), *a.* (and *n.*) *Gastron.* [Russ., abbrev. of *malosol'niy*, f. *malo* little + *sol* salt.] Of caviare: lightly salted. Also *absol.* as *n.*
1959 W. HEPTINSTALL *Hors d'Oeuvre & Cold Table* i. 29 Beluga Malossol Caviar.. has the largest grain and.. the highest price. **1964** A. LAUNDY *Caviare and After* i. 20 The best quality caviare is always slightly salted and is known as *malossol*... The best malossol caviare is prepared from the spring fishing of sturgeon. **1975** *Harpers & Queen* May 64/3 The best Russian [caviar].. is the Malossol, a term applied to the grading of spring fish roes. **1985** *New Yorker* 16 Dec. 117/1 He..forks over $295..for fourteen ounces of fresh premier beluga caviar... Malossol is the process whereby salt is added to the freshly caught roe ('malossol' means 'little salt').

maloti *n. pl.*: see *LOTI *n.*

Malungeon *n.*, var. of *MELUNGEON *n.*

Malus (ˈmɑːləs, ˈmæləs), *n.* *Astron.* Now chiefly *Hist.* [a. L. *mālus* mast.] The southern constellation Pyxis.
[**1679** E. HALLEY *Catalogus Stellarum Australium* sig. B4ᵛ, Argo Navis... In medio mali duarum.] **1845** *Rep. Brit. Assoc. Adv. Sci. 1844* 41 As regards the southern constellations, the following are the principles proposed to be adhered to: viz...5°. That Argo be divided into four separate constellations, as partly contemplated by Lacaille; retaining his designations of *Carina*, *Puppis* and *Vela*; and substituting the term *Malus* for *Pixis Nautica*, since it contains four of Ptolemy's stars that are placed by him in the *mast* of the ship. **1937** A. P.

NORTON *Star Atlas* (ed. 6) 1 La Caille..sub-divided the unwieldly Argo into Carina, Malus (now Pyxis), Puppis, and Vela.

mamma, *n.*¹ Senses a–e in Dict. become 1 a–c, 3, 4. Add: **2.** (With pronunc. (ˈmɑːmə).) In more general senses (orig. *Black English*). **a.** As a title or term of address for a woman, esp. an older woman. *U.S.* and *W. Indies colloq.*
In many instances a term of respect.
1810 J. LAMBERT *Trav. L. Canada & U.S.* II. xxxvii. 414 An old negro woman is called *momma*, which is a broad pronunciation of *mama*. **1835** A. B. LONGSTREET *Georgia Scenes* 110 'Aunt' and 'mauma', or 'maum', ..are terms of respect, commonly used by children, to aged negroes. *a*1843 SOUTHEY *Comm. -pl. Bk.* (1851) IV. 4 Mango Capac and Mama Oella his sister-wife. **1956** in Cassidy & Le Page *Dict. Jamaican Eng.* (1967) 283/1 /*Mama*/, a term of address used in speaking (familiarly) to any woman;..a term of address used to a strange woman. **1982** *Dict. Bahamian Eng.* 129/2 *Mama*,..a term of address for an older, respected woman (especially by Haitians).
b. A wife or girlfriend; a sexually attractive woman; a promiscuous woman. See also *red-hot momma* s.v. RED-HOT *a.* 2 a, *sweet mama* s.v. SWEET *a.* and *adv.* C. 1 a. *slang* (chiefly *U. S.*).
1925 *College Humor* Aug. 100/2 It is the picture of a red-headed mama, and the reader is supposed to identify her with the heroine, Minnie, herself. The author..claims that Min is a comely damsel..whose only equipment for stardom is beauty. **1926** C. VAN VECHTEN *Nigger Heaven* 286 *Mama*, mistress or wife. **1927** WODEHOUSE *Meet Mr. Mulliner* vi. 179 What would I do supposing the Jane on whom I had always looked as a steady mamma had handed me the old skimmer? **1980** *Times* 20 June 4/4 She denied ever being at an impromptu or organized gathering where there was a 'mama' present, someone available to the whole group for sexual intercourse. **1984** A. LURIE *Foreign Affairs* (1985) ii. 34 When I meet a mama who turns me on, I lay it on the line.

mammary, *a.* and *n.* Add: **B.** *n. pl.* A woman's breasts; also (*rare*), those of a man. *colloq.* (*joc.*).
1976 P. CAVE *High Flying Birds* i. 8 Her quite magnificent mammaries pointed upwards, gazing sightlessly at the ceiling. **1981** *Times Lit. Suppl.* 26 June 719/3 Most of the women Harnforth comes into contact with aren't much more than mobile mammaries. All that stands out about them is their breasts. **1985** MCCONVILLE & SHEARLAW *Slanguage of Sex* 175/1 Do you think she should be pregnant? It might damage the mammaries. **1990** *Sky Mag.* Apr. 45/2 Kurt Russell is Cash, a rougher cop but with equally large mammaries.

mammotroph (ˈmæməʊtrəʊf), *n.* *Histol.* [f. MAMMOTROPH(IC *a.*] A cell of the mammalian adenohypophysis which secretes prolactin.
1966 H. D. PURVES in Harris & Donovan *Pituitary Gland* I. iv. 186 It would therefore be appropriate to call prolactin secreting cells in mammals 'mammotrophs'. The name 'lactotroph' is suggested as one suitable for use in any vertebrate. **1972** *Amer. Jrnl. Anat.* CXXXV. 96/2 A lysosomal mechanism has been described..in mammotrophs following cessation of lactation. **1990** *Jrnl. Neuroendocrinol.* II. 823/2 Estrogen-induced transformation of somatotrophs into mammotrophs in the rat.

man, *n.*¹ Add: [IV.] [**20.**] **man-rem**, a unit of radiation exposure equal to one rem incident on one person.
1973 J. DUNSTER in *New Scientist* 18 Oct. 194/1 The collective dose..is the sum of the products of a level of radiation dose and the number of people exposed at that level. The collective dose has the unit '*man-rem' and is a useful measure of the total dose to a community or population. **1975** *Science* 14 Feb. 509 The total

future cost of one man-rem in terms of health costs paid in present dollars, is between $12 and $120. **1977** *Health Physics* XXXIII. 155/1 An additional concept was considered [by the American Nuclear Society]; that of the man-rem. Current guidelines detail the dose limit projection for individuals, but fail to consider the number of individuals—the integrated effect considered in man-rem... The work group expended considerable effort in attempting to incorporate a man-rem limit into research reactor siting criteria. **1979** *Washington Post* 31 Mar. A8/2 Studies.. show 10,000 to 20,000 man-rems would result in one to two excess cases of cancer in future years. **1983** *Financial Times* 8 Jan. 4/2 The collective radiation dose of 50,000 man-rems accumulated by that work-force 'may be increasing this number [of deaths from cancer] to 505 per year'.

manage, *v.* Add: [4.] **b.** To organize the activities of (a person or group of people), esp. in the fields of sport and entertainment; to act as manager to (*MANAGER *n.* 3 b (*b*)).

1928 *Weekly Dispatch* 20 May 14/4 Nowadays the potential star has to be managed and publicised. **1930** *Daily Express* 6 Oct. 11/5 Francois Descamps, who will in future manage him, told me later.. that Jeans looks.. like a potential champion. **1975** *Economist* 3 May 28/3 Fulham are managed by an elderly asthmatic who.. sold his two best players for £250,000 at the end of 1973. **1989** *Q* Dec. 12/3 McVey has managed Cherry throughout the year.

manager, *n.* Sense 3 in Dict. become 3a. Add: [3.] **b.** One who manages or organizes the activities of a person or group of people, in the fields of sport and entertainment; *spec.*, †the captain of a cricket team (*Obs.*). **team manager**: see TEAM *n.* 11.

1843 'WYKHAMIST' *Pract. Hints Cricket* p. vi, There should be one Captain, or Manager of the 'field', and one only. **1880** *N.Y. Herald* 12 July 8/3 He was manager during 1879 of the Providence Club, which.. is now flying the championship pennant of the League. **1885** *James Lillywhite's Cricketers' Compan.* (ed. 41) 59 George Alexander.., the successful manager.., only played as an emergency. **1897** N. INNES *Ring Rec. & Fistic Facts* I. 21 Mr. Tuohey has long been identified with boxers as backer and manager. **1946** E. O'NEILL *Iceman Cometh* I. 12 Dem tarts.. dey're just a side line to pick up some extra dough... Like dey was fighters and I was deir manager, see? **1969** B. JAMES *England v. Scotland* x. 217 Spurs manager Bill Nicholson has an interesting postscript to that decision. **1989** *Looks* Dec. 102/4, I get on the blower to the press officers and managers and make sure that the acts arrive at the studio on time.

mandarin, *n.*[1] Sense 4 in Dict. becomes 5. Add: **4.** *Ornith. ellipt.* for *mandarin duck*, sense 5 a below.

1860 G. BENNETT *Gatherings of Naturalist in Australasia* viii. 190 The old Mandarin male began to change his plumage. **1890** in *Cent. Dict.* **1925** J. C. PHILLIPS *Nat. Hist. Ducks* III. 74 The Mandarin is a strictly East Asian species. **1952** C. SAVAGE *Mandarin Duck* iii. 19 The virtues of the Mandarin.. must have also contributed to the early history of the duck. **1965** P. A. JOHNSGARD *Handbk. Waterfowl Behavior* 116 Mandarins are gregarious and tend to be most active in the evening. **1985** *Birds* Winter 14/1 By 1981, it was estimated that there were more wild mandarins living in the south of England than in the whole of China.

mandate, *v.* Add: **5.** To require (some action) by legal mandate or other formal process; more generally, to make mandatory or compulsory; (with abstract subject) to necessitate. chiefly *U.S.*

1967 *National Observer* (U.S.) 3 July 13 Mr. Reagan must raise the money to pay off that deficit and to pay for mandated new programs. **1975** P. GERBER *Willa Cather* iii. 84 Cather had found that dedication mandates loneliness. *Ibid.* 88 The adoption of Jim's point-of-view not only explains but actually mandates the episodic structure of the novel. **1976** *National Observer* (U.S.) 10 Jan. 10/1 Until the Government began mandating better auto safety, it was difficult if not impossible to buy American-made cars with such things as crash-resistant bumpers. **1981** *Observer* 6 Sept. 16/9 No single carrier could have unilaterally reduced its services. But the strike mandated a 20 to 25 per cent reduction in operations generally. **1991** *South* Aug. 48/1 Zionist ideology mandates free entry for any Jew wishing to settle in Israel.

Mandelbrot ('mænd(ə)lbrɒt), *n. Math.* [The name of Benoit B. *Mandelbrot* (b. 1924), Polish-born American mathematician, who investigated the concept.] **Mandelbrot set**, the set of all complex numbers *c* for which the Julia set of the mapping $z \rightarrow z^2 + c$ is connected, where z is a complex variable; the set of all complex numbers *c* such that under repeated application of the mapping $z \rightarrow z^2 + c$ any complex number z remains within a bounded region of the complex plane.

1984 *Bull. Amer. Math. Soc.* XI. 127 Many important open questions regarding quadratics are best phrased in terms of the Mandelbrot set. *Ibid.* 129 This computer evidence strongly suggests that the Mandelbrot set is also a fractal and that the dynamics always bifurcates according to the same 'pattern'. **1985** *Sci. Amer.* Aug. 8/1 The boundary of the Mandelbrot set is a fractal, but it is also much more. **1986** *Nature* 16 Oct. 590/2 Peitgen and Richter present high-resolution computer-generated images of the Julia and Mandelbrot sets, vividly coloured to illustrate their important mathematical properties. **1988** *Bookseller* 23 Sept. 1221 Yuval Fischer introduces the fundamentals of a new, extremely efficient algorithm for the Mandelbrot set. **1994** J. BARTH *Once upon Time* 180 History is a Mandelbrot Set, infinitely subdivisible.

mandelonitrile (mæn,dɛləʊ'naɪtraɪl), *n. Chem.* [f. MANDEL(IC *a.* + -*o* + NITRILE, after G. *Mandelnitril.*] Benzaldehyde cyanohydrin, $C_6H_5CH(OH)CN$, a yellow oily liquid which is the nitrile of mandelic acid and of which amygdalin is a glucoside.

1898 *Jrnl. Chem. Soc.* LXXIV. II. 509 When silicon tetrachloride is heated with mandelonitrile or lactonitrile, silicic acid and complex tarry products are formed. **1912** *Proc. R. Soc.* B. LXXXV. 360 It.. will be convenient to use the name Prunasin in speaking of the glucoside (d-mandelonitrile glucoside) which, hitherto, we have termed Fischer's glucoside. **1936** W. STILES *Introd. Princ. Plant Physiol.* v. 106 The prunasin is now hydrolysed by means of prunase into glucose and mandelonitrile. **1956** I. L. FINAR *Org. Chem.* II. vii. 244 The enzyme zymase hydrolyses amygdalin into one molecule of glucose and a glucoside of (+)-mandelonitrile (this compound is identical with prunasin, a naturally occurring glucoside). **1986** *Arch. Biochem. & Biophysics* CCXLVII. 440 Five multiple forms.. of mandelonitrile lyase.. which catalyze the decomposition of mandelonitrile to benzaldehyde and hydrogen cyanide have been extensively purified from seeds of black cherry.

Mandevilla (mændə'vɪlə), *n. Bot.* [mod.L., f. the name of Henry John *Mandeville* (1773-1861), British minister: see quot. 1840.] A tropical American genus of plants (mostly lianas) of the family Apocynaceae, some of which are grown as ornamentals in tropical and subtropical regions and including the Chilean jasmine; (also **mandevilla**) a plant of this genus; *esp.* the cultivar M. × *amabilis*, with red flowers having a strong fragrance.

1840 J. LINDLEY in *Edwards's Bot. Reg.* XXVI. 7 Mandevilla suaveolens, Sweet Scented Mandevilla... This new climber was sent from Buenos Ayres, by H. J. Mandeville, Esq., H. M. Minister in that place, to the Hon. W. F. Strangways, by whom seeds were presented to the Horticultural Society. It had been collected by Mr. Tweedy, and sent home under the name of the Chile Jasmine. [*Note*] I have much pleasure in naming this beautiful twiner after Henry John Mandeville, Esq. **1896** T. W. SANDERS *Encycl. Gardening* (ed. 2) 224 Mandevilla (Chili Jasmine). **1940** A. J. MACSELF *Concise Dict. Gardening* 309/2 Mandevilla... Plant Feb. in a mixture of equal parts peat and loam. **1985** PRANCE & LOVEJOY *Amazonia* ix. 179 (*caption*) A Mandevilla vine with clear central nectar guide. **1987** *Courier-Mail* (Brisbane) 7 Feb. 15/3 Closely related to dipladenia is the beautiful Mandevilla Alice Dupont, with attractive corrugated foliage and large bright pink trumpet blooms.

Mandingo, *n.* and *a.* Add: [A.] [b.] The form **Manding** is freq. used *spec.* to denote (*a*) the Malinke language, (*b*) a group of closely related and mutually intelligible Mande languages including Malinke. (Further examples.)
   1952 WESTERMANN & BRYAN *Lang. W. Afr.* ii. 31 The name *Mande* or *Mandingo* is a general term applied by Europeans and others to all the tribes speaking Mande languages. The name (other versions of which are *Mandi, Male, Mali, Mele.., Manding*) is properly applied only to the people commonly known as *Malinke* and to their speech. **1969** MORGAN & PUGH *W. Afr.* I. i. 24 The Senoufo are a Voltaic community who have adopted many Manding and Akan customs. They live well to the south, in sub-Sudanic and sub-Guinean environments. **1983** I. F. HANCOCK in I. R. Dihoff *Current Approaches to Afr. Linguistics* I. xv. 249 Ethnic groups speaking dialects of the Manding language in Sierra Leone include the *Bambara, Dyula, Kuranko, Mandinka, Maninka* and *Manyaka.* By far the most widely represented of these is the Maninka, usually referred to as Mandinka or Mandingo in reference to Sierra Leone.

maneb ('mænɛb), *n. Agric.* [Acronym f. the initial letters of *manganese ethylene bisdithiocarbamate*, the systematic name. Cf. earlier ZINEB *n.*] A yellowish-brown organosulphur compound, $Mn(S_2C\cdot NH\cdot C_2H_4\cdot NH\cdot CS_2)$, used as a protective fungicidal powder on vegetables and fruit.
   1954 *Chem. Abstr.* XLVIII. 11315/2 (Index), Maneb. **1956** *Ibid.* L. 524 (*heading*) Tolerances for residues of maneb. **1966** *McGraw-Hill Encycl. Sci. & Technol.* V. 563/2 Organic fungicides have become increasingly important since 1934... Examples are.. nabam, zineb, and maneb, the sodium, zinc, and manganese salts, respectively, of ethylenebis (dithiocarbamic acid). **1976** *Homes & Gardens* June 131/2 Tulips are particularly susceptible to tulip fire... Apply a fungicide such as maneb or dineb at seven- to 10-day intervals until flowering. **1986** *Canad. Jrnl. Plant Path.* VIII. 323 Fungus diseases.. were controlled by maneb.

manganese, *n.* Add: [3.] [a.] **manganese nodule** *Geol.*, a nodular concretion consisting primarily of manganese and iron oxides, such as occur in large quantities on the floors of oceans and the Great Lakes.
   1876 *Proc. R. Soc.* XXIV. 507 The trawl brought up many *manganese nodules or concretions and two shark's teeth; these nodules had in most cases a nucleus of pumice. **1912** MURRAY & HJORT *Depths of Ocean* iv. 157 Sulphate of barium has been found to be present in most marine deposits and in manganese nodules in small quantities. **1989** *Encycl. Brit.* XXV. 172/2 An estimated 1,500,000,000,000 tons of manganese nodules are on the Pacific Ocean floor alone.

mango, *n.*[1] Add: [6.] **mango fly**, (*a*) = *mangrove fly* s.v. MANGROVE *n.*[1] 3; (*b*) = TUMBU FLY *n.*
   1910 CASTELLANI & CHALMERS *Man. Trop. Med.* xvi. 424 It has been thought by Manson that the further stages of the life-history will be found in the *mango-fly (Chrysops dimidiatus*), but others suspect not merely Tabanidæ, but *Glossinæ* and *Stomoxys.* **1962** GORDON & LAVOIPIERRE *Entomol. for Students of Med.* xxxi. 195 *Cordylobia anthropophaga*, locally known as the 'tumbu fly' or 'mango fly' is distributed in Africa from Senegal and Ethiopia in the North to Natal in the South. **1972** M. PUGH *Murmur of Mutiny* iii. 21 The heat built up and the high whine of mango flies arose. **1980** M. W. SERVICE *Guide Med. Entomol.* xiii. 114/1 This species [sc. *Cordylobia anthropophaga*] is known as the tumbu or mango fly and is found only in Africa. **1987** C. R. SCHULL *Common Med. Probl. in Tropics* xxxii. 367/1 The adult produces microfilaria which circulate in the blood. These infect *Chrysops* ('mango' or 'softly-softly' flies) which then give the infection back to man.

manhood, *n.* Add: [2.] c. *spec.* The sexual potency of a man; virility. **d.** The male genitalia; the penis.
   1640 H. GLAPTHORNE *Hollander* v. sig. I. 4, You have excellent salves and unguents sir... Have you never a one that will eat off the wen of manhood, make all whole before that will eunuchise a man, I would faine be a Hermaphrodite, or a woman to escape this match. **1689** *Upon King's Voy. to Chatham* in *Coll. Poems on Affairs of State* 19, I wish this sad Accident don't spoil the young Prince, Take off all his Manhood and make him a Wench. *a*1704 T. BROWN tr. Beroaldus *Declam. in Defence Gaming* in *Wks.* (1708) III. 134 A Man depriv'd of his Manhood.. by an Inundation of *Claret.* **1709** E. WARD *Secret Hist. Clubs* xxviii. 325 They make themselves merry, when they are met o'er their Claret, interposing now and then, either extraordinary Commendations of their Husbands Manhood, or some witty Reflections on their slender Qualifications. **1749** J. CLELAND *Mem. Woman Pleasure* I. 168 On my first stirring, which was not till past ten o'clock, I was oblig'd to endure one more trial of his manhood. **1809** 'D. KNICKERBOCKER' *Hist. N. Y.* II. VI. i. 69 To manhood roused, he spurns the amorous flute. **1967** T. W. BLACKBURN *Good Day to Die* xix. 145, I have but one living son... If I do not speak the truth, let the white man's pox strike him and his manhood rot in his clout. **1975** I. McEWAN *First Love* (1976) 21 My blood pounding, my manhood proudly stirring. **1991** *Sun* 28 Feb. 19/2 Topless kissogram girl Linzi Berry went on sick leave suffering from shock — after a naked miner coshed her with his manhood.

manically ('mænɪkəlɪ), *adv.* [f. MANIC *a.*: see -ICALLY.] As if affected with mania; maniacally.
   *a*1963 C. S. LEWIS *Poems* (1964) 100 And all his famed Elysium Worthless, if former joys in all their earthliness Are there repeated, manically, dizzily. **1977** *Economist* 31 Dec. 24/2 And we didn't tell Brian Beedham why we were laughing so manically until we landed, safe and shaken, in Wuhan. **1988** G. SWIFT *Out of this World* 127 On Sunday evenings the whole town suddenly swarms into the streets and starts walking up and down, just walking manically up and down. **1991** J. SAYERS *Mothering Psychoanalysis* v. vi. 241 He manically wrapped himself up in a Union Jack and triumphantly sang the national Anthem.

‖**manicotti** (mani'kotti, anglicized mænɪ'kɒtɪ), *n. pl.* [It., pl. of *manicotto* muff, f. *manica* sleeve (cf. MANICA *n.*).] Large tubular pasta shells; also, a dish consisting of these, usu. stuffed with cheese, tomatoes, meat, etc., and served with a sauce.
   1948 R. W. DANA *Where to eat in N.Y.* 54 There is a large selection of pastas, of course, such as.. manicotti. **1965** H. KANE *Other Sins only Speak* iv. 25 That man makes the wildest manicotti. **1974** H. L. FOSTER *Ribbin'* iv. 163 Politicians are notorious for

winning votes by.. eating pizza, lasagna, or manicotti at an Italian block party. **1978** *Tucson Mag.* Dec. 117/1 The Baked Manicotti was also more paste than polish. **1983** J. FAMULARO & L. IMPERIALE *Joy of Pasta* i. 22 We offer here two recipes: one for gnocchi..; and crespelle, or manicotti shells, which you can use to stuff as you would the classic manicotti. **1993** *Santa Fe* (New Mexico) *Jrnl. Reporter* 3–9 Feb. 28/2 Screenwriter Todd Graff throws a little manicotti onto the table with the gefilte fish.

manifold, *a.*, *adv.*, and *n.*[1] [C.] [3.] Substitute for def.: [tr. G. *Mannigfaltigkeit* (B. Riemann *Grundlagen für eine Allgemeine Theorie der Functionen* (1867) 26).] A topological space each point of which has a neighbourhood homoeomorphic to the interior of a sphere in a Euclidean space of given dimension; = MANIFOLDNESS *n.* 2.
1878 *Mind* III. 213 The space-representation might still be the necessary *a priori* form in which every co-extended manifold is perceived. **1886** *Trans. & Proc. N.Z. Inst.* XVIII. 59 The manifold I described in my paper is not a space. [*Note*] This term is now generally used instead of the more cumbrous 'manifoldness'. **1897** B. RUSSELL *Ess. Found. Geom.* i. 14 Riemann's epoch-making work.. was written, and read to a small circle, in 1854.. it remained unpublished till 1867... The two fundamental conceptions.. are that of a manifold, and that of the measure of curvature of a manifold. **1926** *Proc. Sect. Sci. Kon. Akad. Wetensch. Amsterdam* XXIX. 618 It will be shewn that bounded and unbounded *n*-manifolds are in fact bounded and unbounded *n*-arrays in the sense already defined. **1945** E. T. BELL *Devel. Math.* (ed. 2) ix. 203 A 'real' space or 'manifold' of *n* dimensions is the set, or class, of all ordered *n*-ples $(x_1, x_2, .. , x_n)$ of *n* real numbers. each of which ranges over a prescribed class of real numbers. **1966** *Mathematical Rev.* XXXI. 33/2 (*title*) Some growth and ramification properties of certain integrals on algebraic manifolds. **1981** A. SALAM in J. H. Mulvey *Nature of Matter* v. 119 Einstein found that the gravitational charge could be represented in terms of curvature in a four-dimensional manifold of space and time. **1986** *New Scientist* 12 June 48/2 The space-time in which we live is expected to be a manifold because the neighbourhood of any point resembles flat space-time.

manipulandum (mə‚nɪpjʊˈlændəm), *n.* *Anthropol.* and *Psychol.* Pl. **manipulanda.** [Either med.L. *manipulandum*, gerund of *manipulare* to take by the hand, or f. MANIPULA(TE *v.* + -*ndum* L. gerund suffix (see -AND²).] An object or feature designed for or capable of manipulation, esp. in a psychological test or experiment.
1951 S. F. NADEL *Found. Social Anthropol.* xii. 365 Reason and logic perhaps merely guide our search for *manipulanda.* **1960** HINSIE & CAMPBELL *Psychiatric Dict.* (ed. 3) 399/2 [The capacities] to respond to such differentiated apperceptions by internal and external reactions of various degrees of finesse, versatility, and efficiency [are called] 'manipulanda' capacities. **1969** *Daily Colonist* (Victoria, B.C.) 9 Oct. 38/4 Much of the research will relate to complex forms of stimulus control [such as] controlled locomotion and operation of manipulanda while flying. **1972** *Science* 9 June 1126/1 Rats learned to press an isometric, force-sensing manipulandum to obtain food pellets. **1974** *Nature* 25 Oct. 705/2 The enriched condition consisted of a large, clear, lucite box (75 × 40 × 20 cm high) divided diagonally in two containing various manipulanda. **1982** *Sociol. Abstr.* Aug. (Suppl. 16) 173/1 Observations were made in the child's home under conditions of exposing the child to unfamiliar objects and manipulanda.

manipulate, *v.* Add: [2.] **b.** *spec.* in *Computing.* To carry out operations on (data) automatically or with the aid of a machine.

1962 *Technical Memo* (System Development Corp., Calif.) TM-WD-16/007/00. i. 5 It is necessary to define the characteristics of a data base to the Data Base System so that when instructed to manipulate data, the system can recognize the format and positioning of item information in the entries. **1967** *Proc. 21st Nat. Conf. Assoc. Computing Machinery* 465 (*heading*) META 5: a tool to manipulate strings of data. **1984** *Which Micro?* Dec. 26 (Advt.), There is a.. set of commands for.. manipulating text. **1990** *Atlantic* Apr. 18/2 To retrieve data from a CD-ROM disk and manipulate it, a user will need a CD-ROM player.

mannerless, *a.* Add: Hence '**mannerlessness** *n.*
1947 C. AMORY *Proper Bostonians* xi. 238 In a single line which he wrote with evident pride about his father Wendell managed what would seem to be a summary of Boston's First Family mannerlessness. **1984** *New Republic* 27 Feb. 34/2 He was.. dogmatic.., and far from conventionally polite; as one of his employers expressed it, 'He had the mannerlessness of genius.'

Mannesmann ('mænəs‚mæn), *n. Manuf.* [The name of Reinhard M. *Mannesmann* (1856–1922), German industrialist and inventor.] Used *attrib.* with reference to a method of making thick-walled seamless metal tubes by drawing a heated cylinder of metal between two inclined rollers that cause it to separate and flow round a pointed mandrel aligned with its axis.
1920 *Jrnl. Iron & Steel Inst.* CI. 736 The method of manufacture of seamless tubes by the Mannesmann process is described. **1960** D. J. O. BRANDT *Manuf. Iron & Steel* (ed. 2) xliii. 345 Before considering in detail the Automatic Mill Process and the Pilger Process of tube-making we may first examine the Rotary Piercing Process or Mannesmann Process.. which is the first stage in both these methods of tubemaking. **1978** *Jrnl. R. Soc. Arts* CXXVI. 612/1 It was hoped to directly produce tubes by electrodeposition, but the process was dropped with the successful development of the Mannesmann piercing and rolling techniques. **1984** E. P. DEGARMO et al. *Materials & Processes in Manuf.* (ed. 6) xiv. 367 The Mannesmann-type mill is used to produce tubing up to about 300 mm (12 inches) in diameter.

Mann–Whitney (mæn'wɪtnɪ), *n. Statistics.* [The names of Henry Berthold *Mann* (b. 1905), Austrian-born U.S. mathematician, and Donald Ransom *Whitney* (b. 1915), U.S. statistician.] Used *attrib.*, esp. in **Mann–Whitney (U) test**, with reference to a method of testing whether the difference between independent observations from two populations has zero median, and hence whether the populations are in fact the same.
1951 *Ann. Math. Statistics* XXII. 165 The large sample power of these tests and of the Mann-Whitney test are obtained by means of a theorem of Hoeffding. **1970** *Jrnl. Gen. Psychol.* LXXXIII. 90 Mann-Whitney *U* comparisons.. between all possible pairs of these groups shows [*sic*] all pairs significantly different save for Groups III. **1978** *Nature* 8 June 470/1 The mean channel conductance in cells at 37°C was 38.8 ± 4.7 pS (6 cells, −70 mV) which is not significantly different from the value at room temperature (Mann-Whitney test, $P > 0.10$). **1980** *Brit. Med. Jrnl.* 29 Mar. 895/2 The results were analysed statistically with the Mann-Whitney U test for small samples or the paired *t* test. **1991** *Lancet* 9 Mar. 592/2 Statistical testing was done with both the Student's *t* test and the Mann-Whitney U test for categorical variables.

manpower ('mænpaʊə(r)), *v. Austral.* and *N.Z. colloq.* ?Now *Hist.* [f. *man-power* s.v. MAN *n.*[1] 20 a.] *trans.* To conscript for non-military service as part of the war effort. Freq. in *pass.*

1959 D. Hewett *Bobbin Up* (1961) ii. 22 I've worked in the mill ever since they manpowered me durin' the war. **1976-7** *Art N.Z.* Dec./Jan. 43/1 Pacifists were sent to camps or manpowered to essential industries. **1984** J. Frame *Angel at my Table* iv. 35 During the summer of that year other students and I were 'manpowered' to pick raspberries on Whittakers' farm at Millers Flat.

man-powered ('mænpaʊəd), *a.* (Formerly at MAN *n.*¹ 19 e). [f. MAN *n.*¹ + POWERED *a.*] Driven by human rather than mechanical effort.

1959 *Times* 27 July 7/6 A purely private effort..to achieve a man-powered 'ornithopter'. **1973** *Nature* 16 Nov. 173/3 A book largely concerned with a theoretical synthesis of man-powered ornithopters. **1992** *Tour de France* 92 19 A fast ride on a racing bicycle is the nearest thing in this world to man-powered flight.

mansard, *n.* Senses a–c in Dict. become 1 a, 2, 3. Add: Also **mansarde**. [1.] **b.** A storey or apartment under a mansard roof.

1886 A. T. Ritchie *Lett.* (1924) x. 197 A remarkable lady who managed Normandy and who received emperors in her mansarde. **1938** S. Beckett *Murphy* ix. 162 The garret that he now saw was not an attic, nor yet a mansarde, but a genuine garret. **1945** E. Bowen *Demon Lover* 121 Glazed-in balconies and French-type mansardes. **1973** T. Pynchon *Gravity's Rainbow* (1975) I. 161 They'd lived in the same drafty mansarde in the Liebigstrasse in Munich.

mantissa, *n.* Add: [2.] **b.** *Computing.* A number, usually of a fixed number of digits and between 0 and 1, by which a power of the base (e.g. 2 or 10) is multiplied to represent a number in floating-point representation.

1959 M. H. Wrubel *Primer of Programming for Digital Computers* ii. 19 The second representation employs a mantissa, containing the significant digits, multiplied by 10 raised to a power. **1960** M. G. Say et al. *Analogue & Digital Computers* v. 142 After multiplication has been completed the digit following the binary point must be examined and, if this digit is 0, a corrective shift must be applied to the mantissa together with an adjustment of the exponent. **1979** *Sci. Amer.* Dec. 87/3 In most computers the decimal point in the mantissa of a floating-point number is by convention placed at the far left, so that the number 3.24×10^6 would be represented in floating-point form as $.324 \times 10^7$, or the pair of numbers 7, 324. **1985** *Pract. Computing* Aug. 102/4 Single-precision variables use a three-byte mantissa and a one-byte exponent.

mantric ('mæntrɪk), *a.* [f. MANTR(A *n.* + -IC.] Of, pertaining to, resembling, or characteristic of a mantra.

1923 *Glasgow Herald* 16 Oct. 6 Reading recently a critical article on the musical compositions of a modern, I encountered the reasonable-looking word 'mantric'. **1965** A. Bharati *Tantric Tradition* v. 102 Such secondary instruction is very frequently couched in *sandhā*-terms and works as a sort of mantric meta-language. **1978** P. Griffiths *Conc. Hist. Mod. Mus.* ix. 139 His [*sc.* Stockhausen's] *Mantra* for two pianos and electronics..is an attempt to create that 'mantric music' which can..'bring the gods into our life'. **1982** *N.Y. Times* 26 Dec. 1. 60/2 Jane Adler, a mime, created visual mantric repetitions. **1987** *New Republic* 5 Oct. 30/3 Minimalism..is music not of structural drama, but of repetitive mantric pulse.

Manu ('mɑːnuː), *n. Hindu Mythol.* Also 8 **Mǎnǒǒ.** [a. Skr. *Manu*, archetypal use of *manu* man.] The father of the human race, and the legendary author of the Laws of Manu (*Manu-smṛti*), an important Sanskrit legal code. Also, one of a series of fourteen cosmic deities, each of which presides over one of the manvantaras.

1785 C. Wilkins tr. *Bhăgvăt Gēētā* x. 83 The seven Măhărshĕĕs and the four Mǎnǒǒs..were born of my mind, of whom are descended all the inhabitants of the earth. **1839** *Penny Cycl.* XIV. 394/2 Manu..was the son or grandson of the creating deity Brahmă, the first of rational beings, and the progenitor of mankind. **1859** Max Müller *Hist. Sanskrit Lit.* Introd. 62 The different dates ascribed to Manu, as the author of our Law-book. **1887** W. J. Wilkins *Mod. Hinduism* 463 At Shrădhas, Manu and other writers distinctly enjoin eating of flesh. **1959** *Chambers's Encycl.* III. 158/2 These distinctions appear in one of the later books of the *Rigveda* and are stereotyped by the code of Manu. **1977** M. & J. Stutley *Dict. Hinduism* 181/2 The Manu myth gradually expanded, and..culminated in his appearance as Vaivasvata, the seventh Manu of the *manvantara* cosmic evolutionary theory.

manual, *a.* and *n.* Add: [B.] [1.] **c.** A set of instructions or procedures (not necessarily concise) for carrying out a particular operation or for using a particular piece of equipment.

1843 J. Jones (*title*) Manual for the use of Jones's multiplying and equalizing hive, containing also hints useful for the management of bees in all sorts of hives. **1858** H. Busk (*title*) Rifleman's manual; or, Rifles, and how to use them (ed. 2). *Ibid* p. xii, A rifle which has successfully stood the test of deer-stalking will generally prove a valuable adjunct in war. Such a weapon will be found fully described in this Manual. **1903** *Lanchester Motor & Carriage* (Lanchester Engine Co.) II. 71 Our present Driving Manual..is primarily a book on the 'Lanchester' Car. **1925** *Manual of Morris Oxford & Cowley Cars* (Morris Motors Ltd.) 2 In case of trouble, first study this Manual; then, if still puzzled, write to the works. **1961** *Computing Rev.* II. 187/1 This hefty, though well-indexed, manual is the most detailed account of a programming system which has come to the reviewer's attention. **1978** R. V. Jones *Most Secret War* iii. 24, I got out the appropriate manual so that we could go through the correct test sequence. **1986** *Shetland Times* 7 Nov. 12/3 Altogether 80 copies of the manual have been distributed outlining what action would need to be taken within a three mile radius of the plant. **1988** *Pract. Motorist* Jan. 11/3 The manual is very comprehensive and is in three volumes.

[4.] **c.** *ellipt.* A manual typewriter. *colloq.*

1972 J. Gores *Dead Skip* (1973) x. 67 One [woman] was..typing on an old manual. **1984** *Runner* (U.S.) Oct. 4/1 He hates computers. He still writes his articles on a beaten up old manual.

manufacturable, *a.* Add: Hence **manufactura'bility** *n.*

1972 *Sci. Amer.* Aug. 14/2 In judging alternative power plants the automobile manufacturer will give weight to the following major considerations.. manufacturability, cost, size, weight. **1983** *Production Engin.* Jan. 16/2 Review part designs carefully for manufacturability on a machining center.

map, *v.*¹ Sense 1 f in Dict. becomes 4 a. Add: [1.] **g.** To plan or devise (a course of action, etc.); to project. *U.S.*

1950 M. Culver *Black Water Blues* in *Atlantic Monthly* May 35/1 Bump Roxy was a great drummer and a great musician. He told them when they overdid it or underdid it; he mapped the order of the solos. He held the band together. **1957** V. Packard *Hidden Persuaders* vi. 62 Our small fears and anxieties, like our guilt feelings, offered many openings for the depth manipulators to map successful campaigns for enterprising merchandisers. **1986** *Philadelphia Inquirer* 11 July D1/2 A spring fund-raising event netted nearly \$500,000 for AIDS research, and more are being mapped.

3. b. *Genetics.* To have a specified position on a genetic map.

1961 *Proc. Nat. Acad. Sci.* XLVII. 408 If there exists space to the right of segment B10, a mutation in that segment might map as if it were in segment B7. **1967** *Bacteriol. Rev.* XXI. 341/2 Both succinate-requiring mutants (which map at the *suc* locus near *gal*) and lipoic acid-requiring mutants are phenotypically similar. **1975** *Nature* 5 June 447/2 Mutations affecting the structure of this enzyme in terms of electrophoretic mobility changes..all map within 5×10^{-3} map units. **1990** *Nucleic Acids Res.* XVIII. 4143/1 A gene in *Drosophila melanogaster* that maps cytologically to 2C1-3 on the distal portion of the X-chromosome encodes a member of the steroid/thyroid hormone receptor superfamily.

4. b. *Linguistics.* To convert (an abstract model of underlying linguistic elements, e.g. a deep structure) *into* a corresponding model at another level (e.g. a surface structure) by the application of transformational rules. Also const. *on to.*

1955 N. CHOMSKY *Theory of Linguistic Struct.* (microfilm, Mass. Inst. Technol.) ii. 64, Φ is a mapping which, in particular, maps μ into the set of grammatical utterances. **1963** N. CHOMSKY in R. D. Luce et al. *Handbk. Math. Psychol.* II. xii. 346 We call *M* a *transducer*, which maps input strings into output strings and, correspondingly, input languages into output languages. **1964** —— *Current Issues in Linguistic Theory* i. 13 The second (transformational) subcomponent consists of a partially ordered set of complex operations called (*grammatical*) *transformations*, each of which maps a full Phrase-marker..of some terminal string..into a new *derived* Phrase-marker of a *T-terminal string.* **1973** *Archivum Linguisticum* IV. 49 Frequently, they [*sc.* suffixes] are 'mapped' onto the verb as a kind of shorthand equivalent of a periphrastic form comprising personal pronoun + postposition of case. **1976** J. S. GRUBER *Lexical Struct. Syntax & Semantics* II. i. 242 The class of verbs that manifests only a *to*-phrase can be said to be characterized by a lexical attachment rule by which the underlying *from*-phrase is mapped into the verb itself. **1991** D. CRYSTAL *Dict. Linguistics & Phonetics* (ed. 3) 211 In transformational grammar, the term is used specifically to refer to the process whereby a particular stage in the derivation of a sentence is formally related to a subsequent stage, e.g. an input phrase is 'mapped' by a set of transformations on to a derived phrase-marker.

c. *Computing.* To associate (an item of data) with a specified location in memory; to associate (a memory location) with a data item. Const. *into, on to, to.*

[**1963** *IBM Systems Jrnl.* II. 113 When several records map the same address, those records in excess of the addressed area..are sometimes chained to a separate overflow area.] **1971** BULL & PACKHAM *Time-Sharing Syst.* iii. 59 With paging, instead of the whole user program being mapped into main memory, only a few of the currently active pages are in memory at one time. **1981** *Byte* Nov. 511/2 A mapping command allows the user to map program memory to PROM/EPROM. **1983** *Austral. Microcomputer Mag.* Aug. 22/3 The most interesting part of the design is the implementation of the 40/80-column text display, which uses a second page of static RAM mapped over the top of the usual 40-column text screen. **1986** D. DEUTSCH in T. C. Bartee *Digital Communications* v. 212 Its name is mapped into its address. **1991** *Personal Computer World* Feb. 170/2 All Sbus based memory is mapped onto on-board memory which itself is mapped onto the cache.

mape ('maːpeɪ), *n.* Also mapé. [Polynesian.] The ivi tree (IVI *n.*).

1888 W. HILLEBRAND *Flora Hawaiian Islands* 109 Here [among the Caesalpinieae] also must be given a place to the anomalous *Inocarpus edulis*, Forst., or Tahitian Chestnut, the Ivi or Mapé. **1928** B. P. BISHOP *Museum Bull.* (Honolulu) XLVIII. 46 The mape or Tahitian chestnut (*Inocarpus edulis*) was formerly called *ràtà*, as it is named in the old writings, both names signifying 'kidney', which the nut resembles in shape. **1952** R. FINLAYSON *Schooner came to Atia* 74 Roast mape nuts threaded on slivers of bamboo. **1969** J. H. VANCE *Deadly Isles* (1970) iii. 27 A clump of *mape*, the Tahitian chestnut.

Mapharsen (mæˈfɑːsən), *n. Pharm.* (chiefly *U. S.*). Also **mapharsen.** [f. the initial letters of *meta*-amino *para*-hydroxyl + ARSEN(IC *n.*[1]] A proprietary name in the U.S. for an organic arsenical drug formerly given intravenously in the treatment of syphilis; the hydrochloride of 3-amino-4-hydroxyphenyloxoarsine, (HO)-(H₂N)C₆H₃·AsO.

1932 TATUM & COOPER in *Science* 20 May 541/2 We have been designating this drug as '158', or more or less tentatively by the name *Mapharsen* from (m)eta-(a)mino-(p)ara-(h)ydroxy (ars)ine oxide. **1934** TATUM & COOPER in *Jrnl. Pharmacol. & Exper. Therapeutics* L. 198 The drug, meta-amino para-hydroxyl phenyl arsine oxide, we designate as Drug No. 158 or, by name, Mapharsen. **1946** *Jrnl. Venereal Dis. Information* XXVII. 9/1 Penicillin and mapharsen are synergistic in the treatment of experimental syphilis. **1985** *Jrnl. Hist. Med.* XL. 187 Mapharsen..provided physicians with a comparatively safe and effective treatment for syphilis for several years until it was replaced by penicillin.

mapped (mæpt), *ppl. a.* [f. MAP *v.*[1] + -ED[1].] That has been mapped (in various senses of the verb). Also as *mapped-out.*

1606 W. WARNER *Albions Eng.: Contin.* (1612) XV. xcviii. 388 What are these but the mapped Orbs of all Hypocrisie? **1849** A. H. CLOUGH *Ambarvalia* (1849) 46 My station, whence the circling land Lies mapped and pictured wide below. **1866** C. KINGSLEY *Hereward* I. i. 71 Not to him, as to us, a world circular, round, circumscribed, mapped, botanized. **1937** *Mind* XLVI. 165 The novelty of Serialism lies in this: in a Serial Universe it is permissible to rotate the geometrically mapped-out axis of a time-dimension (T₂) until its divisions coincide with those of a time (T₁) one dimension lower. **1950** F. W. SINNOTT et al. *Princ. Genetics* (ed. 4) ix. 226 The most extensively mapped species, after *Drosophila melanogaster*, is the maize plant. **1955** N. CHOMSKY *Theory of Linguistic Struct.* (microfilm, Mass. Inst. Technol.) vii. 343 In stating these mappings we may refer to the constituent structure of the mapped string. **1979** *Nature* 7 June 491/1 A single arcuate (folded?) and fault-bounded block of plagiogranite is present in the much-faulted northern part of the mapped area.

mapping, *vbl. n.* Add: **3.** *Linguistics.* The (degree of) correspondence between associated elements of different types or at different levels within a linguistic process or scheme. Cf. *MAP v.* 4 b.

1955 N. CHOMSKY *Theory of Linguistic Struct.* (microfilm, Mass. Inst. Technol.) ii. 63[1] The relations between L and other levels can be presented as a set of mappings defined on L. *Ibid.* 64 Φ is a mapping which, in particular, maps μ into the set of grammatical utterances. **1971** *Language* XLVII. 8 This overwhelming predominance of many-one mapping over one-many, as we move from semantics to phonetics, can then be seen as further evidence of language's directionality. **1987** *Multilingua* VI. 319 The more syntax is more often ambiguous or vague, the mapping between expression and meaning more often indirect. **1992** *Lit. & Linguistic Computing* 234/2 A sentence in English may have one-to-many mapping to many different structures in Chinese.

maprotiline (məˈprəʊtiliːn), *n. Pharm.* [f. *mapro-*, of unkn. origin + *-tiline* var. of *-tyline* (in AMITRIPTYLINE *n.*, PROTRIPTYLINE *n.*, etc.).] A tetracyclic antidepressant structurally related to the tricyclics, and usually administered in tablet form as the hydrochloride; 3-(9,

10-dihydro-9,10-ethanoanthracen-9-yl)propyl-(methyl)amine, $C_{20}H_{23}N$.
1970 *WHO Chron.* XXIV. 130 Maprotiline. **1976** *Lancet* 18 Dec. 1357/1 We have seen a patient with a rash and severe neutropenia probably associated with maprotiline hydrochloride ('Ludiomil'), a tetracyclic antidepressant. **1983** STAFFORD-CLARK & SMITH *Psychiatry for Students* (ed. 6) vii. 118 Maprotiline (Ludiomil) has a different structure but it is not very different from nortriptyline in properties, dosage and side-effects. **1989** *Jrnl. Psychopharmacol.* XXX. IV. 36P Second generation atypical antidepressants produce a lesser incidence of poisoning fatalities than tricyclics and maprotiline.

Mapuche (mæˈpʊtʃɪ), *n.* and *a.* Pl. unchanged or with -s. [Native name f. Mapuche *mapu* land, country + *che* people.] **A.** *n.* **1.** A member of any of the Araucanian Indian peoples of central Chile and Argentina.
Early Spanish settlers in Chile identified three distinct groups of Araucanian Indian peoples; the *Picunche* in the north, the *Huilliche* in the south, and the *Mapuche*. Only the *Mapuche* survive unassimilated, and, consequently, their name has become almost synonymous with *Araucanian*.
1922 L. E. ELLIOTT *Chile Today & Tomorrow* ii. 26 The 'Changos' of the coastal border took up a permanent position as friends just as the Mapuches (Araucanians) took up a permanent position as enemies. **1929** A. EDWARDS *Peoples of Old* 9 From Aconcagua to the Chacao Channel and the Gulf of Reloncaví the Kingdom of Chile was inhabited by the Mapuches, the indigenous race who regarded themselves as autochthonous. **1973** *Black Panther* 20 Oct. 14/1 At the Mapuche Indian reservation, all the male Mapuches the military could catch were killed or severely beaten. **1974** *Encycl. Brit. Macropædia* XVII. 120/2 In response to the colonists' demands for more Indian labour, Spanish troops attempted to conquer the southern Araucanians, the Mapuche and Huilliche. **1985** R. A. CROESE in Klein & Stark *S. Amer. Indian Lang.* xxi. 784 The Spanish conquistadores called the Mapuches *Araucanians.* **1988** *Nat. Geographic* July 67 Most Chileans are surprised when I tell them that at least 400,000 of us are Mapuche. *Ibid.* In 1541 he [*sc.* conquistador Pedro de Valdivia] proclaimed Spanish rule, founded Santiago, and demanded land and gold of the Mapuche and related tribes, collectively called Araucanians.
2. The language of these peoples. Cf. ARAUCANIAN *n.* 2.
1941 M. W. NICHOLS *Bibliogr. Guide Materials Amer. Spanish* 65/2 Vol. I..contains a list of 134 words entering Chilean Spanish from Mapuche. **1977** *Word* 1972 XXVIII. 241 Lenz investigated the indigenous Indian language of Chile—Araucan or Mapuche, as it is sometimes called. **1977** C. F. & F. M. VOEGELIN *Classif. & Index World's Lang.* 287 Araucanian = Araukan.. = Mapuche. 200,00. Chile..; also Argentina.
B. *adj.* Of or pertaining to the Mapuche or their language.
1961 L. C. FARON (*title*) Mapuche social structure. **1974** *Encycl. Brit. Macropædia* I. 662/1 The Mapuche culture, also in Chile, relates tales characterized by fairly long narratives about.. supernatural characters. **1977** *Language* LIII. 264/2 The Araucanian or Mapuche language is currently spoken by about 200,000 Indians in Chile and 40,000 in Argentina. **1985** R. A. CROESE in Klein & Stark *S. Amer. Indian Lang.* xxi. 785 The active use of the Mapuche language is greatly diminished, if not totally gone in some areas.

‖**maquiladora** (makiaˈdora, anglicized məˌkilə ˈdɔːrə), *n.* [Mexican Sp., f. *maquilar* to assemble.] In Mexico, a factory or workshop owned by a foreign company, which employs low-cost local labour to assemble goods (esp. electronic

equipment or clothing) from imported components, and exports the completed products to the company's country of origin.
1978 *Washington Post* 26 Mar. A11/1 Clusters of twin factories known as maquiladoras dot the border region. **1988** D. BURSTEIN *Yen!* v. 155 The electronic components made at a Matsushita *maquiladora* in Tijuana..disappear completely from the U.S.-Japan trade picture. **1991** *Newsweek* 20 May 43/1 Since the mid-1960s U.S. companies have been setting up maquiladoras in Mexico and shipping the tariff-free products back to American markets.

‖**maquillé** (makije), *a.* Also fem. **maquillée**. [Fr.: see MAQUILLAGE *n.*] Wearing cosmetics; made up.
1893 MRQ. LANSDOWNE *Let.* 18 Nov. in Ld. Newton *Lord Lansdowne* (1929) iii. 116 Funny little maidens in tight pink silk petticoats, like a trouser with one leg, much *maquillées*, and with absurd gestures. **1919** C. MACKENZIE *Sylvia & Michael* iv. 127 My friend..was very *maquillée*. Too much paint. **1959** N. MAILER *Advts. for Myself* (1961) 408 The sniffs I get from the ink of the women are always fey,..tiny,..*maquillé* in mannequin's whimsy. **1966** *New Statesman* 14 Jan. 58/3 Miss Krafftowna's unfashionably *maquillée* mouth.

marabi (məˈrɑːbi), *n.* S. *Afr. Mus.* Also **Maraba**, **Marabi**, **maraba**. [Etym. disputed: perh. f. the name of *Marabastad*, a township in Pretoria + -1^2.
Other commentators have derived the term from the Sotho *ho raba raba*, lit. 'to fly around' (supposedly a reference to the accompanying dance), or from the Sotho *lerabi* (pl. *Marabi*), a slang term meaning 'criminal, gangster'. For a fuller discussion see D. B. Coplan *In Township Tonight* (1985) 94-5.]
A style of popular music, originating in the townships of Pretoria during the 1930s, with a keyboard- (and usu. brass-)dominated sound which reflects the strong influence of both ragtime and indigenous folk musics; also, the dance associated with this music.
1941 W. M. B. NHLAPO in *Bantu World* 15 Mar. 9 The Jazz Maniacs..were regarded as a 'marabi' or 'Tsaba-Tsaba' band. **1945** P. ABRAHAMS *Song of City* 73 The tom-tom beat of the Maraba..danced away the seething bitterness that is attendant with repression. **1948** O. WALKER *Kaffirs are Lively* xi. 178 Children scavenge the streets, learning the lore of the faro-dens, *marabi* beer-drink dances, the prostitutes' hide-outs. **1973** M. DIKOBE *Marabi Dance* i. 2 George..was the pianist at the Marabi parties run by Ma-Ndlovu which were very popular but not favoured by respectable people. **1992** *Jazz* No. 12. 56/2 The learned elements of style and arrangement are applied to indigenous material, such as the repetitive *marabi* progressions that would flow through 'township jive' into the sax-dominated instrumentals of the Seventies and Eighties.

Marangoni (mærænˈɡəʊnɪ), *n. Physics.* [The name of Carlo G. M. *Marangoni* (1840-1925), Italian physicist.] Used *attrib.* to designate concepts arising from Maragoni's investigation of surface tension, as **Marangoni effect**, the phenomenon of longitudinal motion in, and small-scale turbulence at, a liquid interface owing to local variations in surface tension; **Marangoni instability**, instability in a liquid interface associated with local variations in surface tension; **Marangoni number**, a dimensionless number associated with a liquid, equal to the ratio of surface tension gradient to the product of viscous drag and the rate of heat diffusion.
1948 J. J. BIKERMAN *Surface Chem.* i. 81 If, on a contaminated surface of water, some ignited talc is

spread and the film of contamination + talc is removed by a scoop or blotting paper from a part of the surface, it is seen that the talc covered area rapidly invades that from which the film has been removed. The cleaner surface has a higher surface tension and reacts against the lower surface tension of the contaminated surface. This phenomenon may be called the Marangoni effect, as C. Marangoni..apparently was the first to explain movements in the surface by local variations of surface tension. **1959** STERNLING & SCRIVEN in *Jrnl. Amer. Inst. Chem. Engin.* V. 521/2 That the authors' simplified model is subject to Marangoni instability is now established. **1966** *Physics of Fluids* IX. 615/1 That convection cells can be induced by surface tension variations in the presence of temperature or concentration gradients was first established by Pearson...Pearson showed that this mode of instability..is governed by the magnitude of a new dimensionless group B (often referred to as the Marangoni number). **1980** *Sci. Amer.* July 87/1 Bénard convection sets in when the Marangoni number exceeds a critical value. **1983** *Jrnl. Colloid & Interface Sci.* XCIII. 392 The influence that various factors (dynamic interfacial tension, Marangoni instability, and natural convection) have to produce spontaneous pulsation of liquid drops in binary systems and [etc.]. **1988** *Physical Rev. Lett.* LX. 964/2 It is possible that the Marangoni effect is inhibited because of the presence of an adsorbed film on the surface of the water.

marathon, *n*. Add: '**marathoner** *n*., one who competes in a marathon.
1925 *Lit. Digest* 9 May 68/2, I knew I was tackling the best bunch of Marathoners that ever took part in such a race. **1962** G. MacEwan *Blazing Old Cattle Trail* xi. 72 The minister preached and prayed with the stamina of a marathoner. **1985** *Times* 3 Apr. 13/2 Virgin marathoners have no sense of competition with their fellow runners, only with themselves.

marbleized ('mɑːb(ə)laɪzd), *ppl. a.* orig. *U. S.* [f. MARBLE *n*. + -IZE + -ED¹.] Having a variegated appearance like that of marble, esp. as a result of an artificial process; made to look like marble, marbled.
1851 H. MELVILLE *Moby Dick* III. xlvii. 268 For an instant his whole marble-ized body formed a high arch. **1881** C. C. HARRISON *Woman's Handiwork* III. 169 The cheap and tawdry mantel-piece of marbleized slate. **1884** *Advt.*, All white and marbleized.. wrought-iron hollow ware. **1888** W. D. HOWELLS *Annie Kilburn* xi. 114 The marbleised iron shelf.. supported two glass vases. **1909** GALSWORTHY *Fraternity* vii. 60 She had before her.. two little books. One of these was bound in marbleized paper. **1974** *State* (Columbia, S. Carolina) 3 & 4 Mar. 13-G/6 She was more than happy to pay the extra baggage fees on two dozen heavy gold-and-white marbleized candles. **1992** *Nauset Calendar* Aug. 21/2 Among items of interest are large sheets of antique marbleized papers once commonly used as end papers in fine leather bound books.

Marburg ('mɑːbɜːɡ), *n. Med.* [The name of the city in central Germany where the first major outbreak occurred.] Used *attrib.* to designate the virus of an acute, often fatal, haemorrhagic febrile disease orig. transmitted to man from the green monkey.
1968 *Lancet* 29 June 1434/1 (*heading*) Human disease from monkeys (Marburg virus). **1969** *Trans. R. Soc. Trop. Med. & Hygiene* LXIII. 324 The isolates were made from human beings with the Marburg disease and not from monkeys. **1975** *Nature* 15 May 185/1 The first task of the laboratory will be to build up a bank of diagnostic sera against the rare haemorrhagic fevers such as Bolivian and Congo haemorrhagic fevers, and other exotic tropical virus diseases, such as Marburg disease. **1976** *Scotsman* 20 Nov. 4/5 He became infected when a syringe containing the

Marburg-type virus penetrated his protective glove. **1983** *Oxf. Textbk. Med.* I. v. 127 Marburg infection was confirmed serologically.

Marcomanni (ˌmɑːkəʊˈmænɪ), *n. pl. Hist.* [a. L. *Marcomanni*, of Germanic origin: cf. MARK *n*.¹, MAN *n*.¹] An ancient Germanic people of the Suevian group who inhabited parts of central Europe to the north of the Danube.
1598 R. GRENEWEY tr. Tacitus *Descr. Germanie* in *Annales* vi. 269 Neere unto the Hermundarians dwell the Narisci, the Marcomani, and Quadi. **1611** CORYAT *Crudities* 444 The people called *Marcomanni* (which are now those of Morauia). **1738** CHAMBERS *Cycl.* II. f. 12 L/2, The expedition of the emperor Marcus Aurelius against the Sarmatæ, Quadi, and Marcomanni. **1776** GIBBON *Decl. & F.* I. p. xxxix/2, A king of the Marcomanni, a Suevic tribe. **1856** C. MERIVALE *Hist. Romans under Empire* V. xliii. 63 The Marcomanni.. had kept Tiberius himself at bay, and sent him back unlaurelled across the Danube. **1935** H. A. L. FISHER *Hist. Europe* I. viii. 84 In 161 A.D. a horde of barbarians, the Marcomanni from Bohemia, the Quadi from Moravia,.. besieged Aquileia. **1976** KING & McLINTOCK *Knight Bostock's Handbk. Old High German* (ed. 2) ii. 21 The Marcomanni are last heard of in Pannonia at the end of the fourth century, where they presumably became subjects of the Huns, who occupied Pannonia in 433.
Hence **Marco'mannic** *a*.
1661 D. BLONDEL *Treat. Sibyls* I. xix. 50 Nor can we, lastly, derive any recommendation.. from the Letter, which the Emperour Aurelian, engaged in the Marcomannick War, writ to the Senate. **1911** *Encycl. Brit.* XXVI. 20/2 The Semnones and Langobardi were at one time subject to the dominion of the Marcomannic king Maroboduus, and at a much later period we hear of Langobardic troops taking part against the Romans in the Marcomannic War.

‖**maréchaussée** (mareʃose), *n.* Chiefly *Fr. Hist.* Also with capital initial. [Fr.: see MARSHALCY *n*.] A French military guard under the command of a marshal. In mod. use, *joc.* or *iron.* (in French contexts), the police, the constabulary.
1775 T. BLAIKIE *Diary Scotch Gardener* (1931) 29 There is a garde called the Maréchaussée which padrols [*sic*] the roads. **1777** P. THICKNESSE *Year's Journey* I. vi. 41 There was a guard of the *Marechaussée*, to prevent the prisoners' escape. **1879** *Encycl. Brit.* X. 142/1 It [*sc.* the word gendarmerie] has been since that time employed to denote a military police, whose duties are to watch over the public safety, keep order,.. [etc.] This police force superseded the old *maréchaussée*. **1955** J. THOMAS *No Banners* v. 43 If we disappear now.. we'll have the whole *Maréchaussée* after us. **1974** N. FREELING *Dressing of Diamond* 202 The *maréchaussée*.. reappeared.. in freshly pressed khaki gabardines.

mareograph ('mærɪəʊɡrɑːf), *n.* [f. L. *mare* sea + -O¹ + -GRAPH.] = MARIGRAPH *n*.
1895 in *Funk's Stand. Dict.* **1941** *Bull. Geol. Soc. Amer.* LII. 726 In using the data from mareographs, two major questions arise: What is the minimum number of yearly means needed to furnish useful results, and how are they to be combined? **1964** *Fennia* LXXXIX. I. 15 The main part of the network.. consists of 18 closed loops, as well as branch lines to the twelve mareographs on the coast and three other branch lines. **1984** *Annales Geophysicae* II. 593 The relative subsidence of the land on the region of the Betts, Sound and Darss Sill.. has been proved by means of the mareograph recordings of the last 100 years.

margarite, *n*.² Add: **2.** *Petrogr.* [a. F. *margarite* (adopted in this sense by H. Vogelsang 1870, in *Arch. Néerl. des Sciences* V. 173).] A line of globulites resembling a string of pearls, commonly occurring in glassy igneous rocks.

1890 in *Cent. Dict.* **1895** A. HARKER *Petrol.* xi. 133 From the partial coalescence of a series of globulites arranged in a line result margarites, resembling a string of pearls.] **1910** *Encycl. Brit.* VII. 568/2 They [*sc.* globulites] may..arrange themselves into rows like strings of beads—margarites. **1930** A. HOLMES *Petrogr. Methods* (rev. ed.) ix. 336 When globulites are aligned and in contact, like a string of beads, the aggregates are called margarites. By the complete coalescence of the globulite beads, longulites, or cylindrical rods with rounded ends, are formed. **1972** WHITTEN & BROOKS *Penguin Dict. Geol.* 122 *Devitrification*, the development of crystals, initially on a very small scale, in a glassy igneous rock...Many of the initial crystal growths have special names, such as globularites, margarites, belonites, etc.

margin, *n.* Add: [**2.**] **f.** *Austral.* An increment or payment made in addition to a basic wage, esp. for skill or extra responsibility.
　　1939 F. W. EGGLESTON et al. *Austral. Standards of Living* 75 Workers who possess skill, or other qualifications, necessary for their work, receive an amount over and above the basic wage...This..is known as the secondary wage, or a margin. **1942** *Commonwealth Arbitration Rep.* XLVIII. 584 What Powers *J.* did was to take the junior officer's margin (above the basic wage), as awarded in 1920..as being equivalent to £6 3s. 9d. per month. **1961** J. L. K. GIFFORD *Wages, Inflation, Productivity* 147 Neglect of margins during inflation could result in injustice to some skilled workers and salary earners. **1965** *Austral. Encycl.* I. 447/2 All courts award 'margins' or 'loadings', for skill, overtime, week-end work, danger, and dirt. **1986** *Age* (Melbourne) 10 Oct. 13/2 The 1967 total wage ruling..combined the basic wage and margin for skill.

marginalization (ˌmɑːdʒɪnəlaɪˈzeɪʃən), *n.* [f. MARGINALIZ(E *v.* + -ATION, or ad. F. *marginalisation*.] The process or result of becoming or making marginal, esp. as a group within a larger society.
　　1973 *Universities Q.* Summer 283 This process of inpoverishment [*sic*]..Latin American investigators have rightly described as the *marginalization* of the masses. This process takes various forms: proletarianization of farmers...and of craftsmen; semi-proletarianization; [etc.]. **1984** *Listener* 16 Feb. 10/3 A wholesale exclusion of, or, at best, a marginalisation of foreign thinking, both past and present. **1987** *New Internationalist* May 14/1 In the U.S...the 'underclass' is largely black and isolated in urban ghettos, so its marginalization is much less disturbing to prosperous Americans than are the visible unemployed within more homogeneous European countries. **1990** D. WALDER in *Lit. in Mod. World* (1991) II. v. 233 McGrath reminds his Cambridge undergraduate audience of his position, as a product of the northern English working class; and of the relevance of such reminders when considering questions of assimilation and marginalization.

marginalize, *v.* Restrict *rare* to sense in Dict. and add: **2.** *trans.* [Prob. after F. *marginaliser*, which occurs slightly earlier in this sense.] To render or treat as marginal; to remove from the centre or mainstream; to force or confine (an individual, social group, activity, etc.) to the periphery of any sphere of influence or operation; *gen.* to belittle, depreciate, discount, or dismiss.
　　1978 *Dædalus* Summer 33 That Rousseau was self-taught..seemed to discredit and marginalize him all the more. **1980** *Times* 11 Mar. 12/6 They [*sc.* Czech dissidents] have been labelled as subversive and marginalized by the authorities for trying to do what should be normal and natural in any social order that values free thought and the maintenance of cultural traditions. **1984** *Listener* 24 May 10/3 Local music will become marginalised and ghetto-ised in the manner of folk and avant-garde music. **1985** *Sunday Times* 24 Feb. 17/7 Because an unpopular minority appeared at risk, its spokesmen's early warnings about the disease were 'marginalised' and discounted. **1987** *Ecologist* Mar./June 60/2 What safeguards can possibly enable you to set up one of the biggest mining and industrial complexes ever conceived of in a tropical forest without destroying it and marginalising its tribal inhabitants? **1992** *Countryside Campaigner* (CPRE) Spring 7/1 The environment has been marginalised to questions of superficial landscaping and design.
So **'marginalized** *ppl. a.* (also *absol.*), **'marginalizing** *ppl. a.* and *vbl. n.*
　　1970 *Times* 31 Oct. 12/3 Towering economic and social problems which effectively leave half the populations marginalized. **1985** *Community Librarian* Aug. 13 The marginalising effect of Urban Aid and Section 11 funding..should be recognised. **1985** *Rev. Eng. Stud.* Aug. 461 This account resists the marginalizing of the literary. **1987** *Christian Aid News* 7 Jan. 5/2 We all have work to do to put the marginalised, the hungry..and the homeless on the election agenda. **1992** *Bomb* Winter 18/3 You work with what are often called 'marginalized' people, such as African-Americans and people of color.

marginate, *v.* Add: **3.** = *MARGINALIZE *v.* 2. Chiefly in *passive*.
　　1969 G. G. MERINO in *In Search of Theol. of Devel.* (Sodepax Conf.) 152 The 'poor' today are the oppressed, marginated by society. **1986** *Los Angeles Times* 28 May 1. 20/1 An 'ever-growing number of Hispanics marginated and alienated from the church'.

margo (ˈmɑːɡəʊ), *n. Bot.* [a. L. *margo* (see MARGIN *n.*), adopted in this sense in Ger. by A. Frey-Wyssling et al. 1956, in *Planta* XLVII. 119.] The network of cellulose strands surrounding the torus of the pit membrane in a bordered pit of a gymnosperm.
　　[**1896** *Jrnl. R. Microscopical Soc.* Oct. 551 Herr K. Starbäck proposes the following terminology for the various parts of the Discomycetes:—The entire outer layer is the *pars parietis excipuli*; the portion which surrounds the hymenium and the epithece is the *margo excipuli* and *pars marginalis excipuli*.] **1965** K. ESAU *Plant Anat.* (ed. 2) iii. 54 The microfibrillar structure of the margo of the bordered pits of conifers has been studied in considerable detail. **1974** *Wood Sci. & Technol.* VIII. 252 This method of enzyme treatment indicates that the embedding substances of the margo in the differentiating pit membranes are composed of hemicelluloses. **1981** J. R. BARNETT *Xylem Cell Devel.* ii. 73 The microfibrils are certainly deposited after those of the margo since they obscure the latter where they pass through the torus. **1986** WILSON & WHITE *Anat. Wood* iv. 56 Once a pit has become aspirated it tends to remain in this condition; the margo adheres closely to the inside of the pit border—hydrogen bonding..is thought to be involved here.

Marie Celeste (ˌmɑrɪ sɪˈlɛst), *n.* Also (more accurately) **Mary** (ˈmɛərɪ). [Altered form of *Mary Celeste*, the name of an American cargo ship which in December 1872 was found mysteriously abandoned in the North Atlantic with sails set.] Used allusively of a place suddenly and inexplicably deserted.
　　1937 E. WHARTON *All Souls'* in *Ghosts* 20 It's like the Mary Celeste—a Mary Celeste on *terra firma*...No one ever knew what happened on board the Mary Celeste. And perhaps no one will ever know what has happened here. **1969** M. ALLINGHAM *Case-bk.* 27 The newspapers were calling the McGill house..'the villa *Marie Celeste*' before Chief Inspector Charles Luke noticed the similarity between the two mysteries. **1976** T. HOOPER *Guide to Bees & Honey* III. ix. 184, I always think that this must be the way in which what I call 'Marie Celeste' hives are produced—a hive which is

completely empty of bees, stores and brood, but in which every cell is cleaned up and in perfect condition. **1984** J. BEDFORD *Titron Madness* iii. 30 'No sign of life, you say?' Delaney shook his head... 'Our very own Marie Celeste, eh? Interesting.' **1989** *Sunday Tel.* 31 Dec. 38/2 The rooms.. have the fascination of a Marie Celeste on dry land. Everything is as she left it.

Marielito (mæriɛˈliːtəʊ, ‖marieˈlito), *n. U. S.* Also with lower-case initial. [a. Amer. Sp. *marielito*, f. the name of the Cuban port of *Mariel* + -*ito* Sp. diminutive: see quot. 1980.] Any of the tens of thousands of Cuban refugees who sailed from Mariel to Florida in 1980 as a result of a temporary relaxation of emigration restrictions by the Cuban government.

A number of those permitted to leave Cuba were inmates of prisons or mental institutions. The adverse publicity occasioned by this has led to the term being used sometimes pejoratively.

1980 *N.Y. Times* 18 Dec. B14/3 There is even a slightly patronizing neologism, 'marielitos', meaning roughly 'the poor little ones from Mariel', used by Cuban-Americans to describe the new refugees. **1983** A. HOLLERAN *Nights in Aruba* vi. 190 Mother, I would never allow you to come here now. First, God knows some Marielito would hijack the plane. **1986** *New Yorker* 17 Feb. 52/3 There was a police report saying that two Marielitos had begun arguing on the street and the argument had ended with one shooting the other dead. **1991** J. SAYLES *Los Gusanos* xx. 173 There is a Marielito in housekeeping at the hospital.

marinara (mæriˈnɑːrə), *a.* (and *n.*) [a. It. (*alla*) *marinara* sailor-fashion, f. *marinaro* seafaring: cf. MARINER *n.*] Applied to various Italian dishes or sauces (*esp.* a spicy tomato sauce traditionally made in Naples), apparently so named because their ingredients are suggestive either of food formerly served on-board ships (by the absence of fresh produce such as cheese or cream, or by the liberal use of herbs, spices, etc.), or of the sea itself (by the use of seafood). Freq. used postpositively. Also *absol.* as *n.*

[**1905** M. GIRONCI *Italian Recipes* 28 Eggs alla Marinara.] **1948** R. W. DANA *Where to eat in N.Y.* 50 Would you prefer some linguine marechiare.. that has just a touch of marinara? [**1954** E. DAVID *Italian Food* 60 (*heading*) Caponata alla marinara. *Ibid.*, A primitive fisherman's and sailor's dish... Ship's biscuits are soaked about 10 minutes in water, broken into pieces.. and generously moistened with olive oil. Garlic, stoned black olives, anchovies, origano, or basil are added.] **1969** P. WEST *Words for Deaf Daughter* ii. 56 Marinara sauce is the insignia most usually to be found on your blouses. **1978** *Chicago* June 243/2 We recommend the seafood combination.. of mussels, shrimp, and clams in spicy marinara sauce. **1981** *Cook's Mag.* Jan./Feb. 42/3 The mill comes with.. a coarse screen for ricing potatoes or for preparing tomatoes for a marinara sauce. **1992** *Pasta Cookbk.* (Australia) 48 Pasta Marinara.. 500g marinara mix.

marinize (məˈriːneɪz), *v.* [f. MARINE *a.* + -IZE.] *trans.* To modify, convert, or adapt for marine use. Also *loosely*, to adapt for use on a boat.

1975 I. NICOLSON (*title*) Marinize your boat. **1986** *Waterways World* July 49/3 Do you know a supplier of a kit to marinize a Mercedes engine? Only 8,000 miles ago I had my 2.4 Mercedes diesel engine rebuilt and I'd like to transfer it into a 71 ft narrowboat that I'm having built.

So **ma'rinized** *ppl. a.*

1967 E. DELMAR-MORGAN *Maintenance of Inboard Engines* v. 84 The marinized vehicle gear-box has no hydraulic pump. **1990** *Flight Internat.* 25 July 19/3 For use in the French Navy testing of the prototype marinised Rafale aircraft in catapult launching.

Maritimer (ˈmærɪtaɪmə(r)), *n.* Also with lower-case initial. [f. MARITIME *n.* + -ER[1].] A native or inhabitant of the Maritime Provinces of Canada.

1931 *Canad. Geogr. Jrnl.* II. 391/1 Labrador, that terra incognito [*sic*] even to the Maritimers. **1967** *Economist* 30 Sept. p. v/1 A Maritimer earning three-quarters of the average income of all Canadians.. has a different perspective from a Quebecois. **1973** *Telegraph-Jrnl.* (St. John, New Brunswick) 28 July 5/3 The Toronto Citizen columnist would have interviewed some of these Maritimers if only he had spoken their language. **1987** E. WRIGHT *Body surrounded by Water* v. 67 Toronto, where all the English-speaking maritimers go when there's no work around here.

mark, *n.*[1] Add: [II.] [8.] **b.** *spec.* in *Athletics*, a time, distance, etc., achieved by an athlete, esp. one which represents a record or personal best; hence, an official record. Also in other competitive sports. orig. *U. S.*

1900 *N.Y. Times* 5 Oct. 8/4 (*heading*) New York Athletic Club sprinter also lowers the time for 300 and 400 yard marks. **1906** *Ibid.* 31 May 8/6 The new figures made by Gilbert are over an inch and one half better than the previous mark. **1915** *Globe* (Toronto) 13 Nov. 11/6 George Goulding gave the two-mile walk record a severe jolt, lowering it from 13.39, his own mark, to 13.27 1-5. **1932** *Scholastic Coach* Mar. 7/2 He had to relinquish the laurels to Lundquist of Sweden, who then in trials attained the best mark of his life. **1967** *N.Y. Times* 11 Feb. 36/3 Sjoeberg.. broke the mark on the opening day of the international ski-jumping week. **1974** *Cleveland* (Ohio) *Plain Dealer* 27 Oct. 1-C/4 The victory was the third straight for Cleveland, which concluded its first six games.. with a 3-3 mark. **1986** *Swimming Times* Sept. 25/1 The England/Wales squad of 21 swimmers achieved 17 World marks, and brought home 22 gold, 4 silver and 3 bronze medals.

[9.] **b.** Hence, a fishing ground located by means of prominences on shore or sea-marks.

[**1921** F. D. HOLCOMBE *Mod. Sea Angling* 7 The good sea fisherman should be able.. to do everything for himself;.. manage his own boat, put her on to the marks.] **1965** E. J. F. WOOD in A. Wrangler *Newnes Compl. Guide Sea Angling* 81/2 Most angling clubs have a log or chart displayed in the club room. These show the recognised local fishing marks, and almost invariably these marks are pinpointed by lining up a series of various conspicuous objects. **1971** *Country Life* 18 Feb. 347/3, I mentioned the changes reported by some of the fishermen along the coast, the poverty of some of the hitherto good fishing marks, the absence of fish in places in which they had once been plentiful. **1976** *Eastern Daily Press* (Norwich) 19 Nov. 21/5 Stronger tides this week-end should improve prospects for cod, especially if the weather permits boats to fish the deeper marks well offshore. **1990** *Angler's Mail* 28 July 17/2 When you're casting over rocky, weedy marks.

[III.] [11.] [c.] Phr. *mark of Cain*, the sign placed on Cain after the murder of Abel, in the original version denoting divine protection (see Gen. iv. 15 and CAIN *n.*[2] 1 a), but now commonly used *fig.* to mean a token of infamy.

1878 HARDY *Return of Native* I. i. ix. 173 Reddle.. stamps unmistakably, as with the mark of Cain, any person who has handled it half-an-hour. **1925** *Blackw. Mag.* Dec. 786/1 He saw himself objectly as a felon with the mark of Cain. **1987** 'E. ANTHONY' *No Enemy but Time* 107 Tweedy, lipsticked matrons, with 'sporting type' branded on their foreheads like the mark of Cain. **1995** *Guardian* 3 Mar. (Friday Suppl.) 6/1 The Artist wears brown sunglasses. Underneath them is his personal Mark of Cain, the word Slave scrawled, rather tastefully, in black across one cheek.

k. *Horse-racing.* In full *handicap mark.* The official assessment of a horse's form, expressed as a figure between 0 and 140, and used as the basis for calculating the weight the horse has to carry in a race. Freq. in *on* or *off a* (specified) *mark*.

1978 FLINT & NORTH *Why You lose at Racing* xii. 121 An initial handicap mark of, say 45, does not mean that this horse retains that mark throughout the season.   **1985** J. ADAMS *Sprint Handicapping Explained* ii. 14 Horses with a 4 lbs difference in their rating.. will each be listed on the same mark if they happen to come within the same 5 lbs group.   **1994** *Times* 30 Sept. II. 35/2 James Fanshawe's progressive filly is running off a handicap mark 16 lb lower than when beaten.. at Ascot last Friday.

[12.] f. Phr. *on the mark* (*Racing slang*), likely to win or succeed; in with a chance.

1890 *Daily News* 10 Dec. 3/7 Backers were also well on the mark in standing Alfred for the Park selling Hurdle.   **1987** *Evening Tel.* (Grimsby) 13 Nov. 19 The trainer, on the mark with Deep South.. saddles Tickite Boo in the.. Gold Cap.   **1992** *Sporting Life* 9 Oct. 10/1 John Gosden's good run has slowed down somewhat but he can still be on the mark with Correspondence.

mark, *v.* Senses I. 2 e–f become I. 2 i–j. Senses II. 11–III. 16 become II. 12–III. 17. Add: [I.] [1.] e. Phr. *to mark off trans.*, to measure off, demarcate.

1803 T. JEFFERSON *Address to Brothers of Choctaw Nation* 17 Dec. in *Writings* (1903) XVI. 402 You have spoken, brothers, of the lands which your fathers formerly sold and marked off, to the English.   **1879** R. A. STERNDALE *Afghan Knife* III. xvii. 289 The English officer took out a case map and unfolded it, marking off the distances with a pair of compasses.   **1911** *Encycl. Brit.* XXIII. 853/2 The course for sprinting races.. is marked off in lanes for the individual runners by means of cords stretched upon short iron rods.   **1992** *Nat. Trust Mag.* Spring 34/2 The remains of a 'ring-garth' wall, which, in medieval times, marked off the open, grazed fell from the enclosed.. land.

[2.] e. *to mark off trans.*, to cancel with a mark or line as passed, dealt with, etc. Also *fig.*

1875 H. JAMES *Roderick Hudson* in *Atlantic Monthly* XXXV. 423/2 The monotonous days.. seemed to Rowland's fancy to follow each other like the tick-tick of a great time-piece, marking off the hours.   **1919** G. B. SHAW *Great Catherine* i, in *Heartbreak House* 126 He marks off the items of his statement with ridiculous stiff gestures.   **1945** H. DOOLITTLE in *Life & Letter To-day* May XLV. 67, I counted the days and marked them off, calculating the weeks.   **1984** *New Yorker* 9 Apr. 43/1 My time was good only for marking off the calendar, and I lived for his return.

f. *trans.* (in *fig.* use). Of experiences, etc.: to affect (a person) deeply, to leave a lasting impression on; now freq. in phr. *to mark for life*.

1879 H. JAMES *Confidence* in *Scribner's Monthly* Nov. 68/2 He saw that Gordon.. looked older.. and more serious, more marked by life. He looked as if something had happened to him.   **1942** W. FAULKNER *Go Down, Moses* 202 Even Uncle Ash went, the cook,.. who did little else save cook for Major de Spain's hunting.. parties, yet who had been marked by the wilderness from simple juxtaposition to it.   **1989** A. BROOKNER *Lewis Percy* x. 147 The stamp of a suburban childhood, he reflected, probably marked one for life.

g. Chiefly *Educ.* To assign a mark to (an examination paper or other piece of work). Also *absol.*, and with the pupil as obj. esp with adv., in *mark down*, *up*, etc.

1877 H. LATHAM *On Action of Examinations* ix. 478 Two Mathematical Examiners, independently marking a set of papers, will usually agree within a few marks.   **1912** *Collier's* 12 Oct. 24/4 A writer and college instructor in Harvard whom Roosevelt did not like because 'he marked too hard'.   **1950** C. S. FORESTER *Randall & River of Time* (1951) viii. 111 Mr. Randall settled himself wearily at the cleared dining-room table to mark a pile of mathematical exercises.   **1960** G. W.

TARGET *Teachers* 220 She appeared to have arranged her desk to look as if she had been marking several sets of exercise books.   **1984** *Guardian* 21 July 5/1 Troops would be posted at all examination centres, assessment centres where the papers will be marked, and at the university headquarters where the results will be compiled.   **1987** *Sunday Mail* (Brisbane) 5 July 11/5 A high school student is suing school officials for being marked down in her class because she refused to dissect a frog.   **1990** *Independent* 29 July (Sunday Rev.) 50/1 The examiner has to attend a 'standardisation' meeting, which ensures that all examiners mark in exactly the same way.

h. Phr. *to mark to* (*the*) *market Stock Market*: to adjust (an account) on a regular basis to reflect the actual market value of (securities, etc.). Also with the vb.-stem used *attrib.* and *absol.* in *mark-to-*(*the*)-*market* and with pres. pple. in *marking-to-*(*the*)-*market*.

1925 S. STRUBLE *Brief Rev. Changes 1925 Revision Const. N.Y. Stock Exchange* 39 Provision was made for.. 'marking to the market.'   **1927** *Const. N.Y. Stock Exchange Rules* v. 94 The holder or maker of said due-bill may require that it shall.. be kept marked to the market.   **1938** H. ST. CLAIR PACE *Brokerage Accounting* III. 7 A transaction to bring to market value the amount of the cash loan on stocks.. is called a mark to market. Settlement of marks to market are made through the Day Branch of the Stock Clearing Corporation.   **1981** *Econ. Recovery Tax Act 1981* (U.S. Senate Rep. No. 144) 157 The committee bill adopts a mark-to-market system for the taxation of commodity futures contracts... All futures contracts must be mark-to-market at year end.   *Ibid.* Marking-to-market requires daily cash adjustments through the exchange clearing association to reconcile exchange members' net gains and losses.   **1993** *Virginia Tax Rev.* Summer 80 The existence of margins is by no means an essential element of mark-to-market taxation.

[7.] h. *Stock Market.* To make a record of (a transaction), noting the price at which trading takes place.

1911 *Encycl. Brit.* XXV. 931/2 [At the Stock Exchange] bargains are 'marked', that is, the prices at which they are 'done' are recorded in the official list.   **1963** H. D. BERMAN *Stock Exchange* (ed. 4) iii. 18 Bargains can be 'marked' by either broker or jobber (or both) but only one mark at any particular price is recorded, and that not necessarily in the order in which the bargains have been done.   **1978** *Times* 6 Sept. 22/1 Jobbers marked stocks better before the official opening.

marked, *ppl. a.* Add: **4.** With *advbs.* That has been marked *off*, *out*, *up*, etc. See also *marked-down* ppl. adj. s.v. MARK *v.* 2 c.

1838 tr. *Kant's Critique Pure Reason* 143 They.. do not therefore belong to our marked-out field of investigation.   **1914** W. OWEN *Let.* 24 May (1967) 254 Enormously [have I advanced] in some fields [of study], but not along the marked-out high-roads.   **1947** *Life* 17 Nov. 11/2 One of the chief reasons for this marked-down bonanza is, ironically, the fact that Peru is economically less self-sufficient than many countries.   **1965** J. A. MICHENER *Source* (1966) 580 When Luke saw that one third of the town's houses stood in the marked-off area he protested.   **1986** *Computer Jrnl.* XXIX. III. 194/2 It is against this that the marked-up document is checked to ensure that it conforms.

marker, *n.* Senses 3 a–b in Dict. become b–c. Sense 3 c in Dict. becomes 3 e. Sense 8 in Dict. becomes 9. Add: [1.] k. *Sport* (esp. *Association Football*). A player assigned to mark or shadow an opposing player (see MARK *v.* 15 c).

1928 *Daily Express* 12 Dec. 11/1 Aarvold,.. the one player whom every Oxford man had vowed to 'mark' relentlessly.. was away at once.., defying his markers, running in and out, shepherded towards the touch-line; but brushing past this man and that, till he .. was across the line. **1947** *Sun* (Baltimore) 8 Nov. 12/2 The Bryn Mawr girls added another marker when Mrs. Menzies, the center forward, put another ball into the corner of the net. **1976** C. BRACKENRIDGE *Women's Lacrosse* v. 50 To be free from a marker can mean .. different things. **1976** *Sunday Mail* (Glasgow) 28 Nov. 47/1 One wonders if Killie would have been better to use McCulloch less as a marker of Kenny Dalglish and more as an attacking midfield player. **1982** R. WIDDOWS *Hamlyn Bk. Football* (1983) 40 Trapping the ball on the move involves .. a wide variety of techniques, depending mainly on whether you're stealing away from a marker to get to the ball .. or literally aiming to take the high ball in your stride. **1987** *Times* 2 Apr. 44/3 The majority of successful teams played with only three defenders—a sweeper and two markers.

[3.] **a.** An object or indicator which acts as a guide to direction, position, or route, or which marks a boundary, limit, etc.; also *fig.*

1832 *Prop. Reg. Instr. Cavalry* III. 46 Any fixed object or marker upon which a body of troops is directed to commence its formation into line. **1890** E. CUSTER *Following Guidon* Pref. 13 A small .. flag .. mounted on a standard with a metal point so that it can be thrust into the ground when in use as a marker. **1946** D. R. BROWER *Manual Ski Mountaineering* 198 Equipment for rock and ice (for party of four) .. 16 route markers. **1978** *Detroit Free Press* 16 Apr. D 3/1 In using this increase on a raglan line, try this: Knit to within one stitch of a marker, make an arrow increase, knit one, pass marker, knit two, make an arrow increase. **1988** G. ADAIR *Holy Innocents* 77 The only marker of time was a rare visit to a luxury supermarket.

d. *(a)* A distinctive object, feature, characteristic, etc., esp. one which aids recognition.

1919 *Summary of Operations, Calif. Oil Fields: Ann. Rep. State Oil & Gas Supervisor* (Calif. Dept. Petroleum & Gas) V. 1. 9 *Marker*, a distinctive stratum that can readily be identified during the process of drilling through it. **1973** R. D. SYMONS *Where Wagon Led* III. xi. 203, I counted all the 'markers', that is, old lead cows and distinctly marked steers and heifers and found them all, but no Blue. **1990** *Lit. & Linguistic Computing* 124/1 Whenever possible Justus used typographic and syntactic markers in the recognition programs.

(b) *spec.* in *Path., Biochem.,* etc. Freq. *attrib.* Cf. sense 6 below.

1961 *Lancet* 16 Sept. 629/1 Detailed analysis of ten cells disclosed the three marker chromosomes. *Ibid.* Of ninety-five metaphases examined, all three types of markers were clearly observed. **1980** *Jrnl. R. Soc. Arts* Jan. 99/1 The availability of good tumour marker substances in the blood .. would help. **1988** *Daily Tel.* 31 Oct. 19/1 Doctors would like to find a biological 'marker' for the disease [*sc.* schizophrenia], a physiological sign which would help make a diagnosis more objective. **1990** *Jrnl. Exper. Bot.* XLI. 1045 Proliferation of transgenic cells .. has been observed using the enzyme activity of β-glucuronidase as a marker.

8. Something serving as a standard of comparison or as an indication of what may be expected; a benchmark. Usu. in phr. *to put* (or *lay*) *down a marker.*

1979 *Policy Rev.* (Heritage Foundation, U.S.) Summer 110 The succession battle is already on. In the coming months others will start to lay down markers. **1982** S. CROSLAND *Tony Crosland* xxxvii. 314 If he stood he would be 'putting down a marker'. **1991** N. FOWLER *Ministers Decide* ix. 168 At the heart of the 1982 dispute was a so-called pay factor for public services of 4 per cent, which was intended as a marker for pay rises to those working in all public services. **1993** *Scotsman* 16 Mar. 19/1 The US

Transportation Secretary laid down a warning marker on the type of negotiations to come.

[9.] **marker crude** *Oil Industry,* a grade of (usu. light) crude oil the price of which is fixed by agreement between oil producers and used as a guideline for the setting of other oil prices.

[**1974** *Oil & Gas Jrnl.* 14 Oct. 52/3 The Organization for Economic Cooperation and Development .. estimates future energy consumption on the basis of two possible crude prices, taking Arabian Light (34°) crude as its marker.] *Ibid.* 4 Nov. 46/1 The Iranians would set the base price at $9.84/661 for Arabian Light '*marker*' crude ... This would do away with such things as posted prices and tax-reference prices. **1978** *Oil Supply Pattern* (Shell Internat. Petroleum Co.) 1 Since October 1973 the basic prices of crude oils from most export sources have been established by producer governments with reference to the Arabian Light marker crude price which has been set by the Organization of Petroleum Exporting Countries (OPEC). **1986** *Auckland Star* 7 Feb. A9 Oil producer Santos Ltd said the Government should use the criterion of 'minimum possible change' to the local crude oil pricing system, including retention of Saudi Light as the marker crude.

market, *v.* Add: [2.] **b.** Of a manufacturer, advertiser, etc.: to place or establish (a product) on the market; *esp.* to seek to increase sales of (a product) by means of distribution and promotion strategies. Freq. *transf.* Cf. SELL *v.* 3 h.

1922 A. P. MILLS *Materials of Construction* (ed. 2) I. iv. 30 The ground grappiers are also separately marketed as a special cement known as grappier cement. **1927** R. BARSODI *Distribution Age* i. 4 The problem which industry today is trying to solve is no longer *how to produce,* but *how to market profitably what it can produce.* **1950** A. GROSS *Sales Promotion* ii. 24 If the product is well accepted and is being marketed successfully, there may be no need to vary from the original product. **1975** *Cleveland* (Ohio) *Plain Dealer* 23 Mar. 7-c/1 Seghi's insistence that he is not 'marketing' Perry. **1980** *Morning Post* 19 May 2/4 His most successful single product by far was Sunlight Soap, which he marketed and promoted on methods learnt in the U.S. **1989** *Spectator* 15 Apr. 34/3 When the time comes for Freemasonry to have to market itself, stories such as McKinstry's will provide brilliant copy.

marketeer, *n.* Add: **4.** A specialist in marketing.

1983 *InfoWorld* 3 Oct. 27/1 Aggressive marketeers are chasing this new target market. **1985** *Times* 8 Mar. 22/2 An historian rather than a technical man by training, he started as a marketeer. **1987** *Sunday Times* 18 Oct. 75/2 Saunders was seen as one of the finest marketeers in British industry. **1988** *Financial Times* 22 Sept. 28/5 Analysis of the over-55s—a group of consumers currently much observed by marketeers—shows that they can be segmented into four distinct sub-groups.

marketer, *n.* Add: **b.** One who markets a product (see *MARKET *v.* 2 b).

1957 V. PACKARD *Hidden Persuaders* ii. 14 Second, some marketers concluded, you can't assume people will tell you the truth about their wants and dislikes even if they know them. **1971** *Sci. Amer.* Sept. 171/3 The marketers of gas usually have to arrange some kind of local storage. **1973** *Daily Tel.* 15 Jan. 15/1 Texaco, the leading marketer of petrol for cars .., announced it was rationing supplies to customers. **1978** *Detroit Free Press* 16 Apr. (Detroit Suppl.) 4/2 The contest, an annual affair held in New York, is sponsored by DeBeers Consolidated Mines Limited, the world's largest marketer of rough diamonds. **1985** *Sydney Morning Herald* 27 July 29/5 (Advt.), Our client, a major marketer and distributor of agricultural chemicals, requires two outgoing, experienced and successful sales representatives. **1987** *Holiday Which?*

Sept. 172/1 Some unscrupulous marketers still sell timeshare as an investment in property.

marking, *vbl. n.* Add: [4.] *marking pen.*
  1956 *Official Gaz.* (U.S. Patent Office) 4 Dec. TM5/2 Felt tip *marking pens.. having felt tips at their ends for marking. **1994** *Star Tribune* (Minneapolis) 6 May (State ed.) 1B/6 During an unusual two-month investigation.. officers seized marking pens and shoe polish and observed suspects comparing sketches of proposed graffiti.

marmalize ('mɑːməlaɪz), *v. Brit. slang.* [Of uncertain origin: perh. fanciful blend of MARMALADE *n.* and PULVERIZE *v.*] *trans.* To thrash; to crush or destroy. Also *fig.*, to defeat decisively.
  1966 F. SHAW et al. *Lern Yerself Scouse* 73 I'll marmalise yer. **1980** 'J. GASH' *Spend Game* xvi. 160 They are real aggro men who'll marmalize anybody for a few quid. **1989** *Victor* 14 Oct. 18/2 'I'll marmalize you, moggie!' 'I'll pulverize you, pooch!' **1993** *Sunday Times* 5 Dec. VIII. 16/1 It was.. a complicated allegation...'How will you deal with it?'...'In the words of Ken Dodd, our great national comedian, I shall marmalise 'em.'

Marmande ('mɑːmɒnd), *n.* Also **marmande**, **Marmont**. [The name of *Marmande*, a town in Lot-et-Garonne, south-west France.] *attrib.* Denoting a large firm variety of tomato.
  1967 I. DIQS *Bedouin Boyhood* xviii. 170 Some of my students started small projects—rabbit-breeding for example, or planting the newly introduced Marmont tomato. **1978** J. GRIGSON *Vegetable Bk.* 381 The tomatoes must be the huge craggy kind, Marmande or Eshkol are sometimes to be bought in the shops. **1986** G. SLOVO *Death by Analysis* viii. 136, I was just finishing off the marmande tomato I'd had to accompany my cheese when the doorbell rang. **1991** *Shepherd's Garden Seeds Catal.* 62/1 A vigorous.. variety, Marmande bears a very prolific crop of large, firm and meaty lobed tomatoes.

marmem ('mɑːmɛm), *n. Metallurgy.* [f. MAR(TENSITE *n.* + MEM(ORY *n.*] = *shape memory* s.v. SHAPE *n.* 17. Usu. *attrib.*
  1972 WAYMAN & SHIMIZU in *Metal Sci. Jrnl.* VI. 175/2 The present authors comment on the shape memory effect with particular regard to the crystallography of martensitic transformations. Since the balance of experimental evidence indicates that it is the *martensitic* phase which exhibits a *memory*, the term 'marmem' is introduced as descriptive of the general behaviour. **1979** *Guardian* 18 June 3/1 A technological revolution called the 'marmem effect' in which a shape can be built into a metal component and 'remembered' at any chosen temperature. **1979** *Sci. Amer.* Nov. 70/3 In the marmem alloy of copper, zinc and aluminium four variants of martensite form out of the parent beta phase, each with a crystal orientation displaced by 60 degrees from the others. **1986** *Materials Sci. & Technol.* II. 496 The influence of parent phase chemistry on the marmem behaviour of Cu-Al-Ni and Cu-Zn-Al alloys has been studied.

Marmont *n.*, var. *MARMANDE *n.*

marmoreal, *a.* Add: **mar'morealize** *v. trans.* (in *fig.* use), to commemorate, immortalize.
  1948 W. DE LA MARE *Chardin* 22 The love that.. stilled Rupert Brooke's whole universe in his poem, 'Dining-room Tea'; marmorealized his cup; 'hung' the 'amber stream' of the tea itself 'on the air' [etc.]. **1993** *Times-Picayune* (New Orleans) 2 July (Metro section) B7/1 There is no law that says every milestone in the city's history should be marmorealized on the street.

marmot, *n.* Add: [1.] **c.** The fur or skin of a marmot. Also *attrib.*

1865 MILTON & CHEADLE *N.W. Passage by Land* xiii. 241 They [*sc.* Shuswap Indians] were clothed merely in a shirt and marmot robe, their legs and feet being naked. **1911** *Encycl. Brit.* XI. 355/2 Marmot, dyed... Sold as mink or sable. **1988** D. VERNON *Tiller's Girls* 95 My friend had a leopard skin [coat] and I had a coney seal with a mink marmot collar.

marocain, *n.* (*a.*) Add: **2.** *attrib.* or as *adj.* Made of marocain.
  1975 G. HOWELL *In Vogue* 80/1 Jean Patou's new sports department sells jersey and marocain bathing suits. **1986** *Times* 24 July 1/2 Mrs Hector Barrantes, mother of the bride, sat with the Ferguson family in golden yellow marocain silk. **1988** *Women's Wear Daily* 7 Nov. 4/1 (*caption*) Isaac Mizrahi's white silk Gazar duffel coat and marocain jumpsuit.

Marotic (mə'rɒtɪk), *a.* [f. the name of Clément Marot (see below) + -IC; cf. Fr. *marotique* (1585).] Of or relating to the French poet Clément Marot (1496–1544), whose work is noted for its light, graceful style; characteristic of Marot or his style.
  1728 CHAMBERS *Cycl.* II. *Marotic Style*, in French Poetry, denotes a peculiarly gay, merry, yet simple and natural Manner of Writing, introduced by *Marot.* **1904** A. TILLEY *Lit. Fr. Renaissance* I. I. v. 90 Eustorg de Beaulieu.. wrote poems of the usual Marotic type. **1967** D. B. WILSON *Descr. Poetry in France* i. 52 The marotic blason was to die out during the second half of the sixteenth century.

Marplan ('mɑːplæn), *n. Pharm.* [Origin unkn.: perh. after MARSILID *n.*] A proprietary name for isocarboxazid.
  [**1956** *Trade Marks Jrnl.* 18 Apr. 229/2 Marplon.] **1959** *Official Gaz.* (U.S. Patent Office) 1 Dec. TM10/1 *Marplan*... For product useful in the treatment of mental depression and angina pectoris. **1963** *Jrnl. Amer. Med. Assoc.* 16 Mar. 952/1 Isocarboxazid (Marplan), a monoamine oxidase inhibitor, is effective as an antidepressant agent. **1965** J. POLLITT *Depression & its Treatment* iv. 56 The monoamine oxidase inhibitors include several members, among them phenelzine (Nardil), iproniazid (Marsilid), isocarboxazid (Marplan). **1982** *Psychiatry Res.* VI. 41 A 6-week, double-blind, placebo-controlled study of the MAO inhibitor isocarboxazid (Marplan).

Marpol ('mɑːpɒl), *n.* Also **MARPOL**. [Acronym f. initial syllables of *mar*ine *pol*lution.] In full, *Marpol Convention.* Any of the successive conventions on marine pollution adopted by the International Maritime Organization. Freq. *attrib.*
  1978 *Marine Pollution Bull.* Apr. IX. 85/2 When MARPOL 1973 was adopted, it was praised above all for its comprehensiveness. MARPOL.. was the first convention to regulate all forms of marine pollution from ships, except dumping. **1980** *Jrnl. R. Soc. Arts* July 518/1 The two conventions having the major impact on the tanker industry at the present time are: the 1974 SOLAS (Safety of Life at Sea) Convention, and the 1973 MARPOL (Marine Pollution) Convention. **1992** *World* (BBC) Apr. 6/1 They may now be prosecuted under the Marpol.. regulations brought in at the end of 1988 which rule that it is illegal to dump any sort of plastic into the sea.

marquee, *n.* Senses a, b in Dict. become 1, 3. Add: **2.** orig. and chiefly *U.S.* **a.** A canopy projecting over the main entrance to a building, *spec.* one at a theatre, cinema, etc., on which details of the entertainment or performers are featured. (Orig. in circus use). **b.** *transf.* and *fig.* The roster of performers, etc., so displayed; the billing.
  [**1926** *Amer. Speech* I. 283/2 *Marquee*, the front door or main entrance of the big top.] **1931** *Amer. Mercury*

Nov. 353/1 *Marquee*, the canopy at the main entrance [of a circus]. **1933** *Billboard* 8 July 24/1 The marquee of the Rivoli, where *Samarang* is playing, reads: 'One of the most exciting films ever shown'. **1938** D. BAKER *Young Man with Horn* (1978) 84 There was a small marquee extending out over some steps, . . and there was a door man, a bright-looking negro boy in a red bell-hop's uniform. **1967** *Boston Globe* 5 Apr. 56/5 British actors mean little on an American movie marquee and Sherlock Holmes always seems old-fashioned. **1977** *Islander* (Victoria, B.C.) 19 Dec. 3/4 The Capitol Theatre remains . . unaltered, apart from a new marquee some years ago. **1979** *Washington Post* 14 Jan. C4/2 With him in the NBA, Philadelphia became the league's biggest road draw and now, three years later, his name tops the arena marquees. **1981** L. R. BANKS *Writing on Wall* v. 40 It was a big, tall building with lots of fancy-work on the front, and a marquee like a cinema. **1991** R. BERGAN *Dustin Hoffman* xii. 73 Every time Dustin saw his name in block letters on the marquee of a movie house, he was assailed with thoughts of his own mortality. **1993** *Daily Tel.* 15 July 21/3 At the Hubbard Dianetics Foundation there's an electric marquee that goes through this routine: Low Self Esteem? Failed Marriage? Tired Of Losing? Relationship Difficulties? Come In Now!

c. *attrib.* or as *adj.* Chiefly *Entertainment* and *Sport.* (Of a name, etc.) appearing or fit to appear on a marquee; so, headlining; starring; leading, pre-eminent. In *Comb.* as **marquee name,** *player,* **star,** etc; **marquee value,** the ability to attract a large audience, pulling power.

1978 *Washington Post* 2 Apr. K6/1 It's very difficult to run a jazz club successfully unless you have a great many marquee names, . . and these marquee names cost too much now. **1980** *N.Y. Times* 16 June C6/3 He has marquee-value looks, a gentle, friendly face. He is personable, friendly, attractive, witty, a family man. **1984** *Christian Science Monitor* 27 Mar. 20/2 Whenever Jack Nicklaus, whose name still has enormous marquee value, plays a major tournament . . , ratings reportedly go up 3 percent. **1986** *Los Angeles Times Mag.* 30 Nov. 28/3 A major factor in the rise of the league has been an influx of marquee players. **1990** *Independent* 17 May 15/2 'Surprisingly restrained' might be the most appropriate marquee quote to describe it, even if this appears to damn the film with faint praise. **1990** J. PARK *Brit. Cinema* ii. 34 [British film-makers] judged it worthwhile incurring the expense of bringing over American stars . . in order to increase their films' marquee value at home and abroad. **1992** *Syracuse Herald-American* 13 Dec. G5/3 Fans called for the Oilers to ink a long-term deal with a marquee player. **1994** *Post* (Denver) 16 Jan. A13/1 The case capped her rise to prominence as . . one of the few women in the nation to attain marquee status in criminal law.

marquenching ('mɑːkwɛntʃɪŋ), *vbl. n. Metallurgy.* [f. MAR(TENSITE *n.* + QUENCHING *vbl. n.*] A process similar to martempering but with the constant-temperature stage kept too short to allow isothermal transformation; also = *martempering* vbl. n. s.v. MARTEMPER *v.* So '**marquench** *v. trans.*

1947 *Iron Age* 3 July 52/1 Martempering consists of quenching from the austenitizing temperature to the M_s temperature . . and holding this temperature until transformation from the austenite is complete . . . Marquenching is the term which is usually applied to interrupted quench only, without involving isothermal transformation. *Ibid.* 53/2 The specimen which was held at 475°F for only 1 min was really marquenched rather than martempered, since it was removed from the bath at about the time transformation would have had a chance to begin. **1956** *Jrnl. Iron & Steel Inst.* CLXXXIII. 332/1 The author discusses the difference between marquenching and martempering and explains the trend of Bain's curve in case hardened steels for the differing carbon contents encountered. **1974** *Industrial Heating* July 33 Marquenching instead of oil

quenching resulted in the smallest growth . . and the narrowest growth spread. **1984** E. P. DeGARMO et al. *Materials & Processes in Manuf.* (ed. 6) vi. 148 If the piece is stabilized and then slowly cooled through the martensite transformation, the process is known as martempering or marquenching. **1985** L. C. LOVE *Princ. Metall.* vii. 216 (*caption*) Schematic diagram of rapidly quenching austenite to an elevated temperature and allowing the entire cross section to transform at the same time. This is called marquenching.

marquise, *n.* Add: [**4.**] **b.** = NAVETTE *n.* Freq. *attrib.*

1898 E. W. STREETER *Precious Stones & Gems* (ed. 6) v. 38 A curious old Marquise ring which formerly belonged to Marie Antoinette, has in the centre an oblong Diamond engraved with her name, Marie: this is now in the collection of Streeter & Co., Ltd. **1903** W. R. CATTELLE *Precious Stones* vi. 66 The 'marquise' rose, and . . the 'pendeloque' rose, both having twenty-four facets. **1945** A. SELWYN *Retail Jeweller's Handbk.* xv. 217 Fancy shapes, such as the three-cornered, the marquise or navette . . , the pear-shaped . . or pendeloque, make unusual jewels, and are generally suggested by the natural form of the diamond itself. **1965** J. Y. DICKINSON *Bk. Diamonds* iii. 63 The marquise and oval cuts are elongated to fit the finger better. **1994** *Sunday Tel.* 24 Apr. 28/1 The vast diamond ring . . her own design of two hearts set each side of a marquise central stone.

‖**marraine** (marɛn), *n. Hist.* [Fr., lit. 'godmother', f. med.L. *matrina,* f. L. *matr-* stem of *mater* mother.] In the war of 1914–18, a woman who befriended a soldier at the front, giving him moral and material support, as by letters, food parcels, etc.

1916 E. V. LUCAS *Vermilion Box* xc. 104 Over here there is that wonderful institution the marraine. A marraine is literally a godmother. Her special duty is to take charge of, and be responsible for, a poilu both in action and on leave. **1941** W. FORTESCUE *Trampled Lilies* v. 59 *Mademoiselle* suggested that Fanny should be the *marraine* of this orphan soldier, send him a parcel of our comforts, in her name, and, above all, write him a letter. **1991** *Times* 18 Feb. 1/6 French women are also reportedly taking up their first world war role as *marraines,* or godmothers, who traditionally adopted frontline soldiers they had never met, serving as pen pals and sending them provisions.

marriage, *n.* Add: [**4.**] **b.** *spec.* An antique object assembled from components differing in provenance, date, etc.; the assembling of such an object. Cf. *MARRIED ppl. a.* 1 c.

1959 L. GROSS *Housewives' Guide to Antiques* ii. 24 Parts of broken furniture may be saved and rebuilt into other or smaller pieces. Some of these late 'marriages' may contain parts which are, in themselves, quite original. **1980** *Times Lit. Suppl.* 1 Aug. 878/1 Many of the blades are joined to luxurious hilts of a different provenance, which may have been antique at the time of the marriage. **1985** *Times* 20 Nov. 5/2 Three elegantly curved legs . . support it, but Mr Glennie thinks it may be a 'marriage', eighteenth-century legs supporting a later top. **1986** J. BLY *Is it Genuine?* 52 Provided both parts are of the same period and as long as they are sold today as a marriage no harm is done. **1990** *Orientations* Apr. 45/3 This suggests a 'marriage' of the rondels—perhaps freshly cut from their original strips—to the plain red cape just prior to Stoke's purchase.

married, *ppl. a.* Add: [**1.**] **c.** *spec.* Of an antique object: assembled from parts of two or more distinct pieces.

1949 T. H. ORMSBEE *Care & Repair of Antiques* iii. 48 Be certain that the piece under consideration is not a 'married' one, assembled from stray bottom and top sections, as indicated with secretaries. **1967** 'A. K.

COLE' *Golden Guide Amer. Antiques* 11 A 'married' piece, made up of parts of two or more similar old pieces, is acceptable if you know what you are getting and paying for. **1973** *Washington Post* 13 Jan. E16/4 A 'married' piece is one in which two or more partial sections are skillfully joined to form one piece, such as a corner cupboard. *Ibid.*, In married pieces, all components are of the same period, but they might be so mismatched as to require extensive recarving or scrolling. **1989** *Antique Collecting* Mar. 5/1 A married case and movement will never be as good an investment as a genuine clock.

marry, *v.* Add: [5.] **e.** *trans.* To assemble (an antique object) by joining two or more components differing in provenance, date, etc.; to join (distinct components) in this way.

1949 [implied at *MARRIED ppl.a.* 1 c]. **1958** *Connecticut Hist. Soc.* Apr. 53 This last piece..was once offered to several dealers and collectors, but was turned down as suspect. The chest itself is undoubtedly old and so are the feet, though the two are obviously married. **1973** *Washington Post* 13 Jan. E16/4 Outright fakery is less prevalent than misrepresentation—such as marrying pieces. **1986** J. BLY *Is it Genuine?* 53 The presence of veneer does not necessarily mean that the two parts have been married, but the absence of veneer is always a good sign.

Mars, *n.* Add: [3.] **b. Mars bar** [rhyming slang], a scar.

1971 S. HOUGHTON *Current Prison Slang* (manuscript) 14 *Mars bar*, scar. **1973** J. PATRICK *Glasgow Gang* xiii. 117, I return..to rhyming slang...Scars were 'Mars Bars' and Mods were 'Sods'. **1987** *Observer* 27 Dec. 3/6 He said 'J' had given the doctor a Mars bar (slang for scar).

marsh, *n.*[1] Add: [4.] [a.] **marsh Arab**, a member of a semi-nomadic people inhabiting marshy areas of the flood plain between the rivers Tigris and Euphrates, in the Basra region of south-eastern Iraq; also *attrib.*

1917 *Handbk. Mesopotamia* (Admiralty) II. 67 The banks on both sides of the river [Tigris] are inhabited by..Arab tribes, the largest being, perhaps, the *Beni Mūlik*.., and by *Ma'adan* or marsh Arabs. **1921** *Indian Antiquary* L. 289 Occasional mounds..are conspicuous, and are sometimes occupied by Marsh Arab villages. **1993** *Washington Post* 18 Oct. A1/3 The Baghdad government is waging an aggressive campaign to crush the 'Marsh Arab' people of southern Iraq and destroy their habitat, according to State Department officials.

marshal, *n.* Add: [5.] **d.** An official (often one of several) at a sporting event responsible for supervising arrangements for competitors, controlling spectators, etc.

1927 *Autocar* 19 Aug. 339/1 Two particularly drenched pit marshals' lives were saved by whisky sent out by their friends. **1931** *Ibid.* 2 Jan. 34/2 In the control a naughty travelling marshal shamelessly jacked up one wheel of his car. **1934** B. LYNDON *Circuit Dust* i. 10 The Fascisti proved willing to act as marshals along the course, obliging non-competitors to keep to the correct side of the road. **1962** *Track & Field Guide* (Amer. Assoc. Health) 75 Suggested officials for a meet...1 clerk of course, 1 marshal, 1 scorer, [etc.]. **1975** I. McEWAN *First Love* 19 Long after the judges, marshals and time-keepers had gone home I remained at the finishing line. **1986** *Road Sport* Aug. 14/3 Fewer spectators and more marshals might have helped as several controls went unmanned. **1992** *Bicycle* Feb. 63/3 You will have a whirlwind affair with a race marshal which cause..your marriage to go down the pan.

Marshallian (mɑːˈʃælɪən), *a. Econ.* [f. the name of Alfred *Marshall* (1842–1924), British political economist, + -IAN[1].] Of or pertaining to the theories or work of Alfred Marshall, esp. to his concepts of marginal utility and elasticity of demand.

1937 *Economic Jrnl.* XLVII. 25 Of these five so-called Marshallian assertions it is quite certain that Marshall would have repudiated the first two and the last two. **1952** *Economica* XIX. 115 The Marshallian world assumes the validity of Say's Law—above all it assumes that the whole volume of *ex ante* saving is converted..into an equivalent amount of *ex post* investment. **1967** *Economist* 28 Jan. p. xxix/1 How does one explain Marshallian theories of value to native growers who have seen the price halved since they first planted coffee? **1975** *Times* 6 Jan. 12/5 To sustain industrial civilizations, we must focus on the Marshallian long period factors. **1987** *Financial Times* 10 Oct. p. xx/7 The earlier Marshallian view of a natural long-run equilibrium..once again appears a la mode.

marshmallow, *n.* Add: Hence **marsh'mallowy** *a.*, soft; esp. *fig.*, cloying, sentimental.

1907 *Smart Set* XXI. Mar. 4/1, [I] watched a pack of emotional matinée-girls crowd round him and coo about their Over-Souls and all that sort of marshmallowy rubbish. **1984** *Listener* 17 May 35/2 Such a pose appeals to her marshmallowy romanticism. **1993** *Coloradoan* (Fort Collins) 12 Sept. C1/2 Or maybe an image of those marshmallowy moon boots that lie forgotten in the back of the closet?

Marsquake (ˈmɑːzkweɪk), *n. Astron.* Also **marsquake.** [f. MARS *n.*, after EARTHQUAKE *n.*: cf. MOONQUAKE *n.*, QUAKE *n.*] A tremor or violent shaking of part of the surface of Mars.

1968 R. A. LYTTLETON *Mysteries Solar Syst.* iii. 87 It would clearly be of the greatest interest and importance to know whether moonquakes, marsquakes, and so on, occur on these other bodies. **1976** *Globe & Mail* (Toronto) 6 Sept. 1/2 Viking 2, at rest in the plains of a Martian Utopia, began 'feeling' the rocky slopes for signs of Marsquakes yesterday. **1978** PASACHOFF & KUTNER *University Astron.* xviii. 470 Viking 2 had the additional scientific value that its seismograph could measure marsquakes...Some marsquakes have been detected. **1993** G. BEAR *Moving Mars* 452 While I read the plaque, the ground shivered with a small marsquake.

marten, *n.* Add: [4.] *marten trap.*

1865 MILTON & CHEADLE *N.W. Passage by Land* xv. 310 Old *marten-traps set at intervals informed us that we had at last touched..an old trapping path. **1912** E. T. SETON *Arctic Prairies* 344 He stated that the squirrels are occasionally taken in marten traps, but are rare. **1992** *Vancouver Sun* 6 Apr. B1/4 Minutes away from his riverside cabin, Anderson shows us a marten trap, rigged in such a way that when the animal is trapped the whole mechanism swings off the ground on a pole.

martial, *a.* and *n.* Add: [A.] **10.** Special collocation: **martial eagle**, a large brown and white crested eagle, *Polemaetus bellicosus*, of central and southern Africa, which preys on game birds and some mammals.

1861 *Ibis* III. 129 (*heading*) Aquila bellicosa (Daud.). *Martial eagle. **1908** HAAGNER & IVY *Sk. S. Afr. Bird-Life* iii. 55 The Martial Eagle..is dark sepia above and below, except the abdominal regions. **1947** J. STEVENSON-HAMILTON *Wild Life S. Afr.* xxxiii. 279 The martial eagle or lammervanger (*Polemaetus bellicosus*).—This is one of the handsomest, as well as the largest of the tribe found in Africa. **1973** *Sci. Amer.* Dec. 103/3 The African martial eagle..uses thermals in much the same way that smaller eagles and hawks use a rocky crag or a telephone pole. **1986** *Daily Tel.* 29 Apr. 4/3 [He] pleaded guilty to importing the eggs of three crowned eagles, four martial eagles and two Verreaux's eagles.

marveller ('mɑːvələ(r)), *n.* Also 6 **maruelour**. [f. MARVEL *v.* + -ER[1].] A person who is inclined to marvel or wonder.

1551 R. ROBYNSON tr. T. More *Utopia* (1895) II. sig. Niᵛ, The curyous and diligent beholder and vewere of his woorke, and maruelour at the same. **1616** H. WOTTON *Let.* 11 Oct. in L. P. Smith *Life & Lett. Sir H. Wotton* (1907) II. 105 It is worthy of wonder, even among sober marvellers. **1969** B. HEAD *When Rain Clouds Gather* xii. 185 That's all that Solomon wants—a lot of gapers and marvelers. **1989** J. UPDIKE *Just Looking* 18, I moved to New England, yet often returned, a visitor now among the swelling tourist crowd, yet still a marveller.

Mary, *n.* Add: [1.] [c.] **Mary blue** [from the blue colour commonly used for the Virgin Mary's cloak in devotional images], a light or medium blue colour.

1943 J. LEES-MILNE *Diary* 9 May in *Ancestral Voices* (1975) 193 Little girls in white veils, little boys with Mary blue sashes. **1962** S. PLATH *Heavy Women* in *Poetry* (Chicago) Mar. 350 They step among the archetypes. Dusk hoods them in Mary-blue. **1980** *Church Times* 29 Mar. 14/2 The..choir's new cassocks..are 'Mary' blue.

6. *slang.* **a.** Sometimes more fully as **Mary Ann.** An effeminate man; a male homosexual; = NANCY *n.*[2] *derog.*

1880 *Pearl* Oct. 159 Girl to Ponce—Go along, you, bloody Mary Ann, and tighten your arsehole with alum. **1881** (*title*) The sins of the Cities of the Plain; or, The recollections of a Mary-Ann. **1936** 'G. ORWELL' *Diary* 5 Mar. in *Coll. Ess.* (1968) I. 195 The woman continues to do all the housework...The man would lose his manhood if, merely because he was out of work, he became a 'Mary Ann'. **1972** B. RODGERS *Queens' Vernacular* 131 Don't push the panic button—it's just another mary safariing through David's Darkest Baths. **1974** P. WRIGHT *Lang. Brit. Industry* v. 51 A *Mary-Ann* is one who helps his wife unduly with housework, shopping and children. **1981** *Verbatim* Autumn 6/2 We refer here only to first names that have acquired meanings of their own or that..have acquired special connotations...*Mary*,..3. male homosexual. **1988** A. HOLLINGHURST *Swimming Pool Library* ii. 41 Falling to bits, of course, ga-ga as often as not, and a coachload of absolute Mary-Anns, I won't deny it.

b. Used *joc.* among (chiefly *U.S.*) male homosexuals as a form of address, and also as an *int.* expressing (mock) amazement.

1941 G. LEGMAN in G. W. Henry *Sex Variants* II. 1171 Note also that male homosexuals will call most anyone Bessie or Mary, e.g. 'Oh, Bessie, you're a camp!' **1968** M. CROWLEY *Boys in Band* II. 141 Oh, Mary, it takes a fairy to make something pretty. **1973** *Amer. Speech 1970* XLV. 52 Mary! I really read *that* girl's beads! **1985** W. DYNES *Homolexis* 150 In America in the 1950s,..Mary was often used in the vocative to address any fellow homosexual ('Well, Mary...'). **1991** *ff Mag.* Spring 28/2 What about every lisping mincing queen doused in Paco Rabane who's called you 'Mary'?

Mary Celeste *n.*, var. *MARIE CELESTE *n.*

marzipan, *n.* Add: **3.** *transf.* or *fig.* A layer, filling, or covering, *esp.* one which resembles marzipan in colour or texture, or which conceals an underlying structure.

1945 *Hansard Commons* 17 Oct. 1223 You only have to look at the fretful fronts stretching along the great roads leading from London—belonging to what I think one cynic called the 'marzipan period'—to see the monstrous crimes committed against aesthetics by..speculators. **1981** *Event* 9–15 Oct. 29/1 *Marzipan, n.* (*motor trade*). The filler used to patch up bodywork damaged by a crash or corrosion. **1989** *Mod. Painters* Autumn 111/1 Yet Mr. Hutchinson condemns

post-modernism as 'Bimbo architecture' and so much marzipan over honest concrete frames.

4. Special Comb. **marzipan layer** or **set** *Stock Market slang*, the stockbroking executives ranking immediately below the partners in a firm.

1984 *Economist* 17 Nov. 72/3 And what of the so-called *marzipan set, the layer of managers too junior to get the icing but too senior for the cake crumbs? Will they be prepared to work if they feel their future has been sold off? **1985** *Listener* 6 June 8/3 The 'marzipan layer' is the bright, younger people just below the partners. **1987** *Observer* 26 Apr. 8/3 Graduate scientists take (often non-scientific) jobs in industry and commerce. Many of the best and brightest go into the City and join the Marzipan Set (above the cake but below the icing). **1992** *Sunday Tel.* 29 Mar. 40/4 Britain's 'Marzipan layer' already spend far more of their disposable income on housing and education than their German and French peers.

'marzipanned *ppl. a.*, covered with a layer of marzipan (also *fig.*); **'marzipan** *v. trans.* (as *pa. pple.*).

1974 R. RENDELL *Face of Trespass* ii. 25 The large home-made Dundee, marzipanned and iced. **1986** T. BARLING *Smoke* xxii. 486 A single boa of cloud feathered out from the Buddhist temple on the high western tor, the thinning outer strands marzipanned by brazen sunlight. **1987** *Los Angeles Times* 15 Feb. (Calendar) 88/4 Produced by that baroque prince of pop Todd Rundgren, the album is marzipaned with ornate embellishments and liberally sprinkled with quotes from the post-acid Beatles. **1994** *Interzone* July 39/3 Just another layer of ironic icing on an already heavily-marzipanned cake.

mas' (mas), *n.*[3] *orig W. Indies.* Also without apostrophe. [Abbrev. of MASQUE *n.*] In Trinidad (and subsequently elsewhere), a masquerade, *spec.* one held as part of an annual carnival parade; more generally, carnival activity. Also *quasi-adv.,* esp. in phr. *to play mas'.*

1956 *Caribbean Q.* IV. III/IV. 194 In local pronunciation both [*sc.* 'masque' and 'mask'] are 'mas' but are clearly differentiated concepts in the minds of the masquers. [*Note*] It is often so spelled. A costume received for the Carnival Exhibition was carefully labelled 'beas mas'. *Ibid.* 228 Obscenity commonly distinguished the Old Mas' costume. **1968** R. D. ABRAHAMS in W. M. Hudson *Tire Shrinker to Dragster* 127 A Tobago variation on this type of Carnival activity is 'Speech Mas' or 'Speech Band.' (*Mas*' is West Indian for *masquerade.*) **1973** *Express* (Trinidad & Tobago) 1 Feb. 6/5 The Queen's Park Cricket Club is having its ole mas' competition and dance at the Oval on Saturday, February 17. **1974** *Sunday Advocate-News* (Barbados) 17 Feb. 1/2 Hundreds of Barbadian children yesterday got their chance to 'play mas', when the Trinidad Women's Club of Barbados staged its annual children's carnival at Culloden Farm. **1977** *Westindian World* 3 June 1/1 It is looking increasingly more and more unlikely that there will be mas on the streets of Notting Hill this year. **1982** *Christian Science Monitor* 14 Dec. 16/1 For almost a year Trinidad prepares for two days..when *mas,* or carnival, takes over this green Caribbean island. **1992** *Canad. Living* Aug. 72/1 (caption) From springtime on, every spare moment is spent at 'mas camp' (masquerade camp), as participants call the warehouses where the [Caribana parade] costumes are made. **1995** *Guardian* 26 Aug. 29/4 Think traditional Notting Hill Carnival and you think of extravagant mas floats and costumes, parades, steel bands, reggae, a huge and colourful party on the move.

‖**masa** ('masa), *n.* [Sp., ult. f. L. *massa* (see MASS *n.*[2]): cf. Pg. *massa* dough.] In Central and South American cuisine, a type of dough made from cornmeal, used in the making of tortillas, etc.

1914 B. HAFFNER-GINGER *Calif. Mexican-Spanish Cook Bk.* 43 Add to the corn dough (masa) rounding tablespoon of lard to four cups dough, little salt. **1927** D. H. LAWRENCE *Mornings in Mexico* 44 A yard with shade round. Women kneading the maize dough, *masa*, for *tortillas*. A man lounging. And a little boy beating a kettledrum sideways. **1949** C. P. LEAHY *Spanish-Mexican Cookbk.* 60 Masa may be purchased by the pound in some Mexican grocery stores and at all tortilla factories. **1975** R. L. BEALS *Peasant Marketing Syst.* iv. 63 Both [chickens and turkeys] are fed household scraps and usually some maize or *masa* (maize dough). **1990** *California* Apr. 51/1 Locals and tourists alike feast on chile rellenos or handmade traditional masa corn-husk tamales.

masala (məˈsɑːlə, ‖məˈsɑːlə), *n.* (and *a.*) Also 8 (in early use) marsall, 9 missala, mussala, 9-masalah, 20 massala(h, etc. [ad. Urdu *maṣālaḥ*, f. Pers. and Urdu *masāleḥ* ingredients, materials; compound of various spices, etc., ult. f. Arab. *maṣāliḥ*, pl. of *maṣlaha* benefit, source of improvement.] **1.** A mixture of spices ground into a paste or powder for use in Indian cookery. Also used quasi-*adj.* (esp. postpositively), and occas. *absol.*, to designate a dish prepared with such a mixture. Cf. *GARAM MASALA n.*

1780 I. MUNRO *Let.* in *Narr. Mil. Operations against French* (1789) ix. 85 A dose of marsall, or purgative spices. **1809** M. GRAHAM *Jrnl. Residence in India* (1812) 20 At the next hut the woman was grinding missala or curry-stuff, on a flat smooth stone, with another shaped like a rolling-pin. **1815** M. M. SHERWOOD *Little Henry & Bearer* 74 Some grinding their *mussala*. **1868** B. H. POWELL *Hand-bk. Econ. Products Punjab* I. III. 273/2 Pickles are either prepared with vinegar . . or else with oil, or else with some 'masálah', as mustard seeds ground up with salt, &c., which being moistened with a little oil or water, is rubbed over the vegetable to be pickled, and left until it becomes sour. *Ibid.* (Index) p. lxx/1 *Masálá*, properly spice or spices compounded; also used to mean any compound or substance used in any manufacture or operation. **1943** in Cassidy & Le Page *Dict. Jamaican Eng.* (1967) 295/1 Mazala, . . Massalah, . . Masala, māsawla, a dish, curry. **1952** S. SELVON *Brighter Sun* ix. 177 Grind the massala yourself, don't buy curry powder from Tall Boy. **1954** S. CHOWDHARY *Indian Cooking* 21 The fragrance and taste of home-made masāla is well worth the trouble taken. **1974** R. A. K. HEATH *Man come Home* ii. 7 Apart from the acrid scent of massala from one of the rooms there was nothing to disturb his reflections. **1978** J. PASSMORE *All Asian Cookbk.* (1979) 21/1 *Egg Masala* . . . Peel eggs and cut in halves . . . Place in the masala and simmer for 3 minutes. *Ibid.* 17/2 Prawns in Green Masala. **1991** *N.Y. Times Mag.* 20 Oct. II. 33/2 Servers who are cruising the restaurant bearing large metal containers of papadum . . , rice, chicken and mutton masala.

2. *fig. Indian Eng.* **a.** Piquancy, pep, 'spice'.

1986 *Stardust* (Bombay) Oct. 2 (Advt.), The . . Casseroles sure put the *masala* back in our marriage. **1992** *Pioneer on Sunday* (Delhi) 13 Sept. 9/3 'The Prime Minister . . said he wanted to have vigilant MPs like me in Parliament. I still have a lot of *masala*,' Jain cackles into the telephone.

b. A mixture of backgrounds, influences, etc.

1986 *Time* (Austral. ed.) 10 Nov. 33/1 While filmmakers elsewhere have developed genres . . nearly all commercial Indian films mix these elements into one big *masala*. *Ibid.* 33/3 Most Bombay producers still crank out variations on the *masala* theme. **1991** *Bomb* Summer 48/1 She is a masala—a mixture—someone who is genuinely from everywhere, yet living within an Indian context. **1992** *Maclean's Mag.* 9 Mar. 52/3 Choudhury, an Indian who grew up with a masala of influences in England, Jamaica, Mexico, Italy and Canada . . , is a striking presence. **1993** *Times Lit. Suppl.* 23 Apr. 22/4 The complicated and bizarre milieu of the *masala* picture, a type of blockbuster Indian film named after mixed spice because of its variety and supposed steaminess.

mascarpone (mæskɑːˈpəʊnɪ, ‖maskarˈpoːne), *n.* Also **mascherpone**. [a. It. *mascarpone*, *mascherpone*, f. earlier *mascarpa*, *mascherpo* a type of ricotta + -*one* augmentative suffix.

C. Battisti (*Dizionario Etimologico Italiano* III, 1975) suggests a possible derivation from L. **manuscarpere* 'to take in the hand, to masturbate', comparing a S. It. phr. *far ricotta* 'to masturbate' (lit. 'to make ricotta').]

A soft, very mild cream cheese originating from the Lombardy region of Italy.

1936 A. L. SIMON *Catechism concerning Cheeses* 35 *Mascher[p]one*, a white, soft and delicate Italian cheese made from fresh cream; made mostly in Lombardy and chiefly in the autumn and winter. **1970** *House & Garden* May 105/1 But they do have *mascarpone*, officially a cream cheese, but in fact totally lacking any cheesy taste and not unlike clotted cream. **1977** E. DAVID *Italian Food* (rev. ed.) 308 *Mascherpone* or *mascarpone* are the fresh little double-cream cheeses sold in white muslin parcels, to be eaten with sugar or fruit. **1986** *Toronto Star* 28 May B7/1 An appetizer one day could be a swordfish paillard with garlic, scallions, tomatoes and smoked salmon mascarpone. **1989** *Homes & Gardens* Dec. 126/3 Beat the egg yolks with the sugar until pale and foamy, then fold in the mascarpone, a tablespoon at a time.

masculinist, *n.* and *a.* Senses 1–2 in Dict. become A. *n.* 1–2. Delete sense 3 in Dict. and quot. 1951. Add: **B.** *adj.* Of, designating, or containing attitudes, values, etc., held to be typical of men; macho.

1912 R. WEST in *Daily Dispatch* (Manchester) 26 Nov. 6/6 Mr. Edgar takes the usual masculinist standpoint of regarding women as incompetent weaklings except for their maternal functions. **1951** R. CAMPBELL *Light on Dark Horse* xvii. 257 Bloomsbury still awaits its 'masculinist' Messiah. **1980** *Washington Post* 18 Feb. B5/3 He was 'really hooked into macho' during a lengthy stint in the Green Berets. He is writing a book on masculinist theory. **1992** *Jrnl. Women & Relig.* XI. 5 Feminism teaches us that no one perspective, no one representation constitutes truth—although masculinist European perspectives have been accorded the value of 'objectivity' for many centuries.

masculism (ˈmæskjʊlɪzm), *n.* [f. MASCUL(INE *a.* + -ISM.] = MASCULINISM *n.*

1895 W. D. MORRISON in Lombroso & Ferrero *Female Offender* Introd. p. xvi, Sexual peculiarities, such as feminism in men, masculism in women, and infantilism in both. **1982** *Bulletin* (Sydney) 30 Mar. 58/3 Masculism aims to change all that by bringing men together in male consciousness-raising groups.

masculist (ˈmæskjʊlɪst), *n.* and *a.* [f. MASCUL(INE *a.* + -IST, after FEMINIST *a.* and *n.*, perh. ad. Fr. *masculiste*, which is recorded from 1974 (*Datations et Documents Lexicographiques* 2me Sér. 24, 1984).] **A.** *n.* = MASCULINIST *n.* **B.** *adj.* Advocating men's rights; also, anti-feminist.

[**1974** A. BOUDARD *Cinoche* 76 On coupe assez de forêts pour vous imprimer toutes ces revues féministes, masculistes et familiales.] **1978** S. MAITLAND *After Ball was Over* in *Fireweed* Oct. 83 'They are *not* radical feminists.' 'Well, they bloody looked like it.' 'You're one to talk. Who wouldn't join a Marxist reading group because he was an antiquated masculist, who couldn't recognise the glory of women in struggle?' **1980** *Logophile* IV. 1. 53/2 'Semantic space' had to be secured in order for women to construct new expressions and neologisms like . . 'masculist'. **1982** *Bulletin* (Sydney) 30 Mar. 58/1 There are no Australian masculist voices as cheeky or challenging as that of Germaine Greer. **1986** *Observer* 27 July 23/1 What this book would call the masculist critic should not reject these essays out of hand. **1989** *Guardian* 23 Nov. 38/6 It does not matter if the cartoon is insulting to men. The number of such cartoons is so small that, set against the insults to women broadcast by every newsagent and television channel, only a loony masculist would object to them.

mash, *v.*[1] Add: **6.** *U.S. colloq.* **a.** *intr.* Freq. const. *down.* To apply pressure, to press down, esp. forcefully (*on*).

1903 *Dialect Notes* II. v. 320 Mash down on the trunk lid so I can lock it. **1936** R. JOHNSON *Terraplane Blues* (song) in P. Oliver *Screening Blues* (1968) vi. 189 And when I mash down on your little starter, then your spark plug will give me fire. **1951** W. FAULKNER *Requiem for Nun* II. ii. 182 He knows that all he's got to do is, just wait and keep his hand on you and maybe just mash hard enough with it, and you'll get another passel of money and diamonds too out of your husband or your pa. **1987** *Fortune* 2 Feb. 98/3 Drivers are mashing down on the accelerator when they think they are hitting the brakes. **1994** *St. Petersburg* (Florida) *Times* (City ed.) 18 May 3/1 Everyone in the car was saying, 'Slow down,..for the red light!'.. Yet he mashed on the gas.

b. *trans.* To press down, esp. forcefully; to squeeze. Also *fig.*, to stifle.

1931 F. HURST *Back Street* II. xxviii. 169 She began to mash her hand against her mouth, to mash back the growing laughter. **1972** C. BUCHANAN *Maiden* ii. 19 He mashed her hand a final time and bounded off into the neon night. **1985** *New Yorker* 18 Nov. 49/1 Trying to get out in a hurry, I mash the gas and spin the wheels. **1994** *Washington Times* 19 Apr. E19/3 There's none of that jump off the line you get with most other cars, unless you're willing to mash the pedal.

mashed, *ppl. a.* Add: **3.** Special Combs. **mashed potato(es)**, (*a*) boiled peeled potatoes, mashed usu. with the addition of butter and milk or cream, and served as an accompaniment; (*b*) (in form **Mashed Potato**) a popular dance of the early 1960s, originating in the U.S.

1747 H. GLASSE *Art of Cookery* ix. 199 Mashed Potatoes...Boil your potatoes, peel them, and..mash them well; to two pounds of potatoes put a pint of milk, a little salt.., a quarter of a pound of butter, stir it in, and serve it up. **1824** M. RANDOLPH *Virginia House-Wife* 120 Potato Balls. Mix mashed potatoes with the yelk of an egg, roll them into balls. **1960** SHELDON & BRIANHERT (song-title) Mashed potato time. **1963** *Punch* 6 Mar. 347/1 The Mashed Potato..remains as much of a mystery as the Hully-Gully and the Loco-Motion. **1989** *Independent* 9 Dec. 32/8 The Sixties, the Silver Age of Dance Crazes where would-be teen queens in America entered competitions to display their prowess at bizarre refinements of the Frug, Watusi or Mashed Potato. **1994** *Guardian* 15 Oct. (Weekend Suppl.) 49/4 My ribeye of beef with mashed potato, shallots cooked in duck fat and a red wine sauce.

mashgiach (mæʃˈgiːax), *n.* Also **mashgiah**. Pl. **mashgichim**, **mashgihim**. [a. Heb. *maśgīaḥ* supervisor.] A person authorized to inspect or supervise premises where food is kept or prepared, in order to ensure compliance with Jewish dietary laws (Kashrut).

1961 WEBSTER, *Mashgiah, Mashgiach.* **1962** *Stand. Jewish Encycl.* 1278/2 *Mashgiah*,..overseer appointed to supervise the observance of *kashrut* laws in the preparation of food. **1967** *Boston Sunday Herald* 26 Mar. VI. 5/4 On request, both the 23,000-ton Olympia and the 26,300-ton Queen Anna Maria offer kosher cuisine from special kitchens supervised by a 'mashgiach'. **1973** *Jewish Chron.* 7 Dec. 21/1 The glatt kosher butchers and caterers..do not make use of..mashgichim, rabbis who are kashrut supervisors. *Ibid.* The mashgiach may declare [the animal] kosher if, after snipping away at the lesion, he finds that there is no sign of disease. **1994** *Atlanta Jrnl. & Constitution* 26 Mar. E6/2 Although there's always plenty of work for a *mashgiach*, or kosher inspector, the time around Passover is particularly busy.

Mason ('meɪsən), *n.*[3] (MASON *n.*[3] in Dict. becomes MASON *n.*[4]) *Ceramics.* [The family name of Staffordshire china manufacturers Miles *Mason* (1752–1822), and his sons William (1785–1855), George Miles (1789–1859), and Charles James (1791–1856).] *absol.* or (usu.) in the possessive. Designating ware originally made in the factories of the Mason family, esp. a form of ironstone china patented by Charles James Mason in 1813.

Mason's Ironstone is a proprietary name in the U.K.

1804 *Morning Herald* 15 Oct. [1]/1 MASON'S CHINA...Miles Mason..has established a Manufactory at Lane Delph...The articles are stamped on the bottom of the large pieces, to prevent imposition. **1863** W. CHAFFERS *Marks & Monograms on Pottery & Porcelain* 127 Mason's Iron Stone China. Staffordshire. Leek. A recent manufacture belonging to Mr. Mason. **1911** O. ONIONS *Beckoning Fair One* in *Widdershins* 16 The tall lattice-paned china cupboard with its Derby and Mason and Spode. **1960** *Connoisseur's Handbk. Antique Collecting* 176/2 *Mason's bone china*: Miles Mason..started to make porcelain at a factory in Market Street, Fenton, in 1800. **1988** R. FEILO *Which? Guide to Buying Antiques* (rev. ed.) 89/1 Mason's Patent Ironstone China was extremely popular, mass-produced, brought pseudo-Oriental polychromatic designs to the general public who had only been able to buy monochrome transfer-printed wares. **1989** *Antique Collecting* XXIII. Feb. 70/3 Mason's ironstone, wide selection.

mass, *n.*[1] Add: [**7.**] **mass card** *R.C. Church*, a card informing the recipient that a mass will be offered for a specified person (esp. one recently deceased) or purpose.

1930 *Irish Times* 1 Dec. 1/1 (Advt.), Numerous kind friends..who sent *Mass cards, wreaths, letters. **1994** *Independent on Sunday* 19 June (Sunday Review) 6 Between two bricks, I discovered a photograph of Cardinal Alojzije Viktor Stepinac printed on a mass card.

mass, *n.*[2] Add: [**10.**] *mass democracy.*

1934 H. G. WELLS *Exper. Autobiogr.* I. v. 264 Lenin conjured government by *mass-democracy out of sight..by his reorganization of the Communist Party so as to make it a directive élite. **1990** *Current Hist.* Dec. 417/2 The Bulgarian Agrarian National Union (BANU) became Bulgaria's party of mass democracy, aiming to bring Bulgaria's peasant majority into full participation in the country's political life.

[**d.**] **mass extinction** *Biol.*, an episode of extinction involving numerous species or higher taxa.

1956 *Evolution* X. 101/1 Perhaps it is futile to search for a single cause for all of the great *mass extinctions. **1990** M. J. BENTON *Vertebr. Palaeont.* iv. 100 The biggest mass extinction of all time took place at the end of the Permian.., and the tetrapods were involved. Of the 37 families that were present in the last 5 Myr of the Permian.., 27 died out (a loss of 73%).

mass line, in Maoist China: a system of arriving at policy decisions, based on direct and repeated consultation between leaders and led.

1950 *People's China* 1 July 7/1 The General Programme and detailed provisions of the Party Constitution lay particular stress on the Party's *mass line...Our mass line is a class line, a mass line of the proletariat. **1964** KANG CHAO in D. J. Dwyer *China Now* (1974) xiii. 261 The factors that impaired the morale of managerial and technical personnel were different. Under the slogans 'politics takes command' and 'reliance on the mass line', the administrative system within an enterprise underwent considerable disruption...Experts had to listen to non-experts in technical matters. **1981** J. B. GRIEDER *Intellect. & State in Mod. China* viii. 333 The strategy of the Mass Line—that is, the idea that 'educating the people' and 'learning from the people' are inseparable dimensions of the same dialectical process.

mass transit chiefly *N. Amer.* [TRANSIT *n.* 1 c (b)], a large-scale coordinated system of public transport in a city.

1972 *Village Voice* (N.Y.) 1 June 10/2 They piously explain how electricity is needed to save the environment through sewage treatment plants and *mass transit. **1992** *Air Canada en Route* Aug. 50/2 The streetcars rumbling past are probably the only reminder that this is a place big enough to warrant mass transit.

massacre, *n.* Add: **4.** In weakened sense (esp. in *Sport*): an occasion or event in which one side is defeated comprehensivey; a complete and decisive defeat.

1940 *Evening Star* (Washington, D.C.) 9 Dec. C3/1 The boys and girls at the Washington massacre yesterday saw what will probably turn out to be the finest old feud in football history. **1959** *Charlotte* (N. Carolina) *Observer* 27 Nov. D1/2 It was the worst defeat in Duke's storied football history... Some 30,000 Duke Stadium fans and a nation-wide television audience sat in on the massacre. **1974** *Times* 20 Apr. 11/1 The crucial [bridge] match was expected to be close... Within a few hours the Americans had suffered the biggest massacre since Pearl Harbour. **1991** *Athlon's Eastern Football 1991* Ann. 60/2 Nance let Klingler's numbers speak for themselves, countering the backlash from that Eastern Washington massacre by pointing out that Klingler's statistics were better than any other Heisman-winning quarterback.

massacre, *v.* Add: **4.** In weakened sense (esp. in *Sport*): to defeat decisively.

1940 *Washington Post* 9 Dec. II. 19/2 The Chicago Bears massacred the Washington Redskins, 73–0, yesterday which more than evens up that little Custer incident. **1976** *Scotsman* 27 Dec. 10/8 Ipswich.. should massacre Norwich on Wednesday at home in the East Anglian derby. **1988** *Financial Times* 11 June (Weekend Suppl.) p. xxiv/6 Last time the West Indies were here they massacred England.

massage, *v.* Add: **b.** To apply (lotion, shampoo, etc.) by means of massage; to restore (warmth or sensation) by rubbing. Usu. const. *into*.

1966 J. S. Cox *Illustr. Dict. Hairdressing* 49/2 Dry shampoo,.. a shampoo in powder form which is applied to the head as a powder, massaged in and then brushed out. **1979** J. RABAN *Arabia through Looking Glass* iv. 144 German businessmen and their wives were massaging suntan lotion into each other's brown backs. **1982** L. CODY *Bad Company* xiii. 96 She massaged some warmth into her cramped fingers. **1987** *Pract. Hairstyling & Beauty* June/July 21 Massage the cream into hair and scalp..and leave on for 10 minutes. **1989** *Looks* Dec. (Calendar Suppl.), Massage in your facial scrub to slough off dead cells and flaky bits.

massive, *a.* Add: **[1.]** **g.** Chiefly *Astron.* Possessing (much) mass.

1917 F. R. MOULTON *Introd. Astron.* (ed. 2) xiii. 509 The discussions..led him to the conclusion that probably in all cases the brighter star is the more massive. **1927** H. N. RUSSELL et al. *Astron.* II. xvii. 551 After colliding with the far more massive atom the electron may be found moving at the same speed as before. **1957** QUADLING & RAMSAY *Elem. Mech.* I. iii. 32 A massive body is one which takes a large force to make it change its motion. **1959** SPITZ & GAYNOR *Dict. Astron.* 399 The curvature of space existing in the vicinity of a massive body, like the sun. **1980** J. W. HILL *Intermediate Physics* ii. 10 The force of gravity exerted by the moon is less than that exerted by the earth because it is less massive.

h. *Physics.* Of a particle: having non-zero mass, not massless.

1963 K. W. FORD *World of Elem. Particles* v. 115 The massless particles definitely belong to the family of particles and resemble the massive particles in more ways than they differ. **1968** *Progress Theoret. Physics* XXXIX. 494 (*heading*) Gauge theories of massive and massless tensor fields. **1984** *Nature* 19 Jan. 297/3 If the electronic neutrino is also massive (with an expected mass of 10^{-8}GeV), the range is even more staggering.

massotherapy (mæsəʊˈθɛrəpɪ), *n.* [f. MASS(AGE *n.* + -O[1] + THERAPY *n.*] The treatment of disorders by massage.

1890 J. S. BILLINGS *Nat. Med. Dict.* II. 115/2 *Massotherapy*,..use of massage in therapeutics. **1994** *Plain Dealer* (Cleveland, Ohio) 24 May 11-E/1 They want herbs, acupuncture, massotherapy. They want guided imagery and other alternative therapies.

Hence **masso'therapist** *n.*, a person who practises massotherapy.

1932 *Who's Who* 754/2 Crow, William Bernard... Hon. Vice-President National Association of Masso-Therapists. **1990** *Gazette* (Montreal) 4 Mar. D3 (*caption*) Holistic therapist works Betty Wallace Simoneau works to invigorate senses of patient Kathleen Hansen at Aromatherapy Clinic. Hansen is also a massotherapist at the clinic.

mass production, *n.* Add: **mass-pro'ducible** *a.*

1975 *Sci. Amer.* Nov. 57/1 The JPL study emphasizes that a major effort will be required to achieve 'mass-producible' versions of the gas-turbine and Stirling power plants. **1991** *Electronic Design* 22 Aug. 30/3 An inexpensively mass-producible means of achieving a small, light package that frees designers from the spatial constraints of planar circuit boards.

massy, *a.* Sense 5 in Dict. becomes 6. Add: **5.** *Physics.* Having significant or non-zero mass. Cf. MASSIVE *a.* 1 *g, *h.

1961 in WEBSTER. **1962** V. LOWE *Understanding Whitehead* I. iv. 18 In the Newtonian physics a massy particle had its location altered by other particles in the universe, but not its essential nature. **1978** *Ann. Physics* CXV. 78 Quantum creation of massy particles can occur in the cosmological context without cost of energy. **1979** *Sci. Amer.* Jan. 100/1 Like a springy support, a massy support does not damp the motion of the string. **1980** *Ibid.* Apr. 100/2 Radiation theorists were able to calculate a new fundamental quantity: the ratio of the number of photons (the massless particles of electromagnetic radiation) in the universe to the number of nucleons (the massy protons and neutrons).

mast, *n.*[1] Add: **[1.]** **c.** *Astron.* (With capital initial.) (The English name of) the southern constellation Pyxis (formerly called Malus).

1883 J. B. HARBORD *Gloss. Navig.* (ed. 2) 22 A very extensive constellation of the southern hemisphere, of which several parts are named, *Carina*, 'the Keel'; *Puppis*, 'the Poop'; *Malus*, 'the Mast'; and *Vela*, 'the Sails'. **1915** M. A. ORR *Stars of Southern Skies* ii. 7 For convenience this large constellation [*sc.* Argo] has been divided into four—the Keel, the Poop, the Mast, and the Sails. **1952** E. J. WEBB *Names of Stars* v. 71 Ptolemy catalogued no fewer than forty-five stars in the group, and modern astronomers have felt compelled to split it up into lesser groups—Keel, Poop, Mast, Sails.

[4.] **[b.]** **mast foot** *Windsurfing*, a part of a sailboard whose top fits into the lower end of the mast and which contains a universal joint.

1976 B. WEBB. tr. V. Mares & R. Winkler *Windsurfing* i. 37/2 As soon as you are under way, take your front foot just aft of the *mast foot, and brace your leg against the foot of the mast. **1988** *Boardsailor* (Glenashley, S. Afr.) June 22/1 The Mistral adjustable mastfoot is also included.

master, *n.*[1] Add: [I.] [3.] **a.** Also in conjunctive phrases, as *master-servant relationship.*

1963 AUDEN *Dyer's Hand* 111 The master-servant relationship..is contractual. **1989** *Independent* 25 Nov. 49/6 Mr Freeman finds the Miss Daisy story a perfect microcosm of Southern mystique, which had blacks and whites glued together in a master-servant relationship.

[8.] **b.** *Bridge.* [Abbrev. of *master card*, sense 30 below.] The highest card still unplayed in any suit.

1962 *Listener* 15 Nov. 836/1 After three rounds of trumps had left North with the master, he led a diamond. **1992** D. ROTH *Why Women win at Bridge* x. 60 Any diamond allows South to complete the drawing of trumps on dummy after which she can enjoy the master spade.

[II.] [14.] **b.** So *master's degree*, a degree of this type. In *U.S.* (and later elsewhere) freq. *ellipt.* as *master's* (also without apostrophe).

1774 J. WOODFORDE *Diary* 14 Jan. (1924) I. 122 Cooke Junᵣ went also to the Convocation House to take his Master's degree. **1856** EMERSON *Eng. Traits, Universities in Wks.* (Bohn) II. 91 Seven years' residence is the theoretic period for a master's degree. **1960** B. BERELSON *Graduate Educ. in U.S.* 4, I concentrate somewhat more on the arts and sciences than on the professional field and much more on the doctorate than the Master's. **1975** W. ALLEN *Without Feathers* (1976) 33 She's a madam, with a master's in comparative lit. **1988** *Independent* 31 Aug. 19, I got..a masters in..screen writing.

[16.] **d.** *Golf. Masters*(') *Tournament*, an international golf tournament for invited competitors, held annually since 1934 at Augusta, Georgia. Freq. *ellipt.* as *the* (*U.S.*) *Masters.* Now also *transf.* in the name of some other sporting tournaments.

1933 *Augusta* (Georgia) *Chron.* 17 Oct. 9/8 Mr. Whitman believes that the Masters Golf tournament to be played here will attract visitors from all sections of the United States. **1948** H. COTTON *This Game of Golf* v. 220/2, I had only played on one occasion with him until my visit to his club at Augusta for the Master's [*sic*] in 1948. **1957** *Encycl. Brit.* X. 502/2 Television enhanced the popularity of golf, such tournaments as the Open, Masters,..and several others being given network coverage on the final day. **1980** *Ann. Reg. 1979* 458 Sam Snead, who first won the US Masters thirty years ago. **1986** *Bowls Internat.* July 56/2 Scotland, Ireland and Wales have all competed in past Masters without actually winning it.

e. *pl.* In *Swimming*, and subsequently in other sports, a class for competitors over the usual age for open competition. Chiefly *attrib.*

1972 *N.Y. Times* 9 Apr. 96/4 The first Masters Swimming Meet in New Jersey, for competitive swimmers over 25 years old — some of them well over 25 — is being held this week-end. **1974** *Sunday Times* 18 Aug. 25/5 'Masters' athletics..known less graciously [in Britain] as Veteran athletics, is for the more mature athletes. You have to be at least 40-years-old to compete. **1986** *Runner* Mar. 12/1 I'd like to get back into my old sport, with the hope of becoming a serious masters runner in a few years. **1986** *Swimming Times* Sept. 44/1, I anticipated bringing over a plane load of Masters swimmers. **1989** *Times* 9 Sept. 10/1 One of the obscure but intriguing races in athletics is for the first 'masters' runner to do a four-minute mile. Masters runners are 40 and over.

[V.] [26.] [a.] *master copy* (cf. sense 10 c above).

1960 L. C. NANASSY & W. SELDEN *Business Dict.* 128 *Master copy*, the original stencil..from which quantities of copies are made. **1989** *Adbusters Q.* Winter 18/1 The Media Foundation will provide one-inch video master copies of all the commercials.

master suite.

1966 R. STANDISH *Widow Hack* vi. 71 There is a lovely curved staircase leading from the hall to the two *master suites.* **1992** *Better Homes & Gardens Building Ideas* Spring 27/2 The 1,000-square-foot master suite 'is like a cocoon', a remote and cozy apartment.

[30.] **master disc**, a disc from which copies of a recording, text, etc., are made or copies of a program are read; *spec.* = sense 10 b.

1951 M. McLUHAN *Let.* 18 June (1987) 225 The *master discs were sent to Lib. of Congress from Harvard. **1980** M. ROSS-TREVOR in Gammond & Horricks *Music goes Round & Round* vi. 117 The relationship between producer and engineer is a close one..right up until the final master-disc is cut. **1992** *CU Amiga* May 124/1 Next comes the installation program, a lengthy process which involves copying and unpacking the *Easy AMOS* files from the two master disks and dumping them on to three blank floppies.

master, *v.* Add: **8.** *Sound Recording.* To record the master disc or tape for (a record or recording); to make a recording of (a performance) from which a master tape or disc can be created. Also *absol.*

1960 [implied in *MASTERING *vbl. n.* 3]. **1967** *DB* Nov. 8/1 Monophonic lateral recordings are commonly mastered with variable ground pitch. **1978** *Gramophone* Mar. 1573 (Advt.), We fully appreciate the vital need for top quality pressings and, therefore, all records are now being mastered and manufactured for us in the Netherlands by a leading manufacturer specialising in really high quality. **1984** *Sounds* 1 Dec. 3/5 Utopia will be mastering and cutting the single, Phonogram will be pressing and distributing it. **1986** *Studio Week* July 13/3 Since we've begun mastering digitally the noise floor has dropped.

mastering, *vbl. n.* Add: **3.** *Sound Recording.* [Partly f. MASTER *n.*] The process of making a master disc or tape.

1960 *Jrnl. Audio Engin. Soc.* VIII. 251/2 For mastering purposes, where maximum signal-to-noise ratio is necessary, wide tracks are desirable. **1982** *New Scientist* 14 Jan. 85/2 Mastering and pressing of discs can take up to three months. **1988** *Studio News* Apr. 19/3 Jones sees the machine being used for ENG (Electronic News Gathering) applications as well as for music mastering. **1990** *Compact Disc* 7 Aug. 5/2 Even when flaws in sonic performance are detectable, they can often be traced to the recording itself, or to the mastering process.

mastic, *n.* Add: [8.] **mastic asphalt**, a dense mixture of bitumen and powdered limestone, to which gravel, stone chips, etc., are often added, used chiefly for surfacing footpaths and roofs.

1930 *Jrnl. Soc. Chem. Industry* 18 Apr. 182T/1 The great distinction between rock and *mastic asphalts is that, while in the former the incorporation of the bitumen and the mineral base has been effected by nature, in the latter it takes place by human agency. **1991** *Better Roads* Nov. 7/2 It's interesting to note the recent touting of the wonders of stone mastic asphalt.

masticate, *v.* Add: [1.] **c.** *intr.* To perform the action of prolonged chewing.

1802, etc. [implied in MASTICATING *ppl. a.*]. **1935** *Chambers's Encycl.* III. 822/1 Many animals can hardly be said to masticate; such are the carnivora..and they are not provided with grinding teeth. **1965** E. J. HOWARD *After Julius* II. viii. 115 He would..subside into a trance-like stillness, unable even to masticate — food froze in his mouth. **1992** *Face* Oct. 110/3, I made a wad out of the young leaves and twigs and tried to masticate slowly. It tasted like a privet hedge.

mastoid, *a.* and *n.* Sense B. b in Dict. becomes B. c. Add: [B.] **b.** = MASTOIDITIS *n. colloq.*

1934 in WEBSTER. **1956** C. P. SNOW *Homecomings* x. 76 He had been trying all ways to get into uniform, but he kept being turned down because he had once had an operation for mastoid. **1987** R. ELLMANN *Oscar Wilde* (1988) i. 10 Even today surgeons use the terms 'Wilde's incision' for mastoid.

Masurian (mæ'zʊərɪən), *a.* [f. Ger. *Masur(en* Mazury (see below) + -IAN.] Of or pertaining to Mazury, a region of N.E. Poland (formerly East Prussia) containing numerous glacial lakes. Chiefly in *Masurian Lakes.*

1914 *Times* 29 Sept. 9/1 Germany had only to fight upon Russian ground, and if repulsed to fall amid the Masurian lakes and woods. **1927** PEAKE & FLEURE *Hunters & Artists* iii. 30 In some parts of the northern plain the drainage is still imperfect, and we find vast extents of marsh and lakes; of this type are the historic 'Masurian Lakes' in East Prussia. **1968** R. W. FAIRBRIDGE *Encycl. Geomorphol.* 1139/1 One of the extensive areas where the lakes remain is the historic Masurian Lakes of eastern Poland and White Russia. **1989** *Encycl. Brit.* XXV. 915/1 The Masurian Lakeland (Pojezierze Mazurskie), east of the lower Vistula.

mat, *v.*[1] Add: **5.** *trans.* To reprimand or admonish as a superior; = CARPET *v.* 4. Usu. in *pass.* Cf. MAT *n.*[1] 1 g. *colloq.*

1948 *Sunday Pictorial* 29 Aug. 7/3 *Carpet*, a three month sentence; *carpeted*, on a charge for misbehaviour (also 'cased' or 'matted'). **1969** 'W. HAGGARD' *Doubtful Disciple* iv. 44 The interviewer had been matted and now he was uncertain. **1982** *Sunday Times* 10 Oct. 1/1 He'd been cornered and couldn't approve because he'd be matted by the bishops if he did.

match, *a.* Add: **[1.]** **match-needle** *a. Photogr.*, designating or pertaining to a technique for obtaining the correct exposure by varying the shutter-speed setting of a camera until two needles, one of which is controlled by a built-in light meter, are seen to coincide in the viewfinder.

1970 *SLR Yearbk. 1970* 169/3 Semi-automatic, match-needle system. **1991** *Buying Cameras* Mar. 33 The match-needle metering is simplicity itself to use and provides correct exposures almost every time.

match, *v.*[1] Add: **[5.]** **[b.]** Also *to match up* (*U. S. Sport*), to assign (one player) to another, esp. of equal strength or ability, so as to form a competing pair; to arrange for (a person) to compete with another. Const. *with, against.*

1959 F. McGUIRE *Defensive Basketball* i. 11 We assign (match up) players to particular opponents on the basis of height, speed, weight, and other characteristics. **1969** R. M. DAVIS *Aggressive Basketball* vi. 122 Wherever the offensive man goes, the defense will match up a man and move with him. **1977** *Washington Post* 1 Jan. D5/2 Here's Washington's own matched up with Bjorn Borg's roommate, Mariana Simonescu, in the Virginia Slims at GW's Smith Center Sunday. **1988** *N. Y. Times* 20 June C7/1 Scott went to the second option, posting up Abdul-Jabbar against Bill Laimbeer, who was matched up against him.

matched, *ppl. a.* Add: **5.** **matched guise** *adj. phr. Sociolinguistics*, designating a method of comparing people's reactions to the same passage spoken in different language varieties.

1971 *New Society* 14 Oct. 714/2 In order to find out whether RP really did have more prestige than regional varieties, I used the 'matched-guise' technique. This consisted of playing tape recordings of speakers with different accents..to listeners who we asked to rate these voices on certain dimensions, including status. **1991** *Eng. World-Wide* XII. 288 This work..included an exploratory matched-guise test to investigate the children's attitude to standard language and dialect.

matching, *vbl. n.*[1] Sense 3 in Dict. becomes 4. Add: **[1.]** (Further examples in various senses.)

1967 D. G. HAYS *Introd. Computational Linguistics* viii. 156 Matching proceeds segment by segment. **1970** O. DOPPING *Computers & Data Processing* iv. 70 Matching means that the machine compares cards from the two input hoppers, pair by pair, with respect to the punching in a certain field. **3.** *Math.* A subset of the set of edges of a (usu. bipartite) graph which contains no two adjacent edges; a subgraph of a graph which may be constructed by selecting a subset of the set of vertices and assigning a distinct adjacent vertex to each member of this subset.

1955 O. ORE in *Duke Math. Jrnl.* XXII. 629 Let us now say generally that a subset A of V is (graph) matched to a subset A' of V' if there exists a one-to-one correspondence between A and A' such that the corresponding elements are edge connected. We shall also call such a matching as a partial matching of V upon V'. **1968** C. L. LIU *Introd. Combinatorial Math.* xi. 281 A matching defines a one-to-one correspondence between the vertices in a subset of X and the vertices in a subset of Y. **1979** PAGE & WILSON *Introd. Computational Combinatorics* vii. 164 Within this rather loose framework there are many types of assignment problems. Alternative names for such problems are matchings (used mainly in graph theory) or marriages.

match-up, ('mætʃʌp) *n. U.S. Sport.* Also **matchup**. [f. the vbl. phr. *to match up* (*MATCH *v.* 5 b).] A pairing of competitors in a game or contest; a game or contest between two people. Also *transf.*

1959 F. McGUIRE *Defensive Basketball* viii. 212 Many a game has been won by careful match-ups. While striving for good match-ups defensively, it is also smart to try to force the opponents into bad match-ups. **1969** R. M. DAVIS *Aggressive Basketball* vi. 121 The match-up is a very effective defense to use when an offensive team shifts to a zone offense from a man-to-man defense. **1975** *Business Week* 14 Apr. 54/3 'Imagine the matchups at the trading post', says the arbitrageur. 'A million shares on the sell side, 10,000 on the buy side.' **1979** *Tucson* (Arizona) *Citizen* 20 Sept. 10A/1 With a lively race for mayor, there should be a healthy spillover effect on three potentially close council match-ups. **1981** J. LEHANE *Basketball Fund.* iv. 170 The taller opponent is usually the winner in this matchup. **1987** *Los Angeles Times* 4 Oct. (Television Times Suppl.) 3/3 Another November match-up pits 'Perry Mason' against the 'Mayflower Madam'.

mate, *v.*[2] Add: **[3.]** **[b.]** *spec.* To copulate (*with* another animal). Also *transf.* (Later examples.)

1922 D. H. LAWRENCE *England, my England* 8 Dark, like a lair where strong beasts had lurked and mated. **1924** W. B. YEATS *Heart Replies in Dial* June 501 Let the cage bird and the cage bird mate and the wild bird mate in the wild. **1968** A. STORR *Human Aggression* iii. 24 A snake who has been vanquished by a rival will crawl away and remain sexually inactive for some weeks, whereas his triumphant adversary will, on achieving victory, immediately mate. **1976** T. HOOPER *Guide to Bees & Honey* I. ii. 45 The drone's only function as far as we know is mating with the young queen. **1986** D. MADDEN *Hidden Symptoms* (1988) 18 How strange and arbitrary it all seemed to be, people marrying, mating and mixing sexes. **1995** *Time Out* 9 Aug. 16/1 Even the potentially edifying sex education classes were spent teaching us how amoebas mate. 'Well, that's very useful in Birmingham,' comes the monumentally deadpan reply.

matehood ('meɪthʊd), *n.* [f. MATE *n.*[2] + -HOOD.] The condition or fact of being a mate; companionship, fellowship. Cf. MATESHIP *n.*

1924 S. STEVENSON *Surplus* xxiv. 298 To limit the fullest manifestation..to beings, between whom the physical tie of matehood or parenthood exists, is like declaring that electricity can only be generated by one particular kind of dynamo. **1965** M. FRAYN *Tin Men* xiii. 68 His belief in the universal matehood of man. **1986** *Act* Feb. 4/1 Philip goes to visit Steve who makes overtures to him for renewed matehood.

material, *a.* and *n.* Add: [A.] [2.] [b.] Also, **material equivalence** *Logic*, the relationship between two propositions in which, for the compound proposition to be true, either both must be true or both false; a case in which such a relationship obtains.
1918 C. I. LEWIS *Survey Symbolic Logic* 293 *Material equivalence*, (p≡q) = (p>q)(q>p). **1932** LEWIS & LANGFORD *Symbolic Logic* iv. 88 Since the relation p≡q is a reciprocal implication, it shares the peculiarities of material implication and is called 'material equivalence'. It does not represent equivalence of logical force or meaning, but only equivalence of truth-value. **1933** *Mind* XLII. 33 Suppose we try 'material equivalence'... It is symmetric, and so satisfies F, for the significance of F lies in making < symmetric. **1982** I. M. COPI *Introd. Logic* (ed. 6) vii. §5. 314 Two statements are said to be *materially equivalent*, or *equivalent in truth value*, when they are either both true or both false. This notion is expressed by the symbol '≡'. Material equivalence is a truth function and can be defined by the following truth table.

maternalism (mə'tɜːnəlɪz(ə)m), *n.* [f. MATERNAL *a.* + -ISM. Cf. PATERNALISM *n.*] Behaviour or attitudes characteristic of a mother; the practice of acting as a mother does towards her child.
*a*1961 in WEBSTER s.v., Remarkable for her benevolent maternalism. **1971** H. GUNTRIP *Psychoanalytic Theory* I. v. 100 These splitting processes begin certainly as soon as the mother's primary maternalism begins to fail the baby. **1980** *Christian Science Monitor* 19 May 19/3 Miss Foster conveys..the emotional depth of Mother Courage's fierce maternalism. **1985** *New Scientist* 14 Feb. 10/1 Lactation has created the myth of maternalism: that only the mother is suited to taking care of the offspring. **1987** *Church Times* 10 Apr. 9/2 Both paternalism and maternalism can take a wrong turning if the attitude includes a desire to keep the other person in a state of dependence.
So **materna'listic** *a.*, characteristic of or exhibiting maternalism; maternal.
1941 *Federal Reporter* (U.S.) 2nd Ser. CXXI. 339/1 The 'mercantilist' system was profoundly paternalistic (or maternalistic). **1974** HAWKEY & BINGHAM *Wild Card* x. 99 She felt..maternalistic concern for him. **1985** *New Scientist* 14 Feb. 12/1 Primates outdo even the carnivores when it comes to 'maternalistic' males.

mateship, *n.* Add: **2.** *Zool.* The condition of having a mate; a pairing of one animal with another.
1927 F. ALVERDES *Social Life in Animal World* v. 47 Permanent mateships within a larger unit are of special interest since human marriages must be classified under this heading. **1972** T. McHUGH *Time of Buffalo* xvii. 193 A single bull with a single cow is the rule, a union zoologists refer to as 'temporary monogamous mateship'. **1977** D. MORRIS *Manwatching* 283 Even after establishing a mateship such individuals may continue to play the human beauty-game, when assessing film stars, pin-ups, or passers-by in the street.

Mateus (mæ'teɪəs, 'mæteɪəs), *n.* [a. Pg. *Mateus*, the name of an estate at Vila Real, northern Portugal.] A proprietary name for a semi-sparkling rosé wine first made on the Mateus estate and subsequently more widely in northern Portugal. More properly *Mateus Rosé*

(since the brand is also used for white and red wines).
1949 *Official Gaz.* (U.S. Patent Office) 24 May 1008/1 *(in figure) Mateus...* For wines. **1951** S. SITWELL in *Sunday Times* 22 Apr. 4/6 The most delicious *vin rose* [*sic*] that I have ever tasted.. is called Mateus, and it may be that the view of the lovely villa of that name, near Vila Real, which is upon the label, makes the wine taste even better... Mateus is delicious beyond words. **1967** *House & Garden* Mar. 103/1 The river Douro, with its.. beautiful valley, is.. primarily the land of port... From this valley also comes the extremely popular Mateus Rosé. **1974** 'G. BLACK' *Golden Cockatrice* ii. 25, I was having dinner.. and drinking a little Mateus with it. **1991** *Decanter* Mar. 90/1 The Chardonnay-based lightly sparkling Prime Rose, aimed at the Mateus Rosé sector of the market.

mathematicize, *v.* Add: **mathe'maticized** *ppl. a.*
1834 *Knickerbocker* Aug. 120 Ladies were invited.. to prepare themselves for future honors.. by becoming Latinized, Græcised, mathematicized and at length diplomatized. **1983** *Sci. Amer.* Mar. 25/1 It presents an exhibit of the detailed, mathematicized, ambitious (and still incomplete) state of field biology today.

mathematize, *v.* Add: Hence **'mathematized** *ppl. a.*
1956 E. H. HUTTEN *Lang. Mod. Physics* vi. 239 The highly developed (i.e. mathematized) theories of physics. **1985** A. C. GRAHAM *Reason & Spontaneity* 64 Since colour theory is mathematized, with the absence of light as black and the mixture of all wavelengths as white, it would be simpler to deduce that light of all wavelengths will become mixed when reflected in all directions from the spherical bubbles, and therefore foam will be white.

Mathieu (mɑ'tjø, *U.S.* 'mædjuː), *n. Math.* [The name of Emile Léonard *Mathieu* (1835–90), French mathematician.] Used *attrib.* and in the possessive to designate concepts and entities mentioned by Mathieu or arising out of his work, as **Mathieu('s) equation**, a differential equation arising in connection with elliptically symmetrical systems, having the form $d^2y/dx^2 + (a + b \cos 2x)y = 0$, where a and b are constants; **Mathieu function**, any even or odd periodic function satisfying Mathieu's equation.
1915 WHITTAKER & WATSON *Course Mod. Analysis* (ed. 2) xix. 399 $d^2u/dz^2 + (a + 16q \cos 2z)u = 0$, where a and q are constants.. is known as *Mathieu's equation and.. particular solutions of it are called Mathieu functions. *Ibid.* xix. 413 *(heading)* A second method of constructing the Mathieu function. **1957** L. Fox *Numerical Solution Two-Point Boundary Probl.* vii. 184 As a second example we consider the evaluation of an eigenvalue and eigenfunction of Mathieu's equation. **1962** *Jrnl. Soc. Industr. & Appl. Math.* X. 314 *(heading)* General perturbational solution of the Mathieu equation. **1973** *Jrnl. Math. Physics* XIV. 199/2 We recommend that numerical integration of the Schrödinger equation for a $-f^2/r^4$ potential be avoided and that, instead, one makes use of linear combinations of Mathieu functions to represent the desired function for the appropriate region of space. **1987** *SIAM Jrnl. Math. Anal.* XVIII. 1616 *(heading)* On a simplified asymptotic formula for the Mathieu function of the third kind.

matinée, *n.* Add: [3.] **matinée jacket** = *matinée coat* s.v. MATINÉE *n.* 3.
1964 *Baby Goods Trade Jrnl.* July 13/1 *(caption)* Quilted brushed Bri-Nylon is used by Billikin for this *matinee jacket and matching bonnet. **1986** *Auckland Star* 6 Feb. A2 She believes the baby's jacket.. is the matinee jacket worn by her daughter.. when she disappeared.

matreshka *n.*, var. *MATRYOSHKA *n.*

matrilineal, *a.* Add: matriline'ality *n.*

1961 D. F. ABERLE in Schneider & Gough *Matrilineal Kinship* xvii. 656 Seldom do they raise the question of the circumstances which give rise to or perpetuate matrilineality—or any other form of descent system. **1970** K. MILLETT *Sexual Politics* (1971) I. ii. 25 Matrilineality..does not constitute an exception to patriarchal rule.

matrioshka *n.*, var. *MATRYOSHKA *n.*

matrist ('mætrɪst, 'meɪtrɪst), *n.* and *a.* *Psychol.* [f. MATR(I- + -IST.] **A.** *n.* A person whose behaviour or attitude is influenced or dominated by the mother. Cf. PATRIST *n.*[2] **B.** *adj.* Pertaining to or exhibiting such influence or domination.

1949 G. R. TAYLOR *Conditions of Happiness* vi. 114 Social history is, in fine, a story of the struggle of matrists (if I may borrow a word and provide it with a feminine form) against the rigid, authoritarian, puritanical, guilt-burdened rule of patrists. **1953** — *Sex in Hist.* iv. 77 It would be tedious to refer continually to persons who have modelled themselves on their fathers. I shall therefore speak of them as *patrists*, while those who have modelled themselves on a mother-figure I shall call *matrists*. **1958** *Times Lit. Suppl.* 11 June 390/1 Matrist and patrist tendencies appear in all periods of history. **1968** P. B. AUSTIN *On being Swedish* xx. 142 Sweden today..bears all the hallmarks of a matrist society.

matroid ('meɪtrɔɪd), *n.* *Math.* [f. MATR(IX *n.* + -OID.] An entity consisting of a non-empty finite set together with a collection of subsets, none of which contains another, and such that if an element of one subset in the collection is replaced by an element of another subset in the collection, the resulting subset is also in the collection.

1935 H. WHITNEY in *Amer. Jrnl. Math.* LVII. 509 Let $C_1, C_2, .., C_n$ be the columns of a matrix M. Any subset of these columns is either linearly independent or linearly dependent; the subsets thus fall into two classes. These classes are not arbitrary; for instance, the two following theorems must hold: (a) Any subset of an independent set is independent. (b) If N_p and N_{p+1} are independent sets of p and $p + 1$ columns respectively, then N_p together with some column of N_{p+1} forms an independent set of $p + 1$ columns...Let us call a system obeying (a) and (b) a 'matroid'. **1958** *Trans. Amer. Math. Soc.* LXXXVIII. 144 By a matroid on a finite set M we understand a class **M** of non-null subsets of M which satisfies the following axioms: [etc.]. **1966** *Math. Rev.* Jan. 16/1 This is strikingly analogous to Tutte's characterization of graphic matroids. **1972** R. J. WILSON *Introd. Graph Theory* i. 7 Matroid theory is merely the study of sets with 'independence structures' defined on them, generalizing not only properties of linear independence in vector spaces but also several of the results in graph theory obtained earlier in the book. **1979** *Q. Jrnl. Math.* XXX. 271 (*heading*) Binary matroid sums.

matron, *n.* Add: [3.] **b.** A female prison officer. Cf. *police matron* s.v. POLICE *n.* 6. orig. and chiefly *U. S.*

1931 *Amer. Mercury* Apr. 392/2 A large slate, hung on her by the matron, showed her name, age, crime, sentence, and nativity. **1950** *Collier's* 3 June 37/2 The prison superintendent told me that, of her staff of 60 matrons, there were only five whom she trusted. **1970** *Notes for Guidance of Inmates* (Arohata (N.Z.) Borstal Inst.) 6 Matrons are responsible to the superintendent for the overall control of the institution. **1981** *Time* 22 June 70/1 The dispute..originated in Washington County, Ore., where women prison guards, called 'matrons', received 30%..less than their male counterparts.

matryoshka (mætrɪ'ɒʃkə, ‖ma'trjoʃkə), *n.* Also **matreshka, matrioshka**, etc. [a. Russ. *matrëshka*.] In Russia, (one of) a set of hollow and usu. decorated wooden doll figures of differing sizes, each one made so as to nest inside the next largest. Chiefly *attrib.* (in *sing.*) in *matryoshka doll*. Cf. *Russian doll* s.v. RUSSIAN *a.* 2 e.

The Russian plural form *matryoshki* is unrecorded in English use.

1948 L. GORDON *Pageant of Dolls* II. 80 Most typically Russian of all are the Matreshka, the nested dolls. **1964** *Punch* 16 Dec. p. xii, Gifts at the Russian Shop..include..Matrioshka nested and swaying dolls. **1982** H. KISSINGER *Years of Upheaval* vii. 281 What emerged was like a Russian *matryoshka* doll that has progressively smaller models nested each inside the other. **1986** B. FREEMANTLE *Kremlin Kiss* vi. 48 Three sets..of *matroyshka* [sic], the traditional Russian doll, one of which lifts from a replica of the other until a whole family is disclosed. **1992** *Holiday Which?* Mar. 74/3 One of the things they sell, popular with western tourists, is a Yeltsin *matryoska* which unscrews to reveal a sad Gorbachov and grinning Brezhnev and finally a devilish Stalin.

Matthew ('mæθjuː), *n.* [The name of the evangelist St. *Matthew.*] **Matthew effect**, a term coined by Robert K. Merton (b. 1910), U.S. sociologist, to describe a tendency whereby more is given to those who already have, *spec.* whereby established individuals, causes, institutions, etc., receive continued or excessive recognition to the detriment of their less well-established counterparts. Also **Matthew principle**.

The allusion is to *Matt.* xxv. 29: 'Unto every one that hath shall be given, and he shall have abundance; but from him that hath not shall be taken away even that which he hath.'

1968 R. K. MERTON in *Science* 5 Jan. 58/2 This complex pattern of the misallocation of credit for scientific work must quite evidently be described as 'the Matthew effect'... The Matthew effect consists in the accruing of greater increments of recognition for particular scientific contributions to scientists of considerable repute and the withholding of such recognition from scientists who have not yet made their mark. **1976** *Conc. Oxf. Dict.* 625/2, Matthew principle. **1985** *Nature* 13 June 529/2 Such industrial funds as there may be will probably be distributed on the Matthew principle ('to him that hath...') and will be concentrated among the better off. **1987** *Amer. Sociol. Rev.* LII. 146 Merton's (1968) notion of the 'Matthew effect' is a reminder that honor begets honor. **1989** *Brit. Med. Jrnl.* 3 June 1498/2 The Matthew effect may be manifested in small ways even in the doctor's outpatient clinic. The well educated, richer sections of the community understand and can comply with the doctor's instructions more easily. The less well educated patients, unable to follow instructions, end up irritating the health personnel.

maturase ('mætjʊreɪz), *n.* *Biochem.* [a. F. *maturase* (coined by C. Jacq et al. 1980, in *Compt. Rend. D* CCXC. 90): see MATURE *a.*, -ASE.] Any of a group of enzymes which catalyse the excision of introns from mRNA, and may themselves be coded for by intronic sequences.

1980 *Nature* 20 Nov. 211/2 A different mediator of splicing was proposed by P. Slonimski..for the transcript of the yeast mitochondrial gene for cytochrome *b*. He proposes that certain introns are spliced out with the help of proteins ('maturases') encoded in the introns themselves. **1981** *Ibid.* 5 Feb. 440/1 Two further observations make it clear that maturase is a chimaeric protein, containing the first 143 amino acid residues of cytochrome *b* fused to the I2 reading frame. **1986** *Current Genetics* XI. 55/2 This action of an intron encoded maturase on the splicing of another intron located in a different gene could represent an interesting control mechanism between two enzymes of the same biochemical pathway.

maturationist (mætjʊˈreɪʃənɪst), *n.* and *a.* *Psychol.* and *Linguistics* (chiefly *N. Amer.*). [f. MATURATION *n.* + -IST.] **A.** *n.* One who holds that genetic factors are more important than environmental ones in determining a child's development, esp. with regard to the acquisition of language. **B.** *adj.* Of, pertaining to, or advocating such a view.

1967 *Canad. Med. Assoc. Jrnl.* 12 Aug. XCVII. 325/1 The 'maturationists'..consider the intrinsic biological mechanisms of the child of such importance [as a factor in enuresis] as to render environmental factors relatively inconsequential. 1985 *Jrnl. Humanistic Educ. & Devel.* XXIV. Sept. 10 The maturationist believes knowledge is the consequence of innate patterning. 1991 *Canad. Jrnl. Linguistics* XXXVI. 431 The developmental problem is particularly relevant to the issues addressed by Matthews and Demopoulos, since..maturationist solutions depend on an even stronger hypothesis of innateness. 1992 *Developmental Psychol.* XXVIII. 377/2 A further important way in which the maturationist principles of Gesell recur in current developmental work is through the search of genetic continuity in individual differences.

mature, *a.* and *n.* Add: [**A.**] [**1.**] **e.** Of cheese: that has attained a full flavour.

1935 O. BURDETT *Little Bk. Cheese* ii. 21 In spite of the grocer's assurance that the Stilton was perfectly mature, we waited a month. 1970 SIMON & HOWE *Dict. Gastron.* 119/2 When it [*sc.* Canadian Cheddar] is mature it is very good and some say it equals English farmhouse Cheddar. 1984 *Washington Post* 12 Dec. E16/3 Specialty shops..prefer mature cheeses. 1990 *Country Homes* June 132/2 At the local hostelry..we drank white wine with hobelkase, a strong cheese like a cross between a mature Cheddar and Parmesan.

f. *Econ.* and *Comm.* Pertaining to or designating an economy, industry, or company which has developed to the point where business investment and the application of technology no longer account for a large proportion of its income. Of a product: no longer subject to substantial development or investment.

Some economic theorists have associated the mature stage of a national economy with increasing unemployment, or with increasing expenditure on consumer goods.

1939 *Economist* 3 June 545/1 The final and most elaborate and abstruse argument for fresh public spending is based on what is called the 'mature economy' theory...The theory is a variant of the oversavings theory: according to it, maturity in the economy means a lack of investment opportunities adequate to absorb savings; savings accumulate and economic stagnation results. 1939 A. H. HANSEN in *Hearings Temp. Nat. Econ. Comm. U.S. Congress* (1940) IX. 3513 When a revolutionary new industry.., after having initiated in its youth a powerful upward surge of plant expansion in all the basic industries which serve its needs, after such an industry reaches maturity and ceases to grow..the whole economy must experience a stagnation, unless indeed new developments equally far-reaching take its place...It is not enough that a mature industry continues its activity at a high level on a horizontal plane. 1960 W. W. ROSTOW *Stages Econ. Growth* ii. 10 As societies achieved maturity in the twentieth century..the structure of the working force changed in ways which increased..the proportion of the population..aware of and anxious to acquire the consumption fruits of a mature economy. 1970 *Sci. Amer.* Mar. 35/2 The debt capacity of safe, mature businesses. 1975 *Dun's Rev.* Apr. 77/3 Because of our youth, it will take a little longer than in the mature industries for the personnel man to reach the top. 1975 *Aviation Week & Space Technol.* 10 Nov. 92/3 $80,000 may be..the figure for this relatively mature product [*sc.* the Boeing Arinc

561]. 1982 *Amer. Banker* 15 Nov. 21/4 In a mature economy like that of the U.S., profit margins tend to be thin. 1991 *MBI* Feb. 59/1 Observers warn that the rate of growth is likely to slow down in relatively 'mature' CD markets such as Germany and Holland. 1992 *Pixel* Mar.-Apr. 33/1 While Khoros is reasonably mature, there are small bugs and design flaws scattered throughout the package.

[**2.**] [**a.**] Also used euphemistically for 'middle-aged' or 'old'. (Further examples.)

1867 W. D. HOWELLS *Ital. Journeys* 120 A matron of mature years. 1907 CONRAD *Secret Agent* vi. 153 Two mature women with a matronly air of gracious resolution. 1911 G. B. SHAW *Getting Married* Pref. 150 Use your own mature charms to attract men to the house. 1922 JOYCE *Ulysses* 398 The lover in the heyday of reckless passion and the husband of maturer years. 1963 *Guardian* 12 July 9/6 Mature matrons..now..wear kiss-me-quick hats. 1992 *En Route* (Toronto) July 9/1 Today many Canadians 60 years of age and over are healthy, adventurous and in pursuit of new ways to enjoy their leisure time...In focus groups we conducted this year, mature Canadians gave their travel priorities: value for money, security and safety.

e. *Estate agents' jargon.* Of a property: old, but not so old as to be of special interest.

1975 *Irish Times* 9 May 21/7 (Advt.), Mature 3 bedroom semi-detached house. 1976 *Milton Keynes Express* 28 May 39 (Advt.), A beautifully maintained mature semi detached house. 1990 *Harrogate Advertiser* 6 Apr. (Classified Supermart section) 6/1 (Advt.), A most impressive mature detached residence occupying delightful corner site..in this favoured residential location.

B. *n.* A mature student.

1973 *Times* 4 July 12/2 Matures are..more highly motivated than younger students.

maturity, *n.* Add: **7.** Special Comb. **maturity-onset** *a.* *Path.*, designating forms of diabetes that typically develop in overweight, middle-aged patients, esp. non-insulin-dependent diabetes.

1965 FAJANS & CONN in Leibel & Wrenshall *Nature & Treatment of Diabetes* (Excerpta Medica Internat. Congr. Ser. LXXXIV) xlvi. 648 The asymptomatic '*maturity-onset type' of diabetes was first recognized in 10 children..by the demonstration of mildly to grossly abnormal glucose tolerance tests. 1990 *Health Guardian* May/June 3/2 Free radicals are increasingly linked with a wide range of degenerative diseases such as cancer, heart disease, maturity-onset diabetes, cataracts and Alzheimer's disease.

matzah, *n.* Add: **2. b.** Special Combs. **matzah ball**, a small dumpling made of seasoned matzah meal bound together with egg and chicken fat, typically served in chicken soup; cf. KNAIDEL *n.*

[1846 'A. LADY' *Jewish Man.* i. 9 *Matso soup*...Ten minutes before serving, throw in the balls, from which the soup takes its name.] 1950 G. ACE *Let.* in *Groucho Lett.* (1967) 103 Would Lupowitz and Moskowitz serve black *matzo balls? 1986 L. COLWIN *My Mistress* in *Another Marvelous Thing* (1987) 47 Billy wolfed down her pastrami sandwich and was watching Francis, a slow eater, slowly finish his matzoh ball soup.

matzah brie or **brei** (braɪ) [Ger. *Brei* porridge, pulp], pieces of matzah soaked in seasoned egg and water and fried.

1949 L. W. LEONARD *Jewish Cookery* vi. 45 *Matzo Brie* or Fried Matzo. 1969 P. ROTH *Portnoy's Complaint* 80 Here is the message I take in each Passover with my mother's *matzoh brei.* *Ibid* 82 His superior Jewish brain might as well be *made* of *matzoh brei*! 1993 *Jewish Exponent* 9 Apr. 18x/B I'm looking forward to maybe having some matza brie backstage.

‖**maudit** (modi, anglicized məʊˈdiː), *a.* [Fr., pa. pple of *maudire* to curse, damn. Cf. MALEDICT *a.* (*n.*)]

Although *maudit* has various senses in French, its uses in English seem to derive exclusively from (and are often explicitly analogous with) the earlier borrowing *poète maudit*.]

Of creative artists or their work: insufficiently appreciated by contemporaries; unsung, undeservedly neglected. Usu. postpositive with nouns (sometimes other Fr. rather than Eng. nouns). Cf. POÈTE MAUDIT *n.*

1963 K. WIDMER *Henry Miller* iv. 113 Miller, of course, pours less of his feelings through Oriental love-and-wisdom than through the literary hysterias of Celine, Patchen, and other *prophètes maudits* that he imitates. **1971** 'E. CANDY' *Words for Murder Perhaps* vi. 76 A poet *manqué*—but hardly *maudit*. **1972** *Guardian* 10 May 14/3 The unsurpassed film maudit of this genre is 'The Cabinet of Dr. Caligari', an expressionistic nightmare. **1987** *Financial Times* 6 Nov. I. 21/1 The novelist's 1914 *roman maudit* about homosexuality now gets the treatment. **1991** *Vanity Fair* Sept. 162/3 It was the period when he was working with writer Charles Bukowski, the *maudit* chronicler of marginal lives in American society.

Maunder ('mɔːndə(r)), *n. Astron.* [The name of E. Walter *Maunder* (1851–1928), English astronomer.] **Maunder minimum**, the period of extremely low sunspot activity between about 1645 and 1715, which coincided with the Little Ice Age in the northern hemisphere.

1975 *Nature* 27 Feb. 686/1 A period of almost complete absence of sunspots which occurred from about 1645 to 1715. This 'Maunder minimum' was discovered in the early years of the century. **1980** *Ibid.* 31 Jan. 427/2 Nineteen different *fang chih* contribute 21 previously unknown naked-eye sunspot records from the seventeenth century, of which six fall into the period claimed by Eddy as the time of the Maunder Minimum. **1992** S. P. MARAN *Astron. & Astrophysics Encycl.* 521/1 An extreme example of sunspot influence may be a persistent period of abnormally low temperatures in Europe coincident with a near absence of sunspots in the Maunder Minimum.

maw (mɔː), *n.*[5] *dial.* (chiefly *U.S.*). [Repr. regional pronunc.] = MA *n.* a. Cf. PAW *n.*[4]

1826 A. ROYALL *Sk. Hist., Life, & Manners U.S.* 121 Here too you have the 'paw and maw'. . and 'tote', with a long train of their kindred. *a*1911 D. G. PHILLIPS *Susan Lenox* (1917) I. ix. 154 You'll find some calikers that belonged to maw in a box under the bed in our room. **1925** E. O'NEILL *Desire under Elms* III. ii. 204 'Twas yer Maw's folks aimed t'steal my farm from me. **1942** G. ADE *Let.* 1 Feb. (1973) 228 The little red school-house is a thing of the past but don't forget that it turned out some of our best people, including possibly your paw and maw, and, certainly, your grandparents. **1962** M. RICHLER in R. Weaver *Canad. Short Stories* (1968) 2nd Ser. 177 She rushed up to Mervyn and kissed him. 'Maw just told me.' **1973** 'J. PATRICK' *Glasgow Gang Observed* xii. 108 Benny was a target for their vilest abuse: 'Yir maw does press-ups oan a carrot field.' **1981** *N.Y. Times Mag.* 13 Dec. 16/3 Paw could whop the errant son with Maw out of earshot. **1991** J. KELMAN *Burn* (1992) 150 She's been dead for fifteen years. Fifteen years. A long time without your maw, eh?

max (mæks), *n.*[2], *a.*, and *adv.* [Abbrev. of MAXIMUM *n.*] **A.** *n. colloq.* **1.** *U.S.* At certain colleges, a maximum score or achievement, esp. in an examination; so, a student who has obtained or is likely to obtain such a mark. *rare.*

1851 B. H. HALL *Coll. College Words* 197 At Union College, he who receives the highest possible number of marks. . is said to *take Max* (or maximum); to be a *Max scholar. Ibid.*, On the Merit Roll all the *Maxs* are clustered at the top. **1862** G. C. STRONG *Cadet Life at West Point* 64 [He was] working out an unmistakable 'max' in the mathematical section-room. **1937** K.

BANNING *West Point Today* 296 *Cadet Lingo*. . . *Max, n.*, a complete success in recitation; a maximum mark of 3.0.

2. *gen.* = MAXIMUM *n.* 2; esp. in phr. *to the max*, to the limit, totally. Chiefly *U.S.*

1911 *Chem. Abstr.* iv. 402 This [fact] and the occurrence of the max. are indications of the existence of genuine complexes in solu. **1942** BERREY & VAN DEN BARK *Amer. Thes. Slang* §24/4 *Max and min*, maximum and minimum. **1950** J. D. MACDONALD *Brass Cupcake* iv. 32 The car continued to increase speed. . . I held it at max. . then dropped it back to eighty. **1980** L. BIRNBACH et al. *Official Preppy Handbk.* 223/1 *To the max.*, . . all the way. **1985** R. SCHLEEH in Yeager & Janos *Yeager* (1986) 186 In the sky and on the ground, we lived to the max. **1986** *Daily News* (N.Y.) 23 May (Suppl.) 3/3 An outstanding cast. . consistently get the max from the material. No ragged edges here. **1988** *New Yorker* 18 Jan. 65/1 By about 1973, when we were at our max, the one plant in Ozone Park had four hundred and fifty people.

3. A maximum security prison.

1968 *Current Slang* (Univ. S. Dakota) III. II. 34 *Max, n.*, maximum amount in prison for a narcotics offense; a maximum security prison. **1984** A. F. LOEWENSTEIN *This Place* 1 Max aint no different than here. They both prison aint they? Just more quiet up there. **1990** J. WELCH *Indian Lawyer* 272 He had learned to live in an eight-by-ten cell in the new max.

B. *adj.* **1.** (Usu. with point.) In *attrib.* use (esp. as a written abbrev.): maximum.

1886 *Dict. Abbrevs.* 63 *Max.*, maximum (Latin), highest. **1911** *Chem. Abstr.* IV. 402 The temp. coeff. of viscosity. . increases progressively up to the max. point. **1968** A. DIMENT *Bang Bang Birds* x. 192 It was hot in the cabin even with the heater to max cold. **1985** *Dirt Bike* Mar. 7/1 (Advt.), The ultimate four-stroke exhaust system featuring our exclusive straight-through aluminum silencer for max power throughout the rpm range. **1990** *Family Album Catal.* Spring & Summer 814 (*caption*) Hot and cold fill. 1.95kW max. loading.

2. max q *Aeronaut.*, the maximum dynamic pressure exerted on an aircraft or spacecraft in the course of its flight; also, the part of a flight during which this is encountered.

1962 J. GLENN in *Into Orbit* 190 At T + 1 minute 16 seconds, Al confirmed that I had passed through '*Max. Q*'. **1979** T. WOLFE *Right Stuff* xii. 318 He was entering the area of 'max q', maximum aerodynamic pressure.

C. Hence parenthetically as *adv.* At the maximum, at the most.

1976 *New Yorker* 15 Mar. 86/2 Another two hundred metres out from that L.P., max. **1985** T. O'BRIEN *Nuclear Age* (1986) viii. 147 In a week or two I'd get the hang of it. A month, max. **1991** *U.S. News & World Rep.* 11 Mar. 35/3 Our information can be in the commander's hand in half an hour, max.

max (mæks), *v. U.S. colloq.* [f. *MAX *a.* and *n.*[2]] **a.** *intr.* To achieve or attain a maximum in something, esp. a test of ability or skill (orig. an examination); to reach a limit of performance, endurance, capacity, etc. Usu. const. *out.* Also *trans.* with the area of achievement as obj., or occas. with *it.* **b.** *intr.* with *out.* To serve the full length of a prison sentence.

1871 O. E. WOOD *West Point Scrap Bk.* 339 *To max it*, to make a perfect recitation. **1930** E. COLBY in *Our Army* Feb. 43/2 *Max*, to secure the highest possible grade, or to do a thing perfectly. . . If the instructor can find no fault with your answers to an examination or with your solution of a tactical problem, you are said to 'max' the examination or to 'max' the problem, or perhaps to 'max it cold'. **1937** K. BANNING *West Point Today* 296 *Max, v.*, to make a 3.0 in recitation; to do a thing perfectly. **1971** *Black Scholar* June 53/2 Most of the other brothers here will be maxing out and home before this year is out, or being shipped to other prisons. **1974** *Guidelines to Volunteer Services* (N.Y. State Dept. Correctional Services) 41 *Max out*, complete maximum sentence. **1977** *New Yorker* 24 Oct. 56/3 Only 2.8 per cent 'max out'—serve until the maximum expiration dates of their sentences. *Ibid.* 68/3 Men are paroled from Green Haven, or get out on C.R., or max out. **1980** *Washington Post* 27 Feb. B11/2 In '76 I gave $2,000—I maxed out—and didn't worry about it. **1981** *N.Y. Times* 31 May (Westchester Weekly section) 2/4 'I squat 195 to 200,' Miss Mayers proudly proclaimed of the number of pounds she could lift. 'But I never really maxed on it.' **1982** *Washington Post* 3 Oct. F9/6 Scott has just finished maxing the push-up test at 68, where he was ordered to stop. **1990** *Annapolitan* July 95/1 The message here is that George and Maureen are maxing their sailing season. **1992** *Smithsonian* Jan. 132/2, I maxed out about three months ago, but I still can't get this damned knob off my hip.

maxed (mækst), *ppl. a. U.S. colloq.* [f. *MAX *v.* + -ED[1].] Stretched, extended, etc., to the maximum degree; *spec.* (*a*) exhausted; (*b*) full to capacity. Usu. const. *out*.

1980 *Washington Post* 21 Apr. C3/2 It's been a terrible week. Everybody's maxed out. **1983** *Maledicta 1982* VI. 252 'And your ears are maxed to the onions,' comments the Hood. **1984** *Marathon & Distance Runner* Oct. 16/3 Health problems aside, he was obviously maxed at running 1:44.81 off a 50.50 bell in his semi. **1987** *BMX Plus!* Sept. 43/1 (Advt.), This maxed-out scoot is available in the tropical colors Coral Reef and Tahiti Green. **1991** *N.Y. Times* 10 Nov. 1. 26/5 We've been in a 10-year depression here, and now it's going to get worse...Everyone is maxed out on credit. Everyone is on the edge, and they're just angry.

maxi, *comb. form* and *n.* Add: **b.** In full *maxi boat*, *yacht*, etc. A racing yacht of between approximately 15 and 20 metres in length; the class of such yachts, currently the largest permitted under International Offshore Rule. Usu. *attrib.* orig. and chiefly *Austral.* and *N.Z.*

1974 *Australian* 26 Dec. 6/9 The new Ondine may do to the 'maxi' end of international ocean racing fleets what Dr Jerome Milgram did to the smaller boats with his controversial Cascade. **1975** *Austral. Seacraft* Feb. 28 Maxi boats are anything over 15 m (50 ft) overall. **1977** *National Times* (Austral.) 17 Jan. 36/6 Rose recently crewed aboard Jack Rooklyn's California Cup and Sydney-Hobart maxi-racer Ballyhoo. **1979** J. STURROCK *Classic Racing Yachts Austral. Waters* 144 A special race for visiting maxis over a 40 nautical mile course from Sydney. **1986** *Auckland Star* 7 Feb. A1/1 Yesterday's..maxi racing..was madness. *Ibid.* 1/3 The maxis had lots of attendant spectator boats. *Ibid.*, His warning follows yesterday's..maxi-race in which all six..yachts had near-misses. **1987** *Courier-Mail* (Brisbane) 30 Nov. 13/1 With only a moderate fleet due to contest this year's AWA Sydney-Hobart Yacht race, the maxis again look set to attract the most interest. **1990** *Daily Tel.* (Colour Suppl.) 4 Aug. 39/1 Of the many things for which President Gorbachev has been responsible during his tempestuous five years in power, one of the least likely is the building of an 82-foot aluminium maxi yacht.

maximand ('mæksɪmænd), *n.* Chiefly *Econ.* [f. MAXIM(IZE *v.* + -AND[2].] A quantity which is to be maximized.

1954 *Jrnl. Pol. Econ.* LXII. 147/1 This should be done by taking as the maximand not profits alone but the sum of the profits yielded and the pecuniary external economies created by the investment. **1980** W. A. GALSTON *Justice & Human Good* vii. 281 On this interpretation, Aristotle was an ideal utilitarian, taking the human good as his maximand. **1987** *Amer. Econ. Rev.* LXXVII. 379/2 The maximand reflects the regulator's goal of maximizing the expected level of consumers' surplus. **1991** *Oxf. Econ. Papers* XLIII. 286 For brevity, the ungainly maximand obtained by doing so and using (14) in (13) is omitted.

maximum, *n.* Add: **[5.]** **[b.]** **maximum likelihood** *Statistics*, the highest value attained by a likelihood function as the population parameters vary; freq. used *attrib.* with reference to a method of estimating parameters by maximizing the likelihood or likelihood ratio.

1922 R. A. FISHER in *Phil. Trans. R. Soc.* A. CCXXII. 323 For the solution of problems of estimation we require a method which for each particular problem will lead us automatically to the statistic by which the criterion of sufficiency is satisfied. Such a method is, I believe, provided by the Method of *Maximum Likelihood. **1937** L. H. C. TIPPETT *Methods of Statistics* (ed. 2) iii. 95 The maximum likelihood estimate of σ is found to be the standard deviation. **1976** *Biometrika* LXIII. 438 Table 3 shows the maximum likelihood fits, obtained by iterative search for various choices of x_0. **1990** *Brain* CXIII. 490 A cumulative Gaussian curve was fitted to each set of frequency-of-seeing data by a maximum-likelihood procedure.

Hence '**maximumly** *adv.*

1949 M. MEAD *Male & Female* xiii. 275 Maximumly efficient and pleasant plumbing. **1981** *Christian Science Monitor* 25 Feb. 21/2 Every door and window was maximumly secure.

Maxina (mæk'siːnə), *n.* Also with lower-case initial. [Origin unknown.] A type of ballroom dance in common time, introduced in England in 1917.

1917 *Dancing Times* Sept. 379/2 The dance competition on Thursday was somewhat shorter than usual...The result was: 'Maxina', first certificate: Madame Low Hurndall (London); 'The Jutland', second certificate. **1936** 'R. HYDE' *Passport to Hell* 84 The pre-war dances—..the Maxina, the Valeta. **1949** V. SILVESTER *Old Time Dancing* 80 The Maxina was introduced at a competition for a new dance organised by the British Association of Teachers of Dancing in 1917, and was awarded the first prize. **1977** *N.Z. Herald* 8 Jan. 1-10/4 Bob Cunis' veleta—or should it be maxina?—footwork on his approach at the crease may have originated in 'Bluey's' subsequent footwork on the mat.

mayhem, *n.* Restrict *Old Law* to sense in Dict. and add: **2.** In weakened sense (orig. *U.S.*): violent behaviour, *esp.* physical assault.

1870 'MARK TWAIN' in *Territorial Enterprise* 20 Jan. 1/1 This same man..pantingly threatened me with permanent disfiguring mayhem, if ever again I should introduce his name into print. **1930** *Times* 11 Jan. 9/5 Murderous gang feuds and 'racketeering', a form of business brigandage which makes free use of mayhem [mutilation] and murder, are increasing to an alarming extent in New York and its vicinity. **1949** 'H. ROBBINS' *Dream Merchants* (1950) 89 If Borden had known what was to be done with his picture, he would have committed mayhem. **1952** *Manch. Guardian Weekly* 25 Sept. 5/1 In the United States..'Smena' tells its readers, 'It [*sc.* baseball] is a beastly battle, a bloody fight with mayhem and murder.' **1985** *Mail on Sunday* 3 Mar. (Colour Suppl.) 19/2 *City Heat*, a tale of murder and mayhem. **1992** M. MEDVED *Hollywood vs. Amer.* v. xv. 247 Many titles..contained more than sixty moments of mayhem per hour—or one each minute.

3. Rowdy confusion; chaos, disorder.

1976 *Daily Mirror* 15 Mar. 24/4 (*caption*) Without wishin' to cast nasturtiums on your worm—I feel he's not goin' to make much mayhem today. **1976** *Economist* 20 Mar. 12/1 Thus were the trade unions tacitly egged on..to the inflationary mayhem in 1970-74. **1978** H. CARPENTER *Inklings* I. i. 11 He developed the ability to work at his desk in the middle of domestic mayhem. **1980** *Times* 2 Sept. 17/4 There is a plentiful supply of receptions, cocktail evenings, and general mayhem. **1982** L. CODY *Bad Company* xv. 107 Bernie avoided the scented mayhem of the ground floor at Peter Jones. **1987** R. MANNING *Corridor of Mirrors* xv. 156 The dragon..moors himself in the harbour and creates his usual mayhem. **1989** *Daily Express* 9 Jan. 1/1 It was mayhem on the motorway, which was blocked off to allow emergency services to reach the scene.

Mazahua (məˈzɑːwə), *n.* and *a.* Pl. **Mazahuas.** [Sp.] **a.** (A member of) a Central American Indian people inhabiting an area of Mexico to the north and west of Mexico City. **b.** The language of the Mazahuas; also *attrib.* or as *adj.*

1787 C. CULLEN tr. *Clavigero's Hist. Mexico* I. II. 105 The Mazahuas were once a part of the nation of the Otomies, as the languages of both nations are but different dialects of the same tongue. **1876** G. HENDERSON tr. *A. Garcia Cubas's Republic of Mexico* xix. 121 The Mazahuas, who in the time of the Aztec empire pertained to the kingdom of Tlacopan, and whose dominions were bordered by Michoacan, consist of some 50,000. **1949** E. A. NIDA *Morphol.* (ed. 2) 36 Problem 27 (data from Mazahua, a language of Mexico). **1952** J. R. SWANTON *Indian Tribes N. Amer.* 627 Mazahua, a tribe of the Otomian linguistic family living in the western portion of the state of México and probably occupying some adjoining territory in Michoacán. **1971** A. IWAŃSKA *Purgatory & Utopia* i. 19 Archeologists and historians agree that unlike many other Indian groups now living in Central Mexico, Mazahuas have been among the oldest inhabitants of this territory. **1972** *Language* XLVIII. 847, 6b is given by Hockett for..Bulgarian, Mazahua, Otomi nasal vowels. **1977** T. A. SEBEOK *Native Langs. Americas* II. 146 Otomí has over 180,000 speakers and Mazahua over 84,000.

‖**mazar** (məˈzɑː(r)), *n.* Freq. **Mazar.** [Arab. *mazār* place which one visits, f. *zāra* to visit.] A Muslim tomb, *esp.* one revered as a shrine.

1900 G. BELL *Let.* 4 May (1927) I. vi. 93, I went first to a Mazar close to my tent—a Mazar is generally the tomb of a saint or a sheikh. **1975** *Bangladesh Observer* 27 July 1/2 The Agriculture Minister Mr Abdus Samad and State Minister for Commerce Dewan Farid Gazi placed floral wreaths at the mazar of the deceased. **1979** *Morning News* (Karachi) 24 May 3/4 An exquisite silver embroidered velvet green 'Chadar'..will be flown..from Lahore for laying at the Mazar of Hazrat Khwaja Moeenuddin Chishti. **1988** *Times of India* 23 Feb. 1. 3/6 The Vice-President..today led various dignitaries in offering 'fatiha' to Maulana Abul Kalam Azad at his mazar in Jama Masjid here on his 30th death anniversary.

‖**mbila** (mˈbila), *n.* Pl. **timbila.** [Venda: see *MBIRA *n.*] Any of various types of African xylophone with wooden keys and hollow gourd resonators.

1928 G. P. LESTRADE in A. M. Duggan-Cronin *Bantu Tribes S. Afr.* I. I. PL. xv, The *mbila*, the finest and most perfect of the Venda musical instruments, consists of a number of carved wooden slabs of from three to four inches wide and of various thicknesses, which are beaten with india-rubber hammers by one or two players. **1931** H. A. STAYT *Bavenda* 320 Players of the *mbila* are becoming increasingly rare; formerly every chief had a player in his village. **1934** P. R. KIRBY *Mus. Instruments Native Races S. Afr.* iii. 52 The old maker of my own specimen reduced the price..because, as he said, I was a *mbila* player. **1964** S. MARCUSE *Mus. Instruments* 335/1 The mbila has resonator gourds with spider-web membrane covering a small hole bored in each one, a mirliton device. **1991** P. SWEENEY *Virgin Directory World Mus.* 60 Orchestras of timbila..are still prevalent, usually attached to village or provincial administrations or local political party officials.

‖**mbira** (mˈbira, anglicized əmˈbɪərə), *n.* Also **ambira, mambira.** [Shona (and other Sintu languages of southeastern Africa), f. *-imba* to sing, prob. by metathesis of *rimba* (*limba*) a note. Often confused with the Venda *mbila*.]

1. = *MBILA *n.* rare.
1876 STAINER & BARRETT *Dict. Mus. Terms* 455/1 Zanze...Known also by the names of mambira, ambira, marimba, ibeka, vissandschi, in different parts of Africa. **1901** G. M. THEAL tr. *J. dos Santos's Ethiopia Oriental* in *Rec. S.-E. Afr.* VII. 202 The best and most musical of their instruments is called the *ambira*...It is composed of long gourds..held close together and arranged in order. **1948** *Newslet. Afr. Mus. Soc.* 20 We met a group of musicians, six mbira players...Mr. Tracey got three of the mbiras to be played without their gourd resonators and the other three to be played with resonators.
2. Any of several small hand-held musical instruments of southern Africa, consisting of a series of wooden or metal keys attached to a resonator, with one end of each key free to be plucked with the thumb and forefingers. Cf. SANSA *n.*

1951 H. TRACEY in *Afr. Drum* Apr. 18 The Mbira is the only instrument of quality which is unique and peculiar to Africa alone. It is of small size, being held comfortably between the palms of the hands. **1961** *Afr. Mus.* II. IV. 20 All the instruments of this family of plucked idiophones share the same generic name of *Mbira* within the South Eastern territories of Africa. **1966** *New Yorker* 4 June 27/3 He was making music with a mbira, a kind of African hand-piano. His brother..was accompanying him on a kalimba..which is a modern version of the mbira. **1975** M. HARTMANN *Game for Vultures* iii. 35 From the kraal there came the blurred, repetitive rhythm of an mbira. A penny whistle joined in. **1992** *Option* July–Aug. 111/3 Maraire's voice and mbira, and an African-American gospel choir combine magnificently.

McArdle (məˈkɑːd(ə)l), *n. Path.* [The name of Brian *McArdle* (b. 1911), British physician who identified the disease in 1951 (*Clin. Stud.* X. 13).] **McArdle's disease** or **syndrome**, a rare congenital metabolic disorder in which, owing to the absence of the enzyme phosphorylase, an abnormal storage of glycogen occurs in the muscles, resulting in pain and stiffness associated with exertion, and often leading to weakness and wasting.

1957 LILIENTHAL & ZIERLER in Thompson & King *Biochem. Disorders in Human Dis.* xi. 480 *McArdle's syndrome.* McArdle (1951) described a myopathy attributed to a defect in muscle glycogen breakdown. **1963** *New England Jrnl. Med.* 17 Jan. 136/2 The 2 cases presented appear to constitute a new..variety of skeletal-muscle phosphorylase deficiency..in contrast to previous cases of 'McArdle's disease' with symptoms beginning in childhood. **1982** T. M. DEVLIN *Textbk. Biochem.* vii. 385 Also called type V glycogen storage disease, McArdle's disease is caused by an absence of muscle phosphorylase. **1984** *Tampa Tribune* 5 Apr. 20 A/2 She describes her suffering from McArdle's Syndrome, a rare muscle disease.

McClellan (məˈklɛlən), *n.* Also **M'Clellan,** (*misspelt*) **McLellan.** [The name of George B. *McClellan* (1826–85), U.S. army officer, who invented this type of saddle.] Used *attrib.* with reference to a type of saddle with a wooden leather-covered frame and a high pommel and cantle, long used by the U.S. cavalry. Also *absol.*

1866 J. E. COOKE *Surry* xxii. 83 His saddle was a plain 'McClellan tree' strapped over a red blanket for saddle cloth. **1885** W. D. HOWELLS *Rise S. Lapham* ii. 47 A burly mounted policeman, bulging over the pommel of his M'Clellan saddle, jolted by. **1901** F. NORRIS *Octopus* (1903) I. I. v. 161 In the corners of the room were muddy boots, a McClellan saddle, a surveyor's transit, and empty coal hod, and a box of iron bolts and nuts. **1940** W. VAN T. CLARK *Ox-Bow Incident* ii. 124 He didn't have a stock saddle either, but a little, light McLellan. **1976** V. RANDOLPH *Pissing* *in Snow* lvi. 85 The McClellan is an old-style army saddle, and there ain't no horn on it. **1981** E. HARTLEY-EDWARDS *Country Life Bk. Saddlery & Equipment* 98/3 The earliest McClellan saddles did not have panels.

McCune–Albright (məkjuːn'ɔːlbraɪt), *n. Path.* [The names of Donovan J. *McCune* (b. 1902), U.S. paediatrician, and Fuller *Albright* (see *ALBRIGHT *n.*).] **McCune–Albright('s) syndrome** = *Albright's syndrome* s.v. *ALBRIGHT *n.* a.

1966 *Amer. Jrnl. Dis. Children* CXI. 647/2 Sexual precocity, which forms part of the McCune-Albright syndrome in girls, is rarely noted in boys. **1968** *Jrnl. Pediatrics* LXXIII. 89 The syndrome is now known as McCune-Albright's syndrome or Albright's syndrome. **1993** *Pediatric Radiol.* XXIII. 15/1 McCune-Albright syndrome is characterized by the triad of polyostotic fibrous dysplasia.., skin hyperpigmentation, and precocious puberty.

McGovernite (məˈɡʌvənaɪt), *n.* [f. the name of George *McGovern* (b. 1922), U.S. Democratic politician + -ITE[1].] A supporter of George McGovern or his policies, esp. as candidate in the 1972 U.S. presidential election.

1972 *Guardian* 26 June 1/4 The capture of the [Democratic] party by the McGovernites. **1977** *Time* 11 Apr. 40/1 Onetime McGovernite Warren Beatty observed that somebody ought to put in a good word for Ronald Reagan. **1992** *New Republic* 10 Aug. 42/1 Monday night's boozy reunion of old McGovernites.

McGuffin (məˈɡʌfin), *n. Cinematogr.* Also **MacGuffin**, **Maguffin**, and with lower-case initial(s). [Scottish surname (see MAC *n.*[1]), allegedly borrowed by Alfred Hitchcock (1899-1980), English film director, from a humorous story involving a diversion of this kind: see quot. 1967. Prob. unrelated to GUFFIN *n.*] In a film or work of fiction: a particular event, object, factor, etc., which assumes great significance to the characters and acts as the impetus for the sequence of events depicted, although often proving tangential to the plot as it develops.

1939 A. HITCHCOCK *Lect. at Univ. Columbia* 30 Mar. (Typescript, N.Y. Mus. Mod. Art: Dept. Film & Video) In regard to the tune, we have a name in the studio, and we call it the 'MacGuffin'. It is the mechanical element that usually crops up in any story. In crook stories it is always the necklace and in spy stories it is always the papers. We just try to be a little more original. **1949** *Theatre Arts* May 34/2 An outgrowth of this near-surrealism of detail is what Hitchcock chooses to call the McGuffin. The McGuffin is the gimmick, an object which holds a hidden key to the plot. **1967** F. TRUFFAUT *Hitchcock* vi. 98 [Alfred Hitchcock *loq.*] The theft of secret documents [in Kipling's stories] was the original MacGuffin. So the 'MacGuffin' is the term we use to cover all that sort of thing: to steal plans or documents, or discover a secret, it doesn't matter what it is... You may be wondering where the term originated. It might be a Scottish name, taken from a story about two men in a train. **1980** *Jewish Chron.* 25 Apr. 10/2 In *The Formula* by Steve Shagan..the McGuffin is a method of producing artificial oil that will render OPEC redundant. **1984** *Washington Post* 7 Aug. D6/1 Here is a thriller that transcends the 'maguffin', Alfred Hitchcock's word for the item everybody wants—the plans, the isotope, the negatives, the cipher. **1991** *Flash Art* Jan.-Feb. 121/1 The macguffin is the thing that the spies are after, but the audience doesn't care.

McKenna (məˈkɛnə), *n.* [The name of Reginald *McKenna* (1863-1943), British Liberal politician.] **McKenna duties**, customs duties imposed on imports of 'luxury' items such as

cars by McKenna, then Chancellor of the Exchequer, in his wartime budget of 1915.

1923 *Hansard* (Commons) 12 June 322 In 1913..the total value of the commodities which are now subject to the McKenna duties amounted to £2,600,000 odd. **1949** *Dict. National Biogr.* [Snowden] abolished the protective 'McKenna duties'. **1985** H. OXBURY *Great Britons* 228/1 In his first budget, he..imposed duties on articles such as motor cars, clocks, and watches, which were regarded as luxurious. These, the famous McKenna duties, were intended to be temporary, but they were continued when the war ended.

McKenzie (məˈkɛnzɪ), *n. Law.* Also **MacKenzie**, **Mackenzie**. [The name of the litigants in the case of *McKenzie v. McKenzie*, in which the English Court of Appeal ruled that any party in a trial is entitled to non-professional assistance in court.] A person who attends a trial as a non-professional helper or adviser to a litigant without other legal representation. Also *attrib.* in **McKenzie friend, man**, etc.

[**1970** *All Eng. Law Rep.* III. 1034 McKenzie v McKenzie... Any person, whether he be a professional man or not, may attend a trial as a friend of either party, may take notes, and may quietly make suggestions and give advice to that party.] **1973** *Civil Liberty* July 4/1 Unable to afford lawyer's fees Miss Fogarty enlisted the services of a McKenzie. **1974** *Observer* 15 Sept. 22/3 A defendant may have a friend beside him..to give moral support, take notes, and generally give a helping hand. Known as McKenzie men.., these helpers can be either lay or legally qualified people. **1979** *Internat. Jrnl. Sociol. of Law* Feb. 115 The Centre should adopt a more aggressive role by developing the legal competence of clients..by encouraging the use of MacKenzie men, and by demystifying the law. **1982** J. PRITCHARD *Penguin Guide to Law* lix. 871 Every DIY litigant should..exercise his right to have a McKenzie man. **1990** *Daily Tel.* 24 July 2/5 Mr Dave Nellist, MP for Coventry, said he intended to appear before Coventry magistrates as a 'McKenzie friend'.

McKinley (məˈkɪnlɪ), *n. U.S. Econ.* Also **M'Kinley**. [The name of William *McKinley* (1843-1901), U.S. Republican politician, Governor of Ohio 1892-96, and President of the United States 1897-1901, who sponsored the legislation.] **McKinley tariff**, a name given to the legislation sponsored by McKinley and enacted in 1890, creating a protective tariff notable for the high duties it imposed; the tariff itself.

1890 *Times* 3 Oct. 7/1 The blow aimed at British industry by the M'Kinley Tariff is an entirely unprovoked act of unfriendliness. **1916** *Economist* 4 Mar. 460/1 The Morrill tariff introduced by the United States in 1881..was gradually developed into the McKinley Tariff, which was Protection naked and unashamed. **1967** J. M. ROBERTS *Europe 1880-1945* ii. 42 It took the McKinley tariff in the U.S.A. and the enormous Russian protective duties to convert the German rulers to protection for their manufacturers.

McMahon (məkˈmɑːn), *n.* [The name of Sir (Arthur) Henry *McMahon* (1862-1949), British foreign secretary to the government of India and commissioner at the Simla Conference.] **McMahon line**, a line proposed by the British under Sir Henry McMahon at the Simla Conference (1913-14) as the frontier between Tibet and the North East Frontier Agency.

The demarcation was accepted by Tibet, but not recognized by China.

1936 O. CAROE *Let.* 6 Feb. in P. Mehra *McMahon Line & After* (1974) xxxv. 422 The whole of the hill country upto the 1914 McMahon Line is within the frontier of India. **1950** J. NEHRU *Let.* 17 Nov. in *Lett. to Chief Ministers* (1986) 268 About our frontier, the MacMahon [*sic*] Line, we are adamant and we are not going to tolerate any breach of it. **1962** E. SNOW *Other Side of River* (1963) lxxvii. 589 The agreement would also have settled the Indo-Tibetan border on the basis of the so-called McMahon line. **1991** *Hindu* (Madras) 6 Dec. 8/6 Beijing has accepted the highest watershed principle—that forms the basis of the McMahon Line signed by British India and independent Tibet—with both Nepal and Burma.

me, *pers. pron.*[1] Add: [**I.**] [**6.**] [a.] Also in *W. Indies* use.

1918 E. C. PARSONS *Folk-Tales of Andros I., Bahamas* (Mem. Amer. Folklore Soc. XIII) 36 Me no tiger. **1943** in Cassidy & Le Page *Dict. Jamaican Eng.* (1967) 298/1 *Migarn,* I am going. **1966** D. J. CROWLEY *I could talk Old-Story Good* 53 And me go down. **1977** *Westindian World* 3–9 June 4/1 All me can say is that all dis revelation come too late, from days gone when me use fe tek me home work back to school. **1981** *Ibid.* 31 July 4/1 (*heading*) Me hear dem say. **1986** B. GILROY *Frangipani House* iii. 11 We all have cross to bear. You got. Me got.

mean, *v.*[1] Senses 3 b, c in Dict. become 3 c, d. Sense 7 in Dict. becomes 8. Add: [**1.**] **g.** *you don't mean to say* (or *to tell me*), etc. (with following clause referring to the person addressed): expressing the speaker's surprise or scepticism at the conclusion in the following clause. Also with other speech act verbs. *do you mean to say* (or *to tell me*): used similarly, but inviting confirmation more strongly. *colloq.*

1838 DICKENS *Nicholas Nickleby* (1839) xix. 181 Do you mean to tell me that your pretty niece was not brought here as a decoy..? **1839** *Ibid.* xxix. 288 Why, he don't mean to say he's going!.. Hoity toity! nonsense. **1841** —— *Barnaby Rudge* xxxix, in *Master Humphrey's Clock* III. 163 You don't mean to say their old wearers are all dead, I hope?' said Mr. Tappertit, falling a little distance from him, as he spoke. 'Every one of 'em.' **1885** 'E. GARRETT' *At Any Cost* ii. 34 You don't mean to tell me that those outlandish old things are still in actual use? **1899** R. BROUGHTON *Game & Candle* 129 You do not mean to imply..that Mrs. Grundy is going to interpose between you and me? **1908** L. M. MONTGOMERY *Anne of Green Gables* xx. 230 Anne Shirley, do you mean to tell me you believe all that wicked nonsense of your own imagination? **1929** M. CALLAGHAN in Atwood & Weaver *Oxf. Bk. Canad. Short Stories* (1988) 56 You mean to say you never step out? **1986** F. PERETTI *This Present Darkness* ix. 87 Do you mean to say you've uncovered something new?

h. *I mean to say*: used parenthetically or as an exclamation, usu. to emphasize the speaker's sincerity or concern. *Brit. colloq.*

1923 WODEHOUSE *Inimitable Jeeves* i. 7 So dashed competent in every respect. I've said it before, and I'll say it again. I mean to say, take just one small instance. **1963** D. LESSING *Man & Two Women* 141, I mean to say, you've got to take the rough with the smooth. **1984** B. MACLAVERTY *Cal* 96 I've a good mind to pay you off here and now...I mean to say, you're working here a fortnight and you break into our property and scare the living daylights out of us. **1991** M. KILBY *Man at Sharp End* 261 'Well it's fairly obvious that you can't go back to the plant, innit?' agreed his platinum blonde flatmate Deirdre. 'Well I mean to say..it stands to reason like..don't it?' she added.

[**2.**] **d.** To be in earnest in saying; esp. in *to mean what one says*, to speak truthfully, sincerely, or with determination; *to mean it*, to be in earnest regarding one's words or (*transf.*) actions.

1749 FIELDING *Tom Jones* II. v. vi. 164 Pardon me if I have said anything to offend you. I did not mean

it. **1840** J. H. NEWMAN *Parochial Sermons* V. iii. 51 Let us aim at meaning what we say, and saying what we mean. **1854** DICKENS *Hard T.* II. viii. 213 'The Bank's robbed!' '*You don't mean it!*' **1876** H. JAMES *Roderick Hudson* III. xi. 398, I was unkind yesterday, without meaning it. **1906** R. E. KNOWLES *Undertow* xxiii. 299 'What do you mean, Hiram?'.. 'I mean what I say.' **1908** L. M. MONTGOMERY *Anne of Green Gables* xiii. 126 When I tell you to come in at a certain time I mean that time and not half an hour later. **1925** F. SCOTT FITZGERALD *Great Gatsby* vi. 124 'I mean it,' she insisted. 'I'd love to have you. Lots of room.' **1952** E. O'NEILL *Moon for Misbegotten* I. 65 It's good to hear him laugh as if he meant it. **1973** J. WAINWRIGHT *Pride of Pigs* 158 It was a very *special* room...Fireproof. And I *mean* fire-proof. Built to contain a furnace. **1987** 'A. T. ELLIS' *Clothes in Wardrobe* 76 He still listened, but now..not believing that I meant what I said.

e. The phr. *I mean* used parenthetically in speech has in some cases lost the function of introducing an explanation or expansion of what has already been said, and become a conversational filler.

1892 I. ZANGWILL *Childr. Ghetto* I. 223 Tank Gawd! I mean, can I see him? **1938** N. MARSH *Artists in Crime* ix. 122, I mean, it was only *once* ages ago, after a party, and I mean I think men and women ought to be free to follow their sex-impulses anyway. **1951** J. D. SALINGER *Catcher in Rye* xi. 92, I knew her like a book. I really did. I mean, besides checkers, she was quite fond of all athletic sports. **1972** G. CHAPMAN et al. *Monty Python's Flying Circus* (1989) II. xxvii. 50 Well I mean a lot of these things that are happening, well they just don't quite ring true. **1988** J. MCINERNEY *Story of my Life* iv. 56 Hey, I go, I'm just being realistic. I mean, really. I'm trying to tell her what life is really like. **1992** L. WOIDWODE *Indian Affairs* vi. 120 You know, like, uh, hey, man, I mean, cool, huh?

[**3.**] **b.** To require, entail, necessitate; to produce as an effect or result.

1841 E. MIALL in *Nonconformist* I. 228 Protection means shutting out the best chapman and the best food. **1851** *Tait's Mag.* XXI. 490 Resurgent Poland, he says, means resurgent Hungary, and even resurgent Italy. **1894** *Times* 5 Feb. 8/2 That would mean taking up all the streets in South London. **1927** *Passing Show* Summer 23/3 Kendal Brown, sorrowfully realising that this would mean a lifer for Bristola Birdseye, ducked his head. **1958** R. NARAYAN *Guide* i. 5 It'd have meant walking home at nearly midnight. **1978** G. GREENE *Human Factor* I. iii. 43 A suicide always means an inquest, and that might lead to a question in the House. **1985** 'J. HIGGINS' *Confessional* (1986) viii. 137 His arm..really needed stitching, but to go to the hospital would have meant questions. **1994** *Maclean's* 17 Oct. 12/1 A third option would be to sharpen the targeting of the child tax benefit, but that would mean less money going to middle-income Canadians.

7. pass. Const. *to* with infin. To be reputed, considered, said (to be). Cf. SUPPOSE *v.* 8 d.

1878 R. SIMPSON *School of Shakspere* I. 34 It is confessed that Hawkins and Cobham were meant to be buccaneers, and it is absurd to deny the like of Stucley. **1945** *Queen* 18 Apr. 17/1 'Such and such a play,' they [*sc.* my children] will say, 'is meant to be jolly good.' **1972** *Listener* 9 Mar. 310/1 America..is meant to be a great melting-pot. **1988** *Sunday Tel.* (Colour Suppl.) 25 Sept. 10/1 Even in normal times, there's one rider who is meant to make £500 a week. **1989** *Times* 30 Mar. 15/1 It [*sc.* evening primrose oil] is also meant to be good for arthritis.

measurable, *a.* Add: [**3.**] **d.** *Math.* [ad. F. *mesurable* (E. Borel *Leçons sur la Théorie des Fonctions* (1898) iii. 46).] Of a set: having a defined measure (*MEASURE n.* 2 g). Of a real-valued function *f*: such that for any real number *a* the set of all *x* for which $f(x) > a$ is measurable.

1905 *Phil. Trans. R. Soc.* A. CCIV. 243 Let the fundamental set be divided into measurable components in any conceivable way, and let the content of each component be multiplied by the upper (lower) limit of the values of the function at points of that component, and the sum of all such products be formed; then the outer (inner) measure of the integral is defined to be the lower (upper) limit of all such summations. **1906** W. H. & G. C. YOUNG *Theory of Sets of Points* xii. 260 The points at which $X(x) \geqslant k$ form a measurable set. **1968** P. A. P. MORAN *Introd. Probability Theory* iv. 199 From now on we choose a definite σ-field of sets, B, in the space R and since we shall later associate with it a σ-additive measure, we call a set 'measurable' if and only if it belongs to the σ-field B. **1986** *Nonlinear Analysis* X. 1160 $C(\cdot)$ is a measurable, closed-valued multifunction from $[a\text{-}\nabla, a]$ to $\mathbb{R}^n$.

measure, *n.* Add: [2.] **g.** *Math.* [ad. F. *mesure* (E. Borel *Leçons sur la Théorie des Fonctions* (1898) iii. 46; H. Lebesgue 1902, in *Annali di Matematica* VII. 236).] A non-negative number assigned to a set of points in a metric space as an evaluation of its content and for comparison with that of other sets, analogous to the area of a plane figure or the volume of a solid figure, and generalized to spaces of any dimension in such a way that the number assigned to the union of disjoint sets is equal to the sum of the numbers assigned to each individual set.
1905 *Phil. Trans. R. Soc.* A. CCIV. 243 Let the fundamental set be divided into measurable components in any conceivable way, and let the content of each component be multiplied by the upper (lower) limit of the values of the function at points of that component, and the sum of all such products be formed; then the outer (inner) measure of the integral is defined to be the lower (upper) limit of all such summations. **1908** *Trans. Amer. Math. Soc.* IX. 237 Lebesgue's theory of integration is based on the notion of the measure of a set of points, a notion introduced by Borel and subsequently refined by Lebesgue himself. **1929** *Encycl. Brit.* XVIII. 117/2 If we are given two intervals which have no point in common, it is not natural to speak of the length of the set of points which they represent...In this case we shall use the word 'measure'. **1954** L. J. SAVAGE *Found. Statistics* iii. 33 A probability measure on a set S is a function $P(B)$ attaching to each $B \subset S$ a real number such that: 1. $P(B) > 0$ for every B. 2. If $B \cap C = 0$, $P(B \cup C) = P(B) + P(C)$. 3. $P(S) = 1$. **1968** E. T. COPSON *Metric Spaces* ix. 141 We do not distinguish between two equivalent functions, two functions which differ only on a set of zero measure. **1976** *Sci. Amer.* July 92/2 Similarly, a two-dimensional measure is a function that assigns to each set a number called its area. **1980** Y. N. MOSCHOVAKIS *Descriptive Set Theory* ii. 111 Prove that the σ-ideal $Z\mu$ of sets of measure D is regular from above relative to the Borel sets. **1985** *Ann. Probability* XIII. 1051 Let μ_1, μ_2 be finitely additive measures on $(D, \mathcal{D})$ where $\mathcal{D}$ is a field on D. Then μ_1 is said to be absolutely continuous wrt [*sc.* with respect to] μ_2 if [etc.].

meat, *n.* Sense 3 f in Dict. becomes 3 g. Add: [3.] **f.** The substance of one's body; flesh; fat. *colloq.* (orig. *U.S.*).
1829 P. EGAN *Boxiana* 2nd Ser. I. 702 Both men, on *peeling*, seemed *prime meat*. **1834** W. A. CARUTHERS *Kentuckian in N.Y.* I. 27 If I hadn't had so many inches, he'd have been into my meat. **1847** J. S. ROBB *Streaks of Squatter Life* 59 Old Tom Jones' *yell*..gives my meat a slight sprinklin' of ager whenever I think on it. **1906** J. LONDON in *Woman's Home Compan.* Sept. 7/3 Nothing the matter with him...Badly debilitated, that's all. Not much meat on his bones. **1965** F. O'CONNOR *Everything that Rises* 226 He liked women with meat on them, so you didn't feel their muscles, much less their old bones. **1978** S.

BRILL *Teamsters* viii. 300 There was a lot of meat on his chest that hadn't yet dropped to his paunch.

mechanic, *a.* and *n.* Add: [B.] [2.] **e.** A hired killer. *slang.*
1973 W. P. MCGIVERN *Reprisal* (1974) 163 There's somebody looking for me. A mechanic name of Nick Lye...That's what the Syndicate calls an executioner. **1986** J. GARDNER *Nobody lives Forever* iv. 37 Bernie Brazier was Britain's top mechanic, a polite name for a hired killer. **1986** J. WAINWRIGHT *Portrait in Shadows* xi. 98 Three hit men — icemen, mechanics, what the hell the present slang calls them.

mechanize, *v.* Add: [1.] **b.** Also *absol.* or *intr.* To introduce machinery or mechanization into an industry, etc.
1976 *New Society* 10 June 562/3 But the labour intensive character of the Post Office could be reduced with a more zealous drive to mechanise. **1989** P. DANIEL in Wilson & Ferris *Encycl. Southern Culture* 49/1 Only in the 1960s did the flue-cured tobacco culture mechanize to any extent.

mechanosensitive (ˌmɛkənəʊˈsɛnsɪtɪv), *a. Biol.* [f. MECHANO- + SENSITIVE *a.*] Responsive to mechanical stimuli.
1959 *Nature* 20 June 1726/2 The receptor membrane of a mechano-sensitive nerve ending resembles..the postsynaptic membrane of skeletal muscle. **1976** *Pain* II. 5 The remaining 11 units could, in addition, be excited by sensitive cutaneous mechanosensitive afferent units. **1990** *Biophysical Jrnl.* Feb. 320a/1 The activities of the large-conductance mechanosensitive channel reported in wild-type *E. coli* spheroplasts..were studied in excised inside-out patches from these mutant cells.
Hence ˌmechanosensiˈtivity *n.*
1976 *Jrnl. Physiol.* CCLVI. 551 The mechanosensitivity of this afferent pathway can be modulated by noradrenergic hormones. **1978** *Nature* 1 June 377/2 In the analogous lateral line organ of submammalian species, the mechanosensitivity of the hair cells is related directly to the external calcium concentration at their specialised receptor poles.

mechatronics (mɛkəˈtrɒnɪks), *n. pl.* (const. as *sing.*). *Engin.* Also **mecha-tronics**. [f. MECHA(NICS *n.* + ELEC)TRONICS *n.*] The branch of technology which combines mechanical engineering and electronics. Used chiefly with reference to Japan.
1982 *Daily Tel.* 12 Feb. 16/6 The Japanese, who lead the world in what they call 'methatronics' [*sic*], are developing such skilled robots that the large, tribal-like firms..are bound to shed men. **1982** *Ibid.* 16 Aug. 11/8 Combining elements of mechanics and electronics advanced enough to be termed mecha-tronics, Hitachi's system is accurate to ±0.01 micron! **1984** *Bulletin* (Sydney) 23 Oct. 25 (Advt.), This has all been made possible because of Epson's specialisation in 'mechatronics' — the art of combining precise mechanical and electronic technologies. **1986** *Times* 20 May 32/7 An unattended operation requires the construction of a computer control system and the introduction of technology related to mechatronics and robots. **1991** *New Scientist* 26 Jan. 48/1 (Advt.), Advancements and applications of mechatronics design in textile engineering.

mecholyl (ˈmɛkəlaɪl, ˈmɛkəlɪl), *n. Pharm.* Also †**Mecholyl**. [f. ME(THYL *n.* + CHOL(INE *n.* + -YL.] = *METHACHOLINE *n.*
1934 *Official Gaz.* (U.S. Patent Office) 28 Aug. 789/1 Mecholyl. **1938** *Amer. Jrnl. Med. Sci.* CXCV. 88 The drugs selected for study have been ancetyl-beta-methylcholine chloride (mecholyl), benzedrine sulphate, atropine, and prostigmin, a drug related to physostigmin. **1946** *Jrnl. Pharmacol. & Exper. Therap.* LXXXVII. 31 A range of doses of eleven

parasympathomimetic drugs (acetylcholine, mecholyl, [etc.]..) was administered subcutaneously. **1952** H. BECKMAN *Pharmacol. in Clin. Pract.* 119 Chief representatives of this group of 'parasympathomimetic' (parasympathetic-stimulating) agents are Mecholyl [etc.]. **1987** *Oxf. Textbk. Med.* (ed. 2) II. xx. 61/2 Intradermal injection of mecholyl (10 μg/0.5 ml saline) reproduces the lesions of cholinergic urticaria.

Meckel's diverticulum (ˈmɛkəlz daɪvəˈtɪkjʊləm), *n. Anat.* and *Path.* [f. the name of the younger J. F. *Meckel* (see MECKELIAN *a.*).]
a. A sacciform remnant of the vitello-intestinal duct found in some individuals, situated in the ileum about one metre from the iliocaecal valve.
b. Any of several pathological conditions associated with this.
1849 E. SIEVEKING tr. Rokitansky *Man. Path. Anat.* II. 1. i. 46 Meckel's diverticulum verum.. is a dilatation of the small intestine, representing a hollow appendix. **1876** *Jrnl. Anat. & Physiol.* X. 617 (*heading*) Note on an example of Meckel's diverticulum. **1890** E. OWEN *Man. Anat. for Senior Students* iv. 325 A special outgrowth, Meckel's diverticulum, is found about 2 ft. above the ileo-cæcal valve. **1961** R. D. BAKER *Essent. Path.* xvi. 399 Meckel's diverticulum is a remnant of the omphalomesenteric duct. **1975** C. C. ROY et al. *Pediatric Clin. Gastroenterol.* (ed. 2) v. 130/2 The infant or young child who has a massive, painless bout of bright red or dark red rectal bleeding most likely has Meckel's diverticulum. **1977** *Lancet* 16 July 145/2 At operation 18 cm of dilated plum-coloured small bowel was removed together with a Meckel's diverticulum. **1987** *Oxf. Textbk. Med.* (ed. 2) I. xII. 143/2 The use of this technique should lead to an earlier and more accurate diagnosis of Meckel's diverticulum.

medallion, *n.* Add: [**2.**] **b.** *Cookery.* = MÉDAILLON *n.*
1907 G. A. ESCOFFIER *Guide Mod. Cookery* II. xvi. 538 Set a medallion on each roundel of *mousse*.. and arrange the medallion prepared in this way on a square dish. **1969** H.-P. PELLAPRAT *Everyday Fr. Cooking for Amer. Home* 156, 8 medallions of pork cut from the fillet, each weighing about 2 oz. **1972** Y. MALEY in G. W. Turner *Good Austral. Eng.* iv. 77 In frypan, saute drained medallions gently in hot olive oil for 10 minutes on each side, until golden brown. **1988** *Observer* (Colour Suppl.) 17 Jan. 51/1 Venison may be sold as medallions, bone-free. **1991** *Food & Wine* Apr. 20/1 Next came rich intensely flavored pork medallions with *girolle* mushrooms and a puree of celeriac and parsnip.

c. *U.S.* A licence to operate a taxi in a city or particular locality, usu. issued in the form of a small metal plaque fastened to the hood or bonnet.
1960 *N.Y. Times* 4 June 47/3 'Bootleg', or illegal cabs do not have medallions. **1970** *New Yorker* 26 Sept. 56/1 A government contract is awarded to the bidder who will best serve the government's interest... The theory is extended to taxicab medallions and turnpike concessions. **1977** *Time* 29 Aug. 47/1 That is about $8,000 more than the price of a medallion to operate a taxi on the streets outside the exchange.

medfly (ˈmɛdflaɪ), *n. Agric.* (chiefly *U.S.*). Also **Medfly.** [f. MED *n.²* + FLY *n.¹*] = *Mediterranean fruit-fly* s.v. *MEDITERRANEAN n.* 1 b.
1956 *Time* 18 June 71/1 Southern Florida was in something like a state of emergency last week... Cause of the uproar: the Mediterranean fruit fly... The 'Medfly' is no laughing matter. Its last visit in 1929 cost millions. **1969** *Bull. Atomic Sci.* XXV. 34/2 The millions of dollars in damage caused by the Mediterranean fruit fly or medfly. **1981** *Business Week* 19 Jan. 34/1 After months of haphazard attempts to thwart the pest, commonly called the medfly, California governor Edmund G. Brown Jr. declared a state of emergency on Christmas Eve. **1990** *Time* 8 Jan. 51/3

An ecoterrorist organization.. which claimed to be breeding and releasing its own medflies.

media, *n.² pl.* Add: **2.** Special Comb. **media studies** *n. pl.* (freq. const. *sing.*; also occas. found in the *sing.* form), analysis or study of the mass media.
1968 *Audiovisual Instruction* Jan. 12/2 Experience gained in the nascent film study and screen education programs can provide guidelines for *media study, which is actually an extension and coordination of these programs and of existing programs in literature, the arts, and the humanities. **1975** *Times Educ. Suppl.* 4 Apr. 54 (*heading*) Stephen Thomas and Brian Thomas on introducing media studies into primary schools. **1977** *Gay News* 24 Mar. 23/2 Dennis.. went to the University of Massachusetts, where he received a BA in media studies. **1994** *Daily Tel.* 27 Aug. 15/4 It has been an uphill struggle to persuade universities to accept entrants with A-level subjects such as media studies.

mediagenic (ˌmiːdɪəˈdʒɛnɪk), *a.* orig. *U.S.* [f. MEDIA *n.² pl.* + -GENIC b, after PHOTOGENIC *a.*] Of a person, subject, etc.: popular with the mass media or their audiences, media-friendly; creating a favourable impression when presented in the media. Cf. TELEGENIC *a.*
1973 *Britannica Bk. of Year* (U.S.) 732/2 *Mediagenic, adj.*, likely to appeal to the audiences of the mass media and especially television. **1978** *N.Y. Times* 8 Jan. IV. 6/1 Carol Bellamy, the new City Council President and the first woman elected to citywide office in New York, moved into City Hall last week, and while she was overshadowed by the mediagenic new Mayor, she served notice that she expected to get some attention of her own. **1986** *Internat. Business Week* 26 May 9/1 Gorbachev is.. mediagenic. **1987** *New Internationalist* May 8/3 The trade-off between 'mediagenic' short-term actions and long-term movement-building does not have to be so direct—one can complement the other. **1991** *Time* 17 June 77/1 Aaron.. spent much of his career overshadowed by mediagenic players.. like Mickey Mantle.

median, *a.¹* and *n.¹* Add: [**B.**] **5.** = *median strip*, sense A. 1 b above. *U.S.*
1944 *Policy on Grade Separations for Intersecting Highways* (Amer. Assoc. State Highway Officials) 36 It is practicable to span four lanes and a narrow median without a central pier. **1976** *N.Y. Times* 25 Sept. 18 There is much.. benefit to be gained by refashioning the old highway into a promenade with a grass median bracketed by bicycle lanes. **1985** *New Yorker* 18 Nov. 49/1, I take a corner too fast, bump into a curb, then bounce up on the median. **1992** *Albuquerque* (New Mexico) *Jrnl.* 27 Dec. A5/5 A state Highway Department fence in the median prevented him from crossing over.

mediastino-, *comb. form.* Add: **mediasti-ˈnoscopy** *Med.*, the visual examination of the mediastinum through an incision.
1959 *Dis. Chest* XXXVI. 348 The operability of the tumor was questioned, but to permit more detailed investigation of the nature of the mediastinal change *mediastinoscopy was done. **1979** L. SHAINBERG *Brain Surgeon* (1980) vi. 154 Just a note concerning Mrs. Mannes, who underwent mediastinoscopy.
mediastiˈnotomy *Surg.*, incision of the mediastinum; an instance of this.
1903 *Therapeutic Gaz.* Jan. 59/1 In such cases esophagotomy is indicated, if the foreign body is situated no deeper than 24 to 26 centimeters from the upper incision; if deeper, gastrotomy or posterior *mediastinotomy is called for. **1987** *Arch. Surg.* CXXII. 1352/1 Occult thymomas were accessible through the transcervical approach, with some operations necessitating a complementary mediastinotomy.

Medibank ('mɛdɪbæŋk), *n.* Now *Hist.* [f. MEDI(CAL *a.* + BANK *n.*[3]] A national scheme of health insurance which operated in Australia between 1974 and 1978. Freq. *attrib.*
1975 *Facts on File* 22 Mar. 184/3 Social Security Minister William Hayden said March 16 that the cost of the federal government's Medibank health program would total about $A1.4 billion in the next fiscal year. **1975** *Courier-Mail* (Brisbane) 24 May 9/5 After July 1, the cards will identify pensioners as patients eligible for free medical and optometrical services under Medibank. **1976** *Lancet* 30 Oct. 952/2 Under Medibank, introduced by the late Labour Government, free accommodation and treatment in public (State-supported) hospitals was available in all States for anyone who desired it. **1979** *Ann. Reg. 1978* 308 The federal commitment to public health expenditure was reduced by finally abolishing the already much modified Medibank system for paying hospital and medical accounts.., and with it any compulsion to carry health insurance or an equivalent payment to government. **1984** *Financial Times* 3 Feb. 4/4 The Health Minister.. added that many Labor supporters 'bitterly resented the (former) Fraser Government's complete dismantling of all the programmes of the Whitlam years, especially those like Medibank (Medicare's predecessor)'.

medicalize ('mɛdɪkəlaɪz), *v.* [f. MEDICAL *a.* and *n.* + -IZE: cf. F. *médicaliser.*] *trans.* To give a medical character to; to involve medicine or medical workers in; to view or interpret in (esp. unnecessarily) medical terms.
1970 [implied in **medicalized* ppl. a. below]. **1975** I. ILLICH *Med. Nemesis* ii. 47 The public acceptance of iatrogenic labelling multiplies patients faster than either doctors or drugs can medicalize them. **1976** — *Limits to Med.* 83 She will thus be marginally medicalized by two sets of institutions, the one designed to socialize her among the blind, the other to medicalize her decrepitude. **1979** *Daily Mail* 27 Jan. 7/7 The drug industry, the Government, the chemist, the taxpayer and the doctor all have vested interests in 'medicalising' problems that should not really belong in the sphere of medicine at all. **1984** *Observer* 2 Sept. 16/3 Changing an individual's personality is not the business of psychological medicine. But not only is it wrong to medicalise the issue. It is also wrong to make demands for a group tiny in size. **1991** G. GREER *Change* 3 This is one book that seeks neither to trivialize nor to medicalize the menopause.
So **'medicalized** *ppl. a.*; **medicali'zation** *n.*
1970 *New Eng. Jrnl. Med.* 24 Sept. 709/1 (*heading*) 'Medicalized' sex. *Ibid.*, Sexually active teen-age girls have a physical examination by a pediatrician, a pelvic examination by a gynecologist, a blood count, urinalysis.. followed by home visits... Such an effort.. represents a 'medicalization' of sex that is probably self-defeating. **1977** *Spare Rib* June 45/3 A female profession up against the male medicalisation of birth. **1983** J. N. KATZ *Gay/Lesbian Almanac* 156 The medicalization of 'sexual inversion' meant that many individuals internalized a new 'scientific' negation, becoming the social agents of their own self-denial. **1991** S. FALUDI *Backlash* ii. viii. 203 Beauty became medicalized as its lab-coated army of promoters.. prescribed physician-endorsed potions.

medication, *n.* Add: **3.** A drug or drugs prescribed or given as medical treatment.
1934 in WEBSTER. **1955** B. SPOCK *Baby & Child Care* 35 The doctor may recommend some medication to apply after nursing. **1965** *Illinois Med. Jrnl.* CXXVIII. 414/1 Resistance to anticonvulsant medications. **1983** J. HENNESSY *Torvill & Dean* 28 Chris had taken little or no medication, because of the fear of becoming ensnared in a drug test. **1987** *My Weekly* 21 Feb. 28/2 The patients at Burford can take their own medication. **1994** *Health Naturally* (Nobel, Ont.) Feb.–Mar. 12/1 The most common medications

prescribed for pain are aspirin and other nonsteroidal anti-inflammatory drugs.

medieval, *a.* and *n.* Add: [A.] **c.** Showing the severity or illiberality ascribed to a former age; cruel, barbarous. *colloq.*
[**1883** *Mem. Vol. Rev. A. Maclean* 231 A curious mixture of mediæval rigidity and modern spasmodism.] **1917** *Church Times* 26 Oct. 335/4 When military officers inflict upon him cruelties almost mediæval, our sympathy goes with him. **1954** T. LEHRER *I wanna go back to Dixie* (song) in *Tom Lehrer Song Bk.* 19 The land of the boll weevil, Where the laws are medieval, Is callin' me to come And never more roam. **1963** M. McCARTHY *Group* xiv. 330 It was medieval of Macy's to fire her because she'd had a breakdown. **1979** P. THEROUX *Old Patagonian Express* (1980) vi. 122 The medieval sight of small children binding up bouquets of flowers with bleeding fingers and being shouted at by cruel old men. **1982** A. N. WILSON *Wise Virgin* (1984) viii. 162 They're trying to give Piers the sack... For driving a motor-car, for God'sake. I mean, it's medieval. **1988** *Financial Times* 8 June 1. 44/3 He stressed he was not seeking vengeance or punishment but a deterrent. Hanging was 'medieval and barbaric' and there were more humane methods. **1994** Q. TARANTINO *Pulp Fiction* 131, I ain't through with you by a damn sight. I'm gonna git Medieval on your ass.

mediocracy (miːdɪ'ɒkrəsɪ), *n.* [Blend of MEDIOCRE *a.* and *n.* and -OCRACY.] Government by the mediocre; a system within which mediocrity is rewarded.
1909 *Daily Chron.* 12 July 4/4 We are all at heart agreed upon one political creed. This is that the only really adequate form of government is a 'mediocracy'... We are happy in our firm belief that.. the greatness of the British Empire rests.. upon the mediocrity of the middle-classes. **1937** D. JERROLD *Georgian Adventure* iv. 124 A professional officer corps.. reinforcing itself from a mediocracy of successful careerists and yes-men. **1972** H. J. EYSENCK *Psychol. is about People* iv. 198 The conscious cultivation of a mediocracy, in which the bright, the original, the innovators, the geniuses are held back in order to spare the mediocre the spectacle of outstanding success is to me an abomination. **1984** A. HEARNDEN *Red Robert* xiv. 254 He had a sharp eye for the point at which a meritocracy becomes a mediocracy. **1990** I. MacDONALD *New Shostakovich* (1991) vii. 233 He was simply furious with the Soviet mediocracy and the morally rotten art it brandished as exemplary.
So **'mediocrat** *n.*
1909 *Daily Chron.* 12 July 4/4 Our style and title is 'The Mediocrats', and our aim may be expressed in a sentence as the promotion, by every means within our members' power, of the great principle of mediocrity. **1928** N. BARTLEY (*title*) The mediocrat. **1995** *Daily Tel.* 16 Jan. 21/6 The cult of mediocrity or 'classlessness' has spread to every aspect of public administration and most areas of industry and commerce. The only thing these mediocrats are good at is keeping better candidates out.

Mediterranean, *a.* and *n.* Add: [B.] [1.] [b.] **Mediterranean fruit-fly**, a fruit-fly, *Ceratitis capitata*, whose larvae cause considerable damage to citrus fruit.
1899 *Agric. Gaz. New South Wales* X. 497 All the specimens bred at this office have been the Western or Mediterranean Fruit-fly (*Halterophora capitata*)... This is quite a modern importation. In 1897 it was discovered in orchards near Perth, Western Australia... Though unknown previous to this in the Colonies, it had a well known record in Europe as far back as 1826, when it was described by Wiedman [*recte* Wiedemann] as an orange pest under the name of *Citriperda capitata.* **1912** *Circular U.S. Dept. Agric. Bureau of Entomol.* No. 160. 1 The recent establishment in Hawaii of the Mediterranean fruit-fly.. and the

quarantine restrictions against Hawaiian fruit imposed by the State of California have aroused considerable interest in this very destructive insect. **1923** *Jrnl. Agric. Res.* XXV. 1 Control by parasites has been the only method of combating the Mediterranean fruit fly (Ceratitis capitata..) in Hawaii that has met with any success. **1970** *Age* (Melbourne) 22 June 12/5 The introduced Mediterranean fruit-fly..belong[s] to the family Tephritidae. **1987** *Los Angeles Times* 17 July 11. 1/3 The pest..is considered the second most destructive fly to agriculture—trailing the Mediterranean fruit fly.

medium, *n.* and *a.* Add: [**B.**] [**1.**] **f.** Of an item of merchandise (esp. a garment): having a size intermediate between large and small.

1866 *Rural Amer.* (Utica, N.Y.) 15 Mar. VI. 94/3 (Advt.), Early white flat dutch, size medium, grows quick. **1895** *Montgomery Ward Catal.* Spring & Summer 283/2 Ladies' combination or union suits..small, medium and large. **1917** *Harrods Gen. Catal.* 1238/2 Truffles...Med[ium] tin. *Ibid.* 1380/5 Spun silk spencers...Medium 10/6. Pure silk knickers...Medium 37/6. Large size 38/6. **1953** *Woman's Home Compan.* June 69/1 Men's clothes are marked in many different ways, including those rather vague designations, 'small, medium, large' and A, B, C, D. **1966** H. YOXALL *Fashion of Life* xiv. 134 We have a medium tube [of shaving cream] called 'king size'. **1981** J. BLUME *Tiger Eyes* (1982) xxi. 89 They decide to split a medium pizza. **1989** S. KERSLAKE *An Old Night* in *Blind Date* 26 He passes a room with shelves of folded white coats and jackets. He chooses a three quarterlength coat size medium.

meeja ('miːdʒə), *n.* (sometimes *pl.*). Chiefly *Brit. colloq.* (*joc.* and *iron.*). Also **meejer**. [Repr. colloq. pronunc. of MEDIA *n.*[2] Cf. the similar respellings *Cajun*, *eejit*.] The media; the members of the media, regarded as an identifiable social group. Freq. *attrib.*

1983 *Guardian Weekly* 17 July 21/4 Part of the reason Mailer is such fun is his self-appointed mission to smash the consensual tea party held by the cultural bureaucrats and 'meeja' liberals. **1984** *Spectator* 20 Oct. 6/3 The reason that no democratic government will decriminalise this fairly agreeable short cut to oblivion and death is nothing to do with agitation in the meejer. **1985** *Listener* 31 Jan. 38/1 The meeja loves a good row. **1988** J. NEEL *Death's Bright Angel* v. 41 We aren't middle-class poor anymore, you know. I am part of the rich *meeja*. **1989** *Observer* 15 Jan. v. 3/4 The cheeky 'model'-cum-nightclub singer-cum-meeja star.

mefenamic (mɛfɪ'næmɪk), *a.* *Pharm.* [f. ME(THYL- + *fen-* (alteration of PHEN-) + AM(INO- + -IC.] **mefenamic acid**, a drug which inhibits prostaglandin synthesis and is used as an anti-inflammatory agent and analgesic; 2-[(2,3-dimethylphenyl)amino]benzoic acid, $C_{15}H_{15}NO_2$.

1962 *Jrnl. Pharmacol. & Exper. Therap.* CXXXVIII. 405/1 N-(2,3-xylyl)anthranilic acid (CI-473; mefenamic acid), prepared by the copper-catalyzed condensation of *o*-chlorobenzoic acid and 2,3-dimethylaniline, has a molecular weight of 241.3. **1967** *New Scientist* 27 Apr. 217/3 Anti-inflammatory drugs such as phenylbutazone, mefenamic acid and flufenamic acid. **1977** *Lancet* 11 June 1239/2 Other pharmacological agents which might be released into the uterus to reduce the bleeding and pain include..the prostaglandin-synthetase inhibitors, mefenamic acid and flufenamic acid. **1987** M. J. NEAL *Med. Pharmacol.* xxviii. 63/2 Fenamates (e.g. mefenamic acid) have the disadvantage of causing diarrhoea.

meg (mɛg), *n.*[4] *slang.* [Abbrev.] = MEGAPHONE *n.* Now *rare*.

1937 'C. McCABE' *Face on Cutting-Room Floor* vii. 53 Vic took the meg and shouted something at the

camera people. **1942** BERREY & VAN DEN BARK *Amer. Thes. Slang* §75/1 *Meg, megger*, a megaphone. **1961** in Partridge *Dict. Slang* Suppl. 1181/2.

meg (mɛg), *n.*[5] *Electronics colloq.* [Abbrev.] = *megohm* s.v. MEGA- b.

1975 *Physics Bull.* Oct. 460/1 (Advt.), It measures voltages to 1200 volts, currents to 2 amps. and resistances to 2000 megs. **1982** *Giant Bk. Electronics Projects* x. 463 Each player control consists of a 1 meg pot and .1 microfarad capacitor.

meg (mɛg), *n.*[6] *Computing colloq.* [Abbrev.] = *megabyte* s.v. MEGA- b.

1983 *Electronic News* 4 Apr. 1 A 3081K with 48 megs of real storage..can achieve an additional throughput improvement of 10 per cent. **1987** *Byte* Dec. 133/2 The card holds 2 megs when fully populated. **1992** *Tucson Weekly* 23-29 Sept. 3/2, I type on a 386PC with 80-meg hard drive, 5 megs of RAM, color VGA monitor,..and much more.

mega ('mɛgə), *a.* *colloq.* [Absol. use of MEGA-.] **1. a.** Usu. *attrib.* Huge, enormous; great, substantial. Also used quasi-*adv.* as an intensifier.

1982 *Guardian* 26 Oct. 8/4 Valspeak is..the funnest, most totally radical language, I guess, like in the whole mega gnarly city of Los Angeles. **1983** *Times* 25 Mar. 2/6 Contracts that forced them to produce 'mega bore' reports that satisfied less than 1 per cent of their customers. **1984** *Gainesville* (Florida) *Sun* 3 Apr. 14 B/5 (Advt.), Professionally oriented apt....Screened Fla. room, utility room, mega storage, low utilities. **1985** M. MIDDLES *Smiths* (1988) xiv. 97 These people constantly told the band to think big, to think mega, to evolve into a major international unit. **1989** *Fast Forward* 18-24 Oct. 25/3 The mega famous classical *Sorcerer's Apprentice* music. **1990** *Mountain* Nov.-Dec. 14/2 This cave is a dark dungeon of mega hard moves and superior climbing. **1991** *Sassy* Aug. 22/1 River seemed to have a mega chip on his shoulder. **1993** *Marketing* 28 Jan. 3/2 Whether they jump or play safe is a knife-edge decision...The implications are mega.

b. Of a person: highly successful or celebrated. Usu. in predicative use.

1987 *Music Week* 12 Sept. 22/1 Already mega in Ireland, O'Donnell has been the subject of a highly successful promotion for his two Ritz label albums. **1989** *Q* Mar. 25/2 If he'd been managed by Malcolm McLaren he'd have been mega. **1992** *Time Out* 22 Apr. 23/1, I got Eddie Murphy for '48 Hrs', Bruce [Willis] for 'Die Hard' and Mel [Gibson] for 'Lethal Weapon' when none of them were [*sic*] particularly mega.

2. Excellent, brilliant, great. Usu. in predicative use.

1985 *New Yorker* 25 Mar. 41/1, I was mega, but not mega enough for the job. **1986** R. SPROAT *Stunning the Punters* 119 'It's a laugh,' says the Captain,..'really mega. Free music and you get to hit people *and* they pay you.' **1987** *New Musical Express* 14 Feb. 23/3 It's a crap record but I had to have it. Look at it. Isn't it mega? What a great sleeve! **1988** *Dirt Bike Rider* Sept. 15/2 Qualifying was mega, the track was mega, and Thorpey wasn't going too bad either. **1989** *Fast Forward* 15-21 Nov. 8 (*heading*) Introducing the megarest music competition since the record was invented. **1994** *Fast Forward* 26 Oct. 30/1 Sam convinces Fisher that it's a mega idea to join in the 40-hour famine.

mega-, *comb. form.* Add: [**a.**] '**megaphyll** *n.* *Bot.* [ad. Da. *megafyl* (coined by C. Raunkiaer 1917, in *Bot. Tidsskr.* XXXIV. 229), f. Gr. φύλλ-ον leaf], a type of leaf, found in ferns and some higher plants, which is usu. large and has a complex vascular system with leaf gaps in the stem stele; opp. *microphyll* n. s.v. *MICRO- 1 a.

1932 *Proc. Linn. Soc.* CXLV. 26 There is an early differentiation between..the simple microphylls and the branch systems or 'telomes' which later evolved into the *megaphylls of the higher plants. **1983** E. C. MINKOFF *Evolutionary Biol.* xxvi. 451/1 Megaphylls of this type occur in ferns, where they bear the sporangia on their lower surfaces. **1989** *Plant Systematics & Evol.* CLXV. 147 It is striking that there is nothing particularly primitive or pre-fern about these plants, they have all the assets of modern Filicalean ferns with bilaterally organized megaphylls and biseriate pinnae.

'**megastore** *n.*, a very large retail store, often one specializing in a particular type of product.

1982 *Times* 14 May 15/4 By then also more than 30 so-called *megastores, [or] factory stores, are expected to be established. **1985** *Investors Chron.* 1-7 Nov. 42/1 Virgin and HMV have set up megastores. **1991** *Bicycling* Feb. 50/2 Though many of these shops have provided character and expertise,..they'll..be replaced by megastores featuring slick merchandising and one-stop shopping.

megaflop ('mɛgəflɒp), *n. Computing.* [Back-formation f. *megaflops*, f. MEGA- b + acronym f. *floating-point operations per second, -s* being taken as a plural ending.] A unit of computing speed equal to one million or 2^{20} floating-point operations per second.

1976 *IEEE Spectrum* Oct. 69/1 Users of large, fast, number-crunching computers often talk in terms of megaflops (millions of floating-point operations per second). **1985** *Science* 26 Apr. 421/1 On a powerful sequential computer that operates at a rate of 1 megaflop.., this formidable task would take about 70 hours of computing. **1991** *UNIX World* Jan. 27/2 On the Iris Vision boards is a proprietary 20-megaflop geometry engine, six custom VLSI (very large-scale integration) chips, and a Weitek accelerator.

megastar ('mɛgəˌstɑː(r)), *n.* [f. MEGA- + STAR *n.*[1] 5.] An exceptionally famous, well-publicized, or successful superstar, esp. in the world of entertainment.

1978 *Business Week* 22 May 77/2 With the number of movie roles declining, and such megastars as John Wayne succumbing to big advertising dollars, the stigma of making commercials has faded. **1979** *Radio Times* 5 May 17/2 Robin Bailey says it was never his ambition to be a megastar. **1983** *Listener* 8 Dec. 12/2 In poetry terms Heaney is something of a mega-star these days. **1986** *Sun* (Melbourne) 26 Dec. (Leisure Suppl.) 6/3 Last week, Spanish megastar tenor Placido Domingo was booked for a Wembley Arena concert. **1993** *Albuquerque* (New Mexico) *Jrnl.* 11 Feb. A17/1 Pop megastar Michael Jackson revealed he has a disorder that destroys his skin pigmentation.

Hence **megastardom** *n.*, the condition of being a megastar; the world of megastars.

1985 *Music Week* 2 Feb. 46/1 Lionel Richie..has been carving out his own slice of megastardom. **1989** *Face* Jan. 20/2 Sandra Bernhard: only a year or a scandal away from megastardom. **1993** *Sports Illustr.* 27 Dec. 62/2 Fed up with the demands of megastardom, Jordan stunned western civilization by retiring from the NBA [National Basketball Assoc.] on Oct. 6.

melanoma, *n.* Delete ‖ and add: Pl. also **melanomas**. Also, the condition of having a melanoma or melanomas. (Further examples.)

1916 *Ann. Surg.* LXIV. 215 The great majority of melanomas have their origin in a pigmented mole. **1920** *N.Y. Med. Jrnl.* CXII. 252/1 (*heading*) Report of a case of melanoma. **1959** S. DUKE-ELDER *Parsons' Dis. Eye* (ed. 13) xxv. 376 Malignant melanoma is the only neoplasm of importance met with in the iris. **1977** *National Observer* (U.S.) 15 Jan. 6/3 The 21-year-old Roth thinks so despite a flare up of melanoma, a type of cancer that caused him to have an operation 2½ years ago. **1987** *Oxf. Textbk. Med.* (ed. 2) II. xx. 79/2 In general, sunlight exposure accounts for the incidence of malignant melanoma in white skins.

Melbournite ('mɛlbənaɪt), *n.* Also (*rare*) **Melbourneite**. [f. *Melbourne*, the name of the capital city of the Australian state of Victoria + -ITE[1].] A native or inhabitant of Melbourne.

1872 W. C. TAYLOR *Jottings on Austral.* 2 Adelaide wheat is very fine, and has led to the city being called by the Melbournites 'the farinaceous village'. **1878** *Age* (Melbourne) 17 June 7/4 The defence of the Melbourneites proved too good. **1898** H. MATTHEWS *Chat about Austral.* 11 Victorians in general, and Melbournites in particular, take the palm from all Australians for their partiality to holidays and sports. **1955** 'S. RUDD' *Far & Near* 11 We reached the famous Sydney Harbour Bridge, or as Melbournites call it, the Coathanger. **1989** *Courier-Mail* (Brisbane) 6 Oct. 4/3 A group of Melbournites,..holidaying on Bedarra Island, sent out an SOS to Melbourne this week, asking for a video of the VFL grand final.

Melburnian (mɛl'bɜːnɪən), *n.* Also **Melbournian**. [f. *Melbourne* (see *MELBOURNITE *n.*), Latinized as *Melburnia* + -IAN[1].] A native or inhabitant of Melbourne.

1838 *Melbourne Advertiser* 1 Jan. 1 The future fortunes of the rising Melbournians will be much accelerated by the dissemination of intelligence. **1876** *Melburnian* (Melbourne Ch. of Eng. Grammar Sch.) 22 Mar. 15 The diphthong, 'ou' is not a Latin diphthong: hence, we argued this way, *Melburnia* would be Latin form of name, and from it comes *Melburnian*. **1911** E. M. CLOWES *On Wallaby* x. 263 If the gardens had to be watered with champagne the wealthy Melbournian would not hesitate. **1965** G. McINNES *Road to Gundagai* xii. 210 'Under the clocks' was the favourite trysting place of Melburnians. **1991** *Outrage* Feb. 3/2 While Melburnians were crying for Argentina.., Sydney theatre audiences were watching choirboys being castrated in *The Choir*.

melittin (mə'lɪtɪn), *n. Biochem.* [a. G. *Melittin* (E. Habermann 1954, in *Arch. exper. Path. u. Pharm.* CCXXII. 173), f. Gr. μέλιττα (Attic form of μέλισσα) bee: see -IN[1].] A polypeptide, $C_{131}H_{229}N_{39}O_{31}$, present in bee venom and used experimentally as an antibacterial agent, esp. against penicillin-resistant bacteria.

1961 *Biochem. Zeitschr.* CCCXXXV. 60 An improved chromatographic method is described for the preparation of mellitin [*sic*], the main compound of the bee venom. **1965** *Ibid.* CCCXLIII. 192 The two basic bee venom polypeptides melittin and apamin. **1968** *Proc. Soc. Exper. Biol. & Med.* CXXVII. 707/1 It was noted that one of the fractions, melittin, possesses potent antibacterial properties. **1987** *Nature* 6 Aug. 478/1 The peptide melittin, for example, is the main toxic component of honeybee venom and its structure has been studied in detail.

mellow, *v.* Add: [3.] c. *intr.* With *out.* To become less intense, to relax, esp. under the influence of a drug. Also (*occas.*) *trans.* or *refl. slang* (orig. *U.S.*).

1974 *Rolling Stone* 14 Feb. 38/1 Critics..were saying he'd mellowed out..'drained the venom from his voice'. **1977** C. McFADDEN *Serial* (1978) ix. 25/2 How about we all smoke a little dope and mellow out, okay? **1979** N. MAILER *Executioner's Song* (1980) I. xx. 342 Even with two Valiums to mellow her out, she felt crazy inside every time she thought about Barrett selling her car. **1985** R. SILVERBERG *Tom O'Bedlam* (1986) v. iii. 178 A tranquilizer whenever you felt the need to mellow yourself out. **1991** *Holiday Which?* Mar. 106/3 A place to stop off at, stay awhile and mellow out. **1995** J. MILLER *voXpop* viii. 125 Now I just smoke grass, I've mellowed out.... I couldn't keep going flat out for life!

mellowed, *ppl. a.* Add: Also with *out* (see *MELLOW *v.* 3 c).

1977 *N.Y. Times Mag.* 20 Nov. 117/1 All suggest that the laid-back, mellowed-out speaker achieves a perfect relation with the universe while in a state of passivity. **1979** *Time* 10 Sept. 82/3 After a lengthy period of mellowed-out serenity.., Vonnegut is mad again. **1988** *Sports Illustr.* 16 May 12/3 'You told me on the phone that the highest rock climb would be 15 feet.' 'Ah, did I?' he said in his most mellowed-out tones.

mellowing, *vbl. n.* Add: Also with *out* (see *MELLOW v.* 3 c).
   1977 C. McFADDEN in *N.Y. Times Mag.* 20 Nov. 117/1 Words and phrases in the Bay Area vocabulary that describe mental inertia: 'mellowing out'. **1993** *Rolling Stone* 18 Feb. 58/2 Jagger.. seems determined to cede nothing to age, dismissing the idea of mellowing out as anathema.

mellowspeak ('mɛləʊspiːk), *n. U.S. colloq.* [f. MELLOW *a.* + -SPEAK.] Language that is bland, unaggressive, and euphemistic, orig. used to characterize a vogueish, self-absorbed argot associated with psychotherapy and New Age philosophy.
   1979 G. B. TRUDEAU in *Washington Post* 14 May DI3/1 'Well, it's really a great context for sharing energy!' 'Huh?' 'That's "mellow-speak", Joanie. We've been studying Dr. Dan Asher's new book!' **1985** *Computer Decisions* 19 Nov. 64/2 Each of these has.. an 'upper' or 'downer' effect. Translation of this.. 'mellowspeak': Some of the negative dependencies act as stimulants, others devitalize. **1989** *U.S. News & World Rep.* 26 June 9 The aging Chinese Communist leaders might listen in on Abdul-Jabbar's new mellow-speak.

melodia (mɪ'ləʊdɪə), *n. Mus.* (chiefly *N. Amer.*). [a. late *L. melodia* melody: see MELODY *n.*] An organ stop of the same type as the hohl-flute, flute-like in tone and closely resembling the clarabella.
   1886 *Daily News* 14 Dec. 7/2 (Advt.), All of the following are reed stops... Diapason, melodia, viola, celeste. **1908** *Sears, Roebuck Catal.* 225 Beckworth Organs... Eleven necessary stops, as follows: Principal, Diapason, Dulciana, Melodia, Celeste, [etc.]. **1944** W. APEL *Harvard Dict. Mus.* 527/1 The open Flutes, such as the Melodia, Claribel Flute, and Concert Flute.. are characterized by a broad mellow flute tone. **1966** H. & H. J. NORMAN *Organ Today* xii. 155 A still purer sound is obtained by a German type block having a recessed space below the flue level. This is the Wald Flute or Melodia.

melon, *n.*[1] Sense 4 in Dict. becomes 5. Add: **4.** *pl. colloq.* Large breasts.
   1972 *Pussycat* XXXIII. LIX. 10/2 She released the catch on her bra and slipped it off... Her full and shapely melons swung and swayed and drooped as she moved. **1991** G. KEILLOR *WLT, Radio Romance* xiii. 107 The ones with the melons, they get a little old on the hoof, and you have to throw a flag over them feedsacks so they don't bang you on the head, so you want a woman with nice little titties.

melphalan ('mɛlfə‚læn), *n. Pharm.* [f. ME(THYL *n.* + L 8 c (ii) + PH(ENYL)ALAN(INE *n.*] A nitrogen mustard given intravenously in the treatment of myelomatosis and other neoplasms; 4-bis(2-chloroethyl)amino-L-phenylalanine, $C_{13}H_{18}N_2O_2Cl_2$.
   1960 *Cancer Chemotherapy Rep.* Feb. 61 Melphalan. **1962** *Surgery* LI. 583/1 Phenylalanine mustard exists in two forms. One is the DL form called Sarcolysin; the other is the L form called melphelan [*sic*]. **1974** R. M. KIRK et al.. *Surgery* v. 73 When excision is not possible.. it is worth trying the effects of.. systemic chemotherapy with phenylalanine mustard drugs, or melphalan given systemically. **1977** *Lancet* 18 June 1307/1 In our similar studies of 8

patients menstruating regularly plasma œstradiol and androgens were measured frequently at random before and after five-day pulses of melphalan. **1992** *Sci. News* 27 June 420/2 Melphalan, seldom used anymore in adjuvant therapy, poses roughly 10 times the leukemia risk.

meltdown, *n.* Senses a, b in Dict. become 1a, 2. Add: [**1.**] **b.** *fig.* Any uncontrolled and usu. disastrous transformation with far-reaching repercussions; a collapse or reversal of fortune; *spec.* in *Comm.*, a sudden rapid drop in the value of a specified currency or of assets, shares, etc.; a crash.
   1983 S. & M. TOLCHIN *Dismantling Amer.* vi. 189 (*chapter title*) Political meltdown. **1986** *Washington Post* 2 June 3/1 They did this mostly, sources say, out of fear of the alternative—a mass fire sale of the EPIC properties. Such a 'meltdown', as it was referred to by lawyers on the case, could have had catastrophic repercussions in the nation's mortgage markets. **1986** *Times* 13 Nov. 10 (*heading*) Brasilia attempts to halt economic melt-down. **1988** *New Yorker* 21 Mar. 25/1 A recent warm spell.. had caused a 'winter meltdown'. Last October's stock-market collapse.. was a 'market meltdown'. A novelist wrote that his central character's fraying nerves had brought about a 'mental meltdown'. **1990** *Vanity Fair* (N.Y.) Aug. 160/1 If women are alienated, homosexuals have reached the meltdown stage. **1991** *Premiere* Dec. 68/3 Julia Roberts experienced a fame melt-down on the order of Marilyn Monroe. **1992** *Financial Times* 11-12 Apr. 11. 2/7 Talk of a meltdown in Japan plunging Wall Street into crisis and the US economy back into recession.

melty ('mɛltɪ), *a.* [f. MELT *v.*[1] or MELT *n.*[3] + -Y[1].] Liable to melt; reminiscent of something which is melting.
   c **1921** D. H. LAWRENCE *Mr. Noon* iii, in *Mod. Lover* (1934) 217 She was startled, jarred in her rather melty mood. **1970** *Honey* June 124/1 (Advt.), For melty young eyes, Run Proof Mascara at 4/9. **1980** *Washington Post* 21 Feb. DC10/3 The quesadillas were superbly prepared, however: outside, crackling crisp but not greasy: inside, melty, mellow cheese enhanced by onions, chillis and spices. **1985** *Cincinnati Enquirer* 18 Oct. A9/2 The original smooth, melty mints in 16-ounce bags. **1992** T. MORRISON *Jazz* 63 Dorcas.. was enchanted by the frail, melty tendency of the flesh.

Melungeon (mɪ'lʌndʒən), *n. U.S.* Also **Malungeon.** [Of uncertain origin, but perh. related to F. *mélange* mixture.] A member of a North American people of mixed white, black, and Amerindian descent inhabiting the southern Appalachian mountains in the eastern U.S.
   1889 *Boston Traveller* 13 Apr. 6/5 They resented the appellation Melungeon, given to them by common consent by the whites, and proudly called themselves Portuguese. **1948** H. L. MENCKEN *Amer. Lang.* Suppl. II. 235 There are many similar groups of mixed bloods, always of low economic status.. notably.. the Malungeons of southwestern Virginia, eastern Kentucky and Tennessee. **1951** *Geogr. Rev.* XLI. 257 The Melungeons are said to have been disfranchised by the restrictions placed on free persons of color in the Tennessee Constitution of 1834. **1967** L. PENNINGTON *Dark Hills of Jesse Stuart* vii. 116 The Melungeons were always a free people. Although they were often of dark complexion, they.. were never enslaved. **1970** *Times* 20 Oct. 8/5 One of the tribes which seems to have a Mediterranean background and which has puzzled scholars for generations are the Melungeons.

Melvillian (mɛl'vɪlɪən), *a.* Also **Melvillean.** [f. the name of Herman *Melville* (1819-91), American novelist + -IAN[1].] Of, pertaining to, or characteristic of Melville or his work.

1947 V. W. Brooks *Times of Melville & Whitman* viii. 169 The castaway crowd of tinkers, watch-makers, doctors and farmers who formed the crew in *White-Jacket*..sprang into life, a vivid Melvillean life, at the author's summons. **1950** M. Lowry *Let.* 6 Mar. (1967) 201 The *Sun* published only a few syndicated lines that called it a turgid novel of self-destruction...This at least is Melvillean anyway; though it went very well in the States. **1950** E. Blunden *Chaucer to 'B.V.'* 256 Even now, when American writing is so multifarious and so capricious, the highest and best track that it takes is Melvillian. **1961** *Amer. Speech* XXXVI. 199 Bartleby is a true Melvillian hero—courageous and uncompromising. **1975** *New Yorker* 26 May 98 (Advt.), Altogether, over 150,000 words spring vividly to life. Including 22,000 new ones like 'bummer' and 'dashiki' as well as the grand old Melvillian polysyllables. **1992** *New Yorker* 14 Dec. 134/1 The book can be read as a monument to a New York that has mostly vanished—a raffish, romantic city of colorful, hard-drinking eccentrics..and of solitary Melvillean types who never venture far from the waterfront.

membership, *n.* Add: [**2.**] **b.** *collect.* The body of members of a society, institution, etc.
1926 Fowler *Mod. Eng. Usage* 347/2 The employers' proposals may be distasteful to a large section of our m[embership]. **1939** *Sat. Rev. Lit.* (U.S.) 23 Dec. 12/1 Its membership could hardly be said to be in a snit. **1975** *Aviation Week* 24 Feb. 23/1 If the UAW membership does not approve the offer, the union has scheduled a strike. **1990** *Physiotherapy* LXXVI. 782/1 Enabling them to provide a higher standard of lectures and education for their membership.

membrane, *n.* Sense 3 in Dict. becomes 4. Add:
3. *gen.* Any thin, extended, sheetlike barrier of material, *esp.* one resembling a biological membrane in being (*a*) permeable to some substances, or (*b*) elastic or taut.
1876 A. G. Bell in *Proc. Amer. Acad. Arts & Sci.* (1877) XII. 8, I placed the membrane of the telephone near my mouth. **1891** *Jrnl. Chem. Soc.* LX. 140 A solution of cupric sulphate superposed on a solution of potassium ferrocyanide precipitates at the dividing surface an exceedingly fine membrane of cupric ferrocyanide. **1958** J. S. Scott *Dict. Civil Engin.* 225 *Membrane*.., a thin film or skin, such as the skin of a soap bubble or a waterproof skin. **1975** *Audubon* May 22/1 A tank structure 80 to 90 feet deep from the deck and almost a quarter of a mile long, over which a thin membrane of steel, a mere 35 millimeters..thick, has been drawn. **1981** P. Davies *Edge of Infinity* (1983) i. 18 The surface of a balloon..is a membrane of rubber. **1986** *Do it Yourself* June 57/2 It is basically a standard 100mm concrete slab with a polythene sheet damp proof membrane laid over it.

‖**membrum virile** (ˌmɛmbrʊm vɪˈriːleɪ, ˌmɛmbrʊm vɪˈraɪlɪ, ˌmɛmbrəm vɪrˈiːleɪ), *n. arch.* or *euphem.* [L., lit. 'male member': see MEMBER *n.*, VIRILE *a.*]
In classical L. *membrum* was used both alone and with other adjectives in this sense.]
The penis.
*a***1732** P. Skippon *Jrnl.* in A. & J. Churchill *Coll. Voy.* VI. (1732) A Frenchman, that seeing the postboy fall down dead with the extremity of cold, opened his codpiece, and rub'd his *Membrum virile* with snow, till he recovered him. **1833** Dunglison *Dict. Med. Sci.*, *Penis*,..Membrum virile,..male organ. **1858** R. G. Mayne *Expos. Lex. Med. Sci.* (1860) 928/2 *Phallalgia*.., term for pain in the *membrum virile*. **1982** *N.Y. Times* 27 Sept. c16/1 Monica is fond of talking about, though not experiencing, what they choose to call the membrum virile until they realize that it might be 'unscholarly' to assume that all membra are virile. **1991** J. Barnes *Talking it Over* v. 64 There we stood, two rivals as yet quite unaware they were rivals, each grasping his *membrum virile*—should I offer the groom some tips as to its deployment?

meme (miːm), *n. Biol.* [Shortened from *mimeme* (see quot. 1976), f. Gr. μίμημα that which is imitated, after GENE *n.*[1]] An element of a culture that may be considered to be passed on by non-genetic means, esp. imitation.
1976 R. Dawkins *Selfish Gene* xi. 206 The new soup is the soup of human culture. We need a name for the new replicator, a noun which conveys the idea of a unit of cultural transmission, or a unit of *imitation.* 'Mimeme' comes from a suitable Greek root, but I want a monosyllable that sounds a bit like 'gene'. I hope my classicist friends will forgive me if I abbreviate mimeme to *meme*...It should be pronounced to rhyme with 'cream'. Examples of memes are tunes, ideas, catch-phrases, clothes fashions, ways of making pots or of building arches. **1976** *New Scientist* 9 Dec. 619/2 A rational person who hasn't acquired any variety of the God meme described by Richard Dawkins. **1980** *Ibid.* 3 July 50/2 The mutant reading (a meme as some sociobiologists might call it) appears to have had at least three independent origins. **1986** W. A. Koch *Genes vs. Memes* iii. 40 Although genes and memes are interconnected in one direction (genes create memes), their circular embrace is disrupted at one point. **1986** *Canad. Jrnl. Zool.* LXIV. 1576 Congruence of the patterns of morphometric and cultural evolution in these islands suggests..that the differentiation has been influenced by a colonization history involving restricted gene and meme flow between archipelagos, subsequent drift, and possibly founder effects. **1988** *Ecology* LXIX. 104 (*heading*) Biological and cultural success of song memes in indigo buntings. **1993** *Wired* Feb. 132/2 I'm not sure what happens to such a culture when radical Maoism is replaced by the far more seductive meme of Western consumer culture.

memorabilia, *n. pl.* Add: **2.** *concr.* Objects serving as reminders of memorable times, people, events, etc.; souvenirs. orig. *U.S.*
1890 in *Cent. Dict.* **1900** *Dialect Notes* II. 46 *Memorabil*, i.e. *memorabilia..n.*, photographs, programmes, old examination papers, and the like, collected during college days, and kept as souvenirs. **1950** S. J. Perelman *Swiss Family Perelman* v. 79 The very room Captain Bligh occupied after his epochal longboat voyage from the South Pacific to Timor, containing some exceptional memorabilia. **1974** *Times* 4 Jan. 2/6 The exhibition has been augmented by material from private collections of Colditz memorabilia. **1987** *Cornwall Rev.* July 3/4 Inside the house can be seen photographs, press cuttings and other memorabilia giving an insight to the artist's personal and professional life.

memory, *n.* (Sense 12: *memory-cell* now defined as below.) Add: [**12.**] **memory board**, (*a*) a noticeboard or other board intended as an aid to the memory or as a record of past events, etc.; (*b*) *Computing*, a board (*BOARD *n.* 2 h) containing (additional) memory.
1974 *Times Lit. Suppl.* 13 Dec. 1407/2 The tales vary from the complex and flowery to summaries so sparse they look like jottings on some medieval comic's *memory-board. **1976** *Laurel* (Montana) *Outlook* 30 June 1/4 Various 'memory boards' that were provided by the classes will contain pictures, newspaper clippings, etc of memorable events that occurred during the high school years of that particular class. **1979** *Personal Computer World* Nov. 3 (Advt.), Just add S100 Memory Boards—S100 disk controller boards—[etc.]. **1984** *Daily Tel.* 3 Sept. 9/2 Most 16-bit business microcomputers are supplied with 256k bytes of memory as standard, but you will still need an additional 128k memory board slotted inside the computer.

memory cell, †(*a*) a nerve cell concerned with memory (*obs.*); (*b*) *Computing* = *CELL *n.* 9 g; (*c*) *Physiol.*, a long-lived lymphocyte capable of responding to a particular antigen on its reintroduction, long after the exposure that prompted its production.

1892 VAN LIEW & BEYER tr. *Ziehen's Introd. Physiol. Psychol.* 156 These numerous sensory cells transmit their excitation further to one other ganglion-cell, a *memory-cell. **1952** *Proc. IRE* XL. 475 (*heading*) A coincident-current magnetic memory cell for the storage of digital information. **1982** *Sci. Amer.* Feb. 59/2 Each memory cell of the chip can be addressed independently. **1985** C. R. LEESON et al. *Textbk. Histol.* (ed. 5) v. 157/1 Memory cells may live for years without growing or dividing. **1994** *Sci. News* 28 May 344/2 Once the immune system's T cells and B cells, which make antibodies, are activated, some of them turn into memory cells.

memory chip *Computing*, a semiconductor chip made as a memory (e.g. a ROM or a RAM) containing many separately addressable locations.

1969 *IEEE Jrnl. Solid-State Circuits* IV. 295/1 Address selection of present semiconductor *memory chips is based on using the 2^n combinations of n binary address bits. **1979** *Maclean's* 2 Apr. 38/3 In 1978 IBM unveiled a semiconductor memory chip containing 64,000 transistors. **1987** *Oxf. Mag.* No. 18. 9/2 It may even be possible one day for the whole *New OED* to be engraved on a single memory chip inside a computer.

ménage, *n.* Sense 4 in Dict. becomes 4 a. Add: [4.] **b.** Hence, a romantic or sexual relationship, an affair; *collect.*, the parties involved in such a relationship. Also *fig.*

1949 P. HASTINGS *Cases in Court* v. 264 He was a good-looking young man and she was said to be very fond of him although the menage was punctuated by repeated altercations. **1959** *Economist* 4 Apr. 17/2 Instead of bilateral relationships between Britain and Europe and between Britain and the Commonwealth, the objective must be a triangular ménage. **1980** *Daily Tel.* 6 June 15/1 He turns up on what appears to be a regular visit from Milan with his 'friend', Picchio, the two being accepted as a ménage.

Menapian (mɪˈnæpɪən, mɪˈneɪpɪən), *n.* and *a.* [f. L. *Menapii*, the name of this people + -IAN.]
A. *n.* **1.** *Roman Hist.* A member of the Menapii, a Celtic people of northern Gaul.

1565 A. GOLDINGE *Eyght Bookes of Caesar* Gloss. p. Mmv, *Menapians*, the people of Gelderlande and Cleveland, or as some suppose the people of Juliers in Belgicke. **1776** GIBBON *Decl. & F.* I. xiii. 363 Gessoriacum, or Boulogne, in the narrow straights of the British channel, was chosen by the emperor for the station of the Roman fleet; and the command of it was intrusted to Carausius, a Menipean of the meanest origin. **1819** J. LINGARD *Hist. Engl.* I. i. 46 The Menapian [*sc.* Carausius] unexpectedly fortified Boulogne, concluded an alliance with the barbarians, sailed to Britain,..and, assuming, with the imperial purple, the name of Augustus, set at defiance the whole power of Rome. **1993** P. SALWAY *Oxf. Illustr. Hist. Roman Britain* 200 In charge of his countermeasures, Maximian put an officer called M. Mausaeus Carausius, by origin a Menapian from the Low Countries.
2. *Geol.* The Menapian glaciation.

1983 T. NILSSON *Pleistocene* x. 138 Recent results also point to a potential split-up of the Menapian into two cold portions, separated by a warm interlude. **1990** A. & M. ALLABY *Conc. Oxf. Dict. Earth Sci.* 170/2 The Günz may correlate with the Menapian of northern Europe.
B. *adj.* **1.** *Roman Hist.* Of or pertaining to the Menapians. *rare.*

1757 J. DYER *Fleece* III. 107 On Albion's coast, the exil'd band, From rich Menapian towns, and the green banks of Scheld alighted.
2. *Geol.* Of, pertaining to, or designating the first major Pleistocene glaciation in northern Europe (possibly corresponding to the Günz of the Alps) or its deposits.

1957 W. H. ZAGWIJN in *Geol. en Mijnbouw* XIX. 235/2 The basal glacial has been named by the author Eburonian, the following interglacial Waalian or Waal Interglacial, and the next glacial Menapian. **1983** T. NILSSON *Pleistocene* x. 137 Strata intermediate between the Eburonian and the Menapian cold stages provide evidence of a genial climate.

menarche, *n.* Add: Hence **meˈnarcheal** (also occas. **meˈnarchial**) *a.*, of or at menarche.

1936 *Jrnl. Pediatrics* VIII. 55 Scheyer studied the relation between body build and menarcheal age in 300 adult patients. [**1942** MAZER & ISRAEL *Diagn. & Treatm. Menstrual Disorders* ii. 35 A study of 175 postmenarchial and 175 premenarchial girls.] **1962** P. BLOS *On Adolescence* i. 6 The mean menarchial age of 13.5 in the United States. **1991** *Utne Reader* July–Aug. 36/1 Celebrations elevate the menarcheal girl to a position of great respect in the society.

mengovirus (ˈmɛŋɡəʊvaɪrəs), *n. Biol.* Also **Mengo virus**. [f. the name of *Mengo* District, Buganda, Uganda, where the virus was first isolated.] A picornavirus originally found in monkeys but capable of infecting other species, the infection in humans being characterized by encephalomyelitis.

[**1948** G. W. A. DICK et al. in *Lancet* 21 Aug. 286/1 Mengo encephalomyelitis virus was originally isolated from a paralysed rhesus monkey..which had been captive in the outside monkey runs in the compound of the Yellow Fever Research Institute in Entebbe.] **1949** *Jrnl. Immunol.* LXII. 375 The UR 22 monkey strain..of Mengo virus was employed in these experiments. **1962** *Biochim. et Biophys. Acta* LV. 241 These experiments suggest that mengovirus RNA may be synthesized in the cytoplasm. **1972** *Nature* 18 Aug. 369/1 Early studies with vaccinia, mengovirus and Semliki Forest virus all indicated that interferon acts at a translation level. **1988** *Jrnl. Gen. Virol.* LXXIX. 275 Interferon (IFN) response mutants were selected from mouse L929 fibroblast cells and their specific resistance to *is*-1, an IFN-sensitive mutant of mengovirus, were studied.

Menippean (mɪˈnɪpɪən), *a.* [f. the name of *Menippus* of Gadara (fl. 3rd cent. B.C.), Cynic philosopher and writer + -EAN.] Characteristic of or resembling the style of satirical writing associated with Menippus. Usu. in *Menippean satire*.

1728 CHAMBERS *Cycl.* s.v., *Menippean, or Satyra Menippea*. It is thus call'd from Menippas, a Cynic Philosopher, who delighted in composing Satyrical Letters, &c. **1797** *Encycl. Brit.* XI. 388/1 *Menippean*, ..a kind of satire consisting of prose and verse intermixed. It is thus called from Menippus a cynic philosopher. **1813** *Pantologia* VII. s.v. *Menippus*, He wrote some snarlish satires, for which reason writings of that stamp have been sometimes called Menippean. **1908** W. P. DICKSON tr. *T. Mommsen's Hist. Rome* V. 488 It resulted both from the nature of the Cynical philosophy and from the temperament of Varro, that the Menippean lash was very specially plied round the ears of the philosophers. **1976** M. McLUHAN *Let.* 3 Feb. (1987) 517 Most of my writing is Menippean satire, presenting the actual surface of the world we live in as a ludicrous image. **1985** *Rev. Eng. Stud.* Feb. 131 The book is enlivening because of the consciously unstuffy 'menippean' quality in its 'clashes of genre and changes of tone'.

mento (ˈmɛntəʊ), *n. Jamaica.* [Of uncertain origin.
Cassidy & Le Page (*Dict. Jamaican Eng.*) merely suggest African provenance; O. Lewin (in *New Grove Dict. Mus.*) suggests a derivation from Old Spanish *mentar* to mention, presumably with reference to the conversational nature and anecdotal or topical content of such songs.]

Orig., a traditional dance in duple time, or a song sung to accompany this; later also, the style of Jamaican folk music associated with this dance. Cf. CALYPSO n.

1910 H. G. DE LISSER *In Jamaica & Cuba* vi. 109 Known as the *mento*, the *bamboula*, the *chica*, you will find this dance wherever the African was taken as a slave. **1954** R. MAIS *Brother Man* ii. 64 The tune of that mento kept going through her head...They sometimes sat on the step, when the evenings were warm, and sang mentos together. **1976** BOOT & THOMAS *Jamaica* 32/2 Jamaican calypso, what's called *mento*, is crude and simple, and back in the fifties the Baptists and the Church of God saw to it that the best *mento*, the lewd stuff, never got out of the backyard. **1980** *Black Perspective in Music* VIII. 46/1 The urbanization of Jamaican folk music from mento to ska. **1989** *Guitar Player* Mar. 36/3 Ska, the uptempo predecessor of reggae, combined the earlier *mento* style with an R & B backbeat. **1992** *Times* 15 Feb. (Sat. Rev. Suppl.) 35/1 Reared on the Bible, the Caribbean *mento* tradition and the spontaneous lyricism of the reggae artists, this is tersely pointed contemporary folk poetry of the highest order.

menudo (mɪˈnuːdəʊ, ‖meˈnudo), *n.* *U.S.* [a. Mexican Sp. (cf. the earlier Sp. *menudos* giblets, offal), substantive use of *menudo* adj. small, ult. f. L. *minutus* MINUTE *a*.] A thick, spicy Mexican soup, traditionally made with tripe, calf's feet, hominy, and seasoning.

1964 G. C. BOOTH *Food & Drink of Mexico* 23 Menudo is a favorite of Mexicans all over the country. **1973** R. L. SIMON *Big Fix* viii. 62 'Take some menudo,' she said, nodding toward the soup. **1977** *Time* 4 July 37/1 In Los Angeles the proliferating Mexican food stands will turn out not just tacos but also burritos, chorizos, carnitas and menudo (a milky-white soup made from the lining of a cow's stomach). **1986** B. FUSSELL *I hear Amer. Cooking* i. i. 33, I was once snowed in for a week and lived entirely on a single large pot of *menudo*, which improved with each reheating. **1994** C. McCARTHY *Crossing* 365 She had brought him some menudo hot from the fire.

merbromin (mɜːˈbrəʊmɪn), *n.* *Pharm.* [f. MER(CURY *n.* + BROM(O- + -IN[1].] A fluorescein derivative containing bromine and mercury, $C_{20}H_8Br_2HgNa_2O_6$, obtained as greenish iridescent scales which dissolve in water to give a red solution used as an antiseptic.

1941 *Bull. Nat. Formulary Comm. Amer. Pharm. Assoc.* IX. 296 Merbromin is the disodium salt of 2, 7-dibrom-4-hydroxymercurifluorescein. **1958** H. BECKMAN *Drugs* lxix. 567/1 Compounds..much used for skin disinfection..are merbromin (Mercurochrome), nitromersol (Metaphen) and thimerosal (Merthiolate). **1974** M. C. GERALD *Pharmacol.* ii. 27 Less irritating antiseptics commonly used in the home today include..merbromin (Mercurochrome). **1982** *Clin. Pediatrics* XXI. 446/1 Four deaths have been reported directly due to and one related to merbromin toxicity.

Merc (mɜːk), *n.*[1] *colloq.* [Abbrev. of *Mercedes*, the brand name of a range of vehicles (esp. luxurious private cars) manufactured in Germany, originally by the Daimler motor company.] A Mercedes vehicle, *esp.* a large saloon car.

1933 M. LINCOLN *Oh! Definitely* xv. 230 Geoffrey and I are going down in the 'Merc'. **1961** 'W. HAGGARD' *Arena* xv. 127 'There's a Merc on our tail...Wave it by.'.. He waved the Mercedes on. **1974** J. WAINWRIGHT *Hard Hit* 33 There is a pale blue Merc parked not far from the club entrance. **1989** *Truck & Driver* Feb. 40/1 The 1729 gets a slightly restyled cab exterior, with greater use of plastics and sloping door windows to echo the smaller Mercs. **1995** *Observer* 19 Mar. (Business section) 13/4 You would still be a couple of thousand pounds in pocket over three years with the budget Merc.

merc (mɜːk), *n.*[2] *colloq.* [Abbrev.] = MERCENARY *n.* 2.

1967 *Time* 11 Aug. 28/2 Zambesi Club 'mercs' are white Rhodesians and South Africans from Colonel 'Mad Mike' Hoare's Fifth Commando. **1976** *National Observer* (U.S.) 10 Jan. 6/4 If you've got 10 mercs going against 20 guerrillas, you've got to have it all together. **1988** B. STERLING *Islands in Net* ix. 284 Any dumbass merc will fight for pay for Grenada or Singapore, or some jungle-jabber African regime.

mercado (məːˈkɑːdəʊ, ‖merˈkaðo), *n.* Pl. mercados (məːˈkɑːdəʊz, ‖merˈkaðos). [a. Sp., f. L. *mercatus*: see MARKET *n.*] In Spain and Spanish-speaking countries: a market, a market place.

1841 G. BORROW *Zincali* I. ii. ii. 239 In Madrid the Gitános chiefly reside in the neighbourhood of the 'mercado', or the place where horses and other animals are sold. **1898** *Baedeker's Spain & Portugal* 105 Along the E. side of the mercado runs the wide Calle de Toledo.., one of the chief arteries of traffic in the S.W. part of old Madrid. **1976** *National Observer* (U.S.) 14 Aug. 13/1 It does help if you go to the *mercado*—the central market—and pick out a Panama hat woven in a nearby cave. **1985** *Supermarket News* 6 May 11. 116/4 We do a good job with seafood now,..but we're not up to the selection the local mercados offer.

merchandiser, *n.* Add: **2.** *Comm.* A display stand for merchandise.

1965 *Quick Frozen Foods* Apr. 108 (*caption*) Rossi's Pizza is displayed near an ice cream case, with promotional material on and above the Star Cooler spot merchandiser...In addition to displaying the product in a spot merchandiser..Rossi's promotes its pizzas with in-store demonstrations. **1976** *Bookseller* 3 July 9 (Advt.), The Dictionary is available in this attractive merchandiser which contains 10 copies. **1982** *DIY Trade* Mar. 41/2 Each merchandiser includes a working door in situ, whereby the prospective customers can try the door as it would be in their own home. **1990** *Gifts Internat.* Nov.-Dec. 41/1 New from Mill Studios is this attractive rotating display merchandiser which can be supplied either as a free-standing unit..or housed in a variety of cabinets tailored to customers' requirements.

meridian, *n.* Add: [4.] **f.** *Acupuncture.* Any of the pathways in the body along which energy is said to flow, *esp.* each of a set of twelve associated with specific organs.

1959 D. LAWSON-WOOD *Chinese Syst. Healing* 33 There is general agreement on the *numbering*, *order* and *naming* of the twelve lines of flow of Vital-Force called by Stiefvater 'Meridiane', by Soulie de Morant 'Meridiens', and by de la Fuÿe 'Kings' or 'Tsings'...After some discussion with Leslie O. Korth, D.O., M.R.O., one of the very few practising acupuncturists in this country, it was decided to use the term 'Meridian' rather than to use the Chinese word. **1964** F. MANN *Meridians of Acupuncture* i. 19 Each of the twelve main meridians has a Luo point and an associated Luo meridian. **1973** *Lancet* 14 July 58/1 In modern acupuncture the meridians are considered to be no more real than are the geographic meridians on the surface of the earth. **1976** *National Observer* (U.S.) 18 Dec. 1/2 The ancient chinese practice of inserting needles at points along the body's 12 'meridians' to treat disease and reduce pain. **1988** *Here's Health* May 14/4 Joannah's treatment involved stimulating the liver meridian in order to correct the blood disturbance.

merino, *n.* Add: [3.] **b.** Chiefly *W. Indies*. An undershirt, orig. one made of merino.

c **1915** in Cassidy & Le Page *Dict. Jamaican Eng.* (1967) 299/2 I've torn my merino. **1936** C. L. R.

JAMES *Minty Alley* iii. 19 A tall, heavily-built, quiet-looking youth of about twenty—dressed in a patched and dirty pair of blue trousers and an old jacket without shirt or merino. **1953** R. MAIS *Hills were Joyful Together* II. iii. 163 He was dressed only in his merino and drawers. **1973** S. SELVON *Ways of Sunlight* I. 75 Once a merino was so torn that the owner's wife asked her if it was a net to catch fish in the river. **1985** I. KHAN *Jumble Bird* vi. 75 The old man took a merino and pair of trousers from the line which Menna had hung across the front of his room.

Merlot ('mɜːləʊ, ‖mɛrləʊ), *n.* Also 9 **murleau**, (rare) **Merlau**, and with lower-case initial. [a. F. *merlot*, *merlau*, in same sense, dim. of *merle* blackbird (see MERLE *n.*).] A variety of vine of the species *Vitis vinifera* yielding black grapes used in wine-making; the grape of this variety, widely grown throughout France, esp. around Bordeaux, in California, and in other temperate regions. Also, the soft-textured, distinctively fruit-flavoured red wine made from this grape.

1825 J. BUSBY *Treat. Culture Vine* ii. 71 The *murleau*. This variety announces much vigour, by the strength of its wood. **1833** C. REDDING *Hist. & Descr. Mod. Wines* v. 141 The vine plants most cultivated in the canton of Bourg are the *merlot*, the *carminet*, the *mancin*, the *teinturier*, the *petit chalosse noire*, and..the *prolongeau*. **1888** *Encycl. Brit.* XXIV. 604/2 The vines of the Cabernet species..are not so greatly used as the Merlot, which is very productive, and not so liable to attacks from *Oidium*. **1978** *Amer. Poetry Rev.* Nov./Dec. 22/3 Two or three empty bottles of Merlot, Avant-garde of the gallons that are to come. **1986** J. ROBINSON *Vines, Grapes & Wines* 91 Merlot, or more properly Merlot Noir since there is a distinctly different variety called Merlot Blanc, is one of the wine world's great underdogs. **1992** *Air Canada en Route* Aug. 58/3 A seductive compote of merlot, blackberries and pecans.

mero-, *comb. form*[1]. Add: **mero'diploid** *a.* *Genetics*, having second copies of only part of the normal chromosome complement; incompletely diploid; also as *n.*, a merodiploid organism.

1961 JACOB & WOLLMAN *Sexuality & Genetics Bacteria* xii. 209 From such heterogenotes, whether *merodiploid as in limited transduction by λdg or meropolyploid as in sexduction, all possible segregants may be obtained, whether haploid or merodiploid (or meropolyploid) homogenotes or heterogenotes. **1980** *Nature* 7 Feb. 599/1 We compared the transcription of r-protein mRNA in haploid and merodiploid strains. **1983** J. R. S. FINCHAM *Genetics* x. 266 Strains harbouring F[1]-elements are partial diploids (or merodiploids).

merogamy (mɛ'rɒgəmi), *n. Biol.* [ad. F. *mérogamie* (coined by P. A. Dangeard 1900, in *Botaniste* VII. v. 265): see MERO-[1], -GAMY.] A mode of sexual reproduction, found in certain protozoa and algae, characterized by the fusion of merogametes formed by fission of vegetative cells. Cf. HOLOGAMY *n.*

1901 *Jrnl. R. Microsc. Soc.* 56 Reduced autophagy or merogamy, which does not require the participation of the whole of a second gamete, but only either of its cytoplasm or of its nucleus. **1965** POLJANSKIJ & CHEJSIN *Dogiel's Gen. Protozool.* (ed. 2) vii. 310 The number of gametes arising from the vegetative forms may vary from two (paired merogamy) to several hundred (multiple merogamy). *Ibid.* 322 The comparative rarity of cases of paired merogamy..is perhaps partly due to its being unsuitable for rapid reproduction. **1979** *Tsitologiya* XXI. 270 Such forms of gametogenesis as transformation of vegetative cells into gametes and merogamy have become prohibited in Ciliophora.

Hence **mero'gamete** *n.*, a gamete produced by fission of a vegetative cell, which is usually smaller than the parent cell.

1932 BORRADAILE & POTTS *Invertebrata* ii. 84 In the male gamont the nucleus divides several times, and the daughter nuclei are set free with portions of the cytoplasm as biflagellate male gametes, which are thus merogametes. **1967** G. A. KERKUT *Borradaile & Potts's Invertebr.* (ed. 4) ii. 36 C[*hlamydomonas*] *brauni* and other species..form merogametes of two sizes and are definitely anisogamous.

Meroite ('mɛrəʊˌaɪt), *n.* and *a.* [f. *Mero-ë* (see MEROITIC *a.* and *n.*) + -ITE[1].] **A.** *n.* An inhabitant of the ancient Nubian kingdom of Meroë. **B.** *adj.* Of or pertaining to this kingdom.

1852 tr. *Lepsius's Discoveries in Egypt* xviii. 164 This may be the barbarous god mentioned by Strabo, which the Meroites revered besides Herakles, Pan, and Isis. **1911** *Encycl. Brit.* XXVI. 14/2 Many of the pyramids have a small shrine on the eastern side inscribed with debased Egyptian or Meroite hieroglyphics. **1911** F. L. GRIFFITH *Karanòg* ii. 20 The titles of the Meroite kings in Meroite hieroglyphic are modelled on those of the later Ptolemaic kings or the Roman emperors. **1973** *Times* 27 Mar. (Sudan Suppl.) p. vii/5 The Meroites..appear to have been surprisingly literate, and..their pottery is of exceptional artistic quality.

mesangial (miː'sændʒɪəl), *a. Anat.* [f. *MESANGI(UM *n.* + -AL[1].] Of or pertaining to the mesangium; *spec.* pertaining to or designating cells found in glomeruli of the kidney between the capillary endothelium and the basement membrane.

1941 *Arch. Path.* XXXII. 46 Möllendorff's impression that where the mesangial tissue apposes the capillary basement membrane the two may be indistinguishable. **1951** H. W. SMITH *Kidney* i. 5 In acute glomerulonephritis, both the capillary and mesangial cells suffer inflammatory changes. **1976** EDINGTON & GILLES *Path. in Tropics* (ed. 2) ii. 29 We have seen haemozoin in the mesangial cells of the glomeruli in two [malaria] patients with a proliferative nephritis. **1980** *Sci. Amer.* July 48/1 (*caption*) Very large [immune] complexes (*A, B*) tend to be disposed of by mesangial cells and circulating phagocytes. **1987** *Oxf. Textbk. Med.* (ed. 2) II. XVIII. 82/1 Diffuse mesangial sclerosis or focal glomerular sclerosis may be found on renal biopsy of children with congenital nephrotic syndrome.

mesangium (miː'sændʒɪəm), *n. Anat.* [mod.L. (coined in Ger. by K. W. Zimmermann 1933, in *Zeitschr. f. mikroskopisch-anat. Forschung* XXXII. 251) f. Gr. ἀγγεῖον vessel: see MESO-.] The part of a glomerulus of the kidney where the afferent and efferent arterioles are closest together, situated towards the outer end of the vascular pole of the glomerular capsule.

1934 *Bull. Johns Hopkins Hosp.* LV. 420 Zimmermann..speaks of the 'Polkissen' as a mass of connective-tissue cells applied to the afferent arteriole at its entry and extending a short way along it...This connective tissue..is especially to be seen in a central position in the lobule, between the capillaries and is spoken of as the 'mesangium'. **1948** in *Biol. Abstr.* (1949) XXIII. 761/2 Certain infrequent stroma cells of the mesangium. **1980** *Sci. Amer.* July 43/1 When these deposits were limited to the mesangium, there was either minimal evidence or none of proteinuria. **1987** *Amer. Jrnl. Path.* CXXVII. 149/1 A number of studies have demonstrated an increase of mononuclear phagocytes in the mesangium in glomerulonephritis.

mesiodistal (ˌmiːzɪəʊ'dɪstəl), *a. Dentistry.* [f. MESIO- + DISTAL *a.*] Situated in or pertaining to the line of the dental arch.

1908 G. V. BLACK *Wk. Operative Dentistry* II. 15 The axio-mesio-distal plane, or the mesio-distal plane, ..passes through the tooth mesio-distally parallel with its long axis. **1949** H. SICHER *Oral Anat.* iv. 217 The pulp chamber or coronal pulp cavity is..narrow in mesiodistal, wide in buccolingual direction. **1963** J. OSBORNE *Dental Mech.* (ed. 5) ix. 171 Clasp arms that encirle the mesiodistal convexity of one or more teeth are useful in this respect. **1988** *Oral Surg., Oral Med. & Oral Path.* LXV. 343/2 This article describes three cases of mesiodistal root fracture with the histopathologic findings in each case.

So **mesio'distally** *adv.*, in the direction of the line of the dental arch.

1900 C. N. JOHNSON *Princ. & Practice filling Teeth* v. 137 The width of the cavity bucco-lingually or mesio-distally in the decayed portion must be great enough to insure strong, well-supported walls. **1963** C. R. COWELL et al. *Inlays, Crowns, & Bridges* ix. 100 A uniform amount should be removed mesiodistally following the incisal contour of the tooth. **1986** *Nature* 7 Aug. 520/1 The one complete tooth crown, right P3, is 11.5 mesiodistally by 16.2 buccolingually.

meso-, *comb. form.* Add: **meso'limbic** *a. Anat.*, situated in or designating the middle of the limbic system of the brain.

1971 *Acta Physiol. Scand.* Suppl. CCCLXVII. 1 The course of the nigro-striatal and the *meso-limbic DA pathways is presented in detail. **1973** *Psychopharmacologia* XXXII. 167 Neuroleptic agents have been shown to increase the turnover of dopamine in the mesolimbic brain areas in a very similar manner to their effects on the extrapyramidal system. **1978** *Nature* 7 Dec. 618/1 It is proposed that the substance P innervation of the VTA is part of a descending feedback loop which modulates the mesolimbic and mesocortical dopaminergic systems.

mesosphere *n.* (*b*) *Geol.*, the inner layer of the earth's mantle.

1939 in B. Gutenberg *Internal Constitution of Earth* v. 92 There would be some advantage in using the terms *kentrosphere* for the core or nucleus, *mesosphere* for the intermediate shell and *perisphere* for the uppermost layer or crust. **1968** *Jrnl. Geophysical Res.* LXXIII. 5856/2 The lithosphere and the mesosphere have relatively high seismic velocities and propagate seismic waves without great attenuation. **1971** I. G. GASS et al. *Understanding Earth* xvi. 248 (*caption*) The lithosphere and mesosphere are thought to have appreciable strength. **1980** *Nature* 14 Feb. 636/2 These heterogeneities may result from original regional heterogeneities in the mesosphere if the plumes are derived from the mesosphere.

mesospheric *a.* (earlier and later examples).

1940 R. A. DALY *Strength & Struct. of the Earth* xii. 355 The strength of the sub-asthenospheric shell and an assumed deviation of its surface from the shape of a rotation-spheroid will be given hypothetical explanation. For this layer we have Washington's convenient name 'mesosphere' or, better, 'mesospheric shell'—a coinage more logically conceived than the older synonym 'centrospheric shell'. **1980** *Nature* 14 Feb. 636/2 These heterogeneities may result..from mixing of mesospheric (lower mantle) and upper mantle components.

mesocyclone ('miːsəʊˌsaɪkləʊn), *n. Meteorol.* [f. MESO- + CYCLONE *n.*] A rotating column of rising air associated with a small area of low pressure, which may develop into a tornado.

1963 T. FUJITA in *Meteorol. Monogr.* Sept. 85/2 A mesolow which is found to accompany a definite circulation pattern is called a 'mesocyclone'. *Ibid.* 89/2 The existence of a mesocyclone is first seen by radar as a pendant echo which soon curls around the circulation center. **1976** *Ottawa Citizen* 7 Dec. 41/1 Twisters appear to be preceded by peculiar rotating motions within thunderstorms... These rotating features [are] called mesocyclones. **1978** *N.Y. Times* 29 Mar. A15/4 Observing the wind and rain movement five to six miles up in a thundercloud, a Doppler radar detects the formation of mesocyclones, the parents of tornadoes. **1984** *Sci. Amer.* Apr. 60/3 First the entire thunderstorm updraft begins to rotate; the spinning column of rising air, 10 to 20 kilometers in diameter, is called a mesocyclone. (If it goes on to generate a tornado, which the majority of mesocyclones do not, it is called a tornado cyclone.)

mesozoan (mɛsəʊ'zəʊən, miːzəʊ-), *a.* and *n. Zool.* [f. MESOZO(A *n. pl.* + -AN.] **A.** *adj.* Of or pertaining to mesozoa or the group Mesozoa. **B.** *n.* A member of the group Mesozoa, comprising minute animals with no organs or body cavity which are parasitic on marine invertebrates.

1909 WEBSTER, Mesozoan, *a.* **1924** *Jrnl. Parasitol.* XI. 59 The type species, *Haplozoon armatum*, was originally described by Dogiel..as a mesozoon, and for the genus..he established a new mesozoan class, the Catenata. **1940** L. H. HYMAN *Invertebrates* I. iv. 245 From the rather complete description of *Salinella* given by Frenzel it is evident that this animal is not a mesozoan and does not fit into any other animal phylum. **1972** *Sci. Amer.* Dec. 95/1 The adult mesozoan, whose natural habitat is the urine of cephalopods, is a long, slender organism. **1988** R. S. K. BARNES et al. *Invertebrates* iii. 94/2 The simplicity of the mesozoan anatomy has been interpreted in terms of such parasitic degeneration.

messenger ('mɛsɪndʒə(r)), *v.* [f. MESSENGER *n.*] *trans.* To send by messenger, esp. within an organization.

[**1687** R. L'ESTRANGE *Brief Hist. Times* I. 84 No other way to Save our Prince, and our Religion..but by a Fair Riddance of all the Kings English Subjects of That Persuasion [*sc.* Roman Catholic]; which by Pursuivanting, Messengering, Sergeanting, Cooping-up, Squeezing, Rifling, Plundering, and Oppressing, they had well-nigh Effected already.] **1822** C. LAMB *Lett.* (1935) II. 351 Can I have a revise of Philelia..*sent by post*. Don't trouble yourself to messenger it. **1979** *Washington Post* 6 Mar. B8/2 A copy of the letter was received from the White House..and of course immediately messengered to the FTC hearings and ABC witnesses. **1985** R. LOURIE *First Loyalty* (1986) xxi. 202, I told him that I would need a letter on his stationery messengered up to me, and then I would messenger the film down to him.

Messier ('mɛsɪə(r)), *n. Astron.* [The name of Charles *Messier* (1730–1817), French astronomer.] Used (*a*) *attrib.* and in the possessive (as *Messier('s) catalogue, Messier number, object*) with reference to Messier's catalogue of diffuse non-stellar objects visible in the northern sky, first published in 1774; (*b*) with a following numeral to denote a particular object in this catalogue (more commonly as the abbrev. M).

1861 *Monthly Notices R. Astron. Soc.* XXI. 33 The cluster known as 80 *Messier* changed, *apparently*, from a pale cometary looking object, to a well-defined star..and then returned to its usual and original appearance. **1899** *Astrophysical Jrnl.* X. 255 The cluster *Messier* 5..contains about 900 stars on the photographs made with the 13-inch Boyden refractor. **1917** *Publ. Astron. Soc. Pacific* XXIX. 177 Most of the Messier numbers, however, have been identified with numbers of Dreyer's *New General Catalogue.* **1929** *Astrophysical Jrnl.* LXIX. 104 Messier 31, the great nebula in Andromeda, is the most conspicuous of all the spirals and the only one which can be seen easily with the naked eye. **1943** H. SHAPLEY *Galaxies* iv. 86 Many a modern amateur and some professional astronomers have since come upon one of these Messier objects and have excitedly telegraphed the supposed discovery of a new comet to the information bureau at the Harvard Observatory. **1947** *Jrnl. R. Astron. Soc. Canada* XLI. 268 This last is the complete list, and is the document usually referred to as Messier's Catalogue. **1964** V. BAROCAS tr. *Abetti & Hack's Nebulae & Galaxies* i. 23 After the Messier catalogue and John Herschel's general catalogue of 1864 and the others already mentioned. **1968** K. G. JONES *Messier's Nebulae & Star Clusters* i. 29 Many of the Messier Objects, being on the whole, easily visible, have played a large part in revealing much of our present knowledge of stellar evolution and general cosmology. **1978** *Sci. Amer.* Dec. 127/1 Their Messier numbers.., together with their popular names, are M8, the Lagoon Nebula; M16, the Eagle Nebula; [etc.]. **1987** *New Yorker* 2 Feb. 26/2 Messier 1 turned out to be the Crab nebula in Taurus.

messily ('mɛsɪlɪ), *adv.* [f. MESSY *a.* + -LY².] In a messy manner, so as to make a mess.
  1920 K. BURKE *Let.* 6 Sept. in P. Jay *Sel. Corr. Kenneth Burke & Malcolm Cowley* (1988) 778, I detest messy things, but so far it has been my fate to write messily, as much as I try to avoid it. **1925** A. HUXLEY *Those Barren Leaves* IV. iii. 291 Miss Elver.. was eating chocolate éclairs and meringues, messily, with an expression of rapture on her cream-smeared face. **1949** J. D. CARR *Life of Sir A. Conan Doyle* xix. 282 At moated Birlstone Manor, a man is messily murdered with a shotgun amid curious clues. **1969** V. NABOKOV *Ada* II. iii. 356 A cauliflowered candle was messily burning in its tin cup on the window ledge. **1987** I. MCEWAN *Child in Time* v. 95 He put his hands over his face and cried briefly and messily. **1991** *N.Y. Times Mag.* 8 Dec. 81/1 His rare personal appearances at home often as not ended up messily, the police required at least once.

mesterolone (mɛ'stɛrələʊn), *n. Pharm.* [Prob. f. ME(THYL *n.* + STEROL *n.* + -ONE.] A synthetic androgen which is given orally in the treatment of male hypogonadism, male infertility, and similar conditions; 17β-hydroxy-1α-methyl-5α-androstan-3-one, $C_{20}H_{32}O_2$.
  1965 *WHO Chron.* XIX. 452 Mesterolone. **1966** *Arzneimittel-Forschung* XVI. 458/2 Mesterolone has a weak progestational activity, like testosterone. **1987** *Oxf. Textbk. Med.* (ed. 2) I. x. 98/2 There is no sound evidence to prove that the various non-specific therapies that have been employed such as.. mesterolone or cooling the scrotum do anything more for the patient than put off the time when he must learn that he is infertile. **1989** COLLIER & LONGMORE *Oxf. Handbk. Clin. Specialties* (ed. 2) i. 58 Oligospermia (<20 million sperm/ml) may respond to tamoxifen 10 mg/12h PO or mesterolone 50 mg/24h PO for three months or the use of clomiphene.

meta-, *comb. form.* Add: [**1.**] [**b.**] *meta-condition.*
  1972 Z. BAR-LEV in *Glossa* VI. 180 The assumption that a definition of the notion 'meaning' as a linguistic level—a definition consisting of a set of 'semantic *metaconditions*' that specify the way in which semantic properties and relations must be represented in semantic structure—is crucial to linguistic theory. **1977** *Canad. Jrnl. Ling.* XXII. 9 Kim.. proposes a meta-condition involving eight phonetic degrees of aperature which manifests itself in several phonological rules in Korean. **1985** *Byte* Aug. 52/2 Metaconditions, metaprograms, tail-recursive definitions, and user-created modules let you experience the full power of Prolog.

metabolize, *v.* Add: Hence **me'tabolizer** *n.*, an individual or organism that metabolizes a particular substance.
  1970 *Nature* 11 July 193/1 These precursors of normal excretory products in mammals are found in measurable quantities in known metabolizers. **1977** *Lancet* 17 Sept. 586/1 Since the mother must carry the n allele for two sons to be nn and must also carry the e allele for the third son and herself to be extensive metabolisers [of debrisoquine], then she herself can

only be heterozygous (en). **1988** *Nature* 14 Jan. 185/2 For this analysis, I identified as sulphur metabolizers the three eocytes.

metacercaria (ˌmɛtəsɜː'kɛərɪə), *n. Zool.* Pl. -iae. [f. META- 4 + CERCARIA *n.*] The (usu. encysted) final larval form of a trematode into which a cercaria develops prior to assuming the adult form in the definitive host.
  1927 *Jrnl. R. Microsc. Soc.* XLVII. 169 Metacercariæ of Strigeidæ have been found parasitic in the eyes of a large number of fish such as the sturgeon. **1930** E. C. FAUST *Human Helminthol.* ii. 32 After the cercaria emerges from the mollusc and discards its tail it is spoken of as the metacercaria or adolescaria. **1978** *Nature* 21 Sept. 216/1 Resistance.. operates against intraperitoneally implanted metacercariae, juvenile or adult flukes as well as against orally administered metacercariae. **1988** J. C. BELL et al. *Zoonoses* 148 Cercariae develop into metacercariae, which migrate into the bile ducts of definitive hosts after they eat the fish.

metacyclic, *a.* and *n.* Add: [**A.**] **2.** *Biol.* and *Med.* [ad. F. *métacyclique* (coined by E. Brumpt 1913, in *Bull. de la Soc. de Path. Exotique* VI. 168).] Designating the form that some trypanosomes attain in the intermediate, invertebrate host, in which they are infective for the vertebrate host.
  1926 C. M. WENYON *Protozool.* I. 344 In the case of the development of trypanosomes in the invertebrate, the final infective forms which pass back to the vertebrate have the trypanosome structure, and have been developed from attached or haptomonad forms of the crithidia type. These infective forms have been termed metacyclic trypanosomes by Brumpt (1913). **1964** M. HYNES *Med. Bacteriol.* (ed. 8) xxi. 323 After this interval large numbers of slender metacyclic forms appear in the body cavity of the louse, which remains infective for life. **1978** *Nature* 22 June 613/1 The trypanosomes causing the various forms of this disease.. are transmitted by tsetse flies (*Glossina* spp.) in whose internal organs they undergo a complicated cycle of development before they reach the infective metacyclic stage in the fly's saliva. **1987** *Oxf. Textbk. Med.* (ed. 2) I. v. 515/2 Trypanosomes of the *T. brucei* group are elongated parasites... Metacyclic trypanosomes are similar to the blood forms.
  B. *n. Biol.* and *Med.* A metacyclic trypanosome.
  1947 *Ann. Trop. Med. & Parasitol.* XLI. 11 We have seen metacyclics with two kinetoplasts and two nuclei, but we have not seen further evidence of splitting and separation. **1955** P. A. BUXTON *Nat. Hist. Tsetse Flies* xv. 642 Only 4 of the 19 developed an infection; they had received doses estimated to be 170, 284, 389, and 455 metacyclics. **1988** *Parasitology* XCVI. 26 The repertoire of variant antigen types displayed by the metacyclics.. is both limited and conserved.

metafiction ('mɛtəfɪkʃ(ə)n), *n. Lit. Theory.* Also **meta-fiction.** [f. META- + FICTION *n.*] (A work of) fiction in which the author self-consciously alludes to the artificiality or literariness of a work by parodying or departing from novelistic conventions (esp. naturalism) and traditional narrative techniques.
  1960 *Times Lit. Suppl.* 17 June 381/3 *All or Nothing*.. can be regarded as a metaphysical discourse, a mockery of rationalism, meta-fiction or space poetry. **1970** W. H. GASS *Fiction & Figures of Life* I. i. 25 Many of the so-called antinovels are really metafictions. **1980** B. W. ALDISS *Life in West* viii. 154 They are worthy of a serious study as metafiction or socio-economic artform. **1994** *Observer* 18 Sept. (Rev. Suppl.) 19/1 Metafiction, fiction which self-consciously signals its status as fiction, is usually a pain... Austin Wright's *Tony and Susan* is a rarity—a metafiction that ingeniously comments on the experience of reading it,

but which, as fiction, retains a feverish psychic grip. Hence **meta'fictional, meta'fictive** *adjs.*

1982 *N.Y. Times* 7 Nov. VII. 12/3 At this level of metafictional farce the book's interest depends less on storytelling than on Mr. Federman's ability to generate a continuous stream of rhetorical energy. **1988** L. HUTCHEON *Canad. Postmodern* vi. 130 The language of the novel makes the metafictive level overt: 'He is the author of those maps but he has never known their ultimate affirmation, the consummation of the pact between traveler and traveled. He can only draw them.' **1991** *Amer. Bk. Rev.* Apr.-May 23/3 This would involve not only the use of metafictive techniques similar to those employed by male-oriented avant-gardes of the past, but also a feminist irony that would help us achieve critical distance from various cultural myths. **1993** *Rev. Eng. Stud.* May 291 His account of spatiality in Walter Abish, and of the problematics of gender relations in Robert Coover's *Spanking the Maid*. . is fully alive to the metafictional procedures worked out by these writers.

metal, *n.* (and *a.*) (*metal detector*: formerly at sense 13b in Dict.). Add: [**1.**] **g.** *ellipt.* for *heavy metal* s.v. HEAVY *a.*[1] (*n.*) 20 d. Freq. *attrib.*, or as the second element in Combs. denoting types of music which incorporate aspects of heavy metal.

1975 'L. REED' (*title of record*) Metal machine music. **1980** *N.Y. Times* 19 Dec. C19/3 The definitive album of postpunk rock and the year's most compelling slice of metal machine music. **1984** *Sounds* 29 Dec. 14/2 You must have metal madmen. **1986** *Courier-Mail* (Brisbane) 28 Aug. (Blitz Suppl.) 3/3, I like to take a break from metal, I don't always listen to it. **1987** *Guardian* 20 Mar. 19/2 Punk and metal are mingling into a hybrid variously called 'speed', 'thrash' or even 'death' metal. **1989** *Q* Dec. 110/3 By side two's live bonanza.., the onus is back on crunching power-trio metal. **1994** *Hypno* I. 20/2 They can do all the Sex Pistols' covers they want, but they are still just a lame-o metal band.

[**14.**] **metal-detecting** *n.*, the practice of searching for buried metallic objects by means of a metal detector.

1977 *Treasure Hunting* I. 44/1 The Shrewsbury and District *Metal Detecting Club. **1986** *Rescue News* Summer 6 (*heading*) The National Council for Metal Detecting. **1992** *Jrnl.* (Milwaukee) 25 July G4/1 (Advt.), Joshua. . is an honor student and a member of the softball and track teams. He enjoys drawing, movies and metal detecting.

metal detector, any of various electronic devices that detect and signal the presence of metallic objects from their magnetic effects; *spec.* (*a*) a portable device for locating buried metal objects; (*b*) a hand-held or walk-through security apparatus for identifying concealed weapons, etc.

1946 *Wireless World* Dec. 402/1 (*caption*) 'Cintel'. *metal detector, an adaptation of the wartime mine detector produced by Cinema-Television Ltd . . . It is claimed to locate accurately . . pipes, etc. buried . . below the surface. **1971** B. ST. J. WILKES *Naut. Archaeol.* vi. 120 Metal detectors are sold quite extensively in the US and Canada to amateur 'prospectors' to aid their hunt for gold. **1975** *Guardian* 1 Oct. 2/1 Chicago police will be using hand-held metal detectors on all crowds who come near President Ford. **1984** D. LODGE *Small World* II. i. 103 He passes through the electronic metal detector, first handing over his spectacle case, which he knows from experience will activate the device, . . and proceeds to the waiting lounge by Gate 5. **1991** *Treasure Hunting* Oct. 51, I moved forward a few paces, switched on my metal detector and started swinging it in an arc before me. At first there was . . just background hum of ironisation in the soil.

So **metal detectorist**, a person who engages in metal-detecting.

1987 *Sunday Tel.* 29 Nov. 11/1 David Loriboad . . wrote the article entirely from the archaeological point of view and scarcely made any reference to the metal detectorists' case. **1989** *Independent* 1 July 1 About 55 per cent of Britain's foreshore is owned by the Crown, including the spot where metal detectorist Ken Willcox found the mount in September 1987. **1994** *Kent Archaeological Rev.* Spring 105 A great deal of Romano-British building material was observed on the surface. (This had been observed as well by members of a metal detectorist club.)

metalaxyl (mɛtə'læksɪl), *n.* *Agric.* and *Pharm.* [f. META- 6 a + A)LA(NINE *n.* + XYL(ENE *n.*] A fungicide effective against mildew on some crops; (±)-methyl-*N*-(2-methoxyacetyl)-*N*-(2, 6-xylyl)alaninate.

1979 *B.S.I. News* May 20/1 The following names have been provisionally adopted . . . Metalaxyl. **1979** *Plant Dis. Reporter* LXIII. 986 (*heading*) Control of Sugarcane downy mildew of maize with metalaxyl. **1984** ROBERTS & BOOTHROYD *Fund. Plant Path.* (ed. 2) xxvi. 325 Metalaxyl has proved highly effective against blue mold. **1986** *Grower* 6 Nov. 23/1 Mildew resistance to metalaxyl-based fungicide . . has . . spread throughout the country.

metallic, *a.* and *n.* Restrict *pl.* to existing senses B. a and b. Add: [**B.**] **c.** A metallic colour; also, a metallic surface or finish, esp. on a motor vehicle.

1976 *Industrial Furnishing* Apr. 46/1 Disadvantages include: . . poor properties with light-colored metallics. **1976** *Liverpool Echo* 6 Dec. 14/4 (Advt.), New Cherry 100 A 2 door, big selection of colours including metallics. **1987** *Lancaster Guardian* 2 Oct. 31/5 (Advt.), Audi 100 CD in Titan red metallic, has done 54,547 miles. **1988** *Oxford Star* 23 June 37/2 (Advt.), 340 GL 3 door . . finished in light green metallic. **1991** *Artpost* Summer 20/1 (Advt.), For metallics, interference and pearlescent colours, try Daniel Smith Luminescent Oil Colours.

metallicity, *n.* Add: **2.** *Astron.* The relative abundance in a celestial object of elements heavier than helium.

In practice the relative abundance of iron relative to hydrogen, as inferred from their line strengths, is usually taken as a measure of this.

1969 *Astron. & Astrophysics* II. 226/2 How can we explain the very high metallicity of the field star τ UMa, and the very different chemical composition amongst the stars of one and the same cluster such as the Hyades? **1980** *Astrophysical Jrnl.* CCXLII. 242/1 The age-metallicity relation (AMR) for the disk is an important constraint on theoretical models of galactic evolution. **1989** R. A. MEYERS *Encycl. Astron. & Astrophysics* 653/2 The usual means of quoting metallicity for these clusters . . is in terms of the Fe/H ratio. This is normally quoted as a differential measure relative to the sun, as [Fe/H] = log (Fe/H) − log (Fe/H)⊙. **1992** *Astronomy* May 32/2 Another study of LSB galaxies shows they have very low metallicities, meaning they are made almost exclusively of hydrogen and helium.

metalliding ('mɛtəlaɪdɪŋ), *vbl. n.* *Manuf.* [f. METALL(O- + -ID(E + -ING[1].] A form of electroplating in which the electrodes are immersed in a bath of molten fluoride salts from which metal ions diffuse into the cathode to form a surface layer whose composition varies continuously from the surface inwards.

1967 *Iron Age* 22 June 71/1 Metalliding is a high temperature electrolytic technique in which an anode and a cathode are suspended in a molten salt bath. As a direct current is passed from anode to the cathode, the anode material diffuses into the surface of the cathode, putting on a uniform pore-free coating. **1971**

Corrosion XXVII. 55/1 Metalliding involves the electrolytic deposition of a variety of diffusion coatings on metal surfaces.

Hence (as a back-formation) 'metallide *v. trans.*, to deposit by this process; 'metallided *ppl. a.*

1967 *Aviation Week* 3 July 55/2 Metallided coating can also be produced from yttrium .. and the rare earth elements. **1967** *Sci. News* 15 July 66 Molybdenum, for example, is a relatively soft metal; when boron is metallided into it, the resulting surface alloy is apparently second in hardness only to diamond.

metallo-, *comb. form.* Add: me‚tallo'genesis *n. Geol.* = metallogeny.
1923 *Econ. Geol.* XVIII. 105 One of the most important problems of *metallogenesis at the present day is that of the existence of a definite arrangement in space of the ore deposits of metalliferous regions. **1947** *Ibid.* XLII. 725 Scientific basis of metallogenesis was introduced by Daubrée, Scheerer and Élie de Beaumont over a century ago. **1975** *Chem. in Brit.* XI. 167/1 Submarine metallogenesis on a large scale has been found in the Red Sea. **1978** *Sci. Amer.* Feb. 60/3 The study of ophiolites .. confirms the validity of the model of hydrothermal metallogenesis.

metallothionein (mɪˌtælǝʊ'θaɪǝniːn) *n. Biochem.* [THION-, -EIN], any of a class of cysteine-rich proteins which are capable of binding heavy metal ions and which may thus be involved in the detoxification of cells.
1960 KÄGI & VALLEE in *Jrnl. Biol. Chem.* CCXXXV. 3460/1 A protein from equine renal cortex which contains 2.9% of cadmium, 0.6% of zinc, and 4.1% of sulfur per g dry weight .. has been termed metallothionein in view of its metal and sulfur content. **1975** *Nature* 11 Sept. 136/1 Induction of hepatic metallothionein (a cadmium-binding protein) is considered to be a protective mechanism in mammals against the toxic cadmium ion. **1982** *Sci. Amer.* Aug. 50/3 In the marine blue-green alga *Synechococcus* a comparatively small cadmium-binding metallothionein can bind an average of 1.28 atoms of cadmium per molecule of protein. **1986** *Science* 14 Feb. 704/1 Metallothioneins and their genes have several potential kinds of physiological activity.

metallocarborane (mɪˌtælǝʊ'kɑːbǝreɪn), *n. Chem.* [f. METALLO- + CAR(BON *n.* + BORANE *n.*] A compound consisting of metal ions complexed with ligands containing carbon, boron, and hydrogen.
1969 *Inorg. Chem.* VIII. 2080 (*heading*) Crystal structure of .. a salt of a three-icosahedral-fragment metallocarborane. **1976** *Nature* 11 Mar. 176/3 Although work on various metallocarboranes is reported, there is almost no coverage of carboranes *per se.* **1984** GREENWOOD & EARNSHAW *Chem. of Elements* (1986) vi. 212 Numerous variants are possible including the insertion of a second metal centre into an existing metallocarborane. **1987** *Inorg. Chem.* XXVI. 3117/2 In the negative ion spectra, the parent group is the most intense in the spectrum (typical for metallocarboranes).

metalware ('mɛtǝlwɛǝ(r)), *n.* Also metal-ware, metal ware. [f. METAL *n.* + WARE *n.*³] Chiefly *collect. sing.* Articles, esp. utensils, made of metal.
1907 *N.E.D.* s.v. *Planish v.*, To flatten (sheet-metal or metal-ware) on an anvil by blows of a smooth-faced hammer, or by [etc.]. **1908** H. N. VEITCH *Sheffield Plate* 12 The earliest Sheffield Platers naturally employed the established methods of making metal wares. **1938** W. H. B. COURT *Rise of Midland Industries* ix. 134 The seventeenth century appears to have seen .. a change in the position of London, the largest single market for metal-wares in the country. **1958** *Jrnl. Roman Stud.* XLVIII. 14 Silver, gold and bronze metalware .. was brought home by victorious Roman

generals. **1981** P. HORNSBY *Arthur Negus Guide to Pewter, Copper & Brass* 8 We opened our first shop .. where we specialise in antique metalware. **1994** *Pop. Crafts* July 72 (*heading*) The ancient art of Bidriware, a form of decorating metalware, is still practised in India.

metamessage ('mɛtǝmɛsɪdʒ), *n.* Also meta-message. [f. META- + MESSAGE *n.*¹] An underlying meaning, a hidden message; *spec.* in *Advertising*, a statement intended to persuade through implication rather than direct exhortation.
1977 *Addictive Dis.* III. 279 Advertisers also make capital of the meta-message—the innuendo, the unstated point that seems innocuous enough on the surface. **1984** T. A. SEBEOK *Communication Measures to bridge Ten Millennia* (Techn. Rep. ONWI-532) v. 27 The 'atomic priesthood' would be charged with the added responsibility of seeing to it that our behest, as embodied in the cumulative sequence of metamessages, is to be heeded. **1991** *New Scientist* 24 Aug. 37/2 His tone was patronising. Its 'metamessage', as Tannen puts it, was that everything baffling her was obvious to him.

metaphor *n.* Senses a,b in Dict. become 1,3. Add: **2.** Something regarded as representative or suggestive of something else, esp. as a material emblem of an abstract quality, condition, notion, etc.; a symbol, a token. Freq. const. *for, of.*
1864 W. ARNOT *Parab. our Lord* iv. 119 The serpent, as a metaphor, was in practice as completely thirled to the indication of evil, as leaven had been. **1881** H. JAMES *Washington Square* xxxii. 241 If your leg is a metaphor for young Townsend, I can assure you he has never been crushed ... He is alive and perfectly intact. **1909** J. LONDON in *Sat. Even. Post* 22 May 3/1 North of the Slot were the theaters, hotels, and shopping district ... South of the Slot were the factories, slums, laundries, machine-shops, boiler works, and the abodes of the working class. The Slot was the metaphor that expressed the class cleavage of Society. **1962** *Times* 20 Dec. 11/1 The great joy of a novelist is that .. he can create his own metaphor of the universe. **1978** P. GRIFFITHS *Conc. Hist. Mod. Mus.* viii. 121 *Mahagonny* is thus a parable of modern society, a work in which the bitter, commercialized sounds of jazz .. stand as a metaphor for the corrupt condition of the capitalist state. **1984** H. JACOBSON *Peeping Tom* (1985) I. iv. 113 The central metaphor for Tess's confusions is the threshing-machine. **1991** *Art in Amer.* Apr. 160/3 The Rococo style becomes a metaphor about the denial through prettification of our often exploitative relationship to nature.

meta-talk ('mɛtǝtɔːk), *n.* [f. META- + TALK *n.*] Underlying messages or hidden significance in a conversation, etc. Cf. METACOMMUNICATION *n.*
1953 *Mind* LXII. 378 The meta-talk abounds in contextual and behavioural terminology. **1974** NIERENBERG & CALERO (*title*) Meta-talk: guide to hidden meanings in conversation. *Ibid.* 9 For those meanings behind our ordinary talk we have coined the word 'meta-talk'. **1982** P. DICKSON *Words* (1983) xlvii. 275 'Meta-talk' .. amounts to the silent messages that are generated when we talk. **1992** *Vancouver Sun* 10 Dec. D3/1 Without warning, the couple sometimes talk in overlapping dialogue as they offer their innermost but unvoiced thoughts as they express, in meta-talk, what they think is acceptable to the other.

metavolcanic (mɛtǝvɒl'kænɪk), *n.* and *a. Petrogr.* (Formerly at META- 5 b.) [f. META- 5 b + VOLCANIC *a.* (and *n.*).] **A.** *n.* A volcanic rock which has been subjected to metamorphism. **B.** *adj.* Designating such rock.
1942 M. P. BILLINGS *Struct. Geol.* xii. 215 Metasediments, metavolcanics, and meta-igneous rocks

are metamorphic rocks derived, respectively, from sedimentary, volcanic, and igneous rocks. **1962** *Mineral. Abstr.* XV. 381/1 The granite gneisses, amphibolites, and metavolcanics of the southern Klodzko metamorphic zone are described. **1964** *Ibid.* XVI. 657/2 Thirteen planimetric and 22 chemical analyses elucidate the composition of the conglomerates, graywacke schists, mica schists, and basic metavolcanic rocks. **1971** *Bull. Volcanologique* XXXIV. 778 Nearly all workers concerned with the stratified rocks have acknowledged that there are probably some metavolcanic rocks in the predominantly metasedimentary formations. **1979** *Canad. Mineralogist* XVII. 198/1 Field relationships suggest that the metavolcanic and metasedimentary rocks may be coeval. **1989** *Jrnl. Petrol.* XXX. 178 The igneous component is represented by amphibolites and intercalated felsic meta-volcanics.

met-enkephalin (ˌmɛtɛnˈkɛfəlɪn), *n. Biochem.* Also **metenkephalin**. [ad. F. *met-enképhaline* (coined by R. Guillemin et al. 1976, in *Compt. Rend.* D. CCLXXXII. 784): cf. METHIONINE *n.*, ENKEPHALIN *n.*] The enkephalin whose peptide chain ends with a methionine unit.
1976 *Proc. Nat. Acad. Sci.* LXXIII. 2156/1 The newly isolated peptides met-enkephalin..and α-endorphin. **1976** *Brit. Jrnl. Pharmacol.* LVIII. 459P/1 We have found that iontophoretically applied met-enkephalin..is predominantly depressant. **1985** *Sci. Amer.* Oct. 119/1 Many features of neuropeptides are exemplified by the two enkephalins... One, called met-enkephalin, ends with methionine and the other, leu-enkephalin, with leucine.

meter, *n.*[3] Add: Hence '**meterless** *a.*, having no meter; also, done without the aid of a meter.
1978 *Taxi* 16 Feb. 3/4 No one..is going to go along to the Public Carriage Office and demand the passing of a meterless cab. **1979** *Mod. Photogr.* Dec. 21/1 Is a meterless camera a bit too pedestrian for you? O.K., go add a meter. **1986** *Courier-Mail* (Brisbane) 11 Oct. 17/2 The North Queensland Electricity Board had submitted a proposal for 'meterless' billing or 'agreed demand' billing.

metformin (mɛtˈfɔːmɪn), *n. Pharm.* [f. MET(HYL *n.* + FORM(ALDEHYDE *n.* + IM)IN(O(-): cf. PHENFORMIN *n.*] A white crystalline solid, 1,1-dimethylbiguanide, $C_4H_{11}N_5$, or its hydrochloride, which has been used in the oral treatment of diabetes mellitus.
1961 *Lancet* 24 June 1368/1 Effectiveness and better gastrointestinal tolerance have been claimed for dimethyldiguanide metformin. **1977** *Ibid.* 22 Jan. 191/2 Metformin is replacing phenformin as the biguanide of choice in the treatment of obese maturity-onset diabetics. **1991** *Longevity* Jan. 46/3 Metformin and buformin are in the same class of drugs, but do not have serious side effects.

methacholine (mɛθəˈkəʊliːn), *n. Pharm.* [f. METH- + -*a*- + CHOLINE *n.*] A parasympathomimetic choline derivative which can produce bronchoconstriction in hypersensitive patients and is used as a challenge in diagnostic tests for subclinical or incipient asthma; *O*-acetyl-β-methylcholine, $C_8H_{18}ClNO_2$.
1952 *Jrnl. Amer. Med. Assoc.* 17 May 271/1 The pharmacologic properties of methacholine chloride resemble those of acetylcholine, except for the less pronounced nicotinic effect on autonomic ganglions. **1961** A. GOTH *Med. Pharmacol.* iv. 51 Bethanechol (Urecholine) and methacholine (Mecholyl) have many of the actions of acetylcholine on glands. **1987** *Oxf. Textbk. Med.* (ed. 2) II. xv. 78/2 Patients with asthma have similar responses to histamine and methacholine while normal subjects are more sensitive to histamine. **1989** *Nat. Med. Jrnl. India* II. 265/1 Two millilitres of sequentially doubling

concentrations of methacholine.. were nebulized.. and delivered through a mouthpiece to the subjects.

methanal ('mɛθənæl) *n. Chem.* [f. METHAN(E *n.* + -AL[2].] = FORMALDEHYDE *n.*
1894 G. M'GOWAN tr. *Bernthsen's Text-bk. Org. Chem.* (ed.2) v. 146 Formic Aldehyde (Methanal)...This may also be regarded as the oxide of the diatomic radicle methylene. **1967** *Tetrahedron* XXIII. 1029 In the previous paper the computed properties of methyl cation using EHT theory were compared with two model systems: methanal and borane. **1983** NORMAN & WADDINGTON *Mod. Org. Chem.* (ed. 4) xii. 171 Methanal is a gas, other aldehydes and ketones of relatively low formula weight are liquids and the remainder are solids.

methanogen (mɪˈθænəʊdʒən), *n. Biol.* [Back-formation f. *METHANOGENIC *a.*] A methanogenic micro-organism.
1977 *Bacteriol. Rev.* XLI. 541/1 My purpose here is both to describe certain features of methanogens..and to review the biology of this group. **1977** *Globe & Mail* (Toronto) 5 Nov. 6/3 We might never have made the acquaintance of archaebacteria or methanogens, which evolved 3.5 to 4 billion years ago. **1980** S. J. GOULD *Panda's Thumb* (1982) xxi. 222 Methanogens are not bacteria at all. **1984** *Science* 9 Mar. 1021/3 Several taxonomically identified species of methanogens have now been isolated and studied in pure culture. **1989** *BioFactors* II. 117/1 Most methylotrophic methanogens contain sarcinapterin.

methanogenesis (ˌmɛθənəʊ-, mɪˌθænəʊˈdʒɛnəsɪs), *n. Biol.* [f. METHAN(E *n.* + -O[1] + GENESIS *n.*] The production of methane by living organisms, esp. archaebacteria.
1969 *Biochim. & Biophys. Acta* CXCII. 420 (*heading*) ATP requirement for methanogenesis in cell extracts of Methanobacterium strain M.o.H. **1976** *Ann. Rev. Microbiol.* XXX. 268 Methane may even be 'mined' from city dumps where methanogenesis has taken place under the fill. **1983** *Science* 4 Nov. 500/2 Methanogenesis in lake sediments. **1985** WOESE & WOLFE in Sokatch & Ornston *Bacteria* VIII. p. xxii, It is through methanogenesis that we have been introduced to the biochemical uniqueness of archaebacteria.

methanogenic (ˌmɛθənəʊ-, mɪˌθænəʊˈdʒɛnɪk), *a. Biol.* [f. METHAN(E *n.* + -O[1] + -GENIC.] Producing methane; of, pertaining to, or involving methanogenesis; *spec.* designating organisms, esp. archaebacteria, which reduce carbon dioxide to methane.
1968 *Jrnl. Bacteriol.* XCVI. 2178/1 Occurrence of methane in gas from the human intestine is evidence that methanogenic organisms grow in the human alimentary tract. **1976** *Appl. Environmental Microbiol.* XXXI. 99/1 Methanogenic activity in its sediments was first reported in 1932. **1982** M. J. DRING *Biol. Marine Plants* (1986) ix. 175 Therefore, anaerobic methanogenic bacteria replace those dependent on sulphate, and methane becomes the dominant product of decomposition in old, deep sediments.

methanoic (mɛθəˈnəʊɪk), *a. Chem.* [f. METHAN(E *n.* + -OIC.] **methanoic acid** = *formic acid* s.v. FORMIC *a.* 1.
1894 G. M'GOWAN tr. *Bernthsen's Text-bk. Org. Chem.* (ed.2) vi. 168 Formic Acid, (Methanoic acid), acidum formicum CH_2O_2. **1937** *Chem. Abstr.* XXXI. 9978/2 (subject index), *Methanoic acid*, see formic acid. **1972** NORMAN & WADDINGTON *Mod. Org. Chem.* xiii. 183 Methanoic acid and ethanoic acid are miscible with water. **1981** J. W. BUTTLE et al. *Chemistry* (ed. 4) xx. 443 Elimination of water follows..the formation of methanoic acid (formic acid) from trichloromethane.

methanotroph (mɛ'θænətrəʊf), *n. Microbiol.* [f.
METHAN(E *n.* + -O¹ + TROPH(IC *a.*] A micro-
organism, esp. an archaebacterium, that can
utilize methane as a source of carbon and energy.
   1976 Y. A. TROTSENKO in H. G. Schlegel et al.
*Symposium on Microbial Production & Utilization of
Gases* 334 No activity of pyruvate dehydrogenase could
be detected in any of the type II methanotrophs. **1979**
Soc. Gen. Microbiol. Q. VI. 71 The capacity to
dechlorinate is an unexpected property of a
methanotroph. **1989** *Nature* 28 Sept. 315/2
Laboratory studies indicate that oxidation of CH₄ by a
variety of methanotrophs is competitively inhibited by
nitrogen.
   Hence **methano'trophic** *a.*
   1975 *Mikrobiologiya* XLIV. 850 Pure cultures of
obligate methanotrophic bacteria were isolated from
natural habitats and cultivated on media containing
silica gel. **1979** I. J. HIGGINS in J. R. Quayle *Microbial
Biochem.* vii. 301 Natural gas contains gaseous
hydrocarbons other than methane and at least some will
be partially oxidized by methanotrophic cooxidative
metabolism. **1991** BARNES & MANN *Fund. Aquatic
Ecol.* (ed. 2) x. 207/2 Like the sulphur-oxidizing
bacteria, these methanotrophic bacteria are aerobic.

methapyrilene (mɛθə'pɪrɪliːn) *n. Pharm.* [f.
METH- + -*a*- + alteration of *pyr(id)yl* s.v.
PYRIDINE *n.* + -ENE.] A bicyclic pyridine
derivative which was formerly used as an
antihistamine agent and in sleeping aids;
dimethyl-2-(*N*-2-pyridyl-*N*-2-thenylamino) ethylamine, C₁₄H₁₉N₃S.
   1949 *Jrnl. Amer. Med. Assoc.* 23 July 1023/2 The
fatal poisoning of a healthy girl 16 months of age was
caused by the accidental ingestion of 100 mg. of
methapyrilene hydrochloride. **1965** *Appl.
Therapeutics* VII. 832/2 Double blind studies in
asthmatic children revealed that an antihistamine drug,
methapyrilene hydrochloride, enhanced the effect of
the bronchodilator drug. **1974** M. C. GERALD
Pharmacol. ii. 20 Nonprescription..sleep-facilitating
products,..have capitalized on the drowsiness induced
by methapyrilene. **1979** *Tucson* (Arizona) *Citizen* 20
Sept. 2E/1 HEW officials felt that a recall of these
products which contain methapyrilene would be 'an
appropriate action'. Methapyrilene has been shown to
be cancerous when fed to test animals.

methimazole (mɛ'θɪməzəʊl), *n. Pharm.* [f.
METH(YL *n.* + IM(ID)AZOLE *n.*] An imidazole
derivative with antithyroid properties, given
orally in the treatment of hyperthyroidism;
1-methylimidazole-2-thiol, C₃H₂N₂(CH₃)(SH).
   1951 *Amer. Jrnl. Med. Sci.* CCXXII. 140/1 The
relatively short period of methimazole therapy required
to produce euthyroidism after initial iodine
treatment. **1968** J. H. BURN *Lect. Notes Pharmacol.*
(ed. 9) 86 Thiouracil has been used to treat
thyrotoxicosis but it is now replaced by methimazole
and carbimazole. **1977** *Lancet* 21 May 1105/1
Treatment with 60 mg of methimazole and 60 mg
propranolol daily resulted in a clearing of his psychotic
and hypomanic symptoms. **1988** *Jrnl. Neural
Transmission* LXXI. 201 Desipramine binding was
decreased in thyrotoxicosis and increased in rats treated
with methimazole.

methiocarb (mɪ'θaɪəʊkɑːb), *n. Agric.* [f.
ME(THYL *n.* + THIO- + CARB(AMATE *n.*] An
insecticide, molluscicide, and acaricide,
C₁₁H₁₅NO₂S, widely used in garden
preparations such as slug pellets; 4-methylthio-
3,5-xylyl-*N*-methylcarbamate.
   1969 *Recommended Common Names for Pesticides
(B.S.I.)* 61 (*table*) Methiocarb. **1974** *Country Life* 24
Oct. 1228/1 Work at the Terrington EHF has compared
metaldehyde and methiocarb pellet baits. **1977** *Homes*

& Gardens Nov. 41 With metaldehyde..the slugs
recovered in damp or humid conditions, with
methiocarb, a stomach poison, there is no dependence
on weather conditions. **1988** *Bull. Environmental
Contamination & Toxicol.* XL. 147 (*heading*)
Laboratory evaluation of the hazard to wood mice,
Apodemus sylvaticus, from the agricultural use of
methiocarb molluscicide pellets.

‖**méthode champenoise** (metɔd ʃãpənwɑːz), *n.*
Also without accent. [Fr., lit. 'champagne
method'.] In wine-making, the process whereby
sparkle (dissolved carbon dioxide) is produced
in a bottled wine by inducing a second alcoholic
fermentation to take place within the bottle, as
with champagne, rather than being introduced
into the wine artificially or by transferring
naturally carbonated wine from a different
bottle or from a larger container; a sparkling
wine or other drink produced in this way.
   From 1994, under a European Union ruling, the
designation *méthode champenoise* was to be replaced
by one of four prescribed categories: *fermentation en
bouteille selon la méthode champenoise*, *méthode
traditionnelle*, *méthode classique*, and *méthode
traditionnelle classique*.
   1928 E. I. ROBSON *Wayfarer in Fr. Vineyards* i. 7 It
was also decided.. that 'champagnized wines' may bear
the title 'Méthode Champenoise'. This at least tells
the buyer how the wine has been treated. **1951** R.
POSTGATE *Plain Man's Guide to Wine* v. 92 Not one of
the 'mousseux', 'méthode champenoise' or 'gazifiés'
possesses the clean, hard flinty taste of
champagne. **1958** A. L. SIMON *Dict. Wines* 48/1 Other
wines, red, white and rosés, can be made and are made
'sparkling' by the *méthode champenoise*. **1976** *National
Observer* (U.S.) 4 Dec. 8/2 A bottle will sell . . for $7.80,
a price competitive with other first quality California
sparkling wines made by the traditional *methode
champenoise*. **1987** *Independent* 11 July 14/1 Bucks
Fizz... You don't have to use champagne, a decent
méthode champenoise sparkling white wine will
do. **1995** *Independent on Sunday* 22 Jan. (Sunday Rev.
Suppl.) 46/2 In the 1980s he experimented with an
English sparkling wine, a Méthode Champenoise, with
the help of a friend from Epernay in the heart of
Champagne country.

methohexital (mɛθəʊ'hɛksɪtæl), *n. Pharm.*
Chiefly *U.S.* [f. METH- + -O¹ + HEX(A- +
BARB)IT(URIC *a.* + AL(LYL *n.*] Methohexitone
sodium. More fully *methohexital sodium*,
sodium methohexital.
   Methohexital sodium is the U.S. Approved Name: cf.
*METHOHEXITONE *n.*
   1958 *Oral Surg.* XI. 604 Methohexital sodium is
the high-melting-point isomer of Compound 22451
(1-methyl-5-allyl-5-[1-methyl-2-pentynyl]) barbituric
acid, sodium salt, and is an ultra-short-acting barbituric
acid. **1961** *Anesthesia & Analgesia* XL. 573/1
Methohexital sodium..is a new intravenous
barbiturate. **1965** *Ibid.* XLIV. 494 (*heading*)
Preanesthetic sedation of children with intramuscular
methohexital sodium. **1978** *Nature* 2 Feb. 446/2
Anaesthesia is induced with Fluothane, a vein is
cannulated, and anaesthesia is maintained with Brevital
(sodium methohexital). **1987** *Anesthesia Progress*
XXXIV. 211/1 A conscious sedation regimen consisting
of alphaprodine, hydroxyzine, and methohexital..was
evaluated in an open pilot study for patients undergoing
minor gynecologic surgery.

methohexitone (mɛθəʊ'hɛksɪtəʊn), *n. Pharm.* [f.
METHOHEXIT(AL *n.* + -ONE.] A derivative of
barbituric acid given intravenously as an
anaesthetic in medical and veterinary use; also
(more fully *methohexitone sodium*), the sodium
salt of this. (1-methyl-5-allyl-5-[1-methyl-2-
pentynyl]) barbituric acid, C₁₄H₁₈N₂O₃.

Methohexitone is the British Approved Name for the compound: cf *METHOHEXITAL *n.*

1961 *Brit. Jrnl. Anaesthesia* XXXIII. 296/2 The incidence of grade 1 induction (complete absence of all complications) decreased with increasing dosage of methohexitone. **1963** *Ibid.* XXXV. 48/1 Methohexitone sodium when compared with other intravenous anaesthetic agents shows a greater potency and a shorter duration of action. **1966** *Brit. Dental Jrnl.* CXXI. 468/2 In the older child, if premedication is necessary we use methohexitone (Brietal) or the new agent propanidid (Epontal) intravenously for induction prior to inhalation anæsthesia. **1980** *Daily Tel.* 22 Sept. 3/2 The manufacturers of methohexitone wrote to all dentists within the past three months asking us to check our stocks for a batch of the drug which they believed was below par.

methoprene ('mɛθəʊpriːn) *n. Agric.* [f. METH- + IS)OPRENE *n.*] A derivative of an isoprene polymer which has the effect on some insects of arresting development at an early (esp. larval) stage and is widely used in insecticidal preparations; propyl 2-(3,7,11-trimethyl-11-methoxydodec-2-4-dien)oate, $C_{19}H_{34}O_3$.

1974 *Jrnl. Econ. Entomol.* LXVII. 386/2 Methoprene effectively inhibited the development of horn flies in cattle manure at all 3 concentrations tested. **1978** *Nature* 22 June 605/2 Several firms..have been interested in developing juvenile hormone mimics and one (methoprene) has been on the market for several years. **1979** *Ibid.* 24 May 280/3 The flour beetle, Tribolium, has not only developed multiple resistance to conventional pesticides but also acquired significant cross-resistance to the growth inhibitor, methoprene. **1986** C. A. HEATON *Chem. Industry* v. 279 Great success has been achieved with juvenile hormones in the laboratory but in the field it is much more difficult to judge the precise timing of application of the IGR [*sc.* insect growth regulator] to achieve maximum efficiency. The best-known commercial product is methoprene.

methylbenzene (ˌmiːθaɪl'bɛnziːn), *n. Chem.* Also as two words. [f. METHYL *n.* + BENZENE *n.*] = *toluene* s.v. TOLU-.

1921 J. S. CHAMBERLAIN *Text-bk. Org. Chem.* II. i. 479 This proves that toluene is methyl benzene. **1964** N. G. CLARK *Mod. Org. Chem.* xix. 376 The first homologue is methylbenzene, $C_6H_5.CH_3$, known as 'toluene'. **1981** J. W. BUTTLE et al. *Chemistry* (ed.4) xix. 415 The reaction of benzene with bromomethane yields some 1,2- and 1,4-dimethylbenzenes as well as methylbenzene.

metiamide (mɪ'taɪəmaɪd), *n. Pharm.* [f. MET(H- + -iamide, perh. f. a rearrangement of IMIDA(ZOL)E *n.*] An imidazole derivative with histamine H₂-receptor blocking properties which was formerly used to treat peptic ulcers; 1-methyl-3-(2-[5-methylimidazol-4-ylmethylthio]ethyl)thiourea, $C_9H_{16}N_4S$.

1973 *Gut* XIV. 424/1 Metiamide, an analogue of burimamide, has been given intravenously to seven volunteers. **1977** *Lancet* 10 Sept. 555/2 The bone-marrow toxicity of metiamide might be related to the compound's ability to block the histamine H₂-receptor associated with the pluripotent bone-marrow stem cell. **1981** M. C. GERALD *Pharmacol.* (ed. 2) xxv. 498 Burimamide, ineffective when taken by mouth.., was succeeded in clinical trials by the orally active metiamide; trials were discontinued when metiamide was found to cause agranulocytosis. **1987** *Agents & Actions* XXII. 220/2 The TTX [*sc.* tetrodotoxin]-resistant responses to histamine were sensitive to mepyramine, but not metiamide.

metical (meti'kal, anglicized 'mɛtɪkæl), *n.* Pl. **meticais** (meti'kaɪʃ), anglicized **meticals**. [Pg. (cf. Sp. *metical*, old Pg. *mitigal*), f. Arab. *miṯkāl*:

see MISKAL *n.*] The basic monetary unit in Mozambique since 1980, equivalent to 100 centavos.

1980 *Times* 17 June 17/1 Mozambique closed its borders..yesterday to change the country's national currency from the old escudo to the metical (35 to the dollar). **1981** *Britannica Bk. of Year 1980* 550/2 Monetary unit: metical (new currency introduced in June 1980 to replace the former escudo at par), with (Sept. 22, 1980) a free rate of 28 meticals to U.S. $1 (68 meticals = £1 sterling). **1989** *New Yorker* 22 May 66/2 The value of the metical..was such that, to pay for a few small items..I had to count out seven large piles of bills. **1991** *Times Lit. Suppl.* 26 July 10/2 He flourished his pay-slip. 110,000 meticais a month, or about 110 US dollars.

metoclopramide (mɛtəʊ'kləʊprəmaɪd), *n. Pharm.* [a. F. *métoclopramide* (coined by L. Justin-Besançon et al. 1964, in *Compt. Rend.* CCLVIII. 4385): cf. METHOXY(-), CHLORO-², PROCAINAMIDE *n.*] A benzamide derivative with dopamine-receptor blocking properties, which is given orally and by injection (usually as the hydrochloride) as an antiemetic; 4-amino-5-chloro-N-(2-diethylaminoethyl)-2-methoxybenz-amide, $C_{14}H_{22}ClN_3O_2$.

1964 *Semaine des Hopitaux de Paris* 14 Oct. 2345/1 An intravenous injection of ten milligrams metoclopramide produces within six minutes a gastric hyperkinesia. **1977** *Lancet* 19 Nov. 1088/2 Metoclopramide, an antidopaminergic drug, stimulates thyroid-stimulating hormone in hypothyroid patients and prolactin in healthy people. **1983** *Listener* 15 Dec. 9/3 He was prescribed..metoclopramide for the vomiting. **1987** *Brit. Med. Jrnl.* 4 July 30/2 The long term use of phenothiazines, butyrophenones, and metoclopramide for dizziness, nausea, and night sedation is inappropriate and must be avoided to prevent extrapyramidal reactions.

me-too, *n. phr.* Add: **2.** *Comm.* Used of a product (esp. a pharmaceutical) designed to emulate or rival another which has already been commercially successful. Also used of (the policies or techniques of) a company which develops or markets such a product. Usu. *attrib.*

1967 *Rep. Comm. Enquiry Relationship of Pharm. Industry with Nat. Health Service* vi. 58 in *Parl. Papers 1966-67* (Cmnd. 3410) XLV. 687 The imitation of existing products by the minimum of molecular manipulation required to circumvent patents has clearly proved profitable and the number of 'me-too' products that follow a new therapeutic fashion shows that it is widely used. **1974** M. C. GERALD *Pharmacol.* iv. 72 All too often 'me, too' products are..promoted..on the basis of some dubious advantage over a competing product. **1976** *S9* (N.Y.) May/June 109 (Advt.), Radio Shack is not a 'me too' company with the same line carried by other stores in town. **1984** *Austral. Microcomputer Mag.* Jan. 60/3 We will introduce new products..and not just take a 'me too' approach. **1993** *Canad. Business* (Toronto, Ont.) Mar. 66/2 MDS hasn't won its reputation by playing it safe. 'We don't do anything that's me-too,' says Rygiel. 'We're looking for major changes in the way things are done in health care.'

metoprolol (mɪ'tɒprəlɒl), *n. Pharm.* [f. MET(H + -O¹ + PRO(PRANO)LOL *n.*] A beta-adrenergic blocking agent which is given orally (usually as the tartrate) and intravenously in the treatment of hypertension and angina; 1-isopropylamino-3-*p*-(2-methoxymethyl)phenoxypropan-2-ol, $C_{15}H_{25}NO_3$.

1974 *Jrnl. Pharmacokinetics & Biopharmaceutics* II. 363 The present study has shown that metoprolol, a new selective β₁-receptor antagonist, is rapidly and completely absorbed when administered orally in solution. **1977** *Lancet* 16 Apr. 843/1 With metoprolol

Davidson et al. found a rise in heart-rate with only a small and insignificant increase of diastolic pressure. **1986** C. W. THORNBER in C. A. Heaton *Chem. Industry* iv. 173 Astra and Ciba-Geigy both sell metoprolol but under the trade marks Betaloc and Lopressor. **1993** *Alert Driver* Jan.-Feb. 9/2 Drugs designed to reduce or limit heart rate (Inderal, Labetalol, Metoprolol) could affect driver capacity.

metre, *n.*[1] Sense 6 in Dict. becomes 7. Add: **6.** *Mus.* The basic rhythmic pattern of beats in a piece of music (or part thereof), usu. denoted at the beginning by a time signature; = MEASURE *n.* 18 a.
    1873 H. C. BANISTER *Text-bk. Mus.* xxxiv. 170 Rhythm.. or metre has to do with the symmetrical arrangement of music, with regard to time and accent. **1888** *Bookseller* 5 Sept. 920 Two-timed metre is identified with the octave or root, three-timed metre with the fifth, and four-timed metre—the last of the uncompounded metres..—is identified with the third. **1947** A. EINSTEIN *Mus. Romantic Era* xvii. 320 Many of these dances show evidence of great age and uninterrupted tradition—the leaping dance (*springar*) in $\frac{3}{4}$ meter and the *halling* in duple meter. **1969** *Rolling Stone* 28 June 17/3 In those days country music was very loose in both meter and lyrics... No one had ever heard of a ninth chord. **1990** *Opera Now* May 83/4 Her obviously thorough preparation on more than one occasion helped singers less at home with Prokofiev's complex metres.

metronidazole (mɛtrəʊ'naɪdəzəʊl), *n. Pharm.* [f. ME(TH- + -*tron*- (perh. f. rearrangement of N(I)TRO-) + IM)IDAZOLE *n.*] A pale yellow crystalline imidazole derivative given orally and as a vaginal pessary in treating infections with anaerobic bacteria or protozoa (e.g. trichomoniasis); 2-(2-methyl-5-nitroimidazol-1-yl)ethanol, $C_3HN_2(CH_3)(CH_2CH_2OH)(NO_2)$.
    1960 *Brit. Med. Jrnl.* 24 Sept. 903/1 In an attempt to determine the clinical efficacy of metronidazole a trial was arranged in St. Mary's Hospital for Women, Manchester. **1965** I. M. ROLLO in Goodman & Gilman *Pharmacol. Basis Therapeutics* (ed.3) liv. 1141/1 In 1959, Cosar and Julou reported the trichomonacidal activity.. of 1-(β-hydroxyethyl)-2-methyl-5-nitroimid-azole... Subsequent experience.. has indicated that the oral administration of the drug, now called *metronidazole*, will cure a high proportion of infected individuals. **1974** R. M. KIRK et al. *Surgery* ii. 24 Symptomatic disease is treated with metronidazole.. given orally. **1980** *Brit. Med. Jrnl.* 29 Mar. 882/2 In general metronidazole seems the most useful prophylactic for anaerobic organisms. **1991** *Saudi Med. Jrnl.* XII. 117/2 These strains.. have a biochemical profile similar to that of *Peptostreptococcus intermedius* which is resistant to metronidazole.

metropolitanize, *v.* Add: Hence **metro,politaniz'ation** *n.*, the process of giving a metropolitan character to a person or area.
    1939 L. HOGBEN *Dangerous Thoughts* v. 95 The distributive aspect of population best described as *metropolitanization*. **1989** *Dynamic West* (U.S. Council of State Govts.) 20/2 The primary reason growing metropolitanization is a key trend is that it connotes such a dramatic change in regional character.

mews, *n.* Add: [2.] [c.] Also, a row of town houses similar to or built in the style of a mews.
    1979 *Arizona Daily Star* 22 July H4/1 The news is the new mews: a row of attached houses with a name redolent with chic. **1986** *Home Finder* Nov. 36/1 The new development programme also includes a stylish new London mews in Fulham.

Mexicano (mɛksɪ'kɑːnəʊ), *n.* and *a.* Also ‖Mejicano (mexi'kano), fem. **Mexicana**, and with lower-case initial. Pl. **Mexicanos**. [Sp. *mexicano* (now *mejicano*) MEXICAN *a.* and *n.*] A. *n.* 1. a. A native or inhabitant of Mexico; = MEXICAN *n.* 1. b. A person of Mexican descent, *esp.* a Mexican-American.
    [**1706** J. STEVENS *New Spanish & Eng. Dict.* sig. Kk3 *Méxicáno*, a native of *Mexico*, or anything of that City.] **1891** D. G. BRINTON *Amer. Race* iii. 152 The name *Tews*,.. was applied to the conquered Nahuatl population around Michoacan. In some old glossaries *teco* is explained by *Mexicano*. **1914** *Dialect Notes* IV. 163 *Mexicano*, anyone from Mexico. **1929** A. MACLEISH *Let.* 11 Mar. in R. H. Winnick *Lett. Archibald MacLeish* (1983) 225 A Spaniard named Barrera who was fine with the cape but.. couldn't kill bulls and got the rasberry (*sic*) from the brave Mexicanos. **1963** *Look* 8 Oct. 68/2 Then there is the other Texas: income-poor, opportunity-poor, equality-poor for most of the state's 1.5 million slow-burning Mexicanos—Americans of Mexican descent. **1972** *La Luz* June 61/2 In the Southwest.. a Spanish Colonial who would object to being called a Mexican, frequently refers to himself culturally as a Mejicano. **1985** J. A. MICHENER *Texas* vi. 321 He was a striking figure, somewhat large for a mexicano. **1986** C. L. BRIGGS *Learning how to Ask* 31 Their ancestry includes a significant Native American element, but the Mexicanos consider themselves to be culturally hispanic.
    2. A Uto-Aztecan language of Southern Mexico; = NAHUATL *n.* b.
    1900 *Mexico* (U.S. Bureau Amer. Republics) iii. 24 Linguistic Families in Mexico... Pimentel's list.. Mexicana. *Ibid.* 25 Following the Bureau of American Ethnology in keeping the Piman as a separate family leaves the Nahuatlan free to include only Pimentel's Mexicana. **1946** C. OSGOOD *Ling. Structures Native Amer.* 368 In Mexico however the term Aztec is little used, the language being called in Spanish usually Mexicano, and in Aztec itself Malsewalkopa. **1971** *Language* XLVII. 737 The language as a whole, once called Mexicano, has been more recently referred to as Nahuatl (in some cases Nahuat). **1986** J. & K. HILL *Speaking Mexicano* i. 1 The modern Mexicano of the Malinche Volcano towns is a syncretic language. **1991** S. CISNEROS *Woman Hollering Creek* 99, I.. said a prayer in *mexicano* to the old gods, an Ave María in Spanish to La Virgen, and gave thanks.
    B. *attrib.* or as *adj.* **a.** Pertaining to or designating a Mexicano; Mexican; Mexican-American (see MEXICAN *a.* a and c.). **b.** Pertaining to or designating the Mexicano language; = NAHUATL *a.*
    1963 *Look* 8 Oct. 68/2 Real nice people pay a Mexicano maid $15 a week and two meals a day. **1965** P. ESPARZA *Mexicano in Valley of Magic* 7 That Mexicano problem didn't come up for discussion. **1981** *N.Y. Times* 22 May A15/4. When Mrs. Sausedo was asked why she had voted for Dr. Casso her only answer was that he was 'Mexicano'. **1985** J. A. MICHENER *Texas* vi. 321 Most of Austin's famous Old Three Hundred, the earliest anglo settlers, were content to remain mexicano citizens. **1991** S. CISNEROS *Woman Hollering Creek* 149 All complementary forces occur in pairs. 'Ah,' said Flavio, 'like the *mexicano* word "sky-earth" for the world.'

mexiletine (mɛk'saɪlətiːn), *n. Pharm.* [f. ME(TH- + XIL- (alteration of XYL(ENE *n.*) + ET(HYL *n.* + AM)INE *n.*] A cyclic derivative of propanol given orally (frequently as the hydrochloride) and intravenously in the treatment of some ventricular arrhythmias; 1-(2,6-dimethylphenoxy)-2-propanamine, $C_6H_3(CH_3)_2(OCH_2 \cdot CH(CH_3)NH_2)$.
    1973 *Lancet* 25 Aug. 400/1 In this paper we describe preliminary work with mexiletine (KÖ 1173), a new antiarrhythmic drug which suppresses experimental

ventricular arrhythmias. **1977** *Ibid.* 16 Apr. 859/1 The arrhythmia responded to lignocaine infusion but oral mexiletine in full doses (250 mg four times a day) failed to achieve control. **1980** *Brit. Med. Jrnl.* 18 Oct. 1072/3 A supraventricular tachycardia with aberrant conduction was mistaken for ventricular tachycardia and lignocaine was given without effect followed by mexiletine, which terminated it. **1988** *Clin. Cardiol.* XI. 132 (*heading*) Chronic mexiletine therapy for suppression of ventricular arrhythmias.

mezzanine, *n.* Add: **3.** *Comm.* Used *attrib.* (orig. in connection with venture capital) to designate an intermediate level or stage in a financial enterprise; used *spec.* (*a*) of the last phase of a firm's development or funding prior to flotation; (*b*) of a method of funding (esp. for a leveraged buyout or a recapitalization) by means of unsecured, high-interest yielding loans that are subordinate to bank loans and secured loans but which rank above equity. Esp. in *mezzanine bracket, debt, finance*, etc. Also *transf.*

1976 *Forbes* (N.Y.) 1 Nov. 71/3 We're a major in municipal bond offerings; we're the only firm outside Wall Street that's in the new mezzanine bracket of corporate underwritings. **1983** *Times* 21 June 16/1 It [*sc.* the company] will principally invest in debt securities, generally on a subordinated basis, in return for interest income and a significant participation in the equity of the borrower. This is generally referred to herein as 'mezzanine investment'. **1986** *Observer* 23 Nov. 37 Before.. 1983, potential raiders looked to venture capitalists and major insurance companies to provide mezzanine finance. **1988** *Investors Chron.* 26 Aug. 63/2 The fashionable phrase now for junk bonds is 'mezzanine debt'. Undoubtedly a politer title but it means the same thing. **1989** *Banker* Feb. 80/3 Drexel Burnham Lambert, king of the junk bond market, proved irresistible as lead manager for the arrangement of fixed-rate mezzanine funding. **1991** *Sight & Sound* Oct. 6/3 The company plans to release a more balanced slate, with a few 'mezzanine' movies in the $20 to $25 million range, and some low-budget 'quality' films.

Miami (maɪˈæmɪ), *n.* and *a.* [a. Fr. *Miami* f. Illinois *miamioua*.]

Hodge (1907) posited a speculative derivation from Chippewa (Ojibwa) *omaumeg* lit. 'people who live on the peninsula'.]

A. *n.* **1.** (A member of) an Algonquian people formerly resident in the north-eastern United States (principally in Illinois, Indiana, and Wisconsin) and, in more recent times, inhabiting areas of Ohio, Kansas, and Oklahoma.

1698 tr. *Hennepin's New Discovery Amer.* xxxv. 141 The *Miamis* arriv'd much about that time, and danced the *Calumet* with the *Illinois*. **1771** SMOLLETT *Humph. Cl.* 26 Oct., A little traffic he drove in peltry during his sachemship among the Miamis. **1877** L. H. MORGAN *Anc. Society* II. vi. 169 The Shawnees had a practice, common also to the Miamis and Sauks and Foxes, of naming children into the gens of the father or of the mother or any other gens. **1907** F. W. HODGE *Handbk. Amer. Indians* I. 853/2 According to the early French explorers the Miamis were distinguished for polite manners, mild, affable, and sedate character, and their respect for and perfect obedience to their chiefs. **1970** B. ANSON *Miami Indians* 11 The Miami had no legends or myths of previous migrations. **1992** A. W. ECKERT *Sorrow in our Heart* Prologue 11 The Miamis, though currently the most powerful tribe in the northwest, suddenly found themselves.. being attacked on the west by their mortal enemies, the Sioux, and now threatened in the east by the Iroquois.

2. The (now extinct) Algonquian language of this people, a dialect of the same language as that spoken by the Illinois, sometimes referred to jointly as *Miami-Illinois*.

1804 C. F. VOLNEY *View of Soil & Climate U.S.A.* 430 (*heading*) Miami after the French Orthography. **1845** R. G. LATHAM in *Trans. Philol. Soc.* II. xxviii. 33/1 English *ear*... *Miami* tawakeh. **1899** *Amer. Anthropologist* I. 156 The form *inini* is represented in Peoria, Miami, and other dialects also, but not as a substantive. **1938** C. F. VOEGELIN *Shawnee Stems* 63 Comparative evidence.. suggests that Miami contains some pre-aspiration and vocalic length not recorded in the manuscript. The manuscript dictionary is given in the order English-Miami. **1992** I. GODDARD in W. Bright *Internat. Encycl. Linguistics* I. 44 [The Algonkian family includes] several languages whose speakers have moved south and west from the Upper Great Lakes in the historical period, namely Potawatomi, Fox-Kickapoo, Shawnee, and Miami-Illinois.

B. *attrib.* or as *adj.* Of or pertaining to the Miami or their language.

1792 G. IMLAY *Topogr. Descrip. W. Territory N. Amer.* 68 The vigorous measures which their depredations have obliged Congress to adopt, must end with a permanent peace, or in a few years their provocations will lead to the extirpation of the whole of the Miami and Illinois tribes. **1804** C. F. VOLNEY *View of Soil & Climate U.S.A.* 427, I shall here add a vocabulary of the Miami tongue. **1818** M. BIRKBECK *Notes Journey Amer.* 100 One young man.., of the Miami nation, had a clear light blue cotton vest with sleeves. **1907** F. W. HODGE *Handbk. Amer. Indians* I. 853/1 There was a Miami village at Detroit in 1703. **1938** C. F. VOEGELIN *Shawnee Stems* (Indiana Hist. Soc.) 63 Since contrastive forms are generally lacking, I do not attempt an editorial analysis of Miami compounds. **1989** *Encycl. Brit.* VIII. 88/3 The staple of the Miami diet was a particular type of maize (corn) that was considered superior to that cultivated by their neighbours.

mianserin (maɪˈænsərɪn), *n.* *Pharm.* [f. *mian-* + SER(OTON)IN *n.*] A tetracyclic compound, $C_{18}H_{20}N_2$, with serotonin blocking properties, given orally (usually as the hydrochloride) in the treatment of depression.

1970 *Jrnl. Med. Chem.* XIII. 36/1 Compound 5 (mianserin) proved to have.. a less pronounced sedative effect and a lower acute toxicity as shown in pilot experiments on animals. **1983** STAFFORD-CLARK & SMITH *Psychiatry for Students* (ed. 6) vii. 118 Mianserin (Norval, Bolvidon) has a kind of tetracyclic structure. **1986** C. W. THORNBER in C. A. Heaton *Chem. Industry* iv. 189 Further chemical modifications have led to variants such as mianserin.. which have additional properties as a serotonin antagonist. **1989** *New Scientist* 18 Mar. 31/2 The Committee on Safety of Medicines.. declared that doctors' reports of adverse reactions in the blood to the antidepressant drug mianserin (Bolvidon) confirmed its own earlier warnings that the elderly are abnormally susceptible to these reactions. **1991** *Pulse* 6 Apr. 74/4 The only other antidepressants which have been attended by any significant degree of success are mianserin, maprotiline, imipramine, and dothiepin.

miasm, *n.* Add: **2.** *Homoeopathy.* [a. G. *Miasm*, first used in this sense by S. Hahnemann 1810, in *Organon der Heilkunst* 35.] Any of a group of supposed predispositions to particular diseases, originally comprising three inherited traits (those of syphilis, sycosis, and psora) but later extended to include various acquired susceptibilities.

1833 DEVRIENT & STRATTEN tr. *Hahnemann's Organon* 165 The diseases of mankind resolve themselves into two classes.. acute diseases.. and.. chronic diseases.. produced by infection from a chronic miasm. **1905** J. H. CLARKE *Homœopathy Explained* viii. 59 By 'miasm' Hahnemann means an infectious principle, which, when taken into the organism, may set up a specific disease. According to Hahnemann, there were not only miasms of acute diseases, like the infectious principle of scarlatina, for example, but also of chronic diseases. **1936** H. A. ROBERTS *Princ. & Art of Cure by Homœopathy* iv. 43 Physical signs and symptoms appear; and all because the vital functions are disturbed either from external impressions having a depressing effect..or from some hidden miasm coming into its full expression in its impress on the vital force. **1974** *Homoeopathy* June/July 87 Homoeopathic treatment can minimise the malign influence of the miasms, but I think it unlikely that it can eradicate them. **1980** G. VITHOULKAS *Sci. of Homoeopathy* I. ix. 130 It is clear that there are a large number of miasms, and that the total number is constantly increasing with the advent of suppressive therapies. **1987** S. & R. GIBSON *Homoeopathy for Everyone* vii. 114 Miasms are now recognized to be both inherited and acquired.

Michaelis (mɪˈkeɪlɪs), *n.* *Biochem.* [The name of Leonor *Michaelis* (1875-1949), German-born American chemist.] **Michaelis constant**, the concentration of a given enzyme which catalyses the associated reaction at half the maximum rate.
1930 J. B. S. HALDANE *Enzymes* iii. 39 We thus have two constants available for fitting a series of results, but V should be (and is found to be) proportional to the enzyme concentration, while K_m, which is generally called the Michaelis constant, is a characteristic of the enzyme. **1955** *New Biol.* XVIII. 63 The concentration of substrate that just gives the maximum rate [of reaction] is difficult to determine exactly, but the concentration giving the half-maximum rate, which is known as the Michaelis constant, can be determined with precision and is important in the characterization of enzymes. **1968** *New England Jrnl. Med.* CCLXXVIII. 475/1 Starch substrate concentrations of 1.00, 0.70, 0.40, 0.25 gm per 100 ml were used to determine the Michaelis constants. **1987** C. G. SINCLAIR in Bu'lock & Kristiansen *Basic Biotechnol.* iv. 91 E_s is the total amount of enzyme, k_m is the Michaelis constant, and S is the substrate concentration.

Michaelis–Menten (mɪˌkeɪlɪsˈmɛntən), *n.* *Biochem.* [f. the name of Leonor *Michaelis* (see *MICHAELIS *n.*) + the name of Maud Lenore *Menten* (1879-1960), American physician.] Used *attrib.* to designate (*a*) a model of enzyme action which assumes the formation of an intermediate complex of enzyme and substrate; (*b*) a rate equation associated with this model.
1947 SUMNER & SOMERS *Chem. & Methods Enzymes* (ed. 2) i. 20 The Michaelis-Menten hypothesis has also been extended to include equilibria involving enzyme, coenzyme, substrate, and hydrogen ions. **1954** H. B. BULL in McElroy & Glass *Symp. on Mechanism of Enzyme Action* II. 141 The Michaelis-Menten rate expression is a composite equation combining zero- and first-order kinetics. **1984** S. D. SHORVON *Epilepsy* 21/2 The best example of this is that of phenytoin, which exhibits Michaelis-Menten kinetics, often with a steeply rising curve at serum levels which are clinically important. **1990** *Jrnl. Exper. Bot.* XLI. 930/1 The deterioration in photosynthetic performance can be predicted from simple Michaelis-Menten kinetics..for two competitive substrates.

micro-, *comb. form.* Add: [**1.**] [**a.**] *microcar.*
1980 *N.Y. Times* 3 Oct. C35/1 The opening show looks at *microcars, which just might relieve urban traffic congestion. **1991** *Economist* 14 Sept. 98/1 Japan's unique micro-car market (with engines under 660cc) is one of the most cut-throat in the car business.
'**microfilament** *n.*, a very fine filament; *spec.* in *Cytol.*, any of the rodlike structures, about 4-7 nanometres in diameter, that are present in the cytoplasm of many eukaryotic cells and are thought to have a structural function and to be involved with cell motility.

1965 *Jrnl. Cell Biol.* XXVII. 39A/2 *Microfilaments are more prominent in non-motile pinocytosing cells. **1970** *New Scientist* 30 Apr. 228/3 Microfilaments have been made in a wide variety of metals, alloys, silicides, borides, oxides and mixed oxides. **1974** D. & M. WEBSTER *Compar. Vertebr. Morphol.* ix. 182 The axon contains microtubules, microfilaments, and a few mitochondria. **1984** HOLTZMAN & NOVIKOFF *Cells & Organelles* (ed. 3) II. xi. 282 The term *microfilament*, originally used for many types of cytoplasmic filament, has increasingly come to be used solely for the 5- to 6-nm actin filaments.
hence **microfila'mentous** *a.*
1970 *Diabetologia* VI. 638/2 The beta cell of the islets of Langerhans has been shown to contain a microtubular-*microfilamentous system. **1975** *New Scientist* 5 June 553/2 But if the actin and myosin of the microfilamentous system interacted with each other while floating just under the membrane, they could hardly be expected to affect the cell's shape, let alone motility. **1989** *Microbial Pathogenesis* VII. 330 This inhibition was not associated with a blockage of local microfilamentous refoldings previously shown to be associated with the internalization of *Shigella* by epithelial cells.

'**microphyll** *n.* *Bot.* [ad. Da. *mikrofyl* (C. Raunkiaer 1917, in *Bot. Tidsskr.* XXXIV. 229), f. Gr. φύλλ-ον leaf], a type of leaf, characteristic of the clubmosses, which is usu. short and whose vascular system is rudimentary; opp. *megaphyll n.* s.v. *MEGA- *a.*
1932 *Proc. Linn. Soc.* CXLV. 26 In most cases there is an early differentiation between..the simple *microphylls and the branch systems or 'telomes' which later evolved into the megaphylls of the higher plants. **1957** *Ann. Bot.* XXI. 434 In the manner of their inception, there is no essential difference between microphylls and macrophylls though very marked differences become evident during their further development. **1983** E. C. MINKOFF *Evolutionary Biol.* xxvi. 451/1 Microphylls are typically small and simple, but some extinct lycopods had unusually large microphylls.

microvillus *n.*: hence **micro'villar** *a.*, pertaining to or consisting of microvilli; also **micro'villous** *a.*, characterized by or consisting of microvilli.
1966 *Jrnl. Clin. Investigation* XLV. 1001/2 (*heading*) Intrinsic factor-mediated attachment of Vitamin B_{12} to brush borders and *microvillous membranes. **1968** *Zeitschr. für Zellforschung* LXXXV. 253 The photoreceptors are of the *microvillar type, yet show some traces of an original cilium. **1975** *Nature* 10 Apr. 522/1 Each photoreceptor or retinula cell gives rise to a microvillar fringe, called the rhabdomere, which consists of parallel tubules containing light-absorbing visual pigments. **1976** *Lancet* 18 Dec. 1319/2 These [abnormalities] included microvillous changes, increase in theliolymphocytes and epithelial lysosomes, [etc.]. **1984** HOLTZMAN & NOVIKOFF *Cells & Organelles* (ed. 3) III. viii. 451 In numerous species, at dusk the microvillar system undergoes expansion through addition of membrane. **1990** *Jrnl. Developmental Physiol.* XIV. 50/1 Microvillous membrane vesicles were isolated from 5 min-preperfused blood-free placentas.

[**b.**] '**micropropa,gation** *n.*, (a technique for) the propagation of plants by growing plantlets in tissue culture and then planting them out.
1973 H. E. STREET *Plant Tissue & Cell Culture* xv. 424 It is this capacity of cell, callus and meristem cultures to regenerate whole plants that has been exploited to obtain virus-free stocks of a number of horticultural plants..and to effect the *micropropagation of orchids and some ornamentals and vegetables. **1977** *Jrnl. Amer. Soc. Hort. Sci.* CII. 48/1 Shoot tip culture, a form of micropropagation, has been used successfully to produce pathogen-free plants. **1986** *Forestry* LIX. 169 Work currently in progress..is examining the possibility of introducing an initial micropropagation stage into the rooted cutting

system developed for Sitka spruce. **1991** *Independent* 5 Jan. 41/4 Dr Wilde's answer was to persuade York University to clone one million plants in 12 months through micropropagation.

hence (as a back-formation) **micro'propagate** *v. trans.*, to propagate by means of micropropagation; **micro'propagated** *ppl. a.*

1977 *Jrnl. Amer. Soc. Hort. Sci.* CII. 53/2 A real difference in mutation rates between conventionally propagated and *micropropagated carnation plants was not proven. **1979** *Farm & Food Res.* X. 75/3 (*heading*) Some plants that have been successfully *micropropagated. **1991** *Gardener* Jan. 6/2 The kit consists of..three houseplants, all of which are micropropagated and supplied growing in a special gel. **1992** *Guardian* 12 May 33/1 (Advt.), The project will investigate the potential of V-A mycorrhizal fungi for crop-protection of micropropagated strawberry plants.

microsimu'lation *n.* *Econ.*, (a method for producing) a statistical model of microeconomic activity, esp. based on detailed demographic profiles of individuals, businesses, etc.

1966 *Public Health Service Publ.* (U.S. Dept. Health) No. 1000 (Ser. 2, No. 13) (*title*) Computer simulation of hospital discharges; micro-simulation of measurement errors in hospital discharge data reported in the Health Interview Survey. **1972** *Times* 8 Sept. 21/5 Papers on the socioeconomic *microsimulation of the United States household sector. **1989** *Surv. Current Business* Mar. 62/1 These data have been used in microsimulation models to provide us with increasingly detailed insights into the effects of government policy changes on economic behavior.

[2.] [a.] micro-engi'neering *n.*, engineering on a very small scale, esp. combined with microelectronics.

1967 *Punch* 4 Jan. 1/2 We live in an age of computers, *micro-engineering and microelectronics and it is becoming a positive disadvantage to have large limbs and digits. **1981** *Business Week* 6 July 49/3 To shrink the circuitry on a chip to that degree will demand prodigious feats of micro-engineering. **1988** *Nuclear News* 1 Apr. 61 The company's involvement in atomic technologies, including fusion energy, nuclear reactors and reactor fuel, microengineering of advanced materials, [etc.].

[4.] micro'nodular *a.* *Med.*, characterized by the presence of small nodules; chiefly in *micronodular cirrhosis*; cf. *macronodular* s.v. *MACRO- 1 d.

1960 *Amer. Jrnl. Path.* XXXVI. 248 (*heading*) Nutritional cirrhosis (alcoholic, fatty, *micronodular, Laennec's cirrhosis). **1976** EDINGTON & GILLES *Path. in Tropics* (ed. 2) xi. 542 The terms portal and postnecrotic would probably be better expressed morphologically as micronodular and macronodular respectively. **1985** *Brit. Med. Jrnl.* 14 Sept. 708/1 Various liver diagnoses were entered, including cirrhosis, micronodular cirrhosis, and nutritional cirrhosis.

[5.] [a.] *micro-amp*.

1960 *Pract. Wireless* XXXVI. pii/1 (Advt.), Complete with 15 valves, 500 *microamp check and tuning meter, circuit and instruction book. **1971** *Nature* 3 Dec. 243/1 A beam of several hundred microamps of electrons. **1991** G. H. TOMLINSON *Electr. Networks & Filters* 213 The requirement for input bias current, which is in the range of picoamps to microamps, depending upon the device type, imposes a restriction on the choice of *RC* impedances for the forward and feedback paths.

[6.] *microsensor*.

1962 F. I. ORDWAY et al. *Basic Astronautics* xii. 486 Basically each *microsensor is a small transmitter. **1984** *Chem. Engin. News* 4 June 8/2 Wohltjen classifies all microsensors into two categories. **1993** *Independent on Sunday* 15 Aug. (Business section) 26/4 In the future MEMMS are expected to be used, for example, as toxic gas sensors

that fit on to workers' belts, and medical micro-sensors and micro-tools.

[8.] c. *Econ.* = *microeconomic* adj. s.v. MICROECONOMICS *n. pl.*

[**1946** *Econometrica* XIV. 94 Let us assume the theory of micro- and of macroeconomics and then construct aggregates..which are consistent with the two theories.] **1961** G. ACKLEY *Macroecon. Theory* xx. 572 Had the micro slopes been identical, the changing distribution of profits would have made no difference. **1965** SELDON & PENNANCE *Everyman's Dict. Econ.* 282 Income concepts are not ignored in micro-theory. **1970** *Globe & Mail* (Toronto) 26 Sept. 9/5 More attention will be given to the ubiquitous 'micro' problems in non-sugar sectors of the [Cuban] economy. **1974** *Times Lit. Suppl.* 8 Mar. 242/5 The forms and methods of economic management, both micro and macro. **1984** *Nat. Westm. Bank Q. Rev.* Feb. 42 These policies amounted to a straightforward Keynesian expansion with some minor additions of a more micro nature such as the shortening of the working week. **1992** *Unesco Courier* Mar. 41/2 Linking the experience of women at the level of their daily lives (the micro level) to economic trends and their global environmental impacts (the macro level).

microballoon ('maɪkrəʊbəluːn), *n.* Also **Microballoon.** [f. MICRO- 1 a + BALLOON *n.*] An artificial hollow microsphere, usu. of glass or synthetic resin, *esp.* one of a kind used in bulk as an insulating material.

A proprietary term in the U.S.

1954 *Official Gaz.* (U.S. Patent Office) 27 Apr. 873/1 *Microballoon.* For hollow, finely divided, hole-free, low density particles of synthetic resins and/or similar film-forming materials for general use in the industrial arts. Claims use since about Sept. 11, 1950. **1967** *Amer. Ceramic Soc. Bull.* XLVI. 442/2 Glass microballoon particles are tiny, hollow, hole-free spheres having a true particle density of about 22 lbs/cu ft and a bulk density of 15 lbs/cu. ft. *Ibid.* 594/2 The microballoons varied in form from perfect spheres to a teardrop shape. **1977** *Offshore Engineer* June 72/3 Developed as a deepsea buoyancy material, Eccofloat FL..is a composite of hollow epoxy macrospheres (average diameter 9.5mm) and matrix of glass microballoon spheres (average diameter 60 microns) mixed with epoxy resin. **1980** BENT & MCKINLEY *Aircraft Maintenance & Repair* (ed. 4) ix. 262/2 The effect of microballoons added to potting resin is to produce a lighter-weight and more resilient repair. **1989** *WoodenBoat* Dec. 33/1 Unlike dry, 'fly-away' fillers like microballoons,..particles are treated with a special coating that allows them to blend with the epoxy quickly and easily.

microbenthos ('maɪkrəʊˌbɛnθɒs), *n.* *Zool.* [f. MICRO- + BENTHOS *n.*] The microfauna of the benthos; *spec.* bottom-dwelling marine organisms less than 0.1 mm long.

1942 M. F. MARE in *Jrnl. Marine Biol. Assoc.* XXV. 519 A new terminology is needed, and these groups are here designated the macrobenthos, meiobenthos, and microbenthos. **1967** *Oceanogr. & Marine Biol.* V. 501 According to Laubier, this endolithic fauna..includes not only several macrobenthonic species..but also an important animal microbenthos chiefly consisting of very small polychaetes..and harpacticoid copepods. **1988** *Nature* 26 May 316/2 Biosedimentary structures attributable to the mat-building activities of prokaryotic microbenthos ('stromatolites').

Hence **micro'benthic** *a.*

1974 *Biol. Abstr.* LVIII. 1992/1 (*title*) Diet variation in oxygen production and uptake in a microbenthic littoral community of a nutrient-poor lake. **1975** G. A. COLE *Textbk. Limnol.* iii. 44/1 The study of benthic forms has generally involved the use of sieves in separating organisms from the sediments...The macrobenthic forms are retained by the meshes of a sieve, while the microbenthic species pass through the interstices of a no. 40 screening device.

microbore ('maɪkrəʊbɔː(r)), *a.* (*n.*) [f. MICRO- 1 a + BORE *n.*[1]] Designating (the pipework of) a central heating system with very narrow pipes. Also as *n.*, such a system.

1968 *Domestic Heating News* Apr. 22/1 Considerable publicity has already been accorded minibore systems—or microbore, as some sections of the heating trade prefer to call it. Employment of minibore—¼ or ⅜ in tubing—is a quite natural development from the use of standard small bore pipe. **1969** *Domestic Heating* Summer 12/1 An important item in any microbore installation is, of course, the microbore tube itself. **1970** *Heating & Ventilating Engineer* Nov. 227 Microbore has shown itself less prone to air locks than the conventional ring system. **1976** *Scotsman* 25 Nov. 22/1 (Advt.), Detached stone-built family house to let... Micro-bore central heating, etc. **1986** *Home Finder* Nov. 16/2 A pumped microbore circuit serves high output Thermalrad radiators in all rooms.

microchiropteran (ˌmaɪkrəʊkaɪˈrɒptərən), *a.* and *n.* *Zool.* [f. mod.L. name of suborder *Microchiroptera* (coined by G. E. Dobson 1875, in *Ann. & Mag. Nat. Hist.* XVI. 345): see MICRO- 1 a, CHEIROPTERA *n. pl.*, -AN.] **A.** *adj.* Of or pertaining to the chiropteran suborder Microchiroptera, which comprises all bats other than megachiropterans, most of them insectivorous and using echolocation. **B.** *n.* A microchiropteran bat.

1890 *Cent. Dict.* 3748/3 *Microchiropteran, a.* and *n.* **1945** A. S. ROMER *Vertebr. Paleont.* (ed. 2) xvii. 333 Middle Eocene deposits in both Europe..and North America have yielded skeletons of microchiropterans with well-developed wings. **1967** *Compar. Biochem. & Physiol.* XXII. 371 Ambient temperatures of 50°C and above commonly occurred in parts of a barn loft used as a summer roost by three species of microchiropteran bats. **1976** *Nature* 15 Apr. 626/2 We have assayed livers of 34 species of New World microchiropteran bats for L-gulonolactone oxidase. **1984** D. MACDONALD et al. *Encycl. Mammals* II. 793 Probably all microchiropterans use ultrasound which they produce with their larynxes. **1984** J. E. HILL *Bats* ii. 6 The length of the thumb varies considerably among bats, being very short in some microchiropteran families. **1990** *Jrnl. Zool.* CCXXII. 577 Most African microchiropterans are considered to be strictly monotocous and the birth of twins in these species is extremely unusual.

microcode ('maɪkrəʊkəʊd), *n.* *Computing.* Also **micro-code.** [f. MICRO- + CODE *n.*[1]] Microinstructions collectively, *esp.* those incorporated into a microprocessor; a microinstruction or sequence of microinstructions.

1958 *Communications Assoc. Computing Machinery* Jan. 3 The present codes should be considered to be micro-codes. **1970** A. CHANDOR et al. *Dict. Computers* 254 *Micro-code,* synonymous with micro instruction. *Ibid.,* *Micro instruction,*..also known as microcode. **1979** KRAFT & TOY *Mini/Microcomputer Hardware Design* iii. 130 A macroinstruction residing in program memory is fetched into the instruction register, and its operation code is used to derive a pointer to the starting address of a microcode segment located in the control ROM. **1987** *Electronics & Wireless World* Jan. 103/1 In the 68020 microcode within the device takes care of coprocessor interfacing. **1989** *Nature* 16 Feb. 591/2 Although computer programs were added to the US Copyright Act by Congress in 1980, the status of microcode—the set of instructions determining how a processor's components will perform a specific function—was unclear. **1992** *Computing* 5 Nov. 3/3 Tandem fault-tolerant systems around the world were brought to a shuddering halt on Sunday by a bug in the microcode.

microcoding ('maɪkrəʊkəʊdɪŋ), *vbl.* *n.* *Computing.* Also **micro-coding.** [f. MICRO- 2 a + *coding* *vbl.* *n.* s.v. CODE *v.*] = MICROPROGRAMMING *vbl.* *n.* Also, microcode.

1958 *Communications Assoc. Computing Machinery* June 17 This machine would be a continual challenge..due to its 'infinite' variations which look somewhat like microcoding. **1970** A. CHANDOR et al. *Dict. Computers* 254 *Micro-coding,* the process of simulating a program instruction not normally part of an instruction set by means of a series of simple program steps. A section of micro-coding forms a macro instruction. **1977** *Dun's Rev.* Apr. 27/1 The company will either boost the capacity and reduce the price of the 370-168 or convert some of its software into the mainframe hardware, via a process known as microcoding. **1985** *Austral. Personal Computer* Sept. 81/2 We guessed that it [*sc.* the compiler chip] would probably rely heavily on microcoding: that is, the functionality would not be designed at the level of the logic gates which comprise integrated circuits.

Hence **'microcoded** *ppl.* *a.*, employing microcode; (as a back-formation) **'microcode** *v.* *trans.*

1974 *IBM Jrnl. Res. & Devel.* XVIII. 344/2 The microcoded modem transmitter described in the preceding section can be programmed to operate in a variety of modes and speeds. **1979** *Amer. Banker* 11 Apr. 12/3 The consulting group said impressive price-performance standards, powerful new IBM software, interface links and microcoded extensions could create an 'iron curtain' for IBM's competitors. **1985** *Datamation* 1 May 35/2 Today the company is shipping thousands of lines of code for VM as well as microcoding its systems. **1989** *DEC Professional* Feb. 39/3 CISC computers include hundreds of microcoded instructions.

microdrive ('maɪkrəʊdraɪv), *n.* [f. MICRO- + DRIVE *n.*] **1.** Chiefly *Med.* A small stepping motor or motor-driven system for the manipulation of microelectrodes.

1956 *Science* 27 July 179/2 A small micrometer drive for controlling the depth of insertion of the electrode is directly mounted on the glass window, which is movable. Thus the electrode, which is mounted in the shaft of the microdrive, may be located over any desired point on the exposed cortex..by sliding the window. **1979** *Electroencephalogr. & Clin. Neurophysiol.* XLVII. 752/1 The present report introduces the design for a subminiature microdrive..which offers precision and stability of electrode placements in the brain of freely-moving rats. **1989** *Jrnl. Neurosci. Methods* XXVIII. 219/2 We have devised a hybrid microdrive—incorporating both stepper motors and a hydraulic system—which..is relatively cheap and easy to manufacture.

2. *Computing.* A miniature tape drive at one time used as a peripheral storage device in some microcomputers.

1982 T. TOMS *Spectrum Pocket Bk.* 117 Microdrive owners can save the instructions in a disk file which can be read back into the assembler. **1984** *Which Micro?* Dec. 7/4 The..Zx Expansion System (..incorporating a microdrive, Interface 1 and four microdrive cartridges). **1985** *Austral. Personal Computer* Jan. 16/2 The microdrives used for backing up the memory are a visible reminder of Sinclair's involvement, but the predominant influence is clearly ICL's. **1986** *What Micro?* Nov. 8/4 The One Per Desk..has tape 'microdrives' for data and program storage.

microfilmer ('maɪkrəʊfɪlmə(r)), *n.* [f. MICROFILM *v.* + -ER[1].] One who or that which microfilms; *spec.* a camera used for recording documents, etc., on microfilm.

1959 H. BALLOU *Guide to Microreproduction Equipment* 67 Junior Microfilmer, Model JD. **1967** D. M. AVEDON *Gloss. Terms Microphotogr.* (ed. 4) 40

Microfilmer. **1971** *Sci. Amer*. Aug. 43/1 (Advt.), We are pleased to announce a computer-output microfilmer of lower price. **1975** *Forbes* (N.Y.) 1 Mar. 11/1 Counterintelligence cannot be confined to cloak-and-dagger microfilmers or film-y blondes bobbing about behind the curtains of foreign chancelleries. **1985** *Bank Admin*. Oct. 84/1 The microfilmer features an interchangeable film head, convenient operating controls, [etc.]. **1993** *Business Wk*. 25 Oct. 19/2 (Advt.), Each Kodak Office Imaging Product—from a single copier, printer, or microfilmer to scanners, optical disk libraries, and writable CD—must be compatible. Each must enable migration to future technologies.

microfloppy ('maɪkrəʊˌflɒpɪ), *n. Computing*. Also **micro-floppy**. [f. MICRO- + FLOPPY *a*. and *n*.] A floppy disc less than 5¼ inches in diameter; *esp*. one 3½ inches in diameter. Also *microfloppy disc*.

   1977 *Electronic Design* 11 Oct. 198/1 Dual index and file protect sensors permit recording of data on both sides of a microdiskette on the Wang co Model 82 Micro-Floppy. **1983** *Observer* 19 June 21/4 The use of the new 3in microfloppy disks looks set to become a standard on the transportables. **1986** *Austral. Personal Computer* Sept. 76/2 The drive is a 2.5 inch microfloppy, and is the smallest capacity microfloppy around, holding a meagre 64k.

micrographics (ˌmaɪkrəʊˈɡræfɪks), *n.pl.* (const. as *sing*.). [f. MICROGRAPHIC *a*.: see -IC 2.] The production of photographically reduced texts.

   1968 *Nat. Microfilm Assoc. Jrnl*. II. 1. 29/1 Keeps abreast of all current and new systems methods, techniques, micrographic equipment and materials, in order to approach all systems studies and problems with a comprehensive understanding of micrographics. **1971** *Jrnl. Documentation* XXVII. 295 The history of microform systems and techniques (henceforth the emergent term 'micrographics' will be used in place of this ponderous phrase). **1979** *Amer. N. & Q.* XVII. XI. 174 The information techniques of reprography, computers, communications, networks, micrographics, and other elements of information transfer. **1984** *Australian* 6 Nov. 21/3 (Advt.), We can..show you how today's micrographics can expand..into a complete..system. **1989** *Information Technol. for Devel*. IV. 48 As we live in the part of the world where books and library resources reach with difficulty, we should be able to put many of the rare ones on micrographics.

microinject (ˌmaɪkrəʊɪnˈdʒɛkt), *v*. Chiefly *Biol*. [Back-formation f. *MICROINJECTION *n*.] **1.** *trans*. To inject into a microscopic object, esp. a living cell.

   1974 *Nature* 4 Oct. 388/1 The *Xenopus* oocyte (into which the mRNA is microinjected). **1976** *Sci. Amer*. Aug. 71/3 Both of these small eggs can be microinjected. **1984** L. W. BROWDER *Developmental Biol*. (ed. 2) vii. 305 Attempts to induce maturation by microinjecting progesterone directly into oocytes. **1994** *Sci. Amer*. Mar. 38/1 We knew the machinery was fairly efficient because we could microinject more than 100 DNA molecules of the same sequence, and the cell would stitch them all together in the same orientation.
   2. *trans*. To subject (a cell, etc.) to microinjection *with*.

   1975 *Nature* 21 Aug. 677/2 Cells microinjected with tRNA^Phe contain more than 500 times the normal concentration of this specific tRNA. **1988** *Ibid*. 20 Oct. 736/1 Fibres were microinjected with a solution of 27.5 mM fura-2.., 66 mM potassium gluconate, 5 mM CaCl₂, 5mM HEPES.

So **microin'jected**, **microin'jecting** *ppl. adjs*.

   1951 *Nature* 5 May 734/2 The first condition could be fulfilled with many of the micro-injecting devices now on the market. **1987** *Biochem. Jrnl*. CCXLI. 793 (*heading*) Studies with microinjected purified glycolytic enzymes. **1988** *Mouse News Let*. Nov. 168 Microinjected antibody also localizes to the Golgi.

microinjection (ˌmaɪkrəʊɪnˈdʒɛkʃən), *n*. (Formerly at MICRO- 2 a in Dict.) Chiefly *Biol*. Also **micro-injection**. [f. MICRO- 2 a + INJECTION *n*.] Injection involving microscopic objects, quantities, etc.

   1921 *Science* 28 Oct. 411/2 The microdissection and microinjection of marine ova and of animal and plant cells. **1925** *Proc. R. Soc*. B. XCVIII. 263 The best method of attacking this problem seemed..to be the use of the technique of micro-injection. **1970** *Nature* 22 Aug. 857/2 For micro-injection we used a hydraulic system of mineral oil with the micro-pipette tip filled with tracer solution. **1976** *Ann. Rev. Microbiol*. XXX. 110 Since this alga has exceptionally large cells, it is well-suited for transmission studies by microinjection. **1988** *Nature* 11 Feb. 479/3 Photobleaching studies after microinjection of fluorescently labelled tubulin show that the kinetochore microtubules shorten from their plus ends.

micro level ('maɪkrəʊ ˌlɛvəl), *n*. Also **micro-level**, **microlevel**. [f. MICRO- + LEVEL *n*.] The most detailed or fundamental level of a concept, process, etc. Cf. *MACRO LEVEL *n*.

   1967 G. WILLS in Wills & Yearsley *Handbk. Managem. Technol*. x. 176 At the macro level, marketing management became concerned with understanding its social environment; at the micro level, the concept of the marketing mix postulated a co-ordinative and integrative activity for product distribution and communication. **1982** *English World-Wide* II. 226 This macro-level analysis is integrated in the thesis with a micro-level analysis of functions. **1989** *Applied Linguistics* X. 450 Durk Gorter describes the results of some microlevel studies of language choice in a Dutch-Frisian bilingual context.

micromanage ('maɪkrəʊmaenɪdʒ), *v*. orig. and chiefly *U.S.* Also **micro-manage**. [Back-formation from *MICROMANAGEMENT *n*.] *trans*. To control and direct (an enterprise or activity) in every particular (esp. in *Pol*.). Occas. *absol*. or *intr*. Cf. *MICROMANAGEMENT *n*.

   1976 *Aviation Week* 7 June 17/1 Our inconsistency and our tendency to micro-manage research and development programs is demonstrably inefficient and detrimental to the cost effectiveness of the programs and products. **1986** *Washington Post* 16 Mar. D2/1 James M. Beggs..promised the NASA field centers..that they would not be 'micromanaged' from headquarters. **1989** *Sunday Tel*. 15 Oct. 15/2 There has been something slightly manic..about his [*sc*. President Bush's] refusal to be ruffled. Accusing Congress of 'micro-managing' foreign policy, and implying that covert actions are hamstrung by the zeal of the Senate Select Committee on Intelligence were not smart moves. **1992** *Spy* (N.Y.) May 11/3 Wayne micro-manages his daughter's life. **1993** *Wall St. Jrnl*. 19 Feb. A1/6 He used construction of his economic plan as a crash course in learning the details of government. 'If it appears he's trying to micromanage, it's temporary and he'll get over it.'

micromanagement (ˌmaɪkrəʊˈmaenɪdʒmənt), *n*. esp. *Comm*. and *Pol*. (chiefly *U.S.*). Also **micromanagement**. [f. MICRO- 1 b + MANAGEMENT *n*.] The control and direction of an enterprise or activity in every particular and to the smallest detail, esp. with the effect of slowing progress or neglecting broader issues of policy or principle.

   [**1975** *Economist* 15 Nov. 102/2 Mr Tun Abdul Rasak's policies in Malaysia are a classic example of good macro, but dismal micro, management of an economy.] **1977** *Aviation Week* 31 Jan. 71/2 Excessive 'micromanagement' by DOR&E and other defense management agencies also contributed to funding delays. **1982** *Maclean's* 22 Feb. 30 Others believe that the Pentagon is too preoccupied with rooting out waste, fraud and abuse..[and] that the obsessive attention being devoted to micromanagement obscures a far greater evil—'the neglect of strategy, the operational art of war, and of tactics.' **1989** W. BELASCO *Appetite for Change* ix. 217 The body was thus like a corporate 'portfolio matrix' requiring ceaseless analysis, rearranging and micromanagement. **1993** *Time* 25 Jan. 28/3 Clinton admits his tendency toward micromanagement..but added, 'As I get more comfortable with it, I'll be able to delegate more and more.'

micromolar (maɪkrəʊ'məʊlə(r)), *a. Chem.* [f. MICRO- 5 + MOLAR *a.*³] Pertaining to, or containing, a quantity of substance of the order of a millionth of a mole; *spec.* containing a specified number of micromoles of solute per litre of solution.
    1970 *Rev. Sci. Instruments* XLI. 475/1 The continuous measurement of changes in micromolar amounts of a gas. **1975** *Nature* 29 May 424/2 When present in micromolar amounts, calcium binds to troponin and releases the inhibition. **1985** *Sci. Amer.* Nov. 53/1 In a typical mammalian cell the concentration of free calcium is about 0.1 micromolar, or four millionths of a gram per liter.

microprogramming, *vbl. n.* Add: **micro'programmable** *a.*, that may be microprogrammed; **microprogramma'bility** *n.*, the property of being microprogrammable.
    1963 *Proc. AFIPS Conf.* XXIV. 212/2 To the casual programmer who has occasion to use only those programming aids and instruction sets that have been devised and provided for him by others, the microprogrammable feature means a larger and more varied instruction repertoire and generally improved performance. **1971** *New Scientist* 7 Jan. 27/1 Such a machine must..be 'microprogrammable', modular, inexpensive, and user-oriented. **1974** *Computer Design* Mar. 86/2 MPS organization has been shown to capitalize on the μP features of low cost, microprogrammability, and infrequent memory references. **1982** *Electronics* 28 July 146/1 In these applications, designers of pipelined microprogrammable systems need not add extra registers.

micropublication (,maɪkrəʊpʌblɪ'keɪʃən), *n.* [f. MICRO- 7 + PUBLICATION *n.*] Publication in microform; = MICROPUBLISHING *vbl. n.*
    1971 *Newsweek* 22 Mar. 77/2 For a complex application of printer's ink, that could be the breakeven press run as against micropublication. **1980** *Times Lit. Suppl.* 25 Apr. 465 Micropublication would make [an edition] seem more difficult and unapproachable than it actually is. **1988** *Los Angeles Times* 10 Sept. II. 7/1 A Northern California firm specializing in what it calls 'micropublication'—miniaturizing printed pages onto single, small cards.

microscreen ('maɪkrəʊskriːn), *n.* Also **microscreen.** [f. MICRO- 1 a + SCREEN *n.*¹] **1.** A screen with a fine mesh, *spec.* one used for filtering liquids.
    A proprietary name (*Micro-screen*) in some applications.
    1959 *Official Gaz.* (U.S. Patent Office) 24 Feb. TM 148/2 *Micro-screen.* For filter assemblies and cartridges therefor for filtering and purifying fluids. **1981** *Engineering News-Record* 19 Feb. 49/1 URS Co...is preparing working drawings for sanitary sewer treatment plant, and operations, service and microscreen buildings. **1988** *Los Angeles Times* 15 Sept. VIII. 37/4 A cone-shaped, 23.7-karat, gold-plated microscreen that filters out bitter-tasting sediments from brewed coffee.
    2. Any small or miniature screen intended for display; *spec.* in *Computing*, a liquid crystal display built into the keyboards of some microcomputers.

1979 *Economist* 1 Sept. 79/1 It was the latest wing-a-ding high-technology product from..Sinclair Radionics when it was launched in January, 1977; the world's first pocket (well, 1½ lb) micro-screen television. **1983** *Austral. Microcomputer Mag.* Sept. 87/2 ACT and Victor claim the major innovation is the built-in microscreen, a two-line 40 column LCD incorporating a digital calendar and clock. **1986** *Byte* Apr. 306/3 Apricot has revived the microscreen for the XEN keyboard, a single-line LCD built into the keyboard that shows the date and time by default.

microspore, *n.* Add: **micro'sporocyte** *n. Bot.*, a mother cell that divides to form four microspores.
    1916 B. D. JACKSON *Gloss. Bot. Terms* (ed. 3) 234/2 *Microsporocyte,* the mother-cell of a microspore or pollen-grain. **1936** J. B. HILL et al. *Botany* xviii. 583 The reduction division in the microsporocytes is followed by an equation division in each of the two nuclei. **1977** K. ESAU *Anat. Seed Plants* (ed. 2) xxi. 405/2 The continuity of the microsporocytes is thought to account for the closely synchronous meiosis within a microsporangium frequently observed in angiosperms.

microteaching ('maɪkrəʊtiːtʃɪŋ), *n. Educ.* (orig. and chiefly *U.S.*). Also **micro-teaching.** [f. MICRO- + TEACHING *vbl. n.*] A method of teacher training, designed to develop specific skills, which typically involves the teaching of a small class for a short time followed by analysis of (a film recording of) the session.
    1964 BUSH & ALLEN in *Micro-teaching* (1967) IV. 1 Micro-teaching is a scaled-down sample of teaching. **1965** *NEA Jrnl.* Dec. 26/2 The most important aspect of microteaching has been its usefulness in predicting eventual success in the normal classroom. **1967** *Jrnl. Teacher Educ.* XVIII. 389/1 Micro-teaching is a scaled-down teaching encounter that has been developed at Stanford University to serve three purposes: (1) as preliminary experience and practice in teaching, (2) as a research vehicle to explore training effects..and (3) as an in-service training instrument for experienced teachers. **1969** ALLEN & RYAN *Microteaching* i.1 Microteaching provides teachers with a practice setting for instruction in which the normal complexities of the classroom are reduced and in which the teacher receives a great deal of feedback on his performance. **1977** P. STREVENS *New Orientations Teaching Eng.* vi. 77 Micro-teaching: the teaching (by the trainee) of specific items or techniques, possibly with the use of closed-circuit television and videotape recordings. **1993** LAWTON & GORDON *Dict. Educ.* II. 61 Aimed at improving teacher performance in the classroom, CBT [*sc.* competency-based teaching] employs many forms of teaching methods, such as games and simulations and microteaching, which seek to promote self-awareness and interaction skills.

microtrabecular (,maɪkrəʊtrə'bɛkjʊlə(r)), *a. Cytol.* [f. MICRO- 4 + TRABECULAR *a.*] Pertaining to or designating a lattice of very fine filamentous strands of protein believed to permeate the cellular cytoplasm and to control the transport of molecules within a cell.
    1976 WOLOSEWICK & PORTER in *Amer. Jrnl. Anat.* CXLVII. 307/2 Upon closer inspection, this three-dimensional lattice resembles the trabecular structure of spongy bone. This microscopic trabecular structure, perhaps better referred to as a *microtrabecular system* (the strands being the trabeculae) or three-dimensional lattice,..is a constant feature in all parts of the cytoplasm. **1980** *Sci. Amer.* Apr. 135/2 In the first model,..materials are moved passively between the microtrabecular elements of the axoplasm. **1984** HOLTZMAN & NOVIKOFF *Cells & Organelles* (ed. 3) II. xi. 289 The overall effect is the integration of the entire cytoplasm into a loosely knit microtrabecular network capable of rapid change and rapid attachment and detachment of the structures linked in it. **1989**

Biochim. et Biophys. Acta CMXCIX. 69/2 Clegg's model should be expanded to include microtubules in addition to actin filaments as interacting components of the microtrabecular lattice.

So ,**microtra'becula** *n.* (pl. -æ), a constituent filament of the microtrabecular lattice.

1976 WOLOSEWICK & PORTER in *Amer. Jrnl. Anat.* CXLVII. 307/1 The fibrous systems are made up of organized bundles of microfilaments,..which are apparently continuous with less organized strands (microtrabeculae) of ground substance, 3-6 nm thick, and with 10-nm filaments. **1977** *Jrnl. Cell Biol.* LXXV. 556/1 It appears that the microtrabeculae are intimately involved in mediating pigment migration. **1987** *Biol. of Cell* LX. 60/1 Incubation with anti-actin antiserum of embedment-free sections of the pars intermedia, followed by IgG-conjugated colloidal gold complexes, resulted in labeling by gold particles of the microtrabeculae suspending the secretory granules.

microwave, *v.* Add: Hence '**microwaved** *ppl. a.*, cooked or heated in a microwave oven.

1982 A. MAUPIN *Further Tales of City* 13 Denny..was eating a microwaved patty melt. **1988** *Daily Tel.* 30 Mar. 21/4 Teachers find that growing numbers of their pupils never sit down to a meal with the rest of the family, but munch microwaved 'telly' snacks instead. **1993** *Options* Aug. 93/1 Leave microwaved food for the recommended standing time and check that food is piping hot throughout before serving.

mictic ('mɪktɪk), *a. Biol.* [f. Gr. μικτ-ός mixed + -IC 1: see also *MIXIS *n.*] Involving or pertaining to mixis; resulting from mixis; hence, of mixed parentage or descent.

1950 *Adv. Genetics* III. 194 In plants we speak of mictic reproduction, its opposite being named apomixis. **1969** *Jrnl. Theoret. Biol.* XXIV. 279 (*heading*) Transformation of mictic indices in components of pedigree. **1975** G. C. WILLIAMS *Sex & Evolution* x. 119 Vegetative multiplication, mictic and apomictic seed..may or may not be present. **1985** G. T. NURSE et al. *Peoples Southern Afr.* ix. 226 Adam Kok's people, now sufficiently mictic to deserve the epithet Bastards (signifying not extramarital but hybridity), were pushed northwards. **1988** *Oecologia* LXXV. 430/1 Throughout their reproductive phase, these parental females retained their potential to produce either mictic or amictic offspring.

midden, *n.* Add: **3.** A receptacle for refuse, a dustbin; also, a small recess in a backyard or basement where domestic rubbish, dustbins, etc., are kept. *Sc. colloq.*

1890 in *Cent. Dict.* **1920** C. YOUNG *Spon's Pract. Builders' Pocket-bk.* (ed. 3) 420 Scottish building terms... Scottish: *Midden*.. English: *Dusthold*. **1958** C. HANLEY *Dancing in Streets* 42 What we called middens, upper-class people described as dustbins. **1981** A. GRAY *Lanark* (1982) xii. 124 He keeked between the stems of sorrel and daisies at the midden, a three-sided brick shed where bins were kept. **1984** J. KELMAN *Busconductor Hines* ii. 79 For every 3 closes you have the 1 midden containing 6 dustbins. **1992** I. PATTISON *More Rab C. Nesbitt Scripts* 9 The ugly side of Govan. We see dogs raking through middens. **1992** J. TORRINGTON *Swing Hammer Swing!* viii. 60 A black one-eyed cat..stared up at me,..dumbly imploring me to tell it why there were no fishheads or meatscraps in the middens anymore.

midfielder ('mɪdfɪːldə(r)), *n. Sport* (esp. *Lacrosse* and *Football*). [f. MID-FIELD *n.* + -ER[1].] A player positioned in midfield; = LINKMAN *n.*[2] b (*c*).

1940 *Official Lacrosse Guide* 23 Macmillan of St. John's is also a finished midfielder. **1940** T. STANWICK *Lacrosse* vi. 61 Midfielders when in possession of the ball play the part of a secondary attack, and when not in possession of it are the first line of defense. **1975**

World Soccer Dec. 21/2 The Honved midfielder, Pinter, battled through the Czech defence early in the second-half. **1978** *Detroit Free Press* 16 Apr. E2/4 Rodney Marsh, the Rowdies' talented midfielder.., is making the trip to Detroit. **1982** R. WIDDOWS *Hamlyn Bk. Football Techniques & Tactics* 45 Turning with the ball is the staple diet of the midfielder, who constantly receives the ball in space facing his own goal and needs to switch the direction of play. **1993** *Sunday Mail* (Brisbane) 7 Mar. 62/4 Young Socceroo midfielder Ante Moric is doubtful for Australia's second game of the world youth championship against Russia in Sydney tomorrow night.

mifepristone (mɪfɛ'prɪstəʊn), *n. Pharm.* [Prob. ad. Du. *mifepriston* (coined by Vervest & Haspels 1985, in *Nederlands Tijdschr. voor Geneeskunde* XXXV. 1680), f. *mefi-* (representing *aminophenol* s.v. AMINO-) + *-pri-* (representing PROPYNE *n.*) + *-st-* (representing OESTRADIOL *n.*) + -ONE.] A synthetic norsteroid, $C_{29}H_{35}NO_2$, which inhibits the action of progesterone and may be given orally in early pregnancy in order to induce abortion.

1985 *Lancet* 2 Nov. 1019/1 Mifepristone (RU486), a new steroid compound which antagonises progesterone and glucocorticosteroid action at the receptor level. **1990** *Sci. Amer.* June 18/1 Under the name mifepristone, RU 486 is administered as a tablet in conjunction with a small dose of a prostaglandin. **1993** *Daily Tel.* 18 Jan. 4/5 The French-made drug, mifepristone..can be used for women who are up to nine weeks pregnant.

MiG (mɪg), *n.*[2] Also MIG, Mig. [Russ. *MIG*, abbrev. f. the names of A. I. *Mikoyan* (+ *i*) and M. I. *Gurevich*, Russian aircraft designers.] Any of various types of Russian fighter aircraft designed by the team of Mikoyan and Gurevich. Also *attrib.* Freq. with following number denoting the specific model.

1942 *Aviation* Aug. 92/3 The Nazis were met by new types of Soviet planes. One in particular, the powerful MIG-3, rapidly won deserved fame and respect. **1949** *Mech. Engin.* LXXI. 417/1 The Mig-7 jet..is powered by probably two German BMW 003 turbojets. **1951** *Aviation Week* 11 June 17/1 They have a jet engine in the MiG 15 that is superior to any jet engine that we have today. **1959** *Listener* 12 Mar. 445/1 We may see the Yemen welcoming Soviet submarines and Indonesia flying nothing but Migs. **1973** E. PACE *Any War will Do* (1974) III. 206 The Nigerian air force was largely a ragtag collection of mercenaries flying newly arrived Mig's. **1986** T. CLANCY *Red Storm Rising* (1988) xxviii. 457 When the MiGs got to within sixty miles, the AWACS aircraft shut down their radars and dove for the ground to avoid the attack. **1992** *Daily Star* 2 July 8/4 Our fighter fleet will soon be hopelessly out-dated by Russia's so-sophisticated MIG 29s.

migrate, *v.* Add: [**2.**] **c.** Of a plant: to change or extend its distribution.

1876 A. BLYTT *Ess. Immigration Norwegian Flora* 29 Do plants migrate all at once across large tracts..? **1915** *Ann. Missouri Bot. Garden* II. 87 *Alnus glutinosa* migrated into Norway from the south, while *Alnus incana* came from the east. **1938** WEAVER & CLEMENTS *Plant Ecol.* (ed. 2) vi. 127 In wind-swept areas, such as prairies and plains, many plants or inflorescences migrate for miles as tumbleweeds. **1960** N. POLUNIN *Introd. Plant Geogr.* x. 201 Examples [of climatic relics] are the mesothermic plants to be found in some boreal areas that have cooled at least since the 'postglacial optimum' when such plants presumably migrated to these areas. **1989** *New Scientist* 20 May 31 (*caption*) All eyes are on the lime..which will migrate north as the climate changes.

milieu, *n.* Sense 2 in Dict. becomes 3. Add: **2. a.** *transf.* A group of people with a shared (cultural) outlook; a social class or set.

1952 P. Bowles *Let it come Down* II. xiii. 157 The American milieu in Tangier was peculiarly hermetic, not inclined to mix with the other diplomatic groups. **1954** I. Murdoch *Under Net* ii. 35 It's not easy to find someone whom one has mislaid for years in London, particularly if she belongs to the sort of milieu that Anna belonged to. **1962** A. S. Neill *Summerhill* 96 In their milieu one could not live sexually together unless one was respectable—that is, married. **1970** D. Martin *50 Key Words: Sociol.* 46 *Milieu*..may..designate an age-group with a definable élan such as students. **1975** *Economist* 15 Mar. 123/1 His cantankerous old father's death..exacerbated tensions within the Gladstone clan and allowed William [Ewart Gladstone] to pass finally out of the *arriviste* milieu of Fasque to the graceful life of Hawarden. **1986** *Oxf. Art Jrnl.* Jan. 86/1 This approach does.. point up some of the anomalies between the works of men and women in the Surrealist milieu.

b. Also **Milieu.** In France, the criminal underworld; also, a group or organization belonging to it.

1972 *Guardian* 29 July 11/3 He had already entered small-time crime and made the acquaintance of a future leader of the 'Milieu'. *Ibid.*, The congregation included the biggest representation of the 'Milieu' to have been seen in Paris since the Guerini trial a couple of years ago. **1972** *Times* 4 Sept. 4/3 This is their excuse in Lyons—that they have to keep an eye on..the serious underworld, the *milieu*. **1985-6** *Sight & Sound* Winter 23/1 The eagle eye pinpointing the milieu and the tender one observing the pimp and the prostitute. **1987** N. Rankin *Dead Man's Chest* 210 The principled bravery that would lead..Graham Green [*sic*] to brave *le milieu*—the gangsters—of Nice.

militance ('mɪlɪtəns), *n.* [f. MILIT(ANT *a.* + -ANCE.] The condition of being militant; (an instance of) militancy.

1949 D. Leon *Ruskin* III. ii. 116 On being met by the police, all its leaders' militance suddenly vanished. **1980** *Times* 13 May 2/2 The right wing have no idea how to handle or initiate militancy when militance is required. **1988** *N.Y. Times* 17 June A4/4 Workers.. complain about what they describe as a lack of militance on the part of their union.

milking, *vbl. n.* Add: **[1.] b.** *fig.* The manipulation of funds for (esp. unscrupulous or illicit) financial gain; more loosely, exploitation of resources.

1936 F. Lundberg *Imperial Hearst* x. 326 Hearst's sons were on the payroll for sums in excess of the average paid the top executives ... This is what is known in Wall Street as 'milking'. **1975** *Times* 5 Aug. 15/2 Company inspectors.. are particularly examining what they describe as 'the milking' of Court Line's building interests to support other activities. **1994** *Vancouver Sun* 26 Mar. B1/2 Yann Piat thought that as a member of parliament it was safe for her to fight the extortion rackets, drug trafficking and milking of public funds that flourish on France's most glamorous and shady playground.

mill, *n.*1 Add: **[3.] e.** The part of Charles Babbage's analytical engine where arithmetic operations were performed on data. Now *Hist.*

1837 C. Babbage in B. Randell *Origins Digital Computers* (1973) 17 The calculating part of the engine may be divided into two portions..the *Mill* in which all operations are performed..[and] the *Store*. **1948** *Proc. Symp. Large-Scale Digital Calculating Machinery 1947* (US Navy Dept. & Harvard Univ.) 93 The early designs of Babbage for an Analytical Engine involved a 'mill', in which the formulas were stored and the mathematical operations carried out. **1975** *Nature* 16 Oct. 541/2 Like a modern computer it [*sc.* Babbage's 'analytical engine'] was to have a store in which numbers could be held, and a processor known as the 'mill' in which the arithmetic operations would be performed.

miller, *n.*1 Sense 8 in Dict. becomes 9. Add:
8. = MOUSSERON *n.*

1954 E. M. Wakefield *Observer's Bk. Common Fungi* 63 *Clitopilus prunulus*. Miller (plate 36). Edible. **1967** W. P. K. Findlay *Wayside & Woodland Fungi* xi. 129 *Clitopilus prunulus*: The Miller (L. *prunulus*, little plum). This species owes its English name to the fact that it is white and smells strongly of meal. **1977** C. Conran tr. *M. Guérard's Cuisine Minceur* (1981) 29 Millers... are an opaque dirty white with soft thick white flesh, and are somewhat trumpet-shaped.

milli-, *comb. form.* Add: *millidarwin* (*DARWIN *n.* 2).

1949 J. B. S. Haldane in *Evolution* III. 55/2 It may be found desirable to coin some word, for example a *darwin*, for a unit of evolutionary rate, such as an increase or decrease of size by a factor of *e* per million years, or, what is practically equivalent, an increase or decrease of $\frac{1}{1000}$ per 1000 years. If so the horse rates would range round 40 *millidarwins. **1987** *Paleobiol.* XIII. 138/1 Previous studies have reported relatively high rates of evolution for marine invertebrates.. but these studies have focused..on changes in body size. Our results indicate that shape experiences much greater evolutionary stability (modal 'rate' in the order of 10 millidarwins for any interval of 1 ma or more).

milliprobe ('mɪlɪprəʊb), *n.* [f. MILLI- + PROBE *n.*] Any instrument for analysing small amounts of material; *spec.* a form of spectrometer in which a narrow beam of accelerated protons (or other subatomic particles) is directed at the specimen and the spectrum of the resulting fluorescence is analysed, frequently used to study delicate or valuable objects.

1963 Banks & Hall in *Archaeometry* VI. 31 Both Dr. E. T. Hall and W. J. Young suggested at the I. I. C. Rome Conference in 1961, that many of these difficulties could be overcome if one used a curved-crystal spectrometer arrangement. The Laboratory has put this idea into operation in designing its new X-ray spectrometer, the 'Milliprobe'. **1966** *Ibid.* IX. 131 X-ray fluorescent analysis by a milliprobe. **1970** *Phil. Trans. R. Soc.* A. CCLXIX. 139 A new variation in emission spectrometry has been provided by the development of the 'Laser milliprobe spectrometer'. **1978** *Analytical Chem.* L. 1644/1 X-ray milliprobes used in these studies have been designed specially and fabricated at Bell Laboratories. **1987** *Nature* 16 July 195/2 Using a proton milliprobe, collimated to 1.0 mm × 0.5 mm (because the width of the lines on the map is of the order of 0.5 mm), Cahill and his team carried out 159 analyses of the parchment and ink of the map.

Millon ('mɪlən, ‖mijɔ̃), *n. Biochem.* and *Chem.* [The name of Auguste Nicolas Eugène *Millon* (1812–67), French chemist.] Used *attrib.* and in the possessive in **Millon's base,** a yellow basic powder, $Hg_2NOH.2H_2O$, produced by the action of aqueous ammonia on mercuric oxide (as reported by Millon in *Ann. de Chim. et de Physique* (1846) XVIII. 393); **Millon('s) reaction,** the characteristic reaction of Millon's reagent with phenolic compounds, in which a white precipitate is produced which becomes pink or reddish on heating (described by Millon for a phenolic protein in *Compt. Rend.* (1849) XXVIII. 40); **Millon's reagent,** a clear solution of mercuric nitrate containing some nitrous acid, used in Millon's test; **Millon's test,** Millon's reaction employed as a test for phenols, esp. for proteins containing tyrosine.

1872 *Chem. News* 2 Aug. 59/1 (*title*) Estimation of urea by means of Millon's Reagent. **1875** A. Gamgee tr. *Hermann's Elem. Human Physiol.* I. 32 Mercuric nitrate, in the presence of a little nitrous acid, at 60°C., colours the albuminous bodies red (Millon's reaction). **1883** *Encycl. Brit.* XVI. 34/1 The product is a yellow solid base ('Millon's base') of the composition $N_2H_6 + 4HgO + H_2O = N_2Hg_4O.2H_2O + 2H_2O$. **1891** LARKIN & LEIGH *Outl. Pract. Physiological Chem.* (ed. 2) 11 Millon's test. No reaction if pure. **1951** *Acta Crystallogr.* IV. 156 The structure of Millon's base, $Hg_2NOH.2H_2O$, consists of a three-dimensional framework Hg_2N^+ in an idealized cristobalite type of arrangement. **1960** *Jrnl. Histochem. & Cytochem.* VIII. 4/2 The Millon reaction has been criticized because of the low pH to which tissues are necessarily subjected. **1978** *Acta Chimica Acad. Sci. Hungaricae* XCVIII. 329 Millon's reagent was prepared from mercury (II) nitrate and potassium nitrite. **1987** G. & S. TOOLE *Understanding Biol. for Advanced Level* iii. 32/2 Millon's Test detects the amino acid tyrosine and will therefore only give a positive result with proteins possessing it.

Mills & Boon ('mılz ənd 'buːn), *n. phr.* Also **Mills and Boon**. [The names of Gerald *Mills* (1877-1928) and Charles *Boon* (1877-1943), who together founded the publishing house Mills & Boon Limited in 1908.] **1.** A proprietary name used *attrib.* and *absol.* to designate popular romantic novels published by Mills & Boon Limited.
   1912 *Dundee Courier* 8 Aug., In choosing a 'Mills & Boon' novel readers of fiction can never go very far wrong when in quest of genuine entertainment. **1912** *Pall Mall Gaz.* 9 Aug. 8 (*heading*) The latest Mills & Boon literature. **1952** *W. H. Smith Trade Circular* 26 July 18/3 Without ever having read a Mills & Boon romance I know I can quite safely say to the vague customer in search of 'a nice romance'—'Try a Mills & Boon romance!' **1982** J. SCOTT *Uprush of Mayhem* iii. 23, I reckon she must have been lonely. Read a lot of Mills and Boon. **1985** *Mail on Sunday* 3 Nov. 27/2 Most of them are as idealistically romantic as the blue-eyed heroines of the Mills and Boon novels they swallow like Smarties. **1990** *Sunday Tel.* 18 Feb. 61/4, I found her.., with *Meg and Mog* and a child's mittened paw in one hand and a Mills & Boon in the other.
   2. *transf.* Used *attrib.* and *absol.* to designate material and situations regarded as resembling or typical of the type of fiction published by Mills & Boon Limited; romantic, story-book.
   1982 *Financial Times* 13 Jan. 19/1 It is more boring to make cheap jokes about Barry Manilow, the Mills and Boon of popular music, than to sit through one of his concerts. **1990** *Courier-Mail* (Brisbane) 15 Oct. 2/6 When in-vitro fertilisation pioneer Carl Wood met his future wife it was not a Mills and Boon romance. **1994** *Daily Mail* 18 Feb. 78/2 Long before the XVIIth Winter Olympics became a made-for-TV mini-series starring an American skater called Tonya Harding, they were packaged for a Mills and Boon ending to another sporting soap opera, featuring Torvill and Dean.
   So **Mills and 'Boony** *a.* (*rare*).
   1946 P. LARKIN *Let.* 23 Aug. in A. Thwaite *Sel. Lett. Philip Larkin* (1992) 123, I have remembered a title I thought of soon after starting to write it—'*A Girl in Winter*'—which, though I believe I discarded it on the grounds of sounding Mills & Boony (if you know what I mean) does conjure up a more precise image than the present one does.

Milroy's disease ('mılrɔız dı'ziːz), *n. Path.* [The name of William Forsyth *Milroy* (1855-1942), American physician, who described the disease in 1892 (*N.Y. Med. Jrnl.* LVI. 505).] A hereditary condition characterized by lymphoedema of one or more of the extremities, usually both lower legs.
   1909 W. OSLER in Osler & McCrae *Syst. Med.* VI. xxviii. 654 Certain persons are born with a special susceptibility to exudative skin lesions. There are families all the members of which present these reactions to particular substances; there are families some members of which are liable to attacks of local œdema, a peculiarity which has been traced through six generations; and lastly, there is an hereditary œdema of the legs (Milroy's disease) which has probably nothing to do with the forms under consideration. *Ibid.* 661 (*heading*) Hereditary œdema of the legs (Milroy's disease). [**1928** W. F. MILROY in *Jrnl. Amer. Med. Assoc.* 20 Oct. 1172/2 The condition now under consideration was first designated by my name by Sir William Osler, in his work on the practice of medicine.] **1966** *Surgery* LX. 1098/1 Only a few cases actually qualify as Milroy's disease under the original four points. **1984** TIGHE & DAVIES *Pathology* (ed. 4) xiii. 116 The most likely clinical examples occur..as a result of congenital absence of lymphatics (Milroy's disease).

mimesis, *n.* Restrict *Rhet.* label to sense 1 a. Delete quots 1962-65 from sense 1 a. Add: [**1.**] **b.** Imitation; *spec.* in *Art* and *Lit.*, the representation or reflection of life or the 'real' world in (a work of) art, literature, etc.
   Sometimes used with reference to Aristotle *Poetics* 1447a or Plato *Republic* 598b.
   [**1789** T. TWINING *Aristotle's Treatise on Poetry* 40 Plato drew his idea of the MIMHΣIΣ of poetry from the theatre itself, and from the personal imitations of *represented* tragedy.] **1939** *Classical Q.* XXXIII. 168 The song is a trick, just as in Plato's eyes illusionistic painting is a trick, and this kind of unreal trickery is called *mimesis*. **1941** AUDEN *New Year Let.* 19 Art in intention is mimesis But, realized, the resemblance ceases. **1953** W. R. TRASK tr. E. Auerbach (*title*) Mimesis. The representation of reality in western literature. **1967** G. STEINER *Lang. & Silence* 111 Baudelaire's *Tableaux de Paris*, whose shape is a mimesis of the city. **1989** R. ALTER *Pleasures of Reading* vi. 192 Several schools of criticism have come to regard mimesis as a sham or impossibility.

mimosa, *n.* Sense 4 in Dict. becomes 5. Add: **4.** *U. S.* A cocktail consisting of champagne and orange juice. Cf. BUCK'S FIZZ *n.*
   1936 F. MEIER *Artistry of Mixing Drinks* 74/2 Mimosa or *Champagne Orange*. In a large wineglass: a piece of Ice, the juice of one-half Orange; fill with Champagne stir and serve. **1948** D. A. EMBURY *Fine Art of Mixing Drinks* xi. 308 Mimosa. Orange juice and champagne, half and half. Just another freak champagne mixture. It's not half bad and the ladies usually like it. **1975** *New Yorker* 30 June 32/1 People keep arriving, parking their cars along the road, going up the outside stairs to the deck..to drink Mimosas, a combination of orange juice and champagne. **1987** T. BOYLE *Post-Mortem Effects* xvi. 134 Leaning against the bar on her stool, holding her mimosa glass by the stem. *Ibid.* 137 Another mimosa, okay?

mind, *n.*[1] Add: [**21.**] **[b.] mind-bending** *a.*: so **mind-bendingly** *adv.*
   1982 *Listener* 23/30 Dec. 60/4 Since programming is one of the most fascinating types of puzzle-solving known to man, such a system was *mind-bendingly frustrating. **1990** K. WOZENCRAFT *Rush* ii. 20 Patrol, I'd discovered, was boring, mind-bendingly pedestrian.
   mind-blowing *a.*: so **mind-blowingly** *adv.*
   1977 *Economist* 31 Dec. 78/3 Unless the triggers become *mindblowingly complex. **1985** *Fortune* 4 Feb. 51/1 Somewhat mind-blowingly, much of this work is performed by keyboarders who don't understand English. **1993** LOWE & SHAW *Travellers* 30 We swapped a view of prefabs and helicopters taking off every twenty minutes, which was mind-blowingly noisy, for a view of uninterrupted, unspoiled coast.
   mind-boggling *a.*: so **mind-bogglingly** *adv.*
   1973 *Observer* 2 Sept. 35/1 A cylindrical sea which arches *mindbogglingly above the explorers' heads. **1990** *Times* 29 Oct. 2/1 The extraordinary thing

about chaos is that you can get some mind-bogglingly complex behaviour from simple equations.

mind-game (*a*) a game designed to exercise the mind, a brain-teaser; (*b*) an instance of psychological manipulation, esp. used to gain an advantage over someone else.

1963 P. WEST *Mod. Novel* II. ii. 169 His dithering adolescents personify the French *mind-game. Theorizing is an effective way of cheering ourselves up, but not of constructing principles. **1973** J. LENNON *Mind Games* (song) in *Lennon Solo Years* (1981) 80 We're playing these mind games together. *Ibid.* 84 Were [*sic*] play-ing those mind games for-ev-er pro-ject-ing our im-ag-es in space and in time. **1988** *Oxford Today* I. 1 (Advt., recto rear cover), Mind games for first class minds... A monthly compendium of ever-challenging problems, puzzles and logic questions.. with a chance to sharpen your wits. **1991** *Boston* Apr. 129/3 Among the obvious mind games that jewelers play to maximize their sales is a mental switcheroo that leaves lovers convinced that the size of a gemstone reflects the depth of their feelings and commitment.

mind, *v.* Add: [**11.**] **b.** To act as a bodyguard to (esp. a criminal); to keep watch over (esp. when engaged in a criminal activity).

1924 E. WALLACE *Room 13* vi. 67 I'll cover you; I've got two boys handy that 'mind' me. **1941** V. DAVIS *Phenomena in Crime* iii. 41 Joe's job was to 'mind' the furniture van in front [containing the burglars' tools]. **1986** *Daily Express* 8 Nov. 15/4 Det. Sgt. Graham Sayer had been ordered to 'mind' Roger Dennhardt... Dennhardt was a supergrass.

minder, *n.* Add: [**3.**] **d.** A person employed to accompany or assist another person, either to provide protection or advice, or to monitor that person's movements; *spec.* a bodyguard.

1980 *Telegraph* (Brisbane) 4 Jan. 6/3 The frustrated spy catcher—or as they call it in the trade, rat catcher—was freed, along with various 'minders', a Morgan sports car and a thoroughly confused spy-watching world. **1985** W. GOLDING *Egyptian Jrnl.* i. 11 Another visit to Egypt but this time with a Minder who spoke the language. **1988** *Independent* 16 Sept. 7/2 You were living in luxury, surrounded by minders and assistants. **1992** *Vanity Fair* Dec. 150/2 Caine sat at a table with a trio of minders behind him and a semicircle of press photographers in front.

e. *Pol.* A political adviser; *spec.* an experienced politician assigned to help a candidate during an election campaign.

1982 *Economist* 20 Mar. 17/3 Mrs Helen Liddell, the shrewd secretary of the Labour party in Scotland, has been assigned as his 'minder'. **1984** *Austral. Financial Rev.* 9 Nov. 3/5 Mr. Hawke's minders have decided he should stay in the Boulevard Hotel when in Sydney rather than return to the cosseted environs of Kirribilli House. **1986** *Observer* 20 July 16/5 Labour had decided that Frank Dobson MP would be her minder during the campaign. **1991** *Guardian* 1 Nov. 4/5 The candidate's minder, Borders MP Archie Kirkwood, hinted yesterday that this coyness had been Mr Stephen's idea.

f. *Journalism.* One who safeguards information, either (as a public relations official or censor) to protect an organization, etc., from detrimental reports, or (as a journalist) to prevent a rival newspaper from gaining access to a story.

1982 *N.Y. Times* 8 May 1. 5/4 Censorship works as follows: all articles are submitted to one of the three public relations officers—'minders' or 'thought people' to the reporters—who strike out anything that offends. **1987** *Times* 22 July 28/3 On the face of it, there is nothing special about a minder's job. 'It is simply a matter of a reporter looking after his sources.' **1994** *Post* (Denver) 30 Jan. F9/1 His broadcasts.. almost instantly transmitted via

satellite.., although an Iraqui censor (called a minder) checked his words beforehand.

mine, *v.* Sense 9 in Dict. becomes 10. Delete quot. 1899 from sense 8 in Dict. and add: **9.** *trans. fig.* To exploit (esp. an abundant source); to extract (an item of value) from an abundant source.

1899 *Westm. Gaz.* 2 Aug. 3/1 We must leave the reader to mine this rich quarry for himself. *a* **1961** *Sat. Rev.* (U.S.) in WEBSTER s.v., So far mined only a fraction of the cultural treasures of those times. **1988** *Creative Rev.* Jan. 15/2 The Americans have achieved the ultimate life-style approach, mining images that touch your senses and make you feel successful. **1995** *GQ* Jan. 74/2 The collective medical data of all hospitals will be mined for statistics to monitor the efficiency of drugs and treatments.

Minervois (ˌmɪnɜːˈvwaː), *n.* [Fr., f. *Minerve*, ancient village named after the Roman goddess *Minerva* (MINERVA *n.*).] The name of a district of the Aude département in the south of France, used to designate the (chiefly red) wine produced there.

An officially recognized and controlled appellation, V.D.Q.S. after 1951, A.O.C. since 1985.

1928 P. M. SHAND *Bk. French Wines* ix. 226 Pantagruel drank '*force bon vin de Mirevault*' (Minervois) on his passage through Montpellier. **1957** L. W. MARRISON *Wines & Spirits* viii. 153 The north of Aude and the south of Hérault share the Minervois wines, which are mostly red and have some reputation. **1985** CHILDS & ALEXANDER *Tante Marie Bk. French Cooking* 61 Minervois, a red wine.. lively and full of flavour. Served with stews, casseroles and hamburgers.

mingle, *v.* Add: [**5.**] Also without const.

1901 G. ADE *Forty Mod. Fables* 48 He got into his Long Suit.. and went down to Mingle. **1964** J. GRENFELL *Opera Interval* in *Turn Back Clock* (1983) II. 172 Do you want to go out and mingle a little and see who is here. **1991** *Advocate* 15 Jan. 30/3 Guests are invited to mingle at our weekend hospitality tour.

minibar (ˈmɪnɪbɑː(r)), *n.* Also **mini-bar**. [f. MINI- + BAR *n.*¹] A small lockable refrigerator in a hotel room, stocked with drinks and freq. snacks which guests may consume and have charged to their bills.

1976 P. LARKIN *Let.* 26 Apr. in A. Thwaite *Sel. Lett. Philip Larkin* (1992) 539 The best thing was a little 'mini-bar', a kind of locked drink-cupboard in my hotel room, with ice and everything. **1987** *Los Angeles Times* 20 Sept. VII. 6/1 Sometimes the mini-bar can be in two sections, with the refrigerator unit used for items that have to be kept cold and a separate drawer for non-refrigerated foods. **1991** *Business Traveller* Jan. 63/1 Each guest room is equipped with hairdryer, trouser press, minibar and satellite TV.

‖**minifundio** (mɪnɪˈfʊndɪəʊ), *n.* Pl. **minifundios**. [Sp. or Port.; cf. *MINIFUNDIUM *n.*] = MINIFUNDIUM *n.* Usu in *pl.*

1960 *Américas* Aug. 11/1 In most of the Latin American countries more than half of the agricultural units.. are *minifundios* of less than twenty-five acres—often so small that they can't even be termed subsistence farms. **1970** C. T. RESTREPO in I. L. Horowitz *Masses in Lat. Amer.* xiv. 509 In view of the predominance of minifundio owners and harvest workers within the Colombian peasant population, we can be certain that the individualistic attitude is quite general, especially in more isolated areas. **1987** *N.Y. Times* 10 Sept. A10/1, 50.4 percent of 'minifundios,' under 25 acres, cover just 2.4 percent of land.

‖**minifundista** (mɪnɪfʊnˈdɪstə), *n.* Also anglicized as **minifundist**. [Sp. or Port., f.

*minifund(io *n.* or *minifund(ium *n.* + *-ista*
-ist.] One who owns, works, or lives on a
minifundium.
  1969 C. N. Hewitt in H. A. Landsberger *Latin
Amer. Peasant Movements* ix. 278 The *agreste* is thus
the region of Pernambuco which contains the largest
number of *minifundistas*—holders of very small plots
who often rent land..to support their families. **1970**
J. Cotler in I. L. Horowitz *Masses in Lat. Amer.* xii.
414 The abundance of manpower in the area—due to
a landless or minifundist population—contributes to
make it cheap. **1983** *Science* 22 July 355/2 Bergmann
contrasts small-scale minifundista herders and large-
scale ranchers in Argentine Patagonia. **1991**
Washington Post 22 Dec. E4/1 We passed the tiny stone
farmhouses on the lower slopes occupied by the
minifundista, the small landowners of the Andes.

‖**minifundium** (mɪnɪˈfʊndɪəm), *n.* Pl. **minifundia.**
[mod.L., f. mini- + lati)fundium *n.*; cf.
*minifundio *n.*]   In Latin America: a
smallholding; *esp.* an estate too small to support
a single family. Usu. in *pl.*
  1950 *Basis Devel. Program for Colombia* (Internat.
Bank for Reconstruction & Devel.) v. 63 In many
areas..the problem of 'minifundia', or excessive
parcelization of the land into uneconomic patches,
prevents efficient land use. **1970** S. L. Barraclough
in I. L. Horowitz *Masses in Lat. Amer.* iv. 130 The
minifundia by definition are too small to provide full
employment for the family labor force using customary
techniques. **1988** *New Leader* 21 Sept. 6/2 The vast
majority of [Haitian] natives are as independent and
prideful as their forebears—who threw out the French
in 1805 and then split the land into *minifundia*, making
each peasant master of his domain.

minimalist, *n.* and *a.* Add: **minima'listic** *a.*;
minima'listically *adv.*
  1976 A. Dulles in P. J. McCord *Pope for all
Christians?* 64 Minimalistically, or even strictly,
interpreted, it is hardly more than an emphatic assertion
that the pope's primacy..extends also to his teaching
power. **1991** *Daily Tel.* 21 Mar. 19/8 As an opera it
was a good spectacle. As music, as any kind of
thoughtful insight into present-day philosophy, it might
be forgotten instantly, maybe minimalistically. **1967**
H. Skolimowsky *Polish Analytical Philos.* v. 137 His
[*sc.* Kazimierz Ajdukiewicz's, 1890–1963] philosophy
was always minimalistic, concerned with particular
problems which were closely scrutinized. **1993**
Atlantic Oct. 108/3 Ivey's melodies are slightly woozy
and doggedly minimalistic; a key change is a big event.

minimalize ('mɪnɪməˌlaɪz), *v. trans.* [f. minimal
a. + -ize.] **a.** = minimize *v.* 1 a.
  1978 *Observer* 2 Apr. 4/8 We should start thinking
about how to minimalise the adverse effects of returning
the West Bank. **1988** *Adweek* 6 June 6/1 Last year's
upfront CPM increases were driven by advertiser and
agency eagerness to minimalize cost increases. **1991**
Woman 24 June 13 To minimalize any swelling, I had
to keep my hand in a sling, raised above shoulder
height.
  b. = *minimize *v.* 1 c.
  1979 tr. *Trybuna Ludu* in *Summary of World
Broadcasts: Eastern Europe* (B.B.C.) 5 Jan. ii. A1/5 The
Government response is normally another attempt to
minimalize the problem. **1981** *Church Times* 20 Nov.
6/2 These Oxford men..have no wish to minimalise
Jesus—in contrast with some tendency in *The Myth* to
see Jesus as liberal Jews see him. **1990** *Guardian* 27
June 17/4 Sex offenders tend to minimalise and justify
their behaviour.

minimize, *v.* Add: [1.] **c.** To play down; to
belittle or dismiss.
  1890 in *Cent. Dict., Minimize,*..to depreciate, treat
slightingly. *a***1909** W. C. Brownell in *Webster* s.v.,
The literary importance of Steele and Goldsmith is

exaggerated, and that of Sterne minimized, in
accordance with the personal predilections and
antipathy of the critic. **1910** *Encycl. Brit.* I. 512/1
Albo set the example of minimizing Messianism in the
formulation of Jewish beliefs. **1928** *Punch* 24 Oct.
466/1, I am not minimising the difficulty of Porlock,
where the bus may conk out and be hauled up
ignominiously by ropes. **1949** 'G. A. Birmingham'
Laura's Bishop xxv. 171 To call this, when it comes, a
world war is to minimize its importance. It will be
worse than a world war. **1991** J. Wiltshire *Samuel
Johnson in Med. World* vii. 240 Boswell plays down the
despair and anxiety we glimpse in the prayers, and
has of necessity to minimise his hero's physical and
psychological maladies.

minion, *n.*[1] and *a.* [A.] [1.] [b.] Delete 'Now only
in contemptuous use' and add: Also (without
the connotation 'favoured') one who waits on
another, an underling; a servant, officer,
subordinate, or assistant.
  1819 Keats *Hyperion* I. 197 His winged minions in
close clusters stood, Amaz'd and full of fear. **1901** G.
B. Shaw *Admirable Bashville* III. 326, I rushed to play
the peacemaker, when lo! These minions of the law laid
hands on me. *a***1961** *Books of Month* in Webster s.v.,
Invasion of their homes by governmental
minions. **1983** 'W. Trevor' *Fools of Fortune* I. v. 86
He had a band of minions, stern-faced youths whom
he'd imbued with his puritan zeal and invested with
the authority of prefects. **1992** *Radio Times* 16 May
37/3 I'm glad to say the noble lord is far too busy
making multi-million dollar deals to read anything from
no-hopers, and gets oppressed minions like me to fob
them off as politely as possible.

ministry, *n.* Add: [5.] **c. man from the
ministry** [after the name of a BBC Radio
programme, *The Men from the Ministry*, first
broadcast in 1962], a government official or
bureaucrat, esp. of an officious kind.
  1963 *Listener* 21 Feb. 320/1 The image of
bureaucracy, the man from the ministry, striped pants
and gobbledygook. **1982** *Guardian Weekly* 4 Apr. 10
In the present climate, what manager would dare to do
more than order a new supply of paper clips without
first clearing it with his friendly neighbourhood
commissar and the man from the ministry? **1990**
Newsday (Nassau ed.) 28 Nov. 109/1 A polite young
man from the ministry welcomes me to Iraq and whisks
me through immigration.

minority, *n.* Add: [3.] [b.] Also (*U.S.*), a
member of a minority group.
  1961 G. Green *Heartless Light* 167 She was one of
Eliot Sparling's neutralized minorities, adopting the
rolling *R*'s and constricted vowels of Los
Angeles. **1976** *Time* 20 Dec. 11/1 He was worried
about the need for new young blood in Government,
for more women and minorities. **1985** *Albuquerque
Jrnl.* 11 Dec. A3/3 If all other qualifications are roughly
equal, they should select a minority or a
woman…During the past year, UNM hired six
minorities and 21 women. **1991** D. D'Souza *Illiberal
Education* v. 156 Minority is the late 20th century term
for nigger.

minty (mɪntɪ), *a.*[2] and *n.* *U. S. slang.* Also **mintie.**
[Origin obscure; see quot. 1941.] **A.** *adj.* Of
a man: homosexual, effeminate. Of a woman:
lesbian (esp. in a masculine manner). **B.** *n.* A
homosexual person.
  [**1941** G. Legman *Lang. Homosexuality* in G. W.
Henry *Sex Variants* II. vii. 1171 *Mantee,* a female
homosexual with very masculine characteristics. The
etymology is obscure, although a French origin of an
older form, *mintée,* seems probable.] **1965** A. Lurie
Nowhere City xvii. 187 That guy's so minty he gives
me the creeps. **1974** *Amer. Speech* 1971 XLVI. 81
Female homosexual,..minty. **1975** *Wentworth &*

Flexner's Dict. Amer. Slang Suppl. 723/2 *Mintie, adj.,* homosexual; exhibiting or affecting mannerisms of the opposite sex; 'gay' or 'queer'. *n.* A homosexual, esp. an aggressive or masculine Lesbian. **1981** R. SPEARS *Slang & Euphemism* 254 *Mintie.* 1. A homosexual male, especially an effeminate male. Also *minty.* 2. Pertaining to a homosexual male. 3. A masculine lesbian.

‖**mirabilia** (mɪrə'bɪlɪə), *n. pl. Hist.* [L., neut. pl. of *mirabilis* wonderful.] Wonders, miracles.

 1829 I. TAYLOR (*title*) Mirabilia; or, The wonders of nature and art: comprising three hundred of the most remarkable curiosities and phenomena in the known world. **1952** G. SARTON *Hist. Sci.* I. xix. 491 The legends of a later time.. made of Alexander a supernatural hero and a wizard to whom all the conceivable *mirabilia* could be ascribed. **1975** *Times Lit. Suppl.* 31 Jan. 117/2 *Rome before Avignon* is full of anecdotal material, *mirabilia*, legends, stories, accounts and similar aids to historical imagination. **1991** *UNESCO Courier* Aug–Sept. 18/1 It was also a golden age for sea literature, travellers' tales and descriptions of wondrous things ('Mirabilia') in which the sea had a central part. **1993** P. ACKROYD *House of Doctor Dee* 20, I, Doctor Dee, am come to dazzle your imagination with *mirabilia*; these are my shows and apparitions which draw the eye cunningly.

miracle, *n.* Add: [2.] [a.] In weakened use: a surprising or unexpected phenomenon or event; a remarkably fortunate outcome.

 *a***1616** SHAKESPEARE *Merry W.* III. v. 119 Being thus cram'd in the Basket.. it was a miracle to scape suffocation. **1748** S. RICHARDSON *Clarissa* (1811) III. 273 It would be a miracle if she stood such an attempter. **1819** BYRON *Don Juan* II. l. 144 Half epileptical, and half hysterical:—Their preservation would have been a miracle. **1886** *Pall Mall Gaz.* 13 Nov. 5 It will be a miracle if no one finds out who the trustee is. **1954** W. FAULKNER *Fable* 273 The miracle is that we have anything left after four years of being overrun by foreigners. **1992** *Daily Mail* 17 Aug. 39/3 After conceding four goals in the Charity Shield last weekend, it's a miracle they weren't reduced to a similar shambles.

mirage, *n.* Add: [1.] d. Used to denote a pale colour (in later use, usu. blue, grey, or turquoise), esp. in the textile and fashion industries; freq. *attrib.*

 1927 *Underwear & Hosiery Rev.* Oct. 63 *Mirage* is a shade paler than Grain. **1932** *Index to Color Names* (Textile Color Card Assoc. of U.S.) 34 Mirage Blue... F[all] '31. **1964** *New Yorker* 5 Sept. 86/1 (Advt.), Slip into the Runabout Shift... Desert cloth.. in desert tones.. mirage-aqua, sunset-red [etc.]. **1976** *Scotsman* 20 Nov. 10/1 The pale blue mirage coat with its Lucca lamb shawl collar is a dream. **1976** *Liverpool Echo* 22 Nov. 15/5 (Advt.), Marina.. Coupe.., mirage grey, one owner.

mirror, *n.* Add: [IV.] [7.] d. *Psychoanal.* Used *attrib.*, esp. in *mirror stage* [tr. F. *stade du miroir*], to designate a stage in infant development considered by some Freudian theorists to be typified by a child's reacting to its reflection in a mirror as if the reflection were a real person.

 [**1937** *Internat. Jrnl. Psycho-anal.* XVIII. 78 Report of the Fourteenth International Psycho-analytical Congress... Second Scientific Session 2. Dr. J. Lacan (Paris). The Looking-Glass Phase.] **1949** *Internat. Jrnl. Psycho-Anal.* XXX. 203/1 The theory of the '*mirror-stage*' has already been presented to the International Congress of 1936, but has remained unpublished in its report. **1968** A. WILDEN tr. J. Lacan *Language of Self* (1974) 160 The 'mirror phase' derives its name from the importance of mirror relationships in childhood. The significance of children's attempts to appropriate or control their own image in a mirror.. is

that their actions are symptomatic of these deeper relationships. **1992** *Times Lit. Suppl.* 28 Feb. 26/2 According to Lacan, the earliest game is that of identification with a mirror-image of the body, in what he calls the 'mirror stage'.

mirror, *v.* Delete sense b. and its quots. For def. read: **b.** *fig.* To reflect, imitate; to represent or express (a fact, phenomenon, idea, emotion, etc.).

 1827 DISRAELI *Viv. Grey* III. v. i. 18 Those glorious hours, when the unruffled river of his Life mirrored the cloudless heaven of his Hope. **1891** O. WILDE *Pict. Dorian Gray* i. 2 The painter looked at the gracious and comely form he had so skilfully mirrored in his art. **1925** F. SCOTT FITZGERALD *Great Gatsby* vii. 155 Tom glanced around to see if we mirrored his unbelief. **1961** K. TYNAN *Curtains* I. 175 Idealism is mirrored in Don Quixote, emblem of the pure romantic quest. **1992** *Economist* 4 Jan. 54/3 McKinsey reckons a shortage of hard currency.. means that the east German car boom is unlikely to be mirrored anywhere else in Eastern Europe.

mirrored, *a.*[1] Add: **b.** Having a surface like a mirror; reflective.

 *a***1851** MOIR *Dark Waggon* iv, Till Lythgo shows, in mirrored gold, its palaced loch so fair. **1962** L. S. SASIENI *Princ. & Pract. Optical Dispensing* xiii. 327 They are known as Mirrored lenses. They are produced by vacuum coating [etc.]. **1980** L. BIRNBACH et al. *Official Preppy Handbk.* 77 Mirrored sunglasses. To hide fear while going down slopes completely hung over. **1986** L. CODY *Under Contract* xli. 168 The pavement streamed and light bounced off its mirrored surface in a yellow glare. **1994** *Post* (Denver) 18 Dec. F2/1 The bodyguards of bad guys invariably wear mirrored dark glasses.

misandry (mɪ'sændrɪ), *n.* (Formerly at MISO- in Dict.) [ad. Gr. μισανδρία, after MISOGYNY *n.*: see -Y[3].] Hatred of men as a sex.

 1909 in *Cent. Dict. Suppl.* **1946** *Scrutiny* XIII. 249 In the absence of feminine precedents, she [*sc.* Beatrice] could do no better than what she very sensibly does do: follow masculine example, and answer to their affected misogyny with the affectation of misandry. **1960** B. KAYE *Upper Nankin St.* xii. 232 Such women are common in.. Kwangtung Province, where there is a tradition of misandry. **1991** *New Art Examiner* Apr. 35/3 Although Surrealism could survive the excision of its misogyny, if SisterSerpents shed their 'misandry', their ideological fangs would prove artless.

 Hence **mi'sandrist** *n.*, one who hates men, a man-hater (esp. in feminist usage).

 1978 *Observer* 23 Apr. 8/3 The respectable feminist equivalent for the word misogynist is misandrist. **1993** *Guardian* 3 Dec. II. 4/5 Strictly speaking, neither misogynist nor misandrist specifies the gender of the person who hates: you should be able to be both female and to hate women.

mischievous, *a.* Add: [4.] **b.** In weakened (usu. positive) sense: charmingly roguish; playful; teasing.

 1761 G. COLMAN *Jealous Wife* I. 15 Lady *Freelove* is as mischievous as a Monkey, and as cunning too. **1817** COLERIDGE *Biog. Lit.* 293 The characters in this act frisk about, here, there, and everywhere, as teasingly as the Jack o'Lantern lights which mischievous boys.. throw with a looking-glass on the faces of their opposite neighbours. **1887** *Pall Mall Gaz.* 1 Nov. 1/2 Stories concerning mischievous and prankish children. **1907** G. B. SHAW *John Bull's Other Island* IV. 80 Doran is reeling in an ecstasy of mischievous mirth which has infected all his friends. **1967** P. SHAFFER *Black Comedy* 35 Clea is Brindsley's ex-mistress: late twenties, dazzling, emotional, bright and mischievous. **1987** *Sunday Express Mag.* 15 Feb. 22/4 Robbie's big, dark eyes held a mischievous twinkle.

mischievously, *adv.* Add: **5.** Playfully, teasingly, impishly.

1807-8 W. IRVING *Salmag.* (1824) 228 A shrewd old gentleman, who stood listening by with a mischievously equivocal look. **1869** L. M. ALCOTT *Little Women* xiii. 202 He had..frightened the maidservants half out of their wits, by mischievously hinting that one of his dogs was going mad. **1907** G. B. SHAW *John Bull's Other Island* III. 72 He goes, chuckling mischievously. **1982** J. SIMMS *Unsolicited Gift* i. 45 She grinned, and mischievously spun her ring at me in her old manner. **1991** *Highlife* (Brit. Airways) May 24/1 Some years ago innovatory landscape designer Alex Dingwall Main mischievously depicted lawnmowers of rival companies competing in his fanciful garden plan.

mischievousness, *n.* Add: Also, playfulness, liveliness.

1938 R. K. NARAYAN *Dark Room* i. 17 'That's all you care for us poor folk,' Ramani said with an elaborate mischievousness. **1986** G. JOSIPOVICI *Contre-Jour* i. 63 The intensity of his gaze, its unquenched mischievousness.

misfile (mɪsˈfaɪl), *v.* [f. MIS-[1] + FILE *v.*[3]] *trans.* To file wrongly.

1961 WEBSTER, *Misfile, vt..*, to file in the wrong place. **1975** *Jrnl. Library Automation* July 229 Another block of 0.9 percent of the title entries will be completely misfiled by the use of a simple table lookup approach. **1985** *Inmac Catal.* Spring/Summer 23/2 Misfiling a computer tape can mean costly delays while the right tape is found. **1992** *Accountancy* Nov. 62 The advantages of a DIP system are that images—unlike paper documents—do not have to be physically moved around the office.., and they cannot be lost, misfiled or damaged in the way that paper can.

Hence **misˈfiled** *ppl. a.*; **misˈfiling** *vbl. n.*

1975 *Jrnl. Library Automation* July 221 An empirical study was made of the frequency of misfiling that would occur for each article if simple table lookup procedures were used. **1981** *Amer. Libraries* Sept. 502/1 Trainees test their understanding of that rule by deciding how a set of misfiled cards could be sequenced. **1994** *Arizona Republic* 5 Aug. (2 star ed.) E14/1 Imagine waiting an eternity on a bench as hard as the Rock of Ages for some inefficient clerk to track down your misfiled records. **1994** *N.Y. Law Jrnl.* 9 Sept. 4/4 A system 'which permitted the wrongful termination of a career to go unchallenged based upon an inadvertent and non-prejudicial misfiling would ill deserve and not long collect the revenue which this statute was crafted to secure.'

mixis (ˈmɪksɪs), *n. Biol.* [a. G. *Mixis*, a. Gr. μίξις mixing, (sexual) intercourse.] Reproduction involving the fusion of gametes and (with some writers) the alternation of nuclear phases.

1944 *Hereditas* XXX. 146 The processes given the names amixis, mixis and apomixis by Winkler. **1950** *Adv. Genetics* III. 194 In plants we speak of mictic reproduction, its opposite being named apomixis, which means reproduction without mixis, *i.e.* without both the fusion of two reproductive cells and adjoining alternation of nuclear phases. **1985** *Marine Biol.* LXXXV. 123 Results suggest that salinity conditions leading to optimal parthenogenic reproduction also support mixis. **1987** *Nature* 22 Jan. 307/2 The fusion of similar eukaryotic cells (mixis) probably evolved from cannibalism, because it paid to retain the DNA of an ingested relative, rather than to digest it. *Ibid.*, A regular haplo-diploid cycle, with alternate mixis and meiosis, evolved as an adaptation to a cyclical environment.

M'Kinley *n.*, var. *MCKINLEY *n.

Modoc (ˈməʊdɒk), *n.*[1] and *a.* Also **Mo-dock.** Pl. unchanged.   [Klamath or Modoc, either

directly f. *moˑwatˈaˑk* southern lake (f. *moˑwat* south), the name given by them to Tule Lake (in the region inhabited by the Modoc), or f. *moˑwatˈaˑkkni:* people of the southern lake, Modocs.] **A.** *n.* A member of a North American Indian people living on the Oregon-California border; also, their language. **B.** *adj.* Of or pertaining to the Modoc.

1854 *Rep. U.S. Bureau Indian Affairs* 262 East of this tribe..is a tribe known as the Mo-docks. They speak the same language as the Klamaths. *Ibid.* 263 The country around An-coose and Modoc lakes is claimed and occupied by the Modoc Indians. **1878** A. S. GATSCHET in *Amer. Antiquarian* July 82 The Klamath language..is spoken by two tribes only, the Klamath Lake people and the Modocs, in two dialects which are almost identical and therefore should be called *subdialects.* **1890** —— *Klamath Indians of S.W. Oregon* I. p. xxiii, A smaller pine species, *Pinus contorta* (kápka, in Modoc kúga)..is peeled by the Indians to a height of twenty feet. **1907** F. W. HODGE *Handbk. Amer. Indians* I. 918/1 The Modoc language is practically the same as the Klamath. **1949** *New Yorker* 2 Apr. 25/2 Broncho Charlie's mother and father were killed by Modoc Indians. **1973** A. H. WHITEFORD *N. Amer. Indian Arts* 47 The Modoc and Klamath made tule baskets and hats. **1977** C. F. & F. M. VOEGELIN *Classification & Index World's Lang.* 288 Klamath...D[ialect] also Modoc. **1984** P. MATTHIESSEN *Indian Country* ix. 247 The Modoc Indians north of Pit River rose in revolt. **1992** E. RENFRO *Shasta Indians of California* v. 105 While their traditions and lifeways show many similarities to those of the Shastan tribes, the Klamath and Modoc are more often classified within the Columbia Plateau Culture area rather than the Californian by anthropologists.

modular, *a.* and *n.* Add: [**1.**] **d.** Of a facility, service, system, etc.: divided into a number of discrete stages.

1984 *Times* 24 May 3/1 British Rail's hot meals go 'modular' over the next five years. Food for lunch and dinner will be prepared 'ashore', chilled and stored, then heated in microwave ovens in the restaurant car. **1987** *Grand Rapids Business Jrnl.* 17 Aug. B6/3 The more difficult patients are handled in TRAC III Rehabilitation, modular rehabilitation services for the complex patient with chronic pain. **1993** *Computing* 21 Oct. 48/1 The next generation of operating systems will be written as microkernels, which promise users the benefits of a highly modular operating system well adapted to the needs of distributed computing.

B. *n.* Chiefly *U.S.* The adj. (sense 1 b) used *absol.*

1969 *Automation in Housing* Aug. 61/2 A two-section modular, the home includes kitchen, bathroom, toilet facility, laundry room and five rooms for sleeping, eating and living in its well-organized plan. **1983** *Motor Trend* Jan. 76/1 At the opposite end of the scale are the high-zoot modulars—racing wheels, really. **1994** *Hartford Courant* (ed. 3) B2/5 The connector was intended to provide students with some protection from the weather as they moved between the new modulars and the main school building.

module, *n.* Add: [**4.**] **h.** Any one of a number or series of objects, elements, etc., which go to make up a complete item or set, without themselves conforming to a particular size or pattern.

1977 F. K. BASKETTE *Art of Editing* (rev. ed.) xiv. 293 A *module* is a unit or component of a whole (or a page), in which each unit has a specific function..[and it] clearly separates and features a story inside it. **1977** J. L. HARPER *Population Biol. Plants* p. xiii, The population biology of higher plants needs to take account of..the number of modules of structure that compose each genet. The modules may be leaf plus bud, ramets, tillers or branch units. **1985** *Neat Ideas Mail Order Catal.* Spring 4/1 Perfect for desk and table top literature, letterhead, paper and file organisation. Modules made of tough corrugated board. **1990** *Thames Valley Now* Feb. 13/1 There is the fascinating Thames Valley Time Trail...Six time modules represent the six stages of development, from volcanic eruptions and dinosaurs to gravel and mineral quarrying.

Mogollon (mʌgɪˈjəʊn, məʊgəˈjəʊn), *n.* (*a.*) Pl. **Mogollones, Mogollons**. [f. the *Mogollon* Rim, Arizona, and the *Mogollon* Mountains, New Mexico, from the name of Juan Ignacio Flores *Mogollón*, governor of New Mexico 1712–15.]

1. (A member of) a North and Central American Indian people, eventually a component band of the Chiricahua Apache, formerly living in western New Mexico.

1859 S. MOWRY *Arizona & Sonora* 16 The Apaches..are best classified under their modern names...The Mescaleros..Mogollones, Chir = aca = huis, Coyoteros.., and the Tontos. **1902** *Encycl. Brit.* XXIX. 463/2 The Chiricahua band.., together with 500 Mimbreños, Mogollones, and Mescaleros, were assigned, about 1870, to the Ojo Caliente reserve, New Mexico. **1983** R. ROESSEL in *Handbk. N.Amer. Indians* X. 508/1 Dodge..was killed by a party of Mogollon and Coyote Apaches.

2. An archaeological culture of south-western New Mexico and south-eastern Arizona which flourished *c*100 B.C. to A.D. 1400. Also *attrib.* or as *adj.*

1939 F. H. H. ROBERTS, JR. *Archeol. Remains Whitewater District E. Arizona* I. 15 The Mogollon pattern seems to center in the San Francisco and Mimbres River valleys in south-western New Mexico. **1948** A. L. KROEBER *Anthropol.* (rev. ed.) xviii. 806 Mogollon is much less distinctive and decisive than Anasazi and Hohokam, it faded away earlier, and some authorities still look upon it as only a local variant of Anasazi, or a temporary and regional blend of that and Hohokam. **1957** *Encycl. Brit.* XII. 204/1 The Mogollon occupied the eastern half of that old region, which is in part at least a mountainous country, lying east of the San Pedro river in Arizona. **1974** J. D. JENNINGS in J. Billard *World of Amer. Indian* 56 By 300 B.C. the Tularosa people were making a characteristic brown pottery and living in pit-house villages. From these beginnings a culture called the Mogollon evolved—and probably spread northward to trigger what many call the zenith of southwestern traditions, the Anasazi. **1989** *Nat. Geographic* Mar. 393/1 In New Mexico virtually every site of the Mimbres—a people of the Mogollon culture—has been wrecked by looters seeking their delicately painted black-on-white bowls.

mohajir (ˈmɒhədʒɪə(r), mʊˈhɑːdʒɪə(r), məˈhɑːdʒɪə(r)), *n.* (*a.*) *Islam.* Forms: 16–17 **mohager**, 18 **mohadjer**, 18– **muhajir**, 19– **mohajir**. Pl. **mohajirs, muhajirin, muhajirun**, etc. [a. Arab. *muhājir*, f. *hājara* to emigrate: cf. HEGIRA *n.*] **1.** One of those who accompanied Muhammad in his emigration from Mecca to Medina in 622.

1697 H. PRIDEAUX *Life of Mahomet* in *True Nature of Imposture* 133 The *Mohagerins*, that is, those who accompanied him in his Flight from *Mecca*, would have him carried thither to be buried in the place where he was Born. **1788** GIBBON *Decl. & F.* V. l. 227 The equal, though various, merit of the Moslems was distinguished by the names of *Mohagerians* and *Ansars*, the fugitives of Mecca and the auxiliaries of Medina. **1861** J. M. RODWELL tr. *Koran* ix. 101 As for those who led the way, the first of the Mohadjers and the Ansars,..God is well pleased with them. **1983** M. COOK *Muhammad* ii. 21 The Medinese *ansar* had an abiding suspicion of the Meccan *muhajirun* and their kinship with Muhammad; they readily flared up at the suggestion that the Meccans were taking over.

2. One who emigrates from a country which is, or has become, ruled by non-Muslims; *spec.* one of the Muslim emigrants who left India for

Pakistan at the time of the Indian Partition in 1947, or a descendant of these people. Also *attrib.* or as *adj.*

1930 *Times Lit. Suppl.* 7 Aug. 635/1 Except for a few devoted *muhajirs*, whose loyalty to Islam had prompted them to follow the retreating horse tails of their defeated Caliph, Turkey had lost, with her European provinces her European non-Turkish Moslems..as well as her Christian Albanians, Greeks, Serbs and Bulgars. **1964** K. S. AHMAD *Geogr. Pakistan* xviii. 146 The refugees, or *muhajirs*, have also brought their own culture from various parts of India. **1979** A. RUMBOLD *Watershed in India* xii. 209 Although the hijrat was orderly, it prompted much..excitement in Peshawar..among the Afridis, through whose territory the caravans of 'muhajarin' passed. **1983** S. RUSHDIE *Shame* xii. 254 The pale skin of her *mohajir* ancestry burned and toughened by the sun, bearing like battle scars the lacerations of bushes, animals, her own itch-scratching nails. **1986** *Times* 20 Aug. 6 Like many interior Sind towns the population is largely Urdu-speaking, and not indigenous Sindhi. They are Mohajirs, those immigrants (or their children) who crossed into Pakistan at the time of Partition in 1947. **1992** *Economist* 12 Sept. 79/3 When Islamabad 'stole' the capital, the mohajirs' political disillusion with Pakistan began.

Mohawk, *n.* Add: [1.] **c.** Also **mohawk**. Chiefly *U. S.* A haircut, supposedly resembling that worn by Mohawk Indians, in which the head is shaved except for a brush-like strip of hair over the top of the head to the back of the neck. Cf. MOHICAN *a.* b.

1983 *Miami News* 7 July 1/4 Mr. Elijah Akeem, a menacing black mountain beneath an intimidating mohawk. **1986** *New Yorker* 2 June 25/2 Punks with stiff green Mohawks. **1992** *Time* 27 July 67/3 He tattooed the Olympic rings on his hip and arrived at the '89 nationals with a double Mohawk—one side dyed black, the other white.

[5.] **Mohawk haircut** = sense *1 c above.

1984 *New Yorker* 21 May 36/3 The Mohawk haircuts of the ice skaters. **1993** *Equinox* (Camden East, Ontario) June 85/2, I catch up with..a brisk, dark-haired woman, who is busy settling her 10-year-old son and his new Mohawk haircut into one of the reclining chairs in the lounge.

moi (mwa), *pers. pron.* [Fr. *moi* me.] In humorous or mock self-deprecatory use: me, myself.

1977 *Washington Post Mag.* 4 Nov. 18/2 My wife and my Kiddies and my aspidistra, who appear with the gracious permission of..*moi!* **1979** CLEESE & BOOTH *Compl. Fawlty Towers* (1988) 190 So Harry says, 'You don't like me any more. Why not?' And he says, 'Because you've got so terribly pretentious.' And Harry says, 'Pretentious? *Moi?*' **1988** *Sunday Times* 24 Jan. G3/1, 11 honest men and women, including a headmistress, a rabbi, a newspaper editor, a poet, a professor, a business man, some famous writers and *moi*. **1992** *Zzap 64!* Nov. 58 My, my. What an original plotline. I'm sure this one was around when Moses parted the red sea (sarcastic, moi?). **1995** *Guardian* 26 June 11. 6/5 *Rosa*: You can be ruthless. *Dominic: Moi?* Ruthless?

moil (mɔɪl), *n. Mining.* [Origin unknown; perh. related to MOIL *v.*] A pointed hand-held steel tool used for cutting rock in a mine. Cf. GAD *n.*[1] 2 b.

1871 W. MORGANS *Man. Mining Tools* 156 Fig. 171 shows a 'set' or 'moil', used for cutting ground where it requires to be done evenly, such as in the case of cutting 'hitches', or preparing seatings for pit work. **1933** R. S. LEWIS *Elements of Mining* xiv. 433 The best tool for cutting a sample in hard rock is the moil. Moils are made of $\frac{3}{4}$- or..$\frac{7}{8}$-in. octagonal steel and are usually from 10 to 12 in. long..preferably sharpened to a diamond point having a taper about 2 in. long. **1991** *Construction Weekly* 18 Sept. 20/1 Of the various tools available, the moil point is generally accepted as the universal tool for demolition and quarrying, whereas the flat chisel is more often used for trenching.

moil, *v*. Add: [4.] **d**. *intr*. orig. *dial*. To be restless or anxious; to move around in a state of agitation or confusion; to swirl, eddy; also, to mill about, to circulate.

1889 *N.W. Linc. Gloss.*, *Moil*,..(2) To be fidgetty or restless. 'Theäre's noä gettin' noä rest wi' him at neets; he's tewin' an' moilin' aboot for iver'. **1932** W. FAULKNER *Light in August* xiii. 280 For a short time the dogs moiled, whimpering, then they set off again. *a*1961 R. ELLISON in *Webster* s.v., A crowd of men and women moiled like nightmare figures in the smoke-green haze. **1979** D. ADAMS *Hitch-Hiker's Guide to Galaxy* vii. 58 The Vogon stared down at him as sluggish thoughts moiled around in the murky depths. **1990** *Atlantic* Apr. 106/2 There discreetly attired partners moiled in dignity amid the serene ambience of a British gentlemen's club. **1996** J. SIBERRY *Angel Voyeur* (song) in *Teenager* (record), And on a separate street Well, that man he ceased to moil.

mokopuna (məkɒˈpuːnə, ‖ˈmɔkɔpʊna), *n*. *N.Z.* Pl. **mokopuna, mokopunas**. [a. Maori.] In Maori culture, a grandchild, great-niece, or great-nephew.

1927 H. W. WILLIAMS in P. H. Buck *Material Culture Cook Islands* p. vii, We shall still regard Te Rangi Hiroa as our *mokopuna*. **1958** S. ASHTON-WARNER *Spinster* 58 He was telling me that he trusted me to look after his 'mokopuna'. **1974** W. IHIMAERA *Whanau* v. 21 Only he and four mokopuna live at home. The mokopuna are the children of some of Miriama's nieces. **1991** A. CAMPBELL *Sidewinder* xii. 143 What for you come anyway? I look after Kare. She my family, not yours. The *mokopuna*, I look after her too.

Moldovan (mɒlˈdəʊvən, ˈmɒldəvən), *a*. and *n*. Also 9 **Moldowan**. [f. Romanian *Moldova*, the name adopted in 1990 by the former Soviet republic previously known as Moldavia (see MOLDAVIAN *a*. and *n*.) + -AN.] **A**. *n. a*. Orig. = MOLDAVIAN *n*. a; now *spec*. a native or inhabitant of Moldova (formerly Moldavia), an independent state since 1991. **b**. The official language of Moldova (formerly MOLDAVIAN *n*. b.). **B**. *adj*. Of or relating to Moldova or its inhabitants.

1835 *Penny Cycl.* IV. 341/1 The majority of the Bessarabians are Moldowans or Moldavians. **1990** *Summary of World Broadcasts: Soviet Union* (B.B.C) 30 July B1 The session of the Supreme Soviet of the Moldovan SSR ended today. **1990** *Independent* 26 Oct. 10/2 The Gagauz, who declared UDI in August, appealed to President Gorbachev to protect them from the Moldovans, who, they said, were preparing to send troops to their capital of Komrat. **1992** *Ibid*. 20 Oct. 8/7 The idea seems to have Mr Yeltsin's backing, and the Moldovan conflict gives a foretaste of what it could mean in practice. **1992** *Economist* 6 June 46/1 Both Moldovans and Russians say that the matter will not lead to war between Russia and Romania. **1994** *Whitaker's Almanack 1995* 959/1 Moldovan was made the official language (written in Latin script) in 1989 but the use of Russian and Ukranian in official business is permitted.

mole, *n*.[2] Add: [5.] **b**. *Mining*. A remotely operated or automatic machine capable of tunnelling or crawling underground.

1960 *Engineering & Mining. Jrnl.* Mar. 86/1 Several years ago, when the first Robbins Mechanical Mole was able to bore a 29.5-ft dia tunnel in shale at about 10 ft per hr, it was seen that here was a tunneling method potentially competitive with present day cyclic operations...It appears that the Mole will be suited for a wider range of rock types than at first thought possible. **1975** D. BEATY *Electric Train* 99, I don't exactly wield the shovel...I'm on the boring machine. The mole. **1993** *Harrowsmith* Dec. 43/2 (*caption*) Alcan's $1 billion project boasts some hefty equipment, including a 600-tonne 'mole' with a cutter head the size of a two-lane highway. It is drilling a 16-kilometre water tunnel at Kemano.

[9.] [a.] **mole drain**: so **mole drainage**.
1939 in WEBSTER Add. **1950** *N.Z. Jrnl. Agric.* Apr. 365/3 A considerable amount of mole, tile, and open drainage is required. **1992** C. CULPIN *Farm Machinery* (ed. 12) xxii. 369 A type of implement favoured where mole drainage is regularly practised has a long (3.7 m) floating beam with skids at front and rear, a pneumatic-tyred carriage and hydraulic (or winch) lift.

molecular, *a*. Sense 5 in Dict. becomes 6. Add: **5**. Concerned with or pertaining to a basic level or limited aspect of a subject, society, etc., rather than the aggregate whole.

1953 C. W. MILLS in *Philos. of Sci.* XX. 266 The other way of sociological research might be called the molecular. It is..characterized by its usually small-scale problems and by its generally statistical models of verification. **1964** A. RAPOPORT in I. L. Horowitz *New Sociol.* vi. 95 In particular, he [*sc*. C. Wright Mills] distinguishes between 'macroscopic' and 'molecular' social inquiry. **1977** A. J. CHAPMAN et al. in H. Giles *Lang., Ethnicity & Intergroup Relations* vi. 165 At a more molecular level of analysis, the data from children in the alone conditions have not been mentioned to date. **1982** *N.Y. Times* 6 Oct. A26/4 The day when any distinction [between blacks and whites] is no longer useful..will come much sooner..if we do not re-ify [*sic*] our cultural distinctions at the molecular level.

molest, *v*. Add: [2.] **c**. *spec*. To harass, attack, or abuse sexually.

1895 T. HARDY *Jude the Obscure* III. iv. 182 No average man—no man short of a sensual savage—will molest a woman by day or night, at home or abroad, unless she invites him. [**1929** *Statutes Calif.* ccclxxvi. 697 Every person who annoys or molests any school child..is a vagrant. **1951** *Session Laws State Arizona* cx. 261 If such subsequent conviction is for petit larceny, molesting a school child, contributing to the delinquency of a minor, or an offense involving lewd or lascivious conduct.] **1958** G. GREENE *Our Man in Havana* IV. i. 150 A notice in Spanish and bad English forbade the audience to molest the dancers. **1972** A. SILLITOE *Raw Material* v. 21 She would carry a bag of pepper to throw in the face of any man who might try to molest her. **1992** *Globe & Mail* (Toronto) 3 Dec. A1/1 An Ontario woman awarded $284,000 in damages against the father who molested her from the time she was 5.

molestation, *n*. Add: [1.] **c**. (An act of) sexual abuse or harassment.

1956 *Pacific Reporter* CCXC. 250/1 Such offense [*sc*. indecent exposure] was punishable under either Code section relating to molestation of children. **1977** *Washington Post* 30 Jan. C2/1 Child molestation and exploitation, including prostitution, pornography, sex perversion and the furnishing of narcotics, are extensive in this city. **1993** *Guardian* 21 Aug. 21/1 A nation so obsessed with the sexual molestation of children that one hesitates to coo at a good-looking infant-in-arms.

molester, *n*. Add: **b**. *spec*. One who harasses, attacks, or abuses someone (esp. a woman or child) sexually.

1968 *Illinois Med. Jrnl.* CXXXV. 731/1 The child molester is an ever present danger in all communities. **1977** K. E. WOODIWISS *Shanna* (1978) ii. 44 You vulgar beggar, they should hang you for a molester of women! **1988** P. GAY *Freud* ii. 94 The Freud of the 1890s was not disposed to idealize his father..but to include Jacob Freud among the child molesters struck him as absurd. **1995** *New Yorker* 27 Mar. 108/2 Oh, great, precisely what we need: not just a molester but a molestation *expert*, an incest wonk.

moling ('məʊlɪŋ), *n. Agric.* [f. MOLE *n.*² + -ING ¹.] The action or process of making mole drains.
   1943 J. W. DAY *Farming Adventure* xii. 138 The land was drained by tiling and moling. **1960** *Times* 5 July (Agric. Suppl.) p. v/3 The pace of ditching and moling work under grant has diminished. **1988** LOCKHART & WISEMAN *Introd. Crop Husbandry* (ed. 6) ii. 38/1 Reasonably dry weather after moling will allow the surface of the mole to harden and so it should last longer.

molinology (məʊlɪ'nɒlədʒɪ), *n.* [f. late L. *molīna* mill + -OLOGY.] The study of mills and milling.
   1965 J. M. DOS SANTOS SIMÕES in *Trans. 1st Internat. Symp. Molinology* (1977) 41, I..propose that..the term *molinology*..shall be adopted to define the study and knowledge of windmills and watermills. **1965** A. JESPERSEN *Stand. Proposals Mill Survey Work* 5 Molinology knows no national borders. **1980** *Who's Who* 1230/2 Hooker, Prof. Morna Dorothy... *Recreations:* Molinology. **1986** *Times* 15 Jan. 16/7 In 1965, he represented Britain at the first International Symposium of Molinology in Portugal.
   Hence ˌmolino'logical *a.*; moli'nologist *n.*
   1965 A. JESPERSEN *Stand. Proposals Mill Survey Work* 10 The Molinologist will not have studied his subject for very long before realizing the need for a system of identifying his mills—beyond the mere name. **1977** *Antiquaries Jrnl.* LVII. 412 (*title*) Windmills and watermills in Iceland. International Molinological Society, 1976. **1979** *Daily Tel.* 14 Apr. 21/7 The revival of interest in mills and milling was demonstrated last week when a four-day molinological conference at Bromsgrove attracted millers and enthusiasts from all over the world. **1989** MILLS & RIEMER *Mills of Gloucestershire* 103 Below Sandford's came *Barretts Mill*,..the site of what must have been one of the longest running water disputes in molinological history. **1989** *Sunday Tel.* 26 Feb. 21/4 Peter Wenham is a keen molinologist (a mill buff to the rest of us).

mollock ('mɒlək), *v. colloq.* [Invented by Stella Gibbons (see quot. 1932), prob. an alteration of *marlock* vb. s.v. MARLOCK *n.*, perh. infl. by *rollock*, dial. form of ROLLICK *v.*] *intr.* To cavort, *esp.* to engage in sexual intercourse; also *fig.* Hence 'mollocking *vbl. n.*
   1932 S. GIBBONS *Cold Comfort Farm* v. 70 He's off a-mollocking somewhere in Howling. **1959** *Sunday Times* 23 Aug. 21/3 There was that little bit of trouble about the carefree mollocking in the London parks. **1978** *Economist* 26 Aug. 91/3 The NEB is mollocking with its own chosen newly-installed entrepreneurial management, rather than propping up lame-duck-breeders. **1983** N. BAWDEN *Ice House* II. i. 25 And yet, here they were, not more than a foot away, bedhead to bedhead, merrily mollocking. **1995** *Guardian* 11 Feb. 26 (*caption*) 'Water vole—mollock with me when the sukebind blooms.'.. He's such an old romantic!

molly, *n.*¹ Add: [4.] **molly-house** *hist.*, in 18th- and 19th-century England, a public house, tavern, or (occas.) a private house used as a meeting-place by homosexual men.
   1728 J. DALTON *Narr. Street Robberies* 36 They fell in amongst a Company of Sodomites; one..told *Dalton*..that..if *Dalton* and Susan Haws would go to such a Place, naming a noted *Molly-House*..they would come to them. **1988** *Times Lit. Suppl.* 4 Nov. 1234/4 He overlays the map of our own disco-studded London on the restaurants and molly-houses of Wilde's.

Moluccan (mə'lʌkən), *n.* and *a.* Also 7 Moluccian. [f. MOLUCCA *n.* + -AN.] **A.** *n.* A native or

inhabitant of the Molucca Islands; also, any of the Austronesian languages spoken by them.
   1613 PURCHAS *Pilgrimage* v. xvi. 452 The Moluccians are better proportioned then other Indians. **1853** H. ST. JOHN *Indian Archipelago* I. iv. 86 The Moluccans quickly discovered the character of the wanderers they had welcomed to their towns. **1903** *N.E.D.* s.v. *Lingo*³, lingoa, Moluccan *lenggoa*. **1983** K. BULMER *You'll be all Right* x. 110 Cowley leafed through the file...'Arrested for sedition...Escaped and fled to Amsterdam...That's where most of the refugees seem to have gathered. Strong ties with the South Moluccans.'
   B. *adj.* Of or pertaining to the Molucca Islands, the Moluccans, or the languages spoken by them.
   1853 H. ST. JOHN *Indian Archipelago* I. iv. 85 A hospitality characteristic of the Moluccan race. **1909** A. WRIGHT *20th Cent. Impressions Netherlands India* 60/1 A general movement against Dutch power, in which the Moluccan people were allied with the Kings of Macassar. **1926** *Geogr. Jrnl.* LXVIII. 346 The Moluccan Arc..is of special interest from its resemblance to the Caribbean Arc, having a volcanic line bounding the basin within, and folded sedimentary rocks forming the outer margin. **1951** *Britannica Bk. of Year* 342/2 Some prominent Ambonnese people..on April 25 [1950] seceded and proclaimed a South Moluccan independent republic. **1988** *Christian Science Monitor* 13 May 22/3 It was a Moluccan blue-ringed octopus, whose bite can be deadly.

moment, *n.* Sense 1 d in Dict. becomes 1 e. Add: [1.] **d.** A (usu. brief) period of time characterized by the particular quality of the experience contained in it rather than by its duration.
   1872 'G. ELIOT' *Middlemarch* II. IV. xlii. 370 Here was a man who now for the first time found himself looking into the eyes of death—who was passing through one of those rare moments of experience when we feel the truth of a commonplace. **1907** G. B. SHAW *John Bull's Other Island* I. 19 Why do you select my most tragic moments for your most irresistible strokes of humor? **1931** A. UTTLEY *Country Child* xii. 146 She awoke later and lay holding her happiness, enjoying the moment. **1960** W. PERCY *Moviegoer* IV. ii. 176 There is very little sin in the depths of the malaise. The highest moment of a malaisian's life can be that moment when he manages to sin like a proper human. **1995** *Observer* 5 Feb. (Life Suppl.) 29/1 He recently met Muhammad Ali in LA...'He didn't know who I was. I told him: "You're my hero and you changed my life." And he said: "Now you are all grown up." Then he pulled my head down and pressed his cheek next to mine. That was a moment.'

monarchist, *n.* and *a.* Add: **B.** *adj.* Loyal to a monarch; advocating or supportive of monarchy.
   1926 *Scots Observer* 13 Nov. 19/1 It is France's policy that the sores be kept open even if they give a handle to Monarchist revanchists. **1962** L. NAMIER *Crossroads of Power* iii. 25 In 1789, during the King's illness, Lord Fife's warm monarchist feelings once more became apparent. **1992** *Economist* 7 Mar. 59/2 The two parties most likely to affect the election outcome are the refounded Communist Party and a monarchist party, which wants the return of King Leka.

monastic, *a.* and *n.* Add: [A.] [2.] **b.** Resembling or suggestive of monks, their way of life, or their environment; austere, silent, secluded.
   *a*1631 DONNE *Elegie Mris. Boulstred* in *Poems* (1633) 69 He sinkes the deepe Where harmelesse fish monastique silence keep. **1835** *Fraser's Mag.* XII. 362 Bologna: a piazzaed town; cold, dull, and monastic. **1876** F. KILVERT *Diary* 25 May (1940) III. 318 They [*sc.* the cloisters of New College] have an

air of higher antiquity and a more severely monastic look. **1940** W. FAULKNER *Hamlet* II. i. 102 The lectures, the learning and wisdom.., the ivied walls and monastic rooms impregnated with it. **1989** *Newsday* (Nassau ed.) 2 Oct. II. 11/1 In his final years, Gould lived a life of monastic seclusion on the ground floor of a resort hotel in Toronto.

Monday, *n.*, *adv.*, and *a.* Senses 1 and 2 in Dict. become A. n. 1,2; sense 3 in Dict. becomes C. *attrib.* and *adj.* Add: **B.** *adv.* **a.** In *sing.* (earliest in *the Monday*), on Monday; last Monday, next Monday. *colloq.* in later use. **b.** In *pl.*, on Mondays; each Monday. *colloq.*

c **1300** *S. Eng. Legendary: St. Thomas A Becket* (E.E.T.S., 1956) II. 639 þe Moneday Sein Thomas wel sore sik lay. **1644** *Mercurius Civicus* 19–26 Sept., Monday we had intelligence that Lieutenant General Cromwell [etc.]. **1780** W. FLEMING *Jrnl.* 14 Mar. in N. D. Mereness *Trav. Amer. Colonies* (1916) 634 Monday night there was a smart white frost. **1880** 'M. TWAIN' *Tramp Abroad* App. F. 626 German papers..contain..no rehash of cold sermons Mondays. **1932** W. FAULKNER *Light in August* xiii. 282 The temperature began to rise Monday. **1942** *Go down, Moses* 249 You've got to be back in school Monday. **1970** *New Yorker* 25 July 8/2 Dancing. Closed Mondays. **1991** *Times Daily* (Florence, Alabama) 16 Apr. A6/1 The town council Monday unanimously approved a trash and garbage ordinance.

mondo ('mɒndəʊ), *n.*[3], *adv.*, and *a.* *slang.* (orig. and chiefly *U.S.*). [a. It. *mondo* world: early usages in English are clearly derived from the use of the word in Italian film (see below), but the later adjectival and adverbial uses show the apparent influence of Sp. *mondo* pure, unadulterated, and perh. of the slightly earlier Spanish borrowing *mucho* much, very (see **MUCHO a.* (and *adv.*).)
The phrase *mondo bizarro* reflects the influences of both languages: Italian in the noun phrase, Spanish in the later adjective phrase.]
A. *n.* [After the 1961 documentary film *Mondo cane* (It., lit. 'world for a dog', the English title being *A Dog's Life*), which inspired numerous (often similarly titled) imitations.] **1.** Used *attrib.* and (rarely) *absol.* to designate a film reminiscent or imitative of *Mondo cane*, esp. in its depiction of eccentric forms of human behaviour.

1967 *Time* 20 Oct. 101/3 Among some *aficionados* of the nudies [*sc.* films], the sub-categories are known as 'roughies' (breasts and violence), 'ghoulies' (breasts and monsters), 'kinkies' (breasts and whips) and..'mondos' (breasts around the world.) **1979** *Globe & Mail* 24 Sept. 14/2 Mr. Mike has clearly been influenced by the mondo movies of the sixties, that survived by showing the seedier side of society. **1981** *Washington Post* 3 Apr. (Weekend section) 39/3 Reluctant to take some of the extrinsic attitudes these tracks require, I get the same queasy feeling of voyeurism, even of a sort of moral imperialism, that I used to get watching those 'Mondo' movies in the '60s.
2. a. [With the sense, 'the (strange or secret) world of..'] Used with postmodifying nouns or, more freq., Italian or quasi-Italian adjectives in compounds (orig. film titles) denoting an unexpected, bizarre, or anarchic view of the phenomenon concerned, usu. with a suggestion of salaciousness or questionable taste.
1967 (*film-title*) Mondo Hollywood. **1970** (*film-title*) Mondo trasho. **1975** V. WELNICK et al. (*song-title*) Mondo bondage. **1989** G. WOLFF *Best Amer. Essays* p. xxiv, Who better than a city editor to recognize the limitless bazaar of the bizarre *mondo weirdo* every morning? **1993** *N.Y. Times Bk. Rev.* 18 Apr. 7/3 The most impressive piece in 'Mondo Barbie' is a chapter from Alice McDermott's second novel... In it, Barbie's

truest, deepest character finally became clear to me.
b. Special Comb. **mondo bizarro** *colloq.*, (*a*) as *n. phr.*, the world of the bizarre or surreal; (*b*) *attrib.* or as *adj. phr.*, very bizarre, tastelessly bizarre.
[**1966** (*film-title*) Mondo bizzaro.] **1976** M. P. LOWERY (*song-title*) Mondo bizarro. **1977** M. KATZEN *Moosewood Cookbk.* 69 Mondo [*sic*] sauce—for your spaghetti. **1980** *Washington Post* 19 Apr. C1/1 It was just part of a week in which the news..went further and further into the realm of Mondo Bizarro. **1981** *Ibid.* 25 June F1/5 It was strange. Not the kind of strange that careens along the corroded edge of outrageous, not mondo bizarro, just a little weirdness in the darkening Georgetown night. **1990** *N.Y. Newsday* 23 Oct. I. 11/1 He claims that when Jackson became best friends with 'Webster' star Emmanuel Lewis.., they had an innocent, although mondo bizarro relationship.
B. *adv.* As an intensifier: very, extremely, completely.
1979 *Washington Post* 28 Sept. E3/1 Austin bowls 'em over every time she walks off the tennis court and turns into what by all reports is a bright, affectionate 16-year-old girl. No movie star-weirdo-drug bust-mondo arcane business here. **1982** M. POND *Valley Girls' Guide to Life* 33 It's worth paying more for a good [hair] cut, 'cause if you get a bad one, it's mondo depressing. *Ibid.* 60 O.K., a new dress from Fashion Conspiracy is mondo cool max. **1986** *Stereo Rev.* Apr. 53/2 He's so mondo cool, even though he's not British and doesn't have spiked hair! **1988** J. MCINERNEY *Story of my Life* iv. 58 Then I remember my little problem, which makes me a mondo unhappy unit.
C. *adj.* Considerable, huge; ultimate, total.
1982 M. POND *Valley Girl's Guide to Life* 49 Last weekend Mom let me go visit her and stay in the dorm and everything. It was *Mondo* party time. **1985** *Ibid.* 60 Like totally, like we did a mondo mac-out. **1987** *People Weekly* (U.S.) 22 June 73/1 The freshly painted mural on the side of the Hollywood Plaza apartment building marks the apogee of mondo ego publicity. **1990** *Chicago Tribune* 31 Oct. v. 3/2, I mean, they're all part of mondo corporations and it just seems to me that these guys are living in pretty damn big glass houses. **1991** D. RICHLER *Kicking Tomorrow* xvi. 289 He..felt the great swell suspend him, like a surfer coasting out on his board for the mondo waves. **1993** *Canad. Living* May 11 Mondo bell-bottoms..take '70s style to the limit.

monergy ('mʌnədʒɪ), *n.* [Invented word: a blend of MONEY *n.* and ENERGY *n.*] Expenditure on energy; *spec.* conservation of energy resources (in the form of nuclear or fossil fuels, etc.) viewed as a means of saving money.
1985 *Observer* 29 Sept. 16/2 An energy-saving campaign, with the awful slogan 'Get more for your monergy.' The hideous word, 'monergy',.. was thought up by..Saatchi and Saatchi. **1986** *Times* 16 Jan. 25/1 Mr Walker said: 'Monergy must succeed.' *Ibid.* 27 Mar. 17/4 Inaction on nuclear matters cannot be absolved by an enthusiasm for 'monergy'. **1990** *Planet* 82 Aug./Sept. 60 Efficiency in use [of energy] also requires conservation, lower energy appliances and domestic insulation, and the government's soft pedalling on its 'monergy' campaign is to be regretted.

monetarize ('mʌnɪtəraɪz), *v.* [f. MONETAR(Y *a.* + -IZE.] = MONETIZE *v.* a, **b; so '**monetarized** *ppl. a.*; ,**monetari'zation** *n.*
1957 H. PEARSON in K. Polanyi et al. *Trade & Market Early Empires* 5 A monetarized economy involved a social structure entirely different from that which went with an economy in kind. **1974** B. PEARCE tr. S. Amin *Accumulation on World Scale* I. ii. 145 The pace at which the primitive economy is monetarized is fairly fast. *Ibid.* 142 The transformation of precapitalist economy into peripheral capitalist economy clearly presupposes the 'monetarization', the 'commercialization' of the subsistence economy. **1992** *Economist* 2 May 109/1 The Bank of Portugal was

barred from directly lending to the government. This brought to an end the common practice of monetarising the budget deficit.

monetary, *a.* Add: Hence 'monetarily (also mone'tarily) *adv.*, as regards money, financially.

1895 in *Funk's Stand. Dict.* **1907** *Pennsylvania State Rep.* CCXVII. 221 He is concerned, monetarily, in having the $500,000 applied to the specific purpose for which it was appropriated. **1942** *Rep. US Board Tax Appeals* XLIV. 403 It may have been somewhat difficult to determine the precise amount of the petitioner's liability to pay the principal and interest of its debentures, yet the liability was real and monetarily measurable. **1968** *Punch* 13 Nov. 684/1 There are the financial serendipitists, the men blessed monetarily by a fortunate law. **1992** *Daily Tel.* 17 Sept. 19/3 German money supply is growing too fast for the Bundesbank's liking, and the monetarily correct response is high interest rates.

monetize, *v.* Add: **b.** To assess in terms of money; to convert into money; *spec.* to convert (government debt) from securities into currency through the issue of treasury bills.

1947 *Federal Reserve Bull.* XXXIII. 40 This would mean a resumption of the practice of creating bank reserves through monetizing the debt. **1965** *McGraw-Hill Dict. Mod. Econ.* 327 The debt can also be monetized to create a greater amount of credit in the economy by using the newly created bank reserves to support additional demand deposits. **1968** E. RUSSENHOLT *Heart of Continent* IV. xiii. 247 The immediate loss to Western farm families is monetized at $243 millions. **1975** J. DE BRES tr. *Mandel's Late Capitalism* xi. 375 Increasing dependence on imperialist food exports is monetized on the capitalist world market via higher prices, if necessary by artificially induced shortages. **1988** *Amer. Banker* 10 Aug. 24/1 The practice known as monetizing the debt, whereby the Fed buys new securities issued by the Treasury to finance the budget deficit. **1991** *South* Aug. 33/2 Food is certain to become more expensive as the government..begins to liberalise farm prices and monetise the 'lojas da povo' where essential items have traditionally been sold..at one seventieth the price they fetch in the open markets.
Hence 'monetized *ppl. a.*, (*a*) *Comm.*, converted into money; (*b*) converted to trading based on the exchange of money (as opposed to barter).

1965 *McGraw Hill Dict. Mod. Econ.* 327 The debt becomes monetized when new securities issued by the government are purchased by the banking system to expand reserves. **1982** *Times Lit. Suppl.* 19 Mar. 327/4 Planners in Java plan, intentionally or otherwise, for the Westernized, monetized, segments of society. **1984** *Oxf. Illustr. Hist. Britain* iii. 160 In more rapidly developing and more highly monetized regions, people used a much debased coinage to perform the economic function of small change. **1992** R. M. BONE *Geogr. Canad. North* III. ix. 212 The monetized informal economy is divided into legal activities and illegal ones (the underground economy).

money, *n.* Delete *money supply* and quots 1878 and 1975 from sense 7 a. Add: [**1.**] **e.** One of the four suits in packs of playing cards used in Italy, Spain, and Spanish-speaking countries, and in tarot packs, corresponding to the suit of diamonds.

1593 A. MUNDAY *Def. Contraries* 49 The inuenter of the Italian Cardes..put the Deniers or monyes, and the Bastons or clubs in combate togither. **1848** W. A. CHATTO *Facts Hist. Playing Cards* iv. 191 The earliest writers who mention Tarocchi as a kind of cards, always speak of them as consisting of four suits,—Swords, Cups, Batons, and Money. **1912** M. K. VAN RENSSELAER *Prophetical, Educ. & Playing Cards* i. 54 A gazelle under a palm tree is placed on the knave of

Money. **1966** S. MANN *Collecting Playing Cards* I. i. 45 The ace of money..shows a single-headed, crowned eagle... The king of money holds an axe. **1989** *Encycl. Brit.* XI. 565/2 The Lesser Arcana [in Tarot] comprises four suits of 14 cards each: Bastoni (Batons or Clubs)..; Coppes (cups, later hearts)..; Spade (swords)..; and Denari (money, later diamonds), symbolizing business undertakings, journeys, and messages.

[**8.**] **money supply** *Econ.*, the total amount of money in a country's economy, as measured by various criteria (see M 7).

1878 F. A. WALKER *Money* iv. 76 (*heading*) The importance of the *money supply. **1989** D. A. HAY *Econ. Today* vi. 241 Preferably control of the money supply would be removed from government since governments are tempted to finance expenditure by monetary expansion, rather than by..raising taxes.

monitor, *n.* Senses 3 b-d in Dict. become 3 d-f. Add: [**3.**] **b.** One who uses monitoring equipment to check levels, standards, etc.

1928 *Paramount Studio News* 20 Sept., Monitor, the engineer on the set where the talking picture is filmed. He is in constant telephonic communication with the mixing panel, recording room and amplifying room. **1930** PITKIN & MARSTON *Art of Sound Pictures* x. 226 In the monitor room sits a sound monitor, who mixes the currents from different microphones in such a way that the best possible sound effects are produced. **1973** *Gloss. Terms Nucl. Sci. & Technol.* (*B.S.I.*) 34 *Monitor.* 1. A device whose purpose is to measure the level of ionizing radiation...2. A person who uses a monitor. **1993** *Guardian* 18 Oct. 1. 8/2 A monitor aboard the Greenpeace vessel, stationed about 50 yards from the Russian tanker..said he had measured radiation levels in the air that were more than 10 times the normal level.

c. A monitoring loudspeaker, either in a recording studio or placed on stage within earshot of the performers. Also *monitor speaker*.

1929 F. GREEN *Film finds its Tongue* xvii. 232 The 'mixer'..has come down out of the monitor booth. **1949** FRAYNE & WOLFE *Elem. Sound Recording* xi. 196 Music is monitored and mixed in a 'monitor booth', which is acoustically insulated from the recording stage and provided with a monitor loudspeaker. *Ibid.*, In disk recording for manufacture of phonograph records and transcriptions, the monitor booth is usually used...Less emphasis is placed on checking..by means of the monitor than in film recording. **1960** O. SKILBECK *ABC of Film & TV* 86 *Monitor speaker*, loudspeaker used as a check in dubbing, or as an alternative to headphones by recordists. **1975** *Independent Broadcasting* Aug. 11/1 The technical area with two mixing desks..and two monitor speakers. **1989** *Guitar Player* Mar. 27/2 (Advt.), There's even a 'wet' stage monitor mix for your singer, using a reverb-to-monitor feature.

e. Hence, a VDU connected to a computer to display its output.

1977 *Computer Design* Apr. 151/2 The color monitor within the case can be driven simultaneously with a separate black and white monitor and video hardcopy printer. **1982** S. BELLOW *Dean's December* i. 5 On the electronic screen of the monitor, symbols and digits shimmied and whirled. **1990** *Inmac* Nov. 28/1 The VGA monitor produces high resolution VGA graphics, with excellent image definition and colour.

f. Also, a computer program which controls the running of other programs; an operating system.

1962 in *IBM Systems Jrnl.* (1963) II. 161 (*title*) IBM 7090/7094 operating systems: basic monitor (IBSYS). **1963** *IBM Systems Jrnl.* II. 155 The FORTRAN II monitor system..was developed by North American Aviation Inc...and introduced in 1959. **1979** *Personal Computer World* Nov. 82/1 Some monitors can support more than one user program simultaneously. **1989** *Byte* Aug. 142/3 The monitor program will power down these selections of the computer to conserve battery power.

monkey, *n.* Add: [I.] [1.] **e.** The fur of any of certain monkeys, as dressed and used in garments. Freq. *attrib.*

c **1896** R. DAVEY *Furs & Fur Garments* xii. 92 Up to the time of the great Exhibition of 1851, monkey was an unknown fur. **1920** E. WHARTON *Age of Innocence* I. xvii. 151 She had on a black velvet polonaise with jet buttons, and a tiny green monkey muff; I never saw her so stylishly dressed. **1974** *Times* 15 Nov. 21/6 A monkey cloak, tattered at the edges, went for £30. **1987** M. McCARTHY *How I Grew* vi. 148 A skunk jacket and a suit with copious monkey trim.

[IV.] [18.] [a.] **monkey bars** orig. *U.S.*, a piece of playground apparatus consisting of a horizontally mounted overhead ladder from the rungs of which children may swing.

1955 *Jrnl. Health, Physical Educ. & Recreation* Apr. 24/1 Our schools have five pieces of playground apparatus that children and teachers have called '*monkey bars'. **1994** *Toronto Star* 16 July A1/2 She lives in a highrise . . — part of a string of buildings where shards of glass litter the grass around monkey bars and swing sets.

monkeyish, *a.* Add: '**monkeyishly** *adv.*

1923 A. HUXLEY *Antic Hay* 93 Let the nose twitch and the mouth grin and the eyes twinkle as monkeyishly as you like; . . the forehead still knows how to be human. **1984** J. UPDIKE *Witches of Eastwick* ii. 129 She grinned monkeyishly.

monkey-wrench ('mʌŋkɪˌrɛntʃ), *n.* and *v.* Senses 1 and 2 of the noun, and sense 1 of the verb formerly at MONKEY *n.* IV 18 a in a Dict. Also **monkey wrench, monkeywrench.** [f. MONKEY *n.* + WRENCH *n.*[2]]

It has been suggested that the term may derive from a corruption of various proper names. See, for example, G. Stimpson *Bk. about Thousand Things* (1946) 287, and *Amer. Gas Jrnl.* (1927) Aug. 52.]

A. *n.* **1.** A wrench or spanner having an adjustable jaw; an adjustable spanner.

?**1807** in E. S. DANE *Peter Stubs & Lancashire Hand Tool Industry* (1973) 219 Fleetwood, Richard . . Parr, Rainford. Screw plates, lathes, clock engines . . monkey wrenches, taps. **1858** P. L. SIMMONDS *Dict. Trade Products,* Monkey-wrench. **1865** in B. PITMAN *Assassination President Lincoln* 86/1, I did not give them the rope and monkey-wrench. **1894** *Outing* (U.S.) XXIV. 132/2, I luckily had a pair of gas pliers in my valise which I used as a monkey-wrench. **1915** S. LEWIS *Trail of Hawk* II. xiii. 132 He had laughed away the straw boss who tried to make him go ask for a left-handed monkey-wrench. **1973** *Times* 29 Dec. 10/2 The stereotypes of the German as a man born with a monkey wrench in his hand and eating vast quantities of sausage and sauerkraut . . should really be discarded. **1989** G. DROHAN et al. *Plumbing* (ed. 2) i. 50/2 With a monkey wrench, unscrew the nuts that attach the trap to the tailpiece.

2. *fig.* An obstruction or hindrance; esp. in colloq. phr. *to throw* (or *hurl*) *a monkey-wrench into the machinery* and varr., to cause trouble or confusion, to interfere disruptively (cf. *to throw a spanner in the works* s.v. SPANNER *n.*[1] 2 b).

1920 *Everybody's Mag.* May 36/3 Don't throw a monkey-wrench into the machinery! **1931** *Daily Express* 16 Oct. 1/2 Mr. Lloyd George hurled a monkey wrench last night into the creaking and decrepit machinery of Liberalism. **1937** M. ALLINGHAM *Dancers in Mourning* viii. 108 White Walls normally contained an excitable household . . . This morning . . the proverbial monkey-wrench had landed squarely in the middle of the brittle machinery. **1966** D. VARADAY *Gara-Yaka's Domain* xi. 126 Just as I was about to squeeze the trigger an ebb wind threw the

monkey wrench into the works. The rising ill-wind struck the back of our necks, carrying our scent down to the elephant. **1971** *Black Scholar* Apr.-May 30/2 It is the black inmate who throws the monkey wrench into the works. **1975** *Jewish Chron.* 16 May 2/3 Mr Eban has thrown a monkey-wrench into the Israeli information campaign in the United States. **1993** *Globe & Mail* (Toronto) 25 Jan. E7/1 Even a one-day cancellation can throw a real monkey wrench into the schedule.

B. *v.* **1.** *trans.* To force, turn, etc., with a monkey-wrench. Also *absol.*

1904 W. N. HARBEN *Georgians* 267 He . . dug down in the road whar his pipe j'ined the main, till he got to it, an' then he monkey-wrenched it off. **1993** *Westcoast Logger* Feb./Mar. 6/2 The program owns its own machinery, I-D4E Cat . . and a crew-cab. Needless to say there are many hours spent monkey-wrenching and welding to keep this tired iron running.

2. *trans.* [with allusion to the title of E. Abbey's novel *The Monkey Wrench Gang* (1975)] to sabotage, *spec.* to disrupt or damage (ecologically detrimental activity, machinery, etc.) as a form of environmentalist protest; also *absol.*

1986 *Washington Post* 3 Aug. (Parade Suppl.) 9/2 He will monkey-wrench any deal with the Soviets that shows even a molecule of promise. **1987** *Nation* (N.Y.) 2 May 568/2 There are a number of ways to monkey wrench, not all of which involve destruction. 'You could file an injunction against a timber sale,' said Foreman. **1990** *San Francisco Chron.* 1 Jan. B3/4 A proposed freeway through a scenic Carmel canyon may be forever monkey-wrenched by a movement named Noel Mapstead. **1993** *Guardian* 10 July (Outlook section) 27/6 'To an Elf a CAT (earth mover) is just a large chunk of metal, probably from somewhere like Papua New Guinea,' says Elm. 'If you monkey wrench it, you're returning it. Those machines have no right to exist, they've been turned into monsters.'

So '**monkeywrenching** *vbl. n.,* the sabotage of industrial sites or equipment by ecological activists; '**monkeywrencher** *n.*

1985 D. FOREMAN *Ecodefense* i. 10 Monkeywrenching is non-violent resistance to the destruction of natural diversity and wilderness. *Ibid.* 12 Monkeywrenchers are very conscious of the gravity of what they do. **1985** *Chicago Tribune* 20 Aug. 1. 1/2 By night, . . they range about the countryside engaging in 'monkey-wrenching'—sabotaging oil rigs, logging sites, road-building machinery, ranch fences and other efforts to develop natural resources in the West. **1986** *Nation* (N.Y.) 18 Oct. 368/1 This motley collection includes Foreman and his band of monkey-wrenchers; grass-roots activists on issues such as hazardous waste and garbage incineration. **1990** *New England Monthly* Mar. 33/2 Muscular monkeywrenchers showing their ability to . . desurvey a mile of road in under 6 minutes. **1992** *Tucson Weekly* 15 Apr. 5/4 Millett was one of two of the five Earth First! defendants who received jail sentences for monkeywrenching.

monkish, *a.* Add: '**monkishly** *adv.,* in the manner of a monk; also *fig.*

1934 in WEBSTER **1980** *Christian Science Monitor* 2 Apr. 17/4 Freddy, the eponymous author of 'Freddy's Book', is an 8-foot-tall giant of a boy, grotesquely overweight, monkishly reclusive, bookishly self-protective. **1984** *N.Y. Times* 20 May VII. 45/1 Local fiction . . has more and more closeted itself monkishly away in worship of its own liturgies—of its own literariness. **1994** *Observer* 27 Mar. 19/1 An earnest, likeable man, he monkishly declines campaign contributions over $500.

mono, *n.*[2] and *a.* Add: **3.** *colloq.* Abbrev. of MONOCHROME *n.* and *a.*

1977 J. McCLURE *Sunday Hangman* ix 95 The monos are about fifty per cent cheaper, depending on this and that. **1983** *Judge Dredd Annual 1984* 12 For mono I use a Rotring with two points, 0.75 and 0.5, and a brush

No. 6 or 7 with the tip cut. **1988** *Amat. Photographer* 3 Sept. 73/1 A graphic image in mono conjures up the idea of stark blacks and whites. **1995** *Daily Tel.* 3 Jan. 12/6 The older models had a mono screen, and the batteries lasted for eight hours. On the new colour model, the batteries have a maximum life of four hours.

monolith, *n.* and *a.* Add: [A.] [1.] b. *Engin.* A large solid block, generally of concrete, sunk in water, used esp. as a foundation in the building of a harbour or dock wall.
   1878 *Min. Proc. Inst. Civil Engin.* LII. 17 These [concrete] blocks are much heavier than those which form the outer breakwater of the harbour of Marseilles..but they are very much less than the monolith, which was moved at Wick. **1904** B. Cunningham *Princ. & Pract. Dock Engin.* v. 210 The monoliths..were made entirely of concrete in the proportion of 7 to 1—viz., 5 parts river ballast, 2 parts broken limestone..and 1 part Portland cement. **1928** F. M. Du-Plat-Taylor *Design of Docks* vii. 99 Monoliths may be built up of concrete blocks, of mass concrete, of brickwork, or any other suitable material. **1959** *Chambers's Encycl.* IV. 569/1 Walls composed of monoliths are usually constructed at sites where a mass wall is impracticable owing to the unstable qualities of the substrata. **1992** *San Diego Union* 12 July G2/4 Monoliths at the mouth of Cabo San Lucas harbor mark the southernmost tip of Baja California.

monster, *v.* Add: **4.** *trans.* orig. and chiefly *Austral.* To harass, attack, or beset; (esp. in political contexts) to criticize (a person, policy, etc.) vigorously; to defame, disparage.
   1967 *Kings Cross Whisper* (Sydney) xxxvi. 4/2 *Monster*, make unwelcome passes at a girl. **1976** *Courier-Mail* (Brisbane) 12 Feb. 5/3 Capote also has the Lady Ina monstering..people like William S. Paley, Chairman of CBS, [etc.]. **1977** *Ibid.* 15 Dec. 4/2 Burchett..has been monstered of late by the New York Post, which considers him a Communist menace and a bit of a double-dealer. **1983** *Sydney Morning Herald* 5 Mar. 13/6 [He] was in trouble for saying something good about the prices and incomes policy while the Prime Minister was monstering it. **1986** *Auckland Metro* Feb. 5 Who needs to be chased, cut in on, choked with burning rubber and exhaust fumes at the next red/green light and generally monstered to salve some easily pricked self esteem? **1993** *Sun-Herald* (Brisbane) 6 June 22/2 One ferocious socialite monstered him with stories about her wealth, shopping expeditions, friends in high places and suitability for a page of photos in *Hello!*

Monterey, *n.* Add: Also **Monterey cheese**, **Monterey Jack** orig. *U.S.*, a kind of cheese resembling Cheddar.
   1918 C. F. Doane *Var. Cheese* (U.S. Dept. Agric. Bull. no. 608) 29 Jack cheese was first made in Monterey County, Cal., about 35 years ago and was then called Monterey cheese. **1940** J. Beard *Hors D'Oeuvre & Canapés* (1952) ii. 41 Monterey Jack cheese..is mild in flavor. **1957** *Encycl. Brit.* V. 334/1 American Cheddar cheese is frequently..retailed merely as American or 'store' cheese...In California this cheese is known as Jack or Monterey cheese. **1994** *Toronto Life* June 72/1 A tough call, though, between yassoo and the house burger garnished with a delicious eggplant mush, grilled pepper and the tart white Greek cheese that isn't feta and tastes a bit like monterey jack.

-monther ('mʌnθə(r)), *comb. form.* [f. MONTH *n.*[1] + -ER[1].] As the second element (with preceding numeral) in combinations designating something that lasts or is aged the specified number of months.
   1889 E. Dowson *Let.* 18 Oct. (1967) 109 Smith is a fixture..& Tweedy from what he tells me, is a six monther. **1970** J. S. Bruner in K. J. Connolly

Mechanisms of Motor Skill Devel. 88 About a third of the trials of the 1-year-olds are of this pattern and a quarter of the 17 monthers. **1994** *Daily Tel.* 18 Nov. 33/5 Sir Alistair Grant, chairman of supermarket group Argyll, is offering a 24-monther to ensure he enjoys the next annual meeting more than the last.

moo, *n.*[1] Add: **2.** *colloq.* [Abbrev. of MOO-COW *n.*] **a.** A cow. **b.** *derog.* (Applied usu. to a woman.) A stupid or objectionable person; *euphem.* for 'cow' (see COW *n.*[1] 4 b).
   1942 Berrey & Van den Bark *Amer. Thes. Slang* § 120/14 *Cow*, boss, bossy,..moo, moo cow, mooer. **1967** *Listener* 24 Aug. 252/1 Those bells which announce the approach of psychedels like medieval lepers or a herd of moos. **1967** P. Bailey *At Jerusalem* i. 70 Unless she's one of those stupid moos who..look into crystal balls. **1973** J. Speight *Till Death us do Part: Scripts* 30 Course it's tax free—it's a rebate—you silly moo. **1990** *Sun* 1 Mar. 3 Silly council moos sent his cows poll tax forms. **1994** *Courier-Mail* (Brisbane) 1 Jan. 15/8 (*heading*) Famed old moo dies...Dublin: The world's oldest cow, Big Bertha, has died at age 49.

mood, *n.*[1] Senses 3 e–f in Dict. become 3 f–g. Add: [3.] [a.] Also, a general feeling among a group of people, a prevailing temper.
   1902 *Edin. Rev.* July 39 Campbell's 'Soldier's Dream' is the most beautiful rendering in English verse of the war-weary mood. **1972** B. Moore *Catholics* i. 10 There were no miracles, there was no hysteria, there was not even a special fervour. The mood was nostalgic. **1989** *Daily Tel.* 16 Nov. 19/5, I wasn't unhappy to give it [*sc.* modelling] up. There's a different mood now...It's more a celebrity catwalk than a career.
   e. A pervading atmosphere or tone (as of a specific place or event), esp. one which induces a certain state of mind or emotion.
   1906 G. B. Shaw in A. L. Coburn *Alvin Langdon Coburn, Photographer* (1966) iii. 36 In landscape he shows the same power. He is not seduced by the picturesque...His impulse is always to convey a mood and not to impart local information. **1919** E. O'Neill *Moon of Caribbees* 32 Brooding music, faint and far-off, like the mood of the moonlight made audible. **1976** *Outdoor Living* (N.Z.) I. ii. 43/3 (Advt.), You can choose a fence that enhances the general mood of your home. **1990** *Artist's & Illustrator's Mag.* May 25 (*caption*) The sky, which always determines the mood of the landscape is registered using blue green, blue violet, red crimson, yellow gold and grey.
   g. **mood drug** *colloq.*, a psychotropic drug; also **mood control drug**.
   1970 *Time* 10 Aug. 44/2 There is some opposition to the use of *mood drugs for children. **1971** *Sunday Times* 24 Oct. 6/6 Overuse of mood drugs is becoming increasingly acute. **1986** *Sun* 17 June 2/3 He was treated last week by a doctor specialising in *mood-control drugs.
   mood elevator *n. colloq.*, a mood-elevating drug, *spec.* an antidepressant; also, anything which improves one's mood or raises one's spirits.
   1977 *Addictive Dis.* III. 283 *Mood elevators, or antidepressants, are urged upon the aging patient. **1995** *Guardian* 18 Feb. (Weekend Suppl.) 8/1 A welcome act of flirtation can act as a mood elevator, enhancing the recipient's well-being, touching him and making him more receptive, generous and open-minded.

moody, *n.* Add: **2.** A moody temper or period, a fit of moodiness. Freq. as *the moodies*, the sulks. Also in phr. *to pull the moody*, to sulk.
   1969 Fabian & Byrne *Groupie* (1970) x. 73, I was sure he was going to drop me,..leaving me all stranded..while he went through a long withdrawn moody on me. **1983** *Observer* 30 Jan. 7/1, I can't stand people having the moodies. **1986** T. Barling *Smoke*

xii. 246, I gave you Allie, so lay off the moodies. **1986** L. CODY *Under Contract* xx. 75, I don't care what moody the stupid cow pulls. **1989** *Q* Mar. 25/4 He pulls the odd moody.

moody, *a*. Add: **5.** *Criminals' slang.* False, counterfeit.

1958 F. NORMAN *Bang to Rights* III. 74 One day they had a moody ruck and made out that they had a punch up. **1978** N. J. CRISP *London Deal* v. 92 'I don't have to tell you,' Kenyon went on, 'how easy it is to plant moody information about a copper.' **1984** 'D. RAYMOND' *Devil's Home* xx. 91 Those two specialized in .. running moody companies. Those companies were nothing but expensive notepaper and a kosher letterhead.

mooli ('muːliː), *n.* Also **moole, muli.** [ad. Hindi *mūlī* radish, f. Skr. *mūlikā*, f. *mūla* root.] A long white variety of radish, the root of *Raphanus sativus* (var. *longipinnatus*) grown in southern and eastern Asia and used in eastern cooking.

[**1868** B. H. POWELL *Handbk. Econ. Products Punjab* I. III. 260/1 Fresh vegetables .. most in use among natives are — Gájar, carrot ... Múlí, radish (*Raphanus sativus*, L.).] **1969** *Sunday Statesman* 27 July 4/3 Vegetable vendors have lao sag .. pui sag .. note sag .. and lal, moole and kolmi sags. **1981** *N.Y. Times* 1 Feb. (Westchester Weekly section) 17/1 'Particularly delicious was mooli stuffed paratha — rich, flaky and filled with a fragrant grated radish mixture. **1987** D. J. MABBERLEY *Plant-Bk.* 494 Daikon, mula, muli, Chinese or Japanese r[adish]. **1990** *Punch* 20 Apr. 42/2 A mooli is a member .. of the radish family.

moon, *n.*[1] Add: [**16.**] **Moon Festival**, in China and Hong Kong and in Chinese communities elsewhere, a festival celebrated in mid-Autumn, on the fifteenth night of the eighth moon of the Chinese year (cf. *moon-cake* above), orig. a family gathering after completion of the harvest.

[**1892** J. D. BALL *Things Chinese* 13 The Full Moon Festival, when .. moon cakes are seen at every confectioner's stall and shop, is kept gaily.] *Ibid.* 114 The *Moon Festival on the 15th day of the 8th moon, in September or October. **1962** F. D. OMMANNEY *Fragrant Harbour* iv. 83 Chinese shops become illuminated caves of colour on the Moon Festival. **1987** *Atlantic* Apr. T32/1 When candles are placed inside three pagodas on the main lake, as they are for the Moon Festival, the light shining from the small round windows gives an effect as if there were 15 reflections of the moon on the water.

moon flask, a type of Chinese ceramic bottle with a flattened circular body and a rounded handle on either side of the neck, first made in the 15th century.

1974 *Times* 26 Oct. 16/4 A fifteenth-century Chinese blue and white *moon flask, just under 10 in high, was sold for £165,757 .. yesterday. **1989** *Independent* 18 Jan. 3/4 Top price was £294,607 .. for a 10 in early Ming dynasty .. double-gourd moon flask.

moonwalking ('muːnwɔːkɪŋ), *vbl. n.* (Formerly at MOON *n.*[1] 16 in Dict.) Also **moon walking, moon-walking.** [f. MOON *n.*[1] + WALKING *vbl. n.*[1]]

1. *Psychol.* [tr. Ger. *Mondsucht* (lit. 'craving for, obsession with, the moon') somnambulism, sleepwalking.] Sleepwalking by moonlight. *rare.*

1919 *Psychoanal. Rev.* VI. 159 The phenomena of sleep walking and moon walking must be acknowledged .. almost entirely as pathological. **1938** B. L. BURMAN *Blow for Landing* viii. 121 'If Miss Birdie'd just start some moon walking, she'd git over being scared of the river sure,' he declared with solemnity.' .. Jest take off her shoes in the light of the moon and walk up and down in water over her toes.' **1950** WEBSTER Add., Moonwalking, sleepwalking outdoors in bright moonlight.

2. a. The action of walking on the moon.

1981 *Times* 23 Mar. 77/2 Pictorial representations covering every subject from cave painting to moon walking. **1991** *New Scientist* 28 Sept. 57/3 At least the Moon shot entertained. Great TV: 'This is a small step for a man, etc etc.' Moon walking is in a totally different televisual ballpark.

b. *transf.* and *fig.* Any exaggeratedly slow action, dance, or method of proceeding which resembles the characteristic weightless movement of walking on the moon.

1980 *Christian Science Monitor* 12 Sept. B8/3 One hang balloon thrill is 'moon walking': heating the balloon until you are almost weightless and then hopping across the landscape as if gravity were a figment of Sir Isaac Newton's imagination. **1987** *Forbes* (N.Y.) 18 May 130/1 While giving the illusion of moving forward, the firm in fact was all the while sliding backward — the financial equivalent of what street dancers call 'moonwalking'. **1988** *Los Angeles Times* 19 Feb. (Calendar) 25/2 'Kids think they were the first ones to come up with moonwalking and poplocking,' Whitmore said. 'They don't know that those dances came from people with names like Rubber Legs, Snakey and Bubbles, and go all the way back to slave days.'

Hence (as a back-formation) '**moonwalk** *v.* and *n.*; **moonwalker** *n.*

1950 WEBSTER Add., Moonwalker. **1966** WEBSTER Add., *Moonwalk*, an instance of walking on the moon. **1969** *Times* 3 June (Suppl.) p. iii/1 The two moon-walkers will be in the lunar module's upper, or ascent stage. **1969** *Daily Tel.* 16 July 22/2 While on the moon, the astronauts will .. only moon-walk for about 3½ to four hours. **1969** *Observer* 20 July 1/2 Hints that the 'moonwalk' will also be brought forward were strengthened when the astronauts' physician .. said that he did not now expect the two men to go to sleep on the moon. **1991** *Inside Sports* Aug. 20/3 Bob Rubin has been banned by his softball league from moonwalking his way around the bases after he hits a home run. **1992** J. & M. STERN *Encycl. Pop Culture* 247/2 His signature 'moonwalk' in which he seemed to defy the laws of physics by striding forward but moving back, became the single best-known bit of celebrity body language since the four Beatles. **1994** *Guardian* 1 July 11. 28/1 If the Apollo missions had continued and lunar voyages had become commonplace, the moonwalkers themselves would seem no more exotic .. than Concorde pilots.

moral, *a.* Add: [**8.**] **c. Moral Majority**: orig., in the *U. S.* [perh. influenced by the title of Westley & Egstien's book *The Silent Majority* (1969)], a political movement of evangelical Christians, founded in 1979 by the Revd. Jerry Falwell, that advocates an ultra-conservative political and social agenda, esp. on issues such as abortion and religious education (renamed as the Liberty Federation in 1986); now used *transf.* (freq. with lower-case initial) of any group claiming to hold majority views on moral issues.

1979 *Washington Post* 25 Aug. A10 The Washington based The Moral Majority .. have already initiated mass mailing campaigns, produced television ads and begun raising money to fund a number of lobbying efforts. **1986** *Times* 1 Oct. 13/1 Appropriating a term hitherto used by the political right (especially in the United States) .. Mr Kinnock declared himself .. to be speaking for the real 'moral majority' of Britain, broad-minded and compassionate. **1990** *Christianity Today* Mar. 16/3 Liberal Christians will argue that this is what Falwell and his Moral Majority tried to do with their efforts to pack the Supreme Court with 'Right to Life' ideologues. **1991** *New Scientist* 21 Dec. 57/2 Lord Kitchener .. was a strong supporter of the White Cross Society — the 'moral majority' of the day.

mosh (mɒʃ), *v.*[2] *slang* (orig. and chiefly *U. S.*) [Origin obscure: perh. f. MASH *v.*[1]; see also MUSH *v.*[2]] **1.** *intr.* To dance in a violent manner involving jumping up and down and deliberately hitting other dancers, esp. at a rock concert.

1987 *U.S. News & World Rep.* 7 Sept. 51/3 On the floor beside the stage, the boys begin to 'mosh', slamming shoulder to shoulder with abandon. **1991** *Rolling Stone* 28 Nov. 11/2 Half-naked performance artists moshed to tribal percussions. **1993** *Chicago Tribune* 13 Apr. 1. 14/3 It wasn't even clear if the crowd noticed the band was changing songs—they pretty much moshed obliviously through the slow ones and the fast ones, and even between songs. **1994** *Club Scene* (Brisbane) 4 May 18/1 When people are at shows and they're having a good-ass time jumpin' around or moshin' it up, they're losing their minds.
2. The vb.-stem used *attrib.* and in *Comb.*, esp. in **mosh-pit** *n.*, the area in front of the stage where such dancing usually takes place.
1990 *Sounds* 10 Nov. 51/3 The security..helped the more diminutive among the crowd on to the stage if they had problems getting free of the moshpit so that they could take a dive. **1991** *Washington City Paper* 6 Sept. 38/4 Take, for example, seminal thrashers Exodus, whose mosh anthem 'Toxic Waltz' goes something like this. **1993** *Independent* 29 July 17/1 The band appeared on time at 9.30 and faced a mosh-pit of rucking, shirtless fans, extending three-quarters of the way down the Roseland's dance floor. **1994** *Sunday Times* (S. Afr.) 28 Aug. (Metro section) 1/1 After midnight, when people are not sober, we play mosh music and people go wild. Everyone slams and bumps into each other. It is madness.
So ˈ**moshing** *vbl. n.* and *ppl. a.*; ˈ**mosher** *n.*
1987 *Music Making* July 6 Soviet scientists last month reported that 'heavy metal listeners are affected by the psycho-physiological mechanisms of addiction'. According to The Guardian (so it must be true), their laboratory tests on moshin' Russkies showed 'a worsening of memory, loss of attention, a fall in reading speeds, and an increase in aggressiveness and stubbornness'. **1990** *Rolling Stone* 22 Mar. 26/2 Like a recent gig that erupted into a near riot when overeager moshers careened out of the slam pit, felling bystanders. **1991** *Twenty Twenty* Spring 73/3 All funk-metal groups agree that one form of self-abuse is still legitimate: moshing, stage-diving and other forms of lemming-like behaviour are *de rigeur* [*sic*]. **1992** *Option* July-Aug. 113/1 They've recorded an album that appeals to the moshers, the headbangers and the grinders alike. **1996** *Cape Times* 14 May (Health & Beauty section) 1/4 Victims of moshing are increasingly seeking damages for injuries.

muhajir *n.* (*a.*), var. *MOHAJIR *n.* (*a.*)

muli *n.*, var. *MOOLI *n.*

multi (ˈmʌltɪ), *n.* and *a.* Chiefly *colloq.* [f. MULTI- in various compounds, with ellipsis of second element.] **A.** *n.* **1.** = *multimillionaire* n. s.v. MULTI- 2.
1958 *Observer* 25 May 16/7 Schizoid son of over-indulgent multi. **1989** A. BEATTIE *Picturing Will* I. viii. 75 She was the young wife of a sixty-year-old multi.
2. *Bridge.* [Abbrev. of MULTI-PURPOSE *a.*, the original name for this bid.] A multicoloured opening bid of two diamonds: see *MULTICOLOURED *a.* 2. Freq. *attrib.*
1972 *Sunday Tel.* 10 Dec. 14/5, I mentioned the multi-purpose 2◇ opening, a comparatively new weapon used with devastating effect by the young Scottish experts, W. Coyle and V. Silverstone...The Multi, as it has been christened, is a constructive as well as a pre-emptive opening. **1977** *Guardian* 11 June 14/5 A 'Multi' 2D, showing a weak two in either major or a certain type of strong hand. **1991** G. THOMPSON *Bridge Player's Dict.* 33 Dixon, first recognised defence to the Multi, based on the principle that a double

of 2◇ shows a fairly balanced hand of about 13-16 points.
3. A multi-storey block of flats: see MULTI-STOREY *a. Sc.*
1973 *Courier & Advertiser* (Dundee) 7 Aug. 9/1 The collapse of the Ronan Point multi in the East End in 1968 also has contributed to the fall in popularity of this kind of dwelling. **1976** *Sunday Post* (Glasgow) 8/2 Robert now lives in Peebles Court, a multi in Greenock. **1985** M. MUNRO *Patter* 47 It's murder stayin in a multi when the lifts urny workin.
4. = MULTINATIONAL *n.*
1983 *Financial Times* 15 Mar. IV. 19/7 The reasons for Geneva's popularity with multis are given by Du Pont as its central location, its excellent banking..facilities, [etc.]. **1986** *Ibid.* 28 Apr. 23/4 Even a new fall in the dollar would probably have only a limited effect on the Swiss chemical multis. **1993** R. HUGHES *Culture of Complaint* i. 75 There is no Marx left to fight; so forth we go in knightly array against the..hydra-headed Multi.
B. *adj. Trade colloq.* = MULTICOLOURED *a.*
1970 *Kay & Co.* (Worcester) *Catal. 1970–71* Autumn/Winter 142 Multi/Black Catsuit. Floral-printed Tricel Jersey takes on an exotic look with its miscellany of colours on Black. **1980** *Freemans Catal.* Spring/Summer 127/2 Check design in feminine pastel shades...Pink/Multi Overdress. **1990** *Littlewoods Catal.* Spring/Summer 508/5 Hawaiian printed shirt...Multi. Sizes S, M, L. **1992** *Wedding & Home* June/July 128 From Laura Ashley the Botanica wallpaper in terracotta multi white costs £8.95 per roll.

multi-, *comb. form.* Add: [1.] [b.] **multi-** doˈmestic *a. Business*, (of a company) having subsidiaries which operate independently in the markets of the countries where they are based (applied also to the operations of such a company); also *ellipt.* as *n.*, a multidomestic company.
1982 *Harvard Business Rev.* Sept.-Oct. 98/2 An international company may need to change from a *multidomestic competitor, which allows individual subsidiaries to operate independently in different domestic markets, to a global organization. **1985** *Ibid.* July-Aug. 139/3 While Caterpillar views its battle with Komatsu in global terms, CPC International and Unilever may safely consider their foreign operations multidomestic. **1989** *Business Rev. Weekly* 24 Nov. 67/3 The value added to our economy by the Australian multidomestics is unclear. **1991** *Forbes* (N.Y.) 2 Sept. 49/2 Barnevik has developed a highly decentralized corporate structure, which he calls a 'multidomestic corporation'. The idea is for each national subsidiary of ABB to act as a domestic company.
[2.] **multicropping** *n. Agric.*, the practice of raising several crops in one year on the same ground.
1969 *Progress Rep. P* (Oklahoma Agric. Exper. Station) No. 620. 58 Weed control may be a problem in double or *multicropping systems. **1980** *Christian Science Monitor* (Midwestern ed.) 4 Dec. B7/2 The Taiwanese were among the early pioneers of multi-cropping, getting as many as five crops of rice and vegetables per year on the same ground. **1989** WILSON & FERRIS *Encycl. Southern Culture* 533/1 The use of multicropping techniques in house gardens, and the preference for small separated fields in the Upland and Gulf Coastal southern areas.
multi-instrumentalist *n.*, one who can play many different musical instruments.
1969 *Listener* 3 Apr. 470/3 At the Ronnie Scott Club.. we have just had the *multi-instrumentalist and improvising genius, Roland Kirk. **1977** *Rolling Stone* 7 Apr. 32/3 Three members of that entourage—Burnett, guitarist Steven Soles and multiinstrumentalist David Mansfield,..—decided to carry on the revue's impromptu spirit. **1989** C. S. MURRAY *Crosstown Traffic* vii. 174 He was a gifted multi-instrumentalist

who could handle himself on guitar, drums, keyboards, bass and harmonica with equal facility.

[3.] *multi-employer a.*

1955 M. REIFER *Dict. New Words,* *Multi-employer *bargaining,* collective bargaining in which more than one employer participate [*sic*] as distinct from single-employer bargaining. **1974** *Encycl. Brit. Micropaedia* VII. 856/2 In [pension] plans known as multi-employer plans, various employers contribute to one central trust fund. **1985** R. BEAN *Compar. Industrial Relations* iv. 79 Industry-wide and multi-employer agreements. **1991** *Business Week* 12 Aug. 52/1 Companies that participate in multi-employer welfare arrangements, or MEWAs, . . self-insure by depositing premiums in a reserve fund overseen by the administrators.

multi-event a.

1968 *New England Jrnl. Med.* 8 Feb. 309/2 The survival curves [postulated for irradiated cells] always show an initial shoulder . . . '*Multievent' theories, such as the multihit single-target or the multitarget single-hit models, were formulated to explain the observations in such complex systems. **1979** *Washington Post* 10 June C6/5 The Spartakiad is the focal point for multievent competition. **1992** *Time* 6 July 34/2 (Advt.), Multi-event national championships.

multi-faith a. (FAITH *n.* 4 a).

1969 *Learning for Living* Jan. 31/2 All the pupils . . learn to live together in a *multi-faith community. **1978–9** *Brit. Jrnl. Religious Educ.* I. 83/2 A multi-faith area can draw on the marriage rituals of all religions in that area. **1989** *Independent* 4 May 19/3, 75 per cent of Muslim girls questioned were eager to be educated in multi-faith, multi-racial schools.

multi-gun a.

1935 *Discovery* Nov. 326/2 Large *multi-gun sets for painting factories, bridges, etc. **1936** *Aeroplane* 1 July 21/2 The interesting points are the invisibility of the numerous guns carried by the multi-gun fighters, [etc.]. **1977** *Time* 20 June 14/1 Batteries of cannon fired multigun salutes.

multi-kilo a.

1975 *Chicago Sun-Times* 2 Mar. 24/1 The . . policy of pursuing 'big-time, *multi-kilo narcotics traffickers'. **1989** *New Scientist* 17 June 23/1 (Advt.), We are currently producing multikilo quantities of ultra pure phospholipids.

multi-fibre a., pertaining to or consisting of numerous or diverse fibres; esp. *Multi-fibre Arrangement,* an international agreement regulating exports of clothing and textiles.

1973 *Times* 10 Dec. 22/1 A *multi-fibre agreement to replace the existing Gatt long-term arrangement on cotton textiles will be concluded within the next 10 days. **1977** *Arab Times* 7 Dec. 6/5 The 'multifibre' agreement negotiated in 1973, governs international commerce in cotton, woollen, synthetic and artificial fibre textiles and clothing. **1986** I. JACOBS in T. C. Bartee *Digital Communications* i. 12 There are a large variety of cable structures, ranging from simple jacketed single-fiber cables to multifiber cables. **1987** F. & T. THOMPSON *Synthetic Dyeing* 110 Many commercial yarns are available in multifibre combinations mixed either as a chopped and blended staple, or as individual piles. **1989** *Independent* 12 Dec. 21/3 There has been no relaxation in restrictions on textiles trade, mostly governed by the Multi-Fibre Arrangement. **1995** *Economist* 18 Feb. 81/1 One of the first agreements under the auspices of the new World Trade Organisation is to unravel, over ten years, the infamous Multi-Fibre Arrangement, which has limited the import of textiles and clothing from low-wage countries such as China to the rich world.

multicoloured, *a.* Add: **2.** *Bridge.* Designating an opening bid of two diamonds used conventionally to indicate one of three or four types of hand, the nature of the hand being clarified in the second round. Cf. *MULTI *n.* 2, *MULTI-PURPOSE *a.* 2.

1976 *Bridge Mag.* July 30/2 An eccentric multi-coloured two diamond bid gave the ladies

trouble. **1977** *Guardian* 11 June 14/4 Nardin and Lodge love gadgets, and the following deal was a triumph for one of their latest 'toys', the Multi-Coloured 2D opening. **1991** G. THOMPSON *Bridge Player's Dict.* 71 *Multicoloured two diamond opener,* a conventional 2◇ opener used to show two or three distinctly different types of hand, including at least one weak and one strong type.

multidisciplinarian (ˌmʌltɪˌdɪsɪplɪˈnɛərɪən), *n.* and *a.* Chiefly *Med.* [f. MULTI- + DISCIPLINE *n.* + -ARIAN. Cf. MULTIDISCIPLINARY*a.*] **A.** *n.* An advocate of a multidisciplinary approach to treatment. **B.** *adj.* Designating or favouring such an approach.

1955 *Neuropharmacology* I. 197, I am from the Department of Pharmacology of Western Reserve University, and I am a multi-disciplinarian. **1985** *Rehabilitation Counseling Bull.* Dec. 69/1 It is recommended that rehabilitation counselors use a holistic approach to counseling chronically ill and disabled adolescents, with an emphasis on a multidisciplinarian approach. **1986** *Dissertation Abstr. Internat.* B. XLVI. 2824/1 One outpatient diagnostic evaluation clinic which offers thorough multidisciplinarian evaluations for children. **1989** *Ann. Otol., Rhinol., & Laryngol.* XCVIII. 575/1 The author is obviously a strong multidisciplinarian even stating . . that 'audiology . . must be the work of a multidisciplinary team.'

multidisciplinary, *a.* Add: **multiˈdiscipline** *a.* and *n.*

1955 *Neuropharmacology* I. 7 Each meeting is limited to twenty-five participants . . , selected to represent a multidiscipline approach to some urgent problem. **1969** *Mental Retardation* Dec. 57/1 These clinics . . are multi-discipline in staffing. **1985** M. HOUVION in H. Payne *Athletes in Action* 139 Multidiscipline training is needed at a young age. **1992** *Engineering News* Sept. 92 1/5 We will perform better if we see multidiscipline as the norm and not as a tiresome complication.

multi-keyboard (mʌltɪˈkɪːbɔːd), *a.* and *n. Mus.* [f. MULTI- + KEYBOARD *n.*] **A.** *adj.* Making use of or incorporating two or more keyboards. **B.** *n.* An electronic keyboard instrument with two or more keyboards; also, in early use, one with the capacity to produce many different sounds.

1975 *Melody Maker* 4 Oct. 38/2 [Keith] Emerson pioneered the multi-keyboard technique. **1976** *Sounds* 11 Dec. 45/1 The ARP Omni . . has eight presets capable of simulating strings, bass, electric piano, harpsichord and vibes . . . It is cheaper than the Polymoog and not quite as versatile, but is nevertheless a true multi-keyboard. **1986** *Keyboard Player* Mar. 25/1 (Advt.), The new Yamaha MC series multi-keyboards are not just stunning to hear. *Ibid.* Apr. 21/3 These [instruments] can sound more than one voice at the same time . . . They really come into their own when under computer control but they can be used effectively in a multi-keyboard set up. **1987** *Los Angeles Times* 24 July VI. 12/1 A multi-keyboard/percussion assault right out of the Philip Glass school of cascading arpeggios. **1992** *Washington Post* 30 July C5/ Keith Emerson's futuristic multi-keyboard console . . drew cheers from the . . crowd.

multilocal (mʌltɪˈləʊkəl), *a.* Also multi-local. [f. MULTI- + LOCAL *a.*] Present, operating (esp. commercially), or performed in many places simultaneously.

1969 *Arzneimittel-Forschung* XIX. 1716/2 By means of numerous tables compiled in the evaluation of two multilocal trials it is proved that there are not such differences. **1982** K. OHMAE *Mind of Strategist* xiv. 199 All the multinational corporations . . are now consolidating their operations in fewer locations where they can secure large enough local markets. In other words, they are turning into *multilocal* companies (MLCs). **1989** *Communication World* July-Aug. 38/2 The traditional multi-local structure of companies has..created nationally based communication departments which tend not to deal with one another. **1992** *Nature Conservancy* July-Aug. 3/3, I often call the Conservancy a 'multilocal' group, because we combine all the advantages of a strong local presence with a clear sense of international mission.

So **multilo'cality** *n.*, multilocal quality or character.

1935 *Theology* XXXI. 205 There was little left for the schools but to defend philosophically the truths which devotion had decreed,..the totality, the multilocality, the permanence of the presence [of Christ in the Eucharist], etc. **1990** *Mediamatics* Summer (Edge 90 special issue) 171 Rather than courting the gloss of homogeneous internationalism, Edge comes closer to the idea..of multi-locality; the world-wide distribution of subjectivism.

multilocational (ˌmʌltiləʊˈkeɪʃənəl), *a.*   [f. MULTI- + LOCATIONAL *a.* Cf. *multilocation* n. s.v. MULTI- 2.] Present or operating in many locations simultaneously; = *MULTILOCAL *a.*

1974 M. McLUHAN *Let.* 25 July (1987) 504 This is a complete break with visual space which came with cubism or '*multi-locational space'. **1979** *Amer. Banker* 23 Mar. 26 We have been able to assist a number of foreign banks with multi-locational problems. **1992** *Computer Reseller News* 17 Feb. 10/ With WANs that are multilocational and even international, a Fortune company prefers to deal with a single vendor.

multiple, *a.* and *n.* Add: [A.] [4.] [c.] **multiple launch rocket system** *Mil.* (orig. *U. S.*), a long-range rocket launcher capable of firing salvoes of up to 12 rockets, each containing several hundred bomblets.

[**1970** *Army* Nov. 29/1 (*heading*) The case for a multiple rocket launcher system.] **1978** *Washington Post* 25 Apr. A13/5 The multiple launch rocket system..is but one of several alternatives to the neutron warhead, defense officials said. The first generation of the rocket would fall free like an artillery shell. But later versions..could have guidance inside each warhead for pinpoint accuracy. **1983** *Christian Science Monitor* 24 May 23/1 For the 'close-in battle' they propose 'some 1,000 salvos of multiple launch rocket systems with terminally guided warheads'. **1991** *Independent on Sunday* 24 Feb. 2/3 On the Saudi border with Kuwait and Iraq, shelling by British and US multiple-launch rocket systems and howitzers was described as 'the most intense yet'.

mutliple rocket launcher *Mil.* (orig. *U. S.*), a rocket launcher capable of firing salvoes of rockets (abbrev. *MRL* s.v. *M III 6 a*).

1945 *Iron Age* 3 May 104/1 The first multiple rocket launcher mounted on tanks was fired at the Aberdeen Proving Grounds Oct. 27 1943. **1968** E. VILIM tr. I. A. Slukhai *Russian Rocketry* 39 By the middle of 1938..work began on a ground-based multiple-rocket launcher intended for 24 missiles. **1992** N. N. SCHWARZKOPF *It doesn't take Hero* xvi. 300 His arsenal included some of the best weapons the international arms bazaar had to offer: Soviet T-72 tanks, South African 155-mm heavy artillery, Chinese and Soviet multiple rocket launchers,..the list went on and on.

multi-purpose, *a.* Add: **2.** *Bridge.* = *MULTICOLOURED *a.* 2.

1972 *Sunday Tel.* 26 Nov. 7/2 Mainly due to effective use of their new multi-purpose 2◇ opening..Scotland won the first 30 board contest.

munchable (ˈmʌn(t)ʃəb(ə)l), *a.* and *n.* [f. MUNCH *v.* + -ABLE.] **A.** *adj.* That may be munched; suitable for munching, esp. as a snack. **B.** *n.* A munchable food.

1868 'F. FERN' *Folly as it Flies* 342 It meant, we were to sit weary hours..sucking our thumbs..the previous overcrowded train having, like locusts, devoured not 'every green thing', alas! but every other munchable edible. **1966** *Economist* 23 July 385/1 Replacing this branched chain [of carbon atoms] with a straight chain makes the detergent 'soft' — that is, easily munchable by the hard-working bugs. **1980** *Washington Post Mag.* 9 Nov. 44/5 Sushi, thin strips of raw fish wrapped around cold rice or other munchables. **1981** *Ibid.* 14 Oct. B1/6 That's what makes..Planter's Cheese Curls so munchable and yet so steadfastly unsatisfying. **1992** J. & M. STERN *Encycl. Pop Culture* 398/2 After World War II, potato chips popularity soared because they were so handy for..casual entertaining..and..as the munchable best suited for television watching.

‖**mura** (mura), *n.* Pl. unchanged. [Jap.] In Japan, a village or hamlet; also, an administrative division corresponding to such a rural community.

[**1890** B. H. CHAMBERLAIN *Things Japanese* 252 Most names of this class are originally nothing more than the names of the localities in which the families bearing them resided, as..*Matsu-mura*, 'pine-tree village'.] **1922** J. W. R. SCOTT *Foundations of Japan* xxx. 262 The village..is joined administratively to another village,..in order to form a *mura* (commune). **1970** J. W. HALL *Japan from Prehist. to Mod. Times* vii. 130 Village units, called *mura*, were encouraged to develop their own organs of self-government. **1989** *Christian Science Monitor* 30 Mar. 14 He lives outside the tightly woven social structure, the enclosed and supportive world of the *mura* (village), and its extensions into family and company.

myrmecochore (ˈmɜːmɪkəˌkɔː(r)), *n. Bot.* [ad. It. *mirmecocore* (Béguinot & Traversa 1905, in *Nuovo Giornale Botanico Italiano* 30 Nov. 547), f. as MYRMECO-, -*chore*.] An oily seed that is dispersed by ants; also, a plant with such seeds.

1928 C. K. OGDEN tr. A. Forel *Social World of Ants* I. II. iii. 257 Sernander has given the name *myrmecochores* (favourite food of ants) to certain seeds with oily appendages which serve to attract ants towards them or towards their fruit, and thus to secure transportation by these insects. **1972** *Amer. Jrnl. Bot.* LIX. 118/1 The *Vancouveria* species also belong to the most common type of myrmecochore, the *Viola odorata*-type..which is characterized by appendaged seeds. **1988** *Amer. Midland Naturalist* CXIX. 434 Beattie (1983) questions the efficacy of large mound-building ants, such as *Formica* spp., as dispersal agents of myrmecochores because their nests are relatively permanent and deeply excavated, and they may be less capable than some ants he has studied in moving the seed to the nests.

So ˌ**myrmeco'chorous** *a.*, designating or characterized by a myrmecochore; ˌ**myrmeco'chory** *n.*, the dispersal of plant seeds by ants.

1916 B. D. JACKSON *Gloss. Bot. Terms* (ed. 3) 245/1 *Myrmecochorous*, dispersed by means of ants. *Ibid.*, Myrmecochory. **1928** C. K. OGDEN tr. A. Forel *Social World of Ants* I. II. iii. 257 It is chiefly plants and bushes growing in the shade of the forest and hence deprived of transport by wind or birds which have need of myrmecochorous seeds, so as to be sown and spread abroad by ants. *Ibid.* 258 He mixed seeds of an indifferent character with ten others belonging to a plant suspected of myrmecochory, and placed them on an ant-track; he then noticed the time the ants took to transport the second kind, while they entirely ignored the first. **1983** *Jrnl. Ecol.* LXXI. 413 The seeds have no dispersal mechanism once they leave the parent and are not myrmecochorous. **1988** *Amer. Midland Naturalist* CXIX. 434 Myrmecochory of leaf spurge seed may aid the observed spread..and persistence of the plant by integrating the seeds more fully into the invaded habitats.

N

N. Add: **[B.]** **[II.]** **[1.]** **[a.]** **NGO**, nongovernmental organization (see also QUANGO *n.*).

1946 *Rev. Rep. Comm. Arrangements Consultation Non-Govt. Org.* in *U.N. Econ. & Social Council Official Rec.* (1947) 1st Year: 2nd Sess. 320/1 It shall be known as the 'Committee on Arrangements for Consultation with Non-Governmental Organizations' (short title: 'Council *NGO Committee'). **1949** GOODRICH & HAMBRO *Charter of United Nations* (ed. 2) II. x. 403 Applications for consultative status, after being screened by the Secretariat on the basis of criteria adopted by the Council and considered by the [Economic & Social] Council NGO Committee, are finally acted upon by the Council. **1969** PLANO & OLTON *Internat. Relations Dict.* 291 Under the United Nations Charter (Article 71), the Economic and Social Council is empowered to make suitable arrangements for consultation with NGOs on matters within its competence. **1992** *Cultural Survival Q.* Fall 39/3 The association will continue with its present policies and projects, hoping to demonstrate to people inside the reserve and to the government and NGOs that we are responsible and dependable and worthy of support.

N.H.S. trust = *hospital trust* s.v. *HOSPITAL *n.* 7.

1989 *Independent* 4 Nov. 3/1 Hospitals that go self-governing would move out of direct management by health authorities, becoming instead semi-independent *NHS trusts, free to set their own terms and conditions for staff and surviving by selling their services to district health authorities and private patients. **1993** *Private Eye* 4 June 10/1 Crawley and Horsham NHS Trust (motto—'Where people matter') is also two months old, £750,000 in debt and slashing its support services.

nanotechnology (ˌnænəʊtɛkˈnɒlədʒɪ), *n.* [f. NANO- + TECHNOLOGY *n.*] The branch of technology that deals with dimensions and tolerances of 0.1 to 100 nanometres, or (*gen.*) with the manipulation of individual atoms and molecules.

1974 N. TANIGUCHI in *Proc. Internat. Conf. Production Engin.* II. 18/1 From the emergent needs based on these industrial requirements, the system of ultra fine finishing or 'Nano-technology' has been introduced. The usual precision finishing technology has aimed to get the preciseness and fineness of 1 μm, i.e. 10⁻⁶m in length, hence it says 'micro-technology', not so accurate in meaning. Consequently, in contrast, the finishing technology aimed to get the preciseness and fineness of 1nm would be called 'Nano-technology'. *Ibid.* 22/1 In the 'Nano-technology' in materials processing, the processing by one atom or one molecule should be fully utilized. **1986** K. E. DREXLER *Engines of Creation* i. 11 As nanotechnology moves beyond reliance on proteins, it will grow more ordinary from an engineer's point of view. **1988** *New Scientist* 24 Mar. 71/3 Nanotechnology differs from microtechnology, being based on molecular manipulation rather than the miniaturisation of bulk processes. **1992** *Times Higher Educ. Suppl.* 27 Mar. 50/1 (Advt.), Our Electronics Research and Development Centre (ERDC) is managing a LINK Nanotechnology Programme project involving the application of silicon micromachined devices to blood cell analysis.

Hence ˌnanoˈtechnoˈlogical *a.*; nanotechˈnologist *n.*, an expert in or student of nanotechnology.

1986 *Washington Post* 21 Dec. D3/4 These developments still involve the manipulation of huge numbers of atoms, and are crude compared with the manipulations the nanotechnologists hope to achieve—one atom at a time. **1989** *Sunday Times* 17 Sept. D5/6 The idea resembles work towards nanotechnological machines—a vision of tiny molecular kits for fabricating materials, molecule by molecule. **1993** *Nature* 11 Mar. 123/3 Microlithography is ignored,..and astonishingly we are told that the nanotechnological computer will be mechanical, like a Lilliputian version of Babbage's difference engine.

nappy, *n.*³ Add: **[b.]** **nappy liner**, a supplementary absorptive strip of material placed inside a baby's nappy (esp. at night).

1970 *Kay & Co.* (Worcester) *Catal. 1970-71* Autumn/Winter 222/3 *Nappy liners by Marathon are indispensable. **1989** *Woman's Realm* 11 Apr. 11/3 Red bottomed babies may show distinct improvement through changing disposable nappies frequently, and perhaps using a towelling nappy, or a one way nappy liner at night.

national, *a.* and *n.* Add: **[A.]** **[5.]** **national curriculum**, a programme designed to ensure nationwide uniformity of content and standards in education; *spec.* in the U.K., a curriculum that state schools in England and Wales have been required to follow since 1990, involving the teaching of specified subjects and assessment (by testing) of pupils at specified ages.

1964 P. ROSENBLOOM *Mod. Viewpoints in Curriculum* 37 The oldest *national curriculum project, the one which has inspired the others, is that of the Physical Science Study Committee (PSSC) to provide a new high school physics course. **1970** *West African Jrnl. Educ.* Feb. XIV. 5/1 In October 1966 there was to have been a National Curriculum Conference under the auspices of the Nigeria Educational Research Council (N.E.R.C.) but it had to be postponed. From 8 to 12 September 1969 the Conference was held in Lagos. **1989** *Child Educ.* Dec. 16/3 The successful head will recognise that if only written outcomes are expected, then assessment will be too narrow to satisfy the needs of the National Curriculum. **1992** *Artist's & Illustrator's Mag.* Oct. 5/1 The final report of the National Curriculum Art Working Party..makes specific demands on teachers to educate children in the formal elements of art and design, critical and contextual studies, and the development of investigative processes.

negative, *a.* Add: **[II.]** **[8.]** **[c.]** **negative equity** *Comm.*, the indebtedness that occurs when the value of an asset falls below that of the debt outstanding on it, esp. when the outstanding debt on a mortgaged property is in excess of its current market value.

[**1850** *U.S. Reports* XLIX. 604 There is still a further want of equity, or, more precisely speaking, a negative of equity.] **1958** *U.S. Tax Court Reports* XXVIII. 919 The excess of liabilities over assets at the beginning of each such year results in a '*negative' equity capital amount less than zero. **1976** *U.S. News & World Rep.* 22 Mar. 24/2 By the end of this year, we will be saddled with an estimated negative equity of 1.3 billion dollars. **1992** *Daily Mail* 17 Aug. 12/1 'The presence of negative equity seems likely to remain an important feature of the finances of many households for some time to come.' It would need annual house price rises of 10 per cent to free everyone caught in the mortgage trap by the end of 1995.

NICAM ('naɪkæm), *n. Television.* Also **Nicam.** [Acronym f. the initial letters of *near instantaneously companded audio multiplex.*] A digital system used in British television to provide video signals with high-quality stereophonic sound.

1986 *Broadcast Syst. Engineering* Feb. 54/3 As the BBC has shown with its NICAM 3 digital transmission system, non-linear digital compansion can achieve a considerable reduction in the number of bits required with minimal side effects on the audio signal. **1989** *Which?* Sept. 449/1 Most current hi-fi models include a Nicam decoder for the stereo broadcasts which will be starting soon. **1991** *Gramophone* Jan. 1440/1 A few up-market NICAM sets have removable loudspeaker units, which is a rather better arrangement, and some fairly recent mono sets can also be upgraded.

nineteen ninety-two, ('naɪntiːn 'naɪntɪ'tuː) *n. phr.* Usu. written 1992. [The year date.] Used to designate the implications, esp. for Britain, of the creation of a single European market, scheduled for 1992, but fully implemented from 1 Jan. 1993. Cf. *single (European) market* s.v. *SINGLE *a.* 17 a.

1988 *Truck* Dec. 45/1 Looking at 1992, Dutch road hauliers know very well that it will be very hard to retain their advantage in European transport. **1989** *Amer. Banker* 31 July 7/1 According to Mr. Howell, 1992 also will mean the reindustrialization of Europe. **1992** *Independent* 29 Dec. 17/4 On Friday, 1992 arrives. It is a year late, but that is one of the least confusing things about '1992', as the Single European Market process used to be called.

non-, *prefix.* Add: [3.] **non-govern'mental,** not belonging to or associated with a government (abbrev. *NGO* s.v. *N II. 1 b; see also QUANGO *n.*).

1920 A. C. PIGOU *Econ. of Welfare* III. iv. 388 The facts..do not warrant us in supposing that local non-governmental Boards would fail if tried on the less completely unionised soil of the Continent. **1967** A. PIFER in *Ann. Rep. Carnegie Corp. N.Y.* 3 In recent years there has appeared on the American scene a new genus of organization which represents a noteworthy experiment in the art of government... We may call it the *quasi nongovernmental organization.* **1980** *Jrnl. R. Soc. Arts* CXXVIII. 501/2 WWF is an international foundation, wholly non-governmental.

non-insulin-dependent *Path.,* designating or pertaining to a type of diabetes which usually develops in adulthood, and is characterized by the presence of some insulin secretion, and which can therefore frequently be managed by diet and hypoglycaemic agents.

1979 *Diabetes* XXVIII. 1041/2 Type II, noninsulin-dependent diabetes mellitus..frequently presents with minimal or no symptoms referrable to the metabolic aberrations of diabetes. **1990** *Q. Jrnl. Med.* LXXVII. 1209 Femoral neuropathy is more common in non-insulin-dependent diabetic men, on average in their sixties.

non-invasive (nɒnɪn'veɪsɪv), *a.* [f. NON- 3 + INVASIVE *a.*] **1.** *Path.* Of a cell or organism: not characterized by invasiveness.

1968 *Johns Hopkins Med. Jrnl.* CXXII. 271/1 The indirect, non-invasive effects of malignant tumors upon the peripheral and central nervous system. **1988** *Internat. Jrnl. Cancer* XLI. 725/1 The *in vivo* growth of the non-invasive, non-metastatic BW 5147 lymphosarcoma results in the reproducible generation of stable invasive and metastatic BW variants. **1989** *Serodiagnosis & Immunotherapy* III. 337 Lymphocytosis-promoting factor (LPF) is the exotoxin responsible for many of the disease symptoms produced by this non-invasive organism.

2. *Med.* Of a diagnostic or therapeutic procedure: not involving the disruption of body tissues.

1969 [implied in *non-invasively below]. **1971** *Biomed. Sci. Instrumentation* VIII. 61/1 Automatic non-invasive measurement of arterial blood pressure has proved to be a..difficult procedure. **1982** *Listener* 16 Dec. 15/3 There is also strong evidence to indicate..that traditional non-invasive methods of monitoring are in fact superior. **1987** *Oxf. Textbk. Med.* (ed. 2) II. XVIII. 92/1 The non-invasive dissolution of stones in the kidney..by focussed shock waves..is another major therapeutic advance. **1990** *Physiotherapy* LXXVI. 804/1 Thermography is a completely non-invasive and safe diagnostic technique.

Hence (in sense *2) **non-in'vasively** *adv.*

1969 *Proc. 8th Internat. Conf. Med. & Biol. Engin.* i. 8/1 A family of ultrasonic instruments is being developed to make these measurements non-invasively. **1980** *Sci. Amer.* Aug. 75/1 (Advt.), With the introduction of the HP 47210 CO₂ monitor.., the physician can get stable, repeatable, continuous CO_2 measurements noninvasively. **1989** *Lancet* 13 May 1048/1 Pulse oximeters allow arterial oxygen saturation to be continuously measured non-invasively.

O

O, *n*.[1] Add: **4.** *Comb.* **0800 number**, (pronounced (əʊ eɪt 'hʌndrəd nʌmbə(r))), a U.K. telephone number with the prefix *0800* which allows customers to call a business or information service without charge to themselves (cf. *EIGHT HUNDRED NUMBER *n*.; *FREEFONE *n*.).

1988 *Financial Times* 8 Mar. 16/3 BT's services..include the Linkline *0800 number which enables calls from anywhere in the UK to be put through free of charge to the caller. **1993** *Times* 17 July (Mag.) 44/2 You wander up to a phone or payphone, dial an 0800 number, press the transmit button on your little barcode-scanning smartcard, which carries out a brief encrypted conversation with the machine at the other end, and you cast your vote.

octopine ('ɒktəpiːn), *n*. *Biochem.* [ad. G. *Oktopin* (coined by K. Moriwaza 1927, in *Acta Schol. Med. Univ. Imperialis Kioto* IX. 290), f. mod.L. *Octop-us* OCTOPUS *n*.: see -INE[5].] An opine, $C_9H_{18}N_4O_4$, present in octopus muscle and also synthesized by plant cells infected by some tumour-inducing plasmids present in the crown gall pathogen *Agrobacterium tumefaciens*. Cf. *NOPALINE *n*.

1928 *Chem. Abstr.* XXII. 3705 Fraction III was sep[arate]d..into histidine, guanidine, cytosine and a new base, $C_9H_{18}N_4O_4$, which was named octopine. **1957** A. MEISTER *Biochem. Amino Acids* i. 44 Octopine occurs free in scallop and octopus muscle...It may be considered as the hydrogenated Schiff base resulting from condensation of pyruvic acid and arginine. **1980** *Nature* 21 Feb. 794/2 Most Ti plasmids fall into one of two groups, based on whether they code for enzymes for octopine or nopaline utilisation.

Offer ('ɒfə(r)), *n*.[2] Also **OFFER**. [Abbrev.] The Office of Electricity Regulation, a regulatory body set up in 1989 to supervise the operation of the British electricity industry, after its privatization.

1989 *Economist* 25 Feb. 26/2 The appointee will run the Office of Electricity Regulation (Offer), the watchdog that will regulate electricity after its 1990-91 privatisation. **1990** *Ideal Home* Apr. 133/4 OFFER will monitor and control prices charged by all the supply companies; the tariffs charged will be determined by the companies themselves. **1990** *Times* 4 May 33/1 Since September 1 last year, Professor Littlechild has headed the Office of Electricity Regulation (Offer), the body which will monitor the electricity supply industry as it is moved by stages into the private sector. **1991** *Purchasing & Supply Managem.* Apr. 22/3 One would need a licence from the Office of Electricity Regulation, OFFER, to sell surplus electricity direct to another user. **1991** *Guardian* 1 Nov. 5/1 The bill—which will be criticized by Labour for not going far enough to protect the consumer—will give all the regulators the powers of the strongest: Offer, the Office of Electricity Regulation. **1992** *Evening Standard* (London) 28 Sept. 51/6 Friends of the Earth called on Professor Stephen Littlechild, Head of the Office of Electricity Regulations [*sic*] (OFFER) to introduce measures to give the 12 Regional Electricity Companies (RECs) incentives to reduce electricity consumption.

Ofgas ('ɒfgæs), *n*. Also **OFGAS** [Abbrev.] The Office of Gas Supply, a regulatory body set up in 1986 to supervise the operation of the British gas industry, after its privatization.

1985 *Financial Times* 20 May 6/3 The Government regards Oftel as a model for the gas industry and refers to 'Ofgas' in internal documents about the proposed gas regulatory authority. **1990** *Ideal Home* Apr. 132/1 Set up in 1986 as an independent department, Ofgas' role is to ensure British Gas does not misuse its monopoly. As its main concern is gas supply, Ofgas monitors the formula used to calculate domestic gas prices, and general consumer interests. **1992** *Independent* 19 Nov. 29/4 Unigate yesterday called for the creation of a regulator of raw milk supplies along the lines of Ofgas or Oftel to prevent the Milk Marketing Board exploiting its monopoly power when it becomes a national co-operative.

Oftel ('ɒftɛl), *n*. Also **OFTEL**. [Abbrev.] The Office of Telecommunications, a regulatory body set up in 1983 to supervise the operation of the British telecommunications industry, after the privatization of British Telecommunications plc.

1982 *Financial Times* 4 Nov. 11/4 A new body called the Office of Telecommunications (Oftel) is to be created, modelled on the Office of Fair Trading (OFT). **1986** *Times* 5 June 23/1 New ways of charging for private telephone lines are examined in a consultative document published yesterday by Oftel, the telecommunications watchdog. **1990** *Which?* Nov. 604/3 OFTEL, the telephone watchdog, is investigating whether BT's credit-vetting scheme is fair. **1992** *Economist* 22 Feb. 27/1 Seeing the success of regulators like Oftel and Ofgas in getting BT and British Gas to cut their costs and prices and to raise the quality of their services, Labour has realised that not only is nationalisation unaffordable, it is unnecessary.

Ofwat ('ɒfwɒt), *n*. Also **OFWAT**. [Abbrev.] The Office of Water Services, a regulatory body set up in 1989 to supervise the operation of the British water industry, after its privatization.

1986 *Financial Times* 15 Jan. 23/8 If Ministers propose an 'Ofwat', similar to Oftel, the analogy would be false. **1989** *Which?* May 230/1 The Office of Water Services (Ofwat..) should take its important decisions in public. **1991** *New Civil Engineer* 3 Oct. 8/2 Their 'k' factors—the number of percentage points above inflation which they are allowed by Ofwat to raise prices annually—have all stayed the same. **1992** *Private Eye* 13 Mar. 29/3 OFWAT..indicated that filthy water in one of the most popular bathing areas in the country has nothing to do with them.

Omnimax ('ɒmnɪmæks), *n*. *Cinematogr.* [f. OMNI- + MAX(IMUM *n*., after *IMAX *n*.] A proprietary name for a technique of wide-screen cinematography in which 70mm film is projected through a fish-eye lens on to a hemispherical screen. Freq. *attrib*.

1973 *Cinema Canada* Aug./Sept. 36/1 There are also two films made in an associated medium which we've developed called 'Omnimax'. It is a dome show in which the picture is projected on the inside of a dome theatre. **1974** *Official Gaz.* (U.S. Patent Office) 11 June TM103/2 *Omnimax*...For motion pictures projectors, cameras, optical printers, film editing machines and motion picture screens. **1982** *Sports Illustr.* 7 June 84/3 The 360-degree-projection Omnimax theater with its geodesic dome. **1989** *Calendar* (Los Angeles) 27 Aug. 82/2 The Omnimax

Theatre at Caesars Palace will reopen Friday. **1993** *Time* (Internat. ed.) 18 Jan. 2/2 If the 250 interactive exhibits bring on exhaustion, they can sit back and watch breathtaking scenery on the world's largest Omnimax movie screen.

Orimulsion (ɒrɪ'mʌlʃən), *n.* Also **orimulsion**. [f. *Ori(noco* (the bitumen being originally extracted from the Orinoco oil belt in Venezuela) + E)MULSION *n.*] A proprietary name for an emulsion of bitumen in water, which may be used as a fuel.

1987 *Official Gaz.* (U.S. Patent Office) 23 June TM 27/1 *Orimulsion*... For hydrocarbon fuels for use in power plants. First use 9-30-1986. **1990** *Daily Tel.* 16 Aug. 16/4 Oil that was previously thought to be too heavy for commercial use..can now be exploited, thanks to the development by Venezuela and BP of a new fuel called orimulsion. **1992** *Farmers Guardian* 7 Aug. 12/9 A proposal by National Power to switch to burning orimulsion at its Pembroke power station would lead to vastly increased levels of acid rain in Welsh rivers, maintains the River Wye Preservation Trust. **1993** *Guardian* 6 Oct. 1. 15/3 British Petroleum yesterday announced plans to pull out of a joint venture marketing Orimulsion, branded by critics as the world's dirtiest power station fuel.

Ossi ('ɒsɪ), *n. colloq.* (sometimes *depreciative*). Pl. **Ossies. Ossis**. [a. G. *Ossi* (prob. an abbrev. of *Ostdeutsche*), f. *Ost* east.] A term used in Germany (esp. since reunification) to denote a citizen of the former German Democratic Republic; an East German. Cf. *WESSI *n.*

1989 *N.Y. Times Mag.* 17 Dec. 74/2 Everywhere he went he was greeted warmly, once people determined that he was an *Ossi* (East German). **1990** *Marxism Today* Mar. 7/1 The *Ossis* want out. The Wall is down. **1991** *Times Lit. Suppl.* 24 May 12/3 None too subtle hierarchies are beginning to appear, with Wessies and Ossies. **1993** *Economist* 10 July 112/3 She rightly lists the many elements of Germany's post-unity despond—including *Ossi-Wessi* friction, soaring unemployment, record state deficits, an upsurge of violence against foreigners and a rush of asylum-seekers.

P

P. Add: [II.] [a.] **PC, pc,** politically correct; political correctness.

1986 *N.Y. Times* 11 May VI. 39/2 There's too much emphasis on being *P.C.*—politically correct. **1989** *Independent* 11 Nov. (Weekend section) 34/5 We thought we'd be accused of not being pc—politically correct. **1992** *Economist* 18 Jan. 44/2 Subjects like science and engineering where the ravages of PC are unknown (or, at least, rare).

PCNA *Biochem.*, proliferating cell nuclear antigen; orig. called *cyclin* (*CYCLIN *n.* 1).

1978 *Jrnl. Immunol.* CXXI. 2233/1 All these lines of evidence suggest that the nuclear antigen reacting with the newly identified antibody is an antigen associated with proliferating cells. Therefore, it is suggested that this antibody might be termed antibody to proliferating cell nuclear antigen (*PCNA). **1990** *Nucleic Acids Res.* XVIII. 261/1 PCNA, or cyclin..is a known cofactor of DNA polymerase d in *in vitro* replication of SV40 DNA.

PET, polyethylene terephthalate.

1966 *Trans. Faraday Soc.* LXII. 1321 The β relaxation in amorphous polyethylene terephthalate (*PET) was chosen. *Ibid.* 1323 Both samples were cut from the same sheet of PET. **1982** *Times* 13 Dec. 15/2 Half a dozen brewers are already trying out PET packaging for their beers. **1991** *Garbage* Jan.-Feb. 35/1 The..facility, capable of recycling 24 million pounds of PET a year, was an investment of $3.3 million.

PET = *positron emission tomography* s.v. *POSITRON *n.* 2.

[**1975** M. M. TER-POGOSSIAN et al. in *Radiol.* CXIV. 90/2 We call this apparatus a *positron emission transaxial tomograph* (PETT).] **1979** *Brain Res.* (Reviews) CLXXX. 48 The concept of positron emission tomography (*PET). **1993** *Chicago Tribune* 13 Apr. 1. 4/6 Using PET scans..to follow the brain's consumption of sugar..he measured the activity level of brains at all ages.

PTSD = *post-traumatic stress disorder* s.v. *POST-TRAUMATIC *a.* 2.

1982 *Southern Med. Jrnl.* LXXV. 704/2 It should be noted that *PTSD can occur as a result of any severe trauma, such as rape or an automobile accident, and not necessarily from combat. **1993** *Men's Health* Jan.-Feb. 75/2 Gilkin's PTSD symptoms struck him earlier and harder than Michael Hall's. He suffered dizzy spells..and flashbacks.

PVS *Med.*, persistent vegetative state.

1985 *Arch. Neurol* XLII. 1045/1 The clinical syndrome of *PVS has been described in patients who survive severe traumatic and non-traumatic brain damage without improvement in mental function. *Ibid.* Electroencephalograms were normal in three patients with PVS. **1996** *Independent* 24 Jan. II. 28/4 13 Nov. 26/1 Now many patients who, 20 years ago, would have died quick and painless deaths, linger on in PVS.

PWA, person with Aids.

1986 *Guardian Weekly* 26 Jan. 12/1 He found a place to live thanks to the Shanti Project, a charity subsidised by the municipality to help *PWAs. It makes houses available to Aids victims. **1992** *Out* (N.Y.) Summer No. 1. 29/2 Aerosolized pentamidine is now a standard prophylactic treatment for what was then the No. 1 killer of PWAs.

paintball ('peɪntbɔːl), *n.* orig. *U.S.* [f. PAINT *n.* + BALL *n.*[1]] **a.** A war-game in which participants use weapons that fire capsules of brightly coloured paint which burst on impact, any competitor marked in this way being eliminated from the game. **b.** A capsule of paint for such a weapon.

[**1983** *Esquire* Sept. 34/4 Several players running through the woods..trying to reach checkpoints without being shot by the harmless paint-pellet pistols.] **1987** *Times* 25 Aug. 3/1 (*caption*) A California Commander player armed with a paintball gun hunts rivals in the Sussex woods. *Ibid.* 3/3 The basic weapon..fires .68 calibre paintball. **1987** *Chicago Tribune* 18 Dec. v. 3/2 Tucker has found a way to shoot people by playing a war game, Paintball, in which he and squads of weekend guerillas stalk each other through the woods with air guns that fire blobs of paint instead of bullets. **1988** T. MCGINLEY et al. *Paintball Players Handbk.* 7 In just two short years, the sport of paintball has become America's fastest growing new form of recreation activity. **1988** *Survival Weaponry & Techniques* Sept. (Suppl.) 3/2 The undergrowth changes colour as a hail of paintballs cut [*sic*] through the leaves; branches go technicolour and nettles psychedelic. **1990** *Sydney Morning Herald* 15 Mar. 30/7 Paintball? Yes, a curious American pastime which involves would-be Rambos running madly through the bush, shooting at each other with guns, which fire paint pellets. **1992** *Independent* 4 May 2/7 He feared commercial owners would use the wood for pheasant rearing... Other threats included paintball games and motorcycling, he said.

Hence **'paintballer** *n.*, one who plays paintball; **'paintballing** *n.*

1989 *Paintball Games Mag.* Oct. 5/2 Paintballers come from all walks of life and we share a love of excitement and the open air. **1992** *Daily Tel.* 15 Aug. (Weekend Suppl.) p. ii/1 We had come to spend upwards of £30 on a day's paintballing at Toby Hall's Skirmish centre. *Ibid.* ii/2 For sheer cunning, aggression and bravado, it is hard to beat the female paintballer.

palm, *n.*[2] Add: [IV.] [9.] **palm-top** *a.* [after DESK-TOP *n.*, *lap-top* s.v. LAP *n.*[1] 7], (esp. of a computer) small enough to be held and used in the palm of the hand; freq. *ellipt.* as *n.*

1987 *Govt. Computer News* 5 June 55/3 Perhaps artificial intelligence will soon allow us to communicate from a 10 MIPS cellular *palmtop to someone's telephone implant and vice versa. **1990** *Daily Tel.* 15 Jan. 23/3 The latest advertising-generated fad is the 'palm-top computer' which is being sold to busy executives as the ultimate replacement for a competent secretary. **1993** *Computing* 27 May 23/1 Whereas in the old days a portable was simply a PC you could carry (although not necessarily use on the move), now you can take your pick from portables, notebooks, sub-notebooks, palmtops and organisers. **1993** *Esquire* Dec. 48 In this novel.., William Gibson imagines the palmtop TV/telephone of the future: a smooth, oblong shape, like a piece of polished obsidian.

‖**panforte** (panˈforte; anglicized panˈfɔːti), *n.* [It., lit. 'heavy bread', f. *pane* bread + *forte* strong, heavy, solid.] A rich Sienese confection, containing nuts, candied peel, honey, and spices, baked hard to form a round flat cake.

1865 *Dublin Internat. Exhib. Kingdom of Italy Official Catal.* (ed. 2) 26/2 Panforte sweetmeat. Price 3s.4d...This house [h]as been established for half a century; the exhibitor states that he makes 18 tons of panforte annually. **1885** W. D. HOWELLS in *Cent. Mag.* Aug. 539/1 The panforte of Siena fears no competition or comparison, either for the exquisiteness of its flavor or for the beauty of its artistic confection. **1954** E. DAVID *Italian Food* 263 The famous *panforte* of Siena, rich and spicy and oddly reminiscent of plum pudding. **1962** A. GLASFURD *Siena* 19 Visitors fortunate to have teeth..will enjoy *panforte*, a glorious dense sugary slab of nuts and candied peel that has been the pride of confectioners here since the thirteenth century. **1985** J. FRASER *In Place of Reason* xviii. 178 A cake of *panforte* the size of a cartwheel arrived.

persistent, *a.* Add: [**2.**] **c.** *Path.* **persistent vegetative state**, a condition of indefinite duration resulting from brain damage, in which a patient recovering from a coma retains brainstem functions such as reflex responses and may appear wakeful, but has no cognitive functions or other evidence of cerebral cortical activity. Abbrev. *PVS* s.v. *P II. a.

1972 *Lancet* 1 Apr. 734/1 Patients with severe brain damage due to trauma..may now survive indefinitely...Such patients are best described as in a persistent vegetative state. **1987** *Oxf. Textbk. Med.* (ed. 2) II. xxi. 51/1 The question of whether it is appropriate to provide the nutrition and nursing care required to ensure survival once the persistent vegetative state has been diagnosed is now a topic of debate. **1993** *U.S. News & World Rep.* 18 Jan. 78/3 In 1986, at the age of 60, she suffered bleeding on the brain and went into a 'persistent vegetative state' — alive but with essentially no higher brain function.

photo, *n.* Add: [**3.**] **photo op** (occas. **photo opp**) *colloq.* (orig. *U. S.*) = *photo opportunity* s.v. PHOTO *n.* 3.

1982 *N.Y. Times* 14 June B8/4 The regulars in this event [*sc.* a baseball match between Democrats and Republicans]..treat it as a relief from workaday umbrage and possibly even as that rare '*photo op*' celebrating real life. **1987** *Times* 9 May 24/8 She..provided photo-opps, usually wearing tight jeans, in the garden of her Long Island house. **1992** A. MAUPIN *Maybe the Moon* xi. 133 A canny photographer, recognizing a great photo op, deposited the dainty Lya on the not-so-dainty lap of the famous financier.

pindown ('pɪndaʊn), *n.* Also **pin-down, pin down**. [f. vbl. phr. *to pin down*: see PIN *v.*1 6 b.] **1.** *Mil.* The effective grounding of enemy missiles by inflicting sufficient damage to their ground sites to disable their guidance or propulsion systems.

1982 *N.Y. Times* 11 Nov. B14/4 Because the 'boost stages' or rocket portions of missiles attempting to fly out through the pindown would probably be destroyed by X-ray energy, the President would have to delay launching United States ICBM's until the pindown ended. **1986** J. GREEN *A-Z Nuclear Jargon* 130 *Pindown*, the concept of saturating enemy missile bases with so many warheads that the resulting electromagnetic confusion will render their outgoing guidance system useless.

2. In the U.K., a system formerly operated in certain children's homes whereby children considered difficult to deal with were placed in solitary confinement for long periods; (a period of) such confinement.

[**1984** R. CRUDDACE *Log-bk. Entry* 20 Jan. in Levy & Kahan *Pindown Experience* (1991) v. 36 Phil and Tony visited and pinned down J.... confined to his bedroom unless requested staff to come out...to be kept from R.... and all times no contact.] **1985** in *Ibid.* vi. 60 Pindown - no - contact - schooling in his room or Duke's Lodge if Tony requires him. **1989** *High Court Injunction* 13 Oct. in *Ibid.* i. 1 No child or young person in the care of (the local authority) shall be subjected to the regime known as 'pin down' in any form whatsoever without the leave of the court. **1991** *Independent* 28 May 4/8 For the whole of the time in pin down I never saw another resident. My only contact was with the workers when they came to give me food. **1991** *Daily Tel.* 31 May 4/1 He had coined the word pindown after

his repetitive use of the phrase 'we must pin down the problem' while gesturing with his forefinger towards the floor. Children later began to speak of 'being in pindown'. **1993** *Observer* 21 Feb. 11/1 An 18-year old victim of sexual abuse has broken a three-year silence to tell of her ordeal under the infamous pindown regime that operated in Staffordshire children's homes in the Eighties. *Ibid.*, I was in solitary confinement for two months, without any day clothes or footwear or anything to do except stare out of the window...From day one I was put..on pindown.

pink, *n.*4 and *a.*1 Add: [**B.**] [**8.**] [Prob. because of the colour's long-standing feminine associations (in clothing etc.), as opposed to 'masculine' blue. See also *pink triangle*, sense *C. c below.] Of a man: gay, homosexual. Hence applied more generally to anything perceived as having some connection with homosexuals (esp. as an economic or political group, as *pink pound*, etc.). Cf. *LAVENDER *a.* 3. *colloq.*

[**1950** H. E. GOLDIN *Dict. Amer. Underworld Lingo* 158/1 *Pink pants*, (rare) a young passive pederast or male oral sodomist.] **1972** B. RODGERS *Queens' Vernacular* 149 *Pink*, homosexual. 'You can meet a straight on Polk Strasse, but that doesn't make him pink.' **1980** *Maledicta* III. II. 253 *Lavender* has become synonymous with *gay*; also *pink*, from the triangle on gays in Nazi concentration camps. **1984** *Guardian* 14 May 11/1 The first major British company to start an openly gay business and go after the 'pink pound'. **1987** (*title of newspaper*) The pink paper: Britain's only national newspaper for lesbians & gay men. **1989** *Sydney Star Observer* 30 June 1/1 An illegal 'pink list', banning gay or gay-associated actors, is maintained by several leading television casting directors, according to a leading Sydney actor and writer. **1990** *Independent* 4 Sept. 16/6 The economic strength of the 'pink pound'..was important in establishing the idea of a gay community. **1993** *Times* 18 June 7/4 He launched his business after visiting New York and seeing the power of the 'pink dollar'.

[**C.**] [**c.**] **pink triangle**, a triangular piece of pink cloth worn to identify homosexuals in Nazi concentration camps; hence, this symbol, used subsequently as a badge to express homosexuality or support for gay rights.

1950 H. NORDEN tr. *E. Kogon's Theory & Pract. of Hell* iii. 43 Homosexual practices were actually very widespread in the camps. The prisoners, however, ostracized only those whom the SS marked with the *pink triangle. *Ibid.* 44 Criminals wore a green triangle...Jehovah's Witnesses wore purple; 'shiftless elements', black; homosexuals, pink. During certain periods, the Gypsies..wore a brown triangle. **1975** *N.Y. Times* 10 Sept. 45/3 In the concentration camps.., the homosexuals were forced to wear pink triangles, and were treated as the lowest of the low by the Nazis. **1977** J. WEEKS *Coming Out* xvi. 191 You were encouraged to wear badges.., asserting your homosexuality, with slogans..., and with prominent logos from the butterfly or clenched fist of the early badges to the pink triangle (commemorating homosexual victims of the Nazi concentration camps) and the purple lambda of later badges. **1992** *New Republic* 13 Apr. 29/1 Her brother Carl displays a pink slip to the library students he teaches, having been sacked for wearing a pink triangle to class.

political, *a.* Add: [**A.**] [**6.**] **political correctness** orig. *U. S.*, advocacy of or conformity to politically correct views; politically correct language or behaviour (see *POLITICALLY *adv.* 3 b; cf. also *CORRECTNESS *n.* 2).

[**1948** *Amer. Polit. Sci. Rev.* XLII. 997 Although modest and tolerant of other views, [he] is quite certain of the moral, legal, and political correctness of his own policies.] **1979** *Washington Post* 16 Sept. (Book World) 13/3 No matter what criticisms are hurled at this feminist fiction, no doubt the author will be cushioned by her *political correctness. **1986** *Los Angeles Times* 8 Aug. VI. 22/1 The key to this was found not in her message songs—like many of her ilk, she tends toward smug political correctness. **1991** *Times* 4 July 19/1 Despising the republic as they do, these champions of 'political correctness' are presumably scowling today.

political incorrectness orig *U. S.*, language, behaviour, etc., which is not politically correct; failure or reluctance to conform to politically correct views (see *POLITICALLY *adv.* 3 b).

1989 *N. Y. Times* 16 July VII. 1/1 By 1969, what some liberal authors saw as the new *political incorrectness of the Apollo program left them feeling guilty or ambivalent toward it. **1990** T. PYNCHON *Vineland* 83 Just for its political incorrectness alone, Frenesi had at first reacted to Sasha's theory with anger. **1994** *Loaded* Sept. 40/1 Local councils have monitored his act to judge whether it contains material which might be offensive under their Equal Opportunities policies... Manning, the living embodiment of political incorrectness, remains somewhat bemused by all the fuss.

politically, *adv.* Add: [3.] **b.** *Special Comb.* **politically correct** *adj. phr.*, (*a*) [not as a fixed collocation in early use] appropriate to the prevailing political or social circumstances.

1793 J. WILSON in *U.S. Rep.* II. (1798) 462 The *states*, rather than the *people*, for whose sake the states exist, are frequently the objects which attract and arrest our principal attention... Sentiments and expressions of this inaccurate kind prevail in our common, even in our convivial, language... 'The United States', instead of the 'People of the United States', is the toast given. This is not *politically correct. **1936** H. V. MORTON *In Steps of St. Paul* vi. 211 It has often been asked why Paul addressed his converts as 'Galatians'. But is there any other word that could have described so mixed a crowd?.. 'Galatians', a term that was politically correct, embraced everyone under Roman rule. **1955** tr. C. Milosz *Captive Mind* 120 A politically correct theme would not have saved him from the critics' attack had they wanted to apply orthodox criteria, because he described the concentration camp as he personally had seen it, not as one was *supposed to see it*. **1979** *Economist* 6 Jan. 17/2 His judgement that the time and place called for an attack on the quality and efficiency of the municipal government proved to be politically correct.

(*b*) from the early 1970s, *spec.* conforming to a body of liberal or radical opinion, esp. on social matters, characterized by the advocacy of approved causes or views, and often by the rejection of language, behaviour, etc., considered discriminatory or offensive; also *absol.* See *CORRECT *a.* 4. (orig. *U. S.*, sometimes *dismissive*).

1970 T. CADE *Black Woman* 73 A man cannot be politically correct and a chauvinist too. **1975** P. GERBER *Willa Cather* vi. 158 If a literary thesis were unmistakable and politically correct, a favorable reception for the work was assured. **1975** *Facts on File* 31 Dec. 1012/3 On the lesbian issue, she said NOW was moving in the 'intellectually and politically correct direction'. **1978** *National Jrnl.* (U.S.) 7 Jan. 29 Circle the politically correct response(s), if any. **1984** *Women's Stud. Internat. Forum* VII. 323/1 The deformed sexuality of patriarchal culture must be moved.. into an arena for struggle, where a 'politically correct' sexuality of mutual respect will contend with an 'incorrect' sexuality of domination and submission. **1987** *Nation* 6 June 769/3 Some readers are going to be disappointed by Poirier's insistent effort to keep literature from becoming a weapon—he would say casually—of the politically correct or incorrect. **1991** *Village Voice* (N.Y.) 3 Dec. 30/3 I've been chided by a reader for using the word *gringos* and informed that European American is politically correct. **1993** *Utne Reader* Jan.-Feb. 152/1 Killing mosquitoes, black flies, midges, and other summer pests is known to politically correct people as 'speciesism'.

Who can say that humans are more valuable than other creatures?

politically incorrect, not politically correct; illiberal; discriminatory.

1947 V. NABOKOV *Bend Sinister* 168 A person who has never belonged to a Masonic Lodge or to a fraternity, club, union, or the like, is an abnormal and dangerous person... It is better for a man to have belonged to a *politically incorrect organization than not to have belonged to any organization at all. **1977** *Washington Post* 29 May D2/3 The African Liberation Day Coalition explained that both the other groups held politically incorrect positions. **1986** J. STACEY in Mitchell and Oakley *What is Feminism?* 230 Within the [feminist] movement, heterosexuality.. has been considered 'politically incorrect'. **1994** *Esquire* Feb. 88/1 [He] may be shedding his image as an extremist, dropping his tendency to use paranoid, espionage lingo, trying not to make politically incorrect remarks about homosexuals.

positron, *n.* Add: **2.** Special Comb. **positron emission tomography** *Med.*, a form of tomography which employs positron-emitting isotopes introduced into the body as a source of radiation instead of applying X-rays externally; abbrev. *PET*.

1976 *Jrnl. Nuclear Med.* XVII. 546/1 (*heading*) Evaluation of *positron emission tomography for study of cerebral hemodynamics in a cross section of the head using positron emitting gallium 68-EDTA and Krypton-77. **1992** *Economist* 26 Dec. 116/2 Positron emission tomography (PET) enables researchers to watch people think.

post-structural (pəʊst'strʌktʃərəl), *a.* Chiefly *Lit. Theory.* Also **poststructural**. [f. POST- + STRUCTURAL *a.* 5.] Pertaining to or designating an analytical approach which emerged after structuralism; = *POST-STRUCTURALIST *a.* and *n.*

?**1970** *Eastern Anthropologist* XXIII. 285 The Craft of Social Anthropology.. is a product of what may be called the post-structural era in the discipline. **1974** *Lang. & Lang. Behavior Abstr.* VIII. 273/2 The experiment demonstrated that the great concepts of poststructural linguistics and 'text-theory' can be assimilated and even rediscovered by young students very easily. **1978** J. V. NEUSTUPNÝ *Post-Structural Approaches to Lang.* i. 3 The expression 'post-structural'.. refers to a typology of linguistic theories... It appears.. to be a convenient descriptor for studies in grammar and sociolinguistics which took over from structural linguistics in the late 1950s and 1960s. **1990** *Rev. Eng. Stud.* XLI. 139 By the end of Maud Ellmann's book, Pound and Eliot look punch-drunk, reeling under a sustained barrage of post-structural élan.

post-structuralism (pəʊst'strʌktʃərəliz(ə)m), *n.* *Lit. Theory.* Also **poststructuralism**. [f. POST- + STRUCTURALISM *n.* 2. Cf. *POST-STRUCTURAL *a.*] An extension and critique of structuralism, esp. as used in critical textual analysis, which rejects structuralist claims to objectivity and comprehensiveness, typically emphasizing instead the instability and plurality of meaning, and freq. using the techniques of deconstruction to reveal unquestioned assumptions and inconsistencies in literary and philosophical language.

1977 *P.M.L.A.* XCII. 1150/2 A Reassessment of Structuralism.. Panellists: Arthur E. Kunst, Univ. of Wisconsin, Madison (post-structuralism and linguistics). **1979** J. V. HARARI *Textual Strategies* 28 We shall retain the singular notation, but it will become obvious to the reader that we think of it partly in the plural: post-structuralism is also post-structuralisms. **1981** F. JAMESON *Political Unconscious*

i. 21 It is..increasingly clear that hermeneutic or interpretive activity has become one of the basic polemic targets of contemporary post-structuralism in France, which..has tended to identify such operations with historicism. **1984** *Listener* 16 Feb. 10/3 In Britain, Structuralism, post-Structuralism and Deconstructionism have made inroads on the thinking of young intellectuals ghettoed in polytechnics. **1987** *Financial Times* 7 Feb. p. xiv/4 Kuznetsov's..central device owes something to European post-structuralism and the idea that everything can be read as a text. **1988** *New Republic* 29 Feb. 31/2 Most would now agree that its main importance was to usher in various post-structuralisms, of which the most central and most thrilling has been deconstruction. **1992** *English* XLI. 176 Most post-structuralism may appear to say that the text is autonomous and that literary criticism has no ethical dimension.

post-structuralist (pəʊst'strʌktʃərəlɪst), *a.* and *n.* Chiefly *Lit. Theory.* Also **poststructuralist**. [f. POST- + STRUCTURALIST *n.* (and *a.*)] **A.** *adj.* Of or pertaining to a post-structural approach or post-structuralism. **B.** *n.* A practitioner or adherent of post-structuralism.
1967 J. VAN VELSEN in A. L. Epstein *Craft of Social Anthropol.* I. 140, I have contrasted the aims and methods of anthropologists writing in the structuralist tradition with the types of problem in which many anthropologists of a younger, post-structuralist, 'generation' have become familiar. **1976** *Archivum Linguisticum* VII. 152 It should..be pointed out that the structuralist and post-structuralist emphasis on the internal structuring of language was self-imposed (rather than the result of blindness to the properties of language as a social phenomenon). **1977** *French Rev.* LI. 256 The post-structuralist's interest in certain very special phenomena is often transparent. **1982** J. CULLER *On Deconstruction* (1983) Introd. 30 Though numerous post-structuralists are feminists (and vice versa), feminist criticism is not post-structuralist, especially if post-structuralism is defined by its opposition to structuralism. **1988** *Nation* (N.Y.) 9 Jan. 23/2 He goes beyond the useful post-structuralist point that facts about the past are structured like texts. **1993** *Sci.-Fiction Stud.* Nov. 450 In providing a nonlinear, non-hierarchical, and nonpatriarchal reading experience hypertext is inherently deconstructive and delivers almost all of the desiderata of poststructuralist literary theory.

post-traumatic (pəʊsttrɔː'mætɪk), *a. Path.* and *Psychiatry.* (Formerly at POST- B. 1.) Add: **2.** Special collocation: **post-traumatic stress disorder** (or **syndrome**), a condition alleged to develop following exposure to a stressful situation or series of events outside the normal range of human experience, whose symptoms reportedly include recurrent dreams or memories of the traumatic event, withdrawal, difficulties in concentration, and sleep disturbance. Abbrev. *PTSD*.
[**1973** *Comprehensive Psychiatry* XIV. 562 The suggestion has been made that neurasthenia is a stress-intolerance syndrome, thus linking it to post-traumatic syndromes and external stress.] **1982** *Southern Med. Jrnl.* LXXV. 704 Primary care physicians may encounter patients having posttraumatic stress disorder. **1985** *Child Abuse & Neglect* IX. iii. 329 An examination of symptoms presented by 17 adult women who experienced childhood incest suggests that the long-term effects of incest may be a post-traumatic stress disorder (PTSD). **1989** *Spin* Oct. 38/1 He was diagnosed by a court psychiatrist as suffering from 'post-traumatic stress syndrome' and 'seeing things, like gangs of people chasing him'. **1993** *Men's Health* Jan.–Feb. 72/2 All of them agree..on one thing: An enemy that still stalks many veterans is Post-Traumatic Stress Disorder (PTSD).

Prader–Willi (ˌprɑːdə(r)'vɪlɪ), *n. Path.* [The names of Andrea *Prader* (b. 1919) and Heinrich *Willi* (b. 1900), Swiss paediatricians, who with Alexis Lebhardt described the syndrome in *Schweiz. Med. Wochenschr.* (1956) LXXXVI. 1260/2.] **Prader-Willi syndrome**, a congenital disorder caused by a chromosomal defect and characterized by sexual infantilism, mental handicap, obsessive eating, and obesity.
1964 *Acta Pædiatrica* LIII. 75/2 It is true that mentally deficient children are often short, but children with the Prader-Willi syndrome grow disproportionately as well. **1972** *Jrnl. Pediatrics* LXXI. 290/2 These findings indicate that diabetes mellitus is not necessarily a consistent feature of the Prader-Willi syndrome, even in the adult, and that when present at any age it is usually mild. **1988** *Guinness Bk. Records* (ed. 35) i. 10/1 People suffering from the Prader-Willi syndrome, a rare brain disorder which makes them constantly crave for food, have been known to get so fat that they die from asphyxiation. **1992** *Newsweek* (Canad. ed.) 2 Nov. 77/3 If the father's chromosome 15 is missing some DNA..his child will have the rare Prader-Willi syndrome.

propadiene (prəʊpə'daɪiːn), *n. Chem.* [f. PROP(ANE *n.* + DI-² + -ENE.] A gaseous unsaturated hydrocarbon, $CH_2{:}C{:}CH_2$, isomeric with propyne. Also called *allene*.
1926 *Chem. Abstr.* XX. 3685 Propadiene was prepd. by dropping the dibromopropylene into a flask contg. Zn dust and EtOH and heating. **1939** *Jrnl. Amer. Chem. Soc.* LXI. 751/2 Particularly interesting cases are the propane-propene mixtures..or propyne-propadiene mixtures from isomerization studies. **1991** *Inorg. Chem.* XXX. 430/2 This C_3 unit thus corresponds to the carbon skeleton of propadiene, C_3H_4.

pull, *v.* Add: **7. e.** *to pull the lever*: see *LEVER *n.*¹ 2 c.

Q

quick, *a.*, *n.*[1], and *adv.* [D.] **quick-fix** *a.* Add: also as *n.*, a hasty remedial measure which does not take account of the long-term consequences; an expedient but temporary solution.

1966 *New Scientist* 11 Aug. 310/2 The most recent 'quick-fix', suggests the committee, is desalting, about which it expresses concern 'lest too heavy a commitment to a single engineering solution may tend to exclude other alternatives.' **1978** *Time* 16 Oct. 43 At first, Schreiber called Dreyfus' proposal a gimmicky, vote-getting '*quick-fix'. **1993** *U.S. News & World Rep.* 11 Jan. 27/2 Rather than cheering, environmental hard-liners label these advances 'technological quick fixes', because they undermine efforts to get farmers to fight pests with crop rotation and other 'sustainable agriculture'.

Quorn, *n.* Add: **2.** [f. the name of *Quorn Specialities Ltd.* of Leicester.] A proprietary name for a type of textured vegetable protein made from an edible fungus and used as a meat substitute in cooking.

1987 *Financial Times* 7 Jan. 1. 11 Food novelties based on mycoprotein—now trade-named Quorn—should be in the shops during this year. **1989** *New Product News* 7 July 43/3 Crispy Chinese with Quorn and Spicy Indian with Quorn are healthy alternatives to meat. **1991** *Which?* Oct. 556/3 Tasters said the Quorn worked well and that the flaked almonds in the curry gave it a good texture.

R

R. Add: [II.] [2.] **RME**, rape methyl ester.
1991 *South* Aug. 58/2 Bio-diesel is made by mixing rape seed oil (ESO) with Methyl Alcohol to produce Methyl RSO. Glycerol is then added to produce Rape Methyl Ester (*RME). **1993** *New Scientist* 9 Oct. 22/1 Since mid-August, two boats fuelled by RME have been cruising on the Broads—a network of inland lakes in eastern England.

rai (raɪ), *n.* [a. Algerian F. *raï*, of uncertain origin; perh. f. the dial. Arab. expression *ha er-ray* or (*ya ray*) lit. 'here is the view', 'that's the thinking' (cf. literary Arab. *ra'y* opinion, view), which is frequently found in the songs.] A style of Algerian popular music, which combines Arabic and Algerian folk elements with western musical styles and whose lyrics often deal with themes (such as drinking or sexual permissiveness) considered taboo in Muslim society.
1986 *People Weekly* (U.S.) 24 Feb. 29/3 Called 'rai' (pronounced 'rye'), the sound is described as space-age Arabic folk music. Wonder will get an earful of rai when he performs at an Algerian youth festival in July. **1989** *Q* Dec. 121/3 Fadela's last Mango album, You Are Mine, was raw rai—with the Algerian singer, a beat box and instrumental lines made up largely, one suspects, of synthesized battery acid. **1992** *New Perspectives Q.* Spring 56/2 In its street form, *rai* operates in France to keep a community of former North African residents connected; in Algeria it operated for a time as a Berber nationalist medium against the Islamicizing, Arabizing currents.

ram, *n.*[4] Add: [2.] [b.] **ram-raid** *n.*, an instance of ram-raiding.
1987 *Evening Chron.* (Newcastle) 12 Nov. 2/7 Thieves drove through the shutters of a Tyneside warehouse and loaded up with television sets and video recorders. The *ram-raid took place last night. **1991** *Viz* Dec. 38/1 Tango alpha. Victor foxtrott (*sic*). We have a report of a ram raid in progress. **1992** *Independent* 17 Sept. 8/8 A cash-dispensing machine was recovered and five men arrested shortly after a ram raid on a branch of the Abbey National Building Society in Herne Bay, Kent. An earthmover was used to remove the machine. **1994** *Courier-Mail* (Brisbane) 24 Mar. 2/8 Police reported two ram-raids..in Brisbane last night and early this morning.
ram-raid *v. trans.*, to break into (esp. commercial premises) by means of ram-raiding.
1991 *Observer* 22 Sept. 13/5 There is even an electronic *koban* that connects the Japanese citizen, via video, to police headquarters. I fear, though, that if this was transplanted to Tyneside it would be either burnt down or ram-raided and stolen. **1992** *New Musical Express* 4 Apr. 18/1 The club doors are ram-raided and trashed by three reprobates in a stolen car, pissed off at being refused entry.
ram-raider, one who engages in ram-raiding.
1987 *Evening Chron.* (Newcastle) 3 Apr. 1/2 A gang of *ram-raiders smashed into two shops on Tyneside today. **1991** *Today* 12 Sept. 34/2 The Tyneside 'ram raider' killed during a police chase. **1994** *Bristol Jrnl.* 7 Jan. 1/1 Private homes are being targeted by ram raiders in the latest crimewave to hit parts of Northavon and Bristol.
ram-raiding, a form of smash-and-grab robbery in which premises are broken into by ramming a vehicle through a window or wall.

1991 *Independent* 1 May 18/1 *Ram-raiding—using cars as battering rams to break into shops—is the latest threat to stores in the North-east. **1994** *Guardian* 11 Jan. 1. 3/4 Police suspected this car might have been involved in ram-raiding and tried to stop it.

ram, *v.*[1] Add: [5.] **c.** *intr.* To crash or bump heavily *into.* orig. *U. S.*
1961 S. ELKIN in *Nugget* Oct. 26/1 All Deegan had to do was slide, fall away, but instead, he rammed into the catcher. Both fell heavily to the ground. **1972** R. ALLEN *Skinhead Escapes* 106 He slammed a fist into the 'Shed' boy's mouth, drew his revolver. The metal barrel slushed across another face, the muzzle rammed into a set of ivories. **1975** *U.S. News & World Rep.* 10 Mar. 28/3 The last time it was towed in, somebody rammed into it. **1983** R. NARAYAN *Tiger for Malgudi* 19 She..knocked me off my feet by ramming into me. **1985** R. SILVERBERG *Tom O'Bedlam* (1986) VIII. i. 279 They were just ramming helplessly into each other down there, the big vans going right up over some of the small cars. **1990** D. McFARLAND *Music Room* 53 An accident in which a young man, swerving to miss a cyclist in a crosswalk, rammed into a steel lamppost.

rape, *n.*[5] Add: [4.] **rape methyl ester**, a liquid fuel derived from rapeseed oil by the addition of methanol and glycerine and used as an alternative to diesel. Abbrev. *RME* s.v. *R II. 2.
1991 *South* Aug. 58/2 Bio-diesel is made by mixing rape seed oil (ESO) with Methyl Alcohol to produce Methyl RSO. Glycerol is then added to produce Rape Methyl Ester (RME)—known as MRE in Germany and diester in France. **1992** *Farmers Weekly* 14 Aug. 40/1 Within five years 600,000t of the new rape-based bio-fuel rape methyl ester (RME) will be produced on the Continent.

rat, *n.*[1] Add: [7.] **e.** **rat-arsed** *a. slang* [perh. related to sense 2 c above], drunk (cf. *RATTED *a.*[3]).
1984 P. BEALE *Partridge's Dict. Slang* (ed. 8) 961/1 *Rat-arsed, drunk, tipsy: teenagers': early 1980s. **1989** *Number One* 8 Nov. 18/2 It's just a great atmosphere at roadshows, everyone's in that holiday sort of mood—there's no trouble, nobody chucks anything, nobody's rat-arsed. **1991** *Rage* 13 Feb. (Sex Suppl.) 23/2 I've only got one big regret—I got rat-arsed and came round from a drunken stupor to find some revolting bloke's tongue down my throat. **1994** *Computer Weekly* 7 July 46/5 The only danger is of getting rat-arsed on the local brew.

ratted ('rætɪd), *a.*[3] *slang.* [f. RAT *n.*[1] + -ED[2]. Cf. *rat-arsed* s.v. *RAT *n.*[1] 7 e.] Drunk.
1983 *Times* 18 July 9/4, I have to be there at 9 am so I try not to get absolutely ratted (drunk). **1987** *Daily Tel.* 19 Dec. (Weekend Suppl.) p. ii/6 He zipped up his anorak and went out to get ratted with the rest of the ice hockey team. **1989** A. DAVIES *Getting Hurt* vi. 68, I..got mildly ratted at the bar.

rave, *n.*[3] Add: [2.] **d.** (*a*) A large, orig. often illicit party or event, with dancing to fast electronic popular music, and sometimes associated with the recreational use of drugs such as LSD and Ecstasy; (*b*) electronic dance music of the kind played at such events. Freq. *attrib.*, esp. in *rave music, scene.* Cf. *Acid House party* s.v. *ACID

HOUSE *n.* 2; *warehouse party* S.V. *WAREHOUSE *n.* 2.

1989 *Independent* 3 July 3/5 The most extraordinary scenes came after 100 police stopped Berkshire's mammoth party... Jeremy Taylor, one-time organiser of the Gatecrashers' Ball—a Sloanie teenage rave—was behind the party. **1989** *Face* Dec. 63/2 The current rave culture is, in many ways, the revenge of the suburbs... In the suburbs, the car is all... In a club culture where mobility is essential, the suburbs rule. **1991** *Sun* 13 June 26/1 If you want to dress for success on the rave scene you'll need a proper selection of pukka gear. **1991** *Daily Tel.* 4 Nov. 19/5 Now, the music is in the charts, there are licensed raves all over the place, and the punters know they can go and dance the night away in a place which is not a fire hazard. **1992** *Economist* 30 May 34/1 To the uneducated ear, rave music is a bone-jangling din, hurtling along at up to 200 beats a minute. **1993** *Crosswinds* (New Mexico) Jan.-Feb. 18/1 Sampling is.. the only truly new musical form of the Nineties, used in everything from Rap to Rave. **1993** *Gnosis* Winter 56/1 Two years ago, a new burst of recreational use revived interest in Ecstasy in the U.S. Nicknamed the 'acid house' or 'rave' scene, it appears to be a new youth movement both similar to and different from the counterculture of the '60s. **1995** *Guardian* 28 Feb. II. 15/3 For many youngsters, fun doesn't come any better than the raves and nightclubs where Ecstasy, amphetamines and other drugs complement the hypnotic music and incandescent lights.

raver, *n.* Add: **c.** One who attends a rave party (see *RAVE *n.*³ 2 d).

1991 *Sun* 13 June 21/2 Heat can't escape through the material and the raver comes out of the club feeling like a roast chicken. **1991** *New Musical Express* 31 Aug. 18/4 When you're at a rave there's 10,000 ravers going mental—you can't beat the energy. **1992** *Nose* XIII. 21/2 *Hallucinations* are frowned upon by ravers. LSD is used sparingly as a stimulant. More often, 'e'.. is the raver's drug of choice. **1993** *Gnosis* Winter 56/2 To make it a little bit harder for the police to raid, the place where the party is held is kept secret until the very last moment. Then it's up to the raver to find out where it is.

rightsize ('raɪtsaɪz), *v.* orig. and chiefly *U.S.* Also **right-size**. [f. RIGHT *adv.* + SIZE *v.*¹, after DOWN-SIZE *v.*] *trans.* To convert to an appropriate or optimum size; *spec.* (*euphem.*) to reduce the size of (an enterprise) by discharging employees. So **rightsizing** *vbl. n.*

1987 *Black Enterprise* Dec. 59/2 Roberts bristles when he hears the word downsizing; he dubs the process 'rightsizing'. And he plans to 'rightsize' a number of departments by offering white-collar employees salaried separation packages. **1990** *Business Week* 26 Feb. 63/2 He adds that 'we're right-sizing our organisation' by reexamining how work is done. Layoffs could result. **1991** *Daily Commercial News* (Sydney) 13 June 25/2 Australia has sought to rejig its schedules through the winter season in an effort to 'right-size' operations to demand. **1992** *Byte* Oct. 162/1 The current wave of what is variously referred to as reengineering, rightsizing, or downsizing has one immediate goal: to reduce the cost of doing business. **1993** *Computing* 3 June 18/1 No longer willing to take only the technology they are given, organisations across the world are beginning to rightsize systems to suit themselves.

road-kill ('rəʊdkɪl), *n.* N. Amer. colloq. Also **road kill, roadkill**. [f. ROAD *n.* + KILL *n.*¹] **a.** The killing of an animal by a vehicle on a road; also, an animal killed in this way.

1972 R. WRIGHT & R. WRIGHT *Cariboo Mileposts* 40 They [*sc.* magpies].. usually feed on carrion or road-kills. **1979** *Washington Post* 28 Dec. (Weekend section) 40/1 Road kills represent no danger to the deer population, which is larger than it ever has been before. *Ibid.* I've raised three kids and fed two wives on road-kills. **1987** C. HIAASEN *Double Whammy* (1988) iii. 34 'Road kill', Skink said, by way of explanation. 'You hungry, Miami?' **1993** *Virginian Pilot & Ledger Star* (Norfolk, Va.) 6 July D1/1 Tom Squier is out there on the highway every day, staring through the windshield of his Dodge Dakota pickup, looking for road kills. Perhaps a nice snake or frog. Or, if he's lucky, maybe a possum, squirrel or bird.

b. *transf.* and *fig.* A person or thing that is useless or moribund; 'dead meat'.

1992 *Time* 15 June 71/1 His kitchen-knife physique, sour face and a hairdo resembling a road-kill toupée. **1992** *Philadelphia Inquirer* 22 Aug. D1/6 Expected to be little more than road kill for opponents, ..fifth place Houston had managed a 9-14 record on the 28-day trip. **1993** *Esquire* Dec. 72/2 We all know any number of men who can cook a virtuoso.. dish or two, but outside of this they are strictly roadkills in the kitchen. **1994** *Denver Post* 2 Jan. H5/4 To avoid becoming roadkill on the digital highway, get a faster modem.

Hence 'road-killed *ppl. a.*

1979 *Washington Post* 28 Dec. (Weekend section) 40/4 He said he'll never pass up another road-killed deer: 'It's manna from heaven.' **1990** D. KLINE *Great Possessions* (1993) I. 9 Sometimes when feeding on a road-killed rabbit, they will not take flight when passed by a buggy. **1992** *Scope* Sept./Oct. 3/1 Wildlife Division biologists were surprised by a report of a road-killed marten near New Hartford.

Rollerblade ('rəʊləbleɪd), *n.* orig. *U. S.* Also as two words and with lower-case initial. [f. ROLLER *n.*¹ + BLADE *n.*, after ROLLER-SKATE *n.*] A proprietary name for a type of roller-skate with wheels set in one straight line beneath the boot, giving an appearance and action similar to that of an ice-skate.

1985 *Official Gaz.* (U.S. Patent Office) 8 Jan. TM 312/2 Roller Blade... For: Boots equipped with longitudinally aligned rollers used for skating and skiing... First use Mar. 1983; in commerce Mar. 1983. **1985** C. MIDDLEBROOK *Rollerblades Dryland Training for Ice Hockey* p. vii, Rollerblades are a dryland skate developed by Scott Olson, president of Ole's Innovative Sports of Minneapolis. **1989** *Omni* Sept. 16/1 Examples ranged from windsurfing and rollerblade skating to jogging and wallyball. **1991** *Boston* Apr. 66/1 One cruises on a bike, one coasts on roller blades, three ride skateboards. **1992** *Atlantic* Sept. 70/2 A college kid was skating across the four lanes of Mass. Ave. on Day-Glo-blue Rollerblades, wearing electric-camouflage harem pants.

Hence **'rollerblade** *v. intr.*, to roller-skate using skates of this type; **'rollerblader** *n.*, one who rollerblades; **'rollerblading** *vbl. n.*

1988 *Maclean's* (Olympics Issue) Feb. 112/1 A summer and fall of long-distance running and cycling workouts..; sessions of 'roller blading', in which skaters tackle hilly roads on modified roller skates. **1988** *Los Angeles Times* (San Diego County ed.) 21 July III. 9B/3 The hazards are limited to crossing just two streets, avoiding skateboarders, roller-bladers and cyclists. **1989** *USA Today* 25 July 3D/6 When Tuck is not dressing up, she roller blades (roller skates with one line of wheels) around New York's Central Park. **1990** *Egg* Aug. 85/2 Sinuous trails filled with bikers, joggers, .. speed-walkers, skateboarders,.. rollerbladers,.. et al. **1992** *Men's Health* Nov.-Dec. 90/3, I go mountain biking and Rollerblading and I ski-race.

S

S. Add: [4.] [a.] **SAD**, seasonal affective disorder (or depression).

1983 *Chicago Sun-Times* 21 Dec. 11/1 Because of symptoms of *SAD sufferers, scientists in the Mental Health Institute wondered if our ancestors hibernated. **1987** *Daily Tel.* 1 June 13/7 Whereas the winter depressives are helped by using bright artificial lights.., people with summer SAD may alleviate their symptoms by lowering their environmental temperature. **1990** *Health Guardian* Nov.-Dec. 4/1 SAD is caused by a biochemical imbalance in the hypothalamus — due to a lack of sunlight.

SCID *Path.*, severe combined immune deficiency.

1973 *Lancet* 16 June 1393/2 Three patients with both severe combined immunodeficiency (*S.C.I.D) and adenosine-deaminase (A.D.A.) deficiency have been reported. **1983** *Oxf. Textbk Med.* I. IX. 79 The prognosis in ADA deficiency SCID is very poor, death due to infection usually occurring in the first year of life. **1992** *Independent* 16 Jan. 2/1 The Cleveland girl suffered from a rare inherited defect, known as severe combined immune deficiency (SCID), which crippled her immune system.

satellite, *n*. Add: [13.] *satellite dish* (*DISH *n*. 4 b).

1978 *Washington Post* 3 May c8 Services that can be performed by improved television sets or by translators linked to *satellite dishes. **1985** *Investors Chron.* 8 Nov. 88/3 A guide to the equipment in question is the 18 foot satellite dish installed by BT in conjunction with American Telephone and Telegraph, linking Bedford with Dallas. **1989** *Japan Times* 15 May 17/5 Huge garden (over 100 sq. m.), satellite dish, garage, 138 sq.m.

scratch, *n*.[1] Add: [V.] [12.] [b.] **scratch card**, (*b*) a card used in a competition (freq. issued free as a consumer incentive), having a section coated in a waxy substance which may be scratched away to reveal whether a prize has been won.

1982 *U.S. News & World Rep.* 6 Dec. 12/3 In Alabama and Kentucky, Shell dealers offered instant giveaway games involving *scratch cards. **1993** *Independent* 12 May 17/7 He is proposing a form of telebingo involving scratch cards with winning numbers shown on screen during selected ad breaks.

seasonal, *a*. and *n*. Add: [A.] 4. Special collocation: **seasonal affective disorder**, a form of depression which tends to occur during the same season (usu. winter) every year and is characterized by loss of motivation, hypersomnia, and often a craving for foods rich in carbohydrates. Abbrev. *SAD* s.v. *S 4 a.

1983 *Chicago Sun-Times* 21 Dec. 11/1 The dark moods that come with shorter days of winter are called Seasonal Affective Disorder. **1986** *Sci. Amer.* Aug. 57A/1 Two-thirds of people who have a recently recognized syndrome, seasonal affective disorder (SAD), crave carbohydrates and gain weight when they are depressed. **1992** *Atlantic* Sept. 66/1 In the fall and winter Robert receives..two hours of light therapy daily to treat the seasonal affective disorder.

sense, *n*. Add: [29.] c. *attrib.* (quasi-*adj.*) *Biochem.* and *Genetics*. Designating or pertaining to a strand of DNA complementary to that which acts as a template for the synthesis of mRNA in a cell, and so essentially similar to mRNA in its base sequence; also, designating or pertaining to RNA (mRNA) produced by the transcription of antisense DNA.

Although this is the dominant use in the literature, the meanings of 'sense' and 'antisense' as defined are occasionally reversed: see quots. 1972, 1989, and quot. 1979 s.v. *ANTISENSE *a*.

1972 *Molecular & Gen. Genetics* CXVIII. 61 The codogenic or 'sense' DNA strand for various genes is conveniently identified by its ability to specifically hybridize with its complementary messenger RNA. **1988** P. W. KUCHEL et al. *Schaum's Outl. Theory & Probl. Biochem.* xvii. 493 Each strand of the duplex DNA would be functioning as both sense and antisense strands, but for two different RNA transcripts. **1989** *New Scientist* 28 Oct. 50/1 Only one strand of the double helix carries this information in a form that cells can use to make proteins — it is called the sense strand. **1990** *Nucleic Acids Res.* XVIII. 261/2 Using yeast codon usage data, a sense strand 64-fold degenerate 44-mer oligonucleotide was made. **1990** *Embo Jrnl.* IX. 3018/2 If the anti-sense RNA interacts with the sense RNA, a biomolecular reaction has to be postulated.

sente ('sɛnti), *n*. Pl. **lisente** (lɪ'sɛnti). [Sesotho.] Since 1980, a monetary unit of Lesotho, equal to one-hundredth of a loti; also, a coin of this value.

1980 *Statesman's Year-Bk. 1980-81* 787 The currency is the *Loti* (plural *Maloti*) divided into 100 *Lisente*. **1990** *Summary World Broadcasts: Middle East, Afr., Latin Amer.* (B.B.C.) A 3/2 The Lesotho government has announced that..the price of petrol will be increased by 32 lisente per litre.

severe, *a*. Add: [IV.] **severe combined immune deficiency** (also **severe combined immuno-deficiency**) *Path.*, a rare and often fatal congenital immune deficiency which is characterized by abnormally low levels of T lymphocytes and (in most cases) also of B lymphocytes. Abbrev. *SCID* s.v. *S 4 a.

1973 *Lancet* 16 June 1393/2 Three patients with both *severe combined immunodeficiency (S.C.I.D) and adenosine-deaminase (A.D.A.) deficiency have been reported. **1984** M. J. TAUSSIG *Processes in Path. & Microbiol.* (ed. 2) 78 The most extreme forms of primary immunodeficiency in children are (a) the X-linked infantile (Bruton-type) agammaglobulinaemia.., (b) thymic aplasia or Di George syndrome.., and (c) severe combined immunodeficiency, where both T and B systems are deficient due to the absence of stem cells in the bone marrow. **1992** *Independent* 16 Jan. 2/1 The Cleveland girl suffered from a rare inherited defect, known as severe combined immune deficiency (SCID), which crippled her immune system. Most patients with the condition die in infancy from overwhelming infection.

shadow, *n*. Add: [8.] e. = *work-shadow* s.v. *WORK *n*. IV. 34 d. (orig *U. S.*).

1973 H. F. WOLCOTT *Man in Principal's Office* i. 2 The principals whom I met volunteered a number of descriptive titles for my role, such as 'anthropologist in residence', 'assistant without portfolio', 'lap dog', and 'shadow'. Ultimately the last term became my nickname. *Ibid.* 3, I intended to pursue him as his 'shadow'; maintaining a constant written record of what

I observed in behavior and conversation; attending formal and informal meetings, [etc.]. **1985** (*title*) Shadows. Schoolgirls in Industry—helping women reach the top. (Dept. Trade & Industry). *Ibid.* 4 'I learned a great deal, not only about the daily work of a manager, but also the workings of her office..,' Shadow—Lucinda Dalziel. **1988** D. LODGE *Nice Work* I. iii. 54 A genuine, inward understanding of.. work is obtained by the shadow, which could not be obtained by a simple briefing or organized visit. **1989** *Daily Tel.* 6 June 17/7 All the 'shadows' I have had lose their preconceived notion that accountants are men in pinstriped suits lacking any sense of humour.

shadowing, *vbl. n.* Sense 8 in Dict. becomes 9. Add: **8.** = *work shadowing* s.v. *WORK *n.* 34 d. (orig. *U.S.*).

1976 E. ANDREWS *Exploring Arts & Humanities Careers in Community* 15 'Shadowing' is a term used to designate a brief out-of-school experience in which the student spends two to ten hours observing and talking with a selected practitioner. **1979** D. H. MELLOR *Community-Based Career Guidance Practices* 4 Activities include speakers, on-site interviews, and shadowing. **1983** A. A. HUCZYNSKI *Encycl. Managem. Devel. Methods* 181 Manager Shadowing is a less formal type of development than apprenticeship. Here there is no necessry requirement that the newcomer will take over the job of the person he is shadowing. **1986** *Daily Tel.* 29 Sept. 24/7 The value of shadowing is enormous. It breaks down the preconceptions and fear that the young have of business. **1992** *Times Educ. Suppl.* 31 Jan. 3/2 The cornerstone of the partnership now was the activities schools and firms were able to share, such as workplace visits, job shadowing and interviewing.

Shar-Pei (ʃɑːˈpeɪ), *n.* Also **Shar Pei**, **Sharpei**, and with lower-case initial. [ad. Chin. *shā pí*, lit. 'sand fur'.] A breed of compact, squarely built dogs of Chinese origin, with a characteristic loose, deeply wrinkled skin and a short, bristly coat of a cream, fawn, red, or black colour; a dog of this breed.

1976 *Dog Fancy* Oct. 19 (*title*) The Chinese Shar-Pei. *Ibid.* 19/3 The Shar-Pei is an amiable animal unless he is deliberately baited and provoked. **1978** E.T. LINN in D. Myrus *Dog Catalog* 78/2 There are some shar-peis who retain their many wrinkles into adulthood. **1987** *Women's Wear Daily* 25 Sept. 16/4 Claude Montana, who.. brought his dog,.. a Sharpei, there to summer as well. **1989** *Newsday* 23 May III. 11/3 Freud and Darwin are the best exemplars of the value of holding on to an idea with the concentrated tenacity of a Shar Pei gripping a bone. **1993** *Daily Tel.* 20 Jan. 13 Anne Quayle speaks out about the dangerous side of Shar Pei dogs.

single, *a.* Add: [III.] [17.] [a.] **single (European) market**, a free trade association allowing for increasing alignment of fiscal policy and unrestricted movement of goods, capital, etc., between the member states of the European Union (fully implemented from 1 Jan. 1993).

1966 *Bull. European Econ. Community* IV. 20 (*heading*) III. Internal Activities. Establishment of a *Single Market. **1979** *Dun's Rev.* Sept. 117/2 The EEC's prime mandate is to create a single European market, and companies in countries with lax liability laws have a cost advantage over rival members subject to stronger laws. **1987** *Financial Times* 24 Mar. 3/4 The development of the single European market, with the further opening of frontiers providing an important spur to economic growth. **1990** *Marketing* 17 May 1/4 In favour of a total ban are the state monopoly producers—Italy, France, Spain and Portugal. It is in their interests to block tobacco imports and protect their national products, against the spirit of the Single Market.

slam, *n.*[1] Add: [5.] **slam dancing** *vbl. n.* chiefly N. Amer., a form of dancing to rock music (orig.

at punk rock concerts) in which participants deliberately collide violently with one another (cf. *MOSH *v.*[2]); so **slam dance** *n.* & *v. intr.*, **slam dancer** *n.*

1981 *N.Y. Times* 8 July C21/5 The Los Angeles punks.. may get out of hand occasionally, but their widely condemned '*slam dancing', which involves careering into one another like bowling balls plowing into sets of pins, is generally confined to a small area. **1981** *Washington Post* 17 July B7/2 (*heading*) The sounds and the *slamdance. **1981** *Ibid.* 10 Nov. D2/2 She recalls ducking glasses and bottles and toppling to the floor, camera and all when *slam dancers broke through her protective ring of punk bouncers. **1982** *New Yorker* 22 Feb. 31/3 Don't let him dance. He likes to *slam-dance. Don't Adam. You'll knock over a candle and there'll be a fire. **1989** C. HIAASEN *Skin Tight* (1990) xii. 133 As the band was playing a song called *Suck Till You're Sore*, a local skinhead gang went into a slam-dancing frenzy, and fights broke out all over the place. **1991** J. O'CONNOR *Cowboys & Indians* 134 The DJ played some awful glam number from the mid-seventies and Eddie tried to slam dance. **1992** *Option* July-Aug. 31/4 Now that Nirvana has brought slam-dancing to MTV, the mosh pit is getting a lot of attention. **1992** *N.Y. Times* 19 Jan. II. 29/5 Rock bands playing clubs can count on stage-divers and slam-dancers—now part of virtually any loud and uptempo scene. **1994** *Globe & Mail* Toronto 14 June A3/1 The clientele.. includes a disproportionate number of green-Mohawk-coiffed, body-pierced, leather-clad slam dancers.

slam, *v.*[1] Add: **7.** = *slam dance* s.v. *SLAM *n.*[1] 5. Chiefly as *vbl. n.* (see below). *N. Amer. colloq.*

1990 D. GAINES *Teenage Wasteland* viii. 200 For most girls, it was virtually impossible to see a band at a hardcore show because the front of the stage was dominated, always, by muscular, lean, sweaty boys stage-diving and slamming around. **1993** *Screamer* Nov. 5/2, I like to stand in front of the stage where the maniacs slam and dive.

Hence **slamming** *vbl. n.* (examples in sense *7 of the vb.).

1983 *People* 28 Mar. 97/1 While mainly a showcase for adolescent male aggression, the slamming ritual depends on a sense of mutual support from the participants. **1992** *Chicago* Jan. 100/3 The first floor is for dancing and slamming and conversation.. while upstairs thrash bands go to the limit.

slammer, *n.* Add: **4.** = *slam dancer* s.v. *SLAM *n.*[1] 5.

1983 *People* 28 Mar. 96/2 While the slammers tend to be teenage leather boys, the audience is more mixed, with a fair number of suburban kids represented. **1990** D. GAINES *Teenage Wasteland* viii. 200 The audience was half headbanger and half slammer. **1992** *Option* July-Aug. 31/4 The boorish Stuart Maconie of *New Musical Express* responded more strongly to slammers and stagedivers.

snake-bite ('sneɪkbaɪt), *n.* (Sense 1: formerly at SNAKE *n.* 9 a in Dict.) Also without hyphen and as one word. [f. SNAKE *n.* + BITE *n.*] **1.** A bite given by a snake.

1839 *Penny Cycl.* XIII. 161/1 It is also one of their remedies for snake-bites, but is no doubt inefficacious. **1880** *Cassell's Nat. Hist.* IV. iv. 323 The population being dense, it is reasonable to expect that great mortality would occur from Snake bites every year. **1894** A. ROBERTSON *Nuggets* 73 She knows as much about snake-bite as any doctor. **1944** *Living off Land* vi. 125 In looking after a snake bite patient.., remember the three 'dont's'. **1965** R. & D. MORRIS *Men & Snakes* iv. 101 The commonest symptoms are fright and fear of death. Convincing reassurance is vital at all stages. Death from snake-bite is rare. **1989** V. SINGH *Jaya Ganga* 25, I don't mind, sonny, if you die of a snake-bite, but I'd hate it if you died of the fear of a snake-bite.

2. a. Strong alcoholic drink, *esp.* whisky of inferior quality. *U. S. slang.*

1928 *Daily Express* 12 Dec. 10/5 It is not really bad wine...It is an acquired taste, but it is better than the 'snake-bite' contraband whisky or the synthetic gin. **1979** A. BOYLE *Climate of Treason* xi. 434 Only the bottle—'snake-bite' was his word for it—could ease the mysterious pain by drowning it. **1981** *Time* 2 Feb. 78/2 For down-the-hatch topers, Chicago's Rodeo offers a selection of booze that includes Redeye whisky, Rotgut Scotch, Panther gin and Snakebite vodka.

b. A mixed drink of cider and lager. *Brit. colloq.*

1983 *New Society* 2 June 333/1 £13.65 a week to pay for..clothes, 'snake bites' (cider and lager), 'tabs' (cigarettes). **1985** L. LOCHHEAD *True Confessions* 103 Hogmanay saw Frank and me delirious On five pernod and blackcurrants plus four cans Of special plus a snakebite We didny know how to make right. **1989** *Independent* 22 Dec. 15/2 Lads now greying at the temples swapped stories of the best Quo gigs...It was definitely '73 in Malvern, when they drank miles too much snake bite. **1993** *New Scientist* 6 Feb. 21/2 Solvent and substance sniffing first came to prominence in Britain..in the late 1970s, along with 'snakebite'.

social, *a.* and *n.* Add: [A.] [12.] **social chapter**, a social charter forming part of the Maastricht Treaty (see *MAASTRICHT n.*).

1991 *Independent* 5 Dec. 12/6 The treaty's *social chapter is probably the single most difficult area. Because it deals with areas of everyday life that everyone can relate to it is politically high-profile. **1992** *Economist* 28 Mar. 9/2 One example is the social charter (now called the social chapter), which will lay down EC-wide rules on working hours, health and safety at work, maternity leave and so on. **1993** *Times* 1 June 17/1 Mr Major..promised that he would protect British industry from excessive labour market regulation with his famous opt-out from the social chapter.

social charter, a document dealing with social policy, esp. workers' rights and welfare; *spec.* that signed in December 1989 by eleven European Union member states, and later forming the basis of the social chapter of the Maastricht Treaty.

1983 *Washington Post* 18 Aug. B7/1 Barry said the '*social charter' forged during King's 1963 march 'is in serious trouble'. **1989** *Independent* 31 Oct. 1/4 Britain yesterday lost all hope of recruiting last-minute allies in its fight against the European Community's proposed Social Charter after labour ministers voted by 11 to one to forward a final draft for adoption at the December EC summit in Strasbourg. **1991** *Economist* 23 Nov. 124/1 The 11 governments which signed the social charter approve of such worker-employer consultation. The British government, on the other hand, considers it the kind of corporatist claptrap which nearly sank the British economy in the 1960s and 1970s. **1992** *Globe & Mail* (Toronto) 1 Feb. A1/1 Two of Canada's business leaders became unexpected supporters yesterday of a 'social charter' in a rewritten Constitution.

Southern ('sʌðən), *n.*[2] *Biochem.* [The name of Edwin M. *Southern* (b.1938), British biochemist.] Used *attrib.* (chiefly in *Southern blot, blotting*: see *BLOT n.*[1] 1 f, *BLOTTING vbl. n.* 4) with reference to a technique for the identification of specific nucleotide sequences in DNA, in which fragments separated on a gel are transferred directly to a second medium on which assay by hybridization, etc., may be carried out.

1979 *Proc. Nat. Acad. Sci.* LXXVI. 860 (*caption*) Localization of the V and C regions in Ch603a6 by hybridization to Southern blots. *Ibid.* 858/2 Filter hybridizations by the Southern blot procedure. **1979** *Cell* XVI. 797/1 Visualization of such higher order bands was achieved by the use of the Southern blotting

technique. **1981** *Anal. Biochem.* CXVI. 237/1 In the last 5 years, the Southern blot technique..has become one of the most common techniques in molecular biology. **1984** L. W. BROWDER *Developmental Biol.* (ed. 2) iii. 100 Southern blotting is used when one needs to detect specific DNA fragments from a large, heterogeneous mixture of fragments, as, for example, following restriction enzyme treatment of DNA. **1990** *Jrnl. Exper. Bot.* XLI. 1047/2 The presence of the NPTII gene in this tissue was confirmed by Southern hybridization of the product. **1991** *Nature* 9 May 119/2 (*caption*) No band corresponding to *Zfy-1* was seen, demonstrating the lack of a Y chromosome; this result was confirmed by Southern blotting using Y-chromosome probes.

spell-check ('spɛltʃɛk), *v.* and *n. Computing.* [f. SPELL *v.*[2] + CHECK *int.* and *n.*[1]] **A.** *v. trans.* To check the spelling of (a document, etc.) using a program which compares the words in a text file with a stored list of acceptable spellings. Occas. *absol.* or *intr.*

1983 *Mod. Office Technol.* Feb. 120/3 A spelling verification program allows operators to spell-check documents before giving them back to their managers for final proofreading. **1991** *Home Office Computing* June 34/2 Write at your natural level of spelling skill, and then spellcheck afterward. **1991** *New Yorker* 25 Nov. 47/1 A good time tonight would be while the computer's spell-checking my homework. **1994** *Daily Tel.* 19 Dec. 28/6 When I spell-checked a page in DOS, I simply pressed the Alt and F2 keys and then the number 2.

B. *n.* A check of the spelling of words in a text file carried out automatically; a program or facility for doing this. Cf. *spelling checker* s.v. *SPELLING vbl. n.*[2] 3.

1983 *Datamation* May 182/3 The unit's software includes..Lexisoft Spellbinder, Mailmerger, and Spell-check. **1990** *Lit. & Linguistic Computing* V. 43/2 Spell-check, with cascaded dictionaries on-line (including proper names). **1992** *Tucson Weekly* 1 Jan. 2/3, I always wondered if he had a special spell check on his word processor for dirty words.

So **spell checker** *n.* = *spelling checker* s.v. *SPELLING vbl. n.*[2] 3; **spell-checking** *vbl. n.*

1983 *Washington Post* 13 June C9/3, I got to try a spell-checking program..that cost $75. **1983** *Graphic Arts Monthly* Sept. 77/1 The composition and editing package includes..a spell checker. **1989** *Word Ways* XXII. 67 Spelling anxiety is no affliction for writers who use..word processing programs that provide so-called spell checking. **1990** *Managem. Computing* Nov. 102/3 Running the spellchecker scrutinises the whole presentation, not just the currently-selected slide.

spoiler, *n.* Add: [2.] **e.** *Journalism.* A news story or other newspaper item published to spoil the impact of and divert attention from a related item published elsewhere. Also used *transf.* in other news media, or to denote an event which is intended to generate news coverage with a similarly distracting effect.

1985 *Guardian* 20 May 7/8 What we have there is a classic Fleet Street spoiling operation aimed at sinking the Bogdanovitch story...The spoiler is designed to neutralise the enemy's razzmatazz by running the same story, preferably bigger, better and sooner. **1988** *Sunday Times* 17 Apr. C6/4 Not to be outdone, the Mail has run a daily 'spoiler', unprecedented in its length, matching each four-page pull-out in Today with its own centre-page spreads: 'Michael Jackson, Uncensored'. **1989** *Daily Tel.* 30 Dec. (Weekend Suppl.) p. v/1 The speech made the front pages of the Daily Mail, The Times and The Daily Telegraph...The Independent..treated it as a spoiler for Paddy Ashdown's 'green' speech to his party conference a couple of days later.

spongiform, *a*. Add: **3.** Special collocation: **spongiform encephalopathy** *Path.*, any of various degenerative diseases of the central nervous system characterized by histological change in brain tissue, which assumes a sponge-like appearance due to the degeneration and loss of neurones, and the appearance of vacuoles; *bovine spongiform encephalopathy* (see **BOVINE a.* 3).

1960 *Brain* LXXXIII. 546 Some authors regard this condition now under review as a variant of the Creutzfeldt-Jakob disease but we consider that it is fundamentally different and propose now to refer to it as subacute *spongiform encephalopathy or spongiform cerebral atrophy as suggested by Jacob *et al.* (1958). **1979** M. J. TAUSSIG *Processes in Path. & Microbiol.* iii. 370 There are four examples of the chronic degenerative brain disease known as spongiform encephalopathy, two in man (kuru and Creutzfeldt-Jakob disease) and two in animals (scrapie and transmissable mink encephalopathy). **1991** *N.Y. Times* 8 Oct. C12/5 In Britain,..an epidemic of spongiform encephalopathy in cows, known as mad cow disease, has held the nation in thrall for the past five years.

squeegee, *n*. Sense 3 in *Dict.* becomes 4. Add: **3.** A (young) person with a squeegee who cleans the windscreen of a car stopped in traffic and solicits payment from the driver. Orig. and freq. *attrib.* in *squeegee bandit, kid, thug*, etc.

1985 *Washington Post* 28 Apr. B1/1 When rush-hour traffic backs up along the downtown streets here, the ‘*squeegee kids’ are in business. **1986** J. A. FRIEDMAN *Cops & Skells* in *Tales of Times Square* (1993) 137 The squeegee bandits at 42nd and Ninth take a moment's break from their particular contribution to a cleaner New York when the patrol passes. **1991** *Evening Standard* 13 May 7/2 ‘Squeegees’, the growing urban tribe who molest waiting motorists at busy road junctions. **1992** *Crime Beat* Jan. 6/3 The squeegee thugs..have become a scourge of inner-city motorists...The squeegees wait at busy intersections. When cars stop for a red light, the young men carrying long-handled rubber squeegees approach each car in line offering to clean the windshield. **1993** H. STERN *Private Parts* xi. 304 We showed her as a carnival barker, a Hare Krishna, a nun, and a squeegee woman washing car windshields. **1994** *Rolling Stone* 19 May 34/3 She let out a voice so clear one could have made a windshield out of it that would put the squeegeemen out of work for good.

stage, *n*. Add: [IV.] [14.] **stage-diving** *vbl. n.* orig. *U.S.*, the practice (esp. among audience members) of jumping from the stage at a rock concert, etc., to be caught and carried aloft by the crowd below; so as *ppl. a.*; also **stage-dive** *v. intr.*; **stage-diver** *n.*

1984 *Washington Post* 12 Nov. C6/4 Obscured by a cascade of *stage-diving fans, Marginal Man and Government Issue played traditional D.C. hard-core featuring adolescent social comment atop a breathtakingly fast guitar attack. **1985** *Los Angeles Times* 29 June V. 5/3 The spell was soon interrupted when a *stage-diver snatched the radio transmitter from Marr's guitar and returned to the audience, followed closely by Marr and a squad of security men. **1987** *Sounds* 1 Aug. 3/1 Onslaught, the Bristol thrash band, are taking steps to prevent their fans injuring themselves by *stage diving at their gigs. *Ibid.* 3/2 Stage diving isn't violence, it's enthusiasm. **1992** *N.Y. Times* 19 Jan. II. 29/5 Rock bands playing clubs can count on stage-divers and slam-dancers—now part of virtually any loud and uptempo scene. **1993** *New Musical Express* 17 Apr. 26/2 The girls all pogo. There's no crushing, no stage-diving. No-one's hurt. **1994** *Rolling Stone* 16 June 50/3 Midway through Tad's set, a crew member throws open the door of Soundgarden's dressing room and excitedly blurts, 'Tad just stage-dived!'

stalker, *n*. Add: [3.] **b.** A person who pursues another, esp. as part of an investigation or with criminal intent; *spec.* one who follows or harasses someone (often a public figure) with whom he or she has become obsessed.

1947 A. RANSOME *Great Northern?* v. 72 ‘We must just go on, pretending we don't know we're being stalked...’ ‘And then the stalker will get a bit careless and let himself be seen,’ said Roger. **1971** (*film title*) The night stalker. **1982** T. HILLERMAN *Dark Wind* viii. 46 The watcher would have to make a decision: to follow or not. However he made it, Chee would be able to reverse the roles. He'd become the stalker. **1988** *Newsday* (Nassau ed.) 14 Jan. II. 17/1 The worst place to look for insight into a celebrity stalker..is the celebrity stalker himself. **1993** *Guardian* 26 June I. 25/6 The former Wimbledon star once found a stalker who had been living undetected in her wardrobe for three days. **1996** *Independent* 6 Jan. 17/6 For the quarry of a determined stalker, there is no hiding place.

stonker (ˈstɒŋkə(r)), *n. slang.* [Perh. f. STONK *n.* + -ER⁶.] Something which is very large or impressive of its kind; a ‘whopper’.

The narrower sense recorded in quot. 1987 is otherwise unrecorded.

1987 P. YATES *Sex with P. Yates* v. 66 When a man gets very excited, he gets an erection, a.k.a. a hard-on, stonker, etc. **1989** *Guardian* 10 Aug. 15/4 In fact he was driving well and at the 15th, where you are required to let out the braces a bit, produced his No. 1 stonker. **1990** *Sounds* 10 Nov. 43/3 Some might call this album preposterous (several did at the time). But it's a stonker, kicking off with the memorably camp spoken intro ‘Future Legend’. **1994** *i-D* Oct. 113/1 Starts off as a fairly standard X-Press 2 New York rip-off, until half-way through when the mood changes and it becomes an absolute stonker.

stonking (ˈstɒŋkɪŋ), *ppl. a.* and *adv. colloq.* [f. *stonk* v. s.v. STONK *n.* + -ING².] **A.** *adj.* Excellent, amazing; considerable, powerful. **B.** *adv.* Qualifying an *adj.*: extremely, very. Cf. THUNDERING *ppl. a.* (*adv.*).

1980 G. RICHARDS *Red Kill* viii. 66 ‘Here you are, sir,’ said the Australian girl...‘Looks pretty stonking to me,’ she added and Fenner did not know whether this was praise or condemnation. **1990** *Sounds* 10 Nov. 12/2 Snogging tackle for stonking wet smackers, warm and reassuring like a comfy settee. **1991** *Rage* 13 Feb. 43/2 Last year..the gals..decided to hook up for a special concert..and had such a stonkin' good time they decided to reunite for a tour. **1993** *What Hi-Fi?* Oct. 61/3 The Kenwood receiver is..stonking value for anyone wanting to take their first steps into home cinema.

strange, *a.* (*adv.* and *n.*) Senses 10 d, e in *Dict.* become 10 e, f. Add: [III.] **17.** Special collocation: **strange attractor** *Math.*, an attractor that is a fractal set, representing a situation in which the ultimate behaviour of a dynamic system is chaotic.

1971 RUELLE & TAKENS in *Communications Math. Physics* XX. 170 Going back to the vector field X, we have thus a ‘*strange’ attractor which is locally the product of a Cantor set and a piece of two-dimensional manifold. **1987** *Nature* 23 Apr. 753/2 Self-determination may well be compatible with unpredictability and even with randomness, provided that the motions are unstable and possess what are, in modern chaos theory, called strange attractors. **1988** I. PETERSON *Math. Tourist* vi. 146 Under certain conditions, however, nonlinear differential equations generate trajectories in phase space that form peculiar shapes, having none of the regularity associated with the previous examples of attractors. Such objects are called chaotic, or strange, attractors. **1991** *Omni* Feb. 24/4 Physicists..can reduce the turbulence of airflow over a helicopter blade to mathematical values that charted geometrically, settle into a..pattern..called a strange attractor.

stuffer, *n.* Add: **4.** A person who smuggles drugs through Customs by concealment in a bodily passage such as the rectum or vagina. Cf. *SWALLOWER *n.* 1 c. *colloq.*
1983 *Listener* 28 July 3/3 The customs teams delicately refer to such smugglers as 'the swallowers and stuffers'. **1986** *Sunday Times* 26 Oct. 3/2 Investigators at Heathrow Airport have discovered more than 100 Nigerians..attempting to smuggle heroin packed inside contraceptive sheaths, which are swallowed or inserted in anal and vaginal passages. They are known..as 'stuffers and swallowers'. **1992** *Independent* 29 Sept. 13/3 'Stuffers', as opposed to 'swallowers', will use any orifice available.

super-, *prefix.* Add: **[II.] [6.] [c.] supermodel**, a highly successful and internationally famous fashion model.
1977 *Time* 25 July 45/2 *Supermodel Margaux Hemingway dreamed up the idea of posing in high fashion in Jimmy's home town to make people think of plain old Plains as a fashion capital. **1987** *Telegraph* (Brisbane) 3 July 14/4 Supermodel Elle has slipped back home to Sydney for a secret working visit. **1992** *Sun* 16 Sept. 5/5 Supermodel Claudia Schiffer has ditched her boyfriend to wed Prince Albert of Monaco, it was claimed last night.

swallower, *n.* Add: **[1.] c.** A person who smuggles drugs through Customs by swallowing them sealed in a bag which can subsequently be excreted and recovered. Cf. *STUFFER *n.* 4. *colloq.*
1983 *Listener* 28 July 3/3 The customs teams delicately refer to such smugglers as 'the swallowers and stuffers'. **1988** *Independent* 8 Apr. 3/6 Body packers, mules, stuffers and swallowers are becoming more sophisticated at smuggling drugs. **1992** *N.Y. Times* 12 July v. 3/2 Everyone at Kennedy was always on the alert for drug couriers, including 'swallowers'.

swingbeat ('swɪŋbiːt), *n.* Also swing-beat. [f. SWING *n.*² 10 b + BEAT *n.*¹] A form of dance music combining elements of rhythm and blues, soul, hip-hop, and rap music.
1988 *Jocks* Feb. 34/3 Promising new releases..are expected to include the upcoming Rooftop rap compilation entitled 'Rooftop Swings'...The LP includes in addition to the multi-performer swing-beat title track, such artists as Ron Cool. **1989** *Observer* 24

Sept. 37/4 It is the uniform worn by followers of black club music called hip-hop, house, garage or swingbeat. **1990** *Record Mirror* 3 Feb. 33 You could probably count the number of *really* good swingbeat tracks (or New Jack Swing as Americans prefer to call it) on the fingers of one hand..though it seems that British dance music fans have given this new musical cross between hip hop and soul a fairly cool reception. **1993** *Q* Jan. 69/3 Swingbeat maestro Teddy Riley sets up a barrage of rasping drums and skimpy synths, against which the self-styled King of Pop was free to come on all weird and alluring.

swipe, *n.*² Add: **[II.] 7.** An electronic device for reading information magnetically encoded on a credit card, identity card, etc., usu. incorporating a slot through which the card is passed. Chiefly *attrib.*, esp. in **swipe card**, a card for use in such a device. Cf. *SWIPE *v.* 5.
1983 *Amer. Banker* 15 Mar. 17/1 A direct debit system that links a 'swipe' card reader and PIN (personal identification number) pad to an electronic cash register. **1986** *Ibid.* 29 Oct. 7/4 Nixdorf Computer Ltd., Hounslow, England, has announced a new identification unit and swipe card reader for users of its 8812-based retail computer systems. **1990** *Observer* 22 Apr. 35/6 An electronic swipe automatically clears the transaction. **1991** *Flight Internat.* 9 Oct. 28/1 The advent of seatback screens, already being tested by several airlines, will lead to the provision of telephone and fax services with interactive computer screens being used to sell merchandise through credit-card 'swipe' technology. **1992** *Gazette* (Imperial College) June 3/2 The Mechanical Engineering building will only be open to those with the appropriate 'swipe card'.

swipe, *v.* Add: **5.** *trans.* To pass (a credit card, identity card, etc.) through an electronic device in order to read and process data magnetically encoded on it. Cf. *SWIPE *n.*² 7, *WIPE *v.* 1 e.
1986 *Chain Store Age* Jan. 92/2 When a cashier accepts payments by a VISA credit card, for example, he presses the VISA button on the CAT and swipes the card through the automatic card reader. **1989** *Austral. Transport & Distribution Managem.* Dec. 16/2 To order a courier, the terminal operator 'swipes' a special company plastic card through a reader in the terminal which then automatically dials the computer centre. **1991** *Offshore Engineer* Sept. (Norway Offshore Suppl.) 18/2 Platform personnel do not need to take any action—such as swiping cards through readers—in order to be logged by the system. **1993** *Options* Aug. 86/1 Your fitness is assessed and the results transferred by computer to a key card. You then swipe this through the weight machines and they are automatically pre-set for you.

T

techno ('tɛknəʊ), *n.* and *a*[1]. [Absol. use of *TECHNO- 2.] **A.** *n.* A type of popular music characterized by the use of synthesized sounds and having a fast, insistent dance beat. **B.** *attrib.* or as *adj.* Of, pertaining to, or characteristic of this music.

1988 *Q* Oct. 65/2 In 1988 the soulful flavour of 'deep house' remains the closest to early Chicago house, 'techno' is the futuristic, synthesizer-based sound of Detroit..and now acid house is the latest and most fantastic edifice. **1988** *New Musical Express* 24 Dec. 71 The techno cabaret is completed by the barbaric electronics of Martin Rev. **1990** *Music Technol.* Apr. 76/1 *Techno II* focusses on the new generation of Detroit techno musicians who have been inspired by the music of Atkins, May and Saunderson. **1992** *Daily Tel.* 20 Mar. 13/7 There is niche marketing in music too — clubs which draw a rigorous distinction between house, acid-house, techno, rare-groove, swingbeat and so on... The predominant sound has been house and techno music, moving at a frantic 130 beats per minute. **1993** *Utne Reader* Jan.-Feb. 125/1 Techno dance beats hard enough to punch holes in your chest, highlighted by some of the most inventive sampling you've ever heard. **1996** *Face* Sept. 223/1 While England has enjoyed a long affair with commercial handbag house, it is a particularly tinny techno, driven by relentlessly frenetic kick drums and helium vocals..that has been ubiquitous north of the border.

techno ('tɛknəʊ), *a.*[2] [Abbrev. of TECHNO-LOGICAL *a.*] Of, pertaining to, or characterized by technology; technologically advanced.

1989 *Sound Choice* Autumn 12/2 They don't have to worry about paying out of pocket for equipment and supplies in line with the latest techno trends. **1990** J. GRIBBIN *Hothouse Earth* x. 243 The other bright idea of the techno fans [is] that of taking carbon dioxide out of the factory and power station chimneys and getting rid of it underground or in the sea. **1992** *Village Voice* (N.Y.) 7 Apr. 48/1 He drives a Humvee, one of those low-riding Desert Storm jeeps that look so mean and techno. **1992** *N.Y. Times* 19 July VIII. 3/1 The suddenly trendy game [*sc.* pro football] was fast, exciting, in tune with the techno times.

techno-, *comb. form.* Add: **2.** Used in comb. with the names of styles of popular music (as *techno-pop*, *-rock*, *-soul*, etc.) to designate variations of these styles characterized by the use of synthesized sounds and an insistent dance beat. Also in other combs., with more general allusion to this style. See also *TECHNO *n.* and *a.*[1]

[**1977** *Rolling Stone* 21 Apr. 88/3 Such technosheen music requires a detached master to hold the reins.] **1980** *N.Y. Times* 11 July C14/4 On her new 'Come Upstairs' album, Miss Simon extends her musical idiom as far as modified techno-pop. **1983** T. HIBBERT *Rockspeak!* 156 Techno-rock groups amass staggering amounts of expensive electronic devices and complex equipment with which to exhibit their skills. **1983** *People Weekly* (U.S.) 7 Nov. 30/3 Depeche Mode is a techno-pop quartet (three synthesizer players and one vocalist) that started out in Basildon, Essex. **1989** *Sound Choice* Autumn 55/3 The style represented includes pop, techno-rock, industrial, free improvisation, and even more obscure styles. **1990** *Atlantic* Jan. 97/1 The slick techno-funk he [*sc.* Miles Davis] has been recording since *The Man With the Horn*, in 1981. **1991** *Trouser Press Record Guide* (ed.

3) 1 Setting his own Ferry/Bowiesque vocals..mostly to a supple techno-soul disco pulse. **1991** *Source* Dec. 36/1 With dry, pseudo, techno-house cold-flooding the systems. **1992** *I-D* July 62/4 Brooklyn techno-meister Lenny D is enthusing about his new label, Industrial Strength.

tele-, *comb. form.* Add: [**1.**] **'telecottage** [tr. Sw. *telestuga*, f. *stuga* cottage], a room or building, esp. in a rural area, containing computers and telecommunications equipment for use by members of the local community.

1989 *InfoWorld* 27 Mar. 41/3 *Telecottages have been set up in 25 Scandinavian cities, offering computer, telex, and fax services to local companies and residents. 'But another service they offer is language translation, and this is where the Telecottages act as a virtual company,' Adler said. **1989** *Times* 7 Dec. 37/2 The first British telecottage, to be officially opened today week, has been set up in a school at Warslow, Staffordshire. **1993** *Oxford Times* 10 Sept. 2/2 Stonesfield Community Trust has won permission from West Oxfordshire planners for a post office, workshop and telecottage in a former glove factory.

tele'cottaging *n.*, working by means of a telecottage.

1991 *Oxf. Dict. New Words* 285 From Scandinavia in the second half of the decade came the concept of the telecottage... Working from one of these is known as *telecottaging. **1993** *Irish Times* 8 Apr. (Special ed.) 5/6 Telecottaging. Rural enterprise centres where telecommunications would eliminate the problems of peripherality.

teledil'donics *n. pl.* (usu. const. as *sing.*) [f. DILDO *n.*[1] + *-onics*, after *electronics*], the proposed use of virtual reality to mediate sexual interaction between computer users operating in different places.

1990 *Washington Times* 20 Dec. E2/2 So pervasive is the idea of sexual escapades in VR that there's even a name for it — *teledildonics. **1991** *Independent on Sunday* 9 June 23/5 'Teledildonics', new as it is, has already caused a few ripples. You will certainly, in the near future, be able to have simulated sex with a graphically enhanced partner of your choice.

telepresence ('tɛlɪprɛzəns), *n.* [f. TELE- 1 + PRESENCE *n.*] The use of remote control and the feedback of sensory information to produce the impression of being at another location; a sensation of being elsewhere created in this way. Cf. *virtual reality* s.v. *VIRTUAL *a.* 4 g.

1980 *Omni* June 48/1 With telepresences one can as easily work from a thousand miles away as from a few feet. *Ibid.* 48/2 We can employ telepresence in any environment alien to humans. **1982** D. L. AKIN et al. in *Rep. Space Syst. Lab., Mass. Inst. Technol. Lab.* (Mass. Inst. Technol.) *Rep.* No. 18. 1 The following definition of telepresence has been developed by the study group. At the worksite, the manipulators have the dexterity to allow the operator to perform normal human functions. At the control station, the operator recieves [*sic*] sensory feedback to provide a feeling of actual presence at the worksite. **1985** *N.Y. Times* 10 Sept. A1/4 It's the beginning of telepresence, of being able to project your spirit to the bottom, your eyes, your mind, and being able to leave your body behind. **1991** *New Scientist* 23 Mar. 55/4 In telepresence systems, the more real the scene relayed to the remote operator, the more accurately — and so more safely — will they perform.

Tempranillo (tɛmprə'nɪl(j)əu), *n.* Also
Tempranilla. [a. Sp. *Tempranillo*, dim. of
temprano early: see TEMPORANEOUS *a.*
The grape is probably so-named because of its
tendency to ripen early.]
   a. A Spanish variety of black grape, used esp.
in making Rioja. **b.** Red Rioja wine made from
such grapes.
   1896 *Rep. Viticultural Wk.* I. 302 *Palomino...*
Synonyms: Listan; Temprano; Tempranilla; Golden
Chasselas (California). **1962** A. J. WINKLER *Gen.
Viticulture* iii. 49 The Rioja region..produces mostly
red wine—Rioja—made principally from Cabernet
Sauvignon, Grenache, Tempranillo, and Mazuela
grapes. **1981** *N.Y. Times* 13 May c18/3 Most Rioja
reds display the oaky flavor of the American barrel in
which they are aged and of the grapes used to make
them—often the tempranillo, but sometimes with
portions of garnacho, graciano or mazuelo blended
in. **1989** M. KRAMER *Making Sense of Wine* ii. 35 It
is possible to taste of Tempranillo wines that display a
wondrous freshness.

teraflop ('tɛrəflɒp), *n. Computing.* [f. TERA-
after *GIGAFLOP *n.*, *MEGAFLOP *n.*] A unit
of computing speed equal to 1000 gigaflops.
   1984 *Electronics Week* 26 Nov. 21/1 We could easily
make use of machines sustaining speeds of one teraflops
(1 trillion floating-point operations per second). **1986**
Computerworld 22 Dec. 40/4 There's no reason why you
can't have highly parallel processors in the hundreds of
GFLOPS or even a teraflop (trillion) range in use by
the end of this decade. **1992** *Computer Weekly* 30 July
10/1 Teraflop performance is needed to tackle the so-
called grand challenge problems such as global
environmental modelling.

terraforming ('tɛrəfɔːmɪŋ), *vbl. n.* Chiefly
Science Fiction. [f. TERRA *n.* 2 + FORMING
vbl. n.] The process of transforming a planet
into one sufficiently similar to the earth to
support terrestrial life.
   1949 'W. STEWART' in *Astounding Sci. Fiction* Feb.
15/1 I've got the Martian industrial trust interested
in an atomic furnace to make synthetic terraforming
diamonds. **1989** *Daily Tel.* 4 Nov. p. xiii/5 Mars..is
a dry, cold and almost airless world that will need
considerable changes, or 'terraforming', before people
can roam its deserts without protective clothing. **1993**
Sci. Fiction Age Jan. 12/2 Mars-Firsters, or Reds, who
see terraforming as an unrectifiable insult to the
uniqueness of the planet.
   So '**terraform** *v. trans.*, to transform (an
environment or planet) in this way;
'**terraformed** *ppl. a.*
   1949 'W. STEWART' in *Astounding Sci. Fiction* Feb.
37/1 That little terraformed planetoid, outside the
mines and the drift, had been the base of supplies for
Freedonia. *Ibid.*, Once old Bruce O'Banion..hired
Jim Drake to terraform it. **1974** NIVEN & POURNELLE
Mote in God's Eye (1975) I. iv. 33 The middle two
planets are inhabited, both terraformed by First Empire
scientists after Jasper Murcheson. **1992** *Waldenbooks
Hailing Frequencies* 14/1 Venus had been terraformed,
more or less.

Tetrazzini (tɛtrə'ziːnɪ), *n.* orig. and chiefly *U. S.*
Also with lower-case initial. [The name of Luisa
Tetrazzini (1871–1940), Italian operatic
soprano.] A type of pasta dish with a cream
sauce and mushrooms, served esp. as an
accompaniment to poultry. Freq. used
postpositively, as *chicken Tetrazzini*, etc.
   1920 *Toledo* (Ohio) *News-Bee* 15 Nov. 2/7 Paquet
began making 'Spaghetti Tetrazzini' several years ago
when she gave him the recipe she brought from abroad
with her. **1948** I. S. ROMBAUER *Joy of Cooking* (rev.
ed.) 83/1 (*title*) Macaroni and chicken casserole (chicken
Tetrazzini). **1949** M. MILLER *Sure Thing* (1950) 35

Tetrazzini..and two Vichyssoise to start out, large
coffees, later. **1975** *New Yorker* 19 May 45/2 A four-
room, bottom-based underwater motel and laboratory,
which they once occupied for seventeen days, living on
things like freeze-dried turkey tetrazzini. **1990**
Gourmet Nov. 192/2 Combine well the remaining 1/3
cup Parmesan, the bread crumbs, and salt and pepper
to taste, sprinkle the mixture evenly over the Tetrazzini
and dot the top with the remaining 1 tablespoon
butter.

thiomalic (θaɪəu'mælɪk), *a. Chem.* [f. THIO- +
MALIC *a.*]   **thiomalic acid**, a thio derivative,
$HOOC \cdot CH_2 \cdot CH(S) \cdot COOH$, of malic acid used
in biochemical research and in the chemical
industry.
   1905 *Jrnl. Chem. Soc.* LXXXVIII. I. 629 Thiomalic
acid forms crystals melting at 148°, and gives a
characteristic reaction with copper sulphate. **1991**
Lancet 21-8 Dec. 1566/1 If a racemic mixture of
thiomalic acid is used in the manufacture of sodium
aurothiomalate, hexamers with seven chiralities could
be formed.
   Hence **thio'malate** *n.*, a salt or ester of
thiomalic acid.
   1905 *Jrnl. Chem. Soc.* LXXXVIII. I. 740 Sodium
thiolmalate [*sic*] in neutral aqueous solution gives with
cobalt carbonate a brownish-red, with bismuth
carbonate a yellow, coloration. **1940** *Jrnl. Pharmacol.
& Exper. Therap.* LXIX. 364 Auro sodium thiomalate
has a marked bacteriostatic effect against hemolytic
streptococcii 'in vitro.' **1991** *Lancet* 9 Mar. 615/1 Both
D-penicillamine and gold (I) thiomalate..might
directly induce synthesis of the 32 kD protein in vivo.

‖ **tiramisu** (tirami'su, sometimes anglicized
tɪrə'miːsuː), *n.* Also **tira mi sù**. [It., 'pick me up'
f. phr. *tira mi sù.*] An Italian dessert consisting
of layers of sponge cake soaked in coffee and
brandy or liqueur and a filling of mascarpone
cheese, topped with cocoa powder.
   1982 A. DEL CONTE *Good Housek. Italian Cookery*
122/1 (*heading*) Tiramesu [*sic*]...Coffee trifle. **1983**
N.Y. Times 4 Feb. c18/3 Such regional temptations as
'tira mi su'. **1985** *Nation's Restaurant News* (U.S.) 11
Nov. F4/1 Diners in New York and Los Angeles are
getting their first taste of a dessert called
Tiramisu. **1989** *Holiday Which?* Sept. 187/2 For the
sweet toothed, *Tiramisù*—a gooey sponge with cream
and powdered chocolate—is worth trying—though not
on a full or queasy stomach. **1991** *N.Y. Times* 13 Mar.
c7/2 Mr. Borroni of Il Boccalone said he had to eject a
few customers who came in merely to have tiramisù
and cappuccino.

Tourette (tuə'rɛt), *n.²* *Path.* [The name of G.
Gilles de la *Tourette* (1857–1904), French
neurologist.] Used *attrib.* and in the possessive
(esp. in *Tourette('s) syndrome*) to designate a
neurological disorder characterized by tics,
involuntary vocalization, and the compulsive
utterance of obscenities. Also *ellipt.* as
Tourette('s).
   [**1886** *Jrnl. Nerv. & Mental Dis.* XIII. 407 (*title*) On
convulsive tic with explosive disturbances of speech
(so-called Gilles de la Tourette's disease).] **1899** *Syd.
Soc. Lex.*, *Tourette's disease*, motor incoordination with
echolalia and coprolalia. A convulsive form of tic. **1940**
S. A. K. WILSON *Neurology* II. xcii. 1632 Tourette's
disease has certain affinities with the no less curious
lâtah of the Malays. **1973** *Psychosomatic Med.* XXXV.
423/2 If the tics spread or progress, chemotherapy for
Tourette's syndrome should be considered. **1978** A.
K. SHAPIRO et al. *Gilles de la Tourette Syndrome* 409
His son had been diagnosed as a Tourette patient. **1981**
London Rev. Bks. 19 Mar. 3/1 The forgetting of sleepy-
sickness (*encephalitis lethargica*) and the forgetting of
Tourette's have much in common. **1996** *Guardian* 8
Nov. (Friday Rev. section) 26/4 'Tourette's has a

wanton force,' said Sacks astutely. 'It impels Shane towards both brilliance and destructiveness.'

Hence **Tou'rettism** *n.*, behaviour typical of Tourette's syndrome.

1981 *London Rev. Bks.* 19 Mar. 3/1, I started to speak of 'Tourettism', although I had never seen a patient with Tourette's. **1988** *Jrnl. Geriatric Psychiatry & Neurol.* I. 169/1 Acquired Tourettism is a syndrome consisting of multiple tics, both motor and vocal.

traffic, *n.* Add: [6.] **traffic calming** [tr. G. *Verkehrsberuhigung*], the deliberate slowing or restriction of road traffic, esp. through residential areas, by means such as narrowing or obstructing roads, or limiting use of some thoroughfares to certain vehicles (such as bicycles or public transport).

1987 *Abstr. European Conf. Laboratoire Théorie des Mutations Urbaines de l'Inst. Français d'Urbanisme* 29 We also have very limited research on how *traffic calming does affect house prices, rents and retailing in such areas. **1987** *Environment Now* Oct./Nov. 29/1 Traffic calming, as it is known in Britain, also involves reduced speeds and environmental improvements, but here speeds are allowed up to about 20 mph. **1988** *Independent* 19 Dec. 17/3 The introduction of the 'traffic-calming' techniques now widely practised on the Continent. **1991** *Courier-Mail* (Brisbane) 7 Mar. 14/4 Traffic calming works, residents of Red Hill said yesterday.

train-spotter, *n.* Add: **b.** Also *transf.* (freq. *derog.*), a person who enthusiastically studies the minutiae of any subject; a collector of trivial information.

1989 *Q* Dec. 55/1 Dedicated dance persons— 'trainspotters' as they will allow themselves to be called in lighter moments—at first sequestered themselves in the world of rare grooves. **1992** *Face* Feb. 15/1 Containing over 3,000 entries.., and spanning 600 pages, this should settle a good few of those arguments about who starred in what and when. Not just for film train-spotters. **1993** *Ibid.* Apr. 32/2 Is Levi's new fine Bedford cord range as good as its original Cord of way back when? Or is it only trainspotters that can tell the difference?

treble, *n.* Sense 8 in Dict. becomes 9. Add: [II.] **8.** The high-frequency component of (esp. transmitted or reproduced) sound. Freq. *attrib.* Cf. BASS *n.*[5] 6.

1930 *Wireless World* 26 Mar. 333/1 The tone control which emphasises either treble or bass consists of a variable capacity between the input and output of the power valves. **1936** *Ibid.* 28 Feb. 214 Bass and treble controls. **1961** *Melody Maker* 9 Sept. (Suppl.) p. III/3 Tone variation by fully independent bass and treble controls. **1977** *West Briton* 25 Aug. 10/6 This one suffers from.. a loss of treble on some tracks. **1994** *Guitarist* Sept. 169/2 (Advt.), The 2-band EQ outboard preamp gives added bass and treble to any bass guitar.

trophy, *n.* Add: [4.] **trophy wife**, a wife regarded as a status symbol for a (usu. older) man.

1989 *Newsday* (Nassau ed.) 28 Aug. 48/1 Is the '*trophy wife' only an update on the old stereotype of the boss who takes on a girlfriend for a final fling? Is 'trophy wife' code for 'power bimbo'? **1992** O. GOLDSMITH *First Wives' Club* I. xii. 126 These trophy wives make the fifty- and sixty-year old CEOs feel they can compete sexually with younger men.

type, *n.*[1] Add: [10.] **type 1** *Path.*, designating or pertaining to some forms of diabetes, esp. insulin-dependent diabetes (see *insulin-dependent* adj. s.v. *INSULIN *n.* 2).

1977 *Lancet* 19 Mar. 638/1 *Type I includes classic insulin-dependent juvenile-onset diabetes, insulin-dependent diabetes presenting in later life, and diabetes initially adequately controlled.. but with islet-cell antibody (I.C.A.) in the serum. **1986** *New England Jrnl. Med.* 22 May 1366/1 So I believe there is something unique about Type I diabetes. Maybe it is more akin to polymyalgia rheumatica, which responds to some safe therapies that we have now.

type 2 *Path.*, designating or pertaining to some forms of diabetes, esp. the non-insulin-dependent type (see *non-insulin-dependent* adj. s.v. *NON- 3).

1977 *Lancet* 13 Aug. 325/2 Although juvenile-onset diabetes is predominantly type I and adult-onset diabetes is predominantly *type II, the inaccuracies inherent in this oversimplification must have vitiated earlier attempts at genetic analysis. **1987** *Oxf. Textbk. Med.* (ed. 2) I. ix. 53/2 It is probably preferable to use the type I, type II scheme, in that considerable confusion arises from the term 'insulin-dependent', which is often equated in practice with insulin-*treated*, which will depend on clinical practice and the state of the patient at a particular time.

V

V, Add: [III.] [5.] [b.] **VR**, virtual reality.

1989 *PC-Computing* Nov. 96/1 VPL Research proclaimed the occasion a holiday, Virtual Reality Day. Declared its press release, 'Like Columbus Day, *VR Day celebrates the opening of a new world.' **1993** *Guardian* 22 July II. 17/2 The pressure to develop this technology may come from robot control systems or from a desire for better VR arcade games. Further technology will provide physical sensations from the VR world, but this is not required for the posture interpretation suit to become the Dance Suit.

vagrant, *n.* and *a.* Add: [A.] **4.** *Ornith.* A bird that is encountered outside its normal area of distribution or migration; *spec.* (in the U.K.), one that has been recorded fewer than twenty times in the British Isles.

1920 H. F. WITHERBY et al. *Pract. Handbk. Brit. Birds* I. 140 The Lapland Bunting..has occurred [in] many English counties as vagrant. **1953** D. A. BANNERMAN *Birds Brit. Isles* I. 337 The snow finch has occurred as a vagrant in several other countries of eastern Europe. **1983** *Birds* Spring 15/2 The vagrant from the Continent, was found sheltering under a car. Many birds are blown off course during gales. **1988** *Bird Watching* Aug. 46/2 Returning migrants are beginning to appear and by the end of the month we could witness good seabird movements and the first North American vagrant.

vanilla, *n.* (and *a.*) Add: [4.] c. [From the popular perception of vanilla as the ordinary, bland flavour of ice-cream.] Plain, basic, conventional; (esp. of a computer, program, or other product) having no interesting or unusual feature; safe, unadventurous. Used orig. with reference to sexual activity (esp. in *vanilla sex*). Only occas. as *pred. adj. colloq.* (orig. *U.S.*).

1972 B. RODGERS *Queens' Vernacular* 184 *Vanilla bar*, a gay bar that is not SM. *Ibid.* 205 *Vanilla*,..rigid, conforming, goody-goody 'This neighborhood is too vanilla for the licks of us.' **1983** G. L. STEELE et al. *Hacker's Dict.* 129 It's just a vanilla terminal; it doesn't have any interesting features. **1985** W. DYNES *Homolexis* 123 S & M adepts dismiss gays of simpler tastes as mere fluffs, who limit themselves to timid exercises in vanilla sex. **1988** *InfoWorld* 24 Oct. 60/2 In its unmodified, 'vanilla' state Accountmate is an adequate, if unimpressive, system. **1989** *Profession 89* 60/1 The specious appropriation of selected fragments of a prestigious literary theory can even make a species of 'vanilla linguistics'..look enticingly 'postmodern'. **1992** *Guardian* 28 Nov. (Weekend section) 7/2 Since the late Seventies, the lesbian community has also suffered a painful schism between 'S & M dykes' and 'vanilla' lesbians.

virtual, *a.* Add: [4.] [g.] Also in more general use, esp. in **virtual reality**, a notional image or environment generated by computer software, with which a user can interact realistically, as by using a helmet containing a screen, gloves fitted with sensors, etc.

1987 *Whole Earth Rev.* Winter 119/1 Much of the real power of computers..is achieved through multiple maskings, the creation of 'virtual' realities. One on top of another, levels of symbols are built. **1989** *Ibid.* Fall 110/1 Virtual Reality is not a computer. We are speaking about a technology that uses computerized clothing to synthesize shared reality. **1991** *Independent* 3 June 4/1 Wriggling your fingers creates a wriggling 'virtual' hand superimposed on the virtual world you see. **1994** *Independent on Sunday* 26 June (Business section) 8/4 The technique, christened virtual therapy, opens up a new market for virtual reality systems in medicine, where at present they are used in training, allowing doctors to see inside 'virtual' patients.

wack, $n.^1$ and $a.$ Add: **B.** *adj.* Bad; harmful; unfashionable, boring. Esp. in the anti-drug slogan *crack is wack* and varr.

1986 *N.Y. Times* 19 Sept. B3/5 Keith Haring, creator of the 'Crack is Wack' mural in East Harlem. **1989** *Chicago Tribune* 22 Oct. IV. 1/1 A brightly colored mural painted on a handball court carried the succinct message, 'Crack Be Wack, Jack.' **1990** D. GAINES *Teenage Wasteland* vii. 183 Suburbia is filled with second-generation Deadheads, twenty wack years after. **1992** *Vibe* Fall (Preview Issue) 45 That was what sparked us to start the band: seeing all these wack people getting paid.

Wessi ('wɛsɪ, ‖vɛsɪ), *n.* *colloq.* (sometimes *depreciative*). Also **Wessie**. [a. G. *Wessi* (prob. an abbrev. of *Westdeutsche*), f. *West* west.] A term used in Germany (esp. since reunification) to denote a citizen of the former Federal Republic of Germany; a West German. Cf. *OSSI n.

1990 *Independent* 8 Oct. 13/3 A former NVA lieutenant-colonel, now a major, may get paid about DM2,000 (£678) a month, whereas a Wessie may get DM4,500. **1990** *Fortune* 3 Dec. 154/1 West German publishers have acquired interests in newspapers accounting for most of the East's circulation. Wessies captured many offices in October's state elections, including the top post in Saxony—a bit like Mario Cuomo winning the California governorship. **1991** *Times* 3 Oct. 12/6 For the Ossi, the Wessi was an arrogant know-all ruled by an oppressive bureaucracy. *Ibid.* 12/7 For the Wessi, the Ossi was pot-bellied, lacking in initiative and naive. **1993** *Vanity Fair* (N.Y.) May 44/1 In the East, people often speak of arrogant 'Wessis' with fear and loathing; in the West, the idle, scrounging 'Ossis' are mocked.

western, $a.$, $n.^1$, and *adv.* Sense 9 in Dict. becomes 10. Add: [A.] **9.** *Biochem.* **Western blotting** (also with lower-case initial) [punningly after *SOUTHERN $n.^2$], an adaptation of the Southern blot procedure for the identification of specific peptide and amino-acid sequences; **Western blot**, Western blotting (usu. *attrib.*); also, a blot (*BLOT $n.^1$ 1 f) obtained by this method. Also *ellipt.* as **Western**.

1981 W. N. BURNETTE in *Analytical Biochem.* CXII. 196/1 With due respect to Southern..the established tradition of 'geographic' naming of transfer techniques ('Southern', 'Northern') is continued; the method described in this manuscript is referred to as '*Western' blotting. *Ibid.* 201/1 Figure 5 is the Western blot of the 2-DGE of Eδ G2 and C3H cell lysates. **1985** *Sci. Amer.* Dec. 60/3 The routine ELISA..test for AIDS and..the more definitive *Western-blot confirmatory test. **1989** *Brit. Med. Jrnl.* 22 July 225/3 The presence of HIV antibody was confirmed by western blot analysis. **1991** *Nature* 18 Apr. p. xxxvi (Advt.), Watch a one minute Western.

white, $a.$ Add: [12.] [d.] **white-knuckle** *colloq.*, (orig. *N. Amer.*), (esp. of a fairground ride) causing or supposed to cause fear or suspense of such intensity that one's knuckles whiten in an anxious grip; also (of a person), experiencing or showing such fear.

1976 *Business Week* 26 July 119/2 A less extreme, cheaper, and yet often effective course for the '*white knuckle' passenger is to join a fairly new type of therapy group devoted to taking the fear out of flying. **1982** *N.Y. Times* 11 Apr. v. 5/3 Stadler salvaged a stroke with a two-foot birdie putt at the fifth, but it was whiteknuckle time again at the seventh, where he saved par from a bunker. **1985** *Times* 7 June 27/6 Wonderworld would eschew the 'white knuckle' rides but there would be thrills in another mode. **1986** *Woman's Day* (Melbourne) 25 Aug. 35/2 All you white-knuckle flyers will understand why Bob..put his private jet on the market..when the plane lost an engine and had to make an emergency landing. **1992** *Caravan Mag.* Sept. 36/3 It has the usual array of rides, offering everything from the white-knuckle thrills of the Rattlesnake roller-coaster and the Tempest, in which passengers are suspended upside down.

So **white-knuckled** $a.$, having white knuckles; (*transf.* and *fig.*) tense from barely contained emotion, esp. fear or suspense.

1973 *Globe & Mail* (Toronto) 8 Sept. 8/6 He meets local editors, goes on talk shows, flies *white-knuckled in bumpy bush planes. **1989** *Daily Tel.* 16 Sept. 8/2 [They] open the gate for a white-knuckled sailor in a fat rented boat, who shrieks orders at his wife as she nips ashore with the bow rope. **1993** *Saturday Night* (Toronto) June 53/2 It felt like an airplane about to crash. The 180 students..focused on the teacher with white-knuckled concentration.

white-label, designating a music recording for which the fully printed commercial label is not yet available, and which has been supplied, usu. with a plain white label, before any general release of the recording, either for promotional purposes or as a limited-edition pressing to test or stimulate the market.

1927 *Gramophone* Sept. 139/1 The new *white label pressings arrived just in time for me to take them to Paris. **1984** *Southern Rag* No. 22. 30/1 We managed to get hold of an advance white-label copy of this one just as we were going to press. **1991** *New Musical Express* 7 Dec. 7/2 Bumper double dose of chart hits and obscure white label only dance tunes.

wipe, $v.$ Add: [1.] **e.** = *SWIPE $v.$ 5. Also, to pass (a light pen) over a bar code.

1985 *Daily Tel.* 22 June 19/5 The retailer will wipe the card through a card reader and enter the details of the transaction. **1987** *Which?* Dec. 565/1 When you hand over your card to pay, the shop assistant wipes it through the terminal. **1990** *What Satellite* July 23/1 Another simple solution..is a barcode reader—you wipe a light pen over a barcode and—bingo!—the recorder's programmed itself.

wise, $a.$ Add: **9.** Special collocation: **wise use** orig. and chiefly *U.S.*, environmental policy which favours stricter controls on existing methods of exploiting natural resources, as opposed to policies which seek either to find alternative resources or to prevent such exploitation altogether; chiefly *attrib.*, esp. designating (members of) a movement advocating such a policy.

1989 R. ARNOLD in A. Gottlieb *Wise Use Agenda* p. xviii, The *Wise Use Movement argues that such dour anti-people attitudes have no place in an ethical view of mankind. **1989** *USA Today* 3 May 10A/1 For 25 years, environmentalists have driven one ranch after another into non-use classifications such as 'wilderness'. But they've radicalized so many people the Wise Use Movement has arisen to defend commodity production on our federal lands. **1991** *U.S. News & World Rep.*

Nov. 5/3 Now, the exploiters and developers have introduced the euphemism 'wise use' for wilderness destruction. **1992** *St. Louis Post-Dispatch* 10 May A8/1 The timber industry says plenty of old-growth forest still exists, and that the industry has adopted a 'wise use' policy that will maintain the integrity of the region's forests.

work, *n.* Add: [IV.] [34.] [d.] **work shadowing**, training or work experience, or a research technique, which consists of 'shadowing' a person at work (see *SHADOW *v.* 12 d); hence **work-shadow**, (*a*) one who 'shadows' another; (*b*) (chiefly in *attrib.* use) = *work-shadowing*; also as *v. intr.* and *trans.*

1984 *Ilea Contact* 20 Jan. 4/2 'Work Shadowing' was our response...My pupils had..very limited perceptions of work. **1985** *Times* 25 Nov. 11/1 A pilot '*work shadowing' scheme started in the summer. **1986** *Daily Tel.* 16 May 5/3 (*heading*), *Work shadow learns the job. **1986** *Ibid.* 29 Sept. 24/6 If you are offered the chance to work shadow you will almost certainly find it a worthwhile experience. **1987** *Railnews* (Brit. Rail) Oct. 7/3 BR encourages managers to involve themselves in workshadowing..as part of their contribution to the community. **1989** *Daily Tel.* 6 June 17/7 Llewellyn is an enthusiastic supporter of the workshadow schemes in which undergraduates spend two to five days watching a top executive at work. **1990** *New Scientist* 5 May 71/3 Another, more personal, way to encourage possible recruits: I have been 'work-shadowed' by one of the girls. **1995** *Independent* 23 Mar. 19/7 Training courses featured highly,..so did more unusual forms of development such as job moves, secondments, project work, task forces, work shadowing, [etc.].

work, *v.* Sense 16 b in Dict. becomes 16 c. Add: [B.] [I.] [16.] **b.** Of a train or other public service vehicle: to operate along (a specified route). Also used of a company operating such a service. Cf. sense *33 f below.

1869 *Bradshaw's Railway Manual* XXI. 86 The Midland..ought not to work the main line. **1873** *Returns Railways Companies Connections* 11 in *Parl. Papers* LVII. 765 Single Lines of Railway..Worked under the Train Porter System. **1902** *Encycl. Brit.* XXXII. 143/2 A line on this system is worked between Barmen and Elberfeld. **1936** *Railway Mag.* LXXVIII. 43/1 The line was worked by the L.M.S.R. and L.N.E.R., having been built..from Kilsyth junction..to Bonny Water junction. **1976** P. R. WHITE *Planning for Public Transport* viii. 173 The first APTs to enter service will probably work the London–Glasgow run. **1987** *Buses Extra* Oct./Nov. 25/1 During the off-peak season it worked a town route between Swanage Pier and New Swanage, via the railway station.

[II.] [33.] **f.** Of a train or other public service vehicle: to ply *between* specified points of a scheduled route. Also in other const. Cf. senses 16 a, *b above.

1914 *Railway Mag.* XXXIV. 19/1 Some of these [trains], though ranking as expresses and taken by express engines, work to and fro in the manner usually associated with suburban traffic. **1951** *Oxf. Jun. Encycl.* IV. 46/2 More recently..the main Blue Train has worked between Paris and Mentone. **1980** K. WARREN *Fifty Yrs. Green Line* i. 12/1 (*caption*) This coach was based at Alpha Street, Slough, and worked between Charing Cross and Windsor. **1986** *Rail Enthusiast* May (Suppl.) p. v/2 It worked down to Edinburgh and that evening headed back towards Newcastle.

workerless ('wɜːkəlɪs), *a.* [f. WORKER *n.* + -LESS.] Having no workers; *spec.* in *Ent.*, designating social insects which have no caste system.

1905 W. M. WHEELER in *Amer. Museum Jrnl.* V. 146 The queen..may continue to live with their hosts as permanent parasites. This seems to be the case..in the workerless species of *Anergates, Epœcus, Epipheidole* and *Sympheidole.* **1906** *Daily News* 28 Aug. 7 We must transfer the workless to the workerless land. **1929** J. G. MYERS *Lubbock's Ants, Bees & Wasps* (new ed.) 303 Such a workerless parasite as *Anergates.* **1967** J. H. SUDD *Introd. Behaviour Ants* vii. 140 *Anergates atratulus*, the workerless parasite of *Tetramorium caespitum.* **1975** *Economist* 1 Feb. 6/1 The workerless factory, the dockerless port, the driverless transport system, would seem to entail the wageless consumer and the customerless shop. **1988** *New Scientist* 19 Nov. 53/2 A highly analogous phenomenon occurs in some ant colonies, which are invaded by obligately parasitic, workerless queens.

working, *ppl. a.* Add: [8.] **c.** Of a level of knowledge or expertise in a specified area, esp. the use of a language: adequate for the purposes of day-to-day use; that one can work with.

1904 *Westm. Gaz.* 29 Dec. 2/1 A working knowledge of the technique of radio-therapy. **1926** *Glasgow Herald* 28 Feb. 9 The Linguaphone Institute has produced a system by means of which one can, in his own home, from book and gramophone record obtain a working knowledge of languages. **1959** 'A. BURGESS' *Beds in East* vii, in *Malayan Trilogy* (1964) 453 I've no wish to be able to speak any of these languages with fluency: a working knowledge is all I aspire to. **1974** 'S. HARVESTER' *Forgotten Road* i. 11 He had a working acquaintance with dialects of most Kafir valley tribes, even Khowar and the almost extinct Domali language. **1985** *Times* 21 Mar. 33/2 (Advt.), The successful candidate will..be fluent in both written and spoken Spanish. A working knowledge of an additional language would be an added advantage.

workshop ('wɜːkʃɒp), *v.* *Theatr.* [f. WORKSHOP *n.* 2.] *trans.* To present a workshop performance of (a dramatic work), esp. in order to explore aspects of the production before it is staged formally. Also *transf.*

1973 *Courier-Mail* (Brisbane) 17 July 14/7 Most of the new Australian plays that are hitting the market come as the result of the plays being workshopped. **1979** A. GINSBERG in *Coll. Poems* (1988) 717 Have a good time workshopping Bodhicitta in the Bird Room. **1985** *Guardian* 29 Apr. 21/7 What we lack in Britain is any Off-Broadway-style house where you can workshop a musical and lick it slowly into shape. **1990** *Sunday Times* 6 May E1/5 There is no system in the commercial sector for workshopping material, there's no way to stop when you realise that you need to have a think about something.

Hence '**workshopping** *vbl. n.*

1984 *Christian Science Monitor* 22 Aug. 23/2 The only way to see it is in performance. This workshopping is an invaluable process. **1986** *Act* Feb. 10/3, I am a great believer in the workshopping system and fond of non-performance workshops. **1992** *Independent* 22 July 19/1 Barr's play, *Richard IV*, is one of five new plays selected for several days of workshopping with professional actors, directors, and a dramaturg.

world, *n.* Add: [II.] [7.] **a.** *to go* (*get*, etc.) *back to the world* (*U. S. Mil. slang.*): to return to the territorial United States after active service overseas.

1971 *Current Slang* (Univ. S. Dakota) VI. 5 *Get back to the world,*..to be discharged and sent home. **1979** *Tucson* (Arizona) *Citizen* 28 Apr. (Weekender Mag.) 3/1 He was due to rotate back to 'the world', as it was known, in only a few weeks. **1987** D. A. DYE *Platoon* iv. 40 You'll kill boo-coo gooks before you go on back to the World.

[V.] [26.] **world music**, traditional local or ethnic music, esp. from the developing world, or (usu. with cap. initials) a style of commercial pop music incorporating elements of such folk traditions.

[**1977** *Washington Post* 20 Nov. F4/1, I..realized that all we were taught about music being either Western or primitive was a shocking form of colonialism, and that we desperately needed to start thinking in terms of world music.]   **1982** *N.Y. Times* 23 June c23/3 Mr. Berendt is co-producing a 'Jazz and *World Music' program that will take place in Avery Fisher Hall at 7 P.M. Saturday.   **1989** *Daily Tel.* (Colour Suppl.) 4 Feb. p. ii/3 Since the late 1950s, there has been a periodic fascination in the West with music from far-flung parts... In 1987, 11 small independent British record companies agreed to employ the term 'world music' to describe the genre, united only by a common feeling that their diverse forms of global music were under-publicised.   **1991** *One* 55 (U.K. ed.) B6/2 The one 'world music' Brits do have admiration for is Bhangra and Asian pop, since it reminds them of late night delights in Indian restaurants.

worldlet ('wɜːldlɪt), *n.* Chiefly *Science Fiction.* [Cf. WORLD *n.* + -LET.]   A little world; a planetoid.

1926 *Spectator* 11 Sept. 375/1 So in turn we visit the asteroids, that belt of tiny worldlets flinging round the sun.   **1937** O. STAPLEDON *Star Maker* ix. 206 As the aeons advanced, hundreds of thousands of worldlets were constructed.   **1968** S. R. DELANEY *Nova* (1971) 21 He finally got up a party to land on Deimos and explored the tiny moon as only a worldlet can be explored.   **1993** A. C. CLARKE *Hammer of God* 108 Not much larger than a family automobile, it could..allow

them to make a fairly detailed examination of the virgin worldlet.

worm, *n.* Sense 17 in Dict. becomes 18. Add: [III.] **17.** *Computing.* A program designed to sabotage a computer or computer network; *spec.* a self-duplicating program which can operate without becoming incorporated into another program. Cf. *VIRUS *n.* 2 d.

1975 J. BRUNNER *Shockwave Rider* II. 176 I'm just assuming that you have the biggest-ever worm loose in the net, and that it automatically sabotages any attempt to monitor a call to the ten nines.   **1980** *N.Y. Times* 13 Nov. D2/1 That is essentially what a group of scientists at the Xerox Corporation's Palo Alto, Calif., research center did when they created the Worm, a series of programs that moved through a data network almost at will, replicating, or copying itself, into free machines.   **1982** SHOCH & HUPP in *Communications Assoc. Computing Machinery* XXV. 173/1 We have undertaken the development and operation of several real, multimachine 'worm' programs.   *Ibid.*, A worm is simply a computation which lives on one or more machines.   **1988** *PC Mag.* July 114/1 The notion of subversive software began back in the 1970s with a program that ran around the US Defense Department's Arpanet messaging system. Dubbed the Creeper, it was one of the first worm programs.   **1990** *Amer. Banker* 1 Aug. 10/3 About 180 companies in the U.S. market offer services and software to stymie worms and viruses, which can alter or destroy data in a corporation's information systems.

Z

zaitech ('zaɪtɛk), *n. Comm.* Also **zaitek**, ‖**zaiteku** (zaiteku). [ad. Jap. *zaiteku*, f. *zai* wealth + *teku* partial transl. Eng. TECH *n.*[3]] Investment in financial markets by a company as a means of supplementing the earnings which it receives from its principal operations.

1986 *Economist* 28 June 86/3 The Euromarkets have already drawn Japan's banks and securities houses to London. Now the country's companies are arriving—for the Zaiteku. **1986** *Washington Post* 26 Oct. D2/2 Everyone seems to be trying his hand at deftly juggling securities using 'zaitech', or financial engineering. **1988** A. VINER *Emerging Power Jap. Money* v. 155 The word *zaitek* is an amalgam of Japanese and foreign elements. **1989** M. & H. SCHMIEGELOW *Strategic Pragmatism* iv. 110 Big enterprises in banking, transportation, and commerce have maintained extremely labor-intensive services, besides services outstanding in the use of limited numbers of personnel extremely qualified in innovative methods of *Zaitech* as well as of modern electronic communication systems. **1992** *Playboy* Nov. 166/3 About 70 percent of the $135 billion went for *zaitech*, Japanese slang for financial engineering.

zalcitabine (zæl'sɪtəbiːn), *n. Pharm.* [f. *zal-* of unknown origin + *-citabine*, app. f. by arbitrary alteration of CYTIDINE *n.* (perh. after *VIDARABINE *n.*).] = *DIDEOXYCYTIDINE *n.*

1991 *Pharmacotherapy* XI. 438/2 Zalcitabine (2',3' dideoxycytidine, ddC) is one of a number of 2',3' dideoxynucleosides demonstrating activity against HIV. **1992** *Sun* (Baltimore) 23 June A3/6 A new AIDS drug, called zalcitabine or ddC, has been approved by the Food and Drug Administration. **1993** *Jrnl. Pediatrics* CXXIII. 9 HIV-1 from four of six patients receiving zidovudine with zalcitabine developed high-level resistance to zidovudine.

zouk (zuːk), *n.* [a. Antillean Fr. creole *zouk*, lit. 'party' (cf. JUKE *n.*).] A style of popular music, originating in the French Antilles, combining Caribbean and Western elements, and characterized by a strong fast beat derived from traditional Antillean drumming.

1986 *N.Y. Times* 12 Nov. C20/1 Zouk is largely the creation of musicians from the islands of Guadeloupe, but it developed first in Paris recording studios, in the late 1970s. **1987** *Guardian* 24 Mar. 11/3 Tonight, the first-ever zouk on British soil kicks off this year's Camden Festival International Arts programme. **1989** *New Musical Express* 25 Feb. 27 The leading exponents of Caribbean 'Zouk' music, Kassav. **1992** *Caribbean Week* Apr. 8/2 West Indian culture is highly visible here. No politicians, but superstars like the zouk bands Kassav and Malavoi. **1993** J. GUILBAULT *Zouk* p. xvii, Can and will zouk play a role in the regional integration of the Creole-speaking islands, and if so, at what levels?

INDEX

demodulated 1
demodulating 1
demonopolize 1
  demonopolization 1
demonstrate 1
demonstration 1
demonstrator 1
den 1
  den mother 1
denature 1
dendroclimatic 1
dendroid 1
denet 3
  denetted 3
  denetting 3
denial 3
  in denial 3
densely
  densely-scrubbed: see
    SCRUBBED 1
densitometry 1
  densitometric 1
density 1
dent 1
  to make a dent in 1
  to put a dent in 1
dental 3
  dental hygiene 3
  dental hygienist 3
Denticare 1
denturist 1
depigmented 1
deplore 1
deposit 1
deprecate 1
derivative 3
descramble 1
  descrambling 1
descrambler 1
deseed 1
  deseeded 1
  deseeder 1
  deseeding 1
desireless 1
  desirelessness 1
desk 1
  desk dictionary 1
desk-top 3
desmo- 1
  desmosomal 1
  desmosome 1
des res 1
destain 1, 3
  destained 3
  destaining 1
destroy 1
destroying 1
  destroying angel 1
destructuration 1
detached 1
  detached retina 1
detect 1
detectional 1
detectival 1
deter 1
detour 1
detritivorous 1
  detritivore 1
detritus 3
  detritus-feeding 3

deutan 1
deuteranomal 1
deuteranomaly 1
deuteride 3
deutero- 1
  deuterostome 1
devein 1
Devensian 1
deviate 1
deviator 1
  stress deviator 1
deviatoric 1
device 3
  nuclear device 3
devolatilize 1
  devolatilization 1
  devolatilized 1
  devolatilizing 1
Dewar 1
  Dewar benzene 1
deworm 1
  dewormed 1
  deworming 1
dex 3
dexie 3
dhania 1
diadic: see DYADIC 2
diagnostic 1
dialogue 3
  dialogue box 3
diamond 3
  diamond willow 3
diaphthoresis 1
diazomethane 1
dichlorvos 1
dicky 1
  dicky bow 1
dictyosome 1
didanosine 3
didemnid 1
dideoxycytidine 3
  2′,3′-dideoxycytidine 3
dideoxyinosine 3
  2′,3′-dideoxyinosine 3
die 1, 3
  to die for 3
  to die 3
diegesis 1
  diegetic 1
dielectrophoresis 1
diesel 1
diestrum: see DIŒSTRUS 1
diestrus: see DIŒSTRUS 1
dietary 2
  dietary fibre: see FIBRE 2
differently: differently
  abled: see ABLED 3
diffractogram 1
diffusion 1
  diffusional 1
digenean 3
digest 1
digital 3
  digital compact cassette 3
  digital compression 3
  digital signal
    compression 3
digitalization 1
digitization 3
Dilantin 3

diner 1
dinero 1
dingbat 1
dingleberry 1
dink 1
dinky 1
dino- 3
  dinomania 3
  dinomaniac 3
dino 3
dioctahedral 1
diode 3
  diode-transistor logic 3
diœstrus 1
  diœstrous 1
diogenite 1
diol 1
dip 1
diphenoxylate 1
directory 1
disabled 1
  the disabled 1
disablist 1
disassemble 1
  disassemblage 1
disc 1, 3
  disc camera 3
  disc emulator 1
  disc file 1
disconnect 3
  disconnectable 3
discount 1
discourse 1
discover 1
disestablishment 1
  disestablishmentarianism 1
dish 3
  dish aerial 3
dishonourable 1
  dishonourable discharge 1
disinhibit 1
disintermediation 1
dismissive 1
  dismissiveness 1
dispensationalism 1
  dispensationalist 1
displacement 1
  displacement pump 1
disposal 1
dissensus 1
dissertation 1
distal 1
distantiate 1
distantiation 1
distort 1
distorted 1
distractor 1
distribution 1
  distribution function 1
district 1
  district auditor 1
ditto 1
  dittoed 1
  ditto mark 1
div 1
divalent 1
  divalence 1
  divalency 1
dive 1
  to take a dive 1

J

mind 3
  mind-bendingly 3
  mind-blowingly 3
  mind-bogglingly 3
  mind-game 3
minder 3
mine 3
Minervois 3
mingle 3
mini- 3
  minidisc 3
  mini roundabout 3
minibar 3
minifundio 3
minifundista 3
minifundium 3
minimalist 3
  minimalistic 3
  minimalistically 3
minimalize 3
minimize 3
minion 3
ministry 3
  man from the ministry 3
minority 3
minty 3
mirabilia 3
miracle 3
mirage 3
mirror 3
  mirror stage 3
mirrored 3
misandry 3
  misandrist 3
mischievous 3
mischievously 3
mischievousness 3
misfile 3
  misfiled 3
  misfiling 3
mixis 3
M'Kinley: see McKINLEY 3
mobilism 1
  mobilist 1
Modoc 3
modular 3
module 3
Mogollon 3
mohajir 3
Mohawk 3
  Mohawk haircut 3
moi 3
moil 3
mokopuna 3
Moldovan 3
mole 3
  mole drain 3
  mole drainage 3
molecular 3
molest 3
molestation 3
molester 3
moling 3
molinology 3
  molinological 3
  molinologist 3
mollock 3
  mollocking 3
molly 3
  molly-house 3

Moluccan 3
moment 3
monarchist 3
monastic 3
Monday 3
mondo 3
  mondo bizarro 3
monergy 3
monetarize 3
  monetarization 3
  monetarized 3
monetary 3
  monetarily 3
  monetary targetry: see
    TARGETRY 2
monetize 3
  monetized 3
money 3
  money supply 3
Mongolian
  Mongolian fire-pot: see
    FIRE-POT 2
monitor 3
  monitor speaker 3
monkey 3
  monkey bars 3
monkeyish 3
  monkeyishly 3
monkey-wrench 3
  monkeywrencher 3
  monkeywrenching 3
  to throw (or hurl) a
  monkey-wrench into the
  machinery 3
monkish 3
  monkishly 3
mono 3
monolith 3
monster 3
Monterey 3
  Monterey cheese 3
  Monterey Jack 3
-monther 3
Montonero 1
montuno 1
  montuna 1
monument 1
moo 3
mooch 1
mooching 1
mood 3
  mood control drug 3
  mood drug 3
  mood elevator 3
moody 3
  the moodies 3
  to pull the moody 3
mooli 3
moon 1, 3
  Moon Festival 3
  moon flask 3
moonwalking 3
  moonwalk 3
  moonwalker 3
moot 1
mopery 1
moral 3
  moral high ground: see
    HIGH GROUND 2
  Moral Majority 3

morinite 1
mormoopid 1
Morningside 1
morphallaxis 1
  morphallactic 1
morphologization 1
  morphologize 1
  morphologized 1
morphopoiesis 1
  morphopoietic 1
mortise 1
  mortiser 1
Morton 1
  Morton's foot 1
  Morton's metatarsalgia 1
  Morton's toe 1
Moscow
  Moscow Centre: see
    CENTRE 1
mosh 3
  mosher 3
  moshing 3
  mosh-pit 3
Mossad 1
mother 1
  Mother Bell: see BELL 1
motherboard 1
motive 1
moto 1
motorized 1
mount 1
mouse 1
mousse 1
  chocolate mousse 1
mousseline 1
  mousseline sauce 1
  sauce mousseline 1
mousy 1
  mousily 1
mouth 1
  to be all mouth 1
move-in 1
  move-in condition 1
movement 1
mow 1
mucho 1
mucicarmine 1
muco- 1
  mucociliary 1
  mucocyst 1
muddie 1
mudge
  to fudge and mudge: see
    FUDGE 2
muesli 1
  muesli belt 1
muffin 1
  English muffin 1
mug 1
  mug punter 1
muggee 1
muhajir: see MOHAJIR 3
muli: see MOOLI 3
mulloway 1
multi- 3
  multicropping 3
  multidomestic 3
  multi-employer 3
  multi-event 3
  multi-faith 3

stroll 2
  stroll on! 2
stropper 2
structural 2
  structural ambiguity 2
stub 2
  stub equity 2
stuff 2
stuffer 3
stukach 2
stultify 2
  stultifyingly 2
stump 2
stumper 2
stupefy 2
  stupefyingly 2
stupid 2
stuttery 2
styling
  styling wand: see WAND 2
stylometric 2
Stylophone 2
sub- 2
  sub-directory 2
subbie 2
subgum 2
subjunctive
  hypothetical subjunctive:
    see HYPOTHETICAL 2
subjunctivity 2
sublet 2
submarine 2
  submarine charge 2
  submarining 2
submersible 2
  submersibility 2
submittable 2
subscript 2
substance 2
  substance abuse 2
  substance abuser 2
substantialist 2
substantivist 2
  substantivism 2
substantivize 2
  substantivization 2
  substantivized 2
substrate 2
  substrate language 2
subsume 2
  subsumed 2
subtextual 2
subversionist 2
subversive 2
  subversively 2
  subversiveness 2
suchness 2
suckle 2
sucky 2
sucralfate 2
sucrier 2
suffixoid 2
sufuria 2
suicidality 2
suicide 2
  suicided 2
suimono 2
suit 2
suke: see SOOK 1
Sukuma 2

sulindac 2
Sullivan 2
  Sullivan principles 2
Sumerian 2
  Sumerologist 2
sumi-gaeshi 2
sump 2
Sunday
  Sunday sup: see SUP 2
sungum: see SANGAM 1
suni 2
sunnies 2
sup 2
  colour sup 2
  lit. sup. 2
  Sunday sup 2
super 2
super- 2, 3
  supercomputing 2
  supermodel 3
superannuate 2
superimposition 2
superintendent 2
supermarketing 2
supernaturalize 2
  supernaturalized 2
superscripted 2
superscripting 2
superstrate 2
  superstrate language 2
superstring 2
  superstring theory 2
supervision 2
supervisor 2
supinate 2
  supinated 2
supp: see SUP 2
supplement 2
support 2
supportive 2
  supportively 2
supra- 2
  suprachiasmatic 2
suprafix 2
  suprafixal 2
surf 2
  surfing 2
surfable 2
  surfable wave 2
surfaceless 2
sur lie 2
surrogacy 2
surtitle 2
  surtitled 2
  surtitling 2
survival 2
survivalism 2
survivalist 2
sus 2
sustain 2
sustainable 2
  sustainably 2
sutemi-waza 2
Suzuki 2
  Suzuki method 2
  Suzuki recital 2
Svetambara 2
swadge 2
swaggery 2
swallower 3

Swarga 2
swartzite 2
Swedish
  Swedish Vallhund: see
    VALLHUND 2
sweep 2
sweeper 2
sweet bread 2
sweetie 2
swell 2
Swetambar(a): see
  SVETAMBARA 2
swigger 2
swim 2
swimmy 2
swing 2
  to swing a left 2
  to swing a right 2
swingbeat 3
swipe 3
  swipe card 3
switch 2
  Switch card 2
switch-around 2
Swoe 2
swoosh 2
swooshy 2
Sylheti 2
sylviculture 2
  sylviculturalist 2
symplectic 2
  symplectically 2
  symplectic group 2
symptomatic 2
syn- 2
  syndiploidy 2
Synclavier 2
syndicate 2
synecology 2
  synecologically 2
syngnathid 2
syntagmeme 2
  syntagmemic 2
syntaxeme 2
  syntaxemic 2
Syntocinon 2
sysop 2
system 2
  system operator 2
  systems operator 2

T

T 2
  T-bird 2
  TI 2
  Ti plasmid 2
tabbing 2
  tab 2
table 2
  tablescape 2
  tablescaping 2
tablet 2
Taceval 2
tachi 2
tack 2
tactful 2

U